CHILTON'S GUIDE TO
AUTOMATIC TRANSMISSION REPAIR
1984-89 IMPORT CARS & LIGHT TRUCKS

D1560965

Vice President–Finance Barry L. Beck
Vice President–Sales Glenn D. Potere
Vice President & Publisher Dean F. Morgantini, S.A.E.
Manager–Consumer Print Kevin M. G. Maher
Project Managers Will Kessler, A.S.E., Richard Schwartz

PUBLISHED BY **W. G. NICHOLS, INC.**

Manufactured in USA
© 1990 Chilton Book Company
Chilton Way, Radnor, PA 19089
ISBN 0–8019–8053–4
4567890123 6543210987

7933468

Contents

1 AUTOMATIC TRANSMISSIONS AND TRANSAXLES

2 AUTOMATIC TRANSAXLES

3 AUTOMATIC TRANSMISSIONS

Section 1

Automatic Transmissions/Transaxles
General Information

TRANSMISSION/TRANSAXLE NAME CHANGE

Old Designation	New Designation
THM 180C	Hydra-Matic 3L30
THM R-1	Hydra-Matic 4L30-E
THM A-1	Hydra-Matic 3T40-A
THM 125C	Hydra-Matic 3T40
THM 700-R4	Hydra-Matic 4L60
THM 440-T4	Hydra-Matic 4T60
THM 400	Hydra-Matic 3L80
THM 475	Hydra-Matic 3L80-HD
THM 200-4R	THM 200-4R
THM F-7	THM F-7
HM-290 ①	Hydra-Matic 5LM60 ①
HM-282 ①	Hydra-Matic 5TM40 ①
HM-117 ①	HM-117 ①

NOTE: By September 1, 1991, Hydra-Matic will have changed the name designation on various transmission/transaxle assemblies throughout its product line. Units built between 1989 and 1990 will serve as transitional years in which a dual system, made up of the old designation and the new designation will be in effect.
① Manual Units

GENERAL INFORMATION

Introduction

With this edition of Chilton's Professional Transmission Manual- import vehicles, we continue to assist the professional transmission repair trade to perform quality repairs and adjustments for that "like new" dependability of the transmission/transaxle assemblies.

This concise, but comprehensive service manual places emphasis on diagnosing, troubleshooting, adjustments, testing, disassembly and assembly of the automatic transmission/transaxle.

Metric Fasteners and Inch System Fasterners

Metric bolt sizes and thread pitches are used for all fasteners on the automatic transmissions/transaxles now being manufactured. The metric bolt sizes and thread pitches are very close to the dimensions of the similar inch system fasteners and for this reason, replacement fasteners must have the same measurement and strength as those removed.

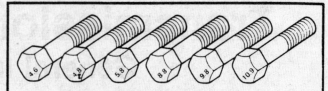

Metric Bolts—Identification Class Numbers Correspond To Bolt Strength—Increasing Numbers Represent Increasing Strength. Common Metric Fastener Bolt Strength Property Are 9.8 And 10.9 With The Class Identification Embossed On The Bolt Head.

Typical metric bolt head identification marks

Do not attempt to interchange metric fasteners for inch system fasteners. Mismatched and incorrect fasteners can result in damage to the transmission/transaxle unit through malfunction, breakage or possible personal injury. Care should be exercised to reuse the fasteners in their same locations as removed when every possible. If any doubt exists in the reuse of fasteners, install new ones.

To avoid stripped threads and to prevent metal warpage, the use of the torque wrench becomes more important, as the gear box assembly and internal components are being manufactured from light weight material. The torque conversion charts should be understood by the repairman, to properly service the requirements of the torquing procedures. When in doubt, refer to the specifications for the transmission/transaxle being serviced or overhauled.

Critical Measurements

With the increase use of transaxles and the close tolerances needed throughout the drive train, more emphasis is placed upon making the critical bearing and gear measurements correctly and being assured that correct preload and turning torque exists before the unit is reinstalled in the vehicle. Should a

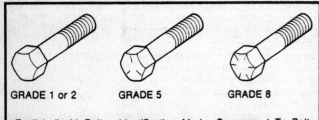

GRADE 1 or 2   GRADE 5   GRADE 8

English (Inch) Bolts—Identification Marks Correspond To Bolt Strength—Increasing Number Of Slashes Represent Increasing Strength.

Typical english bolt head identification marks

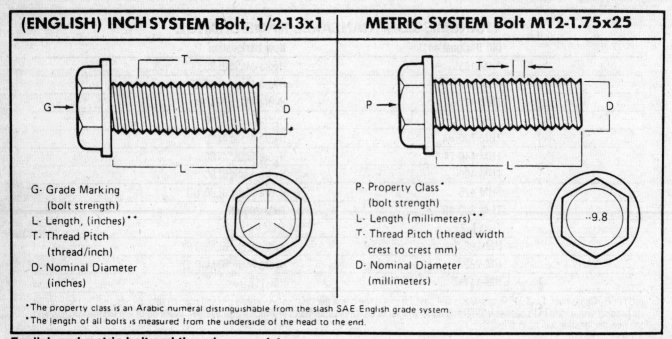

(ENGLISH) INCH SYSTEM Bolt, 1/2-13x1

G- Grade Marking
   (bolt strength)
L- Length, (inches)**
T- Thread Pitch
   (thread/inch)
D- Nominal Diameter
   (inches)

METRIC SYSTEM Bolt M12-1.75x25

P- Property Class*
   (bolt strength)
L- Length (millimeters)**
T- Thread Pitch (thread width
   crest to crest mm)
D- Nominal Diameter
   (millimeters)

*The property class is an Arabic numeral distinguishable from the slash SAE English grade system.
*The length of all bolts is measured from the underside of the head to the end.

English and metric bolt and thread nomenclature

(ENGLISH) INCH SYSTEM		METRIC SYSTEM	
Grade	Identification	Class	Identification
Hex Nut Grade 5	3 Dots	Hex Nut Property Class 9	Arabic 9
Hex Nut Grade 8	6 Dots	Hex Nut Property Class 10	Arabic 10
Increasing dots represent increasing strength.		May also have blue finish or paint daub on hex flat. Increasing numbers represent increasing strength.	

English and metric hex nut strength identification marks

comeback occur because of the lack of proper clearances or torque, a costly rebuild can result. Rather than rebuilding a unit by "feel", the repairman must rely upon precise measuring tools, such as the dial indicator gauge, micrometers, torque wrenches and feeler gauges to insure that correct specifications are adhered to. At the end of each transmission/transaxle section specification data is provided so that the repairman can measure important clearances that will effect the outcome of the transmission/transaxle rebuild.

Electronically Controlled Units

Today transmissions/transaxles are being developed and manufactured with electronically controlled components. The demand for lighter, smaller and more fuel efficient vehicles has resulted in the use of electronics to control both the engine spark and fuel delivery. Certain transmission/transaxle assemblies are a part of the electronic controls, by sending signals of vehicle speed and throttle opening to an on-board computer, which in turn computes these signals, along with others from the engine assembly, to determine if spark occurrence should be changed or the delivery of fuel should be increased or decreased. The computer signals are then sent to their respective controls and/or sensors as required.

Automatic transmissions/transaxles with microcomputers to determine gear selections are now in use. Sensors are used for engine and road speeds, engine load, gear selector lever position, kickdown switch and a status of the driving program to send signals to the microcomputer to determine the optimum gear selection, according to a preset program. The shifting is accomplished by solenoid valves in the hydraulic system. The electronics also control the modulated hydraulic system during shifting, along with regulating engine torque to provide smooth shifts between gear ratio changes. This type of system can be designed for different driving programs, such as giving the operator the choice of operating the vehicle for either economy or performance.

Lockup Torque Converter Units

DESCRIPTION

Most all vehicle transmissions/transaxles are equipped with a lockup torque converter. The lockup torque converter clutch should apply when the engine has reached near normal operating temperature in order to handle the slight extra load and when the vehicle speed is high enough to allow the operation of the clutch to be smooth and the vehicle to be free of engine pulses.

When the converter clutch is coupled to the engine, the engine pulses can be felt through the vehicle in the same manner as if equipped with a clutch and standard transmission. Engine condition, engine load and engine speed determines the severity of the pulsations.

The converter clutch should release when torque multiplication is needed in the converter, when coming to a stop, or when the mechanical connection would affect exhaust emissions during a coasting condition.

The electrical control components consists of the brake release switch, the low vacuum switch and the governor switch. Some transmission/transaxles have a thermal vacuum switch, a relay valve and a delay valve. Diesel engines use a high vacuum switch in addition to certain above listed components. These various components control the flow of current to the apply valve solenoid. By controlling the current flow, these components activate or deactivate the solenoid, which in turn engages or disengages the transmission/transaxle converter clutch, depending upon the driving conditions. The components have 2 basic circuits, electrical and vacuum.

ELECTRICAL CURRENT FLOW

All of the components in the electrical circuit must be closed or grounded before the solenoid can open the hydraulic circuit to engage the converter clutch. The circuit begins at the fuse panel and flows to the brake switch as long as the brake pedal is not depressed. The current will flow to the low vacuum switch on gasoline engines and to the high vacuum switch on diesel engines. These switches open or close the circuit path to the solenoid, dependent upon the engine or pump vacuum. If the low vacuum switch is closed (high switch on diesel engines), the current continues to flow to the transmission/transaxle case connector and then into the solenoid and to the governor pressure switch. When the vehicle speed is approximately 35–50 mph, the governor switch grounds to activate the solenoid. The solenoid, in turn, opens a hydraulic circuit to the converter clutch assembly, engaging the unit.

It should be noted that external vacuum controls include the thermal vacuum valve, the relay valve, the delay valve, the low vacuum switch and a high vacuum switch (used on diesel engines). Keep in mind that all of the electrical or vacuum components may not be used on all engines, at the same time.

VACUUM FLOW

The vacuum relay valve works with the thermal vacuum valve to keep the engine vacuum from reaching the low vacuum valve switch at low engine temperatures. This action prevents the clutch from engaging while the engine is still warming up. The delay valve slows down the response of the low vacuum switch to changes in engine vacuum. This action prevents the low vacuum switch from causing the converter clutch to engage and disengage too rapidly. The low vacuum switch deactivates the converter clutch when engine vacuum drops to a specific low level during moderate acceleration just before a part-throttle transmission downshift. The low vacuum switch also deactivates the clutch while the vehicle is coasting because it receives no vacuum from its ported vacuum source.

The high vacuum switch, on diesel engines, deactivates the converter clutch while the vehicle is coasting. The low vacuum switch used on diesel engines only deactivates the converter clutch during moderate acceleration, just prior to a part-throttle downshift. Because the diesel engine's vacuum source is a vacuum pump, rather than from a carburetor port, diesel engines require both the high and the low vacuum switch to achieve the same results as the low vacuum switch used on gasoline engines.

COMPUTER CONTROLLED CONVERTER CLUTCH

With the use of microcomputers governoring the engine fuel and spark delivery, the converter clutch electronic control has been changed to provide the grounding circuit for the solenoid valve through the microcomputer, rather than the governor pressure switch. Sensors are used in place of the formerly used switches. These sensors send signals back to the microcomputers to indicate if the engine is in its proper mode to accept the mechanical lockup of the converter clutch.

Normally a coolant sensor, a throttle position sensor, an engine vacuum sensor and a vehicle speed sensor are used to signal the microcomputer when the converter clutch can be applied. Should a sensor indicate the need for the converter clutch to be deactivated, the grounding circuit to the transmission/transaxle solenoid valve would be interrupted and the converter clutch would be released.

HYDRAULIC CONVERTER CLUTCH OPERATION

Numerous automatic transmissions/transaxles rely upon hydraulic pressures to sense and determine when to apply the converter clutch function. This type of automatic transmission/transaxle unit is considered to be a self-contained unit with only the shift linkage, throttle cable or modulator valve being external. Specific valves, located within the valve body or oil pump housing, are put into operation when a sequence of events occur within the unit. For example, to engage the converter clutch, most all automatic transmissions require the gear ratio to be in the top gear before the converter clutch control valves can be placed in operation. The governor and throttle pressures must maintain specific fluid pressures at various points within the hydraulic circuits to aid in the engagement or disengagement of the converter clutch. In addition, check valves must properly

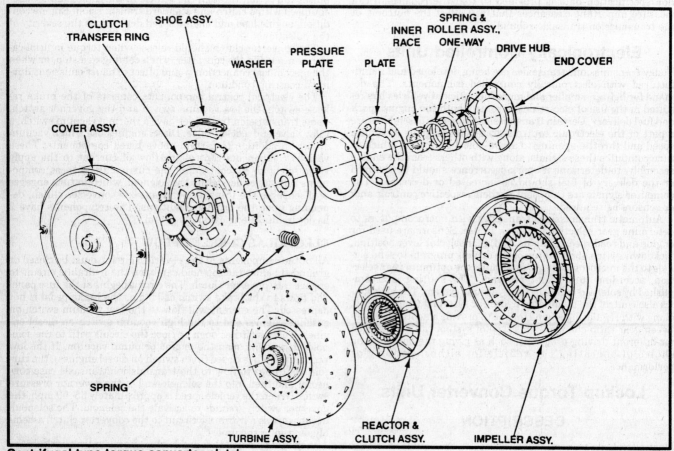

Centrifugal type torque converter clutch

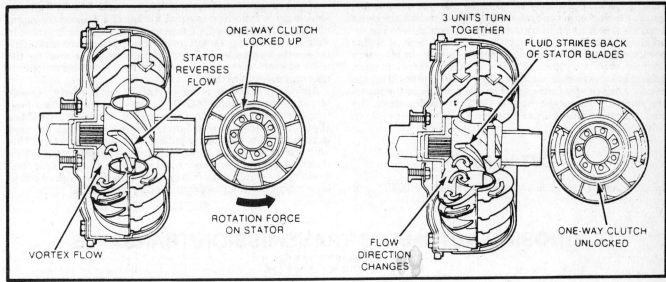

Stator operation in lockup and freewheeling modes

seal and move the exhaust pressurized fluid at the correct time to avoid "shudders" or "chuckles" during the initial application and engagement of the converter clutch.

CENTRIFUGAL CONVERTER CLUTCH

Transmissions/transaxles also use a torque converter that mechanically locks up centrifugally without the use of electronics or hydraulic pressure. At specific input shaft speeds, brake-like shoes move outward from the rim of the turbine assembly, to engage the converter housing, locking the converter unit mechanically together for a 1:1 ratio. Slight slippage can occur at the low end of the rpm scale, but the greater the rpm, the tighter the lockup. Again, it must be mentioned, that when the converter has locked up, the vehicle may respond in the same manner as driving with a clutch and standard transmission. This is considered normal and does not indicate converter clutch or transmission/transaxle problems. Keep in mind if the engine is in need of a tune-ups or repairs, the lockup "shudder" or "chuckle" feeling may be greater.

CONFIRMING CONVERTER LOCKUP

To confirm that the lockup function of the torque converter has occurred, check the engine rpm with a tachometer while the vehicle is being driven. If the torque converter is locked up, the engine rpm will decrease approximately 200–400 rpm, at the time of lockup.

Overdrive Units

With need for greater fuel economy, the automatic transmission/transaxles were among the many vehicle components that have been modified to aid in this quest. Internal changes have been made and in some cases, additions of a fourth gear to provide the overdirect or overdrive gear ratio. The reasoning for adding the overdrive capability is that an overdrive ratio enables the output speed of the transmission/transaxle to be greater than the input speed, allowing the vehicle to maintain a given speed with less engine speed. This results in better fuel economy and a slower running engine.

The automatic overdrive unit usually consists of an overdrive planetary gear set, a roller one-way clutch assembly and 2 friction clutch assemblies, one as an internal clutch pack and the second for a brake clutch pack. The overdrive carrier is splined

to the turbine shaft, which in turn, is splined into the converter turbine.

Another type of overdrive assembly is a separation of the overdrive components by having them at various points along the gear transassembly and also utilizing them for other gear ranges. Instead of having a brake clutch pack, an overdrive band

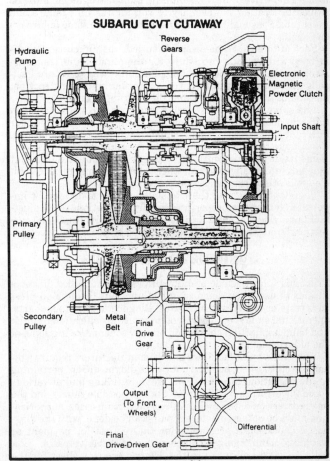

Typical ECVT transaxle assembly

is used to lock the planetary sun gear. In this type of transmission, the converter cover drives the direct driveshaft clockwise at engine speed, which in turn drives the direct clutch. The direct clutch then drives the planetary carrier assembly at engine speed in a clockwise direction. The pinion gears of the planetary gear assembly "walk around" the stationary reverse sun gear, again in a clockwise rotation. The ring gear and output shaft are therefore driven at a faster speed by the rotation of the planetary pinions. Because the input is 100% mechanical drive, the converter can be classified as a lockup converter in the overdrive position.

CVT Units

The continuously variable transmission/transaxle (CVT) is a new type of automatic transmission/transaxle. The CVT offers a vehicle drive ratio that is equal to that of a 5 speed (or more) manual gear box. The CVT transmission/transaxle is lighter in weight than the regular automatic transmission/transaxle. This is because 2 variable sheave pulleys eliminate the need for the mass of gears that are incorporated in the regular automatic transmission/transaxle.

Also in production is an electronic continuously variable transmission/transaxle (ECVT). This transmission uses electronic solenoids to regulate the hydraulic shift controls and has electronic controls mounted on the valve body, which are used to regulate how the sheave pulleys vary their diameters. This unit also incorporates a powder electromagnetic clutch. This clutch consists of a chamber filled with very fine stainless steel powder. The clutch spins free until the coils are energized and in turn magnetize the powder and lockup the clutch.

DIAGNOSING AUTOMATIC TRANSMISSION/TRANSAXLE MALFUNCTIONS

Introduction

Diagnosing automatic transmission/transaxle problems is simplified following a definite procedure and understanding the basic operation of the individual transmission/transaxle that is being inspected or serviced. Do no attempt to short-cut the procedure or take for granted that another technician has performed the adjustments or the critical checks. It may be an easy task to locate a defective or burned-out unit, but the technician must be skilled in locating the primary reason for the unit failure and must repair the malfunction to avoid having the same failure occur again.

Each automatic transmission/transaxle manufacturer has developed a diagnostic procedure for their individual transmissions/transaxles. Although the operation of the units are basically the same, many differences will appear in the construction, method of unit application and the hydraulic control system.

The same model transmission/transaxle can be installed in different makes of vehicles and are designed to operate under different load stresses, engine applications and road conditions. Each make of vehicle will have specific adjustments or use certain outside manual controls to operate the individual unit, but may not interchange with another transmission/transaxle vehicle application from the same manufacturer.

The identification of the transmission/transaxle is most important so that the proper preliminary inspections and adjustments may be done and if in need of a major overhaul, the correct parts may be obtained and installed to avoid costly delays.

Systematic Diagnosis

Transmission/transaxle manufacturers have compiled diagnostic aids to use when diagnosing malfunctions through oil pressure tests or road test procedures. Diagnostic symptom charts, operational shift speed charts, oil pressure specifications, clutch and band application charts and oil flow schematics are some of the aids available.

Numerous manufacturers and re-manufacturers require a diagnosis check sheet be filled out by the diagnostician, pertaining to the operation, fluid level, oil pressure (idling and at various speeds), verification of adjustments and possible causes and the need correction of the malfunctions. In certain cases, authorization must be obtained before repairs can be done, with the diagnostic check sheet accompanying the request for payment or warranty claim, along with the return of defective parts.

It is a good policy to use the diagnostic check sheet for the evaluation of all transmission/transaxle diagnosis and include the complete check sheet in the owners service file, should future reference be needed.

Many times, a rebuilt unit is exchanged for the defective unit, saving down time for the owner and vehicle. However, if the diagnostic check sheet would accompany the removed unit to the rebuilder, more attention could be directed to verifying and repairing the malfunctioning components to avoid costly comebacks of the rebuilt unit, at a later date. Most large volume rebuilders employ the use of dynamometers, as do the new unit manufacturers, to verify proper build-up of the unit and its correct operation before it is put in service.

General Diagnosis

Should the diagnostician not use a pre-printed check sheet for the diagnosing of the malfunctioning unit, a sequence for diagnosis of the gear box is needed to proceed in an orderly manner. During the road test, use all the selector ranges while noting any differences in operation or changes in oil pressure, so that the defective unit or hydraulic circuit can be isolated and the malfunction corrected. A suggested sequence is as follows:

1. Inspect and correct the fluid level.
2. Inspect and adjust the throttle or kickdown linkage.
3. Inspect and adjust the manual linkage.
4. Be sure to properly install a pressure gauge to the transmission/transaxle as instructed in the individual repair section.
5. Road test the vehicle (with owner if possible).

Clutch and Band Or Brake Application Diagnosis

During the road test, operate the transmission/transaxle in each gear position and observe the shifts for signs of any slippage, variation, sponginess or harshness. Note the speeds at which the upshifts and downshifts occur. If slippage and engine flare-up occurs in any gear, clutch band or overrunning clutch problems are indicated and depending upon the degree of wear, a major overhaul may be indicated.

The clutch and band or brake application chart in each transmission/transaxle section provides a basis for road test analysis to determine the internal units applied or released in a specific gear ratio.

NOTE: Some transmissions/transaxles use brake and clutches in place of bands and are usually indicated at B1 and B2 on the unit application chart. These components are diagnosed in the same manner as one would diagnose a band equipped gearbox.

TRANSMISSION/TRANSAXLE NOISE DIAGNOSIS

In diagnosisng transmission/transaxle noises, the diagnostician must be alert to any abnormal noises from the transmission/transaxle area or any excessive movement of the engine or the transmission/transaxle assembly during torque application or transmission/transaxle shifting.

NOTE: Before attempting to diagnose automatic transmission/transaxle noises, be sure the noises do not originate from the engine components, such as the water pump, alternator, air conditioner compressor, power steering or the air injection pump. Isolate these components by removing the proper drive belt and operate the engine. Do not operate the engine longer than 2 minutes at a time to avoid overheating.

1. Whining or siren type noises can be considered normal if occurring during a stall speed test, due to the fluid flow through the converter.
2. A continual whining noise with the vehicle stationary and if the noise increases and decreases with the engine speed, the following defects could be present:
   a. Oil level low
   b. Air leakage into pump (defective gasket, O-ring or porosity of a part)
   c. Pump gears damaged or worn
   d. Pump gears assembled backward
   e. Pump crescent interference
3. A buzzing noise is normally the result of a pressure regulator valve vibrating or a sealing ring broken or worn out and will usually come and go, depending upon engine and the transmission/transaxle speed.
4. A constant rattling noise that usually occurs at low engine speed can be the result of the vanes stripped from the impeller or turbine face or internal interference of the converter parts.
5. An intermittent rattleing noise reflects a broken flywheel or flex plate and usually occurs at low engine speed with the transmission/transaxle in gear. Placing the transmission/transaxle in **N** or **P** will change the rattling noise or stop it for a short time.
6. Gear noise (1 gear range) will normally indicate a defective planetary gear unit. Upon shifting into another gear range, the noise will cease. If the noise carries over to the next gear range, but at a different pitch, defective thrust bearings or bushings are indicated.
7. Engine vibration or excessive movement can be caused by transmission/transaxle filler or cooler lines vibrating due to broken or disconnected brackets. If excessive engine or transmission/transaxle movement is noted, look for broken engine or transmission/transaxle mounts.

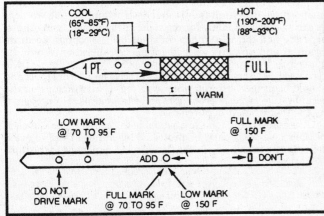

Typical fluid level indicators

NOTE: When necessary to support an engine equipped with metal safety tabs on the mounts, be sure the metal tabs are not in contact with the mount bracket after the engine or transmission/transaxle assembly is again supported by the mounts. A severe vibration can result.

8. Squeal at low vehicle speeds can result from a speedometer driven gear seal, a front pump seal or rear extension seal being dry.
9. The above list of noises can be used as a guide. Noises other than the ones listed can occur around or within the transmission assembly. A logical and common sense approach will normally result in the source of the noise being detected.

Fluid Diagnosis

FLUID INSPECTION AND LEVEL

Most automatic transmissions/transaxles are designed to operate with the fluid level between the **ADD** or **ONE PINT** and **FULL** marks on the dipstick indicator, with the fluid at normal operating temperature. The normal operating temperature is attained by operating the engine assembly for at least 8–15 miles of driving or its equivalent. The fluid temperature should be in the range of 150–200°F when normal operating temperature is attained.

NOTE: If the vehicle has been operated for long periods at high speed or in extended city traffic during hot weather, an accurate fluid level check cannot be made until the fluid cools, normally 30 minutes after the vehicle has been parked, due to fluid heat in excess of 200°F.

The transmission/transaxle fluid can be checked during 2 ranges of temperatures.
1. Transmission/transaxle at normal operating temperature.
2. Transmission/transaxle at room temperature.
During the checking procedure and adding of fluid to the transmission/transaxle, it is most important not to overfill the reservoir in order to avoid foaming and loss of fluid through the breather, which can cause slippage and transmission/transaxle failure.

Transmission/Transaxle at Room temperature
65–95°F – DIPSTICK COOL TO TOUCH

NOTE: The automatic transmissions/transaxles are sometimes overfilled because the fluid level is checked when the transmission/transaxle has not been operated and the fluid is cold and contracted. As the transmission/transxle is warmed to normal operating temperature, the fluid level can change as much as ¾ in.

1. With the vehicle on a level surface, engine idling, wheels blocked or parking brake applied, move the selector lever through all the ranges to fill the passages with fluid.
2. Place the selector lever in the **P** position and remove the dipstick from the transmission/transaxle. Wipe clean the re-insert it back into the dipstick tube.
3. Remove the dipstick and observe the fluid level mark on the dipstick stem. The fluid should be directly below the **FULL** indicator.

NOTE: Most dipsticks will have either one mark or two marks, such as dimples or holes in the stem of the dipstick, to indicate the cold level, while others may be marked HOT or COLD levels.

4. Add enough fluid, as necessary, to the transmission/transaxle, but do not overfill. This operation is most critical, due to the expansion of the fluid under heat.

Transmission/Transaxle at Normal operating Temperature

150–200°F – DIPSTICK HOT TO THE TOUCH

1. With the vehicle on a level surface, engine idling, wheels blocked or parking brake applied, move the gear selector lever through all the ranges to fill the passages with fluid.

2. Place the selector lever in the **P** position and remove the dipstick from the transmission/transaxle. Wipe clean and reinsert and dipstick to its full length into the dipstick tube.

3. Remove the dipstick and observe the fluid level mark on the dipstick stem. The fluid level should be between the **ADD** and the **FULL** marks. If necessary, add fluid through the filler tube to bring the fluid level to its proper height.

4. Reinstall the dipstick and be sure it is sealed to the dipstick filler tube to avoid the entrance of dirt or water.

FLUID TYPE SPECIFICATIONS

The automatic transmission fluid is used for numerous functions such as a power-transmitting fluid in the torque converter, a hydraulic fluid in the hydraulic control system, a lubricating agent for the gears, bearings and bushings, a friction-controlling fluid for the bands and clutches and a heat transfer medium to carry the heat to an air or cooling fan arrangement.

Because of the varied automatic transmission/transaxle designs, different frictional characteristics of the fluids are required so that one fluid cannot assure freedom from chatter or squawking from the bands and clutches. Operating temperatures have increased sharply in many new transmissions/transaxles and the transmission/transaxle drain intervals have been extended or eliminated completely. It is therefore most important to install the proper automatic transmission fluid into the automatic transmission/tranaxle design for its use.

FLUID CONDITION

During the checking of the fluid level, the fluid condition should be inspected for color and odor. The normal color of the fluid is deep red or orange-red and should not be a burned brown or black color. If the fluid color should turn to a green/brown shade at an early stage of transmission/transaxle operation and have an offensive odor, but not a burned odor, the fluid condition is considered normal and not a positive sign of required maintenance or transmission/transaxle failure.

With the use of absorbent white paper, wipe the dipstick and examine the stain for black, brown or metallic specks, indicating clutch, band or bushing failure, and for gum or varnish on the dipstick or bubbles in the fluid, indicating either water or antifreeze in the fluid.

Should there be evidence of water, antifreeze or specks of residue in the fluid, the oil pan should be removed and the sediment inspected. If the fluid is contaminated or excessive solids are found in the removed oil pan, the transmission/transaxle should be disassembled, completely cleaned and overhauled. In addition to the cleaning of the transmission/transaxle, the converter and transmission/transaxle cooling system should be cleaned and tested.

SYSTEM FLUSHING

Much reference has been made to the importance of flushing the transmission/transaxle fluid coolers and lines during an overhaul. With the increased use of converter clutch units and the necessary changes to the internal fluid routings, the passage of contaminated fluid, sludge or metal particles to the fluid cooler is more predominate. In most cases, the fluid returning from the fluid cooler is directed to the lubrication system and should the system be deprived of lubricating fluid due to blockage premature unit failure will occur.

Procedure

1. Disconnect both fluid lines from the transmission/transaxle assemblies, leaving the lines attached to the cooler.

2. Add a length of hose to the return line and place in a container. Flush both lines and the cooler at the same time.

NOTE: When flushing the cooling components, use a commercial flushing fluid or its equivalent. Reverse flush the lines and cooler with the flushing fluid and pulsating air pressure. Continue the flushing process until clean flushing fluid appears. Remove the flushing fluid by the addition of transmission fluid through the lines and cooler.

Special Tools

There are an unlimited amount of special tools and accessories available to the transmission rebuilder to lessen the time and effort required in performing the diagnosing and overhaul of the automatic transmission/transaxles. Specific tools are necessary during the disassembly and assembly of each unit and its subassemblies. Certain tools can be fabricated, but it becomes the responsibility of the repair shop operator to obtain commercially manufactured tools to insure quality rebuilding and to avoid costly "come backs".

The commercial labor saving tools range from puller sets, bushing and seal installer sets, compression tools and presses (both mechanically and hydraulically operated), holding fixtures, oil pump aligning tools, degreaser tanks, steam cleaners, converter flushing machines, transmission/transaxle jacks and lifts, to name a few. For specific information concerning the various tools, a parts and tool supplier should be consulted.

The use of the basic measuring tools has become more critical in the rebuilding process. The increased use of front drive transaxles, in which both the automatic transmission/transaxle and the final drive gears are located, has required the rebuilder to adhere to specifications and tolerances more closely than ever before.

Bearings must be torqued or adjusted to specific preloads in order to meet the rotating torque drag specifications. The end play and backlash of the varied shafts and gears must be measured to avoid excessive tightness or looseness. Critical tensioning bolts must be torqued to specification.

Dial indicators must be protected and used as a delicate measuring instrument. A mutilated or un-calibrated dial indicator invites premature unit failure and destruction. Torque wrenches are available in many forms, some cheaply made and others, accurate and durable under constant use. To obtain accurate readings and properly applied torque, recalibration should be applied to the torque wrenches periodically, regardless of the type used. Micrometers are used as precise measuring tools and should be properly stored when not in use. Instructions on the recalibration of the micrometers and a test bar usually accompany the tool when it is purchased.

Other measuring tools are available to the rebuilder and each in their own way, must be protected when not in use to avoid causing mis-measuring in the fitting of a component to the unit.

Section 2
Automatic Transaxle Applications

Vehicle Manufacturer	Year	Vehicle Model	Transaxle Manufacturer	Transaxle Identification
Honda, Acura/Sterling	1986–89	Civic, Accord, Integra, Legend, 825	Honda	CA-4, F4-4, LU-4, G4-4, P1-4, L5-4
Isuzu	1985–89	I-Mark	Jatco	KF100
Mazda	1984–88	GLC, 323, and 626	Jatco	F3A
	1987–89	323, 626 and MX-6	Mazda	G4AEL, G4AHL and FU-06
Mitsubishi, Hyundai	1985–89	Galant, Galant Sigma	Mitsubishi	KM175 and KM177
Nissan	1984–89	Sentra, Pulsar, Stanza	Jatco	RE4F02A, RL4F02A
Porsche	1984–89	928	—	A28
	1984–89	924, 944	—	087N
Saab	1985–89	9000	ZF	ZF-3HP18, ZF-4HP18
Subaru	1989	Justy	Subaru	ECVT
	1987–89	XT Coupe, XT 4WD, Legacy	Subaru	MP-T
Suzuki	1989	Swift	Aisin-Seiki	880001
Toyota	1987–89	Tercel	Aisin-Warner	A132L

AUTOMATIC TRANSAXLES

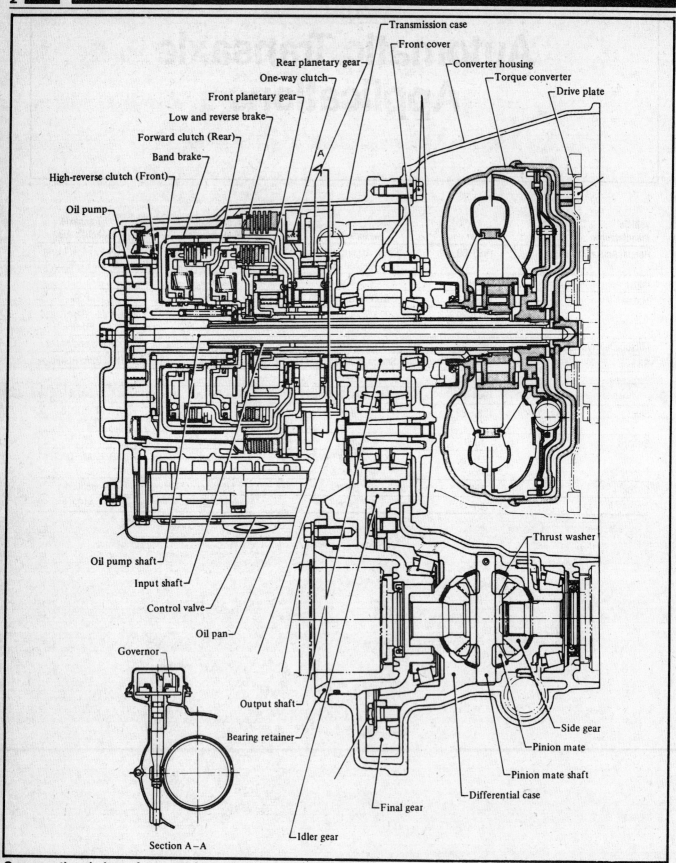

Transmission case

Front cover

Rear planetary gear

Converter housing

One-way clutch

Torque converter

Front planetary gear

Drive plate

Low and reverse brake

Forward clutch (Rear)

Band brake

High-reverse clutch (Front)

Oil pump

A

Thrust washer

Oil pump shaft

Input shaft

Control valve

Oil pan

Governor

Output shaft

Bearing retainer

Side gear

Pinion mate

Pinion mate shaft

Differential case

Final gear

Idler gear

Section A–A

Crosssectional view of an automatic transaxle

Section 2

CA-4, F4-4, G4-4, K4-4, L5-4, LU-4 and P1-4 Transaxles
Honda and Acura/Sterling

APPLICATION

HONDA TRANSAXLE IDENTIFICATION

Year	Vehicle	Engine	Transaxle
1986	Civic	1.3L/1.5L	CA-4
	Accord	2.0L	F4-4
	Prelude	2.0L	F4-4
1987	Civic	1.3L/1.5L	CA-4
	Accord	2.0L	F4-4
	Prelude	2.0L	F4-4
1988	Civic	1.5L/1.6L	LU-4
	Accord	2.0L	F4-4
	Prelude	2.0L	K4-4
1989	Civic	1.5L/1.6L	LU-4
	Accord	2.0L	F4-4
	Prelude	2.0L	K4-4

ACURA TRANSAXLE IDENTIFICATION

Year	Vehicle	Engine	Transaxle
1986	Integra	1.6L	CA-4
	Legend	2.5/2.7	G4-4
1987	Integra	1.6L	CA-4
	Legend	2.5L	G4-4
	Legend Coupe	2.7L	G4-4
1988	Integra	1.6L	P1-4
	Legend	2.5L	L5-4
	Legend Coupe	2.7L	L5-4
1989	Integra	1.6L	P1-4
	Legend	2.5L	L5-4
	Legend Coupe	2.7L	L5-4

STERLING TRANSAXLE IDENTIFICATION

Year	Vehicle	Engine	Transaxle
1987	825S	2.5L	G4-4
	825SL	2.5L	G4-4
1988	825S	2.5L	G4-4
	825SL	2.5L	G4-4
1989	825S	2.5L	G4-4
	825SL	2.5L	G4-4

GENERAL DESCRIPTION

The CA–4, LU–4, F4–4, G4–4 and P1–4, 4 speed automatic transaxles. These units are a combination of 3 element torque converter and a dual shaft automatic transaxle which provides 4 forward speeds and 1 reverse speed. The entire unit is placed in line with the engine assembly.

These automatic transaxles are equipped with a lockup torque converter. When the transaxle is in D4 and at speeds above 43 mph, the torque converter will utilize the lockup function. Lockup of the torque converter is prevented by a servo valve, which unless the throttle is opened sufficiently, the torque converter will not engage.

The L5–4 and K4–4 are basically the same as the other transaxles, except that they use an electronic control unit, sensors and 4 solenoids to control shifting and converter lockup.

Transaxle and Torque Converter Identification

TRANSAXLE

The automatic transaxle identification numbers are stamped on a plate, which is located on top of the automatic transaxle assembly. This plate can be viewed from the top of the engine compartment.

TORQUE CONVERTER

Torque converter usage differs with the type of engine and the type of vehicle that the automatic transaxle is being used in. Some torque converters can be disassembled. However, should problems exist within the torque converter replacement of the unit is recommended.

Electronic Controls

The L5–4 and K4–4 transaxles utilize an electronic control system. This system consists of an electronic control unit, sensors and 4 solenoid valves. Shifting and lockup are electronically controlled for comfortable driving under all conditions.

For shift control, the electronic control unit recieves a signal from each sensor and detects the appropriate gear shifting, it then activates the shift valves acordingly.

For lockup control, the sensors send data to the control unit which in turn detects wether to turn the lockup on or off. The lock is controlled by the lockup control solenoid.

The electronic control unit is located under the drivers seat and the solenoid control valves are located on the transaxle. Various sensors include; vehicle speed signal, throttle angle, shift position, brake light switch, coolant temperature, engine rpm and cooling fan control unit.

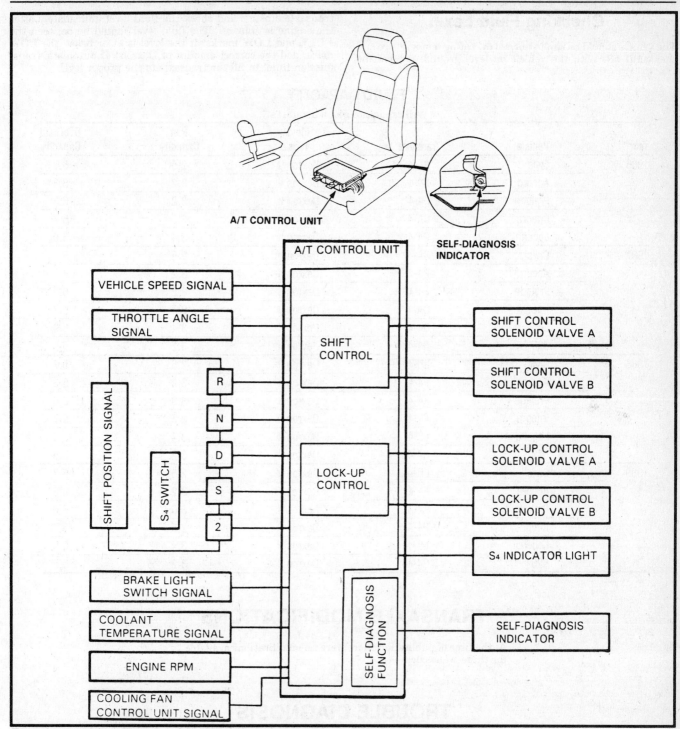

Electrical system diagram—L5-4 and K4-4 transaxles

Metric Fasteners

Metric tools will be required to service this transaxle. Due to the large number of alloy parts used in this transaxle, torque specifications should be strictly observed. Before installing capscrews into aluminum parts, dip the bolts into clean transmission fluid as this will prevent the screws from galling the aluminum threads, thus causing damage.

Metric fastener dimensions are very close to the dimensions of the familiar inch system fasteners. For this reason replacement fasteners must have the same measurement and strength as the original fastener.

Do not attempt to interchange metric fasteners for inch system fasteners. Mismatched or incorrect fasteners can cause damage to the automatic transaxle unit and possible personal injury. Care should be taken to reuse fasteners in their original locations.

Checking Fluid Level

The vehicle should be run to normal operating temperature and then shut off. With the vehicle on level ground, remove the transaxle dipstick and check the fluid level immediately after the engine is shut off. The fluid level should be between the **FULL** and **LOW** marks. If the level is at or below the **LOW** mark, add the correct amount of Dexron® II automatic transmission fluid, to fill the transaxle to the proper level.

FLUID CAPACITY
All capacities given in quarts

Year	Vehicle	Transaxle	Fluid Type	Pan Capacity	Overhaul Capacity
1986	Civic	CA-4	Dexron II	2.5	5.7
	Accord	F4-4	Dexron II	3.2	6.3
	Prelude	F4-4	Dexron II	3.2	6.3
	Integra	CA-4	Dexron II	2.5	5.7
	Legend	G4-4	Dexron II	3.4	6.9
1987	Civic	CA-4	Dexron II	2.5	5.7
	Accord	F4-4	Dexron II	3.2	6.3
	Prelude	F4-4	Dexron II	3.2	6.3
	Integra	CA-4	Dexron II	2.5	5.7
	Legend	G4-4	Dexron II	3.4	6.9
	825	G4-4	Dexron II	3.2	6.5
1988	Civic	LU-4	Dexron II	2.5	5.7
	Accord	F4-4	Dexron II	3.2	6.3
	Prelude	K4-4	Dexron II	3.0	6.6
	Integra	P1-4	Dexron II	2.5	5.7
	Legend	L5-4	Dexron II	3.4	6.9
	825	G4-4	Dexron II	3.2	6.5
1989	Civic	LU-4	Dexron II	2.5	5.7
	Accord	F4-4	Dexron II	3.2	6.3
	Prelude	K4-4	Dexron II	3.0	6.6
	Integra	P1-4	Dexron II	2.5	5.7
	Legend	L5-4	Dexron II	3.4	6.9
	825	G4-4	Dexron II	3.2	6.5

TRANSAXLE MODIFICATIONS

At the time of publication there were no modifications available for these transaxles.

TROUBLE DIAGNOSIS

CLUTCH AND BRAKE APPLICATION
CA-4, F4-4, G4-4, LU-4, P1-4 Transaxles

Range	1st Gear 1st Clutch	1st Gear One-way Clutch	2nd Gear 2nd Clutch	3rd Gear 3rd Clutch	4th Gear	4th Clutch	Reverse Gear	Parking Gear
P	—	—	—	—	—	—	—	Applied
R	—	—	—	—	—	Applied	Applied	—
N	—	—	—	—	—	—	—	—

CLUTCH AND BRAKE APPLICATION
CA-4, F4-4, G4-4, LU-4, P1-4 Transaxles

Range		1st Gear 1st Clutch	1st Gear One-way Clutch	2nd Gear 2nd Clutch	3rd Gear 3rd Clutch	4th Gear	4th Clutch	Reverse Gear	Parking Gear
D3	1st	Applied	Applied	—	—	—	—	—	—
	2nd	Applied ①	—	Applied	—	—	—	—	—
	3rd	Applied ①	—	—	Applied	—	—	—	—
D4	1st	Applied	Applied	—	—	—	—	—	—
	2nd	Applied ①	—	Applied	—	—	—	—	—
	3rd	Applied ①	—	—	Applied	—	—	—	—
	4th	Applied ①	—	—	—	Applied	Applied	—	—
2	2nd	—	—	Applied	—	—	—	—	—

① Although the 1st clutch engages, driving power is not transmitted as the one-way clutch races

CLUTCH AND BRAKE APPLICATION
L5-4 and K4-4 Transaxles

Range		1st Gear 1st Clutch	1st Gear One-way Clutch	2nd Gear 2nd Clutch	3rd Gear 3rd Clutch	4th Gear	4th Clutch	Reverse Gear	Parking Gear
P		—	—	—	—	—	—	—	Applied
R		—	—	—	—	—	Applied	Applied	—
N		—	—	—	—	—	—	—	—
S3	1st	Applied	Applied	—	—	—	—	—	—
	2nd	Applied ①	—	Applied	—	—	—	—	—
	3rd	Applied ①	—	—	Applied	—	—	—	—
S4 or D	1st	Applied	Applied	—	—	—	—	—	—
	2nd	Applied ①	—	Applied	—	—	—	—	—
	3rd	Applied ①	—	—	Applied	—	—	—	—
	4th	Applied ①	—	—	—	Applied	Applied	—	—
2	2nd	—	—	Applied	—	—	—	—	—

① Although the 1st clutch engages, driving power is not transmitted as the one-way clutch slips

CHILTON'S THREE C'S TRANSAXLE DIAGNOSIS
CA-4, LU-4, F4-4, P1-4, G4-4, L5-4 and K4-4

Condition	Cause	Correction
Engine runs but vehicle won't move	a) Fluid level low	a) Check and adjust
	b) Damaged oil pump	b) Repair or replace oil pump
	c) Mainshaft damaged	c) Repair or replace mainshaft
	d) Damaged final gear	d) Check final gear. Replace as needed
	e) Control cable damaged	e) Replace control cable
	f) Damaged drive plate or improper transaxle installation	f) Correct transaxle alignment or replace drive plate
	g) Regulator valve stuck	g) Repair valve
	h) Oil filter clogged	h) Remove and replace

CHILTON'S THREE C'S TRANSAXLE DIAGNOSIS
CA-4, LU-4, F4-4, P1-4, G4-4, L5-4 and K4-4

Condition	Cause	Correction
Vehicle moves in 2, but not in S or D	a) 1st gear worn or damaged b) Countershaft one way clutch seized or damaged c) 1st clutch faulty d) Control cable misadjusted e) Blockage in orifice	a) Check 1st gear and replace b) Check clutch and replace as needed c) Repair or replace d) Correct adjustment e) Clear orifice
Vehicle moves in S or D, but not in 2	a) 2nd gear worn or damaged b) 2nd clutch faulty c) Control cable misadjusted d) Blockage in separator orifice	a) Check 2nd gear and replace as needed b) Repair or replace c) Correct cable adjustment d) Clear separator orifice
Vehicle moves in S, D, or 2 but not in R	a) 4th gears worn or damaged b) Reverse gears worn or damaged c) 4th clutch faulty d) Control cable misadjusted e) Servo shaft stuck f) 1-2 shift valve faulty g) Electrical system faulty	a) Check and replace gears as needed b) Check and replace gears as needed c) Check clutch and replace d) Correct adjustment e) Clean shaft and check f) Replace shift valve as needed g) Check system and repair as needed
Poor acceleration	a) Fluid level low b) Oil pump damaged c) Control cable misadjusted d) Regulator valve stuck or spring damaged e) Torque converter check valve faulty f) Countershaft one way clutch damaged g) 1st clutch faulty h) 2nd clutch faulty i) Poor engine performance	a) Check and adjust b) Check pump and replace as needed c) Correct adjustment d) Check valve and spring. Replace or repair e) Repair or replace check valve f) Check clutch operation and repair or replace g) Check clutch and replace as needed h) Check clutch and repair or replace i) Check engine for tune-up, idle adjust. Correct as needed
Excessive idle vibration	a) Oil pump damaged or seized b) Drive plate faulty or transaxle improperly installed c) Engine performance poor	a) Repair or replace oil pump b) Repair or readjust transaxle alignment c) Check and repair as needed
Shift up speed is too fast or slow	a) Electrical system faulty	a) Repair as required
Jumps from 1st to 3rd in S	a) Electrical system faulty	a) Repair as required
Jumps from 1st to 4th in D	a) Electrical system faulty	a) Repair as required
Shift up point too early/late	a) Electrical system faulty	a) Repair as required
Harsh upshift from 1st to 2nd	a) 2nd clutch faulty b) Modulator valve faulty c) Clutch clearance incorrect d) 1-2 shift valve faulty e) Throttle valve B faulty f) 2nd accumulator faulty g) Clutch pressure control valve faulty h) Foreign material stuck in check ball i) Shift control solenoid valve "A" faulty	a) Repair or replace clutch assembly b) Repair or replace valve c) Check and adjust clearance d) Repair or replace e) Repair or replace throttle valve B f) Repair or replace accumulator g) Repair or replace valve h) Clean passage or replace check ball i) Repair or replace solenoid valve assembly
Harsh upshift from 2nd to 3rd	a) 3rd clutch faulty b) Modulator valve faulty c) Clutch clearance incorrect d) 2-3 shift valve faulty e) 3rd accumulator faulty f) Clutch control valve faulty g) Clutch pressure control valve faulty	a) Repair or replace clutch b) Repair or replace c) Check and adjust d) Repair or replace e) Repair or replace accumulator f) Repair or replace clutch control valve g) Repair or replace pressure valve

CHILTON'S THREE C'S TRANSAXLE DIAGNOSIS
CA-4, LU-4, F4-4, P1-4, G4-4, L5-4 and K4-4

Condition	Cause	Correction
	h) Foreign material stuck in separator orifice	h) Check and clean separator orifice
Harsh upshift from 3rd to 4th	a) 4th clutch faulty	a) Repair or replace clutch
	b) Modulator valve faulty	b) Repair or replace
	c) Clutch clearance incorrect	c) Check and adjust
	d) 3-4 shift valve faulty	d) Repair or replace valve
	e) Throttle valve "B" faulty	e) Repair or replace valve
	f) 4th accumulator faulty	f) Repair or replace
	g) Clutch pressure control valve faulty	g) Repair or replace valve
	h) Foreign material stuck in separator orifice	h) Check and clean separator
	i) 3rd orifice control faulty	i) Clean orifice
	j) Shift solenoid valve "A" faulty	j) Repair or replace
	k) Electrical system faulty	k) Repair
Car creeps forward in neutral	a) Fluid level too high	a) Adjust level
	b) 1st clutch faulty	b) Repair or replace
	c) 2nd clutch faulty	c) Repair or replace
	d) 3rd clutch faulty	d) Repair or replace
	e) 4th clutch faulty	e) Repair or replace
	f) Needle bearing seized	f) Replace bearing
	g) Washers/collars seized	g) Replace
	h) Clutch clearance incorrect	h) Check and adjust
Excessive time lag from N to S/D	a) 1st clutch faulty	a) Repair or replace clutch
	b) Foreign material stuck in separator orifice	b) Check and clear separator
	c) Foreign material in check ball orifice	c) Check and clean check ball orifice
Excessive time lag from N to R	a) 4th clutch faulty	a) Repair or replace clutch
	b) Servo shaft stuck	b) Repair or replace servo
	c) 1-2 shift valve faulty	c) Repair or replace shift valve
Abnormal noise in all gears	a) Oil pump seized	a) Repair or replace
	b) Mainshaft damaged	b) Replace as needed
	c) Mainshaft ball bearing	c) Replace bearing
	d) Drive plate faulty	d) Replace drive plate
	e) Control cable misadjusted	e) Adjust or replace cable
	f) Manual valve faulty	f) Repair or replace valve
	g) Electrical system faulty	g) Repair as required
	h) Torque converter check valve faulty	h) Repair or replace check valve
Harsh shift to lockup	a) Lockup shift valve faulty	a) Repair or replace shift valve
	b) Lockup piston faulty	b) Repair or replace
	c) Lockup control solenoid valve A faulty	c) Replace solenoid valve A
	d) Electrical system faulty	d) Check and repair
Vibration in lockup	a) Lockup timing valve "B" faulty	a) Repair or replace timing valve assembly
	b) Lockup control valve faulty	b) Repair or replace lockup control valve
	c) Lockup solenoid valve B faulty	c) Repair or replace solenoid assembly
	d) Electrical system faulty	d) Check and repair
Lockup clutch does not engage	a) Torque converter check valve faulty	a) Repair or replace check valve
	b) Lockup shift valve faulty	b) Repair or replace shift valve
	c) Lockup timing valve B faulty	c) Repair or replace timing valve B
	d) Lockup control valve faulty	d) Repair or replace lockup control valve
	e) Electrical system faulty	e) Check or repair

NO.	DESCRIPTION OF PRESSURE	NO.	DESCRIPTION OF PRESSURE	NO.	DESCRIPTION OF PRESSURE	NO.	DESCRIPTION OF PRESSURE
1	LINE	6	MODULATOR	40	4TH CLUTCH	94	TORQUE CONVERTER
2	LINE	6'	MODULATOR	41	4TH CLUTCH	95	LUBRICATION
3	LINE	10	1ST CLUTCH	42	4TH CLUTCH	96	TORQUE CONVERTER
3'	LINE	20	2ND CLUTCH	55	THROTTLE **B**	97	TORQUE CONVERTER
3''	LINE	21	2ND CLUTCH	90	TORQUE CONVERTER	99	SUCTION
4	LINE	22	2ND CLUTCH	91	TORQUE CONVERTER	X	BLEED
4''	CLUTCH PRESSURE CONTROL	30	3RD CLUTCH	92	TORQUE CONVERTER		
5	CLUTCH PRESSURE CONTROL	31	3RD CLUTCH	93	OIL COOLER		

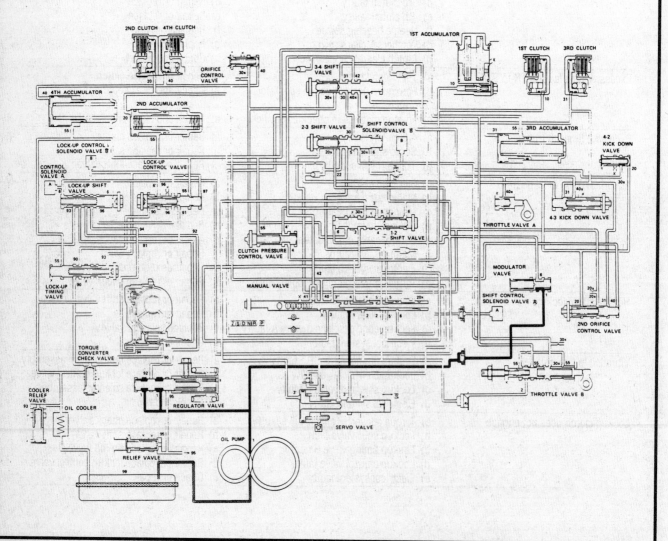

Hydraulic system flow – L5–4 and K4–4 transaxles

No.	DESCRIPTION OF PRESSURE	No.	DESCRIPTION OF PRESSURE	No.	DESCRIPTION OF PRESSURE	No.	DESCRIPTION OF PRESSURE
1	LINE	10	1ST CLUTCH	41	4TH CLUTCH	91	TORQUE CONVERTER
2	LINE	11	1ST CLUTCH	42	4TH CLUTCH	92	TORQUE CONVERTER
3	LINE	20	2ND CLUTCH	50	THROTTLE A	93	OIL COOLER
3'	LINE	21	2ND CLUTCH	51	THROTTLE A	94	TORQUE CONVERTER
3"	LINE	23	2ND CLUTCH	55	THROTTLE B	95	LUBRICATION
4	LINE	24	2ND CLUTCH	56	THROTTLE B	96	TORQUE CONVERTER
4'	LINE	30	3RD CLUTCH	60	GOVERNOR	97	TORQUE CONVERTER
5	LINE	31	3RD CLUTCH	61	GOVERNOR	99	SUCTION
6	MODULATOR	40	4TH CLUTCH	90	TORQUE CONVERTER		

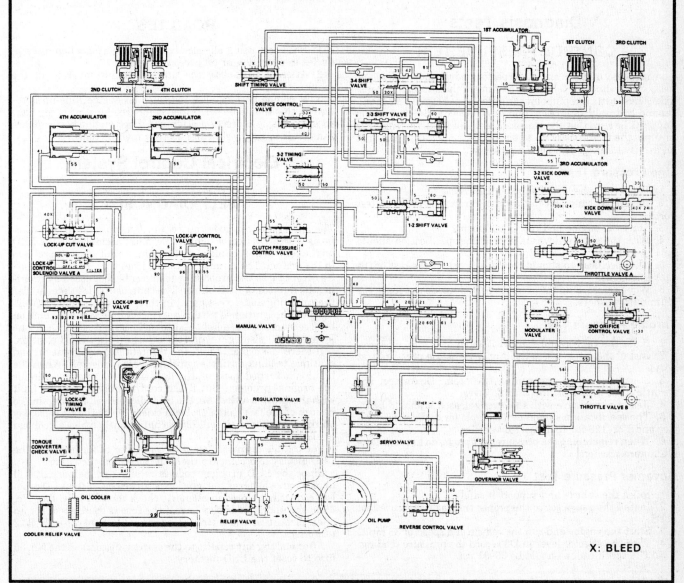

X: BLEED

Hydraulic system flow – CA-4, LU-4, F4-4, P1-4 and G4-4 transaxles

Hydraulic Control System

The valve assembly includes the main valve body, secondary valve body, servo valve body, modulator valve body, regulator valve body and lockup shift valve body, through their respective separator plates. They are bolted to the torque converter case as an assembly.

The main valve body contains the manual valve, 1–2 shift valve, 2–3 shift valve, 3–4 shift valve, pressure relief valve, 2nd orifice control valve and oil pump gear

The secondary valve body includes the CPC valve, REV control valve, lockup cut valve, kickdown valve, 3–2 timing valve and shift timing valves.

The servo valve body contains the accumulator pistons, 3rd orifice control valve, throttle A and B valves and the modulator.

The regulator valve body contains the lockup timing valves, pressure regulator valve and lockup control valve. Fluid from the regulator passes through the manual valve to the various control valves.

The lockup shift valve body contains a lockup timing valve and lockup shift valve. The 1st, 3rd, and 4th clutches receive oil from their feed pipes.

Diagnosis Tests

CONTROL PRESSURE TEST

Control pressure tests should be performed whenever slippage, delay or harshness is felt in the shifting of the automatic transaxle. These tests can pinpoint the differences between mechanical and hydraulic failures within the transaxle. Before making any tests be sure that the transaxle is full of fluid, the engine is in tune, the transaxle is up to operating temperature and that all external linkage is adjusted properly.

Line Pressure Test

1. Raise the vehicle and support it safely.
2. Install the gauge set to the proper transaxle pressure test ports.
3. Start the engine and run at 2000 rpm.
4. With the selector lever in **N** or **P** the specification should be 114–121 psi.
5. The specification should be 114–121 psi for the rest of the gear selections.
6. When reinstalling the pressure port plugs, do not reuse the aluminum washers.

Throttle Pressure Test

1. Raise the vehicle and support it safely.
2. Install the gauge set to the proper transaxle pressure test ports.
3. Start the engine and run at 1000 rpm. Disconnect the throttle control cable at the throttle lever.
4. Read the pressure with the lever released it should be 0.
5. The specification should be 73–75 psi for carbureted vehicles and 121–128 for fuel injected vehicles.
6. When reinstalling the pressure port plugs, do not reuse the aluminum washers.

Governor Pressure Test

1. Raise the vehicle and support it safely.
2. Install the gauge set to the proper transaxle pressure test ports.
3. Start the engine and run the vehicle at a speed of 38 mph.
4. With the selector lever in **D3** record the pressure reading.
5. The specification should be 30–31 psi.

6. When reinstalling the pressure port plugs, do not reuse the aluminum washers.

Stall Speed Test

1. Raise the vehicle and support it safely.
2. Connect an engine tachometer and start the engine.
3. Once the engine has reached normal operating temperature, position the selection lever in **D3**.
4. Fully depress the accelerator pedal for 6–8 seconds and note the engine speed.

NOTE: To prevent damage to the automatic transaxle, do not test stall speed for more than 10 seconds at a time.

5. Allow 2 minutes for the transaxle to cool and then repeat the test in **D4**, **2** and **R**.
6. All stall speed readings must be the same in all selector positions. The specification should be 2750 rpm for all transaxles except the L5–4 and K4–4. On these transaxles the specification should be 2600 rpm.

ROAD TEST

1. Road test using all selective ranges, noting when discrepancies in operation or oil pressure occur.
2. Attempt to isolate the unit or circuit involved in the malfunction.
3. If engine performance indicates an engine tune-up is required, this should be performed before road testing is completed or transaxle correction attemped. Poor engine performance can result in rough shifting or other malfunctions.

Electrical Control System

SELF DIAGNOSIS

The automatic transaxle control unit has an built in, self diagnosis. The S3 indicator light in the gauge asembly and the LED on the control unit blink when the control unit senses a problem in the system. The number of blinks from the LED display varies according to the problem, which can be diagnosed by counting the number of LED blinks. The control unit is located under the carpeting and access panel in the passengers side footwell.

When the ignition is turned on, the S3 indicator will come on for 2 seconds, this is a light test to make sure it is working. The indicator will also light when the selector is in the S3 position.

If there is a system fault, the S3 indicator will come on and continue to blink until the ignition key is turned off. When the ignition is turned back on, the light will not come on again for the original problem. But if the control unit senses the fault with the ignition switch on, the S3 indicator will flash again. To be sure of the fact that a problem exists, check the LED display on the control unit, it will blink continuously when a problem exists.

For trouble diagnosis, count the number of flashes from the LED display and compare them to the diagnostic chart.

Since the LED problem code is retained in memory, it will blink again whenever the ignition is turned on. If the LED problem code is not stored in memory, check the EFI ECU fuse No. 35 in the underhood relay box. If the fuse is good, check for an open circuit in the automatic transaxle control unit B12 terminal.

After making any repairs to the system, disconnect the No. 35 fuse to reset the LED memory.

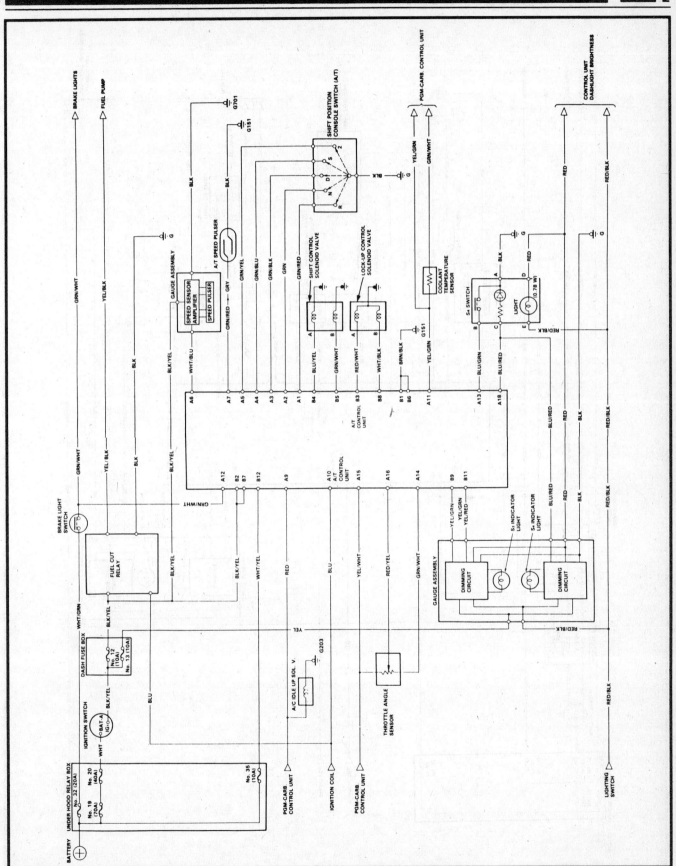

Electrical circuit diagram for carbureted engines—L5–4 and K4–4 transaxles

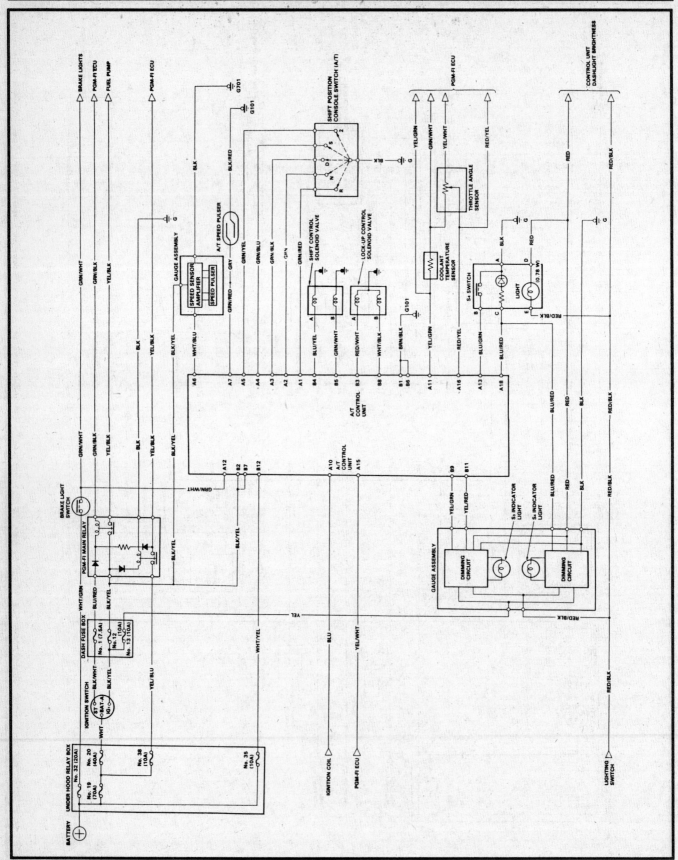

Electrical circuit diagram for fuel injected engines — L5–4 and K4–4 transaxles

INDICATOR DIAGNOSIS

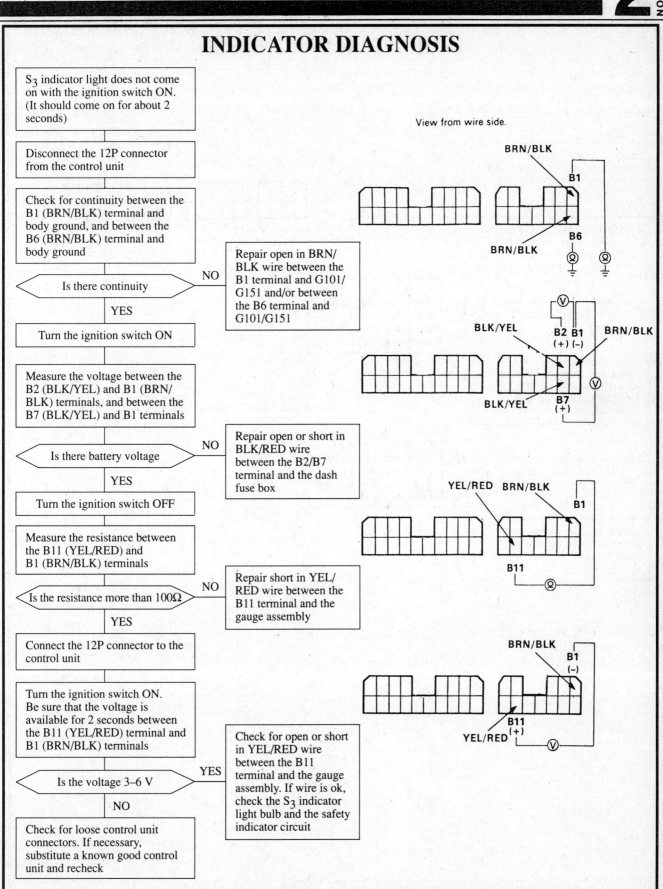

S3 indicator light does not come on with the ignition switch ON. (It should come on for about 2 seconds)

↓

Disconnect the 12P connector from the control unit

↓

Check for continuity between the B1 (BRN/BLK) terminal and body ground, and between the B6 (BRN/BLK) terminal and body ground

↓

Is there continuity — NO → Repair open in BRN/BLK wire between the B1 terminal and G101/G151 and/or between the B6 terminal and G101/G151

YES

↓

Turn the ignition switch ON

↓

Measure the voltage between the B2 (BLK/YEL) and B1 (BRN/BLK) terminals, and between the B7 (BLK/YEL) and B1 terminals

↓

Is there battery voltage — NO → Repair open or short in BLK/RED wire between the B2/B7 terminal and the dash fuse box

YES

↓

Turn the ignition switch OFF

↓

Measure the resistance between the B11 (YEL/RED) and B1 (BRN/BLK) terminals

↓

Is the resistance more than 100Ω — NO → Repair short in YEL/RED wire between the B11 terminal and the gauge assembly

YES

↓

Connect the 12P connector to the control unit

↓

Turn the ignition switch ON. Be sure that the voltage is available for 2 seconds between the B11 (YEL/RED) terminal and B1 (BRN/BLK) terminals

↓

Is the voltage 3–6 V — YES → Check for open or short in YEL/RED wire between the B11 terminal and the gauge assembly. If wire is ok, check the S3 indicator light bulb and the safety indicator circuit

NO

↓

Check for loose control unit connectors. If necessary, substitute a known good control unit and recheck

View from wire side.

BRN/BLK

B1

B6

BRN/BLK

BLK/YEL   B2 B1   BRN/BLK
           (+) (−)

BLK/YEL   B7
           (+)

YEL/RED BRN/BLK

B1

B11

BRN/BLK

B1
(−)

B11
YEL/RED (+)

INDICATOR DIAGNOSIS

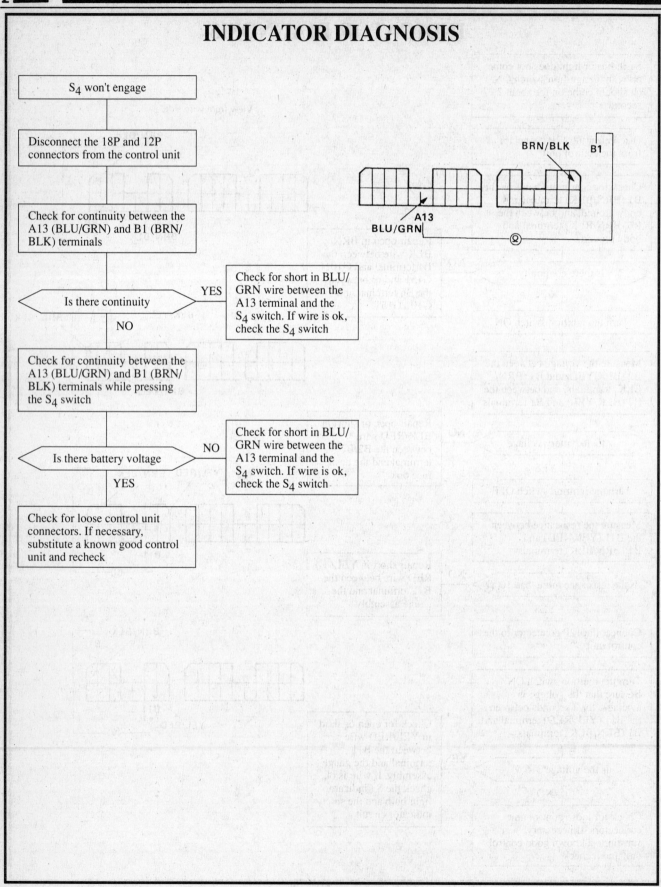

2ND GEAR SHIFT DIAGNOSIS

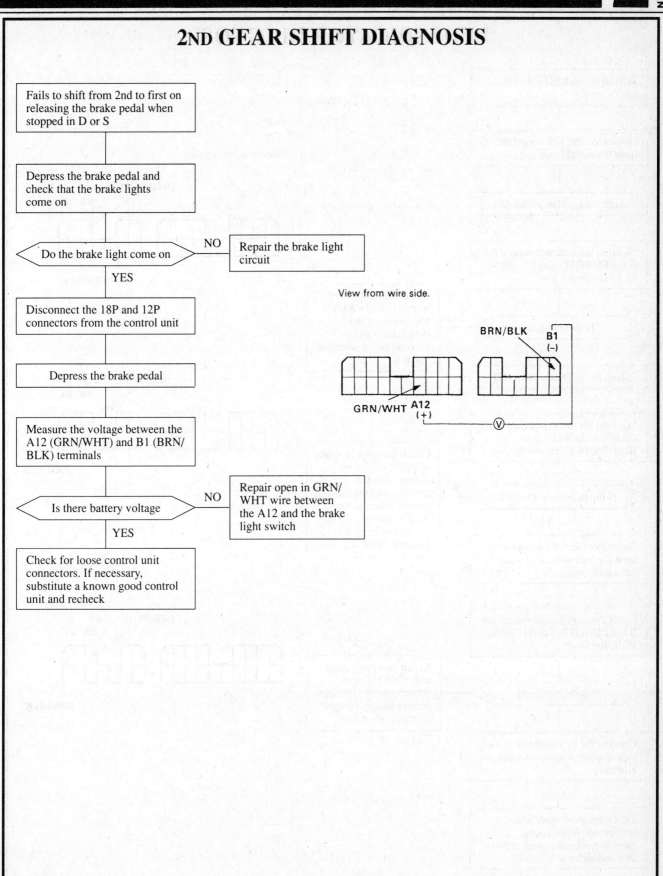

View from wire side.

2-17

LED INDICATOR DIAGNOSIS

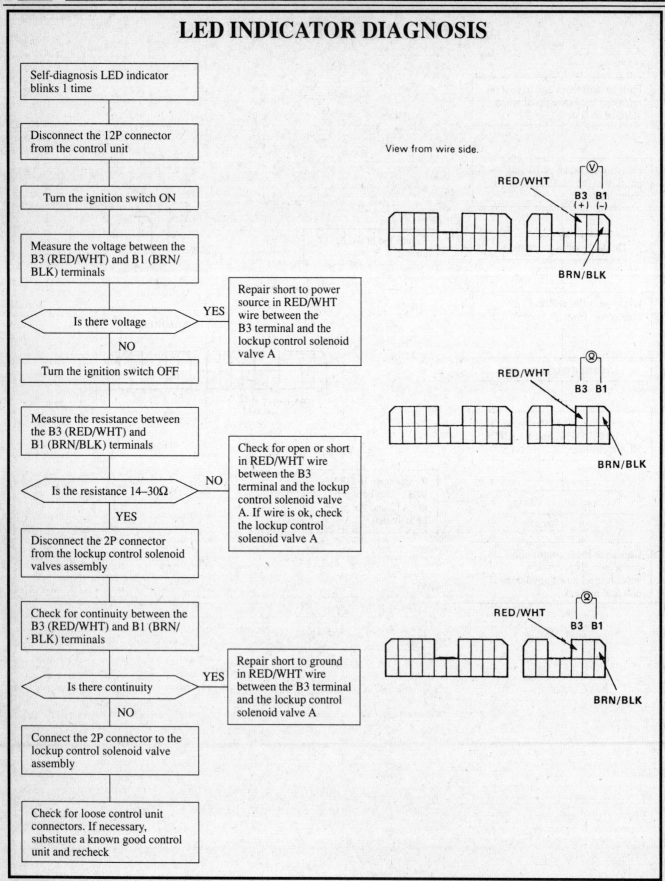

Self-diagnosis LED indicator blinks 1 time

Disconnect the 12P connector from the control unit

Turn the ignition switch ON

Measure the voltage between the B3 (RED/WHT) and B1 (BRN/BLK) terminals

Is there voltage — YES → Repair short to power source in RED/WHT wire between the B3 terminal and the lockup control solenoid valve A

NO

Turn the ignition switch OFF

Measure the resistance between the B3 (RED/WHT) and B1 (BRN/BLK) terminals

Is the resistance 14–30Ω — NO → Check for open or short in RED/WHT wire between the B3 terminal and the lockup control solenoid valve A. If wire is ok, check the lockup control solenoid valve A

YES

Disconnect the 2P connector from the lockup control solenoid valves assembly

Check for continuity between the B3 (RED/WHT) and B1 (BRN/BLK) terminals

Is there continuity — YES → Repair short to ground in RED/WHT wire between the B3 terminal and the lockup control solenoid valve A

NO

Connect the 2P connector to the lockup control solenoid valve assembly

Check for loose control unit connectors. If necessary, substitute a known good control unit and recheck

View from wire side.

RED/WHT
B3 B1
(+) (−)
BRN/BLK

RED/WHT
B3 B1
BRN/BLK

RED/WHT
B3 B1
BRN/BLK

LED INDICATOR DIAGNOSIS

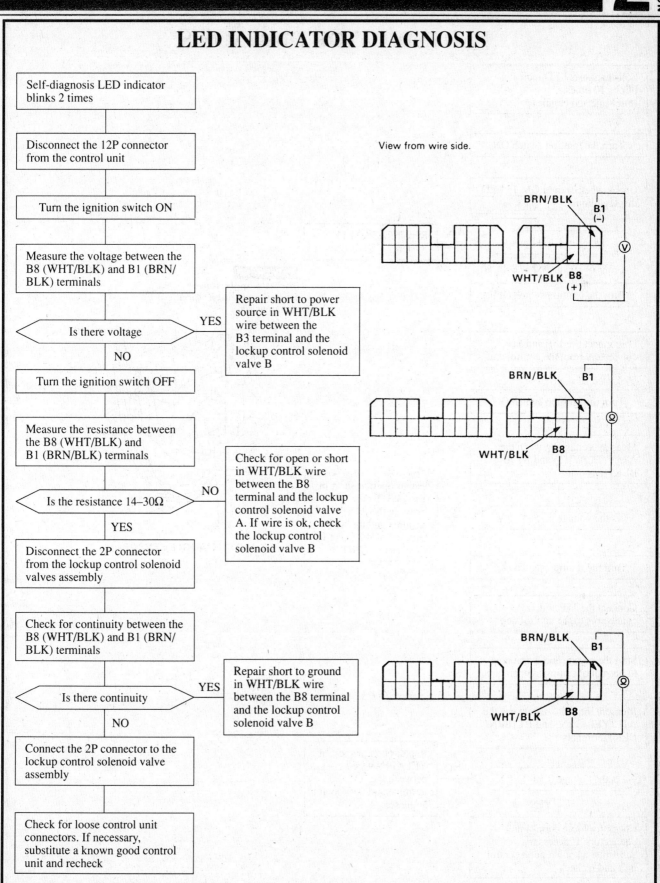

Self-diagnosis LED indicator blinks 2 times

↓

Disconnect the 12P connector from the control unit

↓

Turn the ignition switch ON

↓

Measure the voltage between the B8 (WHT/BLK) and B1 (BRN/BLK) terminals

↓

Is there voltage — YES → Repair short to power source in WHT/BLK wire between the B3 terminal and the lockup control solenoid valve B

NO

↓

Turn the ignition switch OFF

↓

Measure the resistance between the B8 (WHT/BLK) and B1 (BRN/BLK) terminals

↓

Is the resistance 14–30Ω — NO → Check for open or short in WHT/BLK wire between the B8 terminal and the lockup control solenoid valve A. If wire is ok, check the lockup control solenoid valve B

YES

↓

Disconnect the 2P connector from the lockup control solenoid valves assembly

↓

Check for continuity between the B8 (WHT/BLK) and B1 (BRN/BLK) terminals

↓

Is there continuity — YES → Repair short to ground in WHT/BLK wire between the B8 terminal and the lockup control solenoid valve B

NO

↓

Connect the 2P connector to the lockup control solenoid valve assembly

↓

Check for loose control unit connectors. If necessary, substitute a known good control unit and recheck

View from wire side.

BRN/BLK — B1 (−)

WHT/BLK — B8 (+)

BRN/BLK — B1

WHT/BLK — B8

BRN/BLK — B1

WHT/BLK — B8

LED INDICATOR DIAGNOSIS

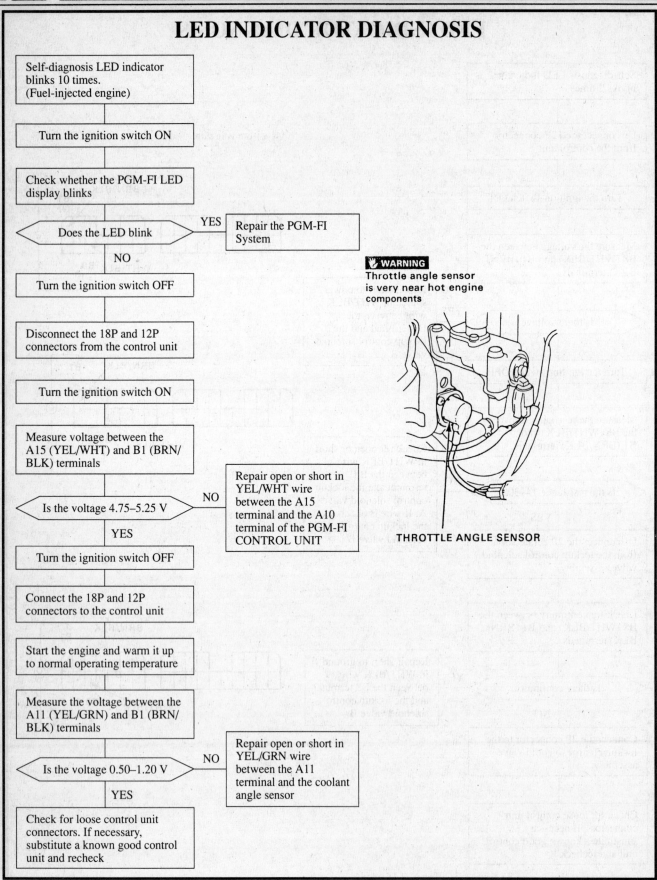

Self-diagnosis LED indicator blinks 10 times. (Fuel-injected engine)

Turn the ignition switch ON

Check whether the PGM-FI LED display blinks

Does the LED blink — **YES** → Repair the PGM-FI System

NO

Turn the ignition switch OFF

Disconnect the 18P and 12P connectors from the control unit

Turn the ignition switch ON

Measure voltage between the A15 (YEL/WHT) and B1 (BRN/BLK) terminals

Is the voltage 4.75–5.25 V — **NO** → Repair open or short in YEL/WHT wire between the A15 terminal and the A10 terminal of the PGM-FI CONTROL UNIT

YES

Turn the ignition switch OFF

Connect the 18P and 12P connectors to the control unit

Start the engine and warm it up to normal operating temperature

Measure the voltage between the A11 (YEL/GRN) and B1 (BRN/BLK) terminals

Is the voltage 0.50–1.20 V — **NO** → Repair open or short in YEL/GRN wire between the A11 terminal and the coolant angle sensor

YES

Check for loose control unit connectors. If necessary, substitute a known good control unit and recheck

⚠ WARNING
Throttle angle sensor is very near hot engine components

THROTTLE ANGLE SENSOR

LED INDICATOR DIAGNOSIS /CONT.

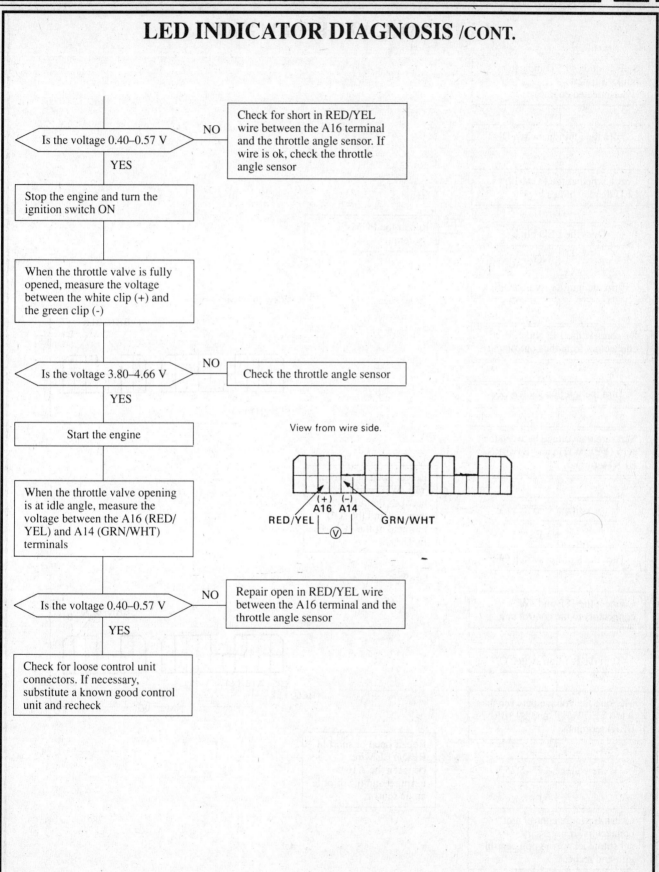

Is the voltage 0.40–0.57 V — **NO** → Check for short in RED/YEL wire between the A16 terminal and the throttle angle sensor. If wire is ok, check the throttle angle sensor

YES

Stop the engine and turn the ignition switch ON

When the throttle valve is fully opened, measure the voltage between the white clip (+) and the green clip (-)

Is the voltage 3.80–4.66 V — **NO** → Check the throttle angle sensor

YES

Start the engine

View from wire side.

(+) (-)
A16 A14
RED/YEL   GRN/WHT
Ⓥ

When the throttle valve opening is at idle angle, measure the voltage between the A16 (RED/YEL) and A14 (GRN/WHT) terminals

Is the voltage 0.40–0.57 V — **NO** → Repair open in RED/YEL wire between the A16 terminal and the throttle angle sensor

YES

Check for loose control unit connectors. If necessary, substitute a known good control unit and recheck

LED INDICATOR DIAGNOSIS

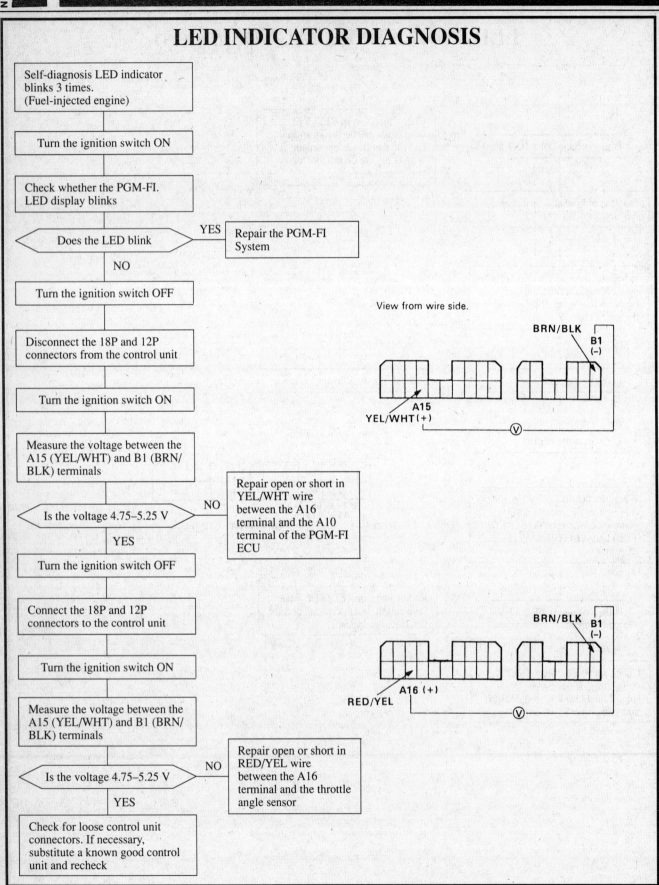

Self-diagnosis LED indicator blinks 3 times. (Fuel-injected engine)

Turn the ignition switch ON

Check whether the PGM-FI. LED display blinks

Does the LED blink — YES → Repair the PGM-FI System

NO

Turn the ignition switch OFF

Disconnect the 18P and 12P connectors from the control unit

Turn the ignition switch ON

Measure the voltage between the A15 (YEL/WHT) and B1 (BRN/BLK) terminals

Is the voltage 4.75–5.25 V — NO → Repair open or short in YEL/WHT wire between the A16 terminal and the A10 terminal of the PGM-FI ECU

YES

Turn the ignition switch OFF

Connect the 18P and 12P connectors to the control unit

Turn the ignition switch ON

Measure the voltage between the A15 (YEL/WHT) and B1 (BRN/BLK) terminals

Is the voltage 4.75–5.25 V — NO → Repair open or short in RED/YEL wire between the A16 terminal and the throttle angle sensor

YES

Check for loose control unit connectors. If necessary, substitute a known good control unit and recheck

View from wire side.

BRN/BLK
B1 (–)
A15
YEL/WHT (+)

BRN/BLK
B1 (–)
A16 (+)
RED/YEL

LED DIAGNOSIS INDICATOR

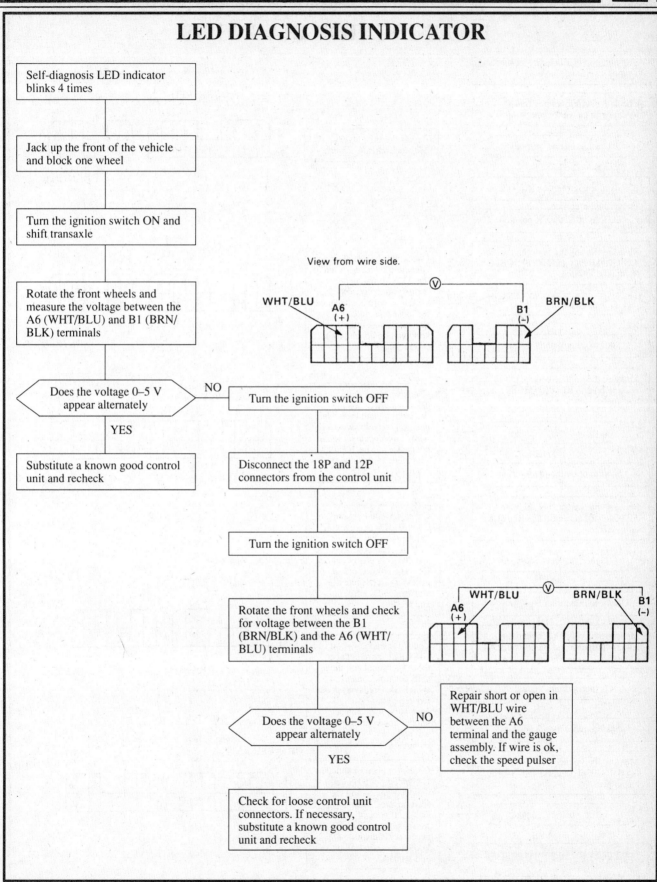

Self-diagnosis LED indicator blinks 4 times

Jack up the front of the vehicle and block one wheel

Turn the ignition switch ON and shift transaxle

Rotate the front wheels and measure the voltage between the A6 (WHT/BLU) and B1 (BRN/BLK) terminals

View from wire side.

WHT/BLU — A6 (+) — V — B1 (−) — BRN/BLK

Does the voltage 0–5 V appear alternately → NO → Turn the ignition switch OFF

YES

Substitute a known good control unit and recheck

Disconnect the 18P and 12P connectors from the control unit

Turn the ignition switch OFF

Rotate the front wheels and check for voltage between the B1 (BRN/BLK) and the A6 (WHT/BLU) terminals

A6 (+) — WHT/BLU — V — BRN/BLK — B1 (−)

Does the voltage 0–5 V appear alternately → NO → Repair short or open in WHT/BLU wire between the A6 terminal and the gauge assembly. If wire is ok, check the speed pulser

YES

Check for loose control unit connectors. If necessary, substitute a known good control unit and recheck

LED INDICATOR DIAGNOSIS

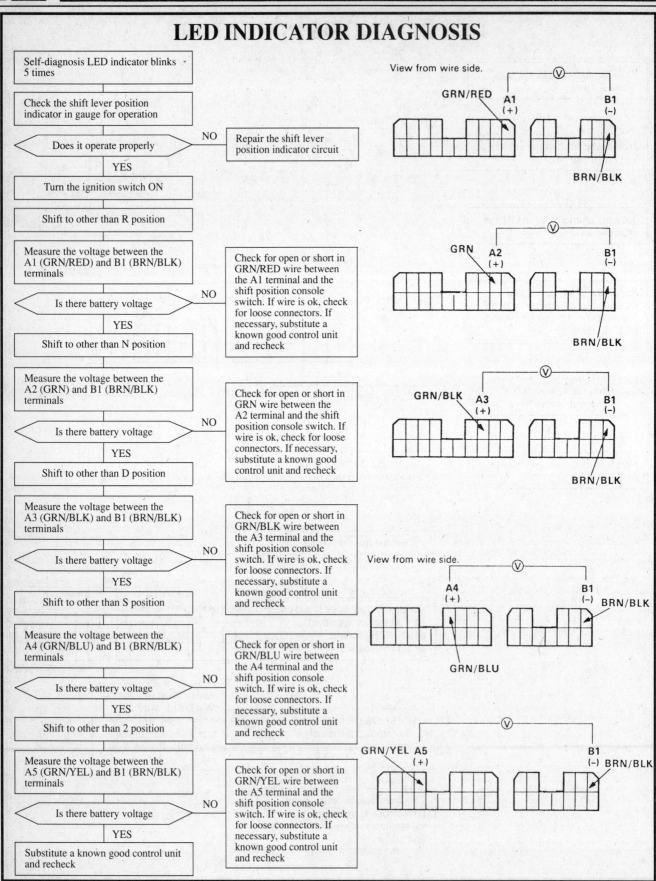

LED INDICATOR DIAGNOSIS

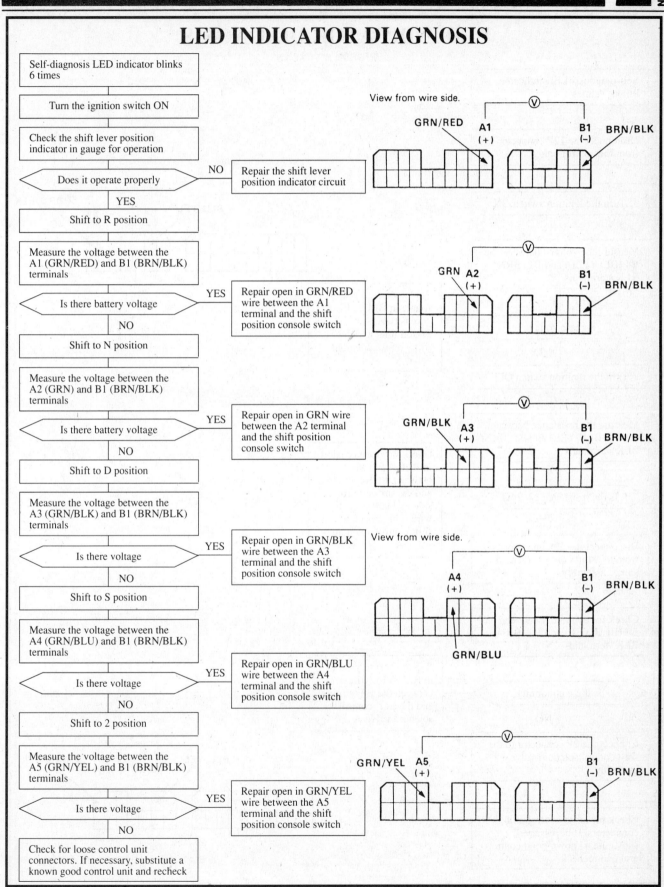

LED INDICATOR DIAGNOSIS

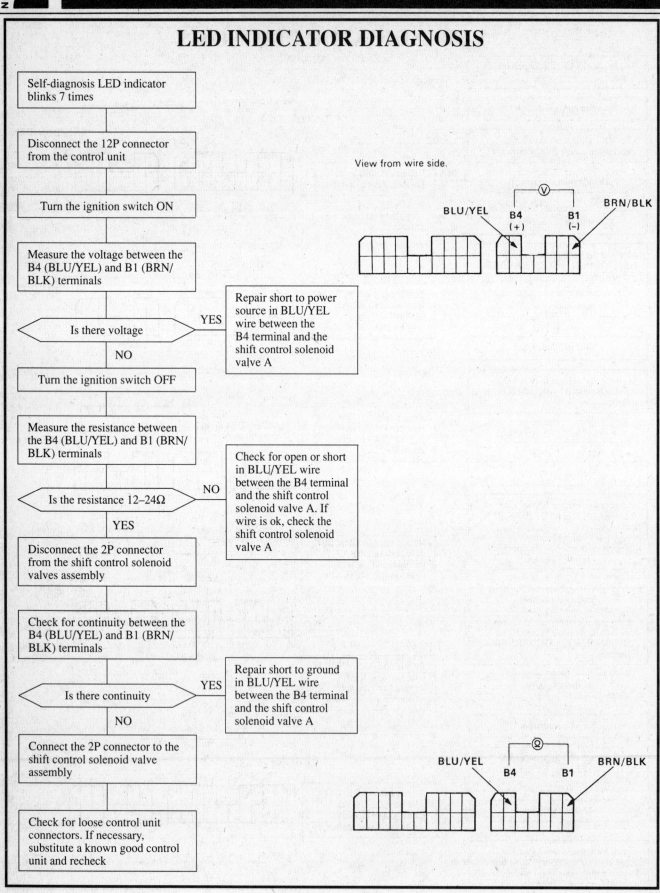

Self-diagnosis LED indicator blinks 7 times

Disconnect the 12P connector from the control unit

Turn the ignition switch ON

Measure the voltage between the B4 (BLU/YEL) and B1 (BRN/BLK) terminals

Is there voltage — YES → Repair short to power source in BLU/YEL wire between the B4 terminal and the shift control solenoid valve A

NO

Turn the ignition switch OFF

Measure the resistance between the B4 (BLU/YEL) and B1 (BRN/BLK) terminals

Is the resistance 12–24Ω — NO → Check for open or short in BLU/YEL wire between the B4 terminal and the shift control solenoid valve A. If wire is ok, check the shift control solenoid valve A

YES

Disconnect the 2P connector from the shift control solenoid valves assembly

Check for continuity between the B4 (BLU/YEL) and B1 (BRN/BLK) terminals

Is there continuity — YES → Repair short to ground in BLU/YEL wire between the B4 terminal and the shift control solenoid valve A

NO

Connect the 2P connector to the shift control solenoid valve assembly

Check for loose control unit connectors. If necessary, substitute a known good control unit and recheck

View from wire side.

BLU/YEL   B4 (+)   B1 (−)   BRN/BLK

BLU/YEL   B4   B1   BRN/BLK

LED INDICATOR DIAGNOSIS

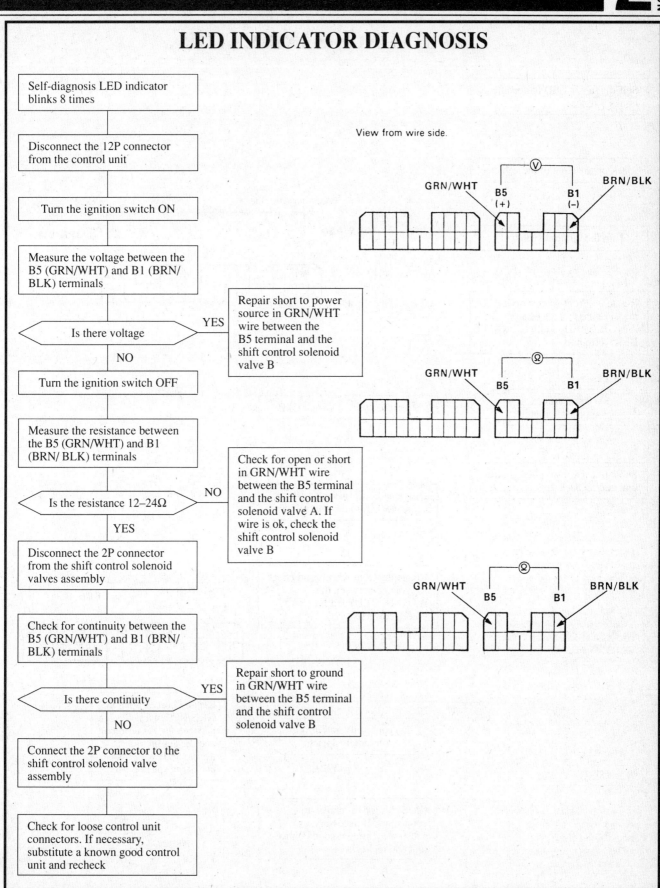

Self-diagnosis LED indicator blinks 8 times

↓

Disconnect the 12P connector from the control unit

↓

Turn the ignition switch ON

↓

Measure the voltage between the B5 (GRN/WHT) and B1 (BRN/BLK) terminals

↓

Is there voltage → **YES** → Repair short to power source in GRN/WHT wire between the B5 terminal and the shift control solenoid valve B

NO

↓

Turn the ignition switch OFF

↓

Measure the resistance between the B5 (GRN/WHT) and B1 (BRN/ BLK) terminals

↓

Is the resistance 12–24Ω → **NO** → Check for open or short in GRN/WHT wire between the B5 terminal and the shift control solenoid valve A. If wire is ok, check the shift control solenoid valve B

YES

↓

Disconnect the 2P connector from the shift control solenoid valves assembly

↓

Check for continuity between the B5 (GRN/WHT) and B1 (BRN/ BLK) terminals

↓

Is there continuity → **YES** → Repair short to ground in GRN/WHT wire between the B5 terminal and the shift control solenoid valve B

NO

↓

Connect the 2P connector to the shift control solenoid valve assembly

↓

Check for loose control unit connectors. If necessary, substitute a known good control unit and recheck

View from wire side.

GRN/WHT   B5 (+)   B1 (−)   BRN/BLK

GRN/WHT   B5   B1   BRN/BLK

GRN/WHT   B5   B1   BRN/BLK

LED DIAGNOSIS INDICATOR

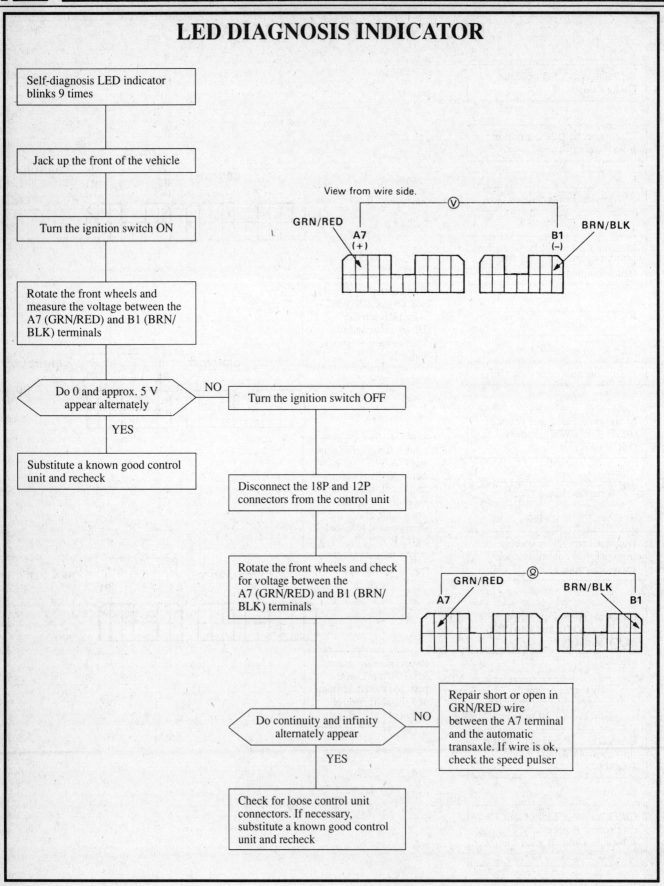

Self-diagnosis LED indicator blinks 9 times

Jack up the front of the vehicle

Turn the ignition switch ON

Rotate the front wheels and measure the voltage between the A7 (GRN/RED) and B1 (BRN/BLK) terminals

Do 0 and approx. 5 V appear alternately → NO → Turn the ignition switch OFF

YES

Substitute a known good control unit and recheck

View from wire side.
GRN/RED A7 (+) B1 (−) BRN/BLK

Disconnect the 18P and 12P connectors from the control unit

Rotate the front wheels and check for voltage between the A7 (GRN/RED) and B1 (BRN/BLK) terminals

GRN/RED A7 B1 BRN/BLK

Do continuity and infinity alternately appear → NO → Repair short or open in GRN/RED wire between the A7 terminal and the automatic transaxle. If wire is ok, check the speed pulser

YES

Check for loose control unit connectors. If necessary, substitute a known good control unit and recheck

LED INDICATOR DIAGNOSIS

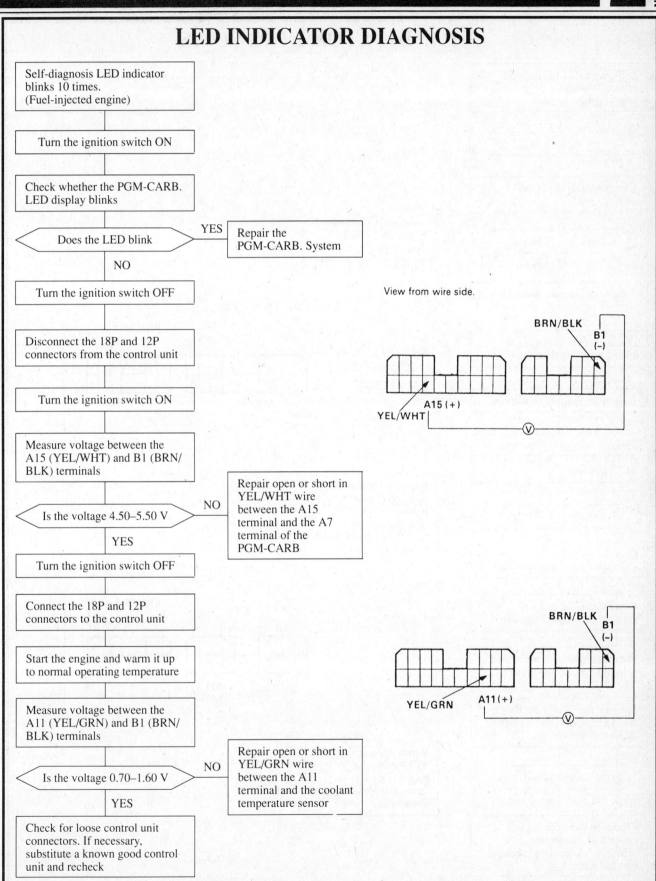

Self-diagnosis LED indicator blinks 10 times. (Fuel-injected engine)

Turn the ignition switch ON

Check whether the PGM-CARB. LED display blinks

Does the LED blink — YES → Repair the PGM-CARB. System

NO

Turn the ignition switch OFF

Disconnect the 18P and 12P connectors from the control unit

Turn the ignition switch ON

Measure voltage between the A15 (YEL/WHT) and B1 (BRN/BLK) terminals

Is the voltage 4.50–5.50 V — NO → Repair open or short in YEL/WHT wire between the A15 terminal and the A7 terminal of the PGM-CARB

YES

Turn the ignition switch OFF

Connect the 18P and 12P connectors to the control unit

Start the engine and warm it up to normal operating temperature

Measure voltage between the A11 (YEL/GRN) and B1 (BRN/BLK) terminals

Is the voltage 0.70–1.60 V — NO → Repair open or short in YEL/GRN wire between the A11 terminal and the coolant temperature sensor

YES

Check for loose control unit connectors. If necessary, substitute a known good control unit and recheck

View from wire side.

BRN/BLK
B1 (−)
A15 (+)
YEL/WHT

BRN/BLK
B1 (−)
YEL/GRN
A11 (+)

LED INDICATOR DIAGNOSIS

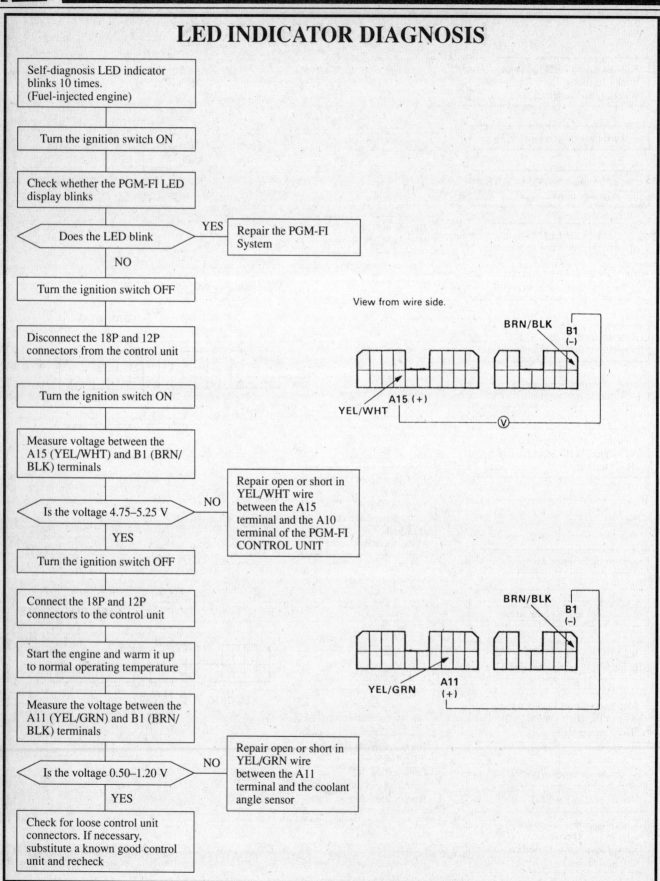

Self-diagnosis LED indicator blinks 10 times. (Fuel-injected engine)

Turn the ignition switch ON

Check whether the PGM-FI LED display blinks

Does the LED blink — YES → Repair the PGM-FI System

NO

Turn the ignition switch OFF

Disconnect the 18P and 12P connectors from the control unit

Turn the ignition switch ON

View from wire side.

BRN/BLK
B1 (−)
A15 (+)
YEL/WHT

Measure voltage between the A15 (YEL/WHT) and B1 (BRN/BLK) terminals

Is the voltage 4.75–5.25 V — NO → Repair open or short in YEL/WHT wire between the A15 terminal and the A10 terminal of the PGM-FI CONTROL UNIT

YES

Turn the ignition switch OFF

Connect the 18P and 12P connectors to the control unit

BRN/BLK
B1 (−)
YEL/GRN   A11 (+)

Start the engine and warm it up to normal operating temperature

Measure the voltage between the A11 (YEL/GRN) and B1 (BRN/BLK) terminals

Is the voltage 0.50–1.20 V — NO → Repair open or short in YEL/GRN wire between the A11 terminal and the coolant angle sensor

YES

Check for loose control unit connectors. If necessary, substitute a known good control unit and recheck

LED INDICATOR DIAGNOSIS

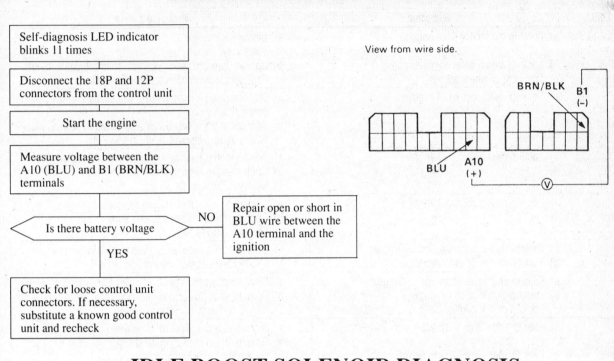

Self-diagnosis LED indicator blinks 11 times

Disconnect the 18P and 12P connectors from the control unit

Start the engine

Measure voltage between the A10 (BLU) and B1 (BRN/BLK) terminals

Is there battery voltage — NO → Repair open or short in BLU wire between the A10 terminal and the ignition

YES

Check for loose control unit connectors. If necessary, substitute a known good control unit and recheck

View from wire side.

BRN/BLK B1 (–)

BLU   A10 (+)

IDLE BOOST SOLENOID DIAGNOSIS

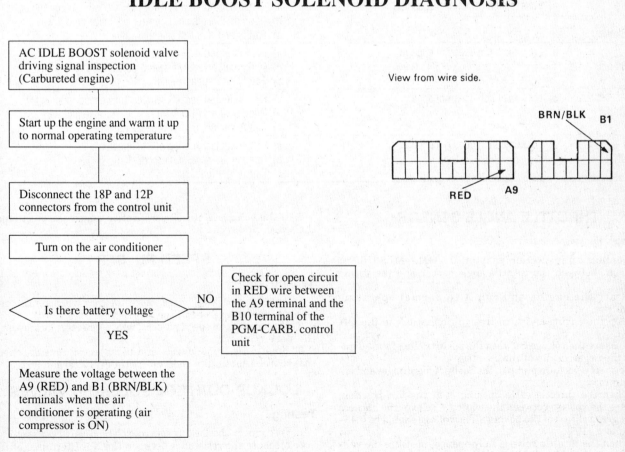

AC IDLE BOOST solenoid valve driving signal inspection (Carbureted engine)

Start up the engine and warm it up to normal operating temperature

Disconnect the 18P and 12P connectors from the control unit

Turn on the air conditioner

Is there battery voltage — NO → Check for open circuit in RED wire between the A9 terminal and the B10 terminal of the PGM-CARB. control unit

YES

Measure the voltage between the A9 (RED) and B1 (BRN/BLK) terminals when the air conditioner is operating (air compressor is ON)

View from wire side.

BRN/BLK B1

RED   A9

SELF DIAGNOSIS TEST INFORMATION

S_3 indicator light	Symptom	Probable Cause
Blinks	a) Lockup clutch does not engage b) Lockup clutch does not disengage c) Frequent engine stalling	a) Disconnected lockup control solenoid valve A connector b) Open or short in lockup control solenoid valve A wire c) Faulty lock-up control solenoid valve A
Blinks	a) Lockup clutch does not engage	a) Disconnected lockup control solenoid valve B connector b) Open or short in lockup control solenoid valve B wire c) Faulty lockup control solenoid valve B
Blinks or off	a) Lockup clutch does not engage	a) Disconnected throttle angle sensor connector b) Open short in throttle angle sensor wire c) Faulty throttle angle sensor
Blinks	a) Lockup clutch does not engage	a) Disconnected speed pulser connector b) Open or short in speed pulser wire c) Faulty speed pulser
Blinks	a) Fails to shift other than 2nd↔4th gear b) Lockup clutch does not engage	a) Short in shift position console switch wire b) Faulty shift position console switch
Off	a) Fails to shift other than 2nd↔4th gear b) Lockup clutch does not engage c) Lockup clutch engages and disengages alternately	a) Disconnected shift position console switch connector b) Open in shift position console switch wire c) Faulty shift position console switch
Blinks	a) Fails to shift other than 1st↔4th, 2nd↔4th, or 2nd↔3rd gears b) Fails to shift (stuck in 4th gear)	a) Disconnected shift control solenoid valve A connector b) Open or short in shift control solenoid valve A wire c) Faulty shift control solenoid valve A
Blinks	a) Fails to shift (stuck in 1st gear or 4th gear)	a) Disconnected shift control solenoid valve B connector b) Open or short in shift control solenoid valve B wire c) Faulty shift control solenoid valve B
Blinks	a) Lockup clutch does not engage	a) Disconnected A/T speed pulser b) Open or short in A/T speed pulser wire c) Faulty A/T speed pulser
Blinks	a) Lockup clutch does not engage	a) Disconnected coolant temperature sensor connector b) Open or short in coolant temperature sensor wire c) Faulty coolant temperature sensor
Off	a) Lockup clutch does not engage	a) Disconnected ignition coil connector b) Open or short in ignition coil wire c) Faulty ignition coil

THROTTLE ANGLE SENSOR

Testing

1. Connect an inspection adapter, 07–GMJ–ML80100 or equivalent, between the throttle angle sensor and the wiring harness.
2. Start the engine and run it to normal operating temperature.
3. Stop the engine and turn the ignition switch to the **ON** position.
4. Measure the voltage between the positive clip of the adapter and the negative clip of the adapter.
5. Connect a vacuum pump to the dashpot diaphragm and apply vacuum.
6. When the throttle valve opening is at the idle position, meassure the voltage between the white (+) clip of the harness and the green clip (-) of the harness. The voltage should be 0.48–0.52 Volts ± 10%.
7. When the throttle valve is fully opened, measure the voltage between the white clip (+) of the adapter and the green clip (-) of the adapter. The voltage should be 3.80–4.66 Volts.

8. If the voltage is out of specification adjust the position of the sensor and recheck.

SPEED PULSER

Testing

1. Apply the parking brake, block the rear wheels, raise and safely support the front of the vehicle.
2. Disconnect the speed pulser 2 wire connector, located near the starter.
3. Rotate the front wheels and using an ohmmeter, check that there is continuity then no continuity, alternately.

LOCKUP CONTROL SOLENOID VALVES

Testing

1. Disconnect the lockup control solenoid valve connector.
2. Measure the resistance between the No. 1 terminal of the solenoid valve connector and body ground. Measure the resistance between the No. 2 terminal and body ground.

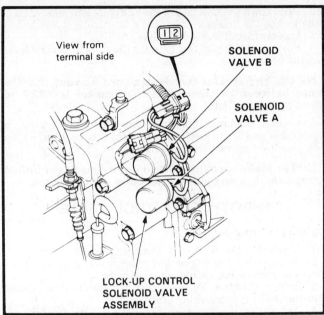

Solenoid valve location and connector identification – L5–4 and K4–4 transaxles

3. The resistance should be between 14–30 Ohms for each.
4. If the resistance is out of specification replace the solenoid valve assembly.
5. If not check for continuity between the harness and body ground. If continuity exists, replace the solenoid assembly.

SHIFT CONTROL SOLENOID VALVE

Testing

1. Disconnect the connector from the shift control solenoid valve.
2. Measure the resistance between the No.1 terminal of the solenoid valve connector and body ground. Measure the resistance between the No. 2 connector and the body ground.
3. Resistance should be 12–24 Ohms. If the resistance is out of specification, replace the shift control solenoid valve assembly.
4. Connect the No. 1 terminal of the solenoid valve connector to the battery positive terminal and the No. 2 connector to the battery positive terminal. A clicking sound should be heard each time the connection is made.
5. If no clicking sound is heard, check for continuity between the harness and body ground. If continuity exists, replace the solenoid assembly.

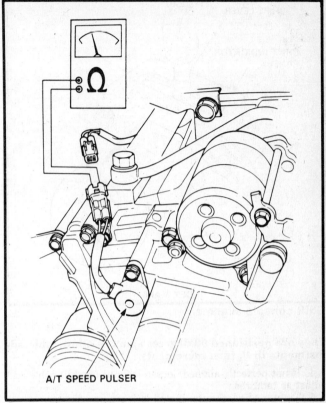

Connecting an ohmmeter to the speed pulser – L5–4 and K4–4 transaxles

Converter Clutch Operation

When the transaxle is in **D** and at speeds above 43 mph, pressurized fluid is drained from the back of the torque converter through an oil passage causing the lockup function of the torque converter to occur. As this takes place the mainshaft rotates at the same speed as the engine crankshaft.

The pressure control valve body is bolted to the top of the regulator body and includes the pressure control shift valve and pressure control timing valve. The pressure control shift valve controls the range of lockup according to vehicle speed and throttle pressure. The timing valve senses when the transaxle is in 4th gear.

The clutch pressure control valve is bolted to the top of the servo valve and prevents the lockup function from taking place when the throttle is not opened sufficiently.

ON CAR SERVICES

Adjustments

SHIFT INDICATOR

1. Check that the index mark of the indicator aligns with the **N** mark of the shift indicator panel when the transaxle is in **N**.
2. If not aligned, remove panel mounting screws and adjust by moving panel.

SHIFT CABLE

1. Remove the console assembly.
2. Shift the selector lever into the **D** detent. Remove the lock pin from the cable adjuster.
3. Check that the hole in the adjuster is in line with the hole in the shift cable.

NOTE: There are 2 holes in end of the shift cable.

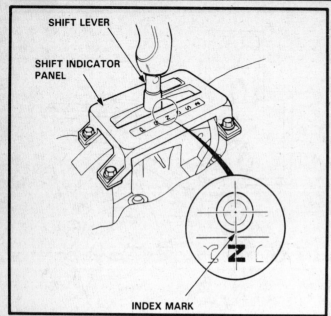

Shift console alignment

They are positioned 90 degrees apart to allow cable adjustments in ¼ turn increments.

4. If not perfectly aligned, loosen locknut on shift cable and adjust as required.

5. Tighten the locknuts. Install lock pin on adjuster.

NOTE: If the lock pin binds as it is being reinstalled, the cable is still out of adjustment and must be readjusted.

6. Start engine and check shift lever in all gears.

THROTTLE CONTROL CABLE BRACKET

1. Disconnect the throttle control cable from the throttle control lever.

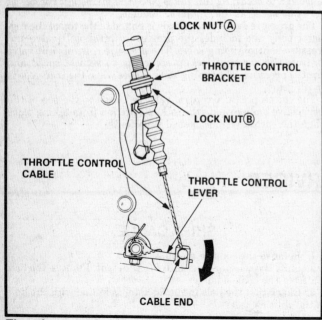

Throttle control cable adjustment points

2. Bend down the lock tabs of the lock plate and remove the 2 bolts to free the bracket.

3. Loosely install a new lock plate.

4. Position the special tool between the throttle control lever and the bracket.

NOTE: The special tool is designed so that the distance between the lever and the bracket is 3.287 in. when it is installed.

5. Position the bracket so that there is no binding between the bracket and the tool. Then tighten the 2 bolts, bend up the lock plate tabs against the bolts heads.

NOTE: Make sure the control lever doesn't get pulled toward the bracket side as the bolts are tightened.

THROTTLE CONTROL CABLE

Carbureted Engine

1. Check that the carburetor throttle cable play is correct.

2. Be sure that the engine has reached operating temperature. The electric fan should come on twice.

3. Be sure that the idle speed is within specification. Check that the choke is functioning properly.

4. Be sure that the distance between the throttle control lever and the throttle control bracket is correct.

5. With the engine off, disconnect the throttle control cable from the throttle control lever.

6. Disconnect the vacuum tube from the dash pot and connect the vacuum pump and keep vacuum applied.

7. Attach a weight of about 2.6 lbs. to the accelerator pedal. Raise the pedal, then release it, this will allow the weight to remove the normal free play from the throttle cable. Secure the cable.

8. Lay the end of the throttle control cable on the battery.

9. Adjust the distance between the throttle control cable end and the locknut to 3.3 in.

10. Insert the end of throttle control cable in the groove of the throttle control lever.

11. Insert the throttle control cable in the bracket and secure it with the locknut. Be sure that the cable is not kinked or twisted.

12. Check that the cable moves freely by depressing the accelerator.

13. Remove the weight on the accelerator pedal and push the pedal to make sure that there is the specified play at the throttle control lever.

14. Start the engine and check the synchronization between the carburetor and the throttle control cable.

NOTE: The throttle control lever should start to move as engine speed increases.

15. If the throttle control lever moves before engine speed increases, turn the cable locknut counterclockwise and re-tighten the other locknut.

16. If the throttle control lever moves after engine speed increases, turn the lock nut clockwise and re-tighten the other locknut.

Fuel Injected Engine

1. Loosen the locknuts on the throttle control cable.

2. Press down on the throttle control lever until it stops.

3. While pressing down on the throttle control lever, pull on the throttle control link to check the amount of throttle control cable free play.

4. Remove all of the throttle control cable free play by turning the top locknut until no movement can be felt in the throttle link.

5. While continuing to press down on the throttle control le-

ver, pull open the throttle link. The control lever should begin to move at precisely the same time as the link.

6. Press the accelerator to the floor, while depressed, check that there is play in the throttle control lever.

Services
FLUID CHANGE

The conditions under which the vehicle is operated is the main consideration in determining how often the transaxle fluid should be changed. Different driving conditions result in different transaxle fluid temperatures. These temperatures affect change intervals.

If the vehicle is driven under severe conditions, change the transaxle fluid every 15,000 miles. If the vehicle is not used under severe conditions, change the fluid and replace the filter every 30,000 miles.

Do not overfill the transaxle. It takes about a pint of automatic transaxle fluid to raise the level from the **ADD** to the **FULL** mark on the indicator dipstick. Overfilling the unit can cause damage to the internal components of the automatic transaxle.

1. Raise the vehicle and support safely.
2. Remove the transaxle drain plug and allow the fluid to drain into a waste container. Remove the dipstick to aid in the draining.
3. When the fluid draining is complete, install the drain plug and tighten securely.
4. Fill with new fluid through the dipstick opening.

NOTE: The fluid refill may be less because of the fluid remaining in the units and the recesses of the case.

SPEED PULSER

Removal and Installation

1. Disconnect the negative battery cable. Disconnect the electrical connector from the speed pulser.
2. Remove the bolt retaining the speed pulser.
3. Pull the speed pulser assembly out of the converter cover.
4. Use a new O-ring on the pulser assembly and install it in the converter cover.
5. Tighten the mounting bolt to 9 ft. lbs. and connect the electrical lead.

LOCKUP CONTROL SOLENOIDS

Removal and Installation

1. Disconnect the negative battery cable. Disconnect the electrical lead from the solenoid assembly.
2. Remove the 4 mounting bolts from the assembly.

NOTE: The lockup control solenoids A and B must be replaced as an assembly.

3. Remove the lockup control solenoid assembly from the transaxle case.
4. Remove the old gasket. Clean the mounting surface and the oil passages.
5. Install a new gasket and install the solenoid assembly in position. Tighten the mountng bolts to 9 ft. lbs.
6. Reconnect the electrical leads.

REMOVAL AND INSTALLATION

TRANSAXLE REMOVAL

CIVIC

1. Disconnect the negative battery cable.
2. Position the selector lever in the **N** detent.
3. Disconnect the battery cable from the starter. Disconnect the transaxle ground cable.
4. Disconnect and plug the transaxle oil cooler lines at the transaxle.
5. Remove the 2 starter mounting bolts. Remove the top 3 transaxle mounting bolts.
6. Loosen the front wheel nuts. Raise the vehicle and support it safely.
7. Drain the transaxle and reinstall the drain plug.
8. Remove the throttle control cable.
9. Remove the cable clip and then pull the speedometer cable out of the holder.
10. Do not remove the holder or the speedometer gear will fall into the transaxle housing.
11. Remove the engine and wheel splash shields from the front end of the frame.
12. Remove the exhaust header pipe.
13. Disconnect the right and left lower arm ball joints and tie rod end ball joints using the ball joint remover.

NOTE: Make sure a floor jack is positioned securely under the lower control arm, at the ball joint. Otherwise torsion bar tension on the lower control arm may cause the arm to jump suddenly away from the steering knuckle as the ball joint is being removed.

14. Turn the right steering knuckle outward as far as it will go. Position a suitable tool against the inboard CV-joint, pry right axle out of the transaxle housing approximately ½ in. (to force its spring clip out of groove inside differential gear splines), then pull it out the rest of the way. Repeat on opposite side.
15. Attach a chain hoist to the bolt near the distributor, then lift the engine slightly to unload the mounts.
16. Raise a transmission jack or equivalent and secure it against the transaxle assembly.
17. Remove the bolts from the front transaxle mount.
18. Remove the transaxle housing bolts from the engine torque bracket.
19. Remove the torque converter housing bolts from the rear transaxle mount.
20. Remove the torque converter cover plate.
21. Remove the drive plate bolts.
22. Remove the cotter pin from the shift cable control pin, then pull out the control pin.
23. Remove the cable holder and carefully remove the shift cable.

NOTE: Be careful not to lose the shift cable bushing.

24. Remove the remaining transaxle mounting bolt from the engine side.
25. Pull the transaxle away from the engine to clear the dowel pins, then lower the jack.
26. Remove torque converter from the transaxle.

ALL EXCEPT CIVIC

1. Disconnect the negative battery cable.
2. Position the selector lever in the **N** detent.
3. Disconnect the battery cable from the starter. Disconnect the wire from the solenoid.

4. Disconnect and plug the transaxle oil cooler lines at the transaxle.

5. Remove the starter mounting bolt on the transaxle side and the top transaxle mounting bolt.

6. Loosen the front wheel nut. Raise the vehicle and support it safely.

7. Drain the transaxle. Reinstall the transaxle drain plug.

8. Remove the throttle control cable.

9. On some vehicles it may be necessary to remove the right front wheel well fender shield.

10. If the vehicle is not equipped with power steering, remove the cable clip and pull the speedometer cable out of the housing. Do no remove the holder because the speedometer gear may fall into the transaxle housing.

11. If the vehicle is equipped with power steering, remove the speed sensor along with the speedometer cable and hoses.

12. Remove the transaxle-side starter motor mounting bolt and upper transaxle mounting bolts.

13. Place transmission jack securely beneath transaxle and hook hanger plate with hoist; make sure hoist chain is tight.

14. Remove subframe center beam.

15. Remove the ball joint pinch bolt from the right side lower control arm, then use a lead or brass hammer to tap the control arm free of the knuckle.

16. Remove the right side radius rod.

17. Disconnect the stabilizer bar at the right side lower control arm.

18. Detach stabilizer spring from radius rods.

19. Remove front self-locking nuts from radius rods on each side.

20. Remove lower arm bolt from both sides of sub frame.

21. Turn right side steering knuckle to its most outboard position. Pry CV-joint out approximately ½ in., then pull CV-joint out of transaxle housing.

NOTE: Do not pull on the driveshaft or knuckle since this may cause the inboard CV-joint to separate; pull on the inboard CV-joint.

22. Remove engine-side starter motor bolt. Detach starter motor and lower through chassis.

23. Remove the transaxle damper bracket located in front of torque converter cover plate.

24. Remove torque converter cover plate.

25. Disconnect the shift cable from transaxle.

26. Wire the shift cable away from the transaxle assembly.

27. Remove both bolts and pull shift cable out of housing.

28. Unbolt torque converter assembly from drive plate by removing the 8 bolts.

29. Remove the rear engine mounting bolts from the transaxle housing. Remove the rear engine mount.

30. Remove the lower transaxle mounting bolts.

31. Pull the transaxle assembly away from the engine in order to clear the dowel pins.

32. Pry the left side CV-joint out about ½ in. Pull the transaxle out and lower the assembly on the transmission jack.

33. Remove the torque converter assembly from the transaxle.

TRANSAXLE INSTALLATION

CIVIC

1. Slide the torque converter onto mainshaft.

2. Position the transaxle on the transmission jack and raise to engine level.

3. Check that the dowel pins are installed in torque converter housing.

4. Align the dowel pins with holes in block; align the torque converter bolt heads with holes in drive plates.

5. Insert left axle (with new spring clip on the end) into differential as the transaxle moves up to the engine.

NOTE: New 26mm spring clips must be used on both axles.

6. Secure the transaxle-to-engine with the engine side mounting bolt and torque to 50 ft. lbs.

7. Attach the torque converter to drive plate with the retaining bolts and torque to 9 ft. lbs. Rotate crank as necessary to tighten bolts to ½ of the torque specification, then to final torque, in a criss-cross pattern. Check for free rotation after tightening last bolt.

8. Install the shift cable.

9. Remove the transmission jack.

10. Install the torque converter cover plate.

11. Install the rear transaxle mount and torque its bolts to 47 ft. lbs.

12. Install the engine torque bracket and torque the retaining bolts to 33 ft. lbs.

13. Loosely install the front transaxle mounting bolts.

14. Install the starter mounting bolts and torque to 33 ft. lbs.

15. Install a new 26mm spring clip on end of each axle.

16. Turn right steering knuckle fully outward, and slide axle into differential until you feel its spring clip engage side gear. Repeat on left side or, if left axle is already in, check to be sure spring clip has engaged side gear.

17. Reconnect the lower arm ball joints and torque to 33 ft. lbs.

18. Reconnect the tie rod end ball joints and torque to 33 ft. lbs.

19. Install the splash shields and exhaust header pipe.

20. Install the front wheels. Lower the vehicle.

21. Remove the chain hoist.

22. Insert the speedometer cable into the gear holder and secure it with the clip. Install the boot.

23. Install the top transaxle mounting bolts. Torque to 42 ft. lbs.

24. Connect the transaxle oil cooler lines.

25. Attach the shift control cable to the shift lever with the retaining pin and clip. Install the center console as required.

26. Connect all electrical wiring.

27. Connect the negative battery cable. Fill the transaxle with the proper grade and type automatic transmission fluid.

28. Start the engine and check for proper shift cable adjustment. Adjust the cable as required.

29. Install and set the throttle control cable as required.

30. Road test the vehicle and check for leaks.

ALL EXCEPT CIVIC

1. Attach the shift cable to the shift arm with the retaining pin. Secure the cable to the edge of the transaxle housing with the cable holder and bolt. Torque the bolt to 9 ft. lbs.

2. Install torque converter on the transaxle.

3. Place the transaxle on transmission jack and raise to engine level.

4. Hook hanger plate with hoist and make hoist chain tight.

5. Check that the dowel pins are installed in the transaxle housing.

6. Install new 26mm spring clips on the end of each axle.

7. Align dowel pins with holes in block; align torque converter bolt head with holes in drive plate.

8. Fit the left axle into the differential as the transaxle moves up to the engine.

9. Secure the transaxle-to-engine with the lower mounting bolts.

10. Install rear and front engine mounts on the transaxle housing, torque to 28 ft. lbs.

11. Install the front transaxle mount bolts and torque them to 28 ft. lbs.

12. Attach torque converter to drive plate with the retaining bolts and torque to 9 ft. lbs. Rotate crank as necessary to tighten bolts to ½ of the torque specification, then to the final torque, in a crisscross pattern. Check for free rotation after tightening the last bolts.

13. Remove the transmission jack.

14. Install torque converter cover plate, torque the bolts (in oil pan flange). Torque bolts to 9 ft. lbs.

15. Install damper bracket, torque nuts to 40 ft. lbs. and bolts to 22 ft. lbs.

16. Remove the hoist from the transaxle assembly.

17. Install the starter mount bolts and torque them to 33 ft. lbs.

18. Install the rear torque rod and bracket.

19. Turn right steering knuckle fully outward and slide axle into differential until you feel its spring clip is engaged in its side gear.

20. Reconnect ball joint to knuckle, then torque its bolt to 32 ft. lbs.

21. Install the speedometer cable. Align the tab on the cable end with the slot in the holder. Install the clip so the bent leg is on the groove. After installation pull the cable to be sure that its secure.

22. Install the front tires and wheels. Lower the vehicle to the ground.

23. Install the transaxle side starter mounting bolts. Torque to 33 ft. lbs. Install the top transaxle mounting bolt and torque to 33 ft. lbs.

24. Connect the transaxle oil cooler lines to the transaxle assembly.

25. Connect all necessary wiring and electrical connectors.

26. Connect the negative battery cable. Fill the transaxle with the proper grade and type automatic transmission fluid.

27. Install and connect the shift cable. Install the console assembly as required.

28. Start the engine and shift the transaxle through all the gears. If the shift cable is out of adjustment correct it.

29. Install the throttle cable and adjust it as required. Road test the vehicle.

BENCH OVERHAUL

Before Disassembly

Cleanliness is an important factor in the overhaul of the automatic transaxle. Before opening up this unit, the entire outside of the transaxle assembly should be cleaned, preferable with a high pressure washer such as a car wash spray unit. Dirt entering the transaxle internal parts will negate all the time and effort spent on the overhaul. During inspection and reassembly all parts should be thoroughly cleaned with solvent then dried with compressed air. Wiping cloths and rags should not be used to dry parts since lint will find its way into the valve body passages.

Wheel bearing grease, long used to hold thrust washers and lube parts, should not be used. Lube seals with clean transaxle fluid and use ordinary unmedicated petroleum jelly to hold the thrust washers and to ease the assembly of seals, since it will not leave a harmful residue as grease often will. Do not use solvent on neoprene seals, friction plates if they are to be reused, or thrust washers. Be wary of nylon parts if the transaxle failure was due to failure of the cooling system. Nylon parts exposed to water or antifreeze solutions can swell and distort and must be replaced.

Before installing bolts into aluminum parts, always dip the threads into clean transaxle fluid. Antiseize compound can also be used to prevent bolts from galling the aluminum and seizing. Always use a torque wrench to keep from stripping the threads. Take care when installing new O-rings, especially the smaller O-rings. The internal snaprings should be expanded and the external rings should be compressed, if they are to be reused. This will help insure proper seating when installed.

Transaxle Disassembly
CONVERTER

Removal

1. Place the transaxle in a suitable holding fixture.

2. Using converter removal handles, remove the converter by pulling it up.

3. Remove the O-ring from the input shaft.

TRANSAXLE HOUSING

Removal

1. Remove the transaxle dipstick. Remove the end cover retaining bolts. Remove the end cover.

2. Shift the transaxle into the **P** position. Lock the mainshaft in place by using the mainshaft holder.

3. Remove the end cover gasket, dowel pins and O-rings.

4. Pry the staked edge of the locknut flange out of the notch in the 1st clutch.

5. Remove the mainshaft locknut. Be careful as the mainshaft locknut is left hand threaded.

6. Remove the 1st clutch assembly. Remove the thrust washer, needle bearing and the 1st gear from the transaxle.

7. Remove the needle bearing and the thrust washer from the mainshaft.

8. Pry the staked edge of the locknut out of the notch in the parking gear. Remove the counter shaft locknut and the parking pawl stop pin.

9. Remove the parking pawl, shaft and spring from the transaxle case.

10. Remove the parking gear and 1st gear countershaft as a complete unit.

11. From the countershaft, remove the needle bearing and the 1st gear collar. From the mainshaft, remove the O-ring and the 1st gear collar.

12. Remove the reverse idler bearing holder.

13. Bend down the tab on the lock plate which is under the parking shift arm bolt. Remove the bolt. Remove the parking shift arm spring.

14. Bend down the tab on the throttle control lever bolt lock plate, then remove the bolt. Remove the throttle control lever and spring from throttle valve shaft.

15. Remove the retaining bolts.

NOTE: Retaining bolt number one will not come all the way out of the transaxle housing because the throttle control cable bracket is in the way. Just unscrew the bracket so that it is free of the threads in the converter housing and leave it in place. If the bracket is removed, it will have to be readjusted it upon installation.

16. Align the control shaft spring pin with the cutout in the transaxle housing.

17. Install the transaxle housing puller. Screw in the puller and separate the transaxle housing from the rest of the transaxle assembly.

18. Remove the puller from the transaxle housing.

MAINSHAFT AND COUNTERSHAFT

Removal

1. Remove the gasket and the dowel pins. Remove the reverse gear collar and the needle bearing.
2. Bend down the tab on the lock plate and remove the bolt from the reverse shift fork. Remove the reverse shift fork.
3. Remove the selector hub, countershaft fourth gear and the needle bearing.
4. Remove the mainshaft and the countershaft assembly together.

GOVERNOR

Removal

1. Bend down the lock tabs on the lock plate.
2. Remove the retaining bolts holding the governor assembly to the torque converter housing.
3. Remove the governor assembly.

MAIN VALVE BODY

Removal

1. Remove the 1st, 3rd and 4th clutch feed pipes. Remove the 2nd accumulator body, spring and piston from the torque converter housing. Remove the accumulator cover.

NOTE: The accumulator cover is spring loaded. To prevent stripping the threads in the torque converter housing push down on the cover while removing the retaining bolts.

2. Remove the accumulator springs. Remove the lockup valve body mounting bolts.

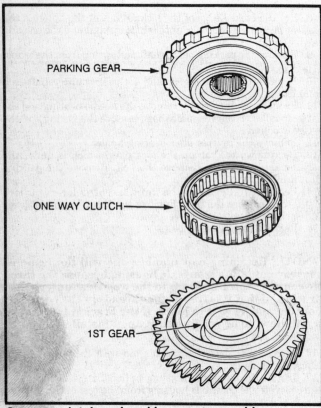

One way clutch and parking gear assembly

3. Remove the oil pipes by 1st moving the lockup valve body upward.
4. Remove the 1st, 3rd and 4th clutch pipes. Remove the clutch pressure control valve body. Remove the oil pipes.
5. Remove the E-clip from the throttle control shaft. Remove the servo valve body retaining bolts.
6. Remove the throttle control shaft from the servo valve body. Remove the separator plate and the dowel pins.
7. Remove the steel balls and the spring from the valve body oil passages. Do not use a magnet to remove the steel balls. Remove the filter screen.
8. Remove the steel ball from the regulator valve. Do not use a magnet to remove the steel ball.
9. Remove the regulator valve retaining bolts.
10. Remove the stator shaft arm, dowel pins, stop pins and the retaining bolts holding the valve body to the torque converter housing.
11. Remove the cotter pin, washer, rollers and pin from the manual valve. Remove the vavle body assembly. Be careful not to loose the torque converter check valve and spring.
12. Remove the pump gears and shaft. Remove the separator plate, dowel pins check valve and spring. Remove the secondary filters and suction pipe.

CONTROL SHAFT

Removal

1. Remove the cable holder. Remove the cotter pin. Remove the control pin and control lever roller from the control lever.
2. Bend down the tab on the lock plate. Remove the retaining bolt in the control lever. Remove the lever.
3. Turn the torque converter housing over and remove the control rod.

Unit Disassembly and Assembly

ONE WAY CLUTCH AND PARKING GEAR

Disassembly

1. Separate the countershaft 1st gear from the parking gear by turning the parking gear assembly counterclockwise.
2. Remove the one way clutch assembly by prying it upward, using a suitable tool.

Inspection

1. Inspect the parking gear for wear or scoring.
2. Inspect the one way clutch for wear or faulty movement.
3. Inspect the countershaft 1st gear for wear or scoring.
4. Replace all damaged components before assembly.

Assembly

1. Assemble the components in the reverse order of the disassembly procedure.
2. Once the components are assembled, hold the countershaft 1st gear and turn the parking gear in a counterclockwise direction; it must turn freely.

MAIN VALVE BODY

Disassembly

1. Position the valve body assembly in a suitable holding fixture.
2. Remove the retaining bolts securing the shift valve covers.
3. Remove the internal components from inside the valve body after removing each of the shift valve covers.
4. Remove the torque converter check spring and valve from the top of the valve body.

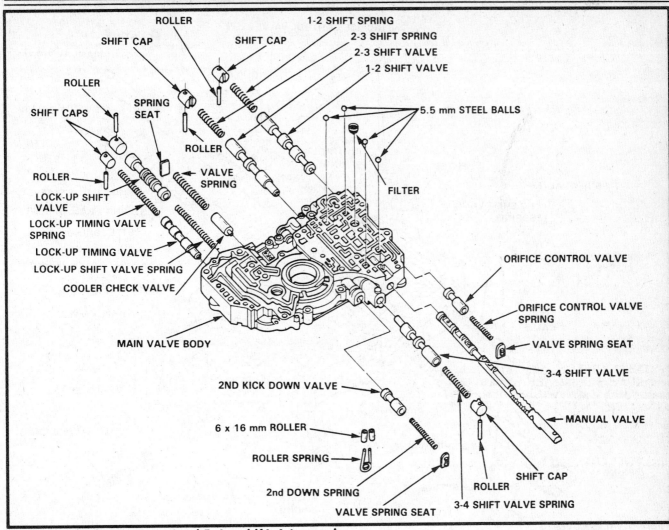

Main valve body components—L5–4 and K4–4 transaxles

5. Remove the pump driven gear and the drive gear from the valve body.

6. Remove the valve spring cap, relief valve spring and the valve.

7. Remove the orifice control spring seat, spring and the second gear orifice control valve.

8. Remove the detent spring, rollers and manual valve from the valve body assembly.

Inspection

1. Clean all parts thoroughly in solvent and blow dry with compressed air.

2. Check all valves for free movement in their bores.

3. Check all springs for damage.

4. Check the valve body for warping or scoring. Check all passages for blockage.

5. Replace all defective components.

Assembly

1. Before reassembly coat all parts with clean automatic transmission fluid.

2. Slide the spring into the hole in the big end of the shift valve. While holding the steel balls in place, position the sleeve over the valve.

3. Position the shift spring in the valve. Install the assembly into the valve body and retain it in place with the valve cover.

4. Position the relief spring into the relief valve. Install the assembly into the valve body. Be sure to install the relief valve 1st.

5. Compress the relief valve spring and then slip the check valve cap into place with the recessed side facing the spring.

6. Install the manual valve, detent rollers and spring into the valve body.

7. Install the pump gears and shaft into the valve body. Measure the thrust clearance of the driven gear to the valve body. It should be 0.001–0.002 in. The service limit specification is 0.003 in.

8. Measure the side clearance of the drive and driven gears. It should be 0.0083–0.0104 in. for the drive gear and 0.0014–0.0025 for the driven gear.

9. Lay the valve body assembly aside until the transaxle is ready to be reassembled.

REGULATOR VALVE BODY

Disassembly

1. Hold the retainer in place while removing the lock bolt. Once the lock bolt is removed, slowly release the retainer.

2. Remove the spring and the control valve.

3. Hold the lockup valve in place and remove the screws, while removing the spring and the control valve.

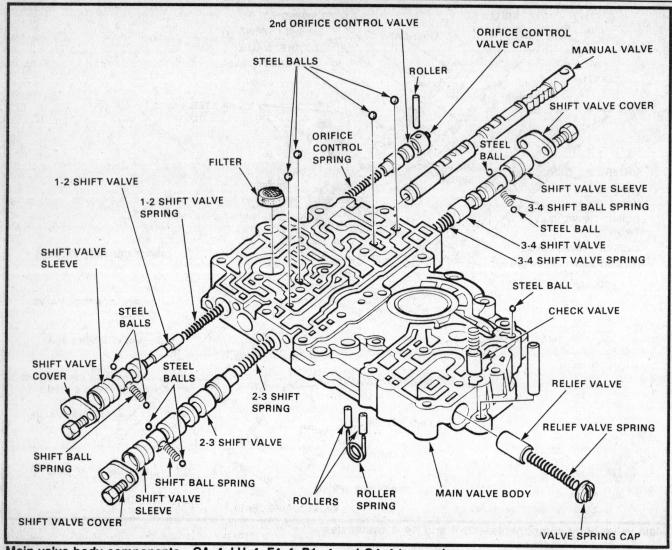

Main valve body components — CA-4, LU-4, F4-4, P1-4 and G4-4 transaxles

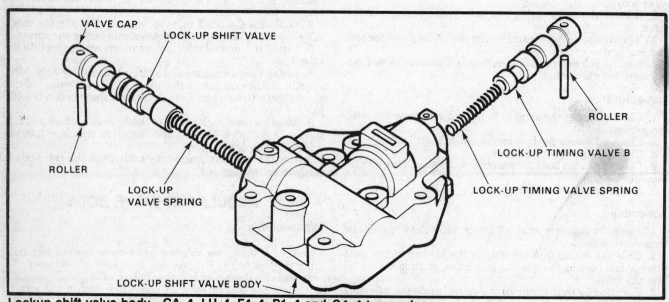

Lockup shift valve body — CA-4, LU-4, F4-4, P1-4 and G4-4 transaxles

Inspection

1. Clean all parts in solvent and dry with compressed air.
2. Check all parts for wear or damage, if any parts are worn, replace the entire valve body as an assembly.
3. Check all valves for free movement in their bores.

Assembly

1. Install the pressure regulator valve along with the inner and outer springs.
2. Install the reaction spring, spring seat and the retainer.
3. Align the hole in the retainer with the hole in the valve body. Press the retainer into the valve body and tighten the lock bolt to 9 ft. lbs.

LOCKUP SHIFT VALVE BODY

Disassembly

1. Remove the shift valve cover retaining bolts. Remove the shift valve sleeve, valve and spring.
2. Remove the clutch pressure control valve plug. Remove the roller, spring and control valve.
3. Remove the clutch pressure control valve separator plate.

Inspection

1. Clean all parts in solvent and blow dry with compressed air.
2. Replace the valve body as an assembly if any parts are worn or damaged.
3. Check all valves for free movement in their bores.
4. Coat all parts with clean transmision fluid before reassembly.

Assembly

1. Assemble the lockup valve body in the reverse order of the disassembly procedure.
2. Install the assembly onto the regulator valve body. Set the unit aside until the transaxle is ready to be reassembled.

SERVO VALVE BODY

Disassembly

1. Remove the throttle valve retainer. Remove the outer throttle valve B, spring B and the inner throttle valve B. Remove the outer throttle valve A, spring A and the inner throttle valve A.
2. Remove the modulator valve spring, retainer plate and spring and the modulator valve.
3. Remove the 2nd and 3rd accumulator cover. Remove the pistons and their related components.
4. Remove the 4th accumulator cover. Remove the pistons and their related components.
5. Remove the servo valve along with the servo return spring.
6. Do not adjust or remove the throttle pressure adjustment bolt, it has been pre-set at the factory for the proper shift points.
7. Remove the 3rd and 4th clutch pipes. Remove the clutch pressure control valve body and its related components.

Inspection

1. Clean all parts with solvent and dry with compressed air.
2. Check all valves for free movement in their bores.
3. Check all components for wear or damage, if nay wear or damage is found, replace the valve body as an assembly.

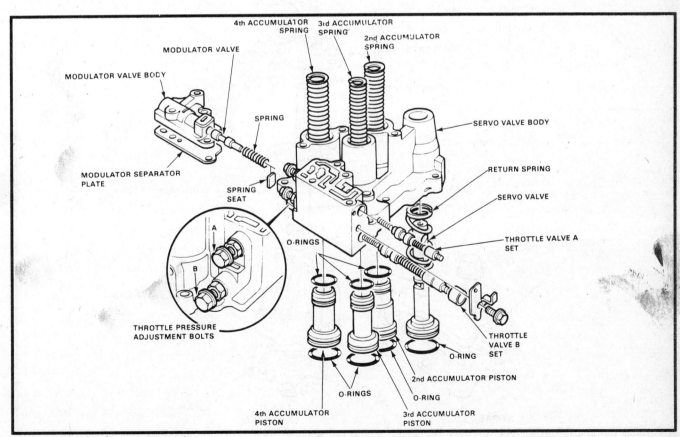

Servo valve body components

Assembly

1. Assemble the servo valve in the reverse order of the disassembly procedure.

2. Once the component has been assembled, set it aside until the automatic transaxle is ready to be assembled.

GOVERNOR VALVE

Disassembly

1. Remove the governor housing retaining bolts, by bending back the lock tabs.

2. Remove the governor housing E-clip and remove the governor housing internal components.

3. Remove the snapring and gear from the governor holder.

4. Remove the key and the dowel pins along with the pipe from the governor assembly shaft.

Inspection

1. Clean all parts in slovent and blow dry with compressed air.

2. Check the operation of the governer, if it does not rotate freely, replace it.

Assembly

1. Inspect the inside of the governor housing where the secondary weight sits for smoothness, correct as required.

2. Assemble the governor in the reverse order of the disassembly procedure. Be sure to use new lock tabs.

3. Set the governor aside until the transaxle is ready for reassembly.

MAINSHAFT

Disassembly

1. Remove the snapring from the rear of the mainshaft assembly. Remove the needle bearing, spacer collar and the metal sealing rings. Discard the metal sealing rings.

2. Remove the snapring from the front of the mainshaft assembly.

3. Remove the ball bearings, thrust needle bearing, snapring, washer and the fourth gear assembly.

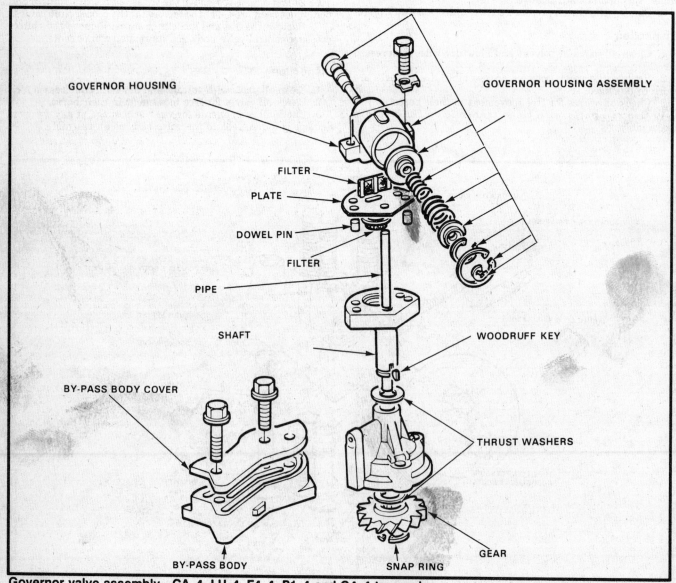

Governor valve assembly — CA–4, LU–4, F4–4, P1–4 and G4–4 transaxles

4. Remove the needle bearings, thrust needle bearing, fourth gear collar, thrust washer and the second and fourth clutch assembly.

5. Remove the remaining washers, gears, bearings and O-rings from the mainshaft assembly. Discard the O-rings.

Inspection

1. Check the shaft splines for burrs or uneven wear.
2. Check the bearing surfaces for scoring or signs of excess heat.
3. Inspect all bearings for freedom of movement and check for galling.
4. Replace all damaged components.
5. Check all bearing clearances on reassembly.

Assembly

1. Assemble the mainshaft by installing the gears, bearings and snaprings in position. Install the needle bearings and the clutch assemblies.
2. Check the mainshaft clearance measurement and replace the thrust washers as required.
3. Set the mainshaft assembly aside until the automatic transaxle is ready for reassembly.

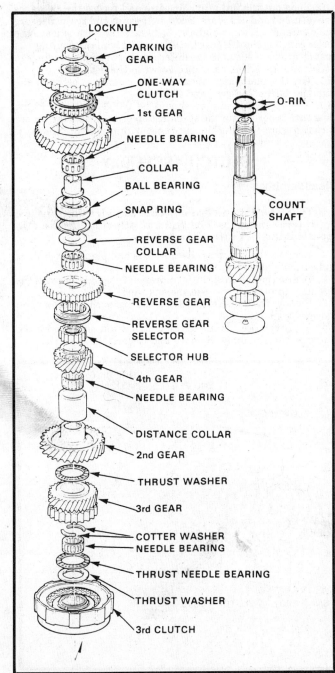

Exploded of countershaft assembly

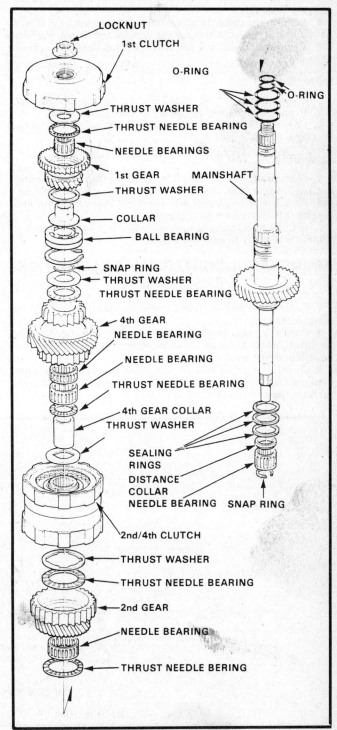

Exploded view of mainshaft assembly

COUNTERSHAFT

Disassembly

1. Remove the snapring. Remove the roller bearing, reverse gear collar and the needle bearings.
2. Remove the reverse gear, reverse gear selector and the selector hub from the countershaft.
3. Remove the 4th gear, needle bearing, spacer collar and 2nd gear.
4. Remove the cotter washers, thrust needle bearing and the 3rd gear assembly.
5. Remove the third clutch assembly, by removing the thrust needle bearing, needle bearing and the splined thrust washer.
6. Remove and discard the O-rings from the countershaft assembly.

Inspection

1. Clean and inspect all parts for wear, damage and scoring.
2. Repair or replace defective components as required.
3. Coat all parts with clean automatic transmission fluid before reassembly.

Assembly

1. Assemble the countershaft by installing the roller bearings and the reverse gear. Install the 3rd and 4th gear assemblies.
2. Check the countershaft clearance measurement and repalce thrust washers as required.
3. Set the countershaft assembly aside until the automatic transaxle is ready to be reassembled.

MAINSHAFT/COUNTERSHAFT CLEARANCE MEASUREMENTS

1. Remove the mainshaft and the countershaft bearings from the transaxle housing.
2. Assemble the mainshaft and the countershaft together. On all thrust needle bearings the unrolled edge of the bearing cage faces the thrust washer.
3. Install the mainshaft assembly into the torque converter housing. Install the mainshaft holder to prevent the shafts from turning. Torque the locknut to 25 ft. lbs.

4. Hold the parking gear on the countershaft and torque the retaining nut to 35 ft. lbs.
5. Measure the thrust washer clearances using the proper feeler gauge. Make all measurements before changing the thrust washers.
6. On the countershaft, measure the clearance between the shoulder on the selector hub and the shoulder on the 4th gear.
7. The clearance should be 0.003–0.006 in. If the clearance is not within the specification given, select the proper thrust washer to bring the clearance to within specification.
8. Leave the feeler gauge in the 4th gear measurement position while measuring 2nd gear.
9. Second gear clearance should be 0.003–0.006 in. If clearance is not within specification select the proper thrust washer to bring the clearance within specification.
10. Slide out the 3rd gear. Measure and record the clearance between 2nd and 3rd gears. Slide 3rd gear in and again measure the clearance between 2nd and 3rd gears. Be sure to leave the feeler gauge in the 4th gear measuring slot while measuring 2nd gear clearance. Calculate the difference between the readings to determine the actual clearance between the gears.
11. On the mainshaft, measure the clearance between the shoulder of the 2nd gear and 3rd gear.
12. The correct clearance should be 0.003–0.006 in. If the clearance is not within the specification given, select the proper thrust washer to bring the clearance within specification.

CLUTCH ASSEMBLY

Disassembly

NOTE: The 1st and 3rd clutches are identical but are not interchangeable. The 2nd and 4th clutches are also identical but not interchangeable.

1. Remove the snapring. Remove the end plate, clutch discs and clutch plates from the clutch assembly.
2. Install the clutch spring compressor tool and compress the assembly in order to remove the snapring.
3. Remove the tool. Remove the snapring, spring retainer and the spring.
4. Apply compressed air to the clutch drum and remove the clutch piston assembly. Remove and discard the O-ring seals.

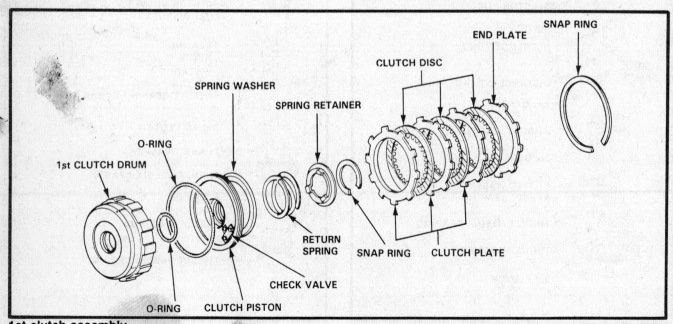

1st clutch assembly

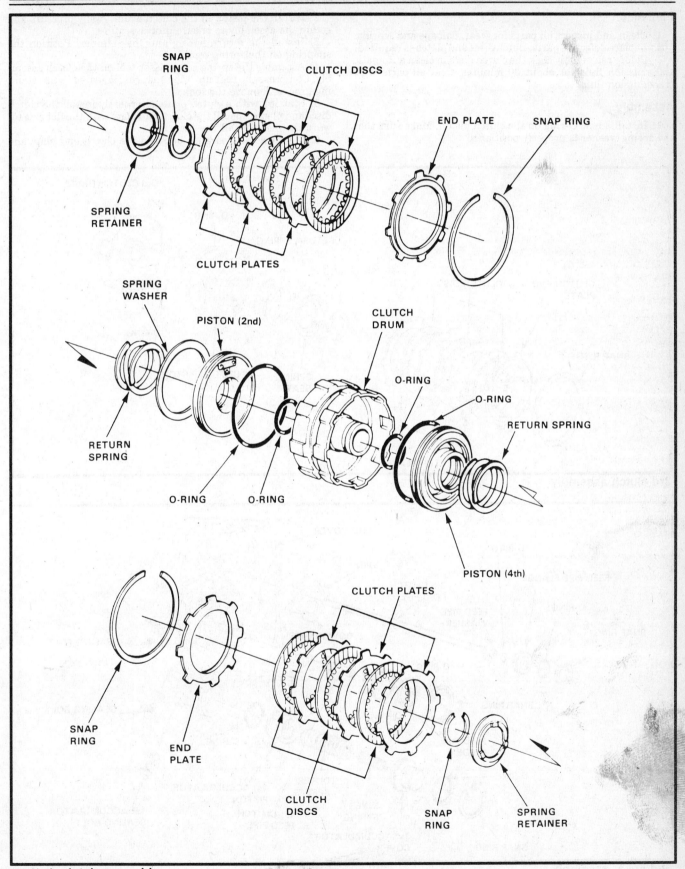

SNAP RING

CLUTCH DISCS

END PLATE

SNAP RING

SPRING RETAINER

CLUTCH PLATES

SPRING WASHER

PISTON (2nd)

CLUTCH DRUM

O-RING

O-RING

RETURN SPRING

RETURN SPRING

O-RING

O-RING

PISTON (4th)

CLUTCH PLATES

SNAP RING

END PLATE

CLUTCH DISCS

SNAP RING

SPRING RETAINER

2nd/4th clutch assembly

Inspection

1. Clean and inspect all parts for wear, damage and scoring.
2. Replace defective parts, clutch discs and plates as required.
3. Before reassembly soak the clutch discs in clean automatic transmission fluid for about 30 minutes. Coat all parts with transmission fluid.

Assembly

1. Install a new O-ring on the clutch piston. Make sure that the spring washer is properly positioned.

2. Install the piston in the clutch drum. Apply pressure and rotate the assembly to ensure proper seating.
3. Install the return spring and the retainer. Position the snapring on the spring retainer.
4. Assemble the spring compressor tool on the clutch assembly. Compress the unit until the snapring is seated in tis retaining groove. Remove the tool.
5. Starting with a clutch plate, alternately install the clutch discs and plates. Install the clutch end plate with the flat side toward the disc. Install the snapring.
6. Measure the clearance between the clutch end plate and

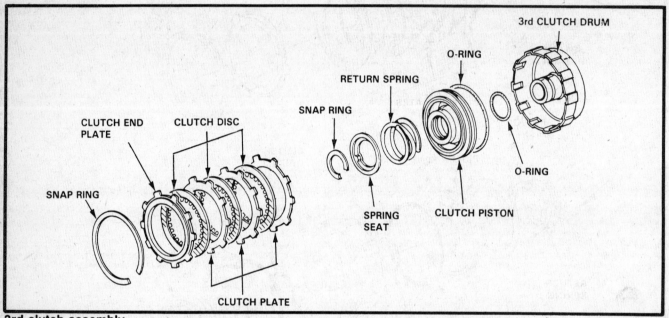

3rd clutch assembly

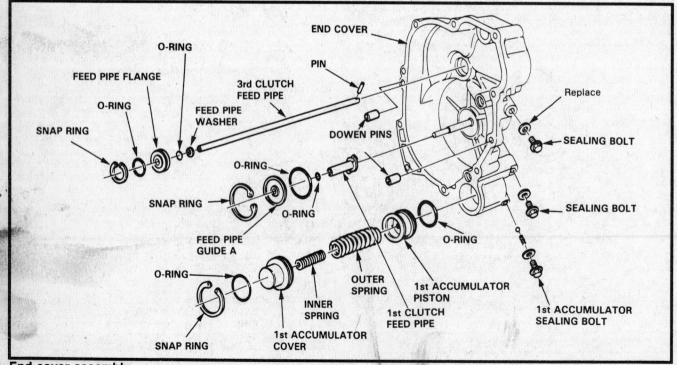

End cover assembly

the top clutch disc. It should be 0.016–0.028 in. for the 1st clutch, 0.026–0.031 in. for the 2nd clutch and 0.016–0.023 in. for the 3rd and 4th clutch.

7. If the reading is not within specification select a new clutch end plate as required.

8. Check for clutch engagement by blowing compressed air into the oil passage of the clutch drum hub. Remove air pressure and check that the clutch releases.

END COVER

Disassembly

1. Remove the snaprings. Remove the dowel pins, feed pipes, washers and O-rings.
2. Remove the 1st accumulator spring and piston.
3. Remove the 1st clutch feed pipe.
4. Remove the cover selaing bolts.

Inspection

1. Inspect the transaxle end cover for wear, scoring and damage.
2. Repair or replace as required.
3. Discard all O-ring seals and replace defective parts and components as required.
4. Coat all components with automatic transmission fluid before reassembly.

Assembly

1. Assemble the transaxle end cover by installing the dowel pins, feed pipes, washers and O-rings. Install the 1st accumulator spring and piston.
2. After the end cover has been assembled, set it aside until the transaxle is ready to be assembled.

REVERSE IDLER GEAR

Disassembly

1. Remove the retaining bolt, washers and spring, if used.
2. Remove the idler bearing holder, shaft and bearing assembly from the transaxle case.
3. Remove the idler gear.

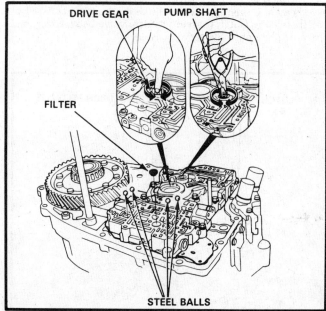

Checking pump gear rotation and installing check balls

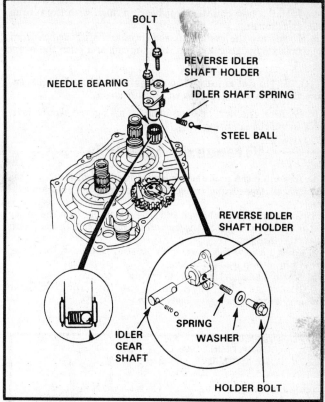

Reverse idler components

Inspection

1. Inspect the case for nicks or burrs.
2. Inspect the dgear for uneven wear or for signs of excess heat.
3. Inspect the idler shaft for damage.

Assembly

1. Install the reverse idler gear so that the larger chamfer on the shaft bore faces the torque converter housing.
2. Install the idler holder and bearing.
3. Install the assembly into the transaxle case.

DIFFERENTIAL SEAL

Replacement

1. Drive out the old seals in the transaxle housing and the torque converter housing using the proper seal removal tools.
2. Check the seal surface for wear, burrs or damage correct as required.
3. Coat the new seals with clean automatic transmission fluid. Install the seals using the proper seal installation tools.

MAINSHAFT/COUNTERSHAFT BEARING AND SEAL

Replacement

1. Remove the mainshaft bearing and seal from the torque converter housing. Drive in the new mainshaft bearing until it bottoms in the torque converter housing.
2. Install the mainshaft seal flush with the torque converter housing using the proper seal installation tool.
3. Position the torque converter housing and remove the countershaft bearing.

4. Be sure that the oil guide plate is installed in the bearing hole. Install a new countershaft bearing flush with the torque converter housing.

5. To remove the mainshaft and countershaft bearings from the transaxle housing, expand the snapring and push the bearing out.

NOTE: Do not remove the snaprings unless it is necessary to clean the grooves in the housing.

6. Position the new bearing in the housing and secure it in place using the snapring.

Transaxle Assembly

1. Assemble the manual lever onto the control shaft.
2. Install the torque converter housing onto the transaxle case.
3. Install the control lever and a new lock plate on the other end of the shaft. Tighten the bolt and torque it to 9 ft. lbs. Bend down the lock tab.
4. Install a new filter assembly. Install the separator plate, dowel pin, pump gears and shaft.
5. Install the check valve and spring.
6. Install the valve body assembly onto the torque converter housing. Torque the valve body bolts to 9 ft. lbs.

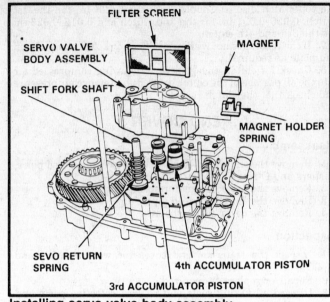
Installing servo valve body assembly

7. Be sure that the pump drive gear rotates smoothly in the normal operating direction and that the pump shaft moves smoothly in both axial and normal operating directions.
8. Install the stator shaft arm, stop pin and the dowel pins.
9. Install the regulator valve and torque the retaining bolts to 9 ft. lbs.
10. Install the steel ball or balls into the valve body oil passage or passages.
11. Install the separator plate. Install the throttle control shaft and the dowel pins.
12. Install the servo assembly. Be sure to use the proper retaining bolts in the proper retaining holes. Torque the retaining bolts to 9 ft. lbs.
13. Put the roller on each side of the manual valve stem. Attach the valve to the lever with the pin. Secure the assembly in place using the lock pin.
14. Install the clutch pressure control separator plate onto the servo body and then install the clutch pressure control body.
15. Install the clutch pressure control valve body, cover, and separator plate onto the servo body.

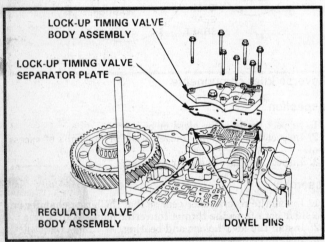
Installing lockup timing valve assembly

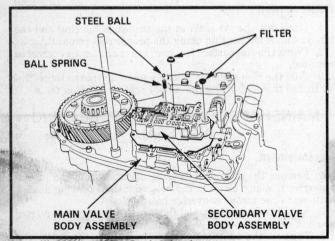
Installing secondary valve body

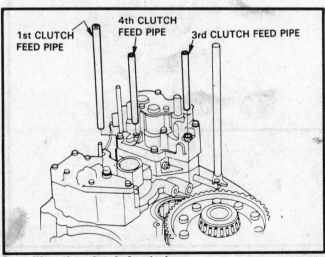
Installing the clutch feed pipes

16. Install and torque the clutch pressure control valve body to 9 ft. lbs. Install the 1st, 3rd and 4th clutch feed pipes. Install the separator plate.

17. Position the oil feed pipes between the pressure control valve and the clutch presure control valve body and slide the assembly into place.

18. Install the pressure control valve body bolts and torque them to 9 ft. lbs.

19. Install the accumulator springs. Install the accumulator cover and torque the retaining bolts to 9 ft. lbs., in a criss cross method.

20. Install the 4th accumulator cover and torque the retaining bolts to 9 ft. lbs.

21. Install the governor valve using new lock plates. Torque the retaining bolts to 9 ft. lbs. and bend the lock tabs.

22. Position the countershaft in palce. Position the mainshaft in place. Do not tap on the shafts with a hammer to drive them in place.

23. Install the countershaft second gear. Install the countershaft fourth gear and the needle bearing.

24. Assemble the reverse shift fork and the selector sleeve. Install these components as an assembly on the countershaft.

NOTE: Install the sleeve with the grooved side down and the unmarked side up. Check for wear on the surface of the sleeve and the shift fork.

25. Install the reverse shift fork over the servo valve stem. Align the hole in the stem with the hole in the fork. Install the bolt and the lock plate. Torque the bolt to 10 ft. lbs. and bend down the lock tab.

26. Install the countershaft reverse gear, needle bearing and reverse gear collar.

27. Install a new gasket, the dowel pins and the oil feed pipes into the torque converter housing.

28. Position the automatic transaxle housing on the torque converter housing.

NOTE: Be sure main valve control shaft lines up with hole in housing and that the reverse idler gear meshes with mainshaft and countershaft, or housing will not go on.

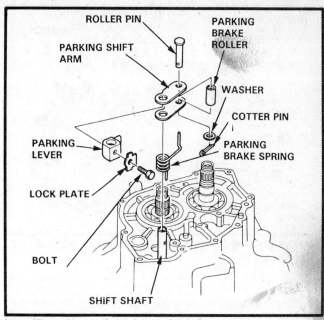

Installing the park lock mechansim

29. Install the retaining bolts and torque in 2 steps, 1st to 30 ft. lbs. and then to 40 ft. lbs in the correct sequence.

NOTE: When tightening the transaxle housing bolts, take care not to distort or damage the throttle control brackets; distortion or damage to bracket will change the transaxle shift points.

30. Install the throttle control lever and spring on the throttle control shaft. Install the bolt and a new lock plate. Torque the retaining bolt to 6 ft. lbs. and bend down the lock plate.

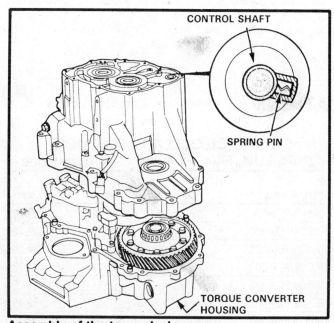

Assembly of the transmission case

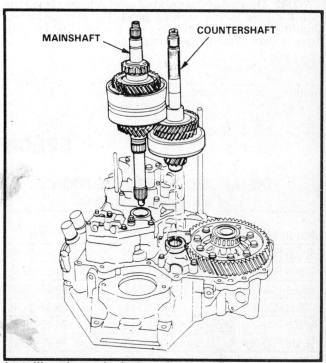

Installing the mainshaft and countershaft

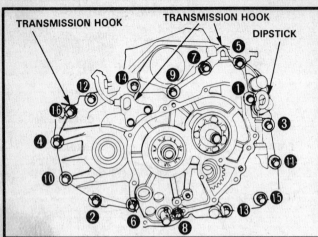

Torque the transaxle housing bolts in numerical sequence

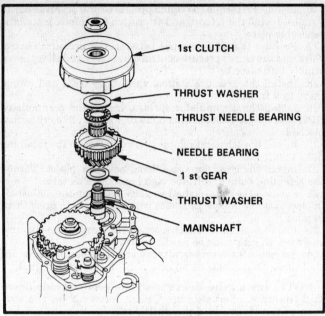

Installing the 1st clutch assembly

31. Install the parking shift arm and spring on the shift shaft with the retaining bolt and a new lock plate. Torque the bolt to 10 ft. lbs. and bend down the lock tab.

   NOTE: The spring should put clockwise tension on the shift arm and force it against the stop pin.

32. Install the 1st gear collar and needle bearing on the countershaft. Install the collar on the mainshaft.
33. Install the reverse idler bearing holder. Install the O-rings on the mainshaft assembly.
34. Install the countershaft 1st gear and the parking gear on the counter shaft.
35. Install the stop pin, parking pawl shaft and the pawl release spring.

   NOTE: The end of the parking pawl release spring fits into the hole in the parking pawl. The release spring should put clockwise tension on the pawl which will force it away from the parking gear.

36. Shift the transaxle into the **P** position. Install the countershaft locknut. Stake the locknut flange into the gear groove.
37. Install the needle bearing and the thrust washer onto the mainshaft. Install the 1st gear, needle bearing and thrust washer onto the mainshaft.
38. Install the 1st clutch ssembly on the mainshaft. Install the mainshaft locknut. This nut has left hand threads. Stake the locknut flange into the groove of the 1st clutch.
39. Install the gasket, dowel pins and O-rings on the transaxle housing. Install the end cover and torque the retaining bolts to 9 ft. lbs.
40. Install the transaxle cooler line fittings on the transaxle assembly.
41. Install the torque converter on the mainshaft assembly.
42. Install the solenoid valve assemblies and the speed pulser.

SPECIFICATIONS

DISTANCE COLLAR SELECTION
L5-4 and K4-4 Transaxles

Part Number	Thickness	
	in.	mm
90503-PC9-000	1.534–1.535	38.97–39.00
90508-PC9-000	1.536–1.537	39.02–39.05
90504-PC9-000	1.538–1.539	39.07–39.10
90509-PC9-000	1.540–1.541	39.12–39.15
90505-PC9-000	1.542–1.543	39.17–39.20
90510-PC9-000	1.544–1.545	39.22–39.25
90507-PC9-000	1.547–1.546	39.27–39.30

DISTANCE COLLAR SELECTION
CA-4, LU-4, F4-4, P1-4 and G4-4 Transaxles

Part Number	Class	Thickness	
		in.	mm
90503-PC9-000	1	1.535	39.00
90504-PC9-000	2	1.539	39.10
90505-PC9-000	3	1.534	39.20
90507-PC9-000	4	1.547	39.30
90508-PC9-000	5	1.537	39.05
90509-PC9-000	6	1.541	39.15
90510-PC9-000	7	1.545	39.25

THRUST WASHER SELECTION
L5-4 and K4-4 Transaxles

Part Number	Thickness	
	in.	mm
90441-PL5-000	0.156–0.157	3.97–4.00
90442-PL5-000	0.158–0.159	4.02–4.05
90443-PL5-000	0.160–0.161	4.07–4.10
90444-PL5-000	0.162–0.163	4.12–4.15
90445-PL5-000	0.164–0.165	4.17–4.20
90446-PL5-000	0.166–0.167	4.22–4.25
90447-PL5-000	0.168–0.169	4.27–4.30
90448-PL5-000	0.170–0.171	4.32–4.35
90449-PL5-000	0.172–0.173	4.37–4.40

THRUST WASHER SELECTION
CA-4, LU-4, F4-4, P1-4 and G4-4 Transaxles

Part Number	Class	Thickness	
		in.	mm
90441-PC9-010	A	0.137–0.138	3.47–3.50
90442-PC9-010	B	0.139–0.140	3.52–3.55
90443-PC9-010	C	0.141–0.142	3.57–3.60
90444-PC9-010	D	0.143–0.144	3.62–3.65
90445-PC9-010	E	0.145–0.146	3.67–3.70
90446-PC9-010	F	0.147–0.148	3.72–3.75
90447-PC9-010	G	0.149–0.150	3.77–3.80
90448-PC9-010	H	0.151–0.152	3.82–3.85
90449-PC9-010	I	0.153–0.154	3.87–3.90

ACCUMULATOR SPRING FREE LENGTH
CA-4, LU-4, F4-4, P1-4 and G4-4 Transaxles

Spring	Length		Limit
	in.	mm	(in.)
2nd Accumulator	3.020	76.7	2.980
3rd Accumulator	3.150	80.0	3.102
4th Accumulator	3.083	78.3	3.035

ACCUMULATOR SPRING FREE LENGTH
L5-4 and K4-4 Transaxles

Spring	Length		Limit (in.)
	in.	mm	
2nd Accumulator	3.31	84.1	3.26
3rd Accumulator	3.08	78.3	3.04
4th Accumulator	3.07	78.0	3.02

TORQUE SPECIFICATIONS

Part	ft. lbs.	Nm
Valve body-to-case	9	12
Separator-to-case	9	12
Regulator valve body-to-main valve body	9	12
Accumulator cover	9	12
Reverse idler retainer	20	27
Parking gear nut	70	95
Case bolts	25	34
End cover bolts	9	12
Idler bearing holder	9	12
Case plugs	13	17.5
Drain plug	29	40
Upper mount bracket	40	55
Engine-to-transaxle	50	68
Driveplate-to-converter	9	12
Front-transaxle mount	29	40
Side transaxle mount	40	55

SPLINED THRUST WASHER SELECTION
L5-4 and K4-4 Transaxles

Part Number	Thickness	
	in.	mm
90411-PF4-000	0.117–0.118	2.97–3.00
90412-PF4-000	0.119–0.120	3.02–3.05
90413-PF4-000	0.121–0.122	3.07–3.10
90414-PF4-000	0.123–0.124	3.12–3.15
90415-PF4-000	0.125–0.126	3.17–3.20
90416-PF4-000	0.127–0.128	3.22–3.25
90417-PF4-000	0.128–0.130	3.27–3.30
90418-PF4-000	0.131–0.132	3.32–3.35
90419-PF4-000	0.133–0.134	3.37–3.40

SPLINED THRUST WASHER SELECTION
CA-4, LU-4, F4-4, P1-4 and G4-4 Transaxles

Part Number	Thickness	
	in.	mm
90411-PA9-010	0.117–0.118	2.97–3.00
90412-PA9-010	0.119–0.120	3.02–3.05
90413-PA9-010	0.121–0.122	3.07–3.10
90414-PA9-010	0.123–0.124	3.12–3.15
90415-PA9-010	0.125–0.126	3.17–3.20
90418-PA9-010	0.127–0.128	3.22–3.25
90419-PA9-010	0.129–0.130	3.27–3.30
90420-PA9-010	0.131–0.132	3.32–3.35
90421-PA9-010	0.133–0.134	3.37–3.40

SPECIAL TOOLS

SERVICE TOOL SELECTION

Description	Number
Mainshaft holder	07923–6890202
Clutch spring compressor set	07GAE–PG40001
Housing puller	07HAC–PK40100
Gauge set	07406–0020003
Low pressure gauge	07406–0070000
Bearing remover	07736–A01000A
Driver	07749–0010000
Oil seal driver	07947–6340201
Gear installer	07HAF–PK40100

KF100 Transaxle
Isuzu

APPLICATION

1985–89 Isuzu I-Mark with 1.5L engine.

GENERAL DESCRIPTION

The KF100 is a Jatco type automatic transaxle designed for front wheel drive vehicles. It is a compact type transaxle, consisting of a transmission and differential in 1 unit. The transaxle is designed so that the preload on the tapered roller bearings can be adjusted by the use of shims. The final gear in the transaxle is a helical type design requiring no tooth contact adjustment. The unit is designed so that the transmission portion and differential use Dexron® II automatic transmission fluid.

Transaxle and Converter Identification

TRANSAXLE

The transaxle identification is stamped on the flange at the front of the transaxle bell housing, on the top left hand side.

TORQUE CONVERTER

The torque converter is a welded unit and cannot be disassembled for repairs. Should this unit need to be replaced, both new and rebuilt units are available.

Metric Fasteners

This transaxle has metric bolts, nuts and threads. Do not replace metric size components with inch size equivalents. Do not use inch size tools to loosen, tighten, adjust or remove the metric size component parts.

Replacement fasteners must have the same measurement and strength as those removed. Mismatched or incorrect fasteners can result in damage to the transaxle unit through malfunctions, breakage or possible personal injury.

Capacities

The fluid capacity for the KF100 automatic transaxle is 6.1 qts. (5.8L) of Dexron® II automatic transmission fluid.

Checking Fluid Level

The vehicle must have been driven so that the engine and transaxle are at normal operating temperature (fluid temperature 158–176° F). If the fluid smells burnt or is black, replace it.

1. Park the vehicle on a level surface and set the parking brake.
2. With the engine idling, shift the selector into each gear from **P** range to **L** range and return to **P** range.
3. Pull out the transaxle dipstick and wipe it clean.
4. Push the dipstick back fully into the tube.
5. Pull out the dipstick and check that the fluid is in the **HOT** range.
6. If the level is low, add fluid. Do not overfill.

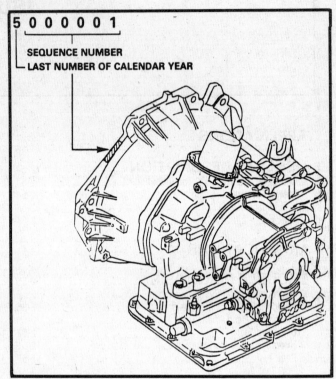

Transaxle identification

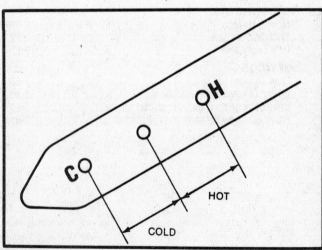

Dipstick

TRANSAXLE MODIFICATIONS
Automatic Transaxle Slip

Some 1986–1988 vehicles (VIN G41111154-J7560740), may experience a momentary engine flare of approximately 50 rpm during a forced downshift from third to second gear. Installing a new band servo return spring part number 8-94140-726-0 will correct this condition.

TROUBLE DIAGNOSIS
CLUTCH AND BAND APPLICATION

Shift Position		Gear Ratio	Clutch Front	Clutch Rear	Low and Reverse Brake	Band Servo Operation	Band Servo Release	One-way Clutch
P		—	—	—	Applied	—	—	—
R		2.400	Applied	—	Applied	—	①	—
N		—	—	—	—	—	—	—
D	1st	2.841	—	Applied	—	—	—	Applied
	2nd	1.541	—	Applied	—	Applied	—	—
	3rd	1.000	Applied	Applied	—	①	①	—
2nd		1.541	—	Applied	—	Applied	—	—
1	2nd	1.541	—	Applied	—	Applied	—	—
	1st	2.841	—	Applied	Applied	—	—	—

① Part is operating under normal line pressure, but not transmitting power

CHILTON THREE "C" TRANSAXLE DIAGNOSIS

Condition	Cause	Correction
Fluid discolored or smells burnt	a) Fluid contaminated b) Torque converter faulty c) Transmission faulty	a) Replace fluid b) Replace torque converter c) Disassemble and inspect transmission
Vehicle does not move in any forward range or reverse	a) Transaxle manual control cable out of adjustment b) Valve body or primary regulator valve faulty c) Transmission faulty	a) Adjust control cable b) Inspect valve body c) Disassemble and inspect transmission
Vehicle does not move in any range	a) Parking lock pawl faulty b) Valve body or primary regulator valve faulty c) Torque converter faulty d) Converter drive plate broken e) Oil pump intake strainer blocked f) Transmission faulty	a) Inspect park pawl b) Inspect valve body c) Replace torque converter d) Replace torque converter e) Clean strainer f) Disassemble and inspect transmission
Shift lever position incorrect	a) Transaxle manual control cable out of adjustment b) Manual valve and lever faulty c) Transmission faulty	a) Adjust control cable b) Inspect valve body c) Disassemble and inspect transmission
Harsh engagement into any drive range	a) Throttle cable out of adjustment b) Valve body or primary regulator valve faulty c) Accumulator pistons faulty d) Transmission faulty	a) Adjust throttle cable b) Inspect valve body c) Inspect accumulator pistons d) Disassemble and inspect transmission
Delayed 1-2, 2-3 or 3-OD upshift, or downshifts from OD-3 or 3-2 then shifts back to OD or 3	a) Throttle cable out of adjustment b) Governor faulty c) Valve body faulty	a) Adjust throttle cable b) Inspect governor c) Inspect valve body
Slips on 1-2, 2-3 or 3-OD upshift; or slips or shudders on take-off	a) Transaxle manual control cable out of adjustment b) Throttle cable out of adjustment c) Valve body faulty d) Transmission faulty	a) Adjust control cable b) Adjust throttle cable c) Inspect valve body d) Disassemble and inspect transmission
Drag, binding or tie-up on 1-2, 2-3 or 3-OD upshift	a) Transaxle manual control cable out of adjustment b) Valve body faulty c) Transmission faulty	a) Adjust control cable b) Inspect valve body c) Disassemble and inspect transmission

CHILTON THREE "C" TRANSAXLE DIAGNOSIS

Condition	Cause	Correction
Harsh downshift	a) Throttle cable out of adjustment b) Accumulator pistons faulty c) Valve body faulty d) Transmission faulty	a) Adjust throttle cable b) Inspect accumulator pistons c) Inspect valve body d) Disassemble and inspect transmission
No downshift when coasting	a) Governor faulty b) Valve body faulty	a) Inspect governor b) Inspect valve body
Downshift occurs too quick or too late while coasting	a) Throttle cable out of adjustment b) Governor faulty c) Valve body faulty d) Transmission faulty	a) Adjust throttle cable b) Inspect governor c) Inspect valve body d) Disassemble and inspect transmission
No OD-3, 3-2 or 2-1 kick-down	a) Throttle cable out of adjustment b) Governor faulty c) Valve body faulty	a) Adjust throttle cable b) Inspect governor c) Inspect valve body
No engine braking in "2" range	a) Valve body faulty b) Transmission faulty	a) Inspect valve body b) Disassemble and inspect transmission
Vehicle does not hold in "P"	a) Transaxle manual control cable out of adjustment b) Parking lock pawl and rod	a) Adjust control cable b) Inspect lock pawl and rod

Hydraulic Control System

PUMP ASSEMBLY

The hydraulic pressure system requires a supply of transmission fluid and a pump to pressurize the fluid. The KF100 transaxle uses an internal-external gear type pump with its oil intake connected to a screen assembly.

The oil pump is designed to deliver fluid to the torque converter, lubricate the planetary gear unit and supply operating pressure to the hydraulic control system. The drive gear of the oil pump and the torque converter pump are driven by the engine. The pump has a sufficient capacity of oil to supply the necessary fluid pressure throughout all forward speed ranges and reverse.

MANUAL VALVE

The manual valve is linked to the gear shift lever and directs the fluid to the gear range circuit that the lever is positioned at.

PRIMARY REGULATOR VALVE

The primary regulator valve varies the hydraulic line pressure to each component in order to conform with engine power and operate all transaxle hydraulic systems.

SECONDARY REGULATOR VALVE

This valve regulates the converter pressure and lubrication pressure. Spring tension in the valve acts in an upward direction. Converter fluid pressure and lubrication pressure are determined by the spring tension.

THROTTLE VALVE

The throttle valve acts to produce throttle pressure in response to accelerator pedal modulation or engine output. When the accelerator pedal is depressed, the downshift plug is pushed upward by the throttle cable and throttle cam. The throttle valve also moves upward by means of the spring, opening the pressure passage for creation of throttle pressure.

THROTTLE MODULATOR VALVE

This valve produces throttle modulator pressure. It reduces throttle pressure when the throttle valve opening angle is high. It causes throttle modulator pressure to act on the primary regulator valve so that line pressure performance is close to engine power performance.

GOVERNOR VALVE

The governor valve is driven by the drive pinion worm gear and produces governor pressure in response to the vehicle speed. It balances the line pressure from the primary regulator valve and the centrifugal force of the governor weights to produce hydraulic pressure in proportion to vehicle speed.

ACCUMULATORS

The accumulators act to cushion the shifting shock. There are 3 accumulators: 1 each for the forward clutch (C_1), direct clutch (C_2) and the 2nd brake (B_2). The accumulators are located in the transaxle case. Accumulator control pressure is always acting on the back pressure side of the C_2 and B_2 pistons. This pressure along with spring tension, pushes down on the 2 pistons.

When line pressure is applied to the operating side, the pistons are pushed upward and shock is cushioned as the fluid pressure gradually rises. Operation of the C_1 piston is basically the same as that for C_2 and B_2. However the force pushing the piston downward is accomplished by spring tension only.

1–2 SHIFT VALVE

This valve automatically controls the 1–2 shift according to governor and throttle pressure. To improve the valve sliding characteristics, a 3 piece valve is used. When governor pressure is low and throttle pressure is high, the valve is pushed down by throttle pressure and because the 2nd brake circuit closes, the transaxle shifts into 1st gear.

When governor pressure is high and throttle pressure low, the valve is pushed up by governor pressure and the circuit to the 2nd brake piston opens so the transaxle will shift into 2nd gear. When the throttle pressure passage is closed, downshifting into

1st gear is dependant on spring tension and governor pressure only.

Unless the downshift plug actuates and allows the detent pressure to act on the 1–2 shift valve, downshifting into 1st gear will take place at a set vehicle speed. In the **L** range, there is no upshifting into 2nd gear because low modulator pressure is acting on the low coast shift valve.

2–3 SHIFT VALVE

This valve performs shifting between 2nd and 3rd gears. Control is accomplished by opposing throttle pressure and spring tension against governor pressure. When governor pressure is high, the valve is pushed up against the resistance of the throttle pressure and spring tension. This opens the passage to the direct clutch (C$_2$) piston to allow the shift into 3rd gear.

When governor pressure is low, the valve is pushed down by throttle pressure and spring tension to close the passage leading to the direct clutch piston, causing a downshift to 2nd gear. In the event of kickdown, the detent pressure acts on the 2–3 shift valve to permit a quicker downshift to 2nd gear. valve movement occurs due to the different size areas where pressure is applied. Since the area is larger for downshift than for upshift, manual **2** range, line pressure from the manual valve acts on the intermediate shift valve. The valve descends and shifting into 2nd gear is accomplished but there is no upshifting into 3rd gear. Line pressure passes through the 2nd modulator valve and 1–2 shift valve and acts on the 2nd coast brake to provide engine braking.

Diagnosis Tests

HYDRAULIC TESTS

1. Run the engine until it reaches normal operating temperature.
2. Raise the vehicle and support it safely.
3. Remove the transaxle case test plugs and install hydraulic pressure gauges.

LINE PRESSURE

1. Apply the parking brake.
2. Start the engine.
3. Apply the brake pedal while manipulating the accelerator pedal and measure the line pressure at the engine speeds as specified:
   D range—idling 43–57 psi
   D range—stall 128–156 psi
   2 range—idling 114–171 psi
   2 range—stall 114–171 psi
   R range—idling 57–110 psi
   R range—stall 228–270 psi
4. In the same manner, perform the test for the **R** range.
5. If the measured pressures are not up to specified values, recheck the throttle cable adjustment and retest.
6. If the measured values at all ranges are higher than specified, check the following:
   a. Throttle cable out of adjustment
   b. Throttle valve defective
   c. Regulator valve defective
7. If the measured values at all ranges are lower than specified, check the following:
   a. Throttle cable out of adjustment
   b. Throttle valve defective
   c. Regulator valve defective
   d. Oil pump defective
8. If the pressure is low in **D** and **2** range only, check the following:
   a. **D** and **2** range circuit fluid leakage
   b. Rear clutch governor defective

9. If the pressure is low in **R** range only, check the following:
   a. **R** range circuit fluid leakage
   b. First and reverse brake defective

GOVERNOR PRESSURE

1. Apply the parking brake.
2. Start the engine.
3. Shift into **D** range and measure the governor pressure at the speeds specified in the following chart:
   Vehicle speed 20 mph—gauge reading 17–21 psi
   Vehicle speed 35 mph—gauge reading 30–35 psi
   Vehicle speed 45 mph—gauge reading 58–64 psi
4. If the governor pressure is not to specification, check for the following:
   a. Line pressure not to specification
   b. Fluid leakage in the governor pressure cuircuit
   c. Improper governor valve operation

STALL SPEED TEST

The object of this test is to check the overall performance of the transaxle and engine by measuring the maximum engine speeds in the **D** and **R** ranges.
1. Run the engine until it reaches normal operating temperature.

NOTE: Do not continuously run this test longer than 5 seconds.

2. Apply the parking brake and block the front and rear wheels.
3. Connect an engine tachometer.
4. Shift into the **D** range.
5. While applying the brakes, step all the way down on the accelerator. Quickly read the highest rpm at this time. The stall speed should be 2050–2350 rpm and the main line pressure should be 128–156 psi.
6. Perform the same test in the **R** range.
7. If the engine speed is the same for all ranges, but lower than the specified value, check for the following:
   a. Engine output insufficient
   b. Stator one-way clutch not operating properly
8. If the engine speed is the same for all ranges and within the specified value, the speed control elements in the transaxle are all normal. Check for a faulty engine.
9. If the stall speed in **D** range is higher than specified, check for a slipping one-way clutch.
10. If the stall speed in **2** range is higher than specified, check for a slipping brake band.
11. If the stall speed in **D**, **2** and **1** is higher than the specified value, check for a slipping rear clutch.
12. If the stall speed in **R** range is higher than specified, check for the following:
   a. Line pressure too low
   b. Front clutch slipping
   c. Low and reverse brake slipping
13. If the stall speed is the same in all ranges, but higher than the specified value, check for the following:
   a. Line pressure too low
   b. Oil pump is weak
   c. Oil leaks from the oil pump control valve or the transaxle case.
   d. Pressure regulator valve is sticky.

ROAD TEST

NOTE: This test must be performed with the engine and transaxle at normal operating temperature.

DRIVE RANGE TEST 1

Shift into **D** range and while driving with the accelerator pedal

Check shift points under following conditions:

Throttle Valve Opening	Completely Closed	Speed Changing Point
Wide open throttle (Kickdown) (0 — 100 mm-Hg, 0 — 3.94 in-Hg)	$D_1 \longrightarrow D_2$ $D_2 \longrightarrow D_3$ $D_3 \longrightarrow D_2$ $D_2 \longrightarrow D_1$	51 — 60 km/h (32 — 37 mph) 101 — 110 km/h (63 — 68 mph) 90 — 99 km/h (56 — 62 mph) 40 — 49 km/h (25 — 30 mph)
Half throttle (200 ± 10 mm-Hg, 7.87 ± 0.39 in-Hg)	$D_1 \longrightarrow D_2$ $D_2 \longrightarrow D_3$ $D_3 \longrightarrow D_2$ $D_2 \longrightarrow D_1$	12 — 21 km/h (8 — 13 mph) 55 — 63 km/h (34 — 39 mph) 28 — 36 km/h (17 — 22 mph) 10 — 18 km/h (6 — 11 mph)
Fully closed throttle Manual "1"	$1_2 \longrightarrow 1$	40 — 48 km/h (25 — 30 mph)

SHIFT SCHEDULE

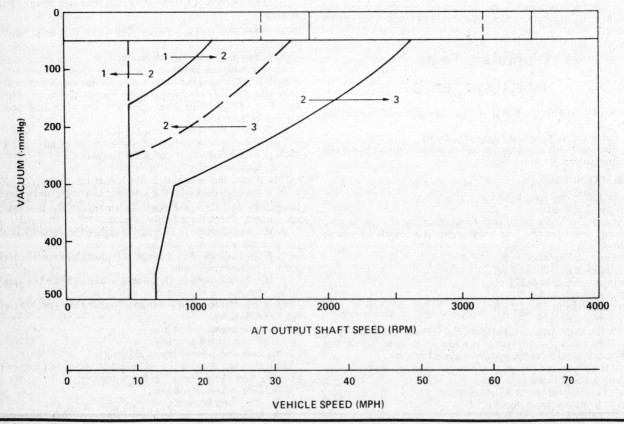

Road test chart

held constant (throttle valve opening 50% and 100%) check the following points:

1. At each of the throttle openings, check that the 1–2 and 2–3 upshifts take place and that the shift points conform to those shown in the automatic shift diagram.

2. If there is no 1–2 upshift, the governor valve may be defective or the 1–2 shift valve stuck.

3. If there is no 2–3 upshift, the 2–3 shift valve is stuck.

4. If the shift point is defective, the throttle cable is out of adjustment or the throttle valve, 1–2 shift valve and the 2–3 shift valves are defective.

DRIVE RANGE TEST 2

Check for harsh shift or soft shift slip at 1–2 and 2–3 upshifts. If the shock is severe, the line pressure is too high, the accumulator is defective or the check ball is defective.

DRIVE RANGE TEST 3

1. While driving in **D** range, 3rd gear, check for abnormal noise and vibration. This condition could also be caused by unbalance in the differential, tires or the torque converter.
2. While driving in **D** range, 2nd and 3rd gears, check the kickdown vehicle speed limits for the 2–1, 3–1 and the 3–2 kickdowns conform to the automatic shift diagram.
3. While driving in **D** range, 3rd gear, shift to **2** and **L** ranges and check the engine braking effect at each of these ranges. If there is no engine braking effect at **2** range, the 2nd coast brake is defective. If there is no engine braking effect at **L** range, 1st and reverse is defective.

DRIVE RANGE TEST 4

While driving in **D** range, release the accelerator pedal and shift into **L** range. Check to see if the 3–2 and 2–1 downshift points conform to those given in the automatic shift diagram.

2 RANGE TEST

1. Shift to **2** range and drive with the throttle valve opening at 50% and 100% respectively. Check the 1–2 upshift points at each of the throttle valve openings to see that it conforms to those indicated in the automatic shift diagram.
2. While driving in **2** range, 2nd gear, release the accelerator pedal and check the engine braking effect.
3. Check the kickdown from **2** range. Check the 2–1 kickdown vehicle speed limit.
4. Check for abnormal noise at acceleration and deceleration and harshness at upshift and downshift.

L RANGE TEST

1. While driving in **L** range, check that there is no upshift to 2nd gear.
2. While driving in **L** range, release the accelerator pedal and check the engine braking effect.
3. Check for abnormal noise during acceleration and deceleration.

R RANGE TEST

Shift into **R** range and while starting at full throttle, check for slipping.

P RANGE TEST

Stop the vehicle on a slight hill and after shifting into **P** range, release the parking brake. Check to see that the parking lock pawl prevents the vehicle from moving.

ON CAR SERVICES

Adjustments

MANUAL LINKAGE

1. When shifting the select lever from **P** to **1**, a clicking should be felt at each shift position. Make sure that the gear corresponds to that of the position plate indicator.
2. Check that the lever can be shifted between **D** and **N** without depressing the push button.
3. Shifting from **D** to **R** cannot be done without depressing the push button. If the lever can be shifted from **D** to **R** without depressing the push button, or if the push button is loose, adjust it by unscrewing the locknut and twisting the selector lever knob.

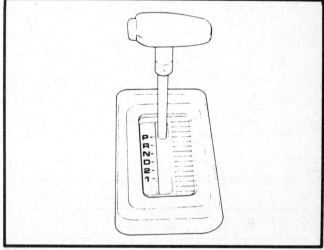

Shifter

SHIFT CONTROL CABLE

1. Loosen the 2 adjusting nuts at the control rod link and connect the shift cable to the link on the transaxle.
2. Shift the transaxle into the neutral detent.
3. Place the shifter lever in the **N** position.
4. Rotate the link assembly clockwise to remove the slack in the cable.
5. Tighten the rear adjusting nut until it makes contact with the link.
6. Tighten the front adjusting nut until it makes contact with the link and then tighten the nuts.

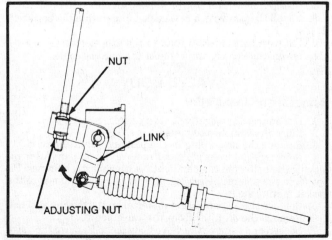

Shift cable adjustment

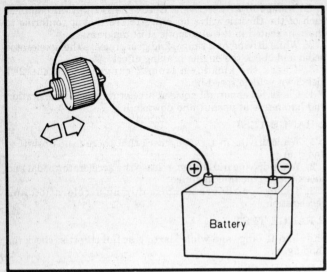

Kickdown solenoid

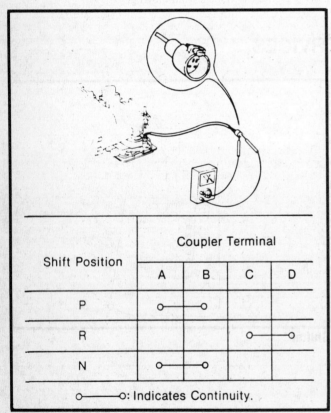

Shift Position	Coupler Terminal			
	A	B	C	D
P	o———o			
R			o———o	
N	o———o			

o———o: Indicates Continuity.

Inhibitor switch

PARK LOCK CABLE

1. Place the ignition key in the **LOCK** position.
2. Place the shifter lever in the **P** position.
3. Pull the cable forward at the shifter bracket and tighten the forward nut until it makes contact with the bracket.
4. Tighten the rear nut until it makes contact with the bracket and then tighten the nuts.

KICKDOWN SOLENOID

1. Make sure the rod functions properly when 12 volts is applied to the kickdown solenoid.
2. Connect a circuit tester to the solenoid terminals. Check if continuity exists when depressing the pedal fully.
3. If continuity does not exist, adjust the kickdown switch by turning the switch so that continuity exists when depressing the pedal more than 7/8 of its stroke.

NEUTRAL SAFETY SWITCH

1. Check that the engine starts only in the **P** and **N** detents.
2. Check that the back-up light is **ON** when the selector lever is in the **R** detent.
3. If the neutral safety switch is faulty, disconnect the switch and check the continuity between each terminal.

Services
FLUID CHANGES

The conditions under which the vehicle is operated is the main consideration in determining how often the transaxle fluid should be changed. Different driving conditions result in different transaxle fluid temperatures. These temperatures effect the change intervals.

If the vehicle is driven under severe service conditions, change the fluid and filter every 15,000 miles. If the vehicle is not used under severe service conditions, change the fluid and replace the filter every 50,000 miles.

Do not overfill the transaxle. It takes 1 pint of fluid to change the level from **ADD** to **FULL** on the transaxle dipstick. Overfilling the unit can cause damage to the internal components of the automatic transaxle.

OIL PAN

Removal and Installation

1. Disconnect the negative battery cable.
2. Raise the vehicle and support it safely.
3. Remove the drain plug in the pan and drain the fluid.
4. Reinstall the drain plug and remove the oil pan. After removing the bolts, tap the pan lightly with a plastic hammer. Do not force the pan off by prying. This may cause damage to the gasket mating surface.
5. Remove the oil pan gasket material on the mating surface.
6. Remove the oil filter from the valve body.
7. Clean the inside of the oil pan before installation.
8. Install a new filter on the valve body.
9. Install the pan with a new gasket and torque the bolts to 5 ft. lbs. (7 Nm).
10. Fill with transmission fluid to the proper level.
11. Lower the vehicle and connect the battery cable.

VALVE BODY

Removal and Installation

1. Disconnect the negative battery cable.
2. Raise the vehicle and support it safely.
3. Remove the drain plug in the pan and drain the fluid.
4. Reinstall the drain plug and remove the oil pan. After removing the bolts, tap the pan lightly with a plastic hammer. Do not force the pan off by prying. This may cause damage to the gasket mating surface.
5. Remove the oil pan gasket material on the mating surface.
6. Remove the oil filter from the valve body.
7. Loosen and remove the valve body bolts. Remove the valve body.

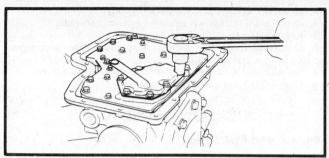

Valve body assembly

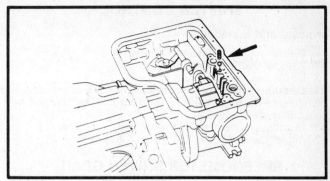

Steel ball and detent spring

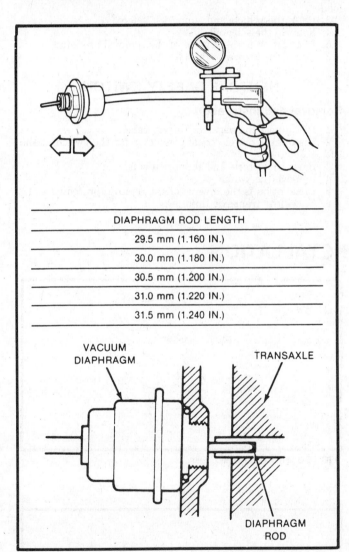

DIAPHRAGM ROD LENGTH
29.5 mm (1.160 IN.)
30.0 mm (1.180 IN.)
30.5 mm (1.200 IN.)
31.0 mm (1.220 IN.)
31.5 mm (1.240 IN.)

Vacuum diaphragm

8. Remove the spring and steel ball from the oil passage.
9. On installation, install steel ball and spring in the oil passage.
10. Install the valve body with the bolts finger tight.
11. Align the manual valve with the shift lever arm and torque the bolts to 7.2 ft. lbs. (8 Nm).
12. Clean the inside of the oil pan before installation.
13. Install the oil pan with a new gasket and torque the bolts to 5 ft. lbs. (7 Nm).

SERVO ASSEMBLY

Removal and Installation

1. Disconnect the negative battery cable.
2. Raise the vehicle and support it safely.
3. Remove the left front wheel and tire assembly.
4. Remove the left lower control arm tension rod assembly.
5. Disconnect the tie rod from the left steering arm.
6. Remove the oil pan bolt nearest to the servo cover.
7. Install tool J–35278 and compress the servo cover. Remove the cover retaining ring and then the cover.
8. Remove tool J–35278 and the servo assembly from the transaxle.
9. Installation is the reverse of the removal procedure. Check the fluid level.

GOVERNOR

Removal and Installation

1. Disconnect the negative battery cable.
2. Raise the vehicle and support it safely.
3. Remove the governor cover retaining bolts.
4. Remove the governor assembly.
5. Installation is the reverse of the removal procedure.

SHIFT CONTROL CABLE

Removal and Installation

1. Disconnect the negative battery cable.
2. Remove the floor console.
3. Disconnect the cable at the shifter.
4. Pull the floor carpet rearward and remove the screws attaching the cable to the floor.
5. Raise the vehicle and support it safely.
6. Disconnect the cable from the transaxle.
7. Remove the cable from the vehicle.
8. Installation is the reverse of the removal procedure.

PARK LOCK CABLE

Removal and Installation

1. Disconnect the negative battery cable.
2. Remove the floor console.
3. Disconnect the cable and the shifter and remove the adjusting nuts.
4. Remove the lower trim cover from the steering column.
5. Pull the floor carpet rearward and remove the cable.
6. Installation is the reverse of the removal procedure.

SHIFTER CONTROL

Removal and Installation

1. Disconnect the negative battery cable.
2. Remove the floor console.
3. Disconnect the shift cable at the control.
4. Disconnect the park lock cable at the shifter.
5. Remove the bolts attaching the control to the floor and remove the control assembly.
6. Installation is reverse of the removal procedure.
7. Adjust the shift cable and the park lock cable.

SPEEDOMETER DRIVEN GEAR

Removal and Installation

1. Disconnect the negative battery cable.
2. Raise the vehicle and support it safely.
3. Disconnect the speedometer cable at the transaxle.
4. Remove the retainer bolt, retainer, speedometer driven gear and the O-ring seal.
5. Installation is the reverse of the removal procedure.
6. Use a new O-ring seal and check the fluid level.

VACUUM DIAPHRAGM

Removal and Installation

1. Disconnect the negative battery cable.
2. Disconnect the kickdown solenoid wire connector at the left fender.
3. Raise the vehicle and support it safely.
4. Remove the kickdown solenoid at the transaxle.
5. Remove the vacuum diaphragm.
6. Make sure that when vacuum is applied to the diaphragm, the diaphragm rod moves properly.
7. Installation is the reverse of the removal procedure.
8. Check the transaxle fluid level.

KICKDOWN SOLENOID

Removal and Installation

1. Disconnect the negative battery cable.
2. Disconnect the electrical connector for the solenoid at the fender.
3. Raise the vehicle and support it safely.
4. Remove the solenoid.
5. Installation is the reverse of the removal procedure.
6. Check the transaxle fluid level.

NEUTRAL SAFETY SWITCH

Removal and Installation

1. Disconnect the negative battery cable.
2. Disconnect the electrical connector for the switch at the left fender.
3. Raise the vehicle and support it safely.
4. Remove the switch.
5. Installation is the reverse of the removal procedure.
6. Check the transaxle fluid level.

REMOVAL AND INSTALLATION

TRANSAXLE REMOVAL

1. Disconnect the negative battery cable.
2. Remove the air cleaner duct.
3. Disconnect the control cable assembly from the transaxle.
4. Disconnect the ground cable from the transaxle. Remove the upper transaxle-to-engine mounting bolts.
5. Disconnect and plug the cooler hoses.
6. Raise and safely support vehicle.
7. Drain the fluid and reinstall the pan.
8. Disconnect the kickdown solenoid and the neutral safety switch.
9. Pull the vacuum hose off of the modulator.
10. Take note of where the speedometer cable is routed and disconnect the cable.
11. Remove both axles.
    a. Disconnect the tension rod from the control arm.
    b. Remove the cotter pin, axle nut and flat washer from the axle end.
    c. Pull the knuckle assembly away from the wheel well and separate the axle from the knuckle.
    d. Using a suitable prying tool, pry the axle from the transaxle.
12. Remove the left side tension arm and bracket.
13. Support both the engine and transaxle safely and firmly with their respective holding fixtures. Use blocks of wood to prevent any bending of either pan. Remove the center support.
14. Remove the converter under cover, matchmark the converter to the flywheel and unbolt the converter from the flywheel. There are 4 converter bolts.
15. Unbolt the engine mounts.
16. Remove any remaining bolts connecting the engine to the transaxle.
17. Tilt the entire assembly downward and remove the transaxle.

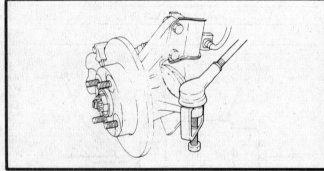

Tie rod end removal

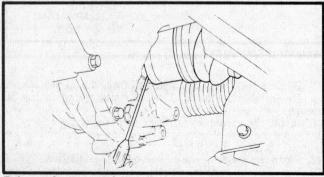

Drive axle removal

TRANSAXLE INSTALLATION

1. Using a lifting device, raise the transaxle, align the engine housing dowels and install the assembly. Be sure that the torque converter is properly aligned with the flex plate. Torque the engine to transaxle bolts to 56 ft. lbs. (76 Nm).

2. Install the engine mounts. Torque the bolts to 61 ft. lbs. (83 Nm).

3. Bolt the torque converter to the flywheel. Install the bolts using loctite® on the threads. Torque the bolts to 30 ft. lbs. (41 Nm). Install the converter under cover.

4. Install the center support. Torque bolts to 51 ft. lbs. (69 Nm). Remove the holding fixtures.

5. Install both axles to the transaxle being careful not to damage the axle seals when installing.

6. Complete the axle installation.

    a. Insert the axle into the hub.

    b. Apply grease to the threads of the axle nut, the flat washer and the axle threads and torque the nut to 137.4 ft. lbs. (187 Nm).

    c. Install a new cotter pin; if the split pin holes are not aligned, tighten the nut just enough to align them.

    d. Torque the tension rod nuts to 80 ft. lbs. (109 Nm).

7. Install the left side tension arm. Torque the bolts that attach the bracket to the body to 48 ft. lbs. (65 Nm).

8. Connect the speedometer cable.

NOTE: Route the speedometer away from hot or moving parts. Do not allow it to kink when installing and do not install in a kinked position.

9. Connect the vacuum hose to the modulator.

10. Connect the kickdown solenoid.

11. Connect the neutral safety switch.

12. Install a new pan gasket.

13. Lower the vehicle.

14. Connect the cooler lines.

15. Connect the ground cable to the transaxle. Install any upper transaxle to engine bolts that were not installed from underneath. Torque to 56 ft. lbs. (76 Nm).

16. Install the control cable and adjust correctly.

17. Install the air cleaner duct.

18. Connect the negative cable to the battery.

19. Install the hood if it was removed.

20. Replenish the fluid to the correct level. Check to see that the reverse lights come on in **R** range and that the neutral safety switch is working. Road test the vehicle and check for leaks.

BENCH OVERHAUL

Before Disassembly

Before opening up the transaxle, the outside of the unit should be thoroughly cleaned, preferably with high pressure cleaning equipment. Dirt entering the transaxle internal parts will negate all the effort and time spent on the overhaul. During inspection and reassembly, all parts should be thoroughly cleaned with solvent and then dried with compressed air. Cloths and rags should not be used to dry the parts since lint will find its way into the valve body passages.

Lube the seals with Dexron® II automatic transmission fluid and use unmedicated petroleum jelly to hold the thrust washers and ease the assembly of the seals. Do not use solvent on neoprene seals, friction plates or thrust washers. Be wary of nylon parts if the transaxle failure was due to a cooling system problem. Nylon parts exposed to antifreeze solutions can swell and distort, so they must be replaced. Before installing bolts into aluminum parts, dip the threads in clean oil.

Converter Inspection

Make certain that the transaxle is held securely. If the torque converter is equipped with a drain plug, open the plug and drain the fluid. If there is no drain plug, the converter must be drained through the hub after pulling the converter out of the transaxle. If the oil in the converter is discolored but does not contain metal bits or particles, the converter is not damaged. Color is no longer a good indicator of fluid condition.

If the oil in the converter contains metal particles, the converter is damaged internally and must be replaced. If the cause of the oil contamination was burned clutch plates or overheated oil, the converter is contaminated and should be replaced. If the pump gears or cover show signs of damage, the converter will contain metal particles and must be replaced.

Transaxle Disassembly

1. Position the transaxle in a suitable holding fixture. Remove the drain plug and drain the fluid from the transaxle.

2. Remove the neutral safety switch and the kickdown solenoid.

3. Remove the vacuum diaphragm and the rod.

4. Remove the dipstick and tube.

5. Remove the speedometer driven gear.

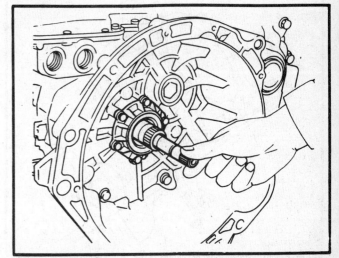

Oil pump shaft

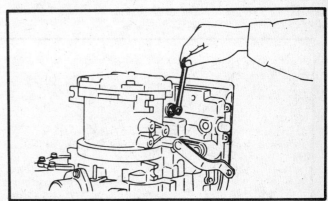

Anchor end bolt

6. Remove the oil pump shaft and then the turbine shaft by pulling outward.

7. Remove the oil pan.

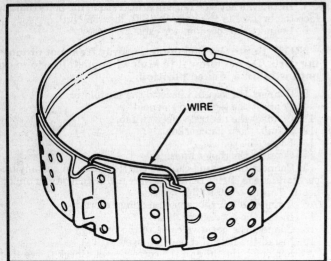

Retaining brake band

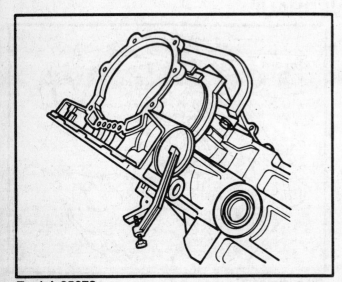

Tool J–35278

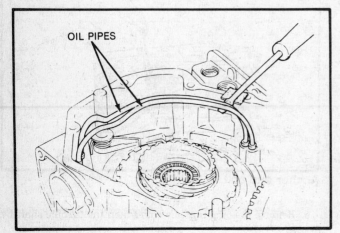

Oil pipes

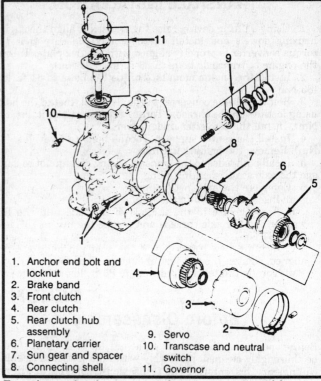

1. Anchor end bolt and locknut
2. Brake band
3. Front clutch
4. Rear clutch
5. Rear clutch hub assembly
6. Planetary carrier
7. Sun gear and spacer
8. Connecting shell
9. Servo
10. Transcase and neutral switch
11. Governor

Front/rear clutch, servo and governor assembly

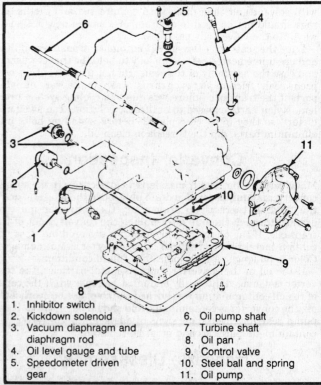

1. Inhibitor switch
2. Kickdown solenoid
3. Vacuum diaphragm and diaphragm rod
4. Oil level gauge and tube
5. Speedometer driven gear
6. Oil pump shaft
7. Turbine shaft
8. Oil pan
9. Control valve
10. Steel ball and spring
11. Oil pump

External controls

8. Remove the valve body assembly.
9. Remove the spring and steel check ball from the case.
10. Remove the oil pump assembly. If the oil pump is difficult to remove, tighten the anchor end bolt and lock the front clutch with the brake band.

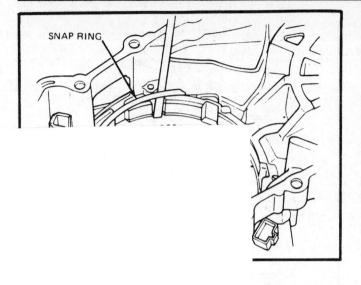

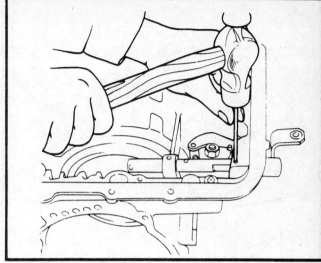

Control rod removal

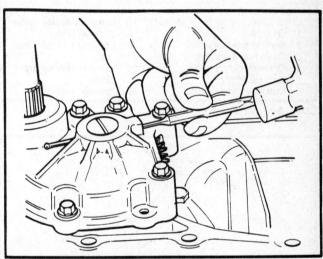

Idler gear roll pin removal

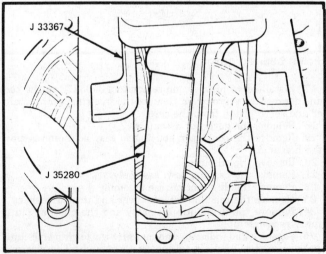

Differental bearing race removal

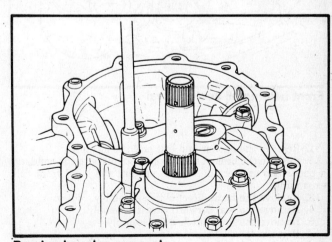

Bearing housing removal

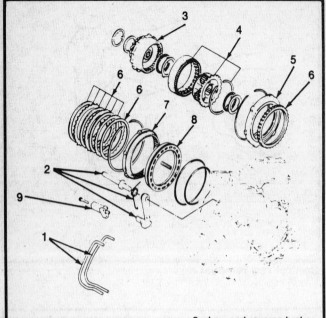

1. Oil pipe
2. Parking pawl assembly
3. Drum hub assembly
4. One-way clutch inner race assembly
5. One-way clutch
6. Low and reverse brake plate assembly
7. Low and reverse brake hub
8. Low and reverse brake piston
9. Actuator support

Low/reverse clutch assembly

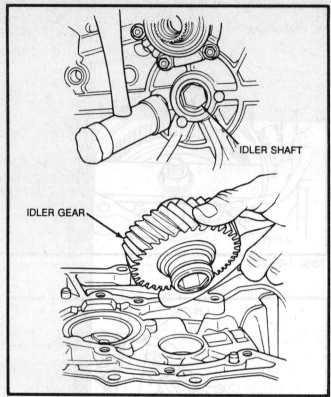

IDLER SHAFT

IDLER GEAR

Idler shaft removal

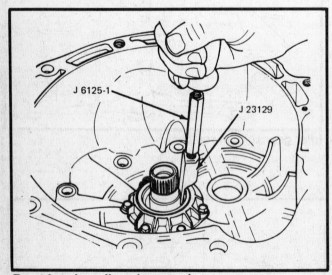

J 6125-1

J 23129

Front bearing oil seal removal

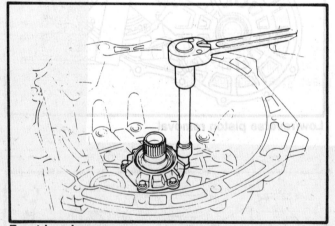

Front bearing cover

11. Remove the anchor end bolt and the locknut.
12. Remove the brake band. To avoid damage to the band, use a paper clip or piece of wire to prevent the band from fully expanding.
13. Remove the front/direct clutch assembly.
14. Remove the rear/forward clutch assembly.
15. Remove the rear clutch hub assembly.
16. Remove the planetary carrier, sun gear with the spacer and the connecting shell.

17. Install servo piston compressor tool J–35278 to the case and depress the servo cover. Remove the snapring, servo retainer and servo piston from the case.
18. Remove the governor assembly.
19. Remove the converter housing to case bolts and remove the housing.
20. Remove the oil pipes.
21. Remove the parking pawl assembly.
22. Remove the differential case assembly.
23. Remove the reaction internal gear and thrust washer.
24. Remove the drum/hub assembly and the one-way clutch inner race assembly.
25. Attach a dial indicator and measure the low/reverse clutch pack clearance. Use air to engage the clutch. The clearance should be 0.031–0.040 in.

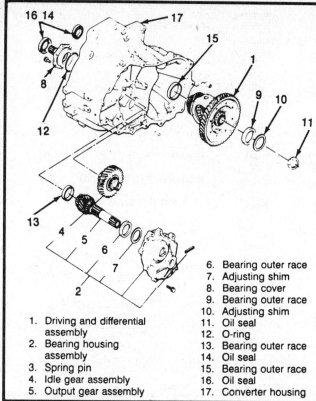

Final drive assembly

1. Driving and differential assembly
2. Bearing housing assembly
3. Spring pin
4. Idle gear assembly
5. Output gear assembly
6. Bearing outer race
7. Adjusting shim
8. Bearing cover
9. Bearing outer race
10. Adjusting shim
11. Oil seal
12. O-ring
13. Bearing outer race
14. Oil seal
15. Bearing outer race
16. Oil seal
17. Converter housing

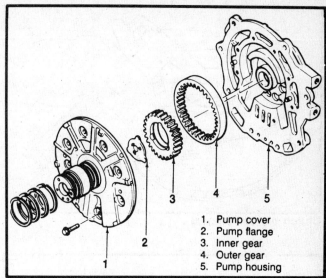

Oil pump exploded view

1. Pump cover
2. Pump flange
3. Inner gear
4. Outer gear
5. Pump housing

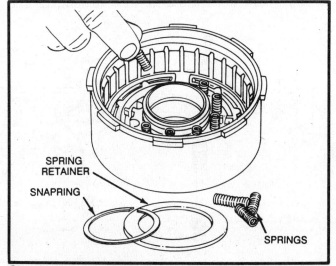

Clutch piston springs

SPRING RETAINER

SNAPRING

SPRINGS

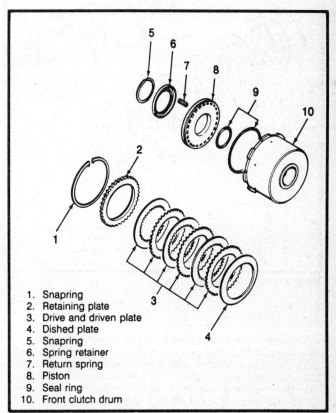

Front clutch exploded view

1. Snapring
2. Retaining plate
3. Drive and driven plate
4. Dished plate
5. Snapring
6. Spring retainer
7. Return spring
8. Piston
9. Seal ring
10. Front clutch drum

28. Install tool J–35279 and thread the 4 small bolts included through the bar and into the piston. Tighten the center bolt to pull the piston from the case.

26. Remove the snapring retaining the one-way clutch assembly and remove the one-way clutch from the case.

27. Install tool J–35279, or equivalent and tighten the bolt to compress the clutch return springs. Remove the snapring from the clutch return spring retainer. Remove tool J–35279 or equivalent, the spring retainer and the springs from the case.

29. Remove the roll pin retaining the manual shaft to the case and remove the manual shaft from the case.

30. Remove the differential side bearing outer race and shim from the case using puller J–33367 and J–35280 bearing race puller.

31. Using a drift and hammer, remove the roll pin retaining the idler gear to the bearing housing.

32. Remove the bolts retaining the bearing housing to the converter housing. Remove the bearing housing.

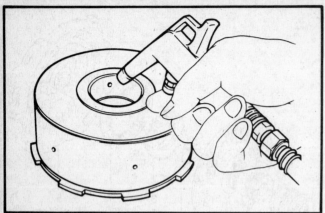

Clutch piston removal

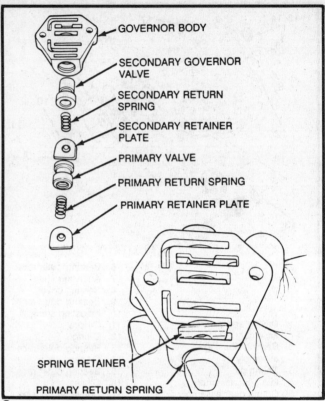

Governor body
Secondary governor valve
Secondary return spring
Secondary retainer plate
Primary valve
Primary return spring
Primary retainer plate

Spring retainer

Primary return spring

Governor springs and retainers

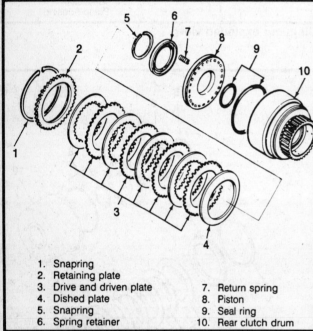

1. Snapring
2. Retaining plate
3. Drive and driven plate
4. Dished plate
5. Snapring
6. Spring retainer
7. Return spring
8. Piston
9. Seal ring
10. Rear clutch drum

Rear clutch exploded view

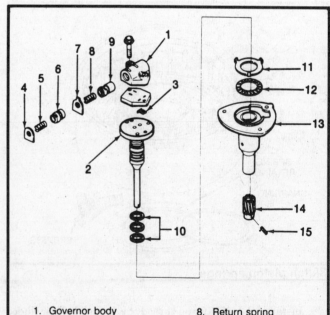

1. Governor body
2. Governor shaft assembly
3. Filter
4. Retainer plate
5. Return spring
6. Primary governor
7. Retainer plate
8. Return spring
9. Secondary governor
10. Seal ring
11. Bearing outer race
12. Bearing
13. Sleeve
14. Governor driven gear
15. Roll pin

Governor assembly

33. Remove the output gear from the housing.
34. Remove the idler gear from the housing. Tap the idler shaft from the converter side of the housing.
35. Remove the bearing outer race from the bearing housing.
36. Remove the oil seal from the front bearing cover using J–23129 seal remover and J–6125–1 slide hammer.
37. Remove the bearing race from the converter housing.
38. Remove the front bearing cover from the converter housing.

Unit Disassembly and Assembly

OIL PUMP

Disassembly

1. Remove the 7 bolts from the pump cover.
2. Separate the cover and hub from the pump body.

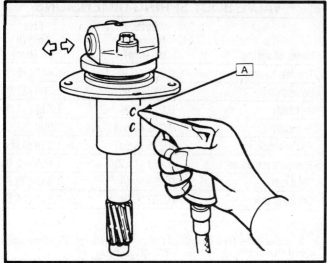

Checking valve operation

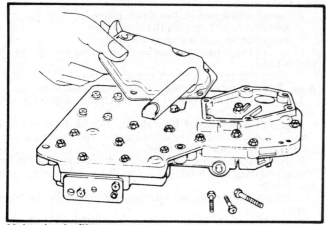

Valve body filter

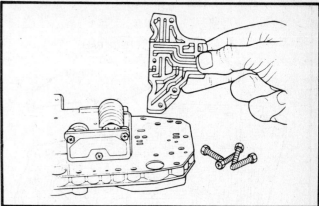

Valve sub-body

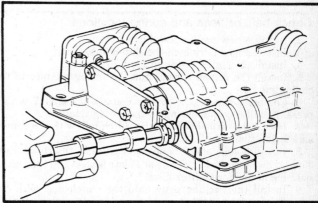

Manual valve

2. Install the pump front cover and hub on the pump body.
3. Install the 7 bolts and tighten them to 17 ft. lbs.(23 Nm).

FRONT/DIRECT CLUTCH

Disassembly

1. Remove the large snapring from the front clutch pack.
2. Remove the multiple disc clutch pack including the dish plate from the hub.
3. Position the front/direct clutch in a press. Use spring compressor J–23327 and adapter J–25018–A to compress the piston return springs.
4. Remove the spring retainer and springs from the piston.
5. Apply air to the clutch hub to remove the piston.
6. Remove the O-ring from the clutch hub.

Inspection

1. Use a micrometer to measure the drum bushing inside diameter. The maximum inside diameter is 0.068 in. (1.735mm). If the bushing is out of specification, replace the drum.
2. Inspect the O-ring for wear. Replace as necessary.
3. Inspect the clutch plates, snaprings and spring retainer for wear.
4. Check the free length of the piston springs. The free length should be 0.992–1.071 in. (25.2–27.2mm).

Assembly

1. Apply Dexron® II automatic transmission fluid to the seals and seal surfaces.

Inspection

1. Place a metal straight edge across the pump face. Use a feeler gauge to measure the inner gear to pump cover clearance. The clearance is 0.001–0.002 in. (0.02–0.04mm). The maximum clearance is 0.003 in. (0.08mm). Measure the outer gear to pump clearance in the same manner.
2. Use a feeler gauge to measure the head of the outer gear teeth to crescent clearance. The clearance is 0.006–0.008 in. (0.14–0.21mm). The maximum clearance is 0.010 in. (0.25mm).
3. Measure the outer gear to housing clearance. The clearance is 0.002–0.008 in. (0.05–0.20mm). The maximum clearance is 0.010 in. (0.25mm).
4. Use a feeler gauge to measure the pump hub seal ring to seal ring groove clearance. The clearance is 0.002–0.006 in. (0.04–0.16mm). The maximum clearance is 0.016 in. (0.40mm).
5. Use a micrometer to measure the pump housing sleeve outer diameter. The diameter should be 1.492 in. (37.900mm) minimum.
6. Use a micrometer to measure the inner gear bushing diameter. The diameter should be 1.499 in. (38.075mm) maximum.

Assembly

1. Reinstall the pump gears in the pump body.

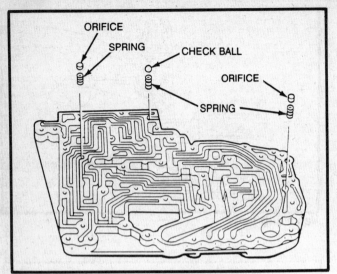

Check ball, orifices and spring locations

2. Install a new seal on the clutch piston.
3. Install a new O-ring on the clutch hub.
4. Install the clutch piston in the hub.
5. Install the return springs and the spring retainer in the clutch hub.
6. Compress the return springs using tool J-23327 with a press. Install a new snapring on the spring retainer.
7. Install the dished plate in the clutch hub with the convex side facing the piston.
8. Install 3 steel and 3 fiber clutch discs in the clutch hub. The 1st disc installed on the dished plate is steel and then alternate metal discs with fiber discs.
9. Install the backing plate onto the clutch disc with the smooth side down. Install a new snapring in the clutch hub.
10. Install the assembled front/direct clutch on the pump hub.
11. Install a dial indicator with the pin resting on the backing plate to measure the clutch pack travel.
12. Engage the clutch by applying air to the pump. The dial indicator measurement should be 0.063–0.071 in. (1.6–1.8mm).
13. If the dial indicator reading is not within specification, change the thickness of the retaining plate. The following is a list of the retaining plate sizes:

0.205 in. (5.2mm)
0.213 in. (5.4mm)
0.220 in. (5.6mm)
0.228 in. (5.8mm)
0.236 in. (6.0mm)
0.244 in. (6.2mm)

REAR/FORWARD CLUTCH

Disassembly

1. Remove the large snapring from the rear clutch pack.
2. Remove the clutch pack from the clutch hub.
3. Position the rear/forward clutch in a press. Use spring compressor J-23327 and adapter J-25018–A to compress the piston return springs.
4. Remove the spring retainer and springs from the piston.
5. Apply air to the clutch hub to remove the piston.
6. Remove the O-ring from the clutch hub.

Inspection

1. Inspect the O-ring for wear. Replace as necessary.
2. Inspect the clutch plates, snaprings and spring retainer for wear.

VALVE BODY SPRING DIMENSIONS

Name of spring	Outer Diameter in. (mm)	Free Length in. (mm)
Throttle backup	0.287 (7.3)	1.417 (36.0)
Downshift	0.218 (5.55)	0.866 (22.0)
2–3 shift	0.272 (6.9)	1.614 (41.0)
1–2 shift	0.258 (6.55)	1.260 (32.0)
Second lock	0.218 (5.55)	1.319 (33.5)
Pressure regulator	0.461 (11.7)	1.693 (43.0)
Steel ball	0.256 (6.5)	1.516 (26.8)
Orifice check	0.197 (5.0)	0.846 (21.5)

3. Check the free length of the piston springs. The free length should be 0.992–1.071 in. (25.2–27.2mm).

Assembly

1. Apply Dexron® II automatic transmission fluid to the seals and seal surfaces.
2. Install a new seal on the clutch piston.
3. Install a new O-ring on the clutch hub.
4. Install the clutch piston in the hub.
5. Install the return springs and the spring retainer in the clutch hub.
6. Compress the return springs using tool J-23327 with a press. Install a new snapring on the spring retainer.
7. Install the dished plate in the clutch hub with the convex side facing the piston.
8. Install 4 steel and 4 fiber clutch discs in the clutch hub. The 1st disc installed on the dished plate is steel and then alternate metal discs with fiber discs.
9. Install the backing plate onto the clutch disc with the beveled edge facing the clutch discs. Install a new snapring in the clutch hub.
10. Install the assembled rear/forward clutch on the pump hub.
11. Install a dial indicator with the pin resting on the backing plate to measure the clutch pack travel.
12. Engage the clutch by applying air to the pump. The dial indicator measurement should be 0.031–0.059 in. (0.8–1.5mm).
13. If the dial indicator reading is not within specification, replace the clutch discs.

GOVERNOR

Disassembly

1. Remove the bolts from the governor body.
2. Remove the body and spacer from the governor shaft assembly.
3. Remove the spring retainers from the governor body by pressing the primary return spring.
4. Remove the secondary retainer and return spring in the same manner.
5. Remove the roll pin from the governor driven gear and remove the gear from the shaft.
6. Remove the governor shaft, bearing and outer race from the sleeve.

Inspection

1. Inspect the valve and return springs for wear or damage.
2. Check the valve operation by applying air in the governor hole. The valve should vibrate and make a buzzing noise.
3. Check for a clogged filter.

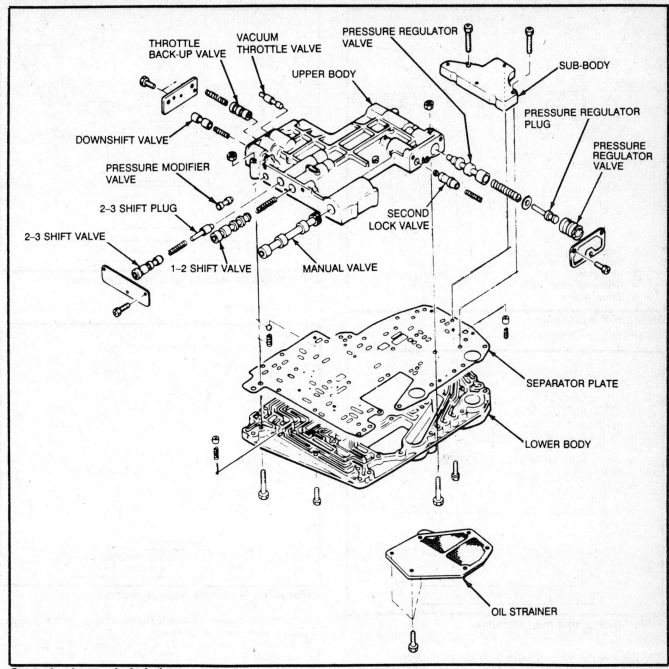

THROTTLE BACK-UP VALVE

VACUUM THROTTLE VALVE

PRESSURE REGULATOR VALVE

UPPER BODY

SUB-BODY

PRESSURE REGULATOR PLUG

DOWNSHIFT VALVE

PRESSURE MODIFIER VALVE

PRESSURE REGULATOR VALVE

2-3 SHIFT PLUG

SECOND LOCK VALVE

2-3 SHIFT VALVE

1-2 SHIFT VALVE

MANUAL VALVE

SEPARATOR PLATE

LOWER BODY

OIL STRAINER

Control valve exploded view

Assembly

1. Install the 3 seal rings on the shaft.
2. Install the bearing and the outer race on the sleeve.
3. Install the governor shaft in the sleeve.
4. Install the governor driven gear on the shaft and retain the gear with a roll pin.
5. Install the secondary valve, rerturn spring and retainer plate in the governor body.
6. Install the primary valve, return spring and retainer plate in the governor body.
7. Install a new filter, spacer and governor body on the shaft.
8. Install the retaining bolts and tighten to 5 ft. lbs. (7 Nm).

VALVE BODY

The control valve is one of the highest precision parts used in the automatic transaxle and it should be handled with the utmost care. If the clutch has been overheated or the brake band has been burnt, be sure to disassemble, clean and inspect the valve body.

Disassembly

1. Remove the 3 bolts retaining the filter to the valve body.
2. Remove the 4 bolts retaining the valve sub-body and remove the sub-body from the valve body.

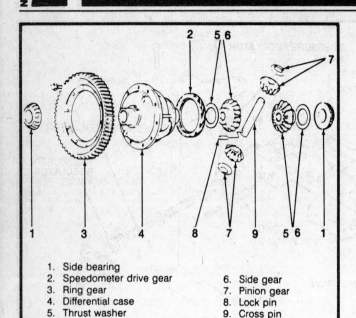

1. Side bearing
2. Speedometer drive gear
3. Ring gear
4. Differential case
5. Thrust washer
6. Side gear
7. Pinion gear
8. Lock pin
9. Cross pin

Differential assembly

LIMIT	27.35 mm (9.358 IN.)

Differential case/drive axle shaft clearance

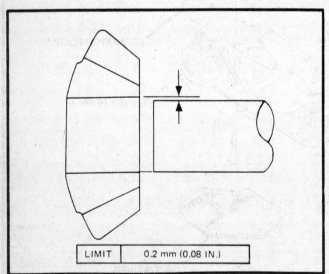

LIMIT	0.2 mm (0.08 IN.)

Pinion gear/cross pin clearance

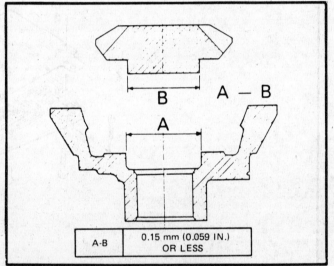

A-B	0.15 mm (0.059 IN.) OR LESS

Differential case/side gear clearance

3. Remove the manual valve from the valve body.

4. Remove the bolts retaining the upper and lower valve bodies. Separate the upper body from the lower body and remove the separator plate.

5. Remove the orifices, check ball and springs from the lower valve body.

6. Disassemble the upper valve body.

Inspection

1. Inspect each valve for damage or wear.
2. Check for damage in the oil passages.
3. Check each valve body for cracks.
4. Check the valve operations.
5. Check for spring fatigue.

Assembly

1. Assemble the upper valve body. When installing the side plate, align the center of the hole that is arrowed with the center of the vacuum throttle valve.

2. Install the springs, orifices and check ball in the lower valve body.

3. Position the separator plate and the upper valve body on the lower valve body.

4. Install the manual valve in the upper valve body.

5. Position and align the valve sub-body on the separator plate and install the retaining bolts.

6. Install the valve body filter and the retaining bolts.

DIFFERENTIAL CASE

Disassembly

1. Remove the side bearings from the differential case using bearing puller J–22888 with J–35288 pilot.

2. Remove the speedometer drive gear. Heat the gear with a heat gun before pulling the gear off.

3. Remove the ring gear from the differential case. The ring gear bolts are not reusable.

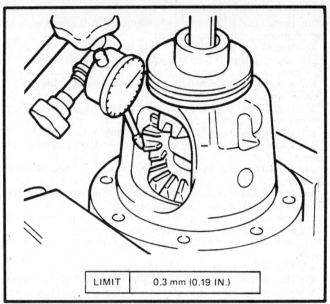

LIMIT	0.3 mm (0.19 IN.)

Side gear/pinion gear backlash

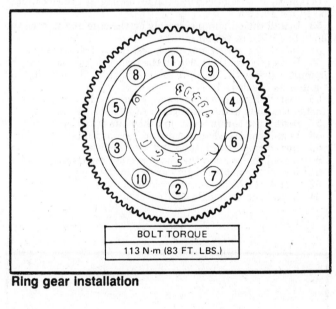

BOLT TORQUE
113 N·m (83 FT. LBS.)

Ring gear installation

4. Remove the lock pin used to retain the cross pin.
5. Remove the cross pin from the differential case.
6. Remove the pinion gears, side gears and thrust washers from the differential case.

Inspection

1. Measure the clearance between the pinion gear and the cross pin. The clearance is 0.08 in. (0.2mm).
2. Measure the clearance between the differential case and the side gear. The clearance is 0.059 in. (0.15mm) or less.
3. Measure the diameter in the differential case of the drive axle shaft. The clearance is 9.358 in. (27.35mm).
4. Measure the backlash between the side gear and the pinion gear. The limit is 0.19 in. (0.3mm). If the backlash is beyond the limit, install new thrust washers.

Assembly

1. Install the thrust washers in the case.
2. Install the side gears in the case.
3. Install the pinion gears in the case. Align the cross pin hole of the pinion gear with the cross pin hole of the differential case.
4. Install the cross pin. After installation of the pin, stake the edge of the lock pin hole in the case with a punch to prevent the loss of the lock pin.
5. Install a new speedometer drive gear. Heater the gear with a heat gun before installing. Do not use hot water to heat the gear.
6. Install both differential side bearings.
7. Install a new ring gear and tighten the bolts following the sequence to 83 ft. lbs. (113 Nm). Use new ring gear bolts if the ring has been removed.

Transaxle Assembly

1. Install the differential side bearing race in the converter housing.
2. Install the differential case assembly in the converter housing.
3. Set the shim selector gauge J–35284 bridge and leg assembly, with J–35284–4 gauge cylinder and J–35284–8 differential gear gauge pin on the transaxle case over the differential bearing housing.
4. Loosen the thumb screw allowing the gauge pin to rest on the bearing race seat. Tighten the thumb screw to remove the tool from the case.
5. Install the other side bearing race on the exposed side bearing. Set the shim selector gauge on the converter housing over the differential case.
6. Loosen the thumb screw allowing the gauge pin to rest on the bearing race and them tighten the thumb screw.
7. Select the appropriate side bearing shim according to the remaining gap in the gauge pin.
8. Install the selected shim into the side bearing race bore of the transaxle case. Install the bearing race.
9. Install a new O-ring on the bearing cover and install the cover on the converter housing. Tighten the bolts to 9 ft. lbs. (13 Nm).
10. Install a new oil seal in the bearing cover.
11. Install the bearing race in the bearing cover.
12. Set the shim selector gauge J–35284 bridge and leg assembly, with J–35284–4 gauge cylinder and J–35284–8 differential gear gauge pin on the bearing housing.
13. Loosen the thumb screw allowing the gauge pin to rest on the output shaft bearing race and shim seat. Tighten the thumb screw to remove the tool from the bearing housing.
14. Install the output gear in the converter housing with the bearing race on the exposed bearing.
15. Place the bridge assembly on the converter housing. Loosen the thumb screw so that the gauge pin rests on the output shaft bearing race. Tighten the thumb screw.
16. Select the appropriate output gear bearing shim according to the remaining gap in the gauge pin. The following is a list of available shim sizes:
   0.004 in. (0.10mm)
   0.005 in. (0.12mm)
   0.006 in. (0.14mm)
   0.007 in. (0.16mm)
   0.008 in. (0.20mm)
   0.020 in. (0.50mm)
17. Install the selected output gear shim into the bearing race bore of the bearing housing. Install the bearing race.
18. Install the idler gear assembly in the converter housing. Tap the idler shaft to seat the gear assembly.
19. Install the output gear assembly in the converter housing.

20. Install the bearing housing on the converter housing and tighten the bolts to 17 ft. lbs. (23 Nm).

21. Align the idler gear shaft roll pin hole with the bearing housing roll pin hole. Install the idler gear roll pin.

22. Install the low/reverse piston in the transaxle case.

23. Install the springs into the spring pockets on the low/reverse piston. Install the spring retainer plate on the springs. Install the snapring and make sure that it is seated in the groove.

24. Install the multiple disc clutch pack. Install the dish plate first with the concave side facing the piston, then alternate the clutch discs: 4 steel, 4 fibers starting with the steel disc first.

25. Install the backing plate on the clutch discs with the smooth flat side facing the discs. Install the one-way clutch on the backing plate with the machined surface facing the backing plate and retain it with a new snapring.

26. Measure the low/reverse clutch clearance by setting a dial indicator on the case with the gauge pin on the clutch plate.

27. Apply air through the oil passage to engage the clutch.

28. The clutch clearance is 0.031–0.041 in. (0.8–1.05mm). If the dial indicator reading is not within the clearance specification, change the thickness of the retaining plate. The following is a list of the available retaining plate sizes:

    0.307 in. (7.8mm)
    0.315 in. (8.0mm)
    0.323 in. (8.2mm)
    0.331 in. (8.4mm)
    0.339 in. (8.6mm)
    0.346 in. (8.8mm)

29. Install the low/reverse clutch pack spacer between the case and bottom disc.

30. Install the one-way clutch inner race assembly with the thrust washer.

31. Install the drum hub gear assembly with the thrust bearings on the one-way clutch inner race.

32. Install the parking rod assembly in the case.

33. Install the control rod in the case after the spring and detent ball has been installed.

34. Install the manual shaft with a new O-ring into the case. Install the manual plate lever on the end of the manual shaft and install the retaining nut.

35. Connect the manual plate lever to the parking rod assembly and install the retaining clip.

36. Install the actuator support in the transaxle case. Tighten the bolt to 10 ft. lbs. (14 Nm).

37. Install the parking pawl assembly.

38. Install the oil pipes in the transaxle case.

39. Install the differential case assembly in the case with the speedometer gear facing upward.

40. Install the governor assembly with a new gasket in the case, aligning thge tab on the governor plate with the mark on the case. Install the governor cover with a new gasket on the governor assembly. Install the bolts the bolts and tighten to 5 ft. lbs. (7 Nm).

41. Install the converter housing on the transaxle case. Tighten the retaining bolts to 30 ft. lbs. (40 Nm).

42. Install the servo and spring assembly into the case.

43. Install the servo cover using a new snapring to retain the cover.

44. Install the thrust bearing and washer on the planetary carrier.

45. Install the spacer and sun gear into the connecting shell. Install the shell in the transaxle case.

46. Install the planetary carrier assembly on the sun gear. Install the thrust washer and bearing on the carrier.

47. Install the rear clutch hub with the thrust bearing in the case.

48. Install the lube oil seal in the case.

49. Install the rear clutch assembly in the case. Make sure the tabbed thrust washer is in place on the back side of the clutch.

50. Install the front clutch assembly in the transaxle case.

51. Install the brake band with the strut in the case.

52. Install the anchor end bolt and tighten the bolt to 10 ft. lbs. (14 Nm) then loosen the bolt 2 full turns. Tighten the locknut to 50 ft. lbs. (68 Nm).

53. Install the oil pump assembly on the case and tighten the bolts to 17 ft. lbs. (23 Nm).

54. Install the spring and check ball in the transaxle case.

55. Install the control valve on the transaxle case aligning the manual valve with the shift lever arm. Install the bolts and tighten to 7 ft. lbs. (10 Nm).

56. Install the oil pan with a new gasket on the transaxle case. Install the bolts and tighten them to 5 ft. lbs. (7 Nm).

57. Install the turbin shaft and then the oil pump shaft.

58. Install the speedometer driven gear assembly.

59. Install the dipstick tube and the dipstick.

60. Install the rod and the vacuum diaphragm in the case.

61. Install the neutral safety switch in the case.

62. Install the kickdown solenoid in the case.

64. Install the drive axle shaft seals.

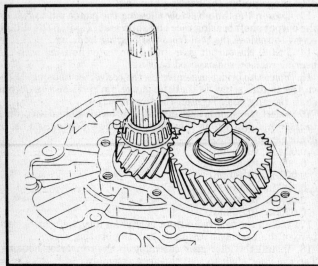

Installing the output gear

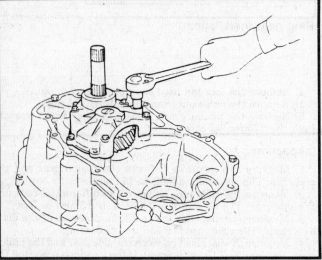

Installing the bearing housing

SPECIFICATIONS

GENERAL SPECIFICATIONS

Characteristics of torque converter	Stall capacity	3000 rpm
Planetary gear ratio	1st	2.841
	2nd	1.541
	3rd	1.000
	Reverse	2.400
	Number of front clutch plate	3
	Number of rear clutch plate	4
Hydraulic unit	Number of low and reverse brake plates	4
	Servo diameter	①
Speedometer gear ratio	—	0.857 (30/35)
Final gear ratio	—	3.526
Number of output gear teeth	—	19
Number of idler gear teeth	—	36
Number of ring gear teeth	—	67
Oil used	Type	ATF Dexron® II
	Capacity	5.8 liters (6.1 U.S. quarts)

① Piston outer diameter—2.520 in. (64 mm)
Retainer inner diameter—1.811 in. (46 mm)

OIL PUMP SHIM SPECIFICATIONS

in.	mm
0.051	1.3
0.059	1.5
0.067	1.7
0.075	1.9
0.083	2.1
0.091	2.3
0.098	2.5
0.106	2.7

DIFFERENTIAL SIDE BEARING SHIM SPECIFICATIONS

in.	mm	in.	mm
0.04252	1.08	0.06142	1.56
0.04409	1.12	0.06299	1.60
0.04567	1.16	0.06457	1.64
0.04724	1.20	0.06614	1.68
0.04882	1.24	0.06772	1.72
0.05039	1.28	0.06929	1.76
0.05197	1.32	0.07087	1.80
0.05354	1.36	0.07244	1.84
0.05512	1.40	0.07402	1.88
0.05669	1.44	0.07559	1.92
0.05827	1.48	0.07717	1.96
0.05984	1.52	0.07874	2.00

DIFFERENTIAL THRUST WASHER SPECIFICATIONS

in.	mm
0.03019	0.765
0.03228	0.820
0.03465	0.880
0.03701	0.940

REAR CLUTCH HUB BEARING OUTER RACE SPECIFICATIONS

in.	mm
0.047	1.2
0.055	1.4
0.063	1.6
0.071	1.8
0.079	2.0
0.087	2.2

IDLER GEAR BEARING PRELOAD SHIM SPECIFICATIONS

in.	mm
0.004	0.10
0.005	0.12
0.006	0.14
0.007	0.16
0.008	0.20
0.020	0.50

SPECIFICATIONS

OUTPUT GEAR BEARING SHIM SPECIFICATIONS

in.	mm
0.004	0.10
0.005	0.12
0.006	0.14
0.007	0.16
0.008	0.20
0.020	0.50

FRONT CLUTCH RETAINING PLATE SPECIFICATIONS

in.	mm
0.205	5.2
0.213	5.4
0.220	5.6
0.228	5.8
0.236	6.0
0.244	6.2

CLUTCH CLEARANCE SPECIFICATIONS

	in.	mm
Low and reverse brake	0.031–0.041	0.8–1.1
Front clutch	0.063–0.071	1.6–1.8

LOW/REVERSE BRAKE RETAINING PLATE SPECIFICATIONS

in.	mm
0.181	4.6
0.189	4.8
0.197	5.0
0.205	5.2
0.213	5.4
0.220	5.6
0.307	7.8
0.315	8.0
0.323	8.2
0.331	8.4
0.339	8.6
0.346	8.8

TORQUE SPECIFICATIONS

Part	ft. lbs.	Nm
Transaxle to engine bolts	56	76
Center support bolts	51	69
Engine mount bolts	61	83
Tension rod bracket bolts	48	65
Tension rod to control arm bolts	80	109
Lug nuts	65	88
Ring gear bolts	83	113
Idler gear shaft locknut	94–130	128–177
Converter housing to case bolts	30	41
Converter to flywheel bolts	30	41

SPECIAL TOOLS

Tool	Description
J 3289-20	Holding fixture base
J 35276	Holding fixture
J 35263	Output shaft bearing remover pilot
J 25695-10	Oil pressure gauge adapter
J 21867	Oil pressure gauge
J 35278	Servo piston compressor
J 35279	Low/reverse spring compressor
J 35280	Bearing outer race puller
J 26941	Bearing race puller
J 33367	Puller bridge
J 35281	Output gear bearing remover
J 29184	Front cover seal installer
J 35283	Output gear bearing installer
J 35286	Idler gear shaft holder
J 35287	Bearing outer race installer

Tool	Description
J 8092	Driver handle
J 35288	Differential side bearing puller pilot
J 22888	Differential side bearing puller
J 35290	Differential side bearing outer race installer
J 35291	Differential side bearing installer
J 35259	Bearing preload checker
J 544-01	Spring tension scale
J 35513	Low/reverse clutch pack support
J 35284	Shim selector
J 23327-A	Clutch spring compressor
J 25018-A	Clutch spring compressor adapter
J 29130	Axle seal installer
J 23129	Seal remover
J 6125-1	Slide hammer

SPECIAL TOOLS

ILLUSTRATION	NO.	NAME
	J-35290	Differential side bearing installer
	J-35291	Differential side bearing installer
	J-35259	Bearing preload checker
	J-35284	Shim selector
	J-23327-A	Clutch spring compressor
	J-25018-A	Clutch spring compressor adapter
	J-29130	Axle seal installer
	J-23129	Seal remover
	J-6125-1	Slide hammer

SPECIAL TOOLS

ILLUSTRATION	NO.	NAME
	J-3289-20	Holding fixture base
	J-35276	Holding fixture
	J-25695-10	Oil pressure gauge adapter
	J-21867	Oil pressure gauge assembly
	J-35278	Servo piston compressor
	J-35279	Low/reverse spring compressor
	J-35280	Bearing outer race puller
	J-33367	Bearing puller bridge
	J-26941	Bearing outer race puller

Section 2
F3A Transaxle
Mazda

APPLICATION

Year	Vehicle	Engine
1984	Mazda GLC	1.5L
	Mazda 626	2.0L
1985	Mazda GLC	1.5L
	Mazda 626	2.0L
1986	Mazda 323	1.6L
	Mazda 626	2.0L
1987	Mazda 323	1.6L
1988	Mazda 323 ①	1.6L

① Station Wagon only

GENERAL DESCRIPTION

The torque converter is located on the engine side and the oil pump is located on the other end of the transaxle. The front clutch, the rear clutch, front planetary and rear planetary gears are arranged in the respective order from the front, or oil pump end of the transaxle. During the section outline, the oil pump end will be referred to as the front and the converter end, or engine end, will be referred to as rear of the transaxle.

The control valve is located under the front clutch and the rear clutch assemblies. The governor is located on the outside of the case and responds to the speed of the output shaft to control operating oil pressure.

The low and reverse brake band is located on the outside of the rear planetary gears to shorten the total length of the transaxle.

The 3 shafts that are contained within the case are the oil pump driveshaft which transmit engine speed directly to the oil pump via a quill shaft inside the input shaft, the input shaft which transmits power from the torque converter turbine and drives the front clutch cover. The 3rd shaft is the output shaft which transmits power from the front planetary gear carrier and the rear planetary gear annulus, through the main drive idler gear to the differential drive gear.

Both the transaxle and the differential use a common sump with ATF fluid as the lubricant.

Transaxle and Converter Identification

TRANSAXLE

Identification tags are located on the front of the transaxle, under the oil cooler lines and identify the transaxle type and model.

CONVERTER

The torque converter is a welded unit and cannot be disassembled unless special tools are available for the purpose. A lockup torque converter is utilized, which consists of a lockup drive plate containing centrifugally operated shoe, bracket and spring assemblies and a one-way clutch.

Metric Fasteners

Metric bolt sizes and thread pitches are used for all fasteners on the Jatco transaxle. The metric fastener dimensions are close to the dimensions of the familiar inch system fasteners and for this reason, replacement fasteners must have the same measurement and strength as those removed. Do no attempt to interchange metric fasteners for inch system fasteners. Mismatched or incorrect fasteners can result in damage to the transaxle unit through malfunctions, breakage or possible personal injury. Care should be taken to reuse the fasteners in the same locations as removed whenever possible.

Capacities

The use of Dexron®II type automatic transaxle fluid or its equivalent, is recommended for use in the F3A automatic transaxle models.

The capacity of the F3A transaxle is 6.0 U.S. quarts (5.7 L).

Checking Fluid Level

With the engine/transaxle assemblies up to normal operating temperature, move the quadrant through all the selector positions and finish in the **P** position. The correct level is between the **F** and **L** marks on the dipstick. It is important to keep the level at, or slightly below, the **F** mark on the dipstick. Do not overfill the assembly.

Transaxle oil level should be checked, both visually and by smell, to determine that the fluid level is correct and to observe any foreign material in the fluid. Smelling the fluid will indicate if any of the bands or clutches have been burned through excessive slippage or overheating of the transaxle.

It is most important to locate the defect and its cause and to properly repair them to avoid having the same problem recur.

TRANSAXLE MODIFICATIONS

Low and Reverse Clutch Hub Snapring

Transaxles which have not been previously disassembled do not have a low and reverse clutch hub snapring. This clutch hub snapring will be install on all transaxles during the rebuilding process.

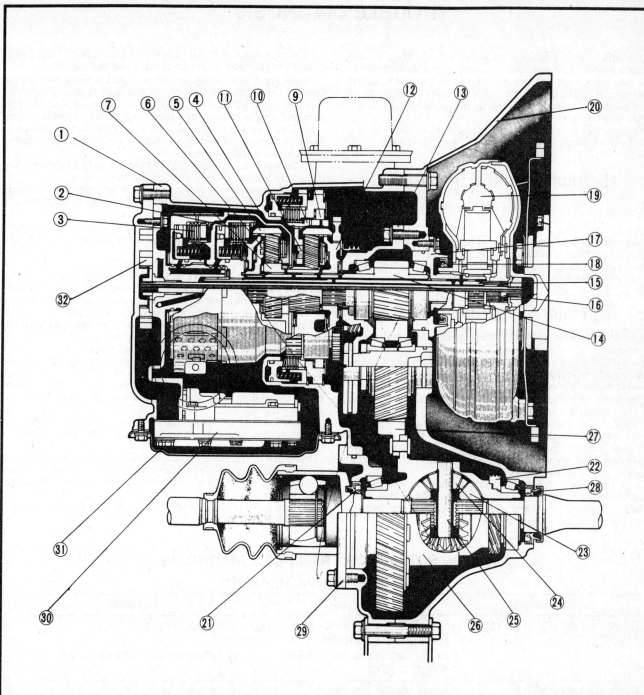

1. Transmission	10. One-way clutch inner race	18. Oil seal	26. Differential gear case
2. Rear clutch	11. Planetary carrier	19. Torque converter	27. Ring gear
3. Front clutch	12. Drum hub assembly	20. Converter housing	28. Oil seal
4. Connection shell	13. Bearing housing	21. Oil seal	29. Side bearing housing
5. Rear clutch hub assembly	14. Output gear	22. Speedometer drive gear	30. Control valve
6. Planetary carrier	15. Turbine shaft	23. Side gear	31. Oil pan
7. Sun gear	16. Oil pump shaft	24. Pinion gear	32. Oil pump
8. Low and reverse brake	17. Bearing cover	25. Pinion shaft	
9. One-way clutch			

Cross-section of the F3A transaxle

TROUBLE DIAGNOSIS

A logical and orderly diagnosis outline and charts are provided with clutch and band applications, shift speed and governor pressures, main control pressure and oil flow circuits to assist the repairman in diagnosing the problems, causes and extent of repairs needed to bring the automatic transaxle back to its acceptable level of operation.

Preliminary checks and adjustments should be made to the manual valve linkage, accelerator and downshift linkage.

Hydraulic Control System

Hydraulic pressure, clutch and band applications control the changing of gear ratios in the automatic transaxle. The clutches and bands are applied by the force of fluid pressure controlled by a system of valves and control mechanisms.

Major Components

The hydraulic control system consists of the following major components:

Main control pressure system which supplies pressure to the transaxle and converter when the engine is operating.

Converter and lubrication system which regulates converter fluid pressure, provides gear train lubrication and fluid cooling while the transaxle is operating.

Forward clutch pressure and governor pressure system applies the forward clutch, which is applied in all forward speeds and applies pressure to the governor valve. The governor valve supplies regulated pressure to the rear side of the shift valves, dependent upon the road speed of the vehicle.

Low and reverse brake apply system applies the low and reverse brake in **1** and **R** selector lever positions and locks out the 2nd and 3rd gears by directing pressure to the appropriate valves to prevent them from shifting.

First gear lock out system allows the transaxle to shift directly to 2nd speed and locks out the 1st and 3rd gears.

Brake band servo apply system applies the servo to hold the band to the surface of the reverse and high clutch cylinder.

Reverse pressure booster system increases control (line) pressure and applies reverse and high clutch in the reverse range.

Shift valve train system applies and exhausts the fluid pressures to servos and clutch assemblies for upshifts and downshifts automatically on demand.

Kickdown system (downshift) forces downshift by overriding governor/throttle valve control of the shift valves.

Governor provides a varying pressure proportional to engine vacuum to help control the timing and quality of the transaxle shifts.

Throttle T.V. system provides a varying pressure proportional to engine vacuum to help control the timing quality of the transaxle shifts.

Throttle backup system compensates for a lower rate of engine vacuum at ½ or more of throttle opening.

Pressure modifier system adjusts the control (line) pressures and 2-3 shift timing valve operation to insure smoother shifting under various engine load and vacuum conditions.

Fluid filter screens the fluid and cleans foreign material from the oil supply before entering the oil pump.

Oil pump supplies oil pressure to transaxle.

Converter pressure relief valve prevents converter pressure build up.

Transaxle fluid cooling system removes heat from torque converter by sending the transaxle fluid through a cooler in the engine cooling system.

Throttle control valve regulates throttle pressure in relation to the engine manifold vacuum through vacuum diaphragm (modulator).

Pressure modifier valve uses throttle pressure, controlled by governor pressure, to modify the main line pressure from the regulator valve. This prevents harsh shifting caused by excessive pump pressure.

Manual control valve moves with the shift selector and directs the line control pressure to the various oil passages.

CHILTON'S THREE C's TRANSAXLE DIAGNOSIS
Jatco F3A Automatic Transaxle

Condition	Cause	Correction
Engine does not start in any range	a) Neutral start/backup lamp switch wiring disconnected or damaged b) Neutral start/backup lamp switch sticking or failed	a) Replace, service b) Perform neutral start switch check
Engine does not start in P	a) Range selector and linkage	a) Service or adjust linkage
Engine starts in ranges other than P and N	a) Range selector linkage b) Neutral start/backup lamp switch loose c) Neutral start/backup lamp switch wiring short circuited	a) Perform linkage check b) Check and retighten c) Check for damage
Vehicle moves in P or parking gear not disengaged when P is disengaged	a) Range selector and linkage b) Parking linkage	a) Perform linkage check b) Check for proper operation
Vehicle moves in N	a) Range selector linkage b) Dirty or sticking valve body c) Rear clutch	a) Perform linkage check b) Clean, service or replace valve body c) Check for clutch not disengaging

CHILTON'S THREE C's TRANSAXLE DIAGNOSIS
Jatco F3A Automatic Transaxle

Condition	Cause	Correction
No drive in any gear	a) Valve body loose	a) Tighten to specification
	b) Sticky or dirty valve body	b) Clean, service or repair valve body
	c) Improper rear clutch application or damaged, worn clutch	c) Service as required
	d) Low rear clutch application pressure	d) Perform line and pressure test
	e) Internal leakage	e) Check pump seals
	f) Valve body loose	f) Tighten to specification
	g) Broken pump or turbine shaft	g) Perform stall test
Vehicle does not move in D (moves in 1, 2 and R)	a) Range selector linkage	a) Perform linkage check
	b) Oil pressure control system	b) Perform line and governor pressure tests
	c) Dirty or sticking valve body	c) Clean, service or repair valve body
	d) One-way clutch	d) Service as required
Vehicle does not move in forward ranges, reverse OK	a) Dirty or sticking valve	a) Clean, service or repair valve body
	b) Improper rear clutch application or oil pressure control	b) Check rear clutch for proper operation. Perform line pressure test
	c) Damaged or worn rear clutch	c) Check and service as required
Vehicle does not move in reverse. Forward OK	a) Improper oil pressure	a) Perform line pressure test
	b) Dirty or sticking valve body	b) Clean, service or replace valve body
	c) Damaged or worn low reverse clutch	c) Check and service as required
Vehicle does not shift out of 1st gear in D	a) Dirty or sticking valve body	a) Check 1-2 shift valve operation. Clean, service or replace valve body
	b) Damaged or worn governor	b) Check governor valve for free movement. Service or replace governor
	c) Improper oil pressure control	c) Perform line pressure cut-back point and governor pressure test
Vehicle does not shift from 2 to 3 in D	a) Dirty or sticking valve body	a) Check 2-3 shift valve operation. Clean, service or replave valve body
	b) Governor valve	b) Check governor valve for free movement. Service or replace governor
	c) Front clutch	c) Check for proper applicaton and for a worn clutch
	d) Improper oil pressure control	d) Perform line pressure, cut-back point and governor pressure tests
Shifts from 1 to 3 in D	a) Improper fluid level	a) Perform fluid level check
	b) Dirty or sticking valve body	b) Check 1-2 shift valve for free movement. Clean, service or replace valve body
	c) Governor valve	c) Check governor valve for free movment. Clean, service or replace governor valve
	d) Band servo	d) Check for seal leakage
	e) Polished or glazed band or drum	e) Service or replace as required
Engine overspeeds on 2-3 shift	a) Improper fluid level	a) Perform fluid level check
	b) Vacuum diaphragm and piping	b) Service or replace
	c) Governor valve	c) Check governor valve for free movement. Clean, service or replace governor valve
	d) Improper front clutch application	d) Check front clutch operation. Check fluid pressure line and governor
	e) Damaged or worn front clutch	e) Service as required
	f) Improper oil pressure	f) Perform line pressure and cut-back point tests

CHILTON'S THREE C's TRANSAXLE DIAGNOSIS
Jatco F3A Automatic Transaxle

Condition	Cause	Correction
Practically no shift shock or slippage while 1-2 shifting	a) Improper fluid level b) Dirty or sticking valve body c) Oil pressure control d) Vacuum diaphragm and piping e) Band servo f) Polished or glazed band or drum	a) Perform fluid level check b) Clean, service or replace valve body c) Perform fluid pressure check line and governor d) Perform vacuum diaphragm test. Service a required e) Check for leaking seal, service as required f) Service or replace as required
Shift points incorrect	a) Kickdown switch, kickdown solenoid and wiring b) Vacuum diaphragm and piping c) Damaged or worn governor d) Improper clutch or band application or oil pressure control e) Damaged vacuum diaphragm	a) Check for loose connection, continuity and proper operation b) Check for proper operation and clogged or disconnected mline c) Perform governor pressure test. Check for free movement of governor valve or dirty governor d) Perform line pressure and cut-back point test. Check clutches and bands for proper engagement e) Perform vacuum diaphragm check
No forced downshifts in D	a) Improper band application or oil pressure control b) Dirty or sticking valve body c) Dirty or sticking governor valve d) Vacuum diaphragm and piping e) Kickdown solenoid kickdown switch and wiring	a) Perform line pressure test. Service or adjust as required b) Check for free movment of all valves. Clean, service or replace valve body c) Check governor valve for free movement. Service or replace governor valve d) Perform vacuum diaphragm test. Check for plugged vacuum line. Service or replace as required e) Perform kickdown switch and circuit test. Service or replace as required
Does not shift from 3-2 on D to 2 shift	a) Dirty or sticking valve b) Oil pressure control system c) Band servo d) Damaged or worn band, glazed or polished drum	a) Clean, service or replace valve body b) Perform line and governor pressure tests c) Check for proper operation. Service or replace as required d) Service or replace as required
Does not shift from 3 to 2 on D to 1 shift	a) Dirty or sticking valve body b) Oil pressure control system c) Band servo d) Damaged or worn band, glazed or polished drum	a) Clean, service or replace as required b) Perform line and governor pressure tests c) Check for proper operation. Service or replace as required d) Service or replace as required
Kickdown operates or engine overruns when depressing pedal in 3 beyond kickdown vehicle speed limit	a) Vacuum diaphragm and piping b) Dirty or sticking valve body c) Improper front clutch application or oil pressure control	a) Check for sticking vacuum diaphragm and throttle valve b) Clean, service or replace as required c) Check front clutch for proper application. Perform line and governor pressure test

CHILTON'S THREE C's TRANSAXLE DIAGNOSIS
Jatco F3A Automatic Transaxle

Condition	Cause	Correction
Runaway engine on 3-2 downshift	a) Improper fluid level b) Improper band application or oil pressure system c) Band servo d) Polished or glazed band drum	a) Perform fluid level check b) Check band for proper application. Perform line pressure, cut-back point and governor pressure test c) Check for proper operation and seal leak d) Replace or service as required
No engine braking in 1	a) Improper fluid level b) Damaged or improperly adjusted manual c) Oil pressure control system d) Dirty or sticking valve body e) Low reverse brake	a) Perform fluid level check b) Perform linkage check linkage c) Perform line pressure test d) Clean, service or replace as required e) Service as required
Slow initial engagement	a) Improper fluid level b) Contaminated fluid c) Dirty or sticking valve body d) Improper clutch application or oil control pressure	a) Perform fluid level check b) Check fluid for proper condition. Check for clogged filter c) Clean, service or replace valve body d) Check rear clutch for proper application Perform line and governor pressure test
Harsh initial engagement in either forward or reverse	a) High engine idle b) Looseness in halfshafts, CV joints or engine mounts c) Vacuum diaphragm and piping d) Improper rear clutch application or oil pressure control e) Sticking or dirty valve body	a) Adjust idle to specifiaction b) Service as required c) Service as required d) Check rear clutch for proper operation. Perform line and governor pressure test e) Clean, service or replace as required
Harsh 1-2 shift	a) Weak engine performance b) Dirty or sticking body c) Vacuum diaphragm and piping d) Improper brake band application or oil pressure control	a) Tune and adjust engine to specification b) Check for free movement of 1-2 shift valve. Clean, service or replace valve body c) Perform vacuum diaphragm test. Service or replace as required d) Check band for proper operation. Perform line and governor pressure tests
Harsh 2-3 shift	a) Dirty or sticking valve body b) Improper front clutch application or oil pressure control c) Band servo d) Brake band	a) Clean, service or replace valve body b) Perform line pressure, cut-back point and governor pressure tests c) Check for proper release d) Check for proper release
Vehicle braked when shifted from 1-2	a) Dirty or sticking valve body b) Improper front clutch application or oil pressure control c) Low reverse brake d) One-way clutch	a) Clean, service or replace valve body b) Check front clutch for proper engagement. Perform line and governor pressure tests c) Check for proper disengagement or dragging clutch d) Check for seized clutch
Vehicle braked when shifted from 2-3	a) Dirty or sticking valve body b) Brake band and servo	a) Clean, service or replace valve body b) Check for proper disengagement
Noise severe under acceleration or deceleration. OK in P or N or speed	a) Speedo cable grounding out b) Shift cable grounding out c) Engine mounts bound up	a) Install and route cable as specified b) Install and route cable as specified c) Neutralize engine mounts

CHILTON'S THREE C's TRANSAXLE DIAGNOSIS
Jatco F3A Automatic Transaxle

Condition	Cause	Correction
Noise in P or N. Does not stop in Drive	a) Loose flywheel to converter bolts b) Pump c) Torque converter	a) Torque to specification b) Examine, service pump c) Examine, service converter. Perform stall test
Noise in all gears, changes power to coast	a) Final drive gearset noisy	a) Examine, service final drive gearset
Noise in all gears, does not change power to coast	a) Defective speedo gears b) Bearings worn or damaged	a) Examine, replace speed drive or driven gear b) Examine, replace
Noise in Low	a) Planetary gearset noisy	a) Service planetary gearset
Transaxle noisy in D, 2, 1 & R	a) Improper fluid level b) Improper fluid pressure control c) Rear clutch d) Oil pump e) One-way clutch f) Planetary gears	a) Perform fluid level check b) Perform line and governor pressure tests c) Check and repair as necessary d) Check, repair or replace e) Check, repair or replace as necessary f) Check or replace as necessary
Transaxle noisy, (valve noise) NOTE: Gauges may aggravate any hydraulic noises. Remove gauge and check for noise level	a) Improper fluid level b) Improper band or clutch application or oil pressure control system c) Cooler line grounding d) Dirty or sticking valve body e) Internal leakage or pump cavitation	a) Perform fluid level check b) Perform line pressure test c) Free cooler lines d) Clean, service or replace valve body e) Service or replace as required
Transaxle overheats	a) Improper fluid level b) Incorrect engine performance c) Improper clutch or band application or oil pressure control d) Restriction in cooler lines e) Dirty or sticking valve body f) Seized converter one-way clutch	a) Perform fluid level check b) Adjust according to specifications c) Perform line and pressure governor pressure tests d) Check cooler lines for kinks and damage. Clean, service or replace cooler lines e) Clean, service or replace valve body f) Replace converter

Diagnosis Tests

OIL PRESSURE CIRCUITS

In order to more fully understand the Jatco automatic transmission and to diagnose possible defects more easily, the clutch and band applications charts and a general description of the hydraulic control system is given.

To utilize the oil flow charts for diagnosing transaxle problems, the repairman must have an understanding of the oil pressure circuits and how each circuit affects the operation of the transaxle by the use of controlled oil pressure.

Control (line) pressure is a regulated main line pressure, developed by the operation of the front pump. It is directed to the main regulator valve, where predetermined spring pressure automatically moves the regulator valve to control the pressure of the oil at a predetermined rate, by opening the valve and exhausting excessive pressured oil back into the sump and holding the valve closed to build up pressure when needed.

Therefore, it is most important during the diagnosis phase to test main line control pressure to determine if high or low pressure exits. Do not attempt to adjust a pressure regulator valve spring to obtain more or less control pressure. Internal transaxle damage may result.

The main valve is the controlling agent of the transaxle which directs oil pressure to 1 of 6 separate passages used to control the valve train. By assigning each passage a number, a better understanding of the oil circuits can be gained from the diagnosis oil flow schematics.

CONTROL PRESSURE SYSTEM TEST

Control pressure tests should be performed whenever slippage, delay or harshness is felt in the shifting of the transaxle. Throttle and modulator pressure changes can cause these problems also, but are generated from the control pressures and therefore reflect any problems arising from the control pressure system.

The control pressure is initially checked in all ranges without any throttle pressure input and then checked as the throttle pressure is increased by lowering the vacuum supply to the vacuum modulator with the use of the stall test.

CLUTCH AND BAND APPLICATION CHART
Jatco F3A Automatic Transaxle

Range		Front Clutch ①	Rear Clutch ②	Low & Reverse Brake Clutch	Brake Band Servo ③ Operation	Release	One-Way Clutch	Parking Pawl
Park		—	—	On	—	—	—	On
Reverse		On	—	On	—	On	—	—
Neutral		—	—	—	—	—	—	—
Drive	Low D1	—	On	—	—	—	On	—
	Second D2	—	On	—	On	—	—	—
	Top D3	On	On	—	(On)	On	—	—
2	Second	—	On	—	On	—	—	—
1	Second 1₂	—	On	—	On	—	—	—
	Low 1₁	—	On	On	—	—	—	—

① Reverse and high clutch
② Forward clutch
③ Intermediate band

Clutch and band applications for the F3A transaxle

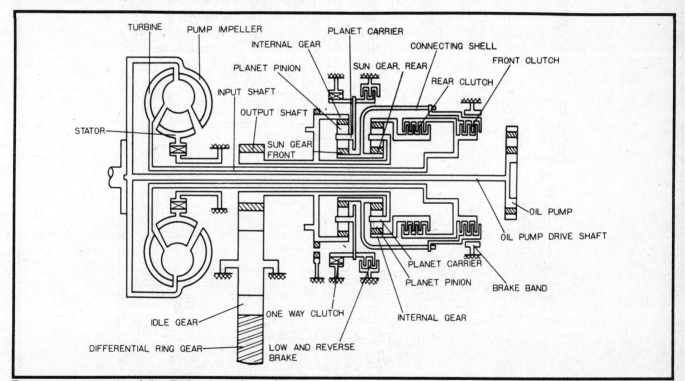

Power components of the F3A transaxle

The control pressure tests should define differences between mechanical or hydraulic failures of the transaxle.

Testing

1. Install a 0–400 psi pressure gauge to the main line control pressure tap. This may be marked ML on the side of the transaxle case.
2. Block wheels and apply both parking and service brakes.
3. Operate the engine/transaxle in the ranges on the following charts and at the manifold vacuum specified.

4. Record the actual pressure readings in each test and compare them to the given specifications.

Results

LOW PRESSURE AT IDLE IN ALL RANGES CAUSED BY:
1. EGR system, if equipped
2. Vacuum modulator
3. Manifold vacuum line
4. Throttle valve or control rod
5. Sticking regulator boost valve (pressure modifier valve)

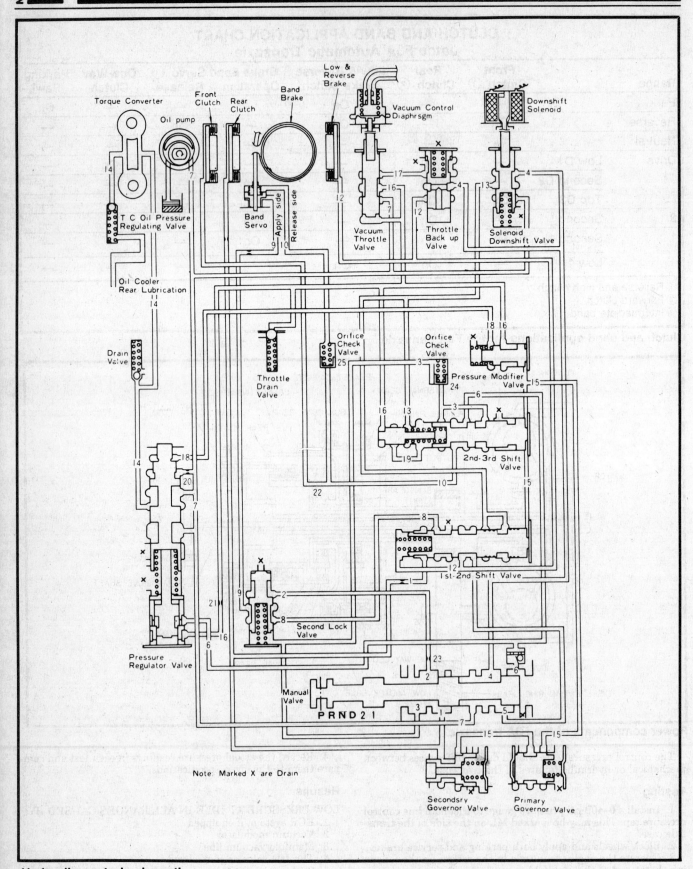

Hydraulic control schematic

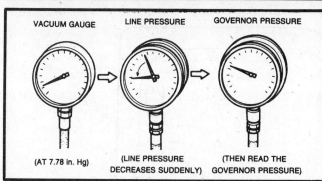

Gauges needed to test the hydraulic circuits

Labels within figure: VACUUM GAUGE | LINE PRESSURE | GOVERNOR PRESSURE

(AT 7.78 in. Hg) | (LINE PRESSURE DECREASES SUDDENLY) | (THEN READ THE GOVERNOR PRESSURE)

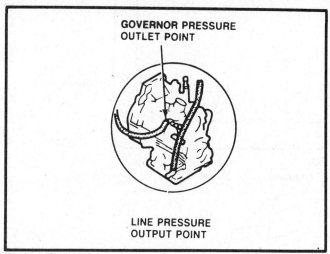

Hydraulic pressure test points

Labels within figure: GOVERNOR PRESSURE OUTLET POINT | LINE PRESSURE OUTPUT POINT

OK AT IDLE IN ALL RANGES, BUT LOW AT 10 IN. OF VACUUM IS CAUSED BY:
1. Excessive leakage
2. Low pump capacity
3. Restricted oil pan screen or filter

PRESSURE LOW IN P RANGE IS CAUSED BY:
Valve body

PRESSURE LOW IN R IS CAUSED BY:
1. Front clutch
2. Low and reverse brake

PRESSURE LOW IN N RANGE IS CAUSED BY:
Valve body

PRESSURE LOW IN D RANGE IS CAUSED BY:
Rear clutch

PRESSURE LOW IN 2 RANGE IS CAUSED BY:
1. Rear clutch
2. Brake band servo

PRESSURE LOW IN 1 RANGE IS CAUSED BY:
1. Rear clutch
2. Low and reverse brake

HIGH OR LOW PRESSURE IN ALL TEST CONDITIONS IS CAUSED BY:
1. Modulator control rod broken or missing
2. Stuck throttle valve
3. Pressure modifier valve or regulator valve

POSSIBLE LOCATIONS OF PROBLEMS DUE TO LINE PRESSURE

Malfunctions

1. Low pressure when in **D**, **2**, or **R** positions could be the re-

sult of a worn oil pump, fluid leaking from the oil pump, control valve or transaxle case, or the pressure regulator valve sticking.

2. Low pressure when in **D** and **2** only could result from fluid leakage from the hydraulic circuit of the 2 ranges selected. Refer to the hydraulic fluid schematics.

3. Low fluid pressure when in the **R** position could result from a fluid leakage in the reverse fluid circuit. Refer to the hydraulic fluid schematic.

4. High pressure when idling could be the result of a broken or disconnected vacuum hose to the modulator or a defective vacuum modulator assembly.

Main Line Pressure Cut-Back Point Test

1. Connect the fluid pressure test gauge to the line pressure test port outlet of the transaxle case.

2. Connect a fluid pressure test gauge to the governor pressure test port on the transaxle case.

3. Position the gauges so that each can be seen from the driver's seat.

4. Disconnect the vacuum hose to the vacuum modulator and plug the hose.

5. Connect a vacuum pump to the vacuum modulator and position the pump so it can be operated from the driver's seat.

6. If the line pressure drops abruptly when the engine rpm is increased gradually while the selector lever is in the **D** position. Measure the governor pressure.

7. Measure the governor pressure when the vacuum is at 0 in. Hg. and at 7.9 in. Hg. The specifications are: 0.0 in. Hg – 14–23 psi (98–157 Kpa) and 7.9 in. Hg (200mm–Hg) – 6–14 psi (39–98 Kpa).

8. If the specifications are not met, check to see that the diaphragm rod has been installed or that it is more than standard. Check for a sticking valve inside the control valve assemble if the rod is correct.

Governor Pressure Test

1. Connect the fluid pressure gauge to the governor test port on the transaxle case. Position the gauge so that it is accessible to the operator.

2. Drive the vehicle with the selector lever in the **D** position.

3. Measure the governor pressure at the following speeds: The governor pressure should be 11.9–17.1 psi at 20 mph, 19.9–28.4 psi at 35 mph and 38.4–48.3 psi at 55 mph.

4. If the test results do not meet the specifications, the following should be checked:
    a. Fluid leakage from the line pressure hydraulic circuit.
    b. Fluid leakage from the governor pressure hydraulic circuit.
    c. Governor malfunctions.

AIR PRESSURE TEST

The control pressure test results and causes of abnormal pressure are to be used as a guide. Further testing or inspection could be necessary before repairs are made. If the pressures are found to be low in a clutch, servo or passageway, a verification can be accomplished by removing the valve body and performing an air pressure test. This test can be used to determine if a malfunction of a clutch or band is caused by fluid leakage in the system or is the result of a mechanical failure and also, to test the transaxle for internal fluid leakage during the rebuilding and before completing the assembly.

1. Obtain an air nozzle and adjust for 25 psi.
2. Apply air pressure (25 psi) to the passages.

Vacuum Modulator Test

The modulated throttle system, which adjusts throttle pressure for the control of the shift valves, is operated by engine manifold

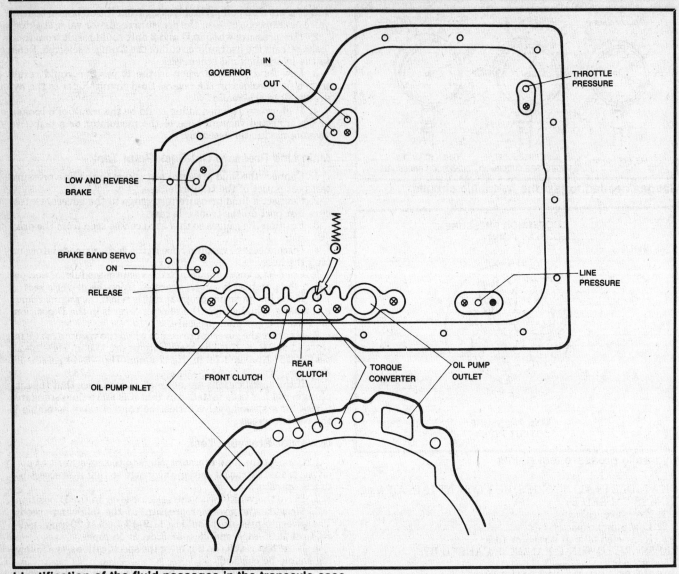

Identification of the fluid passages in the transaxle case

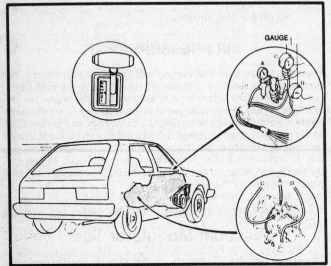

Line pressure cut back point

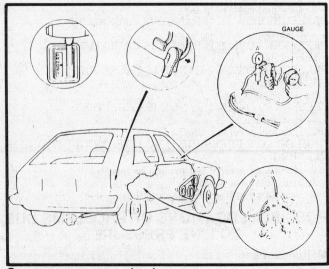

Governor pressure check

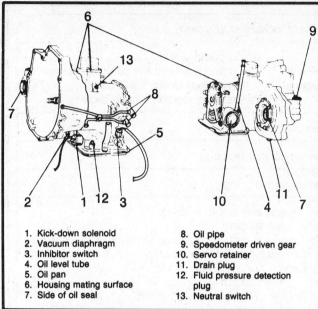

1. Kick-down solenoid
2. Vacuum diaphragm
3. Inhibitor switch
4. Oil level tube
5. Oil pan
6. Housing mating surface
7. Side of oil seal
8. Oil pipe
9. Speedometer driven gear
10. Servo retainer
11. Drain plug
12. Fluid pressure detection plug
13. Neutral switch

Possible fluid leakage locations

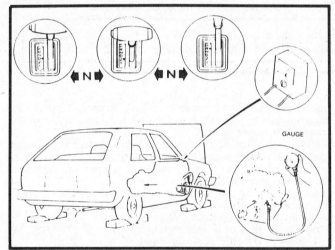

Line pressure test

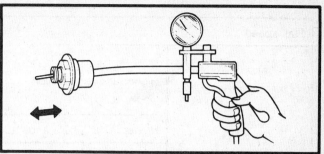

Testing the modulator with a hand vacuum pump

from the modulator nipple and check the hose end for the presence of engine vacuum with an appropriate gauge.

2. If vacuum is present, accelerate the engine and allow it to return to idle. A drop in vacuum should be noted during acceleration and a return to normal vacuum at idle.

3. If manifold vacuum is not present, check for breaks or restrictions in the vacuum lines and repair.

VACUUM MODULATOR CHECK

1. Apply at least 18 in. Hg. to the modulator vacuum nipple and observe the vacuum reading. The vacuum should hold.

2. If the vacuum does not hold, the diaphragm is leaking and the modulator assembly must be replaced.

NOTE: A leaking diaphragm causes harsh gear engagements and delayed or no up-shifts due to maximum throttle pressure developed.

On Vehicle Test

The vacuum modulator is tested on the vehicle with the aid of an outside vacuum source, which can be adjusted to maintain a certain amount of vacuum. Apply 18 inches Hg. to the vacuum modulator vacuum nipple, through a hose connected to the outside vacuum source. The vacuum should hold at the applied level without any leakdown. If the vacuum level drops off, the vacuum diaphragm is leaking and must be replaced.

Remove the vacuum hose and check transmission fluid in the hose. If the diaphragm has a leak, engine vacuum may draw transmission fluid through the hose and into the engine where it will be burned with the fuel.

Off Vehicle Test

With the vacuum modulator removed from the automatic transaxle, apply 18 in. Hg. to the modulator vacuum nipple.

The vacuum level should remain and not drop off. If the vacuum level drops, the diaphragm is leaking and the unit should be replaced.

Another test can be made with the modulator removed from the transaxle. Insert the control rod into the valve end of the diaphragm and apply vacuum to the nipple. Hold a finger over the control rod and release the vacuum supply hose. The control rod should be moved outward by the pressure of the internal return spring. If the control rod does not move outward, a broken return spring is indicated.

STALL TEST

The stall test is an application of engine torque, through the transaxle and drive train to lock up the rear wheels, which are held by the vehicle's brakes. The engine's speed is increased until the rpms are stabilized. Given ideal engine operating conditions and no slippage from transaxle clutches, bands or torque converter, the engine will stabilize at a specified test rpm.

vacuum through a vacuum diaphragm and must be inspected whenever a transaxle defect is apparent.

Before the vacuum modulator test is performed, check the engine vacuum supply and the condition and routing of the supply lines.

With the engine idling, remove the vacuum line at the vacuum modulator and install a vacuum gauge. There must be a steady, acceptable vacuum reading for the altitude at which the test is being performed.

If the vacuum is low, check for a vacuum leak or poor engine performance. If the vacuum is steady and acceptable, accelerate the engine sharply and observe the vacuum gauge reading. The vacuum should drop off rapidly at acceleration and return to the original reading immediately upon release of the accelerator.

If the vacuum reading does not change or changes slowly, check the vacuum supply lines for being plugged, restricted or connected to a vacuum reservoir supply. Repair the system as required.

MANIFOLD VACUUM CHECK

1. With the engine idling, remove the vacuum supply hose

Stall speed		Possible location of problem	
Higher than standard	Higher at every position	Low line pressure	a) Oil pump weak b) Oil leakage from the oil pump control valve body or transaxle case c) Pressure regulator valve sticking
	Higher in "D", "2", and "1"	Rear clutch slipping	
	Higher only in "D"	One-way clutch slipping	
	Higher only in "2"	Brake band slipping	

	Higher only in "R"	Low and reverse brake slipping
		Front clutch slipping
		  Perform road test to determine whether problem is low and reverse brake or front clutch
		a) Engine brake applied in 1st
		   .....Front clutch
		b) Engine brake not applied in 1st
		   .....Low and reverse brake	

Within standard		Speed control elements in transaxle all normal	
Lower then standard		Faulty engine One-way clutch in torque converter slipping	

Stall speed trouble chart

Procedure

1. Check the engine oil level. Run the ngine until it reaches operating temperature.

2. Check the transaxle fluid level and correct as necessary. Attach a calibrated tachometer to the engine and a 0–400 psi oil pressure gauge to the transaxle control pressure tap on the right side of the case.

3. Mark the specified maximum engine rpm on the tachometer cover plate with a grease pencil to easily check if the stall speed is over or under specifications.

4. Apply the parking brake and block both front and rear wheels.

— CAUTION —

Do no allow anyone in front of the vehicle while performing the stall test. Secure vehicle with parking brake and blocking wheeling wheels or anchoring with chains.

5. While holding the brake pedal with the left foot, place the selector lever in **D** position and slowly depress the accelerator.

6. Read and record the engine rpm when the accelerator pedal is fully depressed and the engine rpm is stabilized. Read and record the oil pressure reading at the high engine rpm point. Stall speed – 2200–2450 rpm.

NOTE: The stall test must be made within 5 seconds.

7. Shift the selector lever into the **N** position and increase the engine speed to approximately 1000–1200 rpm. Hold this engine speed for 1–2 minutes to cool the transaxle and fluid.

8. Make similar tests in the **2**, **1** and **R** positions.

Results

HIGH ENGINE RPM

If a slipping condition occurs during the stall test, indicated by high engine rpm, the selector lever position at the time of slippage provides an indication as to what holding member of the transaxle is defective.

If at any time the engine rpm races above the maximum as per specifications, indications are that a clutch unit or band is slipping and the stall test should be stopped before more damage is done to the internal parts.

By determining the holding member involved, several possible causes of slippage can be diagnosed.

1. Slips in all ranges, control pressure low
2. Slips in D, 1 or 2, rear clutch
3. Slips in D1 only, one-way clutch
4. Slips in R only, front clutch or low and reverse brake

Perform a road test to confirm these conditions.

LOW ENGINE RPM

When low stall speed is indicated, the converter one-way clutch is not holding or the engine is in need of a major tune-up. To determine which is at fault, perform a road test and observe the operation of the transaxle and the engine. If the converter one-way clutch does not lock the stator, acceleration will be poor up to approximately 30 mph. Above mph the acceleration will be normal. With poor engine performance, acceleration will be poor at all speeds. When the one-way clutch is seized and locks the stator from turning either way, the stall test rpm will be normal. However, on a road test the vehicle will not go any faster than 50–55 mph because of the 2:1 reduction ratio in the converter.

If slippage was indicated by high engine rpm, the road test will help identify the problem area observing the transaxle operation during upshifts, both automatic and manual.

Road Test

The road test is used to confirm that malfunctions do exist within the transaxle unit, or that repairs have been accomplished

STALL TEST HOLDING MEMBER CHART

Selector Lever Position	Holding Member Applied
"D" 1st Gear	Rear clutch One-way clutch
"1" Manual	Rear clutch Low and reverse brake clutch
"2" Manual	Rear clutch Rear band
Reverse	Front clutch Low and reverse brake clutch

Line Pressure At Stall Speed	
"D" Range	128 to 156 psi
"2" Range	114 to 171 psi
"R" Range	228 to 270 psi

Line Pressure Before Stall Test—At Idle	
"D" Range	43 to 57 psi
"2" Range	114 to 171 psi
"R" Range	57 to 110 psi

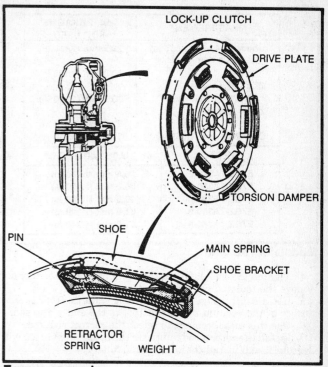

Torque converter

and the transaxle unit is either operating properly or will require additional adjustments or repairs. The road test must be performed over a pre-determined drive course that has been used before to evaluate transaxle and/or transaxle operations.

Should malfunctions occur during the road test, the selector range and road speed should be noted, along with the particular gear and shift point. By applying the point of malfunction in the operation of the transaxle, to the Clutch and Band Application Chart and the Chilton's Three "C's"; diagnosis chart, the probable causes can be pinpointed.

Some of the points to be evaluated during the road test are as follows:

1. The shift point should be smooth and have a positive engagement.
2. The shifts speed are within specifications.
3. All shifts occur during the upshifts and downshifts when in the selector lever detents, as required.
4. All downshifts occur when a forced downshift is demanded.
5. No upshift to 3rd when the selector lever is in the **2** position and the transaxle is in the 2nd speed.
6. Only 1 upshift from the 1st speed when the selector lever is in the **1** position.
7. The vehicle is firmly locked when the lever is in the **P** position.

Converter Clutch Operation and Diagnosis

TORQUE CONVERTER CLUTCH

A lockup torque converter is utilized. This eliminates the slip which is inherent in conventional torque converters. The no slip characteristics are achieved by automatically locking the converter into direct mechanical drive at high engine speed.

The lockup converter consists of a lockup drive plate containing centrifugally operated shoe, bracket and spring assemblies and a one-way clutch.

The lockup drive plate assembly is attached to the splined turbine shaft and is located inside the torque converter between the turbine and the converter cover. Torque is transmitted when the centrifugal clutch linings contact the machined inner surface of the converter housing. Torsion dampers are provided in the drive plate to absorb shock when the clutch is engaged.

NOTE: Whenever a transaxle has been disassembled, the converter and oil cooler must be cleaned.

ON CAR SERVICES

Adjustments
VACUUM MODULATOR

The vacuum modulator has no adjustments other than the replacement of the diaphragm rod. The rods are available in varied lengths as follows.

1. Raise and support the vehicle safely. Remove the vacuum modulator from its mounting.
2. Insert the vacuum diaphragm rod gauge into the mounting hole, with the beveled side out, until the tool bottoms.
3. Place the rod through the opening of the vacuum diaphragm tool until the rod bottoms out against the valve.

MEASUREMENT	DIAPHRAGM ROD USED
Under 25.4 mm (1.000 in)	29.5 mm (1.160 in)
25.4 ~ 25.9 mm (1.000 ~ 1.020 in)	30.0 mm (1.180 in)
25.9 ~ 26.4 mm (1.020 ~ 1.039 in)	30.5 mm (1.200 in)
26.4 ~ 26.9 mm (1.039 ~ 1.059 in)	31.0 mm (1.220 in)
Over 26.9 mm (1.059 in)	31.5 mm (1.240 in)
PART NO.	**DIAPHRAGM ROD**
E7GZ-7A380-E	29.5 mm (1.160 in)
E7GZ-7A380-C	30.0 mm (1.180 in)
E7GZ-7A380-D	30.5 mm (1.200 in)
E7GZ-7A380-B	31.0 mm (1.220 in)
E7GZ-7A380-A	31.5 mm (1.240 in)

Modulator rod chart

4. Tighten the lock knob on the vacuum modulator tool and remove the tool and rod from the transaxle case.
5. Use a depth gauge to measure the distance from the flat surface of the vacuum modulator tool to the end of the rod.
6. Use this measurement to select the correct size rod.
7. Install the correct rod, lubricate the modulator O-ring with Dexron®II and install the vacuum modulator.

NOTE: The transaxle will have to be partially drained before the vacuum modulator is removed. Add the necessary fluid and correct the level as required.

KICKDOWN SWITCH

1. Move the ignition switch to the **ON** position.
2. Loosen the kickdown switch to engage when the accelerator pedal is between ⅞–¹⁵/₁₆ in. of full travel. The downshift solenoid will click when the switch engages.
3. Tighten the attaching nut and check for proper operation.

NEUTRAL SAFETY SWITCH

No adjustment is possible on the neutral safety switch. If the engine will not start while the selector lever is in the **P** or **N** positions and the back-up lamps do not operate, check the shift control cable for proper adjustment. If shift cable adjustment is correct, the switch is defective and must be replaced.

Services

MANUAL SHIFT LINKAGE

REMOVAL AND INSTALLATION

1. Position the gear selector lever in the **N** position.
2. Remove the spring clip and pin attaching the shift cable trunnion to the transaxle shift lever.
3. Rotate the transaxle shift lever fully counterclockwise. This is the park position.
4. Rotate the transaxle shift lever clodkwise 2 detents. This is the neutral position. As the lever is rotated, position it between the ends of the shift cable trunnion.
5. If the hole in the shift lever aligns with the holes in the trunnion, the cable is properly adjusted. If the holes do not align proceed to the next step.
6. Remove the shift quadrant bezel. Lift the front of the bezel to disengage it from the console.
7. Lift and rotate the quadrant to provide access.
8. Loosen the adjuster nuts on the shift cable.

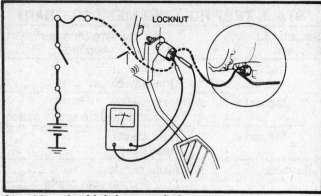

Checking the kickdown switch

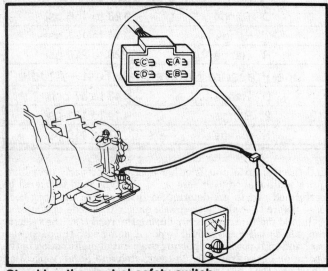

Checking the neutral safety switch

9. Position the gear selector lever in **P** position and inspect the position of the detent spring roller.
10. Loosen the attaching screws and move the detent spring forward or backward to center it in the detent.
11. Position the quadrant and install the attaching screws.
12. Position the selector lever in the **N** position.
13. Screw the adjuster nuts up or down the cable until the holes in the transaxle shift lever and the shift cable trunnion are aligned.
14. Torque the adjuster nut to 69–95 inch lbs. (8–11 Nm).
15. Check the alignment of the holes to make sure alignment was not disturbed.
16. Install the transaxle shift lever to shift cable attaching pin and retainer clip.
17. With an assistant, note the amount of freeplay when moving the shifter from **N** to **D** and compare to amount of freeplay between **N** and **R**. Adjust as necessary for equal amount of play in shifter and torque adjuster nut to 69–95 inch lbs. (8–11 Nm).

— **CAUTION** —

Make sure the linkage adjustment has not affected operation of the neutral safety switch. With the parking brake and service brake applied, try to start the engine in each gearshift position.

18. Position the shift quadrant bezel and install the attaching screws.

FLUID CHANGES

The Jatco transaxles do not have a specific or periodic fluid

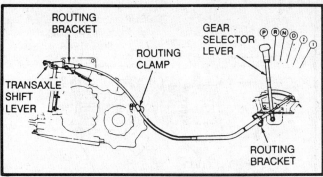

Manual shift linkage

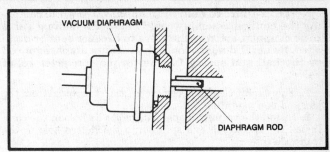

Installation of the modulator assembly

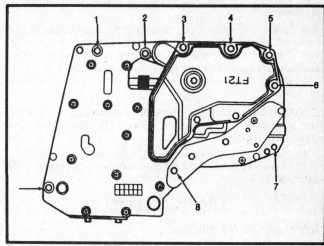

Bolt removal and torque sequence

change interval for the normal maintenance of the units. However, at the time of any major repairs or when the fluid has been contaminated, the converter, cooler and lines must be flushed to remove any debris and contaminated fluid. If the vehicle is used in continuous service or driven under severe conditions (police or taxi type operations), the transaxle should be drained, flushed and refilled at mileage intervals of 18,000–24,000 or at time intervals of 18–24 months.

NOTE: The time or mileage intervals given are average. Each vehicle operated under severe conditions should be treated individually.

1. Raise and support vehicle safely.
2. Remove the undercover and side cover to gain access to the transaxle pan and drain plug.
3. Remove the drain plug at the bottom of the transaxle case.
4. Allow the fluid to drain completely and reinstall the drain plug. Torque drain plug to 29–40 ft. lbs. (39–54 Nm).
5. Add Dexron®II type fluid to the transaxle until the desired level is reached. Approximately 3 quarts if the transaxle, not including the torque converter, was drained.

VACUUM MODULATOR

Removal and Installation

NOTE: Drain the transaxle before removing the vacuum modulator.

1. Raise the vehicle and support safely. Disconnect the vacuum hose from the modulator unit.
2. Turn the threaded modulator unit to remove it from the transaxle case.
3. Pull the actuating pin and the throttle valve from the transaxle case.
4. Remove the O-ring from the assembly.
5. Install a new O-ring on the modulator unit.
6. Install the throttle valve, the actuating pin and the vacuum modulator tubes toward the transaxle case and install the assembly into the case.
7. Tighten the vacuum modulator unit securely.

OIL PAN

Removal and Installation

1. Raise and support vehicle safely.
2. Remove the undercover and side cover to gain access to the transaxle pan and drain plug.
3. Remove the drain plug at the bottom of the transaxle case.
4. Allow the fluid to drain completely.
5. Remove the pan from the transaxle case.
6. Thoroughly clean the oil pan and filter screen.
7. Install a new washer on the drain plug and torque to 29–40 ft. lbs. (39–54 Nm).

8. Install a new pan gasket and replace pan. Torque pan bolts to 4–6 ft. lbs. (5–8 Nm).

NOTE: Do not overtighten bolts. Do not use any type of gasket sealer, RTV, etc., on the transaxle pan gasket. If necessary, soak the gasket in clean Dexron®II automatic transaxle fluid.

9. Install the undercover and side cover.
10. Remove the dipstick and add 3 quarts of Dexron®II transmission fluid.
11. Start and run engine until normal operating temperature is reached. Apply service brake and move selector through all the shift positions.

NOTE: Do no overspeed the engine during warm-up.

12. Place shift back in **P** and add fluid as necessary so reading is between the **F** and **L** marks on dipstick.

NOTE: Make certain fluid is just below the F mark. Do not overfill.

VALVE BODY

Removal and Installation

1. Disconnect the negative battery cable.
2. Raise and safely support the vehicle.
3. Remove the undercover and side cover.
4. Drain the transaxle fluid.
5. Remove the pan attaching bolts, pan and gasket.
6. Remove the valve body-to-case attaching bolts. Hold the manual valve to keep it from sliding out of the valve body and remove the valve body from the case.

NOTE: Failure to hold the manual valve while removing the control assembly could cause the manual valve to be dropped, causing the valve to become bent or damaged. Be careful not to loose the vacuum diaphragm rod or the ball and spring for the torque converter relief valve.

7. Thoroughly clean and remove all gasket material from the pan and pan mounting face of the case.
8. Install the vacuum diaphragm rod to its hole in the case. Install the check ball and spring into the slotted hole in the transaxle case.

NOTE: The ball is inserted first and then the spring. Use petroleum jelly to retain the spring and ball, if necessary.

9. Install the valve body, mating the groove of the manual valve with the driving pin of the shift rod.
10. Position the valve body to the case and install the attaching bolts. Torque the bolts to 70–95 inch lbs. (8–11 Nm).
11. Install the oil pan and torque the bolts to 43–69 inch lbs. (5–8 Nm).

NOTE: Do not use any type of gasket sealer or RTV on the pan gasket. If necessary, soak the gasket in clean transaxle fluid.

12. Install the undercover and side cover.
13. Lower vehicle. Refill the transaxle with the proper grade and type fluid.

SERVO ASSEMBLY

Removal and Installation

1. Raise and support the vehicle safely. Remove pan and valve body.
2. Remove left front wheel.
3. Remove the left lower ball joint bolt and separate the lower arm from the knuckle.
4. Separate the left drive shaft from the transaxle by prying with a bar inserted between the shaft and the case.

NOTE: A notch is provided in the side bearing housing to accommodate the bar. Do not insert the bar too far or damage to the lip of the oil seal may occur.

5. Support the halfshaft with a wire.
6. Loosen the anchor end-bolt and nut.
7. Remove the band strut.
8. Use a C-clamp and socket to compress the servo piston into the transaxle case.

――――――― **CAUTION** ―――――――
Eye protection should be worn during servo removal.

9. Remove the servo snapring.
10. Remove the servo retainer, piston and spring by slowly loosening the C-clamp.
11. Lubricate the piston and spring with Dexron®II transmission fluid.
12. Replace the return spring. Replace the O-ring piston seal.
13. Use a C-clamp and socket to compress the assembly.
14. Install the snapring to the snapring groove.
15. Install the band strut to the band.
16. Install the anchor end-bolt to the band and torque to 8.7–10.8 ft. lbs. (12–15 Nm).
17. Back off the end-bolt 2 complete turns on carburetor equipped vehicles and 3 complete turns on EFI equipped vehicles.
18. Install the anchor end-bolt locknut and torque to 41–59 ft. lbs. (55–80 Nm).
19. Replace the clip at the end of the halfshaft with a new clip and install shaft with the clip gap at the top of the groove.

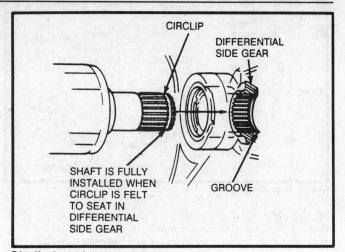

CIRCLIP
DIFFERENTIAL SIDE GEAR
SHAFT IS FULLY INSTALLED WHEN CIRCLIP IS FELT TO SEAT IN DIFFERENTIAL SIDE GEAR
GROOVE

Circlip location and installation

NOTE: Do not reuse the old clip. A new clip must be installed.

20. Slide the halfshaft horizontally into the transaxle differential, supporting it at the CV joint to prevent damage to the oil seal lip. Apply even pressure to the hub until the circlips are heard to engage.

NOTE: After installation, pull both front hubs outward to confirm that the drive shafts are retained by the circlips.

21. Install the lower arm ball joint to knuckle and torque nut to 32–40 ft. lbs. (43–54 Nm).
22. Install the underside covers.
23. Install the front wheel assembly and torque lugnuts to 65–87 ft. lbs. (90–120 Nm).
24. Refill the transaxle with the proper grade and type fluid.

GOVERNOR

Removal and Installation

1. Note the position of the governor, remove the 3 retaining bolts from the governor cover assembly. Lift the governor assembly from the transaxle case.
2. Remove the 2 governor retaining screws from the governor sleeve. Remove the governor valve body.
3. Disassemble the governor valve body as required.
4. Reassemble the governor valve body.
5. Install the governor valve body to the governor sleeve.
6. Mount the governor to the transaxle case in position noted during removal.
4. Install the 3 cover/governor retaining bolts and tighten to 69–95 inch lbs. (7.8–10.8 Nm).

DIFFERENTIAL OIL SEALS

The left and right axle seals can be installed with the axles removed. Conventional seal removing and installing tools can be used. Care must be exercised to prevent damage to the seals as the axles are reinstalled into the transaxle case.

Removal and Installation

1. Support vehicle safely, remove wheel assembly and underbody covers.
2. Remove the stabilizer bar to control arm bolts, washers and bushings.
3. Remove the lower ball joint bolt and separate the lower arm from the knuckle.

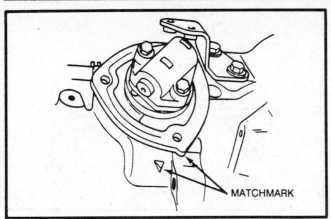

MATCHMARK

Aligning projection with mark on case

4. Partially drain the transaxle.
5. Separate the halfshaft from the transaxle by prying with a bar inserted between the shaft and the case. Tap the bar lightly to help loosen it from the differential gear.

NOTE: A notch is provided in the side bearing housing to accommodate the bar. Do not insert the bar too far or damage to the lip of the oil seal may occur.

6. Pull the halfshaft from the transaxle and support the it with a wire.
7. Pry the seal from the transaxle case using an appropriate tool.
8. Lubricate the new seal with transmission fluid and install using an appropriate tool.
9. Replace the clip at the end of the halfshaft with a new clip and install shaft with the clip gap at the top of the groove.

NOTE: Do not reuse the old clip. A new clip must be installed.

10. Slide the halfshaft horizontally into the transaxle differential, supporting it at the CV-joint to prevent damage to the oil seal lip. Apply even pressure to the hub until the circlips are heard to engage.

NOTE: After installation, pull both front hubs outward to confirm that the driveshafts are retained by the circlips.

11. Install the lower arm ball joint to knuckle and torque nut to 32–40 ft. lbs. (43–54 Nm).
12. Install the underside covers.
13. Install the front wheel assembly and torque lugnuts to 65–87 ft. lbs. (90–120 Nm).
14. Check and add Dexron®II transmission fluid as needed.

REMOVAL AND INSTALLATION

TRANSAXLE REMOVAL

GLC VEHICLES

1. Disconnect the negative battery cable. Raise and support the vehicle safely. Drain the transaxle fluid. Properly support the rear end of the engine.
2. Disconnect the the speedometer cable and EGR pipe.
3. Disconnect all electrical wiring connections and control linkages from the transaxle.
4. Remove the front tire and wheel assemblies. Disconnect the lower ball joints and pull the lower arm downward. Separate the lower arms from the knuckles.
5. Remove the axle shafts from the transaxle by prying with a suitable pry bar inserted between the shaft and the case. Be sure not to damage the oil seals.
6. Remove the undercover. Install the engine support tool 49-E301-025 or equivalent on the engine hanger and hoist the engine up slightly. Remove the crossmember. Disconnect and plug the cooler lines.
7. Remove the starter motor. Remove the end cover and remove the bolts holding the torque converter to the drive plate.
8. Using a suitable jack, support the transaxle. Remove the transaxle to engine mounting bolts. Remove the transaxle from the vehicle.

626 VEHICLES

1. Disconnect the negative battery cable and drain the transaxle. Disconect the speedometer cable.
2. Remove the shift control cable from the transaxle.
3. Disconnect the ground wire, the inhibitor switch and the kickdown solenoid.
4. Remove the starter motor.
5. Attach the engine support tool 49-G030-025 or equivalent and suspend the engine.
6. Remove the line connected to the vacuum diaphragm.
7. Remove the 5 upper transaxle-to-engine attaching bolts.

8. Remove the transaxle cooler lines from the transaxle. Plug the ends to prevent leakage.
9. Raise and support the vehicle safely.
10. Remove the front tire and wheel assemblies. Remove the left and right splash shields.
11. Remove the stabilizer bar control link. Remove the undercover.
12. Remove the pinch bolt and separate the ball joint from the steering knuckle.
13. Remove the left axle shaft from the transaxle by inserting a chisel between the axle shaft and the bearing housing. Tap the end of the chisel lightly in order to separate the axle shaft from the transaxle.
14. Pull the front hub outward and remove the axle shaft from the transaxle. Support the axle shaft during and after removal to avoid damaging the CV-joints and boots.
15. Pull the right axle shaft from the transaxle by inserting a prybar between the axle shaft and the joint shaft and force the axle shaft coupling open.
16. Pull the front hub out and remove the axle shaft from the joint shaft. Support the axle shaft during and after removal to avoid damaging the CV-joints and boots. Remove the joint shaft assembly from the transaxle.
17. Remove the transaxle undercover and torque converter to drive plate bolts. Support the transaxle assembly. Remove the crossmember and the left side lower arm together as an assembly.
18. Attach a safety chain to the transaxle mounting brackets in 2 places and secure the rope over the engine support bar.
19. Remove the lower 2 transaxle-to-engine bolts. Lower the transaxle to the floor.

323 VEHICLES

1. Disconnect the negative battery cable. Remove the air cleaner.
2. Disconnect the speedometer and throttle cable from the

transaxle. Disconnect the shift control cable from the transaxle.

3. Remove the ground wire. Remove the water pipe bracket. Remove the secondary air pipe and the EGR pipe bracket.

4. Remove the wire harness clip. Disconnect the inhibitor switch, the kickdown solenoid and any other necessary solenoids or switches.

5. Remove the upper transaxle mounting bolts. Disconnect the neutral switch connector and the vacuum line from the vacuum diaphragm. Disconnect and plug the transaxle oil cooler lines. Mount the engine support tool 49-ER301-025A or equivalent to the engine hanger.

6. Raise and support the vehicle safely. Drain the transaxle oil and remove the front wheel and tire assemblies.

7. Remove the engine under cover and side covers.

8. Remove the lower arm ball joints and the knuckle clinch bolts, pull the lower arm downward and separate the lower arms from the knuckles.

9. Separate the axle shafts from the transaxle by prying with a suitable pry bar inserted between the shaft and the case. Be sure not to damage the oil seals.

10. Support the transaxle assembly. Remove the transaxle crossmember. Remove the starter motor and electrical connection.

11. Remove the end plate. Lean the engine toward the transaxle side and lower the transaxle by loosening the engine support hook bolt. Support the transaxle with a suitable floor jack.

12. Remove the necessary engine brackets. Remove the remaining transaxle mounting bolt. Lower the jack and slide the transaxle out from under the vehicle.

TRANSAXLE INSTALLATION

GLC VEHICLES

1. Install the transaxle to the engine assembly in the correct position and torque the retaining bolts to 70 ft. lbs.

2. Install the torque converter to drive plate and torque the retaining bolts to 25-36 ft. lbs.

3. Install the starter motor. Install the end cover.

4. Install the crossmember and reconnect the cooler lines. Lower the engine and remove the support tool. Install the undercover.

5. Install the axle shafts to the transaxle and torque the axle shaft retaining nut to 116-174 ft. lbs., if axle shaft was removed from the vehicle. Reconnect the lower ball joints and install the front wheel and tire assemblies.

6. Reconnect all electrical wiring connections and control linkages to the transaxle.

7. Connect the the speedometer cable and EGR pipe.

8. Lower the vehicle. Reconnect the negative battery cable. Refill the transaxle and road test for proper operation.

626 VEHICLES

1. Install the transaxle mount bracket if removed. Install the transaxle to the engine assembly in the correct position and torque the upper retaining bolts to 66-86 ft. lbs.

2. Install the crossmember and the transaxle mount nuts. Torque the mount nuts to 31-40 ft. lbs.

3. Install the torque converter to drive plate and torque the retaining bolts to 25-36 ft. lbs.

4. Install the under cover.

5. Install the axle shafts with new circlips (gap at the top of the groove) in the transaxle. After installing the the axle shaft pull the front hub outward to make sure the axle shaft does not come out. Mount the joint shaft bracket if necessary.

6. Install the ball joints to the steering knuckle and torque to 32-40 ft. lbs.

7. Install the stabilizer bar control link. Torque the stabilizer bar control link bolt so that 1.00 in. (25mm) bolt is exposed.

8. Install the splash shields and wheel and tire assemblies.

9. Lower the vehicle. Reconnect the transaxle cooler lines.

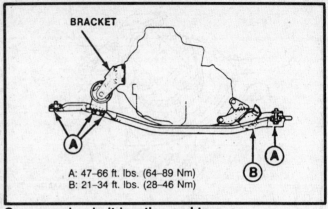

A: 47–66 ft. lbs. (64–89 Nm)
B: 21–34 ft. lbs. (28–46 Nm)

Crossmember bolt location and torque

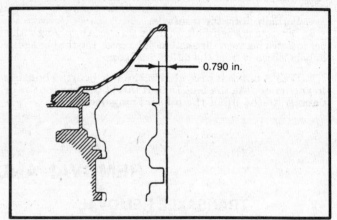

0.790 in.

Checking converter clearance

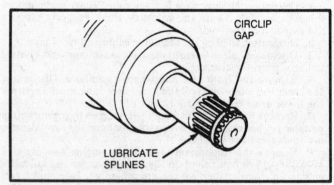

CIRCLIP GAP

LUBRICATE SPLINES

Circlip location and installation

10. Install the lower transaxle retaining bolts and torque to 66-86 ft. lbs.

11. Install the vacuum diaphragm line.

12. Install the starter and electrical connection.

13. Reconnect the wiring to the inhibitor switch, kickdown solenoid and ground wire.

14. Reconnect the change control cable and speedometer cable.

15. Refill the the transaxle with the correct fluid and reconnect the battery cable.

16. Road test the vehicle for proper operation.

323 VEHICLE

1. Install the transaxle to the engine assembly in the correct position and torque the retaining bolts to 47-66 ft. lbs.

2. Install the torque converter to drive plate and torque the retaining bolts to 25-36 ft. lbs.

3. Install the starter motor. Install the end cover.

4. Install the crossmember and reconnect the cooler lines.

5. Install the axle shafts with new circlips (gap at the top of the groove) in the transaxle. After installing the the axle shaft pull the front hub outward to make sure the axle shaft does not come out.

6. Install the lower ball joint to the steering knuckle.

7. Install the under and side covers. Install the wheel and tire assemblies.

8. Lower the vehicle. Reconnect all electrical wiring connections and control linkages to the transaxle.

9. Connect the the speedometer cable, throttle cable, secondary air pipe, water pipe bracket and EGR pipe.

10. Install the air cleaner and engine ground wire.

11. Reconnect the negative battery cable. Refill the transaxle and road test for proper operation.

BENCH OVERHAUL

Before Disassembly

Before removing any of the sub-assemblies, thoroughly clean the outside of the transaxle to prevent dirt from entering the mechanical parts during the repair operation.

CAUTION

Eye protection should be worn during procedures involving air pressure, when using spring compression tools or when removing snaprings.

During the repair of the subassemblies, certain general instructions which apply to all units of the transaxle must be followed. The instructions are given here to avoid unnecessary repetition.

Handle all transaxle parts carefully to avoid nicking or burring the bearing or mating surfaces.

Lubricate all internal parts of the transaxle before assembly with clean automatic transaxle fluid. Do not use any other lubricants except on gaskets and thrust washers which may be coated with petroleum jelly to facilitate assembly. Always install new gaskets when assembling the transaxle.

Converter Inspection

1. If the converter is to be reused, inspect the outer area of the converter for crack, inspect the bushing and seal surfaces for worn areas, scores, nicks or grooves.

2. The converter must be cleaned on the inside with cleaning solvent, dried, flushed with clean transmission fluid and drained until ready for installation.

3. Measure the converter bushing inside diameter.

4. Replace converter if bushing diameter is greater than 1.302 in. (33.075mm).

NOTE: Whenever a transaxle has been disassembled, the converter and oil cooler must be cleaned.

Transaxle Disassembly

CONVERTER AND OIL PAN

Removal

1. Remove the torque converter from transaxle by pulling it straight out of the housing.

2. If not already drained, remove the drain plug at the bottom of the transaxle case and allow the fluid to drain completely.

3. Remove the pan from the transaxle case.

VALVE BODY

Removal

1. Remove the vacuum modulator, taking care not to loosen vacuum diaphragm rod.

2. Remove the kickdown solenoid.

3. Remove the neutral safety switch.

4. Remove the valve body-to-case attaching bolts, note the position of each bolt for installation reference.

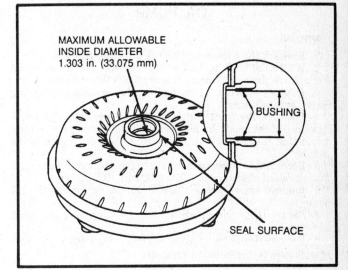

Torque converter bushing

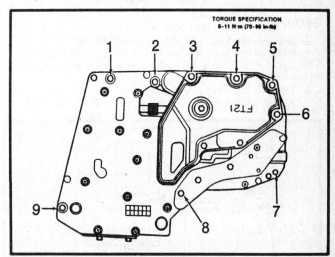

Bolt removal and torque sequence

NOTE: Be careful not to loose the ball and spring, located in the slotted hole.

5. Hold the manual valve to keep it from sliding out of the valve body and remove the valve body from the case.

NOTE: Failure to hold the manual valve while removing the control assembly could cause the manual valve to become bent or damaged. Be careful not to loose the vacuum diaphragm rod or the ball and spring for the torque converter relief valve.

6. If complete disassembly is to be done, remove the dipstick tube, speedometer driven gear, oil pump shaft and input shaft.

GOVERNOR

Removal

1. Note the position of the governor.
2. Remove the 3 retaining bolts from the governor cover assembly.
3. Lift the governor assembly from the transaxle case.
4. Remove the 2 governor retaining screws from the governor sleeve.
5. Remove the governor valve body.

OIL PUMP

Removal

1. Position the transaxle with the oil pump facing down.
2. With a flat blade tool inserted in the wide slot between the front clutch drum and connecting shell, pry down on the drum.
3. Rotate the drum 2 complete revolutions while repeating Step 2 several times.
4. Measure the front clutch drum endplay by checking the clearance of the small slot between the front clutch tabs and the connecting shell slots. This clearance is the front clutch drum endplay.
5. Record this measurement for reference upon assembly. The standard clearance is 0.020–0.031 in. (0.5–0.8mm).
6. Remove the oil cooler lines from the outside of the oil pump.
7. Secure the front clutch in place by tightening the band adjuster.
8. Remove the oil pump attaching bolts and note the position of each bolt for installation reference.

FRONT UNIT

Removal

1. Remove the band adjuster bolt and locknut.
2. Remove the band adjuster strut from inside the case.
3. Remove the band from the transaxle case from the oil pump side.
4. Remove the front clutch assembly.
5. Remove the needle bearing located on the rear clutch.

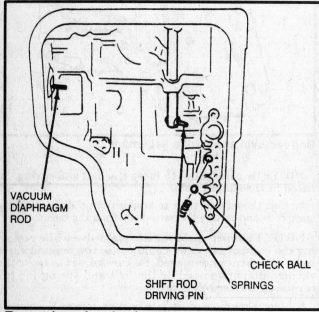

Transaxle and spring location

VACUUM DIAPHRAGM ROD

SHIFT ROD DRIVING PIN

CHECK BALL

SPRINGS

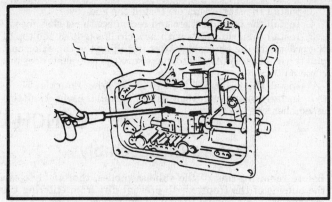

Prying clutch drum to check clearance

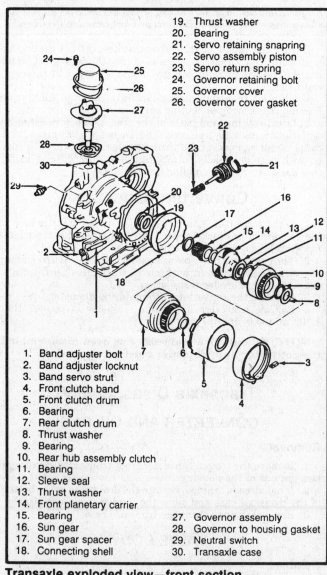

19. Thrust washer
20. Bearing
21. Servo retaining snapring
22. Servo assembly piston
23. Servo return spring
24. Governor retaining bolt
25. Governor cover
26. Governor cover gasket

1. Band adjuster bolt
2. Band adjuster locknut
3. Band servo strut
4. Front clutch band
5. Front clutch drum
6. Bearing
7. Rear clutch drum
8. Thrust washer
9. Bearing
10. Rear hub assembly clutch
11. Bearing
12. Sleeve seal
13. Thrust washer
14. Front planetary carrier
15. Bearing
16. Sun gear
17. Sun gear spacer
18. Connecting shell
27. Governor assembly
28. Governor to housing gasket
29. Neutral switch
30. Transaxle case

Transaxle exploded view – front section

6. Remove the rear clutch drum.
7. Remove the oil pump thrust washer, if washer did not stay on pump.
8. Remove the needle bearing located on the rear clutch hub assembly.

9. Remove the needle bearing and thrust washer from the planetary.

10. Remove the planetary carrier.

11. Remove the sun gear and spacer.

12. Remove the connecting shell.

13. Remove the thrust washer and needle bearing.

14. Use a C-clamp and socket to remove the servo piston into the transaxle case, if not already removed.

—————————— **CAUTION** ——————————

Eye protection should be worn during servo removal.

15. Remove the servo snapring.

16. Remove the servo retainer, piston and spring by slowly loosening the C-clamp.

INTERMEDIATE AND REAR UNIT

Removal

1. Remove the bolts attaching the transaxle case to the torque converter housing.

2. Carefully pry cases apart to separate the housings.

3. Pry oil lines away from case to remove.

4. Note the position of the parking pawl shaft and spring for installation reference. Remove pawl assembly by pulling the shaft straight out.

5. Remove the drum hub assembly from the case.

6. Remove the one-way clutch inner race assembly and planetary carrier from the case.

7. Remove the needle and thrust washer bearings from the planetary gear.

8. Before removing the one-way clutch, measure the clearance of the low and reverse clutch retaining plate and the one-way clutch, by using a feeler gauge. The clearance should be 0.032–0.041 in. (0.8–1.05mm).

9. Remove the snapring securing the one-way clutch and the retaining plate to the case.

10. Remove the clutch pack assembly.

11. Using a clutch compressor, place the recessed side of the large plate over the low and reverse clutch hub.

12. Place the small plate on the opposite side of the case. Insert the bolt through to clutch compressor plate and tighten the nut until the tension is relieved from the snapring.

NOTE: Transaxles which have not been previously disassembled do not have a low and reverse clutch hub snapring.

13. Remove the snapring from groove, if equipped.

14. Remove the clutch compressor tool.

15. Remove the low and reverse clutch hub.

16. Remove the springs from the low and reverse clutch piston.

17. To remove the low and reverse clutch piston, hold a wood block over the low and reverse clutch piston and apply a short burst of air to the piston application orifice in the transaxle case.

—————————— **CAUTION** ——————————

Wear eye protection and keep fingers out from between wood block and piston. Do not exceed 60 psi.

MANUAL LINKAGE

Removal

1. Remove the bolts attaching the parking pawl actuator guide to the case and remove the actuator guide.

2. Remove the lower nut at the end of the manual shaft assembly, hold the shaft with an open-end wrench.

3. Remove the 2 circlips from the manual shift linkage.

4. Remove the shift shaft linkage from the manual shaft.

1. Oil lines	24. Parking pawl actuator
2. Parking pawl	support retaining bolt
3. Parking pawl return spring	25. Parking pawl actuator
4. Parking pawl shaft	support
5. Drum hub assembly	26. Circlip parking pawl
6. Needle bearing	actuator ferrule
7. Thrust washer	27. Parking pawl actuator rod
8. One-way clutch inner race	28. Clevis-pin
9. Planetary carrier	29. Flat washer
10. Retaining snapring	30. Spring
11. Needle bearing	31. Ferrule
12. Thrust washer	32. Lower manual shaft
13. One-way clutch snapring	retaining nut
14. One-way clutch	33. Manual shaft
15. One-way clutch retaining	34. O-ring
plate	35. Control rod actuating lever
16. Internal spline clutch plate	36. Circlip
17. External spline clutch plate	37. Actuating lever
18. Dished plate	38. Pivot pin
19. Low-reverse retaining	39. Upper manual shaft
snapring	retaining nut
20. Low-reverse clutch hub	40. Lock washer
21. Low-reverse piston	41. Manual shaft arm
22. Outer piston seal	42. Control rod
23. Inner piston seal	43. Detent ball
	44. Detent spring

Transaxle exploded view—intermediate section

5. Remove the bolts from the upper shaft support and slide the manual shaft out of the transaxle case.

6. Remove the parking pawl actuator rod from the transaxle case.

7. Position the transaxle with the oil pan opening up.

8. Remove the roll pin securing the control rod to the transaxle case by lightly tapping the roll pin with a $^3/_{32}$ in. pin punch and a hammer.

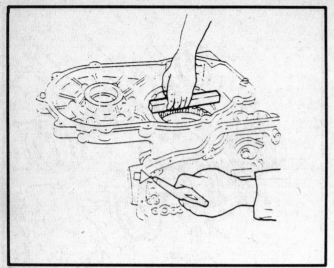

Testing low reverse clutch piston

9. Carefully slide the control rod out of the transaxle case, making sure not to lose the detent ball and spring.
10. Remove the detent ball.
11. Remove the spring.

FINAL DRIVE

Removal

1. Remove the differential assembly, by lifting it out of the case.
2. Remove the bolts attaching the output bearing and idler support to the converter housing.
3. Remove the support housing from the converter housing by lightly tapping the idler shaft with a brass drift and hammer.
4. Place the support assembly into a vise and remove the roll pin from the housing by tapping with a pin punch and hammer.
5. Carefully remove the bearing housing assembly from the vise.
6. Remove the idler gear assembly from the bearing cover.
7. Use the bearing remover to remove the bearing race from the support housing. Remove the adjustment shim from the housing. Separate or mark each shim for installation reference.
8. Using a puller and slide hammer remove the differential side bearing races from both the differential bearing housing and from the converter housing.
9. Remove the bolts and side bearing housing from the transaxle.
10. Remove the shim from the differential side bearing housing and drive out the oil seal.
11. Remove the O-ring from the differential side bearing housing.
12. Remove the oil seal from the output shaft bearing/stator support, using a puller and slide hammer.
13. Remove the output shaft bearing race from the bearing support, using a puller and slide hammer.
14. Remove the bolts and output shaft bearing/stator support by pressing it out of the case, using appropriate step plate tool.

Unit Disassembly and Assembly

NOTE: Allow all new clutch plates to soak in Dexron® II transmission fluid for a minimum of 2 hours before assembly.

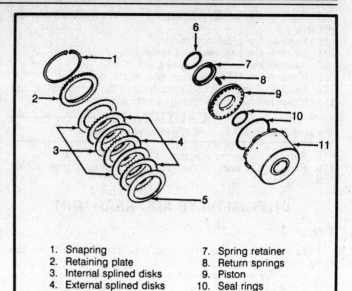

1. Snapring	7. Spring retainer
2. Retaining plate	8. Return springs
3. Internal splined disks	9. Piston
4. External splined disks	10. Seal rings
5. Dished plate	11. Rear clutch drum
6. Snapring	

Front clutch

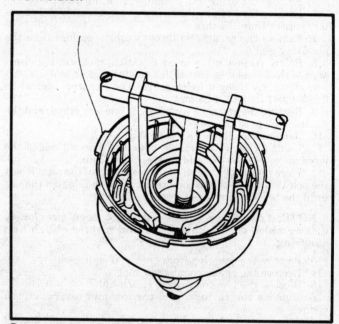

Compressing clutch plates

FRONT CLUTCH

Disassembly

1. Remove the retaining snapring from the drum.
2. Remove the retaining plate and the clutch plate assembly.
3. Remove the dished plate, noting the direction of the dish.
4. Remove the snapring from the drum hub with the use of a compressing tool.
5. Remove the piston from the drum by blowing compressed air into the apply hole in the drum. Remove the oil seals from the piston and drum hub.

Inspection

1. Inspect for damaged or worn drive plates, broken or worn

snaprings, deformed spring retainer, or weakened return springs.

NOTE: The free length of the return springs is 0.992–1.071 in. (25.2–27.2mm). If any spring is out of specification, replace all springs.

2. Inspect the drum bushing for being worn. Maximum inside diameter is 1.735 in. (44.075mm).

Assembly

1. It is good practice to install new clutch plates, both drive and driven, during the overhaul of the unit and not reuse the original plates.
2. Install the oil seals on the piston and the clutch drum hub. Lubricate the seals and grooves with vaseline or clean fluid.
3. Install the piston into the drum, being careful not to cut or damage the seals.
4. Install piston return springs to their mounting pegs on the clutch piston.
5. Place the spring retainer over the return spring.
6. Install the compressing tool and install the snapring holding the springs and spring retainer.
7. Install the dished plate with the protruding side facing the piston. Starting with a steel plate next to the dished plate, alternate with the lined plate and steel plate until 3 of each are installed.
8. Install the retaining plate and the retaining snapring.
9. Measure the front clutch clearance between the retaining plate and the snapring. The standard clearance is 0.063–0.071 in. (1.6–1.8mm). If the clearance is not correct, adjust it with the proper sized retaining plate.
10. After assembly, position the front clutch drum on the oil pump. Check clutch operation by applying air pressure to the application orifice.

REAR CLUTCH

Disassembly

1. Remove the clutch drum snapring, using an appropriate tool.
2. Remove the retaining plate, clutch plates, spacers and the dished plate from the clutch drum.
3. Place a "T" handled clutch spring compressor through the clutch drum. Install and tighten the nut of the compressor tool until the tension is relieved from the hub snapring.
4. Remove the clutch hub snapring, using an appropriate tool.
5. Remove the clutch compressor tool.
6. Place a wood block over the front of the front clutch drum. Remove the piston by applying compressed air into the fluid hole of the pump housing with the front and rear clutch assembly positioned on the oil pump extension.

——————————— **CAUTION** ———————————

Wear eye protection and keep fingers out from between wood block and piston. Do not exceed 60 psi.

7. Remove the inner and outer piston seal rings.

Inspection

Inspect for damaged or worn drive plates, broken or worn snaprings, deformed spring retainer, or weakened return springs.

NOTE: The free length of the return springs is 0.992–1.071 in. (25.2–27.2mm). If any spring is out of specification, replace all springs.

Assembly

1. Install the clutch piston into the clutch drum by pushing evenly, taking care not to damage the seals.

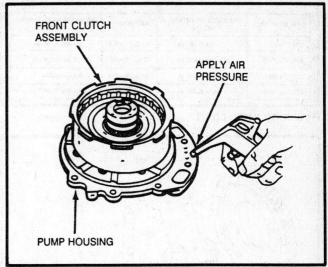

FRONT CLUTCH ASSEMBLY

APPLY AIR PRESSURE

PUMP HOUSING

Testing front clutch assembly

PART NUMBER	THICKNESS OF RETAINING PLATE	PART NUMBER	THICKNESS OF RETAINING PLATE
E7GZ-7B066-B	5.2 mm (0.205 in)	E7GZ-7B066-E	5.8 mm (0.228 in)
E7GZ-7B066-C	5.4 mm (0.213 in)	E7GZ-7B066-F	6.0 mm (0.236 in)
E7GZ-7B066-D	5.6 mm (0.221 in)	E7GZ-7B066-G	6.2 mm (0.244 in)

Retaining plate chart

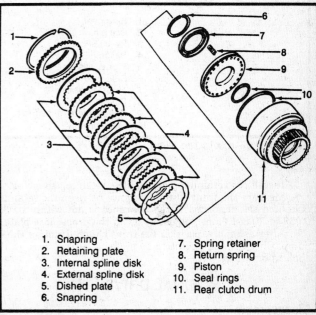

1. Snapring
2. Retaining plate
3. Internal spline disk
4. External spline disk
5. Dished plate
6. Snapring
7. Spring retainer
8. Return spring
9. Piston
10. Seal rings
11. Rear clutch drum

Rear clutch

2. Install the piston return springs to their mounting pegs on the clutch piston.
3. Place the spring retainer over the return springs.
4. Using the clutch spring compressor, press the clutch to gain access to the inner hub snapring groove.
5. Install the inner hub snapring, making certain it is fully seated in the groove. Remove compressor tool.
6. Install the dished plate with the protruding side facing the piston. Starting with a steel plate next to the dished plate, alternate with the lined plate and steel plate until 3 of each are installed.

PART NUMBER	THICKNESS OF RETAINING PLATE	PART NUMBER	THICKNESS OF RETAINING PLATE
E7GZ-7B066-A	5.0 mm (0.197 in)	E7GZ-7B066-E	5.8 mm (0.228 in)
E7GZ-7B066-B	5.2 mm (0.205 in)	E7GZ-7B066-F	6.0 mm (0.236 in)
E7GZ-7B066-C	5.4 mm (0.213 in)	E7GZ-7B066-G	6.2 mm (0.244 in)
E7GZ-7B066-D	5.6 mm (0.221 in)	E7GZ-7B066-H	4.8 mm (0.189 in)

Retaining plate chart

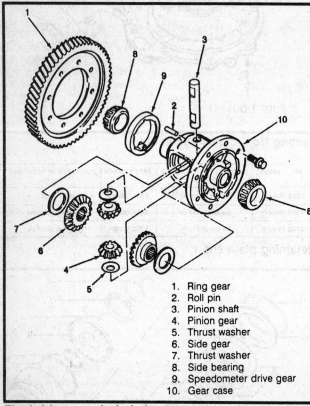

1. Ring gear
2. Roll pin
3. Pinion shaft
4. Pinion gear
5. Thrust washer
6. Side gear
7. Thrust washer
8. Side bearing
9. Speedometer drive gear
10. Gear case

Final drive – exploded view

7. Install the retaining plate and the retaining snapring.
8. Measure the front clutch clearance between the retaining plate and the snapring. If the clearance is not within 0.031–0.039 in. (0.8–1.0mm), adjust by using the proper size plate.
9. After assembly, position the front clutch drum on the oil pump. Check clutch operation by applying air pressure to the application orifice.

FINAL DRIVE

Disassembly

1. Install the halfshafts on differential and support unit in "V" blocks.
2. Measure and record the backlash of both pinion gears. Standard backlash is 0.000–0.004 in. (0.0–0.1mm).
3. Remove the ring gear.
4. Remove the pinion shaft roll pin, using a $^5/_{32}$ in. diameter punch or rod at least 3 in. long.
5. Press the front bearing from the differential case, using a puller tool.

NOTE: If differential bearing is removed, it must be replaced with a new bearing and race.

6. Remove the rear bearing from the differential case, using a puller.
7. Remove the pinion shaft by sliding it out of the gear case.
8. Remove the pinion gears and thrust washers by rotating them out of the gear case.
9. Remove the side gears from the case.
10. Remove the speedometer drive gear from the case.

Inspection

1. The inspection of the components consists of checking for broken teeth, worn gears and thrust washers, or a cracked carrier housing.
2. The roller bearing must be pressed from the carrier housing and new ones pressed back on. New races must be used with new bearings.
3. The backlash of the pinion gears is 0.0–0.039 in. (0.0–0.1mm).
4. If the backlash of the pinions are not correct, replace all the thrust washers with new and recheck. If excessive clearance still exists, check the carrier for wear.

Assembly

1. Install the speedometer drive gear, align the locating tang on the gear with the groove in the gear case.
2. Install the front and rear differential bearings to the gear case with a press.
3. Locate and record the identification number on each side gear thrust washer. This information may be used when setting the backlash of the side and pinion gears. If backlash was measured when disassembled, use proper thickness thrust washer to obtain necessary backlash.
4. Coat the side gear thrust washers with Dexron®II transmission fluid and install washers and gears into the case.
5. Coat the pinion gear thrust washers with Dexron®II transmission fluid and install pinion gear and washers into the case.
6. Align pinion shaft with gears and install pinion shaft, with flat on the shaft up and the roll pin hole entering case last.
7. Install the pin through the gear case and into the pinion shaft, using an appropriate tool, until $^1/_{16}$ in. below the surface of the gear case.
8. After installing the pin, stake the gear case to prevent the pin from coming out.
9. Install the ring gear to case, with the depression on the gear toward the case.
10. Align the holes in the gear with holes in case and install the bolts hand tight.
11. Tighten the bolts in a diagonal pattern in stages until torqued to 52–62 ft. lbs. (67–83 Nm).
12. Install the halfshafts on differential and support unit in "V" blocks.
13. Measure the backlash of both pinion gears. Standard backlash is 0.000–0.004 in. (0.0–0.1mm).
14. If the backlash is more than allowable, adjust by using different thickness thrust washers. Thrust washers should be the same thickness at each gear.

OUTPUT SHAFT

1. To disassemble, press off bearings.
2. Check for worn bearings or gears.
3. To reassemble, press bearing onto shaft.

IDLER GEAR

Disassembly

1. Insert hex torque adapter T87C–77000–E into the end of idler gear shaft and place the assembly into a vise.
2. Remove the locknut, using a 1½ in. socket.
3. Remove the idler gear and idler gear bearing.

Identification mark	Thickness
0	2.0 mm (0.079 in)
1	2.1 mm (0.083 in)
2	2.2 mm (0.087 in)

Pinion thrust washer identification

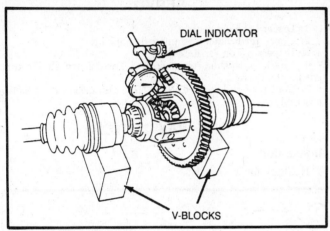

Checking backlash

4. If necessary, pull bearing race from gear, using appropriate puller.
5. Press other bearing race from gear, if necessary.

Inspection

Check for worn bearings or gears.

Assembly

1. Press the races into the idler gear, using a hydraulic press and appropriate adapters.
2. Assemble bearings, shims and locknut on the shaft and torque nut to 94 ft. lbs. (128 Nm).
3. Reposition the assembly in a vise, while protecting gear.
4. Using torque adapter tool and an inch lbs. wrench, measure the bearing preload. The correct amount of preload is 0.26–7.8 inch lbs. (0.3–9.0 Nm) while rotating tool.
5. Adjust shims as necessary to obtain proper preload.
6. When preload in correct, torque locknut to 94–130 ft. lbs. (128–177 Nm).

OIL PUMP

Disassembly

1. Remove the bolts that retain the pump cover to the pump housing.
2. Remove the pump cover, being careful not to allow the gears to fall out of the housing.
3. Mark the inner and outer gears with an indelible marker, prior to removing them.

NOTE: Do not mark the gears by pin-punching, or otherwise stressing the gear.

4. Remove the pump flange and inner and outer gears.

Inspection

1. Check the housing and cover for cracks or worn areas.

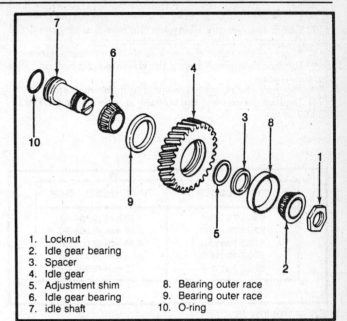

1. Locknut
2. Idle gear bearing
3. Spacer
4. Idle gear
5. Adjustment shim
6. Idle gear bearing
7. idle shaft
8. Bearing outer race
9. Bearing outer race
10. O-ring

Idler gear – exploded view

Using torque adapters

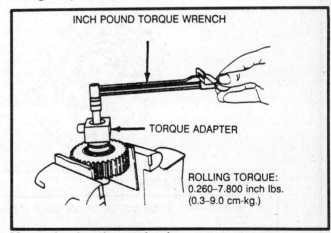

ROLLING TORQUE: 0.260–7.800 inch lbs. (0.3–9.0 cm-kg.)

Measuring bearing preload

2. Check the gears for wear, broken or damaged gear teeth.
3. Check the inner gear bushing of the pump housing sleeve for being worn or damaged.
4. Check the clearance of the inner gear to the pump cover and the outer gear to the pump cover.
5. Check the clearance of the outer gear teeth head to the crescent dam.

6. Check the clearance between the outer gear to the housing.

7. Check the clearance between the new seal rings and the seal ring groove in the pump cover hub.

8. Measure the outer diameter of the pump flange sleeve.

9. Replace the pump flange if the sleeve is worn beyond 1.492 in. (38.075mm).

10. Measure the pump cover bushing inside diameter.

11. Replace the cover if the bushing is worn beyond 1.499 in. (38.075mm).

PART NUMBER	THICKNESS OF SHIM
E7GZ-7N112-A	0.10 mm (0.004 in)
E7GZ-7N112-B	0.12 mm (0.005 in)
E7GZ-7N112-C	0.14 mm (0.006 in)
E7GZ-7N112-D	0.16 mm (0.007 in)
E7GZ-7N112-E	0.20 mm (0.008 in)

Shim thickness chart

Assembly

1. Assemble the gears to flange so the marks on the inner and outer gears are aligned and facing out.

2. Coat the gears with Dexron®II transmission fluid.

3. Install the pump cover to the pump housing.

4. Install the bolts and torque to 95–122 inch lbs. (11–14 Nm).

5. Install the oil pump shaft and make sure the gears turn easily.

SERVO

1. Discard the old seals.

2. Check for broken or damaged snapring.

3. Inspect piston for damage.

4. Check for weaken return spring. The free length of return spring should be 1.870 in. (47.5mm).

5. Coat new seals with Dexron®II transmission fluid before assembly.

ONE-WAY CLUTCH

Inspection

1. Check for worn parts.

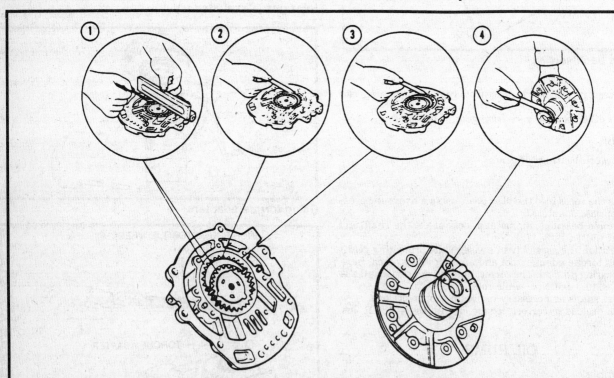

	MEASURED LOCATION	STANDARD VALUE	LIMIT
1	INNER GEAR ~ PUMP COVER: OUTER GEAR ~ PUMP COVER	0.02 ~ 0.04 mm (0.001 ~ 0.002 in)	0.08 mm (0.003 in)
2	HEAD OF OUTER GEAR TEETH ~ CRESCENT DAM	0.14 ~ 0.21 mm (0.006 ~ 0.008 in)	0.25 mm (0.010 in)
3	OUTER GEAR ~ HOUSING	0.05 ~ 0.20 mm (0.002 ~ 0.008 in)	0.25 mm (0.010 in)
4	SEAL RING ~ SEAL RING GROOVE	0.04 ~ 0.16 mm (0.002 ~ 0.006 in)	0.40 mm (0.016 in)

Checking pump and gear clearance

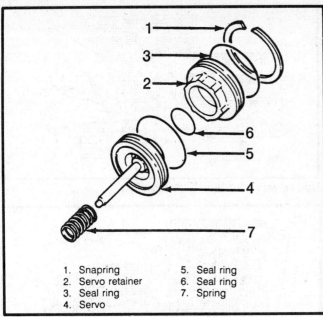

1. Snapring
2. Servo retainer
3. Seal ring
4. Servo
5. Seal ring
6. Seal ring
7. Spring

Servo – exploded view

2. Check for proper one-way operation.
3. Measure bushing, replace if greater than 5.121 in. (130.063mm).

LOW AND REVERSE CLUTCH

Inspection

1. Check for worn parts.
2. Check for weakened or damaged returned springs.
3. If any spring length is less than 1.07–1.11 in. (27.2–28.2mm), replace all springs.

DRUM HUB

Disassembly

1. Remove the parking gear spring.
2. Remove the parking gear by pushing the 2 pins which project from the drive hub.
3. Remove the snapring, the internal gear and the drive hub.

Inspection

Inspect the components for broken or worn snaprings, damaged or worn gears, or broken teeth.

Assembly

1. Assembly of the drum hub is in the reverse of its disassembly procedure.
2. Make certain the snapring and parking gear spring are in their proper positions.

PLANETARY UNITS

Disassembly

Remove snapring from one-way clutch inner race and separate planetary. The following procedures and measurements are the same for all planetary units.

Inspection

1. Inspect for worn snapring.

2. Inspect for binding, loose or rough rotation of gears.
3. Measure the clearance between the pinion washer and the planetary carrier, by using a feeler gauge. If the clearance exceeds 0.031 in. (0.8mm), replace the planetary unit.

Assembly

Clean and replace components in the reverse order of the removal procedure.

CONTROL VALVE BODY

The valve body is a high precision unit. It should be handled very carefully. Since many parts look alike, they should be kept in a well arranged order. If the clutches have been overheated or the band has been burn, make certain to disassemble, clean and inspect the valve body.

Disassembly

1. Remove the manual valve from the upper valve body.
2. Remove the bolts attaching the oil screen to the valve body and remove the oil screen.
3. Remove the 2-3 valve cover.
4. Remove the bolts attaching the upper and lower valve body, noting the position of each bolt.

NOTE: Keep the separator plate attached to the lower valve body to prevent losing the check ball, orifices and springs. If valve body is disassembled, note the locations of check ball, orifices and springs for reference during reassembly.

5. Carefully lift the lower body from the upper valve body, keeping the separator plate attached to the lower body.
6. Turn the assembly over, carefully remove the separator plate and remove the check ball and spring, 2 orifices and springs from the valve body, noting their locations.
7. Remove the orifice from the upper valve body with a magnet.
8. Note the location and position of each valve as the body is disassembled.
9. Carefully remove the side plates of the upper valve body to gain access to the valves.

NOTE: Keep the parts for each valve separated to prevent interchanging of springs that look alike.

Inspection

1. Check the valve body bores and valves for varnish or minor scoring.
2. Clean all parts, use carburetor cleaner to remove varnish.
3. If varnish or scoring is excessive, replace valve assembly.
4. Remove burrs from valves, using 600–800 grit finishing paper wet with Dexron®II transmission fluid.
5. Insert each valve separately into its bore. Do not lubricate at this time.
6. Check free movement of each valve, by tipping the valve body. Each valve should slide freely when valve body is shaken slightly.

Assembly

1. Lubricate all the components in Dexron®II transmission fluid.
2. Install the valves and springs in their correct bores.
3. Install the side plates at their correct positions and tighten the bolts to 22–30 inch lbs. (2.5–3.5 Nm).
4. Install the orifice in the upper half of the valve body.
5. Install the check ball and spring and the other 2 orifices and springs into their correct positions in the lower valve body.
6. Place the separator plate over the lower valve body. Hold-

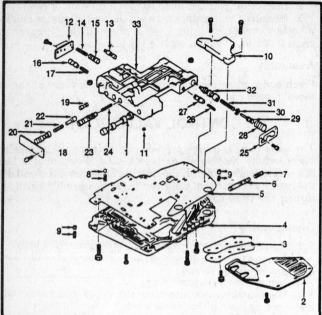

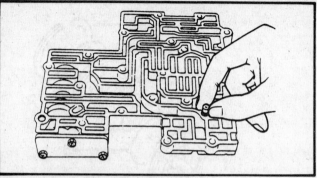

Upper valve body orifice location

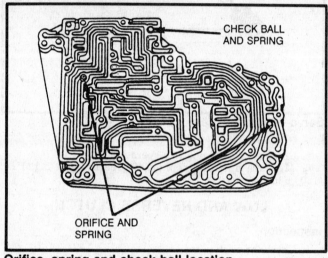

Orifice, spring and check ball location

1. Manual valve	18. Side plate
2. Oil strainer	19. Modifier valve
3. 2–3 valve cover	20. 2–3 shift valve
4. Lower valve body	21. Spring
5. Separator plate	22. 2–3 shift plug
6. 3–2 timing valve	23. 1–2 shift plug
7. Spring	24. Spring
8. Check ball and spring	25. Side plate
9. Orifice check valve and spring	26. Spring
10. Sub-body	27. 2nd lock valve
11. Orifice check valve	28. Pressure regulator sleeve
12. Side plate	29. Pressure regulator plug
13. Vacuum throttle valve	30. Spring seat
14. Spring	31. Spring
15. Throttle backup valve	32. Pressure regulator valve
16. Downshift valve	33. Upper valve body
17. Spring	

Valve assembly – exploded view

ing the separator plate and valve body together, turn the assembly over and place it onto the upper valve body.

7. Align the upper and lower valve body. Install attaching bolts and tighten to proper torque.

8. Install the 3-2 valve cover and torque the bolts to 26–35 inch lbs. (3–4 Nm).

9. Place valve body aside in a clean area, for installation at a later time.

GOVERNOR

Disassembly

1. Remove the governor body from the separator plate.
2. Remove the separator plate from the shaft.
3. Remove the filter from the separator plate.

NOTE: Cover the bore hole when removing the retainer plate to prevent losing the primary governor spring.

4. Remove the retainer plate for the primary governor spring by applying light pressure against the retainer plate and spring and sliding the plate out of the slot of the machined surface.

5. Remove the primary governor spring.

NOTE: Cover the bore hole when removing the retainer plate to prevent losing the secondary governor spring.

6. Remove the retainer plate for the secondary governor spring by applying light pressure against the retainer plate and spring and sliding the plate out of the slot of the machined surface.

7. Remove the secondary governor spring.

8. Remove the governor driven gear roll pin, using a pin punch and hammer.

9. Remove the governor driven gear and separate the governor shaft from the sleeve.

10. Remove the seal rings from the governor shaft.

11. Remove the bearing outer race from the governor shaft.

12. Remove the needle bearing from the sleeve.

Inspection

1. Inspect the valves for scoring or sticking.

NOTE: Minor scoring or varnish may be removed with fine 600–800 grit finishing paper wet with Dexron®II transmission fluid.

2. Inspect return springs.

3. Replace the primary spring, if the diameter is not 0.34–0.87 in. (8.7–9.3mm) or free length is not 0.66–0.70 in. (16.7–17.7mm).

4. Replace the secondary spring, if the diameter is not 0.35–0.38 in. (8.95–9.55mm) or free length is not 0.50–0.54 in. (12.7–13.7mm).

5. Inspect driven gear for damaged teeth.

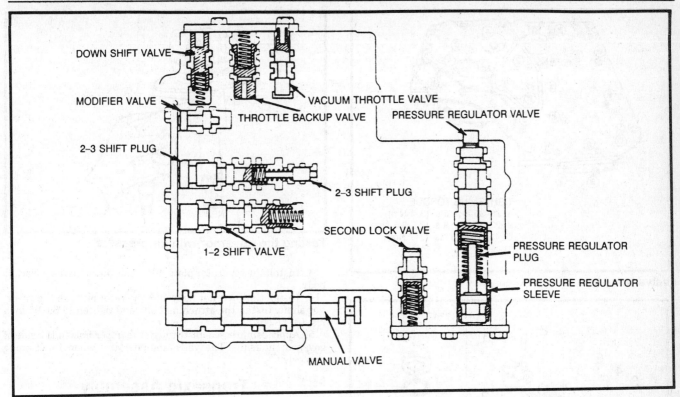

Valve location

NAME	OUTER DIA. mm (in)	FREE LENGTH mm (in)	NO. OF COILS	WIRE DIA. mm (in)
THROTTLE BACK UP	7.3 (0.287)	36.0 (1.42)	16.0	0.8 (0.031)
DOWN SHIFT	5.5 (0.217)	21.9 (0.862)	14.0	0.55 (0.022)
2-3 SHIFT	6.4 (0.252)(carb.) 6.9 (0.272)(EFI)	39.2 (1.54)(carb.) 41.0 (1.61)(EFI)	20.0	0.7 (0.028)
1-2 SHIFT	6.55 (0.258)	32.0 (1.26)	18.7 (carb.) 18.0 (EFI)	0.55 (0.022)
SECOND LOCK	5.55 (0.219)	33.5 (1.32)	18.0	0.55 (0.022)
PRESSURE REGULATOR	11.7 (0.461)	43.0 (1.69)	15.0	1.2 (0.047)
THROTTLE RELIEF	7.0 (0.276)	11.2 (0.44)	6.0	0.9 (0.035)
ORIFICE CHECK	5.0 (0.197)	15.5 (0.61)	12.0	0.23 (0.009)
3-2 TIMING	7.5 (0.295)	22.1 (0.870)	13.0	0.8 (0.031)

Valve spring size chart

6. Inspect needle bearings and thrust washer for wear.
7. Inspect for clogged or torn filter.

Assembly

1. Coat all parts with Dexron®II transmission fluid.
2. Install the seals.

3. Install the needle bearing into sleeve with the exposed bearing facing up.
4. Install the thrust washer on the governor shaft, making certain the tangs of the washer are inserted into the holes of the governor shaft.
5. Install the governor shaft into the sleeve.

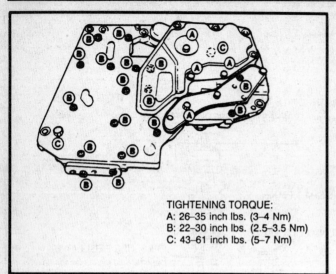

TIGHTENING TORQUE:
A: 26–35 inch lbs. (3–4 Nm)
B: 22–30 inch lbs. (2.5–3.5 Nm)
C: 43–61 inch lbs. (5–7 Nm)

Valve body torque chart

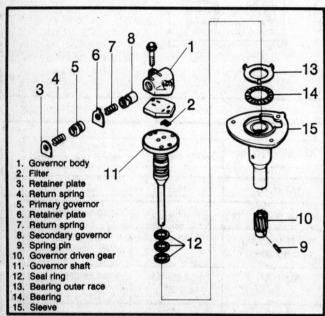

1. Governor body
2. Filter
3. Retainer plate
4. Return spring
5. Primary governor
6. Retainer plate
7. Return spring
8. Secondary governor
9. Spring pin
10. Governor driven gear
11. Governor shaft
12. Seal ring
13. Bearing outer race
14. Bearing
15. Sleeve

Governor assembly – exploded view

6. Install the governor driven gear to the governor shaft and install the roll pin, using a pin punch and hammer.

7. Install the secondary governor valve, narrow land first, into the large bore end of the governor body.

NOTE: The valve is fully seated when the narrow valve and extends out of the governor body case.

8. Install the secondary governor spring into the governor body until the spring end is seated in the recess of the secondary valve.

9. Compress the secondary spring. Install the retainer plate through the slot of the machined surface.

10. Install the primary governor valve, notched land last, into the large bore end of the governor body. The primary governor valve is fully seated when it contacts the retainer plate of the secondary valve.

11. Compress the primary spring. Install the retainer plate through the slot of the machined surface.

12. Install the filter onto the separator plate.

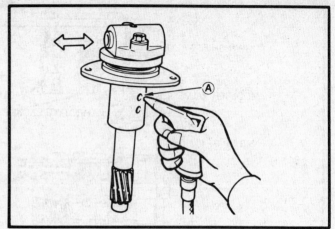

Testing the governor with air pressure

13. Install the separator plate, filter side down, to the governor body.

14. Install the governor body and separator plate on the governor shaft. Install the attaching bolts and tighten to 69–95 inch lbs. (8–11 Nm).

15. Apply compressed air through the upper hole in the side of governor housing. The valve should rattle when functioning properly.

Transaxle Assembly

CONVERTER HOUSING

Assembly

1. Install the differential output seal, using an appropriate tool.

2. Install the differential side bearing outer race in housing, using an appropriate tool.

3. Using guide pins, position output bearing/stator support in converter housing. Install and torque bolts to 8–10 ft. lbs. (11–14mm).

4. Using a driver and appropriate step plate press outer race for output shaft into bearing support.

5. Install the seal into stator support.

6. Using a new O-ring, install output bearing support in the transaxle case and torque bolts to 14–19 ft. lbs. (18–26 Nm).

DIFFERENTIAL BEARING PRELOAD

1. Position differential side bearing outer race in the recessed end of the gauge tool T87C–77000J. Screw the gauge tool on unit no clearance remains.

3. Place the differential in the converter housing. Place the gauge tool, with the outer race installed, over the differential side bearing.

4. Position the spacer collars in position and assemble the case halves. Torque bolts to 27–39 ft. lbs. (36–53 Nm).

5. Use the gauge wrench pins to unscrew the gauge tool and establish preload on the differential. Measure the preload using an inch lbs. torque wrench. Extend the gauge tool until the turning torque (drag) reads 4.3–6.9 inch lbs. (0.5–0.8 Nm).6. Measure the clearance at the separation of the gauge tool in order to determine the shim thickness.

7. Disassembly the gauge assembly. Install the necessary shims and bearing race in the transaxle housing and assemble the housing halves.

NOTE: Measure the clearance around the entire circumference and select shims equivalent to the maximum clearance. Do not use more than 5 shims.

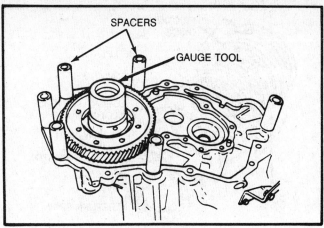

Installing bearing preload gauge

8. Test the bearing turning torque (drag) with housing assembled. If the turning torque is not 18–25 inch lbs. (2.1–2.9 Nm), repeat Steps 7 through 13.

9. Separate housing halves and install output shaft seals.

OUTPUT SHAFT BEARING PRELOAD

1.

Position the output gear and shaft into the converter housing.2.Position the 4 spacer collars.3.Insert the output shaft outer bearing race into the recessed end of the gauge tool and place the tool over the output gear shaft. Screw the halves of the gauge tool together so no clearance exists.4.Assemble the converter housing to the side bearing housing, using tool spacer bolts and torque bolts to 14–19 ft. lbs. (19–26 Nm).5.Unscrew the gauge tool, using gauge tool pins, until all the freeplay is removed and the bearing is seated.

6. Measure the drag on the output gear, by using the torque adapter tool.

7. Adjust drag to 0.36–0.65 inch lbs. (0.5–0.8 Nm), by adjusting shim thickness as necessary.

8. Disassemble the assembly tool and install selected shims and bearing race, using the appropriate tool and step plate.

9. Assembly output gear and bearing support. Torque bolts to 14–19 ft. lbs. (19–26 Nm).

10. Remeasure preload, if preload is not 0.26–7.81 inch lbs., repeat Steps 15 through 24.

11. After proper preload has been obtained, remove the bearing housing and install the idler gear assemble into the bearing housing. Replace the O-ring on the idler gear shaft.

12. Reinstall the bearing cone.

13. Torque the bearing housing bolts to 14–19 ft. lbs. (19–26 Nm).

MANUAL LINKAGE

Installation

1. Install the manual valve control rod, spring and ball detents.

2. Install the roll pin to retain the control rod.

3. Install the parking pawl actuator support and torque bolts to 8.7–11.6 ft. lbs. (12–16 Nm).

4. Install the actuating arm to the pawl rod and install circlips.

5. Install a new O-ring on the manual shaft.

6. Install the manual shaft to the transaxle case.

7. Install the manual shaft support to the transaxle case and torque the bolts to 8.7–11.6 ft. lbs. (12–16 Nm).

8. Install the shifter actuating arm to the manual shaft and align with the manual valve control rod.

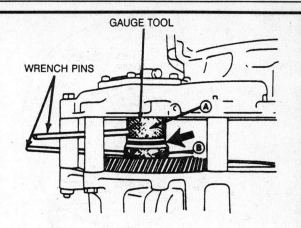

PART NUMBER	THICKNESS OF SHIM
E7GZ4067A	0.10 mm (0.004 in)
E7GZ4067A	0.12 mm (0.005 in)
E7GZ4067B	0.14 mm (0.006 in)
E7GZ4067C	0.16 mm (0.007 in)
E7GZ4067B	0.20 mm (0.008 in)
E7GZ4067C	0.30 mm (0.012 in)
E7GZ4067D	0.40 mm (0.016 in)
E7GZ4067E	0.50 mm (0.020 in)
E7GZ4067F	0.60 mm (0.024 in)
E7GZ4067G	0.70 mm (0.028 in)
E7GZ4067H	0.80 mm (0.032 in)
E7GZ4067J	0.90 mm (0.036 in)

Adjusting bearing preload

PART NUMBER	THICKNESS OF SHIM
E7GZ-7F405-A	0.10 mm (0.004 in)
E7GZ-7F405-B	0.12 mm (0.005 in)
E7GZ-7F405-C	0.14 mm (0.006 in)
E7GZ-7F405-D	0.16 mm (0.007 in)
E7GZ-7F405-E	0.20 mm (0.008 in)
E7GZ-7F405-F	0.50 mm (0.020 in)

TEST PRELOAD: 0.5 ~ 0.9 N·m (0.05 ~ 0.09 m-kg, 0.36 ~ 0.65 ft-lb)

ASSEMBLED PRELOAD: 0.03 ~ 0.9 N·m (0.3 ~ 9.0 cm-kg, 0.26 ~ 7.81 in-lb)

CAUTION
A) MEASURE THE CLEARANCE AROUND THE ENTIRE CIRCUMFERENCE, AND SELECT SHIMS EQUIVALENT TO THE MAXIMUM CLEARANCE.
B) MAXIMUM ALLOWABLE NUMBER OF SHIMS: 7

Adjusting shim chart

9. Install the nut on manual shaft and torque to 22–29 ft. lbs. (29–39 Nm).

INTERMEDIATE UNIT

Installation

1. Install new seals in the low and reverse piston and install piston in bore taking care not to damage seal.

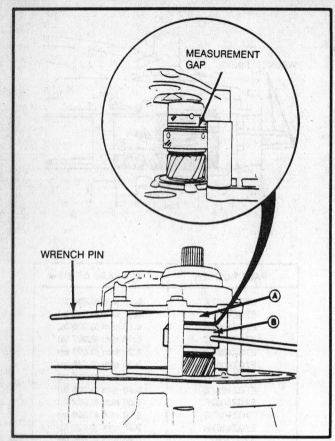

Check preload

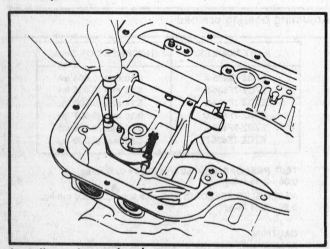

Install arm to pawl rod

2. Place the return spring and low and reverse clutch hub on top of the piston.

3. Install the clutch compressor and compress the assembly far enough to permit insertion of the retainer ring.

4. Install the dished plate to the low and reverse piston.

5. Install the clutch disc pack starting with a steel disc against the dished plate. Alternate internal and external tooth plates until all discs have been installed.

6. Install the retaining plate.

7. Install the one-way clutch with the bushing against the retaining plate. Compress the clutch assembly enough to install the retaining ring.

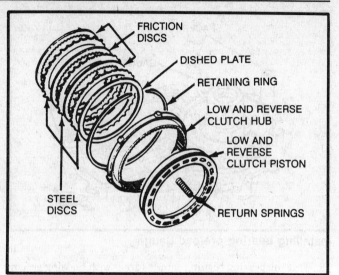

Intermediate clutch pack

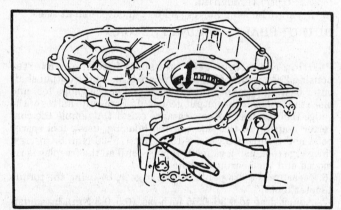

Test clutch pack

PART NUMBER	THICKNESS
E7GZ-7B066-J	7.8 mm (0.307 in)
E7GZ-7B066-K	8.0 mm (0.315 in)
E7GZ-7B066-L	8.2 mm (0.322 in)
E7GZ-7B066-M	8.4 mm (0.331 in)
E7GZ-7B066-N	8.6 mm (0.339 in)
E7GZ-7B066-P	8.8 mm (0.346 in)

Retaining plate thickness chart

8. Using a feeler gauge, measure the clearance between the one-way clutch and the retaining plate.

9. If the clearance is not 0.032–0.041 in. (0.81–1.05mm), adjust shim size as necessary.

10. Apply a burst of air pressure to the application port to test clutch plate action.

CAUTION
Do not allow air pressure to exceed 60 psi. Wear eye protection.

11. Install the parking pawl, spring and anchor pin to the case.

12. Position the converter housing to receive the differential. Install the differential, meshing ring gear with idler gear.

13. Install the thrust washer over output shaft.

14. Install the bearing so that the rollers contact the thrust washer.

15. Install the assembled drum hub onto the output shaft spline.

16. Install a bearing in the recess of the drum hub. Secure the opposing thrust washer to the planetary carrier with petroleum jelly.

17. Install the planetary carrier onto the one-way clutch inner race and secure it in place with the retainer ring.

18. Install the planetary carrier/inner race assembly into the drum hub.

19. Using a plastic mallet, install the governor oil transfer lines into the transfer case.

20. Apply a $^1/_{16}$ continuous bead of gasket eliminator E1FZ–19562–A (non-silicone) onto the converter housing mating surface.

21. Assemble the transaxle halves by rotating the one-way clutch inner race as the transaxle case is lowered onto the converter housing to engage the spline teeth of the inner race with the low and reverse disks.

22. Install the bolts and torque to 22–34 ft. lbs. (29–46 Nm).

23. After the cases are together, make certain all rotating parts rotate without resistance.

FRONT UNIT

Installation

1. Install the bearing to the rear planetary carrier.

2. Install the spacer over the small end of the sun gear and insert the sun gear into the connecting shell.

3. Place the thrust bearing over the end of the sun gear protruding from the connecting shell. Hold the washer in place with petroleum jelly.

4. Install the connecting shell/sun gear assembly into the rear planetary carrier.

5. Place the thrust bearing into the front planetary carrier using petroleum jelly. Face the rollers pointing out.

6. Install the front planetary carrier into the connecting shell.

7. Install the thrust washer and matching bearing to the end of the front planetary carrier. Install the seal sleeve in the center of the front planetary carrier.

8. Install the rear clutch hub assembly over the front planetary carrier.

9. Install the thrust bearing, rollers up, in the rear clutch hub.

10. Coat the matching thrust washer with petroleum jelly. Index the tangs on the washer with the mating holes in the rear clutch and install the washer.

11. Install the rear clutch assembly to the rear clutch hub, while gently rotating the rear clutch.

12. Install the thrust bearing in the rear clutch hub, rollers up. The companion thrust washer will be installed to the end of the oil pump extension later.

13. Place the assembled front clutch over the splines of the rear clutch hub, while gently rotating the front clutch.

14. Install the intermediate band, servo, strut and adjuster bolt. Apply sealant E1FZ–19562–A (non-silicone) to threads and install bolts tight enough to hold components in place, but do not perform adjustments until pump has been installed.

GOVERNOR

Installation

1. Install the governor onto the transaxle case so that the sleeve projection is aligned with the mark on case.

2. Torque bolts to 69–95 ft. lbs. (7.8–10.8 Nm)

SERVO

Installation

1. Install the servo into the transaxle housing.

2. Use a C-clamp and deep socket to compress the servo return spring.

3. Install the retaining ring and remove C-clamp.

OIL PUMP

Installation and Measurement

TOTAL ENDPLAY

1. Remove the oil pump extension and place the housing with gears installed aside.

2. Install the oil pump extension into the front clutch housing, without the plastic adjusting washer.

3. Position a machinist straightedge over the oil pump cover in the transaxle case, be careful not to place the tool on the bolt holes.

4. Use a feeler gauge and measure the clearance between the pump and bar or transaxle and bar. The measurement should not be greater than 0.004 in. (0.10mm) with the pump below the transaxle surface, or 0.006 in. (0.15mm) with the pump cover above the case surface.

5. Replace thrust washer as necessary to obtain proper clearance.

6. Reassemble oil pump and torque the oil pump cover to housing bolts to 95–122 inch lbs. (11–14 Nm).

7. Lubricate pump with Dexron®II transmission fluid and check for free movement by inserting and turning shaft.

FRONT CLUTCH ENDPLAY

1. Use petroleum jelly to install the oil pump gasket to the oil pump.

2. Install the plastic adjusting washer to the oil pump cover using petroleum jelly.

PART NUMBER	THICKNESS OF BEARING RACE
E7GZ-7D014-A	1.2 mm (0.047 in)
E7GZ-7D014-B	1.4 mm (0.055 in)
E7GZ-7D014-C	1.6 mm (0.063 in)
E7GZ-7D014-D	1.8 mm (0.071 in)
E7GZ-7D014-E	2.0 mm (0.079 in)
E7GZ-7D014-F	2.2 mm (0.087 in)

Endplay race selection chart

3. Install the thrust washer onto the end of the pump extension using petroleum jelly.

4. Install the oil pump to the transaxle and torque bolts to 11–16 ft. lbs. (15–22 Nm).

5. Reposition the transaxle with the oil pump facing down.

6. While turning the connecting shell through 2 complete revolutions, push the front clutch down toward the oil pump, using an appropriate tool inserted into the tabs of the clutch drum.

7. Measure the clearance between the tabs of the clutch drum and the connecting shell.

8. If the endplay in not within 0.020–0.031 in (0.5–0.8mm), replace the plastic washer with an appropriate size washer.

9. Reassemble and install the oil pump.

10. Apply sealant E1FZ–19562–A (non-silicone) to threads and torque to 11–16 ft. lbs. (15–22 Nm).

VALVE BODY

Installation

1. Install the steel ball into the transaxle case.

PART NUMBER	THICKNESS OF SHIM
E7GZ-7F373-A	2.1 mm (0.083 in)
E7GZ-7F373-B	2.3 mm (0.091 in)
E7GZ-7F373-C	2.5 mm (0.098 in)
E7GZ-7F373-D	2.7 mm (0.106 in)
E7GZ-7F373-E	1.5 mm (0.059 in)
E7GZ-7F373-F	1.7 mm (0.067 in)
E7GZ-7F373-G	1.3 mm (0.051 in)

Plastic adjustment washer chart

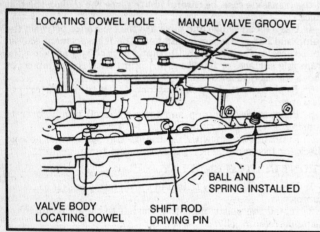

Spring and ball location

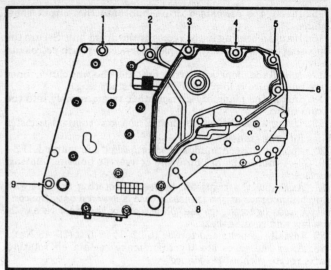

Bolt removal and torque sequence

MEASUREMENT	DIAPHRAGM ROD USED
Under 25.4 mm (1.000 in)	29.5 mm (1.160 in)
25.4 ~ 25.9 mm (1.000 ~ 1.020 in)	30.0 mm (1.180 in)
25.9 ~ 26.4 mm (1.020 ~ 1.039 in)	30.5 mm (1.200 in)
26.4 ~ 26.9 mm (1.039 ~ 1.059 in)	31.0 mm (1.220 in)
Over 26.9 mm (1.059 in)	31.5 mm (1.240 in)

PART NO.	DIAPHRAGM ROD
E7GZ-7A380-E	29.5 mm (1.160 in)
E7GZ-7A380-C	30.0 mm (1.180 in)
E7GZ-7A380-D	30.5 mm (1.200 in)
E7GZ-7A380-B	31.0 mm (1.220 in)
E7GZ-7A380-A	31.5 mm (1.240 in)

Vacuum diaphragm rod selection chart

2. Install the manual valve into the valve body.
3. Align the manual valve land with the pin on the control rod. Mate the dowels in the transaxle case with the holes in the valve body.
4. Install the valve body retaining bolts and torque to 70–90 inch lbs. (8–11 Nm) in proper sequence.

INTERMEDIATE BAND ADJUSTMENT

1. Tighten adjuster bolt to 8.7–10.8 ft. lbs. (12–15 Nm).
2. Apply sealant E1FZ-19562–A (non-silicone) to adjuster screw threads and torque locknut to 41–59 ft. lbs. (55–80 Nm).

CONTROL VALVE DIAPHRAGM ROD

1. Insert the vacuum diaphragm rod gauge into the mounting hole, with the beveled side out, until the tool bottoms.
2. Place the rod through the opening of the vacuum diaphragm tool until the rod bottoms out against the valve.
3. Tighten the lock knob on the vacuum modulator tool and remove the tool and rod from the transaxle case.
4. Use a depth gauge to measure the distance from the flat surface of the vacuum modulator tool to the end of the rod.5. Use this measurement to select the correct size rod.6. Install the correct rod, lubricate the modulator O-ring with Dexron®II and install the vacuum modulator.

OIL PAN AND CONVERTER

Installation

1. Install the kickdown solenoid, coat O-ring with Dexron®II and threads with sealant E1FZ-19562 (non-silicone).

2. Install the speedometer drive gear and torque bolts to 43–49 inch lbs. (5–8 Nm).
3. Lubricate oil filler tube end with Dexron®II and install. Torque retaining bolt to 43–69 inch lbs. (5–87 Nm).
4. Install a new pan gasket and oil pan. Torque pan bolts to 43–69 inch lbs. (5–87 Nm).

NOTE: Do not use any type of sealer or adhesive on the pan gasket. If necessary, soak the gasket in Dexron®II transmission fluid.

5. Coat the neutral safety switch threads with sealant E1FZ-19562 (non-silicone) and install.

NOTE: Switch must to torque to 14–19 ft.lbs. (19–26 Nm) for proper switch operation.

6. Install the turbine and oil pump shafts.
7. Lubricate the inside of torque converter with no more than ½ qt. of Dexron®II transmission fluid and install.
8. Measure the recess from converter to front housing mating surface. If distance is not 0.790 in. (20.0mm), converter is not seated properly.

SPECIFICATIONS

VALVE BODY

Item		EFI in. (mm)	Carburetor in. (mm)
Throttle back-up valve spring	Diameter	0.287 (7.3)	0.287 (7.3)
	Free length	1.417 (36.0)	1.420 (36.0)
Down shift valve spring	Diameter	0.219 (5.55)	0.217 (5.5)
	Free length	0.866 (22.0)	0.862 (21.9)
Throttle relief	Diameter	0.276 (7.0)	0.276 (7.0)
	Free length	0.440 (11.2)	0.440 (11.2)
2–3 shift valve spring	Diameter	0.272 (6.9)	0.252 (6.4)
	Free length	1.614 (41.0)	1.540 (39.2)
1–2 shift valve spring	Diameter	6.258 (6.55)	0.258 (6.55)
	Free length	1.260 (32.0)	1.260 (32.0)
Second lock valve spring	Diameter	0.219 (5.55)	0.219 (5.55)
	Free length	1.319 (33.5)	1.320 (33.5)
Pressure regulator valve spring	Diameter	0.461 (11.7)	0.461 (11.7)
	Free length	1.693 (43.0)	1.693 (43.0)
3-2 timing	Diameter	0.295 (7.5)	0.295 (7.5)
	Free length	0.870 (22.1)	0.870 (22.1)
Orifice check valve spring	Diameter	0.197 (5.0)	0.197 (5.0)
	Free length	—	0.610 (15.5)

SERVO

Item	Specification in. (mm)
Free length of return spring	1.87–1.93 (47.5–49.0)

GOVERNOR SPRINGS

Item		Specification in. (mm)
Primary spring	Outer diameter	0.343–0.366
	Free length	0.65–0.728 (16.5–18.5)
Secondary spring	Outer diameter	0.352–0.376 (8.95–9.55)
	Free length	0.488–0.567 (12.4–14.4)

GEAR ASSEMBLY

Item	Specification in. (mm)
Total endplay at pump	0.004–0.006 (0.1–0.15)
Endplay adjusting race	0.047 (1.2) 0.055 (1.4) 0.063 (1.6) 0.071 (1.8) 0.079 (2.0) 0.087 (2.2)
Idle gear bearing preload	0.3–7.8 (0.03–0.09)①
Preload adjusting shims	0.004 (0.10) 0.005 (0.12) 0.006 (0.14) 0.007 (0.16) 0.020 (0.50) 0.008 (0.20)
Output gear bearing preload	0.26–7.81 (0.03–0.9)①

① inch lbs. (Nm)

VACUUM DIAPHRAGM

Item	Specification in. (mm)
Available diaphragm rods	1.161 (29.5) 1.181 (30.0) 1.200 (30.5) 1.220 (31.0) 1.240 (31.5)

DRIVE AND DIFFERENTIAL

Item		Specification in. (mm)
Final gear	Type	Helical gear
	Reduction ratio	3.631
Side bearing preload		18–25 (2.1–2.9)①
Preload adjusting shims		0.004 (0.1) 0.008 (0.2) 0.012 (0.3) 0.016 (0.4) 0.020 (0.5) 0.024 (0.6) 0.028 (0.7) 0.031 (0.8) 0.035 (0.9) 0.047 (0.12) 0.055 (0.14) 0.063 (0.16)
Backlash of side gear and pinion		0–0.004 (0–0.1)
Backlash adjusting thrust washers		0.079 (2.0) 0.083 (2.1) 0.087 (2.2)

① inch lbs. (Nm)

TORQUE SPECIFICATIONS

Item	ft. lbs (Nm)
Drive plate to crankshaft	96–103 (71–76)
Drive plate to torque converter	25.3–36.2 (35–50)
Converter housing to engine	64–89 (47–66)
Converter halves	29–46 (22–34)
Converter housing to transaxle case	26.8–39.8 (37–55)
Bearing housing to converter housing	13.7–18.8 (19–26)
Side bearing housing to transaxle case	13.7–18.8 (19–26)
Bearing cover to transaxle case	8.0–10.1 (11–14)
Oil pump to transaxle case	11–16 (15–22)
Governor cover to transaxle case	7.8–10.8 (5.8–8.0)
Oil pan	3.6–5.8 (5–8)
Anchor end bolt (when adjusting band brake)	8.7–10.8 (12–15)
Anchor end bolt lock nut	41–59 (56–82)
Control valve body to transaxle case	5.8–8.0 (8–11)
Lower valve body to upper valve body	1.8–2.5 (2.5–3.5)
Side plate to control valve body	1.8–2.5 (2.5–3.5)
Reamer bolt of control valve body	3.6–5.1 (5–7)
Oil strainer of control valve	2.2–2.9 (3–4)
Governor valve body to governor shaft	5.8–8.0 (8–11)
Oil pump cover	8.0–10.1 (11–14)
Inhibitor switch	13.7–18.8 (19–26)
Manual shaft lock nut	21.7–29.0 (30–40)
Oil cooler pipe set bolt	11.6–17.4 (16–24)
Actuator for parking rod to transaxle case	8.7–11.6 (12–15)
Idle bear bearing lock nut	94–130 (130–180)

LINE PRESSURE SPECIFICATIONS

Gear	Condition	Specification psi (kPa)
R	Idling	57–100 (392–687)
	Stall	228–270 (1570–1864)
D	Idling	43–57 (294–392)
	Stall	128–156 (883–1079)
2	Idling	114–171 (785–1177)
	Stall	114–171 (785–1177)

CUT BACK POINT

Vacuum of Vacuum Pump in. Hg. (mm Hg.)	Governor Pressure psi (kPa)
0 (0)	14–23 (98–157)
7.87 (200)	6–14 (39–98)

GOVERNOR PRESSURE

mph	Governor Pressure psi (kPa)
20	13–21 (88–147)
35	27–36 (186–245)
55	58–70 (402–481)

SHIFT POINT SPEED

Throttle Condition		Shift Point mph (km/h)
CARBURETOR		
Wide open throttle	D^1–D^2	30–36 (48–58)
	D^2–D^3	60–68 (96–110)
	D^3–D^2	53–58 (85–93)
	D^2–D^1	24–26 (38–42)
Half throttle	D^1–D^2	10–19 (16–30)
	D^2–D^3	17–37 (28–60)
Fully closed throttle	D^3–D^1	6–9 (10–15)
	1_2–1_1	22–26 (35–42)
ELECTRONIC FUEL INJECTION		
Wide open throttle	D^1–D^2	30–36 (48–58)
	D^2–D^3	60–68 (96–110)
	D^3–D^2	53–58 (85–93)
	D^2–D^1	24–26 (38–42)
Half throttle	D^1–D^2	12–21 (20–34)
	D^2–D^3	37–48 (60–78)
Fully closed throttle	D^3–D^1	6–9 (10–15)
	1_2–1_1	22–26 (35–42)

TORQUE CONVERTER

Item	Specifications
Stall torque ratio	1.95–2.35
Stall torque rpm	2300–2500
Bushing diameter wear limit	1.302 in (33.075mm)

OIL PUMP

Clearance		Specification in. (mm)
Gear end float	Standard	0.0008–0.0016 (0.02–0.04)
	Limit	0.0031 (0.08)
Outer gear and crest	Standard	0.0055–0.0083 (0.14–0.21)
	Limit	0.0098 (0.25)
Outer gear and housing	Standard	0.002–0.0079 (0.05–0.20)
	Limit	0.0098 (o.25)
Oil seal ring and ring groove	Standard	0.0016–0.0063 (0.04–0.16)
	Limit	0.0157 (0.40)

LOW AND REVERSE BRAKE

Item	Specification in. (mm)
Number of friction and steel plates	3
Clearance between retaining plates and stopper	0.8–1.05 (0.032–0.041)
Clearance adjusting retaining plates	0.181 (4.6) 0.189 (4.8) 0.197 (5.0) 0.205 (5.2) 0.213 (5.4) 0.221 (5.6)
Free length of return spring	27.2–28.2 (1.07–1.11)

CLUTCH SPECIFICATIONS

Front Clutch	Specification in. (mm)
Number of driven & drive plates	3
Front clutch clearance	0.063–0.071 (1.6–1.8)
Clearance adjusting retaining plate	0.205 (5.2)
	0.213 (5.4)
	0.220 (5.6)
	0.228 (5.8)
	0.236 (6.0)
	0.244 (6.2)
Return spring free length	0.992–1.071 (2.52–27.2)
Drum bushing inner diameter	
Standard	1.7322–1.7331 (44.0–44.025)
Limit	1.7354 (44.075)
Front clutch drum end prary (clearance between drum and connecting shell)	0.020–0.032 (0.5–0.8)

CLUTCH SPECIFICATIONS

Front Clutch	Specification in. (mm)
Endplay adjusting shim	0.051 (1.3)
	0.059 (1.5)
	0.067 (1.7)
	0.075 (1.9)
	0.083 (2.1)
	0.091 (2.3)
	0.098 (2.5)
	0.106 (2.7)

Rear Clutch	Specification in. (mm)
Number of driven and drive plates	4
Rear clutch clearance	0.031–0.059 (0.8–1.5)
Return spring free length	0.992–1.071 (25.2–27.2)

SPECIAL TOOLS

Tool	Identification
Tool–1175–AC	Seal remover
Tool–4201–C	Dial indicator
D78P–4201–C	Magnetic base for dial indicator
D79P–6000–C	Engine support bar
D80L–630–A	Step plate adapter set
D80L–943–A	Puller
D83L–7059–A	Vacuum pump
D84L–1122–A	Bearing pulling attachment
T50T–100–A	Slide hammer
T57L–500–B	Bench mounted holding fixture
T57L–77820–A	Pressure gauge
T58L–101A	Puller
T65L–77515–A	Front clutch spring compressor
T77F–1217–B	Bearing cup puller
T77F–4220–B1	Differential bearing cap puller
T80T–4000–W	Handle
T80L–77003–A	Gauge bar

Tool	Identification
T86p–70043–A	Jaws (used with T58L–101–A)
T87C–7025–C	Differential plugs
T87C–77000–A	Vacuum diaphragm rod gauge
T87C–77000–B	Clutch compressor
T87C–77000–C	Bearing cone replacer
T87C–77000–D	Bearing cone replacer
T87c–77000–E	Torque adapter
T87C–77000–G	Converter seal replacer
T87C–77000–J	Shim selection tool
014–00456	Transmission tester (Tracer ATX adapter)
014–00028	Torque converter cleaner
D80L–630–3	Plate
D80L–630–7	Plate
D80L–943–A2	Jaw puller
D79P–6000–B	Engine support bar
T86P–70043–A2	Jaw puller
T87C–77000–H	Differential seal replacer

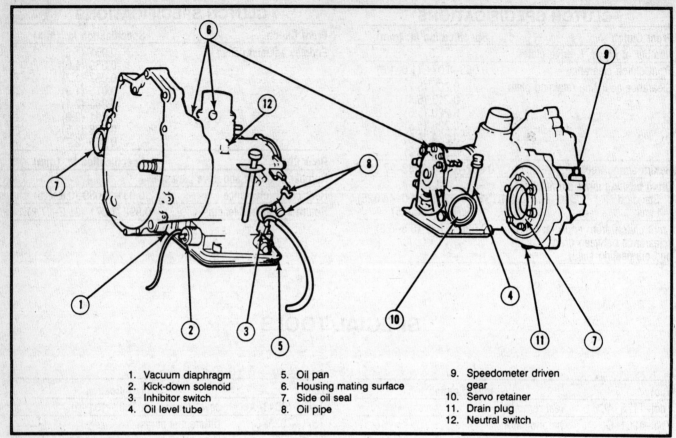

1. Vacuum diaphragm
2. Kick-down solenoid
3. Inhibitor switch
4. Oil level tube
5. Oil pan
6. Housing mating surface
7. Side oil seal
8. Oil pipe
9. Speedometer driven gear
10. Servo retainer
11. Drain plug
12. Neutral switch

Fluid leakage locations

G4AEL, G4AHL and FU06 Transaxles
Mazda

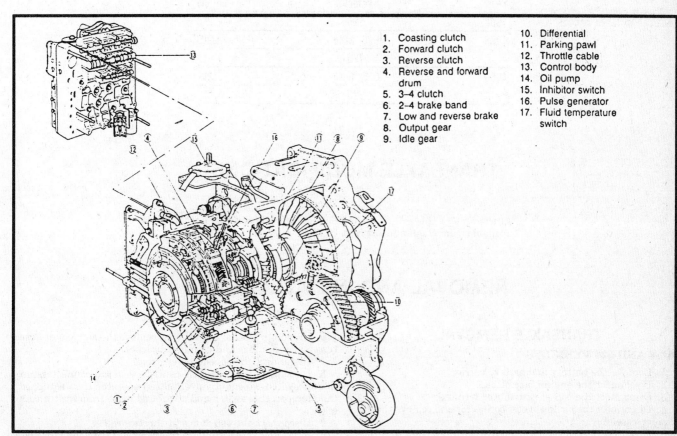

1. Coasting clutch
2. Forward clutch
3. Reverse clutch
4. Reverse and forward drum
5. 3–4 clutch
6. 2–4 brake band
7. Low and reverse brake
8. Output gear
9. Idle gear
10. Differential
11. Parking pawl
12. Throttle cable
13. Control body
14. Oil pump
15. Inhibitor switch
16. Pulse generator
17. Fluid temperature switch

Crossection view of G4AEL transaxle

REFERENCES

APPLICATION

1984–89 Chilton's Professional Automatic Transmission Manual #7959
1984–89 Chilton's Professional Transmission Manual—Import Vehicles #7960

GENERAL DESCRIPTION

1984–89 Chilton's Professional Automatic Transmission Manual #7959

MODIFICATIONS

1984–89 Chilton's Professional Automatic Transmission Manual #7959
1984–89 Chilton's Professional Transmission Manual—Import Vehicles #7960

TROUBLE DIAGNOSIS

1984–89 Chilton's Professional Automatic Transmission Manual #7959

ON CAR SERVICES

1984–89 Chilton's Professional Automatic Transmission Manual #7959

REMOVAL AND INSTALLATION

1984–89 Chilton's Professional Automatic Transmission Manual #7959
1984–89 Chilton's Professional Transmission Manual—Import Vehicles #7960

BENCH OVERHAUL

1984–89 Chilton's Professional Automatic Transmission Manual #7959

SPECIFICATIONS

1984–89 Chilton's Professional Automatic Transmission Manual #7959
1984–89 Chilton's Professional Transmission Manual—Import Vehicles #7960

SPECIAL TOOLS

1984–89 Chilton's Professional Automatic Transmission Manual #7959

APPLICATION

Year	Vehicle	Engine
1987	626	2.2L
1988	626, MX6	2.2L
	323	1.6L
1989	626, MX6	2.2L
	323	1.6L

TRANSAXLE MODIFICATIONS

At the time of this printing, modification information was not available from the manufacturer.

REMOVAL AND INSTALLATION

TRANSAXLE REMOVAL

MX-6 AND 626 VEHICLES

1. Remove the battery and battery carrier.
2. Disconnect the engine fuse block.
3. Disconnect the center distributor terminal.
4. Disconnect the airflow meter connector and remove the air cleaner assembly.
5. On turbocharged vehicles, remove the intercooler to throttle body hose and the air cleaner to turbocharger hose.
6. On non turbocharged vehicles remove the air cleaner hose, resonance chamber and chamber bracket.
7. Disconnect the speedometer cable.
8. Disconnect the transaxle control electrical connectors, inhibitor switch, solenoid valve, pulse generator if so equipped, fluid temperature switch and all ground wires from the transaxle case.
9. Disconnect the selector and throttle cable.
10. Raise and safely support the vehicle. Drain the transaxle fluid and remove the front wheels.

11. Remove the splash shields. Disconnect and plug the transaxle cooler lines.

12. Disconnect the tie rod ends with a suitable tool. Remove the stabilizer bar control links.

13. Remove the left and right lower arm ball joint retaining bolts and nuts. Pull the lower arms downward to separate them from the steering knuckles.

14. Separate the left axle shaft from the transaxle by carefully prying with a tool inserted between the axle shaft and the transaxle case. Do not damage the transaxle oil seal.

15. Remove the right joint shaft bracket.

16. Remove the right axle shaft from the transaxle by carefully prying with a bar inserted between the axle shaft and transaxle case.

17. Install transaxle plugs 49G030455 or equivalent, into the differential side gears.

NOTE: Failure to install the transaxle plugs may allow the differential side gears to become mispositioned.

18. Remove the exhaust pipe hanger and gusset plates.

19. Remove the torque converter cover.

20. Remove the torque converter retaining nuts.

21. Remove the starter motor and access brackets.

22. Mount an engine support bar, 49G0175A0 or equivalent and attach it to the engine hanger.

23. Remove the center transaxle mount and bracket.

24. Remove the left transaxle mount.

25. Remove the nut and bolt attaching the right transaxle mount to the frame.

26. Remove the crossmember and left lower arm as an assembly.

27. Position a transmission jack under the transaxle and secure the transaxle to the jack.

28. Remove the engine to transaxle bolts.

29. Before the transaxle can be lowered out of the vehicle, the torque converter studs must be clear of the flex plate. Insert a tool between the flex plate and converter and carefully disengage the studs.

30. Lower the transaxle out of the vehicle.

323 VEHICLES

1. Disconnect the negative battery cable. Remove the air cleaner.

2. Disconnect the speedometer and throttle cable from the transaxle. Disconnect the shift control cable from the transaxle.

3. Remove all ground wires from the transaxle case.

4. Remove the wire harness clip. Disconnect the inhibitor switch, the overdrive release solenoid and any other necessary electrical connections.

5. Remove the upper transaxle mounting bolts. Disconnect and plug the transaxle oil cooler lines. Mount the engine support tool 49G0175A0 or equivalent to the engine hanger.

6. Raise and support the vehicle safely. Drain the transaxle oil and remove the front wheel and tire assemblies.

7. Remove the engine under cover and side covers. Remove the torque converter to engine retaining bolts.

8. Remove the left and right lower arm ball joint knuckle clinch bolts. Remove the stabilizer bar control link assemblies. Pull the lower arm downward and separate the lower arms from the knuckles.

NOTE: Install transaxle plugs 49B027006 or equivalent into the differential side gears after axle shaft removal. Failure to install the transaxle plugs may allow the differential side gears to become mispositioned.

9. Separate the axle shafts from the transaxle by prying with a suitable pry bar inserted between the shaft and the case. Be sure not to damage the oil seals.

10. Support the transaxle assembly. Remove the transaxle

crossmember. Remove the starter motor and electrical connection.

11. Remove the end plate. Lean the engine toward the transaxle side and lower the transaxle. Support the transaxle with a suitable floor jack.

12. Remove the necessary engine brackets. Remove the remaining transaxle mounting bolts. Lower the jack and slide the transaxle out from under the vehicle.

TRANSAXLE INSTALLATION

MX-6 AND 626 VEHICLES

1. Place the transaxle on a transmission jack. Be sure the transaxle is secure.

2. Raise the transaxle to the proper height and mount the transaxle to the engine.

NOTE: Align the torque converter studs and flex plate holes.

3. Install the engine to transaxle bolts and tighten to 66–86 ft. lbs.

4. Install the center transaxle mount and bracket. Tighten the bolts to 27–40 ft. lbs. and the nuts to 47–66 ft. lbs.

5. Install the left transaxle mount. Tighten the transaxle to mount attaching nut to 63–86 ft. lbs. Tighten the mount to bracket bolt and nut to 49–69 ft. lbs.

6. Install the crossmember and left lower arm as an assembly. Tighten the bolts to 27–40 ft. lbs. and the nuts to 55–69 ft. lbs.

7. Install the right transaxle mount bolt and nut. Tighten to 63–86 ft. lbs.

8. Install the starter motor and access brackets.

9. Install the torque converter nuts and tighten to 32–45 ft. lbs.

10. Install the converter cover and tighten the bolts to 69–85 inch lbs.

11. Install the gusset plate to transaxle bolts and tighten to 27–38 ft. lbs.

12. Replace the circlip located on the end of each axle shaft.

13. Remove the transaxle plugs and install the axle shafts.

14. Attach the lower arm ball joints to the knuckles.

15. Install the tie rod ends and tighten the nuts to 22–33 ft. lbs. Install new cotter pins.

16. Install the bolts and nuts to the lower arm ball joints. Tighten to 32–40 ft. lbs.

17. Install the stabilizer link assemblies. Turn the nuts on each assembly until 1.0 in. (25.4mm) of bolt thread can be measured from the upper nut. When then length is reached, secure the upper nut and back off the lower nut until a torque of 12–17 ft. lbs. is reached.

18. Connect the oil cooler outlet and inlet hoses.

19. Install the splash shields.

20. Install the front wheel and tire assemblies.

21. Reconnect the throttle cable.

22. Connect the range selector cable to the transaxle case and tighten the bolt to 22–29 ft. lbs.

23. Connect the ground wires to the transaxle case and tighten to 69–95 inch lbs.

24. Connect the transaxle control electrical connectors and attach the control harness to the transaxle clips. On turbocharged vehicles, install the intercooler to throttle body hose and the air cleaner to turbocharger hose.

25. Connect the speedometer cable.

26. Install the resonance chamber and bracket and tighten to 69–95 inch lbs.

27. Install the air cleaner assembly. Tighten the bolt to 23–30 ft. lbs. and the nuts to 69–95 inch lbs.

28. Connect the airflow meter connector.

29. Connect the center distributor terminal lead.

30. Connect the main fuse block and tighten to 69–95 inch lbs. Install the battery carrier and battery and tighten to 23–30 ft. lbs.

31. Remove the engine support bracket.

32. Add the specified transaxle fluid. Check for fluid leakage.

33. Road test vehicle for proper operation.

323 VEHICLES

1. Install the transaxle to the engine assembly and torque the retaining bolts to 41–59 ft. lbs.

2. Install the torque converter to drive plate and torque the retaining bolts to 25–36 ft. lbs.

3. Install the starter motor and bracket. Install the end cover.

4. Install the crossmember and reconnect the cooler lines.

5. Install the axle shafts with new circlips (gap at the top of the groove) in the transaxle. After installing the the axle shaft pull the front hub outward to make sure the axle shaft does not come out.

6. Install the lower ball joint to the steering knuckle.

7. Install the stabilizer link assemblies. Turn the nuts on each assembly until 0.33 in. (8.5mm) of bolt thread can be measured from the upper nut. When then length is reached, secure the upper nut and back off the lower nut until a torque of 9–13 lbs. is reached.

8. Install the under and side cover. Reconnect the oil cooler hoses and install the wheel and tire assemblies.

9. Lower the vehicle. Reconnect all electrical wiring connections and control linkage to the transaxle.

10. Reconnect the speedometer and throttle cable to the transaxle.

11. Install the air cleaner and all ground wires.

12. Reconnect the negative battery cable. Refill the transaxle with the proper amount and type fluid. Road test the vehicle for proper operation.

SPECIFICATIONS

DIFFERENTIAL BEARING SHIM SELECTION

Part Number	Shim Thickness in. (mm)
E92Z-4067-A	0.004 (0.10)
E92Z-4067-B	0.005 (0.12)
E92Z-4067-C	0.006 (0.14)
E92Z-4067-D	0.006 (0.16)
E92Z-4067-E	0.007 (0.18)
E92Z-4067-F	0.008 (0.20)
E92Z-4067-G	0.010 (0.25)
E92Z-4067-H	0.012 (0.30)
E92Z-4067-J	0.014 (0.35)
E92Z-4067-K	0.016 (0.40)
E92Z-4067-L	0.018 (0.45)
E92Z-4067-N	0.020 (0.50)
E92Z-4067-P	0.022 (0.55)
E92Z-4067-Q	0.024 (0.60)
E92Z-4067-R	0.026 (0.65)
E92Z-4067-S	0.028 (0.70)
E92Z-4067-T	0.030 (0.75)
E92Z-4067-U	0.032 (0.80)
E92Z-4067-V	0.034 (0.85)
E92Z-4067-W	0.036 (0.90)
E92Z-4067-X	0.038 (0.95)
E92Z-4067-Y	0.040 (1.00)
E92Z-4067-Z	0.042 (1.05)
E92Z-4067-AA	0.044 (1.10)
E92Z-4067-AB	0.046 (1.15)
E92Z-4067-AC	0.048 (1.20)

3-4 CLUTCH CLEARANCE SPECIFICATIONS

Part Number	Measurement in. (mm)
E92Z-7B066-T	0.157 (4.0)
E92Z-7B066-U	0.165 (4.2)
E92Z-7B066-V	0.173 (4.4)
E92Z-7B066-W	0.181 (4.6)
E92Z-7B066-X	0.189 (4.8)

TORQUE SPECIFICATIONS

Part	ft. lbs.	Nm
Valve body cover to case bolts	6–8	8–11
Main fuse box retaining bolts	6–8	8–11
Oil strainer retaining bolts	6–8	8–11
Oil pan bolts	6–8	8–11
Oil pump to clutch assembly	14–19	19–26
Transaxle to engine	66–86	89–117
Torque converter to engine	32–45	43–61
Lower arm ball joints to knuckles	32–40	43–54
Tie rod end retaining nut	22–30	29–44
Valve body retaining bolts	7.9–10	11–15
Oil cooler retaining bolts	6–8	8–11
Oil pump check valve	17–26	24–35
1–2 accumulator plate to valve body	4–6	6–8
Actuator support bolts	8–10	11–14
Tranxaxle case to converter housing	27–38	37–52

OUTPUT GEAR BEARING SHIM SELECTION

Part Number	Shim Thickness in. (mm)
E92Z-7F405-B	0.004 (0.10)
E92Z-7F405-C	0.005 (0.12)
E92Z-7F405-D	0.006 (0.14)
E92Z-7F405-E	0.006 (0.16)
E92Z-7F405-F	0.007 (0.18)
E92Z-7F405-G	0.008 (0.20)
E92Z-7F405-A	0.020 (0.50)

REVERSE CLUTCH CLEARANCE SPECIFICATIONS

Part Number	Measurement in. (mm)
E92Z-7B066-N	0.260 (6.6)
E92Z-7B066-O	0.268 (6.8)
E92Z-7B066-P	0.276 (7.0)
E92Z-7B066-Q	0.283 (7.2)
E92Z-7B066-R	0.291 (7.4)
E92Z-7B066-S	0.299 (7.6)

FORWARD CLUTCH CLEARANCE SPECIFICATIONS

Part Number	Measurement in. (mm)
E92Z-7B066-A	0.232 (5.9)
E92Z-7B066-B	0.240 (6.1)
E92Z-7B066-C	0.248 (6.3)
E92Z-7B066-D	0.256 (6.5)
E92Z-7B066-E	0.264 (6.7)
E92Z-7B066-F	0.350 (8.9)

IDLER GEAR PRELOAD SHIM SELECTION CHART

Part Number	Shim Thickness in. (mm)
E92Z-7N112-F	0.004 (0.10)
E92Z-7N112-A	0.005 (0.12)
E92Z-7N112-B	0.006 (0.14)
E92Z-7N112-C	0.006 (0.16)
E92Z-7N112-G	0.007 (0.18)
E92Z-7N112-D	0.008 (0.20)
E92Z-7N112-E	0.020 (0.50)

COASTING CLUTCH CLEARANCE SPECIFICATIONS

Part Number	Measurement in. (mm)
E92Z-7B066-M	0.181 (4.6)
E92Z-7B066-G	0.189 (4.8)
E92Z-7B066-H	0.197 (5.0)
E92Z-7B066-J	0.205 (5.2)
E92Z-7B066-K	0.213 (5.4)
E92Z-7B066-L	0.220 (5.6)

LOW AND REVERSE CLUTCH CLEARANCE SPECIFICATIONS

Part Number	Measurement in. (mm)
E92Z-7B066-AD	0.268 (6.8)
E92Z-7B066-Y	0.276 (7.0)
E92Z-7B066-Z	0.283 (7.2)
E92Z-7B066-AA	0.291 (7.4)
E92Z-7B066-AB	0.299 (7.6)
E92Z-7B066-AC	0.307 (7.8)

OIL PUMP TO TRANSAXLE CASE CLEARANCE SHIM SELECTION

Part Number	Shim Thickness in. (mm)	Case Clearance in. (mm)
E92Z-7D014-E	0.047 (1.2)	0.036–0.043 (0.91–1.10)
E92Z-7D014-F	0.055 (1.4)	0.028–0.035 (0.71–0.90)
E92Z-7D014-A	0.063 (1.6)	0.020–0.027 (0.51–0.70)
E92Z-7D014-B	0.071 (1.8)	0.012–0.019 (0.31–0.50)
E92Z-7D014-C	0.078 (2.0)	0.004–0.011 (0.11–0.30)
E92Z-7D014-D	0.047 (2.2)	0.036–0.043 (0.00–0.10)

Section 2
KM175 and KM177 Transaxles
Mitsubishi

APPLICATION

Year	Vehicle	Engine	Transaxle
1985	Mitsubishi Galant	2.4L	KM175
1986	Mitsubishi Galant	2.4L	KM175
1987	Mitsubishi Galant	2.4L	KM175
1988	Mitsubishi Galant Sigma	3.0L	KM177
1989	Mitsubishi Galant	2.0L	KM175
1989	Mitsubishi Galant Sigma	3.0L	KM177

GENERAL DESCRIPTION

The KM175 and KM177 are fully automatic electronically controlled transaxles consisting of a valve body, a planetary gearset, 3 clutch packs, an overrunning clutch, a brake band, an oil pump, a torque converter, a differential assembly and final drive gear set. All of the above components are integrated into 1 compact unit. An oil cooler is built into the bottom of the radiator to cool the transaxle fluid (some 1988–89 vehicles have a separate transaxle oil cooler). Rubber hoses are used to carry the fluid from the transaxle to the cooler.

throughout the vehicle and each has an important function in the operation of the unit.

ACCELERATOR PEDAL SWITCH

The accelerator pedal switch is located behind the accelerator pedal. This switch functions to detect the condition of the accelerator pedal. Since the pedal is not operated during constant speed driving control, the ground circuit is switched OFF during that time only.

TRANSAXLE CONTROL UNIT

The Transaxle Control Unit (TCU) is located underneath the heater unit at the front of the console. The TCU receives signals from various sensors and converts the data signals into usable information. It activates the correct solenoid(s) according to the calculations derived from the signals received, causing the transaxle to shift gears at the correct speed. The engine control

Its operation is controlled by selecting the appropriate position from a console-mounted selector lever mounted on the passenger compartment floor and a push-button overdrive control switch. A power/economy switch was added in 1989 to further increase the driveability of the vehicle. An on-board computer calculates the shift points based upon the input data signals received from various sensors.

1. Torque converter
2. Differential
3. Transfer shaft
4. Pulse generator B
5. Transfer driven gear
6. End clutch
7. Transfer drive gear
8. Transfer idler gear
9. Planetary gearset
10. Low/reverse brake
11. Rear clutch
12. Pulse generator A
13. Kickdown band
14. Front clutch
15. Oil pump

Main components of the KM175 and KM177 automatic transaxles

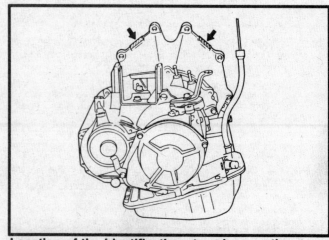

Location of the identification stampings on the KM177

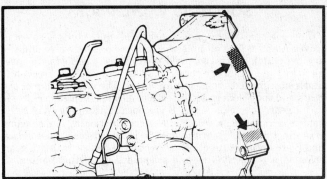

Location of the identification stampings on the KM175

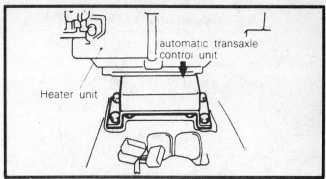

Location of the transaxle control unit

The oil pump pressurizes automatic transaxle fluid regulated by the valve body to various components within the transaxle and in conjunction with the computer, provides the hydraulic pressure needed to obtain the desired gear for all possible driving conditions, optimum engine performance and low fuel consumption. If the transaxle were to fail altogether, the computer would go into its fail-safe system and lock the transaxle in third gear.

The torque converter provides a fluid coupling between the engine and transaxle for optimum power transfer when driving at a constant speed and increased torque when starting, accelerating and climbing an incline. The damper clutch is used in the torque converter (except in the 1989 Sigma with 3.0 V6 engine) to provide a solid coupling for improved fuel mileage when at cruising ranges.

Transaxle and Converter Identification

TRANSAXLE

A vehicle information code plate is riveted to the top of the firewall on all vehicles. The second line contains the engine code and the third line contains the transaxle model number.

In addition, on the KM175, two sets of identification numbers are stamped into the right side of the bell housing. Use the upper set for identifying original equipment parts and the lower set when ordering replacement parts. On the KM177 the two stampings are located on either side of the coolant pipe cutout. The stamping on the right side is for original equipment parts and the left side stamping is for ordering replacement parts.

CONVERTER

The torque converter is a 3 element type and has an internal damper clutch. It is a welded 1 piece unit and cannot be disassembled for inspection purposes.

Electronic Controls

The electronic portion of this transaxle is made up of various sensors, switches, and a control unit. These items are located unit (ECU) is also interconnected with the TCU and is located behind the right side kick panel.

COOLANT TEMPERATURE SENSOR

The coolant temperature sensor is located on the cylinder head near the thermostat housing. This sensor tells the TCU the temperature of the coolant. This is important because the damper clutch torque converter is designed to operate only when the coolant temperature is above 122°F (50°C).

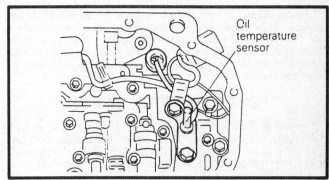

Location of the oil temperature sensor

INHIBITOR SWITCH

The inhibitor switch is located on top of the transaxle case. This switch has the manual control lever attached to it and the selector cable attached to the lever. It provides signals for the TCU so it knows what gear the vehicle is in. Also, it is a neutral safety switch that will prevent the vehicle from starting in any gear except **P** or **N**. The inhibitor switch also completes the reverse light circuit when backing up.

KICKDOWN SERVO SWITCH

The kickdown servo switch is mounted on the kickdown servo. This switch detects the position immediately prior to the application of the kickdown brake (the switch is **ON** until this point). To improve the response during kickdown, high hydraulic pressure is applied just before application of the kickdown brake, then the appropriate pressure is provided to alleviate the shifting impact.

OIL TEMPERATURE SENSOR

The oil temperature sensor is mounted to the bottom of the valve body of 1988–89 vehicles only. This sensor relays the temperature of the transaxle fluid to the TCU so it will activate the fluid cooling fan relay when the temperature of the oil becomes too hot.

OVERDRIVE SWITCH

The overdrive (O/D) switch is mounted on the gear shaft handle. This push-button switch **disengages** 4th (overdrive) when depressed (turned off). The indicator light will illuminate when the switch is turned **OFF.** Automatic shifting will occur in either case, be it to third or fourth gear, according to the position of the switch.

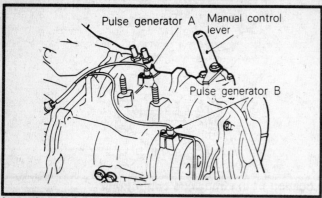

Locations of the pulse generators

Leaving the switch up during high speed driving will allow the transaxle to go into overdrive resulting in more economical driving. However, since automatic shifting into overdrive when climbing or descending a steep grade would decrease the climbing ability or engine braking effectiveness, it is advisable to press the switch under these types of road conditions.

POWER/ECONOMY SWITCH

The power/economy switch was added in 1989. It is located on the console, near the shifter. The indicator light on the dash will light in the power mode only. In the power mode (button pushed down), the shift points are later than in the economy mode, thus increasing the amount of power the vehicle is able to deliver. In the economy mode (button left up), the gears will change faster; high gear will be attained sooner, thus achieving better fuel economy.

PULSE GENERATORS A AND B

The pulse generators A and B are installed on the top of the transaxle. Pulse generator A reads the kickdown drum rpm via four holes provided on the outer circumference of the drum. Pulse generator B reads the speed of the transfer driven gear according to the number of gear teeth. The TCU processes these bits of information and computes the ratio of kickdown drum rpm to transfer driven gear rpm to determine the correct range. In also determines when to shift speed by the change in the ratio provided by the pulse generators.

SELF-DIAGNOSTICS CONNECTOR

The self-diagnostics connector is located behind the glove box in all models except 1989 Galant, in which it is located behind the dash to the lower left of the steering column. This connector enables the technician to utilize electronic equipment to locate a problem or check the electronic function of the transaxle.

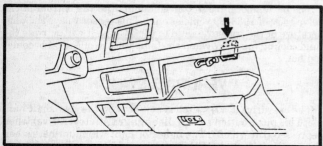

Location of the self-diagnostics connector except 1989 Galant

SOLENOID VALVE PACK

The solenoid valve pack consists of shift control solenoid valves A and B, the oil pressure control solenoid valve and the damper clutch control solenoid valve. These solenoids are energized by the TCU at the correct time to provide the correct shift under any given driving circumstances. The relationship of the gears and the solenoid activity is as follows. When the vehicle is in 1st gear, solenoids A and B are both functioning. When the vehicle is in 2nd gear, solenoid A is not functioning and solenoid B is functioning. When the vehicle is in 3rd gear, solenoids A and B are both not functioning. When the vehicle is in 4th gear, solenoid A is functioning and solenoid B is not functioning.

THROTTLE POSITION SENSOR

The Throttle Position Sensor (TPS) is a rotating type variable resistor. The TPS is connected to the throttle valve shaft and provides signals relative to the amount the throttle is opened. These signals are read by the TCU so it knows how much the engine is being accelerated.

SPEED SENSOR

The vehicle speed sensor is a reed switch located either behind the instrument panel as part of the speedometer assembly or at the port that the speedometer is installed. The speed sensor generates signals that are proportional to the vehicle speed.

Metric Fasteners

Metric tools will be required to service this transaxle. Due to the large number of alloy parts used in this transaxle, torque specifications should be strictly observed. Before installing capscrews into aluminum parts, dip the bolts into clean transaxle fluid as this will prevent the screws from galling the aluminum threads, thus causing damage.

Metric fastener dimensions are very close to the dimensions of the familiar inch system fasteners. For this reason replacement fasteners must have the same measurement and strength as the original fastener.

Do not attempt to interchange metric fasteners for inch system fasteners. Mismatched or incorrect fasteners can cause damage to the automatic transaxle unit and possible personal injury. Care should be taken to reuse fasteners in their original locations.

Capacities

The KM175 and KM177 from 1985–1988 is designed to operate with 6.1 quarts (5.8L) of Dexron®II automatic transaxle fluid. In 1989, the fluid capacity increased to 6.4 quarts (6.1L) of Dexron®II.

Checking Fluid Level

1. Warm up the engine until the fluid is at normal operating temperature (140–180°F/60–80°C).
2. Park the vehicle on a level surface.
3. Move the selector lever sequentially to every position on the scale to fill the torque converter and the hydraulic circuit with fluid and place the lever in **N** while the engine is idling to check the fluid level.
4. Wipe all dirt from the area around the dipstick and remove the dipstick. Inspect the fluid for a burning odor, metal particles, or a particularly dark coloring.
5. Add fluid until the level is in the **HOT** range on the dipstick, or simply between the two lines on earlier dipsticks that do not have a **HOT** range.
6. Road test and recheck the fluid level.

TRANSAXLE MODIFICATIONS

No modifications are available at the time of publication.

TROUBLE DIAGNOSIS

CLUTCH AND BRAKE APPLICATION

Selector Lever Position	O/D Switch	Gear	Front Clutch	Rear Clutch	End Clutch	Kickdown Brake	Low/Reverse Brake	One-way Clutch
P	—	Neutral	—	—	—	—	—	—
R	—	Reverse	Applied	—	—	—	Applied	—
N	—	Neutral	—	—	—	—	—	—
D	On	1st	—	Applied	—	—	—	Applied
	On	2nd	—	Applied	—	Applied	—	—
	On	3rd	Applied	Applied	Applied	—	—	—
	On	OD	—	—	Applied	Applied	—	—
D	Off	1st	—	Applied	—	—	—	Applied
	Off	2nd	—	Applied	—	Applied	—	—
	Off	3rd	Applied	Applied	Applied	—	—	—
2	—	1st	—	Applied	—	—	—	Applied
	—	2nd	—	Applied	—	Applied	—	—
L	—	1st	—	Applied	—	—	Applied	—

CHILTON'S THREE C'S TRANSAXLE DIAGNOSIS

Condition	Cause	Correction
Line pressures are all low or high	a) Oil filter clogged b) Out of adjustment c) Sticky regulator valve d) Valve body bolt loose e) Oil pump faulty	a) Replace filter b) Adjust line pressure or replace valve body c) Repair or replace valve body d) Torque bolts e) Inspect pump
Improper reducing pressure	a) Improper line pressure b) L-shaped oil filter in the valve body clogged c) Out of adjustment d) Sticky reducing valve e) Valve body bolt loose	a) Refer to above b) Disassemble valve body and replace the filter c) Adjust reducing pressure or replace valve d) Repair or replace valve body e) Torque bolts
Improper kickdown brake pressure	a) Servo piston or seals faulty b) Valve body bolt loose c) Valve body faulty	a) Replace faulty parts b) Torque bolts c) Overhaul valve body
Improper front clutch pressure	a) Servo piston or seals faulty b) Valve body bolt loose c) Valve body faulty d) Front clutch faulty	a) Replace faulty parts b) Torque bolts c) Overhaul valve body d) Overhaul transaxle
Improper end clutch pressure	a) End clutch assembly faulty b) Valve body bolt loose c) Valve body faulty	a) Replace faulty parts b) Torque bolts c) Overhaul valve body

CHILTON'S THREE C'S DIAGNOSIS

Condition	Cause	Correction
Improper low/reverse brake pressure	a) O-ring between the valve body and the case damaged	a) Replace O-ring
	b) Center support loose	b) Torque bolts or overhaul transaxle
	c) Valve body bolt loose	c) Torque bolts
	d) Valve body faulty	d) Overhaul valve body
	e) Low/reverse brake assembly faulty	e) Overhaul transaxle
Improper torque converter pressure	a) Sticky DCCSV or damper clutch control valve	a) Repair or replace as necessary
	b) Oil cooler system clogged or leaking	b) Repair system
	c) Damaged input shaft seal sing	c) Overhaul transaxle
	d) Torque converter faulty	d) Replace converter
Not moving in any range	a) Low oil level	a) Add until at correct level
	b) Wrong type of oil	b) Change oil
	c) Converter bolts missing or broken	c) Replace bolts
	d) Valve body faulty	d) Overhaul valve body
	e) Selector cable out of adjustment	e) Adjust cable
	f) Internal linkage parts broken	f) Replace broken parts
	g) Input shaft or output shaft broken	g) Replace shaft(s)
	h) Torque converter faulty	h) Replace converter
	i) Oil pump faulty	i) Inspect pump
	j) Final drive faulty	j) Overhaul final drive assembly
	k) Center support loose	k) Torque bolts or overhaul transaxle
	l) Low line pressure	l) Adjust line pressure or repair leak
	m) Low/reverse brake assembly faulty	m) Overhaul transaxle
	n) PCSV stuck open	n) Repair or replace valve
Not moving in any forward range	a) Valve body faulty	a) Overhaul valve body
	b) Selector cable out of adjustment	b) Adjust cable
	c) Rear clutch not applying	c) Overhaul transaxle
	d) Oil pump faulty	d) Inspect pump
	e) One-way clutch not applying	e) Overhaul transaxle
	f) Torque converter faulty	f) Replace converter
	g) Center support loose	g) Torque bolts or overhaul transaxle
	h) Low line pressure	h) Adjust line pressure or repair leak
	i) PCSV stuck open	i) Repair or replace valve
Not moving in Reverse	a) Valve body faulty	a) Overhaul valve body
	b) Selector cable out of adjustment	b) Adjust cable
	c) Low/reverse brake not holding	c) Overhaul transaxle
	d) Front clutch not applying	d) Overhaul transaxle
	e) Oil pump faulty	e) Inspect pump
	f) Control unit faulty	f) Replace unit
	g) Torque converter faulty	g) Replace converter
	h) Center support loose	h) Torque bolts or overhaul transaxle
	i) Low line pressure	i) Adjust line pressure or repair leak
	j) Pulse generator B malfunction	j) Repair or replace unit
	k) PCSV stuck open	k) Repair or replace valve
Moving in Neutral	a) Selector cable out of adjustment	a) Adjust cable
	b) Wrong type of oil	b) Change oil
	c) Valve body faulty	c) Overhaul valve body
Shudder or slip when starting in Drive	a) Valve body faulty	a) Overhaul valve body
	b) Selector cable out of adjustment	b) Adjust cable
	c) Low oil level	c) Add until at correct level
	d) Wrong type of oil	d) Change oil
	e) Oil pump faulty	e) Inspect pump
	f) Rear clutch faulty	f) Overhaul transaxle
	g) One-way clutch not holding	g) Overhaul transaxle
	h) Transaxle and/or engine mount faulty	h) Replace mount

CHILTON'S THREE C'S DIAGNOSIS

Condition	Cause	Correction
Shudder or slip when starting in Drive	i) Low line pressure j) PCSV stuck open	i) Adjust line pressure or repair leak j) Repair or replace valve
Shudder or slip when starting in Reverse	a) Valve body faulty b) Selector cable out of adjustment c) Low oil level d) Wrong type of oil e) Center support loose f) Oil pump faulty g) Front clutch faulty h) Low/reverse brake faulty i) Transaxle and/or engine mount faulty j) Low line pressure k) PCSV stuck open	a) Overhaul valve body b) Adjust cable c) Add until at correct level d) Change oil e) Torque bolts or overhaul transaxle f) Inspect pump g) Overhaul transaxle h) Overhaul transaxle i) Replace mount j) Adjust line pressure or repair leak k) Repair or replace valve
Engine stalls when shifting from Neutral to Drive or Reverse	a) Valve body faulty b) DCCSV stuck open c) Engine idle incorrect d) Engine performance malfunction	a) Overhaul valve body b) Repair or replace valve c) Adjust idle d) Repair as necessary
Excessive vibration when shifting from Neutral to Drive or Reverse	a) Valve body faulty b) Selector cable out of adjustment c) Low oil level d) Front clutch faulty e) Engine idle too high f) Oil pump faulty g) Rear clutch faulty h) Low/reverse brake not holding i) Engine idle too high j) TPS malfunction k) Accelerator switch malfunction l) Control unit faulty	a) Overhaul valve body b) Adjust cable c) Add until at correct level d) Overhaul transaxle e) Adjust idle f) Inspect pump g) Overhaul transaxle h) Overhaul transaxle i) Adjust idle j) Adjust or replace TPS k) Adjust or replace switch l) Replace unit
Loud noise inside transaxle case	a) Torque converter faulty b) Oil pump faulty c) Final drive faulty d) Broken planetary gear e) Center support loose	a) Replace converter b) Inspect pump c) Overhaul final drive d) Overhaul transaxle e) Torque bolts or overhaul transaxle
Will not shift from second to third	a) Valve body faulty b) PCSV stuck open c) Front clutch not applying d) Control unit faulty	a) Overhaul valve body b) Repair or replace valve c) Overhaul transaxle d) Replace unit
Will not shift into fourth gear (overdrive)	a) Selector cable out of adjustment b) Worn inside diameter of front clutch retainer c) End clutch assembly faulty d) PCSV stuck open e) Overdrive switch malfunction f) Control unit faulty	a) Adjust cable b) Overhaul transaxle c) Replace faulty parts d) Repair or replace valve e) Repair or replace switch f) Replace unit
Shift points at wrong speeds	a) Valve body faulty b) Speed sensor faulty c) Control unit faulty d) TPS faulty e) Pulse generator B malfunction	a) Overhaul valve body b) Replace speed sensor c) Replace unit d) Adjust or replace TPS e) Repair or replace unit
Excessive shift shock when shifting from first to second or third to fourth	a) Valve body faulty b) Pulse generator A malfunction c) Low oil level d) Wrong type of oil e) Servo piston faulty	a) Overhaul valve body b) Repair or replace unit c) Add until at correct level d) Change oil e) Adjust or overhaul brake piston

CHILTON'S THREE C'S DIAGNOSIS

Condition	Cause	Correction
Excessive shift shock when shifting from first to second or third to fourth	f) Kickdown band not holding g) Oil pump faulty h) End clutch assembly faulty i) Kickdown servo switch malfunction j) Control unit faulty	f) Overhaul transaxle g) Inspect pump h) Replace faulty parts i) Adjust or replace switch j) Replace unit
Excessive shift shock when shifting from second to third or fourth to third	a) Valve body faulty b) Pulse generator A malfunction c) Low oil level d) Wrong type of oil e) Front clutch faulty f) Control unit faulty	a) Overhaul valve body b) Repair or replace unit c) Add until at correct level d) Change oil e) Overhaul transaxle f) Replace unit
Starts off in the wrong gear	a) Selector cable out of adjustment b) Torque converter faulty c) Valve body faulty d) Accelerator switch malfunction e) Control unit faulty	a) Adjust cable b) Replace converter c) Overhaul valve body d) Adjust or replace switch e) Replace unit
Increase in engine rpm during upshifts	a) Low line pressure b) Valve body faulty c) Front clutch faulty d) Servo piston faulty e) Kickdown band not holding f) End clutch assembly faulty g) TPS faulty h) Pulse generator A malfunction i) PCSV stuck open j) Control unit faulty	a) Adjust line pressure or repair leak b) Overhaul valve body c) Overhaul transaxle d) Adjust or overhaul brake piston e) Overhaul tranxaxle f) Replace faulty parts g) Adjust or replace TPS h) Repair or replace unit i) Repair or replace valve j) Replace unit
Increase in engine rpm or excessive shudder during 3-2 downshift	a) Oil pump faulty b) Low oil level c) Low line pressure d) Valve body faulty e) Servo piston faulty f) Kickdown band not holding g) TPS faulty h) Pulse generator A malfunction i) PCSV stuck open j) Control unit faulty	a) Inspect pump b) Add until at correct level c) Adjust line pressure d) Overhaul valve body e) Adjust or overhaul f) Overhaul transaxle g) Adjust or replace TPS h) Repair or replace unit i) Repair or replace valve j) Replace unit
Excessive vibration or shock only when cold	a) Engine performance malfunction b) Valve body faulty c) Control unit faulty d) Loss of transaxle oil viscosity factor	a) Repair as necessary b) Overhaul valve body c) Replace unit d) Change oil and filter
Excessive vibration or shock all the time	a) Engine performance malfunction b) Low line pressure c) Valve body faulty d) Kickdown servo out of adjustment e) TPS faulty f) Pulse generator A malfunction g) Coolant temperature sensor malfunction h) Control unit faulty	a) Repair as necessary b) Adjust line pressure or repair leak c) Overhaul valve body d) Adjust servo e) Adjust or replace TPS f) Repair or replace unit g) Repair or replace sensor h) Replace unit
Abnormal vibration in high load region in low gear	a) Engine performance malfunction b) Torque converter faulty c) Valve body faulty d) TPS faulty e) Pulse generator A or B malfunction f) DCCSV stuck open g) Coolant temperature sensor malfunction h) Control unit faulty	a) Repair as necessary b) Replace converter c) Overhaul valve body d) Adjust or replace TPS e) Repair or replace unit(s) f) Repair or replace valve g) Repair or replace sensor h) Replace unit

CHILTON'S THREE C'S DIAGNOSIS

Condition	Cause	Correction
Damper clutch inoperative	a) Torque converter faulty b) Valve body faulty c) TPS faulty d) Accelerator switch malfunction e) Pulse generator A or B malfunction f) DCCSV stuck closed g) Coolant temperature sensor malfunction h) Control unit faulty	a) Replace converter b) Overhaul valve body c) Adjust or replace TPS d) Adjust or replace switch e) Repair or replace unit(s) f) Repair or replace valve g) Repair or replace sensor h) Replace unit
Automatic transaxle fluid leaking	a) Oil level too high b) Cooler hose(s) leaking c) Oil pan cracked or gasket leaking d) Oil pump seal leaking e) Front seal leaking f) Differential seal leaking	a) Drain to correct level b) Replace hose(s) c) Replace pan or gasket d) Replace seal e) Replace seal f) Replace seal
Vehicle will not hold in Park	a) Selector cable out of adjustment b) Parking assembly broken c) Internal linkage parts broken	a) Adjust cable b) Replace broken part c) Replace broken parts
Engine will not start	a) Selector cable of out adjustment b) Inhibitor switch faulty	a) Adjust cable b) Check wiring and switch
Transaxle fluid in antifreeze or antifreeze in transaxle fluid	a) Fluid cooler core in radiator is leaking	a) Replace radiator and change the transaxle fluid and the antifreeze

Hydraulic Control System

OIL PUMP

The oil pump generates the pressure for supplying oil to the torque converter, for lubricating frictional parts throughout the transaxle and for activating the hydraulic control system.

The pump is of the inner-teeth engaging involute gear type. It always generates pressure while the engine is running because the drive gear is driven by the 2 pawls of the pump drive hub welded at the center of the converter.

REGULATOR VALVE

This valve regulates oil pump line pressure according to the accelerator opening. Line pressure is applied to this valve against calibrated spring force and is regulated to correspond with every driving condition.

TORQUE CONVERTER CONTROL VALVE

This valve adjusts the torque converter (when the damper clutch is disengaged) and the hydraulic pressure for lubricating oil to a constant pressure.

DAMPER CLUTCH CONTROL VALVE

This valve is installed in the lower valve body and is used to change the hydraulic pressure which engages or disengages the converter damper clutch.

REDUCING VALVE

Also installed in the lower valve body, the reducing valve produces a constant pressure that is always lower than the line pressure. With this pressure as the hydraulic pressure source, the control pressure is produced by the damper clutch control solenoid valve and the pressure control solenoid valve, thus activating the damper clutch control valve and the pressure control valve.

MANUAL VALVE

The manual valve moving in conjunction with the selector lever operated by the driver provides each valve and control element with the line pressure.

SHIFT CONTROL VALVE AND SHIFT CONTROL SOLENOID VALVES

The line pressure acting upon the shift control valve is controlled by the 2 shift control solenoid valves which are switched **ON** and **OFF** according to the TCU command. The shift control valve is activated according to the shifting gear, thus switching the oil passage to the appropriate component(s).

1-2 SHIFT VALVE

This shift valve is activated by line pressure which is regulated by the shift control valve. This function switches the flow of line pressure during shifting from 1st gear to 2nd gear, or vice versa. In reverse, the 1-2 shift valve controls the hydraulic passage to the low/reverse brake.

2-3/4-3 SHIFT VALVE

This shift valve is activated by line pressure which is regulated by the shift control valve. This function switches the flow of line pressure during shifting from 2nd or 4th gear to 3rd gear.

NEUTRAL TO DRIVE CONTROL VALVE

This valve is used to prevent an impact shock from occurring when shifting from **N** to **D**.

During this particular shift only, hydraulic pressure regulated by the pressure control valve is supplied to the rear clutch. After the shift is complete, the valve switches so that line pressure is supplied to the rear clutch.

NEUTRAL TO REVERSE CONTROL/ ACCUMULATOR VALVE

This valve is used to prevent an impact shock from occurring when shifting from **N** or **P to R**. It regulates the hydraulic pressure applied to the low/reverse brake.

PRESSURE CONTROL VALVE

By control of the pressure control solenoid valve, the pressure control valve makes pressure adjustment of the hydraulic pressure supplied to each clutch and to prevent impact shock during a shift.

PRESSURE CONTROL SOLENOID VALVE

This electro-mechanical device is duty-controlled by commands from the TCU. It converts electronic commands into hydraulic pressure.

END CLUTCH VALVE

The end clutch valve regulates the timing of the hydraulic pressure supply to the end clutch.

REAR CLUTCH EXHAUST VALVE

This shift valve is activated by the line pressure regulated by the shift control valve and discharges the hydraulic pressure of the

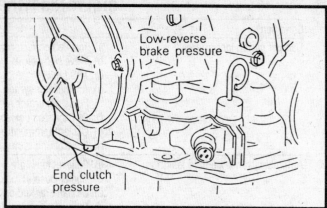

Location of the end clutch and low/reverse brake pressure ports

rear clutch during third to fourth gear shifting. In addition, it also regulates the timing of the hydraulic pressure supplied to the rear clutch during fourth to third gear shifting, thus preventing an impact shock.

Diagnosis Tests

CONTROL PRESSURE TESTS

1. Warm up the transaxle completely.
2. Raise and support the vehicle safely.
3. Connect a tachometer to the engine and position it so it can easily be read.
4. Attach an oil pressure gauge and adaptor to each oil pressure outlet port corresponding to the test being performed.

OIL PRESSURE SPECIFICATIONS
1985-86 KM 175

Selector Lever Position	Approx. Vehicle Speed (mph)	Engine Speed (rpm)	Gear	Reducing Pressure psi (kPa)	Kickdown Brake Pressure psi (kPa)	Front Clutch Pressure psi (kPa)	End Clutch Pressure psi (kPa)	Low/Reverse Brake Pressure psi (kPa)	Torque Converter Pressure psi (kPa)
N	0	idle	Neutral	36–57 (250–390)	0–1.4 (0–9.8)	0–1.4 (0–9.8)	0–1.4 (0–9.8)	0–1.4 (0–9.8)	0–1.4 (0–9.8)
N	0	2500	Neutral	0–1.4 (0–9.8)	0–1.4 (0–9.8)	0–1.4 (0–9.8)	0–1.4 (0–9.8)	0–1.4 (0–9.8)	29–35 (200–240)
D	0	idle	2nd	36–57 (250–390)	15–30 (100–210)	0–1.4 (0–9.8)	0–1.4 (0–9.8)	0–1.4 (0–9.8)	0–1.4 (0–9.8)
D ①	70	2500	Overdrive	36–57 (250–390)	90–100 (620–680)	0–1.4 (0–9.8)	90–100 (620–680)	0–1.4 (0–9.8)	0–1.4 (0–9.8)
D ②	45	2500	3rd	36–57 (250–390)	90–100 (620–680)	90–100 (620–680)	90–100 (620–680)	0–1.4 (0–9.8)	0–1.4 (0–9.8)
2	30	2500	2nd	36–57 (250–390)	90–100 (620–680)	0–1.4 (0–9.8)	0–1.4 (0–9.8)	0–1.4 (0–9.8)	0–1.4 (0–9.8)
L	0	1000	1st	36–57 (250–390)	0–1.4 (0–9.8)	0–1.4 (0–9.8)	0–1.4 (0–9.8)	44–61 (300–420)	0–1.4 (0–9.8)
R	20	2500	Reverse	36–57 (250–390)	0–1.4 (0–9.8)	168–255 (1160–1760)	0–1.4 (0–9.8)	168–255 (1160–1760)	0–1.4 (0–9.8)
R	0	1000	Reverse	36–57 (250–390)	0–1.4 (0–9.8)	168–255 (1160–1760)	0–1.4 (0–9.8)	168–255 (1160–1760)	0–1.4 (0–9.8)

① Overdrive switch on
② Overdrive switch off

OIL PRESSURE SPECIFICATIONS
1987–89 KM175 and KM177

Selector Lever Position	Approx. Vehicle Speed (mph)	Engine Speed (rpm)	Gear	Reducing Pressure psi (kPa)	Kickdown Brake Pressure psi (kPa)	Front Clutch Pressure psi (kPa)	End Clutch Pressure psi (kPa)	Torque Low/Reverse Brake Pressure psi (kPa)	Torque Converter Pressure 1987 psi (kPa)	Torque Converter Pressure 1988 psi (kPa)	Torque Converter Pressure 1989 psi (kPa)
N	0	idle	Neutral	50–70 (350–490)	0–1.4 (0–9.8)	0–1.4 (0–9.8)	0–1.4 (0–9.8)	0–1.4 (0–9.8)	0–1.4 (0–9.8)	50–64 (350–450)	NA
N	0	2500	Neutral	50–70 ① (350–490)	0–1.4 (0–9.8)	0–1.4 (0–9.8)	0–1.4 (0–9.8)	0–1.4 (0–9.8)	50–64 (350–450)	50–64 (350–450)	NA
D	0	idle	2nd	50–70 (350–490)	14–30 (100–210)	0–1.4 (0–9.8)	0–1.4 (0–9.8)	0–1.4 (0–9.8)	0–1.4 (0–9.8)	50–64 (350–450)	NA
D ②	70	2500	OD	50–70 (350–490)	118–128 (830–900)	0–1.4 (0–9.8)	118–128 (830–900)	0–1.4 (0–9.8)	0–1.4 (0–9.8)	50–64 (350–450)	56–84 (392–588)
D ③	45	2500	3rd	50–70 (350–490)	118–128 (830–900)	118–128 (830–900)	118–128 (830–900)	0–1.4 (0–9.8)	0–1.4 (0–9.8)	50–64 (350–450)	56–84 (392–588)
2	30	2500	2nd	50–70 (350–490)	118–128 (830–900)	0–1.4 (0–9.8)	0–1.4 (0–9.8)	0–1.4 (0–9.8)	0–1.4 (0–9.8)	50–64 (350–450)	56–84 (392–588)
L	0	1000	1st	50–70 (350–490)	0–1.4 (0–9.8)	0–1.4 (0–9.8)	0–1.4 (0–9.8)	43–60 (300–420)	0–1.4 (0–9.8)	50–64 (350–450)	NA
R	20	2500	Reverse	50–70 (350–490)	0–1.4 (0–9.8)	230–319 (1640–2240)	0–1.4 (0–9.8)	230–319 (1640–2240)	0–1.4 (0–9.8)	50–64 (350–450)	56–84 (392–588)
R	0	1000	Reverse	50–70 (350–490)	0–1.4 (0–9.8)	215 or more (1500)	0–1.4 (0–9.8)	215 or more (1500)	0–1.4 (0–9.8)	50–64 (350–450)	56–84 (392–588)

① 0–1.4 psi (0.98 kPa)—1987 vehicles
② Overdrive switch on
③ Overdrive switch off

— CAUTION —

When the reverse pressure is tested, use a high-scale gauge (400 psi/3000 kPa). A low-scale gauge could burst under reverse pressure and cause mechanical damage and personal injury.

5. Measure the oil pressure under various conditions and check the results and conclusions against the appropriate chart.

NOTE: Line pressure (kickdown brake pressure) and reducing pressure can both be adjusted if they are incorrect.

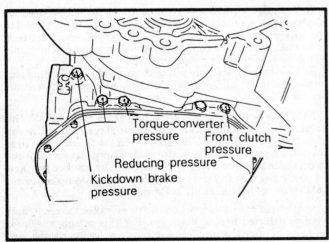

Torque-converter pressure
Front clutch pressure
Reducing pressure
Kickdown brake pressure

Identification of oil pressure outlet ports

STALL SPEED TEST

The stall test consists of determining maximum engine speed obtained at full throttle in **D** and **R** ranges, without allowing the vehicle to move. This test checks the torque converter stator overrunning clutch operation and the holding ability of the clutches and the low/reverse brake.

— CAUTION —

Never allow anyone to stand near — especially in front of or behind — the vehicle when performing a stall test.

1. Warm up the engine sufficiently. The transaxle fluid should be 120–180°F (50–80°C) and the coolant should be 180–190°F (80–90°C). Check the trasnsaxle fluid and bring it to the correct level before proceeding with the test.
2. Block the wheels securely and firmly set the parking brake.
3. Connect a tachometer to the engine.
4. Push down the brake pedal firmly and shift the gear selector to **D**.
5. Gradually depress the accelerator pedal. Do not perform this step for more than 5 seconds.
6. When the engine has stopped increasing in speed, read the tachometer and immediately release the accelerator pedal.
7. Shift into **N** and allow the engine to idle for two minutes.

NOTE: This step is important so that the fluid can cool and to prevent the possibility of overheating.

8. Perform the stall test in **R**, following the same procedure as above.
9. The stall speed specification is 2200 ± 200 rpm for 1985–1987 and 2300 ± 500 rpm for 1988–1989.

Test Results

STALL SPEED HIGHER THAN SPECIFICATION IN DRIVE

If this is the condition, then either the rear clutch or overrunning clutch is slipping. In either case, perform the appropriate hydraulic pressure test to locate the cause of the slippage.

STALL SPEED HIGHER THAN SPECIFICATION IN REVERSE

If this is the condition, then either the front clutch or low/reverse brake is slipping. In either case, perform the appropriate hydraulic pressure test to locate the cause of the slippage.

STALL SPEED LOWER THAN SPECIFICATION IN DRIVE AND REVERSE

If this is the condition, then either the engine is not in tune and has insufficient output or the torque converter is fauly. Check the condition of the engine first. If it checks good, the the converter is suspect.

ROAD TEST

This test is designed to check if upshift and downshift occurs at the correct speeds while actually driving the vehicle. The test should be performed on long, level road, with little or no traffic so that speeds can be chosen and maintained and not forced or altered by others on the road.

Before performing a road test, check to be sure that all sensor wiring connectors and ground connections are correctly and securely in place and all fluid levels are at the correct levels.

Certain shift patterns have been programmed into the computer to provide the driver with optimum shifting performance in accordance with the engine performance.

The upshift points and corresponding downshift points are at different speeds so that frequent up-and-down-shifting will not occur when driving at a speed in the vicinity of the shift point.

When the vehicle is stopped, there is a shift into second gear to obtain a suitable creeping but when the accelerator is depressed, the vehicle does start in first gear.

1. Run the engine until at operating temperature and check the fluid level.

2. Accelerate the engine to 1500 rpm and shift from **P** to **R**. There should be no abnormal feeling of shifting impact.

3. Allow the engine to idle. Then shift from **R** to **N**. There should be no abnormal feeling of shifting impact.

4. Accelerate the engine to 1500 rpm and shift from **N** to **D**. There should be no abnormal feeling of shifting impact.

5. Allow the engine to idle again and observe vehicle creeping in **D**. The vehicle should not move more than 177 in. (4500mm) in 5 seconds.

6. With the O/D switch on (in the up position) and the power/economy switch in the economy mode (in the up position), accelerate at different rates to check the shift points. Also, take note of the operation of the converter clutch. Perform the test again, this time with the power/economy switch in the power mode (switch pushed down), if the vehicle is so equipped.

7. Depress the O/D switch while in fourth gear. It should result in a shift down to third gear and an increase in engine speed.

8. Slow down and shift from **D** to **2**. It should result in a shift down to second gear and an increase in engine speed with engine braking.

9. Slow down some more and shift into **L**. This should produce an increase in engine speed and much engine braking as well as a shift into first gear.

10. Start off in **2** range. Automatic shifting from first to second only should occur and the damper clutch should be operational. Repeat in **L** range; no shifting should occur and the damper clutch should not engage.

11. If any abnormality is found during the road test, compare the findings with the Chilton Three C's Diagnosis Chart.

Electronic Control System

COMPONENT TESTING

Always check fluid level and condition, wiring connections and all pertinent adjustments before performing more complicated procedures.

Diagnostic instruments and techniques are available for diagnosing electrical transaxle problems with the KM175 and KM177. Use of these tools will expedite the diagnostic sequence.

Malfunctions of the electronic control system are detected by the computer itself, stored in its Random Access Memory (RAM) and the malfunction code is indicated and displayed by the device used.

Analog Voltmeter or Diagnosis Checker

1. Connect the checker or voltmeter to the diagostics connector.

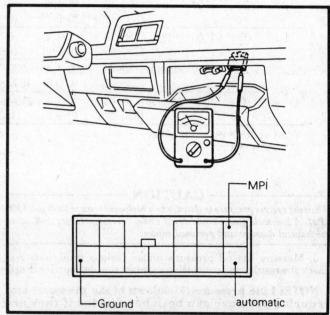

Connecting a voltmeter for self-diagnostics

2. Turn the key to the **N** position. Since the output used for display of the malfunction is cancelled when the key is turned to the **OFF** position, the code will not be displayed even if the tester or voltmeter is still connected. Hence, confirm the malfunction code before turning the key **OFF**.

3. The malfunction code will be displayed by the flashing pattern of the tester LED light or the swing pattern of the voltmeter needle.

NOTE: When the key is switched from OFF to ON, the same display pattern as No. 12 is displayed after the engine has started. (1985–88 only). This is to indicate that the diagnosis function is normal. The pattern is, however, extinguished after it finishes if the engine is started while the display pattern is displayed. Do not confuse this with an actual fault code pattern.

4. If two or more malfunctions occur one after the other, only the one detected first is displayed. For this reason, check for more codes after the problem has been resolved; a second malfunction code may have been hidden by the preceding code.

Malfunction indication code	Diagnosis	Assumed location
ON / OFF — 4 sec. 0.5 1.5 0.5 ... 2 sec. Repeats	Microprocessor (computer) malfunction; not remedied by resetting.	Low power-supply voltage (recharging system) Computer
4 sec. 0.5 1.5 1.5 0.5	First gear signal is detected at high vehicle speed.	Pulse generator B Computer
(waveform)	Vehicle speed detected by pulse generator B is much lower than actual vehicle speed.	Pulse generator B Computer
(waveform)	Operation of shift-control solenoid valve A differs from computer command.	Shift-control solenoid valve A Computer
(waveform)	Operation of shift-control solenoid valve B differs from computer command.	Shift-control solenoid valve B Computer
(waveform)	Kickdown servo switch signal differs from actual gear engaged.	Kickdown servo switch Pressure-control solenoid valve Computer
(waveform)	Shifting doesn't finish.	Pulse generator A Pressure-control solenoid valve Computer
(waveform)	Pressure-control solenoid valve drive differs from computer command.	Pressure-control solenoid valve Computer
(waveform)	Engine speed is judged to be 6,500 rpm or more.	Pulse generator B Ignition coil (ignition signal system) Computer
(waveform)	Kickdown drum rotation speed is judged to be 6,500 rpm or more.	Pulse generators A · B Computer
(waveform)	Damper clutch control solenoid valve is directly connected.	Damper clutch control system Computer
(waveform)	No ignition signal.	Ignition coil Ignition signal system Computer

Self-diagnostics malfunction codes data — 1985–88

5. The malfunction code is repeatedly displayed until the ignition key is switched to **OFF**.

6. Compare the code to the diagnosis table, then follow the flow chart and use the wiring diagram if necessary. After the repair has been completed, road test the vehicle and recheck for codes.

7. The fail-safe system (3rd gear held) operates during all malfunctions except when:

a. Operation of shift-control solenoid valve A differs from computer command.

b. The kickdown servo switch signal differs from actual gear engaged.

c. The damper clutch control solenoid valve is directly connected.

d. There is no ignition signal.

Multi-use Tester

1. Connect the tester to the diagnostics connector and follow the manufacturer's instructions on how to obtain fault codes.

2. A maximum of ten fault codes, in sequence of occurrence, can be stored in the RAM. The same code can be stored three times. If the number of stored codes exceeds 10, already stored codes will start becoming erased, starting with the oldest one first.

3. Do not disconnect the battery until all codes are recorded. All fault codes and patterns will be erased when the battery is disconnected.

Code No.	Output code — Output pattern (for voltmeter)	Description	Fail-safe	Note (relation to fault code)
11	5V / 0V	Malfunction of the microprocessor	Locked in 3rd gear	When code No. 31 is generated 4th time.
12		First gear command during high speed driving	Locked in 3rd (D) or 2nd (2, L) gear	When code No. 32 is generated 4th time.
13		Damaged or disconnected wiring of the pulse generator B system	Locked in 3rd (D) or 2nd (2, L) gear	When code No. 33 is generated 4th time.
14		Damaged or disconnected wiring, or short circuit, of shift control solenoid valve A	Locked in 3rd gear	When code No. 41 or 42 is generated 4th time.
15		Damaged or disconnected wiring, or short circuit, of shift control solenoid valve B	Locked in 3rd gear	When code No. 43 or 44 is gnerated 4th time.
16		Damaged or disconnected wiring, or short circuit, of the pressure control solenoid valve	Locked in 3rd (D) or 2nd (2, L) gear	When code No. 45 or 46 is generated 4th time.
17		Shift steps non-synchronous	Locked in 3rd (D) or 2nd (2, L) gear	When either code No. 51, 52 53 or 54 is generated 4th time.

Self-diagnostics malfunction codes data — 1989

Fault code	Fault code (for voltmeter)	Cause	Remedy
21	5V ----- / 0V ----- (waveform)	Abnormal increase of TPS output	Check the throttle position sensor connector. Check the throttle position sensor itself. Adjust the throttle position sensor. Check the accelerator switch (No. 28: output or not). Check the throttle position sensor output circuit harness.
22	(waveform)	Abnormal decrease of TPS output	
23	(waveform)	Incorrect adjustment of the throttle-position sensor system	
24	(waveform)	Damaged or disconnected wiring of the oil temperature sensor system	Check the oil temperature sensor circuit harness. Check the oil temperature sensor connector. Check the oil temperature sensor itself.
25	(waveform)	Damaged or disconnected wiring of the kickdown servo switch system, or improper contact	Check the kickdown servo switch output circuit harness. Check the kickdown servo switch connector. Check the kickdown servo switch itself.
26	(waveform)	Short circuit of the kickdown servo switch system	
27	(waveform)	Damaged or disconnected wiring of the ignition pulse pick-up cable system	Check the ignition pulse signal line.
28	(waveform)	Short circuit of the accelerator switch system or improper adjustment	Check the accelerator switch output circuit harness. Check the accelerator switch connector. Check the accelerator switch itself. Adjust the accelerator switch.
31	(waveform)	Malfunction of the microprocessor	Replace the control unit.
32	(waveform)	First gear command during high-speed driving	Replace the control unit.
33	(waveform)	Damaged or disconnected wiring of the pulse generator B system	Check the pulse generator B output circuit harness. Check pulse generator B itself. Check the vehicle speed reed switch (for chattering).

Self-diagnostics malfunction codes data – 1989 (cont.)

Fault code	Fault code (for voltmeter)	Cause	Remedy
41		Damaged or disconnected wiring of the shift control solenoid valve A system	Check the solenoid valve connector. Check shift control solenoid valve A itself. Check the shift control solenoid valve A drive circuit harness
42		Short circuit of the shift-control solenoid valve A system	
43		Damaged or disconnected wiring of the shift control solenoid valve B system	Check the solenoid valve connector. Check shift control solenoid valve B itself. Check the shift control solenoid valve B drive circuit harness.
44		Short circuit of the shift control solenoid valve B system	
45		Damaged or disconnected wiring of the pressure control solenoid valve system	Check the solenoid valve connector. Check the pressure control solenoid valve itself. Check the pressure control solenoid valve drive circuit harness.
46		Short circuit of the pressure control solenoid valve system	
51		First gear non-synchronous	Check the pulse generator output circuit harness. Check the pulse generator connector. Check pulse generator A and pulse generator B themselves. Kickdown brake slippage.
52		Second gear non-synchronous	Check the pulse generator A output circuit harness. Check the pulse generator A connector. Check pulse generator A itself. Kickdown brake slippage.
53		Third gear non-synchronous	Check the pulse generator A output circuit harness. Check the pulse generator connector. Check pulse generator A and pulse generator B themselves. Front clutch slippage. Rear clutch slippage.
54		Fourth gear non-synchronous	Check the pulse generator A output circuit harness. Check the pulse generator A connector. Check pulse generator A itself. Kickdown brake slippage.

Self-diagnostics malfunction codes data – 1989 (cont.)

Check items	Check procedures		Probable cause (or remedy) if a malfunction is found
	Check conditions	Normal value	
Pulse generator • Service data • Item No.13	D range; stopped.	0 rpm	• Pulse generator B or circuit harness malfunction. • Pulse generator B shielded line malfunction. • Intrusion of external noise.
	D range; driving at 50 km/h (31 mph) in 3rd gear.	1600 ~ 2000 rpm	
	D range; driving at 50 km/h (31 mph) in 4th gear.	1600 ~ 2000 rpm	
Pulse generator • Service data • Item No.19	D range; driving at 30 km/h (19 mph) in 2nd gear.	0 rpm	• Pulse generator A or circuit harness malfunction. • Pulse generator A shielded line malfunction. • Intrusion of external noise. • Kickdown brake slippage.
	D range; driving at 50 km/h (31 mph) in 3rd gear.	1400 ~ 1800 rpm	
	D range; driving at 50 km/h (31 mph) in 4th gear.	0 rpm	
Throttle position sensor (TPS) • Service data • Item No.21	Accelerator completely closed.	0.5 ~ 0.6 V	• TPS is incorrectly adjusted if voltage is high during fully closed or fully open. • TPS or circuit harness malfunction if there is no change. • TPS or accelerator wire malfunction if the change is not smooth.
	Accelerator slowly depressed.	Changes occur according to degree of opening.	
	Accelerator completely open.	4.5 ~ 5.0 V	
Oil temperature sensor • Service data • Item No.24	Engine cold (before starting).	Corresponding to outside air temperature.	• Oil-temperature sensor or circuit harness malfunction.
	Engine warming up (during driving).	Gradual increase.	
	After engine warmed up.	80 ~ 110°C	
Kickdown servo switch • Service data • Item No.25	L range; idling.	ON	• Kickdown servo improperly adjusted. • Kickdown servo switch or circuit harness malfunction. • Kickdown servo malfunction.
	D range; 1st or 3rd gear.	ON	
	D range; 2nd or 4th gear.	OFF	
Ignition signal line • Service data • Item No.27	N range; idling.	650 ~ 750 rpm	• Ignition system malfunction. • Ignition signal pick-up circuit harness malfunction.
	N range; 2,500 rpm (tachometer reading).	2400 ~ 2600 rpm	
Accelerator switch • Service data • Item No.28	Accelerator fully closed.	OFF	• Accelerator switch incorrectly adjusted. • Accelerator switch or circuit harness malfunction.
	Accelerator slightly depressed.	ON	
Vehicle-speed reed switch • Service data • Item No.33	Vehicle stopped.	0 km/h	• Vehicle-speed reed switch malfunction if high-speed signals emitted while vehicle is stopped. • Otherwise, vehicle-speed reed switch or circuit harness malfunction.
	Driving at 30 km/h (19 mph).	30 km/h (19 mph)	
	Driving at 50 km/h (31 mph).	50 km/h (31 mph)	
Inhibitor switch • Service data • Item No.34	Shift to P range.	P	• Inhibitor switch improperly adjusted. • Inhibitor switch or circuit harness malfunction. • Manual control cable malfunction. o If the shift lever does not move, check the parking shift lock mechanism.
	Shift to R range.	R	
	Shift to N range.	N	
	Shift to D range.	D	
	Shift to 2 range.	2	
	Shift to L range.	L	
Overdrive switch • Service data • Item No.35	Overdrive switch ON.	OD	• Overdrive switch or circuit harness malfunction.
	Overdrive switch OFF.	OD–OFF	
Power/Economy select switch • Service data • Item No.36	Selection of the Power pattern. (including during E pattern control when oil temperature is low)	Power	• Power/Economy select switch or circuit harness malfunction.
	Selection of the Economy pattern.	Economy	
Air conditioner relay signals • Service data • Item No.37	D range; air conditioner idling speed increased.	ON	• Air conditioner power relay ON signal-detection circuit harness malfunction.
	D range; air conditioner switch OFF.	OFF	
T/M gear position • Service data • Item No.38	D range; idling.	C	• TCU malfunction. • Accelerator switch system malfunction. • Inhibitor switch system malfunction. • TPS system malfunction.
	L range; idling.	1ST	
	2 range; 2nd gear.	2ND	
	D range; overdrive–OFF; 3rd gear.	3RD	
	D range; overdrive; 4th gear.	4TH	
PCSV duty • Service data • Item No.45	D range; idling.	50 ~ 70 %	• Duty should become 100% when, while idling in D range, accelerator is pressed even slightly. • TCU malfunction. • TPS system malfunction. • Accelerator switch system malfunction.
	D range; 1st gear.	100 %	
	D range; during shift.	Changes occur according to conditions.	
Damper clutch slippage amount • Service data • Item No.47	D range; 3rd gear. 1,500 rpm (tachometer reading)	200 ~ 300 rpm	• Damper clutch malfunction. • Ignition signal line or pulse generator B system malfunction. • T/M oil pressure not appropriate. • DCCSV malfunction.
	D range; 3rd gear. 3,500 rpm (tachometer reading)	30 ~ 50 rpm	
DCCSV duty • Service data • Item No.49	D range; 3rd gear. 1,500 rpm (tachometer reading)	0 %	• TCU malfunction. • TPS system malfunction. • Pulse generator B system malfunction.
	D range; 3rd gear. 3,500 rpm (tachometer reading)	Changes occur according to load.	

Multi-use Tester Specifications Data

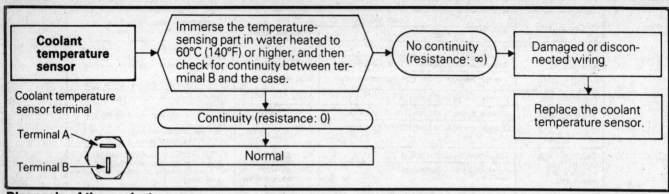

Diagnosis of the coolant sensor

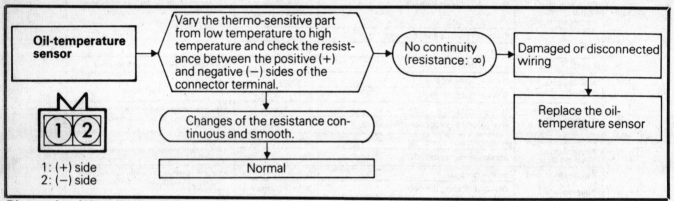

Diagnosis of the oil temperature sensor

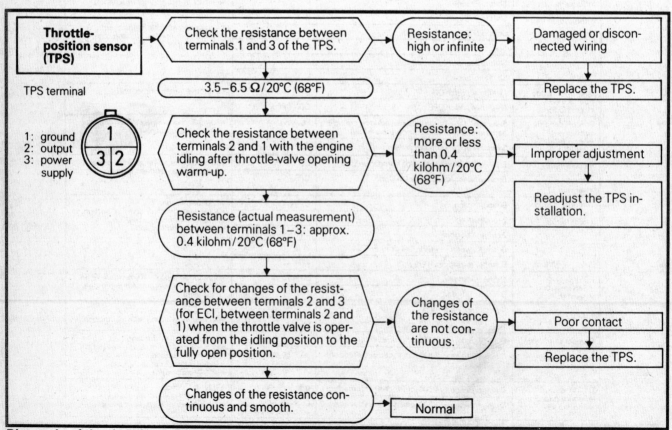

Diagnosis of the throttle position sensor (TPS) — 1985–88

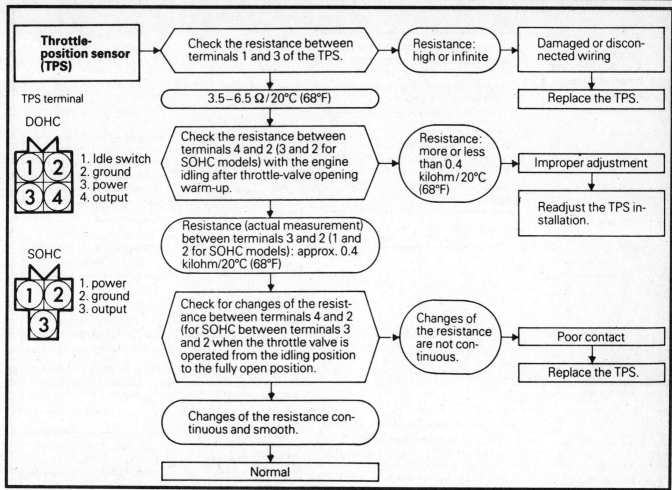

Diagnosis of the throttle position sensor (TPS) — 1989

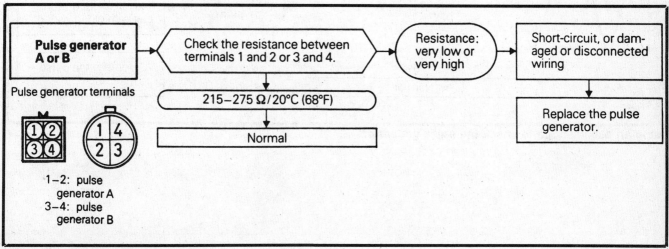

Diagnosis of the pulse generators

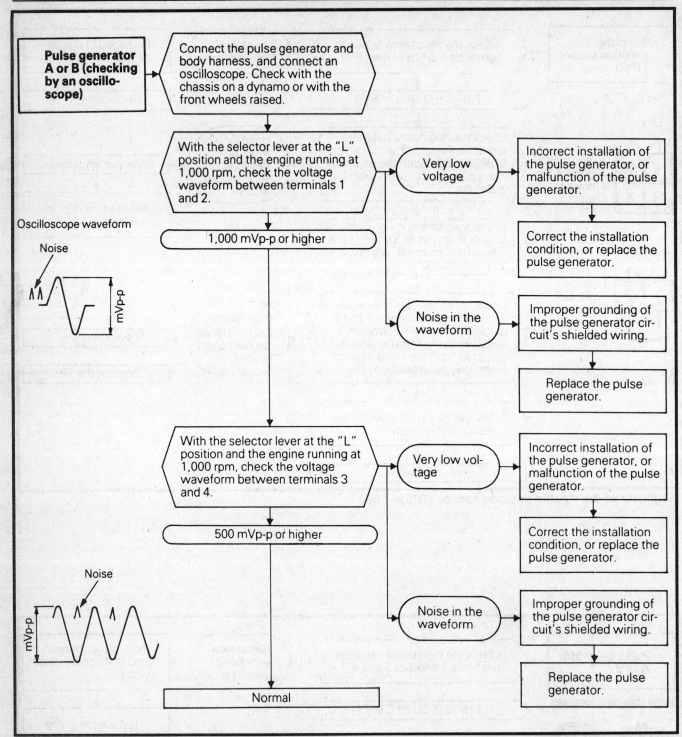

Using an oscilloscope to check the pulse generators

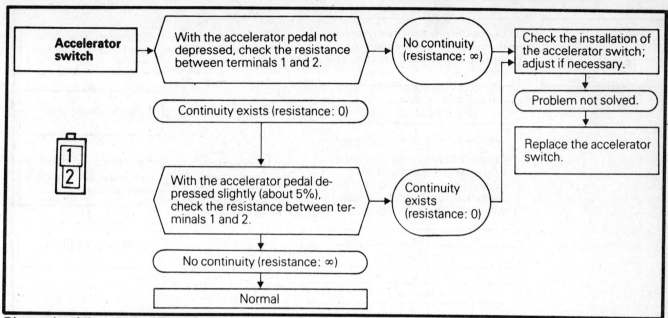

Diagnosis of the accelerator switch

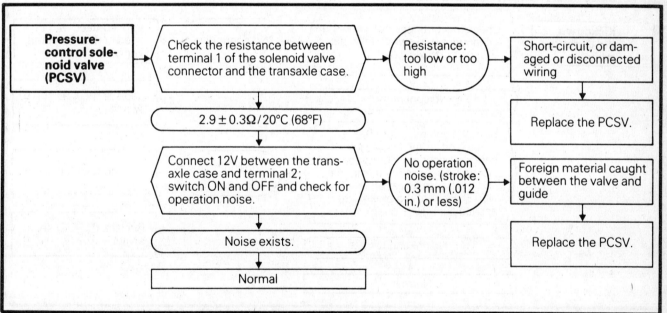

Diagnosis of the pressure control solenoid valve (PCSV)

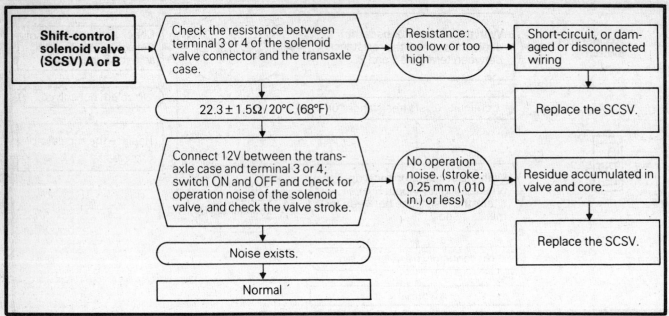

Diagnosis of the shift control solenoid valve (SCSV) A or B

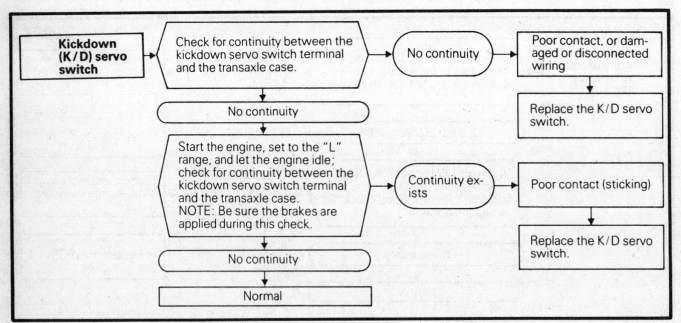

Diagnosis of the kickdown servo switch

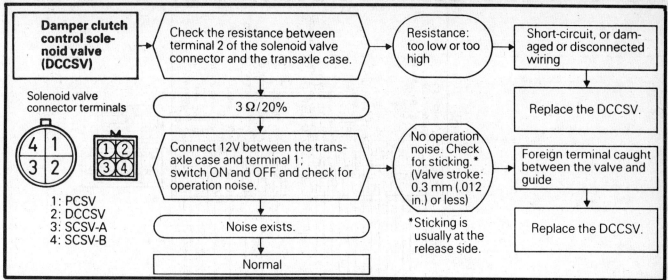

Diagnosis of the damper clutch control solenoid valve (DCCSV)

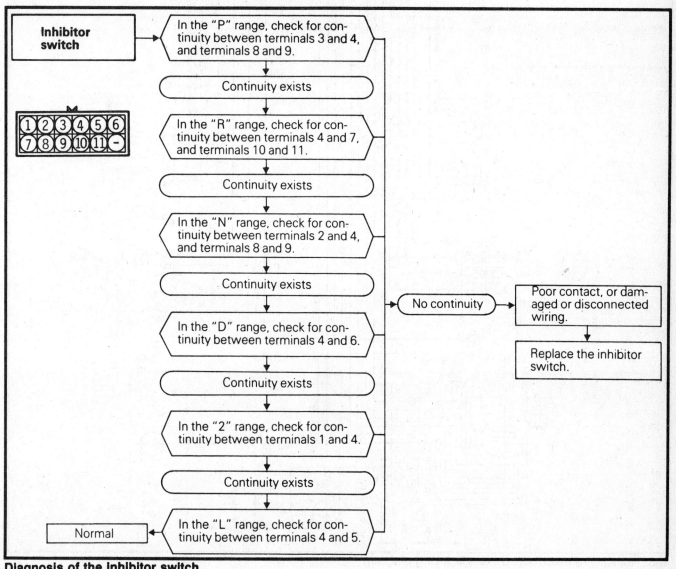

Diagnosis of the inhibitor switch

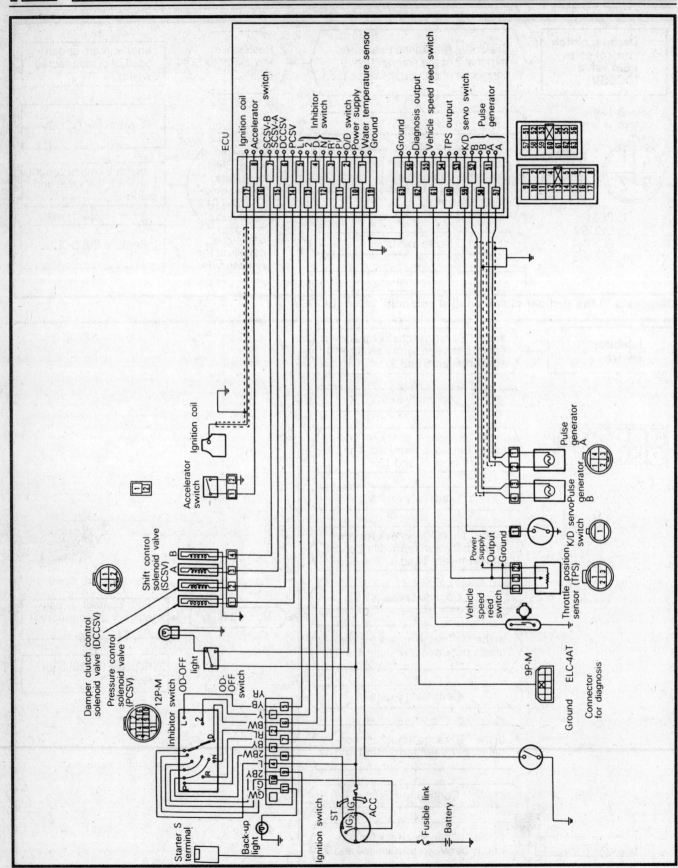

1985–87 KM175 electronic transaxle wiring diagram

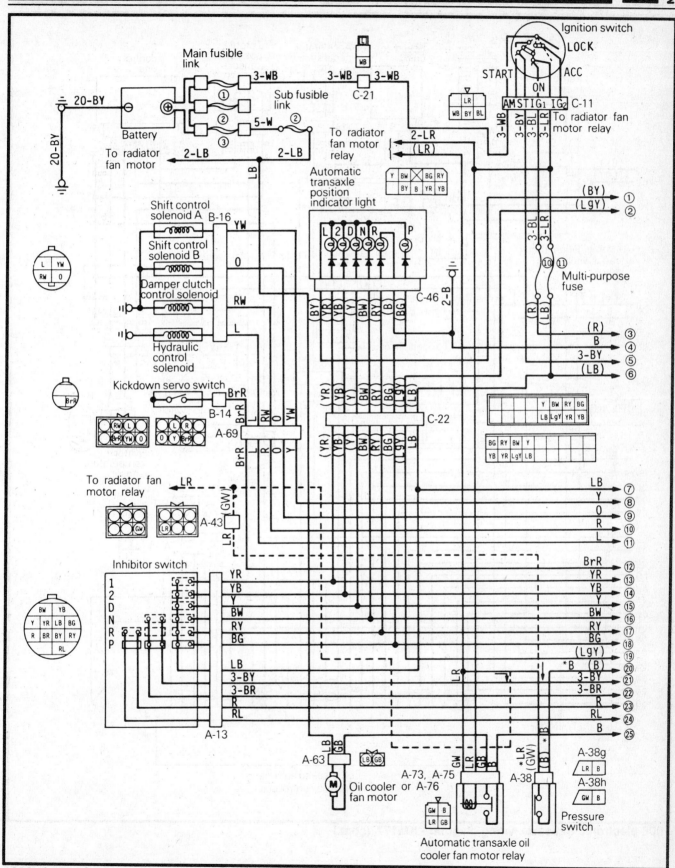

1988 electronic transaxle wiring diagram–KM177

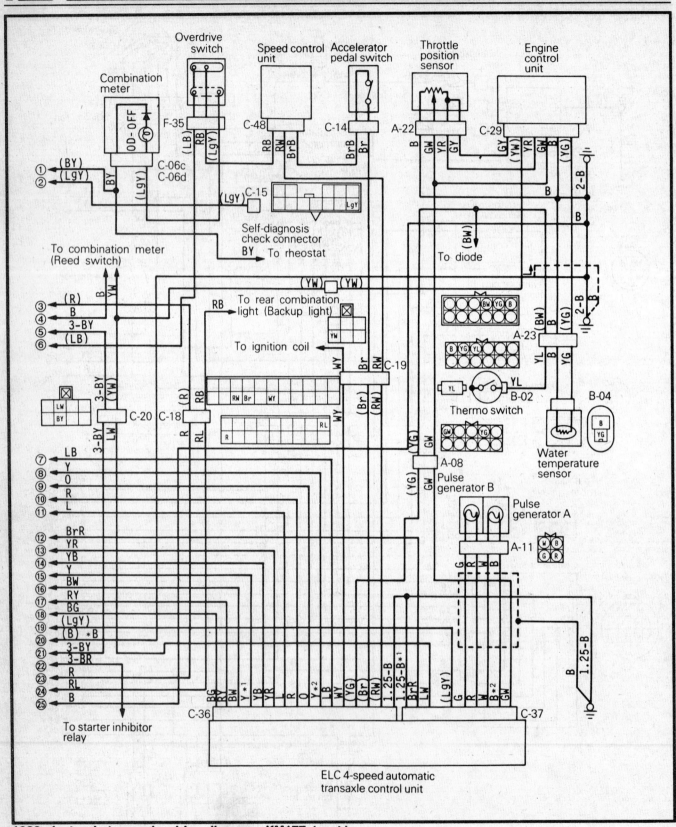

1988 electronic transaxle wiring diagram—KM177 (cont.)

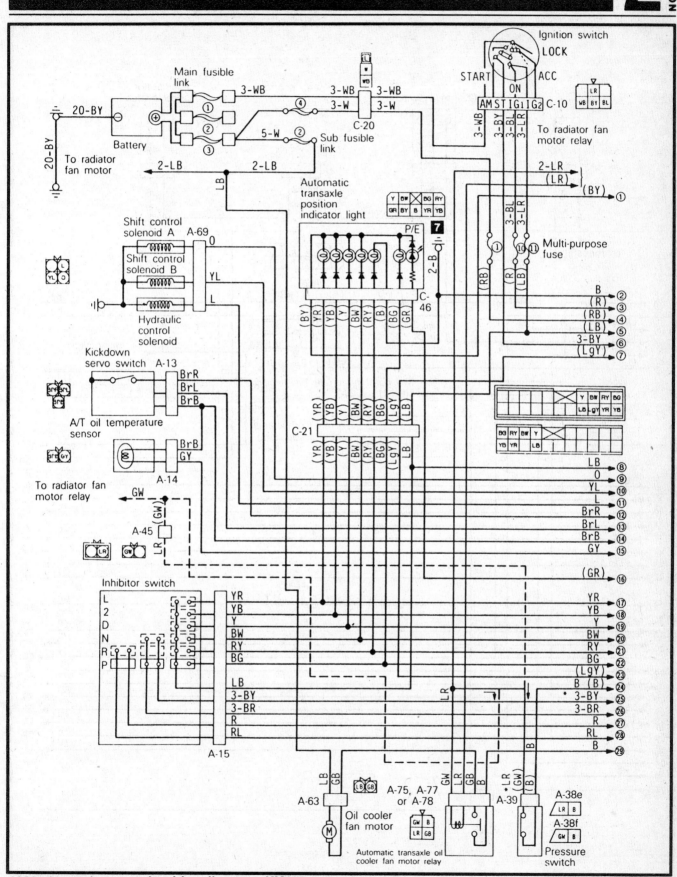

1989 electronic transaxle wiring diagram — KM177

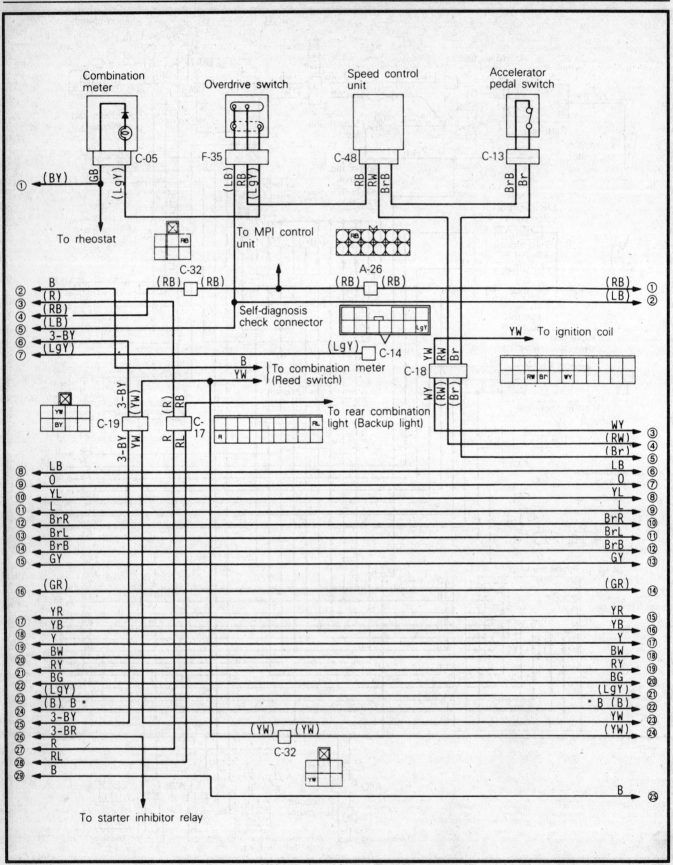

1989 electronic transaxle wiring diagram – KM177 (cont.)

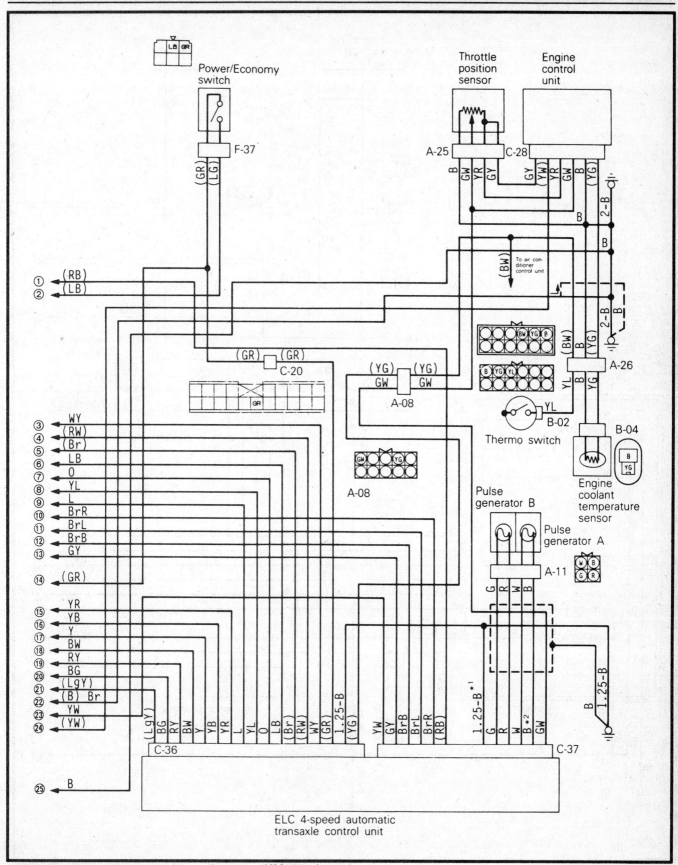

1989 electronic transaxle wiring diagram—KM177 (cont.)

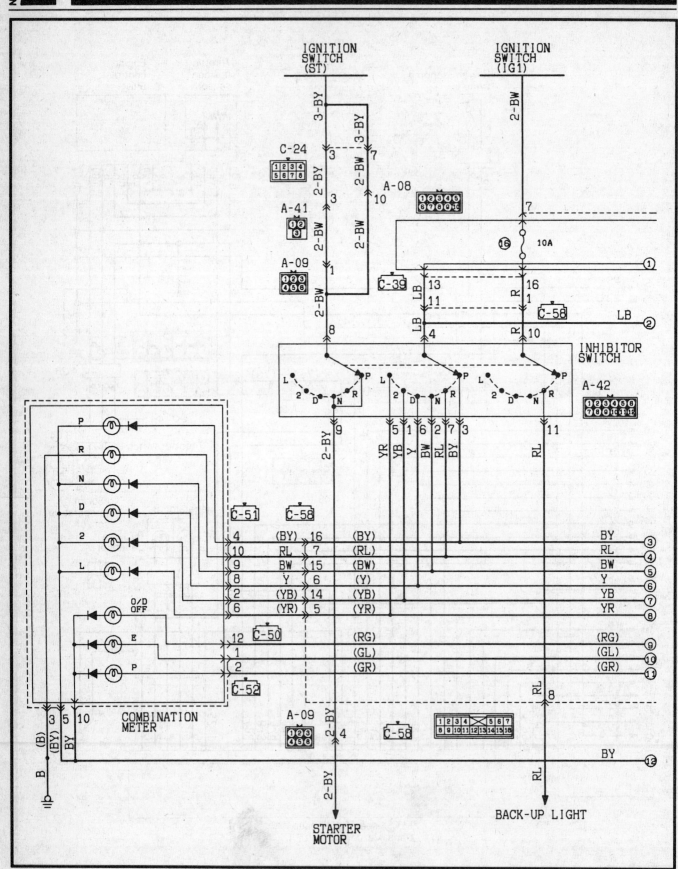

1989 electronic transaxle wiring diagram—KM175

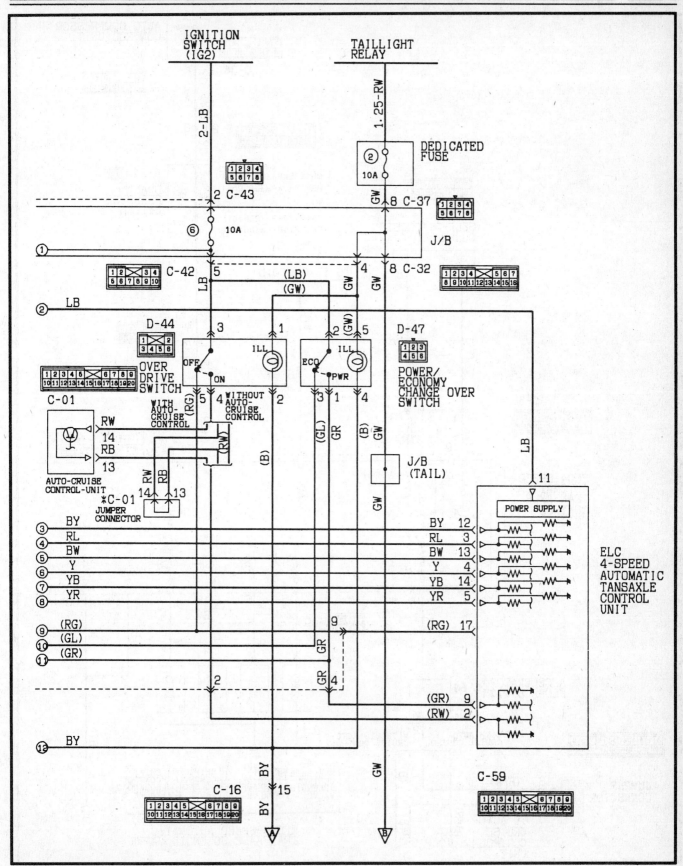

1989 electronic transaxle wiring diagram—KM175 (cont.)

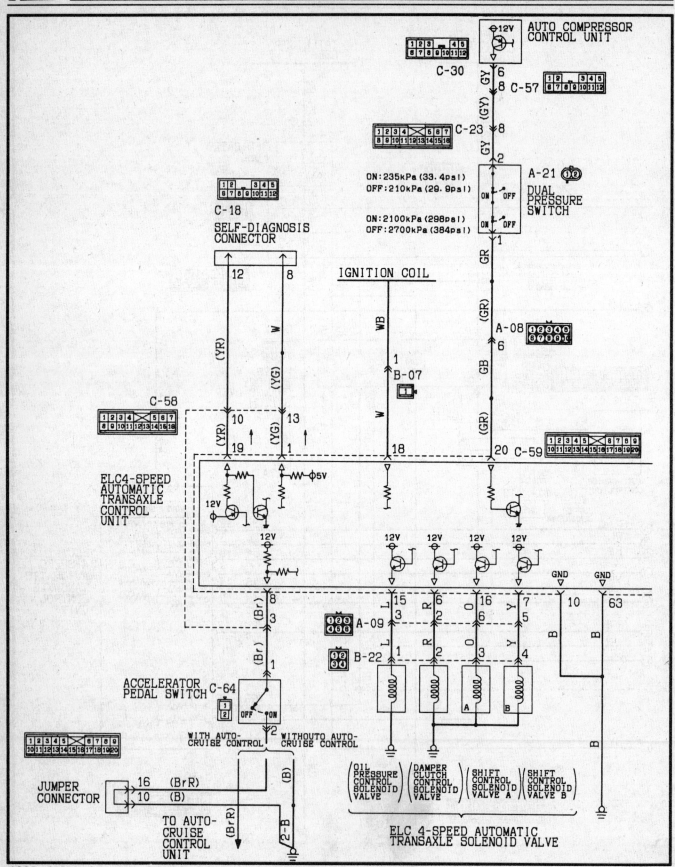

1989 electronic transaxle wiring diagram—KM175 (cont.)

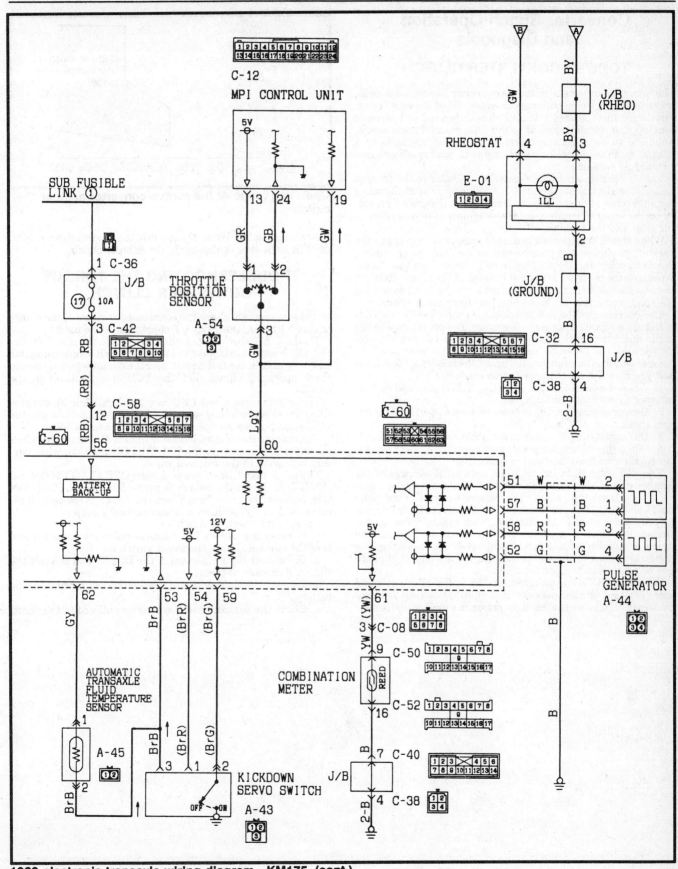

1989 electronic transaxle wiring diagram – KM175 (cont.)

Converter Clutch Operation and Diagnosis

TORQUE CONVERTER CLUTCH

The internal damper clutch torque converter has the same basic construction as a conventional converter. The difference is that this design incorporates a damper clutch operated by hydraulic control. The clutch is similar to that in a manual transaxle. It functions to suppress torque converter losses (slippage) to a minimum, thus increasing direct engine-to-road-speed efficiency and fuel economy.

The damper clutch friction material is similar to the friction material on the transaxle clutches. A lock ring pawl on the outer circumference of the turbine shell engages in the groove provided on the outer circumference of the damper clutch to connect the clutch to the turbine.

When clutch engagement hydraulic pressure is applied to the back of the clutch, it is pressed against the front cover causing the front cover and the turbine to be connected via the clutch. When release pressure is applied in front of the clutch through the input shaft, the clutch is released from the front cover and the solid connection of the turbine and front cover is broken.

The operation of the damper clutch is controlled by the TCU based upon signals from various sensors. The operational range of the clutch depends on the engine rpm and the degree of throttle opening. In order to maintain driving performance, the damper clutch is non-operational under the following conditions and operates like an ordinary torque converter:

1. When starting off and accelerating in first gear and reverse in order to maintain performance.

2. During engine braking in order to prevent deceleration impact shock.

3. During shifting in order to maintain good shift feeling.

4. When the coolant temperature is below 51°F (123°C) in order to allow engine stabilization when cold.

The TCU calculates the optimum amount of slippage of the damper clutch based upon the data received from various sensors. Signals are then sent to the Damper Clutch Control Solenoid Valve (DCCSV). When the DCCSV is activated, the hydraulic pressure applied to the damper clutch control valve is controlled, the valve is activated and line pressure from the oil pump is supplied to the torque converter. By regulating the pressure applied to the damper clutch, the amount of slippage can be controlled to a certain value.

When the DCCSV is switched off, the orifice of the solenoid valve is closed and the pressure applied to the control valve increases until it reaches a constant pressure which is adjusted by

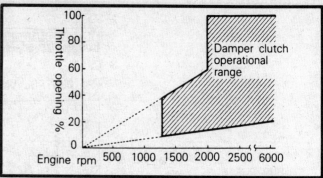

Operating range of the torque converter damper clutch

the reducing valve. When this occurs, the control valve moves, switching the flow to disengage the damper clutch.

TROUBLESHOOTING THE TORQUE CONVERTER CLUTCH

In order to properly check the electronic functions of the damper clutch system, the ELC-A/T checker must be used.

The ELC-A/T checker contains two circuits: the clutch-on circuit which is used to inspect the damper clutch torque converter and its hydraulic control circuit, and the circuit which is used to check operating signal that the TCU is outputting to the DCCSV.

The checker has a red LED monitor light that illuminates when the select switch is set to the CONTROL position and the TCU is outputting an operating signal to the DCCSV.

The checker also has an indicator light that illuminates when the select switch is set to the CLUTCH ON position (when current is flowing to the solenoid valve).

The select switch has three positions: OFF, CLUTCH ON and CONTROL. When the switch is pressed to the CLUTCH ON side, current begins to flow. When the switch is released, it returns to the OFF position and automatically resets.

Connect the checker as follows:

1. Connect the ELC-A/T test lead wires to connectors **A** and **B** of the checker. Leave the select switch off.

2. Disconnect the connectors of the DCCSV and connect the ELC-A/T checker to them.

3. Connect the checker clip to the positive (+) terminal of the battery.

4. Check the damper clutch system as outlined in the chart.

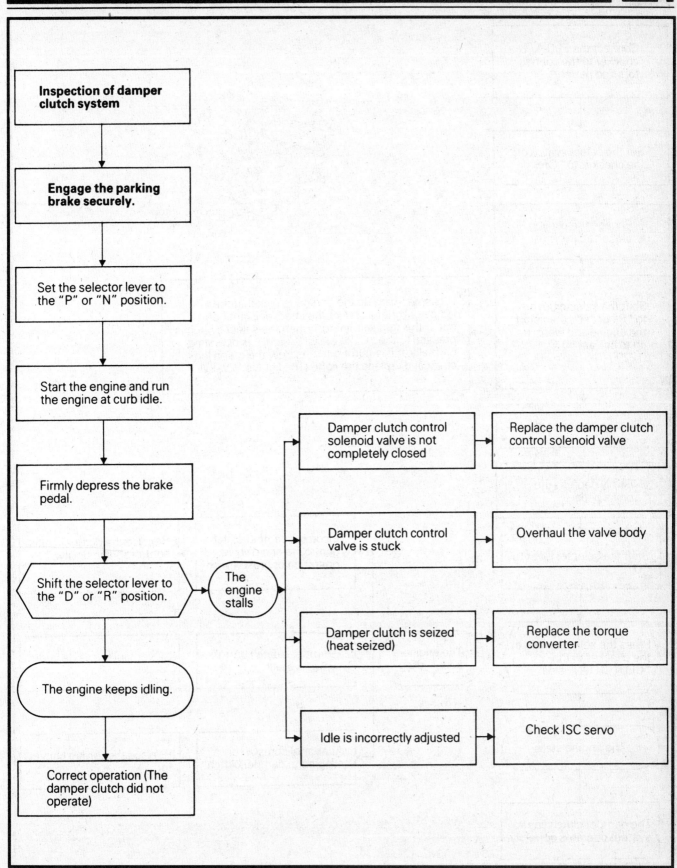

Damper clutch diagnosis chart — engine idling

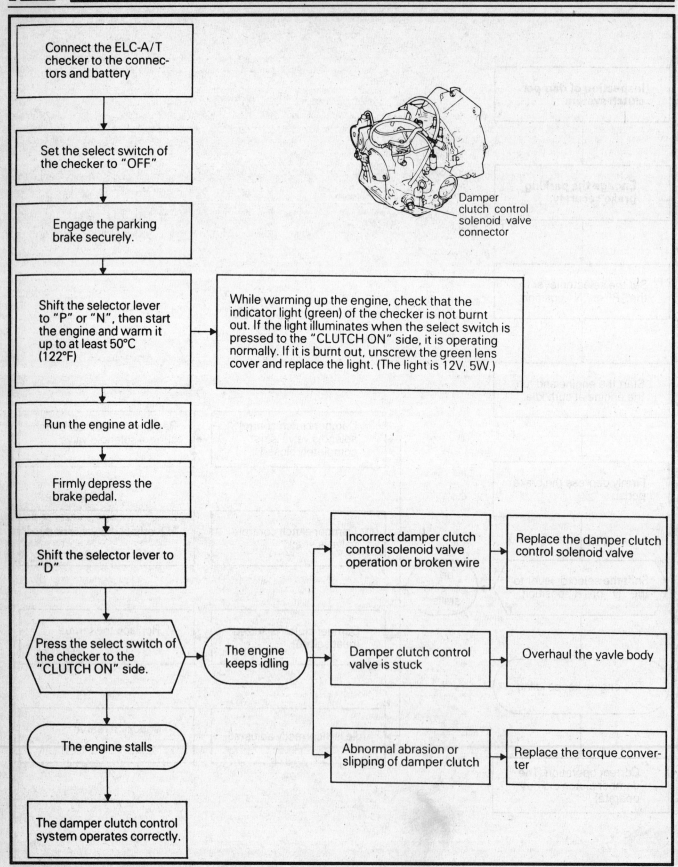

Connect the ELC-A/T checker to the connectors and battery

↓

Set the select switch of the checker to "OFF"

↓

Engage the parking brake securely.

↓

Shift the selector lever to "P" or "N", then start the engine and warm it up to at least 50°C (122°F) → While warming up the engine, check that the indicator light (green) of the checker is not burnt out. If the light illuminates when the select switch is pressed to the "CLUTCH ON" side, it is operating normally. If it is burnt out, unscrew the green lens cover and replace the light. (The light is 12V, 5W.)

Damper clutch control solenoid valve connector

↓

Run the engine at idle.

↓

Firmly depress the brake pedal.

↓

Shift the selector lever to "D"

↓

Press the select switch of the checker to the "CLUTCH ON" side. → The engine keeps idling → Incorrect damper clutch control solenoid valve operation or broken wire → Replace the damper clutch control solenoid valve

→ Damper clutch control valve is stuck → Overhaul the vavle body

→ Abnormal abrasion or slipping of damper clutch → Replace the torque converter

↓

The engine stalls

↓

The damper clutch control system operates correctly.

Damper clutch system – electrical check

ON CAR SERVICES

Adjustments

MANUAL CONTROL CABLE

1. Apply parking and service brakes securely.
2. Place selector lever in **R** range.
3. Set ignition key to the start position.
4. Slowly move the selector lever upward until it clicks into the notch of the **P** range. If the starter motor operates when the lever clicks into place, then **P** position is correct.
5. Next, slowly move the selector lever to **N**; if the starter operates in this gear, then **N** is also correct.
6. Also check to see that the vehicle does not move and the lever does not stop in between gears. If all of the above checks out, the cable is correctly adjusted.
7. Adjust the adjusting nuts where the cable is connected to the manual lever at the inhibitor switch to take up any slack in the control cable.
8. Recheck operation of the selector lever and inhibitor switch.

INHIBITOR SWITCH

1. Place control lever in **N**.
2. Loosen the mounting bolts and turn the inhibitor switch body until the 0.472 in. (12mm) wide end of the manual control lever overlaps the corresponding switch body flange.
3. Torque the two mounting bolts to 8 ft. lbs. (11 Nm) and check the operation of the inhibitor switch.

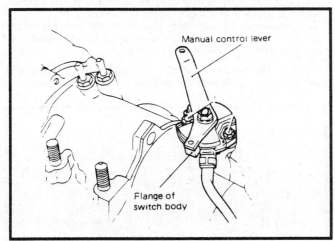

Adjusting the inhibitor switch

KICKDOWN SERVO

1. Disconnect the negative battery cable. Raise and safely support the vehicle. Completely remove all dirt from around the kickdown servo cover.
2. Remove the kickdown servo switch.
3. Remove the snapring and cover.
4. Loosen the locknut.
5. While holding with the special tool (which prevents the kickdown servo piston from turning), use the tightening tool to tighten to 7.2 ft. lbs. (9.8 Nm). Then loosen the adjusting screw two turns and torque the adjusting screw to 3.6 ft. lbs. (4.9 Nm). Finally, back off the adjusting screw 2–2¼ turns or 2½–2¾ turns if equipped with 1989 KM177 transaxle.

NOTE: If using the adaptor available in new kits, do not screw the nut in so far as to push the piston in. Also, when the adaptor is installed to the brake pressure port, tighten it by hand only.

6. Still holding the servo piston with the special tool, torque the locknut to 18–23 ft. lbs. (25–31 Nm).
7. After installing a new seal ring in the groove around the cover, install the cover to the case so that the seal ring won't be twisted. Then install the snapring.
8. Install the kickdown servo switch on the cover. Torque the screws to (8.4–12.0 in. lbs. (1–4 Nm).

LINE PRESSURE

1. Disconnect the negative battery cable. Raise and support the vehicle safely. Drain the transaxle fluid. Remove the pan, filter and valve body.

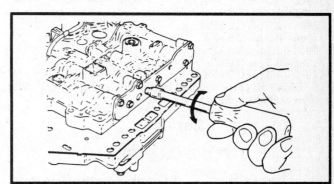

Adjusting the line pressure

2. Turn the adjustment screw of the regulator valve so that the line pressure (kickdown brake pressure) will come to the standard value for the specific year vehicle being worked on. When the adjusting screw is turned clockwise, the line pressure becomes lower; when turned counterclockwise, it increases. For each turn of the adjusting screw the oil pressure will change according to the following list:
   - 1985 — 4 psi (28 kPa)
   - 1986 — 4 psi (28 kPa)
   - 1987 — 5.5 psi (38 kPa)
   - 1988 — 5.5 psi (38 kPa)
   - 1989 — 5.5 psi (38 kPa)
3. Install all parts removed in step No. 1. Torque the valve body installation bolts to 7.5–8.5 ft. lbs. (10–11.5 Nm). Fill the transaxle and recheck the line pressure.

REDUCING PRESSURE

NOTE: This adjustment should be made at an oil temperature of 160–180°F (70–80°C). If the adjustment is made at too high an oil temperature, the line pressure will drop at idle, making accurate adjustment very difficult.

1. Disconnect the negative battery cable. Raise and support the vehicle safely. Drain the transaxle fluid, remove the pan and the filter. The valve body does not need to be removed for this adjustment.
2. Turn the adjustment screw of the valve body so that the reducing pressure will come to the standard value for the specific year vehicle being worked on. When the adjusting screw is turned clockwise, the reducing pressure becomes lower; when

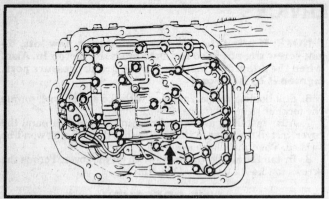

Location of the reducing pressure adjusting screw

turned counter-clockwise, it increases. For each turn of the adjusting screw the oil pressure will change according to the following list:

    1985 — 2.3 psi (16 kPa)
    1986 — 2.3 psi (16 kPa)
    1987 — 3.1 psi (22 kPa)
    1988 — 4.3 psi (30 kPa)
    1989 — 4.3 psi (30 kPa)

3. Install all parts removed in step No. 1. Fill the transaxle and recheck the reducing pressure.

Services

FLUID CHANGES

The conditions under which the vehicle is operated is the main consideration in determining how often the transaxle fluid should be changed. Different driving conditions result in different transaxle fluid temperatures. These temperatures affect change intervals.

If the vehicle is driven under severe conditions, change the transaxle fluid every 15,000 miles. If the vehicle is not used under severe conditions, change the fluid and replace the filter every 30,000 miles.

Do not overfill the transaxle. It takes about a pint of automatic transaxle fluid to raise the level from one line or dimple to the next on the transaxle indicator dipstick. Overfilling the unit can cause damage to the internal components of the automatic transaxle.

OIL PAN

Removal and Installation

1. Disconnect the negative battery cable. Raise the vehicle and support safely. Position a large drain pan under the drain plug and remove the drain plug.
2. After the fluid has drained, reinstall the drain plug. Remove the pan bolts and carefully pull the pan down; try to avoid prying, or the pan may get bent. Excess fluid may drip from the bolt holes, so have the drain pan handy as the bolts are removed.
3. Inspect the strainer and pan for any concentrations of friction material and metal pieces. A small amount of accumulation around the pan magnet or strainer is considered normal, but larger amounts may indicate heavy wear. If metal pieces are present, more serious damage is possible.
4. Clean the pan thoroughly with clean solvent and straighten the mating surface with a block of wood and a mallet if necessary. Pay special attention to the cleanliness of the mating surface.
5. Replace the strainer if necessary.

To Install:

6. Clean and completely dry all bolts and bolt holes with solvent and compressed air.
7. Glue the new gasket to the pan and hold against the case while installing a few bolts finger-tight. Torque the pan bolts to 8.0 ft. lbs.(10.5 Nm) in a crisscross order. Torque the drain plug with gasket to 23.5 ft. lbs. (22 Nm).
8. Lower the vehicle and reconnect the battery. Fill with 4 quarts of Dexron®II. Start the engine and allow it to get to operating temperature and run through the gears.
9. Check the fluid level in **N** and add until between the dimples or marks in the **HOT** range (or simply between the lines) on the dipstick. Make sure the fluid level does not go above the highest line. Road test and recheck the fluid level on level ground.

VALVE BODY

Removal and Installation

NOTE: The valve body is a precisely machined part used in the automatic transaxle. Handle it with care and do not clamp in a vise. The material is fragile and could distort easily. Keep all parts labeled and in a well-arranged order, since many of them look similar. Cleanliness is of the utmost importance when working with valve bodies; even the most minuscule scratch or piece of dirt can restrict valve movement and impair the transaxle's performance.

1. Disconnect the negative battery cable. Raise and safely support the vehicle.
2. Drain the transaxle fluid and remove the pan.
3. Remove the oil filter from the valve body.
4. Take note of the positioning of the notch in the solenoid valves connector and disconnect the connector.
5. Remove the 10 valve body assembly bolts and remove the valve body from the case. These bolts are different lengths, so take note of where each one is located.

NOTE: Be cautious of the manual valve because it could easily fall from the valve body onto the floor.

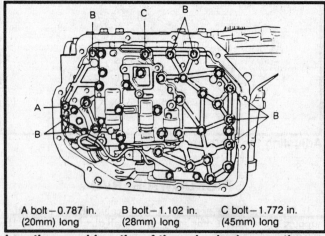

A bolt — 0.787 in. (20mm) long   B bolt — 1.102 in. (28mm) long   C bolt — 1.772 in. (45mm) long

Locations and lengths of the valve body mounting bolts

To Install

6. Make sure the O-ring is installed on the upper surface of the valve body in the correct location.
7. Replace the solenoid valves connector O-ring.
8. Install the valve body assembly to the case being sure to catch the manual valve correctly. Insert the solenoid valves con-

nector into the case. Be sure the notched part of the connector is positioned correctly and the wires are not pinched anywhere.

9. Install the different-length bolts and torque all valve body bolts to 7.5–8.5 ft. lbs. (10–11.5 Nm).

10. Install the oil filter and pan with new gasket. Torque the oil pan bolts to 8 ft. lbs. (11 Nm).

11. Lower the vehicle and reconnect the battery. Replenish the transaxle fluid to the correct level, check and adjust the oil pressures if desired.

12. Road test and recheck the fluid level.

AXLE SEALS

1. Raise and support the vehicle safely.

2. Remove the tire and wheel assemblies. Remove the cotter pin, axle nut and washer from the axle end.

3. Remove the locknut from the ball joint and separate the ball joint from the knuckle.

4. Push the strut assembly away from the wheel well and remove the axle from the transaxle using a puller if necessary. Prying with a large pry bar may be needed to separate the axle from the transaxle.

5. For vehicles with left-side center-support bearing, remove the support with the inner shaft still attached. Disconnect the oxygen sensor connector from the support before removing it.

6. Remove the axle shaft from its mounting. Remove the axle seal.

7. Using the special tool, tap the new seal into place.

8. Apply a coating of Dexron®II or petroleum jelly to the rubber lip of the seal.

9. The assembly of the axle shafts is the reverse of the disassembly procedure. Torque the center support bolts to 29–36 ft. lbs. (40–50 Nm). Torque the ball joint nut to 43–52 ft. lbs. (60–72 Nm) and the axle nuts to 144–188 ft. lbs. (200–260 Nm).

10. Replenish the fluid to the correct level, road test and check for leaks. Recheck the fluid level.

REMOVAL AND INSTALLATION

TRANSAXLE REMOVAL

WITHOUT ENGINE

1. Remove the battery and battery tray.

2. Remove the entire air cleaner assembly including the air intake and breather hoses. Disconnect the air flow sensor connector and the purge control solenoid valve connector and hoses.

3. Remove the ACTIVE-ECS (Electronic Control Suspension) air compressor and its mounting bracket, if equipped.

4. Disconnect the manual control cable. Do not remove the cable by loosening the nuts or the adjustment will be lost.

5. Unplug the connectors to the solenoid valves, inhibitor switch, pulse generators, kickdown servo switch, oil temperature sensor and unplug the engine wiring harness.

6. Remove and plug the oil cooler hoses.

7. Remove the speedometer cable.

8. Support the engine and remove the upper engine-to-transaxle bolts. If it is necessary to remove heater hoses to gain access to the upper bolts, drain the radiator first.

9. Remove the outer cover cap in the right fender shield, if equipped. Remove the mount bolts under it.

10. Remove the transaxle mount bracket and the mount.

11. Remove the starter motor. Raise the vehicle and safely support.

12. Remove the left side under cover.

13. Remove both wheels and both axle-end cotter pins, nuts and washers.

14. Disconnect the front height sensor rod (vehicles with ECS only).

15. Remove the ball joint nuts and separate the ball joints from the knuckles.

16. Remove the axles and the center support bearing, if equipped.

NOTE: If desired, the axles may be left attached to the vehicle. Some technicians prefer to have them out of the way. If left attached, be sure to suspend them with a strong rope or wire; if they hang free, the CV-joints or boots could get damaged.

17. Drain the transaxle fluid.

18. Suport the transaxle with a transaxle jack and remove the transaxle center member (KM175) or stay plates (KM177). Remove the torque converter inspection cover.

19. Remove the 3 torque converter bolts. Push the converter away from the engine to separate it from the crankshaft.

20. Remove the remaining transaxle-to-engine bolts.

21. Slide the transaxle assembly to the right and tilt it down to remove it from the vehicle.

TRANSAXLE INSTALLATION

1. Install the torque converter to the transaxle. The converter is correctly installed when the distance from the ring gear to the bell housing surface is 0.47 in. (12mm).

2. Place the transaxle on the transaxle jack securely and install the transaxle to the engine using the dowls as guides. Make sure all heater tube clamps, wires, etc. are out of the way or it will not be possible to install the transaxle flush with the block.

3. Install the lower transaxle-to-engine bolts. Torque the bolts to specification.

4. Apply Loctite® to the threads and install the torque converter bolts. Torque to 25–30 ft. lbs. (35–42 Nm) for 1985–1986 application and 34–38 ft. lbs. (46–53 Nm) for 1987–1989 applications.

5. Install the torque converter inspection plate.

6. Install the transaxle center mount or stay plates. Torque stay-to-engine bolts to 47–61 ft. lbs. (65–85 Nm) and the stay-to-transaxle bolts to 22–30 ft. lbs. (30–42 Nm). Torque the center mount bolts to 15–19 ft. lbs. (20–26 Nm).

7. Install the axles and the center support bearing, if equipped. Apply Loctite® to the threads and torque the center support bolts to 29–36 ft. lbs. (40–50 Nm). Make sure the axle is completely seated in place and all circlips and snaprings are securely in place. Clip the oxygen sensor connector to the support.

8. Install the ball joints to the knuckles and torque the locknuts to 50 ft. lbs. (68 Nm).

9. Install the height sensor (vehicles with ECS only). Torque the bolts to 15 ft. lbs. (20 Nm).

10. If removed, install the axle-end washers, nuts and cotter pins. Torque the nuts to 145–188 ft. lbs. (200–260 Nm).

11. Install the left-side under cover. Lower the vehicle.

12. Install the starter motor. Torque the bolts to specification.

13. Install the transaxle mount and bracket. Torque the bracket-to-transaxle nuts to 43–57 ft. lbs. (60–89 Nm) and the body bolts to 29–36 ft. lbs. (40–50 Nm). Torque the through bolt of the mount itself to 50 ft. lbs. (60 Nm). Install the cover cap in the right fender shield, if equipped and the right side under cover.

14. Install the upper transaxle to engine bolts. Torque bolts on all KM175 applications to 32–40 ft. lbs. (43–55 Nm) and to 47–61 ft. lbs. (65–85 Nm) on the KM177 transaxle. Remove the en-

gine support fixture. Reconnect any heater hoses that were disconnected.

15. Install the speedometer cable.
16. Install the oil cooler hoses.
17. Plug in all connectors that were unplugged in step No. 5 of the removal procedure.
18. Install the manual control cable and secure the cotter pin.
19. Install the ECS air compressor and mount, if equipped.

20. Install the air cleaner assembly and all items removed in step No. 2 of the removal procedure.
21. Install the battery tray and the battery.
22. Pour about 5 qts. of Dexron®II into the transaxle and run the vehicle through all the gears while still on the lift. Add fluid as needed to the correct level. Check to see that the reverse lights come on in **R** range and that the inhibitor switch is working. Road test the vehicle, check for leaks and recheck the fluid level.

BENCH OVERHAUL

Before Disassembly

Cleanliness is an important factor in the overhaul of the this automatic transaxle. Before opening up this unit, the entire outside of the transaxle assembly should be cleaned, preferable with a high pressure washer such as a car wash spray unit. Dirt entering the transaxle internal parts will negate all the time and effort spent on the overhaul. During inspection and reassembly all parts should be thoroughly cleaned with solvent then dried with compressed air. Wiping cloths and rags should not be used to dry parts since lint will find its way into the valve body passages.

Wheel bearing grease, long used to hold thrust washers and lube parts, should not be used. Lube seals with clean transaxle fluid and use ordinary unmedicated petroleum jelly to hold the thrust washers and to ease the assembly of seals, since it will not leave a harmful residue as grease often will. Do not use solvent on neoprene seals, friction plates if they are to be reused, or thrust washers. Be wary of nylon parts if the transaxle failure was due to failure of the cooling system. Nylon parts exposed to water or antifreeze solutions can swell and distort and must be replaced.

Before installing bolts into aluminum parts, always dip the threads into clean transaxle fluid. Antiseize compound can also be used to prevent bolts from galling the aluminum and seizing. Always use a torque wrench to keep from stripping the threads. Take care when installing new O-rings, especially the smaller O-rings. The internal snaprings should be expanded and the external rings should be compressed, if they are to be reused. This will help insure proper seating when installed.

Converter Inspection

Although the torque converter is a welded unit and cannot be disassembled for inspection, some visible items can be checked.

The converter should be replaced if any cracks or external damage of any sort are found. If any rust is found on the pilot or boss unit, it must be removed completely. If the hub has a deep score where the seal has been rubbing, replace the converter or a leak could result.

Position the converter horizontally on the bench and inspect the stator roller clutch. The inner race should turn freely one way, but should offer considerable resistance when turned the other direction.

Transaxle Disassembly

1. Place the transaxle on the bench right side up.
2. Remove the torque converter.
3. Measuring input shaft endplay and transfer shaft endplay before disassembly will usually indicate when a thrust washer change is required, except when major parts are replaced.
   a. Mount a dial indicator to the bell housing so the pin rests on the input shaft. Measure the endplay by pulling out and pushing in the input shaft with pliers. Record the reading for reference when reassembling. The specification is:
   1985–87 – 0.020–0.055 in. (0.5–1.4mm) 1988–89 – 0.012–0.040 in. (0.3–1.0mm)
   b. Remove the transfer shaft cover and measure the transfer shaft endplay. Mount a dial indicator to the case so the plunger rests on the transfer shaft. Obtain the endplay by pulling out and pushing in the transfer shaft with pliers. Record the reading for reference when reassembling. The specification is:
   0.006–0.008 in. (0.15–0.20mm) if equipped with a snapring.
   0–0.001 in. (0–0.025mm) if equipped with a locknut.
4. Remove the pulse generators.
5. Remove the manual control lever and the inhibitor switch.
6. Remove the kickdown servo switch retaining snapring and the kickdown servo switch.
7. Place the transaxle on a suitable holding fixture.
8. Remove the oil pan and gasket. Remove the filter from the valve body.
9. Remove the oil temperature sensor, if equipped.
10. Remove the solenoid valves connector clip, push the catches in and remove the solenoid valves connector.
11. Disconnect the throttle control cable from the cam on the valve body, if equipped. Remove 10 bolts and remove the valve body.
12. Remove the end clutch cover.
13. Remove the end clutch assembly.
14. Remove the end clutch thrust washer.
15. Remove the end clutch hub and thrust washer.
16. Pull out the end clutch shaft.
17. Remove 13 bolts and remove the converter housing.
18. Remove 6 bolts from the oil pump. Attach the special tools and remove the oil pump assembly, then the adaptor and gasket.
19. Remove the spacer and the differential assembly.
20. Remove the fiber thrust washer from the top of the front clutch retainer.
21. Remove the input shaft, front clutch assembly and rear clutch assembly together.
22. Remove the thrust bearing from on top of the clutch hub.
23. Remove the clutch hub.

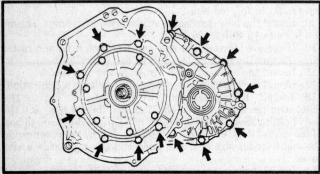

Remove these bolts to separate the converter housing from the case

24. Remove the thrust race and bearing from inside the kickdown drum.

25. Remove the kickdown drum.

26. Remove the kickdown band.

27. Using the valve spring compressor and the special tool, push in the kickdown servo and remove the snapring.

28. Remove the kickdown servo piston and return spring.

29. Remove the anchor rod.

30. Remove the 2 center support bolts, if equipped. Remove the center support retaining snapring, if equipped.

31. Attach the special tool to the center support and pull the center support straight out of the transaxle case.

32. Remove the reverse sun gear and the forward sun gear together.

33. Remove the planet carrier assembly and thrust bearing.

34. Remove the wave spring, return spring, reaction plate, brake disc and brake plate from the case unless these parts come out with the center support as an assembly. If the discs and plates are being reused, do not change the installation order or direction.

35. Remove the 4 screws around the transfer gear bearing. Screw lock paste is applied to these screws from the factory and an impact driver may be needed to remove them. Remove the oil pipe, if equipped.

36. Remove the transfer shaft rear end snapring, if equipped. Install the transfer shaft locknut rotation stopper if equipped with a locknut. Clamp the converter housing side of the transfer shaft in a vise so it will not turn. Remove the left-hand threaded transfer shaft locknut, if equipped.

37. Knock the transfer shaft out to the converter housing side.

38. Pull the bearing from the transfer shaft.

39. Pull the bearing from the transfer driven gear.

40. Remove the 2 bearing outer races.

41. Remove the idler shaft lock plate.

42. Use the special tool to loosen the idler shaft.

43. Pull out the idler shaft. Remove the 2 transfer idler gear bearing inner races and the spacer from inside of the case.

44. Remove the snapring from the transfer gear bearing.

45. Remove the internal gear, output flange, transfer drive gear and bearing as an assembly from the case.

46. Remove the parking sprag rod with retaining plate.

47. Remove the set screw and the manual control shaft assembly. Remove the steel ball, the seat and the spring together.

Unit Disassembly and Assembly

OIL PUMP

Disassembly

1. Remove the O-ring from the oil pump housing.

2. Remove 5 bolts and remove the reaction shaft support from the housing.

3. Remove the steel ball from the housing.

4. Matchmark the drive and driven gears and remove the gears from the pump housing.

5. Remove the seal rings from the reaction shaft support.

Inspection

1. Visually inspect the entire assembly for any type of excessive scoring, damage or wear. Pay close attention to the inner and outer gear tooth surfaces.

2. Inspect the seal ring grooves for wear or burrs.

3. Measure the side clearance of the oil pump gear using a flat edge and feeler gauge. The clearance specification is 0.001–0.002 in. (0.03–0.05mm). Replace any part that is damaged or excessively worn.

Assembly

1. Immerse the gears in fresh Dexron®II and install them in

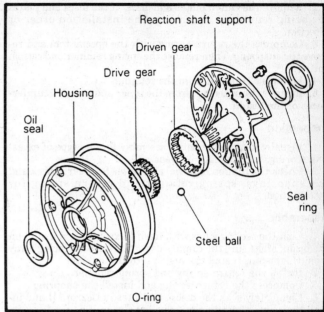

Exploded view of the oil pump assembly

the pump housing with the mating marks properly aligned.

2. Install the new O-ring into the groove at the inner circumference of the drive gear.

3. Install the steel ball in its bore.

4. Coat the seal rings with Dexron®II and install them to the reaction shaft.

5. Install the new O-ring to the groove on the outer circumference of the pump housing and coat it with Dexron®II or petroleum jelly.

6. Install the reaction shaft support to the pump housing and tighten the bolts hand tight.

7. Place the assembly in the special holding tool and torque the bolts to 7.5–8.5 ft. lbs. (10–12 Nm).

8. Remove the pump housing oil seal and use the special tool to install a new seal.

FRONT CLUTCH ASSEMBLY

Disassembly

1. Remove the snapring from the clutch retainer.

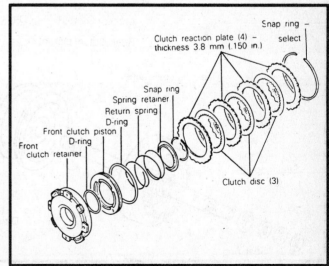

Exploded view of the front clutch assembly

2. Remove the clutch plates and discs. If the discs and plates are being reused, do not change the installation order or direction.

3. Compress the return spring with the special tool and remove the snap ring. Then remove the spring retainer and return spring.

4. Remove the piston from the retainer.

5. Remove the seal rings from the inner and outer circumferences of the piston.

Inspection

1. Visually inspect the entire assembly for any type of excessive scoring, heat damage or wear.

2. Check the friction material and plates for wear. Check and the snaprings, spring retainer and return spring for deformation.

Assembly

1. Coat the sealing rings with fresh Dexron®II and install on the pison. Make sure the round sides of the seals are facing away from the piston. Install the piston into the retainer.

2. Install the return spring and spring retainer.

3. Compress the return spring and install the snapring.

4. Completely soak the discs and plates in Dexron®II and install them into the retainer. Install the snapring.

5. Check the clearance between the snapring and the top clutch plate. Push down on the top plate with 11 lbs. of force to obtain an accurate clearance reading. The clearance specification is:

1985–87 – 0.024–0.031 in. (0.6–0.8mm)
1988–89 – 0.028–0.035 in. (0.7–0.9mm)

Adjust the clearance by selecting the proper snapring. Selective snaprings are available in 0.008 in. (0.2mm) increment sizes from 0.063–0.118 in. (1.6–3.0mm) thick.

REAR CLUTCH ASSEMBLY

Disassembly

1. Remove the snapring and the thrust race.

2. Remove the input shaft from the rear clutch retainer.

3. Remove the clutch reaction plate, clutch plates, clutch

discs and pressure plate from the retainer. If the discs and plates are being reused, do not change the installation order or direction.

4. Compress the return spring using the special tool and remove the snapring.

5. Remove the return spring and the piston.

6. Remove the sealing rings from the piston.

Inspection

1. Visually inspect the entire assembly for any type of excessive scoring, heat damage or wear.

2. Check the friction material and plates for wear. Check and the snaprings and return spring for deformation.

3. Inspect the input shaft for damage. Inspect the splines and seal grooves for burrs or damage.

Assembly

1. Coat the sealing rings with fresh Dexron®II and install them to the piston. Make sure the round sides of the rings face away from the piston. Install the piston into the retainer.

2. Install the return spring on the piston.

3. Compress the return spring with the snapring by pushing down with a suitable tool and setting the snapring in its groove.

4. Completely soak the pressure plate, discs, plates and reaction plate in Dexron®II and install to the rear clutch retainer. Install the snapring.

5. Check the clearance between the snapring and the clutch reaction plate. Push down on the plate with 11 lbs. of force to obtain an accurate clearance reading. The clearance specification is 0.016–0.024 in. (0.4–0.6mm). Adjust the clearance by selecting the proper snapring. The snaprings are the same as those used with the front clutch.

6. Install the input shaft to the retainer.

7. Install the thrust race and the snapring.

8. Install the 3 seal rings to the grooves in the input shaft.

END CLUTCH ASSEMBLY

Disassembly

1. Remove the snapring, then remove the reaction plate,

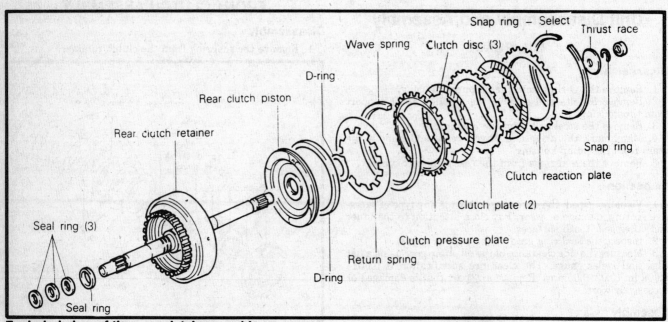

Exploded view of the rear clutch assembly

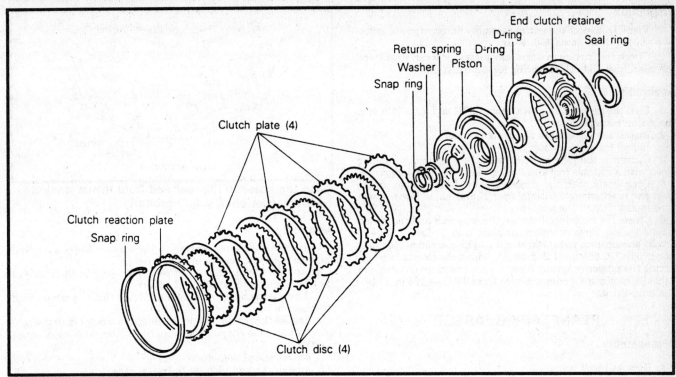

Exploded view of the end clutch assembly

clutch discs and plates. If the discs and plates are being reused, do not change the installation order or direction.

2. Remove the snapring and remove the washer and return spring.

3. Remove the piston. If it is difficult to remove, place the retainer on the bench piston side down and blow low pressure compressed air through the oil hole on the back side of the retainer.

4. Remove the seal rings from the retainer and the piston.

Inspection

1. Visually inspect the entire assembly for any type of excessive scoring, heat damage or wear.

2. Check the friction material and plates for wear. Check and the snaprings and return spring for deformation.

Assembly

1. Coat the new seal rings with Dexron®II and install them to the piston. Install the oil seal to the piston.

2. Install the piston to the end clutch retainer.

3. Install the return spring and washer.

4. Install a new snapring into the guide of the special snapring installer and install the retainer. Fit the snapring as far down on the guide as possible. Attach the installer and press until the snapring enters the groove.

5. Completely soak the clutch plates, discs and reaction with Dexron®II and install in the end clutch retainer. Install the snapring.

6. Check the clearance between the snapring and the clutch reaction plate. Push down on the plate with 11 lbs. of force to obtain an accurate clearance reading. The clearance specification is:

   1985–87–0.016–0.026 in. (0.4–0.65mm) 1988–89–0.024–0.033 in. (0.6–0.85mm)

Adjust the clearance by selecting the proper snapring. Selective snaprings are available in 0.01 in. (0.25mm) increment sizes from 0.04–0.08 in. (1.05–2.05mm) thick.

LOW/REVERSE BRAKE ASSEMBLY

Disassembly

1. Remove the snapring from the center support.

2. Remove the reaction plate, brake discs, plates and pressure plate. If the discs and plates are being reused, do not change the installation order or direction.

3. Compress the return spring and remove the snapring.

4. Remove the return spring and wave spring.

5. Remove the piston. If it is difficult to remove place the center support on the bench with the piston facing down and blow low pressure compressed air through the oil hole to remove.

6. Remove the seal ring from the piston.

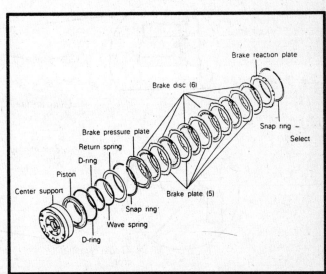

Exploded view of the low/reverse brake assembly

Inspection

1. Visually inspect the entire assembly for any type of excessive scoring, heat damage or wear.
2. Check the friction material and plates for wear. Check and the snaprings and return spring for deformation.

Assembly

1. Coat the new seal rings with Dexron®II and install them to the piston round side out.
2. Install the piston into the center support.
3. Install the wave spring and return spring.
4. Compress the return spring with the snapring by pushing down with a suitable tool and setting the snapring in its groove.
5. Completely soak the pressure plate, brake plates, brake discs and reaction plate with Dexron®II and install into the center support. Install the snapring.
6. Check the clearance between the snapring and the clutch reaction plate. Push down on the plate with 11 lbs. of force to obtain an accurate clearance reading. The clearance specification is 0.047–0.055 in. (1.2–1.4mm). Adjust the clearance by selecting the proper snapring. Selective snaprings are available in 0.008 in. (0.20mm) increment sizes from 0.071–0.126 in. (1.80–3.20mm) thick.

PLANETARY GEARSET

Disassembly

1. Remove the 3 bolts.
2. Remove the overrunning clutch outer race assembly and the overrunning clutch end plate.
3. Remove any 1 of the short pinion shafts.
4. Remove the spacer bushing and 2 front thrust washers.
5. Remove only 1 short pinion. Do not drop the pinion or the 17 rollers could get lost.
6. Remove the thrust bearing.
7. Push the overrunning clutch out of the outer race.

Inspection

1. Inspect the planetary carrier carefully. Turn each pinion to see if it spins freely and smoothly.
2. Check the enire assembly for damage, wear and heat spots.

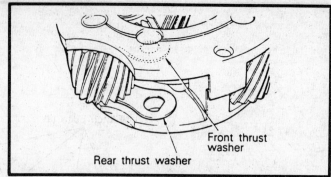

Align the holes in the rear and front thrust washers so the carrier shaft will fit properly

Assembly

1. Install the thrust bearing to the carrier. Make sure that the bearing fits correctly in the carrier.
2. Apply a liberal amount of petroleum jelly to the inside of the short pinion to hold the 17 rollers.
3. Line up the holes in the rear and front thrust washers with the shaft holes.
4. Install the pinion, spacer bushing and 2 front thrust washers and align the holes. Make sure the rollers do not get out of position.
5. Insert the pinion shaft.
6. Install the end plate to the outer race.

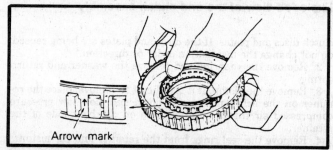

Installing the overrunning clutch

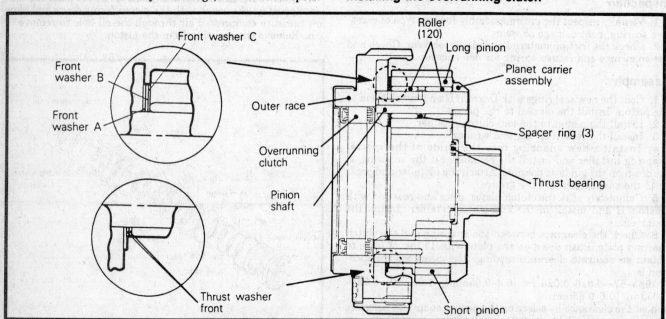

Exploded view of the planetary gearset assembly

7. Push the overrunning clutch onto the outer race. Make sure the arrow on the outside circumference of the cage is directed up when the overrunning clutch is installed.

8. Apply petroleum jelly to the overrunning clutch end plate and install to the clutch.

9. Install the assembly to the carrier and align the bolt holes.

10. Install the 3 bolts and torque to specification.
   1985 models – 6–7 ft. lbs. (8–9.5 Nm)
   1986–87 models – 9–10 ft. lbs. (12–13.5 Nm)
   1988–89 models – 18–25 ft. lbs. (25–35 Nm)

11. Bend new lock plates exactly along bolt heads, if equipped. Do not reuse lock plates.

12. Check the operation of the overrunning clutch. It should turn in one direction and lock up in the other direction.

INTERNAL GEAR AND TRANSFER DRIVE GEAR SET

Disassembly

1. Remove the snapring from the end of the output flange.
2. Using the special puller, pull off the top ball bearing, the transfer drive gear and the other ball bearing from the output flange.
3. Remove the snapring and remove the internal gear from the output flange.

Inspection

1. Check all splines and gears for cracks, wear or damage.
2. Check the ball bearings for smooth rotation and heat damage.
3. Check the snaprings and grooves for deformation

Assembly

NOTE: The output flange and the transfer drive gear should be replaced as a set only.

1. Press the first ball bearing and the transfer drive gear onto the output flange. The groove in the side surface of the transfer drive gear should face up when properly installed.
2. Press the top ball bearing onto the output flange.
3. Install the assembly in the internal gear and secure the snapring.
4. Select the thickest snapring that can fit in the groove in the top of the output flange.

DIFFERENTIAL ASSEMBLY

Disassembly

1. Remove the ring gear from the differential case.
2. If reusing parts, note their locations before removing. Pull off the side bearings with the special puller.
3. Measure the backlash between the side gears and the pinion gears. Record for reference when assembling.
4. Drive out the lock pin.
5. Remove the pinion shaft, gears and spacers.
6. Remove the side gears and spacers.

Inspection

1. Check all gears for cracks, heat damage or abnormal wear patterns.
2. Check the bearings for smooth rotation.
3. Make sure the pinion shaft fits snug in the case.

Assembly

1. Install the side gears with chosen spacers in the differential case. If reusing parts, install them in the same positions as before disassembly. If using new gears, install a spacer of medium thickness.

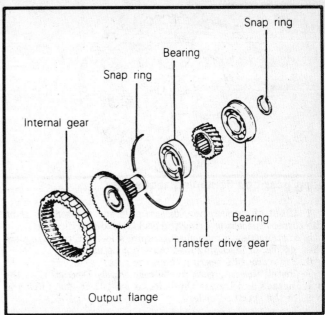

Exploded view of the internal gear and transfer drive gearset

2. Install the pinion gears with washers in the case and install the pinion shaft.

3. Measure the backlash between the side gears and the pinion gears. The right and left hand gear pairs should have the identical reading. The backlash specification is:
   1985–87 – 0–0.0030 in. (0–0.076mm)
   1988–89 – 0.0010–0.0059 in. (0.025–0.150mm).

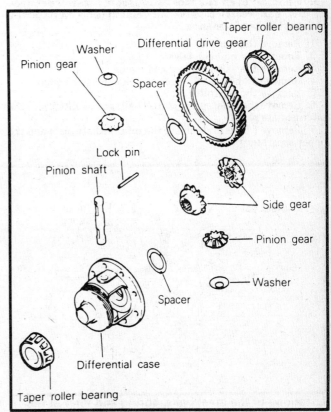

Exploded view of the differential assembly

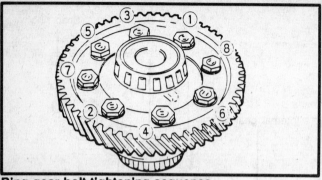

Ring gear bolt tightening sequence

4. If out of specification, disassemble and reassembly using the correct spacers to bring the backlash to specification.

5. Install a new pinion shaft lockpin. A lock pin requiring less than 44 lbs. of installing load must not be used.

6. Press the side bearings onto the case.

7. Install the ring gear to the case. Apply Dexron®II to the bolt threads and torque the bolts to 94–101 ft. lbs. (130–140 Nm) in the specified order.

VALVE BODY

Disassembly

NOTE: **The valve body is a precisely machined part used in the automatic transaxle. Handle it with care and do not clamp in a vise. The material is fragile and could distort easily. Keep all parts labeled and in a well-arranged order, since many of them look similar. Cleanliness is of the utmost importance when working with valve bodies; even the most minuscule scratch or piece of dirt can restrict valve movement and impair the transaxle's performance.**

1. Remove the solenoid valves
2. Remove the manual valve.
3. Remove the valve stopper and clamp.
4. Remove 13 bolts and remove the lower valve body.
5. Remove the separator plate.
6. Remove the relief spring, 2 steel balls and oil filter from the intermediate plate.
7. Remove 8 bolts and remove the intermediate plate and the upper separator plate.

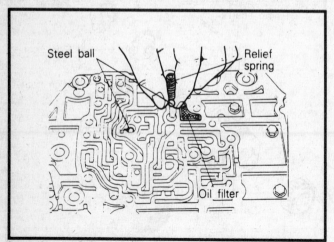

Locations of the steel balls, spring and filter in the intermediate plate

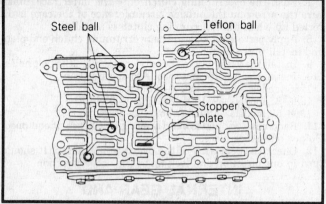

Locations of the 4 check balls in the upper valve body

8. Remove the block.
9. Remove the upper separator plate.
10. Remove 4 steel balls and 2 stopper plates from the upper body. (1989 transaxles have 3 steel balls and 1 teflon ball).
11. Remove the front end cover and the adjustment screw from the upper body. When removing the bolts, hold the front cover against the body to prevent the adjustment screw from popping out.
12. Remove the pressure control spring and valve.
13. Remove the torque converter control spring and valve.
14. Remove the regulator spring and valve.
15. Remove the shift control spring and shift control plug A.
16. Remove the rear clutch exhaust valves A and B and the rear clutch exhaust spring.
17. Remove the 2 – 3/4 – 3 shift spring and valve.
18. Remove the neutral – drive control sleeve and valve from the rear of the upper body.
19. Remove the rear end cover.
20. Remove the 1 – 2 shift spring and valve.
21. Remove the shift control plug B.
22. Remove the shift control valve.
23. Using a magnet, extract the pin from the lower valve body and remove the stopper.
24. Remove the end clutch valve plug, spring and the valve itself.
25. Remove the lower body end cover, the adjustment screw and the reducing spring.
26. Remove the reducing valve.
27. Remove the neutral/reverse control-accumulator valve and spring.
28. Remove the damper clutch control sleeve, valve and spring on all except KM177 transaxle.

Inspection

1. Check the bodies for damage, wear, and cracks.
2. Check the valves and their bores for damage and burrs. Slight burrs may be sanded out with crocus cloth.
3. Check for oil passage damage and restrictions.
4. Check for spring fatigue.

Assembly

NOTE: **Torque all valve body end plate bolts to 3–4 ft. lbs. (4–6 Nm).**

1. Install the damper clutch control spring, valve and sleeve (except KM177) in the lower valve body.
2. Install the neutral/reverse control-accumulator spring and valve.
3. Install the reducing valve.

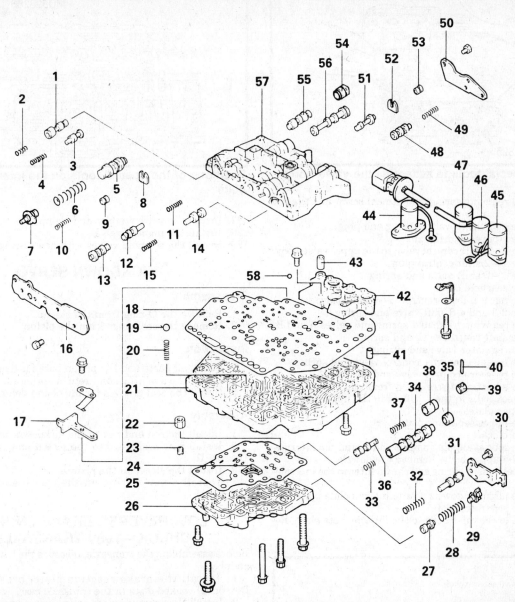

1. Pressure control valve
2. Pressure control spring
3. Torque converter control valve
4. Torque converter control spring
5. Regulator valve
6. Regulator spring
7. Adjusting screw
8. Stopper plate
9. Shift control plug
10. Shift control spring
11. Rear clutch exhaust spring
12. Rear clutch exhaust valve B
13. Rear clutch exhaust valve A
14. 2nd-3rd/4th-3rd shift valve
15. 2nd-3rd/4th-3rd shift spring
16. Front end cover
17. Valve stopper
18. Upper separating plate
19. Steel ball
20. Relief spring
21. Intermediate plate
22. Nut
23. Jet
24. Filter
25. Lower separating plate
26. Lower valve body
27. Reducing valve
28. Reducing spring
29. Adjusting screw
30. End cover
31. Neutral-reverse control/accumulator valve
32. Neutral-reverse control/accumulator spring
33. Damper clutch control spring
34. Damper clutch control valve
35. Damper clutch control sleeve
36. End clutch valve
37. End clutch spring
38. End clutch plug
39. Stopper
40. Pin
41. Dowel bushing
42. Block
43. Pipe
44. Pressure control solenoid valve (PCSV)
45. Shift control solenoid valve B (SCSV-B)
46. Shift control solenoid valve A (SCSV-A)
47. Damper clutch control solenoid valve (DCCSV)
48. 1-2 shift valve
49. 1-2 shift spring
50. Rear end cover
51. Shift control valve
52. Stopper plate
53. Shift control plug B
54. Neutral-drive control sleeve
55. Neutral-drive control valve
56. Manual valve
57. Upper valve body
58. Check ball

Exploded view of the valve body assembly

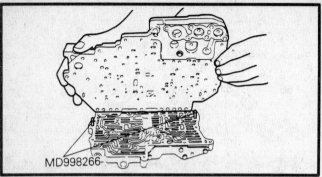

Using the special tools to assemble the valve body

4. Install the reducing spring, adjustment screw and the end cover.
5. Install the end clutch valve, spring and plug.
6. Install the stopper and the pin.
7. Install the 1–2 shift control valve to the upper valve body.
8. Install the 1–2 shift control plug.
9. Install the 1–2 shift valve and spring.
10. Install the rear end cover.
11. Install the neutral-drive control valve and sleeve.
12. Install the 2-3 and 4-3 shift valve and spring.
13. Install the rear clutch exhaust spring and valves A and B.
14. Install the shift control valve and spring.
15. Install the regulator valve and spring.
16. Install the torque converter control valve and spring.
17. Install the pressure control valve and spring.
18. Install the adjustment screw and front end cover.
19. Place 4 check balls in their orifices in the upper body. Install the 2 stopper plates.
20. Install the upper separator plate.
21. Install the block.
22. Install the special aligning dowels and install the intermediate plate to the upper body. Remove the dowels.
23. Place 2 steel balls, 1 spring and the oil filter in the intermediate plate.
24. Install the aligning dowels on the intermediate plate.
25. Install the separator plate.
26. Install the lower valve body to the intermediate plate. Remove the dowels.

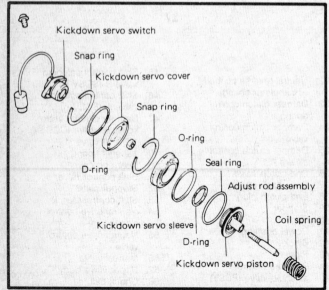

Exploded view of the kickdown servo assembly

Kickdown servo switch
Snap ring
Kickdown servo cover
Snap ring
O-ring
D-ring
Seal ring
Adjust rod assembly
Kickdown servo sleeve
Coil spring
D-ring
Kickdown servo piston

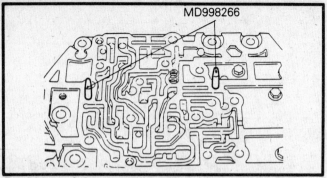

Positions of the special tools on the intermediate plate

27. Install the valve stopper and clamp.
28. Install the manual valve.
29. Install the solenoid valves with new O-rings.

KICKDOWN SERVO

Disassembly

1. Remove the O-ring from the sleeve.
2. Remove the seal rings from the piston.

Inspection

1. Check all parts and the piston bore for damage or wear.
2. Check the snaprings and return spring for deformation.
3. Check the seal grooves for burrs and deformation.

Assembly

1. Install the rod and nut to the kickdown servo piston.
2. Install new seal rings to the piston and coat them with Dexron®II.
3. Install the sleeve to the piston.
4. Install a new O-ring on the sleeve and coat it with Dexron®II.

LOW/REVERSE BRAKE ENDPLAY CHECK – 1989 TRANSAXLES

Before assembling the transaxle, measure the low/reverse brake endplay.

1. Install the brake reaction plate, brake plates and Dexron®II soaked discs in the transaxle case.
2. Install the pressure plate and return spring.
3. Coat the wave spring with petroleum jelly and attach it to the center support.
4. Install the center support using the special tool. Install the snapring.
5. Install a dial indicator so the pin contacts the brake reaction plate through the transfer idler shaft hole.
6. Blow low pressure compressed air through the oil hole and record the dial indicator reading. The clearance specification is 0.04–0.06 in. (1.13–1.44mm). Selective pressure plates are available for adjusting low/reverse brake clearance.
7. Remove the low/reverse brake assembly.

Transaxle Assembly

1. Install the internal gear and output flange assembly with 2 ball bearings and transfer drive gear attached in the transaxle case.
2. Install the snapring on the output flange rear bearing.
3. Coat the transfer idler gear spacer with petroleum jelly and install to the case.

4. Install 2 taper roller bearings to the transfer idler gear.
5. Place the transfer idler gear (grooved side out) into the case. Insert the idler gear shaft from the outer side of the case through the gear and screw it in.
6. Tighten the idler shaft with the special tool.
7. Measure the output flange preload with the special tool and a low-scale torque wrench. The preload specification is 1 ft. lbs. (1.5 Nm). Adjust by tightening or loosening the idler shaft. Install a new O-ring on the idler shaft.
8. After completing the preload adjustment, install the idler shaft lock plate.
9. Eliminate the play between the shaft and the lock plate by loosening the shaft until it contacts the plate. Torque the lock plate bolt to 15–19 ft. lbs. (20–26 Nm) on 1985–87 models. Torque the bolt to 35–43 ft. lbs. (48–60 Nm) on 1988–89 models.
10. Install new O-rings on the oil pipe, if equipped and install in the case.
11. Install a new O-ring into the output flange groove in the rear of the transaxle case.
12. Install the bearing retainer and torque the screws to 13–15 ft. lbs. (17–21 Nm). Apply a 0.2 in. width of sealant (3M Stud Locking No.4176 or similar) to the top of the screws. The sealant should not stick out the top of the screw head. Stake the edges of the screws.
13. Install a new O-ring for the retainer edge.
14. Press the taper roller bearing onto the transfer driven gear and press the outer race onto the transaxle case—end clutch side.
15. Install the transfer shaft assembly to the case.
16. Install the special tool to the case to support the transfer shaft.
17. Install the taper roller bearing to the transfer shaft.
18. Install the outer race to the transaxle case—converter housing side and install the snapring, if equipped.
19. Insert the transfer driven gear spacer. Install the transfer driven gear with the special tool.
20. Measure the endplay of the transfer shaft. The specification is 0–0.001 in. (0–0.025mm), if equipped with a locknut. If equipped with a snapring, the specification is 0.006–0.008 in. (0.15–0.020mm). If necessary, disassemble and install the proper spacer(s) that will bring the endplay to specification. Spacers are available in 0.0012 in. (0.03mm) increment sizes from 0.0472–0.0710 in. (1.20–1.80mm) thick.
21. Install the snapring to the end of the transfer shaft, if equipped. If equipped with a locknut, clamp the converter housing side of the transfer shaft in a vise. Tighten the locknut to 145–166 ft. lbs. (200–230 Nm). Lock the locknut in place using a punch when completed. Install the transfer shaft cover and holder.
22. Install the thrust bearing and race, if equipped and install the planetary carrier assembly on the output flange.

23. Assemble the reverse sun gear and the forward sun gear.
 a. Install the seal ring and the snapring to the reverse sun gear.
 b. Install the thrust race and bearing to the forward sun gear
 c. Assemble the reverse sun gear with snapring and the forward sun gear.
24. Install the sun gear assembly in the planetary carrier.
25. Install the low/reverse brake clutch assembly in the case with the selected pressure plate and install the center support with wave spring. If the low/reverse brake clutches have already been assembled in the center support install the assembly in the case. Make sure to install 2 new O-rings on the pressure plug ports of the center support assembly.
26. Install the snapring if equipped. Install the snapring so that no portion of it is covering the hole for pulse generator A. If the center support is held by bolts, torque them as follows:
 a. Press on the center support firmly and tighten bolt A to 2 ft. lbs. (4 Nm). Back off 1½ turns.
 b. Torque bolt B to 15–20 ft. lbs. (20–27 Nm).
 c. Torque bolt A to 15–20 ft. lbs. (20–27 Nm).

NOTE: For proper alignment of the low/reverse apply port, be sure to tighten bolt A (closest to the transfer idler gear) first.

27. Install the kickdown band anchor rod.
28. Install the servo spring, piston and sleeve with all new O-rings in the case.
29. Press in the servo and spring using the special tools and install the snapring. Install the servo cover, switch and snapring.
30. Install the kickdown band; attach the ends of the band to the anchor rod and the servo piston rod.
31. Install the kickdown drum with its splines in mesh with the sun gear. Place the kickdown band on the drum and tighten the servo adjusting screw enough to keep the band in place.
32. Install the thrust bearing if equipped on the kickdown drum.
33. Install the clutch hub on the sun gear splines.
34. Install the thrust bearing on the clutch hub.
35. Install the rear clutch assembly

INPUT SHAFT THRUST WASHERS

Thickness of metal thrust washer [1] in. (mm)	Thickness of fiber thrust washer [1] in. (mm)
0.031 (0.8)	0.071 (1.8)
0.047 (1.2)	0.087 (2.2)
0.055 (1.4)	0.039 (1.0)
0.055 (1.4)	0.047 (1.2)
0.063 (1.6)	0.102 (2.6)
0.071 (1.8)	0.039 (1.0)
0.071 (1.8)	0.047 (1.2)
0.079 (2.0)	0.118 (3.0)
0.087 (2.2)	0.055 (1.4)
0.087 (2.2)	0.063 (1.6)
0.102 (2.6)	0.071 (1.8)
0.102 (2.6)	0.079 (2.0)
0.118 (3.0)	0.087 (2.2)
0.118 (3.0)	0.095 (2.4)

[1] Input shaft thrust washers must be used in paired sets.

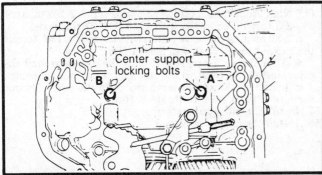
Tighten bolt A first for proper alignment of the low/reverse apply port

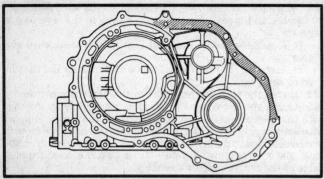

Apply silicone sealer to the hatched area of the case before installing the converter housing

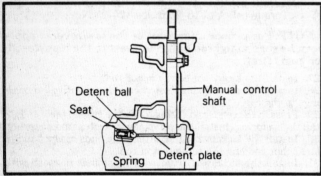

Assembly of the manual control shaft assembly

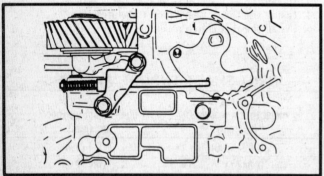

Proper installation of the park sprag rod support

36. Install the fiber thrust washer, the thrust bearing and the metal thrust race to the rear clutch retainer. If the input shaft endplay was not at specification at disassembly, install a metal thrust race that will bring the endplay to specification. If the metal thrust race is changed, the fiber thrust race between the oil pump and the front clutch must be replaced with one that will correspond to the thickness of the metal race.
37. Install the front clutch assembly.
38. Install the fiber washer on the front clutch assembly.
39. Install the differential assembly.

40. Install the special pump alignment pin to the case. Install a new adapter gasket and the adapter, if equipped, a new pump gasket and the pump assembly.
41. Install a new O-ring to the groove in pump housing and coat the outer surface of the ring with Dexron®II. Torque the oil pump bolts to 11–15 ft. lbs. (15–21 Nm) evenly. Remove the special tools.
42. Check input shaft endplay and readjust if necessary. The specification is 0.020–0.055 in. (0.5–1.4mm) for 1985–87. The specification is 0.012–0.039 in. (0.3–1.0mm) for 1988–89.
43. Measure the differential endplay before installing the converter housing. The specification is 0.0031–0.0051 in. (0.08–0.13mm). To adjust replace the taper roller bearing outer race spacer in the converter housing with one that will bring the endplay to specification.
44. Apply silicone sealer to the hatched area of the transaxle case flange and install a new gasket. Install the converter housing and torque the bolts to 14–16 ft. lbs. (19–22 Nm). Replace the axle seals in the transaxle case and converter housing. Install the inhibitor switch.
45. Install the end clutch shaft. Install the end with the longer splines first.
46. Install the end clutch hub thrust washer groove side out to the case. If the end clutch hub uses athrust bearing, install it to the hub. Install the end clutch hub.
47. Install the thrust washer to the return spring at the end clutch side.
48. Install the end clutch assembly.
49. Install the end clutch cover with new seal rings. Torque the bolts to 5 ft. lbs. (7 Nm).
50. Insert the manual control shaft into the case and push it fully towards the manual control shaft. At this time do not install the larger of the 2 O-rings on the shaft because it will interface with the set screw hole.
51. After install a new O-ring on the manual shaft, draw the shaft back into the case and install the set screw and gasket. Install the detent steel ball, seat and spring at the same time.
52. Install parking sprag rod to the detent plate of the manual control shaft. Install the sprag rod support and torque the bolts to 17 ft. lbs. (23 Nm).
53. Install a new O-ring to the brake oil pressure passage at the top center of the valve body. Replace the solenoid valves connector O-ring and insert the connector in the case.
54. Install the valve body assembly to the case. Install the oil temperature sensor, if equipped. Torque all valve body mounting bolts to 7.5–8.5 ft. lbs. (10–11.5 Nm). Install the oil filter and torque the bolts to 5 ft. lbs. (6.6 Nm).
55. Install the magnet in the pan, if equipped and install the pan and new gasket. Torque the bolts to 8 ft. lbs. (11 Nm).
56. Adjust the kickdown servo.
   a. Loosen the locknut.
   b. While holding with the special tool (which prevents the kickdown servo piston from turning), use the tightening tool to tighten to 7.2 ft. lbs. (9.8 Nm). Then loosen the adjusting screw two turns and torque the adjusting screw to 3.6 ft. lbs. (4.9 Nm). Finally, back off the adjusting screw 2–2¼ turns or 2½–2¾ turns if equipped with 1989 KM177 transaxle.
   c. Still holding the servo piston with the special tool, torque the locknut to 18–23 ft. lbs. (25–31 Nm).
   d. After fitting a new seal ring in the groove around the cover, install the cover to the case and install the snapring.
   e. Install the kickdown servo switch to the cover. Torque the screws to (0.7–1.0 ft. lbs. (1–4 Nm).
57. Install the pulse generators.
58. Install the torque converter.

SPECIFICATIONS

FRONT AND REAR CLUTCH SNAPRING SPECIFICATIONS

Part Number	Color	in.	mm
MD955630	None	0.063	1.6
MD955631	Blue	0.071	1.8
MD955632	Brown	0.079	2.0
MD955633	None	0.087	2.2
MD955634	Blue	0.095	2.4
MD955635	Brown	0.102	2.6
MD955636	None	0.110	2.8
MD955637	Blue	0.118	3.0

END CLUTCH SNAPRING SPECIFICATIONS

Part Number	Color	in.	mm
MD715800	White	0.04	1.05
MD715801	Yellow	0.05	1.30
MD715802	None	0.06	1.55
MD715803	Green	0.07	1.80
MD720849	Pink	0.08	2.05

TRANSFER SHAFT SPACER SPECIFICATIONS

Part Number	Identification Mark	in.	mm
MD723160	20	0.0472	1.20
MD723161	23	0.0484	1.23
MD723162	26	0.0496	1.26
MD723163	29	0.0508	1.29
MD723164	32	0.0520	1.32
MD723165	35	0.0531	1.35
MD723166	38	0.0543	1.38
MD723167	41	0.0555	1.41
MD723168	44	0.0567	1.44
MD723169	47	0.0579	1.47
MD723170	50	0.0591	1.50
MD723171	53	0.0602	1.53
MD723172	56	0.0614	1.56
MD723173	59	0.0626	1.59
MD723174	62	0.0638	1.62
MD723175	65	0.0650	1.65
MD723176	68	0.0661	1.68
MD723177	71	0.0673	1.71
MD723178	74	0.0685	1.74
MD723179	77	0.0697	1.77
MD723180	80	0.0709	1.80

LOW/REVERSE BRAKE SNAPRING SPECIFICATIONS

Part Number	Color	in.	mm
MD707413	Blue	0.071	1.8
MD707406	Brown	0.079	2.0
MD707407	None	0.087	2.2
MD707408	Blue	0.094	2.4
MD707409	Brown	0.102	2.6
MD707410	None	0.110	2.8
MD707411	Blue	0.118	3.0
MD707412	Brown	0.126	3.2

TORQUE SPECIFICATIONS

Part	ft. lbs.	Nm
Oil pan bolts	7–9	9.5–12.5
Axle center bearing support bolts	29–36	40–50
Ball joint nuts	43–52	60–72
Axle end nuts	144–188	200–260
8mm transaxle to engine bolts	7–9	9.5–12.5
Transaxle to engine bolt marked "7"	31–40	43–55
Transaxle to engine bolt marked "10"	22–25	30–35
Transaxle to engine flange bolt	58–72	80–100
Transaxle to engine bolt with washer	47–61	65–85
Torque converter bolts (1985–86)	25–30	35–42
Torque converter bolts (1987-89)	34–38	46–53
Transaxle center mount bolts	15–19	20–26
Stay plate to block bolts	47–61	65–85
Stay plate to transaxle bolts	22–30	30–42
Starter bolts (1985–86)	16–23	22–32
Starter bolts (1988–89)	20–25	27–34
Transaxle mount to transaxle nuts	43–57	60–89
Transaxle mount to body bolts	29–36	40–50
Transaxle mount through bolt	46–54	63–73
Upper transaxle to engine bolts (KM175)	32–40	43–55
Upper transaxle to engine bolts (KM177)	47–61	65–85
Oil pump assembly bolts	7.5–8.5	10–12
Differential ring gear bolts	94–101	130–140
Idler shaft lock plate bolt (1985–87)	15–19	20–26
Idler shaft lock plate bolt (1988–89)	35–43	48–60
Oil pump mounting bolt	11–15	15–21
Converter housing to case bolts	14–16	19–22
Valve body mounting bolts	7.5–8.5	10–12

DIFFERENTIAL CASE ENDPLAY

Part Number	Identification Mark	in.	mm
MD710454	J	0.043	1.10
MD700270	D	0.044	1.13
MD710455	K	0.046	1.16
MD710456	L	0.047	1.19
MD700271	G	0.048	1.22
MD710457	M	0.049	1.25
MD710458	N	0.050	1.28
MD706574	E	0.052	1.31
MD710459	O	0.053	1.34
MD710460	P	0.054	1.37
MD706573	None	0.055	1.40
MD710461	Q	0.056	1.43
MD710462	R	0.057	1.46
MD706572	C	0.059	1.49
MD710463	S	0.060	1.52
MD710464	T	0.061	1.55
MD706571	B	0.062	1.58
MD710465	U	0.063	1.61
MD710466	V	0.065	1.64
MD706570	A	0.066	1.67
MD710467	W	0.067	1.70
MD710468	X	0.068	1.73
MD706575	F	0.069	1.76
MD710469	Y	0.070	1.79

DIFFERENTIAL CASE ENDPLAY

Part Number	Identification Mark	in.	mm
MD710470	Z	0.072	1.82
MD700272	H	0.073	1.85
MD710471	AA	0.074	1.88
MD715955	BB	0.075	1.91
MD715956	CC	0.076	1.94
MD715957	DD	0.078	1.97
MD715958	EE	0.079	2.00
MD715959	FF	0.080	2.03
MD715960	GG	0.081	2.06
MD715961	HH	0.082	2.09
MD715962	II	0.083	2.12
MD715963	JJ	0.085	2.15
MD715964	KK	0.086	2.18
MD715965	LL	0.087	2.21
MD715966	MM	0.088	2.24
MD715967	NN	0.089	2.27
MD715968	OO	0.091	2.30
MD715969	PP	0.092	2.33
MD715970	QQ	0.093	2.36
MD715971	RR	0.094	2.39
MD722734	SS	0.095	2.42
MD722735	TT	0.096	2.45
MD722736	UU	0.098	2.48

SPECIAL TOOLS

Tool (Number and name)	Use	Tool (Number and name)	Use
MD998340-01 REMOVER/INSTALLER, center support	Removal and installation of center support	MD998336-01 PIN, guide	Alignment of oil pump housing and reaction shaft support
MD998330 for 3,000 kPa and 980 kPa GAGE, oil pressure	Measurement of the hydraulic pressure [Use with joint (MD998332-01 adapter)]	MD998337-01 COMPRESSOR, spring	Disassembly of front clutch
MD998332-01 ADAPTER, oil pressure gage	Measurement of the hydraulic pressure	MD998348-01 Bearing remover	
MD998333-01 REMOVER, oil pump	Removal of oil pump	MD998266-01 PIN, guide	Alignment of intermediate plate and valve bodies
MD998335-01 BAND, oil pump	Alignment of oil pump housing and reaction shaft support	MD998334-01 INSTALLER, oil pump oil seal	Installation of oil pump oil seal
MD998363-01 ADAPTER, wrench	Preload measurement of transfer idler shaft	MD998349-01 INSTALLER, bearing	Installation of output flange bearings and gear
MD998344-01 ADAPTER "B", wrench	Removal and installation of transfer idler shaft	MD998341-01 ADAPTER, kickdown servo	Removal and installation of kickdown servo

Tool (Number and name)	Use	Tool (Number and name)	Use
MD998345 RETAINER, reverse sun gear	Hold of sun gears	MD998318-01 INSTALLER, bearing	Installation of transfer shaft front bearing (Common to manual and automatic transaxle)
MD998346-01 REMOVER, bearing outer race	Removal of bearing outer race	MD998319-01 RETAINER, transfer shaft	Installation of transfer shaft rear bearing and gear
MD998347-01 INSTALLER, bearing outer race	Installation of bearing outer race	MD998325-01 INSTALLER, differential oil seal	Installation of differential oil seal (Common to manual and automatic transaxle)
MD991194 Multi-use tester		MD998341-01 ADAPTER, kickdown servo	Removal and installation of kickdown servo
MD998405 CHECKER, ELC-A/T	Inspection of damper clutch operation	MIT209038 CHECKER, end play	
MB991113 PULLER, steering linkage	Disconnection of the tie rod Disconnection of the lower ball joint	MD998422 CONNECTOR HARNESS, ELC-A/T	

Section 2

RE4F02A and RL4F02A Transaxles
Nissan

APPLICATION

Year	Vehicle	Engine
1985	Maxima	3.0L
1986	Maxima	3.0L
	Stanza Wagon	2.0L
1987	Maxima	3.0L
	Stanza Sedan and Wagon	2.0L
1988	Maxima	3.0L
	Pulsar	1.8L
	Stanza Sedan and Wagon	2.0L
1989	Maxima	3.0L
	Pulsar	1.8L
	Stanza Sedan	2.0L

GENERAL DESCRIPTION

The RL4F02A and RE4F02A are 3 speed automatic transaxles equipped with an overdrive, driver selected 4th gear. These units have a lockup torque converter that operates only in 3rd and 4th gear.

TRANSAXLE IDENTIFICATION

The automatic transaxle serial number is located on the top of the control body cover pan.

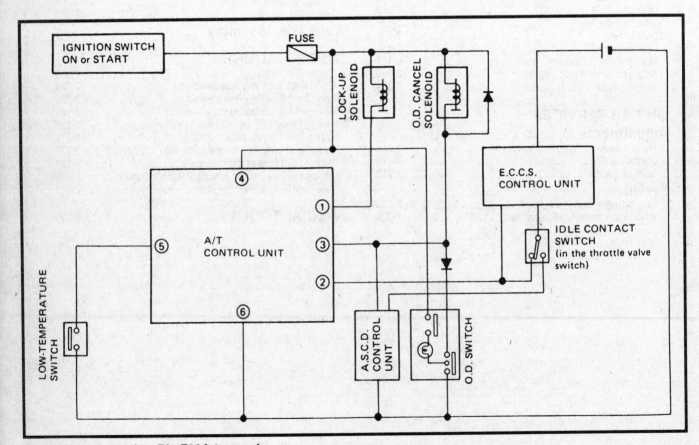

Electrical schematic—RL4F02A transaxle

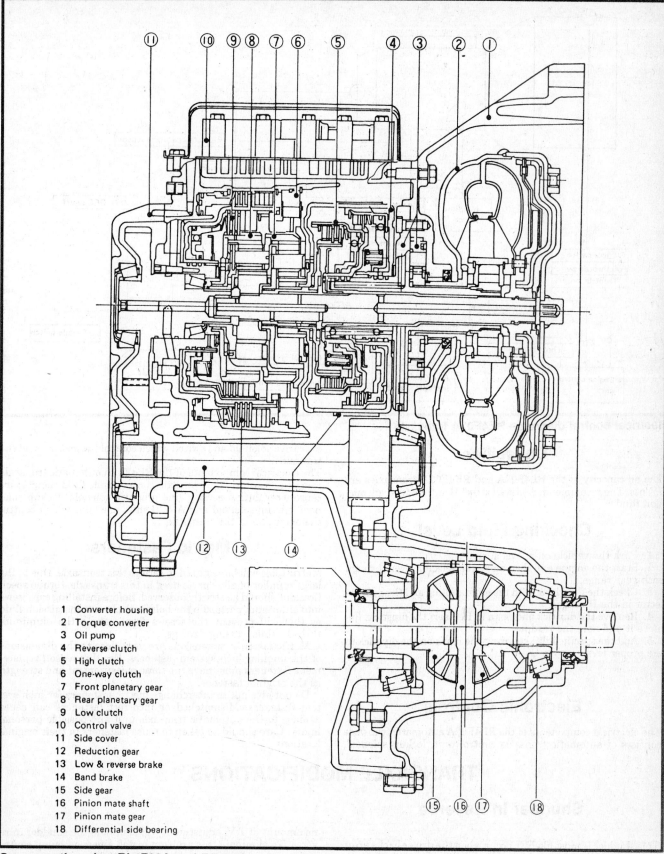

1 Converter housing
2 Torque converter
3 Oil pump
4 Reverse clutch
5 High clutch
6 One-way clutch
7 Front planetary gear
8 Rear planetary gear
9 Low clutch
10 Control valve
11 Side cover
12 Reduction gear
13 Low & reverse brake
14 Band brake
15 Side gear
16 Pinion mate shaft
17 Pinion mate gear
18 Differential side bearing

Cross section view RL4F02A and RE4F02A transaxles

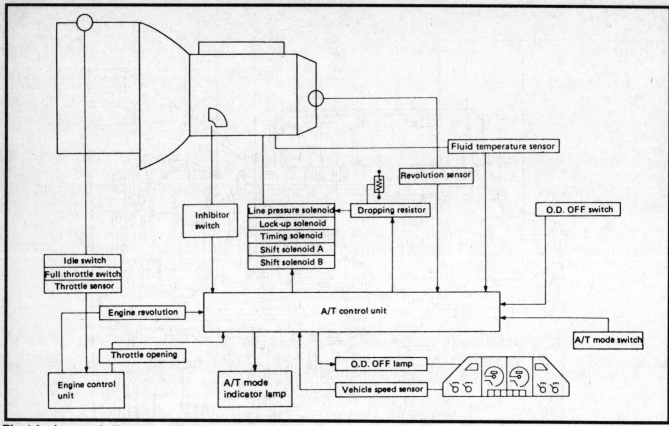

Electrical control diagram – RE4F02A transaxle

Capacities

The oil capacity of the RL4F02A and RE4F02A transaxles are 7¾ qts. The recommended oil is Dexron® II automatic transmission fluid.

Checking Fluid Level

1. Park the vehicle on a level surface.
2. Start the engine and then move the selector lever through each gear range.
3. Check the fluid level with the engine idling and the gear selector in the P range.
4. Remove the dipstick and clean it. Reinsert the dipstick. Remove it and note the reading.
5. Add the specified fluid to bring the mark on the dipstick to the proper level.

Electronic Controls

The electrical components of the RL4F02A automatic transaxle consists of automatic transaxle control unit, lockup solenoid, overdrive solenoid and switch which control the operation of the transaxle.

The electrical components of the RE4F02A automatic transaxle consists of automatic transaxle control unit, fluid temperture sensor, revolution sensor, line pressure solenoid, lockup solenoid, timing solenoid and A & B shift solenoids which control the operation of the transaxle.

Metric Fasteners

Metric tools will be required to service this transaxle. Due to the large number of alloy parts used in this transaxle, torque specifications should be strictly observed. Before installing capscrews into aluminum parts, dip the bolts into clean transmission fluid as this will prevent the screws from galling the aluminum threads, thus causing damage.

Metric fastener dimensions are very close to the dimensions of the familiar inch system fasteners. For this reason replacement fasteners must have the same measurement and strength as the original fastener.

Do not attempt to interchange metric fasteners for inch system fasteners. Mismatched or incorrect fasteners can cause damage to the automatic transaxle unit and possible personal injury. Care should be taken to reuse fasteners in their original locations.

TRANSAXLE MODIFICATIONS

Shudder In Reverse

This shudder is most likely to occur when the driver backs up an incline or accelerates quickly in reverse. On some 1985 Maximas no amount of T.V. adjustment will eliminate the shudder in reverse. To eliminate this problem install a new oil pump control piston assembly part number 31330–21X02.

TROUBLE DIAGNOSIS

CLUTCH AND BAND APPLICATION CHART

Range		Gear Ratio	Reverse Clutch	High Clutch	Low Clutch	Band Operation	Servo Release	Low and Reverse Brake	One-way Clutch	Parking Pawl	Lockup
Park		—	—	—	—	—	—	—	—	Applied	—
Reverse		2.272	Applied	—	—	—	—	Applied	—	—	—
Neutral		—	—	—	—	—	—	—	—	—	—
Drive	D_1 Low	2.785	—	—	Applied	—	—	—	Applied	—	—
	D_2 Second	1.545	—	—	Applied	Applied	—	—	—	—	—
	D_3 Top (3rd)	1.000	—	Applied	Applied	Applied	Applied	—	—	—	Applied ①
	D_4 O.D. (4th)	0.694	—	Applied	—	Applied	—	—	—	—	Applied ②
2	2_1 Low	2.785	—	—	Applied	—	—	—	Applied	—	—
	2_2 Second	1.545	—	—	Applied	Applied	—	—	—	—	—
1	1_1 Low	2.785	—	—	Applied	—	—	Applied	Applied	—	—
	1_2 Second	1.545	—	—	Applied	Applied	—	—	—	—	—

① Lockup operates in 3rd speed (lockup) range when O.D. control switch is "OFF" (Overdrive not allowed).
② Lockup operates in 4th speed (lockup) range when O.D. control switch is "ON" (Overdrive allowed).

CHILTON'S THREE C's TRANSAXLE DIAGNOSIS
RL4F02A and RE4F02A

Condition	Cause	Correction
Engine does not start in N or P	a) Control cable misadjusted b) Defective inhibitor switch or wiring	a) Adjust control cable b) Replace switch or repair wiring
Transaxle noise in P or N ranges	a) Oil level incorrect b) Line pressure problem c) Defective oil pump	a) Correct oil level b) Repair line pressure problem c) Replace oil pump
Vehicle runs in N range	a) Control cable misadjusted b) Oil level incorrect c) Control valve problem d) Low clutch malfunction	a) Adjust control cable b) Correct oil level c) Repair or replace control valve d) Replace low clutch
Excessive creep when vehicle starts out	a) Engine idle speed misadjusted	a) Adjust idle speed
Lockup point is too high or low	a) Control valve problem b) Governor valve problem c) Lockup solenoid malfunction	a) Repair or replace control valve b) Repair or replace governor valve c) Replace solenoid
Torque converter lockup pressure is not normal	a) Throttle cable misadjusted b) Line pressure problem c) Control valve problem d) Oil pump malfunction e) Torque converter	a) Adjust throttle cable b) Repair line pressure problem c) Repair or replace control valve problem d) Replace oil pump e) Replace torque converter
Transaxle shifts to overdrive even if OD switch is turned to off	a) Control switch malfunction b) Switch wiring problem c) Overdrive solenoid problem	a) Replace control switch b) Replace switch wiring c) Replace overdrive solenoid
Lamp inside OD control switch glows even if transaxle is shifted to overdrive	a) Control switch malfunction b) Switch wiring problem c) OD indicator switch problem	a) Replace control switch b) Repair switch wiring c) Replace indicator switch

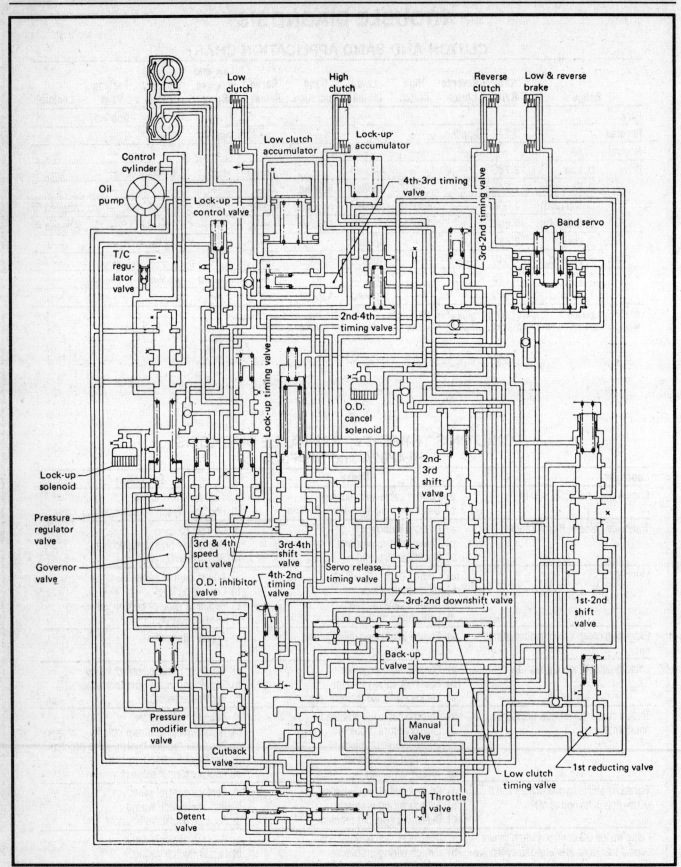

Hydraulic control circuits — RL4F02A transaxle

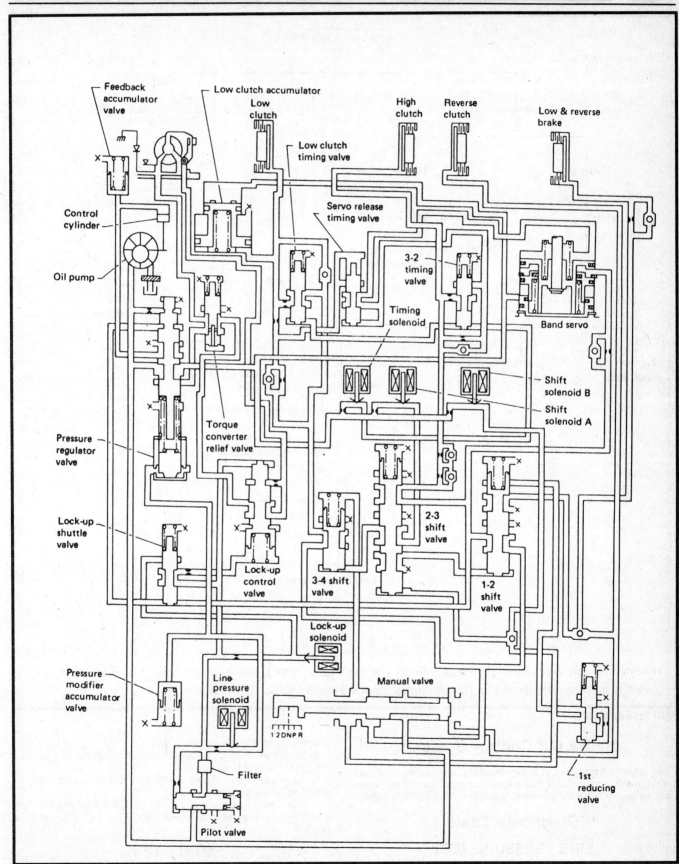

Hydraulic control circuits — RE4F02A transaxle

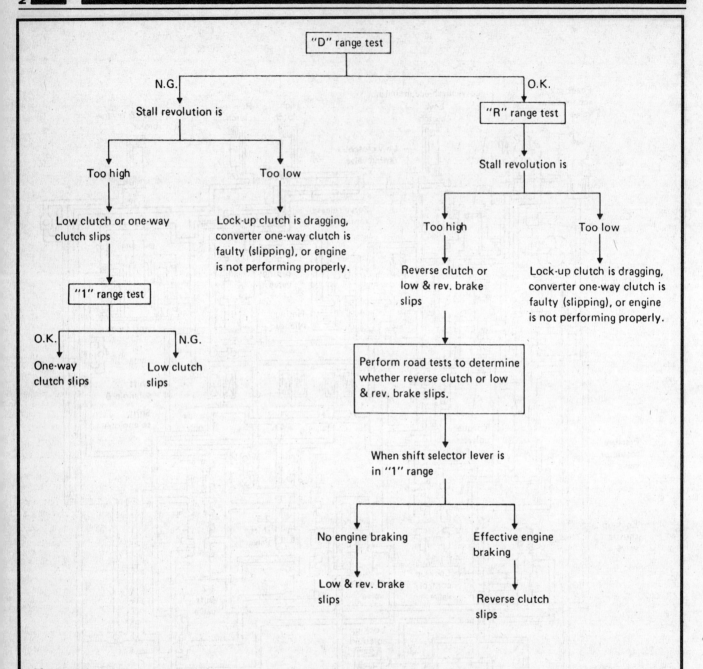

If converter one-way clutch is frozen, vehicle will have poor high speed performance. If converter one-way clutch is slipping, vehicle will be sluggish up to 50 or 60 km/h (30 or 40 MPH).

Stall test analysis

Hydraulic Control System

The major components of the hydraulic control circuit consists of oil pump, accumulator valve, pressure regulator valve, governor valve, lockup control valve, manual valve and shift valves.

Diagnosis Tests

LINE PRESSURE TEST

1. Install pressure gauge to line pressure port. Locate the gauge so it can be seen by the driver.

2. Warm up the engine until the engine oil and transaxle fluid reachs operating temperature.

3. Measure line pressure at idle and at stall points while depressing brake pedal fully.

4. The line pressure at idle should be 54–64 psi at all ranges. The line pressure at stall speed should be 175–198 psi at all ranges.

STALL TEST

NOTE: Do not perform this test for more than 5 sec-

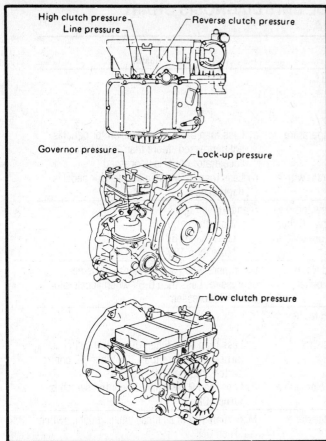

Pressure taps location

High clutch pressure
Line pressure
Reverse clutch pressure
Governor pressure
Lock-up pressure
Low clutch pressure

onds at any shift range. Wait a couple minutes before testing in the next range so that the transaxle fluid temperature decreases.

1. Warm up the engine until the engine oil and transaxle fluid reachs operating temperature.
2. Set parking brake and block wheels.
3. Install tachometer. Locate the tachometer so it can be seen by the driver.
4. Start the engine and place selector lever in the **D** range.
5. Apply foot brake and accelerate to wide open throttle position. Note the stall speed and immediately release the throttle.
6. The stall revolution specification is 2300–2600 rpm for the RL4F02A transaxle. The stall revolution specification is 2350–2650 rpm for the RE4F02A transaxle.
7. Perform stall tests all driving ranges.

LOCKUP TEST

1. Install pressure to port.
2. Position shift lever to **D** range.
3. Record pressure. The torque converter lockup pressure specification should be 7 psi with **ON** condition and 28 psi in **OFF** condition.

Electronic Control System

AUTOMATIC CONTROL UNIT

Testing

RL4F02A TRANSAXLE

1. The automatic control unit is located under the driver's seat. The No. 6 terminal is the terminal at the lower right side of the harness while facing the terminal block.
2. Turn ignition to the **ON** position.
3. Check voltage between the No.6 terminal which is the ground terminal and each terminal in diagnosis chart in the correct order.

RE4F02A TRANSAXLE

The RE4F02A transaxle electronic control system is diagnosis by using the preliminary check charts, self-diagnostic procedure and diagnostic procedures.

AUTOMATIC TRANSAXLE CONTROL UNIT DIAGNOSIS CHART
RL4F02A

Terminal No.	Checking input/ output signal	Checking Method	Result
1	Lockup control signal (G/W) Release signal 1	Connect tester to terminals No. 1 and No. 6. Measure in two situations	
		a) Disconnect connector for Low temperature switch	a) Less than 0.5V when accelerator pedal is not depressed. More than 10V when accelerator pedal is depressed
		b) Jump terminals of harness connector with a lead wire	b) Less than 0.5V when accelerator pedal is depressed
	Lockup control signal (G/W) Release signal 2	Measure while changing OD control switch position from ON to OFF, and vice versa. (When measuring, disconnect low temperature switch and depress accelerator pedal)	Standard voltage More than 10V→ Less than 0.5V→ More than 10V
2	Idle switch signal (Orange)	Connect tester to terminals No. 2 and No. 6. Measure while operating accelerator pedal	8V or more when accelerator pedal is not depressed. Less than 0.5V when accelerator pedal is depressed
3	OD cancel signal (Y/P)	Connect tester to terminals No. 3 and No. 6. Measure in two situations a) Disconnect for Low temperature switch	a) Less than 0.5V when OD control switch is turned OFF. More than 10V when OD control switch is turned ON
		b) Jump terminals of harness connector with a lead wire	b) Less than 0.5V when OD control switch is turned ON
4	Power source (G)	Make ground connections. (Connect tester to terminals No. 4 and No. 6.)	More than 10V at all times while ignition switch is turned ON
5	Low temperature switch (G/B)	Refer to lockup control diagnosis chart	—
6	Ground (B)	Connect tester to terminal 6 and body	Check continuity

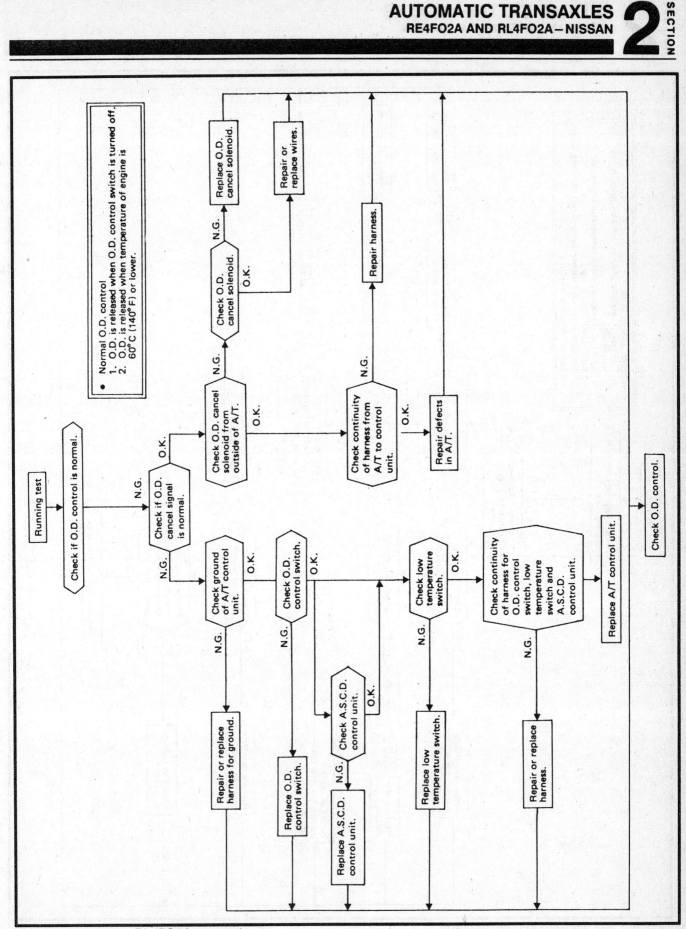

Normal O.D. control
1. O.D. is released when O.D. control switch is turned off.
2. O.D. is released when temperature of engine is 60°C (140°F) or lower.

Running test data — RL4FO2A transaxle

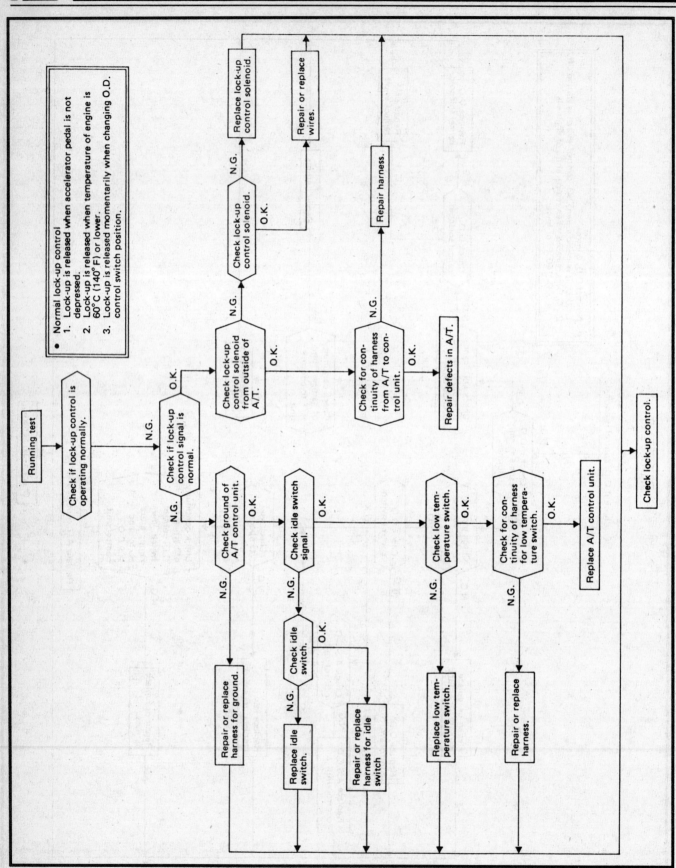

Running test data—RL4FO2A transaxle

PRELIMINARY CHECK 1 – ENGINE NOT STARTED

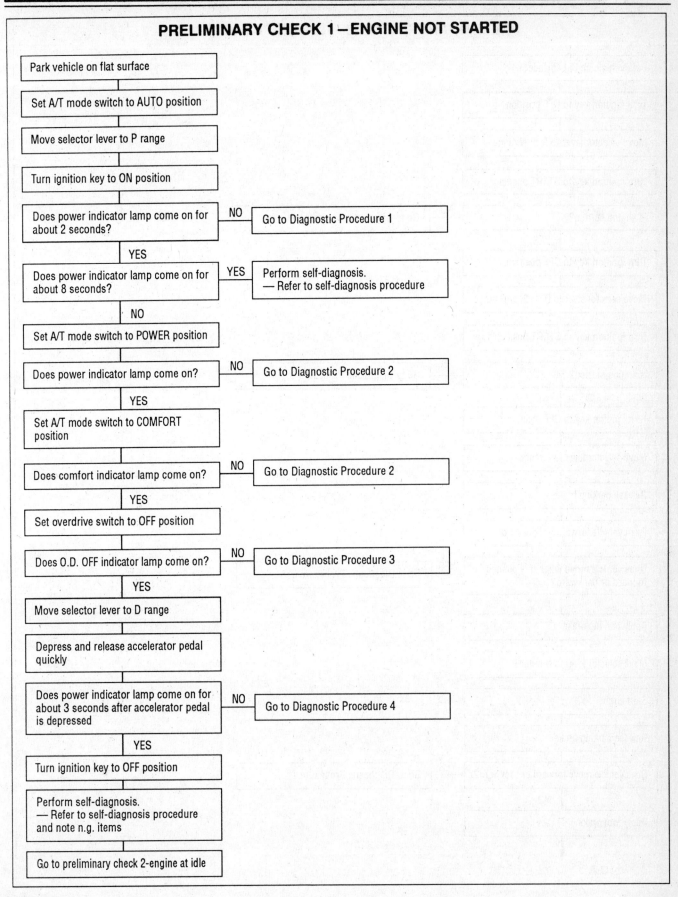

Park vehicle on flat surface

Set A/T mode switch to AUTO position

Move selector lever to P range

Turn ignition key to ON position

Does power indicator lamp come on for about 2 seconds? — **NO** → Go to Diagnostic Procedure 1

YES

Does power indicator lamp come on for about 8 seconds? — **YES** → Perform self-diagnosis.
— Refer to self-diagnosis procedure

NO

Set A/T mode switch to POWER position

Does power indicator lamp come on? — **NO** → Go to Diagnostic Procedure 2

YES

Set A/T mode switch to COMFORT position

Does comfort indicator lamp come on? — **NO** → Go to Diagnostic Procedure 2

YES

Set overdrive switch to OFF position

Does O.D. OFF indicator lamp come on? — **NO** → Go to Diagnostic Procedure 3

YES

Move selector lever to D range

Depress and release accelerator pedal quickly

Does power indicator lamp come on for about 3 seconds after accelerator pedal is depressed — **NO** → Go to Diagnostic Procedure 4

YES

Turn ignition key to OFF position

Perform self-diagnosis.
— Refer to self-diagnosis procedure and note n.g. items

Go to preliminary check 2-engine at idle

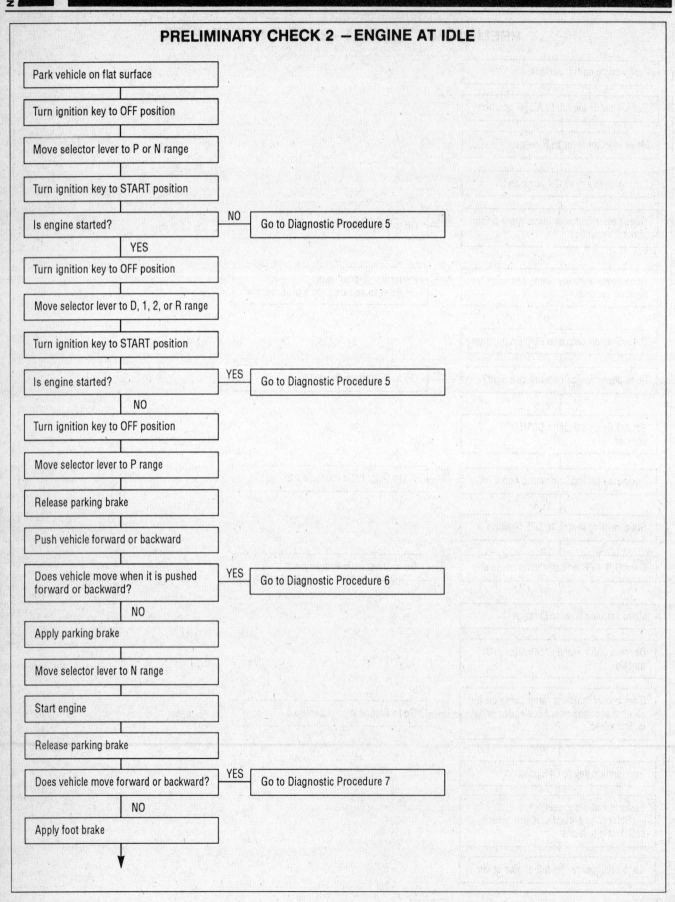

PRELIMINARY CHECK 2 — ENGINE AT IDLE

Park vehicle on flat surface

Turn ignition key to OFF position

Move selector lever to P or N range

Turn ignition key to START position

Is engine started? — **NO** → Go to Diagnostic Procedure 5

YES

Turn ignition key to OFF position

Move selector lever to D, 1, 2, or R range

Turn ignition key to START position

Is engine started? — **YES** → Go to Diagnostic Procedure 5

NO

Turn ignition key to OFF position

Move selector lever to P range

Release parking brake

Push vehicle forward or backward

Does vehicle move when it is pushed forward or backward? — **YES** → Go to Diagnostic Procedure 6

NO

Apply parking brake

Move selector lever to N range

Start engine

Release parking brake

Does vehicle move forward or backward? — **YES** → Go to Diagnostic Procedure 7

NO

Apply foot brake

PRELIMINARY CHECK 2 — ENGINE AT IDLE

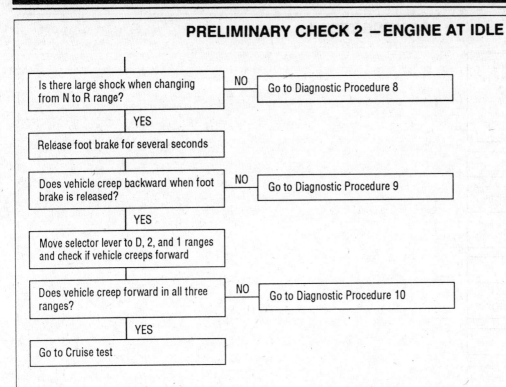

Is there large shock when changing from N to R range?	**NO** → Go to Diagnostic Procedure 8

↓ **YES**

Release foot brake for several seconds

↓

Does vehicle creep backward when foot brake is released?	**NO** → Go to Diagnostic Procedure 9

↓ **YES**

Move selector lever to D, 2, and 1 ranges and check if vehicle creeps forward

↓

Does vehicle creep forward in all three ranges?	**NO** → Go to Diagnostic Procedure 10

↓ **YES**

Go to Cruise test

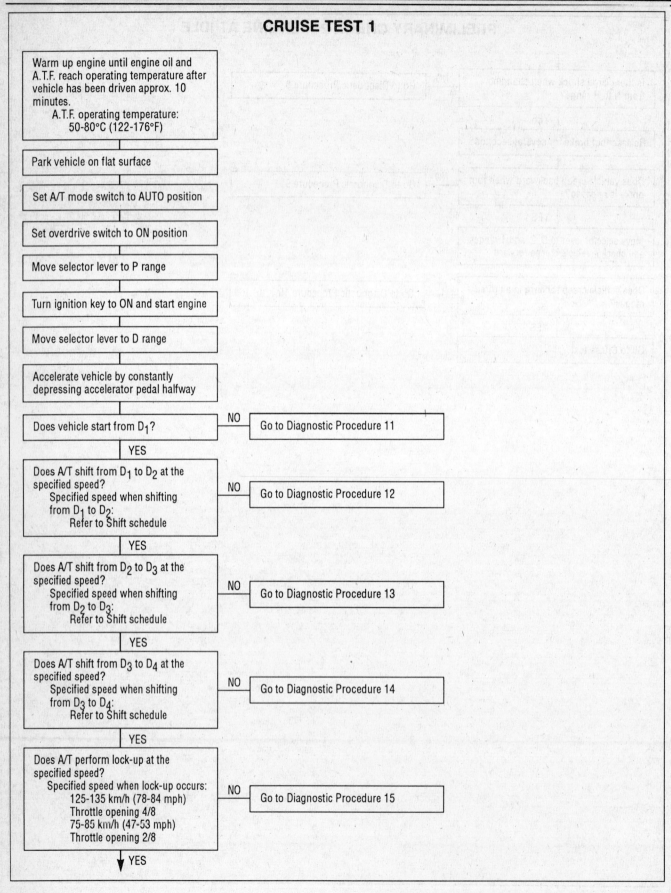

CRUISE TEST 1

Warm up engine until engine oil and A.T.F. reach operating temperature after vehicle has been driven approx. 10 minutes.
   A.T.F. operating temperature:
      50-80°C (122-176°F)

↓

Park vehicle on flat surface

↓

Set A/T mode switch to AUTO position

↓

Set overdrive switch to ON position

↓

Move selector lever to P range

↓

Turn ignition key to ON and start engine

↓

Move selector lever to D range

↓

Accelerate vehicle by constantly depressing accelerator pedal halfway

↓

Does vehicle start from D_1? —NO→ Go to Diagnostic Procedure 11

↓ YES

Does A/T shift from D_1 to D_2 at the specified speed?
   Specified speed when shifting from D_1 to D_2:
      Refer to Shift schedule
—NO→ Go to Diagnostic Procedure 12

↓ YES

Does A/T shift from D_2 to D_3 at the specified speed?
   Specified speed when shifting from D_2 to D_3:
      Refer to Shift schedule
—NO→ Go to Diagnostic Procedure 13

↓ YES

Does A/T shift from D_3 to D_4 at the specified speed?
   Specified speed when shifting from D_3 to D_4:
      Refer to Shift schedule
—NO→ Go to Diagnostic Procedure 14

↓ YES

Does A/T perform lock-up at the specified speed?
   Specified speed when lock-up occurs:
      125-135 km/h (78-84 mph)
      Throttle opening 4/8
      75-85 km/h (47-53 mph)
      Throttle opening 2/8
—NO→ Go to Diagnostic Procedure 15

↓ YES

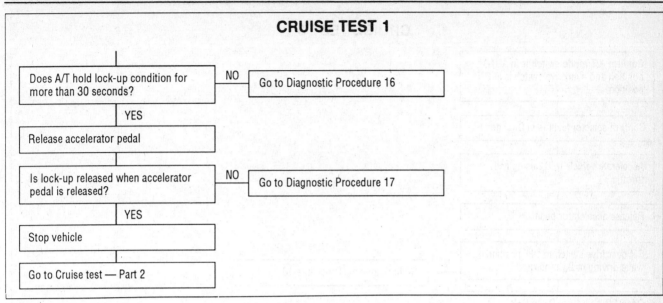

CRUISE TEST 1

Does A/T hold lock-up condition for more than 30 seconds? — NO → Go to Diagnostic Procedure 16

YES

Release accelerator pedal

Is lock-up released when accelerator pedal is released? — NO → Go to Diagnostic Procedure 17

YES

Stop vehicle

Go to Cruise test — Part 2

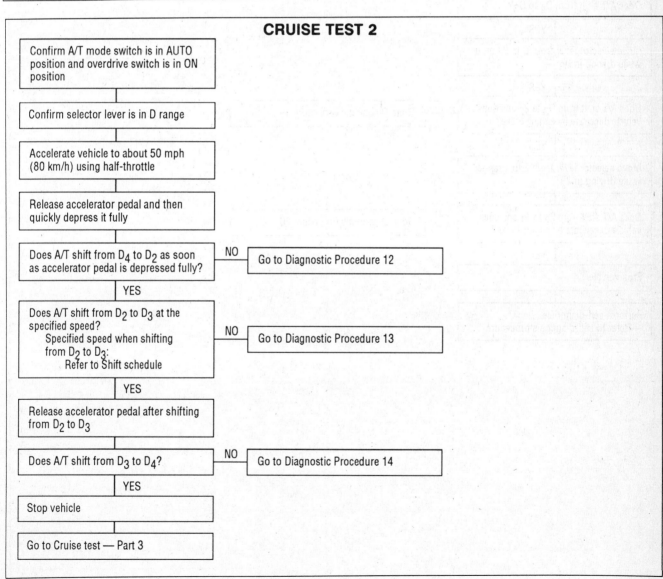

CRUISE TEST 2

Confirm A/T mode switch is in AUTO position and overdrive switch is in ON position

Confirm selector lever is in D range

Accelerate vehicle to about 50 mph (80 km/h) using half-throttle

Release accelerator pedal and then quickly depress it fully

Does A/T shift from D_4 to D_2 as soon as accelerator pedal is depressed fully? — NO → Go to Diagnostic Procedure 12

YES

Does A/T shift from D_2 to D_3 at the specified speed?
Specified speed when shifting from D_2 to D_3:
Refer to Shift schedule — NO → Go to Diagnostic Procedure 13

YES

Release accelerator pedal after shifting from D_2 to D_3

Does A/T shift from D_3 to D_4? — NO → Go to Diagnostic Procedure 14

YES

Stop vehicle

Go to Cruise test — Part 3

CRUISE TEST 3

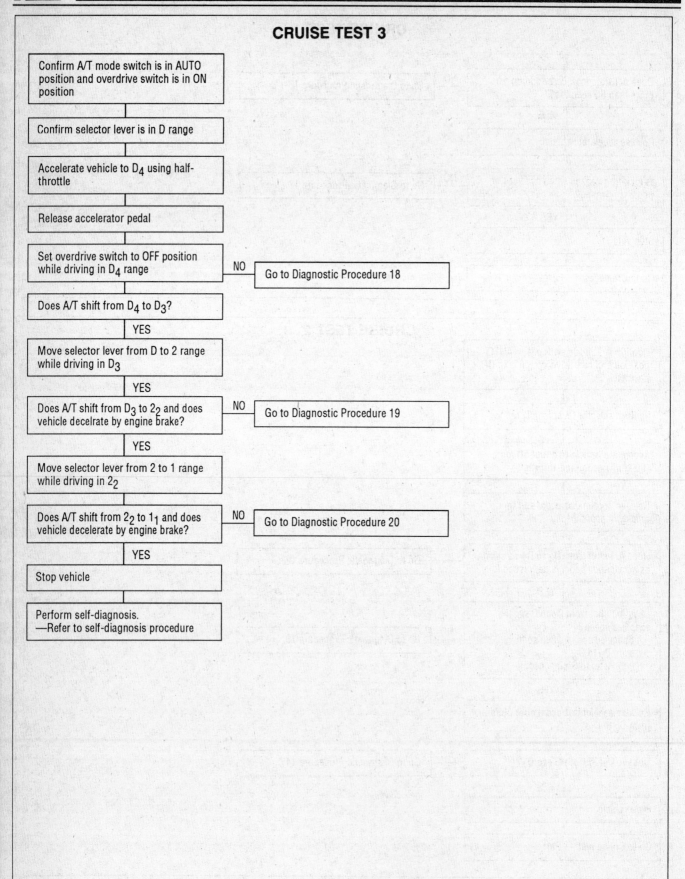

Confirm A/T mode switch is in AUTO position and overdrive switch is in ON position

Confirm selector lever is in D range

Accelerate vehicle to D_4 using half-throttle

Release accelerator pedal

Set overdrive switch to OFF position while driving in D_4 range → **NO** → Go to Diagnostic Procedure 18

Does A/T shift from D_4 to D_3?

YES

Move selector lever from D to 2 range while driving in D_3

YES

Does A/T shift from D_3 to 2_2 and does vehicle decelrate by engine brake? → **NO** → Go to Diagnostic Procedure 19

YES

Move selector lever from 2 to 1 range while driving in 2_2

Does A/T shift from 2_2 to 1_1 and does vehicle decelerate by engine brake? → **NO** → Go to Diagnostic Procedure 20

YES

Stop vehicle

Perform self-diagnosis.
—Refer to self-diagnosis procedure

SELF-DIAGNOSIS PROCEDURE

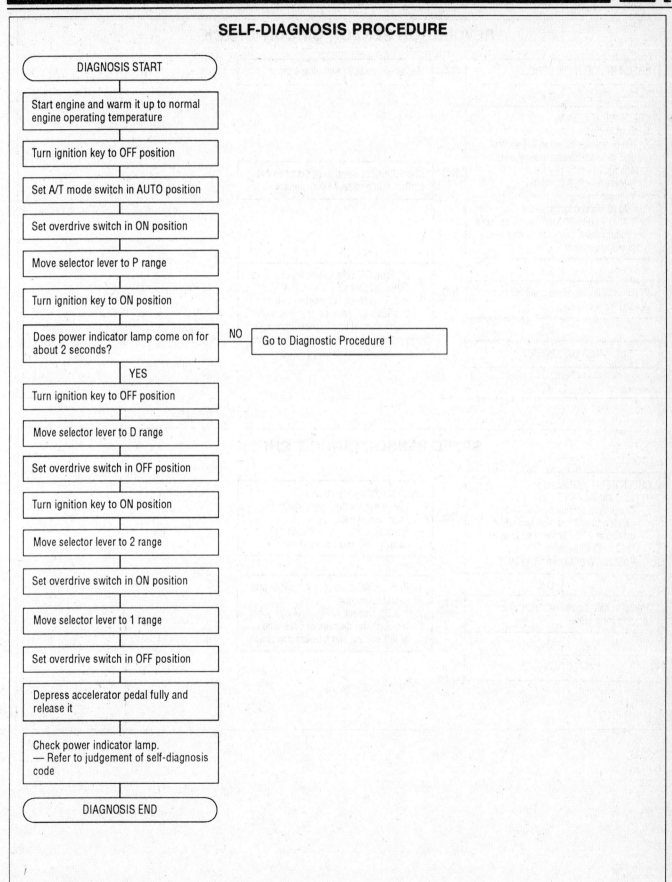

DIAGNOSIS START

Start engine and warm it up to normal engine operating temperature

Turn ignition key to OFF position

Set A/T mode switch in AUTO position

Set overdrive switch in ON position

Move selector lever to P range

Turn ignition key to ON position

Does power indicator lamp come on for about 2 seconds? — NO → Go to Diagnostic Procedure 1

YES

Turn ignition key to OFF position

Move selector lever to D range

Set overdrive switch in OFF position

Turn ignition key to ON position

Move selector lever to 2 range

Set overdrive switch in ON position

Move selector lever to 1 range

Set overdrive switch in OFF position

Depress accelerator pedal fully and release it

Check power indicator lamp.
— Refer to judgement of self-diagnosis code

DIAGNOSIS END

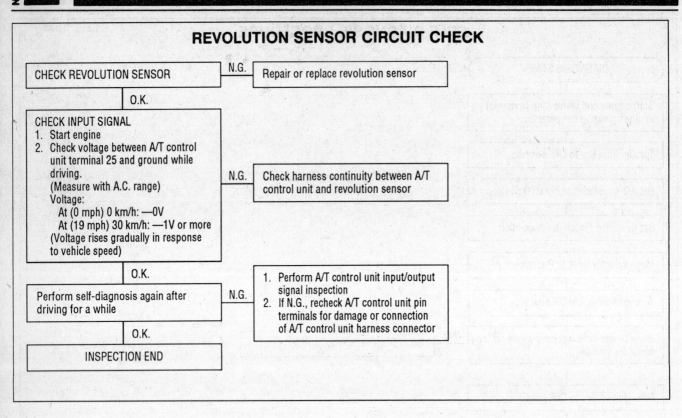

REVOLUTION SENSOR CIRCUIT CHECK

CHECK REVOLUTION SENSOR — N.G. → Repair or replace revolution sensor

O.K.

CHECK INPUT SIGNAL
1. Start engine
2. Check voltage between A/T control unit terminal 25 and ground while driving.
   (Measure with A.C. range)
   Voltage:
     At (0 mph) 0 km/h: —0V
     At (19 mph) 30 km/h: —1V or more
   (Voltage rises gradually in response to vehicle speed)

— N.G. → Check harness continuity between A/T control unit and revolution sensor

O.K.

Perform self-diagnosis again after driving for a while

— N.G. →
1. Perform A/T control unit input/output signal inspection
2. If N.G., recheck A/T control unit pin terminals for damage or connection of A/T control unit harness connector

O.K.

INSPECTION END

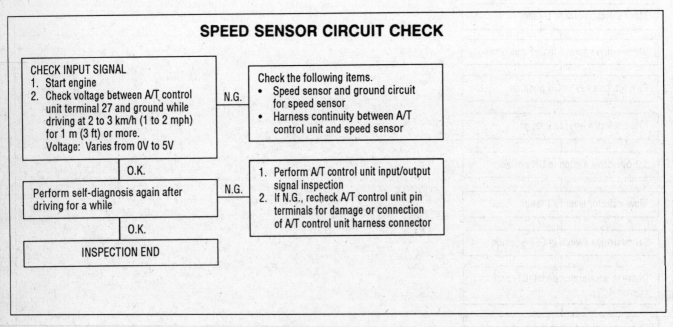

SPEED SENSOR CIRCUIT CHECK

CHECK INPUT SIGNAL
1. Start engine
2. Check voltage between A/T control unit terminal 27 and ground while driving at 2 to 3 km/h (1 to 2 mph) for 1 m (3 ft) or more.
   Voltage: Varies from 0V to 5V

— N.G. →
Check the following items.
• Speed sensor and ground circuit for speed sensor
• Harness continuity between A/T control unit and speed sensor

O.K.

Perform self-diagnosis again after driving for a while

— N.G. →
1. Perform A/T control unit input/output signal inspection
2. If N.G., recheck A/T control unit pin terminals for damage or connection of A/T control unit harness connector

O.K.

INSPECTION END

THROTTLE SENSOR CIRCUIT CHECK

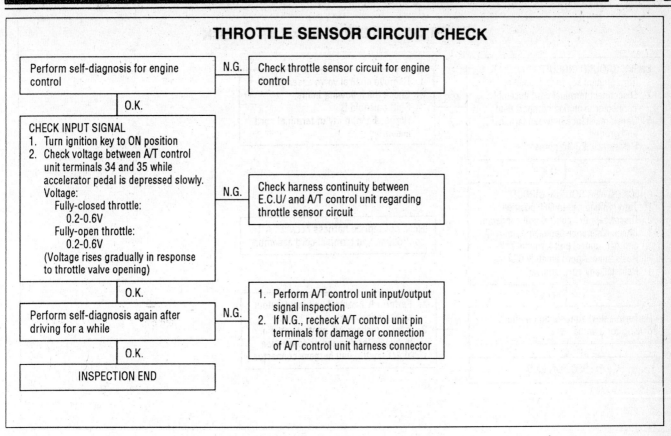

Perform self-diagnosis for engine control

→ **N.G.** → Check throttle sensor circuit for engine control

O.K.

CHECK INPUT SIGNAL
1. Turn ignition key to ON position
2. Check voltage between A/T control unit terminals 34 and 35 while accelerator pedal is depressed slowly.
   Voltage:
   Fully-closed throttle:
   0.2-0.6V
   Fully-open throttle:
   0.2-0.6V
   (Voltage rises gradually in response to throttle valve opening)

→ **N.G.** → Check harness continuity between E.C.U/ and A/T control unit regarding throttle sensor circuit

O.K.

Perform self-diagnosis again after driving for a while

→ **N.G.** →
1. Perform A/T control unit input/output signal inspection
2. If N.G., recheck A/T control unit pin terminals for damage or connection of A/T control unit harness connector

O.K.

INSPECTION END

SHIFT SOLENOID A CIRCUIT CHECK

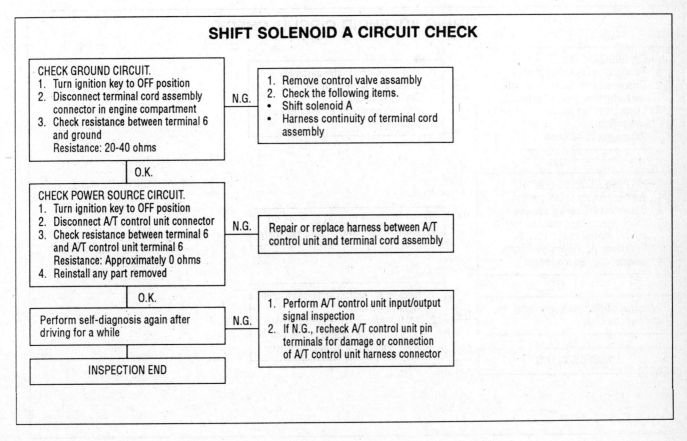

CHECK GROUND CIRCUIT.
1. Turn ignition key to OFF position
2. Disconnect terminal cord assembly connector in engine compartment
3. Check resistance between terminal 6 and ground
   Resistance: 20-40 ohms

→ **N.G.** →
1. Remove control valve assembly
2. Check the following items.
   - Shift solenoid A
   - Harness continuity of terminal cord assembly

O.K.

CHECK POWER SOURCE CIRCUIT.
1. Turn ignition key to OFF position
2. Disconnect A/T control unit connector
3. Check resistance between terminal 6 and A/T control unit terminal 6
   Resistance: Approximately 0 ohms
4. Reinstall any part removed

→ **N.G.** → Repair or replace harness between A/T control unit and terminal cord assembly

O.K.

Perform self-diagnosis again after driving for a while

→ **N.G.** →
1. Perform A/T control unit input/output signal inspection
2. If N.G., recheck A/T control unit pin terminals for damage or connection of A/T control unit harness connector

O.K.

INSPECTION END

SHIFT SOLENOID B CIRCUIT CHECK

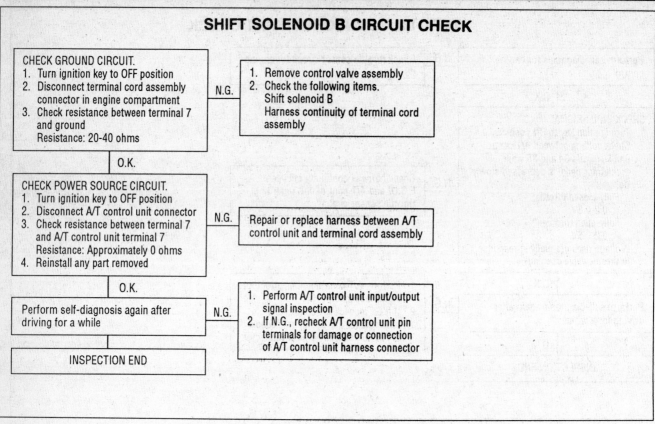

CHECK GROUND CIRCUIT.
1. Turn ignition key to OFF position
2. Disconnect terminal cord assembly connector in engine compartment
3. Check resistance between terminal 7 and ground
   Resistance: 20-40 ohms

→ N.G. →

1. Remove control valve assembly
2. Check the following items.
   Shift solenoid B
   Harness continuity of terminal cord assembly

↓ O.K.

CHECK POWER SOURCE CIRCUIT.
1. Turn ignition key to OFF position
2. Disconnect A/T control unit connector
3. Check resistance between terminal 7 and A/T control unit terminal 7
   Resistance: Approximately 0 ohms
4. Reinstall any part removed

→ N.G. →

Repair or replace harness between A/T control unit and terminal cord assembly

↓ O.K.

Perform self-diagnosis again after driving for a while

→ N.G. →

1. Perform A/T control unit input/output signal inspection
2. If N.G., recheck A/T control unit pin terminals for damage or connection of A/T control unit harness connector

↓

INSPECTION END

TIMING SOLENOID CIRCUIT CHECK

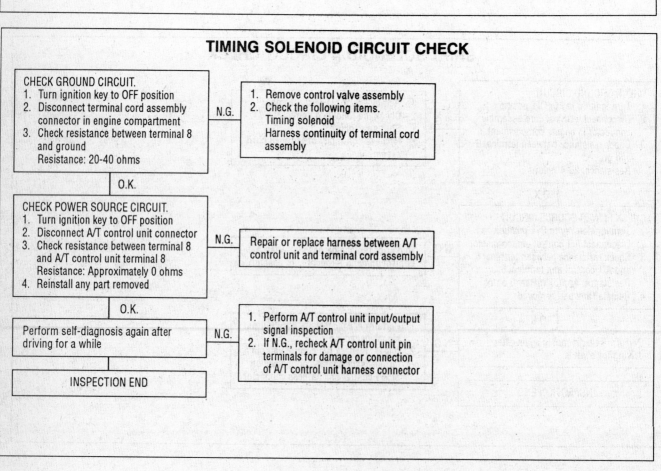

CHECK GROUND CIRCUIT.
1. Turn ignition key to OFF position
2. Disconnect terminal cord assembly connector in engine compartment
3. Check resistance between terminal 8 and ground
   Resistance: 20-40 ohms

→ N.G. →

1. Remove control valve assembly
2. Check the following items.
   Timing solenoid
   Harness continuity of terminal cord assembly

↓ O.K.

CHECK POWER SOURCE CIRCUIT.
1. Turn ignition key to OFF position
2. Disconnect A/T control unit connector
3. Check resistance between terminal 8 and A/T control unit terminal 8
   Resistance: Approximately 0 ohms
4. Reinstall any part removed

→ N.G. →

Repair or replace harness between A/T control unit and terminal cord assembly

↓ O.K.

Perform self-diagnosis again after driving for a while

→ N.G. →

1. Perform A/T control unit input/output signal inspection
2. If N.G., recheck A/T control unit pin terminals for damage or connection of A/T control unit harness connector

↓

INSPECTION END

LOCKUP SOLENOID CIRCUIT CHECK

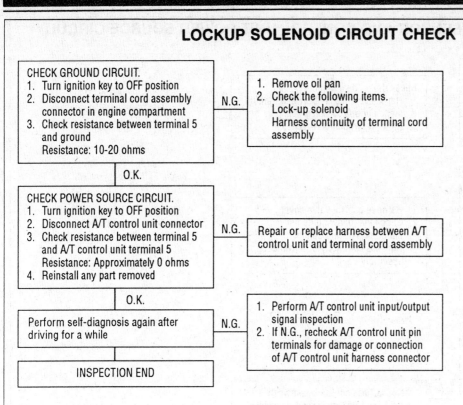

CHECK GROUND CIRCUIT.
1. Turn ignition key to OFF position
2. Disconnect terminal cord assembly connector in engine compartment
3. Check resistance between terminal 5 and ground
   Resistance: 10-20 ohms

→ N.G. →

1. Remove oil pan
2. Check the following items.
   Lock-up solenoid
   Harness continuity of terminal cord assembly

↓ O.K.

CHECK POWER SOURCE CIRCUIT.
1. Turn ignition key to OFF position
2. Disconnect A/T control unit connector
3. Check resistance between terminal 5 and A/T control unit terminal 5
   Resistance: Approximately 0 ohms
4. Reinstall any part removed

→ N.G. →

Repair or replace harness between A/T control unit and terminal cord assembly

↓ O.K.

Perform self-diagnosis again after driving for a while

→ N.G. →

1. Perform A/T control unit input/output signal inspection
2. If N.G., recheck A/T control unit pin terminals for damage or connection of A/T control unit harness connector

↓

INSPECTION END

FLUID TEMPERATURE SENSOR AND CONTROL UNIT POWER SOURCE CIRCUIT CHECK

CHECK A/T CONTROL UNIT POWER SOURCE.
1. Turn ignition key to ON position
2. Check voltage between A/T control unit terminals 4, 9 and ground. Battery voltage should exist

N.G. →
Check the following items
Harness continuity between ignition switch and A/T control unit
Ignition switch and fuse

↓ O.K.

CHECK FLUID TEMPERATURE SENSOR WITH TERMINAL CORD ASSEMBLY.
1. Turn ignition key to OFF position
2. Disconnect terminal cord assembly connector in engine compartment
3. Check resistance between terminals 33 and 35 when A/T is cold
Resistance: Cold [(68°F) 20°C] Approximately 2.5 ohms
4. Reinstall any part removed

N.G. →
1. Remove control valve cover
2. Check the following items
Fluid temperature sensor
Harness continuity of terminal cord assembly

↓ O.K.

CHECK INPUT SIGNAL OF FLUID TEMPERATURE SENSOR
1. Start engine
2. Check voltage between A/T control unit terminal 33 and ground while warming up A/T
Voltage:
Cold [(68°F) 20°C]
Hot [(176°F) 80°C]:
1.56V → 0.45V

N.G. →
Check harness continuity between A/T control unit and terminal cord assembly

↓ O.K.

Perform self-diagnosis again after driving for a while

N.G. →
1. Perform A/T control unit input/output signal inspection
2. If N.G., recheck A/T control unit pin terminals for damage or connection of A/T control unit harness connector

↓ O.K.

INSPECTION END

ENGINE REVOLUTION SIGNAL CIRCUIT CHECK

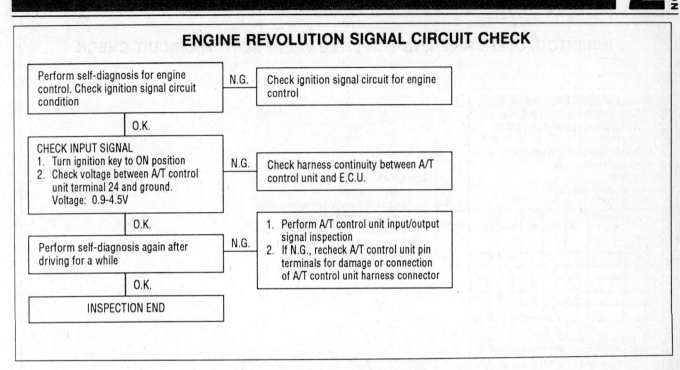

Perform self-diagnosis for engine control. Check ignition signal circuit condition	**N.G.** →	Check ignition signal circuit for engine control
↓ **O.K.**		
CHECK INPUT SIGNAL 1. Turn ignition key to ON position 2. Check voltage between A/T control unit terminal 24 and ground. Voltage: 0.9-4.5V	**N.G.** →	Check harness continuity between A/T control unit and E.C.U.
↓ **O.K.**		
Perform self-diagnosis again after driving for a while	**N.G.** →	1. Perform A/T control unit input/output signal inspection 2. If N.G., recheck A/T control unit pin terminals for damage or connection of A/T control unit harness connector
↓ **O.K.**		
INSPECTION END		

LINE PRESSURE SOLENOID CIRCUIT CHECK

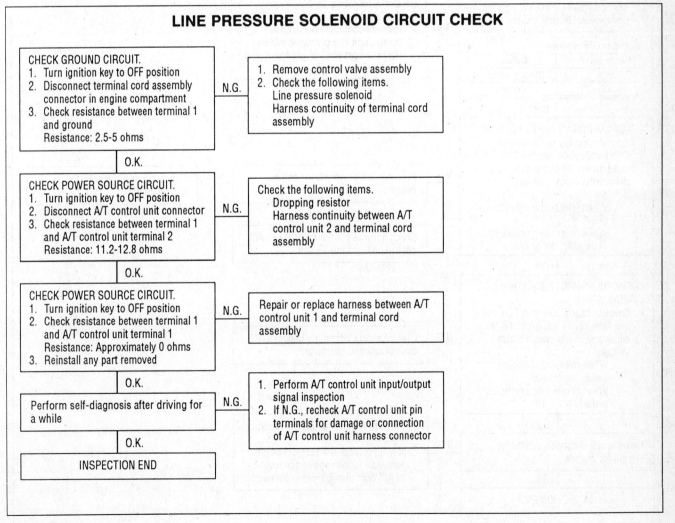

CHECK GROUND CIRCUIT. 1. Turn ignition key to OFF position 2. Disconnect terminal cord assembly connector in engine compartment 3. Check resistance between terminal 1 and ground Resistance: 2.5-5 ohms	**N.G.** →	1. Remove control valve assembly 2. Check the following items. Line pressure solenoid Harness continuity of terminal cord assembly
↓ **O.K.**		
CHECK POWER SOURCE CIRCUIT. 1. Turn ignition key to OFF position 2. Disconnect A/T control unit connector 3. Check resistance between terminal 1 and A/T control unit terminal 2 Resistance: 11.2-12.8 ohms	**N.G.** →	Check the following items. Dropping resistor Harness continuity between A/T control unit 2 and terminal cord assembly
↓ **O.K.**		
CHECK POWER SOURCE CIRCUIT. 1. Turn ignition key to OFF position 2. Check resistance between terminal 1 and A/T control unit terminal 1 Resistance: Approximately 0 ohms 3. Reinstall any part removed	**N.G.** →	Repair or replace harness between A/T control unit 1 and terminal cord assembly
↓ **O.K.**		
Perform self-diagnosis after driving for a while	**N.G.** →	1. Perform A/T control unit input/output signal inspection 2. If N.G., recheck A/T control unit pin terminals for damage or connection of A/T control unit harness connector
↓ **O.K.**		
INSPECTION END		

INHIBITOR, OVERDRIVE AND THROTTLE VALVE SWITCH CIRCUIT CHECK

CHECK INHIBITOR SWITCH CIRCUIT.
1. Turn ignition key to ON position
2. Check voltage between A/T control unit terminals 16, 17, 18, 19, 20 and ground while moving selector through each range
   Voltage:
   B: Battery voltage
   0: 0V

Lever position	Terminal No. 19	20	18	17	16
P,N	B	0	0	0	0
R	0	B	0	0	0
D	0	0	B	0	0
2	0	0	0	B	0
1	0	0	0	0	B

→ **N.G.** → Check the following items.
- Inhibitor switch
- Harness continuity between ignition switch and inhibitor switch
- Harness continuity between inhibitor switch and A/T control unit

↓ O.K.

CHECK OVERDRIVE SWITCH CIRCUIT.
1. Turn ignition key to ON position
2. Check voltage between A/T control unit terminal 39 and ground when overdrive switch is in ON position and in OFF position

Switch position	Voltage
ON	Battery voltage
OFF	1V or less

→ **N.G.** → Check the following items.
- Overdrive switch
- Harness continuity between A/T control unit and overdrive switch
- Harness continuity of ground circuit for overdrive switch

↓ O.K.

CHECK OVERDRIVE SWITCH CIRCUIT.
1. Turn ignition key to ON position
2. Check voltage between A/T control unit terminal 14 and ground while depressing accelerator pedal slowly
   Voltage:
   When releasing accelerator pedal: 8-15V
   When depressing accelerator pedal fully: 1V or less

→ **N.G.** → Perform self-diagnosis for engine control. Check idle switch circuit → **N.G.** → Check idle switch circuit for engine control

↓ O.K.

Check harness continuity between A/T control unit and idle switch

↓ O.K.

CHECK FULL THROTTLE SWITCH CIRCUIT.
- Check voltage between A/T control unit terminal 21 and ground in the same way as idle switch circuit
   Voltage:
   When releasing accelerator pedal: 1V or less
   When depressing accelerator pedal fully: 8-15V

→ **N.G.** → Check harness continuity between A/T control unit and idle switch

↓ O.K.

Perform self-diagnosis again after driving for a while

→ **N.G.** →
1. Perform A/T control unit input/output signal inspection
2. If N.G., recheck A/T control unit pin terminals for damage or connection of A/T control unit harness connector

↓ O.K.

INSPECTION END

DIAGNOSTIC PROCEDURE – No. 1

Power indicator lamp does not come on for about 2 seconds when turning ignition switch to ON

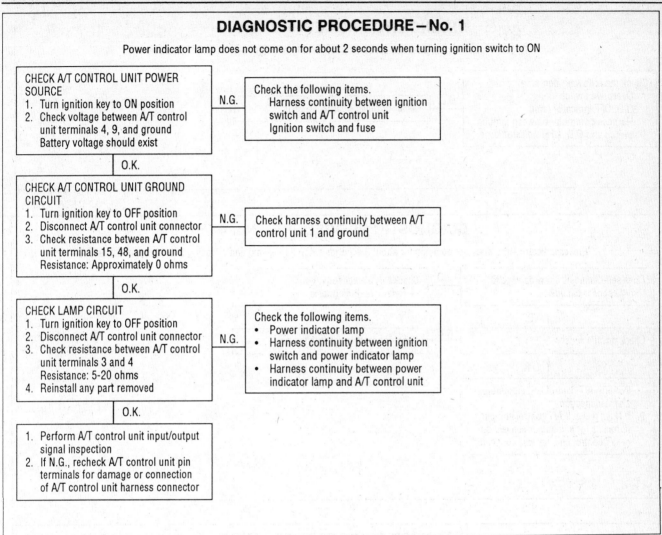

CHECK A/T CONTROL UNIT POWER SOURCE
1. Turn ignition key to ON position
2. Check voltage between A/T control unit terminals 4, 9, and ground
   Battery voltage should exist

N.G. → Check the following items.
   Harness continuity between ignition switch and A/T control unit
   Ignition switch and fuse

O.K.

CHECK A/T CONTROL UNIT GROUND CIRCUIT
1. Turn ignition key to OFF position
2. Disconnect A/T control unit connector
3. Check resistance between A/T control unit terminals 15, 48, and ground
   Resistance: Approximately 0 ohms

N.G. → Check harness continuity between A/T control unit 1 and ground

O.K.

CHECK LAMP CIRCUIT
1. Turn ignition key to OFF position
2. Disconnect A/T control unit connector
3. Check resistance between A/T control unit terminals 3 and 4
   Resistance: 5-20 ohms
4. Reinstall any part removed

N.G. → Check the following items.
   • Power indicator lamp
   • Harness continuity between ignition switch and power indicator lamp
   • Harness continuity between power indicator lamp and A/T control unit

O.K.

1. Perform A/T control unit input/output signal inspection
2. If N.G., recheck A/T control unit pin terminals for damage or connection of A/T control unit harness connector

DIAGNOSTIC PROCEDURE – No. 2

Power indicator lamp or comfort indicator lamp does not come on when turning A/T mode switch to the appropriate position

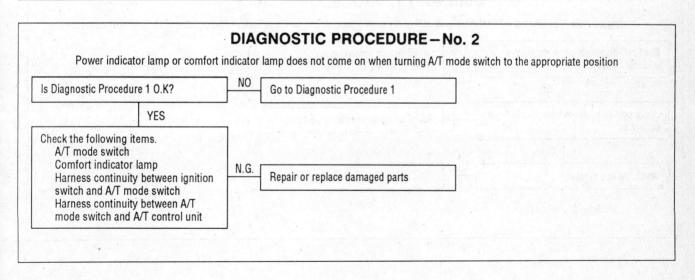

Is Diagnostic Procedure 1 O.K?

NO → Go to Diagnostic Procedure 1

YES

Check the following items.
   A/T mode switch
   Comfort indicator lamp
   Harness continuity between ignition switch and A/T mode switch
   Harness continuity between A/T mode switch and A/T control unit

N.G. → Repair or replace damaged parts

DIAGNOSTIC PROCEDURE — No. 3

O.D. OFF indicator lamp does not come on when setting overdirve switch to OFF position

Check the following items.
    Overdrive switch
    O.D. OFF indicator lamp
    Harness continuity between ignition
    switch and O.D. OFF indicator lamp

N.G. → Repair or replace damaged parts

DIAGNOSTIC PROCEDURE — No. 4

Power indicator lamp does not come on for about 3 seconds when depressing and releasing accelerator pedal fully

Does self-diagnosis show damage to throttle sensor circuit?

NO → Check throttle sensor circuit.
    — Refer to self-diagnosis

YES

Check throttle sensor

N.G. → Repair or replace damaged parts

O.K.

1. Perform A/T control unit input/output signal inspection
2. If N.G., recheck A/T control unit pin terminals for damage or connection of A/T control unit harness connector

DIAGNOSTIC PROCEDURE — No. 5

Engine cannot be started with selector lever in P or N range or engine can be started with selector lever in D, 2, 1, or R range

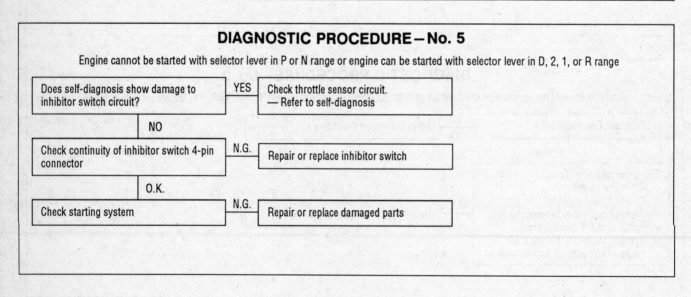

Does self-diagnosis show damage to inhibitor switch circuit?

YES → Check throttle sensor circuit.
    — Refer to self-diagnosis

NO

Check continuity of inhibitor switch 4-pin connector

N.G. → Repair or replace inhibitor switch

O.K.

Check starting system

N.G. → Repair or replace damaged parts

DIAGNOSTIC PROCEDURE – No. 6

Vehicle moves when it is pushed forward or backward with selector lever in P range

Check parking components — N.G. → Repair or replace damaged parts

DIAGNOSTIC PROCEDURE – No. 7

Vehicle moves forward or backward when selecting N range

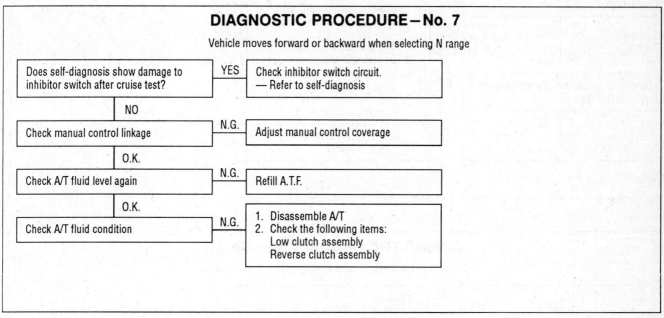

DIAGNOSTIC PROCEDURE – No. 8

There is large shock when changing from N to R range

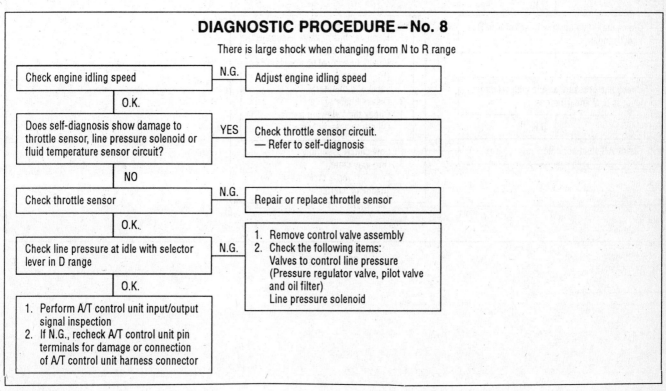

DIAGNOSTIC PROCEDURE – No. 9

Vehicle does not creep backward when selecting R range

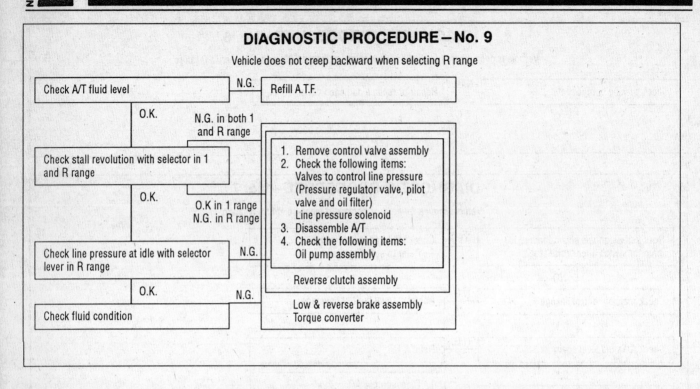

DIAGNOSTIC PROCEDURE – No. 10

Vehicle does not creep forward when selecting D, 2 or 1 range

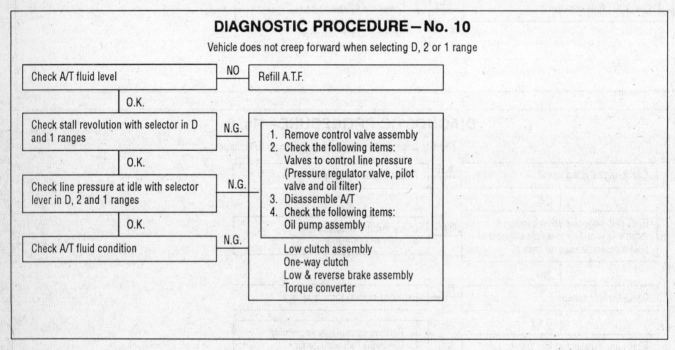

DIAGNOSTIC PROCEDURE—No. 11

Vehicle cannot be started from D_1.

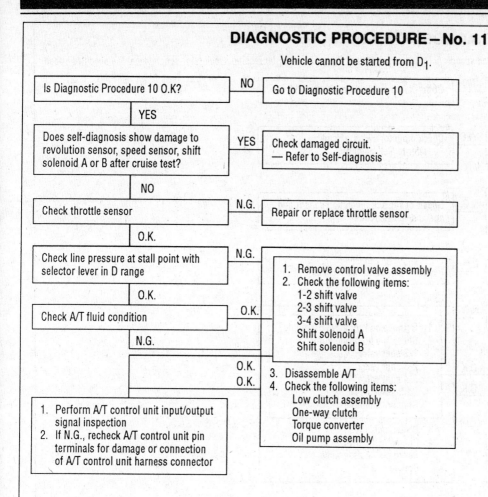

Is Diagnostic Procedure 10 O.K?	**NO** → Go to Diagnostic Procedure 10
YES	
Does self-diagnosis show damage to revolution sensor, speed sensor, shift solenoid A or B after cruise test?	**YES** → Check damaged circuit. — Refer to Self-diagnosis
NO	
Check throttle sensor	**N.G.** → Repair or replace throttle sensor
O.K.	
Check line pressure at stall point with selector lever in D range	**N.G.**
O.K.	
Check A/T fluid condition	**O.K.**
N.G.	

1. Remove control valve assembly
2. Check the following items:
   1-2 shift valve
   2-3 shift valve
   3-4 shift valve
   Shift solenoid A
   Shift solenoid B

O.K.
O.K.

3. Disassemble A/T
4. Check the following items:
   Low clutch assembly
   One-way clutch
   Torque converter
   Oil pump assembly

1. Perform A/T control unit input/output signal inspection
2. If N.G., recheck A/T control unit pin terminals for damage or connection of A/T control unit harness connector

DIAGNOSTIC PROCEDURE — No. 12

A/T does not shift from D_1 to D_2 at the specified speed. A/T does not shift from D_4 to D_2 when depressing accelerator pedal fully at the specified speed.

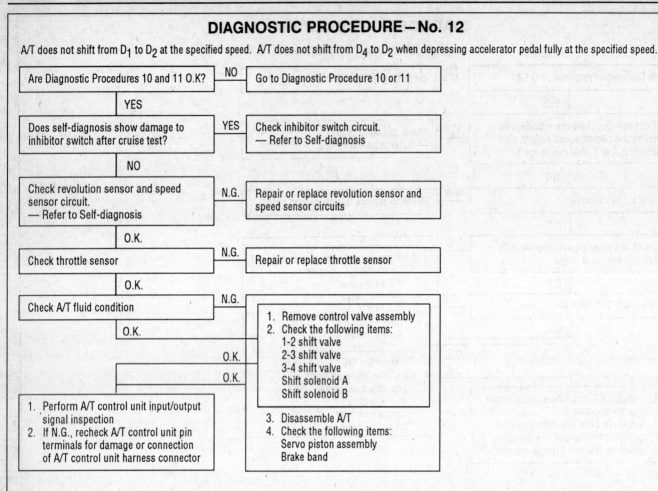

DIAGNOSTIC PROCEDURE — No. 13

A/T does not shift from D_2 to D_3 at the specified speed.

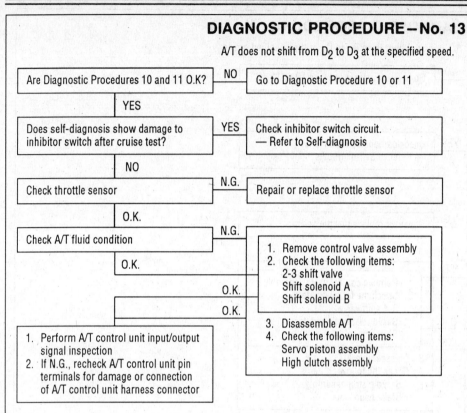

Are Diagnostic Procedures 10 and 11 O.K? — **NO** → Go to Diagnostic Procedure 10 or 11

YES

Does self-diagnosis show damage to inhibitor switch after cruise test? — **YES** → Check inhibitor switch circuit. — Refer to Self-diagnosis

NO

Check throttle sensor — **N.G.** → Repair or replace throttle sensor

O.K.

Check A/T fluid condition — **N.G.** →

O.K.

1. Remove control valve assembly
2. Check the following items:
   2-3 shift valve
   Shift solenoid A
   Shift solenoid B

O.K.

3. Disassemble A/T
4. Check the following items:
   Servo piston assembly
   High clutch assembly

O.K.

1. Perform A/T control unit input/output signal inspection
2. If N.G., recheck A/T control unit pin terminals for damage or connection of A/T control unit harness connector

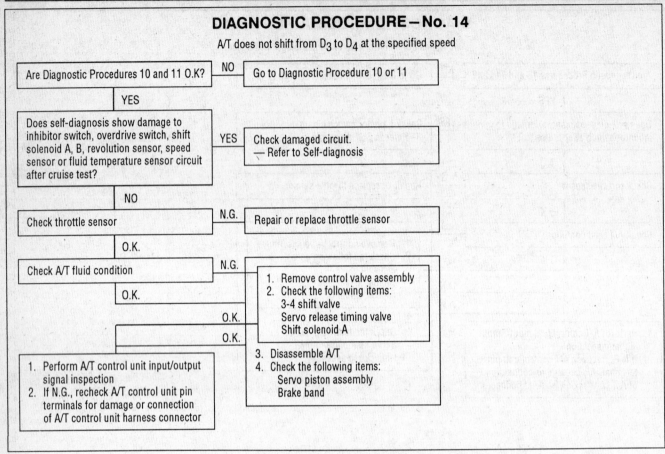

DIAGNOSTIC PROCEDURE—No. 14

A/T does not shift from D_3 to D_4 at the specified speed

Are Diagnostic Procedures 10 and 11 O.K? — NO → Go to Diagnostic Procedure 10 or 11

YES ↓

Does self-diagnosis show damage to inhibitor switch, overdrive switch, shift solenoid A, B, revolution sensor, speed sensor or fluid temperature sensor circuit after cruise test? — YES → Check damaged circuit.
— Refer to Self-diagnosis

NO ↓

Check throttle sensor — N.G. → Repair or replace throttle sensor

O.K. ↓

Check A/T fluid condition — N.G. →
1. Remove control valve assembly
2. Check the following items:
   3-4 shift valve
   Servo release timing valve
   Shift solenoid A

O.K. →
O.K. →
3. Disassemble A/T
4. Check the following items:
   Servo piston assembly
   Brake band

1. Perform A/T control unit input/output signal inspection
2. If N.G., recheck A/T control unit pin terminals for damage or connection of A/T control unit harness connector

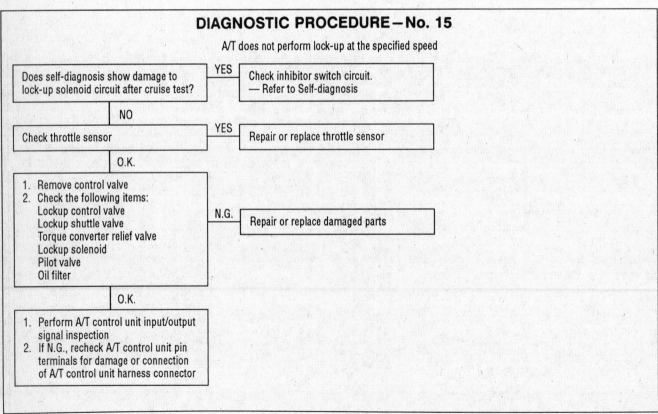

DIAGNOSTIC PROCEDURE—No. 15

A/T does not perform lock-up at the specified speed

Does self-diagnosis show damage to lock-up solenoid circuit after cruise test? — YES → Check inhibitor switch circuit.
— Refer to Self-diagnosis

NO ↓

Check throttle sensor — YES → Repair or replace throttle sensor

O.K. ↓

1. Remove control valve
2. Check the following items:
   Lockup control valve
   Lockup shuttle valve
   Torque converter relief valve
   Lockup solenoid
   Pilot valve
   Oil filter
— N.G. → Repair or replace damaged parts

O.K. ↓

1. Perform A/T control unit input/output signal inspection
2. If N.G., recheck A/T control unit pin terminals for damage or connection of A/T control unit harness connector

DIAGNOSTIC PROCEDURE — No. 16

A/T does not hold lock-up condition for more than 30 seconds

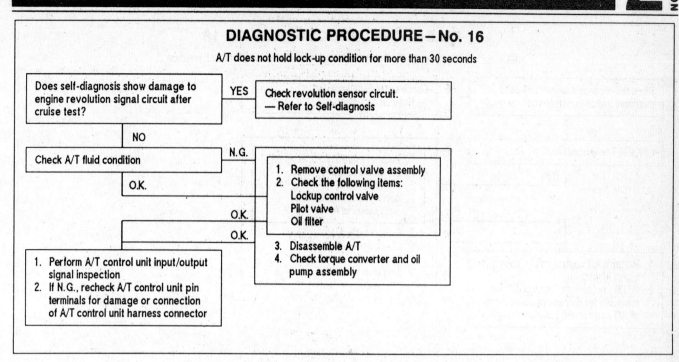

Does self-diagnosis show damage to engine revolution signal circuit after cruise test?

YES → Check revolution sensor circuit.
— Refer to Self-diagnosis

NO

Check A/T fluid condition

N.G. →
1. Remove control valve assembly
2. Check the following items:
   Lockup control valve
   Pilot valve
   Oil filter

O.K.

O.K. →

O.K. →
3. Disassemble A/T
4. Check torque converter and oil pump assembly

1. Perform A/T control unit input/output signal inspection
2. If N.G., recheck A/T control unit pin terminals for damage or connection of A/T control unit harness connector

DIAGNOSTIC PROCEDURE — No. 17

Lock-up is not released when accelerator pedal is released

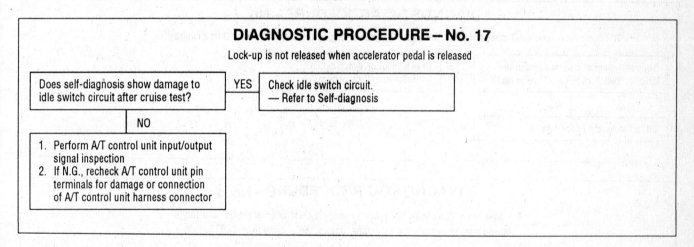

Does self-diagnosis show damage to idle switch circuit after cruise test?

YES → Check idle switch circuit.
— Refer to Self-diagnosis

NO

1. Perform A/T control unit input/output signal inspection
2. If N.G., recheck A/T control unit pin terminals for damage or connection of A/T control unit harness connector

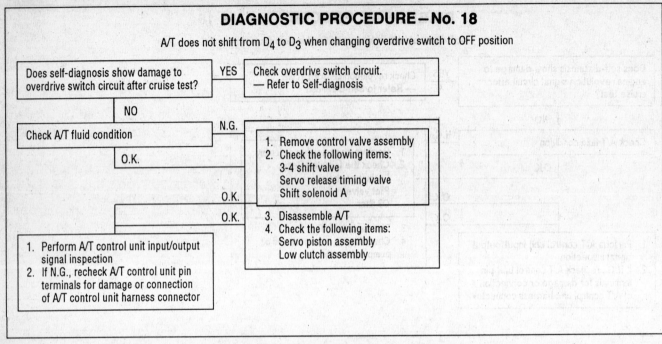

DIAGNOSTIC PROCEDURE — No. 18

A/T does not shift from D_4 to D_3 when changing overdrive switch to OFF position

Does self-diagnosis show damage to overdrive switch circuit after cruise test?

YES → Check overdrive switch circuit.
— Refer to Self-diagnosis

NO

Check A/T fluid condition

N.G. →
1. Remove control valve assembly
2. Check the following items:
   3-4 shift valve
   Servo release timing valve
   Shift solenoid A

O.K.

O.K. →
3. Disassemble A/T
4. Check the following items:
   Servo piston assembly
   Low clutch assembly

O.K.

1. Perform A/T control unit input/output signal inspection
2. If N.G., recheck A/T control unit pin terminals for damage or connection of A/T control unit harness connector

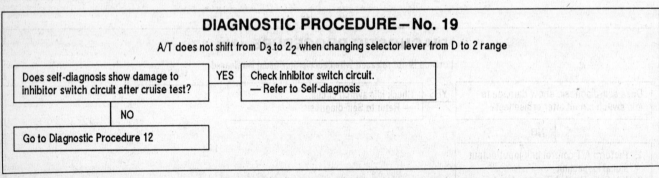

DIAGNOSTIC PROCEDURE — No. 19

A/T does not shift from D_3 to 2_2 when changing selector lever from D to 2 range

Does self-diagnosis show damage to inhibitor switch circuit after cruise test?

YES → Check inhibitor switch circuit.
— Refer to Self-diagnosis

NO

Go to Diagnostic Procedure 12

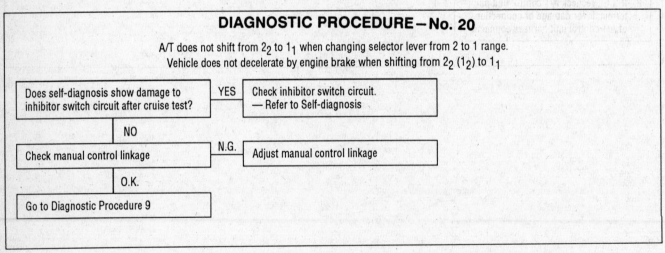

DIAGNOSTIC PROCEDURE — No. 20

A/T does not shift from 2_2 to 1_1 when changing selector lever from 2 to 1 range.
Vehicle does not decelerate by engine brake when shifting from 2_2 (1_2) to 1_1

Does self-diagnosis show damage to inhibitor switch circuit after cruise test?

YES → Check inhibitor switch circuit.
— Refer to Self-diagnosis

NO

Check manual control linkage

N.G. → Adjust manual control linkage

O.K.

Go to Diagnostic Procedure 9

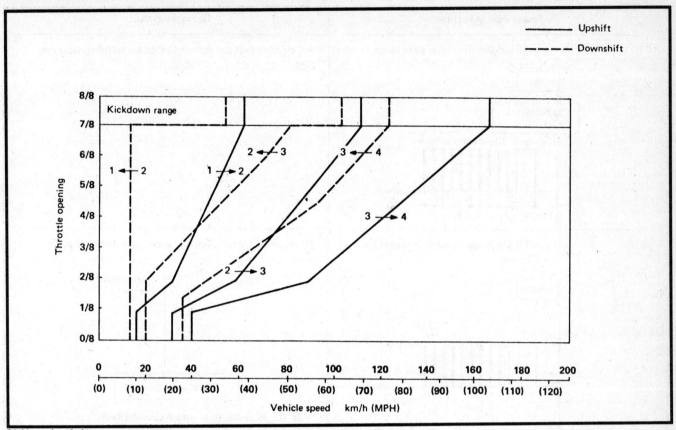

Shift schedule—power pattern

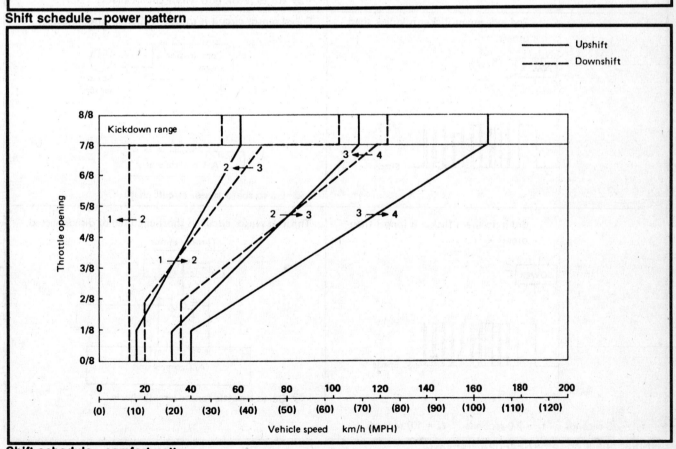

Shift schedule—comfort pattern

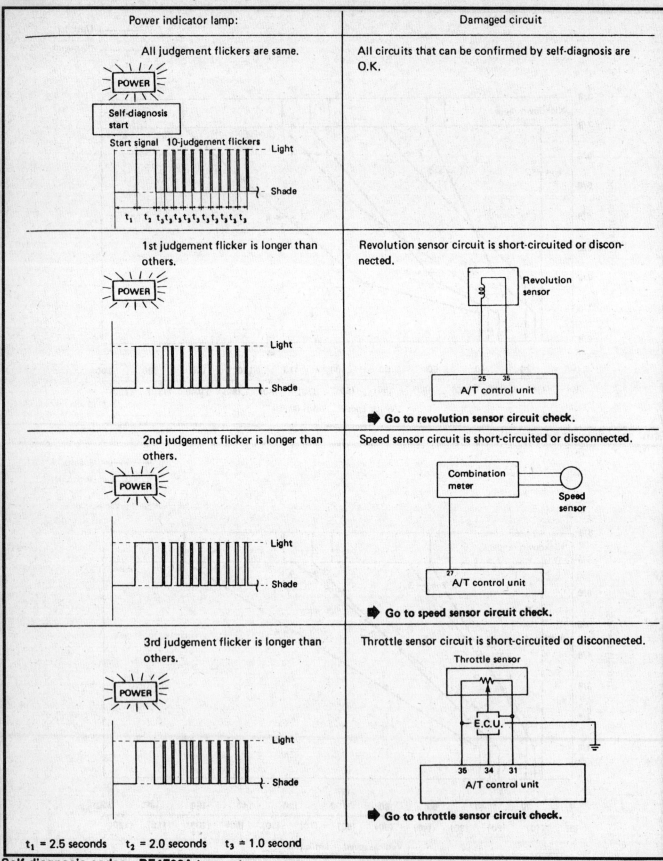

Power indicator lamp:	Damaged circuit
All judgement flickers are same.	All circuits that can be confirmed by self-diagnosis are O.K.
1st judgement flicker is longer than others.	Revolution sensor circuit is short-circuited or disconnected. **Go to revolution sensor circuit check.**
2nd judgement flicker is longer than others.	Speed sensor circuit is short-circuited or disconnected. **Go to speed sensor circuit check.**
3rd judgement flicker is longer than others.	Throttle sensor circuit is short-circuited or disconnected. **Go to throttle sensor circuit check.**

t₁ = 2.5 seconds   t₂ = 2.0 seconds   t₃ ≒ 1.0 second

Self-diagnosis codes – RE4F02A transaxle

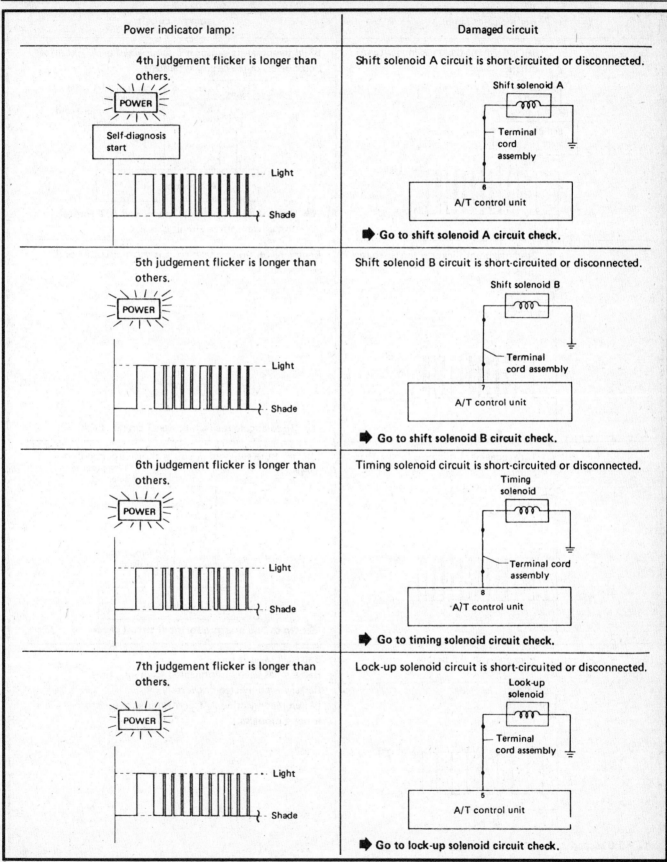

Power indicator lamp:	Damaged circuit
4th judgement flicker is longer than others.	Shift solenoid A circuit is short-circuited or disconnected. Go to shift solenoid A circuit check.
5th judgement flicker is longer than others.	Shift solenoid B circuit is short-circuited or disconnected. Go to shift solenoid B circuit check.
6th judgement flicker is longer than others.	Timing solenoid circuit is short-circuited or disconnected. Go to timing solenoid circuit check.
7th judgement flicker is longer than others.	Lock-up solenoid circuit is short-circuited or disconnected. Go to lock-up solenoid circuit check.

Self-diagnosis codes — RE4F02A transaxle

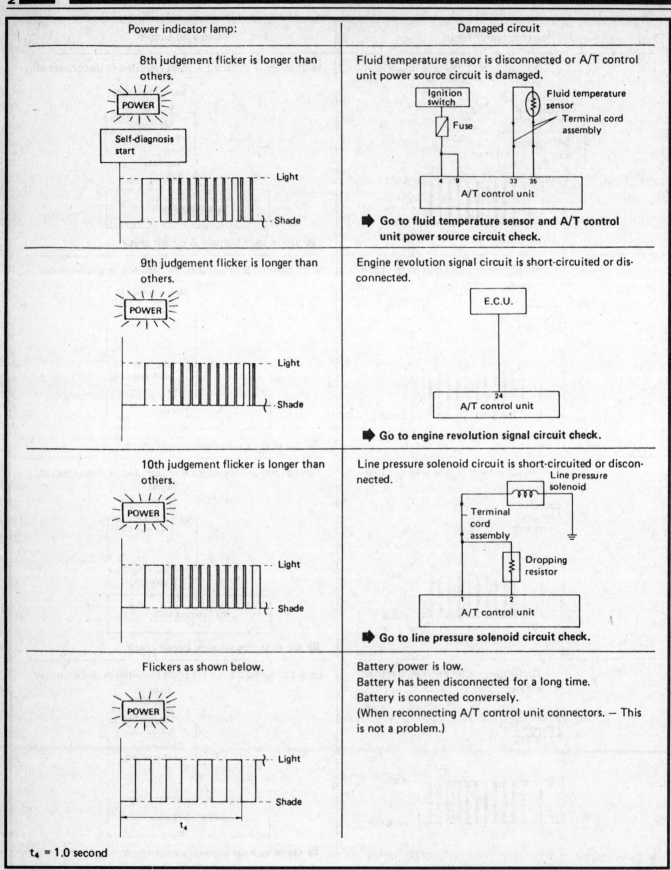

Power indicator lamp:	Damaged circuit
8th judgement flicker is longer than others.	Fluid temperature sensor is disconnected or A/T control unit power source circuit is damaged.
	➡ Go to fluid temperature sensor and A/T control unit power source circuit check.
9th judgement flicker is longer than others.	Engine revolution signal circuit is short-circuited or disconnected.
	➡ Go to engine revolution signal circuit check.
10th judgement flicker is longer than others.	Line pressure solenoid circuit is short-circuited or disconnected.
	➡ Go to line pressure solenoid circuit check.
Flickers as shown below.	Battery power is low. Battery has been disconnected for a long time. Battery is connected conversely. (When reconnecting A/T control unit connectors. — This is not a problem.)

t_4 = 1.0 second

Self-diagnosis codes—RE4F02A transaxle

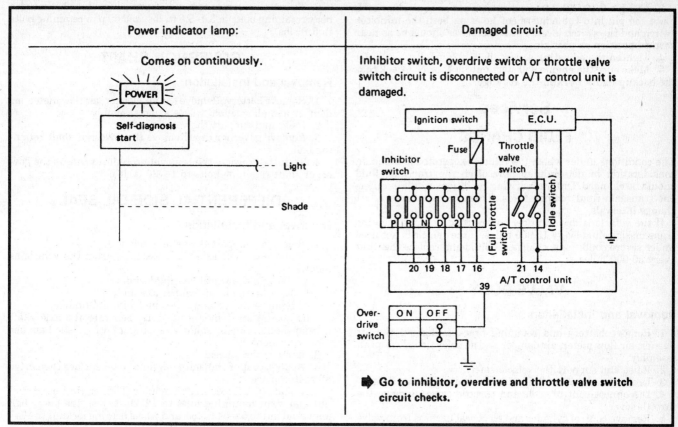

Power indicator lamp:	Damaged circuit

Comes on continuously.

Inhibitor switch, overdrive switch or throttle valve switch circuit is disconnected or A/T control unit is damaged.

➡ Go to inhibitor, overdrive and throttle valve switch circuit checks.

Self-diagnosis codes—RE4F02A transaxle

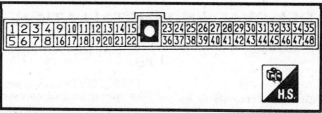

Pin connector terminal layout

ON CAR SERVICES

Adjustments

THROTTLE CABLE

NOTE: The throttle cable is operated via a cam on the throttle shaft of the injection unit. The adjustment is located on the side of the air intake plenum.

1. Loosen the 2 locknuts that position the cable. Open the throttle lever and hold it at the fully open position.
2. Back off both locknuts. Slide the outer cable as far as it will go away from the throttle cam.
3. Turn the nut on the side away from the throttle until it just starts to hold. Then, back it off ¾–1¼ revolutions. Tighten the nut on the throttle side to lock this position securely.

CONTROL CABLE

1. Place selector lever in **P** range. Make sure that control lever locks at **P** range.
2. Loosen lock nuts. Screw front lock nut until it touches select rod end while holding select rod horizontal.
3. Tighten back lock nut. Make sure that selector lever moves smoothly in each range.

INHIBITOR SWITCH

1. Disconnect the negative battery cable. Raise and support the vehicle safely.
2. Loosen the inhibitor switch adjusting screws. Place the select lever in the **N** range.

3. Using a 0.16 inch (4mm) diameter pin or equivalent tool, place the pin into the adjustment holes on both the inhibitor switch and the switch lever. The switch lever should be as near vertical position as possible.

4. Tighten the adjusting screws to 16–22 inch lbs.

5. Make sure the engine will start only in **P** or **N**. Check that the backup lights work in the **R** range.

Services

FLUID CHANGE

The conditions under which the vehicle is operated is the main consideration in determining how often the transaxle fluid should be changed. Different driving conditions result in different transaxle fluid temperatures. These temperatures affect change intervals.

If the vehicle is driven under severe conditions, change the transmission fluid every 15,000 miles. If the vehicle is not used under severe conditions, change the fluid and replace the filter every 30,000 miles.

VALVE BODY

Removal and Installation

1. Remove battery and retaining bracket. Remove the air cleaner, air flow meter, air damper and all solenoid valves as an assembly.

2. Raise and support the vehicle safely.

3. Drain the transaxle fluid. Remove the transaxle oil pan.

4. Disconnect control cable and throttle cable. Remove the throttle lever.

5. Remove control cylinder and electrical harness from valve body.

6. To install reverse the removal procedures torque the valve body retaining bolts to 5.1–6.5 ft. lbs. and oil pan retaining bolts to 5 ft. lbs.

GOVERNOR SHAFT

Removal and Installation

1. Remove battery. Remove the air cleaner, air flow meter, air damper and all solenoid valves as an assembly.

2. Raise and support the vehicle safely.

3. Remove governor cap. Remove the governor shaft retaining bolt.

4. To install reverse the removal procedures torque the governor shaft retaining bolts to 14–20 ft. lbs.

DIFFERENTIAL SIDE OIL SEAL

Removal and Installation

1. Raise and support the vehicle safely.

2. Remove the left axle shaft assembly from the vehicle as follows:

    a. Remove the wheel bearing locknut.

    b. Remove the brake caliper assembly.

    c. Remove tie rod and lower ball joint stud nuts.

    d. Loosen strut mounting nuts. Separate the axle shaft from the knuckle by slightly tapping it with plastic hammer or equivalent.

3. Remove the oil seal.

4. Apply a coat of transmission fluid to oil surface then drive oil seal in place.

5. Install the left axle shaft assembly. Tighten the tie rod stud nut and strut mounting nuts to 22–29 ft. lbs., the lower ball joint stud nut to 52–64 ft. lbs. and wheel bearing locknut to 174–231 ft. lbs.

REMOVAL AND INSTALLATION

TRANSAXLE REMOVAL

MAXIMA

NOTE: **The transaxle and engine are removed as an assembly.**

1. Disconnect the negative battery cable.

2. Matchmark the hood hinges to hood assembly and remove the hood assembly from the vehicle.

3. Relieve the fuel pressure and disconnect the fuel line. Drain cooling system.

4. Disconnect the shift linkage and throttle cable.

5. Remove and mark all electrical wiring and vacuum hoses.

6. Remove all necessary upper components to remove the the engine and transaxle assembly from the vehicle.

7. Raise and safely support the vehicle. Remove the axle shafts.

8. Drain the transaxle fluid from the unit.

9. Disconnect the exhaust system and engine mounting brackets. As required, remove the starter.

10. Lower the vehicle and using a suitable engine slinger support remove the engine and transaxle assembly from the vehicle.

11. Remove the transaxle to engine retaining bolts.

12. Matchmark the relationship between the torque converter and drive plate.

13. Remove the torque converter retaining bolts and seperate the torque converter from the drive plate.

PULSAR AND STANZA

1. Disconnect the negative battery terminal.

2. Raise and safely support the vehicle. Drain the transaxle fluid.

NOTE: **On Stanza wagon, remove air cleaner and airflow meter and disconnect the front exhaust pipe.**

3. Remove the left front wheel assembly and the left front fender protector.4. Remove the axle shafts. Disconnect the speedometer cable, the throttle cable from the throttle lever.

5. Remove the control cable from the rear of the transaxle, then the oil level gauge tube.

6. Place a floor jack or equivalent under the transaxle and a support under the engine.

7. Disconnect and plug the oil cooler hoses from the tubes. Remove the torque converter to drive plate bolts.

NOTE: **When removing the torque converter to drive plate bolts place alignment marks on the converter to drive plate for alignment purposes.**

8. Remove the engine mount securing bolts and the starter motor.

9. Remove the transaxle to engine bolts, pull the transaxle away from the engine and lower it from the vehicle.

TRANSAXLE INSTALLATION

MAXIMA

1. Check drive plate for runout. The maximum allowable runout is 0.020 in. (0.5mm). If the runout is out of specification replace drive plate.

2. Install converter to transaxle. Measure the distance between the torque converter and transaxle housing the distance should be more than 0.709 in. (18.0mm).

3. Install the transaxle to engine. Torque the converter to drive plate bolts in the correct position to 29–36 ft. lbs. and the transaxle to engine bolts 22–30 ft. lbs.

4. Using a suitable engine slinger install the engine and transaxle assembly in the vehicle.

5. Raise and safely support the vehicle.

6. Reconnect the exhaust system and engine mounting brackets.

7. Lower the vehicle. Install all necessary upper components to the engine and transaxle assembly.

8. Reconnect the shift linkage and throttle cable.

9. Install all electrical wiring and vacuum hoses in the correct location.

10. Reconnect the fuel line and refill the cooling system.

11. Matchmark the hood hinges to hood assembly and install the hood assembly to the vehicle.

12. Connect the negative battery cable. Refill transaxle with the correct amount of fluid.

13. Road test the vehicle for proper operation.

PULSAR AND STANZA

1. Check drive plate for runout. The maximum allowable runout is 0.020 in. (0.5mm). If the runout is out of specification replace drive plate.

2. Install converter to transaxle. Measure the distance between the torque converter and transaxle housing the distance should be more than 0.748 in. (19.0mm).

3. Install the transaxle to engine. Torque the converter to drive plate bolts in the correct position to 29–36 ft. lbs. and the transaxle to engine bolts to 32 ft. lbs.

4. Install the control cable to the rear of the transaxle and the oil level gauge tube.

5. Install the axle shafts. Connect the speedometer cable and the throttle cable to the throttle lever.

6. Install all securing bolts, brackets and transaxle cooling lines.

7. Install the starter motor.

NOTE: On Stanza wagon, install air cleaner and air flow meter and reconnect the exhaust pipe.

8. Install the left front wheel assembly and the left front fender protector.

9. Refill the transaxle fluid with the proper type. Connect battery cable and road test for proper operation.

BENCH OVERHAUL

Before Dissassembly

Cleanliness is an important factor in the overhaul of the automatic transaxle. Before opening up this unit, the entire outside of the transaxle assembly should be cleaned, preferable with a high pressure washer such as a car wash spray unit. Dirt entering the transaxle internal parts will negate all the time and effort spent on the overhaul. During inspection and reassembly all parts should be thoroughly cleaned with solvent then dried with compressed air. Wiping cloths and rags should not be used to dry parts since lint will find its way into the valve body passages.

Wheel bearing grease, long used to hold thrust washers and lube parts, should not be used. Lube seals with clean transmission fluid and use ordinary unmedicated petroleum jelly to hold the thrust washers and to ease the assembly of seals, since it will not leave a harmful residue as grease often will. Do not use solvent on neoprene seals, friction plates if they are to be reused, or thrust washers. Be wary of nylon parts if the transaxle failure was due to failure of the cooling system. Nylon parts exposed to water or antifreeze solutions can swell and distort and must be replaced.

Before installing bolts into aluminum parts, always dip the threads into clean transmission fluid. Antiseize compound can also be used to prevent bolts from galling the aluminum and seizing. Always use a torque wrench to keep from stripping the threads. Take care when installing new O-rings, especially the smaller O-rings. The internal snaprings should be expanded and the external rings should be compressed, if they are to be reused. This will help insure proper seating when installed.

Transaxle Disassembly

1. Position transaxle in a suitable holding fixture.

2. Remove the torque converter and draw out the input shaft.

3. Remove control cylinder, throttle lever and valve body cover.

4. Disconnect harness connectors and remove valve body. Remove the terminal assembly.

5. Remove the throttle shaft and return spring.

6. Remove the accumulator, side cover, output gear.

7. Remove idler gear with suitable puller or equivalent.

8. Remove parking pawl asembly.

9. Remove the speedometer case and speedometer gear.

10. Remove the governor cap and pin. Remove governor shaft assembly.

11. Remove the converter housing.

12. Remove the final drive assembly and reduction pinion gear.

13. Remove the oil (filter) strainer.

14. Remove the differential lubrication tube and gutter.

15. Loosen band brake stem lock nut then back off the piston stem.

16. Remove brake band, high clutch, reverse clutch pack.

17. Remove one-way clutch, front and rear carriers and low clutch as an assembly.

18. Remove snapring then low and reverse brake clutches.

19. Remove the low and reverse brake piston with compressed air.

20. Remove the bearing retainer assembly.

21. Remove outer band servo snapring. Remove inner return spring and servo assembly.

22. Loosen manual shaft lock nuts. Remove the manual plate and retaining pin.

Unit Disassembly
OIL PUMP

Disassembly

1. Remove oil pump cover.

2. Remove cam ring spring and assembly. Do not damage converter housing when removing spring.

Inspection

1. Inspect oil pump cover, cam ring, rotor and vanes for wear.

2. Measure the clearance between clutch housing and cam ring, rotor and vanes in 4 places.

3. The wear limit specification is 0.0013 in. (0.034mm).

4. Remove the friction ring and vane ring and measure the clearance between seal ring and ring groove.

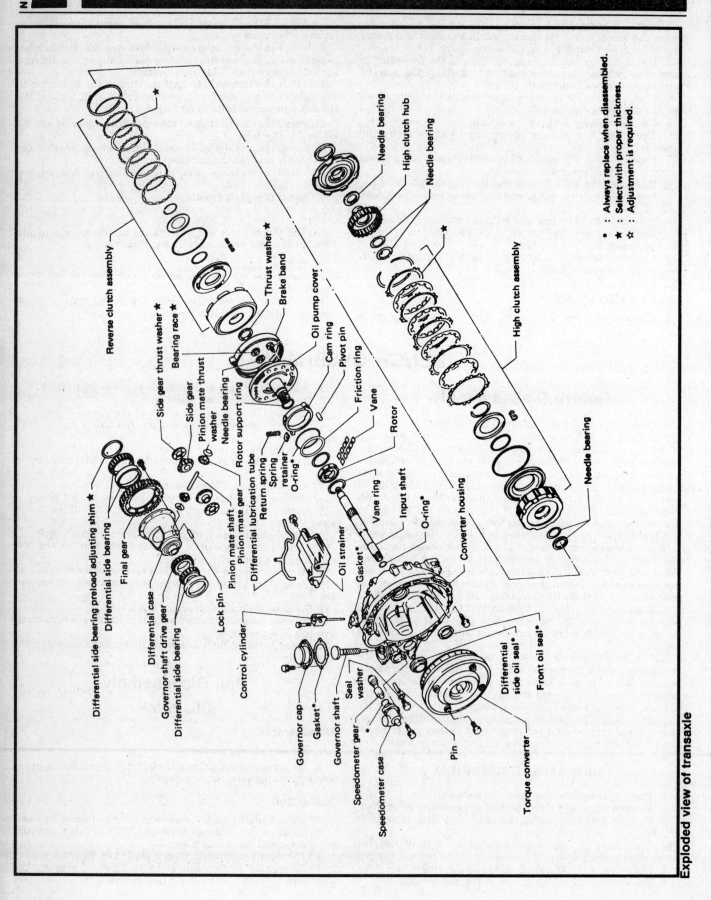

- ★ : Always replace when disassembled.
- ★ : Select with proper thickness.
- ☆ : Adjustment is required.

Reverse clutch assembly

Side gear thrust washer ★

Bearing race ★

Thrust washer ★

Brake band

Oil pump cover

Cam ring

Pivot pin

Friction ring

Vane

Rotor

Input shaft

O-ring*

Vane ring

Converter housing

Rotor support ring

Needle bearing

Pinion mate thrust washer

Side gear

Spring retainer

Return spring

Differential lubrication tube

O-ring*

Gasket*

Oil strainer

Control cylinder

Lock pin

Pinion mate shaft

Pinion mate gear

Differential side bearing

Differential side bearing preload adjusting shim ★

Final gear

Governor shaft drive gear

Differential side bearing

Differential case

Governor cap

Gasket*

Governor shaft

Seal washer

Speedometer gear

Speedometer case

Pin

Differential side oil seal*

Front oil seal*

Torque converter

Needle bearing

High clutch hub

Needle bearing

High clutch assembly

Needle bearing

Exploded view of transaxle

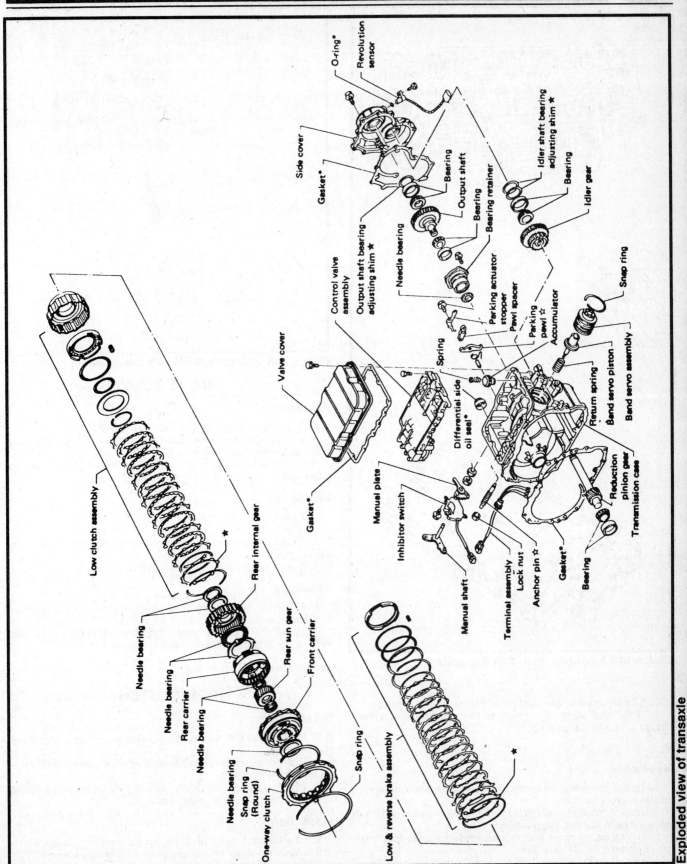

Exploded view of transaxle

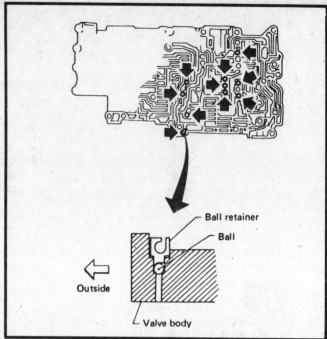

Check ball location—RE4F02A transaxle

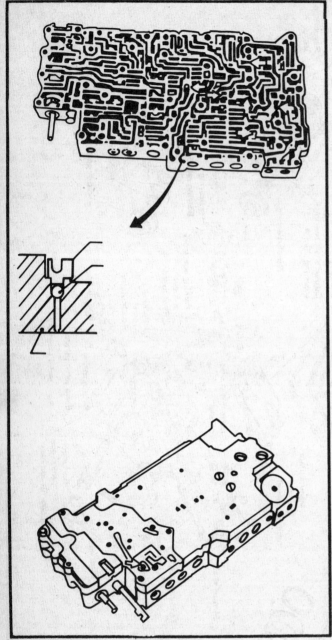

Check ball location—RL4F02A transaxle

5. The wear limit specification is 0.0098 in. (0.25mm).
6. If the clearances are more than the specifications replace the oil pump as an asembly.

Assembly

1. Install cam ring, oil pump spring retainer and cam spring in the correct position.
2. Install rotor vanes, friction ring, rotor support ring and vane rings in the correct position.
3. Install pump cover and tighten retaining bolts in a criss-cross pattern to 12–15 ft. lbs.
4. Install seal rings to oil pump in the correct position (small diameter towards the top).

VALVE BODY

Disassembly

1. Remove all check balls from the valve body.
2. Remove the separator plate and lower valve body retaining bolts from the upper valve body and lockup body.
3. Separate all components and note position of all parts and gaskets.

Inspection

1. Check valves for signs of burning or wear.
2. Check separator plate for scratches or damage.
3. Check oil passages in upper and lower valve bodies for varnish deposits, scratches and damage.
4. Check valve springs for damage.

Assembly

1. Reinstall the steel check balls in the valve body in the correct location.
2. Install the separator plate and lower valve body with gaskets to the upper valve body and lockup body.
3. Install all bolts and harness clamps in the correct location and torque to 2.5–3.3 ft. lbs.

HIGH CLUTCH

Disassembly

1. Using a suitable tool compress clutch springs and remove the snapring.
2. Remove clutch springs. Remove retainer plate and all driven and drive plates.
3. Position the clutch drum onto the oil pump and remove clutch piston using compressed air.

Inspection

1. Check clutch drive plate facing for wear or damage.
2. Check for wear on snaprings or broken coil springs.
3. Check for warped spring retainer.
4. Check clutch drum for damage.

Assembly

1. Lubricate clutch drum bushing. Install inner seal and piston seal in the correct position.
2. Install high clutch piston with lip seal in place. After installing turn piston to ensure there is no binding.
3. Install clutch springs and snapring.
4. Install driven plates, drive plates and snapring.
5. Measure clearance between retainer plate and snapring. The allowable limit is 0.102 in. (2.6mm).
6. Check high clutch operation by using compressed air.

LOW CLUTCH

Disassembly

1. Using a suitable tool compress clutch springs and remove the snapring.
2. Remove clutch springs. Remove retainer plate and all driven and drive plates.
3. Remove low clutch piston using compressed air.

Inspection

1. Check clutch drive plate facing for wear or damage.
2. Check for wear on snaprings or broken coil springs.
3. Check for warped spring retainer.
4. Check clutch drum for wear or damage.

Assembly

1. Lubricate clutch drum bushing. Install inner seal and piston seal in the correct position.
2. Install low clutch piston with lip seal in place. After installing turn piston to ensure there is no binding.
3. Install clutch springs and snapring.
4. Install driven plates, drive plates and snapring.
5. Measure clearance between retainer plate and snapring. The allowable limit is 0.079 in. (2.0mm).
6. Check the low clutch operation by using compressed air.

REVERSE CLUTCH

Disassembly

1. Using a suitable tool compress clutch springs and remove the snapring.
2. Remove clutch springs. Remove retainer plate and all driven and drive plates.
3. Remove the reverse clutch piston using compressed air.

Inspection

1. Check clutch drive plate facing for wear or damage.
2. Check for wear on snaprings or broken coil springs.
3. Check for warped spring retainer.
4. Check clutch drum for wear or damage.

Assembly

1. Lubricate clutch drum bushing. Install inner seal and piston seal in the correct position.
2. Install reverse clutch piston with lip seal in place. After installing turn piston to ensure there is no binding.
3. Install clutch springs and snapring.
4. Install driven plates, drive plates and snapring.
5. Measure clearance between retainer plate and snapring. The allowable limit is 0.047 in. (1.2mm).
6. After assembly, check reverse clutch operation by using compressed air.

LOW AND REVERSE BRAKE

Disassembly

1. Using a suitable tool compress clutch springs and remove the snapring.
2. Remove clutch springs. Remove retainer plate and all driven and drive plates.
3. Remove low and reverse clutch piston.

Inspection

1. Check drive and driven plate facing for wear or damage.
2. Check for wear on snaprings and dished plate or broken coil springs.
3. Check for warped spring retainer.

Assembly

1. Install seals on low and reverse piston.
2. Install clutch springs and snapring.
3. Install driven plates, drive plates and snapring.
4. Measure clearance between retainer plate and snapring. The allowable limit is 0.157 in. (4.0mm).

PLANETARY CARRIER ASSEMBLY

Disassembly

The planetary carrier is a complete unit and not disassembled. Replaced the planetary carrier as an assembly.

Inspection

1. Check planetary gear sets and bearings for damage or wear.
2. Check clearance between pinion washer and planetary carrier with a feeler gauge.
3. Replace the assembly if the clearance exceeds 0.0315 in. (0.80mm)

Assembly

The planetary carrier is a complete unit and replaced as an assembly.

FINAL DRIVE ASSEMBLY

Disassembly

1. Remove the final (ring) gear.
2. Remove the shaft lock pin and draw out the pinion shaft.
3. Remove the governor drive gear.
4. Remove the outer differential side bearing outer race and inner race.

Inspection

1. Check mating surface of differential case, side gears and pinion gears.
2. Check clearance between side gear and differential case as follows:
    a. Position tool KV38106500 or equivalent and dial indicator gauge on the side gear.
    b. Move the side gear up and down. Measure on both sides of gear.
    c. The clearance between the side gear and the differential case should 0.004–0.008 in (0.1–0.2mm).
    d. If clearance exceeds the standard valve replace the necessary parts.
3. Check tapered roller bearings for wear or damage.

Assembly

1. Install the side gear and thrust washer in the differential case.
2. Install the pinion gear and thrust washer in the differential case.
3. Install pinion shaft.
4. Measure clearance between side gear and pinion gear. The clearance betwwen the side gear to pinion gear is 0.004–0.008

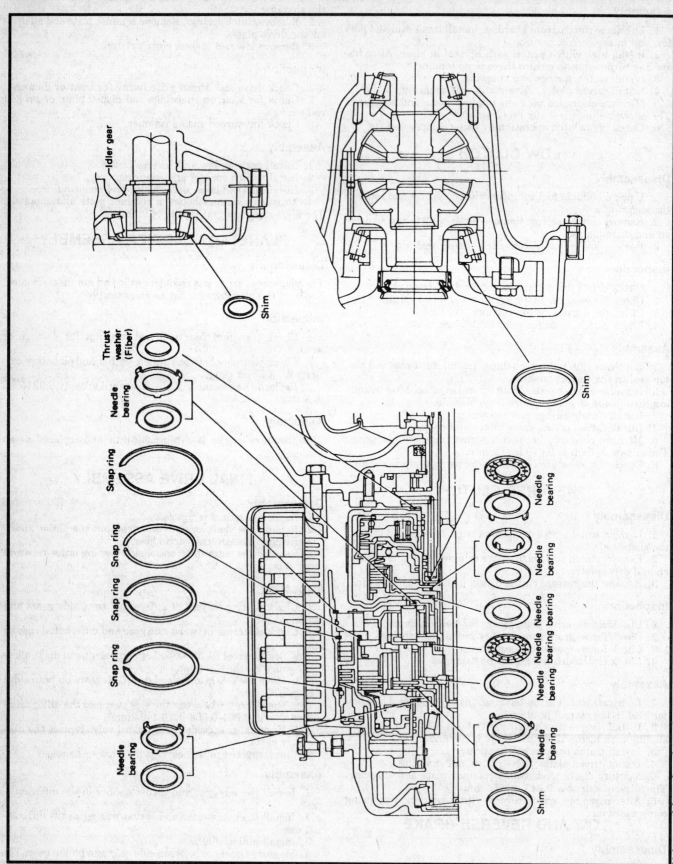

Idler gear

Shim

Shim

Thrust washer (Fiber)

Needle bearing

Snap ring

Snap ring

Snap ring

Snap ring

Needle bearing

Needle bearing

Needle bearing

Needle bearing

Needle bearing

Needle bearing

Needle bearing

Shim

Shim and bearing locations

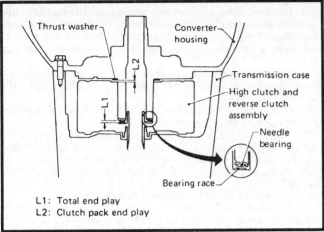

Total endplay and clutch pack endplay adjustment

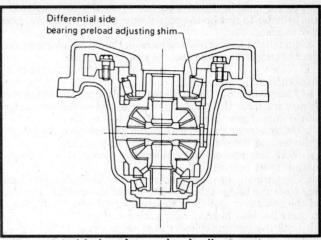

Differential side bearing preload adjustment

in. (0.1–0.2mm), if necessary adjust by selecting the correct thrust washer.

5. Install pinion lock pin using a punch, make sure it is flush with case.

6. Install the governor drive gear.

7. Press on differential side beraring inner and outer race.

8. Install the final (ring) gear.

Transaxle Assembly

1. Install differential lubrication tube and gutter tube to converter housing.

2. Install the oil strainer.

3. Install the detent spring assembly.

4. Position the parking rod in the manual plate than install the manual plate on the manual shaft.

5. Install the band brake servo assembly wtih snapring.

6. Install the low and reverse brake assembly.

7. Assemble the front carrier, rear carrier and low clutch assembly.

8. Install the carrier set.

9. Install the one-way clutch asembly while rotating front carrier by high clutch hub.

10. Remove high clutch hub and install clutch snapring.

11. Install seal rings onto the bearing retainer. Install the bearing retainer asembly.

12. Assemble reverse clutch and high clutch. Install the reverse and high clutch as an assembly.

13. Install brake band and anchor pin. Temporarily tighten anchor bolt by hand.

14. Adjust total endplay as follows:

    a. Remove the thrust bearing race from the high clutch drum.

    b. Install neddle bearing on top of oil pump cover.

    c. Place tool J–34290–1 bridge and J–34290–2 gauging cylinder on the machined surface of the converter housing and on neddle bearings. Lock tool in place.

    d. Insert tool J–34290–7 endplay plunger into the gauging cylinder. Allow the plunger to rest on the surface where the bearing race was removed. Lock tool in place.

    e. Remove the complete tool. Using a feeler gauge measure the gap between the gauging cylinder and the shoulder of the gauging plunger.

    f. Use this reading to select the correct oil pump bearing race thickness.

15. Adjust clutch pack endplay as follows:

    a. Place tool J–34290–1 bridge and J–34290–2 gauging cylinder on the machined gasket surface of the transaxle case and allow the cylinder to rest on the thrust washer surface of the high clutch drum. Lock tool in place.

    b. Insert tool J–34290–6 clutch pack gauging plunger into the gauging cylinder.

    c. Place the complete tool onto the machined surface of the converter housing. Remove the thrust washer and lock the gauging plunger in place.

    d. Using a feeler gauge measure the gap between the gauging cylinder and the shoulder of the gauging plunger.

    e. Use this reading to select the correct thrust washer thickness to give the clutch pack the proper endplay.

16. Adjust the differential side bearing preload as follows:

    a. Remove the left side bearing inner cone and shims from the transaxle case.

    b. Place tool J–34290–1 bridge and J–34290–2 gauging cylinder on the machined gasket surface of the transaxle case and allow the cylinder to rest on the bearing mating surface. Lock tool in place.

    c. Position the differential case assembly into the converter housing, then put side bearing inner cone on the differentail case.

    d. Hold the inner bearing cone in place while spinning the differential case to seat the bearings.

    e. Insert the tool J–34290–3 differential side bearing gauging plunger into the gauging cylinder.

    f. Place the complete tool onto the machined surface of the converter housing and allow the gauging plunger to rest on the surface of the bearing inner cone. Lock tool in place.

    g. Using a feeler gauge measure the clearance between the gauging cylinder and the shoulder of the gauging plunger. With this measurement select the appropriate side bearing preload shim.

    h. Install the selected shim(s) and the left side inner bearing cone onto the transaxle case.

17. Install the reduction pinion gear and the differential case into the transaxle case.

18. Install the converter housing to the transaxle case. The retaining bolts are self-sealing bolts and should always be replaced.

19. Install the parking pawl, return spring, pawl shaft and spacer.

20. Install the idler gear.

21. Lubricate the seal rings of the output gear and install the output gear.

22. Adjust the output shaft and idler gear bearing preload as follows:

    a. Remove the output gear and idler gear bearing outer races and shims. These races must be marked for correct installation.

    b. Place tool J–34290–1 bridge and J–34290–2 gauging cylinder on the machined gasket surface of the side cover and allow the cylinder to rest on the output gear bearing race bore. Lock tool in place.

c. Install the correct bearing races on the output gear and idler gear bearings. Turn the races to seat the bearing.

d. Place tool J-34290-4 output gauging plunger into the gauging cylinder.

e. Place J-342980-1 onto the machined surface of the transaxle case and allow the gauging plunger to rest on the rear surface of the output gear bearing race. Lock tool in place.

f. Using a feeler gauge measure the gap betwwen the gauging cylinder and the shoulder of the gauging plunger.

g. With this measurement select the correct shim(s) for the output shaft bearing preload.

h. To measure for the correct preload shim at idler gear bearing place the bridge tool J-34290-1 onto the machined surface of the side cover and allow the gauging cylinder J-34290-2 to contact the idler bearing race mating surface.

i. Lock the gauging cylinder in place. Insert J-34290-3 gauging plunger into the gauging cylinder and place the bridge onto the machined surface of the case, so that the gauging plunger meets the idler bearing race surface.

j. Lock the gauging plunger inplace and use a feeler gauge to measure the gap between the gauging cylinder and the gauging plunger.

k. Use this measurement to select the correct shim(s) for te the idler gear bearing preload. Install the selected shim(s) and bearing outer races.

23. Install side cover and gaskets. The retaining bolts are self-sealing bolts and should always be replaced.

24. Position manual lever until parking pawl engages the idler gear. Measure the clearance betwwen parking pawl and parking actuator. The clearance specification is 0.0106–0.0240 in. (0.27–0.61mm). If clearance is out of specification replace the parking pawl.

25. Install the input shaft. The correct distance specification from the top of shaft to top of the oil pump is 1.14–1.22 in. (29–31mm).

26. Insert tool J-34284 or equivalent into final drive portion and make sure that it rotates smoothly.

27. Adjust the brake band by torquing anchor end pin to 2.9–4.4 ft. lbs. then backing off anchor end pin 5¼ turns. Tighten locknut to 23–31 ft. lbs. while holding anchor end pin.

28. Install electrical terminal assembly, accumulator and spring.

29. Install the throttle shaft and return spring.

30. Install the manual valve to valve body then assemble valve to the transaxle case. Torque retaining bolts to 5.1–6.5 ft. lbs. and position the throttle shafdt return spring in the correct position.

31. Connect all harness electrical connections and install valve body cover and throttle lever.

32. Install the control cylinder, governor assembly, speedometer assembly, inhibitor switch (adjust switch if necessary), drain plug.

33. Install filled torque converter to converter housing in the correct manner.

SPECIFICATIONS

HIGH CLUTCH RETAINING PLATE SELECTION

Part Number	Shim Thickness in. (mm)
31567-21X00	0.142 (3.6)
31567-21X01	0.150 (3.8)
31567-21X02	0.157 (4.0)
31567-21X03	0.165 (4.2)
31567-21X04	0.173 (4.4)
31567-21X05	0.181 (4.6)
31567-21X06	0.189 (4.8)

REVERSE CLUTCH RETAINING PLATE SELECTION

Part Number	Shim Thickness in. (mm)
31537-21X10	0.181 (4.6)
31537-21X11	0.189 (4.8)
31537-21X12	0.197 (5.0)
31537-21X13	0.205 (5.2)
31537-21X14	0.213 (5.4)

LOW CLUTCH RETAINING PLATE SELECTION

Part Number	Shim Thickness in. (mm)
31597-21X10	0.126 (3.2)
31597-21X11	0.134 (3.4)
31597-21X12	0.142 (3.6)
31597-21X13	0.150 (3.8)
31597-21X14	0.157 (4.0)
31597-21X15	0.165 (4.2)

LOW AND REVERSE RETAINING PLATE SELECTION

Part Number	Shim Thickness in. (mm)
31667-21X00	0.134 (3.4)
31667-21X01	0.142 (3.6)
31667-21X02	0.150 (3.8)
31667-21X03	0.157 (4.0)
31667-21X04	0.165 (4.2)
31667-21X05	0.173 (4.4)
31667-21X06	0.181 (4.6)
31667-21X07	0.189 (4.8)
31667-21X08	0.197 (5.0)

CLUTCH PACK TRUST WASHER SELECTION

Part Number	Thickness in. (mm)
31528-21X00	0.028 (0.7)
31528-21X01	0.035 (0.9)
31528-21X02	0.043 (1.1)
31528-21X03	0.051 (1.3)
31528-21X04	0.059 (1.5)
31528-21X05	0.067 (1.7)
31528-21X06	0.075 (1.9)

OIL PUMP HOUSING BEARING RACE SELECTION

Part Number	Thickness in. (mm)
31429-21X00	0.031 (0.8)
31429-21X01	0.039 (1.0)
31429-21X02	0.047 (1.2)
31429-21X03	0.055 (1.4)
31429-21X04	0.063 (1.6)
31429-21X05	0.071 (1.8)
31429-21X06	0.079 (2.0)

DIFFERENTIAL SIDE BEARING PRELOAD SHIM SELECTION

Part Number	Thickness in. (mm)
38453-21X00	0.0173 (0.44)
38453-21X01	0.0189 (0.48)
38453-21X02	0.0205 (0.52)
38453-21X03	0.0220 (0.56)
38453-21X04	0.0236 (0.60)
38453-21X05	0.0252 (0.64)
38453-21X06	0.0268 (0.68)
38453-21X07	0.0283 (0.72)
38453-21X08	0.0299 (0.76)
38453-21X09	0.0315 (0.80)
38453-21X10	0.0331 (0.84)
38453-21X11	0.0346 (0.88)
38453-21X12	0.0362 (0.92)

OUTPUT SHAFT PRELOAD SHIM SELECTION

Part Number	Thickness in. (mm)
31499-21X00	0.0047 (0.12)
31499-21X01	0.0063 (0.16)
31499-21X02	0.0079 (0.20)
31499-21X03	0.0094 (0.24)
31499-21X04	0.0110 (0.28)
31499-21X05	0.0126 (0.32)
31499-21X06	0.0142 (0.36)
31499-21X07	0.0157 (0.40)
31499-21X08	0.0173 (0.44)
31499-21X09	0.0189 (0.48)
31499-21X10	0.0205 (0.52)
31499-21X11	0.0220 (0.56)
31499-21X12	0.0236 (0.60)
31499-21X13	0.0252 (0.64)
31499-21X14	0.0268 (0.68)
31499-21X15	0.0283 (0.72)
31499-21X16	0.0299 (0.76)
31499-21X17	0.0315 (0.80)
31499-21X18	0.0331 (0.84)
31499-21X19	0.0346 (0.88)
31499-21X20	0.0362 (0.92)
31499-21X21	0.0567 (1.44)
31499-21X22	0.0772 (1.96)

IDLER GEAR PRELOAD SHIM SELECTION

Part Number	Thickness in. (mm)
31499-21X06	0.0142 (0.36)
31499-21X07	0.0157 (0.40)
31499-21X08	0.0173 (0.44)
31499-21X09	0.0189 (0.48)
31499-21X10	0.0205 (0.52)
31499-21X11	0.0220 (0.56)
31499-21X12	0.0236 (0.60)
31499-21X13	0.0252 (0.64)
31499-21X14	0.0268 (0.68)
31499-21X15	0.0283 (0.72)
31499-21X16	0.0299 (0.76)
31499-21X17	0.0315 (0.80)
31499-21X18	0.0331 (0.84)
31499-21X19	0.0346 (0.88)
31499-21X20	0.0362 (0.92)
31499-21X21	0.0567 (1.44)
31499-21X22	0.0772 (1.96)

SIDE GEAR THRUST WASHER SELECTION

Part Number	Thickness in. (mm)
38424-21X00	0.0295–0.0315 (0.75–0.80)
38424-21X01	0.0315–0.0335 (0.80–0.85)
38424-21X02	0.0335–0.0354 (0.85–0.90)
38424-21X03	0.0354–0.0374 (0.90–0.95)

TORQUE SPECIFICATIONS

Part	ft. lbs.	Nm
Drive plate to torque converter	29–36	39–49
Converter housing to engine	29–36	39–49
Case to converter housing	14–17	19–23
Case to side cover	14–17	19–23
Case to valve body cover	3.6–5.1	5–7
Case to bearing retainer	12–15	16–21
Oil pump cover to converter housing	12–15	16–21
Valve body to to case	5.1–6.5	7–9
Governor cap to converter housing	3.6–5.1	5–7
Speedometer case to converter housing	4.6–6.1	6.3–8.3
Lower valve body to upper valve body	2.5–3.3	3.4–4.4
Final drive retaining bolts	54–65	74–88
Governor body to governor shaft	3–5	5–7
Governor shaft bolt	14–20	20–26
Manual shaft locknut	23–31	31–42
Oil strainer-converter housing	4.6–6.1	6.3–8.3
Control cylinder to case	4.6–6.1	6.3–8.3
Piston stem locknut	23–31	31–42
Drain plug to case	11–14	15–20

SPECIAL TOOLS

Tool Number (Kent-Moore No.)	Tool Name
(J2505S001) (J-25695)	Oil pressure gauge set
(J-34282)	Oil pressure gauge adapter
KV38106500 (J-34284)	Preload adapter
(J-34285)	Clutch spring compressor
(J-34286)	Side bearing outer race puller
(J-34290)	Shim selecting tool
(J-26744-A)	Seal installation tool
(J34279)	Automatic transaxle holding fixture
(J3289-20)	Bench mount fixture

Section 2

087N Transaxle
Porsche

APPLICATION

1984–89 Porsche 924 and 944

GENERAL DESCRIPTION

The 087N automatic transaxle is a fully automatic 3 speed unit, containing a 3 piece torque converter, forward and reverse planetary gear sets, 3 multiple disc clutches and band. The final drive unit is part of the transaxle assembly, containing the differential assembly. Shift control is by manually operated linkage.

Transaxle and Converter Identification

TRANSAXLE

Code letters and numbers are stamped on the bottom of the transaxle case, as well as on a pad on the front of the converter housing by the dipstick handle. These code letters and numbers denote the series of the transaxle, the model code and the date of manufacture. These numbers are important when ordering service replacement parts.

CONVERTER

The torque converter has a letter stamped on the outside of one of the lugs. It is important to make note of the letter for parts ordering.

Metric Fasteners

Metric tools will be required to service this transaxle. Due to the large number of alloy parts used in this transaxle, torque specifications should be strictly observed. Before installing bolts into aluminum parts, dip the bolts into clean transaxle fluid as this will prevent the screws from galling the aluminum threads, thus causing damage.

Metric fastener dimensions are very close to the dimensions of the familiar inch system fasteners. For this reason replacement fasteners must have the same measurement and strength as the original fastener.

Do not attempt to interchange metric fasteners for inch system fasteners. Mismatched or incorrect fasteners can cause damage to the automatic transaxle unit and possible personal injury. Care should be taken to reuse fasteners in their original locations.

Capacities

The 087N transaxle has an overhaul fluid capacity of 4.3 qts. of Dexron® automatic transaxle fluid (vehicles built after 1987 use a new fluid, Dexron IID®). The service fluid capacity is 3 qts. The final drive assembly has a fluid capacity of 1 qt. of SAE 90 Hypoid gear oil.

Checking Fluid Level

The fluid should be checked with the vehicle running and the transaxle in N, the fluid should be warm.

The fluid level can be checked visually, by looking through the transparent reservoir, located at the rear of the transaxle housing. The fluid level should be between the **MAX** and **MIN** levels on the reservoir, not over or under. Add fluid to correct the level if needed.

TRANSAXLE MODIFICATIONS

There were no modifications to this transaxle at the time of publication.

TROUBLE DIAGNOSIS

CHILTON'S THREE C's TRANSAXLE DIAGNOSIS
087N

Condition	Cause	Correction
Low oil level	a) Oil leaking from inlet b) Oil leaking from seals	a) Correct inlet leakage b) Replace seals
Oil escaping from inlet piping	a) High oil level b) Clogged transaxle vent valve c) Leak in oil pump suction line	a) Correct oil level b) Clean vent valve c) Correct oil pump suction leakage
Oil leaking at transaxle bell housing	a) Oil leaking from converter b) Transaxle bell housing seal c) Capscrew securing housing to transaxle case	a) Replace or repair converter b) Replace bell housing seal c) Reseal capscrew and torque properly

CHILTON'S THREE C's TRANSAXLE DIAGNOSIS
087N

Condition	Cause	Correction
Oil leakage near transaxle case	a) Selector valve sealing ring b) Oil sump gasket c) Sealing ring on oil inlet piping d) Oil pressure point connector	a) Replace selector valve sealing ring b) Replace oil pan gasket c) Replace sealing ring d) Tighten port plug
Low oil pressure	a) Low oil level b) Clogged oil filter c) Leak in oil pump suction line d) Leak in hydraulic circuit e) Oil pressure regulator valve spring out of adjustment	a) Correct fluid level b) Replace oil filter c) Repair suction line leakage d) Locate hydraulic circuit leakage and repair e) Adjust or replace regulator valve spring
High oil pressure	a) Main pressure regulator valve spring out of adjustment	a) Adjust or replace regulator valve spring
Park difficult to disengage	a) Selector lever linkage jammed	a) Correct binding or jammed condition
No take off with selector lever at Drive, 2, 1 or Reverse	a) Low oil level b) Oil filter clogged c) Selector lever linkage disconnected d) Input shaft failed e) Oil pressure regulator valve stuck open f) Defective oil pump	a) Correct oil level b) Replace oil filter c) Reconnect selector lever linkage d) Install new input shaft e) Correct pressure regulator valve operation f) Replace oil pump
Take off only after repeated movement of selector lever	Selector valve not aligned with valve body ports: a) Distorted or badly adjusted connecting cable b) Nut securing sector to shaft loose	 a) Adjust or replace the connecting cable b) Tighten the retaining nut
No take off after shift from Park to Drive, 2 or 1	a) Parking device stuck in engagement position	a) Correct binding or jammed condition
Sudden take off at high engine rpm	a) Front clutch piston seized b) Low oil level c) Defective oil pump d) Oil filter missing	a) Overhaul unit as required b) Correct fluid level c) Replace oil pump d) Install oil filter
Bumpy take off smooth only in Reverse	a) Low oil pressure b) Pressure regulator valve stuck	a) Correct oil pressure b) Correct pressure regulator valve operation
No take off in Drive or 2, only in 1 and Reverse	a) Defective free wheel	a) Overhaul unit as required
No take off in Drive, 2 and 1 (Reverse only)	a) Defective front clutch	a) Overhaul unit as required
No take off in Reverse	a) Defective front brake b) Defective rear clutch	a) Overhaul unit as required b) Overhaul unit as required
Take off in Neutral	a) Selector lever linkage incorrectly adjusted	a) Adjust linkage correctly
No 1-2 upshift with selector lever at Drive or 2 (transaxle locked in 1st)	a) Centrifugal speed governor valve sticking b) 1-2 shift valve stuck in 1st c) Leaking seals on oil pump hub d) Leaking governor hydraulic circuit e) Clogged governor filter f) Worn brake band	a) Free up governor valve b) Free up 1-2 shift valve c) Replace seals on oil pump hub d) Locate and repair leaking governor hydraulic circuit e) Remove or replace governor filter f) Replace brake band

CHILTON'S THREE C's TRANSAXLE DIAGNOSIS
087N

Condition	Cause	Correction
No 2-3 upshift with selector lever at Drive (transaxle locked in 2nd)	a) 2-3 shift valve stuck in 2nd b) Leaking governor hydraulic circuit	a) Free up 2-3 shift valve b) Locate and repair leaking governor hydraulic circuit
Upshifts in Drive and 2 only with throttle valve completely open	a) Modulator and relief valves stuck b) Kickdown valve or control cable stuck	a) Free up modulator and relief valves b) Free up or replace valve or cable
Upshifts in Drive and 2 only with throttle valve partially open	a) Kickdown valve cable incorrectly adjusted b) Kickdown valve cable failed	a) Correct kickdown cable adjustment b) Replace kickdown cable or adjust
No downshift with kickdown actuated	a) Kickdown valve cable failed b) Kickdown valve cable incorrectly adjusted	a) Replace kickdown cable and adjust b) Correct kickdown cable adjustment
Downshift at high speeds	a) Loss of pressure in governor	a) Correct governor oil pressure loss
Rough 3-2 downshift with kickdown actuated and at high speed	a) Rear brake incorrectly adjusted b) 3-2 shift valve seized or defective spring	a) Correct rear brake adjustment b) Free up 3-2 shift valve or replace spring
During downshift with kickdown actuated, engine idles and revs up	a) Low oil pressure b) Excessive band brake play or loose adjusting screw	a) Correct low oil pressure malfunction b) Adjust band
Engine braking minimal with lever at 1	a) Selector lever linkage incorrectly adjusted b) Front clutch piston and front brake stuck	a) Adjust selector lever linkage b) Overhaul unit as required
Engine braking minimal with lever at 2	a) Selector lever linkage incorrectly adjusted b) Front clutch piston and front brake stuck	a) Adjust selector lever linkage b) Overhaul unit as required
Vehicle not restrained with lever at Park	a) Selector lever linkage incorrectly adjusted b) Parking release spring failed c) Parking pawl stop failed	a) Adjust selector lever linkage b) Replace parking release spring c) Replace parking pawl stop
Excessive noise in all gears	a) Excessive play between sun and planet gears b) Defective thrust bearings c) Worn bushings d) Excessive end float e) Parking release spring unhooked or incorrectly installed f) Nuts securing bell housing to transaxle case	a) Replace necessary gears b) Replace thrust bearings c) Replace bushings d) Correct end play e) Connect parking release spring or install correctly f) Tighten nuts securely
Screech on starting	a) Converter defective	a) Replace converter assembly
Excessive quantity of ferrous deposits in oil	a) Oil pump b) Clutch hub worn	a) Replace oil pump, clean and examine unit for wear b) Replace clutch hub, clean and examine unit for wear
Excessive quantity of aluminum deposits in oil	a) End float adjustment thrust washer	a) Replace thrust washer, clean and examine unit for wear

CLUTCH AND BRAKE APPLICATION
087N

Selector Lever	Gear Engaged	Front Clutch	Rear Clutch	Front Brake	Brake Band	Free Wheel	Parking Device
P	Park	—	—	—	—	—	Applied
R	Reverse	—	Applied	Applied	—	—	—
N	Neutral	—	—	—	—	—	—
D	1st	Applied	—	—	—	Applied	—
	2nd	Applied	—	—	Applied	—	—
	3rd	Applied	Applied	—	—	—	—
2	1st	Applied	—	—	—	Applied	—
	2nd	Applied	—	—	Applied	—	—
1	1st	Applied	—	Applied	—	—	—

Hydraulic Control System

The power flow from the torque converter flows to the planetary gears by means of the turbine shaft, through the hollow drive pinion. All 3 forward gears and reverse are obtained by driving or holding either the sun gear, planetary gear carrier or annulus (internal ring) gear.

The hydraulic control system directs the path and pressure of the fluid so that the proper element can be applied as needed. The valve body directs the pressure to the proper clutch or band servo. There are 3 ways in which these control valves are operated. The manual valve is connected to the selector lever by a cable. Shifting the lever moves the manual valve to change the range of the transaxle. The kickdown valve and the modulated pressure valves are operated and controlled by a mechanical cable, connected to the accelerator linkage. The governor controls the pressure relative to speed and so makes the transaxle sensitive to changes in vehicle speed.

With the engine running, the oil pump supplies the torque converter with fluid. The fluid is passed through the impeller and at low speeds, the oil is redirected by the stator to the converter turbine in such a manner that it actually assists in delivering power or multiplying engine torque. As the impeller speed increases, the direction of the oil leaving the turbine changes and flows against the stator vanes in such a manner that the stator is now impeding the flow of oil. At this point, the roller clutch in the converter releases and the stator revolves freely on its shaft. Once the stator becomes inactive, there is no further multiplication of torque within the converter. At this point, the converter is merely acting as a fluid coupling at approximately a 1:1 ratio.

The converter is attached to planetary gears by the turbine shaft, so that a smooth gear change can be made without interrupting the flow of power from the engine. Various ratios (3 forward and 1 reverse) can be obtained by holding, releasing or driving different parts of the planetary gear set.

To accomplish this, 3 multiple disc clutches, 1 band and a one way clutch are used. The clutches and the band are applied and released by oil pressure, while the one way clutch mechanically prevents the rotation of the front brake/front planetary hub assembly when the transaxle is in the **D** position, 1st speed ratio and under an application of torque from the engine.

The valve body controls the shifting of the transaxle, dependent upon the engine load and the road speed.

Diagnosis Tests

CONTROL PRESSURE TEST

The pressure test port is located near the mid-section of the transaxle housing, next to the band servo. The pressure gauge to be used should have at least a 300 psi capacity.

1. Connect the pressure gauge hose to the pressure port and route the hose so that the gauge can be read from the drivers position.
2. Start the engine and apply the brakes. The engine/transaxle assembly must be at normal operating temperature.
3. Place the selector lever in the **D** position and allow the engine to idle. Observe the pressure reading.
4. Place the selector lever in **R** and allow the engine to idle. Observe the pressure reading.
5. For the full throttle pressure test, the manufacturer recommends the test be done on a dynamometer. However, if the test is done on the road, the pressure hose must be protected from dragging.
6. Establish a speed of 25 mph or higher, apply full throttle and observe the pressure gauge reading.

The pressure tests should be carefully reviewed to help locate the source of the malfunction.

CONTROL PRESSURE TEST SPECIFICATIONS
087N

Selector Lever Position	Accelerator Pedal Position	Main Pressure psi	Test Condition mph
D	Idle (no acceleration)	42–43	Speed greater than 30
D	Full throttle	105–107	Speed greater than 30
R	Idle (no acceleration)	134–143	Vehicle stopped
R	Full throttle	290 or more	At stall speed

AIR PRESSURE TEST

Air can be applied to appropriate passages so that the operation of the bands and clutches can be checked. Use a reduced amount of air pressure and make certain that the air is relatively free from dirt and moisture. Observe the clutch and servo area for excessive leakage. Often the clutch housing can be felt with the finger tips to feel if the clutches are applying as the air is introduced to the apply passage. The bands should move as the air is applied and relax when the pressure is removed.

STALL SPEED TEST

1. Raise the vehicle and support it safely.
2. Connect an engine tachometer and start the engine. Apply the parking brake.
3. Start the engine and run it to normal operating temperature, position the selection lever in **D**.
4. Fully depress the accelerator pedal for 6–8 seconds and note the engine speed.

NOTE: To prevent damage to the automatic transaxle, do not test stall speed for more than 10 seconds at a time.

5. Operate the engine at high idle with the transaxle selector lever in the **N** detent, for about 2 minutes in order for the transaxle to cool. Repeat the test.
6. The specification should be 2600–3000 rpm. If the measured stall speed exceeds the specification by more than 200 rpm, transaxle slip may be present and the transaxle should be checked.
7. If the stall speed drops below specification by 400–700 rpm, converter slippage may be present and should be checked.

ROAD TEST

If the transaxle is operative, the vehicle should be road tested in each gear range and under all possible road conditions. The shift points should be noted and recorded, checked against specifications and malfunction probabilities listed. The shifts should be smooth and take place quickly, without a lag in the acceleration. Listen for any signs of engine flare-up during the shifts, which would indicate a slipping brake band or clutches. Check the transaxle for abnormal fluid leakages.

If the shift points are incorrect or the transaxle does not have a kickdown, check and verify the accelerator cable for proper adjustment.

SHIFT POINT SPECIFICATIONS
087N

Shift Point	Full Throttle mph	Kickdown mph
1–2	21–29	45–47
2–3	52–65	80–82
3–2	37–51	77–79
2–1	15–17	41–44

ON CAR SERVICES

Adjustments

SELECTOR LEVER CABLE

1. Apply the parking brake and move the selector lever to the **P** detent.
2. Check the range selector on the transaxle, make sure it is in the **P** detent.
3. Adjust the ball on the end of the cable at the transaxle until there is no play in the cable.
4. The cable should slide on and off of the range selector with no tension on it.

THROTTLE AND CONTROL PRESSURE CABLE

1. Check the idle speed adjustment and set if necessary.
2. At the throttle body, take up the play in the cable. Do this by turning the adjusting nut.
3. Adjust the round end of the control cable until the cable can be installed or removed without strain.

Services

FLUID CHANGE

The conditions under which the vehicle is operated is the main consideration in determining how often the transaxle fluid should be changed. Different driving conditions result in different transaxle fluid temperatures. These temperatures affect change intervals.

If the vehicle is driven under severe conditions, change the transaxle fluid every 15,000 miles. If the vehicle is not used under severe conditions, change the fluid and replace the filter every 25,000 miles.

Do not overfill the transaxle. It takes about a pint of automatic transaxle fluid to raise the level from the **ADD** to the **FULL** mark on the transaxle fluid reservoir. Over filling the unit can cause damage to the internal components.

OIL PAN

Removal and Installation

1. Run the vehicle until it reaches normal operating temperature. The vehicle must be driven so that the transaxle fluid will also reach operating temperature.
2. Raise and safely support the vehicle.
3. Place a suitable drain pan under the transaxle and disconnect the filler tube at the oil pan.
4. Allow the transaxle to completely drain. Turn the crankshaft until the converter drain plug is visible through the access hole and remove the plug. Allow the converter to completely drain.
5. Remove the oil pan retaining bolts and carefully remove the oil pan.
6. Remove the oil filter retaining bolts and remove the oil filter, discard the O-ring from the filter.
7. Clean the gasket mounting surfaces.
8. Install the new filter in position, using a new O-ring. Install a new oil pan gasket and install the transaxle pan. Tighten the pan bolts to 15.4 ft. lbs.
9. Reconnect the filler tube and fill the transaxle to the correct level with fluid.

VALVE BODY

Removal and Installation

1. Raise and safely support the vehicle.
2. Drain the transaxle fluid and remove the oil pan retaining bolts.

3. Remove the oil pan. Remove the bolts retaining the valve body and carefully remove the valve body.

4. Lower the valve body down and away from the transaxle.

NOTE: When removing the valve body, do not open it, or all of the check balls will fall out.

5. Install the valve body in position.

6. Install the retaining bolts, making sure to install the bolts in their original position.

7. Center the valve body by tightening the corner bolts first then the balance of the bolts. Torque all bolts to 2.5 ft. lbs.

8. Install the oil pan and gasket, tighten the pan retaining bolts, install the oil filler tube and fill the transaxle to the correct level.

GOVERNOR

Removal and Installation

1. Raise and safely support the vehicle.

2. Loosen the intermediate muffler shield and push it aside as far as possible.

3. Disconnect the plug from the starter interlock switch.

4. Press in on the governor cover and remove the snapring. Remove the snapring and cover.

5. Loosen the nut on the axial governor holder.

6. Using a suitable tool, pry the axial holder in a clockwise direction.

7. Slide the governor from the case.

8. Check the governor for freedom of movement, it should rotate easily. Check the driven gear for damage or wear.

9. Slide the governor into the case and rotate the axial holder counterclockwise into position. Tighten the retaining nut.

10. Install the cover and snapring. Connect the electrical lead to the starter interlock switch.

11. Reposition the exhaust shield.

STARTER INTERLOCK AND BACKUP LIGHT SWITCH

Removal and Installation

1. Raise and safely support the vehicle.

2. Remove the range selector lever retaining bolt and remove the lever.

3. Disconnect the electrical lead from the switch.

4. Remove the switch mounting bolts and remove the switch from the transaxle case.

5. Install the switch in the case and install the retaining bolts, do not tighten the retaining bolts.

6. Position the range selector in the **N** detent and install the lever. Tighten the lever retaining bolt to 7 ft. lbs.

7. Tighten the switch mounting bolts and adjust the switch.

8. Connect the electrical lead to the switch and lower the vehicle.

9. Check the operation of the switch.

REMOVAL AND INSTALLATION

TRANSAXLE REMOVAL

1. Disconnect the negative battery cable.

2. Disconnect the battery ground strap from the body.

3. Disconnect the multi-plugs in the spare tire well and pull the wires out from below.

4. Remove the upper and lower air cleaner housings. Remove the upper air guide section.

5. Disconnect the control cable on the throttle housing. Disconnect the oxygen sensor wire on the fuse panel and pull it out from below.

6. Remove the engine air guide. Raise and safely support the vehicle.

7. Remove the complete exhaust system with all of the heat shields.

8. Remove the starter and suspend it out of the way.

9. Place a suitable drain pan under the transaxle and drain the fluid. Remove the fluid reservoir.

10. Disconnect the halfshafts from the rear of the transaxle and suspend them on a piece of wire.

11. Remove the transaxle crossmember suspension mounting bolts. Support the transaxle on the stabilizer bar, using support tool 9164 or equivalent.

12. Mark the position of the toe eccentric and the rear axle crossmember for reinstallation purposes. Remove the rear axle crossmember. Remove the clamp bolt from the central tube.

13. Disconnect the selector lever cable on the transaxle lever, unscrew the cable holder and sleeve.

14. Remove the fluid cooler and return lines. Plug the bores.

15. Pull off the vacuum modulator hose. Disconnect the pressure cable on the transaxle and pull the guide out carefully.

16. Place a universal transaxle jack or equivalent under the transaxle and tighten the retaining strap.

17. Remove the front and rear transaxle reinforcement plates. Lift the transaxle slightly and remove the support tool from the stabilizer.

18. Lower transaxle far enough to so that central tube mounting bolts and control cable bolt can be removed.

19. After removing the central tube-to-transaxle bolts, reposition the central tube in the installed position and loosely install the mounting plate. Place a block of wood under the central tube to keep it in position.

20. Slowly lower the transaxle assembly, pulling back on it as it comes out. Remove the transaxle from under the vehicle.

TRANSAXLE INSTALLATION

1. Coat the splines of the central shaft with and appropriate lubricant.

2. With the transaxle on a suitable lifting device, slowly raise it into an installed position under the vehicle. While raising it slide it onto the central shaft.

3. Install and lightly tighten the central shaft bolts. Lift the transaxle slightly and remove the block of wood and the support from the central shaft.

4. Lower the transaxle slightly and install the remaining central shaft bolts. Tighten all central shaft bolts to 87 ft. lbs. (120 Nm).

5. Mount the guide tube for the control cable on the converter housing. Tighten it to 6 ft. lbs.

6. Push the wiring harness up through the spare tire well.

7. Lift the transaxle up slightly and install the holding tool 9164 or equivalent, to the stabilizer bar.

8. Install the rear axle mount and tighten all bolts. Lift the transaxle and remove the holding tool.

9. Install the transaxle crossmember and bolts, tighten all bolts to 85 ft. lbs.

10. Adjust the transaxle suspension using the following procedure:

   a. Install the transaxle crossmember mounting bolts loosely.

b. Lift the transaxle in the middle of the case far enough so that there is a gap between both transaxle mounts and the crossmember. Measure this gap on both sides and take up the difference with shims.

c. Lower the transaxle and tighten the bolts to 85 ft. lbs.

d. Check the clearance on the transaxle stops after tightening the bolts, there should be at least 1mm clearance between the case stop and the transaxle.

11. Check the selector lever adjustment and the throttle cable adjustment.

12. Reconnect the halfshafts and lower the vehicle.

13. Road test the vehicle and check all gearshift operations.

BENCH OVERHAUL

Before Disassembly

Cleanliness is an important factor in the overhaul of the automatic transaxle. Before opening up this unit, the entire outside of the transaxle assembly should be cleaned, preferable with a high pressure washer such as a car wash spray unit. Dirt entering the transaxle internal parts will negate all the time and effort spent on the overhaul. During inspection and reassembly all parts should be thoroughly cleaned with solvent then dried with compressed air. Wiping cloths and rags should not be used to dry parts since lint will find its way into the valve body passages.

Wheel bearing grease, long used to hold thrust washers and lubricate parts, should not be used. Lubricate seals with clean transaxle fluid and use ordinary unmedicated petroleum jelly to hold the thrust washers and to ease the assembly of seals, since it will not leave a harmful residue as grease often will. Do not use solvent on neoprene seals, friction plates if they are to be reused, or thrust washers. Be wary of nylon parts if the transaxle failure was due to failure of the cooling system. Nylon parts exposed to water or antifreeze solutions can swell and distort and must be replaced.

Before installing bolts into aluminum parts, always dip the threads into clean transaxle fluid. Anti-seize compound can also be used to prevent bolts from galling the aluminum and seizing. Always use a torque wrench to keep from stripping the threads. Take care when installing new O-rings, especially the smaller O-rings. The internal snaprings should be expanded and the external rings should be compressed, if they are to be reused. This will help insure proper seating when installed.

Transaxle Disassembly

1. Remove the converter assembly. Drain all fluid and oil from both the transaxle and final drive units.

2. Mount the transaxle assembly on a suitable holding fixture.

3. Remove the oil pump shaft, the governor and the oil filler tube.

4. Remove the retaining nuts and separate the transaxle unit from the final drive. Remove the input shaft.

5. Remove the bolts retaining the flange and remove the flange and gasket. Remove the oil pan.

NOTE: Endplay between the transaxle and final drive is controlled by a selective shim and must be adjusted to limit the endplay of the reverse planetary ring gear. The shim should be retained for measurement purposes during reassembly.

6. Check that the parking pawl is not engaged and withdraw the parking plate, containing the governor drive gear and front ring gear.

7. Remove the friction washer and thrust bearing. Remove the one way clutch outer race retaining snapring and the locating pin.

8. Remove the one way clutch outer race. If necessary, 2 stiff pieces of wire can be used to help lift the race, if required.

9. Remove the reverse planetary gear set and the thrust washer.

10. Remove the forward planetary gear set/drive shell from the transaxle, along with the thrust bearing.

11. Remove the forward clutch and friction or thrust washer.

12. Remove the 1st/reverse brake clutch plates.

13. Remove the direct/reverse clutch unit. Loosen the band adjusting screw and pushrod. Remove the 2nd gear brake band.

NOTE: A thread sealing compound is used on the band adjusting bolt to case threads. Use care not to damage the case when removing this bolt.

14. Remove the bolts holding the spring holder and the oil pump. Remove the spring plate with the springs attached. Remove the oil pump assembly.

15. Remove the 2nd gear brake piston cover retaining ring. Remove the cover, piston and ring assembly. Remove the piston return spring.

16. Remove the band adjusting screw and pushrod.

17. Remove the 1st/reverse apply shell.

18. Remove the 1st/reverse brake piston.

19. Remove the oil filter and retaining screws.

20. Remove the valve body retaining bolts and carefully remove the valve body from the case.

21. Remove the accumulator piston spring and piston from the bore in the case.

22. Remove the oil pump filter, if equipped.

NOTE: Pistons with moulded seals should be replaced and not be reused during the reassembly of the transaxle components.

Unit Disassembly and Assembly

GOVERNOR

Disassembly

1. Remove the screws and lock plate retaining the governor shaft to the governor body.

2. Remove and discard the oil filter from the circuit plate. Note the position of the circuit plate and remove.

3. Remove the counter weight from the governor housing.

4. Remove the circlip, the flyweight, valve and spring, cap and centralizer shaft.

Inspection

1. Thoroughly flush the governor housing oil passages. Blow compressed air through the passages.

2. Check the governor housing for scoring, burrs or deposits. Replace if required.

3. Check the governor valve spring for damaged or weakened condition.

4. Check the valve for scores or burrs.

5. Check the governor shaft and gear for being bent, worn or damaged. Replace as required.

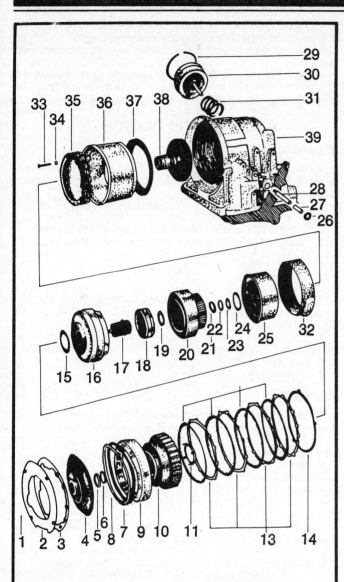

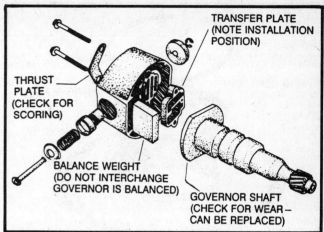

Exploded view of governor assembly

Assembly

1. Install the centralizer shaft, cup, spring and valve into the governor housing. Install the flyweight and retain with the circlip.
2. Install the counter weight and circuit plate. Install the circuit plate in the same position as it was when it was removed.
3. Assemble the shaft assembly to the governor housing and retain it with the 2 screws and the lock plate.

PARKING PLATE AND RING GEAR ASSEMBLY

Disassembly

Remove the retaining ring, separate the drive gear hub from the parking plate and ring gear.

Inspection

1. Inspect the parking plate teeth for damage and side wear.
2. Inspect the drive and ring gear teeth for scores or being worn.
3. Replace the components as required.

Assembly

1. Mate the splines of the drive gear hub and parking plate and ring gear.
2. Install the retaining ring.

ONE WAY CLUTCH

Disassembly

1. Mark the position of the cage to the outer race.
2. Remove the top and bottom retaining rings.
3. Tap the cage lightly and remove the cage from the outer ring.
4. Disassemble the rollers and the springs, noting their direction for assembly.

Inspection

1. Inspect the springs for distortion or breakage.
2. Inspect the rollers and outer race for wear or galling.
3. Replace the worn or damaged parts.

Assembly

1. Position the lower retaining ring in the outer ring.
2. Heat the outer ring to 300°F (150°C) on a hot plate or equivalent.

1. Screw	20. Forward clutch
2. Intermediate plate	21. Bearing ring
3. Gasket	22. Bearing cage
4. Ring gear	23. Bearing ring
5. Axial needle bearing	24. Thrust washer
6. Thrust washer	25. Direct and reverse
7. Circlip	clutch
8. Holding wedge	26. Nut
9. One way clutch	27. Adjusting screw
10. Reverse planetary gear	28. Support
set	29. Circlip
11. Thrust washer	30. Cover with piston
12. Inner plate (1st and	31. Spring
reverse gear brake)	32. Brake band (2nd gear
13. Outer plate (1st and	clutch)
reverse gear brake)	33. Bolt
14. Corrugated washer	34. Lock washer
15. Thrust washer	35. Spring retainer
16. Drive shell	36. Shell
17. Sun gear	37. Piston
18. Forward planetary set	38. Pump
19. Axial needle bearing	39. Transaxle case

Exploded view of main transaxle components

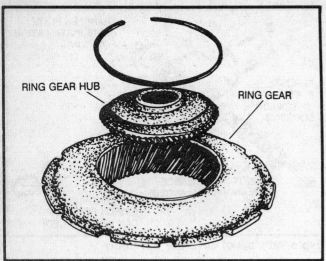

Ring gear assembly

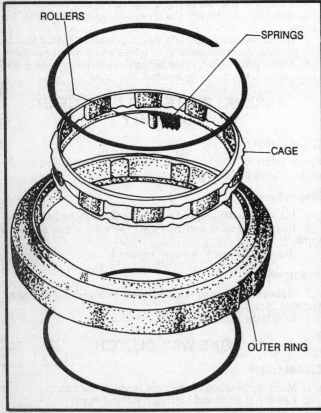

One way clutch assembly

3. Using gloves and 2 sets of pliers, place the cage on top of the outer ring, aligning the previously made marks and install the cage into the outer ring quickly. Be sure the cage is securely inserted into the outer ring quickly and that the cage "dogs" are securely positioned in the appropriate outer ring grooves. Rotate the cage slightly immediately after installation, if necessary.

NOTE: The cage quickly absorbs the heat from the outer ring and will lockup. If the cage is not correctly positioned, do not force it, but remove it and repeat the operation.

4. When the unit has cooled down, install the springs and rollers in the cage. Install the top retaining ring.
5. Install the one way clutch on the reverse planetary gear set.
6. With the one way clutch outer race held by the right hand, the reverse planetary gear set should rotate freely in a clockwise direction and lockup in a counterclockwise direction.

FORWARD CLUTCH

Disassembly

1. Remove the retaining ring. Lift the ring gear, pressure plate and set of clutches from the clutch housing. The thrust plate can then be removed.
2. Remove the lower retaining ring and remove the dished spring.
3. Remove the piston assembly from the clutch housing.
4. Remove the seals from the clutch housing hub and the piston.

Inspection

1. Inspect the clutch drum for wear. Using compressed air, inspect the check ball in the clutch housing for leakage. Air should flow one way, but not the other.
2. The distance between the outer edges of the upper and lower retaining ring grooves should be 1.173 in. (29.8mm).
3. Inspect the clutch piston for wear or damage.
4. Replace any components as required.

Assembly

1. Install the seals on the piston and the clutch housing hub. Lubricate the piston and the seals before installation.
2. Install the piston in the clutch housing, being careful not to damage the seals.
3. Install the dished spring so that the convex end (or smaller diameter), faces towards the base of the clutch housing.
4. Install the retaining ring. Check the dished spring to be sure it is under slight tension. If no tension is present, replace the spring.
5. Soak the friction lined clutch plates in automatic transmission fluid for at least 15 minutes before assembly.
6. Install the thrust plate with the projecting part facing towards the base of the clutch drum. Install the ring gear.
7. Starting with a lined clutch plate, alternate a steel plate and a lined plate. Install the pressure plate next to a line clutch plate and install the retaining ring.
8. After the assembly is complete, check the running clearance of the clutch pack. Using a dial indicator tool, measure the movement of the clutch pack in an up and down motion. The proper clearance should be 0.020–0.035 in. (0.5–0.9mm).
9. Should the measurement be out of specifications, pressure plates of different thicknesses are available to allow clearance adjustment.
10. To test the assembly, install the forward clutch and the direct/reverse with the thrust washers, on the oil pump.
11. Apply compressed air to the forward clutch port.
12. The piston must compress the clutch plates under air pressure and release them when the air pressure is removed.

DIRECT/REVERSE CLUTCH

Disassembly

1. Remove the clutch pack retaining snapring and remove the clutch pack assembly.
2. Install a special spring compressor tool and compress the spring cover in the clutch housing. Remove the retaining ring, release the compressor tool and remove. Remove the spring cover, the springs and the piston.

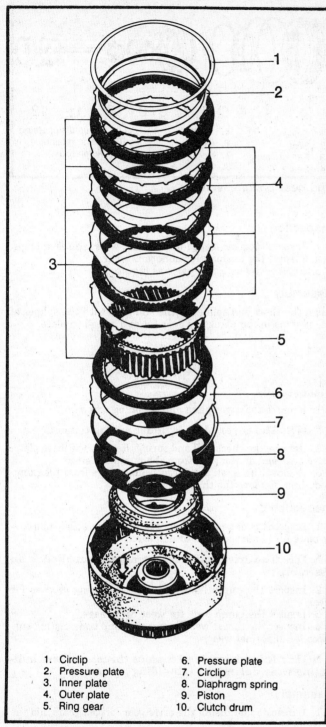

1. Circlip
2. Pressure plate
3. Inner plate
4. Outer plate
5. Ring gear
6. Pressure plate
7. Circlip
8. Diaphragm spring
9. Piston
10. Clutch drum

Forward clutch assembly

Inspection

1. Inspect the clutch drum bushing. The bushing can be replaced, if required. The old bushing can be used to press the new bushing into a measurement of 0.067 in. (1.7mm) below the top edge.

2. Inspect the clutch drum for wear or damage.

3. The distance between the the outer edges of the upper and lower retaining ring grooves should be 1.230 in. (31.25mm).

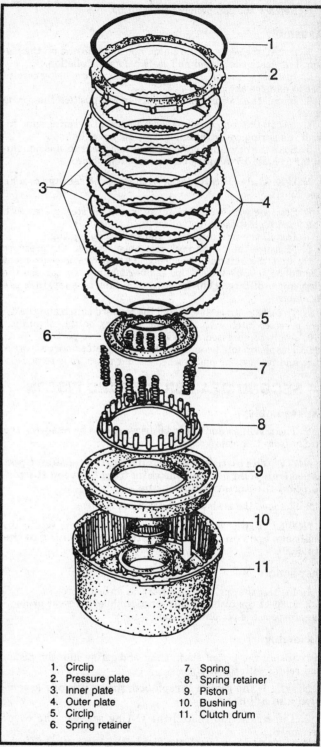

1. Circlip
2. Pressure plate
3. Inner plate
4. Outer plate
5. Circlip
6. Spring retainer
7. Spring
8. Spring retainer
9. Piston
10. Bushing
11. Clutch drum

Direct and reverse clutch assembly

NOTE: If the measurement is out of specifications, different sized clutch drums are available. Install only the clutch drum with the correct dimensions.

4. Inspect the piston and clutch housing bore for wear or damaged surfaces.

5. Using compressed air, inspect the check ball for leakage. Air should flow in one direction, but not the other.

6. Replace the components as required.

Assembly

1. Install the seals on the clutch housing hub and on the piston. Lubricate the piston and seals before installation.
2. Install the piston in the clutch housing bore, being careful not to damage the seals.
3. Install the 24 springs on the piston and position the spring cover.
4. Install the compressing tool. Compress the springs and install the spring cover retaining ring. Remove the tool.
5. Soak the new lined clutches in automatic transmission fluid for at least 15 minutes before installing them.

NOTE: Only clutch plates with grooved facings can be used.

6. Starting with a steel plate, alternate the steel plates with the lined plates, finishing with a lined plate.
7. Install the pressure plate and the retaining ring.
8. Measure the clutch pack clearance between the pressure plate and the retaining snapring. The correct measurement should be 0.0807–0.0984 in. (2.05–2.50mm). To correct the clearance, different thicknesses of retaining snaprings are available.
9. To test the assembly, install the forward clutch and the direct/reverse clutch with the thrust washers, on the oil pump.
10. Apply compressed air to the direct/reverse port.
11. The piston must compress the clutch plates under air pressure and release the plates when the air pressure is removed.

SECOND GEAR BRAKE BAND PISTON

Disassembly

1. The piston assembly can be disassembled by removing the circlip from the piston shaft.

NOTE: The piston shaft is under spring tension. Upon disassembly, do not lose the shim from between the piston and the accumulator spring.

2. Remove the seals from the piston and cover.

NOTE: O-ring seals are used on the cover, while lip seals are used on the piston. Note the positioning of the lip seals.

Inspection

1. Inspect the springs for distortion or being broken.
2. Inspect the piston and cover assemblies for wear or damage. Inspect the piston diameter.

Assembly

1. Install the piston shaft, shim and spring into the piston and retain with the circlip.

NOTE: If the piston is replaced, the unit is pre-assembled and adjusted.

2. Lubricate and install the O-ring seals in the cover assembly.
3. Lubricate and install the lip seals on the piston with the small seal lip facing the bottom of the cover and the large seal lip facing the open end of the cover.

SUN GEAR

Disassembly

Separate the sun gear from the forward planetary gear set. Note short side of sun gear engages the pinion gear.

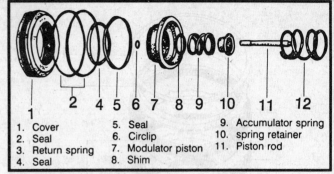

1. Cover	5. Seal	9. Accumulator spring
2. Seal	6. Circlip	10. spring retainer
3. Return spring	7. Modulator piston	11. Piston rod
4. Seal	8. Shim	

2nd gear brake assembly

Inspection

1. Inspect the gear teeth for breakage, wear, scores or chips.
2. Inspect the bushing for abnormal wear.
3. Replace the defective parts as required.

Assembly

Align the short end splines of the sun gear with the splines of the pinions in the planetary gear set and install in place.

OIL PUMP

Disassembly

1. Remove the cover plate and retaining screws.

NOTE: The cover plate is under spring tension.

2. Remove the check ball and spring. Remove the drive plate, drive gear and driven gear from the pump housing.
3. Remove the small and large sealing rings from the pump body hub. Remove the thrust washer.

Inspection

1. Inspect the drive and driven gears, the drive plate and cover plate for abnormal wear or damage.

NOTE: The drive and driven gears are supplied as an assembly.

2. Inspect the pump housing hub sealing ring grooves for wear.
3. Inspect the pump body for wear or damage.
4. Inspect the thrust washer and oil pump body mating surfaces for abnormal wear.

NOTE: It is advisable to replace thrust washers indicating wear during the rebuilding process.

Assembly

1. Lubricate and install the drive gear, driven gears and the drive plate.

NOTE: Install the driven gear with the code letter facing towards the cover plate.

2. Install the springs and check ball in the pump housing.
3. Install the cover plate and retain with the retaining capscrews.
4. Install the thrust washer, the large seal rings and the small seal rings. Be sure the seal rings are hooked together at their ends.
5. After the assembly, insert the oil pumpdrive shaft and check that the gear rotate freely.

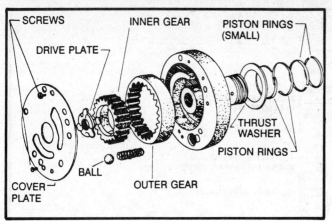

Oil pump assembly

VALVE BODY

NOTE: The valve body should only be disassembled for cleaning or when the transaxle failure was due to dirty fluid or burned friction plate linings. A storage tray is available, to store the valves, springs, balls and screws while the valve body is being cleaned and/or overhauled. The storage tray resembles the valve body in order to maintain the sequence of disassembly and assembly. It is suggested the tray or its equivalent be used.

Disassembly

1. Remove the screws retaining the accumulator cover and kickdown valve control lever detent spring.
2. Remove the retaining screws from the circuit plate and intermediate plate to valve body.
3. Remove the valve plates and retaining screws. Remove the kickdown valve, bushing, spring and modulator valve.
4. Remove the spring, 1–2 shift valve, spring seat and spring.
5. Remove the pressure relief valve for the converter fluid supply, spring, main relief valve, spring and 2–3 shift valve, spring and spring seat and the 3–2 kickdown valve from the valve body.
6. On the opposite side of the valve body, remove the valve plates and retaining screws.
7. Remove the 1–2 shift valve, the plug, adjuster screw, spring and spring seat.
8. Remove the modulated pressure relief valve, plug, adjuster screw, spring and main pressure control valve.
9. Remove the adjuster screw, spring, primary regulator valve, spring, front brake control valve and sleeve.
10. Remove the 2–3 shift valve, 3–2 shift valve and spring.
11. Remove the 5 (6mm diameter) check balls and if equipped, the 6th ball, (3mm diameter). Mark the locations of each ball for reference during the assembly.

Inspection

1. Clean the valve body parts in solvent and air dry with compressed air. Clean the plate and valve body with solvent and blow the passages dry with compressed air.
2. Check that all valves move freely in their bores.
3. Remove small burrs on the valves, using fine emery cloth, but do not remove the sharp edges from the valves.
4. Check the springs for failure or lack of tension.
5. If defects are found on any part of the valve body or components, replace the entire assembly.

NOTE: The valve springs are not interchangeable due to different tension values.

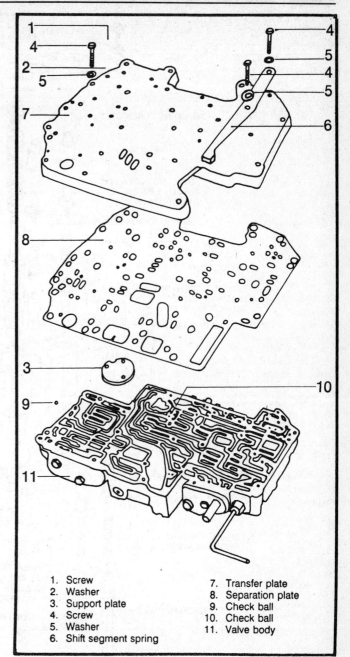

1. Screw	7. Transfer plate
2. Washer	8. Separation plate
3. Support plate	9. Check ball
4. Screw	10. Check ball
5. Washer	11. Valve body
6. Shift segment spring	

Removing transfer and separation plates

Assembly

1. Lubricate the valves, sleeves, springs, adjuster screws and plugs with automatic transmission fluid and install on the one side of the valve body, as they were removed.
2. Install the valves, sleeves, springs, adjuster screws and plugs on the opposite side of the valve body.
3. As each side is assembled, install the retaining plates and retaining screws.

NOTE: Do not attempt to turn the adjusting screws. Their adjustment must be made on a test bench only.

4. Install the 5 check balls (6mm diameter) and if equipped, the 6th check ball (3mm diameter) in their respective pockets in the valve body.

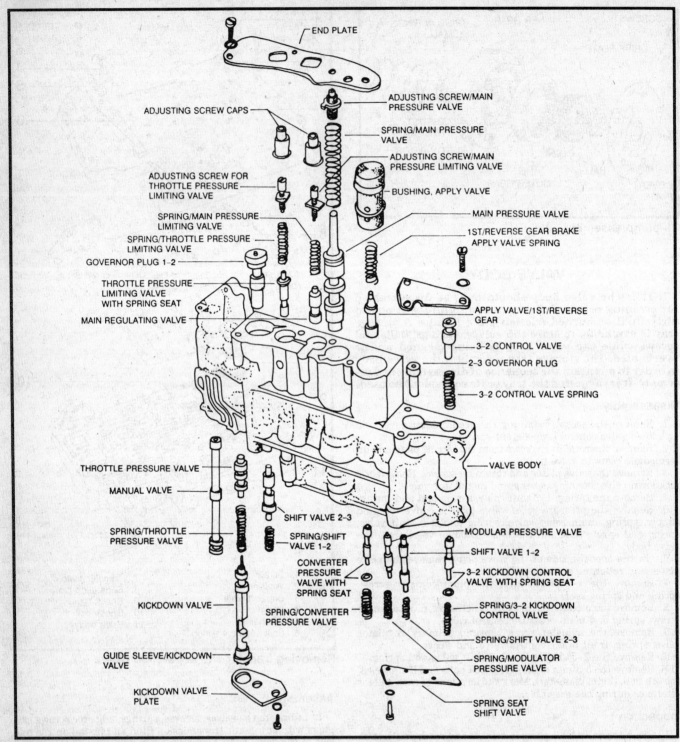

Valve body components

ADJUSTING SCREW CAPS

ADJUSTING SCREW FOR THROTTLE PRESSURE LIMITING VALVE

SPRING/MAIN PRESSURE LIMITING VALVE

SPRING/THROTTLE PRESSURE LIMITING VALVE

GOVERNOR PLUG 1–2

THROTTLE PRESSURE LIMITING VALVE WITH SPRING SEAT

MAIN REGULATING VALVE

THROTTLE PRESSURE VALVE

MANUAL VALVE

SPRING/THROTTLE PRESSURE VALVE

KICKDOWN VALVE

GUIDE SLEEVE/KICKDOWN VALVE

KICKDOWN VALVE PLATE

END PLATE

ADJUSTING SCREW/MAIN PRESSURE VALVE

SPRING/MAIN PRESSURE VALVE

ADJUSTING SCREW/MAIN PRESSURE LIMITING VALVE

BUSHING, APPLY VALVE

MAIN PRESSURE VALVE

1ST/REVERSE GEAR BRAKE APPLY VALVE SPRING

APPLY VALVE/1ST/REVERSE GEAR

3–2 CONTROL VALVE

2–3 GOVERNOR PLUG

3–2 CONTROL VALVE SPRING

VALVE BODY

SHIFT VALVE 2–3

SPRING/SHIFT VALVE 1–2

CONVERTER PRESSURE VALVE WITH SPRING SEAT

SPRING/CONVERTER PRESSURE VALVE

MODULAR PRESSURE VALVE

SHIFT VALVE 1–2

3–2 KICKDOWN CONTROL VALVE WITH SPRING SEAT

SPRING/3–2 KICKDOWN CONTROL VALVE

SPRING/SHIFT VALVE 2–3

SPRING/MODULATOR PRESSURE VALVE

SPRING SEAT SHIFT VALVE

NOTE: Should the valve plugs over the 1–2 shift valve, 2–3 shift valve and converter control valve become loose or dislodged, loss of 2nd or 3rd gear and the lack of proper converter charging can occur.

5. Install the intermediate plate on the valve body and check to see if 3 balls are visible through ports in the upper section of the circuit plate. If not, check to see if the check balls are in their proper location, or replace the valve body.

6. Install the circuit plate on the valve body and torque the screws to 2.9 ft. lbs. Fasten the accumulator cover to the circuit plate and torque the screws to 2.2 ft. lbs.

7. Fasten the kickdown valve control lever detent spring to the valve body.

Transaxle Assembly

1. Install 1st/reverse brake piston into the transaxle case.

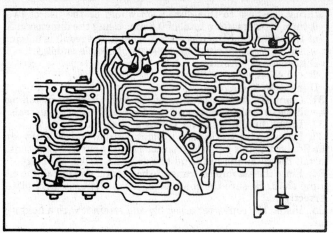

Check ball locations

2. Position the 1st/reverse apply shell in the transaxle case so that the lugs on the shell/housing line up with the grooves in the transaxle case.

3. Install the band actuator rod until it touches the band adjuster screw.

4. Install the spring, 2nd gear brake piston and cover in the transaxle housing. Press the cover/piston assembly inward and install the retaining ring.

5. Position the oil pump into the transaxle case with the oil pump rib facing away from the band actuator rod.

NOTE: The lugs of the thrust washer straddle the oil pump rib and should be on the opposite or top side of the transaxle.

6. Position the springs on the spring plate and attach the spring plate assembly to the oil pump with the retaining bolts. Torque to 61 inch lbs. (7 Nm).

7. Insert the oil pump driveshaft into the oil pump drive pate and rotate the shaft in a clockwise direction, checking for any binding from the oil pump gears. The gears should rotate freely. Remove the driveshaft from the pump.

8. Install the 2nd gear brake band into the transaxle case making sure the actuator rods engage with the lugs on the band.

9. If the forward clutch and the direct/reverse clutch assemblies have not previously been assembled, coat the thrust washers with petroleum jelly and install on the forward clutch drum.

10. Insert the forward clutch drum into the direct/reverse clutch drum, engaging the grooves of the forward clutch drum with the dirct/reverse clutch assembly.

11. Install the input shaft into the clutch assemblies, lift and install the clutch assemblies into the transaxle, engaging the 2 clutch units to the oil pump.

12. Coat the thrust washer with petroleum jelly and install on the forward clutch hub.

13. Install the forward planetary gear set into the forward clutch drum until the planetary gear teeth mesh with the ring gear teeth.

NOTE: The sun gear short splined end must be engaged with the planetary gear teeth when the planetary gear set is installed.

14. Install the drive shell/housing, along with the thrust washer, on the sun gear.

15. Install the reverse-planetary gear set into the transaxle case until the sun gear meshes with the planet gear teeth. Install the thrust washer, coated with petroleum jelly, on the planet carrier hub.

16. Install the 1st/reverse brake plates, starting with the wavy spring washer, a steel plate, followed by lined plate. Alternately install the clutch plates, steel to lined, until all are installed.

17. Coat the thrust washer with petroleum jelly and install. Install the one way clutch into the transaxle case. Rotate the reverse planetary gear set in a clockwise direction while pressing the one way clutch into operating position.

NOTE: To verify the correct operation of the one way clutch position the transaxle in the upright position and while holding the one way clutch outer race stationary, the reverse planetary gear set should rotate freely in a clockwise direction and lockup in a counterclockwise direction.

18. Install the one way clutch outer race locating pin in the housing of the transaxle case.

19. An indicator of correct assembly of the transaxle components, is the installation of the outer race retaining snapring without interference from the assembly.

NOTE: The snapring opening must be opposite the locating pin.

20. Position the transaxle horizontally. Loosen the band adjusting locknut and tighten the adjusting screw to 87 inch lbs. (10 Nm). Loosen and retighten the adjusting screw to 43 inch lbs. (5 Nm). Loosen the adjusting screw exactly 2½ turns and tighten the locknut.

21. Install the reverse planetary ring gear/governor drive gear on the reverse planetary gear set.

22. Install the flange with the 2 gaskets. Install the retaining cap screws.

23. Install the valve body and accumulator piston and spring into its bore in the transaxle case. Install the valve body to the transaxle housing, connecting the manual valve and the kickdown valve. Tighten all bolts diagonally and to a torque of 35 inch lbs. (4 Nm).

24. Install the gasket, oil strainer, cover and attach with the retaining screws. Torque to 26 inch lbs. (3 Nm).

25. Using a new gasket, install the oil pan and install the retaining bolts. Torque to 14 ft. lbs. (20 Nm).

26. Before assembling the transaxle and final drive, the endplay between the transaxle and final drive must be measured and adjusted as required to limit the endplay movement of the reverse planetary ring gear before the units are assembled.

27. To finding the endplay dimension **A** of the final drive unit:

    a. Have the final drive unit in an upright position with the seal, sealing ring and thrust washer removed.

    b. Using a straight edge laid across the face of the final drive unit, measure the distance from the top face of the straight edge to the top of the oil sleeve bushing, with a depth measuring tool. Record the reading.

    c. Measure the distance from the straight edge to the face of the final drive housing and record the measurement.

NOTE: This measurement is the thickness of the straight edge tool.

    d. An example of the measurements and results would be as follows:

From the straight edge to oil sleeve bushing – 18.7mm
From straight edge to final drive surface – 8.0mm
Represents dimension **A** – 10.7mm

28. To find the endplay dimension **B** of the transaxle:

    a. Position the transaxle with its attaching studs upright.

    b. Lay the straight edge tool across the face of the housing and measure the distance from the straight edge to the gasket on the plate.

    c. Measure the distance from the straight edge to the shoulder for the shim on the plate.

    d. An example of the measurements and results would be as follows:

From the straight edge to plate – 19.2mm
From the straight edge to shoulder – 10.0mm
Represents dimension **B** – 9.2mm.

29. To find the endplay dimension **X** – shim thickness:

    a. To determine the shim thickness needed, subtract dimension **B** from dimension **A**. The result would be dimension **X**.

    b. An example of finding dimension **X** would be as follows:

Dimension **A** – 10.7mm
Dimension **B** – 9.2mm
Dimension **X** – 1.5mm

    c. Shims are available in 2 thicknesses, 0.4 and 1.2mm.

    d. From the following chart, determine the shim or shim combination and to be used to correct dimension **X**.

30. An allowable endplay clearance, described as dimension **Y**, is constant and should be between 0.23–0.84mm or 0.009–0.033 in. This measurement must be included in the stacking of the proposed thrust washer(s), as determined in the preceding steps. An example of the inclusion of the endplay clearance is as follows:

    a. As the previous examples explained how to find dimensions **A** and **B**, resulting in dimension **X**, the theoretical use of thrust washers to this dimension would be the use of two 0.4mm washers, for a total of 0.8mm. Using the dimension **X** of 1.5mm and subtracting 0.8mm from it, the result is 0.7mm which falls within the 0.23–0.84mm allowable endplay.

Dimension **X** – 1.5mm
2 × 0.4mm shim – 0.8mm
Dimension **Y** – 0.7mm.

31. Complete the installation of the final drive by installing the oil seal, thrust washer and turbine shaft with O-ring seals.

32. Install final drive outer O-ring seal and lubricate.

33. Have the transaxle in an upright position and carefully set the final drive unit onto the transaxle mating surface and studs. Install the retaining nuts and torque to 22 ft. lbs. (30 Nm).

34. Place the assembled transaxle horizontal and install the oil pump shaft. Be sure the shaft engages the oil pump drive plate correctly.

35. Install the converter assembly and retain it with a holding bar.

SPECIFICATIONS

TORQUE SPECIFICATIONS

Part	ft. lbs.	Nm
Test port plug	11	15
Filter tube to pan	58	80
Fluid supply tank to holder	5	7
Transaxle-to-final drive	21	29
Intermediate plate-to-transaxle case	2.5	3.5
Pump-to-case	5	7
2nd gear brake band adjustment nut	14	19.6
Oil pan bolts	15	20.5
Oil filter-to-valve body	2.5	3.5
Valve body-to-case	2.5	3.5
End plate-to-valve body	2.5	3.5
Support-to-transfer plate	2.5	3.5
Manual lever-to-case	2.5	3.5
Kickdown lever-to-shaft	12	17
Control lever-to-shaft	13	18
Governor cover-to-case	7	9
Governor shaft-to-housing	2.5	3.5
Pinion cover-to-final drive	30	42
Final drive cover-to-case	18	25
Ring gear-to-differential	67	93
Converter-to-drive plate	29	40
Filler tube-to-oil pan	58	80
Lines to transaxle	16	22.5

ENDPLAY SHIM SELECTION

Measured Endplay in.	(mm)	Number and Size of Shims (mm)
0.009–0.033	0.23–0.84	No shim
0.034–0.049	0.85–1.24	1–0.4
0.050–0.065	1.25–1.64	2–0.4
0.066–0.081	1.65–2.04	1–1.2
0.082–0.097	2.05–2.44	1–0.4 and 1–1.2
0.098–0.113	2.45–2.84	2–0.4 and 1–1.2
0.114–0.129	2.85–3.24	2–1.2
0.130–0.145	3.25–3.64	1–0.4 and 2–1.2
0.146–0.155	3.65–3.88	2–0.4 and 2–1.2

SPECIAL TOOLS
SERVICE TOOL SELECTION

Description	Number
Holder plate	VW 351
Seal driver	VW 192
Dial indicator holder	VW 387
Bridge	VW 46013
Thrust pad	VW 433
Thrust plate	VW 402
Punch	VW 411
Puller	US 1078
Adapter	VW 295A
Slide hammer	VW 771
Driving mandrel	VW 2056
Transaxle support	VW 353
Internal puller	US 1108
Storage tray	VW 2008A

Section 2

A28 Transaxle
Porsche

APPLICATION

1984–89 Porsche 928

GENERAL DESCRIPTION

The A28 transaxles are rear mounted units that incorporate a sun and planetary gear set. The transaxle has 4 forward speeds and 1 reverse, the 4th gear is an overdrive ratio. The transaxle is connected to the engine through a driveshaft, that is attached to the rear of the engine. The shaft rides in a central tube, that is a structural part of the drive train. The entire drive train, including the engine, central tube and transaxle assembly are mounted at 4 points with rubber dampers.

Transaxle Identification

The transaxle can be identified by a stamping on a stiffening rib of the rear axle assembly. The first group of 4–5 numbers are the transaxle identification number.

Metric Fasteners

Metric tools will be required to service this transaxle. Due to the large number of alloy parts used in this transaxle, torque specifications should be strictly observed. Before installing capscrews into aluminum parts, dip the bolts into clean transaxle fluid as this will prevent the screws from galling the aluminum threads, thus causing damage.

Metric fastener dimensions are very close to the dimensions of the familiar inch system fasteners. For this reason replacement fasteners must have the same measurement and strength as the original fastener.

Do not attempt to interchange metric fasteners for inch system fasteners. Mismatched or incorrect fasteners can cause damage to the automatic transaxle unit and possible personal injury. Care should be taken to reuse fasteners in their original locations.

Capacities

The A28 transaxles have an overhaul fluid capacity of 19.6 pts. of Dexron automatic transmission fluid (vehicles built after 1987 use a new fluid, Dexron IID). The service fluid capacity is 15.4 pts. The final drive assembly has a fluid capacity of 6.3 pts. of SAE 90 Hypoid gear oil.

Checking Fluid Level

The fluid should be checked with the vehicle running and the transaxle in **N**, the fluid should be warm.

The fluid level can be checked visually, by looking through the transparent reservoir, located at the rear of the transaxle housing. The fluid level should be between the **MAX** and **MIN** levels on the reservoir, not over or under. Add fluid to correct the level if needed.

TRANSAXLE MODIFICATIONS

Kickdown Relay (Speed Relay) with 2 Shift Points

The 1st–2nd gear shift of the early kickdown relay was carried out hydraulically at an engine speed of 5000 rpm. Upshifts from 2nd–3rd gear and 3rd–4th gear, with accelerator in the kickdown position, were introduced by the kickdown relay at an engine speed of 5900 rpm.

The new design relay uses the engine speed and road speed information to determine which gear the vehicle is being driven in. It has 2 shift points, 4950 ± 50 rpm for 1st–2nd gear kickdown and 5950 ± 50 rpm for other kickdown upshifts.

Stronger Central Shaft

Vehicles built before the 1989 use a 25mm central shaft. Vehicles built for 1989 use a 28mm central shaft that is designed to absorb more torsional torque. The splines on both ends of the shaft remain the same and supporting mounts are adapted to the new diameter.

CHILTON'S THREE C's TRANSAXLE DIAGNOSIS

Condition	Cause	Correction
Transaxle slips in all selector positions	a) Incorrect modulating pressure	a) Check and adjust pressure or check modulator valve
	b) Plugged vacuum line to intake branch	b) Replace as needed
	c) Poor operating pressure	c) Disassemble and clean
2nd gear slips or transaxle shifts 1st to 3rd	a) Faulty control valve B1	a) Replace shift valve housing if necessary
	b) B1 brake band piston seal faulty	b) Replace seal
	c) Faulty B1 brake band	c) Replace brake band and pressure element

CHILTON'S THREE C's TRANSAXLE DIAGNOSIS

Condition	Cause	Correction
Transaxle slips in 1st and 2nd gear or no forward movement possible	a) Faulty shift valve B2 b) Faulty B2 brake band piston c) Brake band B2 misadjusted	a) Replace shift housing if necessary b) Replace piston c) Replace band or adjust using longer pin
Transaxle slips during 2nd–3rd shift	a) Poor modulating pressure b) Faulty shift valve housing c) Clutch K1 faulty	a) Adjust as necessary b) Check and replace shift valve housing as required c) Replace clutch K1 components
Transaxle slips during 3rd–4th shift	a) Poor modulating pressure b) Faulty shift valve housing	a) Adjust as necessary b) Check and replace shift valve housing as required
Transaxle has no power flow or fails after brief operation	a) Improper converter installation b) No drive dog engagement in primary pump	a) Check installation and correct as needed b) Check and replace primary pump
No power flow in all selector positions after startup	a) Leaky or defective lubricating ring on converter drive shaft b) Leaky lubricating valve in shift housing	a) Replace lubricating ring b) Check and clean valve
No power flow in reverse gear	a) Faulty plates or seals on brake band 3 b) Faulty one way clutch	a) Check and replace seals, plates or band as needed b) Check and replace clutch in gear set
Harsh engagement of D or R	a) Improper idle or CO adjustment b) Poor modulating pressure c) Poor vacuum connections or blockage d) Pressure piston in shift valve housing stuck	a) Adjust as needed b) Check and adjust as needed c) Check lines and replace or repair as needed d) Check piston or replace shift valve housing
Harsh shifting	a) Poor modulating pressure b) Poor vacuum connections or blockage in line	a) Check and adjust b) Check lines and replace as needed
Harsh 3rd–4th downshift	a) Faulty seal on B2 brake band b) Faulty brake band B2 piston c) B2 pressure element turned	a) Replace seal b) Replace piston c) Replace pressure element
Harsh shift with partial load	a) Control pressure cable misadjusted b) Poor modulating pressure c) Vacuum leak or blockage	a) Check and adjust cable b) Check and adjust c) Check lines and replace as needed
No upshifts	a) No governor pressure b) Dirt in shift valve housing	a) Clean and service governor b) Clean and service housing or replace as needed
Upshifts only in upper speed range	a) Control pressure cable misadjusted b) Poor governor pressure c) Faulty control pressure valve	a) Check and adjust b) Check and replace governor as needed c) Replace valve
Upshifts only in lower speed range	a) Faulty control pressure cable b) Full throttle stop misadjusted c) Governor pressure too high	a) Adjust or replace b) Check and adjust c) Replace governor
No 3rd to 2nd kickdown	a) Control pressure cable misadjusted b) Accelerator cable misadjusted	a) Check and adjust cable b) Check and adjust cable
No downshifts	a) Blown solenoid valve fuse b) Faulty solenoid valve c) Control pressure cable damaged or misadjusted d) Kickdown control slide stuck or damaged	a) Check and replace fuse b) Remove solenoid, check and replace as needed c) Check adjustment and replace cable if needed d) Check operaiton and replace if necessary

CHILTON'S THREE C's TRANSAXLE DIAGNOSIS

Condition	Cause	Correction
No 4th–3rd or 3rd–2nd shifts	a) Control pressure cable misadjusted b) Vacuum leak or blockage c) Brake shift plunger stuck	a) Check and adjust as needed b) Check lines and repair or replace as needed c) Separate shift slider housing and repair or replace plunger
Unwanted downshift	a) Faulty solenoid valve O-ring b) Sticky kickdown switch c) Solenoid valve sticking open	a) Replace O-ring b) Check switch and replace as needed c) Check valve and replace as needed
Poor acceleration when starting out	a) Incorrect stall speed	a) Converter replacement needed
Selector lever won't engage R or P	a) Governor faulty b) Faulty blocking piston in lower cover	a) Clean and service governor b) Clean and service blocking piston or replace if needed
Engine will not start in P and N	a) Selector lever cable misadjusted b) Starter interlock switch faulty	a) Check and adjust cable b) Replace switch
1st and reverse gears loud	a) Damaged front gear set	a) Check and replace gear set
3rd gear loud	a) Damaged rear planet set	a) Replace rear planet set
Whining noise when changing gears under load	a) Clogged oil filter	a) Replace oil filter
Whining noise that increases with engine speed	a) Primary pump damaged	a) Check pump and replace as needed
Rattling noise at or below 1500 rpm	a) Reverse gear plates swinging in transaxle	a) Replace inner plates of reverse gear brake B3

TROUBLE DIAGNOSIS

Hydraulic Control System

The hydraulic system consists of the valve body, torque converter, modulator valve, oil pump and a centrifugal governor.

The pump is driven at engine speed by the shell of the housing of the torque converter. The pump is of the gerotor type and is located in the front of the transaxle case cover. It is the basis of the hydraulic system and delivers the pressure required to operate the brake bands and clutch packs.

Pressure from the pump is considered main pressure, this pressure operates the clutches and brakes. This pressure is regulated by the main pressure control valve in the valve body. Main pressure can be measured but not adjusted. The main pressure is controlled by the modulator pressure, this can be measured and adjusted by adjusting the modulator control valve.

The modulator control valve is driven by vacuum pressure from the engine and this in turn activates the valve in opposition to a control spring thus controlling pressure. This spring force also acts against the governor pressure.

Throttle pressure is controlled by a cable that is linked in conjunction to the accelerator. Pressure is applied to the throttle pressure control valve by the throttle control cable. This causes kickdowns or upshifts depending on throttle position and the relative pressure caused by activating the throttle valve.

Governor pressure is is controlled by the centrifugal governor in accordance with road speed. Governor pressure is used to cause upshifts.

The valve contains all of the various activating valves for the clutches and brakes. The valve body is affected by the pressures developed from accelerating or decelerating as well as selector lever position and road speed.

All transaxle fluid is routed through the filter screen to eliminate any debris or contamination from the fluid before it enters the valve body.

Diagnosis Tests

STALL SPEED TEST

1. Raise the vehicle and support it safely.
2. Connect an engine tachometer and start the engine. Apply the parking brake.
3. Run the engine to normal operating temperature, position the selection lever in **D**.
4. Fully depress the accelerator pedal for 6–8 seconds and note the engine speed.

NOTE: To prevent damage to the automatic transaxle, do not test stall speed for more than 10 seconds at a time.

5. Allow 2 minutes for the transaxle to cool and then repeat the test.
6. The specification should be 2200–2600 rpm. If the measured stall speed exceeds the specification by more than 300 rpm, transaxle slip may be present and the transaxle should be checked.
7. If the stall speed drops below specification by 400–700 rpm, converter slippage may be present and should be checked.

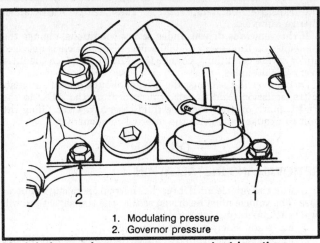

1. Modulating pressure
2. Governor pressure

Modulating and governor pressure test locations

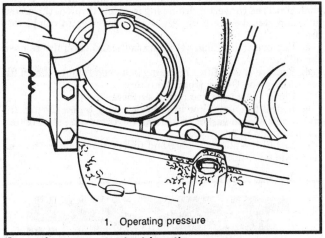

1. Operating pressure

Operating pressure test location

CONTROL PRESSURE TESTS

There are 3 pressure test points on the transaxle. There are test points for modulating pressure, operating pressure and governor pressure. Both modulating pressure and governor pressure can be adjusted, operating pressure is not adjustable, but is directly affected by modulating pressure.

Before perfroming any of the pressure checks, appropriate gauges must be connected to the test ports on the sides of the transaxle. A gauge that will measure up to at least 385 psi. (25 bar) is needed. The modulating and governor pressure ports are on the lower edge of the transaxle on the side opposite of the fluid reservoir. The operating pressure port is just below the fluid reservoir.

Modulating Pressure Test

NOTE: Modulating pressure must be checked and adjusted, if necessary, before any other pressure is checked.

1. Open the hood and disconnect the vacuum line to the intake manifold. Plug the opening.
2. With the gauges correctly installed, run the vehicle to normal operating temperature.
3. Drive the vehicle and accelerate to 30 mph and check the gauge reading for modulator pressure.
4. The correct pressure is 64–70 psi (4.4–4.9 bar).
5. If the pressure is not correct, check the modulator adjustment and adjust as needed.

The modulator pressure can be adjusted by removing the rubber cover from the modulator valve vacuum nozzle. Pull the retainer out slightly on the cover and adjust the setting screw. Turning the adjusting screw a full turn clockwise, will increase the adjustment pressure by 6 psi (0.4 bar); counterclockwise will decrease the pressure adjustment by 6 psi (0.4 bar).

Governor Pressure Test

1. Open the hood and disconnect the vacuum line to the intake manifold. Plug the opening.
2. With the gauges correctly installed, run the vehicle to normal operating temperature.
3. The governor pressure must be checked at various speeds, each speed has its own specific pressure reading; at 13 mph the pressure should be 3 psi (0.2 bar), at 31 mph the pressure should be 16 psi (1.1 bar) and at 62 mph the pressure should be 30 psi (2.0 bar).
4. If the pressure is not at specification or no pressure is evident, the governor is at fault. The only way to correct the pressure, is to remove the governor assembly, disassemble, clean and repair it. If the governor can not be repaired it must be replaced.

Operating Pressure Test

Although not adjustable, operating pressure can be checked. After the modulating pressure is checked and adjusted, check the gauge showing operating pressure it should read approximately 220 psi (15.4 bar). If the gauge reading is not at or near specification, recheck the modulator pressure and the governor pressure.

ROAD TEST

1. Road test using all selective ranges, noting when discrepancies in operation or oil pressure occur.
2. Attempt to isolate the unit or circuit involved in the malfunction.
3. If engine performance indicates an engine tune-up is required, this should be performed before road testing is completed or transaxle correction attemped. Poor engine performance can result in rough shifting or other malfunctions.

ON CAR SERVICES

Adjustments

CONTROL PRESSURE CABLE

1. Check the idle speed adjustment and set if necessary.
2. At the throttle body, take up the play in the cable. Do this by turning the adjusting nut.

3. Adjust the round end of the control cable until the cable can be installed or removed without strain.

SELECTOR LEVEL CABLE

1. Apply the parking brake and move the selector lever to the **N** detent.

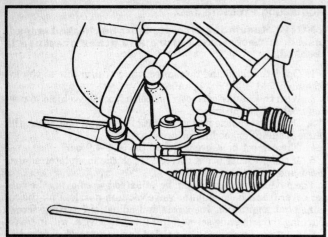

Control pressure cable adjustment point

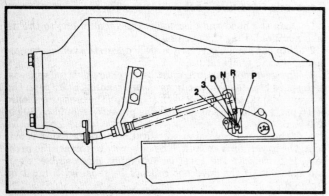

Selector lever adjustment

2. Check the range selector on the transaxle, make sure it is in the **N** position.

3. Adjust the ball on the end of the cable at the transaxle until there is no play in the cable.

4. The cable should go on and off of the range selector with no tension on it.

STARTER INTERLOCK AND BACKUP LIGHT SWITCH

1. Raise and safely support the vehicle.

2. Loosen the mounting bolts on the starter interlock switch and disconnect the electrical lead from it.

3. Using a piece of wire approximately 4 mm in diameter, insert it into the lug locating bore of the starter interlock switch.

4. With the wire installed in the lug opening, tighten the mounting bolts to 7 ft. lbs.

5. Reconnect the electrical plug and remove the locating wire from the lug opening.

6. Lower the vehicle and check the operation of the switch. Readjust if necessary.

Services

FLUID CHANGE

The conditions under which the vehicle is operated is the main consideration in determining how often the transaxle fluid should be changed. Different driving conditions result in differ-

ent transaxle fluid temperatures. These temperatures affect change intervals.

If the vehicle is driven under severe conditions, change the transmission fluid every 15,000 miles. If the vehicle is not used under severe conditions, change the fluid and replace the filter every 25,000 miles.

Do not overfill the transaxle. It takes about a pint of automatic transmission fluid to raise the level from the **ADD** to the **FULL** mark on the transaxle fluid reservoir. Over filling the unit can cause damage to the internal components.

OIL PAN

REMOVAL AND INSTALLATION

1. Run the vehicle until it reaches normal operating temperature. The vehicle must be driven so that the transaxle fluid will also reach operating temperature.

2. Raise and safely support the vehicle.

3. Place a suitable drain pan under the transaxle and remove the drain plug.

4. Allow the transaxle to completely drain. Turn the crankshaft until the converter drain plug is visible through the access hole and remove the plug. Allow the converter to completely drain.

5. Remove the oil pan retaining bolts and carefully remove the oil pan.

6. Remove the oil filter retaining bolts and remove the oil filter, discard the O-ring from the filter.

7. Clean the gasket mounting surfaces.

8. Install the new filter in position, using a new O-ring. Install a new oil pan gasket and install the transaxle pan. Tighten the pan bolts to 5.9 ft. lbs.

9. Install the oil drain plug and fill the transaxle to the correct level with fluid.

Filter removal and installation

VALVE BODY

Removal and Installation

1. Raise and safely support the vehicle.

2. Drain the transaxle fluid and remove the oil pan retaining bolts. Remove the oil pan.

3. Remove the bolts retaining the valve body and remove the valve body slowly.

4. Lower the valve body down and away from the transaxle.

NOTE: When removing the valve body, keep it in a upright position or all of the check balls will fall out.

5. Install the valve body in position, making sure that the check balls are all in position.

6. Install the retaining bolts, making sure to install the bolts in their original position.

7. Center the valve body by tightening the corner bolts first then the balance of the bolts. Torque all bolts to 5.9 ft. lbs.

8. Install the oil pan and gasket, tighten the pan retaining bolts to 5.9 ft. lbs. Install the oil drain plug and fill the transaxle to the correct level.

GOVERNOR

Removal and Installation

1. Raise and safely support the vehicle.

2. Loosen the intermediate muffler shield and push it aside as far as possible.

3. Disconnect the plug from the starter interlock switch.

4. Press in on the governor cover and remove the snapring. Remove the snapring and cover.

5. Loosen the nut on the axial governor holder.

6. Using a suitable tool, pry the axial holder in a clockwise direction.

7. Slide the governor from the case.

8. Check the governor for freedom of movement, it should rotate easily. Check the driven gear for damage or wear.

9. Slide the governor into the case and rotate the axial holder counterclockwise into position. Tighten the retaining nut.

10. Install the cover and snapring. Connect the electrical lead to the starter interlock switch.

11. Reposition the exhaust shield.

STARTER INTERLOCK AND BACKUP LIGHT SWITCH

Removal and Installation

1. Disconnect the negative battery cable. Raise and safely support the vehicle.

2. Remove the range selector lever retaining bolt and remove the lever.

3. Disconnect the electrical lead from the switch.

4. Remove the switch mounting bolts and remove the switch from the transaxle case.

5. Install the switch in the case and install the retaining bolts, do not tighten the retaining bolts.

6. Position the range selector in the **N** detent and install the lever. Tighten the lever retaining bolt to 7 ft. lbs.

7. Tighten the switch mounting bolts and adjust the switch.

8. Connect the electrical lead to the switch and lower the vehicle.

9. Check the operation of the switch.

REMOVAL AND INSTALLATION

TRANSAXLE REMOVAL

1. Disconnect the negative battery cable.

2. Disconnect the battery ground strap from the body.

3. Disconnect the multi-plugs in the spare tire well and pull the wires out from below.

4. Remove the upper and lower air cleaner housings. Remove the upper air guide section.

5. Disconnect the control cable on the throttle housing. Disconnect the oxyqen sensor wire on the fuse panel and pull it out from below.

6. Remove the engine air guide. Raise and safely support the vehicle.

7. Remove the complete exhaust system with all of the heat shields.

8. Remove the starter and suspend it out of the way.

9. Place a suitable drain pan under the transaxle and drain the fluid. Remove the fluid reservoir.

10. Disconnect the halfshafts from the rear of the transaxle and suspend them on a piece of wire.

11. Remove the transaxle crossmember suspension mounting bolts. Support the transaxle on the stabilizer bar, using support tool 9164 or equivalent.

12. Mark the position of the toe eccentric and the rear axle crossmember for reinstallation purposes. Remove the rear axle crossmember. Remove the clamp bolt from the central tube.

13. Disconnect the selector lever cable on the transaxle lever, unscrew the cable holder and sleeve.

14. Remove the fluid cooler and return lines. Plug the lines.

15. Pull off the vacuum modulator hose. Disconnect the pressure cable on the transaxle and pull the guide out carefully.

16. Place a universal transaxle jack or equivalent under the transaxle and tighten the retaining strap.

17. Remove the front and rear transaxle reinforcement plates. Lift the transaxle sligtly and remove the support tool from the stabilizer.

18. Lower transaxle far enough to so that central tube mounting bolts and control cable bolt can be removed.

19. After removing the central tube-to-transaxle bolts, reposition the central tube in the installed position and loosely install the mounting plate. Place a block of wood under the central tube to keep it in position.

20. Slowly lower the transaxle assembly, pulling back on it as it comes out. Remove the transaxle from under the vehicle.

TRANSAXLE INSTALLATION

1. Coat the splines of the central shaft with and appropriate lubricant.

2. With the transaxle on a suitable lifting device, slowly raise it into an installed position under the vehicle. While raising it slide it onto the central shaft.

3. Install and lightly tighten the central shaft bolts. Lift the transaxle slightly and remove the block of wood and the support from the central shaft.

4. Lower the transaxle slightly and install the remaining central shaft bolts. Tighten all central shaft bolts to 87 ft. lbs. (120 Nm).

5. Mount the guide tube for the control cable on the converter housing. Tighten it to 6 ft. lbs.

6. Push the wiring harness up through the spare tire well.

7. Lift the transaxle up slightly and install the holding tool 9164 or equivalent, to the stabilizer bar.

8. Install the rear axle mount and tighten all bolts. Lift the transaxle and remove the holding tool.

9. Install the transaxle crossmember and bolts, tighten all bolts to 85 ft. lbs.

10. Adjust the transaxle suspension using the following procedure:

    a. Install the transaxle crossmember mounting bolts loosely.

b. Lift the transaxle in the middle of the case far enough so that there is a gap between both transaxle mounts and the crossmember. Measure this gap on both sides and take up the difference with shims.

c. Lower the transaxle and tighten the bolts to 85 ft. lbs.

d. Check the clearance on the transaxle stops after tightening the bolts, there should be at least 1mm clearance between the case stop and the transaxle.

11. Check the selector lever adjustment and the throttle cable adjustment.

12. Reconnect the halfshafts and lower the vehicle.

13. Road test the vehicle and check all gearshift operations.

BENCH OVERHAUL

Before Disassembly

Cleanliness is an important factor in the overhaul of the automatic transaxle. Before opening up this unit, the entire outside of the transaxle assembly should be cleaned, preferable with a high pressure washer such as a car wash spray unit. Dirt entering the transaxle internal parts will negate all the time and effort spent on the overhaul. During inspection and reassembly all parts should be thoroughly cleaned with solvent then dried with compressed air. Wiping cloths and rags should not be used to dry parts since lint will find its way into the valve body passages.

Wheel bearing grease, long used to hold thrust washers and lube parts, should not be used. Lube seals with clean transmission fluid and use ordinary unmedicated petroleum jelly to hold the thrust washers and to ease the assembly of seals, since it will not leave a harmful residue as grease often will. Do not use solvent on neoprene seals, friction plates if they are to be reused, or thrust washers. Be wary of nylon parts if the transaxle failure was due to failure of the cooling system. Nylon parts exposed to water or antifreeze solutions can swell and distort and must be replaced.

Before installing bolts into aluminum parts, always dip the threads into clean transmission fluid. Antiseize compound can also be used to prevent bolts from galling the aluminum and seizing. Always use a torque wrench to keep from stripping the threads. Take care when installing new O-rings, especially the smaller O-rings. The internal snaprings should be expanded and the external rings should be compressed, if they are to be reused. This will help insure proper seating when installed.

Transaxle Disassembly

1. With the transaxle in a suitable holding fixture, remove the bolts retaining the final drive assembly and remove the assembly.

2. Remove the rear transaxle case. Remove the front converter case and remove the converter from the transaxle.

3. Remove the bolts retaining the transaxle oil pan and remove the oil pan.

4. Remove the oil filter retaining bolts and remove the oil filter.

5. Remove the valve body retaining bolts and remove the valve body. Use care not to drop the check balls from the valve body.

6. Remove the combination bolts and lift off the lower cover with the backing plate and oil tube.

7. Remove the one way valve, brake band B2 guide, temperature throttle valve and oil wiper.

8. Press in the brake band B2 cover, remove the circlip and cover. Remove the B2 brake band piston.

9. Position the special puller tool 9316 or equivalent, on the case over the brake band piston hole and using the tool remove brake band B1. Remove the tool.

10. Remove the B1 brake band guide and pressure plug.

11. Remove the drive range selector lever and remove the starter interlock switch mounting bolts and switch.

12. Remove the vacuum control unit retaining bolts and remove the vacuum control unit.

13. Remove the modulating pressure control valve. Remove the kickdown solenoid valve and injector tube.

14. Remove the parking lock with pawl and expander ring. Remove the plastic guide and roller.

15. Remove the secondary pump by removing the axial holder retaing bolts and turning the axial retainer.

16. Remove the O-ring and backer from the secondary pump bore. Disconnect the throttle linkage.

17. If equipped, remove the oil tube retaining bolt and remove the oil tube.

18. Press in on the governor cover and remove the snapring. Remove the governor assembly.

19. Remove the helical gear and shims, note the thickness of the shims for reinstallation.

20. Remove the circlip from the input shaft.

21. Remove the front cover retaining bolts, use 2 of the bolts to pull the cover off.

22. Grab the gearset at the front of the input shaft and pull the gearset carefully from the case.

23. Remove the B3 clutch plates and damping spring. Remove the K2 clutch assembly and pressure pin.

24. Tilt the B2 brake band and remove it from the case.

25. Remove the detent plate retaining bolt and remove the detent plate. Remove the thrust washer.

26. Remove the B2 pressure unit. Remove the remaining sealing rings and plugs from the case.

Unit Disassembly and Assembly

PLANETARY GEAR SET

Disassembly

1. Mount the gear set assembly in a suitable holding fixture.

2. Remove the top retaining snapring.

3. Remove the clutch K1 assembly from the shaft. Remove the axial bearing and the front gear set.

4. Remove the sun gear and the inner plate carrier with one way clutch.

5. Remove the K2 clutch assembly from the shaft. Remove the axial bearings and snaprings.

Inspection

1. Inspect the input shaft teeth for burrs or uneven wear.

2. Inspect the surface for signs of bluing from excess heat.

3. Check the bearing surfaces for excess wear or burrs.

4. Check the planetary set for freedom of movement.

5. Check the axial bearings for damage.

6. Clean all bearings and gears.

Assembly

1. Lubricate all components with clean transmission fluid before assembly.

2. Install the one way clutch and carrier in a suitable holding fixture and install the sun gear.

3. Install the axial and radial bearings on the output shaft. Install the drive shaft and axial bearing.

4. Install the front gear set and the retaining snapring.

5. Remove the assembly from the holding fixture and turn it over, reinstall it in the holding fixture.

6. Install the radial bearing on the output shaft using a small amount of petroleum jelly to hold it in position.

7. Install the K2 clutch assembly.

8. Install the final axial bearing on the end of the output shaft, using petroleum jelly to hold it in place.

ONE WAY CLUTCH

Disassembly

1. Remove the snapring from the inner plate cover and remove the inner plate cover.

2. Pull the K2 clutch from the carrier. Pull the roller bearing from the carrier.

3. Turn the inner race of the one way clutch counterclockwise and pull it out.

Inspection

1. Check the bearing surfaces and inner race for wear. If the bearing surfaces show signs of scoring or excess wear, replace the entire one way clutch assembly.

2. Check the carrier plate splines for wear or damage.

3. Replace all damaged components.

Assembly

1. Place the thrust washer and O-ring on inner plate carrier.

2. Install the roller bearings in the roller cage.

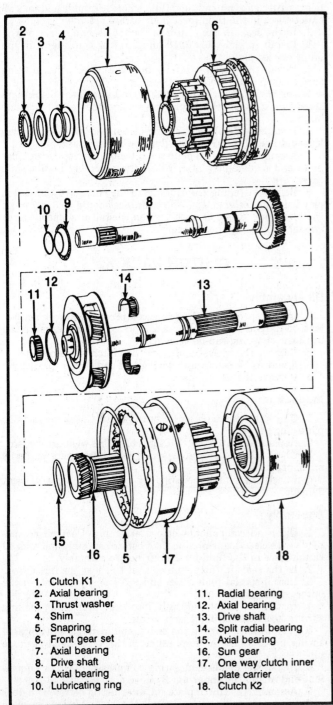

1. Clutch K1	11. Radial bearing
2. Axial bearing	12. Axial bearing
3. Thrust washer	13. Drive shaft
4. Shim	14. Split radial bearing
5. Snapring	15. Axial bearing
6. Front gear set	16. Sun gear
7. Axial bearing	17. One way clutch inner
8. Drive shaft	plate carrier
9. Axial bearing	18. Clutch K2
10. Lubricating ring	

Gear assembly – exploded view

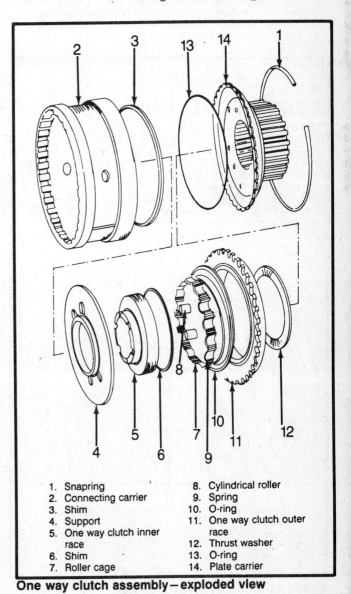

1. Snapring	8. Cylindrical roller
2. Connecting carrier	9. Spring
3. Shim	10. O-ring
4. Support	11. One way clutch outer
5. One way clutch inner	race
race	12. Thrust washer
6. Shim	13. O-ring
7. Roller cage	14. Plate carrier

One way clutch assembly – exploded view

3. Place the outer race of the one way clutch on the inner plate carrier and install the roller bearings into position.

4. Using special tool 9322 or equivalent, insert it to hold the roller bearings in position.

5. Install the one way clutch inner race while turning it counterclockwise.

6. Remove the special bearing holder tool. Install the shim and Check the clutch axial play with a feeler gauge, the play should be 0.007 in. (0.2 mm). Install the one way clutch support, make sure that the support pin engages the outer race.

7. Install the shims on the outer race and install the connecting carrier on the one way clutch.

8. Install the retaining snapring, making sure it seats fully in its groove.

CLUTCH PACK K1

Disassembly

1. Install special clutch spring compressor 9315 or equivalent, on the clutch assembly and compress the diaphragm spring until the snapring can be removed.

2. Remove the special tool from the clutch assembly.

3. Remove the diaphragm spring and the clutch springs.

4. Remove the clutch discs.

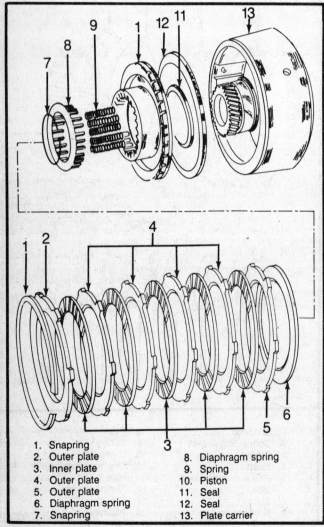

1. Snapring	
2. Outer plate	8. Diaphragm spring
3. Inner plate	9. Spring
4. Outer plate	10. Piston
5. Outer plate	11. Seal
6. Diaphragm spring	12. Seal
7. Snapring	13. Plate carrier

Clutch K1 assembly – exploded view

Inspection

1. Check the clutch plates for burnt spots. Check the metallic plates for bends.

2. Replace all clutch plates if signs of excess wear are evident.

3. Check all of the clutch springs for stretching or badly mishaped coils.

4. Check the clutch housing for scoring or signs of heat damage.

Assembly

1. Clean all components before assembly. Coat all components with clean transmission fluid before assembly and soak all clutch discs in the fluid for 1 hour before assembly.

2. In the seals in the piston so that the seal lips face down.

3. Install special tools 9318 and 9317 or equivalent, in the outer carrier plate.

4. Install the piston carefully into the outer plate, making sure to keep it as straight as possible.

5. Instal the springs in the piston and install the diaphragm spring, making sure the diaphragm spring is centered by a guide pin.

6. Install the diaphragm spring compressor 9315 or equivalent and install the snapring. Remove the special tool.

7. Assemble the clutch plate set, alternating between an fiber plate and a metallic plate. Install the assembly in the plate cover.

8. Before installing the final snapring, measure the clutch play using an feeler gauge. The clearance should be 0.027 in., if the clearance is not at specification, install a snapring large enough to take up the difference.

CLUTCH PACK K2

Disassembly

1. Install special clutch spring compressor 9315 or equivalent, on the clutch assembly and compress the diaphragm spring until the snapring can be removed.

2. Remove the special tool from the clutch assembly.

3. Remove the diaphragm spring and the clutch springs.

4. Remove the clutch discs.

Inspection

1. Check the clutch plates for burnt spots. Check the metallic plates for bends.

2. Replace all clutch plates if signs of excess wear are evident.

3. Check all of the clutch springs for stretching or badly mishaped coils.

4. Check the clutch housing for scoring or signs of heat damage.

Assembly

1. Clean all components before assembly. Coat all components with clean transmission fluid before assembly and soak all clutch discs in the fluid for 1 hour before assembly.

2. In the seals in the piston so that the seal lips face down.

3. Install special tools 9318 and 9317 or equivalent, in the outer carrier plate.

4. Install the piston carefully into the outer plate, making sure to keep it as straight as possible.

5. Install the springs in the piston and install the diaphragm spring, making sure the diaphragm spring is centered by a guide pin.

6. Install the diaphragm spring compressor 9315 or equivalent and install the snapring. Remove the special tool.

7. Assemble the clutch plate set, alternating between an fiber plate and a metallic plate. Install the assembly in the plate cover.

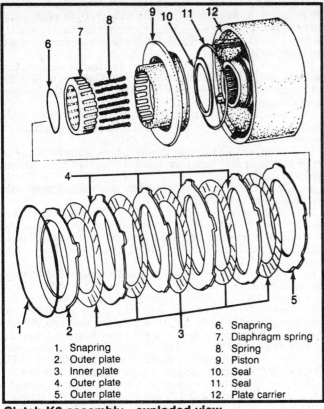

Clutch K2 assembly – exploded view

1. Snapring	6. Snapring
2. Outer plate	7. Diaphragm spring
3. Inner plate	8. Spring
4. Outer plate	9. Piston
5. Outer plate	10. Seal
	11. Seal
	12. Plate carrier

8. Before installing the final snapring, measure the clutch play using an feeler gauge. The clearance should be 0.027 in., if the clearance is not at specification, install a snapring large enough to take up the difference.

VALVE BODY

Disassembly

1. With the valve body removed from the transaxle case, remove the plastic valve and chip screen.
2. Remove the check valve, shift pin and the lock valve K1.
3. Remove the valve body-to-shift valve housing bolts and separate the valve body.
4. Remove all of the check valves and remove the check valve balls.

NOTE: Note the location of all check valves and balls, this will make assembly easier.

Inspection

1. Inspect the passages of the valve body for blockage.
2. Check the valve body casing and the shift valve housing for flatness.
3. If the valve body or the shift valve housing are warped, they must be replaced as an assembly.
4. Check all valves and check balls for damage, replace any that show signs of damage.
5. Clean all components before assembly. Lubricate all components with clean fluid before assembly.

Assembly

1. Install all check balls in the valve body, making sure to install them in their correct bores.
2. Install all of the valves in their bores.

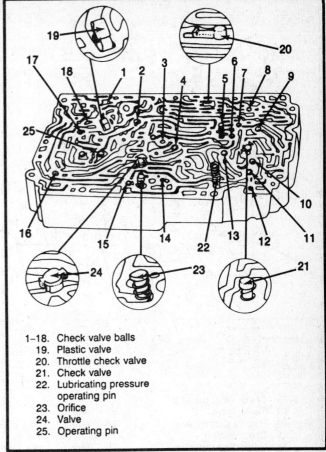

1–18.	Check valve balls
19.	Plastic valve
20.	Throttle check valve
21.	Check valve
22.	Lubricating pressure operating pin
23.	Orifice
24.	Valve
25.	Operating pin

Valve body check ball locations – 1984–87

3. Install the lubricating pressure valve, over-pressure modulating valve and bleed valve K1 in the sensor housing.
4. Carefully install the backing plate on the valve body and check to make sure that the valve ball is in the proper location.
5. Place the shift valve housing in position over the valve body.
6. While holding the valve body together, turn it over and install the retaining bolts. Do not tighten the bolts.
7. Insert the plastic valve in position and install the chip screen.
8. Tighten the valve body bolts.

Transaxle Assembly

1. Coat all bearings and friction surfaces with automatic transmission fluid before assembling. Soak all brake bands in automatic transmission fluid for at least 1 hour prior to assembly.
2. Using special tool 9119 or equivalent, insert the guide ring in the case and drive it in toward the brake band piston cover.
3. Insert new O-rings on the case plugs and install the plugs into the case, tightening to 7 ft. lbs. Place a new O-ring in the support flange opening.
4. Lubricate the grooves in the support flange K2 and install the teflon rings. Press in the rings until the joints are closed.
5. Position the support flange on the case so that the bolt holes are aligned and tighten the bolts to 8 ft. lbs.
6. Position the thrust washer on the back of the support flange so that the lug engages the support flange. Insert the pressure unit B2 with the projection upward.

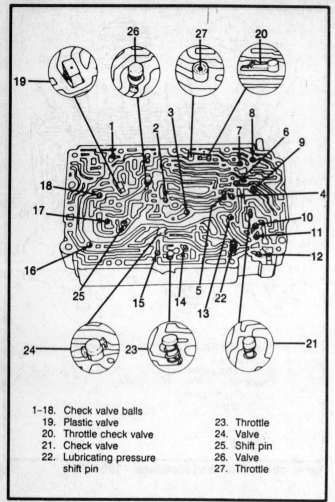

1-18. Check valve balls
19. Plastic valve
20. Throttle check valve
21. Check valve
22. Lubricating pressure shift pin

23. Throttle
24. Valve
25. Shift pin
26. Valve
27. Throttle

Valve body check ball locations — 1988–90

7. Press brake band B2 as close together as possible and insert it into the case. Place the split radial bearing on the output shaft.

8. Push clutch assembly K2 onto the gear set. Place the gearset in the transaxle case, turn the input shaft while inserting it.

9. Rotate the transaxle so that the input shaft is facing upward. Check to make sure that the gearset is in correct position. Install the damping spring in the case.

10. Insert the clutch plates for plate brake B3, check the plate play and correct it using larger clutch plates and shims. The specification is 0.059–0.078 in.

11. Place axial bearing on the planet carrier. Check to make sure that the lubricating pressure rings are in position.

12. Engage the brake band B1 in the locked position. Insert the clutch K1 assembly, turning until the teeth lock. Insert the brake band so that the pin is facing from the assembly lock to the B1 unit.

13. Insert the axial bearing over clutch assembly K1. Push the pressure pin into the pressure unit B1.

14. Insert the pressure unit in the case and tighten the plug to 52 ft. lbs.

15. Insert the brake band guide, the pins must engage the holes n the case. Check the axial play for the K1 clutch assembly by placing the seal on the front cover and using special tool 9313 or equivalent, measure the depth to the seal. This is distance **A**. Place the measuring bridge toll 9313 or equivalent on the trans-

axle face and mesure the depth to the clutch K1, this is distance **B**. Subtract the distance **A** from the distance **B**, this is the axial play fro the clutch K1 assembly. The correct thickness should be 0.14 in. Select axial bearing and shims to correct the distance to this specification.

16. Attach the spacer to the support and install the front cover, with seal, in position. Tighten the retaining bolts to 10 ft. lbs.

17. Insert the circlip on the input shaft. Install the helical gear and the axial holder.

18. Install a new O-ring and then install the goveror assembly. Attach the axial holder to the governor. Install the governor cover and snapring.

19. Install a new O-ring in the secondary pump bore and install the secondary pump in position. Tighten the retaining bolts to 5.9 ft. lbs.

20. Rotate the pump axial holder into position and tighten the retaining bolt to 4.4 ft. lbs.

21. Insert the detent plate and shaft, tighten the retaining bolt to 5.9 ft. lbs. Push the linkage onto the detent plate and install the circlip. Push the roller and plastic guide onto the linkage.

22. Install the shims on the helical gear. Install the parking lock pawl spring and gear.

23. Measure the axial play of clutch K2 using a depth gauge, measure from the rotating ring to the seal. The depth should not exceed 1.3 in., if it does, it must be made up with shims.

24. Install the bearing assembly with shims and tighten all mounting bolts to 24 ft. lbs., then measure the from the case bearing face to the inner race of the roller bearing. Axial play should no be more than 0.19 in. Remove the bearing assembly.

25. Screw in the kickdown solenoid valve and tighten to 15 ft. lbs. Insert the modulating pressure valve and locating pin.

26. Insert the vacuum control unit with holder and and tighten the retaining bolts to 5.9 ft. lbs. Install the starter interlock switch and and tighten the mounting bolt to 5.9 ft. lbs.

27. Insert the sealing ring onto brake band piston B1. Bolt special tool 9316 or equivalent, to the transaxle case and insert the brake band piston B1 with compression springs. Insert the retaining circlip and remove the special tool.

28. Measure and adjust the play **L** of the brake band by inserting the speciall tool 9320 or equivalent, into the bore. Count the number of turns of the tool required to seat it fully. Each turn is equivalent to 1 mm, tighten the tool to 2.3 ft. lbs. The torque must be reached by 3–4 turns of the tool.

29. If the tool takes more than 4 turns to seat, replace the brake band with one using a longer piston pin. Remove the tool.

30. Install the brake band piston cover. Install the brake band pressure pin. Insert the brake band B2, make sure that the pressure pin engages it.

31. Press in the brake band piston cover B2 and insert the circlip.

32. Insert the one way valve and filter. Insert the brake band guide. Insert the temperature throttle until it is flush with the casing. Insert the oil wiper.

33. Install the lower cover with the backing plate and insert the oil tube in the casing bore.

34. Install the combination bolts and lightly tighten. Engage the return spring. Place the leaf spring in position and lightly tighten.

35. Install the shift valve housing, the range selector must engage the carrier on the detent plate.

36. Insert the combination bolts and tighten to 5.9 ft. lbs. Tighten the combination bolts for the leaf spring and the backing plate to 5.9 ft. lbs.

37. Place the filter in position and tighten the screws to 2.9 ft. lbs. Install the oil pan with a new gasket and tighten the bolts to 5.9 ft. lbs.

38. Set the range selector to the **N** detent and adjust the detent position. Tighten the mounting bolts to 5.9 ft. lbs. Install the converter assembly.

39. Install the transaxle into the vehicle and check all adjustments and operation of the linkage and of the trnasaxle.

SPECIFICATIONS

TORQUE SPECIFICATIONS

Part	ft. lbs.	Nm
Primary pump-to-cover	14	20
Converter plug	10	14
Front cover-to-transaxle	9	13
Support flange	8	11
Brake band B1 plug	51	70
Catch plate or range shaft	6	8
Leaf spring-to-transaxle case	6	8
Starter interlock	6	8
Range selector shaft	6	8
Secondary pump	6	8
Governor axial holder	4.3	6
Lower cover	3	4
Test connection plugs	9	13
Kickdown solenoid valve	14	20
Drive housing-to-valve body	1.3 ①	0.15
Filter-to-case	3	4
Pan-to-case	10	14
Converter case to transaxle case	23	17
Carrier plate-to-converter	34	46
Bearing assembly-to-case	24	33
Final-to-transaxle case	34	46

① Inch lbs.

SPECIAL TOOLS

SERVICE TOOL SELECTION

Description	Number
Pressure pad	9180/1
Mandrel	P254
Transaxle holder	9216
Grip plate	9301
Converter mandrel	9310
Assembly stand	9314
Assembly tool	9315
Clutch K1 sleeve	9317
Primary pump guide sleeve	9319
Centering pins	9321

Section 2

ZF 3HP–18 and ZF 4HP–18 Transaxles
Saab

APPLICATION

1985–89 Saab 9000

GENERAL DESCRIPTION

The ZF 3HP-18 is used in the 1985 Saab 9000 and is a 3 speed transaxle. The ZF 4HP-18 is used in the 1986–89 Saab 9000 and is a 4 speed transaxle. Third gear ratio is 1:1 in both transaxles. Fourth gear in the ZF 4HP-18, is an overdrive range providing an 0.74:1 gear ratio. Shifting is controlled by a governor valve, a line pressure valve, a throttle pressure regulator valve and a modulator valve. Valve operation depends on shift lever position, vehicle speed and throttle position.

Transaxle and Converter Identification

TRANSAXLE

The transaxle can be identified by a tag on the left side of the transaxle case just below the valve body cover. The information on the plate consists of the builders sequence number, manufacturers part number and the transaxle type.

CONVERTER

The torque converter diameter is 10.2 in. Identification numbers or symbols, are either stamped into the cover or ink stamped on the cover surface. The torque converter used in this transaxle is not serviceable. If the converter is damaged in any way, it must be replaced.

Metric Fasteners

The transaxle is designed and assembled using metric fasteners. Metric measurements are used to determine clearances within the unit during servicing. Metric fasteners are required to service the unit and torque specifications must be strictly adhered to.

The metric thread is extremely close to the dimensions of the standard inch system threads and for this reason, extreme care must be taken to prevent the interchanging of inch system bolts or screws with metric bolts or screws. Mismatched or incorrect fasteners can result in damage to the transaxle unit. The fasteners should be used in the same location as they were removed from or replaced with fasteners of the same size and grade.

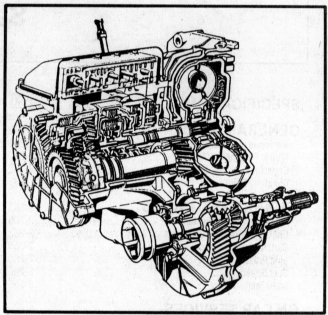

Cutaway view of the ZF 4HP-18 transaxle

Capacities

The dry refill capacity of the transaxle is 8.6 qts. The service capacity is 4.2 qts. Recommended fluid is Dexron®II automatic transaxle fluid.

Checking Fluid Level

1. Check the level when the fluid is cold (at ambient temperature). If the fluid temperature is more than 125°F, allow it to cool before checking the level.
2. Position the vehicle on a level surface. Start and run the engine at idle.
3. Shift the transaxle through every gear range, return it to the **P** position and check the fluid level.
4. Correct level is to the cold fill mark on the dipstick.

TRANSAXLE MODIFICATIONS

There were no modifications to these transaxles at the time of publication.

TROUBLE DIAGNOSIS

CHILTON'S THREE C'S TRANSAXLE DIAGNOSIS

Condition	Cause	Correction
Will not engage or hold in part	a) Shift cable incorrectly adjusted b) Excess clearance on detent plate c) Detent segment out of position d) Park pawl damaged	a) Adjust cable b) Adjust or replace plate c) Correct position or replace segment and rod d) Replace pawl and pin
Engine will not start	a) Neutral start switch inoperative b) Excess clearance on selector shaft	a) Replace switch b) Adjust or replace shaft
No reverse	a) Shift cable incorrectly adjusted b) Oil screen plugged c) Reverse clutch damaged d) First reverse brake damaged. Also engine will not decelerate in position one, 1st gear e) Governor sticking f) Lockup valve 1 and reverse gear sticking	a) Adjust cable b) Replace oil screen c) Replace transaxle d) Replace transaxle e) Replace governor f) Replace valve body
Slips/vibrates when accelerating from stop	a) 1-2-3 clutch damaged b) First-reverse brake damaged c) Turbine shaft O-ring or pump starter malfunction d) Oil leaking into reverse clutch or seat piston ring has scored center plate	a) Replace transaxle b) Replace transaxle c) Replace transaxle d) Replace transaxle
Harsh engagement P to R, or N to R may be accompanied by improper 2-1 downshift	a) Accumulator inoperative	a) Replace valve body
Back-up lights not functioning (electrical feed/ground ok)	a) Neutral start switch malfunction	a) Replace switch
Engine will not start	a) Neutral start switch defective	a) Replace switch
Vehicle creeps in park or neutral	a) Shift cable incorrectly adjusted	a) Adjust cable
No power, poor acceleration in D range	a) Converter valve operation b) Oil screen plugged c) 1-2-3 clutch defective d) Roller clutch slips e) Shift cable incorrectly adjusted f) Throttle or shift valve sticking	a) Replace transaxle b) Replace oil screen c) Replace transaxle d) Replace transaxle e) Correct adjustment f) Replace valve body
Harsh engagement during N to D shift	a) Accumulator sticking or spring broken	a) Replace valve body

No shift in cold or warm condition
  No 1-2 or 2-1 shift
 	
  No 1-2 shift
  No 2-3 or 3-2 shift
 	
  No 2-3 shift
 	
  No 3-4 or 4-3 shift
 	
  No 3-4 shift
	a) Governor sticking
	b) 1-2 shift valve sticks
	c) Forward brake or 2-4 band malfunction
	d) Governor sticking
	e) 2-3 shift valve sticks
	f) 3-4 clutch damaged
	g) Oil supply for 3-4 clutch leaking
	h) Governor sticking
	j) 3-4 shift valve sticks
	j) Forward brake inoperative (1-2 up-shift not ok)
	k) 2-4 band loose
	l) 2-3-4 up-shift valve sticks
	m) Position 3 valve sticks
		a) Replace governor
		b) Replace valve body
		c) Replace transaxle
		d) Replace governor
		e) Replace valve body
		f) Replace transaxle
		g) Replace transaxle
		h) Replace governor
		j) Replace valve body
		j) Replace transaxle
		
		k) Replace transaxle
		l) Replace valve body
		m) Replace valve body

CHILTON'S THREE C'S TRANSAXLE DIAGNOSIS

Condition	Cause	Correction
Vehicle takes off in 2nd gear (will not downshift to 1st)	a) Governor piston sticks	a) Replace governor
	b) 1-2 shift valve sticks	b) Replace valve body
	c) 2-4 band binds	c) Correct adjustment
	d) 2-4 band will not release	d) Replace transaxle
Vehicle takes off in 3rd gear (will not downshift to 1st or 2nd)	e) Center ring of governor flange defective	e) Replace transaxle
	f) Governor piston sticking	f) Replace governor
	g) 1-2 and 2-3 shift valve sticking	g) Replace valve body
	h) Closing cap in center plate leaking (reverse clutch always filled with oil)	h) Replace transaxle
Transaxle shifts 1-3 (no 2nd gear)	i) 2-3 shift valve sticks	i) Replace valve body
	j) 2-3-4 shift valve sticks	j) Replace valve body
	k) 1-2-3 shift valve sticks	k) Replace valve body
Transaxle shifts 1-4 (no 1-2; or 2-3 shift)	l) Engine will not accelerate	l) Replace valve body
Will not downshift to 1st at idle or no kickdown shift. Will not return to 1st gear at idle speed when stopped	a) Governor sticking	a) Replace governor
	b) Leakage in governor assembly	b) Replace transaxle
	c) Shift valve binding	c) Replace valve body
No full throttle kickdown	d) Throttle valve cable incorrectly adjusted	d) Adjust cable
No kickdown shifts	e) Throttle valve cable incorrectly adjusted	e) Adjust cable
	f) Governor sticking	f) Replace governor
Harsh engagement at idle speeds	a) Accumulator malfunction	a) Replace valve body
	b) Modulator pressure too high	b) Replace valve body
	c) Clutch pack damage	c) Replace transaxle
Full throttle kickdown shifts too long	d) Accumulator malfunction	d) Replace valve body
	e) Clutch pack damage	e) Replace transaxle
Full throttle and kickdown shifts too harsh	f) Modulator pressure not ok	f) Replace valve body
	g) Accumulator malfunction	g) Replace valve body
Engine overspeed at 3-4 shift	h) Orifice control valve sticking	h) Replace valve body
	i) 3-4 traction valve binding	i) Replace valve body
	j) 2-4 band slips	j) Replace transaxle
Engine overspeed at 3-4 downshift	k) Time control valve and 4-3 downshift valves not coordinated	k) Replace valve body
	l) 1-2-3 clutch damaged	l) Replace transaxle
	m) Damper function of 1-2-3 clutch and 4-3 traction valve not functioning properly	m) Replace valve body
Manual 2nd gear downshift incorrect or downshift early or late	a) Lockup valve 2 binding	a) Replace valve body
	b) Governor piston binding	b) Replace governor
No overrun braking in D1	a) 2-4 band inoperative	a) Check/replace band piston and cover O-rings if required
	b) 2-4 band damaged	b) Replace transaxle
Manual 2-1 downshift incorrect	a) Lockup valve 1 and reverse gear binding	a) Replace valve body
	b) Governor piston binding	b) Replace governor
No overrun braking in 1st gear	a) 1st/reverse brake damaged	a) Replace transaxle
Throttle valve cable sticks	a) Cable not attached to cam	a) Connect cable to cam
	b) Internal friction in cable	b) Replace cable
	c) Throttle pressure piston sticks	c) Replace valve body
After long drive, noise develops and vehicle will not move in drive or reverse	a) Valve body oil screen plugged	a) Replace oil screen
Transaxle noisy. Will not move in drive or reverse	a) Converter driveplate damaged	a) Replace driveplate
	b) Oil pump gears worn or damaged	b) Replace transaxle
Oil leaking from converter housing seam	a) Torque converter leaking at welded	a) Replace converter
	b) Pump seal leaking	b) Replace pump seal
Leakage between transaxle and oil pan	a) Oil pan bolts loose or pan warped	a) Tighten bolts or replace pan
	b) Oil pan gasket damaged	b) Replace gasket

CHILTON'S THREE C'S TRANSAXLE DIAGNOSIS

Condition	Cause	Correction
Leakage between transaxle housing and differential cover	a) Cover bolts loose	a) Tighten bolts
Leakage at transaxle cooler	a) Cooler attaching bolt loose b) Gasket damaged c) Cooler cracked or split	a) Tighten bolt b) Replace gasket c) Replace cooler
Leakage at 2-4 band piston cover	a) Cover O-rings worn or damaged	a) Replace O-rings
Leakage from 2-4 band retaining shaft	a) Retaining shaft O-ring damaged	a) Remove valve body and replace shaft O-ring
Leakage at output shaft	a) Bolts loose b) Seal rings damaged	a) Tighten bolts b) Replace seal rings
Oil leakage at throttle cable connection in case	a) Cable connector O-ring damaged	a) Replace O-ring; if necessary, replace cable
Leakage at differential	a) Output shaft seals or cover seal damaged	a) Replace seals
Leakage at speedometer sensor	a) Sensor or O-ring damaged	a) Replace O-ring or sensor
Leakage at breather vents in transaxle or differential	a) Transaxle or differential overfilled b) Incorrect fluid or lubricant	a) Correct oil level b) Replace transaxle
Leakage at selector shaft	a) Seal ring damaged	a) Replace seal ring
Noise in all positions	a) Fluid level low b) Valve body leaking internally c) Oil screen plugged	a) Correct level b) Replace valve body c) Replace oil screen
Noise at certain speeds	a) Bearing adjustment of differential b) Bearing adjustment of differential incorrectly set	a) Replace transaxle pinion gear incorrectly set b) Replace transaxle

CLUTCH AND BRAKE APPLICATION
ZF 4HP-18

Selector Position		Clutch A	Clutch B	Brake C	Brake Band C	Brake D	Clutch E	1st one way Clutch	2nd one way Clutch	Parking Gear
P		—	—	—	—	—	—	—	—	Applied
R		—	Applied	—	—	Applied	—	—	—	—
N		—	—	—	—	—	—	—	—	—
D	1	Applied	—	Applied	—	Applied	—	Applied	—	—
D	2	Applied	—	Applied	—	—	—	—	Applied	—
D	3	Applied	—	Applied	Applied	—	Applied	—	—	—
D	4	—	—	Applied	—	—	Applied	—	—	—

CLUTCH AND BRAKE APPLICATION
ZF 3HP-18

Selector Position		Clutch A	Clutch B	Brake C	Brake Band C	Brake D	1st one way Clutch	2nd one way Clutch	Parking Gear
P		—	—	—	—	—	—	—	Applied
R		—	Applied	—	—	Applied	—	—	—
N		—	—	—	—	—	—	—	—
D	1	Applied	Applied	Applied	—	—	Applied	—	—
D	2	Applied	—	Applied	Applied	—	—	—	—
D	3	Applied	—	Applied	—	—	—	Applied	—

These transaxle assemblies are not being overhauled at this time. If diagnosis determines trouble in the transaxle, the entire assembly must be removed and replaced through the factory parts exchange program.

Hydraulic Control System

The hydraulic control system operates by applying hydraulic pressure to various valves and components of the transaxle. The hydraulic control system is affected by various activities of the vehicle, including; selector lever position (line pressure), accelerator position and vehicle speed.

The system incorporates various control valves, these valves include:

Selector Valve—this valve routes the oil flow through the shift and lockup valves, to the clutches and to the brakes. This routing depends on the selector position.

Line Pressure Regulator Valve—this valve will open when the pressure has risen to a certain value, this routes the oil back to the suction side of the pump. It acts as a pressure limiting valve and operates in relation to modulator pressure.

Modulator Valve—the modulator pressure simulates the engine torque, to which the gear shifting carried out by the control elements must be adjusted. At low engine torque the, the closing pressure for engaging the control elements is low and at high pressure, the closing pressure is high. Since the engine torque may be high even at low engine speeds, the function of the modulator pressure is to boost the closing pressure in the control elements at this stage.

Throttle Pressure Valve—this is designed as a pressure reducing valve for adjusting the throttle pressure in relation to the accelerator pedal position.
Diagnosis Tests

LINE PRESSURE TEST

1. Raise and safely support the vehicle.

2. Connect the transaxle gauge set to the pressure outlet port on the side of the transaxle.
3. Start the engine and run the vehicle in the gear positions.
4. Check to see that the pressure readings are within specification.

STALL SPEED TEST

1. Raise the vehicle and support it safely.
2. Connect an engine tachometer and start the engine. Apply the parking brake.
3. Run the engine to normal operating temperature, position the selection lever in **D**.
4. Fully depress the accelerator pedal for 6-8 seconds and note the engine speed.

NOTE: To prevent damage to the automatic transaxle, do not test stall speed for more than 10 seconds at a time.

5. Allow 2 minutes for the transaxle to cool and then repeat the test.
6. The specification should be 2600-3100 rpm. If the measured stall speed exceeds the specification by more than 300 rpm, transaxle slip may be present and the transaxle should be checked.
7. If the stall speed drops below specification by 400-700 rpm, converter slippage may be present and should be checked.

ROAD TEST

Road test using all selective ranges, noting when discrepancies in operation or oil pressure occur. Attempt to isolate the unit or circuit involved in the malfunction. If engine performance indicates an engine tune-up is required, this should be performed before road testing is completed or transaxle correction attempted. Poor engine performance can result in rough shifting or other malfunctions.

LINE PRESSURE SPECIFICATIONS
With Turbocharged Engine

Selector Position	Line Pressure (psi)	Test Condition	Idle Speed rpm
R	149-178	At idle speed	900-950
N	102-114	At idle speed	875
N	178-198	Kickdown cable fully withdrawn	2000
D	102-114	At idle speed	900-950
1	102-114	At idle speed	900-950

LINE PRESSURE SPECIFICATIONS
With Non-Turbocharged Engine

Selector Position	Line Pressure (psi)	Test Condition	Idle Speed rpm
R	149-178	At idle speed	950
N	102-114	At idle speed	875
N	168-188	Kickdown cable fully withdrawn	2000
D	102-114	At idle speed	950
1	102-114	At idle speed	950

ON CAR SERVICES

Adjustments

1. Loosen the cable locknuts and lift the threaded cable shank out of the engine bracket.
2. Place the throttle lever in idle position.
3. Pull cable wire forward and place a 1.55 in. (39.5mm) long gauge block on the wire between the cable connector and cable end.

NOTE: Vernier calipers can be substituted for the gauge block.

4. Pull cable shank rearward to the detent position (but not to the wide open throttle position).
5. The detent position will provide a definite feel, similar to a stop, when it is reached.
6. Hold the shank at the detent position and insert it in the engine bracket. Tighten the locknuts to lock it in place.
7. Remove the gauge block and verify adjustments. Detent position should be reached when travel of the cable wire is 1.55 in. (39.5mm).

Selector lever in N position for adjustment

SELECTOR LEVEL CABLE

1. Apply the parking brake and move the selector lever to the **N** detent.
2. Check the range selector on the transaxle, make sure it is in the **N** position.
3. Adjust the ball on the end of the cable at the transaxle until there is no play in the cable.
4. The cable should go on and off of the range selector with no tension on it.

Services

FLUID CHANGES

The conditions under which the vehicle is operated is the main consideration in determining how often the transmission fluid should be changed. Different driving conditions result in different transmission fluid temperatures. These temperatures affect change intervals.

If the vehicle is driven under severe conditions, change the transmission fluid every 15,000 miles. If the vehicle is not used under severe conditions, change the fluid and replace the filter every 30,000 miles.

Do not overfill the transaxle. It takes about a pint of automatic transmission fluid to raise the level from the **ADD** to the **FULL** mark on the transaxle indicator dipstick. Overfilling the unit can cause damage to the internal components of the automatic transaxle.

1. Raise and safely support the vehicle.
2. Remove the underbody splash shield and loosen the nut that attaches the filler tube to the oil pan. Drain the fluid.
3. When all of the fluid is drained, tighten the nut on the filler tube to 74 ft. lbs. Install the splash shield and lower the vehicle.
4. Remove the transaxle dipstick and add clean automatic transmission fluid.
5. Check and adjust the fluid as necessary.

OIL FILTER

1. Remove the 3 bolts retaining the transaxale filter cover, located on the side of the transaxle.
2. Remove the filter cover and pull the filter from the case.
3. Discard the filter cover O-ring and install a new one on the cover.

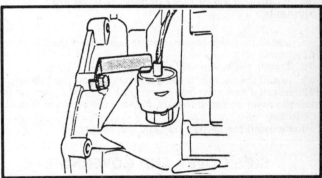

Speedometer gear and sensor location

4. Install a new filter in the case and reinstall the cover. Tighten the cover bolts to 6 ft. lbs.

SPEEDOMETER DRIVE

1. Remove the bracket retaining the electronic speed sensor in the transaxle case.
2. Remove the speedometer drive from the case, by pulling upward on it.
3. Remove the speedometer gear from the sleeve. Remove the O-ring and sealing ring from the sleeve.
4. Install a new O-ring and seal ring on the speedometer gear sleeve.
5. Install the speedometer gear to the speedometer gear sleeve and install the assembly into the case.
6. Install the retaining bracket.

VALVE BODY

1. Disconnect the battery cables and remove the battery.
2. Remove the battery tray.
3. Remove the transaxle dipstick. Remove the 4 bolts retaining the valve body cover.
4. Remove the valve body cover and discard the gasket.
5. Remove the 10 Torx® head screws retaining the valve body.
6. Remove the oil tubes and remove the valve body from the case.
7. To install the valve body, first set the selector lever mechanism to the 1st detent.
8. Set the selector rod in the valve body to the fully inserted position.

Removing the valve body assembly from the transaxle

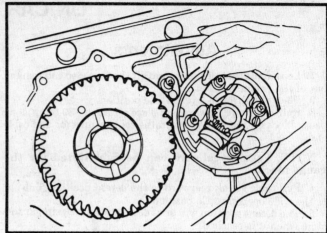

Removing the governor assembly from the transaxle case

9. Install the valve body in the case and insert the 10 retaining screws.
10. Torque the valve body retaining screws to 7.3 ft. lbs.
11. Install the oil tubes, using new O-rings on the tubes.
12. Install a new valve body cover gasket on the cover and install the cover on the transaxle. Tighten the retaining bolts to 4.4 ft. lbs.
13. Reinstall the battery tray and the battery.

SIDE COVER AND GOVERNOR

1. Raise and safely support the vehicle.
2. Remove the left front wheel and tire assembly.
3. Remove the inner fender liner.
4. Place a drain pan under the transaxle and drain the fluid.
5. Remove the 13 bolts retaining the side cover.
6. Remove the side cover and gasket. Remove the screw on the pinion shaft.

7. Remove the gear and inner race of the tapered roller bearing from the pinion shaft.
8. Use a heat gun or equivalent, to heat the outer race of the tapered bearing and remove the outer race.
9. Remove the governor housing from the case.
10. The governor can now be cleaned or serviced.
11. To install the governor, apply petroleum jelly to the seals and install the governor in position. The governor hub should be flush with the pinion shaft splines.
12. Heat the housing with a heat gun or equivalent and install the outer race. Install the gear and bearing to the pinion shaft.
13. Install the pinion shaft bolt and tighten to 110 ft. lbs.
14. Apply a thin coat of petroleum jelly to the gasket and install the gasket on the case.
15. Install the cover and tighten the bolts to 7.3 ft. lbs.
16. Install the inner fender cover and install the wheel and tire assembly.
17. Lower the vehicle and fill the transaxle to the correct level with the correct fluid.

REMOVAL AND INSTALLATION

TRANSAXLE REMOVAL

1. Disconnect the battery cables and remove the battery.
2. Remove the windshield washer fluid reservoir. Plug the outlet to keep the fluid from running out.
3. Open the terminal box and disconnect the cables.

NOTE: When removing the fuel filter, wrap a rag around the line to prevent fuel from spraying out. Use proper caution when working with the fuel system.

4. Release the fuel filter clamp and remove the filter. Remove the battery cable.
5. Disconnect the wiring from the air mass meter and remove the meter.
6. Disconnect the hose from the transaxle and the bypass hose from the turbocharger delivery pipe. Remove the delivery pipe.
7. Disconnect the throttle cable form the throttle housing.
8. Disconnect the gear selector lever cable from the selector lever. Do not separate the ball joint on the cable.
9. Disconnect the inlet hose from the oil cooler on top of the transaxle. Disconnect the selector lever from the transaxle.

10. Remove the return line from the oil cooler. Place a drain pan under the transaxle to collect the oil.
11. Remove the clamp retaining the turbocharger oil supply line to the transaxle, if equipped.
12. Disconnect the speedometer cable from the transaxle. Remove the top retaining bolt for the starter motor.
13. Disconnect the starter motor stay from the intake manifold. Disconnect the top end of the starter stay from the wheel housing.
14. Place engine support yoke 83–93–977 or equivalent, in position on the wheel housing to support the engine when the transaxle has been removed.
15. Raise and safely support the vehicle. Remove the left front wheel and remove the inner fender liner.
16. Remove the starter motor and suspend it out of the way. Remove the bolts retaining the torque converter to the drive plate.
17. Remove the bolts retaining the ball joint to the suspension arm. Remove the anti-roll bar mounting nut from the suspension arm. Remove the 2 bolts retaining the anti-roll bar bearing.
18. Remove the front engine mount bolt.
19. Split the sub-frame at the front and slightly open the joint.

Remove the 2 bolts at the rear of the sub-frame, 1 of the bolts retains the steering gear.

20. Remove the bolts for the rear sub-frame joint and remove the 2 bolts in the front corner. Lower the sub-frame from the vehicle.

21. Remove the clamps from both the left and right CV-joints, separate the joints. Allow the driveshafts to hang down.

22. Position a suitable lifting device under the transaxle and lower it from the vehicle.

TRANSAXLE INSTALLATION

1. Install a suitable converter holding device to prevent the converter from falling out during installation. With the transaxle on a suitable lifting device, raise it into position under the vehicle.

2. Guide the transaxle into position aligning the converter pin as a guide. Install 1 bolt to retain the assembly.

3. Reattach the driveshafts and install the clamps over the CV boots.

4. Install the transaxle mounting bolt through the engine mount.

5. Raise the sub-frame assembly into position. Make sure the engine mount is in position.

6. Install all sub-frame bolts and the engine mount bolt.

7. Install the anti-roll bar and bearing into the suspension arm. Install all of the suspension arm bolts.

8. Install the torque converter-to-driveplate bolts. Use Loctite® 242 on the bolts.

9. Install the starter and stay. Lower the vehicle.

10. Remove the engine support tool. Install the upper starter mount bolts. Connect the speedometer cable.

11. Install the turbocharger oil pipe to the engine block.

12. Reconnect the selector lever cable. The selector should be in the **N** detent. Adjust the selector as needed.

13. Reconnect the oil cooler hose to the transaxle oil cooler.

14. Reconnect the turbocharger delivery pipe. Install the air mass meter.

15. Install the battery tray. Install the fuel filter.

16. Attach the battery cable to the battery tray. Reconnect the cables to the terminal box.

17. Install the winshield washer fluid bottle and connect the electrical leads.

18. Install the battery and reconnect the cables.

19. Raise and safely support the vehicle.

20. Install the inner fender cover. Install the wheel and tire assembly.

21. Lower the vehicle, refill the fluid in the transaxle.

22. Road test the vehicle and check the operation of the transaxle. Adjust the throttle linkage as needed. Check the fluid level.

SPECIFICATIONS

TORQUE SPECIFICATIONS

Part	ft. lbs.	Nm
Selector lever bolt	1.5 ①	2
Valve body cover	4.4	6
Valve body bolts	7.3	10
Park lock plate bolt	7.3	10
Pinion shaft bolt	110	150
Side case cover	7.3	10
Ball joint	56–72	80–100
Anti-roll bar	18–25	25–34
Oil filter cover	5.8	8
Governor housing bolts	7.3	10

① Inch lbs.

SPECIAL TOOLS

SPECIAL SERVICE TOOL

Description	Number
Torque converter holding tool	8791816
Selector arm clearance retainer bar	8791501
Gear position spring holding tool	8791493
Torque converter retainer	8791477
Torque converter retainer sleeve	8791485
Pressure gauge	8791600
Pressure gauge spacer	8791584
Pressure gauge adapter	8791865
Brake piston "C" press tool	8791709
Differential puller	8791642
Sleeve	8791410
Centering tool	8791725
Oil Pipe installation tool (turbocharged engine)	8791782
Oil pipe installation tool (non-turbocharged engine)	8791790
Seal ring drift	8791311
Differential bearing race mandrel	8390189
Dolly	8795177
Selector shaft adjusting wrench	9791758
Converter handle	8791766
Side hammer for oil pipes	8791360
Transaxle flush kit	8791824
Engine support yoke	8393977

APPLICATION

1989 Justy 2WD

GENERAL DESCRIPTION

The ECVT combines an electronically controlled magnetic clutch with a variable transaxle that is driven by steel belt pulleys to provide high running performance, low fuel consumption and ease of control. Hydraulic line pressure can be changed from high to low or vice versa, in response to engine load and output. The engine fuel and the clutch control are optimally controlled by a microcomputer to enhance high transmitting efficiency and excellent driveability. The magnetic clutch is designed for exclusive use with the ECVT. It is a standing start clutch that utilizes magnetic powder and is controlled by a microcomputer which constantly evaluates engine speed, vehicle speed and throttle position signals. The variable transaxle consists of a steel belt and a set of pulleys. Groove width is controlled by hydraulic pressure to provide speed changes from a standing start to maximum speed without shifting problems.

Transaxle Identification

TRANSAXLE IDENTIFICATION NUMBER

The transaxle can be indentified by the 11th letter in the vehicle identification number located on the dashboard. The transaxle identification code is C which indicates Gunma manufacturer-ECVT.

The transaxle serial number is located on the side surface of the case assembly. The number can be used to identify type and manufacture date of the transaxle. The number is alsdo used in conjunction with specific factory information.

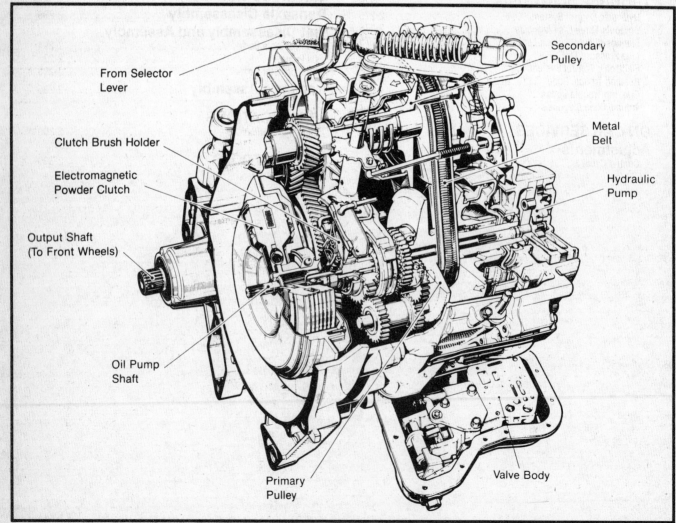

View of ECVT transaxle

Electronic Controls

ELECTROMAGNETIC POWDER CLUTCH

The clutch control is applied and released by controlling the current to the clutch electromagnetic coil. This circuit has a self-diagnosis function and a fail-safe function.

ENGINE REVOLUTIONARY SIGNAL

The ignition pluse from the negative terminal of the ignition coil is detected and a clutch current proportional to the engine speed is obtained.

ACCELERATOR SWITCH

The operation of the accelerator pedal is detected by the movement of a microswitch attached to the accelerator pedal. Once the accelerator pedal is depressed, the electronic clutch is energized.

THROTTLE POSITION SWITCH

The amount the accelerator pedal is depressed is sensed and the current required to direct couple the clutch control is determined.

DRIVE, DRIVE SPORTY AND REVERSE SWITCH

These switches are used to sense the drive, drive sporty and reverse positions.

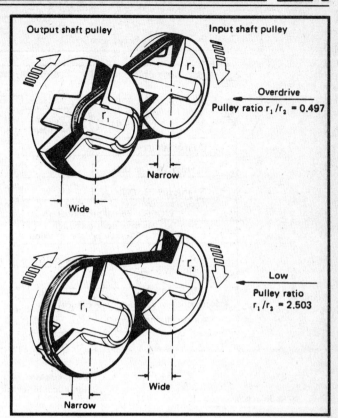

Variable pulleys

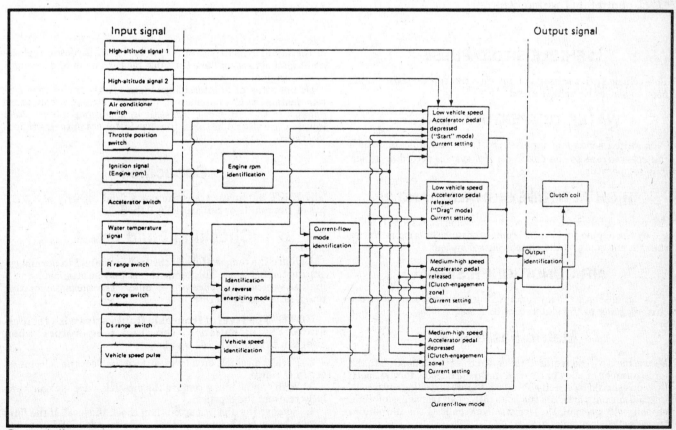

Control diagram

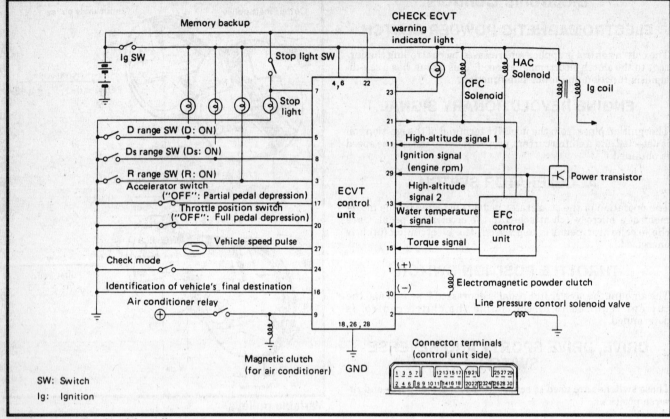

ECVT control unit wiring diagram

VEHICLE SPEED PULSE

The vehicle speed sensor is built into the speedometer and is used to sense the vehicle speed.

WATER TEMPERTURE SWITCH

This switch sends and input signal to the control unit which controls current to the clutch control system according to engine temperature.

HIGH ALTITUDE SIGNALS 1 AND 2

An input signal which varies with atmospheric pressure is emitted by the engine fuel control computer unit. This signal varies the current going to the clutch control system.

AIR CONDITIONER SIGNAL

This signal senses the air conditioning operation and varies the current going to the clutch control system.

Metric Fasteners

Metric tools will be required to service this transaxle. Due to the large number of alloy parts used in this transaxle, torque specifications should be strictly observed. Before installing capscrews into aluminum parts, dip the bolts into clean transmission fluid as this will prevent the screws from galling the aluminum threads, thus causing damage.

Metric fastener dimensions are very close to the dimensions of the familiar inch system fasteners. For this reason replacement fasteners must have the same measurement and strength as the original fastener.

Do not attempt to interchange metric fasteners for inch system fasteners. Mismatched or incorrect fasteners can cause damage to the automatic transaxle unit and possible personal injury. Care should be taken to reuse fasteners in their original locations.

Capacities

The EVCT automatic transaxle has a fluid capacity of 3.3–3.6 qts of Dexron®II or Subaru EVCT fluid.

Checking Fluid Level

1. Raise the temperature of the transaxle fluid to normal operating temperature. This temperature may be attained by driving the vehicle a distance of 3–6 miles. The normal operating temperature is 140–176°F.

NOTE: The level of transaxle fluid varies with temperature. Pay attention to the fluid temperature when checking transaxle oil level.

2. Park the vehicle on a level surface then set the selector lever in **P** range.
3. With engine idling remove the dipstick, wipe it clean, then fully reinsert the dipstick.
4. Remove the dipstick again then check the level. If the fluid level is below **HOT** range, add the recommended fluid up to the correct mark through the dipstick hole.

TRANSAXLE MODIFICATIONS

At the time of this printing there were no modification information available from the manufacturer.

TROUBLE DIAGNOSIS

CHILTON'S THREE C's TRANSAXLE DIAGNOSIS
ECVT

Condition	Cause	Correction
Clutch engages too soon	a) Broken or worn bush assembly b) Brush holder wire faulty	a) Replace brush assembly b) Repair or replace brush holder wire
Transaxle remains in low and does not shift	a) Fluid level low b) Pulley inoperative c) Control valve oil pressure problem	a) Add fluid to correct level b) Replace pulley and belt assembly c) Repair oil circuit leakage
Shifting from N to D or R cannot be made	a) Electromagnetic clutch problem b) Shift mechanism or fork	a) Replace clutch assembly b) Repair or replace shift mechanism or fork
Shock is felt when shifting from D to D_s	a) Accelerator and throttle position switch misadjusted b) Range switch inoperative c) Pulley inoperative	a) Adjust accelerator or throttle position switch b) Replace range switch c) Replace pulley and belt assembly
Engine races while driving	a) Selector cable linkage misadjusted b) Brush holder connection bad brush worn or broken c) Accelerator and throttle position switch misadjusted d) Range switch inoperative e) Clutch malfunction or oil on slip ring f) Oil pump seal ring worn or pump malfunction g) Control valve problem h) Pitot pressure circuit problem	a) Adjust selector cable b) Repair correction or replace brush holder assembly c) Adjust accelerator or throttle position switch d) Replace range switch e) Replace clutch assembly or service slip ring f) Replace oil pump seal ring or pump assembly g) Repair or replace control valve h) Repair Pitot pressure circuit

Hydraulic Control System

OIL PUMP

The oil pump is driven by the engine through a shaft passing through the primary pulley. The pump is an external gear pump.

PRESSURE REGULATOR VALVE

The pressure regulator valve supplies the optimum hydraulic pressure to the secondary pulley when the pulley transmits power through the steel belt.

SHIFT CONTROL VALVE

The shift control valve controls continuous speed changes from low range to the overdrive range in the **D** and **Ds** positions.

ENGINE BRAKE VALVE

The engine brake valve maintains a comparatively high engine speed when the engine braking is necessary for driving down hills.

Diagnosis Tests

LINE PRESSURE TEST

When a slipping belt and pulley system is noted as a result of a road test or when inadquate vehicle speed is encountered during shift operations, check the line pressure.

1. Remove the outlet plug and install a suitable oil pressure gauge. Discard the oil plug after removal and replace with a new one.

2. Disconnect the electrical connector of the line pressure control solenoid valve.

3. Shift the selector lever to the **N** range while idling the engine (after normal operating temperature has been reached) and measure the line pressure.

4. The standard value for line pressure should be 341 psi with the engine idling in the **D** range.

5. To adjust the line pressure drain the transaxle fluid. Remove the oil pan and oil strainer.

6. Loosen the locknut on the pressure regulator valve guide and turn the bolt in or out to adjust the line pressure as required.

NOTE: One rotation of bolt changes line pressure by 14 psi. After measuring the line pressure, connect the electrical connector of the line pressure control solenoid valve.

7. Loosening the bolt a complete rotation increases line pressure by 14 psi and tightening the bolt a complete rotation decreases line pressure by 14 psi.

Electronic Control System

NOTE: When troubleshooting the electronic control system always check basic items and check all adjustment procedures before entering in self diagnostics.

READING TROUBLE CODES

When a problem occurs in the system, the **CHECK ECVT** warning indicator light will illuminate. When there is no problem in the system, the warning indicator light will go out soon after the engine is started. When the warning indicator light illuminates, connect the check mode connector, which will determine the cause of the problem in accordance with the call up procedure and repair the faulty part as per the troubleshooting chart. After a repair has been made, recheck that the problem has been eliminated and then clear the memory. The check mode connector is 2 single electrical connectors from the control unit input harness. The control unit is located under the dash to the left of the brake pedal. The trouble code 3 is a vehicle type identification code to be checked in the D-check mode.

CLEARING TROUBLE CODES

To cancel previous trouble codes stored in the memory and set

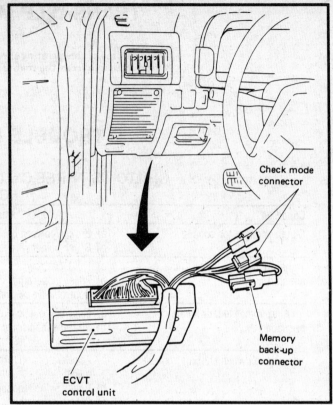

Connector locations

the system diagnostics in the clear memory mode disconnect the memory back-up connector for at least 1 minute. The memory back-up connector is a single electrical connector from the control unit input harness. The control unit is located under the dash to the left of the brake pedal.

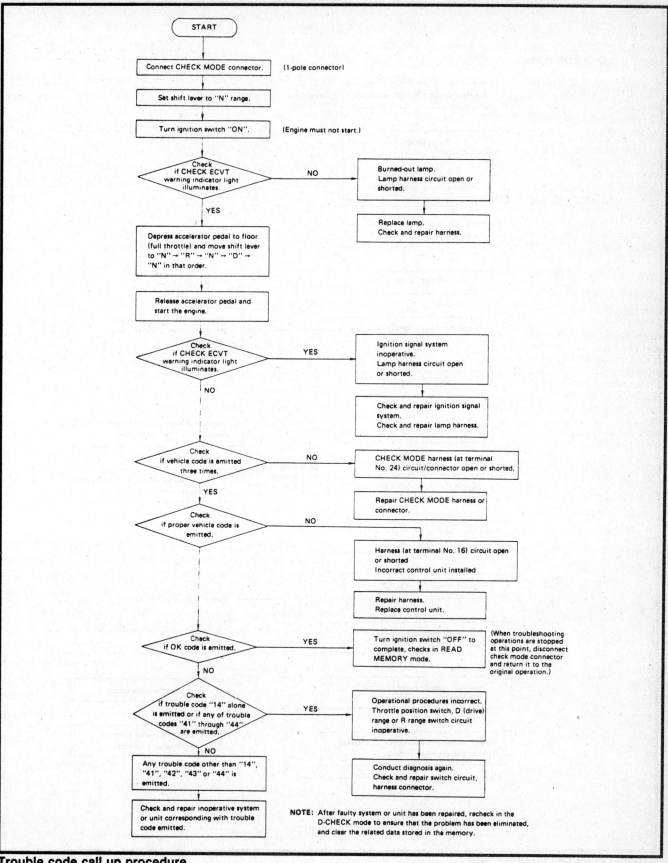

Trouble code call up procedure

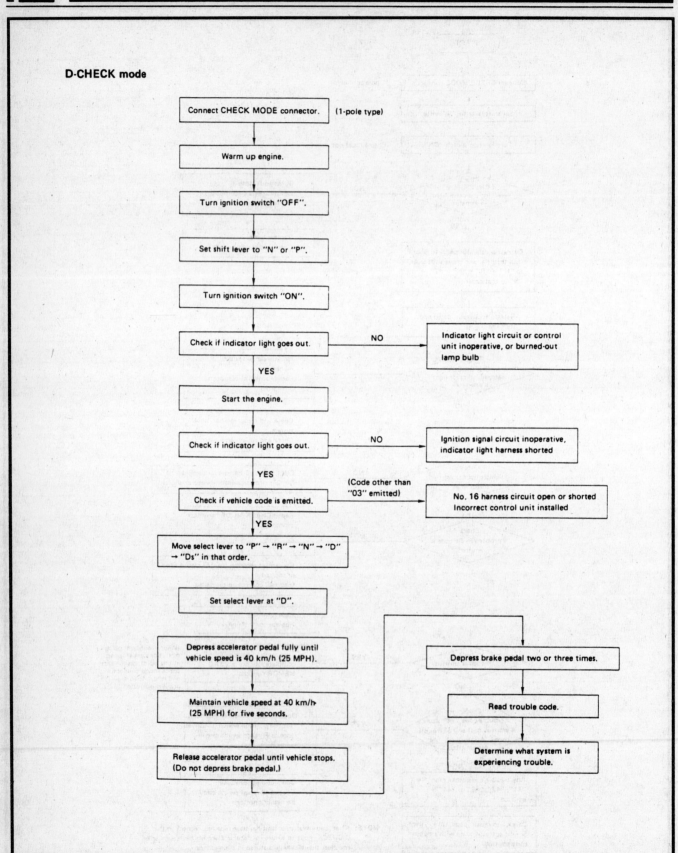

D-CHECK mode

Connect CHECK MODE connector. (1-pole type)

↓

Warm up engine.

↓

Turn ignition switch "OFF".

↓

Set shift lever to "N" or "P".

↓

Turn ignition switch "ON".

↓

Check if indicator light goes out. —NO→ Indicator light circuit or control unit inoperative, or burned-out lamp bulb

↓ YES

Start the engine.

↓

Check if indicator light goes out. —NO→ Ignition signal circuit inoperative, indicator light harness shorted

↓ YES

Check if vehicle code is emitted. —(Code other than "03" emitted)→ No. 16 harness circuit open or shorted Incorrect control unit installed

↓ YES

Move select lever to "P" → "R" → "N" → "D" → "Ds" in that order.

↓

Set select lever at "D".

↓

Depress accelerator pedal fully until vehicle speed is 40 km/h (25 MPH).

↓

Maintain vehicle speed at 40 km/h (25 MPH) for five seconds.

↓

Release accelerator pedal until vehicle stops. (Do not depress brake pedal.)

→ Depress brake pedal two or three times.

↓

Read trouble code.

↓

Determine what system is experiencing trouble.

Trouble code call up procedure

TROUBLE CODES

Trouble code (Blinks)	System in trouble	Probable cause	Parts to check
13	D-range switch signal system	D-range switch signal circuit open or shorted	1. Wire harness and connector 2. D-range inhibitor switch 3. Control unit
14	Ds-range switch signal system	Ds-range switch signal circuit open or shorted	1. Wire harness and connector 2. Ds-range inhibitor switch 3. Control unit
15	R-range switch signal	R-range switch signal circuit open or shorted	1. Wire harness and connector 2. R-range inhibitor switch 3. Control unit
21 ①	Torque signal system	Torque signal remains ON or OFF	1. Wire harness and connector 2. Control unit 3. EFC control unit
22	Water temperature signal system	Signal remains ON or OFF	1. Wire harness and connector 2. Control unit 3. EFC control unit
25	Slow cut solenoid system	Slow cut output circuit open or shorted	1. Wire harness and connector 2. Slow cut solenoid 3. Control unit
31	Accelerator switch signal system	Accelerator switch signal circuit open or shorted	1. Wire harness and connector 2. Accelerator switch 3. Control unit
32	Throttle position signal system	Throttle position signal circuit open or shorted	1. Wire harness and connector 2. Throttle position switch 3. Control unit
33	Vehicle speed signal system	Vehicle speed signal not entered	1. Wire harness and connector 2. Speedometer cable 3. Vehicle speed switch 4. Control unit
34	Clutch coil system	Current control does not occur for at least 3 seconds during standing start	1. Wire harness and connector 2. Brush holder 3. Clutch 4. Control unit
35	Line pressure solenoid system	Line pressure solenoid output circuit open or shorted	1. Wire harness and connector 2. Line pressure solenoid 3. Control unit
41	High altitude signal 1	High altitude signal 1 remains ON or OFF	1. Wire harness and connector 2. Control unit 3. EFC control unit
42	High altitude signal 2	High altitude signal 2 remains ON or OFF	1. Wire harness and connector 2. Control unit 3. EFC control unit
45 ②	Brake switch signal system	Brake signal switch circuit open or shorted	1. Wire harness and connector 2. Brake switch 3. Control unit

① When torque signal circuit becomes inoperative, check EFC control unit sensor system (including pressure sensor, vehicle speed sensor, etc.). Also check air conditioner harness and switch signal connector.

② When vehicle-speed pulse circuit becomes inoperative while driving, brake signal circuit problem may also be stored in memory.

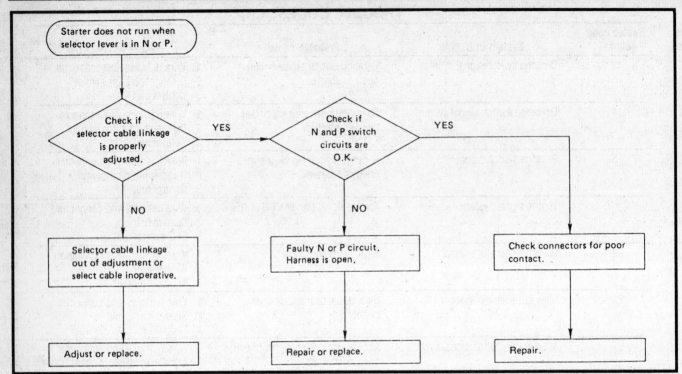

Troubleshooting chart

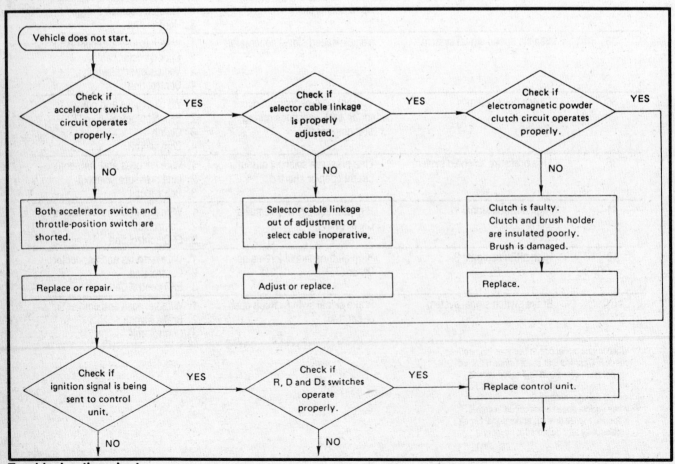

Troubleshooting chart

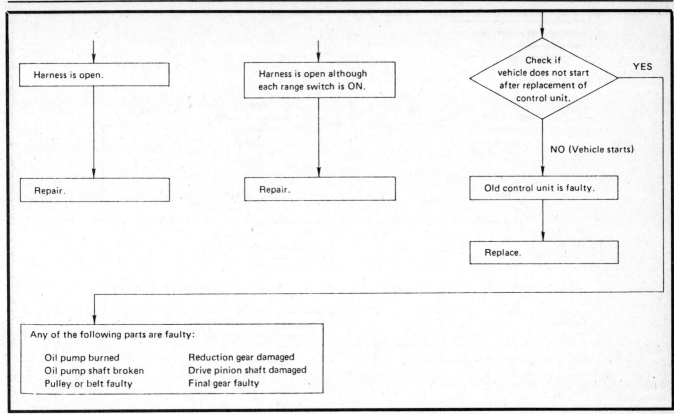

Troubleshooting chart

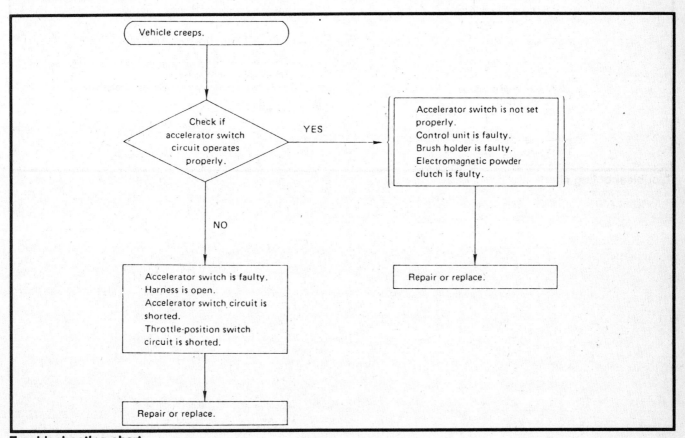

Troubleshooting chart

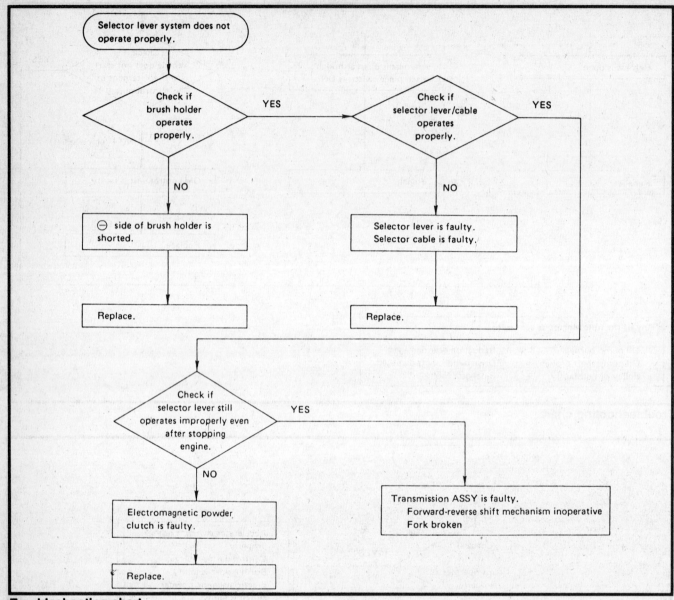

Troubleshooting chart

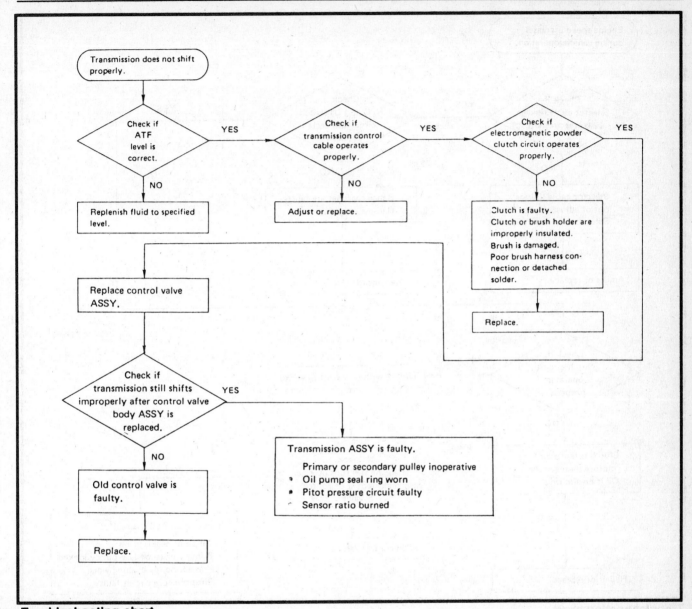

Troubleshooting chart

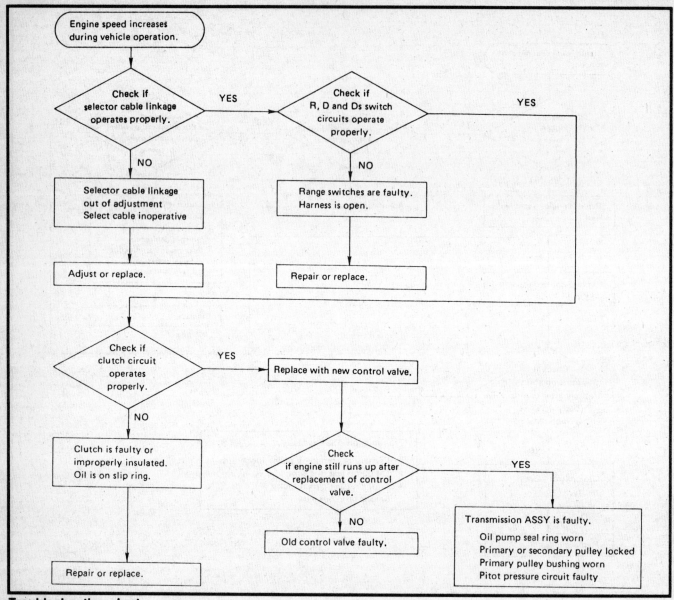

Troubleshooting chart

ON CAR SERVICES

Adjustments

CONTROL CABLE

1. Check the throttle valve to make sure that it open and closes completely. Check that the shift control lever turns fully when the throttle valve is fully opened.
2. While fully opening the throttle valve, lightly pull the control cable to ensure free play is within specified range. The standard valve for cable free play is 0.020–0.098 in.
3. If the freeplay is not within the specified range, loosen the locknuts and adjust length of the control cable.
4. Loosen the locknuts and lightly pull the inner cable with

the throttle valve at the full open position so that free play is zero. Then temporarily tighten locknuts. Loosen the top locknut 1½ turns and tighten bottom locknut. Install the rubber boot after adjustment.

Services

FLUID CHANGE

1. Raise and safely support the vehicle.
2. Place a suitable drain pan under the transaxle.
3. Remove the transaxle drain plug and allow the fluid to drain.

4. When the fluid is completely drained, install the drain plug and tighten it to 18 ft. lbs.

5. Lower the vehicle and fill the transaxle to the correct level with fluid.

CONTROL CABLE

Removal and Installation

NOTE: To facilitate removal of the transaxle oil pan, remove the front grille and radiator if necessary.

1. Raise and safely support the vehicle. Drain the transaxle fluid and remove the oil pan.

2. Remove the end of the cable from the pulley and remove the bolt. Discard the O-ring.

3. Install the new O-ring onto the cable, insert the cable into the hole in the transaxle case and tighten with the bolt and washer to 3.3–4.0 ft. lbs.

4. Route the inner cable along the rib (guide) on the transaxle inner case. Secure the end of the cable hole on the shift control lever and place the cable on the lever.

5. Check that the inner cable moves smoothly without disturbing the rib (guide) of the transaxle case. Make sure that the outer cable does not interfere with the control valve body assembly. Lower the vehicle.

BRUSH HOLDER

Removal and Installation

1. Disconnect the negative battery cable. Remove the starter.

2. Disconnect the brush holder harness and wiring harness connector. Remove the bolts which secure the brush holder and remove the brush holder.

3. Installation is the reverse of the removal procedure. The correct torque for the brush holder retaining bolts is 3.3–4.0 ft. lbs.

NOTE: Be careful not to bend or scratch the seal plate affixed to brush holder. Make sure that the brush is installed in the bursh holder's groove of the housing when the brush holder is installed in clutch housing. Do not forcefully install or tighten the brush holder.

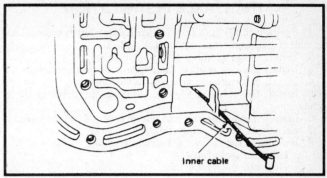

Inner cable installation

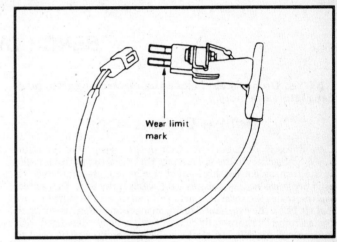

Brush holder assembly

REMOVAL AND INSTALLATION

TRANSAXLE REMOVAL

NOTE: When removing and installing ECVT transaxle, always remove and install the engine and transaxle as an assembly.

1. Disconnect the negative battery cable. Drain the coolant.

2. Remove the grille. Disconnect hoses and electric wiring from radiator and remove the radiator.

3. Remove front hood release cable and remove radiator upper support member. Disconnect horn and remove the air cleaner assembly.

4. Disconnect the following hoses and cables:
   a. Hoses from carburetor
   b. Hoses from the heater unit
   c. Hose for brake booster
   d. Accelerator cable
   e. Choke cable from carburetor if equipped
   f. Speedometer cable
   g. Distributor wiring

5. Disconnect selector cable. Set selector lever at **N** position. Remove clip and detach selector cable from bracket. Remove snap pin, clevis pin and separate selector cable from transaxle.

6. Remove the pitching stopper from the bracket.

7. Disconnect the starter cable, engine wiring harness connectors, ground lead terminals and brush holder harness connector. Rasie and safely support the vehicle.

8. Drain the transaxle fluid. Remove the hanger from the rear of transaxle.

9. Remove under covers and remove the exhaust system.

10. Remove the drive shaft from transaxle.

11. Remove transverse link.

12. Remove the spring pin retaining the axle shaft by using a sutiable tool and separate front axle shaft from the transaxle.

13. Remove engine and transaxle mounting brackets.

14. Raise the engine and remove center member and crossmember. Lower the vehicle.

15. Using a suitable lifting device, lift up the engine and transaxle assembly carefully and remove it from the vehicle.

TRANSAXLE INSTALLATION

1. Position the engine and transaxle assembly in the vehicle. Install engine and transaxle mounting brackets.
2. Install center member and crossmember.
3. Install the axle shaft to transaxle with new spring pin.
4. Install gearshift rod and stay to transaxle.
5. Install the exhaust sustem. Connect the drive shaft to transaxle.
6. Install transverse link and under covers to the vehicle.
7. Reconnect the pitching stopper to bracket.
8. Reconnect the following hoses and cables:
   a. Hoses to carburetor
   b. Hoses to the heater unit
   c. Hose to brake booster
   d. Accelerator cable
   e. Choke cable from carburetor (if so equipped)
   f. Speedometer cable
   g. Distributor wiring
9. Reconnect the starter cable, engine wiring harness connectors, ground lead terminals and brush holder harness connector. Install the air cleaner assembly.
10. Install radiator upper member and connect hood release cable to lock assembly. Reconnect the horn.
11. Install the radiator and connect hoses and electric wiring. Install grille to the vehicle.
12. Refill the coolant and refill the transaxle to the correct level. Reconnect the battery cable.
13. Check all fluid levels. Road test vehicles for proper operation in all driving ranges.

BENCH OVERHAUL

NOTE: Do not steam clean the electromagnetic powder clutch assembly.

Before Disassembly

Cleanliness is an important factor in the overhaul of the automatic transaxle. Before opening up this unit, the entire outside of the transaxle assembly should be cleaned, preferable with a high pressure washer such as a car wash spray unit. Dirt entering the transaxle internal parts will negate all the time and effort spent on the overhaul. During inspection and reassembly all parts should be thoroughly cleaned with solvent then dried with compressed air. Wiping cloths and rags should not be used to dry parts since lint will find its way into the valve body passages.

Wheel bearing grease, long used to hold thrust washers and lube parts, should not be used. Lube seals with clean transmission fluid and use ordinary unmedicated petroleum jelly to hold the thrust washers and to ease the assembly of seals, since it will not leave a harmful residue as grease often will. Do not use solvent on neoprene seals, friction plates if they are to be reused, or thrust washers. Be wary of nylon parts if the transaxle failure was due to failure of the cooling system. Nylon parts exposed to water or antifreeze solutions can swell and distort and must be replaced.

Before installing bolts into aluminum parts, always dip the threads into clean transmission fluid. Antiseize compound can also be used to prevent bolts from galling the aluminum and seizing. Always use a torque wrench to keep from stripping the threads. Take care when installing new O-rings, especially the smaller O-rings. The internal snaprings should be expanded and the external rings should be compressed, if they are to be reused. This will help insure proper seating when installed.

Transaxle Disassembly

1. Separate the engine and transaxle. Place transaxle in suitable workstand or holding fixture.
2. Remove the starter motor and the brush holder from the transaxle assembly.
3. Disconnnect the shift control cable.
4. Remove the electromagnetic powder clutch (do not disassemble the clutch assembly) from the flywheel and do not handle the slip ring.
5. Be careful not to turn over the removed electromagnetic powder clutch, apply an impact to it or handle it improperly. Otherwise, powder may flow out through the powder hole. Always handle or store it with the slip ring facing up. Do not steam clean the electromagnetic powder clutch.

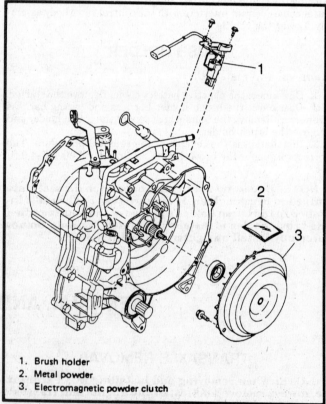

1. Brush holder
2. Metal powder
3. Electromagnetic powder clutch

Electromagnetic clutch and brush holder assembly

6. Position the transaxle with the oil pan facing down. Remove the pitching stopper bracket. Cover the axle shaft (stub shaft) serration with vinyl tape or equivalent.
7. Carefully remove the oil pump shaft by pulling it straight out by hand. Check the oil pump shaft for damage. Discard the clip after removal.
8. Remove the clutch housing section from the transaxle case sections.
9. Remove the differential assembly from the transaxle case section.
10. Remove the shift connecting rod, shift arm and shift cam. Do not reuse the spring pin.

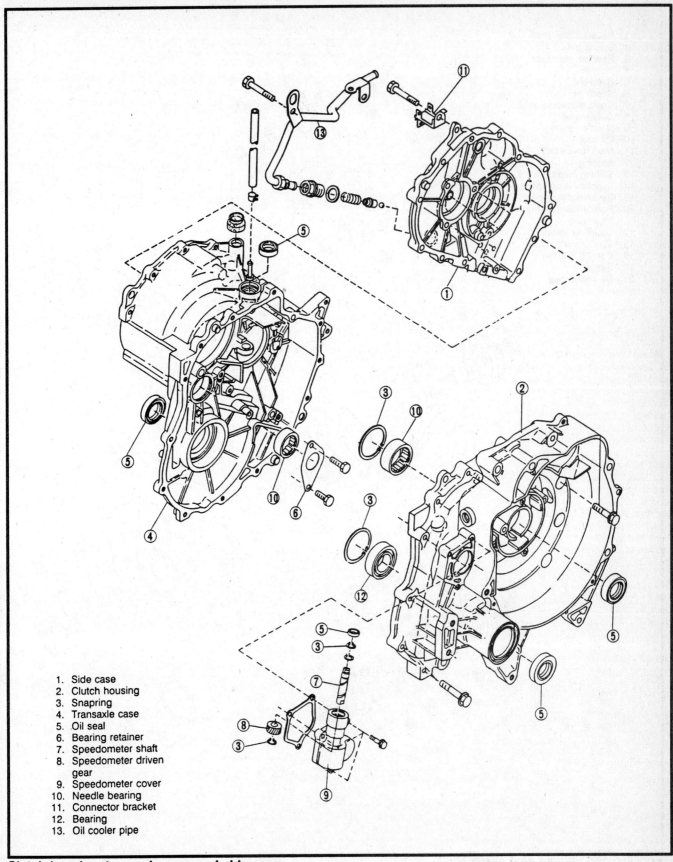

1. Side case
2. Clutch housing
3. Snapring
4. Transaxle case
5. Oil seal
6. Bearing retainer
7. Speedometer shaft
8. Speedometer driven gear
9. Speedometer cover
10. Needle bearing
11. Connector bracket
12. Bearing
13. Oil cooler pipe

Clutch housing, transaxle case and side case

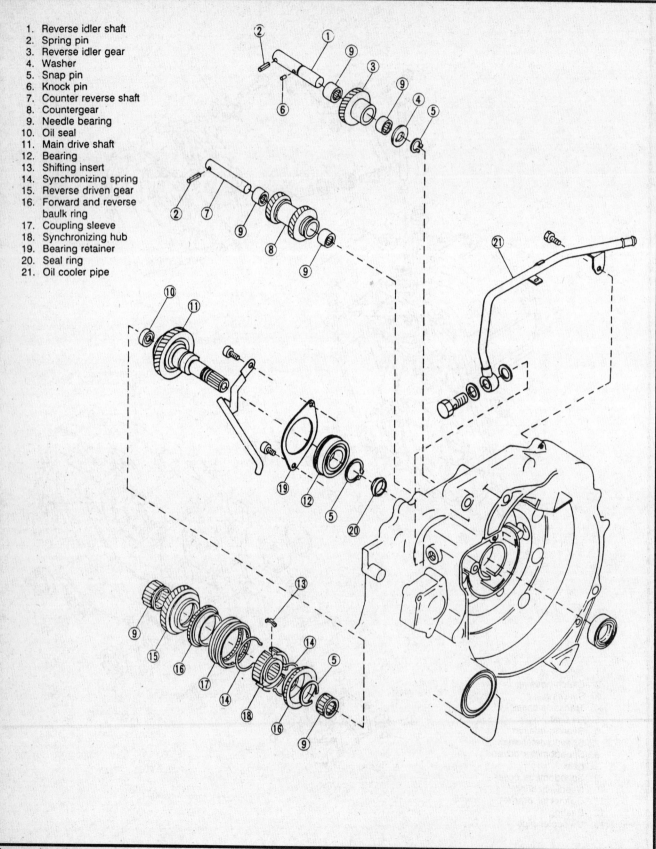

1. Reverse idler shaft
2. Spring pin
3. Reverse idler gear
4. Washer
5. Snap pin
6. Knock pin
7. Counter reverse shaft
8. Countergear
9. Needle bearing
10. Oil seal
11. Main drive shaft
12. Bearing
13. Shifting insert
14. Synchronizing spring
15. Reverse driven gear
16. Forward and reverse baulk ring
17. Coupling sleeve
18. Synchronizing hub
19. Bearing retainer
20. Seal ring
21. Oil cooler pipe

Forward and reverse gear assembly

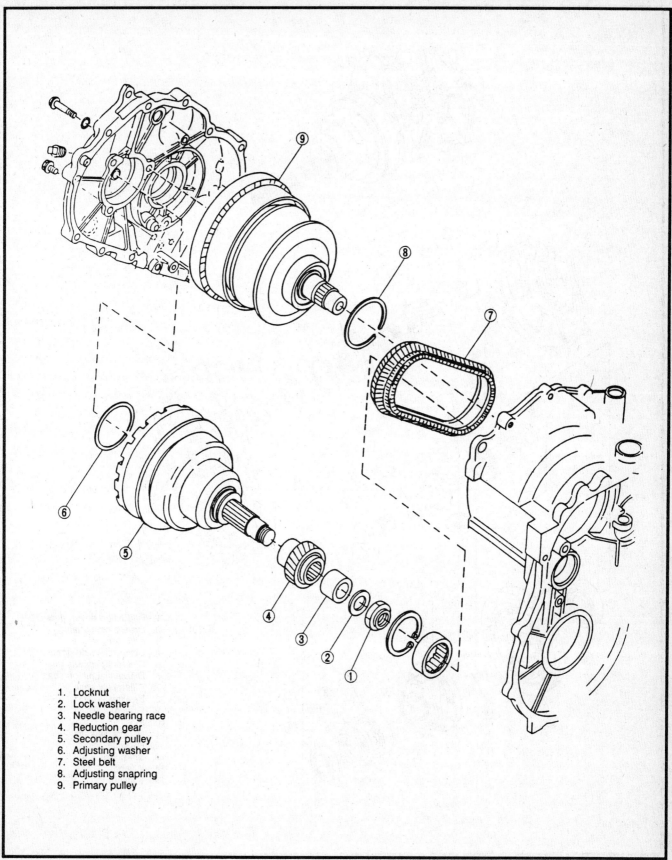

1. Locknut
2. Lock washer
3. Needle bearing race
4. Reduction gear
5. Secondary pulley
6. Adjusting washer
7. Steel belt
8. Adjusting snapring
9. Primary pulley

Steel belt and pulleys assembly

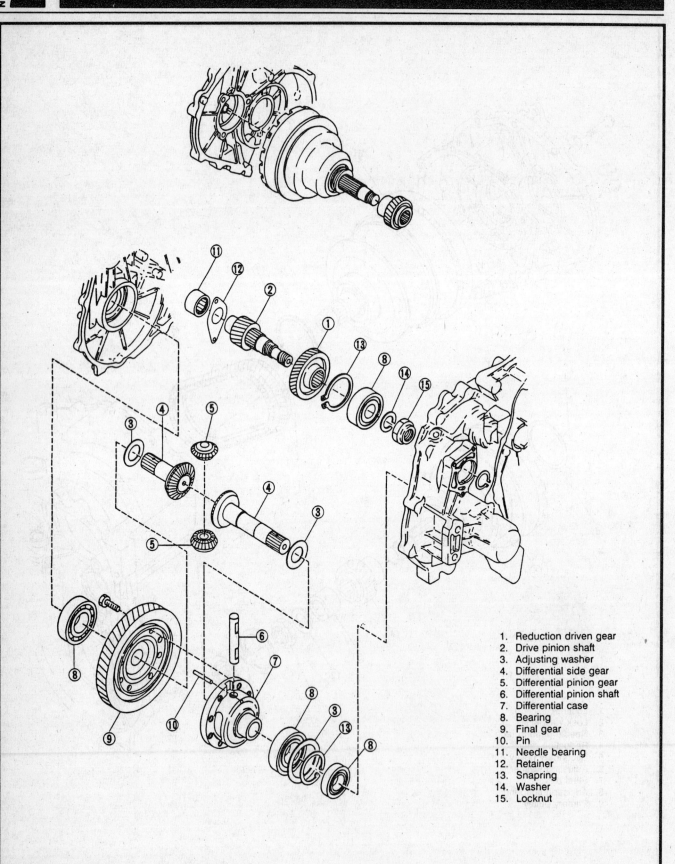

Reduction gear and differential gear assembly

1. Reduction driven gear
2. Drive pinion shaft
3. Adjusting washer
4. Differential side gear
5. Differential pinion gear
6. Differential pinion shaft
7. Differential case
8. Bearing
9. Final gear
10. Pin
11. Needle bearing
12. Retainer
13. Snapring
14. Washer
15. Locknut

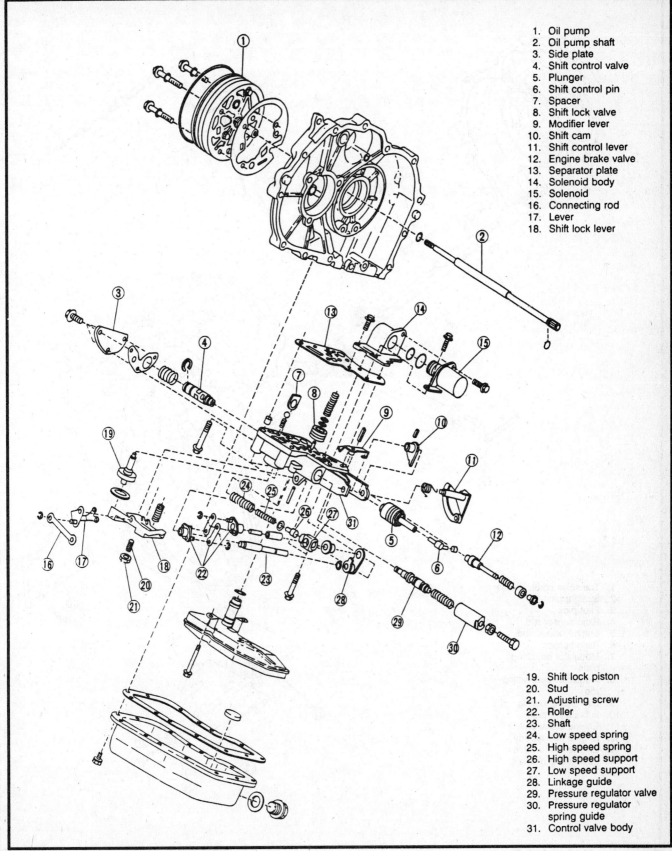

1. Oil pump
2. Oil pump shaft
3. Side plate
4. Shift control valve
5. Plunger
6. Shift control pin
7. Spacer
8. Shift lock valve
9. Modifier lever
10. Shift cam
11. Shift control lever
12. Engine brake valve
13. Separator plate
14. Solenoid body
15. Solenoid
16. Connecting rod
17. Lever
18. Shift lock lever

19. Shift lock piston
20. Stud
21. Adjusting screw
22. Roller
23. Shaft
24. Low speed spring
25. High speed spring
26. High speed support
27. Low speed support
28. Linkage guide
29. Pressure regulator valve
30. Pressure regulator spring guide
31. Control valve body

Oil pump and control valve assembly

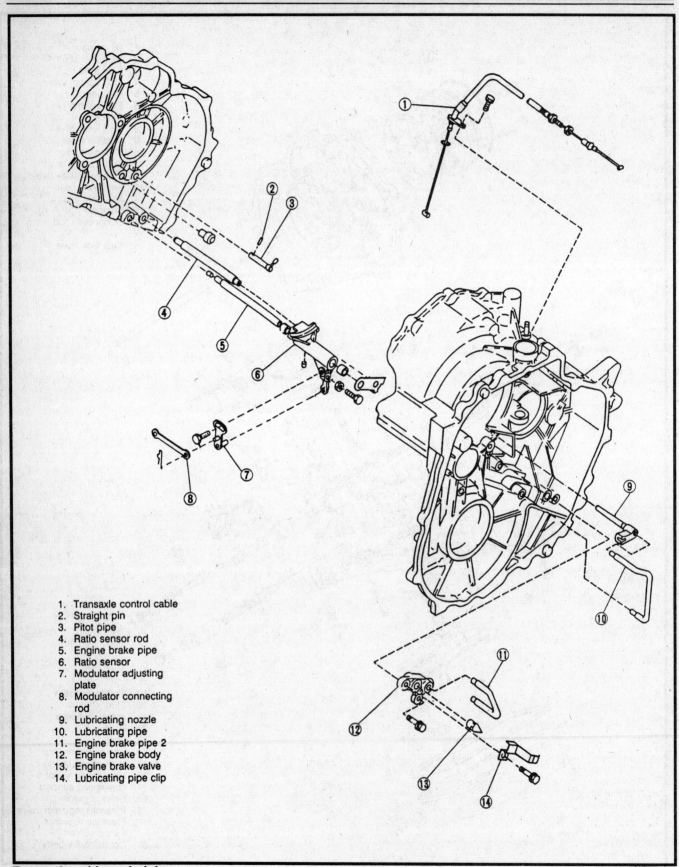

1. Transaxle control cable
2. Straight pin
3. Pitot pipe
4. Ratio sensor rod
5. Engine brake pipe
6. Ratio sensor
7. Modulator adjusting plate
8. Modulator connecting rod
9. Lubricating nozzle
10. Lubricating pipe
11. Engine brake pipe 2
12. Engine brake body
13. Engine brake valve
14. Lubricating pipe clip

Transaxle cable and piping

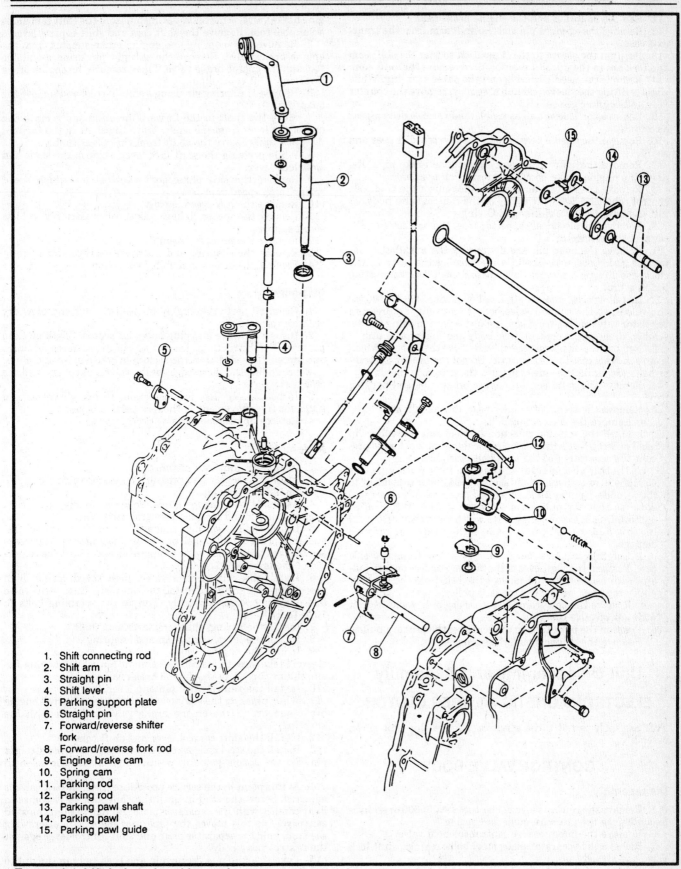

1. Shift connecting rod
2. Shift arm
3. Straight pin
4. Shift lever
5. Parking support plate
6. Straight pin
7. Forward/reverse shifter fork
8. Forward/reverse fork rod
9. Engine brake cam
10. Spring cam
11. Parking rod
12. Parking rod
13. Parking pawl shaft
14. Parking pawl
15. Parking pawl guide

Transaxle shift fork and parking rod

11. Remove snapring and the engine brake cam.

12. Remove the straight pin and the shift arm from the transaxle case.

13. Position the sleeve to the **D** position so that the shift cam and fork are in the upright position then remove the shift cam.

14. Remove the needle bearing and the outer snapring. While slightly lifting the sleeve and hub assembly, remove the counter gear and counter gear shaft.

15. Remove the sleeve/hub assembly and reverse driven gear as a unit.

16. Remove the needle bearing and the reverse idler gear and shaft.

17. Remove the lubricating pipe and engine brake pipe. Remove the engine brake body and lubricating nozzle.

18. Remove the oil pan and gasket. Disconnect the transaxle control cable and from the pulley of the control valve body.

19. Remove the oil strainer and O-ring.

20. Remove the electrical connector from the bracket and disconnect the connector.

21. Remove the snap pin and disconnect the modulator connecting rod. Loosen the bolt. While turning the plate in the clockwise direction, remove the plate and modulator connecting rod as a unit.

22. Install special tool control valve holder 499205600 or equivalent, to the control valve body to prevent the pressure regulator valve spring from popping out when removing the assembly. Remove the control valve body and holder as a unit.

23. Remove the oil pump assembly. Remove the 12 bolts which secure the side case to the transaxle. Do not remove the 3 retainer bolts. Separate the side case from the transaxle case.

24. Remove the ratio sensor, engine brake pipe and parking pawl.

25. Remove the secondary pulley assembly as follows:

    a. Remove the 3 retaining bolts.

    b. Mark the rotation direction of steel belt. Install a clip band or wrap belt with black electrical tape at 2 places to prevent the separation of the steel belt assembly.

    c. Install the special tool secondary pulley puller 499195400 or equivalent and seat 899524105 or equivalent to the secondary pulley and using hand pressure only screw tool down so that the pulley groove width is 2.05–2.09 in. (52–53mm). Do not expand the groove width more than 2.05–2.09 in. (52–53mm). Otherwise the pulley interior may be damaged.

    d. Carefully remove the secondary pulley from the side case. Position the V grooves of the pirmary and secondary pulleys with each other and remove the belt from the primary pulley together with the secondary pulley.

    e. Remove the belt from the secondary pulley and wrap it with a protective covering.

26. Position the pitot tube in the center of the primary pulley.

27. Remove the primary pulley assembly.

Unit Disassembly and Assembly

ELECTROMAGNETIC POWDER CLUTCH

This assembly is not to be serviced. Replace this unit as an assembly.

CONTROL VALVE BODY

Disassembly

1. Remove the control valve holder tool 499205600 or equivalent. Remove the pressure guide and spring.

2. Remove the line pressure control solenoid valve.

3. Remove the spearator plate, steel balls, springs, shift lock valve and straight pin.

4. Being careful not to remove the straight pin from the engine brake valve, remove the spring pin from the shift cam using a suitable tool. Remove the shift cam and shift control lever.

5. Remove the snapring and engine brake support from the engine brake valve. Remove the straight pin using a suitable tool and the engine brake valve. Then, remove the engine brake lever and shift control pin.

6. Remove the spring pin using a suitable tool and remove the snapring.

7. Move the shaft in the forward direction and remove one end of the lever from the shaft. Move the shaft in the forward direction and remove the shaft from the roll assembly.

8. While pressing the shift lock lever, remove the shaft and shift lock lever.

9. Remove the side plate, shift control vlave, high speed spring, high speed support.

10. Remove the low speed spring.

11. Remove the spacer, linkage guide, roller assembly and low speed support.

12. Remove the plunger assembly.

13. Remove the snapring and the pressure regulator valve.

14. Remove the spacer and shift lock piston.

Inspection

1. Clean all parts thoroughly in clean solvent and blow dry with compressed air.

2. Inspect all valve and plug bores for scores. Check all fluid passages for obstructions. Inspect all mating surfaces for burrs and scores. If needed, use crocus cloth to polish valve and plugs. Avoid rounding the sharp edges of the valves and plugs with the crocus cloth.

3. Inspect all springs for distortion. Check all valves and plugs for free movement in their respective bores.

4. Replace any components as necessary.

Assembly

1. Install the shift lock piston.

2. Install the spacer and pressure regulator valve.

3. Install the plunger.

4. Assemble the linkage guide, roller assembly, low speed support, spacer and install on control valve body.

5. Install the low spring using a thin tool (feeler gauge). Install the spring with its small pitched end facing the plunger. Assemble the shift control valve temporarily and adjust the centering of the low speed spring.

6. Install the shift control valve, high speed spring, high speed support, spring and install the side plate. Ensure the valve and plunger operate smoothly. Torque the retaining bolts to 13.2–18 inch lbs.

7. Install the spring, shift lock lever and shaft.

8. Install the lever, spring pin and snapring.

9. Install the engine brake valve, spring and engine brake sleeve. Make sure to install the straight pin while pushing the aluminum portion of the engine brake valve.

10. Install the shift control pin and lever.

11. While pressing the engine brake lever down, install engine brake support in the engine brake valve and lock with the snapring.

12. Install the shift control lever and shift cam.

13. Install the steel balls, springs, shift lock valve and straight pin. Set the spring guide in position and install the solenoid valve.

14. At this point in the service procedure the shift lock valve is adjusted. Screw the stud in until the shift lock valve comes in light contact with the separator plate. Do not tighten the stud excessively as this moves the separator plate. While screwing the stud, hold the separator plate and shift control lever against the control valve body.

15. Turn the stud a 1/8–1/4 turn in and then tighten the nut to 2.2–2.9 ft. lbs.

16. Install the pressure regulator spring and guide. Install the control valve holder tool 499205600 or equivalent and the pressure regulator assembly to the control valve body.

PRIMARY AND SECONDARY PULLEY ASSEMBLIES

These assemblies are not to be serviced. Replace the pulley assemblies in sets.

OIL PUMP

Disassembly

1. Remove the 3 retaining bolts.
2. Install 2 bolts from the inner cover side. While tapping the bolt heads with a plastic hammer, separate the housing and outer cover.
3. Separate the housing from the inner cover by tapping the housing with a plastic hammer.

Inspection

1. Check all parts for abnormal wear, breakage or damage.
2. Replace all defective components.

Assembly

1. Install the lubricating valve on the housing and position the inner cover on the housing.
2. Install the driven gear and spring in place and the outer cover. Apply a thin coat of transmission fluid to the contact surfaces of the gears and parts.
3. Torque the retaining bolts to 4–10 ft. lbs. After tightening the retaining bolts check that the shaft rotates smoothly.
4. Install 2 seal rings on oil pump shaft.

SPEEDOMETER COVER

Disassembly

1. Remove the speedometer cover.
2. Remove the outer snapring from the inside of the cover. Remove the speedometer drive gear.

NOTE: Remove the outer snapring in the direction opposite the oil seal. Otherwise, the contact surface of the oil seal may be damaged.

3. Place the speedomter cover in a vise. Drive the oil seal and speedometer shaft out by lightly tapping the end of the shaft on the gear side.

Inspection

1. Check the speedometer driven gear for wear or damage.
2. Make sure that the shaft rotates smoothly.
3. Replace all defective components.

Assembly

1. Install a new outer snapring on the end of the speedometer shaft on the driven gear side.
2. Install washer under the speedometer shaft and install the speedomter shaft in the cover.
3. Install the speedometer driven gear onto the shaft and secure with a new outer snapring.
4. Using a suitable tool install a new oil seal into place.
5. Install the cover assembly with a new gasket. Tighten bolts with the washers to 4.3–5.1 ft. lbs.

DIFFERENTIAL ASSEMBLY

Disassembly

1. Remove the final drive gear.
2. Remove and mark for correct installation, differential side gear adjusting washer from final drive gear side.
3. Remove straight pin from differential case and remove differential pinion shaft.
4. Remove differential pinions, differential side gears and adjusting washer.
5. Using a suitable tool, remove the left and right bearing assemblies from differential case.
6. Remove the snapring and drive the bearing assembly from the clutch housing.

Inspection

1. Check final gear of differential, drive pinion, differential pinion, differential side gear, washer, differential pinion shaft for damage and wear.
2. Check differential case for cracks and other casting defects.
3. Replace all defective components.

Assembly

1. Install new bearing assembly (mark must face up) onto final gear, using suitable tool.
2. Install new bearing assembly (mark must face up) onto differential case, using suitable tool.
3. Install pinion, washer, side gear, pinion shaft and straight pin on differential case side.
4. Install washer and side gear on final side gear.
5. Install differential case to final gear, tightening torque is 42–49 ft. lbs. for retaining bolts.
6. Measure the backlash at this point of the procedure. The standard valve for backlash is 0.0020–0.0059 in. The backlash is set by selecting the correct adjusting washer. Install adjusting washers with chamfered side of inside diameter toward differential side gear.
7. Install the bearing assembly (mark must face up) into the bore in the clutch housing.
8. Install the snapring.
9. Install the left and right differential gear oil seal into main case using a suitable tool. The seals are marked for correct installation. Press oil seals into place until installer rests everly against main case or clutch housing.

Transaxle Assembly

NOTE: If transaxle was serviced for a contamination problem and belt and pulley assemblies were not replaced, pulley alignment and endplay adjustments are notnecessary.

1. Install the side case to a suitable holding fixture.
2. Install the pitot pipe. Face the pitot straight pin toward the center of the pulleys. Install the seal ring on the secondary guide using a suitable tool.
3. Adjust the pulley alignment and the primary pulley endplay if pulleys are replaced (using good existing side case only) at this point of the procedure.

NOTE: If the shim thickness determined by calculations (alignmemt or endplay) overlap the value in the next range, use a shim in either range.

4. Adjust the pulley alignment as follows:
   a. Remove all traces of liquid gasket from mating surface of the side case.
   b.Install special gauge tool 499575700 or equivalent to the side case using bolts.

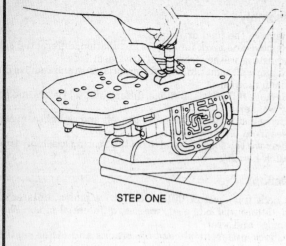

STEP ONE

× mm (Calculated value)	Part Number	t in. (mm) (Shim thickness)
0–0.050	–	0 (0)
0.050–0.150	803054021	0.004 (0.1)
0.150–0.250	803054022	0.008 (0.2)
0.250–0.350	803054023	0.012 (0.3)
0.350–0.450	803054024	0.016 (0.4)
0.450–0.550	803054025	0.020 (0.5)
0.550–0.650	803054026	0.024 (0.6)

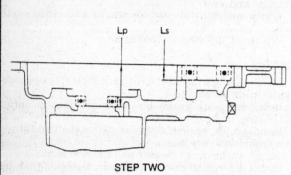

STEP TWO

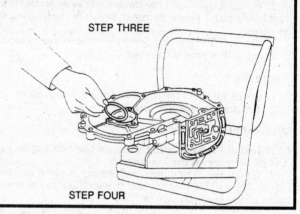

STEP THREE

STEP FOUR

Pulley alignment adjustment procedure

c. Measure the depth between the mating surface of the side case and the mounting portion of the primary pulley bearing and between the mating surface of the side case and the mounting portion of the secondary pulley bearing, using special depth gauge tool 498145400 or equivalent.

d. The depths must be measured at 4 points.

e. Determine the average values of the measurement. The equation, which is in milimeters, for the calculation is $x = A - (B + Lp - Ls) + 0.054mm - 24.45mm$.

f. The symbol t = shim thickness is a result of the calculation of the above equation. Select a suitable shim from the calculated valve (symbol x). The symbol A = indicated primary pulley dimension. The symbol B = indicated secondary pulley dimension. The symbol Lp = depth between side case mating surface and mounting portion of primary pulley bearing average value of 4 different measurements. The symbol Ls = depth between side case mating surface and mounting portion of secondary pulley bearing average value of 4 different measurements. The symbol 24.45mm is a constant figure.

5. Adjust the primary pulley endplay as follows:

a. Remove all traces of liquid gasket from the mating surface of the transaxle case.

b. Install the special gauge tool 499575700 or equivalent to the transaxle case using bolts.

c. Using the special gauge tool 499575700 or equivalent and the special tool depth gauge tool 498145400 or equivalent, measure the depth (distance) betweent the mating surface of the transaxle case and the stepped portion at the 2.76 in. (70mm) diameter hole.

d. The equation, which is in milimeters, for the calculation is $X = C + Lp - D$

e. The symbol T = snapring thickness, select a suitable shim whose thickness is determined by the above calculation

(symbol X). The symbol C = depth or distance between the mating surface of the transaxle case (on the side case side) and the recess for the snapring at the 2.76 in. (70mm) hole average value of 4 different measurements. The Lp = dimension measured under adjusting the pulley alignment. The symbol D = indicated primary pulley dimension.

6. Install the secondary pulley puller tool 499195400 or equivalent and seat tool 899524105 or equivalent to the secondary pulley and using hand pressure only screw tool down so that the pulley groove width is 2.05–2.09 in. (52–53mm). Do not expand the groove width more than 2.05–2.09 in. (52–53mm). Otherwise the pulley interior may be damaged.

7. Place the belt on the secondary pulley and engage the V grooves of the primary and secondary pulleys with each other. While placing the belt on the primary pulley, poisition the primary and secondary pulleys in the side case. Ensure the belt is installed in the proper direction as indicated by the mark (made during removal) or arrow (new belt) on it. Remove clip band or tape after installing belt. Install shim(s) in the proper location for the secondary pulley.

8. Remove the special pulley puller tool and install the retainer. Make sure the bolts and the O-rings are installed as a unit. The torque for the retaining bolts is 10.5–12.7 ft. lbs.

9. Install the ratio sensor in the groove of the primary pulley, pass the rod through the ratio sensor and insert into the side case. Install the engine brake pipe into the side case and the parking pawl into the side case.

10. Remove grease from the mating surfaces and apply a continuous coat of liquid gasket part number 004403007 or equivalent to the mating surfaces. While inserting the ratio sensor rod, engine brake pipe and parking pawl into the hole in the transaxle case, install the transaxle case on the side case. Tighten bolts in crossing pattern to 17–20 ft. lbs.

11. Install the needle bearing assembly.

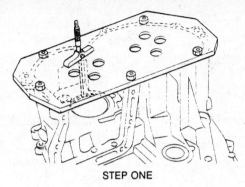

STEP ONE

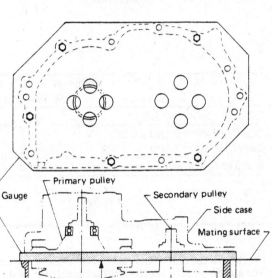

STEP TWO

Gauge — Primary pulley — Secondary pulley — Side case — Mating surface

70 mm (2.76 in) dia.

× mm (Calculated value)	Part Number	T in. (mm) (Snapring thickness)
1.2–1.28	805062022	0.0531 (1.35)
1.28–1.36	805062023	0.0563 (1.43)
1.36–1.44	805062024	0.0594 (1.51)
1.44–1.52	805062025	0.0626 (1.59)
1.52–1.60	805062026	0.0657 (1.67)
1.60–1.68	805062027	0.0689 (1.75)
1.68–1.76	805062028	0.0720 (1.83)

STEP THREE

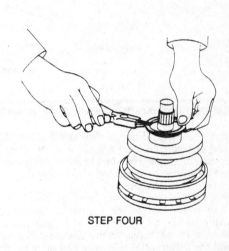

STEP FOUR

Primary pulley endplay adjustment procedure

12. Install the reverse idler gear. Make sure the spring pin is positioned in the groove on the transaxle case by turning the shaft.

13. Install the sleeve/hub assembly, fork and reverse driven gear on the primary pulley as unit.

14. Position the small diameter end of the counter gear downward (toward the belt), install the counter gear onto the shaft.

15. While slightly lifting the sleeve/hub asembly and reverse driven gear, install the counter gear. Make sure the spring pin is positioned in the groove on the transaxle case by turning the shaft.

16. Install the outer snapring and the needle bearing assembly.

17. Install the lubricating pipe, engine brake pipe, engine brake body and lubricating nozzle.

18. Install the parking rod on the shift cam. Make sure the parking rod faces in the correct direction during installation. While inserting the fork pin into the groove in the shift cam, install the parking rod in the hole on the parking cam guide. Pass

the shift arm through the transaxle case and shift cam and insert the straight pin into the case. Install the engine brake cam on the shift arm using the snapring and straight pin. Position the shift arm so that the straight pin is horizontal installed. Secure the shift arm to the shift cam by driving the spring pin into place.

19. Install the differential assembly in the transaxle case.

20. Adjust the thrust clearance of differential assembly at this point of the procedure as follows:

a. Measure the distance (height) between the mating surface of the transaxle case and the bearing assembly using the special gauge tool 499575660 or equivalent and depth gauge tool 498145400 or equivalent.

b. Measure the distance (height) between the mating surface of the clutch housing and the 2.83 in. (72mm) diameter stepped portion using the special gauge tool 499575600 or equivalent and depth gauge tool 498145400 or equivalent.

c. The equation (unit:mm) for calculation is C = H - h. The symbol C = thrust clearance. The symbol H = distance be-

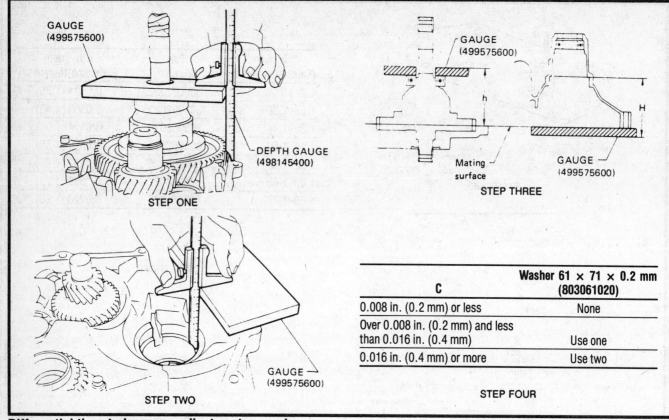

Differential thrust clearance adjustment procedure

tween clutch housing mating surface and 2.83 in. (72mm) diameter stepped portion. The symbol h = distance between transaxle case mating surface and bearing. After determining the thrust clearance by using the above equation, select the number of suitable washers.

21. Apply a continuous coat of liquid gasket, part number 004403007 or equivalent to the mating surfaces. Install the clutch housing on the transaxle case and tighten the bolts in crossing pattern 17–20 ft. lbs. To provide smooth gear engagement, rotate the differential side gear and or main driveshaft during assembly.

22. Install the control valve body assembly with special control valve holder tool 499205600 or equivalent in place.

23. Route the shift control cable along the rib or guide in the transaxle case.

24. Install the valve body assembly on the transaxle assembly. Make sure the valve body pin is inserted into the dowel hole in the control valve body. While lightly pushing the body assembly toward the ratio sensor, align the valve body pin with the hole in the side case. Then install the valve body on the side case. The engine brake lever must come in contact with the back of the ratio sensor bolt's seating surface. Torque retaining bolts 6.1–6.9 ft. lbs.

25. Install the modulator connecting rod to the ratio sensor using a snapring and temporarily fix the modulator adjust plate with bolts. Position the special modualator plate tool 498255600 or equivalent in place.

26. While pushing the modulator adjusting plate in the forward direction (takes out free play) tighten the bolts to 2.2–2.9 ft. lbs.

27. Secure the end of the cable to the hole in the shift control lever and place it along the shift control lever. Make sure that the inner cable is routed through the guide rib in the transaxle case. Pull the inner cable from the outside to ensure it moves smoothly without being interfered with by the inner wall of the case and the control valve body assembly.

28. Reconnect the electrical connector and install the connector in retaining clip.

29. Installing the oil strainer with new O-ring. Torque retaining bolts to 6.1–6.9 ft. lbs.

30. Install the oil pan with new gasket torque bolts to 3.3–4.0 ft. lbs.

31. Install the shift connecting rod.

32. Install the oil pump assembly. Evenly tighten the bolts and push the O-ring in the side case. Turn the pitot pipe tube counterclockwise until it comes in contact with the wall. Torque retaining bolts to 6.9–7.6 ft. lbs.

33. Insert the small diameter spline end of the oil pump shaft. Install the oil pump shaft.

34. Install the oil cooler inlet and outlet pipes.

35. Install the pitching stopper bracket.

36. Install the electromagnetic powder clutch on the flywheel. Torque the retaining bolts to 24–27 ft. lbs.

37. Install the engine to transaxle. Connect the shift control cable to the carburetor.

38. Install the brush holder. Torque the retaining bolts to 3.3–4.0 ft. lbs.

39. Install the starter to transaxle.

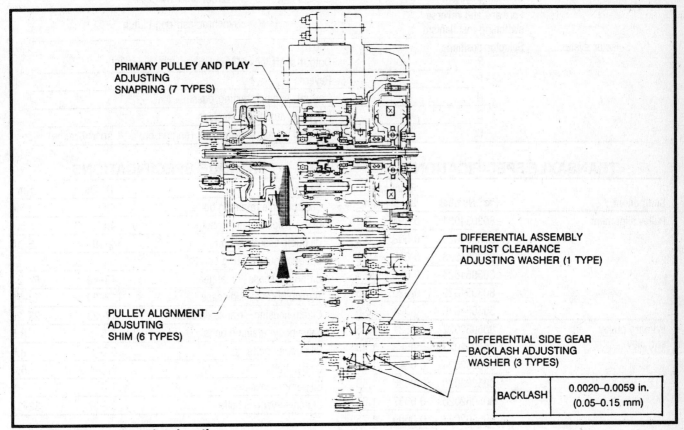

PRIMARY PULLEY AND PLAY ADJUSTING SNAPRING (7 TYPES)

DIFFERENTIAL ASSEMBLY THRUST CLEARANCE ADJUSTING WASHER (1 TYPE)

PULLEY ALIGNMENT ADJSUTING SHIM (6 TYPES)

DIFFERENTIAL SIDE GEAR BACKLASH ADJUSTING WASHER (3 TYPES)

BACKLASH	0.0020–0.0059 in. (0.05–0.15 mm)

Adjusting shim and washer location

SPECIFICATIONS

ELECTROMAGNETIC POWDER CLUTCH

Type	Internal damper rotating coil type
Rated torque	99 ft. lbs. (134 Nm)
Power consumption	31.1 W
Metal powder	2.29 oz. (65 g)
Weight	18.7 lb. (8.5 kg)
Control system	Electronic control

GENERAL TRANSAXLE SPECIFICATIONS

Speed ratio	Forward	2.503–0.497
	Reverse	2.475
Reduction ratio	1st	1.275
	2nd	4.666
Oil pump	Type	External gear pump
	Drive system	Direct drive by engine
Lubricating oil	Quality	Genuine Subaru ECVT fluid or Dexron II
	Amount	3.3–3.6 qts. (3.L–3.4L)

GENERAL TRANSAXLE SPECIFICATIONS

Selector system	Operating system	Direct shift by cable
	Forward and reverse switching mechanism	Synchromesh dog clutch
	Selector positions	
	P	Output shaft locked, engine starting possible
	R	Reverse
	N	Neutral, engine starting possible
	D	Forward, automatic stepless
	Ds	Forward, automatic stepless (engine brake & sporty range)

TRANSAXLE SPECIFICATIONS

Component	Part Number	Thickness in.	mm
Pulley alignment	803054021	0.004	0.1
	803054022	0.008	0.2
	803054023	0.012	0.3
	803054024	0.016	0.4
	803054025	0.020	0.5
	803054026	0.024	0.6
Primary pulley end play	805062022	0.0531	1.35
	805062023	0.0563	1.43
	805062024	0.0594	1.51
	805062025	0.0626	1.59
	805062026	0.0657	1.67
	805062027	0.0689	1.75
	805062028	0.0720	1.83
Differential side gear backlash Washer (27.1×42 ×t mm) thickness	803027041	0.0394	1.000
	803027042	0.0413	1.050
	803027043	0.0433	1.100

TORQUE SPECIFICATIONS

Part	ft. lbs.	Nm
Control cable retaining bolts	4.0	5.4
Brush holder retaining bolts	4.0	5.4
Oil pump assembly bolts	4–10	5–15
Speedometer housing bolts	5.0	7
Differential case—final gear	42–49	57–67
Transaxle case—side case	17–20	23–26
Clutch housing—transaxle case	17–20	23–26
Valve body retaining bolts	6.5	8.5
Oil strainer bolts	6.5	8.5
Oil pan bolts	3.0–4.0	5.4
Oil pump—case bolts	7.0	9
Clutch—flywheel bolts	24–27	32–37

SPECIAL TOOLS

398663600	398791700	399520105	399703600
PLIER	STRAIGHT PIN REMOVER 2	DIFFERENTIAL BEARING PULLER SEAT	PULLER ASSY

Special tools

498145400	498175600	498255600	498415600
DEPTH GAUGE	INSTALLER	MODULATOR PLATE	OIL SEAL DRIFT

498475500	498575400	498895400	498935400
OIL SEAL DRIFT	OIL PRESSURE GAUGE	OIL PRESSURE ADAPTER	HOLDER

499195400	499205600	499305600	499305500
SECONDARY PULLEY PULLER	CONTROL VALVE HOLDER	SEAL RING GUIDE 2	SEAL RING GUIDE

499575600	499575700	499715600	49982700
GAUGE	GAUGE	OIL PUMP REMOVER	SPEEDOMETER OIL SEAL PRESS

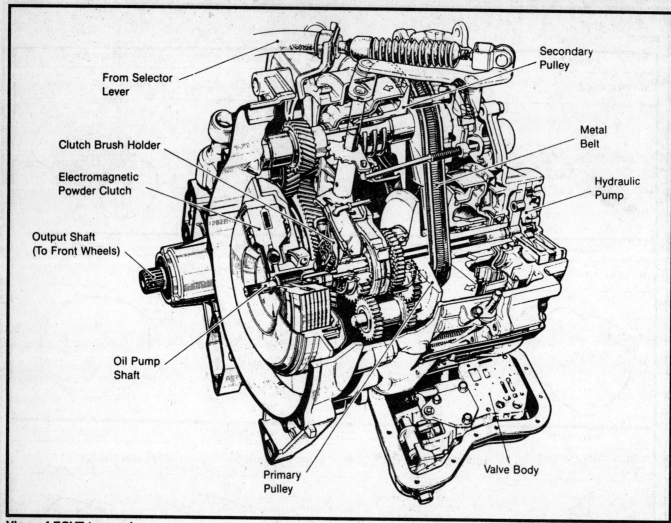

From Selector Lever

Clutch Brush Holder

Electromagnetic Powder Clutch

Output Shaft (To Front Wheels)

Oil Pump Shaft

Primary Pulley

Secondary Pulley

Metal Belt

Hydraulic Pump

Valve Body

View of ECVT transaxle

APPLICATION

Year	Vehicle	Engine
1987	XT Coupe	1.8L
	XT Coupe 4WD	1.8L
1988	XT Coupe	1.8L
	XT Coupe 4WD	1.8L
	XT Coupe	2.7L
	XT Coupe 4WD	2.7L
	STD 4WD	1.8L
1989	XT Coupe	1.8L
	XT Coupe 4WD	1.8L
	XT Coupe	2.7L
	XT Coupe 4WD	2.7L
	STD 4WD	1.8L
	Legacy	2.2L

GENERAL DESCRIPTION

FWD

This transaxle is an electronically controlled, 4 speed fully automatic transaxle. The various control operations such as gear shifting, engine brake application, lockup operation, selection of proper gear shift timing etc. are controlled accurately by a microcomputer according to vehicle operating conditions. This transaxle also features a drive pattern selection. This function automatically selects an optimum driving pattern for the vehicle. It ranges between a normal pattern, suitable for economy driving to a power pattern for driving up hill or accelerating.

4WD

This transaxle is an electronically controlled Multi Plate Transfer (MP-T) system, full time, 4WD automatic transaxle. Its design is based on the 4 speed fully automatic transaxle for FWD vehicles. On this automatic transaxle, self-diagnosis and fail safe functions are used to improve serviceability and reliability.

TRANSAXLE IDENTIFICATION

The transaxle can be indentified by the 11th letter in the vehicle identification number located on the bulkhead panel of the engine compartment.

The transaxle serial number label is either on the converter housing or on the upper surface of the main case assembly.

The automatic transaxle 11th letter code is as follows:
C Gunma manufacture – AT
H Gunma manufacture – Full time 4WD AT
K Gunma manufacture – 4 speed electronic (Legacy)

Electronic Controls

THROTTLE SENSOR

This sensor detects throttle opening and determines shift point, line pressure and lockup vehicle speed according to engine load. The throttle sensor sends a input signal to the control unit.

VEHICLE REVOLUTION SENSOR 1

This sensor detects vehicle speed. This signal is used to control shifting, lockup, line pressure and transfer clutch. The vehicle revolution sensor 1 on FWD vehicles, sends a input signal to the control unit and is mounted internally to the transaxle. On the 4WD vehicles the sensor is externally mounted to the extension case.

VEHICLE REVOLUTION SENSOR 2

This sensor sends an input signal to the control unit and on FWD vehicles is used as backup in case of failure of vehicle revolution sensor 1. On 4WD vehicles this sensor sends an input signal to the control unit and is used to control the transfer clutch. It is also used as a backup in case of failure of vehicle revolution sensor 1. On all vehicles this sensor is built in the speedometer panel or the speedometer.

ENGINE SPEED/IGNITION PULSE SENSOR

This sensor detects the engine speed. This input signal is used for smooth control of the lockup clutch and to prevent engine overracing at 2 range and 1st hold.

NEUTRAL SAFETY SWITCH

This switch allows the vehicle to start in the N or P position only and in the R position, allows the back up lights to come on. This switch also sends an input signal to the control unit detecting the selected range position.

IDLE SWITCH

This switch sends an input signal to the control unit and detects throttle closing. This signal is used for lockup release and for line pressure control.

CRUISE SWITCH

This switch sends an input signal to the control unit and detects

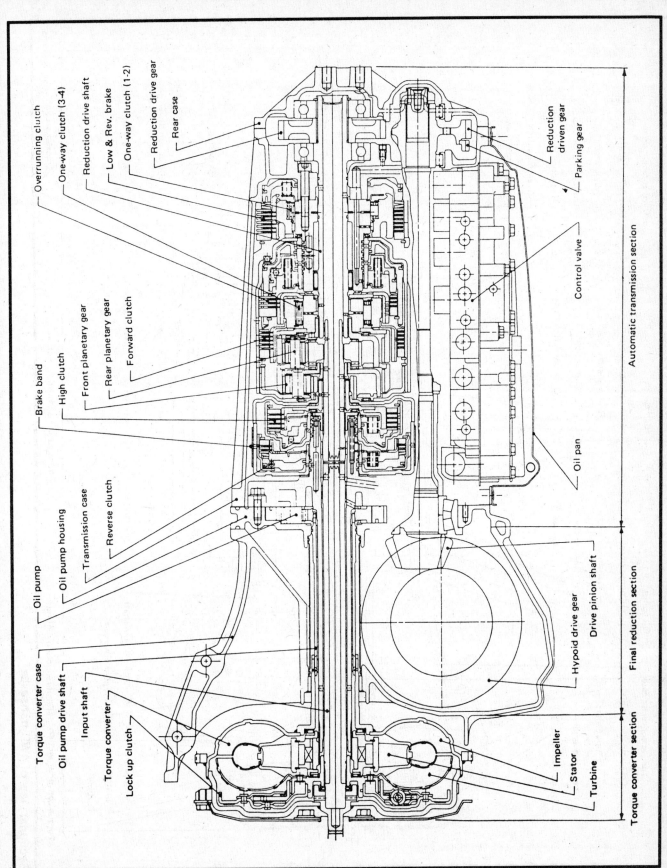

Sectional view of FWD transaxle

Torque converter case
Oil pump drive shaft
Input shaft
Torque converter
Lock up clutch

Oil pump
Oil pump housing
Transmission case
Reverse clutch

Brake band
High clutch
Front planetary gear
Rear planetary gear
Forward clutch

Overrunning clutch
One-way clutch (3-4)
Reduction drive shaft
Low & Rev. brake
One-way clutch (1-2)
Reduction drive gear
Rear case

Reduction driven gear
Parking gear
Control valve
Oil pan

Hypoid drive gear
Drive pinion shaft

Impeller
Stator
Turbine

Automatic transmission section
Final reduction section
Torque converter section

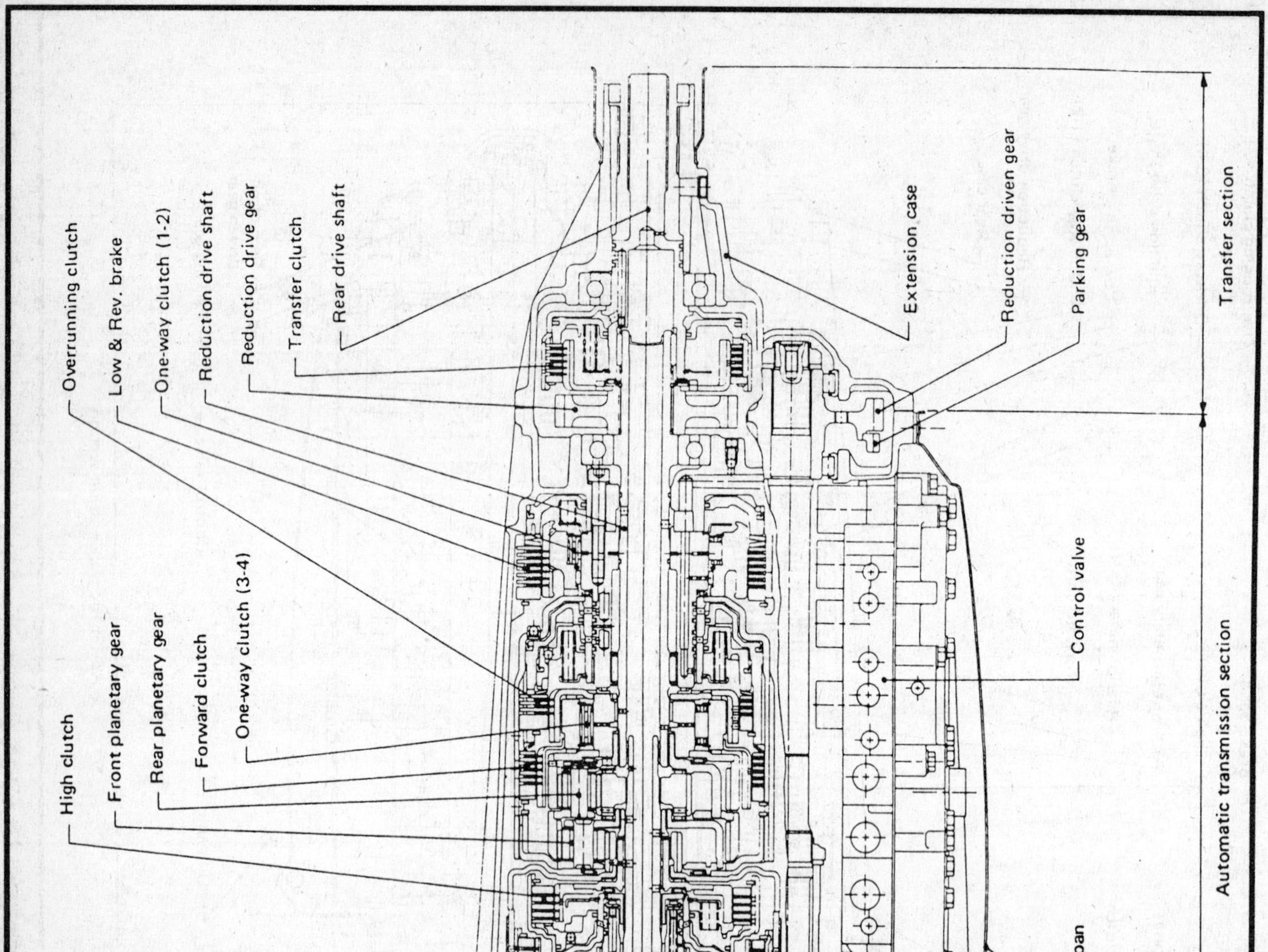

Sectional view of 4WD transaxle

Overrunning clutch

Low & Rev. brake

One-way clutch (1-2)

Reduction drive shaft

Reduction drive gear

Transfer clutch

Rear drive shaft

Extension case

Reduction driven gear

Parking gear

Transfer section

High clutch

Front planetary gear

Rear planetary gear

Forward clutch

One-way clutch (3-4)

Control valve

Automatic transmission section

Oil pump

Oil pump housing

Transmission case

Reverse clutch

Brake band

Oil pan

Torque converter case

Oil pump drive shaft

Input shaft

Torque converter

Lock up clutch

Drive pinion shaft

Hypoid drive gear

Final reduction section

Impeller

Stator

Turbine

Torque converter section

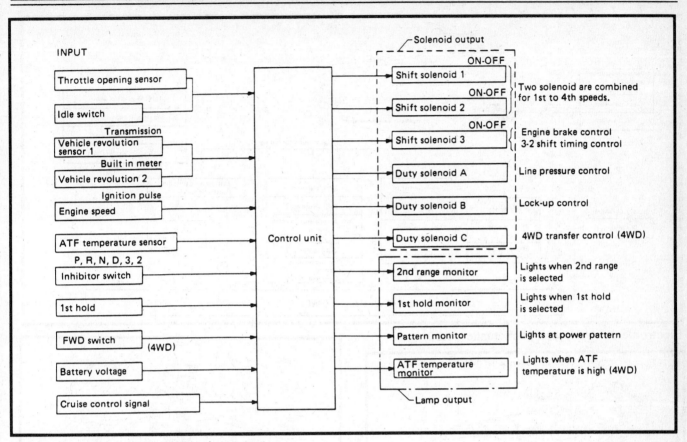

Electronic controls input and output functions

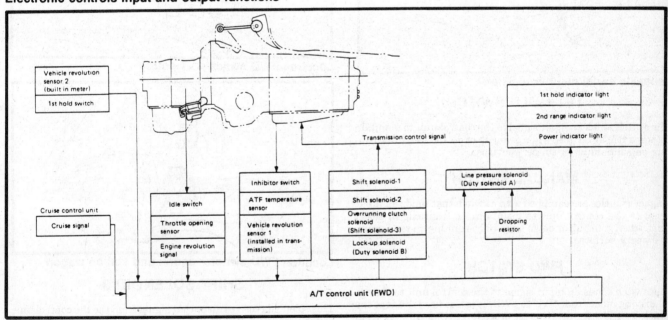

Electronic control system schematic — FWD

operation of cruise control. It also expands 4th gear operating range.

4TH CRUISE CUT OUT SWITCH

This switch sends an input signal to the control unit which causes forced release of 4th gear from the cruise control unit if a large difference exists between set vehicle speed and actual speed when cruise is selected.

AUTOMATIC TRANSAXLE FLUID TEMPERATURE SENSOR

This switch sends an input signal to the control unit which detects the transaxle fluid temperature.

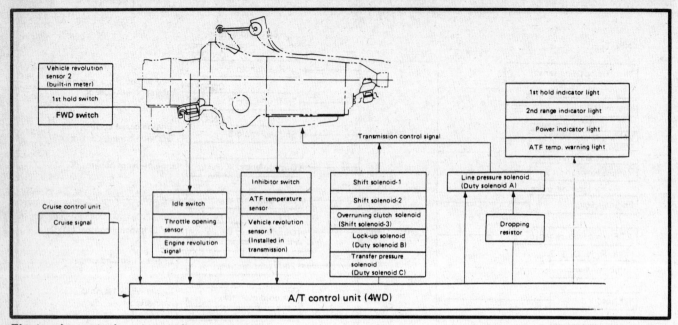

Electronic control system schematic — 4WD

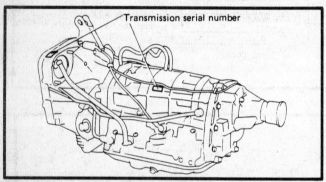

Transaxle serial number location

1ST HOLD SWITCH

This switch sends an input signal to the control unit to maintain the transaxle in 1st gear when going up or down steep hills, running on sand, mud, or slippery surfaces.

MANUAL SWITCH

Leagacy vehicles are equipped with a switch that sends an input signal to the control unit to maintain the transaxle in select range when going up or down steep hills, running on sand, mud, or slippery surfaces.

FWD SWITCH

This switch sends an input signal to the control unit to change the driving mode from 4WD to FWD. It is also used to adapt the vehicle to FWD for service test procedures. Change over from 4WD to FWD can be accomplished by inserting a fuse into the fuse holder located in the engine compartment on 4WD vehicles.

SHIFT SOLENOIDS 1 AND 2

These solenoids receive output signals from the the control unit which determines shift patterns by turning each solenoids on and off. When shifting, timing is controlled for each solenoid to reduce shock.

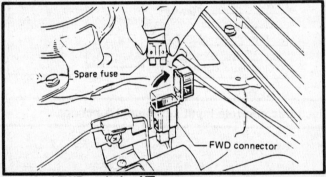

Location FWD switch — XT coupe

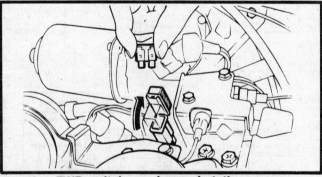

Location FWD switch — sedan and station wagon

SHIFT SOLENOID 3

This solenoid receives an output signal from the the control unit which controls 3–2 shift timing and overrunning clutch operation. Shift timing is controlled by controlling release speed of oil pressure to reduce shock while downshifting. The overrunning clutch is controlled so that it will operate during coasting to apply engine brake.

DUTY SOLENOID A

This solenoid receives an output signal from the control unit which regulates the line pressure according to driving conditions.

DUTY SOLENOID B

This solenoid receives an output signal from the the control unit which regulates the hydraulic pressure of the lockup clutch and operates in 3 modes open, smooth and lockup.

DUTY SOLENOID C

This solenoid receives an output signal from the control unit which regulates the hydraulic pressure of the transfer clutch and controls the driving force to the rear driveshaft.

POWER INDICATOR LIGHT

This circuit receives an output signal from the control unit indicating whether the shift pattern is normal or power. The indicator lights only in the power mode. This light is also used for self-diagnosis on all vehicles.

2ND RANGE INDICATOR LIGHT

This circuit receives an output signal from the control unit which lights when the 1st hold switch is turned off in 2nd range.

1ST HOLD INDICATOR LIGHT

This circuit receives an output signal from the control unit which lights when 1st speed is achieved with the 1st hold switch turned on and shift lever set to 2nd range.

MANUAL INDICATOR LIGHT

Legacy vehicles incorporate a manual indicator light that receives an output signal from the control unit which lights when the manual switch is turned on.

AUTOMATIC TRANSAXLE FLUID TEMPERATURE WARNING LIGHT

This circuit receives an output signal from the control unit which lights when the transaxle fluid exceeds the temperature specification on 4WD vehicles only.

AUTOMATIC TRANSAXLE CONTROL UNIT

The control unit on all vehicles except Legacy is mounted inside the left hand (driver's side) rear quarter panel of the vehicle. On the Legacy the control unit is located under the dash on the driver's side along side of the ECU. It receives various sensor signals and determines the running condition of the vehicle. It then sends control signals to each solenoid according to the preset gearshift characteristic data, lockup operation data and transfer clutch torque data (4WD vehicles only).

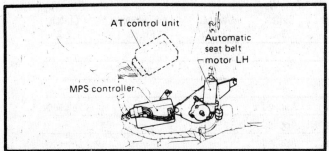

Automatic transaxle control unit

NOTE: If vehicle is equipped with the anti-lock brake system, an input signal is sent to control the transfer clutch torque in order to help eliminate the influence of engine braking and reduce the degree of coupling between front and rear wheels.

Metric Fasteners

Metric tools are required to service this transaxle. Due to the large number of alloy parts used in this transaxle, torque specifications should be strictly observed. Before installing capscrews into aluminum parts, dip the bolts into clean transmission fluid as this will prevent the screws from galling the aluminum threads, thus causing damage.

Metric fastener dimensions are very close to the dimensions of the familiar inch system fasteners. For this reason replacement fasteners must have the same measurement and strength as the original fastener.

Do not attempt to interchange meteric fasteners for inch system fasteners. Mismatched or incorrect fasteners can cause damage to the automatic transaxle unit and possible personal injury. Care should be taken to reuse fasteners in their original locations.

Capacities

The FWD automatic transaxle has a fluid capacity of 9.8 qts. and the 4WD automatic transaxle has a fluid capacity of 10.0 qts. on all vehicles except Legacy. The fluid capacity on 4WD Legacy is 8.8 qts.

Checking Fluid Level

1. Raise the temperature of the transaxle fluid to normal operating temperature. This temperature may be attained by driving the vehicle a distance of 3 to 6 miles. The normal operating temperature is 140–176°F.

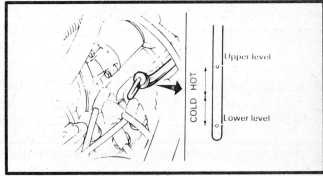

Automatic transaxle dipstick

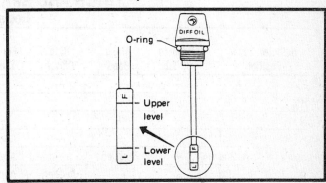

Differential dipstick

NOTE: The level of transaxle fluid varies with temperature. Pay attention to the fluid temperature when checking transaxle oil level.

2. Park the vehicle on a level surface. With the foot brake applied, select all quadrant positions then set the selector lever in **P** range and set the parking brake. Run the engine at idle speed for about 1–2 minutes before taking the measurement.

3. Remove the dipstick, wipe it clean, then fully reinsert the dipstick.

4. Remove the dipstick again then check the level. If the fluid

level is below **HOT** range add the recommended fluid up to the upper mark through the dipstick hole.

DIFFERENTIAL

1. Park the vehicle on a level surface.

2. Turn the oil level gauge knob counterclockwise, remove the dipstick and wipe it clean.

3. Reinsert the dipstick so that the threaded section of the dipstick fits flat against the beveled opening.

4. Remove the dipstick and check the oil level. The upper mark on the dipstick is the correct (full) level for operation.

TRANSAXLE MODIFICATIONS

At the time of this printing there is no modification information available from the manufacturer.

TROUBLE DIAGNOSIS

CLUTCH AND BRAKE APPLICATION
Except Legacy

Selector Lever Position		Reverse Clutch	Brake Band	High Clutch	Forward Clutch	One-Way Clutch 3-4	Overrun Clutch	Low/Reverse Brake	One-Way Clutch 1-2
P		—	—	—	—	—	—	—	—
R		Applied	—	—	—	—	—	Applied	—
N		—	—	—	—	—	—	—	—
D	1st	—	—	—	Applied	Applied	—	—	Applied
	2nd	—	Applied	—	Applied	Applied	—	—	—
	3rd	—	—	Applied	Applied	Applied	—	—	—
	4th	—	Applied	Applied	Applied	—	—	—	—
3	1st	—	—	—	Applied	Applied	—	—	Applied
	2nd	—	Applied	—	Applied	Applied	—	—	—
	3rd	—	—	Applied	Applied	Applied	Applied	—	—
2	1st	—	—	—	Applied	Applied	Applied	Applied	—
	2nd	①	Applied	—	Applied	Applied	Applied	—	—
	3rd	—	—	Applied	Applied	Applied	Applied	—	—
1st Hold ②	1st	①	—	—	Applied	Applied	Applied	Applied	—
	2nd	①	Applied	—	Applied	Applied	Applied	—	—
	3rd	—	—	Applied	Applied	Applied	Applied	—	—

① For prevention of overrevolution   ② Only when lever is in 2 and 1st hold button pressed

CLUTCH AND BRAKE APPLICATION
Legacy

Selector Lever Position		Reverse Clutch	Brake Band	High Clutch	Forward Clutch	One-Way Clutch 3-4	Overrun Clutch	Low/Reverse Brake	One-Way Clutch 1-2
P		—	—	—	—	—	—	—	—
R		Applied	—	—	—	—	—	Applied	—
N		—	—	—	—	—	—	—	—
D	1st	—	—	—	Applied	Applied	—	—	Applied
	2nd	—	Applied	—	Applied	Applied	—	—	—
	3rd	—	—	Applied	Applied	Applied	—	—	—
	4th	—	Applied	Applied	Applied	—	—	—	—

CLUTCH AND BRAKE APPLICATION
Legacy

Selector Lever Position		Reverse Clutch	Brake Band	High Clutch	Forward Clutch	One-Way Clutch 3-4	Overrun Clutch	Low/Reverse Brake	One-Way Clutch 1-2
3	1st	—	—	—	Applied	Applied	—	—	Applied
	2nd	—	Applied	—	Applied	Applied	—	—	—
	3rd	—	—	Applied	Applied	Applied	Applied	—	—
2	1st	—	—	—	Applied	Applied	Applied	—	Applied
	2nd	①	Applied	—	Applied	Applied	Applied	—	—
	3rd	—	—	Applied	Applied	Applied	Applied	—	—
1	1st	①	—	—	Applied	Applied	Applied	Applied	—
	2nd	①	Applied	—	Applied	Applied	Applied	—	—
	3rd	—	—	Applied	Applied	Applied	Applied	—	—

① For prevention of overrevolution

CHILTON'S THREE C'S TRANSAXLE DIAGNOSIS

Condition	Cause	Correction
Noise or shudder is emitted when vehicle starts	a) Fluid level low	a) Add specified fluid
Engine stalls while shifting to any range	a) Control valve in valve body sticking b) Poor engine performance c) Lockup clutch seized	a) Service or replace as necessary b) Correct engine performance c) Replace torque converter
Lengthy time lag when shifting from N to D range	a) Control valve in valve body sticking b) Faulty forward clutch relief ball c) Forward clutch slippage	a) Service or replace as necessary b) Service necessary components c) Replace forward clutch unit
Lengthy time lag when shifting from N to R range	a) Control valve in valve body sticking b) Low and reverse brake slipping c) Reverse clutch slippage	a) Service or replace as necessary b) Replace necessary components c) Replace reverse clutch unit
Engine stalls in all ranges	a) Parking brake mechanism faulty	a) Replace necessary components
Engine stalls in R range	a) Forward clutch seized b) Band seized	a) Replace forward clutch unit b) Replace band
Engine stalls in D, 3 or 2 range	a) Reverse clutch seized	a) Replace reverse clutch unit
Erroneous shift points	a) Faulty control unit b) Control valve in valve body sticking c) Faulty throttle sensor d) Band and servo slippage	a) Replace control unit b) Service or replace as necessary c) Replace throttle sensor d) Replace band and servo unit
No power mode in D range	a) Faulty control unit b) Faulty throttle sensor	a) Replace control unit b) Replace throttle sensor
Power mode not released in D range	a) Faulty control unit b) Faulty throttle sensor	a) Replace control unit b) Replace throttle sensor
Fluid overflow	a) Transaxle fluid level too high b) Differential oil level too high	a) Correct transaxle fluid level b) Correct differential oil level
Shock is felt when accelerator pedal is released at medium speed or above	a) Faulty control unit b) Control valve in valve body sticking c) Faulty throttle sensor d) Poor engine performance e) Faulty lockup damper f) Lockup clutch seized	a) Replace control unit b) Service or replace as necessary c) Replace throttle sensor d) Correct engine performance e) Replace torque converter unit f) Replace torque converter unit
Select lever slips out of detents during acceleration or on rough roads	a) Select cable out of adjustment b) Faulty detent spring c) Faulty manual plate	a) Adjust select cable b) Replace detent spring c) Replace manual plate

Hydraulic Control System

NOTE: Please refer to Section 8 in this manual for oil flow circuits.

PRESSURE REGULATOR VALVE

This valve regulates the pressure of oil delivered from the oil pump to an optimun level (line pressure) corresponding to vehicle running conditions.

PRESSURE MODIFIER VALVE

This valve is an auxiliary valve for the pressure regulator valve. It adjusts the pressure used to regulate line pressure to an optimum level corresponding to running conditions.

PRESSURE MODIFIER ACCUMULATOR PISTON

This piston smoothes the pressure regulated by the pressure modifier valve to prevent pulsation in line pressure thereby reducing gearshift shock.

PILOT VALVE

This valve creates the constant pressure (pilot pressure) necessary to control line pressure, lockup, overrunning clutch, 3–2 timing and gearshift operations from line pressure.

ACCUMULATOR CONTROL PLUG AND SLEEVE

This component adjusts accumulator back pressure to correspond to running conditions.

MANUAL VALVE

This valve delivers line pressure to each circuit corresponding to the selected gear position. When the valve is set in the line pressure no delivery position, the pressure is relieved.

SHIFT VALVE A

This valve simultaneously changes oil pressure to 3 different oil passages, using shift solenoid 1 output pressure and corresponding to operating conditions such as vehicle speed and throttle opening. Combined with shift valve B, this valve permits automatic shifting of all speeds.

SHIFT VALVE B

This valve simultaneously changes oil pressure to 3 different oil passages, using shift solenoid 2 output pressure and corresponding to operating conditions such as vehicle speed and throttle opening. Combined with shift valve A, this valve permits automatic shifting of all speeds.

SHUTTLE SHIFT VALVE S

This valve changes the 3–2 timing control and overrunning clutch control oil passages corresponding to the throttle opening. When the throttle is wide open, the overrunning clutch becomes inoperative to prevent interlocking at 4th speed.

OVERRUNNING CLUTCH CONTROL VALVE

This valve changes oil passages so as to prevent simultaneous operation of the overrunning clutch when the brake band is actuated at 4th speed. Operation of overrunning clutch at D range 4th speed results in interlocking.

4–2 RELAY VALVE

This valve memorizes the 4th speed position and prevents gear shifting from 4th to 3rd to 2nd speeds due to combined operation of the 4–2 sequence valve, shift valve A and shift valve B when shifting down from 4th to 2nd speeds.

4–2 SEQUENCE VALVE

This valve inhibits the release of band servo operating pressure acting at 4th speed until the high clutch operating pressure and band servo release pressure are drained when shifting down from 4th speed to 2nd speed.

SERVO CHARGER VALVE

The 2nd speed band servo actuating hydraulic circuit has an accumulator and one way orifice for relieving shift shock when shifting from 1st speed to 2nd speed. The servo charger valve is installed to ensure sufficient oil flow when shifting down from 4th to 2nd speed, or from 3rd to 2nd speed. It operates at 3rd or higher speeds and supplies the 2nd speed band servo actuating pressure by bypassing the one way orifice.

3–2 TIMING VALVE

When shifting down from D range 3rd to D range 2nd speed, the timing valve retards the release of band servo pressure and creates a temporary neutral conditions so that vehicle speed can be changed smoothly.

NO. 1 REDUCING VALVE

This valve reduces the low and reverse brake operating pressure so as to relieve engine braking shock when changing from 2nd range 2nd speed to 1st speed.

OVERRUNNING CLUTCH REDUCING VALVE

This valve reduces the operating pressure applied to the overrunning clutch so as to relieve engine braking shock. In the 2nd and 3rd ranges, line pressure is applied to the valve to raise the pressure adjusting point, thereby increasing engine braking capacity.

TORQUE CONVERTER REGULATOR VALVE

This valve prevents excessive rise of torque converter pressure.

LOCKUP CONTROL VALVE, PLUG AND SLEEVE

It controls the operation of the lockup function. It also smoothes the transition between the lockup state and release state.

SHUTTLE SHIFT VALVE D

This valve changes the oil passage so that output pressure to the duty solenoid B (lockup) will be applied to the lockup valve in the D range 2nd, 3rd, or 4th speed. lockup at 1st speed is inhibited. lockup control is not actuated if the lockup solenoid does not generate output pressure when singaled from the control unit, even if the vehicle is in the D range 2nd, 3rd, or 4th speeds.

Diagnosis Tests

STALL TEST

The purpose of the stall test is to check the automatic transaxle clutch and brake band, operation of the torque converter and engine performance. Before performing test make sure that the vehicle is at normal operating temperture, throttle valve opens fully and all fluid levels are full.

1. Install an engine tachometer at a location visible from the driver's compartment.
2. Place wheel chocks at the front and rear of all wheels and engage the parking brake.
3. Shift the select lever to the **D** range.
4. While forcibly depressing the foot brake pedal, gradually depress the accelerator pedal until the engine operates at full throttle.
5. When the engine speed is stabilized, read and note the rpm speed then release the accelerator pedal.

NOTE: Shift the select lever to N after each test in each range and cool down the engine by idling it at the normal rpm for 2 minutes. Do not continue the stall test for more than 5 seconds at a time from closed throttle to fully open throttle to stall speed reading, possible damage to the transaxle may result.

6. Perform the stall test in the **3**, **2** and **R** ranges.

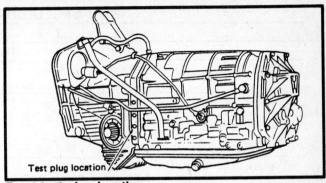
Front test plug location

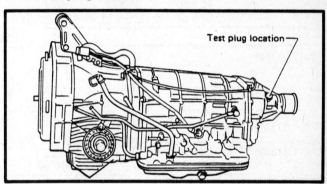
Rear test plug location

LINE PRESSURE

Range	Minimum ① Pressure psi (kPa)	Maximum ① Pressure psi (kPa)
P	64-82 (441-569)	—
R	85-100 (588-686)	206-230 (1422-1589)
N	64-82 (441-569)	—
D	64-82 (441-569)	164-182 (1128-1255)
3	64-82 (441-569)	164-182 (1128-1255)
2	64-82 (441-569)	164-182 (1128-1255)
Accelerator pedal	Fully closed	Fully open

① Stall speed RPM—600-800

TRANSFER CLUTCH LINE PRESSURE

Range	4WD Mode Low Pressure ① Side psi (kPa)	4WD Mode High Pressure ① Side psi (kPa)	FWD Mode High Pressure ① Side psi (kPa)
R	7-11 (49-78)	104-114 (716-785)	(0)
D	7-11 (49-78)	104-114 (716-785)	(0)
Accelerator pedal	Fully closed	Fully open	Fully open

① Stall speed rpm 600-800

7. The stall speed for sedan and wagon equipped with the 1.8L engine is 2750–3150 rpm. The stall speed for the XT coupe equipped with the 1.8L engine is 2450–2850 rpm and for the 2.7L engine is 2400–2800 rpm. The stall speed for the Legacy equipped with the 2.2L engine is 2550–2950 rpm

8. If the stall speed is higher than the specified range, attempt to finish the stall test in as short a time as possible, in order to prevent the automatic transaxle from sustaining damage.

NOTE: If vehicle stall speed is higher than specification, slippage of the automatic transaxle is indicated. If vehicle stall speed is in the specified range, the transaxle control members and engine are in good order. If stall speed is lower than specification, check engine operation or torque converter one way clutch slippage.

TIME LAG TEST

If the shift lever is shifted while the engine is idling, there will be a certain time elapse or lag before the shock can be felt. This test is used for checking the condition of the forward clutch, reverse clutch, low and reverse brake, forward one way clutch and low one way clutch.

1. Start engine and check the idle speed. Correct the idle speed if necessary.

NOTE: Perform the test at normal engine operation temperature. Be sure to allow a 1 minute interval between tests. Take 3 tests and take the average value.

2. Shift the shift lever from **N** to **D** range. Using a stop watch, measure the time it takes from shifting the lever until the shock is felt. The correct specification is less than 1.2 seconds. Shift the shift lever from **N** to **R** in the same manner, measure the time lag it should less than 1.5 seconds.

NOTE: If time lag test results from N to D results are longer than specified check for low line pressure. Check for a worn forward clutch and the low one way clutch

SHIFT SPEED CHART—1.8L ENGINE

		1→2	2→3	3→4	4→3	3→2	2→1
		THROTTLE FULLY OPEN mph (km/h)					
D range	Normal	31 ± 2 (50 ± 2.5)	58 ± 2 (94 ± 2.5)	89 ± 2 (144 ± 2.5)	83 ± 2 (134 ± 2.5)	52 ± 2 (84 ± 2.5)	25 ± 2 (40 ± 2.5)
	Power	35 ± 2 (56 ± 2.5)	65 ± 2 (104 ± 2.5)	96 ± 2 (155 ± 2.5)	90 ± 2 (145 ± 2.5)	58 ± 2 (94 ± 2.5)	28 ± 2 (45 ± 2.5)
3 range	—	35 ± 2 (56 ± 2.5)	65 ± 2 (104 ± 2.5)	—	—	58 ± 2 (94 ± 2.5)	28 ± 2 (45 ± 2.5)
2 range	1st hold S/W off	35 ± 2 (56 ± 2.5)	65 ± 2 (104 ± 2.5)	—	—	58 ± 2 (94 ± 2.5)	28 ± 2 (45 ± 2.5)
	1st hold S/W on	35 ± 2 (56 ± 2.5)	65 ± 2 (104 ± 2.5)	—	—	58 ± 2 (94 ± 2.5)	31 ± 2 (50 ± 2.5)
		THROTTLE FULLY CLOSED mph (km/h)					
D range	Normal	9 ± 2 (15 ± 2.5)	19 ± 2 (30 ± 2.5)	28 ± 2 (45 ± 2.5)	25 ± 2 (40 ± 2.5)	9 ± 2 (15 ± 2.5)	6 ± 2 (10 ± 2.5)
	Power	9 ± 2 (15 ± 2.5)	19 ± 2 (30 ± 2.5)	31 ± 2 (50 ± 2.5)	25 ± 2 (40 ± 2.5)	12 ± 2 (20 ± 2.5)	6 ± 2 (10 ± 2.5)
3 range	—	9 ± 2 (15 ± 2.5)	19 ± 2 (30 ± 2.5)	—	—	12 ± 2 (20 ± 2.5)	6 ± 2 (10 ± 2.5)
2 range	1st hold S/W off	9 ± 2 (15 ± 2.5)	65 ± 2 (104 ± 2.5)	—	—	58 ± 2 (94 ± 2.5)	6 ± 2 (10 ± 2.5)
	1st hold S/W on	35 ± 2 (56 ± 2.5)	65 ± 2 (104 ± 2.5)	—	—	58 ± 2 (94 ± 2.5)	31 ± 2 (50 ± 2.5)

SHIFT SPEED CHART—2.7L ENGINE

		1→2	2→3	3→4	4→3	3→2	2→1
		THROTTLE FULLY OPEN mph (km/h)					
D range	Normal	34 ± 2 (55 ± 2.5)	66 ± 2 (107 ± 2.5)	103 ± 2 (165 ± 2.5)	97 ± 2 (156 ± 2.5)	61 ± 2 (98 ± 2.5)	28 ± 2 (45 ± 2.5)
	Power	34 ± 2 (55 ± 2.5)	66 ± 2 (107 ± 2.5)	103 ± 2 (165 ± 2.5)	97 ± 2 (156 ± 2.5)	61 ± 2 (98 ± 2.5)	28 ± 2 (45 ± 2.5)
3 range	—	34 ± 2 (55 ± 2.5)	66 ± 2 (107 ± 2.5)	—	—	61 ± 2 (98 ± 2.5)	28 ± 2 (45 ± 2.5)
2 range	1st hold S/W off	34 ± 2 (55 ± 2.5)	65 ± 2 (105 ± 2.5)	—	—	62 ± 2 (100 ± 2.5)	28 ± 2 (45 ± 2.5)
	1st hold S/W on	35 ± 2 (57 ± 2.5)	65 ± 2 (105 ± 2.5)	—	—	62 ± 2 (100 ± 2.5)	25 ± 2 (40 ± 2.5)
		THROTTLE FULLY CLOSED mph (km/h)					
D range	Normal	8 ± 2 (13 ± 2.5)	11 ± 2 (18 ± 2.5)	24 ± 2 (38 ± 2.5)	21 ± 2 (33 ± 2.5)	9 ± 2 (15 ± 2.5)	6 ± 2 (10 ± 2.5)
	Power	11 ± 2 (17 ± 2.5)	19 ± 2 (30 ± 2.5)	34 ± 2 (55 ± 2.5)	25 ± 2 (40 ± 2.5)	12 ± 2 (20 ± 2.5)	6 ± 2 (10 ± 2.5)
3 range	—	11 ± 2 (17 ± 2.5)	19 ± 2 (30 ± 2.5)	—	—	12 ± 2 (20 ± 2.5)	6 ± 2 (10 ± 2.5)
2 range	1st hold S/W off	11 ± 2 (17 ± 2.5)	65 ± 2 (105 ± 2.5)	—	—	62 ± 2 (100 ± 2.5)	6 ± 2 (10 ± 2.5)
	1st hold S/W on	35 ± 2 (57 ± 2.5)	65 ± 2 (105 ± 2.5)	—	—	62 ± 2 (100 ± 2.5)	25 ± 2 (40 ± 2.5)

operation. If time lag test results from N to R results are longer than specified also check for low line pressure. Check for a worn reverse clutch and low and reverse clutch problem.

LINE PRESSURE TEST

If the transaxle operation shows signs of slippage or a shifting problem the line pressure should be checked. If excessive shocks during upshifting or shifting takes place, at a higher point than under normal circumstances, it may be due to the line pressure being too high. Line pressure measurement must be taken under no load condition and a heavy load condition.

No Load Condition Check

1. Before measuring line pressure, raise and safely support the vehicle.
2. The engine must be at normal operating temperature.
3. Remove test plug and install oil pressure gauge. Record test results under no load condition.

Heavy Load Condition Check

1. Before measuring line pressure, apply both front and parking brakes with all wheels chocked.
2. The engine must be at normal operating temperature and shift selector through each range.
3. Remove test plug and install oil pressure gauge. Record test results under heavy load condition.
4. Measure line pressure for 5–10 seconds in each range. Before measuring it again, idle the engine for 2–5 minutes.

Transfer Clutch Pressure Check

Check the transfer clutch pressure in the same manner as line pressure, except connect the test gauge at the rear test plug location.

ROAD TEST

The road test should be conducted to properly diagnose the condition of the automatic transaxle. Pay careful attention to ensure the shift is made smoothly and at the proper speed. Check the shift patterns in all ranges and the kickdown for proper operation. Check the 4WD function if tight corner braking occurs when the steering wheel is fully turned at low speed:
1. Determine the applicable trouble code and check the corresponding duty solenoid C (transfer) for proper operation.
2. If the solenoid is operating properly, check the transfer clutch pressure.
3. If oil pressure is normal check the transfer control valve for sticking and the transfer clutch assembly for wear.

Electronic Control System

NOTE: When troubleshooting the electronic control system, always start with the simple easy operations and then proceed to the complicated and difficult operations.

The electronic-hydraulic control system consists of various sensors and switches, a transaxle control unit and the hydraulic controller including solenoid valves. The system controls the transaxle properly including shift control, lockup control, overrunning clutch control, line pressure control, auto pattern select control and shift timing control. It also controls the 4WD transfer clutch. The system detects various operating conditions from various input signals and sends output signals to shift solenoids 1, 2 and 3 and duty solenoids A, B and C a total of 6 solenoids for 4WD vehicles and 5 solenoids for FWD vehicles.

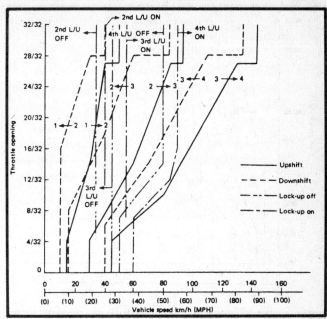
D range (normal pattern) – 1.8L engine

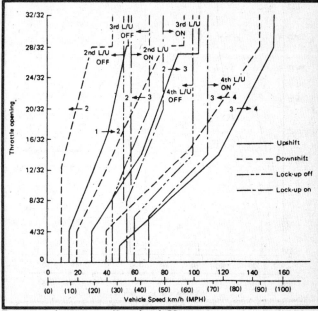
D range (power pattern) – 1.8L engine

The following items can be checked for improper operation using the self-diagnosis (trouble codes) system:
1. Vehicle revolution sensor No. 1 (on transaxle)
2. Vehicle revolution senosr No. 2 (in speedometer)
3. Throttle sensor
4. Shift solenoid No. 1
5. Shift solenoid No. 2
6. Shift solenoid No. 3
7. Duty solenoid B
8. Duty solenoid C
9. Automatic transaxle fluid temperature sensor
10. Ignition pulse
11. Duty solenoid A

NOTE: On Legacy, the atmospheric sensor, which is built in the ECU can also be checked using the self-diagnosis (trouble codes) system.

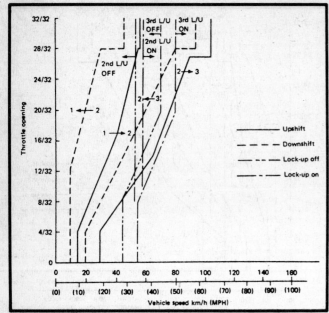

3RD range—1.8L engine

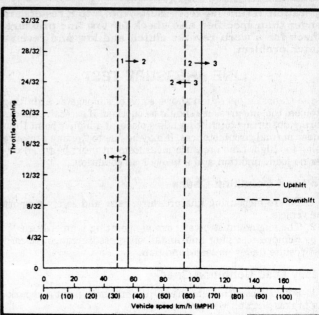

2ND range (1st hold switch on)—   engine

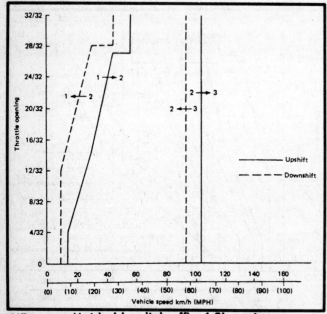

2ND range (1st hold switch off)—1.8L engine

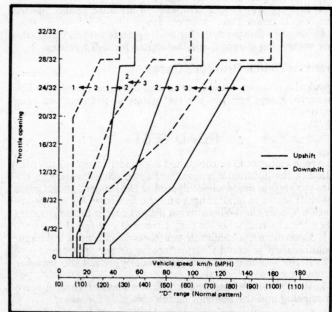

D range (normal pattern)—2.7L engine

RETRIVAL OF TROUBLE CODES

EXCEPT LEGACY

The trouble history and codes of the self-diagnosis items are revealed by **POWER** indicator light flashes. Calling up trouble history or codes for a 4WD vehicle is accomplished by inserting a fuse in the FWD switch. On the FWD vehicles ground the self-diagnosis terminal (LR) of check connector (17 pin connector) or connect terminal (LR) with terminal (BR).

LEGACY

On these vehicles, the diagonstic codes are read with a monitor. The select monitor connector is located under the dash on the driver's side.

NOTE: Low battery voltage will cause faulty operation of the diagnosis system.

READING TROUBLE CODES

EXCEPT LEGACY

In case of malfunction, a trouble code will be observed by the **POWER** indicator light. The sequence of indicator light blinks, show each system fault. A long blink (0.9 seconds) means the system is normal. Blinking at short intervals (0.6 seconds.) means that a system is faulty.

LEGACY

The **POWER** indicator light flashes the code corresponding to the faulty part. A long blink (2 seconds) indicates a normal system and the short blink (0.2 seconds) indicates a problem.

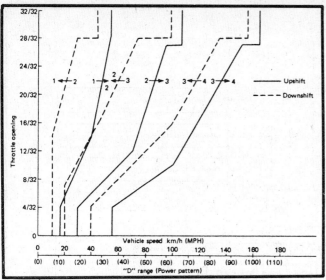

D range (power pattern)—2.7L engine

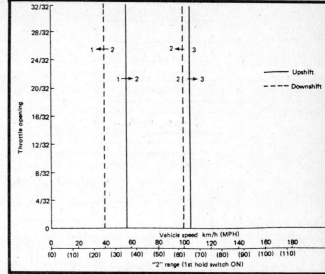

2ND range (1st hold switch on)—2.7L engine

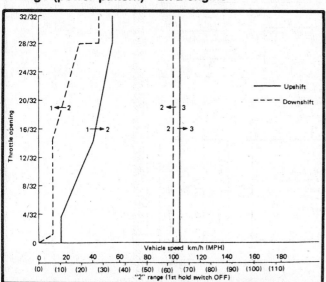

2ND range (1st hold switch off)—2.7L engine

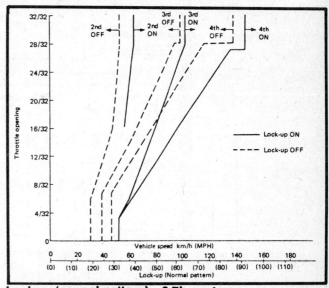
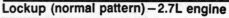

Lockup (normal pattern)—2.7L engine

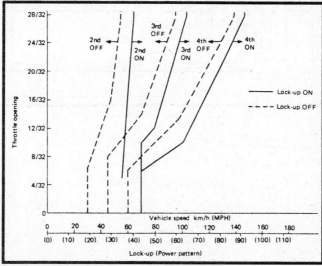

Lockup (power pattern)—2.7L engine

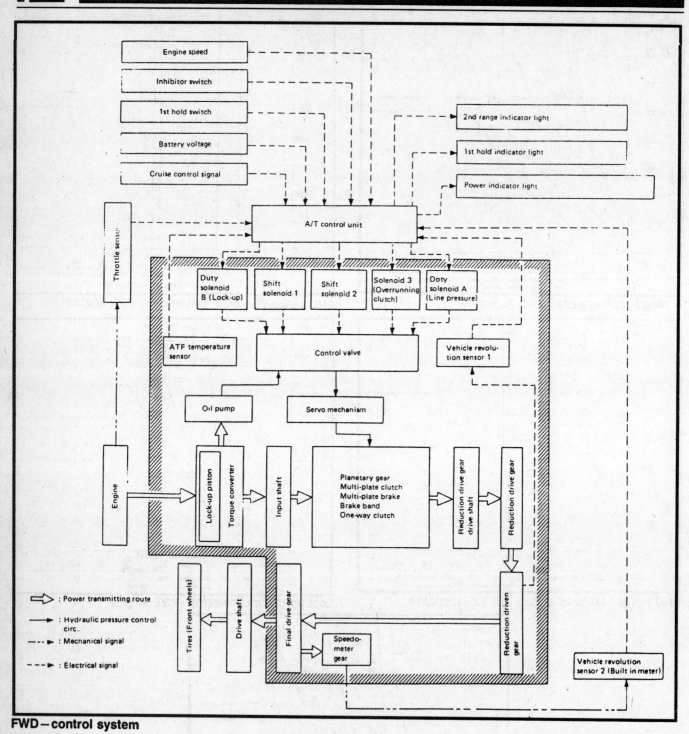

FWD — control system

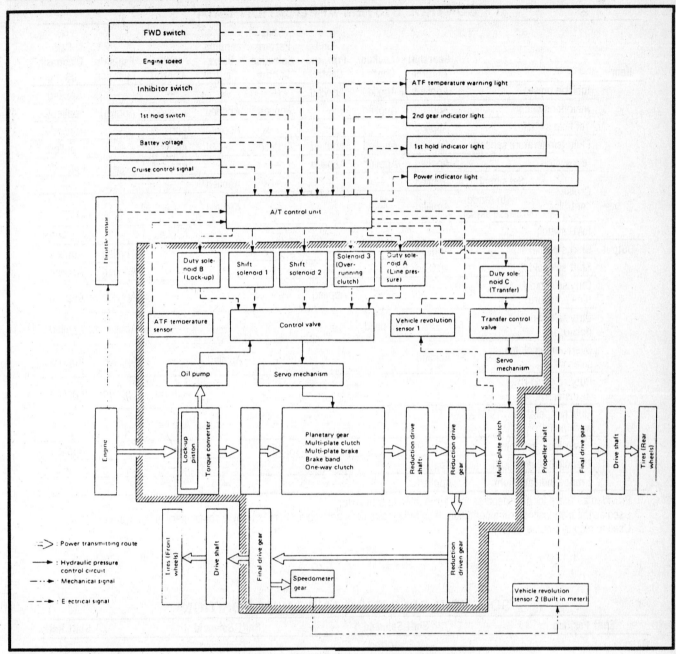

4WD—control system

CONTROL SYSTEM APPLICATION DATA

Item		Gearshift Control	Lockup Control	Line Pressure Control	Shift Pattern Selection Control	Engine Brake Control	4WD Control	Fail-safe Function	Self-Diagnosis Function
Input	Throttle sensor	Applied	Applied	Applied	Applied	Applied	Applied	Applied	Applied
	Vehicle revolution sensor 1 (output shaft revolution sensor mounted to transaxle)	Applied	Applied	Applied	Applied	Applied	Applied	Applied	Applied
	Vehicle revolution sensor 2 (built into meter panel)	Applied①	Applied①	Applied①	Applied①	Applied①	Applied	—	Applied

CONTROL SYSTEM APPLICATION DATA

Item		Gearshift Control	Lockup Control	Line Pressure Control	Shift Pattern Selection Control	Engine Brake Control	4WD Control	Fail-safe Function	Self-Diagnosis Function
	Ignition pulse	Applied	Applied	Applied	—	—	—	—	Applied
	Inhibitor switch	Applied	Applied	—	Applied	Applied	Applied	Applied	Applied②
	1st hold switch	Applied	—	—	—	Applied	Applied	—	Applied②
	Fluid temperature sensor	Applied	Applied	Applied	Applied	—	Applied	—	Applied
	Idle switch	Applied	Applied	Applied	—	—	Applied	—	Applied②
Cruise control	Set signal	Applied	—	—	—	Applied	—	—	—
	4th range release signal	Applied	—	—	—	Applied	—	—	—
	FWD switch	—	—	—	—	—	Applied	—	Applied③
Output	Shift solenoid 1	Applied	—	—	—	—	—	Applied	Applied
	Shift solenoid 2	Applied	—	—	—	—	—	Applied	Applied
	Duty solenoid A (line pressure)	—	—	Applied	—	—	—	Applied	Applied
	Duty solenoid B (lockup)	—	Applied	—	—	—	—	Applied	Applied
	Overrunning clutch solenoid	Applied	—	—	—	Applied	—	Applied	Applied
	Duty solenoid C (transfer)	—	—	—	—	—	Applied	Applied	Applied
	Fluid temperature warning light	—	—	—	—	—	Applied	—	—
	Power indicator light	—	—	—	Applied	—	—	—	Applied
	1st hold indicator light	Applied	—	—	—	—	—	—	—
	2 range indicator light	Applied	—	—	—	—	—	—	—

① Provided as spare for car-speed sensor 1 (mounted to transaxle)
② Used as the diagnosis starting condition. If self-diagnosis does not begin, there is trouble somewhere in the system
③ Used to display trouble history

SOLENOID OPERATION AND SHIFT POSITION

Shift Position		Shift Solenoid 1	Shift Solenoid 2	Shift Ratio
D range		Energized	Energized	1st
		Not energized	Energized	2nd
		Not energized	Energized	3rd
		Energized	Not energized	4th
3 range		Energized	Energized	1st
		Not energized	Energized	2nd
		Not energized	Not energized	3rd
2 range	1st hold released	Energized	Energized	1st
		Not energized	Energized	2nd
	1st hold applied	Not energized	Not energized	3rd
	1st hold applied	Energized	Energized	1st
	1st hold applied	Not energized	Energized	2nd
	1st hold applied	Not energized	Not energized	3rd

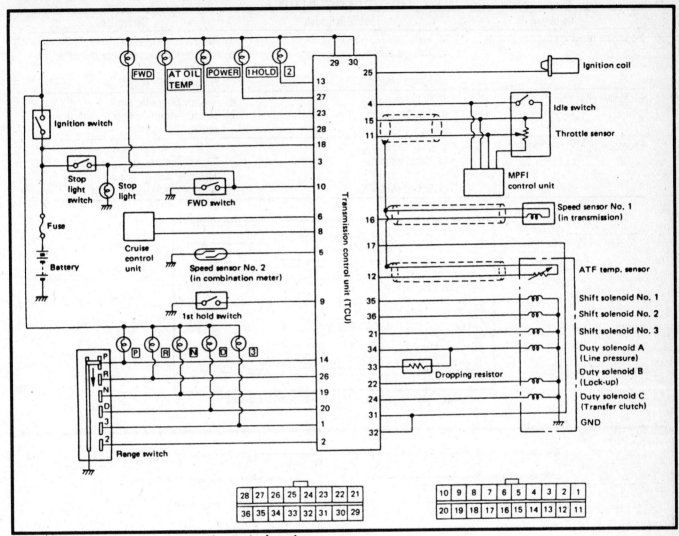

Wiring diagram electronic transaxle control system

TROUBLESHOOTING

Condition	Possible Cause	Correction
No shift	a) Shift solenoid No. 1 and/or No. 2	a) Repair No. 1 and No. 2 shift solenoid circuit
	b) Speed sensor No. 1 and No. 2	b) Replace No. 1 and No. 2 speed sensor or defective wiring
	c) Power source and grounding	c) Repair circuit wiring
Shift point too high or too low	a) Throttle sensor	a) Replace throttle sensor or repair defective wiring
	b) Speed sensor No. 1	b) Replace speed sensor No. 1
No up-shift to overdrive (after warm-up)	a) Range switch	a) Replace range switch
	b) Fluid temp sensor	b) Replace fluid temperature sensor
	c) Cruise control unit	c) Repair or replace cruise control unit
No back-up (after warm-up)	a) Duty solenoid B	a) Replace duty solenoid B
	b) Fluid temp sensor	b) Replace fluid temperature sensor
	c) Ignition pulse	c) Repair circuit or harness for ignition pulse
	d) Idle switch	d) Replace idle switch

TROUBLESHOOTING

Condition	Possible Cause	Correction
No engine braking effect at 3 range	a) Shift solenoid No. 3 b) Throttle sensor c) Range switch	a) Replace shift solenoid No. 3 b) Replace throttle sensor or defective wiring c) Replace range switch
Excessive shift shock	a) Duty solenoid A b) Throttle sensor	a) Replace duty solenoid A b) Replace throttle sensor or defective wiring
Excessive tight corner braking	a) Duty solenoid C b) Throttle sensor c) Speed sensor No. 1	a) Replace duty solenoid C b) Replace throttle sensor or repair defective wiring c) Replace speed sensor No. 1

Check connector.
(17-pole, black)

LR BR

FWD switch

Diagnostic connections – trouble codes

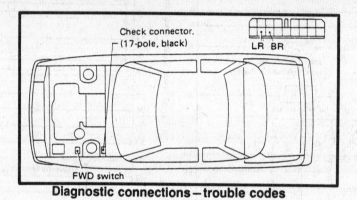

Shift solenoid No. 3 — Duty solenoid B
Shift solenoid No. 2 — Duty solenoid C (4WD only)
Shift solenoid No. 1 — ATF Temp. sensor
Throttle sensor — Ignition pulse
Speed sensor No. 2 — Duty solenoid A
Speed sensor No. 1

ON
OFF
2.5 2 1 1 1 1 1 1 1 1 1 1 1 1 → Repeat

Unit: second

ON
OFF
0.1 0.9
1
Normal system

ON
OFF
0.6 0.4
1
Faulty system
Unit: second

Reading trouble codes – except Legacy

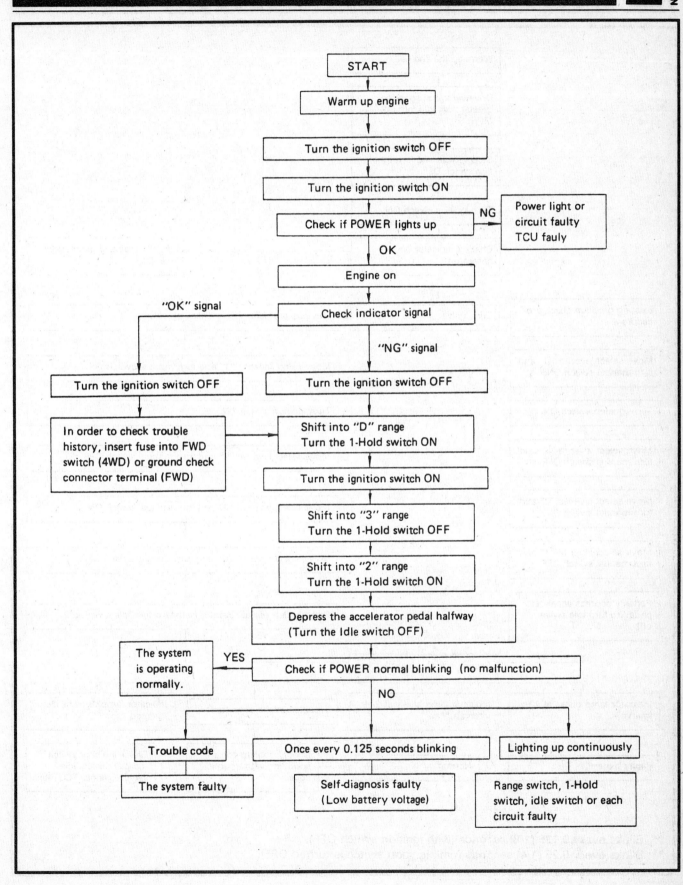

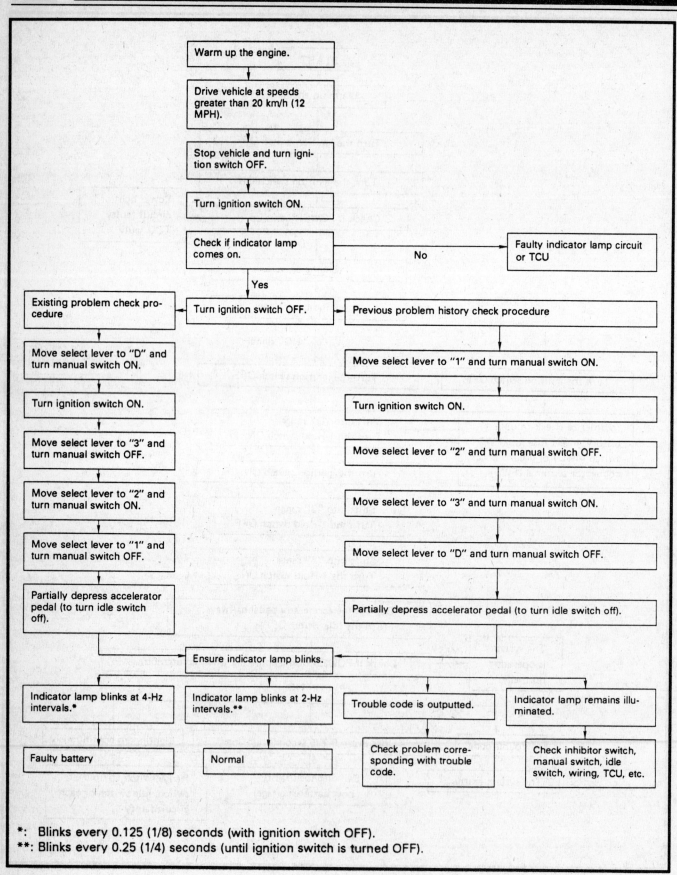

Warm up the engine.

Drive vehicle at speeds greater than 20 km/h (12 MPH).

Stop vehicle and turn ignition switch OFF.

Turn ignition switch ON.

Check if indicator lamp comes on. —— No —→ Faulty indicator lamp circuit or TCU

Yes

Turn ignition switch OFF.

Existing problem check procedure

Move select lever to "D" and turn manual switch ON.

Turn ignition switch ON.

Move select lever to "3" and turn manual switch OFF.

Move select lever to "2" and turn manual switch ON.

Move select lever to "1" and turn manual switch OFF.

Partially depress accelerator pedal (to turn idle switch off).

Previous problem history check procedure

Move select lever to "1" and turn manual switch ON.

Turn ignition switch ON.

Move select lever to "2" and turn manual switch OFF.

Move select lever to "3" and turn manual switch ON.

Move select lever to "D" and turn manual switch OFF.

Partially depress accelerator pedal (to turn idle switch off).

Ensure indicator lamp blinks.

Indicator lamp blinks at 4-Hz intervals.* → Faulty battery

Indicator lamp blinks at 2-Hz intervals.** → Normal

Trouble code is outputted. → Check problem corresponding with trouble code.

Indicator lamp remains illuminated. → Check inhibitor switch, manual switch, idle switch, wiring, TCU, etc.

*: Blinks every 0.125 (1/8) seconds (with ignition switch OFF).
**: Blinks every 0.25 (1/4) seconds (until ignition switch is turned OFF).

Trouble code	Item	Content of diagnosis	Abbr. (Select monitor)
11	Duty solenoid A	Detects open or shorted drive circuit, as well as valve seizure.	PL
12	Duty solenoid B	Detects open or shorted drive circuit, as well as valve seizure.	L/U
13	Shift solenoid 3	Detects open or shorted drive circuit, as well as valve seizure.	OVR
14	Shift solenoid 2	Detects open or shorted drive circuit, as well as valve seizure.	SFT2
15	Shift solenoid 1	Detects open or shorted drive circuit, as well as valve seizure.	SFT1
21	ATF temperature sensor	Detects open or shorted input signal circuit.	ATFT
22	Atmospheric sensor	Detects a faulty atmospheric sensor built into ECU (MPFI).	BARO.P
23	Engine revolution signal	Detects open or shorted input signal circuit.	EREV
24	Duty solenoid C	Detects open or shorted drive circuit, as well as valve seizure.	4WD
31	Throttle sensor	Detects open or shorted input signal circuit.	THV
32	Vehicle speed sensor 1	Detects open or shorted input signal circuit.	VSP1
33	Vehicle speed sensor 2	Detects open or shorted input signal circuit.	VSP2

Reading trouble codes – Legacy

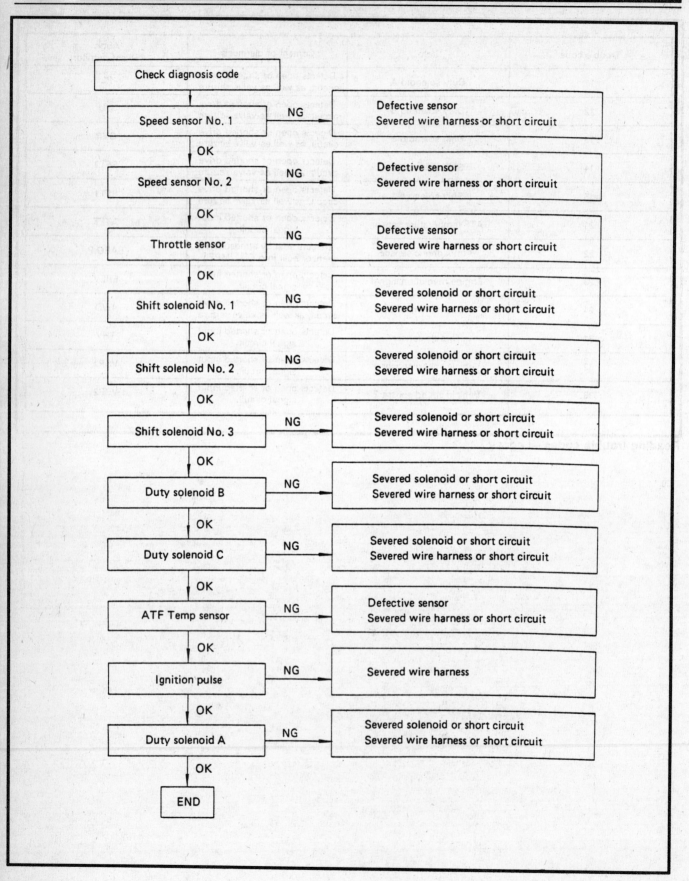

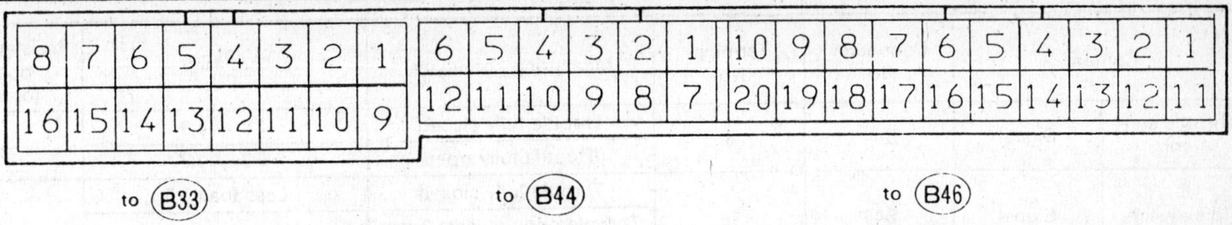

8	7	6	5	4	3	2	1
16	15	14	13	12	11	10	9

to (B33)

6	5	4	3	2	1
12	11	10	9	8	7

to (B44)

10	9	8	7	6	5	4	3	2	1
20	19	18	17	16	15	14	13	12	11

to (B46)

Content			Connector No.	Terminal No.	Measuring conditions	Voltage (V)
Battery supply			B46	14	Ignition switch OFF	10 — 14
Ignition power supply			B33 / B44	1 / 6	Ignition switch ON (with engine OFF)	10 — 14
Inhibitor switch	"P" range switch	Signal (—)	B46	9	Select lever in "P" range	Level than 1
					Select lever in any other than "P" range	9 — 13
	"R" range switch	Signal (—)	B46	10	Select lever in "R" range	Level than 1
					Select lever in any other than "R" range	6 — 10
	"N" range switch	Signal (—)	B46	8	Select lever in "N" range	Level than 1
					Select lever in any other than "N" range	9 — 13
	"D" range switch	Signal (—)	B44	1	Select lever in "D" range	Level than 1
					Select lever in any other than "D" range	4 — 7
	"3" range switch	Signal (—)	B44	2	Select lever in "3" range	Level than 1
					Select lever in any other than "3" range	6 — 10
	"2" range switch	Signal (—)	B44	3	Select lever in "2" range	Level than 1
					Select lever in any other than "2" range	6 — 10
	"1" range switch	Signal (—)	B44	4	Select lever in "1" range	Level than 1
					Select lever in any other than "1" range	6 — 10
Manual switch		Signal (—)	B46	6	Manual switch ON	Level than 1
					Manual switch OFF	6 — 10
Brake switch		Signal (—)	B46	5	Brake pedal depressed	10 — 14
					Brake pedal released	Less than 0.5

Content		Connector No.	Terminal No.	Measuring conditions	Voltage (V)	Resistance to body (ohms)
Throttle sensor	Signal	B44	8	Throttle fully closed	4.0 — 4.8	—
				Throttle fully open	0.7 — 1.7	
Idle switch	Signal	B46	16	Throttle fully closed	Less than 0.5	—
				Throttle open at least 2 degrees	3 — 6	
ATF temperature sensor	Signal (+)	B44	10	ATF temperature 20°C (68°F)	3.0 — 3.5	2.3 k — 2.7 k
				ATF temperature 80°C (176°F)	1.0 — 1.3	280 — 360
Vehicle speed sensor 1	Signal (+)	B44	12	Vehicle stopped	0	450 — 650
				Vehicle speed at least 20 km/h (12 MPH)	Greater than 1 (AC range)	
Vehicle speed sensor 2	Signal (+)	B46	11	When vehicle is slowly moved at least 2 meters (7ft)	Less than 1→↑greater than 4	—
Atmospheric sensor	Signal (+)	B44	9	—	—	—
Cruise set signal	Signal (+)	B46	3	When cruise control is set (SET lamp ON)	Less than 1	—
				When cruise control is not set (SET lamp OFF)	6 — 10	
Shift solenoid 1		B33	14	Select lever in 1st or 4th gear	10 — 14	20 — 30
				Select lever in 2nd or 3rd gear	Less than 1	
Shift solenoid 2		B33	13	Select lever in 1st or 2nd gear	10 — 14	20 — 30
				Select lever in 3rd or 4th gear	Less than 1	
Shift solenoid 3		B33	15	Select lever in "N" range (with throttle fully closed)	Less than 1	20 — 30
				Select lever in "D" range (with throttle fully closed)	10 — 14	
Duty solenoid A		B33	8	Throttle fully closed (with engine OFF) after warm-up	1.5 — 3.0	1.5 — 4.5
				Throttle fully open (with engine OFF) after warm-up	Less than 0.5	
Dropping resistor		B33	7	Throttle fully closed (with engine OFF) after warm-up	5 — 14	9 — 15
				Throttle fully open (with engine OFF) after warm-up	Less than 0.5	
Duty solenoid B		B33	5	When lockup occurs	8 — 14	9 — 15
				When lockup is released	Less than 0.5	
Duty solenoid C		B33	3	Fuse on FWD switch	8 — 14	9 — 15
				Fuse removed from FWD switch (with throttle fully open and with select lever in 1st gear	Less than 0.5	
Sensor ground line 1		B44	7	—	0	Less than 1
Sensor ground line 2		B46	20	—	0	Less than 1
System ground line		B46	1	—	0	Less than 1
Power system ground line		B33	10	—	0	Less than 1
FWD switch		B46	2	Fuse removed	10 — 14	
				Fuse installed	Less than 1	

CLEARING TROUBLE CODES

EXCEPT LEGACY

The trouble codes are cancelled after self-diagnosis and those in the trouble history remain in the memory of the control unit after the ignition switch is turned off. After repairs, a trouble code can be erased by turning the ignition switch off and disconnecting the connector from the control unit.

LEGACY

The No. 14 fuse is located in the line to the memory back up power supply of the TCU and the ECU. Removal of this fuse clears the codes stored in the memory. This fuse must be removed for at least 1 minute.

ON CAR SERVICES

Adjustments

BRAKE BAND

If the following abnormal shifting conditions are noted in a road test, the brake band must be adjusted.

NOTE: Do not excessively loosen the adjustment screw otherwise, the band strut on the servo piston will drop off.

The 2nd gear state and 4th gear state can be achieved but the engine rpm increases excessively when shifting up from 2nd to 3rd or a shift delay (over 1 second) happens at kickdown from 3rd to 2nd. If any of these problems occurs, it is excessive clearance between the reverse clutch drum and brake band. Tighten the adjustment screw by turning it ¾ of a turn clockwise from original state.

The 2nd gear state and 4th gear state can be achieved, but a braking phenomenon is noted when shifting up from 2nd to 3rd. It is attributable to small brake band clearance. Loosen the adjust screw by turning it ¾ of a turn counterclockwise from original state.

When accelerating, direct shift up from 1st to 3rd occurs or when shifting up from 2nd to 3rd, tire slip occurs. Torque the adjustment screw to 6.5 ft lbs. (9 Nm), then back off 3 turns. With the adjusting screw locked, tighten the locknut to 19–21 ft. lbs. (26 Nm.).

NEUTRAL SAFETY SWITCH

1. Loosen the switch securing bolts.
2. Shift the select lever to the N range.
3. Insert stopper pin tool, 499267300 or equivalent as vertical as possible into the holes in the switch lever and switch body.
4. Torque the switch bolts to 1.5 ft lbs.

Services

FLUID CHANGES

The conditions under which the vehicle is operated is the main consideration in determining how often the transaxle fluid should be changed. Different driving conditions result in differ-

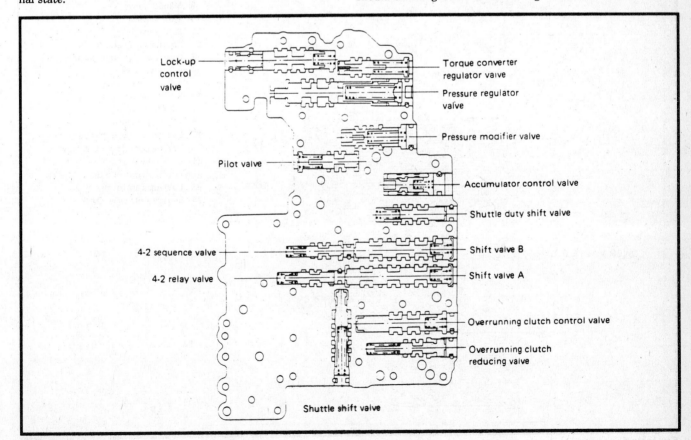

Lock-up control valve — Torque converter regulator valve — Pressure regulator valve — Pressure modifier valve — Pilot valve — Accumulator control valve — Shuttle duty shift valve — 4-2 sequence valve — Shift valve B — 4-2 relay valve — Shift valve A — Overrunning clutch control valve — Overrunning clutch reducing valve — Shuttle shift valve

Upper body

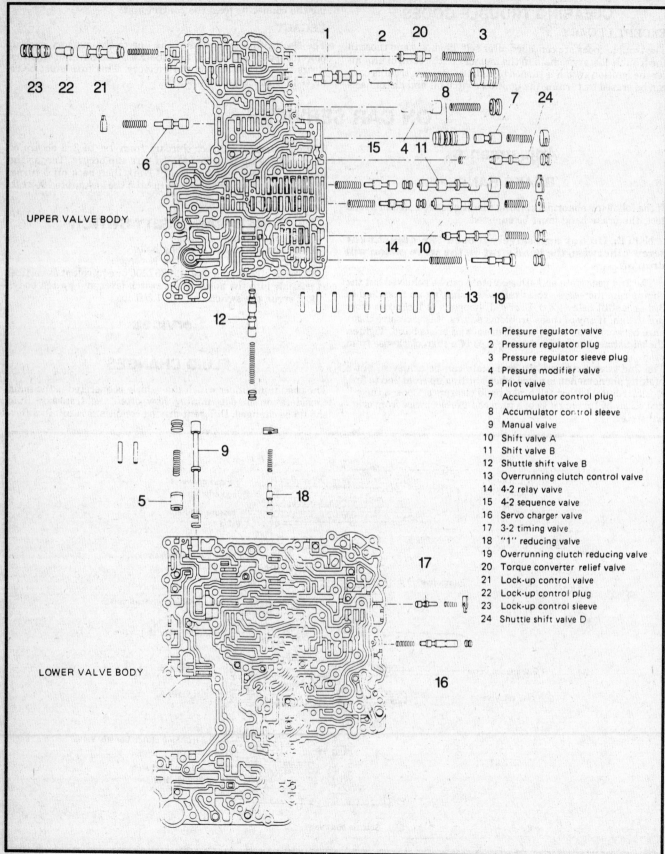

UPPER VALVE BODY

LOWER VALVE BODY

1 Pressure regulator valve
2 Pressure regulator plug
3 Pressure regulator sleeve plug
4 Pressure modifier valve
5 Pilot valve
7 Accumulator control plug
8 Accumulator control sleeve
9 Manual valve
10 Shift valve A
11 Shift valve B
12 Shuttle shift valve B
13 Overrunning clutch control valve
14 4-2 relay valve
15 4-2 sequence valve
16 Servo charger valve
17 3-2 timing valve
18 "1" reducing valve
19 Overrunning clutch reducing valve
20 Torque converter relief valve
21 Lock-up control valve
22 Lock-up control plug
23 Lock-up control sleeve
24 Shuttle shift valve D

Exploded view valve body

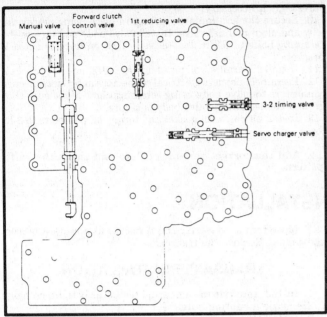

Lower valve body

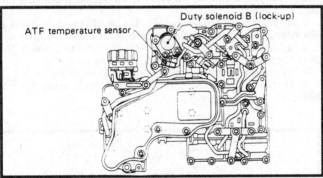

Lower surface of control valve

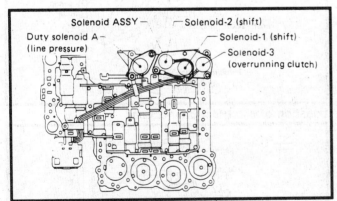

Upper surface of control valve

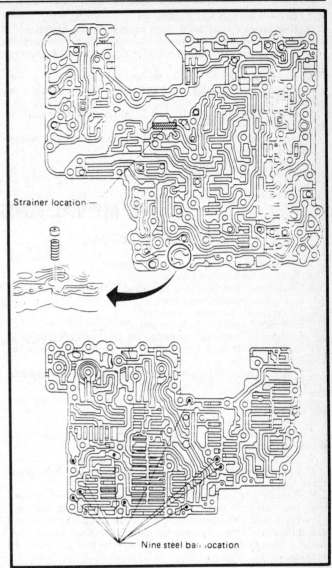

Check ball location

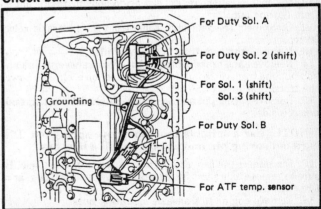

Harness connections

ent transaxle fluid temperatures. These temperatures affect change intervals.

If the vehicle is driven under severe conditions, change the transaxle fluid every 15,000 miles. If the vehicle is not used under severe conditions, change the fluid and replace the filter every 30,000 miles.

Do not overfill the transaxle. Overfilling the unit can cause damage to the internal components of the automatic transaxle.

VALVE BODY AND SOLENOID ASSEMBLIES
Removal and Installation

1. Raise and safely support the vehicle. Drain the transaxle fluid from the unit.

2. Remove oil pan and gasket.

3. Remove electrical connectors from clips and disconnect 5 electrical connectors. Disconnect all solenoid valve connectors.

4. Remove the 4 retaining bolts for duty solenoid B then remove the solenoid.

5. Disconnect the oil pipe by removing the 2 retaining bolts and remove 4 retaining bolts for oil strainer. Remove oil strainer.

6. Remove the 8 long bolts and 11 short bolts for retaining valve body. Remove valve body.

7. Remove shift solenoids 1, 2 and 3 and duty solenoid A from valve body if necessary.

8. Install duty solenoid B with retaining bolts.

9. Install shift solenoids 1, 2 and 3 and duty solenoid A to valve body if necessary.

10. Secure the accumulator springs in place using petroleum jelly and align manual valve. Install valve body and torque the retaining bolts to 5.8 ft. lbs. (8 Nm). Tighten duty solenoid B bracket.

11. Install oil strainer, oil pipe and harness connector bracket.

12. Reconnect harness electrical connectors at 5 places. Secure connectors to valve body using retaining clips. Make sure that ground connection in valve body is secure.

13. Install oil pan with gasket and torque oil pan bolts to 3 ft. lbs.

14. Add the correct amount of fluid and check the shift pattern.

REMOVAL AND INSTALLATION

TRANSAXLE REMOVAL

1. Disconnect the negative battery cable.
2. Remove speedometer cable.
3. Disconnect the following electrical harness connections:
   a. Oxygen sensor connector
   b. Transaxle harness connector
   c. Neutral safety switch connector
   d. Revolution sensor connector on 4WD equipped vehicles
   e. Crankshaft and camshaft angle sensor connector on Legacy
   f. Knock sensor connectors and transaxle ground terminal on Legacy
4. Remove clip band which secures air breather hose to pitching stopper.
5. Remove the starter and air intake boot.
6. Remove timing hole inspection plug and remove the 4 bolts which hold torque converter to drive plate.
7. Disconnect pitching stopper from bracket.
8. Remove engine to transaxle mounting nut and bolt on the right side.
9. Remove the buffer rod from the vehicle. Support the engine assembly with special engine support tool or equivalent.
10. Raise and safely support the vehicle. Drain the transaxle and differential fluid. Remove the exhaust system. Remove exhaust brackets or hangers that attach to the transaxle as necessary.
11. Matchmark and remove the driveshaft on 4WD vehicles. Plug the opening at the rear of extension housing to prevent oil from flowing out.
12. Disconnect the gear shift cable from the transaxle select lever.
13. Remove stabilizer from transverse link.
14. Remove hand brake cable bracket from transverse link and bolt holding transverse link to crossmember on each side. Lower the transverse link.
15. Remove spring pin and separate axle shaft from transaxle on each side.

NOTE: Use a suitable tool to remove spring pin. Discard old spring pin and always install a new one.

16. Disconnect the axle shaft from transaxle on each side. Be sure to remove axle shaft from transaxle by pushing the rear of tire outward.
17. Remove engine to transaxle mounting nuts.
18. Disconnect oil cooler hoses.
19. Place transmission jack or equivalent under transaxle. Always support transaxle case with a transmission jack.

NOTE: Do not place jack under oil pan, otherwise oil pan may be damaged.

20. Remove rear cushion rubber mounting nuts and rear crossmember.

21. Move torque converter and transaxle as a unit away from the engine. Remove the transaxle.

TRANSAXLE INSTALLATION

1. Install transaxle to engine and temporarily tighten engine to transaxle mounting nuts.
2. Install rear crossmember to rear cushion rubber mounts. Align rear cushion guide with rear crossmember guide hole and tighten nuts.
3. Install rear crossmember. Be careful not to damage threads. Torque rear crossmember bolts to 39–49 ft. lbs.
4. Tighten engine to transaxle retaining nuts to 34–40 ft. lbs. Remove transmission jack from the vehicle.
5. Remove the engine support tool and install buffer rod.
6. Install axle shaft to transaxle and install spring pin into place.

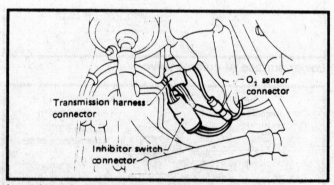

Location of electrical connections

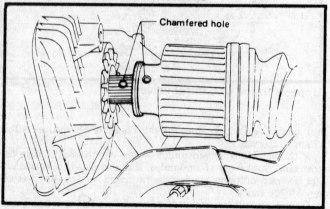

Correct alignment of axle shaft

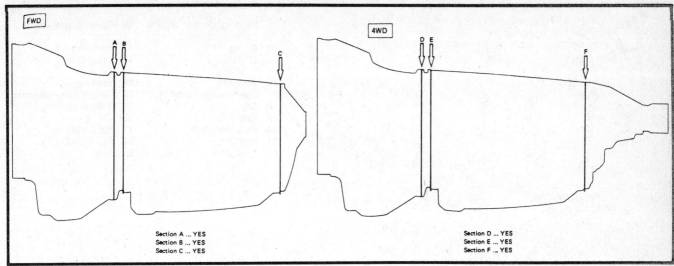

Transaxle sections that can be disassembled on FWD and 4WD vehicles

NOTE: Always use new spring pin. Be sure to align the axle shaft and shaft from the transaxle at chamfered holes and install shaft splines correctly.

7. Install transverse link temporarily to front crossmember by using bolt and self locking nut. Do not complete final torque at this point.

8. Install stabilizer temporarily to transverse link. Install hand brake cable bracket to transverse link.

9. Lower vehicle. Tighten transvere link to front crossmember mounting bolts and tranverse link to stabilizer mounting bolts with the tires placed on the ground when the vehicle is not loaded. Tightening torque for transverse link to front cross-member (self locking nuts) 43–51 ft. lbs. and transverse link to stabilizer 14–22 ft. lbs.

10. Raise and safely support the vehicle. Reconnect the gear shift cable to the select lever. Make sure that the lever operates smoothly all across the operating range.

11. Install drive shaft on 4WD vehicles. Torque drive shaft to rear differential retaining bolts to 17–24 ft. lbs. and center bearing location retaining bolts to 25–33 ft. lbs.

12. Connect oil cooler hoses.

13. Tighten engine to transaxle bolts to 34–40 ft. lbs.

14. Install starter.

15. Install pitching stopper. Be sure to tighten the bolt for the body side first and then the engine or transaxle side. Tightening torque for the body side is 27–49 ft. lbs. and for engine or trans-axle side is 33–40 ft. lbs.

16. Install and tighten torque converter to drive plate mounting bolts to 17–20 ft. lbs.

17. Install timing hole inspection plug, air intake boot and air breather hose to pitching stopper.

18. Reconnect the following electrical harness connections:
    a. Oxygen sensor connector
    b. Transaxle harness connector
    c. Neutral safety switch connector
    d. Revolution sensor connector on 4WD equipped vehicles
    e. Crankshaft and camshaft angle sensor connector on Legacy
    f. Knock sensor connectors and transaxle ground terminal on Legacy

19. Reconnect the speedometer cable. Manually tighten cable nut all the way and then turn it approximately 30 degrees more with a tool.

20. Install exhaust system and exhaust brackets or hangers that attach to the transaxle as necessary.

21. Connect the battery ground cable. Refill and check transaxle oil level.

22. Road test vehicle for proper operation across all operating ranges.

BENCH OVERHAUL

Before Disassembly

Cleanliness is an important factor in the overhaul of the automatic transaxle. Before opening up this unit, the entire outside of the transaxle assembly should be cleaned, preferable with a high pressure washer such as a car wash spray unit. Dirt entering the transaxle internal parts will negate all the time and effort spent on the overhaul. During inspection and reassembly all parts should be thoroughly cleaned with solvent then dried with compressed air. Wiping cloths and rags should not be used to dry parts since lint will find its way into the valve body passages.

Wheel bearing grease, long used to hold thrust washers and lube parts, should not be used. Lube seals with clean transmission fluid and use ordinary unmedicated petroleum jelly to hold the thrust washers and to ease the assembly of seals, since it will not leave a harmful residue as grease often will. Do not use solvent on neoprene seals, friction plates if they are to be reused, or thrust washers. Be wary of nylon parts if the transaxle failure was due to failure of the cooling system. Nylon parts exposed to water or antifreeze solutions can swell and distort and must be replaced.

Before installing bolts into aluminum parts, always dip the threads into clean transmission fluid. Antiseize compound can also be used to prevent bolts from galling the aluminum and seizing. Always use a torque wrench to keep from stripping the threads. Take care when installing new O-rings, especially the smaller O-rings. The internal snaprings should be expanded and the external rings should be compressed, if they are to be reused. This will help insure proper seating when installed.

Transaxle Disassembly

1. Place the transaxle unit on a suitable workbench, with the oil pan facing down.

2. Remove the drain plug and drain differential oil. Tighten the plug temporarily after draining.

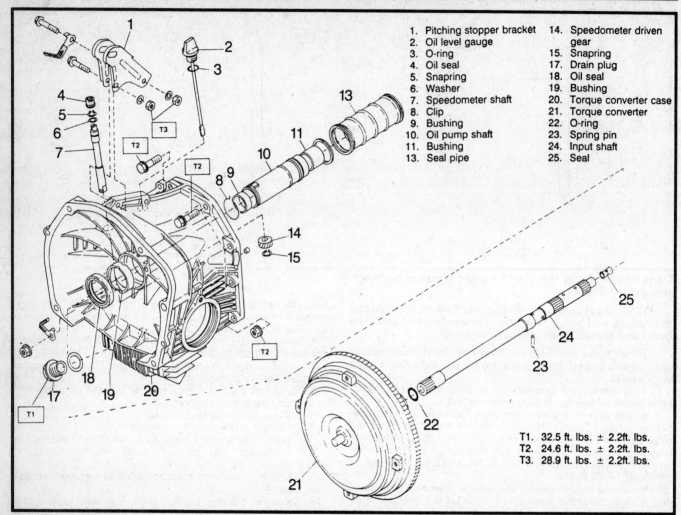

1. Pitching stopper bracket	14. Speedometer driven
2. Oil level gauge	gear
3. O-ring	15. Snapring
4. Oil seal	17. Drain plug
5. Snapring	18. Oil seal
6. Washer	19. Bushing
7. Speedometer shaft	20. Torque converter case
8. Clip	21. Torque converter
9. Bushing	22. O-ring
10. Oil pump shaft	23. Spring pin
11. Bushing	24. Input shaft
13. Seal pipe	25. Seal

T1. 32.5 ft. lbs. ± 2.2ft. lbs.
T2. 24.6 ft. lbs. ± 2.2ft. lbs.
T3. 28.9 ft. lbs. ± 2.2ft. lbs.

Torque converter and converter case

3. Remove the drain plug and drain automatic transaxle fluid. Tighten the plug temporarily after draining.

4. Remove the torque converter and oil pump shaft. Be careful not to scratch the bushing inside the oil pump shaft.

5. Remove the input shaft.

6. Remove the pitching stopper bracket and any hoses that are attached to the unit.

7. Remove the dipstick tube and remove the O-ring from the flange face.

8. Remove the oil cooler inlet and outlet pipes.

9. Separated the converter case from the transaxle case sections by tapping lightly on the housing. Be careful not to damage the oil seal and bushing inside the converter case by the oil pump cover.

10. Remove the revolution sensor on 4WD vehicles.

11. While pulling the extension case slightly away, disconnect the electrical connector for the duty solenoid C and separate the extension section from the transaxle case.

12. Remove the reduction drive gear assembly from the transaxle case.

13. Straighten the staked portion and remove the locknut. Using a puller tool remove the reduction driven gear.

14. Remove the parking pawl, return spring and shaft.

15. Remove the revolution sensor on FWD vehicles.

16. Loosen the taper bearing assembly mounting bolts and stand the transaxle case with its rear end facing down.

17. Remove the transaxle oil pan and gasket. Remove the oil cooler outlet pipe.

18. Disconnect the harness connectors for the solenoids, duty solenoids and the ground connection.

19. Remove the oil strainer with O-ring.

20. Remove the control valve body.

21. Mark and remove the accumulator springs.

22. Loosen the reverse clutch drum by turning the adjusting screw. Then remove the oil pump housing.

23. Loosen the brake band adjusting screw and take out the strut.

24. Remove the brake band and reverse clutch. Keep the brake band contracted with a clip when remove from the transaxle assembly.

25. Remove the high clutch and high clutch hub.

26. Remove the front sun gear and front planetary carrier.

27. Remove the rear planetary carrier and rear sun gear.

28. Remove the rear internal gear, one way clutch outer race, overrunning clutch hub and the forward clutch drum.

29. Remove the low and reverse brake section by removing the snapring. Then remove the retaining plate, drive plates, driven plates and dish plates as a unit. Turning the case upside down, remove one way clutch inner race and spring retainer assembly. Remove the low and reverse piston by applying compressed air to the pressure side.

30. Remove the inner snapring and the servo piston by apply-

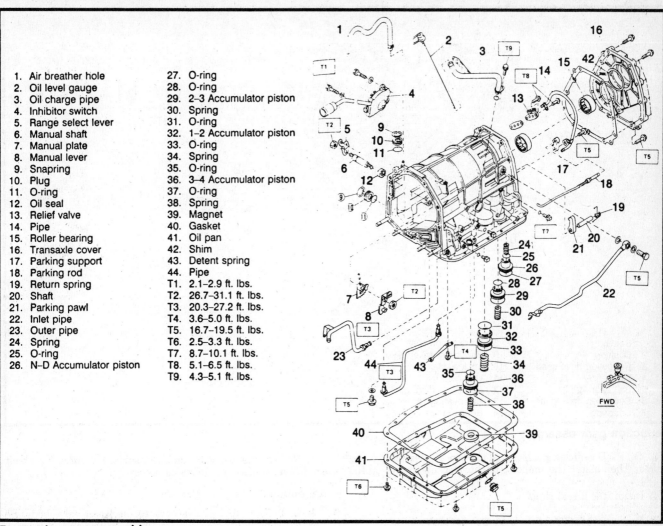

1. Air breather hole
2. Oil level gauge
3. Oil charge pipe
4. Inhibitor switch
5. Range select lever
6. Manual shaft
7. Manual plate
8. Manual lever
9. Snapring
10. Plug
11. O-ring
12. Oil seal
13. Relief valve
14. Pipe
15. Roller bearing
16. Transaxle cover
17. Parking support
18. Parking rod
19. Return spring
20. Shaft
21. Parking pawl
22. Inlet pipe
23. Outer pipe
24. Spring
25. O-ring
26. N–D Accumulator piston
27. O-ring
28. O-ring
29. 2–3 Accumulator piston
30. Spring
31. O-ring
32. 1–2 Accumulator piston
33. O-ring
34. Spring
35. O-ring
36. 3–4 Accumulator piston
37. O-ring
38. Spring
39. Magnet
40. Gasket
41. Oil pan
42. Shim
43. Detent spring
44. Pipe
T1. 2.1–2.9 ft. lbs.
T2. 26.7–31.1 ft. lbs.
T3. 20.3–27.2 ft. lbs.
T4. 3.6–5.0 ft. lbs.
T5. 16.7–19.5 ft. lbs.
T6. 2.5–3.3 ft. lbs.
T7. 8.7–10.1 ft. lbs.
T8. 5.1–6.5 ft. lbs.
T9. 4.3–5.1 ft. lbs.

Transaxle case assembly

ing compressed air from the release pressure side.

31. Apply compressed air from the operating pressure side and remove 3–4 accumlator, 1–2 accumulator, 2–3 accumulator and N–D accumulator.

32. Remove the range select lever and the detent spring.

33. Remove the parking rod together with the manual lever. Then remove the manual shaft by removing the retaining pin. Do not damage the lips of the press fitted oil seal in the case.

34. Remove the neutral safety switch and electrical harness.

35. Remove the differential side retainer from the converter case section. Hold the differential case assembly by hand to avoid damaging the retainer mounting hole of the converter case and speedometer gear.

36. Remove the stub shaft. Do not reuse the circlip.

37. Remove the differential case assembly.

38. Remove snapring and the speedometer driven gear. Tap out the speedometer shaft to the outside of the case and remove the oil seal.

39. Remove the transfer clutch from the extension section by lightly tapping the end of the rear driveshaft. Do not to damage the oil seal in the extension section.

40. Remove the transfer pipe. Remove duty solenoid C and the transfer valve body.

41. Using a suitable tool remove the roller bearing assembly from the extension section.

Unit Disassembly and Assembly

REDUCTION DRIVE GEAR ASSEMBLY

Disassembly

1. Remove the seal rings.
2. Remove the outer snapring.
3. Using a suitable press, remove the reduction drive gear from the reduction shaft.
4. Using a suitable press, remove the bearing assembly from the reduction shaft.

Inspection

1. Check reduction shaft and gears for nicks or damage.
2. Make sure each component is free from dirt or grease.
3. Check bearing assembly for wear or damage.
4. Replace defective components as necessary.

Assembly

1. Using a suitable tool press install the bearing assembly and reduction drive gear to the reduction shaft.
2. On 4WD vehicles, install the snapring securely in the snapring groove on the shaft.

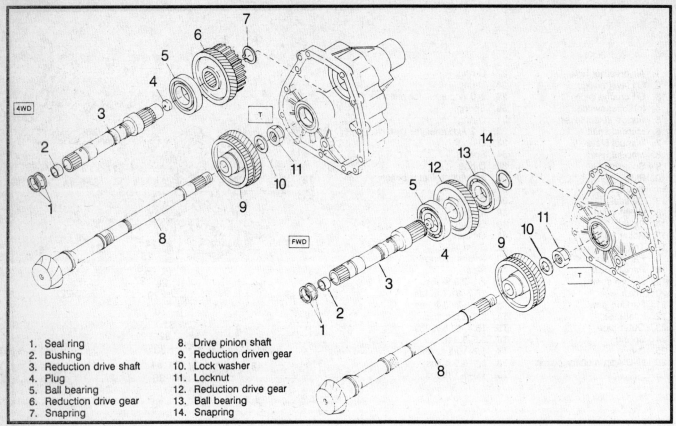

1. Seal ring
2. Bushing
3. Reduction drive shaft
4. Plug
5. Ball bearing
6. Reduction drive gear
7. Snapring
8. Drive pinion shaft
9. Reduction driven gear
10. Lock washer
11. Locknut
12. Reduction drive gear
13. Ball bearing
14. Snapring

Reduction gear assembly

3. On FWD vehicles, press install the bearing assembly using a press, then install the snapring to the snapring groove on the shaft.
4. Install the 2 seal rings.

CONTROL VALVE BODY

Disassembly

1. Remove the shift solenoid assembly (shift solenoid 1, 2 and 3) and duty solenoid A from the upper valve body.
2. Remove the duty solenoid B and fluid temperature sensor from the lower valve body.
3. Separate the upper valve body and lower valve body. Do not lose the 9 steel balls contained in the upper valve body. Do not lose an orifice and a strainer contained in the lower valve body.

NOTE: During ordinary servicing, clean the control valve bodies in this manner, without further disassembly. In the event of a seized clutch or a contamination problem, disassemble the control valve bodies further and clean the component parts.

Inspection

1. Clean all parts thoroughly in clean solvent and blow dry with compressed air.
2. Inspect all valve and plug bores for scores. Check all fluid passages for obstructions. Inspect all mating surfaces for burrs and scores. If needed, use crocus cloth to polish valve and plugs. Avoid rounding the sharp edges of the valves and plugs with the crocus cloth.
3. Inspect all springs for distortion. Check all valves and plugs for free movement in their respective bores.

4. Roll the manual valve on a flat surface to check for a bent condition. Replace any parts as necessary.

Assembly

1. Install the upper valve body to the lower valve body. Be sure to properly position the steel balls, orifice and strainer.
2. Install the duty solenoid B and fluid temperature sensor to the lower valve body.
3. Install the shift solenoid assembly (shift solenoid 1, 2 and 3) and duty solenoid A to the upper valve body.
4. Tighten the locating bolts and the upper-lower valve body retaining bolts to 6.5 ft. lbs.

OIL PUMP

Disassembly

1. Remove the oil seal retainer, O-ring and oil seal.
2. Remove the oil pump cover. Lightly tap the end of the stator shaft to remove the cover.
3. Remove the retainer and return spring. Remove the rotor, 2 van rings and 9 vane assemblies.
4. Remove the cam ring and control piston. Remove the O-ring, friction ring, 2 side seals and plain seal.
5. Remove all seal rings.

Inspection

1. Make sure all components are free from dirt or grease.
2. Using a micrometer, measure the height of the rotor, vanes, control piston and cam ring in at least 4 positions. Measure the height at 1 place for each of the 9 vanes. Remove all seals and friction ring when measuring.
3. Using a depth gauge, measure the depth of the oil pump housing from the contact/sliding surface of component parts.

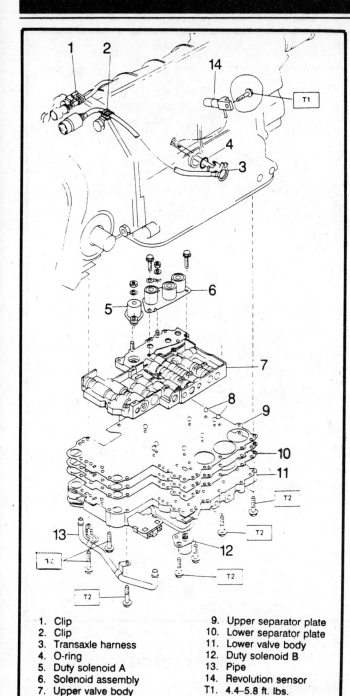

1. Clip
2. Clip
3. Transaxle harness
4. O-ring
5. Duty solenoid A
6. Solenoid assembly
7. Upper valve body
8. Ball
9. Upper separator plate
10. Lower separator plate
11. Lower valve body
12. Duty solenoid B
13. Pipe
14. Revolution sensor
T1. 4.4–5.8 ft. lbs.
T2. 5.1–6.5 ft. lbs.

and attach to the cam ring. Then install them into the oil pump housing.

2. Install the vane ring, rotor, vanes and vane ring into the housing.

3. Install the return spring, retainer between the housing and cam ring.

4. Install the control piston to the oil pump housing. Install the seal in the piston groove, with the red seals facing the top side.

5. Position the rotor at the center of the housing bore. Apply transmission fluid to each vane in the pump housing.

6. Align both pivots with the pivot holes of the cover and install the cover. Torque retaining bolts to 17–19 ft. lbs. Turn the oil pump shaft to check for smooth rotation of the rotor.

7. Install the oil seal retainer and seal rings after adjusting the drive pinion backlash and tooth contact.

DRIVE PINION SHAFT

Disassembly

1. Straighten the staked portion of the locknut and remove the locknut while locking the rear spline portion of the shaft. Remove the drive pinion collar.

2. Using a suitable press, separate the rear roller bearing and outer race from the shaft.

3. Using a suitable press, separate the front roller bearing from the shaft.

Inspection

1. Check shaft and pinion for nicks or damage.
2. Make sure each component is free from dirt or grease.
3. Check bearing assembly for wear or damage.
4. Replace defective components as necessary.

Assembly

1. Measure dimension A of the drive pinion shaft.

2. Using a press, install the roller bearing in position. Do not change the relative positions of the outer race and bearing cone.

3. After installing the O-ring to the shaft, attach the drive pinion collar to the shaft. Do not damage the O-ring.

4. Tighten the lock washer and locknut. Torque locknut to 80–86 ft. lbs. When using special tool 499787100 or equivalent and torque wrench, tighten to 65 ft. lbs.

5. Measure the starting torque of the bearing. Make sure the starting torque is within the specified range. If out of the allowable range, replace the roller bearing. The starting torque specification is 16.4 in. lbs.

6. Stake the locknut securely at 2 places. Measure dimension B of the drive pinion shaft.

7. Determine the thickness of the drive pinion shim. Use the formula of thickness equals 0.256 in. (6.5mm) ± 0.0004 in. (0.0125mm), 0.0024 in. (0.0625mm) on Legacy, subtracted from dimension B minus dimension A. Add the correct amount of shims to attain the correct specification do not use more than 3 shims.

Valve body

4. Make sure that the clearances are within the specified wear limits. If the wear limit is exceeded replace the necessary components.

5. The standard valve and specified wear limits are as follows for the rotor, control piston and vanes 0.0012–0.0017 in. standard valve and 0.0021 in. wear limit.

6. The standard valve and specified wear limit for the cam ring is 0.0004–0.0009 in. standard valve and 0.0013 in. wear limit.

Assembly

1. Coat both the O-ring and friction ring with petroleum jelly

REVERSE CLUTCH

Disassembly

1. Remove the snapring and remove the retaining plate, drive plates, driven plates and dish plate.

2. Using suitable tools remove the snapring and remove the spring retainer and springs.

3. Remove the piston by applying compressed air.

Inspection

1. Check drive plate for wear and damage.

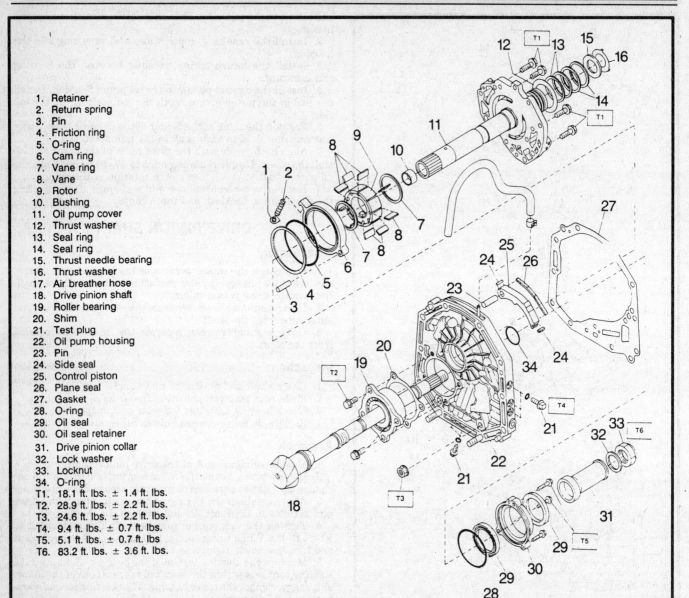

1. Retainer
2. Return spring
3. Pin
4. Friction ring
5. O-ring
6. Cam ring
7. Vane ring
8. Vane
9. Rotor
10. Bushing
11. Oil pump cover
12. Thrust washer
13. Seal ring
14. Seal ring
15. Thrust needle bearing
16. Thrust washer
17. Air breather hose
18. Drive pinion shaft
19. Roller bearing
20. Shim
21. Test plug
22. Oil pump housing
23. Pin
24. Side seal
25. Control piston
26. Plane seal
27. Gasket
28. O-ring
29. Oil seal
30. Oil seal retainer
31. Drive pinion collar
32. Lock washer
33. Locknut
34. O-ring
T1. 18.1 ft. lbs. ± 1.4 ft. lbs.
T2. 28.9 ft. lbs. ± 2.2 ft. lbs.
T3. 24.6 ft. lbs. ± 2.2 ft. lbs.
T4. 9.4 ft. lbs. ± 0.7 ft. lbs.
T5. 5.1 ft. lbs. ± 0.7 ft. lbs
T6. 83.2 ft. lbs. ± 3.6 ft. lbs.

Oil pump

2. Check snapring, return spring and spring retainer for wear.
3. Check seal and seal ring for damage or wear.
4. Check piston check ball for correct operation.

Assembly

1. Using suitable tools assemble piston, return springs, spring retainer and snapring.
2. Install the dish plate, driven plates, drive plates, retaining plate in order and install the snapring.
3. Apply compressed air to the oil hole and check the reverse clutch for smooth operation.
4. Measure clearance for retaining plate selection by placing the same thickness of shim on both sides to prevent retaining plate from tilting.
5. The standard valve is 0.020–0.031 in. and the allowable limit is 0.047 in.

HIGH CLUTCH

Disassembly

1. Remove the snapring and remove the retaining plate, drive plates and driven plates.
2. Using suitable tools remove the snapring and take out the spring retainer assembly.
3. Apply compressed air to the clutch drum to remove the piston.

Inspection

1. Check drive plate for wear and damage.
2. Check snapring, return spring and spring retainer for wear.
3. Check seal and seal ring for damage or wear.
4. Check piston check ball for correct operation.

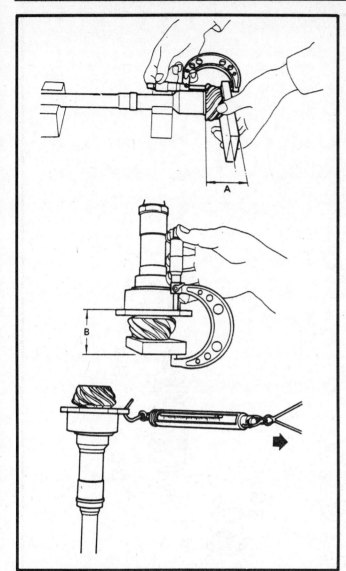

Pinion backlash procedure

Assembly

1. Using suitable tools assemble piston, return springs, spring retainer and snapring.
2. Install the thin driven plate, drive plates, driven plates, retaining plate in order and install the snapring.
3. Apply compressed air to the oil hole and check the reverse clutch for smooth operation.
4. Measure clearance for retaining plate selection by placing the same thickness of shim on both sides to prevent retaining plate from tilting.
5. The standard valve is 0.071–0.087 in. and the allowable limit is 0.102 in.

FORWARD CLUTCH DRUM

Disassembly

1. Remove 2 snaprings from the forward clutch drum.
2. Remove the retaining plate, drive plates, driven plates and dish plate from the forward clutch drum.
3. Remove the inner snapring from the forward clutch drum.
4. Remove the retaining plate, drive plates, driven plates and dish plate from the overrunning clutch assembly.

5. Compress the spring retainer and remove the snapring from the forward clutch assembly.
6. Temporarily install the one way clutch inner race to the forward clutch drum and apply compressed air to remove the overrunning piston and forward piston.
7. Remove the one way clutch assembly and the snapring.
8. Remove the needle bearing assembly and the snapring.

Inspection

1. Check drive plate for wear and damage.
2. Check snapring, return spring and spring retainer for wear.
3. Check seal and seal ring for damage or wear.
4. Check piston and drum check ball for correct operation.

Assembly

1. Position the forward piston and overrunning piston to the forward clutch drum. Align the forward piston cutout portion with the spline of the drum.
2. Install the springs and retainer on the piston with a suitable tool and install the snapring.
3. Install the dish plate, driven plates, drive plates and retaining plate and secure with the snapring for overrunning clutch assembly.
4. Install the dish plates, driven plates, drive plates and retaining plate and secure with the snapring for the forward clutch assembly.
5. Install the snapring for front planetary carrier.
6. Check the forward clutch and overrunning clutch for operation by setting the one way clutch inner race and apply compressed air.

NOTE: Before measuring clearance, place the same thickness of shim on both sides to prevent retaining plate for tilting.

7. When checking clearance for the forward clutch the standard valve is 0.0177–0.0335 in. and the allowable limit is 0.063 in.
8. When checking clearance for the overrunning clutch the standard valve is 0.039–0.055 in. and the allowable limit is 0.079 in.
9. If the clearance is out of the specified range, select a proper retaining plate so that the standard clearance can be obtained.
10. Install the needle bearing and secure with the snapring. Install the 1–2 one way clutch assembly and plate and secure with the snapring.
11. Set the inner race. Make sure that the forward clutch is free in the clockwise direction and locked in the counterclockwise direction, as viewed from the front of the vehicle.

ONE WAY CLUTCH OUTER RACE

Disassembly

1. Remove the snapring.
2. Remove the 3–4 one way clutch assembly.

Inspection

1. Check the sliding surface for nicks or wear also check for proper operation.
2. Check inner race for wear or damage.
3. Replace components as necessary.

Assembly

1. Assemble the 3–4 one way clutch and secure with the snapring.
2. Assemble the rear internal gear and secure the outer race. Make sure that the internal gear is locked in the clockwise direction and free to rotate in the counterclockwise direction.

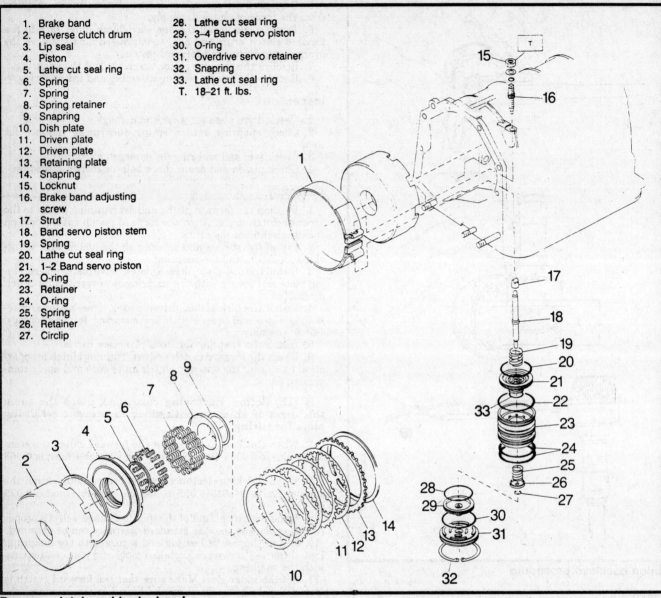

1. Brake band
2. Reverse clutch drum
3. Lip seal
4. Piston
5. Lathe cut seal ring
6. Spring
7. Spring
8. Spring retainer
9. Snapring
10. Dish plate
11. Driven plate
12. Driven plate
13. Retaining plate
14. Snapring
15. Locknut
16. Brake band adjusting screw
17. Strut
18. Band servo piston stem
19. Spring
20. Lathe cut seal ring
21. 1–2 Band servo piston
22. O-ring
23. Retainer
24. O-ring
25. Spring
26. Retainer
27. Circlip
28. Lathe cut seal ring
29. 3–4 Band servo piston
30. O-ring
31. Overdrive servo retainer
32. Snapring
33. Lathe cut seal ring
T. 18–21 ft. lbs.

Reverse clutch and brake band

SERVO PISTON

Disassembly

1. Remove the spring and the 3–4 band servo piston.
2. While compressing the retainer, remove the snapring. Then remove the retainer, spring and stem.
3. Remove the band 1–2 servo piston.

Inspection

1. Check each component for wear or damage.
2. Check the O-ring and seal ring for damage.
3. Replace components as necessary.

Assembly

1. Install the 1–2 band servo piston to the retainer and insert the stem.
2. Install the spring and retainer on the piston. Install the snapring securely while compressing the spring.
3. Install the 3–4 band servo piston.

4. Install the spring securely to the 1–2 band servo piston.

DIFFERENTIAL CASE ASSEMBLY

Disassembly

1. Using a suitable press remove the taper roller bearing. Be careful not to damage the speedometer drive gear.
2. Secure the case in a vise and remove the crown or ring gear bolts, then separate the crown or ring gear from upper and lower differential case.
3. Remove the retaining pin and shaft. Remove the differential bevel gear, washer and differential bevel pinion.

Inspection

1. Make sure all components are free from dirt or grease.
2. Check for damaged or worn gears.
3. Check for a cracked or damaged gear case.
4. Replace components as necessary.

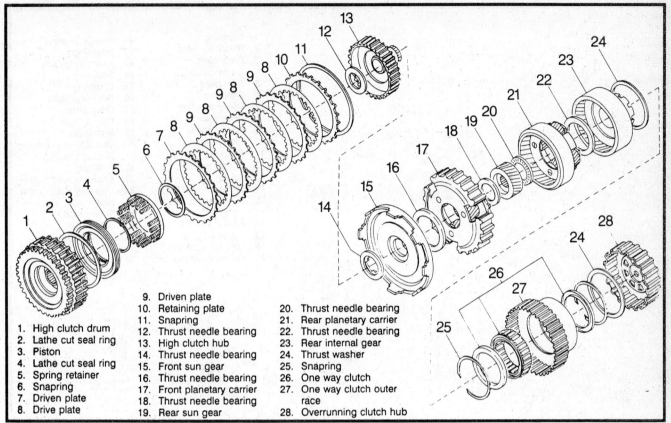

9. Driven plate
10. Retaining plate
11. Snapring
12. Thrust needle bearing
13. High clutch hub
14. Thrust needle bearing
15. Front sun gear
16. Thrust needle bearing
17. Front planetary carrier
18. Thrust needle bearing
19. Rear sun gear

1. High clutch drum
2. Lathe cut seal ring
3. Piston
4. Lathe cut seal ring
5. Spring retainer
6. Snapring
7. Driven plate
8. Drive plate

20. Thrust needle bearing
21. Rear planetary carrier
22. Thrust needle bearing
23. Rear internal gear
24. Thrust washer
25. Snapring
26. One way clutch
27. One way clutch outer race
28. Overrunning clutch hub

High clutch and planetary gear

Assembly

1. Install the washer, differential bevel gear, differential bevel pinion in the upper differential case. Insert the pinion shaft and install the retaining pin.

NOTE: Make sure to stake the retaining pin.

2. Install the washer and differential bevel gear to the lower differential case.

3. Install the upper differential case assembly to the lower differential case assembly.

4. Install the crown gear or ring gear. Torque the crown or ring gear retaining bolts to 42–49 ft. lbs.

5. Measure the gear backlash by inserting a dial gauge through the access window of the case. The standard value specification is 0.0051–0.0071 in.

6. Install the speedometer drive gear and taper roller bearing assembly with a suitable press. Position the locking end of the speedometer drive gear correctly.

TRANSFER CLUTCH

Disassembly

1. Remove the seal ring.
2. Using a suitable press remove the bearing assembly.
3. Remove the snapring, pressure plate, drive plates and driven plates.
4. Remove the snapring and spring retainer assembly.
5. Apply compressed air to the rear stub shaft on the transfer clutch assembly to remove piston.

Inspection

1. Check the drive plate for wear and damage.

2. Check the snapring for wear, return spring for permanent set and breakage.
3. Check spring retainer for deformation.
4. Check the seal ring for damage.

Assembly

1. Install the seal ring to the clutch piston.
2. Install the piston and spring retainer and snapring.
3. Install the driven plates, drive plates, pressure plate and secure with a snapring.
4. Apply compressed air to see if the assembled parts move smoothly. Before measuring clearance, place the same thickness of shim on both sides to prevent pressure plate from tilting.
5. When checking the clearance the standard valve is 0.008–0.035 in. and the allowable limit 0.063 in. If the clearance is not within the specified range, select a proper pressure plate.
6. Using a suitable press install the bearing assembly.
7. Coat the seal ring with petroleum jelly and install it in the seal ring groove of the shaft. Do not expand the seal ring excessively when installing.

Transaxle Assembly

1. Install the washer and snapring to the speedometer shaft and set the oil seal in the converter case section. Install the shaft to the converter case.
2. Install the speedometer driven gear to the speedometer shaft and secure with snapring.
3. Install the front oil seal to the converter case.
4. Install the differential assembly to the case.
5. Install the snapring to the stub shaft, insert the shaft into the differential assembly and tap it into position.

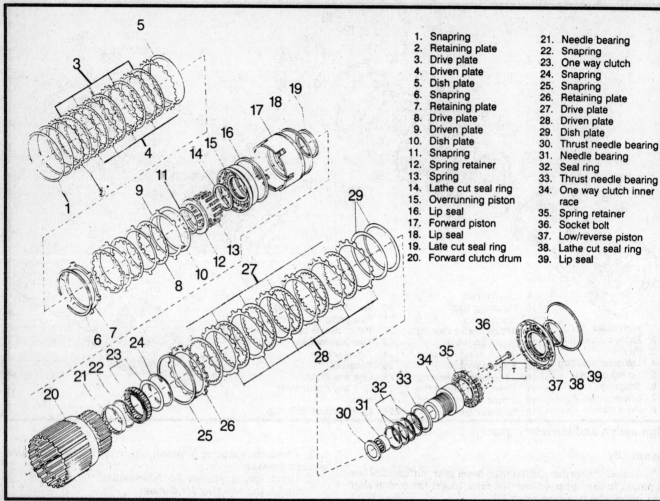

1. Snapring
2. Retaining plate
3. Drive plate
4. Driven plate
5. Dish plate
6. Snapring
7. Retaining plate
8. Drive plate
9. Driven plate
10. Dish plate
11. Snapring
12. Spring retainer
13. Spring
14. Lathe cut seal ring
15. Overrunning piston
16. Lip seal
17. Forward piston
18. Lip seal
19. Late cut seal ring
20. Forward clutch drum
21. Needle bearing
22. Snapring
23. One way clutch
24. Snapring
25. Snapring
26. Retaining plate
27. Drive plate
28. Driven plate
29. Dish plate
30. Thrust needle bearing
31. Needle bearing
32. Seal ring
33. Thrust needle bearing
34. One way clutch inner race
35. Spring retainer
36. Socket bolt
37. Low/reverse piston
38. Lathe cut seal ring
39. Lip seal

Forward clutch and low/reverse brake

6. Check the thrust play. The standard valve is 0.012–0.020 in. If no play is felt, check whether the shaft is fully inserted. If shaft insertion is correct, replace the stub shaft. Be sure to use a new snapring.

7. Wrap vinyl tape or equivalent around the splined portion of the stub shaft.

8. Install the oil seal and outer race (taper roller bearing) to the differential side retainer. Screw in the retainer without O-ring after coating the threads with oil.

9. Using suitable tools, screw in the retainer until light contact is felt. Screw in the righthand side slightly deeper than the lefthand side.

10. Check the gear backlash adjustment and tooth contact check at this point of the procedure as follows:

a. Assemble the drive pinion assembly to the oil pump housing. Be careful not to bend the shims and not to force the pinion against the housing bore.

b. Torque 4 bolts to 27–31 ft. lbs. to secure the bearing assembly.

c. Install the oil pump housing assembly to the converter case and secure evenly by tightening 4 bolts to 23–27 ft. lbs.

d. Rotate the drive pinion several times. Tighten the lefthand retainer until contact is felt while rotating the shaft. Then loosen the righthand retainer. Keep tightening the lefthand retainer and loosening the righthand retainer until the pinion shaft can no longer be turned. This is the zero state.

e. After the zero state is established, back off the lefthand retainer 3 notches and secure it with the locking tab. Then

back off the righthand retainer and retighten until it stops. Repeat this procedure several times. Tighten the righthand retainer 1¾ notches further. This sets the preload, secure the retainer with its locking tab. Turning the retainer by 1 tooth changes the backlash about 0.0020 in. (0.05mm).

f. Turn the drive pinion several rotations and check to see if the backlash is within the standard value. The standard valve is 0.0051–0.0071 in. After confirming that the backlash is correct, check the tooth contact.

g. Apply marking compound (red lead or suitable dye) evenly to surfaces of 3–5 teeth of the crown gear. Rotate the drive pinion in the forward and reverse directions several times. Then remove the oil pump housing and check the tooth contact pattern. If tooth contact is not correct, readjust the backlash or shim thickness.

h. If tooth contact is correct, mark the retainer position and loosen it. After installing the O-ring, screw in the retainer to the marked position. Then tighten the lock plate to the 17–20 ft. lbs.

11. Install the seal pipe with a new seal to the converter case.

12. Install 2 oil seals to the oil seal retainer with a suitable tool.

13. Install the O-ring to the oil seal retainer with petroleum jelly. Install the seal to the oil pump housing bore.

14. Install the oil seal retainer. Torque retaining bolts 4–6 ft. lbs.

15. Apply petroleum jelly to the groove on the oil pump cover, install all seal rings. Install the seal ring after compressing and rub petroleum jelly into the seal ring to avoid expansion. The

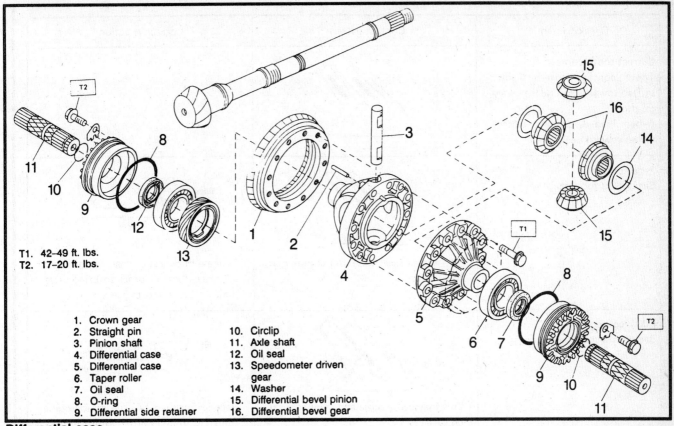

T1. 42–49 ft. lbs.
T2. 17–20 ft. lbs.

1. Crown gear
2. Straight pin
3. Pinion shaft
4. Differential case
5. Differential case
6. Taper roller
7. Oil seal
8. O-ring
9. Differential side retainer
10. Circlip
11. Axle shaft
12. Oil seal
13. Speedometer driven gear
14. Washer
15. Differential bevel pinion
16. Differential bevel gear

Differential case

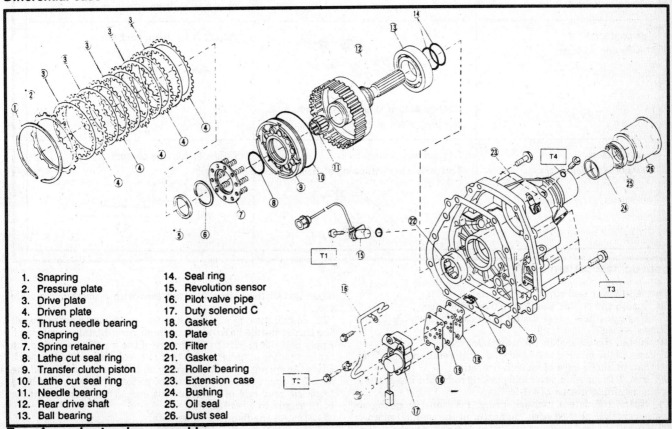

1. Snapring
2. Pressure plate
3. Drive plate
4. Driven plate
5. Thrust needle bearing
6. Snapring
7. Spring retainer
8. Lathe cut seal ring
9. Transfer clutch piston
10. Lathe cut seal ring
11. Needle bearing
12. Rear drive shaft
13. Ball bearing
14. Seal ring
15. Revolution sensor
16. Pilot valve pipe
17. Duty solenoid C
18. Gasket
19. Plate
20. Filter
21. Gasket
22. Roller bearing
23. Extension case
24. Bushing
25. Oil seal
26. Dust seal

Transfer and extension assembly

Checking item	Contact pattern	Corrective action
Correct tooth contact Tooth contact pattern slightly shifted toward toe under no-load rotation. (When loaded, contact pattern moves toward heel.)		
Face contact Backlash is too large.	This may cause noise and chipping at tooth ends.	Increase thickness of drive pinion hight adjusting shim in order to bring drive pinion close to crown gear.
Flank contact Backlash is too small.	This may cause noise and stepped wear on surfaces.	Reduce thickness of drive pinion hight adjusting shim in order to move drive pinion away from crown gear.
Toe contact (Inside end contact)	Contact area is small. This may cause chipping at toe ends.	Adjust as for flank contact.
Heel contact (Outside end contact)	Contact area is small. This may cause chipping at heel ends.	Adjust as for face contact.

Tooth contact pattern chart

upper and lower seal rings are diameter.

16. Install the rubber seal to the converter case.

17. Using suitable press install the bearing assembly to the transaxle case.

18. Install the oil seal in the transaxle case.

19. Install the manual plate and shaft with retaining pin. After installation, make sure of smooth operation.

20. Install the manual lever and parking rod to the inside shaft torque retaining nut to 27–31 ft. lbs.

21. Install the detent manual spring. Position the spring so that is center is aligned with the center of the manual plate.

22. Install the seal ring and seal to the low and reverse piston.

Then install the piston into the case with a press or suitable tool.

23. Install the one way clutch inner race. Using a press, install the thrust needle bearing to the inner race. Install 4 seal rings. Apply petroleum jelly to the groove of the inner race and to the seal ring after installation, so that the seal ring will not expand. Place the spring retainer assembly on the inner race. Install the spring to the recessed portion of the piston. Then tighten 8 bolts from the rear side of the transaxle case. Torque the retaining bolts evenly to 17–19 ft. lbs.

24. Install the band servo assembly.

25. Install the servo retainer into position and secure with a

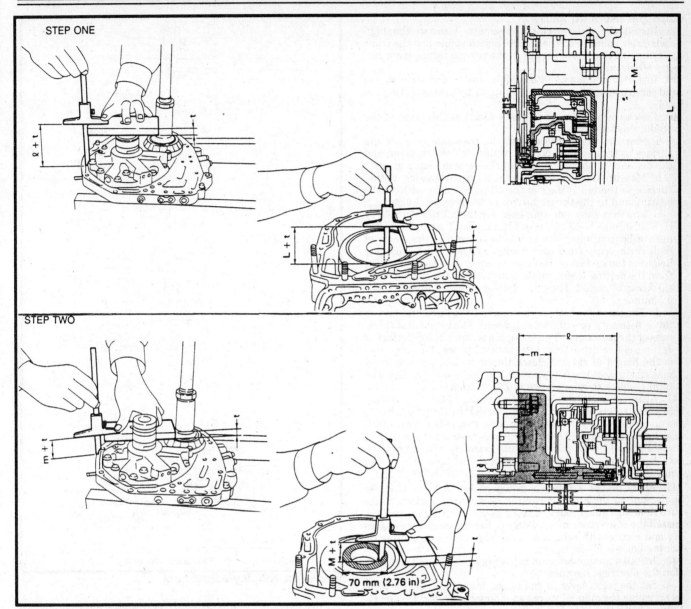

STEP ONE

STEP TWO

70 mm (2.76 in)

Total endplay adjustment procedure

snapring.

26. Install the low and reverse brake assembly. Install 2 dish plates, driven plates, drive plates, retaining plate and secure with a snapring. Be careful of the installation of the dish plate. Apply compressed air to check for correct operation. Before measuring clearance, place the same thickness of shim on both sides to prevent retaining plate from tilting. Check the clearance the standard value is 0.043–0.067 in. and the allowable limit is 0.106 in.

27. Install the thrust needle bearing to the inner race.

28. Install the forward clutch drum assembly. Install carefully while rotating the drum slowly do not damage the seal ring. Installation is complete when the drum recedes 0.098 in. from the inner race surface.

29. Install the overrunning clutch hub. Install the thrust needle bearing and thrust washer with petroleum jelly and then install them together. Make sure that the splines are engaged correctly.

30. Install the one way clutch outer race assembly. Make sure the forward clutch splines are engaged correctly.

31. Install the rear internal gear. Install the thrust needle bearing and thrust washer to the gear with petroleum jelly and install the gear while rotating it. Securely install the bearing to the overrunning clutch hub. Installation is complete when the snapring top surface of the forward clutch drum recedes approximately 0.138 in.

32. Install the rear planetary carrier. Install the thrust needle bearing to the inside of the carrier with petroleum jelly. Then install the carrier while rotating slowly.

33. Install the rear sun gear with the oil hole facing up.

34. Install the front planetary carrier. Position the thrust needle bearings to both sides of the carrier with petroleum jelly. Install the carrier carefully, while aligning with the splines of the forward clutch drum and while rotating the pinion.

35. Install the front sun gear. Position the thrust needle bearing to the gear and install the gear while turning slowly.

36. Install the high clutch hub. Position the thrust needle bearing to the hub with petroleum jelly and install the hub by correctly engaging the splines of the front planetary carrier.

37. Install the high clutch assembly. Correctly install the high

clutch hub and clutch splines.

38. Install the reverse clutch assembly. Position the high clutch outer spline with the reverse clutch spline and the front sun gear with the cutout portion of the reverse clutch drum correctly when installing.

39. Install the brake band assembly. Install the strut to the band servo piston stem tighten it temporarily to avoid tilting the band.

40. Check the adjustment of total endplay at this point of the procedure as follows:

a. Measure the distance from the transaxle case mating surface to the recessed portion of the high clutch drum and the distance to the top surface of the reverse clutch drum.

b. Measure the distance from the oil pump housing mating surface to the top surface of the oil pump cover with needle bearing and to the thrust surface of the reverse clutch.

c. The first equation (unit:mm) for the calculation is T = (L + 0.4mm) – l – (0.25mm–0.55mm). The T symbol is thickness of bearing race. The L symbol is depth of the recess of high cluth drum from case mating surface. The l symbol is height of top surface of the oil pump cover with needle bearing from the mating surface of the housing. The 0.4 symbol is the thickness of gasket. The total endplay standard valve is 0.25–0.55mm.

d. The second equation (unit:mm) for the calculation is t = (M + 0.4mm) – m – (0.55mm–0.9mm). The t symbol is thickness of thrust washer. The M symbol is depth of top surface of reverse clutch drum from case mating surface. The m symbol is the height of reverse clutch thrust surface from housing mating surface. The 0.4 symbol is the thickness of gasket. The total endplay standard valve is 0.55–0.9mm.

41. After completing endplay adjustment, insert the bearing race in the recess of the high clutch. Install the thrust washer to the oil pump cover with petroleum jelly. Install both parts with dowel pins aligned. Make sure no clearance exists at the mating surface. Install the oil pump housing assembly with a new gasket. Any clearance suggests a damaged seal ring. Secure the housing with 2 retaining nuts torque to 23–27 ft. lbs.

42. Apply proper amount of liquid gasket (3 bond 1215) or equivalent to the entire converter case mating surface. Make sure that the rubber seal and seal pipe are installed in position. Install the converter case assembly to the transaxle case assembly and secure with retaining bolts. The correct torque for retaining bolts is 22–26 ft. lbs.

43. Install 4 accumulators in correct position. Install and position the electrical harness.

44. Set the select lever in 2nd range. Install the control valve by engaging the manual valve and manual lever, tighten the retaining bolts evenly to 5–6 ft. lbs.

NOTE: There are 11 short and 8 long control valve retaining bolts.

44. Install the oil strainer to the control valve. Tighten the retaining bolts 5–6 ft. lbs. Secure the 5 electrical connectors and the oil cooler outlet pipe.

45. Position the magnet correctly (righthand corner about 4–6 inches from drain plug) in the oil pan and evenly torque the bolts to 3 ft. lbs.

46. Install the extension case filter in correct position in the extension case section.

47. Install the transfer clutch valve assembly and secure with retaining bolts. The correct torque for retaining bolts is 5–6 ft. lbs.

48. Install the pipe and clamp securely. Install the transfer clutch assembly to the case. Insert the transfer clutch assembly fully into position until the bearing shoulder bottoms.

49. Install the revolution sensor to the transaxle case on FWD vehicles (internal mount).

50. Install the reduction driven gear. Install the parking pawl and shaft, position the select lever in the **P** range and tighten

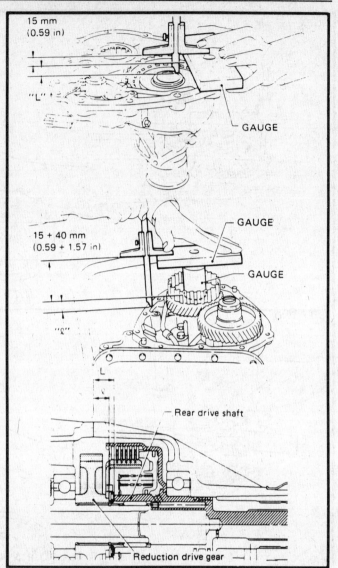

Extension endplay adjustment

the drive pinion locknut. The correct torque is 69–75 ft. lbs. After tightening, stake the locknut securely.

51. Install the reduction drive gear assembly. Insert it fully into position until the bearing shoulder bottoms.

52. Check the adjustment of extension endplay at this point of the procedure as follows:

a. Measure the distance from the transaxle case mating surface to the reduction drive gear end surface. On FWD vehicles measure the distance from the transaxle case mating surface to the bearing end face.

b. Measure the distance from the extension case mating surface to the rear driveshaft end face. On FWD vehicles measure the distance from the cover case mating to the bearing mounting surface.

c. The equation (unit:mm) for the calculation is T = (L + 0.4mm) – l – (0.05mm to 0.25mm). The T symbol is thickness of thrust bearing. On FWD vehicles it is the thickness of the washer. The L symbol is the distance of rear driveshaft end face from extension case mating surface. On FWD vehicles it is the depth of bearing mounting face from the cover case mating surface. The l symbol is the height of reduction drive gear end surface from transaxle case mating surface. On FWD vehicles it is the height of bearing end face from transaxle case mating surface. The 0.4 symbol thickness of gasket. The total endplay standard valve is 0.05–0.25mm.

53. On 4WD vehicles, install the selected thrust needle bearing to the end surface of reduction drive gear with petroleum jelly. Install the parking return spring. Temporarily remove the transfer clutch from the extension case. Install the needle bearing on the reduction driveshaft and then install transfer clutch to the transfer clutch hub. Be sure to engage the spline teeth correctly. With new gasket install the extension case to the transaxle case. Torque the retaining bolts to 17–19 ft. lbs.

NOTE: After inserting the extension case halfway, connect the connector for duty solenoid C. Make sure not to damage wire during installation.

54. On FWD vehicles, install the selected aluminum washer to the cover case with petroleum jelly. Install the parking return spring. With new gasket install the cover case to the transaxle case. Torque the retaining bolts to 17–19 ft. lbs.
55. Install the revolution sensor on the 4WD vehicles (external mount).
56. Install the neutral safety switch to the transaxle case. Install the projecting portion of the switch in the recessed portion of the case and tighten 3 bolts temporarily.
57. Insert the range selector lever in the shaft and tighten the nut to 26–30 ft. lbs.
58. With the selector lever set to **N** adjust the neutral safety switch so that the hole of range selector lever is aligned with the neutral safety switch hole.
59. When adjustment hole is the correct position tighten retaining bolts to 2.5 ft. lbs.
60. Position and clip electrical transaxle harness, neutral safety switch and revolution sensor 4WD vehicles.
61. Install the oil cooler outlet and inlet pipe. Install the oil dipstick tube with O-ring.
62. After tightening the brake band adjusting screw to 6.5 ft. lbs. (9Nm), back it off 3 turns. Torque the locknut to 18–21 ft. lbs.
63. Install the pitching stopper. Tighten the drain plugs.
64. Install the air breather hose.
65. Insert the input shaft.
66. Install the torque converter assembly. Install the oil pump shaft to the torque converter. Make sure the clip fits securely in its groove.

NOTE: Holding the torque converter assembly by hand, carefully install it to the converter case. Be careful not to damage the bushing. Also, to avoid undue contact between the oil pump shaft bushing and stator shaft portion of the oil pump cover. Rotate the shaft lightly by hand to engage the splines securely.

67. Add the specified amount of the correct oil. After adding oil, insert the oil level gauge into the oil dipstick tube.

SPECIFICATIONS

ACCUMULATOR VALVE SPRING SPECIFICATION
Legacy

Accumulator spring	Outer diameter in. (mm)	Free length in. (mm)
1—2	1.122 (28.5)	1.752 (44.5)
2—3	0.807 (20.5)	1.220 (31.0)
3—4	0.681 (17.3)	1.720 (43.7)
N—D	0.701 (17.8)	1.437 (36.5)

TORQUE SPECIFICATIONS

Part	ft. lbs.	Nm
Brake band locknut	19–21	26
Inhibitor switch retaining bolts	1.5	2.5
Valve body retaining bolts	6.0	8
Oil pan bolts	3.0	4
Crossmember bolts	39–49	53–67
Transaxle-engine bolts	34–40	46–54
Transverse link-front crossmember	43–51	59–69
Transverse link-stabilizer	14–22	20–29
Driveshaft-differential	17–24	24–32
Center bracing retaining	25–33	34–44
Torque converter-drive plate retaining bolts	17–20	23–26
Crown (ring) gear bolts	42–49	57–67
Converter case-transaxle case	22–26	30–36
Oil strainer retaining bolts	6	8
Extension case-transaxle case	17–19	23–26

DRIVE PINION SHIM SELECTION
Legacy

Part Number	Thickness in. (mm)
31451AA050	0.0059 (0.15)
31451AA060	0.0069 (0.18)
31451AA070	0.0080 (0.20)
31451AA080	0.0089 (0.23)
31451AA090	0.0098 (0.25)
31451AA100	0.0108 (0.28)

FRONT CLUTCH THRUST WASHER SELECTION
Except Legacy

Part Number	Thickness in. (mm)
31528X0100	0.075 (1.9)
31528X0101	0.083 (2.1)
31528X0102	0.091 (2.3)
31528X0103	0.098 (2.5)
31528X0104	0.106 (2.7)
31528X0105	0.059 (1.5)
31528X0106	0.067 (1.7)

FORWARD CLUTCH RETAINING PLATE
SELECTION
Legacy

Part Number	Thickness in. (mm)
31567AA010	0.315 (8.0)
31567AA060	0.323 (8.2)
31567AA070	0.331 (8.4)
31567AA080	0.339 (8.6)
31567AA090	0.346 (8.8)
31567AA100	0.354 (9.0)

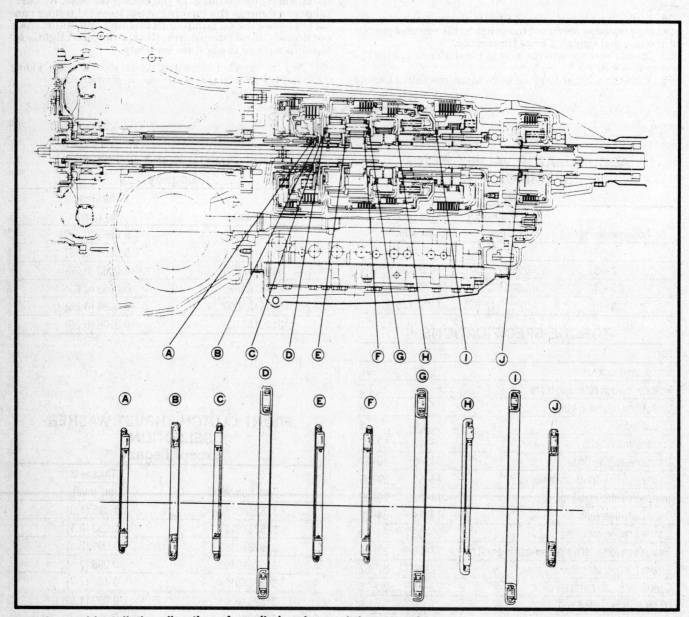

Location and installation direction of needle bearing and thrust washers

398437700	398573600	398603610	398643600
DRIFT	OIL PRESSURE GAUGE ASSY	SOCKET	GAUGE
Front oil seal for converter case.	Oil pressure.	Brake band.	Used to adjust drive pinion. ● Oil pump clearance ● Total end play

398673600	399520105	399703600	399780111
COMPRESSOR	SEAT	PULLER	WRENCH
Snap ring for clutch piston retainer.	Roller bearing (Differential)	● Used to install band servo piston to case. ● Used with COMPRESSOR (498677000).	Axle shaft oil seal holder.

399790110	399893600	498247001	498247100
INSTALLER	PLIER	MAGNET BASE	DIAL GAUGE
Roller bearing (Differential)	Snap ring for spring retainer.	Backlash of gears.	Backlash of gears.

498517000	498627000	498627100	498677000
REPLACER	SEAT	SEAT	COMPRESSOR
Drive pinion front roller bearing.	Snap ring for clutch piston spring retainer.	Used to hold overrunning clutch piston retainer (return spring) when installing snap ring. 4AT	Band servo piston. 4AT

498897100	498937100	499095500	499247300
ADAPTER CP	HOLDER	REMOVER ASSY	INSTALLER
Used when checking oil pressure, etc. 4AT	• Used to tighten/loosen M30 lock nut for drive pinion. • Used when measuring tooth contact pattern. 4AT	• Used to extract axle drive shaft from differential ASSY. • Used with INSTALLER (499247300) 4AT	Drive pinion oil seal. 4AT

499267300	499577000	499787100	499787300
STOPPER PIN	GAUGE	WRENCH ASSY	WRENCH
Used to align range selector lever/inhibitor switch. 4AT	Transfer end play. 4AT	• Used to tighten/loosen M30 lock nut for drive pinion. • Used when measuring hypoid gear backlash. 4AT	Manual shaft. 4AT

99827000	499897000	899524100	899580100
RES.	PL .	PULLER SET	INSTALLER
Speedometer shaft oil seal.	Snap ring.	Reduction driven gear.	Ball bearing for rear drive shaft.
		Puller – Cap	

397471600	398177700	398217700	398227700
HANDLE & DRIFT KIT	INSTALLER	ATTACHMENT SET	WEIGHT
Front and rear bearing cup.	Rear bearing cone.	Differential case.	Side bearing.
1 HANDLE (398477701) 2 DRIFT (398477702) 3 DRIFT 2 (398477703)			

398237700	398417700	398427700	398437700
GAUGE	DRIFT	FLANGE WRENCH	DRIFT
Side bearing.	Oil seal.	Companion Flange	Oil seal.

398457700	398467700	398487700	398507701
ATTACHMENT	DRIFT	DRIFT	GAUGE
Side bearing retainer. 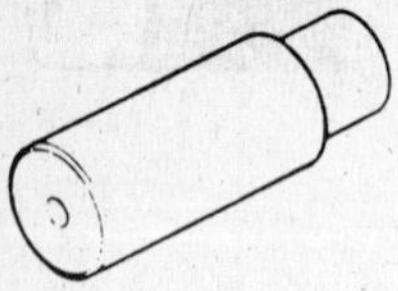	Drive pinion, Pilot bearing, Front bearing cone. 	Side bearing cone. 	Pinion height adjustment. 

398507702	398507703	398507704	398517700
DUMMY SHAFT	DUMMY COLLAR	BLOCK	REPLACER
Pinion height and Preload adjustment. 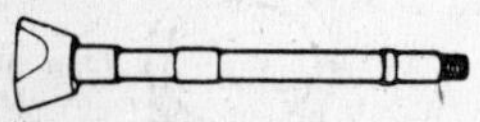	Pinion height and Preload adjustment. 	Pinion height and Preload adjustment. 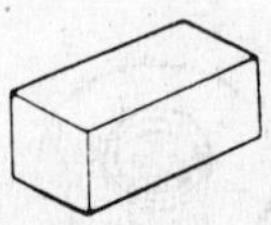	Rear bearing cone. 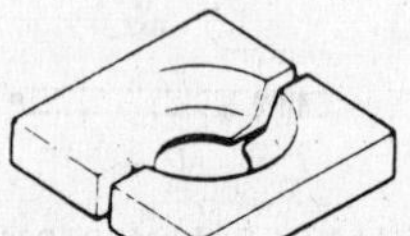
	A14-082		

398527700	399527700	399780104	899580100
PULLEY ASSY	PULLER SET	WEIGHT	INSTALLER
Oil seal, Side bearing cup.	Side bearing cone.	Front bearing cone, Pilot bearing, Companion flange.	Front bearing cone. Pilot bearing.

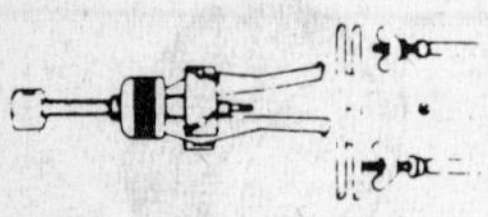

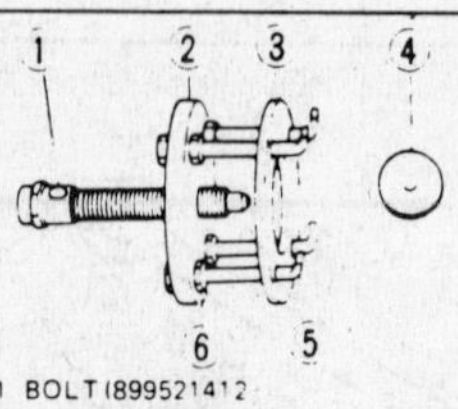

1 BOLT (899521412)
2 PULLER (399527702)
3 HOLDER (399527703)
4 ADAPTER (398497701)
5 BOLT (899520107)
6 NUT (021008000)

OIL FLOW CIRCUIT – P OR N RANGE – MP-T TRANSAXLE

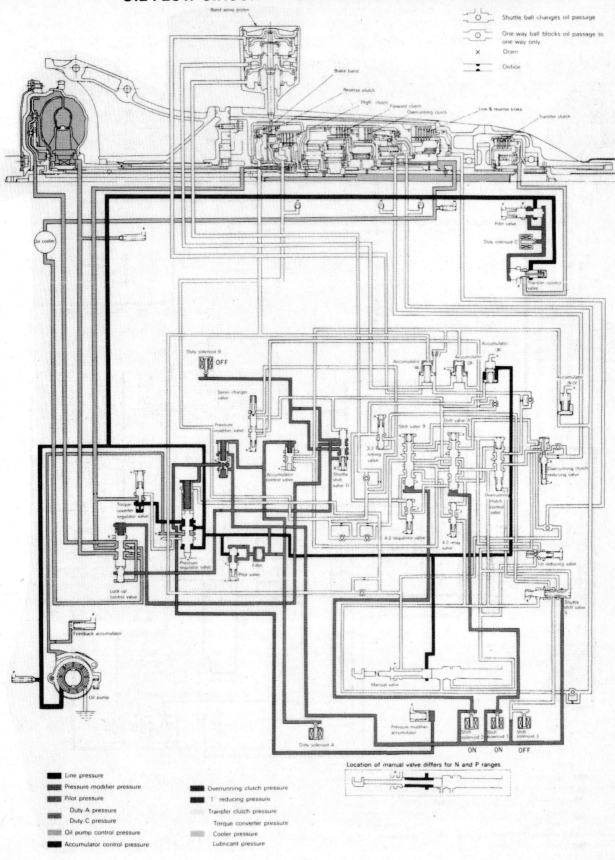

Shuttle ball changes oil passage	
One way ball blocks oil passage to one way only	
Drain	
Orifice	

Line pressure
Pressure modifier pressure
Pilot pressure
Duty-A pressure
Duty-C pressure
Oil pump control pressure
Accumulator control pressure

Overrunning clutch pressure
'1' reducing pressure
Transfer clutch pressure
Torque converter pressure
Cooler pressure
Lubricant pressure

Location of manual valve differs for N and P ranges.

OIL FLOW CIRCUIT — R RANGE — MP-T TRANSAXLE

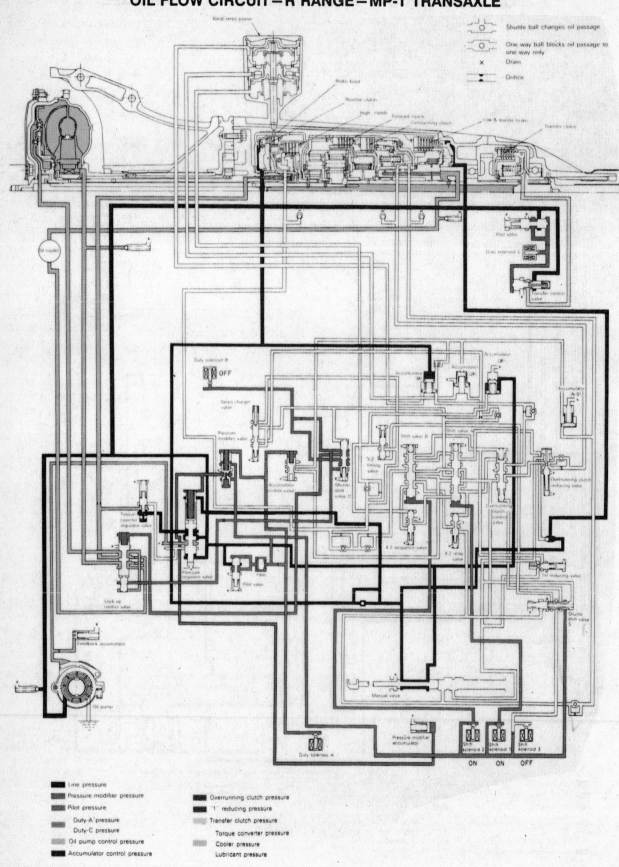

OIL FLOW CIRCUIT—D OR 3 RANGE FIRST SPEED—MP-T TRANSAXLE

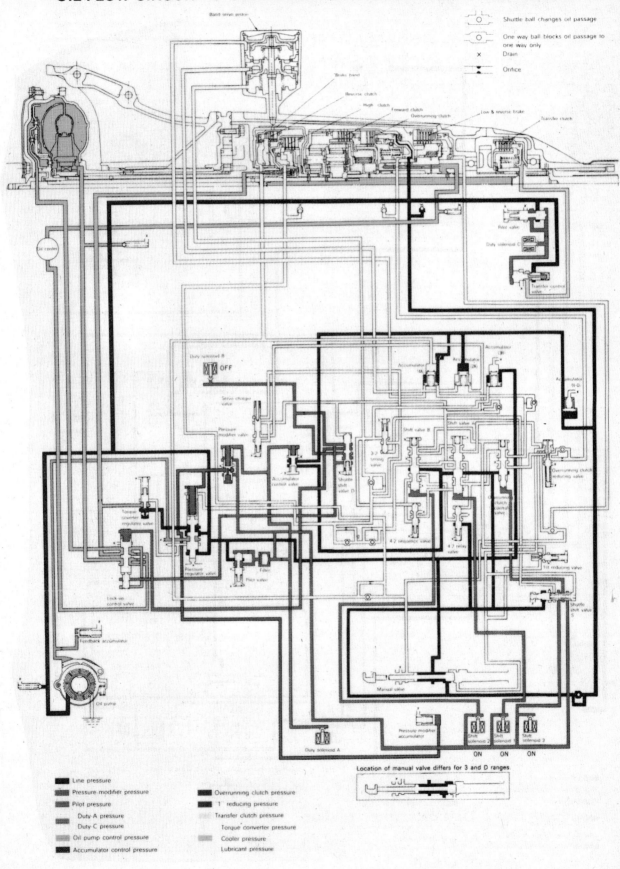

OIL FLOW CIRCUIT – D OR 3 RANGE SECOND SPEED – MP-T TRANSAXLE

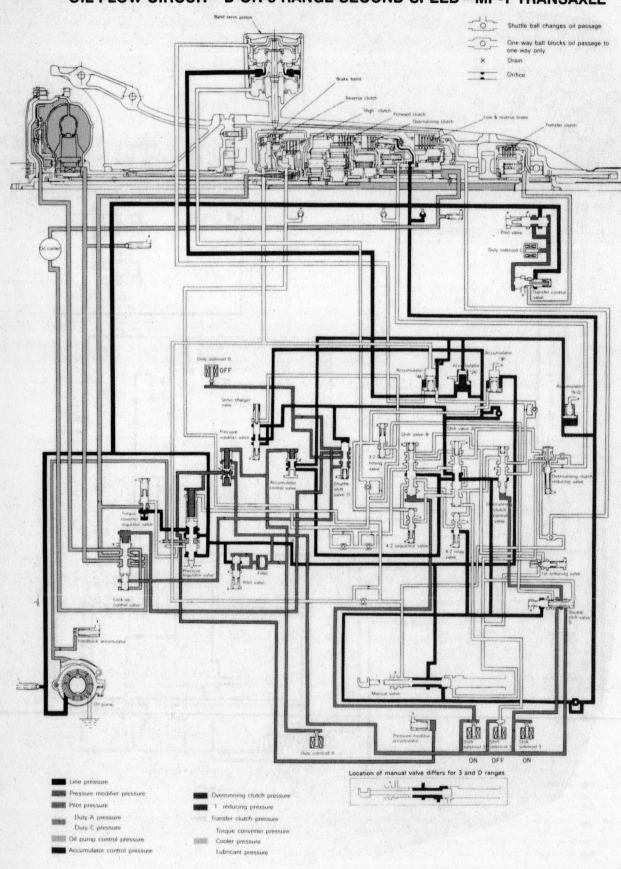

OIL FLOW CIRCUIT – D OR 3 RANGE SECOND SPEED AT LOCKUP – MP-T TRANSAXLE

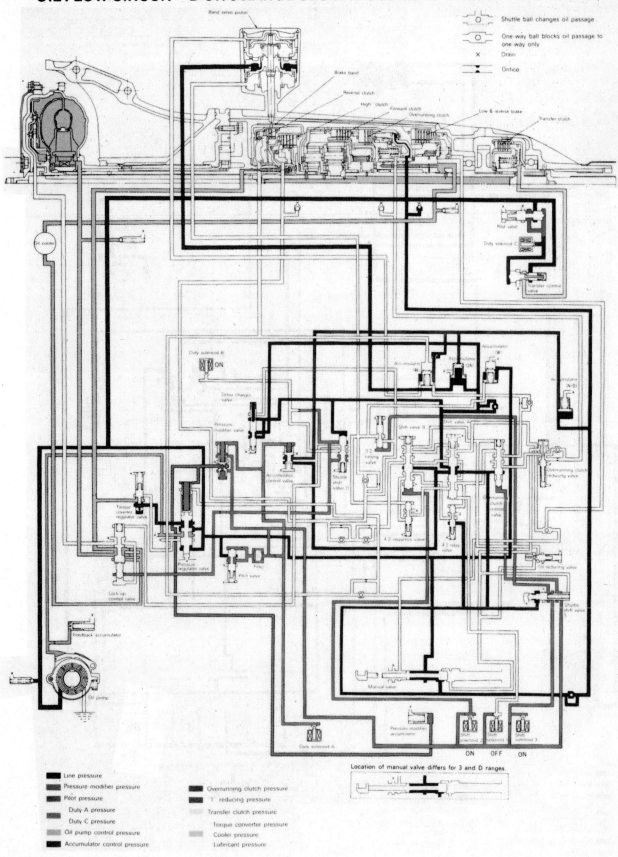

Location of manual valve differs for 3 and D ranges.

OIL FLOW CIRCUIT — D OR 3 RANGE THIRD SPEED — MP-T TRANSAXLE

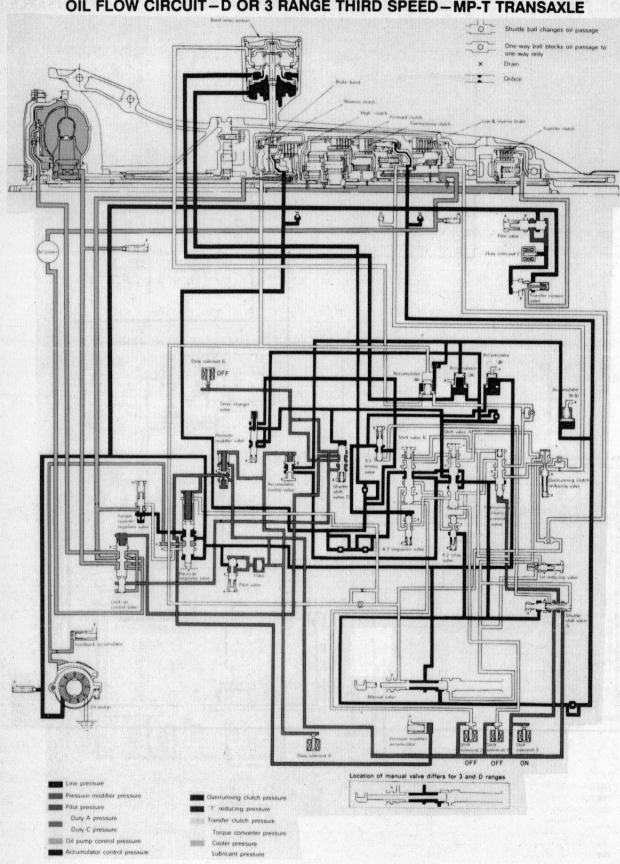

Location of manual valve differs for 3 and D ranges.

OIL FLOW CIRCUIT—D OR 3 RANGE THIRD SPEED AT LOCKUP—MP-T TRANSAXLE

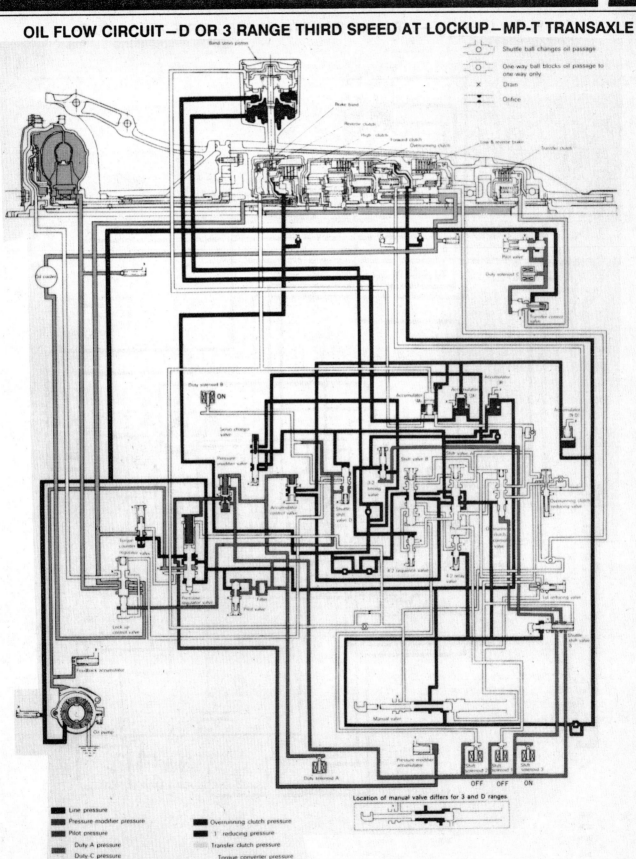

	Shuttle ball changes oil passage
	One-way ball blocks oil passage to one-way only
×	Drain
	Orifice

Location of manual valve differs for 3 and D ranges

■ Line pressure
■ Pressure modifier pressure
■ Pilot pressure
  Duty A pressure
  Duty-C pressure
  Oil pump control pressure
■ Accumulator control pressure

■ Overrunning clutch pressure
■ 1 reducing pressure
  Transfer clutch pressure
  Torque converter pressure
  Cooler pressure
  Lubricant pressure

OIL FLOW CIRCUIT—R RANGE FOURTH SPEED—MP-T TRANSAXLE

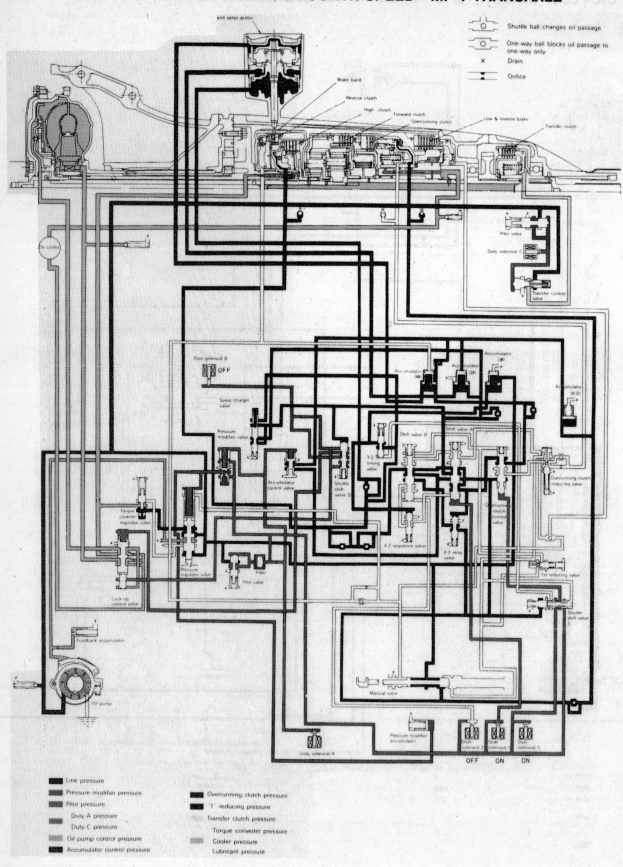

OIL FLOW CIRCUIT — D OR 3 RANGE FOURTH SPEED AT LOCKUP — MP-T TRANSAXLE

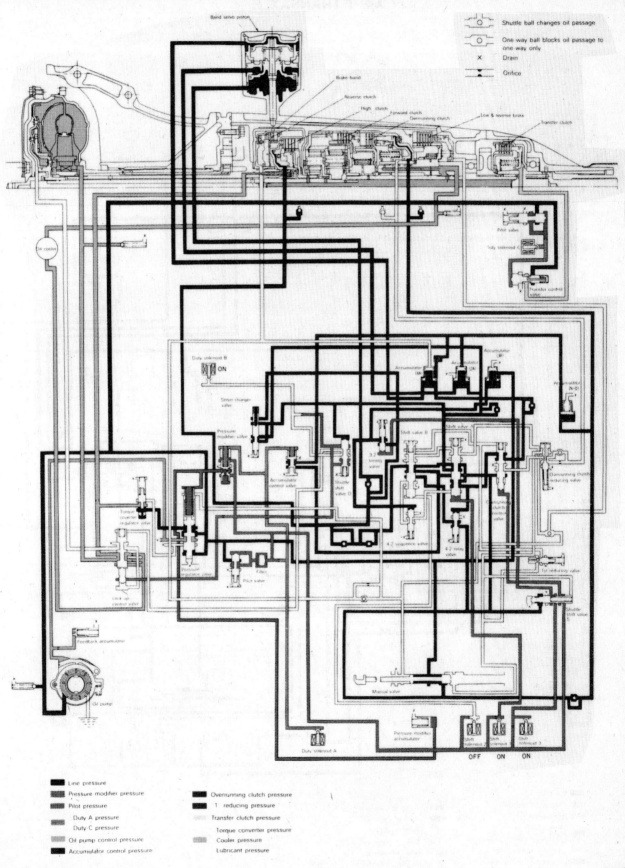

OIL FLOW CIRCUIT — FIRST SPEED OF 2 RANGE OR FIRST HOLD RANGE
MP-T TRANSAXLE

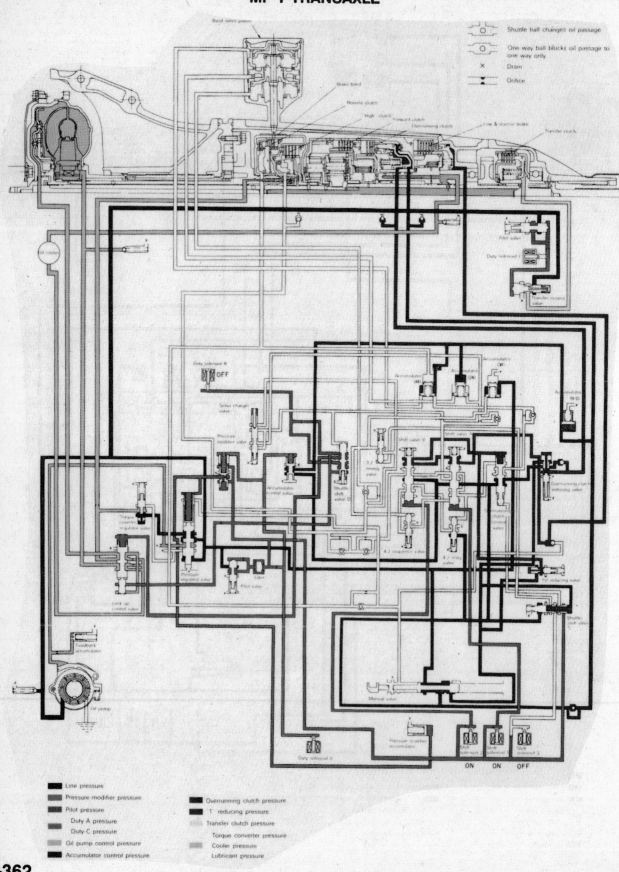

OIL FLOW CIRCUIT—SECOND SPEED OF 2 RANGE OR FIRST HOLD AT LOCKUP
MP-T TRANSAXLE

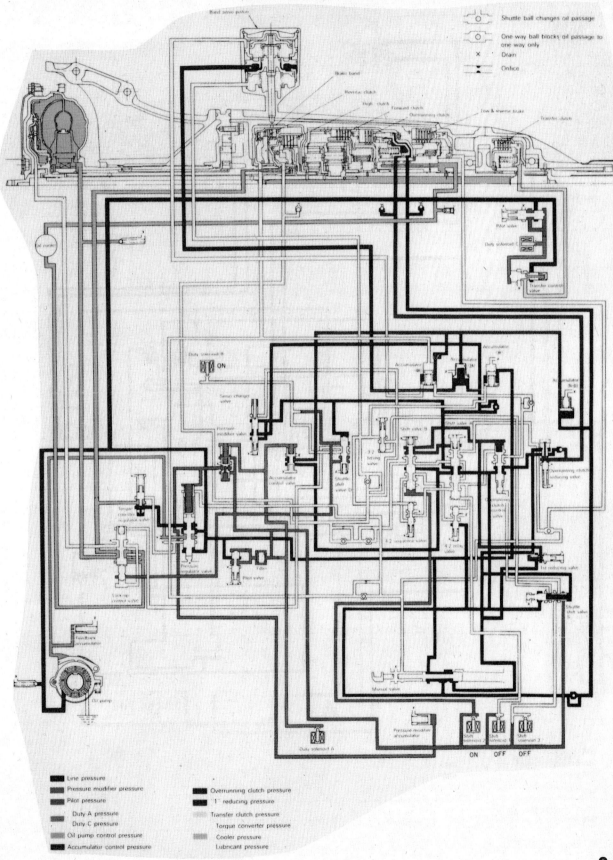

OIL FLOW CIRCUIT—THIRD SPEED OF 2 RANGE OR FIRST HOLD AT LOCKUP

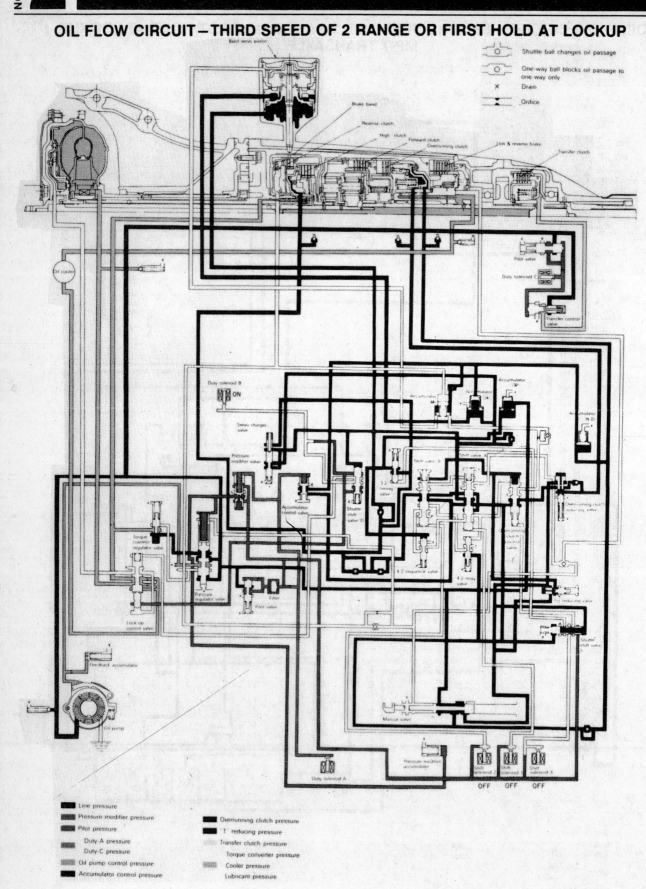

Section 2

Aisin Seiki–880001 Transaxle
Suzuki

APPLICATION

1989 Suzuki Swift with 1.3L engine

GENERAL DESCRIPTION

The Aisin Seiki 880001 automatic transaxle is an electronically controlled 3speed consisting of a valve body, 2 planetary gears, 3 clutch packs, a one-way clutch, a brake band, an oil pump, a torque converter, a differential assembly and final drive gear set. All of the above components are integrated into 1 compact unit. An oil cooler is built into the bottom of the radiator to cool the transaxle fluid. Rubber hoses are used to carry the fluid from the transaxle to the cooler.

Its operation is controlled by selecting the appropriate position from a 6-position selector lever mounted on the passenger compartment floor.

The oil pump pumps automatic transaxle fluid which is regulated by the valve body to various components within the transaxle in order to obtain the desired gear for all possible driving conditions and speeds.

The torque converter provides a fluid coupling between the engine and transaxle for optimum power transfer when driving at a constant speed and increases torque when starting, accelerating and climbing an incline.

TRANSAXLE AND CONVERTER IDENTIFICATION

TRANSAXLE

The identification tag is located on the top of the transaxle case. This tag contains the model number and build date of the transaxle.

TORQUE CONVERTER

The torque converter used is a welded one-piece unit and can not be disassembled for inspection.

Electronic Controls

The electronic control portion of this transaxle is made up of a control module, 2 shift solenoids, a throttle position sensor, a speed sensor and a neutral safety switch.

The control module is located to the right of the steering column. The controller receives signals from various sensors and converts the signals into usable information. Then it sends current to the correct shift solenoid, causing the transaxle to shift gears. Sensors that provide signals for the controller include the throttle position sensor, neutral safety switch and speed sensor.

There are 2 shift solenoids, the second brake solenoid and the direct clutch solenoid. The second brake solenoid and the direct clutch solenoid are energized by the controller and open or close oil passages in the valve body in order to attain the gear shift.

The throttle position sensor (TPS), connected to the throttle valve shaft, provides signals relative to the amount the throttle is opened. These signals are read by the conroller so gears shift at the correct speed.

The neutral safety switch is built into the selector lever. This switch provides signals for the controller so it knows what gear the vehicle is in. Also, it will prevent the vehicle from starting in any gear except **P** or **N**. The neutral safety switch also completes the reverse light circuit when backing up.

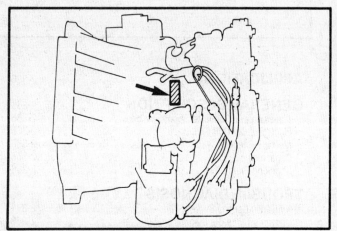
Location of the identification tag

Metric Fasteners

Metric tools will be required to service this transaxle. Due to the large number of alloy parts used in this transaxle, torque specifications should be strictly observed. Before installing capscrews into aluminum parts, dip the bolts into clean transaxle fluid as this will prevent the screws from galling the aluminum threads, thus causing damage.

Metric fastener dimensions are very close to the dimensions of the familiar inch system fasteners. For this reason replacement fasteners must have the same measurement and strength as the original fastener.

Do not attempt to interchange metric fasteners for inch system fasteners. Mismatched or incorrect fasteners can cause damage to the automatic transaxle unit and possible personal injury. Care should be taken to reuse fasteners in their original locations.

Capacities

This transaxle is designed to operate with 4.3 quarts (4.9L) of Dexron® II automatic transaxle fluid. If only the pan is removed then the refill capacity is 3.1 quarts (3.5L).

Checking Fluid Level

Run the engine until at operating temperature and move the gear selector through all ranges. Park the vehicle on level ground and check the level with the shifter in **P**. The fluid level is sufficient when it is between the 2 dimples in the **HOT** range.

NOTE: Only 0.6 qt. (0.35L) of Dexron® II is needed to raise the level from 1 dimple to the next. Be sure the fluid level does not go above the highest dimple or it will be overfull.

A cold check may also be performed at room temperature. Follow the same procedure as above, only bring the level between the 2 dimples in the **COLD** range.

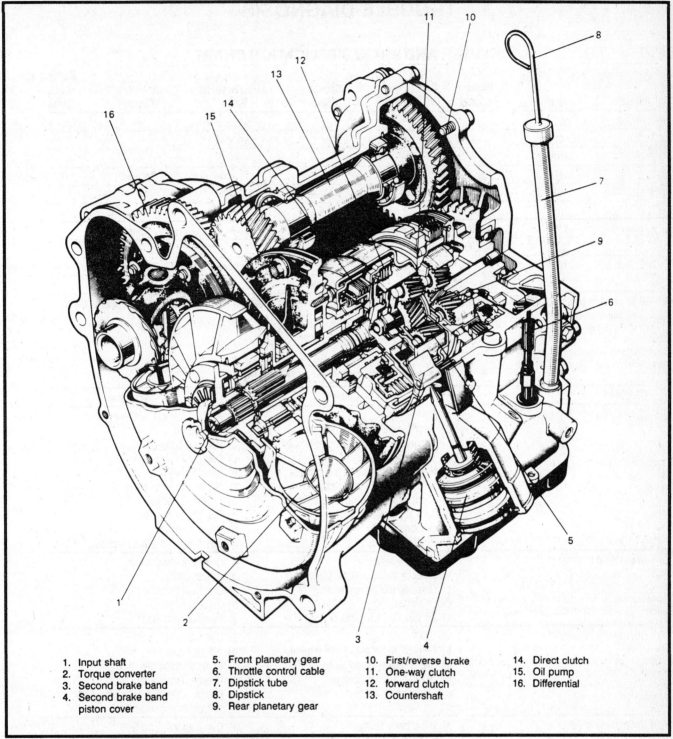

1. Input shaft
2. Torque converter
3. Second brake band
4. Second brake band piston cover
5. Front planetary gear
6. Throttle control cable
7. Dipstick tube
8. Dipstick
9. Rear planetary gear
10. First/reverse brake
11. One-way clutch
12. forward clutch
13. Countershaft
14. Direct clutch
15. Oil pump
16. Differential

Construction of the Aisin Seiki Model 88001

TRANSAXLE MODIFICATIONS

At present, there are no modifications in print for this transaxle.

TROUBLE DIAGNOSIS

CLUTCH AND BRAKE APPLICATION CHART

Range	Gear	Forward Clutch	Direct Clutch	Second Brake	First/Reverse Brake	One-Way Clutch	Parking Lock Pawl
P	Park	—	—	—	Applied ②	—	Applied
R	Reverse	—	Applied	—	Applied	—	—
N	Neutral	—	—	—	—	—	—
D	1st	Applied	—	—	—	Applied	—
D	2nd	Applied	—	Applied	—	—	—
D	3rd	Applied	Applied	—	—	—	—
2	1st	Applied	—	—	—	Applied	—
2	2nd	Applied	—	Applied	—	—	—
L	1st	Applied	—	—	Applied	Applied	—
L	2nd ①	Applied	—	Applied	—	—	—

① To prevent overrevolution of the engine, this 2nd gear is operated only when the selector lever is shifted to L range at speeds higher than 33 mph.
② With the engine running.

CHILTON'S 3 C'S DIAGNOSIS

Condition	Cause	Correction
Not moving in any range	a) Low oil level b) Wrong type of oil c) Converter bolts missing or broken d) Valve body faulty e) Selector cable out of adjustment f) Internal linkage parts broken g) Input shaft or output shaft broken h) Torque converter faulty i) Oil pump faulty j) Final drive faulty	a) Add until at correct level b) Change oil c) Replace bolts d) Overhaul valve body e) Adjust cable f) Replace broken parts g) Replace shaft(s) h) Replace converter i) inspect pump j) Overhaul final drive assembly
Not moving in Drive	a) Valve body faulty b) Selector cable out of adjustment c) One way clutch not holding d) Oil pump faulty e) Forward clutch not applying	a) Overhaul valve body b) Adjust cable c) Overhaul transaxle d) Inspect pump e) Overhaul transaxle
Not moving in Second	a) Valve body faulty b) Selector cable out of adjustment c) Brake piston or rod faulty d) Brake band not holding e) Electrical problem	a) Overhaul valve body b) Adjust cable c) Inspect assembly d) Overhaul transaxle e) Check controller, connectors and second brake solenoid
Not moving in Reverse	a) Valve body faulty b) Selector cable out of adjustment c) First/reverse brake not holding d) Direct clutch not applying e) Oil pump faulty f) Electrical problem	a) Overhaul valve body b) Adjust cable c) Overhaul transaxle d) Overhaul transaxle e) Inspect pump f) Check controller, connectors and direct clutch solenoid
Moving in Neutral	a) Selector cable out of adjustment b) Wrong type of oil c) Forward clutch applying	a) Adjust cable b) Change oil c) Overhaul transaxle

CHILTON'S 3 C'S DIAGNOSIS

Condition	Cause	Correction
Not moving in any forward range	a) Valve body faulty b) Selector cable out of adjustment c) Forward clutch not applying d) Oil pump faulty e) One way clutch not applying	a) Overhaul valve body b) Adjust cable c) Overhaul transaxle d) Inspect pump e) Overhaul transaxle
Loud noise in Neutral or Park	a) Torque converter faulty b) Oil pump faulty c) Final drive faulty	a) Replace converter b) Inspect pump c) Overhaul final drive assembly
Loud noise in first or second gear	a) Broken planetary gear	a) Overhaul transaxle
No shift change from Drive first to Drive second	a) Valve body faulty b) Throttle pressure cable out of adjustment c) Speed sensor faulty d) Brake piston faulty e) Brake band not holding f) Electrical problem	a) Overhaul valve body b) Adjust cable c) Replace speed sensor d) Overhaul brake piston e) Overhaul transaxle f) Check controller connectors and second brake solenoid
No shift change from Drive second to Drive third	a) Valve body faulty b) Throttle pressure cable out of adjustment c) Speed sensor faulty d) Direct clutch not applying e) Electrical problem	a) Overhaul valvebody b) Adjust cable c) Replace speed sensor d) Overhaul transaxle e) Check controller, connectors, and direct clutch solenoid
Shift points at wrong speeds	a) Valve body faulty b) Speed sensor faulty c) Electrical problem d) Throttle pressure cable out of adjustment e) TPS faulty	a) Overhaul valve body b) Replace speed sensor c) Check controller, connectors, and applicable solenoids d) Adjust cable e) Replace TPS
No kickdown	a) Valve body faulty b) Throttle pressure cable out of adjustment c) WOT not possible d) Electrical problem e) TPS faulty	a) Overhaul valve body b) Adjust cable c) Adjust accelerator pedal d) Check controller connectors and applicable solenoids e) Replace TPS
Shock when shifting from Neutral or Park to Drive	a) Valve body faulty b) Selector cable out of adjustment c) Low oil level d) Forward clutch faulty e) Engine idle too high	a) Overhaul valve body b) Adjust cable c) Add until at correct level d) Overhaul transaxle e) Adjust idle
Shock when shifting from Neutral or Park to Reverse	a) Valve body faulty b) Selector cable out of adjustment c) Low oil level d) Oil pump faulty e) Direct clutch faulty f) First/reverse brake not holding g) Engine idle too high	a) Overhaul valve body b) Adjust cable c) Add until at correct level d) Inspect pump e) Overhaul transaxle f) Overhaul transaxle g) Adjust idle
Shudder or slip when starting in Drive	a) Valve body faulty b) Selector cable out of adjustment c) Low oil level d) Wrong type of oil e) Torque converter faulty	a) Overhaul valve body b) Adjust cable c) Add until at correct level d) Change oil e) Replace converter

CHILTON'S 3 C'S DIAGNOSIS

Condition	Cause	Correction
Shudder or slip when starting in Drive	f) Oil pump faulty g) Forward clutch faulty h) One way clutch not holding i) Transaxle and/or engine mount faulty j) Engine idle too high	f) Inspect pump e) Overhaul transaxle h) Overhaul transaxle i) Replace mount j) Adjust idle
Shudder or slip when shifting from Drive first to Drive Second	a) Valve body faulty b) Throttle pressure cable out of adjustment c) Low oil level d) Wrong type of oil e) Brake piston faulty f) Brake band not holding g) Oil pump faulty h) Electrical problem	a) Overhaul valve body b) Adjust cable c) Add until at correct level d) Change oil e) Overhaul brake piston f) Overhaul transaxle g) Inspect pump h) Check controller connectors and second brake solenoid
Shudder or slip when shifting from Drive second to Drive third	a) Valve body faulty b) Throttle pressure cable out of adjustment c) Low oil level d) Wrong type of oil e) Brake piston faulty f) Brake band not holding g) Oil pump faulty h) Direct clutch faulty i) Electrical problem	a) Overhaul valve body b) Adjust cable c) Add until at correct level d) Change oil e) Overhaul brake piston f) Overhaul transaxle g) Inspect pump h) Overhaul transaxle i) Check controller connectors and direct clutch solenoid
Shudder or slip when starting in Low	a) Valve body faulty b) Selector cable out of adjustment c) Low oil level d) Wrong type of oil e) Torque converter faulty f) Oil pump faulty g) Forward clutch faulty h) First/reverse brake faulty i) Transaxle and/or engine mount faulty j) Engine idle too high	a) Overhaul valve body b) Adjust cable c) Add until at correct level d) Change oil e) Replace converter f) Inspect pump e) Overhaul transaxle h) Overhaul transaxle i) Replace mount j) Adjust idle
Shudder or slip when starting in Second	a) Valve body faulty b) Selector cable out of adjustment c) Low oil level d) Wrong type of oil e) Torque converter faulty f) Oil pump faulty g) Forward clutch faulty h) Transaxle and/or engine mount faulty i) Engine idle too high	a) Overhaul valve body b) Adjust cable c) Add until at correct level d) Change oil e) Replace converter f) Inspect pump g) Overhaul transaxle h) Replace mount i) Adjust idle
Shudder or slip when Starting in Reverse	a) Valve body faulty b) Selector cable out of adjustment c) Low oil level d) Wrong type of oil e) Torque converter faulty f) Oil pump faulty g) Direct clutch faulty h) First/reverse brake faulty i) Transaxle and/or engine mount faulty j) Engine idle too high	a) Overhaul valve body b) Adjust cable c) Add until at correct level d) Change oil e) Replace converter f) Inspect pump g) Overhaul transaxle h) Overhaul transaxle i) Replace mount j) Adjust idle

CHILTON'S 3 C'S DIAGNOSIS

Condition	Cause	Correction
Large vibration in Drive	a) Torque converter faulty b) Converter bolts loose c) Transaxle and/or engine mount faulty	a) Replace converter b) Tighten bolts c) Replace mount
Engine will not start	a) Selector cable out of adjustment b) Shift lever switch faulty	a) Adjust cable b) Check wiring and switch
Vehicle will not hold in Park	a) Selector cable out of adjustment b) Parking assembly broken c) Internal linkage parts broken	a) Adjust cable b) Replace broken part c) Replace broken parts
Selector lever trouble	a) Cable binding b) Control valve sticking	a) Lube or replace binding part b) Overhaul valve body
Automatic transaxle fluid leaking	a) Oil level too high b) Cooler hose(s) leaking c) Oil pan cracked or gasket leaking d) Oil pump seal leaking e) Front seal leaking f) Differential seal leaking	a) Drain to correct level b) Replace hose(s) c) Replace pan or gasket d) Replace seal e) Replace seal f) Replace seal
Transaxle fluid in antifreeze or antifreeze in transaxle fluid	a) Fluid cooler core in radiator is leaking	a) Replace radiator and change the transaxle fluid and the antifreeze

Hydraulic Control System

Throttle Valve System

As the throttle valve is linked to the accelerator pedal by a cable, throttle pressure is produced corresponding to the extent the accelerator pedal is depressed which is, in turn relative to engine output.

When the accelerator pedal is depressed, the throttle cam pushes the shift plug in the valve body which then compresses 2 springs to move the throttle valve itself. The line pressure passage is then opened and throttle pressure is produced.

The throttle pressure is also applied to the back of the throttle valve to push the valve back. The amount of throttle pressure is determined by the tension of the springs (which positions the shift plug correctly) and is applied to the primary and secondary regulator valves to regulate the line pressure.

Diagnosis Tests

NOTE: Perform the following tests at operating temperature and with the automatic transaxle fluid at the proper level.

STALL SPEED TEST

—————————— CAUTION ——————————
Never allow anyone to stand near — especially in front of or behind — the vehicle when performing a stall test.

1. Block the wheels securely and firmly set the parking brake.
2. Connect a tachometer to the engine.
3. Push down on the brake pedal firmly and shift the gear selector to **D**.
4. Gradually depress the accelerator pedal. Do not perform this step for more than 5 seconds.
5. When the engine has stopped increasing in speed, read the tachometer and immediately release the accelerator pedal.
6. Shift into **N** and allow the engine to idle for 1 minute.

NOTE: Step 6 is important at this point so that the fluid can cool and to prevent the possibility of overheating.

7. Repeat the stall test in **R** range.
8. The stall speed should be 2000–2500 rpm.
9. If the stall speed is lower than specifications:
   a. Engine output is not sufficient.
   b. The torque converter is defective.
10. If the stall speed is higher than specifications in **D**:
    a. The forward clutch is slipping.
    b. The one-way clutch is not holding.
11. If the stall speed is higher than specifications in **R**:
    a. The direct clutch is slipping.
    b. The first/reverse brake is slipping.

LINE PRESSURE TEST

1. Block the wheels securely and firmly set the parking brake.
2. Connect a tachometer to the engine and an oil pressure gauge to the fitting located in front of and below the left side axle shaft.
3. Shift the gear selector to **D** and read the pressure when idling.
4. Repeat the stall speed test and read the pressure at the stall speed.
5. Allow 1 minute cool-down time and repeat Steps 3 and 4 in **R** range.
6. Install the fitting plug and torque to 5 ft. lbs. (7 Nm).
7. If the line pressure is higher than specification in **D** and **R**:
   a. The regulator valve is defective.
   b. Throttle valve is defective.
   c. Accelerator cable or throttle valve cable is out of adjustment.
8. If the line pressure is lower than specification in **D** and **R**:
   a. The oil pump is defective.
   b. The regulator valve is defective.
   c. Throttle valve is defective.
   d. Accelerator cable or throttle valve cable is out of adjustment.
9. If the line pressure is lower than specification in **D** only:
   a. Oil pressure loss in forward clutch.
   b. Oil pressure loss elsewhere in **D** range oil flow.

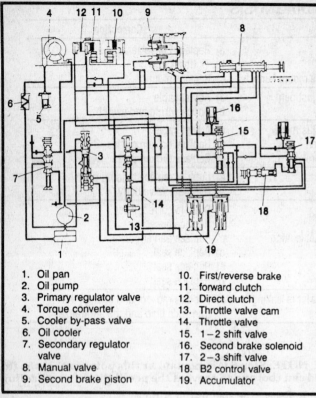

1. Oil pan
2. Oil pump
3. Primary regulator valve
4. Torque converter
5. Cooler by-pass valve
6. Oil cooler
7. Secondary regulator valve
8. Manual valve
9. Second brake piston
10. First/reverse brake
11. forward clutch
12. Direct clutch
13. Throttle valve cam
14. Throttle valve
15. 1—2 shift valve
16. Second brake solenoid
17. 2—3 shift valve
18. B2 control valve
19. Accumulator

Oil circuit in N range

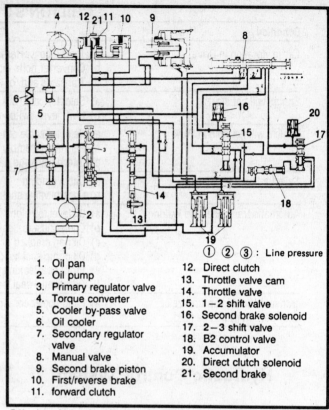

① ② ③ : Line pressure

1. Oil pan
2. Oil pump
3. Primary regulator valve
4. Torque converter
5. Cooler by-pass valve
6. Oil cooler
7. Secondary regulator valve
8. Manual valve
9. Second brake piston
10. First/reverse brake
11. forward clutch
12. Direct clutch
13. Throttle valve cam
14. Throttle valve
15. 1—2 shift valve
16. Second brake solenoid
17. 2—3 shift valve
18. B2 control valve
19. Accumulator
20. Direct clutch solenoid
21. Second brake

Oil circuit in second gear D or 2 ranges

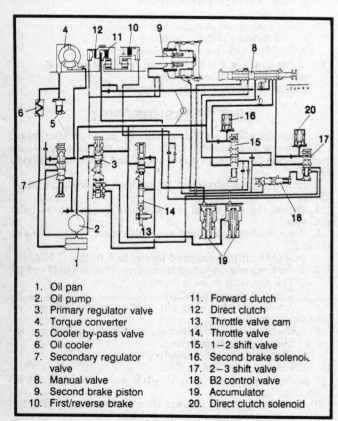

1. Oil pan
2. Oil pump
3. Primary regulator valve
4. Torque converter
5. Cooler by-pass valve
6. Oil cooler
7. Secondary regulator valve
8. Manual valve
9. Second brake piston
10. First/reverse brake
11. Forward clutch
12. Direct clutch
13. Throttle valve cam
14. Throttle valve
15. 1—2 shift valve
16. Second brake solenoid
17. 2—3 shift valve
18. B2 control valve
19. Accumulator
20. Direct clutch solenoid

Oil circuit in first gear D or 2 ranges

LINE PRESSURE SPECIFICATIONS

Model	Engine Speed (rpm)		Line Pressure psi (kPa)	
	Idling Speed	Stall Speed	D Range	R Range
GLI	800–900	—	28.5–56.8 (200–400)	78.2–113.7 (550–800)
		2000–2500	85.3–113.7 (600–800)	170.6–220.4 (1200–1550)
GLX	700–800	—	28.5–56.8 (200–400)	78.2–113.7 (550–800)
		2000–2500	71.1–99.5 (500–700)	149.4–199.1 (1050–1400)

10. If the line pressure is lower than specification in **R** only:
 a. Oil pressure loss in direct clutch.
 b. Oil pressure loss in first/reverse brake.
 c. Oil pressure loss elsewhere in **R** range oil flow.

ROAD TEST

This test is designed to check if upshift and downshift occurs at the correct speeds while actually driving the vehicle. The test should be performed on a long, level road, with little or no traffic so that speeds can be chosen and maintained, and not forced or altered by others on the road.
1. Run the engine until at operating temperature.
2. Accelerate the vehicle very gradually.
3. Check to see that upshift from first to second occurs at 8–9

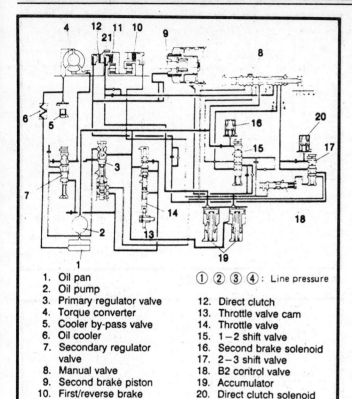

1. Oil pan
2. Oil pump
3. Primary regulator valve
4. Torque converter
5. Cooler by-pass valve
6. Oil cooler
7. Secondary regulator valve
8. Manual valve
9. Second brake piston
10. First/reverse brake
11. forward clutch

① ② ③ ④ : Line pressure

12. Direct clutch
13. Throttle valve cam
14. Throttle valve
15. 1 – 2 shift valve
16. Second brake solenoid
17. 2 – 3 shift valve
18. B2 control valve
19. Accumulator
20. Direct clutch solenoid
21. Second brake

Oil circuit in third gear D range

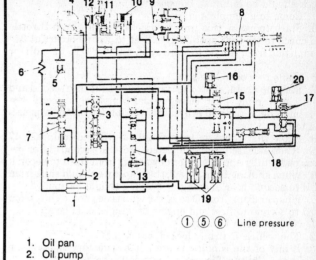

① ⑤ ⑥   Line pressure

1. Oil pan
2. Oil pump
3. Primary regulator valve
4. Torque converter
5. Cooler by-pass valve
6. Oil cooler
7. Secondary regulator valve
8. Manual valve
9. Second brake piston
10. First/reverse brake
11. forward clutch

12. Direct clutch
13. Throttle valve cam
14. Throttle valve
15. 1 – 2 shift valve
16. Second brake solenoid
17. 2 – 3 shift valve
18. B2 control valve
19. Accumulator
20. Direct clutch solenoid
21. Second brake

Oil circuit in R range

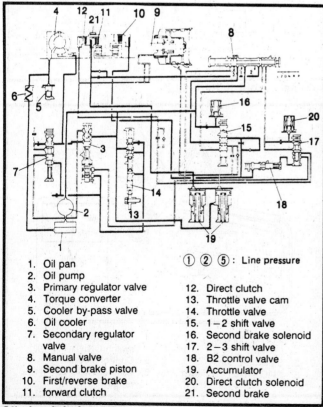

1. Oil pan
2. Oil pump
3. Primary regulator valve
4. Torque converter
5. Cooler by-pass valve
6. Oil cooler
7. Secondary regulator valve
8. Manual valve
9. Second brake piston
10. First/reverse brake
11. forward clutch

① ② ⑤ : Line pressure

12. Direct clutch
13. Throttle valve cam
14. Throttle valve
15. 1 – 2 shift valve
16. Second brake solenoid
17. 2 – 3 shift valve
18. B2 control valve
19. Accumulator
20. Direct clutch solenoid
21. Second brake

Oil circuit in L range

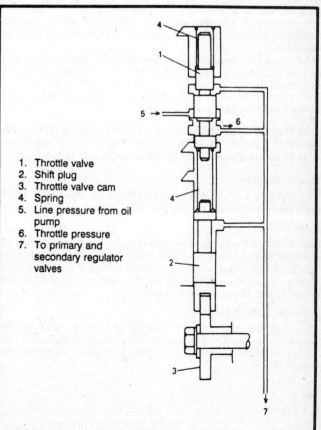

1. Throttle valve
2. Shift plug
3. Throttle valve cam
4. Spring
5. Line pressure from oil pump
6. Throttle pressure
7. To primary and secondary regulator valves

Oil circuit of the throttle valve

mph and from second to third at 19–20 mph. Shift changing shock should be minimal, but positive.

4. Come to a complete stop.

5. Start up again, this time go quickly to wide open throttle and check to see that upshift from first to second occurs at 34–35 mph and from second to third at 65 mph for GTi, 62 mph for GLX.

6. Come to a complete stop.

7. Start up again, allow the transaxle to shift into second and maintain 15 mph. Then release pedal completely. Seceral seconds later, depress pedal fully and check for downshift from second to first.

8. Allow the transaxle to shift into third and maintain 47 mph. Then release pedal completely. Several seconds later depress pedal fully and check for downshift from third to second.

9. When shifting from **D** to **2**, the transaxle should shift from third to second gear and engine braking should be applied.

10. When shifting from **D** to **L**, the transaxle should shift from third to second to first and engine braking should be applied.

11. No upshift in **L** range.

12. The vehicle is firmly locked when in **P**.

13. If any of the conditions are not satisfactory check them against the Chilton Three C's Diagnostic chart.

Electronic Control System

COMPONENT TESTING

All of the electrical components can be checked by using the self-diagnostic mode built into the system. Exercise basic systematic troubleshooting guidelines first, then turn to self-diagnostics.

1. After confirming a problem by road testing, keep the engine running in **P** and apply the parking brake.

2. Connect a voltmeter or a test light to the green monitor connector under the dash panel to the right of the steering column.

3. Using a connector with a length of wire, make a short circuit at the black diagonal switch connector beside the green connector.

4. To read the diagnostic code, count the swings of the voltmeter needle, or blinks of the bulb.

NOTE: All applicable codes will be indicated from the smallest numbered code to the largest. Code memory will be erased when the ignition switch is turned off.

Speed Sensor

The resistance of the sensor itself should be 160–200Ω. At 37 mph the speed sensor should put out 1 volt.

Solenoid Valves

Insert oil into the solenoid being tested, and check to see that oil does not leak out from side holes of solenoids when battery voltage is not being applied. When battery voltage is applied, a click should be heard and the fluid should shoot out hard from the holes. If not, the solenoid is defective.

Neutral Safety Switch

Make sure the engine does not start in any gear except **P** and **N**. Also check to see that the reverse lights are lit when in reverse. If the switch is faulty, check for continuity between the terminals.

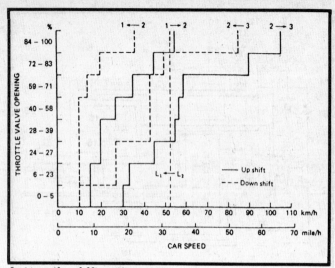

Automatic shift pattern-GLI

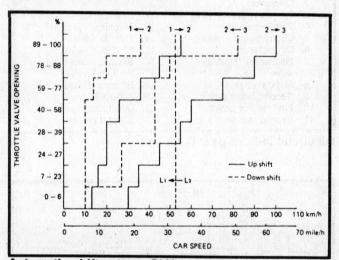

Automatic shift pattern-GLX

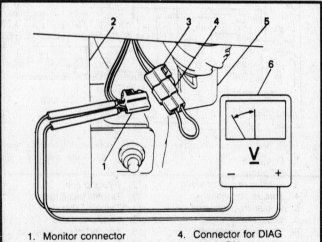

1. Monitor connector (green)
2. Steering column
3. DIAG switch connector
4. Connector for DIAG switch ON
5. Control module
6. Voltmeter (DC 20V range)

Connections for monitoring diagnostic codes

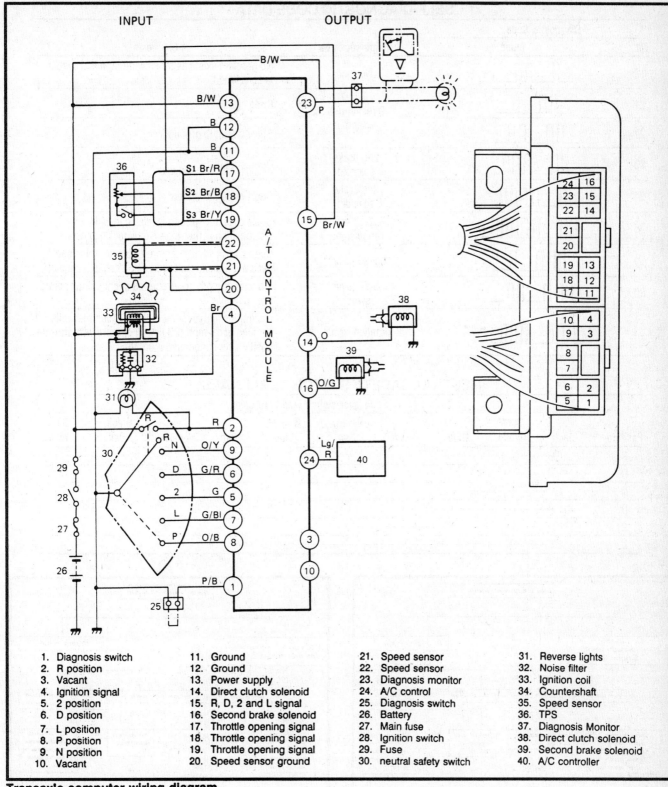

Transaxle computer wiring diagram

INPUT   OUTPUT

1. Diagnosis switch	11. Ground	21. Speed sensor	31. Reverse lights
2. R position	12. Ground	22. Speed sensor	32. Noise filter
3. Vacant	13. Power supply	23. Diagnosis monitor	33. Ignition coil
4. Ignition signal	14. Direct clutch solenoid	24. A/C control	34. Countershaft
5. 2 position	15. R, D, 2 and L signal	25. Diagnosis switch	35. Speed sensor
6. D position	16. Second brake solenoid	26. Battery	36. TPS
7. L position	17. Throttle opening signal	27. Main fuse	37. Diagnosis Monitor
8. P position	18. Throttle opening signal	28. Ignition switch	38. Direct clutch solenoid
9. N position	19. Throttle opening signal	29. Fuse	39. Second brake solenoid
10. Vacant	20. Speed sensor ground	30. neutral safety switch	40. A/C controller

SELF-DIAGNOSTIC CODE DATA

No.	Diagnostic Code Mode	Diagnostic Area	Diagnosis
12	(waveform)	Normal	No problem exists as far as self-diagnosis system is concerned
21	(waveform)	Direct clutch solenoid	Open circuit
22	(waveform)		Short circuit to ground
23	(waveform)	2nd brake solenoid	Open circuit
24	(waveform)	2nd brake solenoid	Short circuit to ground
25	(waveform)	R, D, 2 and L range signal	Short circuit to ground in wiring to ECM. Use positions other than P or N for diagnosis.
31	(waveform)	Speed sensor	Open circuit while running. However, this code does not appear once ignition switch is turned off
32	(waveform)	Shift lever switch	2 points or more are grounded at once or all points are open
33	(waveform)	Ignition signal	No ignition signal for more than 9 seconds while running at 19 mph (30 km/h) or more with throttle position sensor opened more than 28%.

NEUTRAL SAFETY SWITCH TERMINALS

Shift lever switch lead wire color

Position	Black	Blue/White	Blue	Green	Green/Red	Green/Blue	Red	Yellow	Black/Red	Black/Yellow
P	○————○								○————○	
R							○————○			
N	○—————————○								○————○	
D	○——————————————○									
2	○———————————————————————○									
L	○—————————————————————○									

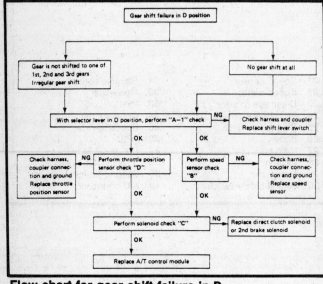

Flow chart for gear shift failure in D

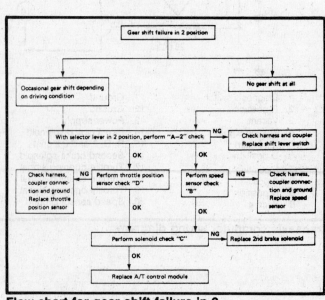

Flow chart for gear shift failure in 2

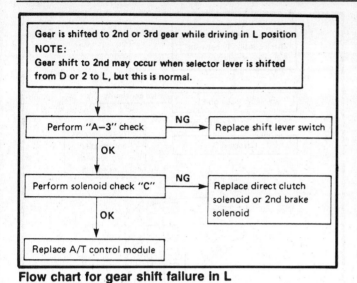

Gear is shifted to 2nd or 3rd gear while driving in L position
NOTE:
Gear shift to 2nd may occur when selector lever is shifted from D or 2 to L, but this is normal.

↓

Perform "A–3" check — NG → Replace shift lever switch

↓ OK

Perform solenoid check "C" — NG → Replace direct clutch solenoid or 2nd brake solenoid

↓ OK

Replace A/T control module

Flow chart for gear shift failure in L

Car does not move backward in R position

↓

Perform "A–4" check — NG → Replace shift lever switch

↓ OK

Perform solenoid check "C" — NG → Replace direct clutch solenoid or 2nd brake solenoid

↓ OK

Replace A/T control module

Flow chart for gear no moving in R

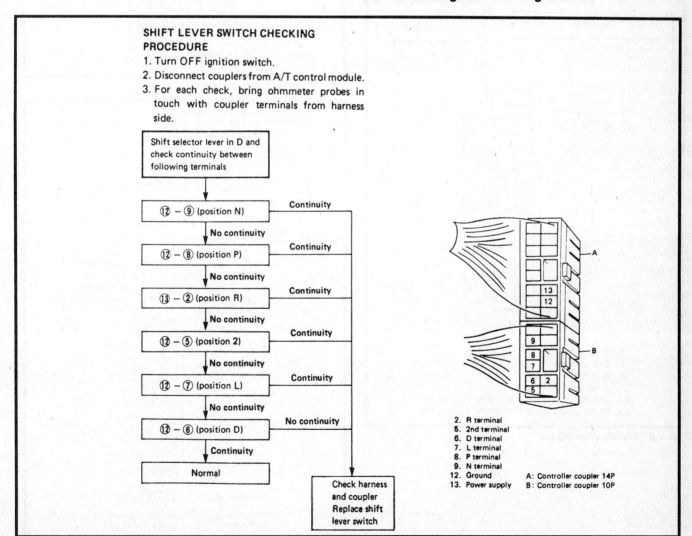

SHIFT LEVER SWITCH CHECKING PROCEDURE
1. Turn OFF ignition switch.
2. Disconnect couplers from A/T control module.
3. For each check, bring ohmmeter probes in touch with coupler terminals from harness side.

Shift selector lever in D and check continuity between following terminals

↓

⑫ – ⑨ (position N) — Continuity

↓ No continuity

⑫ – ⑧ (position P) — Continuity

↓ No continuity

⑬ – ② (position R) — Continuity

↓ No continuity

⑫ – ⑤ (position 2) — Continuity

↓ No continuity

⑫ – ⑦ (position L) — Continuity

↓ No continuity

⑫ – ⑥ (position D) — No continuity

↓ Continuity

Normal

Check harness and coupler Replace shift lever switch

2. R terminal
5. 2nd terminal
6. D terminal
7. L terminal
8. P terminal
9. N terminal
12. Ground
13. Power supply

A: Controller coupler 14P
B: Controller coupler 10P

"A–1" check procedure

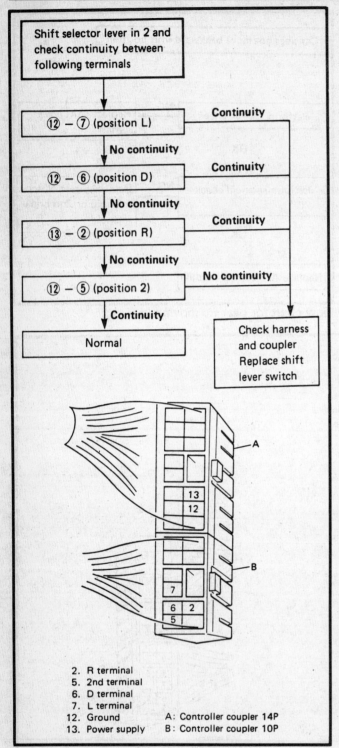

"A–2" check procedure

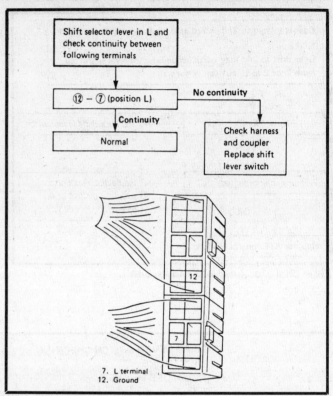

"A–3" check procedure

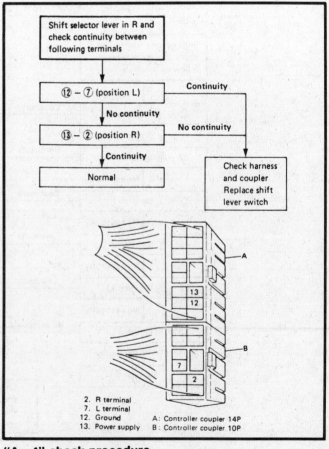

"A–4" check procedure

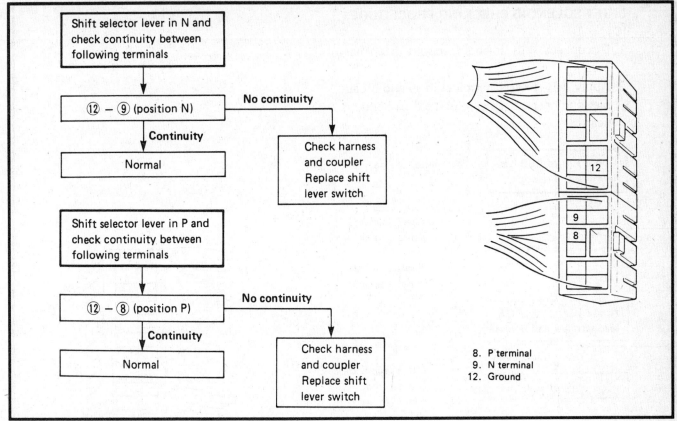

Shift selector lever in N and check continuity between following terminals

↓

⑫ – ⑨ (position N) → **No continuity** → Check harness and coupler Replace shift lever switch

↓ **Continuity**

Normal

Shift selector lever in P and check continuity between following terminals

↓

⑫ – ⑧ (position P) → **No continuity** → Check harness and coupler Replace shift lever switch

↓ **Continuity**

Normal

8. P terminal
9. N terminal
12. Ground

"N−P" check procedure

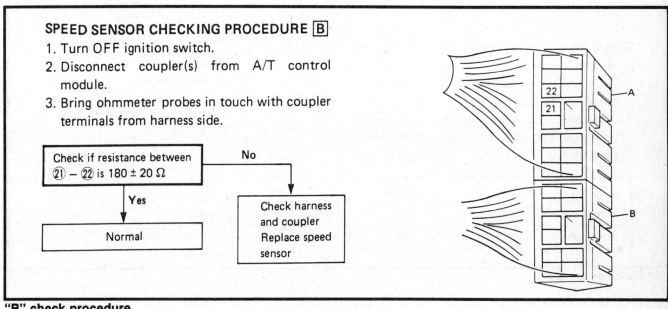

SPEED SENSOR CHECKING PROCEDURE [B]
1. Turn OFF ignition switch.
2. Disconnect coupler(s) from A/T control module.
3. Bring ohmmeter probes in touch with coupler terminals from harness side.

Check if resistance between ㉑ – ㉒ is $180 \pm 20\ \Omega$ → **No** → Check harness and coupler Replace speed sensor

↓ **Yes**

Normal

"B" check procedure

SHIFT SOLENOID CHECKING PROCEDURE

C

1. Disconnect shift solenoid coupler from harness.
2. Apply 12V to each terminal in solenoid coupler and check to be sure that a click sound is heard.

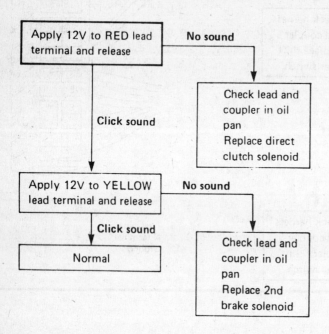

Apply 12V to RED lead terminal and release →(No sound)→ Check lead and coupler in oil pan. Replace direct clutch solenoid

↓(Click sound)

Apply 12V to YELLOW lead terminal and release →(No sound)→ Check lead and coupler in oil pan. Replace 2nd brake solenoid

↓(Click sound)

Normal

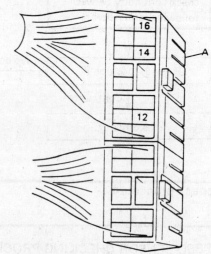

12. Ground
14. Direct clutch solenoid
16. 2nd brake solenoid
 A: Controller coupler 14P

Shift solenoid circuit will be checked by using ohmmeter at controller coupler.

1. With ignition switch turned OFF, disconnect controller coupler.
2. Bring ohmmeter probes in touch with coupler terminals from harness side and measure each resistance.

Solenoid	Terminal	Resistance
Direct clutch	⑭ – ⑫	13 Ω
2nd brake	⑯ – ⑫	13 Ω

"C" check procedure

THROTTLE VALVE OPENING SIGNAL
CHECKING PROCEDURE D

1. Disconnect coupler(s) from A/T control module.
2. Bring voltmeter probes in touch with coupler terminals from harness side.

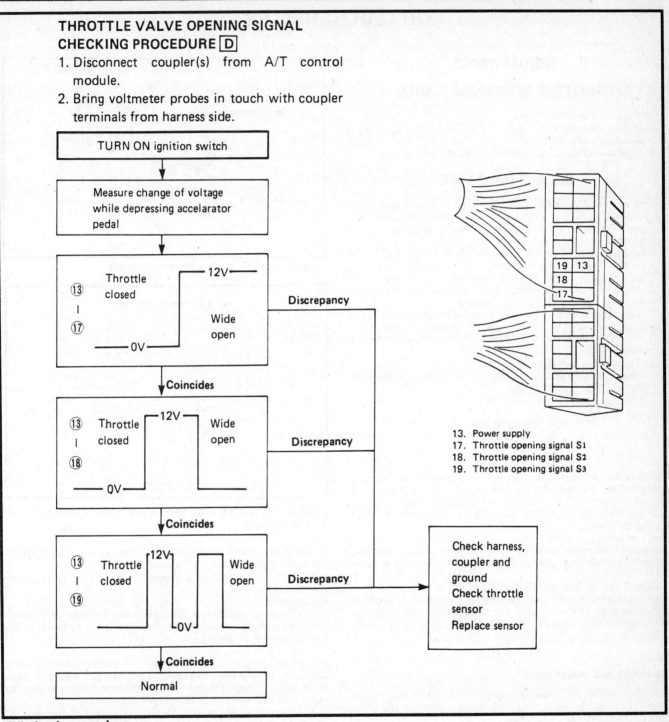

13. Power supply
17. Throttle opening signal S1
18. Throttle opening signal S2
19. Throttle opening signal S3

"D" check procedure

ON CAR SERVICES

Adjustments

THROTTLE PRESSURE CABLE

1. Remove the cable cover.
2. Adjust clearance "A" to 0–0.02 in. (0–0.5mm) by turning the adjusting nuts.
3. Tighten all nuts that were loosened for adjustment.

SELECTOR CABLE

Before adjusting the cable, make sure that when the selector lever is moved down the scale, the detents can be felt and a clicking heard between each shift position. Also, check that the gear corresponds to that shown on the position plate.

The shifter should be able to go from **N** to **R** and **D** to **2** with the knob button pushed halfway in. A shift from **2** to **L** and **R** to **P** should require the button to be pushed all the way in.

1. Make sure the shift cable link on the transaxle is well lubricated, pivots freely and the clip is secure.
2. Loosen the cable end nut, shift the selector lever to **N** and place the manual lever on the transaxle into the N detent.
3. Turn the cable end nut by hand until it just contacts the selector cable joint.
4. Tighten the locknut.
5. Check the operation of the neutral safety switch, the parking gear and the reverse lights.

Services

FLUID CHANGE

The conditions under which the vehicle is operated is the main consideration in determining how often the transaxle fluid should be changed. Different driving conditions result in different transaxle fluid temperatures. These temperatures affect change intervals.

If the vehicle is driven under severe conditions, change the transaxle fluid every 15,000 miles. If the vehicle is not used under severe conditions, change the fluid and replace the strainer every 30,000 miles.

Only 0.6 qt. (0.35L) of Dexron® II is needed to raise the level from one dimple to the next. Be sure the fluid level does not go above the highest dimple or it will be overfilled and damage to the internal components of the automatic transaxle may result.

OIL PAN

Removal and Installation

1. Disconnect the negative battery cable. Raise the vehicle and support safely. Position a large drain pan under the drain plug and remove the drain plug.
2. After the fluid has drained, install the drain plug with a new gasket and torque to 15 ft. lbs. (20 Nm). Remove the 15 pan bolts and carefully pull the pan down; try to avoid prying, or the pan may get bent. Excess fluid may drip from the bolt holes, so have the drain pan handy as the bolts are removed.
3. Inspect the strainer and pan for any concentrations of friction material and metal pieces. A small amount of accumulation around the pan magnet, if equipped or strainer is considered normal, but larger amounts may indicate heavy wear. If metal pieces are present, more serious damage is possible.
4. Clean the pan and magnet thoroughly with clean solvent and straighten the mating surface with a block of wood and a

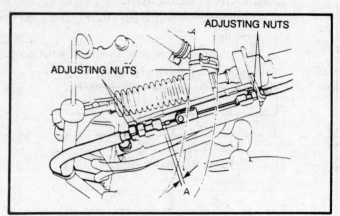

Adjusting the throttle pressure cable

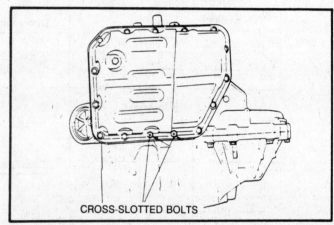

Location of the two cross-slotted bolts; apply sealant to the threads

mallet if necessary. Pay special attention to the cleanliness of the mating surfaces of the pan and case.

5. Replace the strainer if necessary. Torque the bolts to 4 ft. lbs. (5.5 Nm).

To Install:

6. Clean and completely dry all bolts and bolt holes with solvent and compressed air. Place the magnet where it will be directly beneath he strainer.
7. Glue the new gasket to the pan (do not use sealant on the gasket) and hold against the case while installing a few bolts finger-tight. Torque the pan bolts to 3.5 ft. lbs. (5.0 Nm) in a criss-cross order. Two of the bolts are cross-slotted; apply sealant to them and install them in the proper positions.
8. Lower the vehicle and fill with 3 quarts of Dexron® II. Start the engine and allow it to get to operating temperature, running through the gears.
9. Check the fluid level in **P** and add until between the dimples in the **HOT** range on the dipstick. Make sure the fluid level does not go above the highest dimple. Road test, check for leaks and recheck the fluid level on level ground.

VALVE BODY

Removal and Installation

NOTE: The valve body is a precisely machined part. Handle it with great care and do not clamp in a vise. The

material is fragile and could distort easily. If disassembly is necessary, keep all parts labeled and in a well-arranged order, since many of them look similar. Cleanliness is of the utmost importance when working with valve bodies; even the most minuscule piece of dirt can restrict valve movement and impair the transaxle's performance.

1. Disconnect the negative battery cable. Raise and support the vehicle safely. Drain the automatic transaxle fluid and remove the oil pan. Note the positions of the 2 cross-slotted bolts.
2. Unplug the 2 solenoids.
3. Note the positioning of the 2 oil tubes and remove them by gently prying them with a suitable pry bar.
4. Remove pressure control cable from the throttle valve cam.
5. Remove the oil strainer.
6. Remove the 11 valve body bolts (note the different lengths of the bolts) and lower the valve body from within the case. Do not allow the manual valve to fall out of it bore.

NOTE: The accumulator pistons, seals and springs may be serviced at this point if necessary. To remove them, blow low pressure compressed air into the hole in between them and hold them as they come out. The springs will follow immediately, so be wary of them falling out of the case.

To install new parts, install the springs first, coat the seals with Dexron® II or petroleum jelly and push the pistons carefully back into place.

To Install:

7. Align the pin on manual neutral safety with the 2 flanges at the end of the manual valve and position the valve body into place.
8. Install the reamer bolts first, then the rest. Torque all bolts to 6.0–8.5 ft. lbs. (8–12 Nm) in diagonal order.
9. Hold the throttle valve cam down and install the throttle cable into the slot.
10. Install the oil tubes. Seat them fully in their bores using a plastic hammer with a light touch.
11. Install the oil strainer, clamping the second brake solenoid wire in its clamp. Torque bolts to 4 ft. lbs. (5.5 Nm). Plug the 2 solenoid connectors into their respective solenoids.
12. Install the oil pan. Apply sealant to the cross-slotted bolts and install them in the correct positions. Torque the pan bolts to 3.5 ft. lbs.(5.0 Nm) in a crisscross order.
13. Lower the vehicle and fill with 3 quarts of Dexron® II. Start the engine and allow it to get to operating temperature, running through the gears.
14. Check the fluid level in **P** and add until between the dimples in the **HOT** range on the dipstick. Make sure the fluid level does not go above the highest dimple. Road test, check for leaks and recheck the fluid level on level ground.

SHIFT SOLENOIDS

Removal and Installation

1. Disconnect the negative battery cable. Raise and support the vehicle safely. Drain automatic transaxle fluid and remove oil pan. Note the positions of the 2 cross-slotted bolts.
2. Unplug the solenoid(s) being replaced.
3. Replace the faulty solenoid(s) using a new O-ring lubricated with automatic transmission fluid.
4. Plug the solenoid connector(s) into the solenoid(s).
5. Install the oil pan. Apply sealant to the cross-slotted bolts and install them in the correct positions. Torque the pan bolts to 3.5 ft. lbs.(5.0 Nm) in a crisscross order.
6. Lower the vehicle and fill with 3 quarts of Dexron® II. Start the engine and allow it to get to operating temperature, running through the gears.
7. Check the fluid level in **P** and add until between the dim-

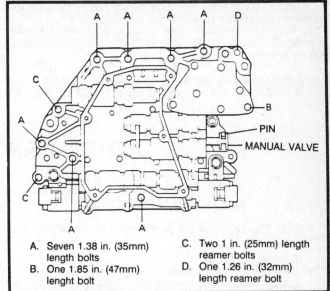

A. Seven 1.38 in. (35mm) length bolts
B. One 1.85 in. (47mm) lenght bolt
C. Two 1 in. (25mm) length reamer bolts
D. One 1.26 in. (32mm) length reamer bolt

Locations and lengths of the valve body bolts

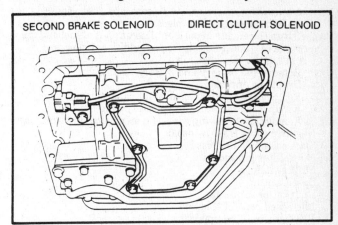

Locations of the two shift solenoids

ples in the **HOT** range on the dipstick. Make sure the fluid level does not go above the highest dimple. Road test, check for leaks and recheck the fluid level on level ground.

AXLE SEALS

Removal and Installation

1. Raise and support the vehicle safely. Drain about 2 quarts of fluid from the pan.
2. Remove the axle.
   a. Remove the axle outer end nut and washer.
   b. Disconnect the stabilizer joint from suspension arm.
   c. Remove the ball joint bolt and nut and separate suspension arm from knuckle.
   d. On the right side, remove the outer axle from the center bearing support. Use a plastic hammer to release the snapring fitting of the joint spline at the center support. Unbolt the center support bearing and remove the axle from the transaxle.
   e. On the left side, pry the axle from the transaxle and remove the axle.
3. Remove the seal using a slide hammer or seal remover tool. In either case, do not damage the seal bore when during removal.

4. Install the new seal using petroleum jelly or Dexron® II to lubricate the rubber sealing lip.

5. Fully seat the axle when installing being careful not to damage the new seal. The axle should snap into place when properly seated.

    a. On the right side, apply loctite to the threads and torque the center support bearing bolts to 35 ft. lbs. (48 Nm).

    b. Install the axle end nut. Torque to 108–145 ft. lbs. (150–200 Nm) and use a blunt end chisel to nick the nut flange into the locking groove on the axle end.

    c. Slip the ball joint stud back into place. Torque the nut and bolt to 36–51 ft. lbs. (50 to 70 Nm).

    d. Torque the stabilizer joint nuts to 13–20 ft. lbs. (18–28 Nm).

6. Replenish the fluid to the correct level and check for leaks.

REMOVAL AND INSTALLATION

TRANSAXLE REMOVAL

NOTE: The engine must be removed with the automatic transaxle.

1. Remove the hood.
2. Relieve the fuel pressure.

    a. Unplug the fuel pump relay located in the main fuse box near the engine coolant reservoir.

    b. Remove the gas cap to release any fuel vapors in the tank. Put the cap back in place.

    c. Run the engine in park until it runs out of fuel and crank a couple of times to dissipate any additional vapors.

    d. Plug the relay back in.

3. Remove the battery and battery tray.
4. Drain the antifreeze.
5. Remove the air cleaner assembly and ducts.
6. Remove the radiator, hoses and cooling fan.
7. Remove the following wires and all applicable wire clamps:
Negative cable from transaxle
Shift solenoids harness
Noise filter ground wire
Shift switch
Speed sensor
Distributor connector
Idle speed control solenoid
REGTS wire if equipped
Water temperature sender
Engine cooling fan thermo switch
Water temperature sensor
Oxygen sensor
Canister purge vacuum switching valve
EGR vacuum switching valve
Ground wire from intake manifold
Throttle position sensor
Fuel injector connector and holding clip
Alternator
Starter motor
Oil pressure sender

8. Disconnect the accelerator cable from the throttle lever and its bracket.
9. Disconnect the gear selector and throttle pressure cables.
10. Disconnect the speedometer cable.
11. Remove the brake booster hose, A/C vacuum switching valve hose and canister purge hose.
12. Disconnect and plug the fuel line hoses.
13. Disconnect the heater hoses.
14. Raise and safely support the vehicle.
15. Remove the exhaust pipe from exhaust manifold.
16. Drain the fluid, remove the torque converter inspection plate.
17. Remove the drive axles.

    a. Remove the axle outer end nut and washer.

    b. Disconnect the stabilizer joint from suspension arm.

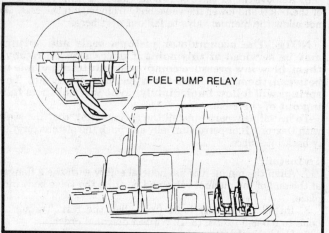

Location of the fuel pump relay and connector

    c. Remove the ball joint bolt and nut and separate suspension arm from knuckle.

    d. On the right side, remove the outer axle from the center bearing support. Use a plastic hammer to release the snapring fitting of the joint spline at the center support. Unbolt the center support bearing and remove the axle from the transaxle.

    e. On the left side, pry the axle from the transaxle and remove the axle.

18. Remove the rear engine torque bracket from the transaxle.
19. Lower the vehicle and attach a lifting device to the engine.
20. Remove the rear engine mount nut.
21. Remove the left side engine mount and bracket.
22. Remove the right side engine mount.
23. Check to see that all hoses, wires and cables are disconnected from the engine and transaxle and using the proper equipment remove the engine and transaxle from the vehicle.
24. Remove the torque converter bolts.
25. Remove the starter motor.
26. Remove the transaxle stiffener.
27. Remove all bolts and nuts fastening the transaxle to the engine and separate both components. Remove the torque converter if necessary.

NOTE: When removing transaxle from engine, move it in parallel with the crankshaft, so as not to apply any excessive force to the driveplate and torque converter.

TRANSAXLE INSTALLATION

1. Install the torque converter. When correctly installed, the distance from the edge of the converter to the front edge of the converter housing is 0.85 in. (21.4mm). If it is less, remove and

reinstall the converter. Apply grease to the cup in the center of the converter.

2. Join the engine and transaxle together and torque the bolts and nuts to 29–43 ft. lbs. (40–60 Nm).

3. Install the transaxle stiffener.

4. Install the starter motor.

5. Install the torque converter bolts. Apply loctite® to the threads and torque the torque converter bolts to 13–14 ft. lbs. (18–19 Nm).

6. Lower the engine and transaxle assembly into the engine compartment, but do not remove the lifting device.

7. Install the right side engine mount. Torque the bolts to 35–45 ft. lbs. (50–60 NM).

8. Install the left side engine mount bracket and engine mount. Torque the bolts to 35–45 ft. lbs. (50–60 Nm).

9. Install the rear engine mount nut and torque to 29–36 ft. lbs. (40–50 Nm). Remove the lifting device.

10. Raise the vehicle and install the drive axles.

   a. Torque the center support bearing bolts to 35 ft. lbs. (48 Nm).

   b. Torque the axle end nuts to 108–145 ft. lbs. (150–200 Nm) and use a blunt-end chisel to nick the nut flange into the locking groove on the axle end.

   c. Slip the ball joint stud back into place. Torque the nut and bolt to 36–51 ft. lbs. (50 to 70 Nm).

   d. Torque the stabilizer joint nuts to 13–20 ft. lbs. (18–28 Nm).

11. Install the engine rear torque bracket. Torque the bolts to 35–45 ft. lbs. (50–60 Nm).

12. Install the torque converter inspection cover.

13. Install the exhaust pipe to the exhaust manifold and lower the vehicle.

14. Connect the heater hoses.

15. Connect the fuel line hoses.

16. Install all wires, hoses and cables.

17. Install the radiator, hoses and cooling fan.

18. Install the air cleaner assembly and ducts.

19. Install the battery tray and battery.

20. Replenish all fluids to their correct levels.

21. Install and align the hood.

22. Road test, check for leaks and recheck fluid levels.

BENCH OVERHAUL

Before Disassembly

Cleanliness is an important factor in the overhaul of this automatic transaxle. Before opening up this unit, the entire outside of the transaxle assembly should be cleaned, preferable with a high pressure washer such as a car wash spray unit. Dirt entering the transaxle internal parts will negate all the time and effort spent on the overhaul. During inspection and reassembly all parts should be thoroughly cleaned with solvent then dried with compressed air. Wiping cloths and rags should not be used to dry parts since lint will find its way into the valve body passages.

Wheel bearing grease, long used to hold thrust washers and lube parts, should not be used. Lube seals with clean transaxle fluid and use ordinary unmedicated petroleum jelly to hold the thrust washers and to ease the assembly of seals, since it will not leave a harmful residue as grease often will. Do not use solvent on neoprene seals, friction plates if they are to be reused, or thrust washers. Be wary of nylon parts if the transaxle failure was due to failure of the cooling system. Nylon parts exposed to water or antifreeze solutions can swell and distort and must be replaced.

Before installing bolts into aluminum parts, always dip the threads into clean transaxle fluid. Antiseize compound can also be used to prevent bolts from galling the aluminum and seizing. Always use a torque wrench to keep from stripping the threads. Take care when installing new O-rings, especially the smaller O-rings. The internal snaprings should be expanded and the external rings should be compressed, if they are to be reused. This will help insure proper seating when installed.

Converter Inspection

Replace the unit if inspection shows cracks, burn spots, or any physical damage of any kind. Check the hub for excessive wear at the oil pump drive cut-outs and on the collar itself. Small amounts of wear in these spots are normal and should not warrant replacement of the converter. If any rust is found on the hub, it must be removed completely.

Position the converter horizontally on the bench and inspect the stator roller clutch by inserting a finger into the splined inner race of the roller clutch and turning the race in both directions. The inner race should turn freely clockwise, but should offer considerable resistance when turning counterclockwise.

If the stator clutch becomes ineffective, the stator assembly freewheels at all times in both directions. With this condition the vehicle tends to lack acceleration from a standstill. If the exhaust system is not blocked, the engine is properly in tune and the transaxle is starting in first gear, then a bad stator clutch is suspect.

If the stator assembly is locked up at all times, then the vehicle speed and rpm of the engine will be limited at high speeds, but, from a standstill, the acceleration will be normal. A blue color resulting from overheating may be evident on a converter that has been operating with a seized stator clutch.

Transaxle Disassembly

1. Remove the torque converter from the transaxle. Position the transaxle in a suitable holding fixture. Remove the left side engine mount bracket. Remove the speed sensor.

2. Unbolt the dipstick tube bracket and remove the tube and dipstick.

3. Tilt the transaxle and drain remaining fluid out through the vacant dipstick tube hole.

4. Remove the oil pan and gasket. If the fluid had not been drained prior to removal, do not flip the transaxle over to remove the pan—this will contaminate the rest of the unit with foreign matter in the pan.

5. Disconnect the direct clutch and second brake solenoids.

6. Remove the 2 oil tubes from the valve body by gently prying with a suitable pry bar. Do not deform the tubes by prying too hard. Note their locations for reassembly.

7. Remove the throttle pressure control cable from the cam and remove the cable.

8. Remove the strainer and valve body. Note the locations and the different lengths of the 11 valve body bolts as they are removed.

9. Remove the accumulator pistons and springs. Use a shop rag to catch the pistons and blow low pressure compressed air through the hole between them to pop the pistons into the rag. Do not push the pistons into their bores as this may spew fluid out.

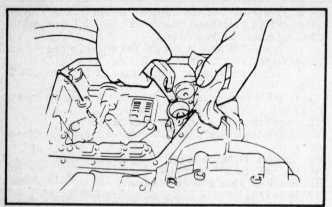

Removing the accumulator pistons

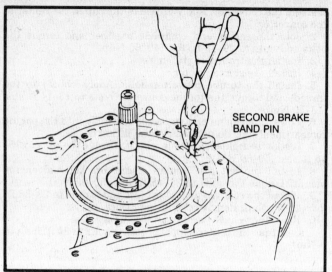

Rmoving the second brake band pin

SECOND BRAKE
BAND PIN

10. Remove the second brake band cover and gasket.
11. After removing the cover, check the second brake piston stroke as follows:

    a. Scribe a mark on the piston where it would be convenient to measure its movement.

    b. Blow low pressure compressed air into the hole and measure the movement.

    c. The stroke specification is 0.06–0.11 in. (1.5–3.0mm). If the stroke is not within specification, replace the band, or try a different piston rod. Piston rods are available in 2 lengths as spare parts:

    Unmarked—4.77 in. (121.3mm)
    Marked—4.83 in. (122.7mm)

12. Use the special valve lifter and a 17mm socket and 8mm bolt assembly to remove the second brake piston. Compress the cover first and remove the snapring. Then remove the tool assembly and tap on the cover lightly to remove it and the remainder of the piston assembly.
13. Remove the solenoid wiring harness.

NOTE: Do not attempt to remove the oil pump without first removing the second brake piston and piston rod. Doing so may cause the second brake band to break.

14. Remove 6 oil pump bolts and use the oil pump removal tool to remove the oil pump.
15. Remove the bolts attaching the converter housing to the case, tap the housing with a plastic hammer and separate the housing from the case.
16. Remove the second brake band pin.
17. Pull the input shaft up. The direct clutch and forward clutches should come up with the input shaft.

NOTE: The ring gear race and bearing may stick to the input shaft; be aware of these items.

18. Separate the direct clutch assembly from the input shaft.
19. Remove the second brake band.
20. Remove the front planetary ring gear and ring gear bearing and race.
21. Remove the planetary gear assembly.
22. Remove the planetary sun gear and front planetary gear bearing.
23. Remove the one-way clutch snapring.
24. Remove the one-way clutch and rear planetary gear. The one-way clutch should only turn in 1 direction and lock the other way.
25. Remove the rear planetary ring gear with the ring gear bearing and washers.
26. Check first/reverse brake clearance at this point. Insert a feeler gauge through the access opening and measure the clearance between the snapring and the flange. The clearance should

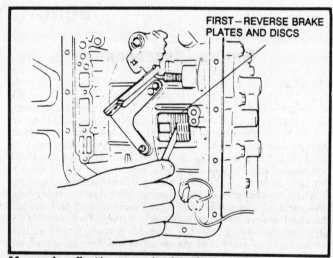

FIRST—REVERSE BRAKE
PLATES AND DISCS

Measuring first/reverse brake clearance

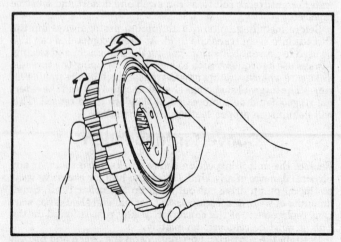

Checking the operation of the one-way clutch. It should turn in the direction of the arrows only

be 0.023–0.075 in. (0.58–1.92mm). If out of specification, the discs and/or plates are worn out.

27. Remove the 2 first/reverse brake snaprings.
28. Remove and inspect the first/reverse brake flange, 8 discs and plates and damper plate. Do not remove the first/reverse brake piston yet.
29. Remove the differential gear assembly.
30. Remove the 10 bolts and 2 nuts fastening the rear cover to the case and remove the rear cover.
31. Shift the manual lever to **P** so the output shaft is locked. Remove the reduction driven gear locknut and pull the gear off of the countershaft.
32. Drive the countershaft out of the case with a plastic hammer.
33. Remove the output shaft by pushing the inner output shaft bearing outer race in with the special remover tool from inside of the case. Do not hit the output shaft with a hammer.
34. Remove the parking pawl, shaft and sleeve.
35. Remove the manual detent spring and manual shift shaft.
36. Push down on first/reverse return spring assembly and remove the snapring.
37. Remove return spring assembly.
38. Carefully blow low pressure compressed air into the hole and push out the first/reverse brake piston

Unit Disassembly and Assembly

OIL PUMP

Disassembly

1. Remove the 2 oil pump cover seal rings.
2. Remove the oil pump cover O-ring.
3. Remove the 11 bolts that attach the cover to the body and separate the 2 pieces.

Inspection

Visually inspect the entire assembly for any type of excessive heat spots, scoring, damage or wear. Pay close attention to the inner and outer gear tooth surfaces. Also inspect the seal ring grooves for wear or burrs. Replace any item that is considered worn or damaged.

Perform the following clearance checks and replace items that do not meet specifications:

1. Measure the clearance between the body and the driven gear. It should be 0.0028–0.0059 in. (0.07–0.15mm) with a service limit of 0.011 in. (0.3mm).
2. Measure the clearance between the tooth tips of both the drive and driven gears and the crescent. It should be 0.0043–0.0055 in. (0.11–0.14mm) with a service limit of 0.011 in. (0.3mm).
3. Using a straight edge and feeler gauge, measure the flatness of the gears and the body. It should be 0.0008–0.0019 in. (0.02–0.05mm) with a service limit of 0.0039 in. (0.1mm).

Assembly

All components should be dipped in fresh Dexron® II before assembling.

1. Replace the body oil seal and coat the rubber lip with petroleum jelly.
2. Install the gears into the pump body.
3. Install the pump cover to the body and torque the 11 bolts to 6.0–8.5 ft. lbs. (8–12 Nm).
4. Replace the 2 pump cover seal rings and coat with automatic transmission fluid.
5. Replace the O-ring around the cover, making sure it is not twisted or extruding anywhere.
6. Check the drive gear for smooth rotation.

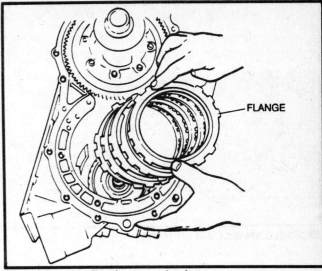

Removing the first/reverse brake

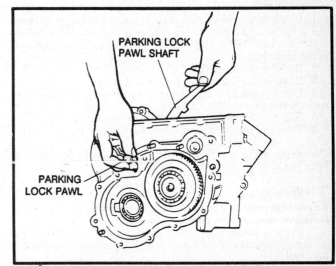

Removing the parking lock pawl and shaft

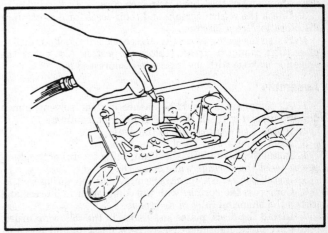

Location of the oil hole to use when removing the first/reverse brake piston

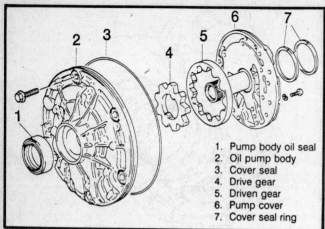

1. Pump body oil seal
2. Oil pump body
3. Cover seal
4. Drive gear
5. Driven gear
6. Pump cover
7. Cover seal ring

Exploded view of the oil pump

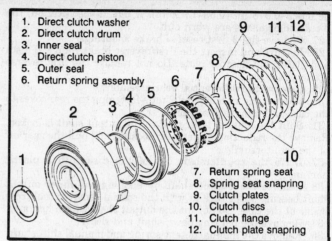

1. Direct clutch washer
2. Direct clutch drum
3. Inner seal
4. Direct clutch piston
5. Outer seal
6. Return spring assembly
7. Return spring seat
8. Spring seat snapring
9. Clutch plates
10. Clutch discs
11. Clutch flange
12. Clutch plate snapring

Exploded view of the direct clutch

DIRECT CLUTCH

Disassembly

1. Check direct clutch clearance. Measure the height between the snapring and clutch flange. The clearance should be 0.098–0.120 in. (2.49–3.06mm). If out of specification, the clutch pack needs servicing.
2. Remove the snapring.
3. Remove the flange and 5 discs and plates.
4. Use a press and the spring compressor to compress the springs and remove the snapring.
5. Remove the spring seat and return spring assembly.
6. Blow low pressure compressed air through the hole in the drum to pop the piston out.
7. Remove the inner seal from the drum and the outer seal from the piston.

Inspection

Visually inspect the entire assembly for cracks, or any type of excessive scoring, heat damage or wear.

1. Dry the plates and inspect them for discoloration. If the surface is smooth and not discolored, that plate can be reused; if not, replace it.
2. Dry the friction plates and inspect them for pitting, flaking, wear, glazing, cracking, charring, or chips of metal particles imbedded in the lining. Replace the entire pack if any of the discs show any of the above characteristics.
3. Check the return springs and their seats for distortion or discoloration from burning.
4. Shake the piston to see that the check ball is not jammed in place. If it cannot be freed, replace the piston. Also check the valve for leakage with low pressure compressed air.

Assembly

1. All components should be washed in clean solvent, blown dry and dipped in fresh Dexron® II before assembling.
2. Install a new inner seal in the drum.
3. Install a new outer seal on the piston.
4. Install the piston into the drum, being careful not to damage or twist the O-rings while doing so.
5. Install the return spring assembly and the spring seat.
6. Compress the springs with the compressor and press and install the snapring fully in its groove.
7. Install the discs, plates and flange in the following order: plate-disc-plate-plate-disc-flange. New discs should be thoroughly soaked with Dexron® II prior to installation.
8. Install the snapring.

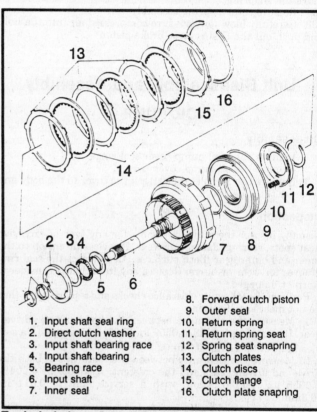

1. Input shaft seal ring
2. Direct clutch washer
3. Input shaft bearing race
4. Input shaft bearing
5. Bearing race
6. Input shaft
7. Inner seal
8. Forward clutch piston
9. Outer seal
10. Return spring
11. Return spring seat
12. Spring seat snapring
13. Clutch plates
14. Clutch discs
15. Clutch flange
16. Clutch plate snapring

Exploded view of the forward clutch

9. Recheck direct clutch clearance. If out of specification after replacing the clutch pack, use a different flange. They are available in 0.118 or 0.132 in (3.00 or 3.37mm) thicknesses. Make sure the clearance is within specification before finishing with the direct clutch.
10. Check the piston for movement by blowing low pressure compressed air through the hole in the drum.

FORWARD CLUTCH

Disassembly

1. Check forward clutch clearance. Measure the height between the snapring and clutch flange. The clearance should be

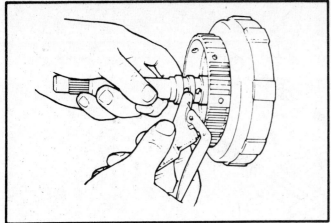

Blow low pressure compressed air through this hole to remove the forward clutch piston

0.079–0.105 in. (2.01–2.68mm). If out of specification, the clutch pack needs servicing.

2. Remove the snapring.

3. Remove the flange and 6 discs and plates.

4. Use a press and the spring compressor to compress the springs and remove the snapring.

5. Remove the spring seat and return spring assembly.

6. Blow low pressure compressed air through the hole in the input shaft to pop the piston out.

7. Remove the inner and outer O-rings from the piston.

Inspection

1. All parts of the forward clutch may be inspected in the identical manner that the direct clutch parts were.

2. All of the same guidelines apply.

3. In addition, inspect the input shaft for any damage.

Assembly

1. All components should be washed in clean solvent, blown dry and dipped in fresh Dexron® II before assembling.

2. Install new inner and outer seals on the piston.

3. Install the piston into the input shaft drum, being careful not to damage or twist the O-rings while doing so.

4. Install the return spring assembly (18 springs) and the spring seat.

5. Compress the springs with the compressor and press and install the snapring fully in its groove.

6. Install the discs, plates and flange in the following order: plate-disc-plate-disc-plate-disc-flange. New discs should be thoroughly soaked with Dexron® II prior to installation.

7. Install the snapring.

8. Recheck direct clutch clearance. If out of specification after replacing the clutch pack, use a different flange. They are available in 0.118 or 0.132 in (3.00 or 3.37mm) thicknesses. Make sure the clearance is within specification before finishing with the forward clutch.

9. Check the piston for movement by blowing low pressure compressed air through the hole in the input shaft.

VALVE BODY

Disassembly

NOTE: The valve body is a precisely machined part. Handle it with great care and do not clamp in a vise. The material is fragile and could distort easily. When disassembling, keep all parts labeled and in a well-arranged

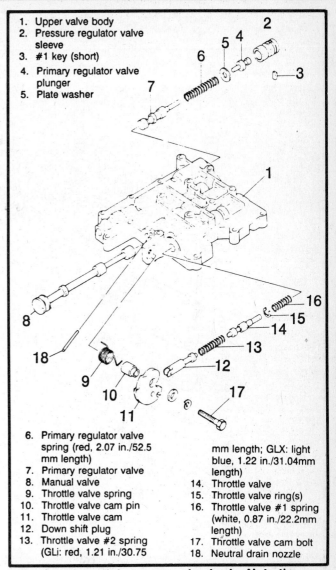

1. Upper valve body
2. Pressure regulator valve sleeve
3. #1 key (short)
4. Primary regulator valve plunger
5. Plate washer
6. Primary regulator valve spring (red, 2.07 in./52.5 mm length)
7. Primary regulator valve
8. Manual valve
9. Throttle valve spring
10. Throttle valve cam pin
11. Throttle valve cam
12. Down shift plug
13. Throttle valve #2 spring (GLi: red, 1.21 in./30.75 mm length; GLX: light blue, 1.22 in./31.04mm length)
14. Throttle valve
15. Throttle valve ring(s)
16. Throttle valve #1 spring (white, 0.87 in./22.2mm length)
17. Throttle valve cam bolt
18. Neutral drain nozzle

Exploded view of the upper valve body. Note the difference between the throttle valve #2 spring in the GLI and the one in the GLX

order, since many of them look similar. Cleanliness is of the utmost importance when working with valve bodies; even the most minuscule piece of dirt can restrict valve movement and impair the transaxle's performance.

1. Unbolt and separate the lower body from the upper body. Watch for the 4 steel balls in the upper body.

2. When disassembling the valve body, keep each valve together with its corresponding spring.

3. Disassemble the unit as completely as desired, depending on the symptoms.

Inspection

1. Check the bodies and accompanying components for damage, wear and cracks.

2. Check the valves and their bores for damage and burrs. Slight burrs may be sanded out with crocus cloth only.

3. Check for oil passage damage and restrictions.

4. Check for spring fatigue or deformation and make sure the retaining keys install well in their keyways.

5. Check the operation of the solenoids if they are suspect.

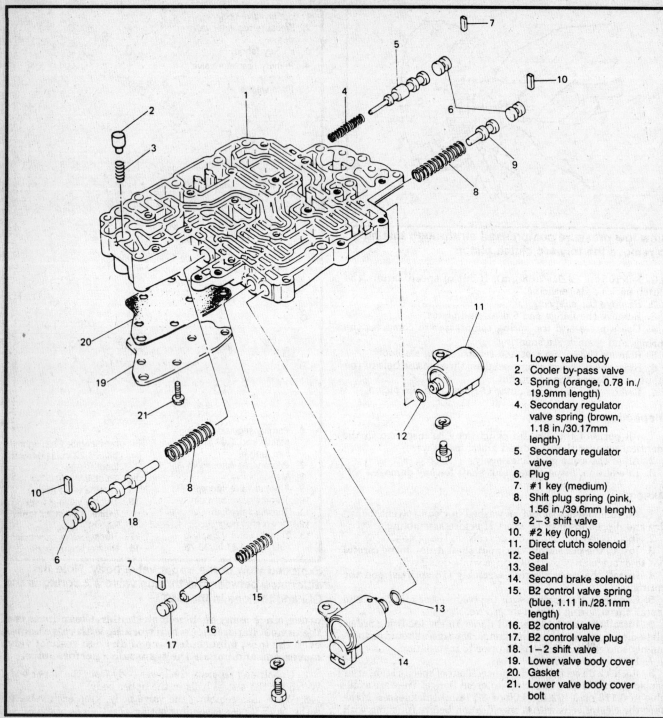

1. Lower valve body
2. Cooler by-pass valve
3. Spring (orange, 0.78 in./ 19.9mm length)
4. Secondary regulator valve spring (brown, 1.18 in./30.17mm length)
5. Secondary regulator valve
6. Plug
7. #1 key (medium)
8. Shift plug spring (pink, 1.56 in./39.6mm lenght)
9. 2–3 shift valve
10. #2 key (long)
11. Direct clutch solenoid
12. Seal
13. Seal
14. Second brake solenoid
15. B2 control valve spring (blue, 1.11 in./28.1mm length)
16. B2 control valve
17. B2 control valve plug
18. 1–2 shift valve
19. Lower valve body cover
20. Gasket
21. Lower valve body cover bolt

Exploded view of the lower valve body

Assembly

1. Wash all parts in clean solvent and blow dry. All components should be dipped in fresh Dexron® II before assembling.

2. Install all valves, plugs, seats, etc. in the reverse order of removal and in the proper installing direction. Install the correct keys after the corresponding parts have been inserted in its bore.

3. Keep all check balls and springs in their orifices with petroleum jelly. They must be in their correct location in order for the overhaul to succeed.

4. Several of the throttle valve rings are used at the throttle valve in the upper body. Install the same number of throttle valve rings as those used before disassembling.

5. Use all new gaskets and seals when assembling the valve body.

6. Install the lower body onto the upper body. Install the 2

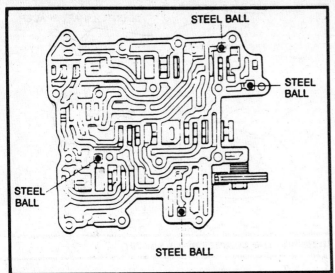

Locations of four steel balls in the upper valve body

A. Six 1.16 in. (29.5mm) length bolts
B. Six 1.49 in. (38mm) length bolts
C. Two 1.73 in. (44mm) length bolts
D. Two reamer bolts

Torque the upper valve body bolts in the order indicated by the circled numbers and to the torques indicated

reamer bolts first, then torque all of the bolts to the specified torque according to the circled numbers.

7. Install the filter onto the lower body. Torque the bolts to the specified torque.

SECOND BRAKE PISTON

Disassembly

1. Remove the piston rod from the piston by removing the E-clip.
2. Remove all sealing rings from the piston cover.
3. Remove all sealing rings from the piston.
4. Remove the sealing ring from the piston rod.

Inspection

1. Check all parts and the piston bore for damage or wear.

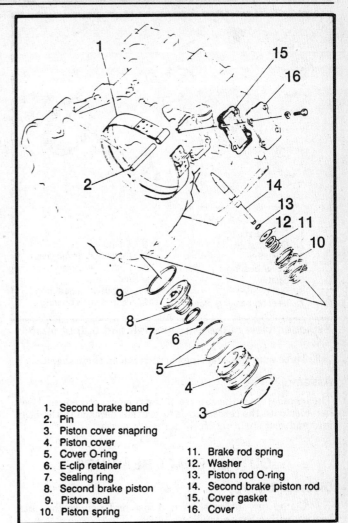

1. Second brake band
2. Pin
3. Piston cover snapring
4. Piston cover
5. Cover O-ring
6. E-clip retainer
7. Sealing ring
8. Second brake piston
9. Piston seal
10. Piston spring
11. Brake rod spring
12. Washer
13. Piston rod O-ring
14. Second brake piston rod
15. Cover gasket
16. Cover

Exploded view of second brake components

2. Check all seal ring grooves for sharp edges or burrs.
3. Check the springs for sufficient tension.

Assembly

1. Coat all new sealing rings with fresh Dexron® II.
2. Install the new O-rings on the piston rod and piston.
3. Assemble the piston and rod assembly with the E-clip. Install the assembly into its bore in the case.
2. Install new O-rings on the piston cover and use the tool to install it. Secure the snapring.

COUNTERSHAFT BEARINGS

Diassembly

1. Remove the snaprings from inside of the case.
2. Remove the bearing backing plate from the rear cover side.
3. Use the bearing puller and slide hammer to remove the bearings, first the ball bearing, then the roller bearing.

Inspection

1. Remove the countershaft gear and check the gear and splines for damage or wear.
2. Check the bearings and spacers for smoothness and wear.

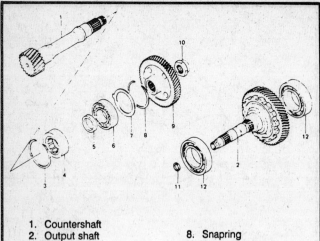

1. Countershaft
2. Output shaft
3. Snapring
4. Roller bearing
5. Spacer
6. Ball bearing
7. Bearing backing plate
8. Snapring
9. Reduction driven gear
10. Reduction driven gear nut
11. Output shaft seal ring
12. Output shaft bearing

Exploded view of the countershaft and output shaft

3. Make sure the snaprings have retained their shape.

Assembly

The installation is the reverse of the removal procedure. Use a hammer with the correct tools to prevent damage to the bearings and seat snaprings fully in their grooves.

OUTPUT SHAFT BEARINGS

Disassembly

1. Clamp the output shaft in a vise and remove the outer bearing with a bearing puller.
2. Flip the assembly over and remove the inner bearing by holding the bearing with a puller and driving the shaft out with a press. Do not hit shaft end with a hammer or the seal ring groove may be damaged.

Inspection

1. Check the output shaft gear splines and parking gear for damage or wear.
2. Check the bearings for smoothness and wear.
3. Check the seal groove for sharp edges or burrs.

Assembly

The installation is the reverse of the removal procedure. Use a press with the correct tools to prevent damage to the bearings.

DIFFERENTIAL ASSEMBLY

Disassembly

1. Remove the ring gear side bearing with a bearing puller.
2. Unbolt 8 ring gear bolts and remove the ring gear.
3. Hold the other side bearing with a puller, set in a vise and drive the case from within the bearing.
4. Remove the speedometer pinion.
5. Remove the side pinion shaft roll pin.
6. Remove the side pinion shaft, differential pinions with washers and differential gears with trashers.

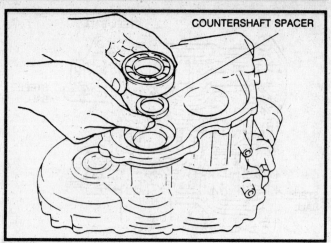

Installing the counter shaft spacer

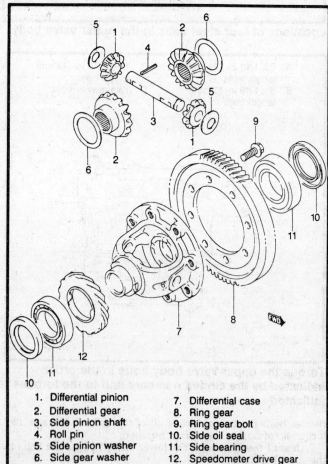

1. Differential pinion
2. Differential gear
3. Side pinion shaft
4. Roll pin
5. Side pinion washer
6. Side gear washer
7. Differential case
8. Ring gear
9. Ring gear bolt
10. Side oil seal
11. Side bearing
12. Speedometer drive gear

Exploded view of the differential assembly

Inspection

1. Visually inspect all parts for excessive wear or damage. Inspect the speedometer gear if the speedometer was faulty.
2. The pinion gears should fit snug on the side pinion shaft.
3. The differential gears should also fit snug in the case.
4. The axle shafts should fit snug into their bores.

Assembly

1. Wash all parts in clean solvent and dry prior to assembly.

2. Assemble the side gears into the case and measure the thrust play.

a. Using a dial indicator, move the gears up and down one at a time and read the dial indicator.

b. The specifications for thrust play is 0.002–0.013 in. (0.05–0.33mm). If out of specification, adjust by selecting the correct washer. They are available in 0.002 in. (0.05mm) increments from 0.035–0.047 in. (0.90–1.20mm) thick.

3. Install the differential pinion washers and pinions, side pinion shaft. Drive the roll pin in from the right side until it is flush with the differential case surface.

4. Install the speedometer pinion.

5. Install the side bearings.

6. Install the ring gear, offset side toward the case. Torque the 8 bolts to 58–65 ft. lbs. (80–90 Nm).

Transaxle Assembly

1. Install the lower washer and parking lock rod to the manual shift shaft. Replace the shift shaft seal and install the shaft to the case; then the detent spring. Torque the nut and bolt to 7 ft. lbs. (9.5 Nm).

2. Install the keyed manual shift lever to the shift shaft and torque the 2 nuts to 21 ft. lbs. (29 Nm). Check the mechanism for smooth rotation.

3. Install the restrictor pin and snapring to the parking pawl sleeve and insert into the case.

4. To install the parking pawl, place the shift lever in any gear except **P**. Install the pawl, shaft and return spring and check for smooth movement when the manual shift lever is moved.

5. Replace the first/reverse brake piston inner and outer seals and insert the piston into the case so the spring holes are facing upward.

6. Place the return spring assembly on the piston, installing all the springs in their holes. Push the assembly down and install the snapring.

7. Using the bearing installer and hammer, carefully install the countershaft into the case. Make sure the spacer is in place above the lower ball bearing.

8. Shift the manual lever into any gear except **P** and install the output shaft in place with the bearing installer.

9. Shift back into **P** and install the reduction driven gear on the countershaft. Torque the nut to 80–108 ft. lbs. (110–150 Nm) and stake it at 2 points.

10. Scrape the rear cover mating surfaces and apply the new gasket. Install the rear cover making sure the output shaft bearing enters into the hole smoothly. Torque the 10 bolts to 14 ft. lbs. (16 Nm) and the 2 nuts to 9 ft. lbs. (12 Nm). Seat the output shaft against the rear cover completely and check the smoothness of the shaft rotation before proceeding.

11. Engage the teeth of the ring gear and countershaft gear and install the differential assembly. Use the bearing installer to seat it in place.

12. Install first/reverse damper plate on return spring assembly with the smaller-diameter side facing upward.

13. Install discs, plates and flange in the following order: plate-disc-plate-disc-plate-disc-plate-disc-flange – flat side downward.

14. Install the snapring in the case.

15. Recheck the first/reverse brake clutch clearance as in Step 26 of the disassembly procedure. Also check the operation of the piston by blowing low pressure compressed air into the oil hole.

16. Install the rear planetary ring gear. Engage the center of the gear to the splines of the output shaft.

17. Install the first ring gear race flange side upward, the bearing and the other race flange side upward.

18. Place the thrust washers on the rear planetary gear, matching the lugs. Install the planetary gear into the case. Make sure the thrust washer did not get misaligned.

19. Install the snapring in the case.

20. Install the one-way clutch on the planetary gear by turning planetary gear clockwise. Confirm rotation of the planetary clockwise and lock up counterclockwise.

21. Install the snapring; the snapring ends must be between lugs.

22. Install the pin in the sun gear and put the thrust washer in place with petroleum jelly to keep in from falling off during installation. Make sure the pin is installed in the thrust washer notch.

23. Push the sun gear in place by engaging it with the rear planetary gear. Make sure the thrust washer is still in place before proceeding.

24. Install the front planetary gear bearing and then the race flange side downward.

25. Install the front planetary gear assembly onto the sun gear.

26. Install the first ring gear race flange side upward, the bearing and the other race flange side downward.

27. Install the front planetary ring gear assembly on to the planetary gear.

28. Install the second brake band.

29. Install a new output shaft seal ring.

30. Install new seal rings on the input shaft.

31 Install the clutch washer on the direct clutch with the grooved face outward and aligning the 3 lugs with the grooves on the drum.

32. Install the direct clutch on the input shaft.

33. Install the first ring gear race – OD: 1.41 in. (35.8mm) – flange side downward. Install first the other race – OD: 1.49 in. (37.9mm) – then the bearing onto the input shaft with plenty of petroleum jelly as they will be upside down in the next step.

34. Insert the input shaft with direct clutch into the case.

35. Measure the distance from the case end surface to the input shaft flange to verify correct installation of all previously installed components. The distance should be 1.962–2.010 in. (49.82–51.06mm). If out of specification, find the problem before proceeding.

36. Dip the brake band pin in Dexron® II, align the hole in second brake band with the case pin hole and insert the pin.

37. Clean the mating surfaces of the case and converter housing and install a new gasket. Apply sealant ot the threads of the 3 Torx® bolts and install them in the proper positions. Torque all bolts to 12–16.5 ft. lbs. (16–23 Nm).

38. If desired, the input shaft position can be measured with the converter housing installed by measuring from the edge of the converter housing to the input shaft flange. The distance this time should be 7.416–7.477 in. (188.37–189.91mm).

39. Place the first input shaft bearing race flange side upward on the input shaft flange and install the bearing into it. Place the other race on the oil pump with plenty of petroleum jelly.

40. Place the direct clutch washer on the oil pump body, aligning the washer flange with the notch in the pump body.

NOTE: Make sure all seals on the pump are new and well lubricated before installing the pump.

41. Align the oil pump bolts holes with those of the case and install the pump carefully. Make sure that both washers and all seals are intact during the installation. Torque the 6 bolts gradually to 13.5–19.5 ft. lbs. (18–27 Nm) in crisscross order. Turn the input shaft to confirm smooth rotation.

42. Position a dial indicator so the pin rests on the end of the input shaft and measure the thrust play. The play should be 0.012–0.035 in. (0.3–0.9mm). Adjust by removing the oil pump and selecting the correct input shaft bearing race. They are available in either 0.031 or 0.055 in. (0.8 or 1.4mm) thick. If replacing the race, recheck the thrust play and reconfirm smooth rotation of the input shaft.

43. Install the solenoid wire harness with new O-ring in the grommet and hold in place with 3 clamps.

44. Check the second band brake and rod for correct installation and recheck rod stroke as in Step 11 of the disassembly. In-

1. Ring gear race
2. Ring gear bearing
3. Ring gear race
4. Snapring
5. Ring gear flange
6. Ring gear race
7. Front planetary ring gear
8. Front planetary gear assembly
9. Front planetary gear race
10. Front planetary gear bearing
11. Input drum snapring
12. Planetary sun gear
13. Sun gear input drum
14. Snapring
15. Planetary thrust washer
16. Rear planetary thrust washer
17. Sun gear pin
18. One-way clutch race snapring
19. One-way clutch snap ring
20. One-way clutch
21. One-way clutch race

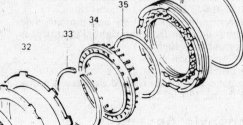

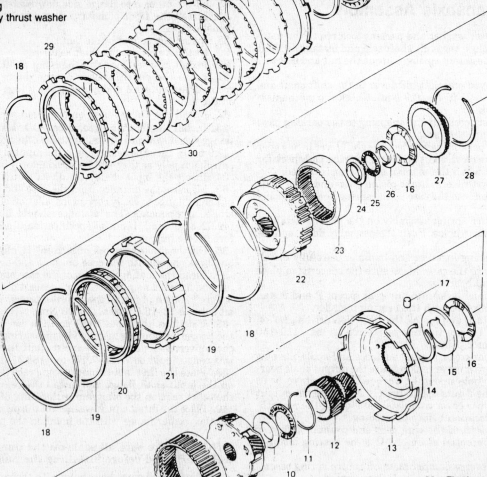

22. Rear planetary gear assembly
23. Rear planetary ring gear
24. Rear ring gear race
25. Ring gear bearing
26. Rear ring gear race
27. Ring gear flange
28. Ring gear snapring
29. First/reverse brake flange
30. First/reverse brake discs
31. First/reverse brake plates
32. First/reverse brake damper plate
33. Return spring snapring
34. First/reverse brake return spring
35. Piston inner seal
36. First/reverse brake piston
37. Piston outer seal

Exploded view of planetary gears and all related parts

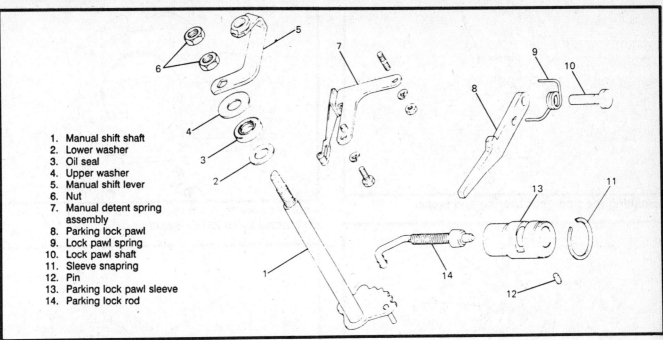

1. Manual shift shaft
2. Lower washer
3. Oil seal
4. Upper washer
5. Manual shift lever
6. Nut
7. Manual detent spring assembly
8. Parking lock pawl
9. Lock pawl spring
10. Lock pawl shaft
11. Sleeve snapring
12. Pin
13. Parking lock pawl sleeve
14. Parking lock rod

Manual shift shaft, parking pawl and related parts

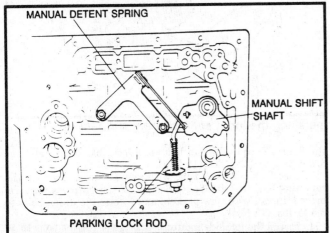

Manual shift shaft and detent spring assembly

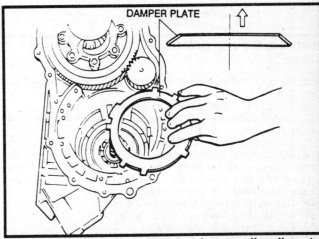

Install the first/reverse damper plate smaller-diameter side facing up of the first/reverse brake piston

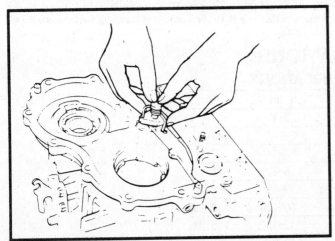

Installing the parking pawl shaft and return spring

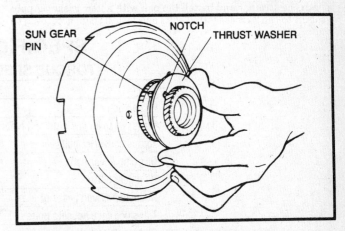

Installing the sun gear pin and thrust washer

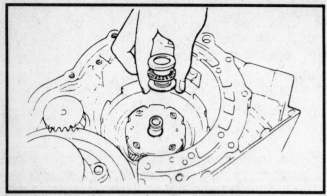

Installing the ring gear bearing and races

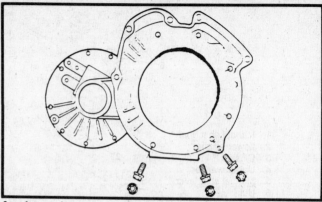

Apply sealant to the threads of these 3 Torx® bolts and install them in the positions shown

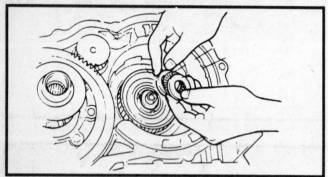

Installing the ring gear bearing and different-size races

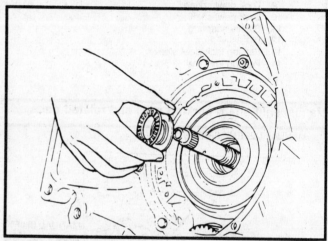

Installing the input shaft bearing and race

stall the cover with a new gasket. Torque the bolts to 5.5–6.5 ft. lbs. (7–9 Nm).

45. Install the throttle pressure cable in the case.

46. Install the accumulator springs and pistons with new seals in their bores.

47. Align the manual shift lever pin with the 2 flanges at the end of the manual shift valve and install the valve body with the correct length bolts at the correct spots. The reamer bolts get torqued first to 6.0–8.5 ft. lbs. (8–12 Nm), then tighten the rest to the same torque in crisscross order.

48. Connect the throttle cable to the cam.

49. Install the tubes to the valve body.

50. Connect the 2 solenoid wires.

51. Install the strainer and second brake solenoid wire clamp. Torque the bolts to 4 ft. lbs. (5.5 Nm).

52. Place the magnet in the oil pan where it will be directly beneath the strainer and install the pan with a new gasket. Apply sealant to the 2 cross-slotted bolts and install them according to

the figure. Torque the pan bolts to 3.5 ft. lbs. (5 Nm) and the drain plug to 14 ft. lbs. (19 Nm).

53. Install the dipstick tube with new O-ring and torque the retaining bolt to 4 ft. lbs. (5.5 Nm). If the oil pipes were removed, install with new gaskets and torque the union bolts to 8.5 ft. lbs. (12 Nm).

54. Install the left side mount bracket. Torque the bolts to 40 ft. lbs. (55 Nm). Install the speed sensor.

55. Install the torque converter and apply grease to the cup in the center of the converter. If correctly installed, the distance from the flange nut to the converter housing surface is 0.85 in. (21.4mm).

SPECIFICATIONS
TORQUE SPECIFICATIONS

Part	ft. lbs.	Nm
Oil pan bolts	3–4	4–6
Transaxle to engine nuts and bolts	29–43	40–60
Torque converter bolts	13–14	18–19
Oil pump cover bolts	6–8.5	8–12
Ring gear bolts	58–65	80–90
Reduction driven gear nut	80–108	110–150
Transaxle case housing bolts	12–16.5	16–23
Oil pipe union bolts	8–9	11–13

Section 2

A132L Transaxle
Toyota

APPLICATION

1987–89 Toyota Tercel Sedan with 1.5L engine

GENERAL DESCRIPTION

The A132L transaxle is a fully automatic 3 speed consisting of a valve body, 2 planetary carriers, 3 brakes, 4 clutch packs, 2 one-way clutches, an oil pump, a torque converter, a differential assembly and final drive gear set. All of the above components are integrated into a single compact unit. An oil cooler is built into the bottom of the radiator to cool the transaxle fluid. Rubber hoses are used to carry the fluid from the transaxle to the cooler.

Power from the engine is transmitted to the input shaft of the direct clutch by the torque converter and is then transmitted to the planetary gears by the operation of the clutch. The operation of the brake or one-way clutch causes either the planetary carrier or the planetary sun gear to be immobilized and changes the speed of the planetary gear unit. Shift changes are carried out by altering the combination of clutch and brake operation.

Each clutch and brake operates by hydraulic pressure which is produced by the rotation of the oil pump. The pressurized fluid is regulated by the valve body and shift change automatically occurs according to throttle opening and vehicle speed.

The torque converter provides a fluid coupling between the engine and transaxle for optimum power transfer when driving at a constant speed and increased torque when starting, accelerating and climbing an incline. The damper clutch is used in the torque converter to provide a solid coupling for improved fuel mileage when at cruising ranges.

Transaxle and Converter Identification

TRANSAXLE

An identification plate is mounted on the right side of the transaxle case which contains the model number and build date of the unit.

CONVERTER

The torque converter is a 3 element type and has an internal damper clutch. It is a welded 1 piece unit and cannot be disassembled for inspection purposes.

Electronic Controls

Since the A132L transaxle is a hydraulically controlled transaxle, its only transaxle related electronic component is the neutral safety switch, which is mounted on the side of the case with the shift control cable lever mounted to it.

It is a conventional neutral safety switch that will prevent the vehicle from starting in any gear except **P** or **N**. The neutral

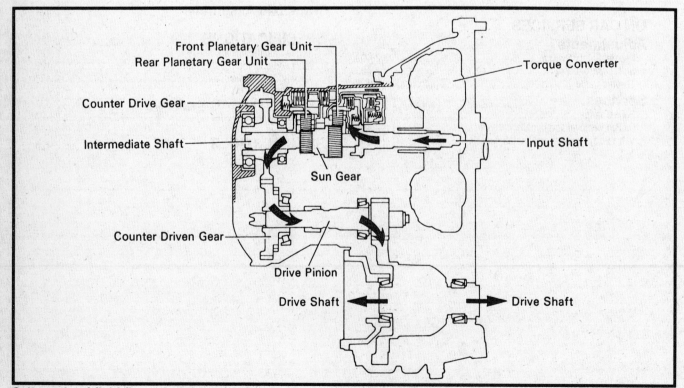

Schematic of fluid flow—A132L transaxle

safety switch also completes the reverse light circuit when backing up.

Metric Fasteners

Metric tools will be required to service this transaxle. Due to the large number of alloy parts used in this transaxle, torque specifications should be strictly observed. Before installing capscrews into aluminum parts, dip the bolts into clean Dexron®II as this will prevent the screws from galling the aluminum threads, thus causing damage.

Metric fastener dimensions are very close to the dimensions of the familiar inch system fasteners. For this reason replacement fasteners must have the same measurement and strength as the original fastener.

Do not attempt to interchange metric fasteners for inch system fasteners. Mismatched or incorrect fasteners can cause damage to the automatic transaxle and possible personal injury. Care should be taken to reuse fasteners in their original locations.

Capacities

When changing the transaxle fluid, drain and refill capacity is 2.3 qts. (2.2L) of Dexron®II. When filling the transaxle dry, capacity is 5.9 qts. (5.6L) of Dexron®II. Differential capacity is 1.5 qts. (1.4L) of Dexron®II.

Checking Fluid Level

Run the engine until at operating temperature and move the gear selector through all ranges. Park the vehicle on level surface and check the fluid level in P range. The fluid level is sufficient when it is within the **HOT** range on the dipstick.

TRANSAXLE MODIFICATIONS

No modifications are available at the time of publication.

TROUBLE DIAGNOSIS

CLUTCH AND BRAKE APPLICATION

Shift lever position	Gear position	Forward Clutch	Direct Clutch	Second Coast Brake	Second Brake	1st/Reverse Brake	Number 1 one-way clutch	Number 2 one-way clutch
P	Parking	—	—	—	—	—	—	—
R	Reverse	—	Applied	—	—	Applied	—	—
N	Neutral	—	—	—	—	—	—	—
D	1st	Applied	—	—	—	—	—	Applied
D	2nd	Applied	—	—	Applied	—	Applied	—
D	3rd	Applied	Applied	—	Applied	—	—	—
2	1st	Applied	—	—	—	—	—	Applied
2	2nd	Applied	—	Applied	Applied	—	Applied	—
L	1st	Applied	—	—	—	Applied	—	Applied
L	2nd	Applied	—	Applied	Applied	—	Applied	—

CHILTON'S THREE C'S TRANSAXLE DIAGNOSIS

Condition	Cause	Correction
Fluid discolored or smells burnt	a) Fluid contaminated b) Torque converter faulty c) Transaxle faulty	a) Replace fluid b) Replace torque converter c) Disassemble and inspect transaxle
Vehicle does not move in any forward range or reverse	a) Shift cable out of adjustment b) Valve body or primary regulator faulty c) Parking lock pawl faulty d) Torque converter faulty e) Converter drive plate broken f) Oil pump intake strainer blocked g) Transaxle faulty	a) Adjust shift cable b) Inspect valve body c) Inspect parking lock pawl d) Replace torque converter e) Replace torque converter f) Clean strainer g) Disassemble and inspect transaxle

CHILTON'S THREE C'S TRANSAXLE DIAGNOSIS

Condition	Cause	Correction
No 1/2 upshift	a) Governor faulty b) 1/2 shift valve stuck c) 2nd brake faulty d) No. 1 one-way clutch faulty	a) Inspect governor b) Inspect valve body c) Disassemble and inspect transaxle d) Disassemble and inspect transaxle
No 2/3 upshift	a) Governor faulty b) 2/3 shift valve stuck c) Direct clutch faulty	a) Inspect governor b) Inspect valve body c) Disassemble and inspect transaxle
Not moving in drive	a) Valve body faulty b) Forward clutch faulty c) No. 2 one-way clutch faulty	a) Inspect valve body b) Disassemble and inspect transaxle c) Disassemble and inspect transaxle
Not moving in second	a) Valve body faulty b) No. 2 one-way clutch faulty	a) Inspect valve body b) Disassemble and inspect transaxle
Not moving in reverse	a) Valve body faulty b) Direct clutch faulty c) 1st/reverse brake faulty	a) Inspect valve body b) Disassemble and inspect transaxle c) Disassemble and inspect transaxle
Not moving in any forward range	a) Valve body faulty b) Forward clutch faulty	a) Inspect valve body b) Disassemble and inspect transaxle
Shift lever position incorrect	a) Shift cable out of adjustment b) Manual valve and lever faulty c) Transaxle faulty	a) Adjust shift cable b) Inspect valve body c) Disassemble and inspect transaxle
Harsh engagement into any drive range	a) Throttle cable out of adjustment b) Valve body or primary regulator faulty c) Accumulator pistons faulty d) Transaxle faulty	a) Adjust throttle cable b) Inspect valve body c) Inspect accumulator pistons d) Disassemble and inspect transaxle
Delayed 1/2, 2/3 or upshift, or downshifts from 3/2 then shifts back to 3rd	a) Throttle cable out of adjustment b) Governor faulty c) Valve body faulty	a) Adjust throttle cable b) Inspect governor c) Inspect valve body
Slips on 1/2, 2/3 upshift, or slips or shudders on takeoff	a) Shift cable out of adjustment b) Throttle cable out of adjustment c) Valve body faulty d) Transaxle faulty	a) Adjust shift cable b) Adjust throttle cable c) Inspect valve body d) Disassemble and inspect transaxle
Drag, binding or tieup on 1/2, 2/3 upshift	a) Shift cable out of adjustment b) Valve body faulty c) Transaxle faulty	a) Adjust shift cable b) Inspect valve body c) Disassemble and inspect transaxle
Harsh downshift	a) Throttle cable out of adjustment b) Accumulator pistons faulty c) Valve body faulty d) Transaxle faulty	a) Adjust throttle cable b) Inspect accumulator pistons c) Inspect valve body d) Disassemble and inspect transaxle
No downshift when coasting	a) Governor faulty b) Valve body faulty	a) Inspect governor b) Inspect valve body
Downshift occurs too quick or too late while coasting	a) Throttle cable out of adjustment b) Governor faulty c) Valve body faulty d) Transaxle faulty	a) Adjust throttle cable b) Inspect governor c) Inspect valve body d) Disassemble and inspect transaxle
No 3/2 or 2/1 kickdown	a) Throttle cable out of adjustment b) Governor faulty c) Valve body faulty	a) Adjust throttle cable b) Inspect governor c) Inspect valve body
No engine braking in 2 range	a) Valve body faulty b) Transaxle faulty	a) Inspect valve body b) Disassemble and inspect transaxle
Vehicle does not hold in park	a) Control cable out of adjustment b) Parking lock pawl and rod	a) Adjust control cable b) Inspect parking lock pawl and rod
Transaxle fluid in antifreeze or antifreeze in transaxle fluid	a) Cooler cone in the radiator leaking	a) Replace radiator and replace the transaxle fluid

Hydraulic Control System

Hydraulic pressure supplied by the oil pump is controlled by the regulator valve and is called line pressure. Line pressure reduces the hydraulic pressure used for throttle pressure and governor pressure. Also, line pressure provides the necessary hydraulic pressure to operate each brake and clutch in the transaxle.

The throttle valve produces throttle pressure which is directly proportional to the amount of throttle opening. The governor valve produces governor pressure which is directly proportional to the vehicle speed.

When shift change occurs in accordance with the difference between throttle and governor pressures, the corresponding shift valve moves, the fluid passages to the correct clutches and brakes are opened and the clutches and brakes are operational

For example, when the vehicle speed increases the governor pressure increases and overcomes throttle pressure and spring tension. The 2/3 shift valve is forced upward and the line pressure passage is opened. Fluid is directed to the direct clutch and the gear is shifted up to 3rd.

Diagnosis Tests

STALL SPEED TEST

--- CAUTION ---

Never allow anyone to stand near — especially in front of or behind — the vehicle when performing a stall test

1. Check the fluid level and condition. Perform the test at normal operating temperature.
2. Block the wheels securely and firmly set the parking brake.
3. Connect a tachometer to the engine.
4. Push down the brake pedal firmly and shift the gear selector to **D**.
5. Gradually depress the accelerator pedal. Do not perform this step for more than 5 seconds.
6. When the engine has stopped increasing in speed, read the tachometer and immediately release the accelerator pedal.
7. Shift into **N**. Allow the engine to idle for 1 minute so the fluid can cool and to prevent the possibility of overheating.
8. Perform the stall test in **R** range.
9. The stall speed specification is 2,100 ± 150 rpm for 1987 vehicles and 2,300 ± 150 rpm for 1988–89 vehicles.
10. If the stall speed is lower than specification in **D** and **R**, then either the engine output is insufficient or the stator one-way clutch is not operating properly.
11. If the stall speed is higher than specification in **D**, then the line pressure is too low, the forward clutch is slipping or one-way clutch No. 2 is not operating properly.
12. If the stall speed is higher than specification in **R**, then the line pressure is too low, the direct clutch is slipping or the 1st/reverse brake is slipping.
13. If the stall speed is higher than specification in **D** and **R**, then either the line pressure is low or the fluid level is incorrect.

TIME LAG TEST

This test is used to check the condition of the forward clutch, direct clutch and the 1st/reverse clutch. When the shift lever is shifted with the engine idling, a time lapse exists before the shift actually occurs and can be felt. The time lag test consists of measuring that time lapse.

1. Check the fluid level and condition. Perform the test at normal operating temperature.
2. Block the wheels securely and firmly set the parking brake.

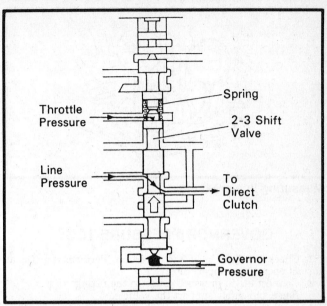

Shift from 2nd to 3rd

3. Set the idle speed to 900 rpm with the cooling fan and air conditioning **OFF**.
4. Shift from **N** to **D** and measure the time it takes from shifting the lever until the shift is felt.
5. Repeat the test twice allowing 1 minute between tests and average the results. The average time lag should be less than 1.2 seconds.
6. Repeat the entire procedure shifting from **N** to **R**. The average time lag should be less than 1.5 seconds.
7. If the neutral to drive time lag is longer than specification, then either the line pressure is too low or the forward clutch is worn.
8. If the neutral to reverse time lag is longer than specification, then the line pressure is too low, or the direct clutch or 1st/reverse brake is worn.

LINE PRESSURE TEST

1. Check the fluid level and condition. Perform the test at normal operating temperature.
2. Connect a tachometer to the engine and an oil pressure gauge to the fitting.
3. Shift the gear selector to **D** and read the line pressure at idle.
4. Repeat the test and read the pressure at the stall speed.
5. Repeat steps 3 and 4 in **R**.
6. The specification in **D** is 53–61 psi (363–422 kPa) at idle and 131–152 (902–1049 kPa) at the stall speed. The specification in **R** is 77–102 psi (530–706 kPa) at idle and 205–239 psi (1412–1648 kPa) at the stall speed.
7. If the pressures are not at the specified values, check the throttle cable adjustment and repeat the test.
8. If the line pressure is high in all ranges, then either the throttle valve or the regulator valve is defective.
9. If the line pressure is low in all ranges, then either the throttle valve or the regulator valve is defective. A defective oil pump will also cause this condition.
10. If the line pressure is low in **D**, then either the **D** hydraulic circuit is leaking somewhere or the forward clutch is defective.
11. If the line pressure is low in **R**, then the **R** hydraulic circuit may be leaking somewhere. A defective 1st/reverse brake or the direct clutch will also cause this condition.

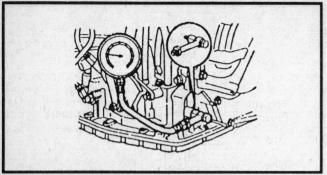

Measuring line pressure

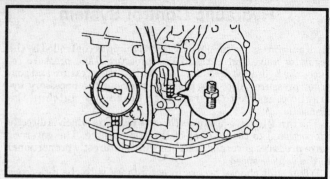

Measuring governor pressure

GOVERNOR PRESSURE TEST

1. Check the fluid level and condition. Perform the test at normal operating temperature.
2. Connect an oil pressure gauge to the fitting.
3. Raise and safely support the vehicle.
4. Start the vehicle, shift into **D** and measure the governor pressure at 20, 35 and 65 mph.
5. If the governor pressure is not within specifications, then there may be a line pressure problem also. If not, then fluid is leaking within the governor hydraulic circuit or the governor valve is defective.

GOVERNOR PRESSURE SPECIFICATIONS

Approximate Vehicle Speed (mph)	Specification psi (kPa)
20	13–24 (88–167)
35	22–35 (154–245)
70	60–78 (412–535)

Converter Clutch Operation and Diagnosis

TORQUE CONVERTER CLUTCH

The torque converter is constructed of the pump impeller which is rotated by the engine, the turbine runner and lockup clutch which are connected to the transaxle input shaft and the stator which is attached to the stator shaft via the one-way clutch.

The rotation of the impeller produces a flow of transaxle fluid inside the converter. This flow strikes the turbine runner and causes it to rotate, thus transmitting torque to the input shaft. The flow of transaxle fluid which has hit the turbine runner rebounds and tries to flow in the direction opposite to the direction of rotation of the pump impeller, but the stator returns the

ROAD TEST

This test is designed to check if upshift and downshift occurs at the correct speeds while actually driving the vehicle. The test should be performed on long, level road, with little or no traffic so that speeds can be chosen and maintained and not forced or altered by others on the road.

1. Run the engine until at operating temperature and check the fluid level.
2. Shift into **D** and check all shift points and any slippage or excessive shock when the transaxle shifts gears. Shifting from 1st to 2nd should occur at 18–25 mph. Shifting from 2nd to 3rd should occur at 40–50 mph. In addition, the converter should lockup shortly after shifting into 3rd gear.
3. While in 3rd gear, check the kickdown mechanism by fully depressing the accelerator pedal. The transaxle should automatically downshift.
4. Allow the transaxle to shift back up to 3rd gear. Release the accelerator pedal and gradually come to a complete stop. Shifting from 3rd to 2nd should occur at 57–68 mph. Shifting from 2nd to 1st should occur at 22–29 mph.
5. Start up again and allow the transaxle to shift ino 3rd gear. Shift into **2** and shortly thereafter into **L**. Engine breaking should occur in both cases. Come to a complete stop.
6. Shift into **2** and start up again. Automatic shifting from 1st to 2nd should occur. Release the accelerator pedal. Engine braking should occur. Come to a complete stop.
7. Shift into **L** and start up again. No automatic shifting should occur. Release the accelerator pedal. Engine braking should occur. Come to a complete stop.
8. Shift into **R** and check for any slippage or excessive shock. Come to a complete stop.
9. Shift into **P** and check the operation of the parking pawl.
10. If any abnormality is found during the road test, compare the findings with the Chilton Three C's Transaxle Diagnosis Chart.

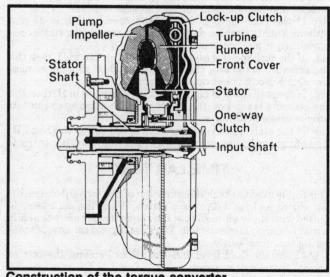

Construction of the torque converter

flow to the original direction of rotation. This action forces the transaxle fluid to support the pump impeller and increases torque.

Although the stator is immobilized by the one-way clutch, should the one-way clutch become defective, the stator will be rotated by the flow of transaxle fluid. In this instance, the flow will not be reversed, torque will not be increased and inadequate acceleration will result.

The lockup clutch is pushed against the front cover by fluid pressure so the engine revolutions are directly transmitted to the input shaft with no loss of revolutions due to torque converter slippage, thus increasing direct engine-to-road-speed efficiency and fuel economy.

TROUBLESHOOTING THE TORQUE CONVERTER CLUTCH

This lockup converter utilizes purely hydraulic means to operate. The lockup control valves in the valve body can be inspected for sticking or clogging of the fluid passages. If this does not solve the problem, replace the torque converter if it does not function properly.

ON CAR SERVICES

Adjustments

THROTTLE CABLE

1. With the engine stopped, depress the accelerator pedal fully and make sure the throttle valve opens fully. If it does not, adjust the accelerator link.
2. With the accelerator pedal fully depressed, loosen the adjustment nuts.
3. Adjust the outer cable so the distance between the end of the rubber boot and the stopper on the cable is 0–0.04 in. (0–1mm).
4. Tighten the adjusting nuts.
5. Recheck the adjustment and road test the vehicle.

SHIFT CONTROL CABLE

1. Loosen the nut on the manual shift lever.
2. Push the manual shift lever fully toward the right side of the vehicle.
3. Return the lever 2 notches into the N position.
4. Set the shift lever to N
5. Tighten the nut and check the adjustment.
6. Check the operation of the neutral safety switch.

NEUTRAL SAFETY SWITCH

1. If the engine starts in any gear except P or R or does not start in P or N and the neutral safety switch is suspect, first check for correct adjustment.
2. Loosen the switch retaining bolts and set the gear selector to N
3. Align the groove in the mounting shaft with the neutral basic line in the switch.
4. Hold the position and tighten the bolts.
5. If the switch is still not operating properly, check for 12V in the black-with-white tracer wire into the switch and 12V in the black wire from the other side of the switch out to the starter relay. Replace the switch if it is defective.
6. If the reverse lights do not illuminate in R and the neutral safety switch is suspect, first check for correct adjustment. Then check for 12V in the red-with-blue-tracer wire into the switch and 12V in the red-with-black-tracer wire from the other side of the switch out to the reverse lights.

Services

FLUID CHANGE

The conditions under which the vehicle is operated is the main

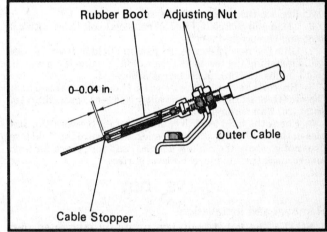

Adjusting the throttle cable

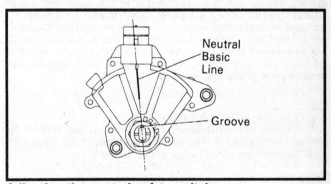

Adjusting the neutral safety switch

consideration in determining how often the transaxle fluid should be changed. Different driving conditions result in different transaxle fluid temperatures. These temperatures affect change intervals.

If the vehicle is driven under severe conditions, change the transaxle fluid every 15,000 miles. If the vehicle is not used under severe conditions, change the fluid and replace the filter every 30,000 miles.

Do not overfill the transaxle. It only takes about a pint of Dexron®II to raise the level from one dimple to the next on the transaxle dipstick. Overfilling the unit can cause damage to the internal components of the automatic transaxle.

OIL PAN

Removal and Installation

1. Raise the vehicle and support safely. Position a large drain pan under the drain plug and remove the drain plug.

2. After the fluid has drained, reinstall the drain plug. Remove the pan bolts and carefully pull the pan down; try to avoid prying, as damage to the pan may result. Excess fluid may drip from the bolt holes, so keep the drain pan handy as the bolts are removed.

3. Inspect the strainer and pan for any concentrations of friction material and metal pieces. A small amount of accumulation around the pan magnet or strainer is considered normal, but larger amounts may indicate heavy wear. If metal pieces are present, more serious damage is possible.

4. Clean the pan thoroughly with clean solvent and straighten the mating surface with a block of wood and a mallet if necessary. Pay special attention to the cleanliness of the mating surface.

5. Replace the strainer if necessary.

6. Clean and completely dry all bolts and bolt holes with solvent and compressed air.

7. Glue the new gasket to the pan and hold against the case while installing the few bolts finger tight. Torque the pan bolts to 43 in. lbs. (5 Nm). in crisscross order.

8. Lower the vehicle. Fill with the proper amount of Dexron®II. Start the engine and allow it to get to operating temperature. Run through the gears.

9. Check the fluid level in **N** and add until between the dimples in the **HOT** range on the dipstick. Make sure the fluid level does not go above the highest dimple. Road test, check for leaks and recheck the fluid level on level surface.

VALVE BODY

Removal and Installation

NOTE: The valve body is a precisely machined part used in the automatic transaxle. Handle it with care and do not clamp in a vise. The material is fragile and could distort easily. Keep all parts labeled and in a well-arranged order, since many of them look similar. Cleanliness is of the utmost importance when working with valve bodies; even the most minuscule scratch or piece of dirt can restrict valve movement and impair the transaxle's performance.

1. Raise the vehicle and support safely. Drain the tranaxle fluid.

2. Remove the oil pan and gasket.

3. Remove the oil strainer. The 2 bolts on one side of the strainer are slightly shorter than the lone bolt on the other side.

4. Remove the tube bracket and 4 tubes.

5. Remove the manual detent spring. One bolt is shorter than the other, so take note of their positions.

6. Remove the manual valve and its body. The 3 bolts on one side are about twice as long as the lone bolt on the other side, so take note of where each one came from.

7. Disconnect the throttle cable from the cam.

8. Remove 14 bolts and remove the valve body. The bolts are different lengths so take note of their locations before removing them.

9. Remove the 2nd brake apply gasket and the governor oil strainer from the case.

NOTE: The accumulator pistons may be removed for service at this point by removing the cover. Remove the cover carefully; there is spring tension behind the pistons. Also, the pistons look similar, so do not confuse them.

10. Install the governor oil strainer and the 2nd brake apply gasket.

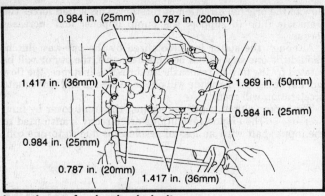

Locations of valve body bolts

11. Lift the valve body into place. Hold the cam down and install the throttle cable end into the slot.

12. Install the valve body bolts in their correct locations finger tight initially. Torque the mounting bolts to 7 ft. lbs. (10 Nm).

13. Align the manual valve with the pin on the manual valve lever. Install the manual valve body into place and tighten the 4 bolts finger tight initially. Torque the bolts to 7 ft. lbs. (10 Nm).

14. Install the detent spring. Make sure the bolts go back in the correct positions. Torque the bolts to 7 ft. lbs. (10 Nm). Make sure the manual valve lever is contacting the center of the roller at the tip of the detent spring.

15. Install the 4 oil tubes and the bracket.

16. Install the oil strainer.

17. Completely clean the pan and magnets and install the magnets in the pan. Install the pan with a new gasket. Torque the bolts to 43 inch lbs. (5 Nm).

18. Fill the transaxle with the proper amount of Dexron®II and road test the vehicle. Check for leaks and recheck the fluid level.

GOVERNOR VALVE

Removal and Installation

1. Raise the vehicle and support safely. Drain the differential fluid.

2. Remove the transaxle dust cover.

3. Remove the engine undercover.

4. Remove the left front tire and wheel assembly.

5. Remove the cotter pin, locknut cap and bearing locknut.

6. Remove the brake caliper and rotor. Disconnect the tie rod end and the strut from the steering knuckle.

7. Use a puller or suitable tool to separate the axle from the steering knuckle.

8. Use the special tool to remove the axle from the transaxle and remove it from the vehicle.

9. Remove the governor bracket.

10. Remove the governor cover with O-ring.

11. Remove the governor body with thrust washer.

12. Remove the plate washer.

13. Remove the governor body adaptor.

14. Install the governor adaptor.

15. Install the plate washer.

16. Install the governor body with thrust washer.

17. Coat the governor cover O-ring with Dexron®II, install it on the cover and install the cover.

18. Install the governor bracket.

19. Install the axle into the transaxle. Check for correct installation. It should not be able to be pulled out by hand.

20. Pull the top of the steering knuckle out and install the other end of the axle into the steering knuckle.

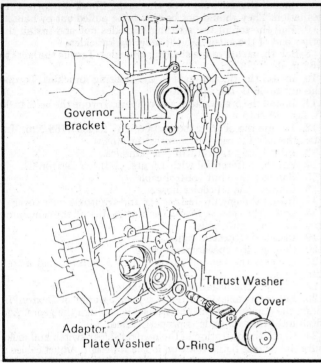

Removing the governor

21. Bolt the strut to the steering knuckle. Torque the bolts to 166 ft. lbs. (226 Nm).
22. Install the tie rod end to the steering knuckle. Torque the nut to 36 ft. lbs. (49 Nm).
23. Install the brake rotor and caliper. Torque the bolts to 65 ft. lbs. (88 Nm).
24. Torque the bearing locknut to 137 ft. lbs. (186 Nm). Install the locknut cap and a new cotter pin.
25. Install the tire and wheel assembly.
26. Fill the differential with 1.5 qts. (1.4L) of Dexron®II.
27. Check wheel alignment, as required.
28. Road test the vehicle and check for leaks.

DIFFERENTIAL AXLE SEAL

Removal and Installation

1. Raise the vehicle and support safely. Drain the differential fluid.
2. Remove the transaxle dust cover.

3. Remove the engine undercover.
4. Remove the tire and wheel assembly.
5. Remove the cotter pin, locknut cap and bearing locknut.
6. Remove the brake caliper and rotor. Disconnect the tie rod end and the strut from the steering knuckle.
7. Use a puller or suitable tool to separate the axle from the steering knuckle.
8. Use the special tool to remove the axle from the transaxle and remove it from the vehicle.
9. Use a suitable tool to pry or pull the leaking seal from the transaxle.
10. Use the special to install the seal to the transaxle. Coat the seal lip with petroleum jelly or Dexron®II.
11. Install the axle into the transaxle. Check for correct installation. It should not be able to be pulled out by hand.
12. Pull the top of the steering knuckle out and install the other end of the axle into the steering knuckle.
13. Bolt the strut to the steering knuckle. Torque the bolts to 166 ft. lbs. (226 Nm).
14. Install the tie rod end to the steering knuckle. Torque the nut to 36 ft. lbs. (49 Nm).
15. Install the brake rotor and caliper. Torque the bolts to 65 ft. lbs. (88 Nm).
16. Torque the bearing locknut to 137 ft. lbs. (186 Nm). Install the locknut cap and a new cotter pin.
17. Install the tire and wheel assembly.
18. Fill the differential with 1.5 qts. (1.4L) of Dexron®II.
19. Check wheel alignment, as required.
20. Road test the vehicle and check for leaks.

THROTTLE CABLE

Removal and Installation

1. Disconnect the throttle cable from the throttle linkage.
2. Raise the vehicle and support safely.
3. Drain the transaxle fluid. Remove the pan. Remove the valve body.
4. Remove the retaining bolt and plate and pull the cable from the transaxle case.
5. Install the cable into the transaxle case. Make sure to push it all the way in. Install the retaining plate and bolt.
6. Install the valve body and oil pan.
7. Connect the throttle cable to the throttle linkage.

NOTE: The stopper is not staked on new cables. Pull the inner cable until a slight resistance is felt and stake it 0.031–0.059 in. (0.8–1.5mm) from the end of the outer cable.

8. Adjust the throttle cable so the distance between the rubber boot and the stopper is 0–0.04 in. (0–1mm).
9. Road test the vehicle.

REMOVAL AND INSTALLATION

TRANSAXLE REMOVAL

1. Disconnect the negative battery cable.
2. Disconnect the neutral safety switch connector and remove the clamp.
3. Disconnect the speedometer cable.
4. Remove the throttle cable from the throttle link.
5. Remove the starter.
6. Remove the upper transaxle to engine bolts.
7. Raise and safely support the vehicle.
8. Drain the transaxle fluid. Drain the differential.

9. Disconnect and plug the oil cooler hoses.
10. Disconnect the shift control cable.
11. Remove the transaxle dust cover.
12. Remove the engine undercover.
13. Remove the tire and wheel assemblies.
14. Remove the cotter pins, locknut caps and bearing locknuts.
15. Remove the brake calipers and rotors. Disconnect the tie rod ends and the struts from the steering knuckles.
16. Use a puller or suitable tool to separate the axles from the steering knuckles.
17. Use the special tool to remove the axles from the transaxle and remove them from the vehicle.

18. Remove the torque converter inspection cover. Remove the torque converter bolts.

19. Disconnect the cable from the left side engine mount bracket.

20. Remove the left side engine mount bolts.

21. Support the engine and transaxle safely with the proper equipment.

22. Unbolt the rear mounting bracket from the body.

23. Remove the rear engine mount bracket.

24. Remove the remaining transaxle to engine bolts.

25. Tilt the transaxle down and remove it from the vehicle.

TRANSAXLE INSTALLATION

1. Make sure the torque converter is correctly installed. Place the transaxle on the transaxle jack securely.

2. Install the transaxle to the engine using the dowls as guides.

3. Install the lower transaxle-to-engine bolts. Torque the bolts to 47 ft. lbs. (64 Nm).

4. Install the left side mounting bracket. Torque the bolts to 32 ft. lbs. (43 Nm). Connect the bond cable.

5. Install the rear engine mount bracket. Torque the bolts to 43 ft. lbs. (58 Nm).

6. Bolt the rear mount bracket to the body. Torque the bolts to 54 ft. lbs. (73 Nm). Remove the support fixtures.

7. Apply Loctite® to the threads and install the torque converter bolts. Install the gray bolt first, then the black bolts. Torque the bolts evenly to 13 ft. lbs. (18 Nm). Install the torque converter inspection cover.

8. Install the axles into the transaxle. Check for correct installation. They should not be able to be pulled out by hand.

9. Pull the top of the steering knuckles out and install the other end of the axles into the steering knuckles.

8 Bolt the struts to the steering knuckles. Torque the bolts to 166 ft. lbs. (226 Nm).

10. Install the tie rod ends to the steering knuckles. Torque the nut to 36 ft. lbs. (49 Nm).

11. Install the brake rotors and calipers. Torque the bolts to 65 ft. lbs. (88 Nm).

12. Torque the bearing locknuts to 137 ft. lbs. (186 Nm). Install the locknut caps and new cotter pins.

13. Install the tire and wheel assemblies.

14. Fill the differential with 1.5 qts. (1.4L) of Dexron®II.

15. Connect the shift control cable.

16. Connect the oil cooler hoses.

17. Install the engine undercover and transaxle dust cover.

18. Lower the vehicle. Install the starter. Install the remaining transaxle to engine bolts.

19. Install the throttle cable.

20. Connect the speedometer cable.

21. Connect the neutral safety switch connector and install the clamp.

22. Connect the negative battery cable.

23. Fill the transaxle with the proper amount of Dexron®II. Start the engine and run the transaxle through the gears. Add fluid until the transaxle is properly filled.

24. Check the operation of the neutral safety switch and make sure the reverse lights come on in the **R** detent. Adjust cables if necessary, road test, check for leaks and recheck the fluid level.

BENCH OVERHAUL

Before Disassembly

Cleanliness is an important factor in the overhaul of the A132L automatic transaxle. Before opening up this unit, the entire outside of the transaxle assembly should be cleaned, preferable with a high pressure washer such as a car wash spray unit. Dirt entering the transaxle internal parts will negate all the time and effort spent on the overhaul. During inspection and reassembly all parts should be thoroughly cleaned with solvent then dried with compressed air. Wiping cloths and rags should not be used to dry parts since lint will find its way into the valve body passages.

Wheel bearing grease, long used to hold thrust washers and lube parts, should not be used. Lube seals with clean transaxle fluid and use ordinary unmedicated petroleum jelly to hold the thrust washers and to ease the assembly of seals, since it will not leave a harmful residue as grease often will. Do not use solvent on neoprene seals, friction plates if they are to be reused, or thrust washers. Be wary of nylon parts if the transaxle failure was due to failure of the cooling system. Nylon parts exposed to water or antifreeze solutions can swell and distort and must be replaced.

Before installing bolts into aluminum parts, always dip the threads into clean transaxle fluid. Antiseize compound can also be used to prevent bolts from galling the aluminum and seizing. Always use a torque wrench to keep from stripping the threads. Take care when installing new O-rings, especially the smaller O-rings. The internal snaprings should be expanded and the external rings should be compressed, if they are to be reused. This will help insure proper seating when installed.

Converter Inspection

1. The converter should be replaced if any cracks or external damage of any sort are found.

2. Insert a turning tool into the inner race of the one-way clutch.

3. Install the stopper so it fits in the notch of the converter hub and outer race of the one-way clutch.

4. Position the converter facing up. The clutch should lock when tuned counterclockwise and rotate freely and smoothly when turned clockwise. Less than 22 inch lbs. (25 Nm) of turning torque should be required to turn the clutch. Replace the converter if it fails the test.

5. Mount the converter to the flywheel. Mount a dial indicator so the pin rest on the converter sleeve. Rotate the engine and

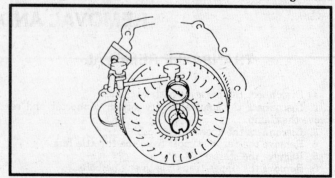

Checking converter sleeve runout

measure the sleeve runout. It should not exceed 0.0118 in. (0.30mm). If not within specification, try to correct it by repositioning the converter on the flywheel and repeating the check. Replace the converter if it fails the test.

Transaxle Disassembly

1. Remove the oil cooler pipes and unions.
2. Remove the neutral safety switch.
3. Remove the oil filler tube and dipstick.
4. Remove the throttle cable retaining plate. Position the transaxle in a suitable holding fixture.
5. Remove the governor bracket, cover, body and thrust washer. Remove the governor plate washer and adaptor.
6. Remove the oil pan and gasket.

NOTE: Do not turn the transaxle upside-down when removing the pan as this could contaminate the components inside the case with foreign matter from the pan.

7. Remove the tube bracket and the oil strainer. Remove the oil tubes.
8. Remove the detent spring. Remove the manual valve body. Remove the manual valve from the body.
9. Disconnect the throttle cable from the cam. Remove the valve body. The bolts are different lengths, so note their locations before removing them.
10. Remove the throttle cable from the case.
11. Remove the 2nd brake apply gasket and the governor oil strainer.
12. Remove the accumulator cover and gasket. Loosen the bolts one at a time until the spring tension is released.
13. Remove the forward and direct clutch accumulators and springs.
14. Remove the remaining accumulator by blowing low pressure compressed air into the hole on the side of its housing..
15. Blow low pressure compressed air into the 2nd coast brake apply hole and measure the piston stroke of the 2nd coast brake. The specification is 0.059–0.118 in. (1.5–3.0mm). If the piston stroke exceeds the limit inspect the brake band.
16. Remove the 2nd coast brake piston cover and O-ring. Remove the piston and outer return spring.
17. Unbolt the oil pump from the case. Use the special tool to separate the oil pump from the case. While holding the input shaft, grasp the pump stator shaft and pull the oil pump and direct clutch out of the case as an assembly.
18. Remove the direct clutch from the oil pump. Remove the bearing race from the pump.
19. Remove the forward clutch. Remove the bearings and races from the forward clutch.
20. Push the 2nd brake band pin and remove it from the oil pump bolt hole. Remove the 2nd brake band.
21. Remove the front planetary ring gear. Remove the bearing races from the ring gear.
22. Remove the planetary gear. Remove the bearings and races from the gear.
23. Remove the sun gear, sun gear input drum, 2nd brake hub and No. 1 one-way clutch.
24. Stand the case up and remove the 2nd coast brake band guide.
25. Remove snapring retaining the 2nd brake drum in the case. Remove the 2nd brake drum.
26. Remove the 2nd brake piston return spring.
27. Remove the clutch plates, discs and flange.
28. Remove the 2nd brake drum gasket.
29. Remove the snapring retaining the No. 2 one-way clutch outer race in the case. Remove the No. 2 one-way clutch and the rear planetary gear.
30. Remove the thrust washers from both sides of the planetary carrier.

31. Remove the rear planetary ring gear. Remove the bearings and races from the ring gear.
32. Remove the snapring retaining the 1st/reverse clutch in the case. Remove the clutch flange, plates and discs.
33. Remove the rear cover. Remove the intermediate shaft.
34. Use the special tool to compress the 1st/reverse brake piston return spring and remove the snapring. Remove the tool and remove the return spring.
35. Remove the piston by blowing low pressure compressed air into the apply passage.
36. Remove the parking lock pawl bracket.
37. Remove the parking lock rod.
38. Remove the pin, spring and parking lock pawl.
39. Remove the manual valve shaft retaining spring. Using the proper tools, pry and turn the collar. Drive out the pin. Slide the shaft out and remove the manual valve lever from the case.
40. Remove the manual shaft oil seal.
41. Remove the governor pressure adaptor torsion spring and the adaptor.
42. Remove the differential cover.
43. Measure and record the total preload by turning the counter driven gear.
44. Measure the backlash of each side gear. The specification is 0.0020–0.0079 in. (0.05–0.20mm). The side gears should have equal backlash.
45. Remove the left side bearing retainer. Remove the side bearing cap, the differential case, the outer race and the adjusting shim from the case.
46. Measure the drive pinion preload by turning the counter driven gear. The specification is 4.3–6.9 in. lbs. (0.5–0.8 Nm). The total preload measured in Step 43 minus the drive pinion preload equals the side bearing preload. If that result is not 1.3–1.7 inch lbs. (0.1–0.2 Nm), then the side bearing preload is wrong.
47. Remove the drive pinion cap
48. Remove the counter driven gear locknut and use the special tool to remove the gear and bearing.
49. Remove the outer race, oil slinger and spacer.
50. Remove the drive pinion snapring. Insert a long brass punch into the hole in the case and tap out the drive pinion.

Unit Disassembly and Assembly

SECOND COAST BRAKE

Disassembly

1. Remove the seal ring from the piston.
2. Remove the E-ring from the top of the piston rod.
3. Remove the spring, washer and piston rod from the piston.

Inspection

1. Inspect the piston and its bore for any damage or scores.
2. Inspect the snapring, E-ring and return springs for deformation.
3. Replace the brake band if the lining is cracked, glazed, discolored or if the printed numbers on the inside surface of the lining are defaced.

Assembly

1. If the piston stroke measured during disassembly of the transaxle was not within specification, a different piston rod may be selected. Piston rods are available in 2.811 in. (71.4mm) and 2.870 in. (72.9mm) lengths.
2. Install the washer and spring to the piston.
3. Install the E-ring while holding the piston down.
4. Apply Dexron®II to the new seal ring and install it to the piston.

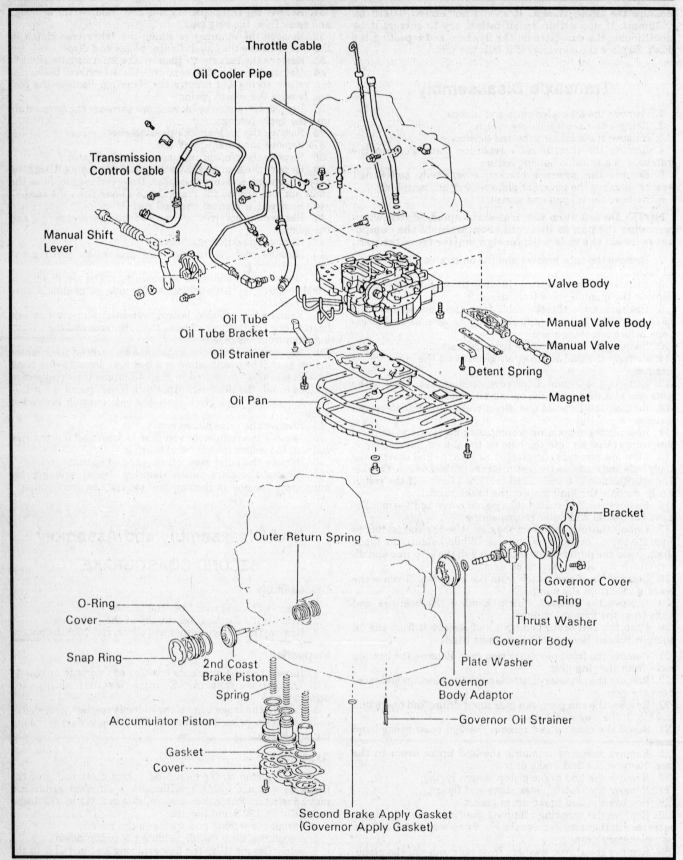

Throttle Cable

Oil Cooler Pipe

Transmission Control Cable

Manual Shift Lever

Oil Tube
Oil Tube Bracket
Oil Strainer

Oil Pan

Valve Body

Manual Valve Body

Manual Valve

Detent Spring

Magnet

Outer Return Spring

O-Ring
Cover

Snap Ring
2nd Coast Brake Piston

Spring

Accumulator Piston

Gasket

Cover

Second Brake Apply Gasket
(Governor Apply Gasket)

Bracket

Governor Cover
O-Ring
Thrust Washer
Governor Body

Plate Washer
Governor Body Adaptor

Governor Oil Strainer

Hydraulic control system and related conponents

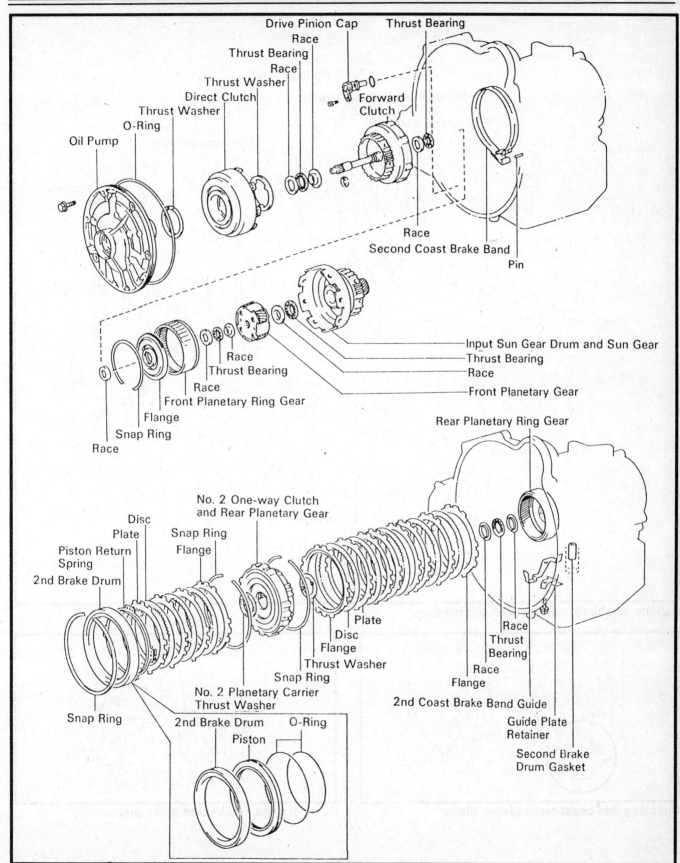

Transaxle clutches, brakes and related components

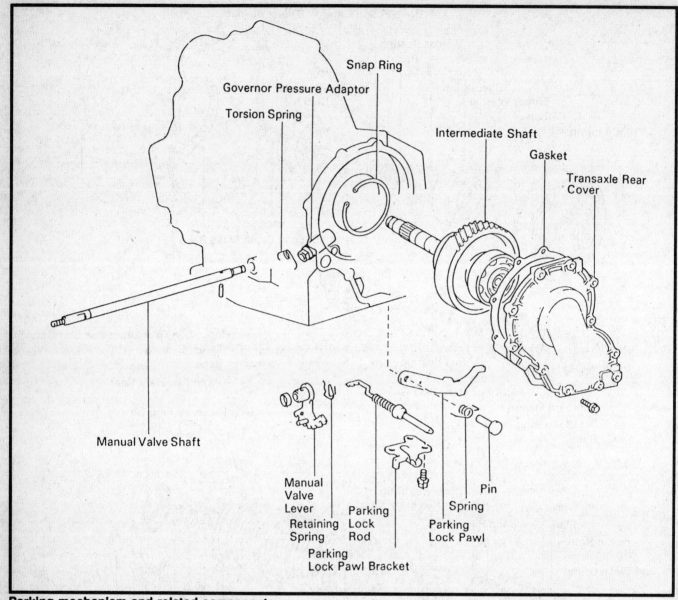

Parking mechanism and related components

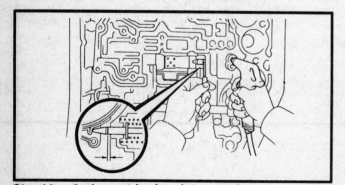

Checking 2nd coast brake piston stroke

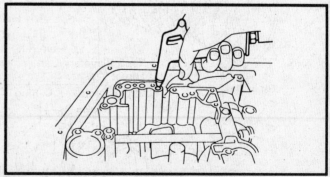

Removing the 1st/reverse brake piston

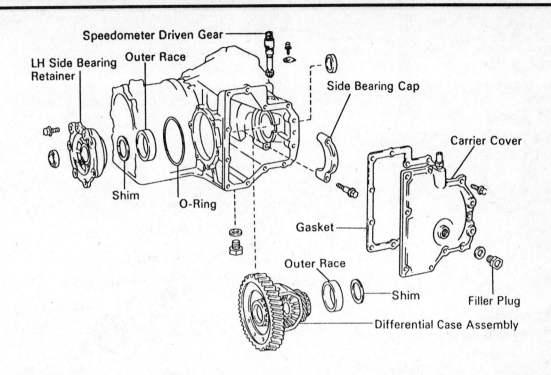

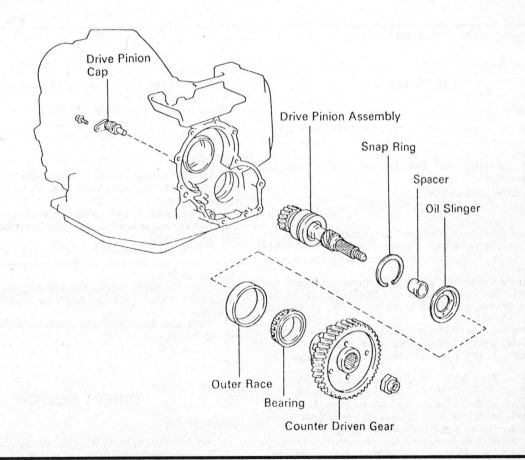

Differential assembly and related components

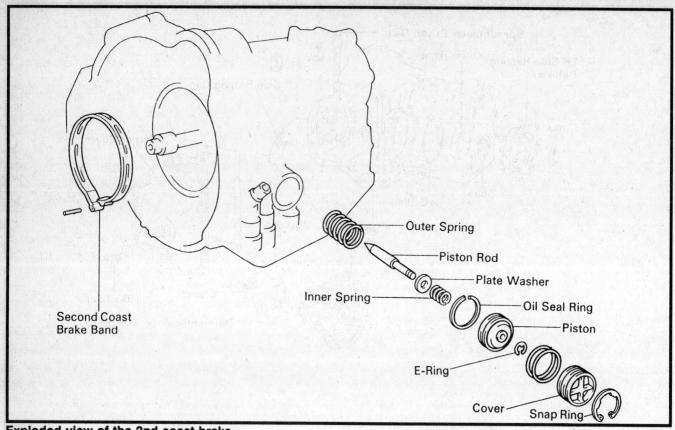

Exploded view of the 2nd coast brake

Labels: Outer Spring, Piston Rod, Plate Washer, Inner Spring, Oil Seal Ring, Piston, E-Ring, Cover, Snap Ring, Second Coast Brake Band

OIL PUMP

Disassembly

1. Remove the 2 seal rings from the rear of the stator shaft.
2. Remove the thrust washer from the rear of the stator shaft.
3. Unbolt the stator shaft from the pump body. Keep the gears in assembled order.
4. Remove the front oil seal.

Inspection

1. Measure the clearance between the outside surface of the driven gear and the pump body. The specification is 0.003–0.012 in. (0.07–0.30mm). If beyond specification, replace the oil pump body subassembly.
2. Measure the clearance between the driven gear teeth and the crescent. The specification is 0.004–0.012 in. (0.11–0.30mm). If beyond specification, replace the oil pump body subassembly.
3. Measure the side clearance of both gears with a straightedge and feeler gauge. The specification is 0.0008–0.0040 in. (0.02–0.10mm). Three different thicknesses of pump gears are available:

Marked A—0.3717–0.3723 in. (9.440–9.456mm) thick
Marked B—0.3723–0.3730 in. (9.456–9.474mm) thick
Marked C—0.3730–0.3736 in. (9.474–9.490mm) thick

If the thickest gear cannot bring the side clearance within specification, replace the oil pump body subassembly.
4. Measure the inside diameter of the oil pump body bushing. The specification is 1.5031 in. (38.18mm). If beyond specification, replace the oil pump body subassembly.

5. Measure the inside diameter of the stator shaft bushings. The specifications are:

Front bushing—0.8492 in. (21.57mm)
Rear bushing—1.0657 in. (27.07mm)

If beyond specification, replace the stator shaft.

Assembly

1. Use the special tool to install a new front oil seal to the pump body. The seal end should be flush with the outer edge of the body.
2. Dip the gears in Dexron®II and install them into the body.
3. Bolt the stator shaft to the pump body. Torque the bolts to 7 ft. lbs. (10 Nm).
4. Coat the thrust washer with petroleum jelly. Align the tab of the thrust washer with the notch in the stator shaft and install the washer.
5. Apply Dexron®II to the new seal rings and install them to the stator shaft. Check the rings for smooth rotation after installation.
6. Turn the drive gear with suitable tools and check for smooth rotation.

DIRECT CLUTCH

Disassembly

1. Remove the snapring from the clutch drum.
2. Remove the flange, discs and plates.
3. Compress the return spring with the special tool and a

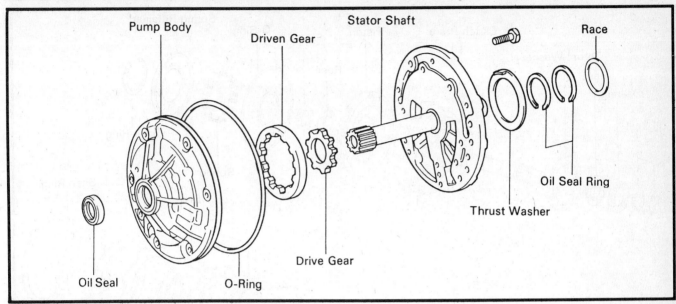

Exploded view of the oil pump

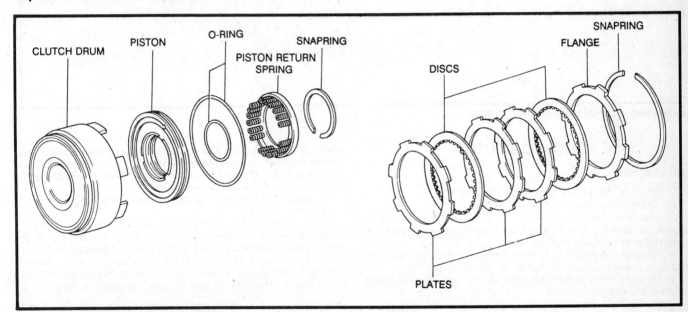

Exploded view of the direct clutch

press. Remove the snapring and the tool. Remove the piston return spring assembly.

4. Install the direct clutch onto the oil pump. Remove the piston by blowing low pressure compressed air into the apply port on the oil pump.

5. Remove the O-rings from the piston.

Inspection

1. Make sure the piston check ball is free. Check for piston valve leakage by applying low pressure compressed air to it.

2. Check the flange, discs and plates for cracks, hot spots and other damage. Replace any part that is worn out.

3. Inspect the drum for any type of damage. The maximum inside diameter of the direct clutch bushing is 1.8531 in. (47.07mm). If beyond specification, replace the drum.

4. Inspect the snaprings, return springs and seats for damage or deformation.

Assembly

1. Install new O-rings on the piston and coat with Dexron®II. Install the piston in the drum with the cup side up.

2. Place the return spring assembly on the piston. Compress the return spring with the special tool and a press. Install the snapring. Do not align the snapring ends with the spring retainer claw. Remove the tool.

3. Install the Dexron®II soaked plates, discs and flange with the flat edge of the flange facing down.

4. Install the snapring. Do not align the snapring ends with any of the cutouts.

5. Position a dial indicator so the pin rests on the top of the piston. Blow low pressure compressed air in the apply port of the oil pump and measure the piston stroke. The specification is 0.054–0.067 in. (1.37–1.70mm). If out of specification change the flange, which is available in 0.1181 in. (3.00mm) and 0.1327 in. (3.37mm) thicknesses and recheck the piston stroke.

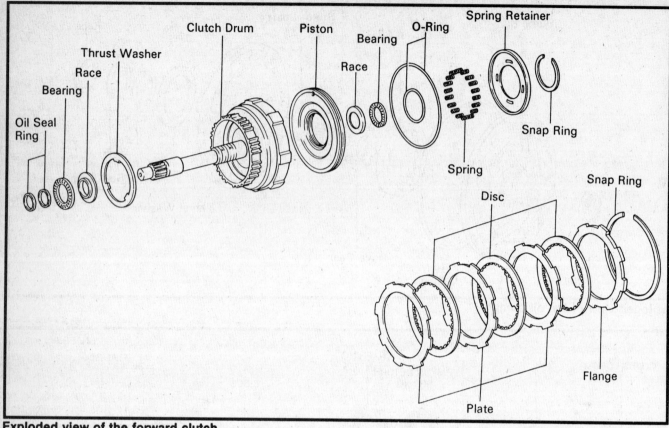

Exploded view of the forward clutch

FORWARD CLUTCH

Disassembly

1. Remove the snapring from the clutch drum.
2. Remove the flange, discs and plates.
3. Compress the return spring with the special tool and a press. Remove the snapring and the tool. Remove the retainer and the piston return springs.
4. Remove the piston by blowing low pressure compressed air into the lower hole on the side of the clutch drum shaft.
5. Remove the O-rings from the piston and the seal rings from the drum shaft.

Inspection

1. Make sure the piston check ball is free. Check for piston valve leakage by applying low pressure compressed air to it.
2. Check the flange, discs and plates for cracks, hot spots and other damage. Replace any part that is worn out.
3. Inspect the drum, bearings, races and thrust washer for any type of damage.
4. Inspect the snaprings, return springs and retainer for damage or deformation.

Assembly

1. Install the seal rings on the clutch shaft and coat with Dexron®II. Check the rings for smooth rotation after installation.
2. Install new O-rings on the piston and coat with Dexron®II. Install the piston in the drum with the cup side up.
3. Place the return springs and the retainer on the piston. Compress the return spring with the special tool and a press. In-

stall the snapring. Do not align the snapring ends with the spring retainer claw. Remove the tool.

4. Install the Dexron®II soaked plates, discs and flange with the flat edge of the flange facing down.
5. Install the snapring. Do not align the snapring ends with any of the cutouts.
6. Position a dial indicator so the pin rests on the top of the piston. Blow low pressure compressed air in the apply port of the oil pump and measure the piston stroke. The specification is 0.044–0.058 in. (1.11–1.47mm). If out of specification change the flange, which is available in 0.1181 in. (3.00mm) and 0.1327 in. (3.37mm) thicknesses and recheck the piston stroke.

FRONT PLANETARY GEAR

Disassembly

1. Check the operation of the one-way clutch. The one-way clutch hub should turn freely clockwise and lock counterclockwise.
2. Remove the 2nd brake hub and one-way clutch from the sun gear.
3. Remove the planetary gear assembly with bearings and races from the drum.
4. Remove the thrust washer from the sun gear input drum.
5. Remove the snapring and the sun gear from the drum.
6. Remove the shaft snapring from the sun gear.
7. Remove the snapring and remove the flange from the ring gear.

Inspection

1. Check all gears and splines for any type of damage.

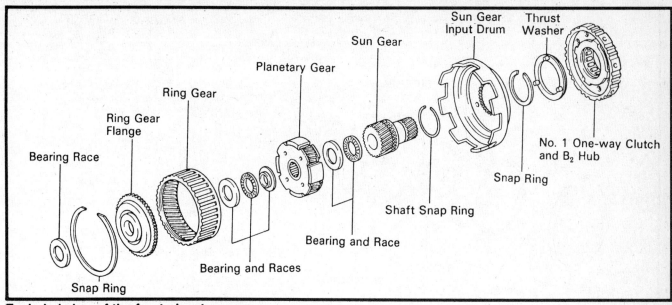

Exploded view of the front planetary gear

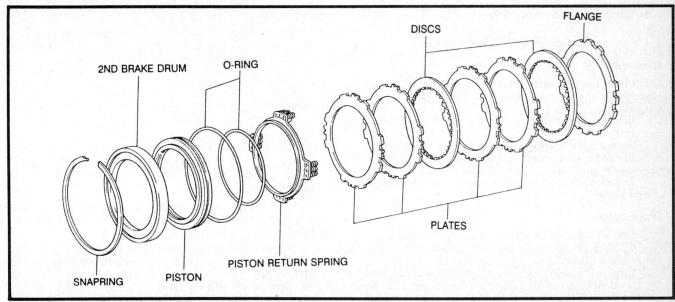

Exploded view of the 2nd brake

2. Check bearings, races and thrust washer for excessive wear. Inspect the snaprings for deformation.

3. The maximum inside diameter of the flange bushing is 0.750 in. (19.05mm). If beyond specification, replace the flange.

4. Inspect the planetary gears for smooth rotation. Measure the thrust clearance of each planetary pinion gear. The specification is 0.0078–0.0197 in. (0.20–0.50mm).

Assembly

1. Install the ring gear flange into the ring gear and install the snapring.

2. Install the snapring on the sun gear.

3. Install the sun gear to the drum. Install the snapring on the back side of the drum. Coat the thrust washer with petroleum jelly and install it on the drum.

4. Install the one-way clutch and 2nd brake hub on the sun gear.

5. Recheck the operation of the one-way clutch.

2ND BRAKE

Disassembly

1. Remove the piston by blowing low pressure compressed air into the apply hole on the side of the drum.

2. Remove the O-rings from the piston.

Inspection

1. Check the piston for any type of damage.

2. Check the flange, discs and plates for cracks, hot spots and other damage. Replace any part that is worn out.

3. Inspect the snaprings, return springs and retainer for damage or deformation.

Assembly

1. Coat new O-rings with Dexron®II and install them on the piston.

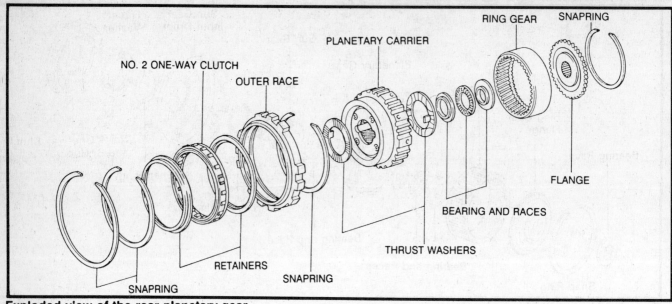

Exploded view of the rear planetary gear

2. Install the piston into the drum.

REAR PLANETARY GEAR

Disassembly

1. Check the operation of the one-way clutch. The one-way clutch hub should turn freely counterclockwise and lock clockwise.
2. Remove the thrust washers from both sides of the planetary gear.
3. Separate the one-way clutch and the planetary gear.
4. Remove the snaprings and retainers from both sides of the one-way clutch. Remove the one-way clutch from the outer race.
5. Remove the snapring and remove the ring gear flange from the ring gear.

Inspection

1. Check all gears and splines for any type of damage.
2. Check bearings, races and thrust washers for excessive wear. Inspect the snaprings for deformation.
3. Inspect the planetary gears for smooth rotation. Measure the thrust clearance of each planetary pinion gear. The specification is 0.0098–0.0197 in. (0.25–0.50mm).

Assembly

1. Install the flange in the ring gear and install the snapring.
2. Install the one-way clutch in the outer race, facing the flanged side of the one-way clutch toward the shiny side of the outer race.
3. Install the 2 retainers and snaprings on both sides.
4. Coat the thrust washers with petroleum jelly. Align the tabs of the thrust washer with the notches in the carrier and install the thrust washers to the planetary carrier. Install the planetary gear into the one-way clutch, facing the inner race of the planetary gear toward the black side of the one-way clutch outer race.
5. Recheck the operaton of the one-way clutch.

1ST/REVERSE BRAKE

Diassembly

Remove the O-rings from the 1st/reverse brake piston.

Inspection

1. Check the piston and its bore for any type of damage.
2. Check the flange, discs and plates for cracks, hot spots and other damage. Replace any part that is worn out.
3. Inspect the snaprings, return springs and retainer for damage or deformation.

Assembly

1. Coat new O-rings with Dexron®II.
2. Install the O-rings on the piston.

VALVE BODY

Disassembly

NOTE: Many of the valve body bolts are different lengths, so take note of their locations before removing them.

1. Remove 9 bolts and remove the upper valve body cover.
2. Remove the strainer, 2 gaskets and plate from the upper valve body.
3. Remove the sleeve stopper.
4. Remove 3 bolts from the upper valve body.
5. Remove 14 bolts from the lower valve body and remove the lower valve body cover and gasket.
6. Remove 3 bolts from the lower valve body.
7. Lift the lower valve body and plate together off of the upper valve body. Do not allow the check balls to fall out of the lower valve body.

UPPER VALVE BODY

Disassembly

1. Remove the throttle valve retainer and check ball.
2. Remove the lockup relay valve retainer, plug, relay valve, spring and control valve. Remove the sleeve retainer and the sleeve.
3. Remove the cut-back valve retainer, plug and valve.
4. Remove the throttle modulator valve retainer, plug, valve and spring.
5. Remove the accumulator control valve retainer, plug, spring and valve.

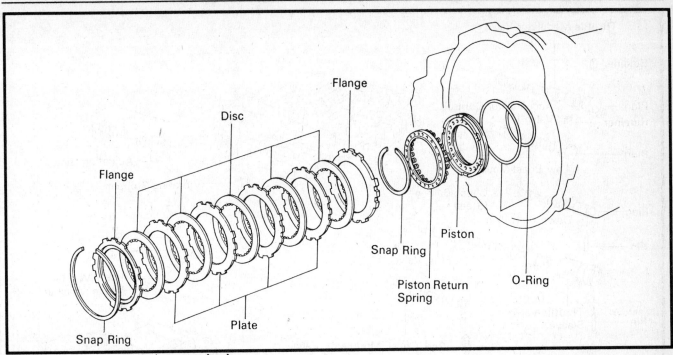

Exploded view of the 1st/reverse brake

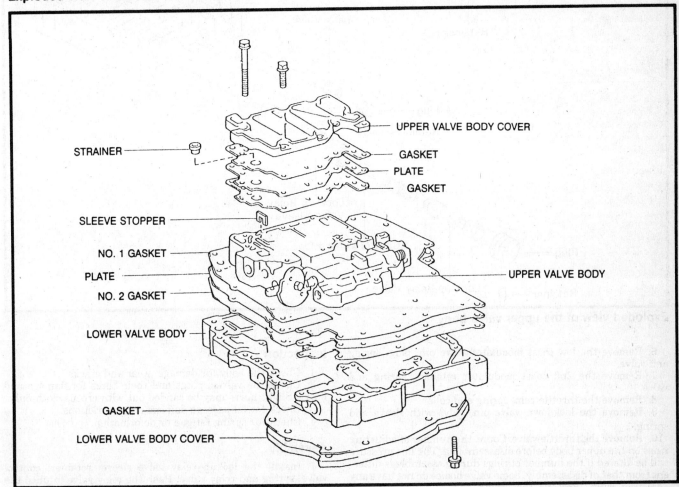

Valve body components

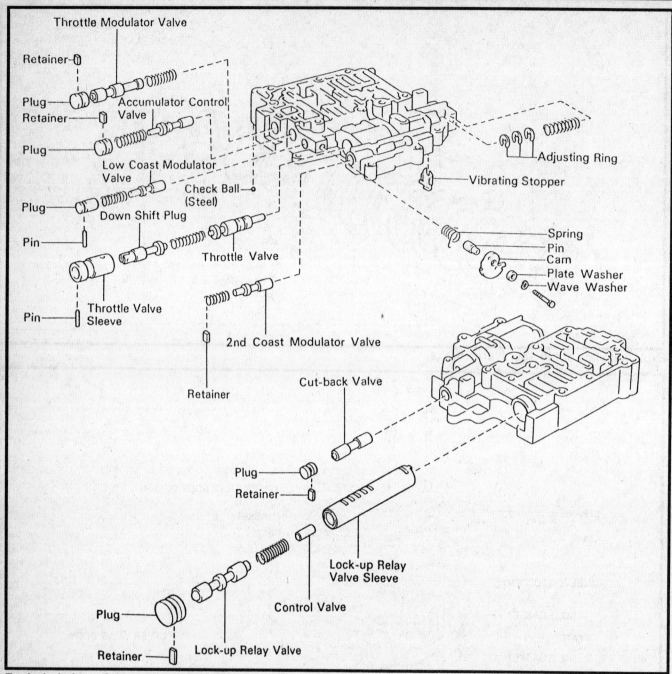

Exploded view of the upper valve body

6. Remove the low coast modulator valve pin, plug, spring and valve.

7. Remove the 2nd coast modulator retainer, spring and valve.

8. Remove the throttle cam, spring and collar.

9. Remove the kickdown valve pin, valve with sleeve and spring.

10. Remove the throttle valve. Count the number of adjusting rings on the upper body before disassembling. The line pressure will be altered if the number of rings during assembly is different from that of disassembly. Some valve bodies do not have any adjusting rings. Remove the spring and adjusting rings, if equipped

Inspection

1. Check the body for damage, wear and cracks.
2. Check the valves, plugs and their bores for damage and burrs. Slight burrs may be sanded out with crocus cloth only.
3. Check for oil passage damage and restrictions.
4. Check for spring fatigue or deformation.

Assembly

1. Install the lockup relay valve sleeve, retainer, control valve, spring and relay valve. Push the relay valve in until the control valve contacts the end of the sleeve. Install the plug and retainer.

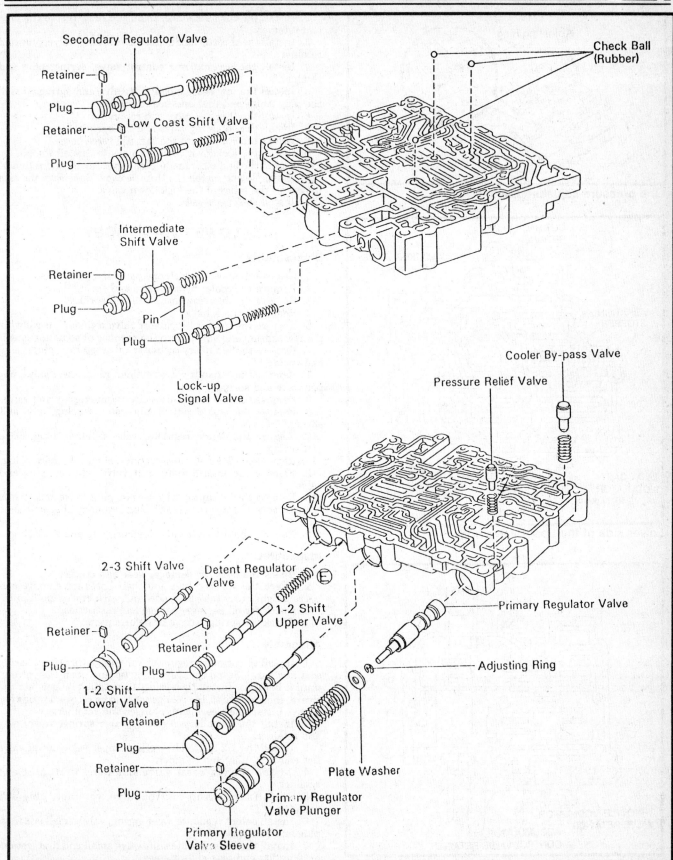

Exploded view of the lower valve body

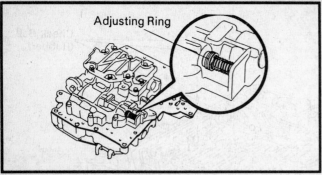

Line pressure adjusting rings

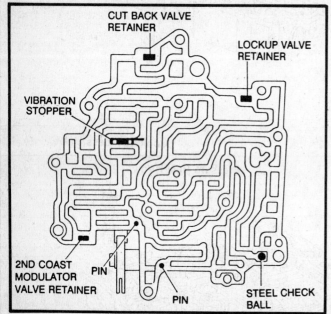

Lower side of the upper valve body

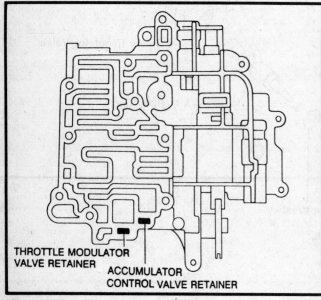

Upper side of the upper valve body

2. Install the cut back valve, small end first. Install the plug and retainer.

3. Install the throttle modulator valve spring, valve, plug and retainer.

4. Install the accumulator control valve, spring, plug and retainer.

5. Install the low coast modulator valve and spring. Install the plug, thick end first and install the pin.

6. Install the throttle valve and retainer.

7. Install the adjusting rings and the spring.

8. Install the spring into the throttle valve bore.

9. Install the kickdown valve with sleeve. Install the pin.

10. Install the 2nd coast modulator valve, spring and retainer.

11. Assemble and install the throttle cam. Make sure the cam moves on the roller of the kick down valve.

12. Install the check balls.

LOWER VALVE BODY

Disassembly

1. Remove the lower valve body plate and gaskets.

2. Remove the cooler bypass valve and spring.

3. Remove the damping check ball and spring.

4. Remove 3 check balls.

5. Remove the primary regulator valve retainer, sleeve with plunger, spring and valve. Note the number of adjusting rings.

6. Remove the secondary regulator valve retainer, plug, valve and spring.

7. Remove the 1/2 shift valve retainer, plug, lower valve, upper valve and spring.

8. Remove the low coast shift valve retainer, plug and valve.

9. Remove the lockup control valve retainer, plug, valve and spring.

10. Remove the detent regulator valve retainer, plug, valve and spring.

11. Remove the 2/3 shift valve retainer, plug, valve and spring.

12. Remove the intermediate shift valve retainer, plug and valve.

13. Remove the lockup signal valve pin, plug, valve and spring.

14. Remove the 3/4 coast shift plug retainer, plug and shift plug.

15. Remove the 3/4 shift plug retainer, plug and shift plug.

Inspection

1. Check the body for damage, wear and cracks.

2. Check the valves, plugs and their bores for damage and burrs. Slight burrs may be sanded out with crocus cloth only.

3. Check for oil passage damage and restrictions.

4. Check for spring fatigue or deformation.

Assembly

1. Install the primary regulator valve adjusting rings, spring seat and valve. Stand the valve body up and push the valve in until it bottoms. Install the spring. Insert the plunger into the sleeve, short end first; the plunger should be recessed inside the sleeve. Install the sleeve with plunger and retainer.

2. Install the secondary regulator valve spring, valve, plug and retainer.

3. Install the 1/2 shift valve spring, upper valve, lower valve flat end first, plug and retainer.

4. Install the low coast valve small end first, plug and retainer.

5. Install the lockup control valve, retainer, plug and retainer.

6. Install detent regulator valve spring, valve, small end first, plug and retainer.

7. Install the intermediate shift valve small end first, retainer, plug flat end first and retainer.

8. Install the 2/3 shift valve spring, valve, plug and retainer.

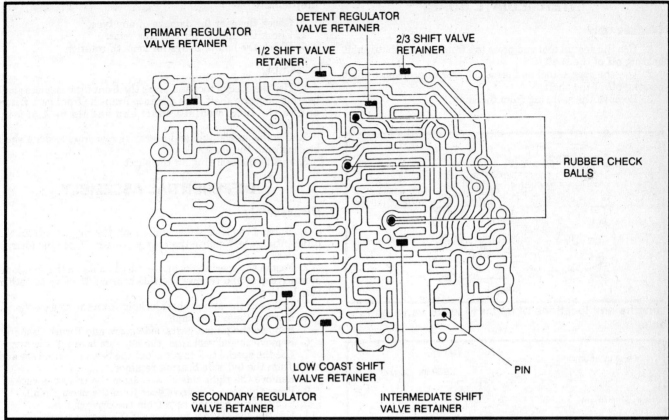

PRIMARY REGULATOR VALVE RETAINER

1/2 SHIFT VALVE RETAINER

DETENT REGULATOR VALVE RETAINER

2/3 SHIFT VALVE RETAINER

RUBBER CHECK BALLS

LOW COAST SHIFT VALVE RETAINER

PIN

SECONDARY REGULATOR VALVE RETAINER

INTERMEDIATE SHIFT VALVE RETAINER

Lower valve body

9. Install the lockup signal valve spring, valve, plug and pin.
10. Install the 3/4 coast shift plug, plug and retainer.
11. Install the 3/4 shift plug, plug and retainer.
12. Install cooler bypass valve spring and valve.
13. Install damping check valve spring and valve.
14. Install check balls and strainer.

VALVE BODY

Assembly

1. Position the new No. 2 gasket, the plate and the new No. 1 gasket on the lower valve body.

NOTE: No. 1 and No. 2 gaskets are very similar. Be very careful not to confuse them.

2. Place the lower valve body, plate and gaskets on the upper valve body as an assembly.
3. Install and finger tighten 3 lower to upper valve body bolts.
4. Install the lower valve body cover over the new gasket.
5. Install and finger tighten 14 lower valve body cover bolts.
6. Install and finger tighten 3 upper to lower valve body bolts.
7. Make sure the sleeve stopper is positioned correctly in the upper valve body.
8. Place a new gasket, plate and another new gasket on the upper body.
9. Install the strainer in the plate.
10. Install the upper valve body cover.
11. Install and finger tighten 9 upper valve body cover bolts.
12. Torque the upper valve body bolts to 48 inch lbs. (5.4 Nm)
13. Torque the lower valve body bolts to 48 inch lbs. (5.4 Nm)

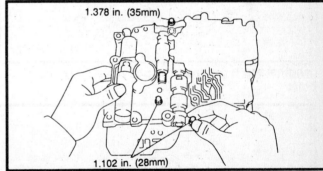

1.378 in. (35mm)

1.102 in. (28mm)

Lengths and locations of lower to upper valve body bolts

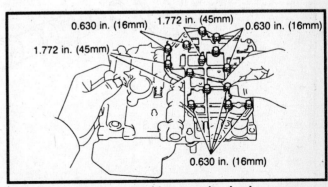

0.630 in. (16mm)   1.772 in. (45mm)   0.630 in. (16mm)

1.772 in. (45mm)

0.630 in. (16mm)

Lengths and locations of lower valve body cover bolts

INTERMEDIATE SHAFT

Disassembly

1. Use the special tool and press the front intermediate shaft bearing off of the shaft.
2. Use the special tool and press the rear intermediate shaft bearing off of the shaft.
3. Remove the seal ring from the shaft.

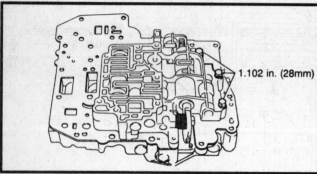

Lengths and locations of upper to lower valve body bolts

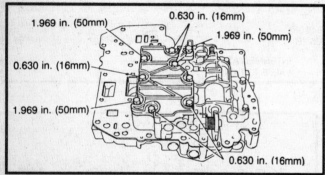

Lengths and locations of upper valve body cover bolts

Inspection

1. Check the gear for damage of any type.
2. Check the splines for chips or wear.
3. Check the ball bearings for smooth rotation.

Assembly

1. Use the special tool and press the front intermediate shaft bearing onto the shaft. The distance from the front gear flange end to the intermediate shaft end should be 4.559 in. (115.8mm).
2. Use the special tool and press the rear intermediate shaft bearing onto the shaft.
3. Install the seal ring on the shaft.

DIFFERENTIAL ASSEMBLY

Disassembly

1. Unbend the lock plates and unbolt the ring gear from the differential case. Remove the ring gear with a brass hammer, if necessary.
2. Fasten the special tool above the cut-outs on the speedometer drive gear and remove the side bearing. Remove the other side bearing.
3. Drive out the pinion shaft lockpin from the ring gear side.
4. Remove the pinion shaft.
5. Remove the pinion gears, side gears and thrust washers.
6. Remove the oil seal from the left side bearing retainer.
7. Use the special tool to press out the bearing outer race and shim from the left side bearing retainer.
8. Remove the right side oil seal from the transaxle case.
9. Press the governor drive gear from the drive pinion.
10. Remove the bearing cage from the drive pinion.
11. Use the special tool to press off the pinion bearing.
12. Use the special tool to press out the oil seals from the bearing cage.
13. Remove the shaft bearing outer race from the cage.
14. Use the special tool to press out the counter driven gear bearing.

Inspection

1. Inspect all gears and splines for damage of any type or unusual waer patterns.

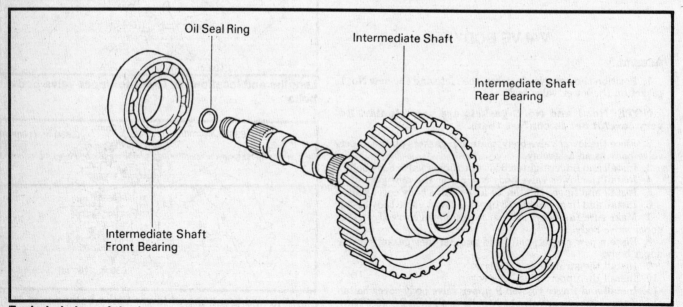

Exploded view of the intermediate shaft

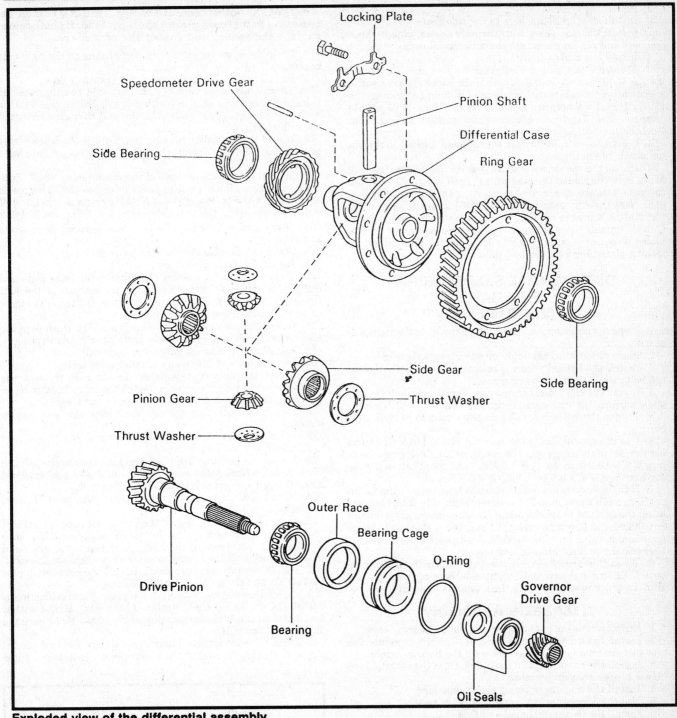

Locking Plate

Speedometer Drive Gear

Pinion Shaft

Side Bearing

Differential Case

Ring Gear

Side Gear

Pinion Gear

Thrust Washer

Side Bearing

Thrust Washer

Drive Pinion

Outer Race

Bearing Cage

O-Ring

Governor Drive Gear

Bearing

Oil Seals

Exploded view of the differential assembly

2. Check the bearings for smooth rotation and the rollers for wear.

3. Check the differential case for damage or wear.

4. Check the thrust washers for wear.

Assembly

1. Use the special tool to install the counter driven gear bearing.

2. Use the special tool to install the 1st oil seal in the cage with the seal facing down. Install the other seal with the lip fac-ing up. The seal end should be flush with the cage surface.

3. Use the special tool to install the shaft bearing outer race in the cage.

4. Use the special tool to install the drive pinion shaft bearing.

5. Install the bearing cage onto the drive pinion shaft.

6. Install the governor drive gear.

7. Install a new oil seal in the case so its end surface is flush with the surface of the case.

8. Place the shim on the bearing retainer. Use the special tool to press the outer race on the retainer.

9. Install the oil seal.

10. Install the thrust washers to the side gears.

11. Install the side gears with thrust washers, pinion thrust washers and pinion gears into the differential case.

12. Install the pinion shaft.

13. Measure the side gear backlash. The specification is 0.0020–0.0079 in. (0.05–0.230mm). If the backlash is not within specification, install thrust washers of different thickness. Selective thrust washers are available in 0.0020 in. (0.05mm) increment sizes. Try to use the same size washers on both sides. Recheck the backlash after reassembling.

14. Install the lockpin through the case and the hole in the pinion shaft. Stake the case.

15. Install the speedometer drive gear on the differential case. Make sure the side of the gear with the tab is facing away from the case. Use the special tool to press on the side bearings.

16. Heat the ring gear to 212°F (100°C) in an oil bath. Clean the mating surfaces of the gear and case with clean solvent. Quickly install the ring gear. Install new bolts and locking plates. Torque the bolts evenly to 91 ft. lbs. (124 Nm). Bend the locking plate tabs over the bolt flats.

DIFFERENTIAL SIDE BEARING PRELOAD ADJUSTMENT

1. Place the outer race and adjusting shim onto the right side bearing.

2. Place differential assembly into the transaxle case.

3. Install the left side bearing retainer. Temporarily tighten the bolts while turning the ring gear.

4. Install the right side bearing cap. Tighten the bolts evenly while turning the ring gear. Torque to 36 ft. lbs. (49 Nm).

5. Torque the left side bearing retainer bolts to 14 ft. lbs. (19 Nm).

6. Use the special tool to measure the preload (starting turning torque) of the ring gear. The specification if using new bearings is 8.7–13.9 inch lbs. (1.0–1.6 Nm). The specification if reusing bearings is 4.3–6.9 inch lbs. (0.5–0.8 Nm).

7. If the preload is not within specification, remove the differential assembly and install the correct right side shim that will bring the preload to specification. Selective shims are available in 0.0020 in. (0.05mm) increment sizes. The preload will change approximately 3.0 inch lbs. (0.35 Nm) with each shim thickness. Recheck the preload after assembling.

8. When the correct shim is selected, remove the bearing retainer, differential assembly, right side bearing retainer and shim in order to proceed with the transaxle assembly.

Transaxle Assembly

1. Install a new outer O-ring on the pinion bearing cage.

2. Install the drive pinion in the case. Tap the cage into the case just far enough so the groove with the bore is visible.

3. Install the snapring. Tap the pinion from the other side to insure proper snapring seating.

4. Install the oil slinger facing the lip outward.

5. Use the special tool to install the outer race.

6. Install a new spacer, small end first.

7. Install the counter driven gear onto the shaft. Drive it on far enough so the nut can be threaded on the shaft.

8. Coat the threads with oil and install the nut. Use the special tool to hold the gear and torque the locknut to 127 ft. lbs. (172 Nm). Measure the preload (starting turning torque) of the drive pinion. The specification if using a new bearing is 8.7–13.9 inch lbs. (1.0–1.6 Nm). The specification if reusing the bearing is 4.3–6.9 inch lbs. (0.5–0.8 Nm).

9. If the preload is greater than specification, replace the bearing spacer. Do not back off the nut to reduce the preload. If the preload is less than specification, torque the locknut 9 ft. lbs. (13 Nm) at a time until the proper preload is obtained.

NOTE: Do not exceed 213 ft. lbs. (289 Nm) when attempting to increase pinion shaft preload. If this occurs, replace the spacer and repeat the procedure.

10. Place the outer race and the selected shim on the right side bearing.

11. Install the differential case in the transaxle case.

12. Thoroughly clean and dry the left side bearing retainer bolts and threads in the case with solvent. Install the retainer with new O-ring. Apply sealant to the bolt threads and install them finger tight.

13. Install the right side bearing cap. Torque the bolts evenly to 36 ft. lbs. (49 Nm). Torque the left side bearing retainer bolts to 14 ft. lbs. (19 Nm).

14. Measure the total preload of the drive pinion shaft. Subtract the drive pinion preload from total preload. The result should be 2.5–3.5 in. lbs. (0.3–0.4 Nm) if using a new bearing. If reusing the bearing, the result should be 1.3–1.7 in. lbs. (0.1–0.2 Nm). If the total preload is not within specification, disassemble and readjust.

15. Stake the counter driven gear locknut.

16. Install the drive pinion cap.

17. Thoroughly clean and dry the differential cover bolts and threads in the case with solvent. Apply sealant to the bolt threads and install the cover and new gasket. Torque the bolts to 18 ft. lbs. (25 Nm).

18. Install the governor pressure adaptor. Align the hole of the adaptor with the hole in the case. Install the torsion spring.

19. Install a new manual valve shaft oil seal.

20. Install a new collar to the manual valve lever.

21. Install the manual valve shaft in the case through the manual lever. Install the roll pin. Match the collar hole to the lever caulking notch and caulk the collar to the lever.

22. Install the retaining spring. Make sure the lever moves smoothly.

23. Install the parking lock pawl, spring and pin.

24. Install the parking lock rod.

25. Install the parking lock pawl bracket. Torque the bolts to 65 in. lbs. (7.4 Nm). Make sure the counter driven gear is locked when the manual valve lever is in the **P** detent.

26. Install the 1st/reverse brake piston with new O-rings, spring seat facing up.

27. Place the return spring on the piston. Use the special tool to compress the return spring. Install the snapring. Make sure the snapring is centered by the 3 lugs on the spring retainer and is not aligned with the spring retainer claw. Remove the tool.

28. Install the intermediate shaft. Install the cover with new gasket. Torque the bolts 18 ft. lbs. (25 Nm).

29. Check the intermediate shaft endplay. The specification is 0.0193–0.0594 in. (0.49–1.51mm). If the play is not within specification, check the installation of the shaft. Make sure the shaft turns smoothly.

30. Install the 1st/reverse brake inner flange, flat end up. Install the Dexron®II soaked discs and plates. Install the outer

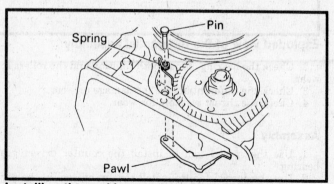

Installing the parking pawl, spring and pin

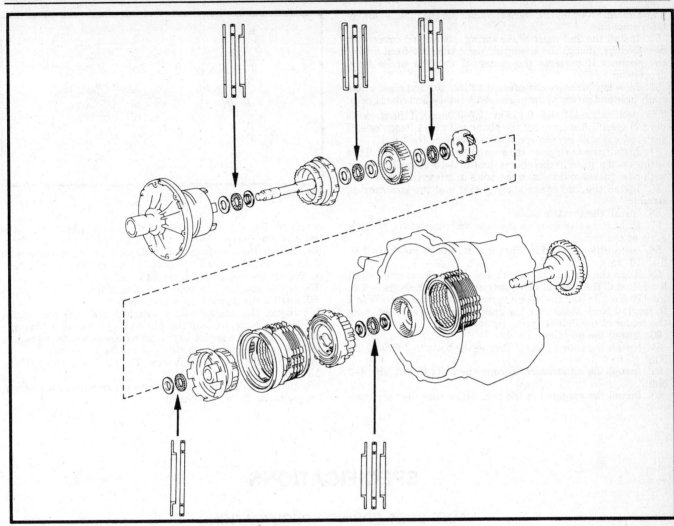

Locations of thrust washers, bearings and races

flange, flat end down. Install the snapring. Do not align the snapring ends with any of the cutouts.

31. Check the operation of the 1st/reverse brake piston by blowing low pressure compressed air into the oil passage in the case.

32. Install the ring gear bearing and races them onto the ring gear. Install the ring gear into the case.

33. Install the rear planetary carrier with thrust washer into the 1st/reverse brake discs.

34. Install the No. 2 one-way clutch into the inner race, shiny side facing up. Install the thrust washer onto the planetary gear. The planetary carrier should turn freely clockwise and lock counterclockwise.

35. Install the snapring. Do not align the snapring ends with any of the cutouts.

36. Install the 2nd coast brake band guides so the tips touch the case.

37. Install the 2nd brake flange, flat end up. Install the Dexron®II soaked discs and plates.

38. Install the piston return spring.

39. Install the 2nd brake drum. Align the groove in the drum with the bolt when installing.

40. Compress the return spring with the proper tools and install the snapring. Do not align the snapring ends with any of the cutouts.

41. Install a new 2nd brake drum gasket.

42. Check the operation of the 2nd brake piston by blowing low pressure compressed air into the oil passage in the case.

43. Install the No. 1 one-way hub into the 2nd brake discs. If correctly installed, the distance between the surfaces of the 2nd brake hub and the rear planetary gear is approximately 0.20 in. (5mm).

44. Install the sun gear and sun gear input drum.

45. Install the bearing and races on the front planetary ring gear. Install the race and bearing on the planetary carrier. Install the planetary carrier into the ring gear.

46. Install the planetary gear assembly onto the sun gear. If correctly installed, the end of the ring gear flange bushing is flush or below the the intermediate shaft shoulder.

47. Install the intrmediate shaft oil seal ring.

48. Install the 2nd coast brake band. Install the pin through the oil pump mounting hole.

49. Install the races and bearings to both side of the forward clutch drum. Install the thrust washer in the direct clutch drum with the grooves facing up. Combine the direct and forward clutch drums and install the assembly into the case.

50. Install the race to the stator shaft. Install the oil pump assembly with new outer O-ring into the case. Torque the mounting bolts to 16 ft. lbs. (22 Nm).

51. Measure the input shaft thrust play. The specification is 0.012–0.035 in. (0.3–0.9mm). If out of specification, use a different stator shaft race, which are available in 0.031 in. (0.8mm)

and 0.055in. (1.4mm) thicknesses. Make sue the input shaft rotates smoothly.

52. Install the 2nd coast brake spring, piston and cover with new O-rings. Install the snapring. Make sure the front end of the piston rod contacts the center of the 2nd brake band depression.

53. Blow low pressure compressed air into the 2nd coast brake apply hole and measure the piston stroke of the 2nd coast brake.

The specification is 0.059–0.118 in. (1.5–3.0mm). If the stroke is beyond specification, replace the piston rod with a longer one. If the stroke is still beyond specification, replace the band.

54. Install new O-rings on the accumulator pistons. Install the springs and pistons in their bores. Install the accumulator cover with new gasket and tighten the bolts in crisscross order.

55. Install the 2nd brake apply gasket and the governor oil strainer.

56. Install the throttle cable.

57. Place the valve body on the case and connect the throttle cable to the cam.

58. Install the valve body. Torque the 14 bolts evenly to 7 ft. lbs. (10 Nm).

59. Align the manual valve with the pin on the manual shaft lever. Install the manual valve body and torque the bolts to 7 ft. lbs. (10 Nm). Install the detent spring and torque the bolts to 7 ft. lbs. (10 Nm). Make sure the manual valve lever is touching the center of the detent spring tip roller.

60. Install the oil tubes.

61. Install the tube bracket. Torque the bolts to 7 ft. lbs. (10 Nm).

62. Install the oil strainer. Torque the bolts to 7 ft. lbs. (10 Nm).

63. Install the magnets in the pan. Make sure they are posi-

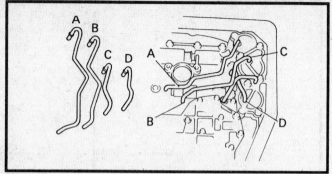

Oil tubes

tioned so they will not interfere with the oil tubes. Install the pan and new gasket. Torque the bolts to 43 in. lbs. (4.9 Nm).

64. Install the governor body adaptor, governor body with plate washer, thrust washer, cover with new O-ring and bracket. Torque the bolts to 9 ft. lbs. (13 Nm).

65. Install the throttle cable retaining plate.

66. Install the dipstick tube and dipstick.

67. Install the neutral safety switch. Install the seal gasket and locking plate. Torque the nut to 61 in. lbs. (6.9 Nm) and stake it. Adjust the switch so the groove lines up with the return neutral line. Torque the bolts to 48 in. lbs. (5.4 Nm).

68. Install the manual shift lever. Torque the nut to 9 ft. lbs. (13 Nm).

69. Install the oil cooler union and elbow with new O-rings. Torque to 20 ft. lbs. (27 Nm).

SPECIFICATIONS

VALVE BODY SPRING SPECIFICATIONS

Item	Free length		Coil Outer Diameter		Number of coils	Color
	in.	mm	in.	mm		
Upper valve body						
Lockup relay valve	1.0457	26.56	0.4016	10.20	11.5	Green
Throttle modulator valve	0.8543	21.70	0.3740	9.50	9.5	Orange
Accumulator control valve	1.3071	33.20	0.4094	10.40	13.5	Red
Low coast modulator valve	0.9213	23.40	0.3110	7.90	11.5	Blue
2nd coast modulator valve	0.8240	20.93	0.3346	8.50	10	Green
Downshift plug	1.1717	29.76	0.3437	8.73	13.5	Yellow
Throttle valve	1.2087	30.70	0.3722	9.20	9.5	Purple
Lower valve body						
Primary regulator valve	2.6240	66.65	0.7323	18.60	12.5	None
1/2 shift valve	1.0697	27.17	0.2516	6.39	15.5	Yellow
Detent regulator valve	1.1701	29.72	0.3110	7.90	12.5	Gray
2/3 shift valve	1.0921	27.74	0.3268	8.30	11	Pink
Lockup signal valve	1.5858	40.28	0.3189	8.10	15.5	Red
Secondary regulator valve	1.7165	43.60	0.4291	10.90	11.5	None
Pressure relief valve	0.4409	11.20	0.2520	6.40	7.5	None
Cooler bypass valve	0.7835	19.90	0.4331	11.00	8.5	None

VALVE BODY RETAINER SPECIFICATIONS

Item	Height in.	Height mm	Width in.	Width mm	Thickness in.	Thickness mm
Upper valve body						
Throttle modulator valve	0.362	9.2	0.197	5.0	0.126	3.2
Accumulator control valve	0.453	11.5	0.197	5.0	0.126	3.2
2nd coast modulator valve	0.591	15.0	0.197	5.0	0.126	3.2
Cutback valve	0.362	9.2	0.197	5.0	0.126	3.2
Lockup relay valve	0.591	15.0	0.197	5.0	0.126	3.2
Lower valve body						
Secondary regulator valve	0.453	11.5	0.197	5.0	0.126	3.2
Low coast shift valve	0.362	9.2	0.197	5.0	0.126	3.2
Intermediate shift valve	0.453	11.5	0.197	5.0	0.126	3.2
2/3 shift valve	0.236	6.0	0.315	8.0	0.126	3.2
Detent regulator valve	0.453	11.5	0.197	5.0	0.126	3.2
1/2 shift valve	0.362	9.2	0.197	5.0	0.126	3.2
Primary regulator valve	0.362	9.2	0.197	5.0	0.126	3.2

ACCUMULATOR SPRING SPECIFICATIONS

Item	Free Length in.	Free Length mm	Coil Outer Diameter in.	Coil Outer Diameter mm	Number of coils	Color
2nd brake (center)	2.6252	66.68	0.6441	16.36	14.5	Orange
Forward clutch (rear)	2.8252	71.76	0.7165	18.20	16.0	None
Direct clutch (front)	2.6181	66.50	0.7051	17.91	13.5	None

RIGHT SIDE DIFFERENTIAL BEARING SHIM SPECIFICATIONS

in.	mm	in.	mm
1.60	0.0630	2.15	0.0846
1.65	0.0650	2.20	0.0866
1.70	0.0669	2.25	0.0886
1.75	0.0689	2.30	0.0906
1.80	0.0709	2.35	0.0925
1.85	0.0728	2.40	0.0945
1.90	0.0748	2.45	0.0965
1.95	0.0768	2.50	0.0984
2.00	0.0787	2.55	0.1004
2.05	0.0807	2.60	0.1024
2.10	0.0827	2.65	0.1043

SIDE GEAR THRUST WASHER SPECIFICATIONS

in.	mm
0.0374	0.95
0.0394	1.00
0.0413	1.05
0.0433	1.10
0.0453	1.15
0.0472	1.20

TORQUE SPECIFICATIONS

Part	ft. lbs.	Nm
Transaxle to engine bolts	47	64
Left side mount bracket bolts	32	43
Rear engine mount bracket bolts	43	58
Rear mount bracket to body volts	54	73
Torque converter bolts	13	18
Axle bearing locknuts	137	186
Oil pump assembly bolts	7	10
Valve body assembly bolts	48 ①	5.4
Ring gear bolts	91	124
Right side differential side bearing retainer bolts	36	49
Left side differential side bearing retainer bolts	14	19
Counter driven gear locknut	127	172
Differential cover bolts	18	25
Intermediate shaft cover bolts	18	25
Oil pump mounting bolts	16	22
Valve body mounting bolts	7	10
Oil pan bolts	43 ①	4.9
Governor cover bracket bolts	9	13
Neutral safety switch bolts	48 ①	5.4

① Inch lbs.

SPECIAL TOOLS

09350-32013	09351-32040	09351-32090	09351-32130
09308-10010	09351-32050	09351-32100	09351-32140
09351-32010	09351-32061	09351-32111	09351-32150
09351-32020	09351-32070	09351-32120	09351-32190
09351-32031			

Section 3
Automatic Transmission Applications

Vehicle Manufacturer	Year	Vehicle Model	Transaxle Manufacturer	Transaxle Identification
Isuzu	1984–89	Impulse, Pick-Up	Aisin-Warner	AW370, AW372
	1988–89	Trooper II, Pick-Up	Aisin-Warner	AW30-80LE
	1984–87	Pick-Up, I-Mark	Aisin-Warner	AW03-55, AW03-75
Mazda	1988–89	929	Mazda	N4A-EL
	1989	MPV	Mazda	R4A-EL, N4A-HL
Nissan	1987–89	Pick-Up, Pathfinder, 240SX	Jatco	RE4R01A
Toyota	1984–89	Land Cruiser	Aisin-Warner	A440F, A440L

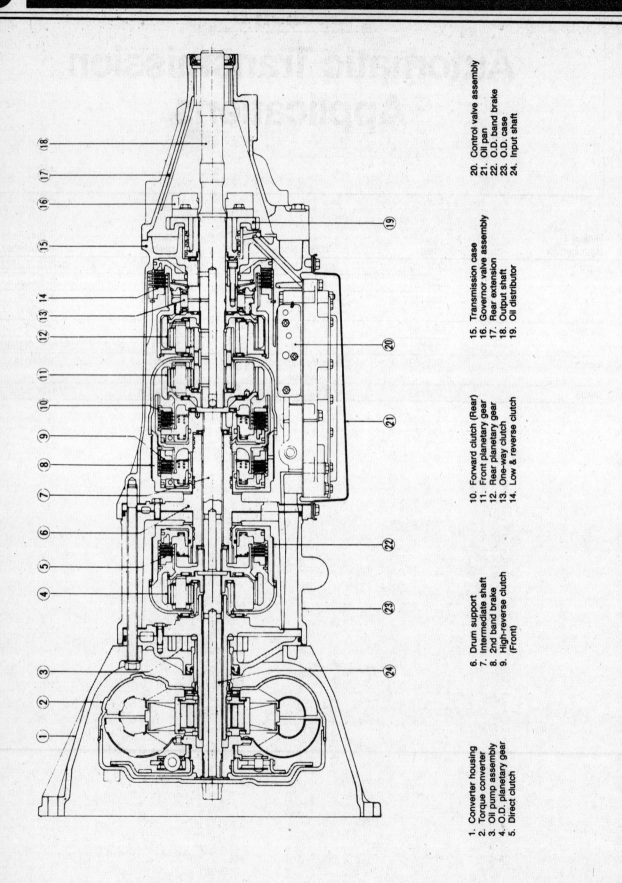

1. Converter housing
2. Torque converter
3. Oil pump assembly
4. O.D. planetary gear
5. Direct clutch

6. Drum support
7. Intermediate shaft
8. 2nd band brake
9. High-reverse clutch
   (Front)

10. Forward clutch (Rear)
11. Front planetary gear
12. Rear planetary gear
13. One-way clutch
14. Low & reverse clutch

15. Transmission case
16. Governor valve assembly
17. Rear extension
18. Output shaft
19. Oil distributor

20. Control valve assembly
21. Oil pan
22. O.D. band brake
23. O.D. case
24. Input shaft

Crosssectional view of an automatic transmission

Section 3

AW370, AW372L and KM148 Transmissions
Isuzu and Mitsubishi

APPLICATION

Year	Vehicle	Engine	Transmission
1984	Isuzu Impulse	1.9L	AW370
1985	Isuzu Impulse	1.9L	AW370
1986	Isuzu Impulse	1.9L	AW370
	Isuzu Impulse	2.0L	AW372
1987	Isuzu Impulse	1.9L	AW370
	Isuzu Impulse	2.0L	AW372
	Mitsubishi Pick-up	2.0, 2.6L	AW372
	Mitsubishi Pick-up	2.6L	KM148
	Mitsubishi Van	2.4L	AW372
1988	Isuzu Impulse	2.3L	AW372
	Isuzu Impulse	2.0L	AW372
	Isuzu Pick-up	2.6L	AW372
	Mitsubishi Pick-up	2.0L	AW372
	Mitsubishi Pick-up	2.6L	KM148
	Mitsubishi Van	2.4L	AW372
1989	Isuzu Impulse	2.3L	AW372
	Isuzu Impulse	2.0L	AW372
	Isuzu Pick-up	2.6L	AW372
	Mitsubishi Pick-up	2.0, 2.6L	AW372
	Mitsubishi Pick-up	2.6L	KM148
	Mitsubishi Van	2.4L	AW372

GENERAL DESCRIPTION

The AW370 and AW372 are fully automatic 4 speed transmissions consisting of 3 clutch packs, 4 brakes, 3 one-way clutches and 2 planetary gearsets which provide 4 forward ratios and 1 reverse.

Power from the engine is transmitted to the input shaft by the torque converter and is then transmitted to the planetary gears by the operation of the clutches. The power flow depends on the engagement or disengagement of the clutches and brakes.

Each clutch and brake operates by hydraulic pressure which is produced by the rotation of the oil pump. The pressurized fluid is regulated by the valve body and shift change automatically occurs according to throttle opening and vehicle speed.

The torque converter provides a fluid coupling between the engine and transmission for optimum power transfer when driving at a constant speed and increased torque when starting, accelerating and climbing an incline. When used, the damper clutch provides a solid coupling for improved fuel mileage when at cruising ranges.

The KM148 transmission combines a 2 speed, part time 4WD transfer case at the rear of an AW372 transmission. The transmission oil sump is separate from the transfer oil sump. Accordingly, the 2 components are filled separately. All 4WD vehicles are equipped with a high/low selector. By operating the transfer control lever, the use of 2 wheel drive high (2H), 4 wheel drive high (4H) and 4 wheel drive low (4L) can be selected freely.

Transmission and Converter Identification

TRANSMISSION

On Mitsubishi vehicles, the transmission number, build date and serial number are indicated on the plate on the left side of the transmission case. In addition, on the Van, the vehicle identification plate is riveted to the front floor pan under a square carpet cutout. On Pick-up trucks, the plate is riveted to the firewall under the hood. In both cases, the third line down identifies the transmission model.

On Isuzu vehicles, stampings on the top and left side of the bellhousing flange identify the transmission. Use the top stamping for production information and the side stamping for service parts information.

CONVERTER

The torque converter is a 3 element, single stage, 2 phase type. The torque converter has an internal damper clutch. The torque converter is a welded 1 piece unit and cannot be disassembled for inspection purposes.

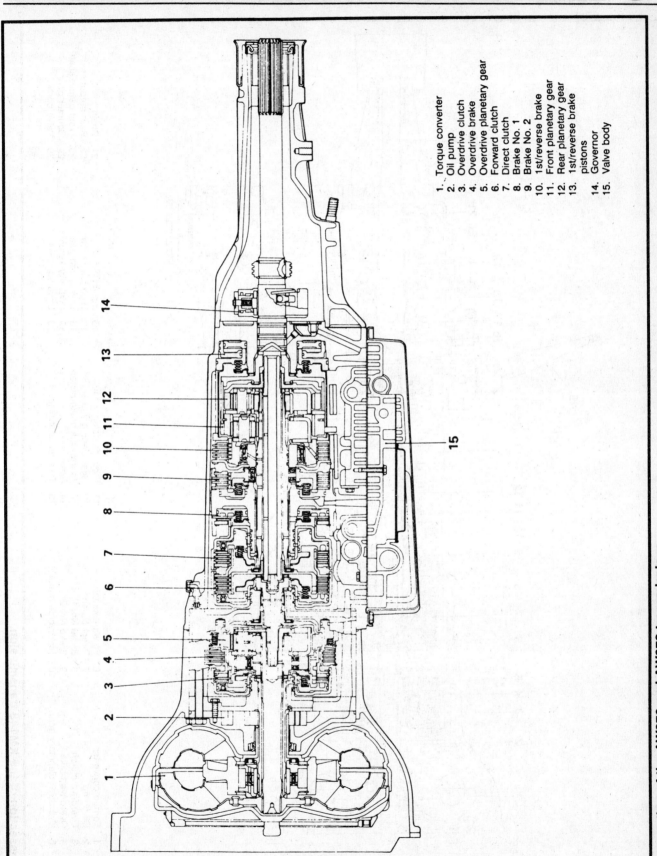

1. Torque converter
2. Oil pump
3. Overdrive clutch
4. Overdrive brake
5. Overdrive planetary gear
6. Forward clutch
7. Direct clutch
8. Brake No. 1
9. Brake No. 2
10. 1st/reverse brake
11. Front planetary gear
12. Rear planetary gear
13. 1st/reverse brake pistons
14. Governor
15. Valve body

Crossection of the AW370 and AW372 transmissions

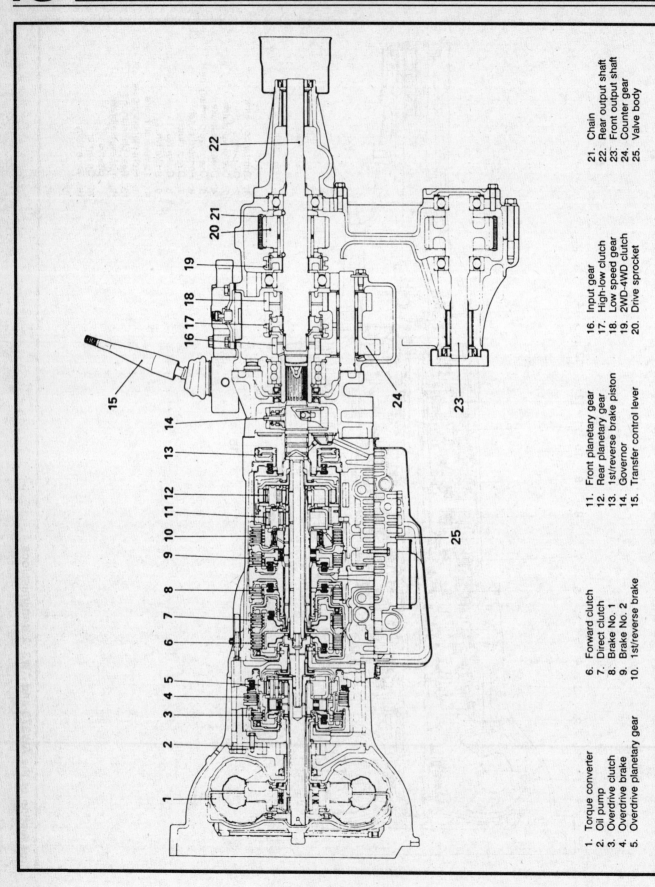

1. Torque converter
2. Oil pump
3. Overdrive clutch
4. Overdrive brake
5. Overdrive planetary gear
6. Forward clutch
7. Direct clutch
8. Brake No. 1
9. Brake No. 2
10. 1st/reverse brake
11. Front planetary gear
12. Rear planetary gear
13. 1st/reverse brake piston
14. Governor
15. Transfer control lever
16. Input gear
17. High-low clutch
18. Low speed gear
19. 2WD-4WD clutch
20. Drive sprocket
21. Chain
22. Rear output shaft
23. Front output shaft
24. Counter gear
25. Valve body

Crossection of the KM148 transmission

FLUID CAPACITY

All capacities given in quarts

Year	Vehicle	Transmission	Fluid Type	Pan Capacity	Overhaul Capacity
1984	Isuzu Impulse	AW370	Dexron® II	4.5	6.7
1985	Isuzu Impulse	AW370	Dexron® II	4.5	6.7
1986	Isuzu Impulse	AW370	Dexron® II	4.5	6.7
	Isuzu Impulse	AW372	Dexron® II	4.5	6.7
1987	Isuzu Impulse	AW370	Dexron® II	4.5	6.7
	Isuzu Impulse	AW372	Dexron® II	4.5	6.7
	Mitsubishi Pick-up	AW372	Dexron® II	5.0	7.2
	Mitsubishi Pick-up	KM148	Dexron® II	5.4	7.6
	Mitsubishi Van	AW372	Dexron® II	5.0	7.2
1988	Isuzu Impulse	AW372	Dexron® II	4.5	6.7
	Isuzu Pick-up	AW372	Dexron® II	4.7	6.9
	Mitsubishi Pick-up	AW372	Dexron® II	5.0	7.2
	Mitsubishi Pick-up	KM148	Dexron® II	5.4	7.6
	Mitsubishi Van	AW372	Dexron® II	5.0	7.2
1989	Isuzu Impulse	AW372	Dexron® II	4.5	6.7
	Isuzu Pick-up	AW372	Dexron® II	4.7	6.9
	Mitsubishi Pick-up	AW372	Dexron® II	5.0	7.2
	Mitsubishi Pick-up	KM148	Dexron® II	5.4	7.6
	Mitsubishi Van	AW372	Dexron® II	5.0	7.2

Electronic Controls

THERMO SWITCH

Located near the thermostat housing, the thermo switch prevents overdrive from engaging when the coolant is below proper operating temperature. This switch is used on Mitsubishi vehicles only.

INHIBITOR SWITCH

Located on the right side of the transmission case, the inhibitor switch prevents the vehicle from starting in any gear except **P** or **N**. The inhibitor switch also completes the reverse light circuit when backing up.

OVERDRIVE SWITCH

A push button switch used to manually choose when to use overdrive (4th gear). Located in the left side satellite switch on Impulse, pushing the button in engages overdrive and illuminates the LED on the switch. Located on the shifter handle on Mitsubishi Van and Isuzu P'up, pushing the button in disengages overdrive and illuminates the O/D OFF lamp in the dash. Located on the end of the column mounted shifter on Mitsubishi Pickup, pushing the button in disengages overdrive and illuminates the O/D OFF lamp in the select indicator.

OVERDRIVE RELAY AND SOLENOID VALVE

The solenoid valve is located on the left side of the transmission case. When the overdrive switch is **ON**, current is sent to the overdrive relay. When the solenoid is energized by the overdrive relay, the plunger is pulled and line pressure to the 3rd coast shift valve is released causing a shift into 4th gear. When the solenoid is off, spring tension pushes the plunger down causing line pressure to be applied to the 3rd coast shift valve preventing a shift into 4th gear.

Metric Fasteners

Metric tools will be required to service this transmission. Due to the large number of alloy parts used in this transmission, torque specifications should be strictly observed. Before installing capscrews into aluminum parts, dip the bolts into clean transmission fluid as this will prevent the screws from galling the aluminum threads, thus causing damage.

Metric fastener dimensions are very close to the dimensions of the familiar inch system fasteners. For this reason replacement fasteners must have the same measurement and strength as the original fastener.

Do not attempt to interchange metric fasteners for inch system fasteners. Mismatched or incorrect fasteners can cause damage to the automatic transmission unit and possible personal injury. Care should be taken to reuse fasteners in their original locations.

Checking Fluid Level

Run the engine until at operating temperature and move the gear selector through all ranges. Park the vehicle on level surface and check the fluid level with the gear selector in **P**. The fluid level is sufficient when it is between the lines or notches in the **HOT** range of the dipstick.

TRANSMISSION MODIFICATIONS

No modifications are available at the time of publication.

TROUBLE DIAGNOSIS

CLUTCH AND BRAKE APPLICATION

Selector lever position	Gear	Overdrive Clutch	Overdrive Brake	Overdrive One-way Clutch	Forward Clutch	Direct Clutch Inner Piston	Direct Clutch Outer Piston	Brake No. 1	Brake No. 2	1st/Reverse brakes Inner Piston	1st/Reverse brakes Outer Piston	No. 1 One-way Clutch	No. 2 One-way Clutch
P	Park	Applied	—	—	—	—	—	—	—	Applied	Applied	—	—
R	Reverse	Applied	—	Applied	—	Applied	Applied	—	—	Applied	Applied	—	—
N	Neutral	Applied	—	—	—	—	—	—	—	—	—	—	—
D	First	Applied	—	Applied	Applied	—	—	—	—	—	—	—	Applied
D	Second	Applied	—	Applied	Applied	—	—	—	Applied	—	—	Applied	—
D	Third	Applied	—	Applied	Applied	—	Applied	—	Applied	—	—	—	—
D	Fourth (Overdrive)	—	Applied	—	Applied	—	Applied	—	Applied	—	—	—	—
2	First	Applied	—	Applied	Applied	—	—	—	—	—	—	—	Applied
2	Second	Applied	—	Applied	Applied	—	—	Applied	Applied	—	—	Applied	—
L	First	Applied	—	Applied	Applied	—	—	—	—	Applied	Applied	—	Applied

CHILTON'S THREE C's DIAGNOSIS

Condition	Cause	Correction
Not moving in any range	a) Low oil level b) Wrong type of oil c) Converter bolts missing or broken d) Valve body faulty e) Gear shifter out of adjustment f) Internal linkage parts broken g) Input shaft or output shaft broken h) Torque converter faulty i) Oil pump faulty	a) Add until at correct level b) Change oil c) Replace bolts d) Overhaul valve body e) Adjust shifter f) Replace broken parts g) Replace shaft(s) h) Replace converter i) Inspect pump
Not moving in Drive	a) Valve body faulty b) Gear shifter out of adjustment c) One-way clutch not holding d) Oil pump faulty e) Forward clutch not applying f) Overdrive clutch not applying	a) Overhaul valve body b) Adjust cable c) Overhaul transmission d) Inspect pump e) Overhaul transmission f) Overhaul transmission
Not moving in Reverse	a) Valve body faulty b) Gear shifter out of adjustment c) 1st/reverse brake not holding d) Direct clutch not applying e) Oil pump faulty f) Torque converter faulty g) Center support loose	a) Overhaul valve body b) Adjust shifter c) Overhaul transmission d) Overhaul transmission e) Inspect pump f) Replace converter g) Torque bolts or overhaul transmission
Moving in Neutral	a) Gear shifter out of adjustment b) Wrong type of oil c) Valve body faulty	a) Adjust shifter b) Change oil c) Overhaul valve body

CHILTON'S THREE C's DIAGNOSIS

Condition	Cause	Correction
Not moving in any forward range	a) Valve body faulty b) Gear shifter out of adjustment c) Overdrive clutch not applying d) Overdrive one-way clutch not applying e) Forward clutch not applying f) Torque converter faulty g) Low line pressure h) Oil pump faulty	a) Overhaul valve body b) Adjust shifter c) Overhaul transmission d) Overhaul transmission e) Overhaul transmission f) Replace converter g) Adjust line pressure or repair leak h) Inspect pump
Loud noise in Neutral or Park	a) Torque converter faulty b) Oil pump faulty	a) Replace converter b) Inspect pump
No shift change from Drive first to Drive second	a) Valve body faulty b) Throttle pressure cable out of adjustment c) No. 2 brake faulty d) No. 1 or 2 one-way clutch faulty e) Governor faulty	a) Overhaul valve body b) Adjust cable c) Overhaul transmission d) Overhaul transmission e) Inspect governor
No shift change from Drive second to Drive third	a) Valve body faulty b) Throttle pressure cable out of adjustment d) Direct clutch outer piston not applying e) No. 1 one-way clutch faulty f) Governor faulty	a) Overhaul valve body b) Adjust cable d) Overhaul transmission e) Overhaul transmission f) Inspect governor
No shift change into Overdrive	a) Overdrive clutch or brake faulty b) Valve body faulty c) Governor faulty d) OD switch faulty e) OD solenoid faulty f) Thermo switch faulty	a) Overhaul transmission b) Overhaul valve body c) Inspect governor d) Replace or repair switch or wiring e) Replace or repair solenoid or wiring f) Replace switch
Shift points at wrong speeds	a) Valve body faulty b) Governor faulty c) Throttle pressure cable out of adjustment d) Line pressure incorrect	a) Overhaul valve body b) Inspect governor b) Adjust cable d) Repair cause of incorrect pressure
No kickdown	a) Valve body faulty b) Throttle pressure cable out of adjustment c) WOT not possible d) Governor faulty	a) Overhaul valve body b) Adjust cable c) Adjust accelerator pedal or linkage d) Inspect governor
Shock when shifting from Neutral or Park to Drive	a) Valve body faulty b) Gear shifter out of adjustment c) Low oil level d) Forward clutch faulty e) Engine idle too high f) Accumulator faulty g) High line pressure	a) Overhaul valve body b) Adjust shifter c) Add until at correct level d) Overhaul transmission e) Adjust idle f) Overhaul accumulator g) Repair cause of high pressure
Shock when shifting from Neutral or Park to Reverse	a) Valve body faulty b) Gear shifter out of adjustment c) Low oil level d) Direct clutch faulty e) 1st/reverse brake faulty f) Engine idle too high g) Accumulator faulty h) High line pressure	a) Overhaul valve body b) Adjust shifter c) Add until at correct level d) Overhaul transmission e) Overhaul transmission f) Adjust idle g) Overhaul accumulator h) Repair cause of high pressure
Shudder or slip when starting in Drive	a) Valve body faulty b) Gear shifter out of adjustment c) Low oil level	a) Overhaul valve body b) Adjust shifter c) Add until at correct level

CHILTON'S THREE C's DIAGNOSIS

Condition	Cause	Correction
	d) Wrong type of oil	d) Change oil
	e) Oil pump faulty	e) Inspect pump
	f) Forward clutch faulty	f) Overhaul transmission
	g) Overdrive clutch faulty	g) Overhaul transmission
	h) Transmission and/or engine mount faulty	h) Replace mount
	i) Low line pressure	i) Adjust line pressure or repair leak
Shudder or slip when shifting from Drive first to Drive second	a) Valve body faulty	a) Overhaul valve body
	b) Throttle pressure cable out of adjustment	b) Adjust cable
	c) Low oil level	c) Add until at correct level
	d) Wrong type of oil	d) Change oil
	e) No. 2 brake faulty	e) Overhaul transmission
	f) No. 1 or 2 one-way clutch faulty	f) Overhaul transmission
	g) Oil pump faulty	g) Inspect pump
Shudder or slip when shifting from Drive second or Drive third	a) Valve body faulty	a) Overhaul valve body
	b) Throttle pressure cable out of adjustment	b) Adjust cable
	c) Low oil level	c) Add until at correct level
	d) Wrong type of oil	d) Change oil
	e) Oil pump faulty	e) Inspect pump
	f) Direct clutch outer piston faulty	f) Overhaul transmission
	g) No. 1 one-way clutch faulty	g) Overhaul transmission
Shudder or slip when starting in low	a) Valve body faulty	a) Overhaul valve body
	b) Gear shifter out of adjustment	b) Adjust shifter
	c) Low oil level	c) Add until at correct level
	d) Wrong type of oil	d) Change oil
	e) Torque converter faulty	e) Replace converter
	f) Oil pump faulty	f) Inspect pump
	g) Forward clutch faulty	g) Overhaul transmission
	h) 1st/reverse brake faulty	h) Overhaul transmission
	i) Overdrive clutch faulty	i) Overhaul transmission
	j) Transmission and/or engine mount faulty	j) Replace mount
	k) Engine idle too high	k) Adjust idle
Shudder or slip when starting in Reverse	a) Valve body faulty	a) Overhaul valve body
	b) Gear shifter out of adjustment	b) Adjust shifter
	c) Low oil level	c) Add until at correct level
	d) Wrong type of oil	d) Change oil
	e) Center support loose	e) Torque bolts or overhaul transmission
	f) Direct clutch faulty	f) Overhaul transmission
	g) 1st/reverse brake faulty	g) Overhaul transmission
	h) Transmission and/or engine mount faulty	h) Replace mount
	i) Low line pressure	i) Adjust line pressure or repair leak
No engine braking in Second	a) Brake No. 1 faulty	a) Overhaul transmission
No engine braking in Low	a) 1st/reverse brake faulty	a) Overhaul transmission
Large vibration in Drive	a) Torque converter faulty	a) Replace converter
	b) Converter bolts loose	b) Tighten bolts
	c) Transmission and/or engine mount faulty	c) Replace mount
Engine will not start	a) Gear shifter out of adjustment	a) Adjust shifter
	b) Inhibitor switch faulty	b) Check wiring and switch
Vehicle will not hold in Park	a) Gear shifter out of adjustment	a) Adjust shifter
	b) Parking assembly broken	b) Replace broken parts
	c) Internal linkage parts broken	c) Replace broken parts

CHILTON'S THREE C's DIAGNOSIS

Condition	Cause	Correction
Transmission fluid in antifreeze or antifreeze in Transmission fluid	a) Fluid cooler core in radiator is leaking	a) Replace radiator and change the transmission fluid and antifreeze

Hydraulic Control System

OIL PUMP

The oil pump is driven by the engine through the torque converter by the 2 pawls of the pump drive hub welded at the center of the converter shell. The pump is the inner teeth engaging involute gear type and provides the hydraulic pressure necessary for supplying the torque converter with fluid, lubricating various parts and forcing fluid into the hydraulic control system.

VALVE BODY

The valve body delivers the hydraulic pressure sent from the oil pump to its components. It also regulates the pressure according to throttle valve opening and vehicle speed to provide automatic gearshifting.

PRIMARY REGULATOR VALVE

The primary regulator valve regulates the line pressure produced by the oil pump according to throttle valve opening and vehicle speed. This eliminates power loss caused by the pump.

Applied to the primary valve are the forces of upward direction by spring tension and downward pressure at the top of the valve generated by the oil pump. As the pressure builds causing the downward pressure to overcome spring tension, the valve starts moving down. This opens the oil passage to the secondary regulator valve, dropping the pressure.

When the pressure is low enough, the valve moves upward and closes the passage to the secondary regulator valve. The line pressure is regulated by the movements of the primary regulator valve.

SECONDARY REGULATOR VALVE

The secondary regulator valve regulates the converter, lubrication and cooler pressures according to throttle valve opening and vehicle speed. This valve operates on pressure supplied by the primary regulator valve and spring tension for upward movement, or throttle pressure that causes downward movement.

When the throttle valve is fully closed, spring tension prevents the valve from operating until the converter pressure reaches about 28 psi (200kPa) and closes the hydraulic circuit from the converter to shut off the supply of oil to the cooler. When the engine is stationary, the valve prevents the transmission fluid from draining out of the converter.

MANUAL VALVE

The manual valve is connected by linkage to the selector lever inside the vehicle. It opens or closes oil passages to start hydraulic pressure movement according to the range selected.

THROTTLE VALVE

The thottle valve provides hydraulic pressure according to throttle opening. It is connected to the throttle valve by a cable.

When the accelerator pedal is depressed, the cam moves the kickdown valve causing the spring to move the throttle valve, thus opening the passage for line pressure to produce throttle pressure. The throttle pressure is applied to the 1/2, 2/3 and 3/4 shift valves to counterbalance governor pressure. The pressure is also applied to the primary and secondary valves to regulate line pressure.

KICKDOWN VALVE

When the accelerator is nearly depressed fully, the kickdown valve moves far enough to open the passage from the detent regulator valve. This applies detent pressure the proper valves in order to provide kickdown.

DETENT REGULATOR VALVE

The detent regulator valve regulates the detent pressure applied via the kickdown valve to the proper shift valves. This sets the vehicles speed limit for kickdown.

LOW COAST MODULATOR VALVE

When the vehicle is in **L** range, the line pressure that is applied to this valve is regulated and applied by the low coast shift valve to the outer piston of the 1st/reverse brake. When in **R** range, the low coast shift valve blocks the passage to the 1st/reverse brake and the line pressure is applied.

INTERMEDIATE MODULATOR VALVE

The intermediate modulator valve regulates the line pressure that is applied to brake No. 1 in order to absorb shocks during engine braking, when the vehicle is in **2** range.

1/2 SHIFT VALVE

The 1/2 shift valve automatically selects between 1st and 2nd gears according to governor and throttle pressures.

Downward pressure is provided by throttle pressure and spring tension. Upward pressure is supplied by the governor. When governor pressure is less than the combined force of throttle pressure and spring tension, the 1/2 shift valve is kept pushed down, which releases brake No. 2 to attain 1st gear. When governor pressure is greater than the downward pressure, the valve is pushed up, which opens the circuit to brake No. 2 to attain 2nd gear.

2/3 SHIFT VALVE

The 2/3 shift valve automatically selects between 2nd and 3rd gears according to governor and throttle pressures.

Downward pressure is provided by throttle pressure and spring tension. Upward pressure is supplied by the governor. When governor pressure is less than the combined force of throttle pressure and spring tension, the 2/3 shift valve is kept pushed down, closing the circuit to the direct clutch to attain 2nd gear. When governor pressure is greater than the downward pressure, the valve is pushed up, which opens the circuit to the direct clutch to attain 3rd gear.

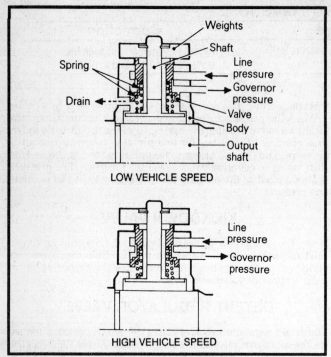

Operation of the governor

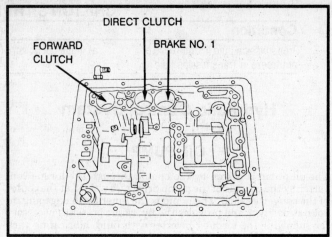

Identifying accumulator pistons

3/4 SHIFT VALVE

The 3/4 shift valve automatically selects between 3rd and 4th gears according to governor and throttle pressures.

Downward pressure is provided by throttle pressure on the top of the valve, line pressure to the middle of the valve and spring tension. Upward pressure is supplied by the governor. When governor pressure is less than the combined force of throttle pressure and spring tension, the 3/4 shift valve is kept pushed down, opening the circuit to the overdrive clutch and at the same time, releasing the circuit to the overdrive brake to attain 3rd gear. When governor pressure is greater than the downward pressure, the valve is pushed up, which opens the circuit to the overdrive brake to attain 4th gear.

When the overdrive switch is **OFF**, the drain circuit of the solenoid is closed. This causes line pressure to be applied to 3rd coast shift valve, pushing down the 3rd coast shift valve and the 3/4 shift valve, preventing a shift into 4th gear.

CUT-BACK VALVE

The cut-back valve applies cut-back pressure to the throttle valve to reduce throttle pressure. It also applies throttle pressure to the primary regulator valve to reduce line pressure. This helps eliminate power losses caused by the oil pump.

REVERSE CLUTCH SEQUENCE VALVE

This valve dampens the shock felt when shifting into **R**. It is controlled by line pressure applied to the inner piston of the direct clutch. The outer piston operates with a lag behind the inner piston and when shifting into 3rd gear. This valve also allows only the inner piston to apply and releases pressure to the outer piston.

D-2 DOWN TIMING VALVE

The D-2 timing valve ensures that engine braking is relatively mild when shifting into **2** when in 4th gear. Gears are shifted from 4th to 3rd to 2nd, instead of directly from 4th to 2nd.

GOVERNOR

Installed on the output shaft, the governor counterbalances the line pressure from the primary regulator valve with the centrifugal force applied to the governor weights. This accounts for the governor pressure in proportion to vehicle speed.

As the output shaft rotates, the governor weights, shaft, valve and spring all move outward allowing the line pressure to enter the governor valve bore. This causes the governor valve to move inward cutting off line pressure.

ACCUMULATOR

Accumulators are provided for the forward clutch, direct clutch and brake No. 2. Their function is to dampen the shock when each is actuated.

When the circuit to the pressure receiving side opens causing the line pressure to be applied to the piston, the piston is slowly pushed downward, thus dampening the shift shock.

OVERDRIVE CLUTCH

The multiple disc overdrive clutch is applied when the transmission is in any gear except 4th. It couples the sun gear to the carrier of the overdrive planetary gearset and transfers the input from the carrier to the forward clutch cylinder via the ring gear.

FORWARD CLUTCH

The multiple disc forward clutch is applied whenever the vehicle is in forward motion. It transfers the input to the rear planetary gearset ring gear via the intermediate shaft.

DIRECT CLUTCH

The multiple disc direct clutch is applied in 3rd and 4th gears and reverse. It transmits the input force to the sun gear, driving the pinion s of the front planetary gearset.

OVERDRIVE BRAKE

The multiple disc overdrive brake is installed in the overdrive case and is applied in 4th gear. The brake holds the sun gear of the overdrive planetary gearset.

BRAKE NO. 1

Brake No. 1, actuated in 2nd gear of **2** range, holds the sun gear stationary.

BRAKE NO. 2

Brake No. 2, actuated in 2nd, 3rd and 4th gears of **D** range and 2nd gear of **2**, holds the outer race of No. 1 one-way clutch, allowing No. 1 one-way clutch to act as an overrunning clutch.

1ST/REVERSE BRAKE

The 1st/reverse brake, actuated in **L** and **R** ranges, brakes the carrier of the front planetary gearset to a standstill.

ONE-WAY CLUTCH

The 3 sets of one-way clutches are sprag type. The overdrive one-way clutch is operated between a 3/4 shift, ensuring smooth selection between the overdrive clutch and brake.

No. 1 one-way clutch functions as an overrunning clutch only when brake No. 2 is actuated and prevents the sun gear from turning counterclockwise. No. 2 one-way clutch prevents the front planetary carrier from turning counterclockwise and is actuated in 1st gear in **D** and **2** ranges.

OVERDRIVE PLANETARY GEAR

The overdrive planeary gear is a single row type planetary gear. It consists of the sun gear, pinion, carrier and ring gear. Input from the overdrive input shaft is transferred to the carrier.

PLANETARY GEARSET

A Simpson type planetary gearset, it is made up of 2 planetary gears. The sun gear is connected to the direct clutch, front carrier and to the 1st/reverse brake. The ring gear is connected to the forward clutch. The front ring gear and the rear carrier are coupled to the output shaft.

Diagnosis Tests

STALL SPEED TEST

─────────── CAUTION ───────────

Never allow anyone to stand in front of or behind the vehicle when performing a stall test

───────────────────────────────

1. Check the fluid level and condition. Perform the test at normal operating temperature.
2. Block the wheels securely and firmly set the parking brake.
3. Connect a tachometer to the engine.
4. Push down the brake pedal firmly and shift the gear selector to the **D** detent.
5. Gradually depress the accelerator pedal. Do not perform this step for more than 5 seconds.
6. When the engine has stopped increasing in speed, read the tachometer and immediately release the accelerator pedal.
7. Shift into the **N** detent. Allow the engine to idle for 1 minute so the fluid can cool and to prevent the possibility of overheating.
8. Perform the stall test in **R** range.
9. If the stall speed is lower than specification in **D** and **R**, then either the engine output is too low or the stator one-way clutch is faulty.
10. If the stall speed is higher than specification in **D**, then either the overdrive clutch is slipping, the overdrive one-way

STALL SPEED SPECIFICATIONS

Year	Vehicle	Stall Speed (rpm)
1984	Isuzu Impulse	2000–2300
1985	Isuzu Impulse	2000–2300
1986	Isuzu Impulse	2000–2300① 2450–2750②
1987	Isuzu Impulse	2000–2300① 2450–2750②
	Mitsubishi Pick-up	1800–2100③ 2100–2400④
	Mitsubishi Van	2050–2350
1988	Isuzu Impulse	2100–2400⑤ 2450–2750⑥
	Isuzu Pick-up	2250–2550
	Mitsubishi Pick-up	1800–2100
	Mitsubishi Van	2050–2350
1989	Isuzu Impulse	2100–2400⑤ 2450–2750⑥
	Isuzu Pick-up	2250–2550
	Mitsubishi Pick-up	1800–2100③ 2100–2400④
	Mitsubishi Van	2050–2350

① with AW 370 Transmission ④ with 2.6L engine
② with AW 372 Transmission ⑤ with 2.3L engine
③ with 2.0L engine ⑥ with 2.0L engine

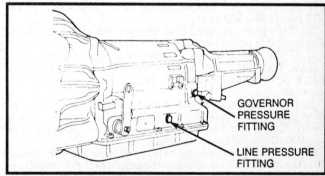

GOVERNOR PRESSURE FITTING

LINE PRESSURE FITTING

Locations of pressure test fittings

clutch is faulty, the forward clutch is slipping, one-way clutch No. 2 is faulty or the line pressure is low.

11. If the stall speed is higher than specification in **R**, then either the overdrive clutch is slipping, the overdrive one-way clutch is faulty, the direct clutch is slipping, the 1st/reverse brake is slipping or the line pressure is low.

LINE PRESSURE TEST

1. Check the fluid level and condition. Perform the test at normal operating temperature.
2. Raise and safely support the vehicle. Connect an oil pressure gauge to the proper fitting. Lower the vehicle. Connect a tachometer to the engine.
3. Block the wheels securely and firmly set the parking brake.
4. Shift the gear selector to **D** and read the line pressure at idle. The specification is 65–77 psi (460–540 kPa).
5. Repeat the test and read the pressure at the stall speed.

GOVERNOR PRESSURE SPECIFICATIONS

Year	Vehicle	Governor Pressure psi (kpa)	Approximate Vehicle Speed (mph)
1984–87	Isuzu Impulse①	13–21 (90–150)	17
		23–33 (160–230)	34
		58–75 (410–530)	58
1986–89	Isuzu Impulse②	13–24 (90–170)	17
		30–40 (210–280)	34
		57–74 (400–520)	58
1987–89	Mitsubishi Pick-up③	19–22 (128–150)	16
		33–38 (226–264)	31
		54–62 (373–431)	50
1987 and 1989	Mitsubishi Pick-up④	20–24 (138–166)	16
		36–41 (246–284)	31
		59–66 (400–460)	50
1987–89	Mitsubishi Van	18–23 (130–160)	16
		33–38 (230–270)	31
		54–63 (380–430)	50
1988–89	Isuzu Pick-up	17–26 (120–180)	17
		33–43 (230–300)	34
		61–78 (430–550)	58

① with AW370 transmission
② with AW372 transmission
③ with 2.0L engine
④ with 2.6L engine

The specification is 144–169 psi (1010–1190 kPa). Allow 1 minute cooling time.

6. Repeat Steps 4 and 5 in **R**. The specification at idle is 100–118 psi (700–830). The specification at the stall speed is 213–270 psi (1500–1900 kPa).

7. If the pressures are not at the specified values, check the throttle cable adjustment and repeat the test.

8. If the line pressure is higher than specification in all ranges, then either the regulator valve is faulty, the throttle valve is faulty or the throttle control cable is incorrectly adjusted.

9. If the line pressure is lower than specification in all ranges, then either the regulator valve is faulty, the throttle valve is faulty, the oil pump is faulty, the overdrive clutch is faulty or the throttle control cable is incorrectly adjusted.

10. If the line pressure is lower than specification in **D**, then either the forward clutch is faulty, the overdrive clutch is faulty or there is a fluid leak in the **D** range hydraulic circuit.

11. If the line pressure is lower than specification in **R**, then either the direct clutch is faulty, the overdrive clutch is faulty, the 1st/reverse brake is faulty or there is a fluid leak in the **R** range hydraulic circuit.

GOVERNOR PRESSURE TEST

1. Check the fluid level and condition. Perform the test at normal operating temperature.

2. Raise and safely support the vehicle. Connect an oil pressure gauge to the fitting. Lower the vehicle to a height at which the wheels can spin freely. Connect a tachometer to the engine.

3. Shift the gear selector to **D** and read the pressure at each speed indicated on the Governor Pressure Specifications chart.

4. If the governor pressure is not within specifications, then either the line pressure is incorrect, there is a hydraulic leak in the governor circuit or the governor is faulty.

TIME LAG TEST

1. Check the fluid level and condition. Perform the test at normal operating temperature.

2. Block the wheels securely and firmly set the parking brake.

3. Shift from **N** to **D** and measure the time it takes from shifting the lever until the shift is felt.

4. Repeat the test twice allowing 1 minute between tests and average the results. The average time lag should be less than 1.2 seconds.

5. Repeat the entire procedure shifting from **N** to **R**.
The average time lag should be less than 1.5 seconds.

6. If the **N** to **D** time lag is longer than specification, then either the line pressure is too low or the forward clutch is worn.

7. If the **N** to **D** time lag is longer than specification, then the line pressure is too low, or the direct clutch or the 1st/reverse brake is worn.

ROAD TEST

This test is designed to check if upshift and downshift occurs at the correct speeds and if slippage or excessive shock is detected while actually driving the vehicle. The test should be performed on a long level road, with little or no traffic so that speeds can be chosen and maintained and not forced or altered by others on the road.

1. Run the engine until at operating temperature and check the fluid level.

2. Shift into **D** and start off with the pedal about half way down. Check all shift points and any clutch slippage when the transmission shifts gears. Shifting from 1st to 2nd should occur at 15–20 mph. Shifting from 2nd to 3rd should occur at 40–45 mph. Shifting from 3rd to 4th should occur at 50–60 mph, providing the overdrive switch is **ON**. In addition, check the operation of the lockup torque converter, on vehicles with the AW372 transmission. The damper clutch should engage at about 45 mph when in 4th gear.

3. Come to a gradual stop. Automatic downshifting through the gears should occur at 10–15 mph less than the corresponding upshift.

4. Start up again. While in 2nd, 3rd and 4th gears, check the kickdown mechanism by fully depressing the accelerator pedal. The transmission should automatically downshift through the gears.

5. While in 3rd or 4th gear, release the accelerator and shift into **L**. Engine braking should be felt. Also automatic shifting from 3rd to 2nd or 4th to 3rd to 2nd should occur immediately and shifting from 2nd to 1st should occur at 28–33 mph.

6. Accelerate back up to 3rd gear and shift into **2**. Engine braking should be felt. Come to a complete stop.

7. Start off in **2** with the pedal depressed about half way down. Shifting from 1st to 2nd should occur at 15–20 mph and kickdown to 1st should operate. Come to a complete stop.

8. Start off in **L** and check that no upshift occurs. Release the accelerator pedal. Engine braking should occur. Come to a complete stop.

9. Shift into **R**. Check for clutch slippage by cautiously making full throttle starts. If possible, check for clutch slippage by depressing the accelerator pedal lightly while in motion. Come to a complete stop.

10. Shift into **P** and check the operation of the parking pawl while on a slope.

11. If any abnormality is found during the road test, compare the findings with the Chilton Three C's Transmission Diagnosis Chart.

Electronic Control System

COMPONENT TESTING

Thermo Switch

If the vehicle will not go into overdrive at operating temperature with the overdrive switch **ON** and the thermo switch is suspect, check for continuity from the terminal to the switch base when the coolant is 122°F (50°C) or more. There should not be continuity when the coolant is below 122°F (50°C).

If necessary, check for continuity between the sensor wire and the brown wire at the overdrive relay.

Inhibitor Switch

1984–86 ISUZU IMPULSE

If the starter circuit of the inhibitor switch is not functioning properly, check for continuity through the switch at the blue and brown wires with the switch in either the **P** or **N** detent.

If the reverse light circuit of the inhibitor switch is not func-

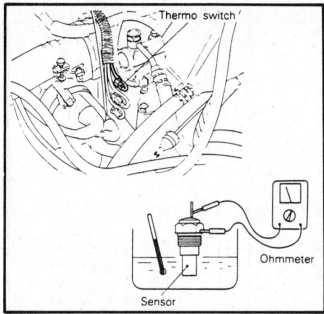

Checking the thermo switch

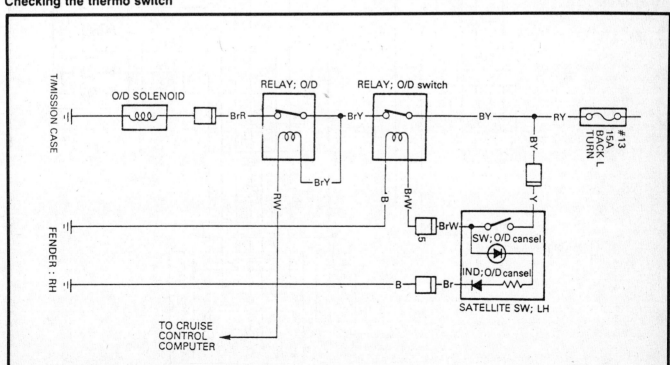

Isuzu Impulse overdrive circuit – typical

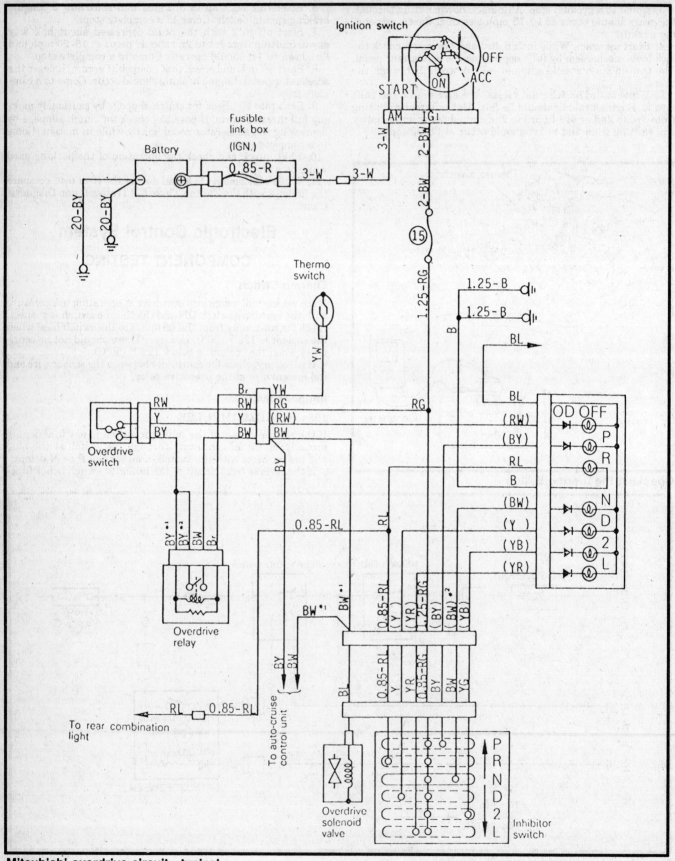

Mitsubishi overdrive circuit—typical

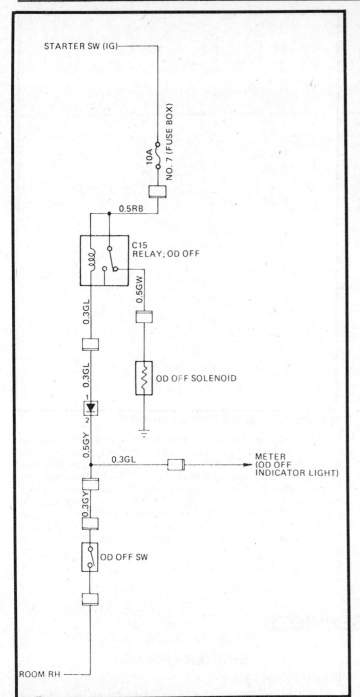

Isuzu P'up overdrive circuit

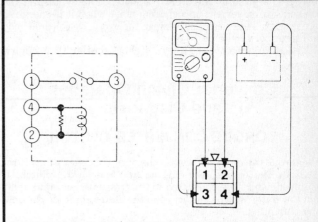

Checking continuity of the overdrive relay

1988–89 ISUZU P'UP

If the starter circuit of the inhibitor switch is not functioning properly, check for continuity through the switch at the black and the black-with-pink-tracer wires with the switch in either the **P** or **N** detent.

If the reverse light circuit of the inhibitor switch is not functioning properly, check for continuity through the switch at the red-with-blue-tracer and the red-with-black-tracer wires with the switch in the **R** detent.

1987–89 MITSUBISHI PICK-UP

If the starter circuit of the inhibitor switch is not functioning properly, check for continuity through the switch at the black-with-yellow-tracer and the black-with-white-tracer wires with the switch in either the **P** or **N** detent.

If the reverse light circuit of the inhibitor switch is not functioning properly, check for continuity through the switch at the red and red-with-blue-tracer wires with the switch in the **R** detent.

1987–89 MITSUBISHI VAN

If the starter circuit of the inhibitor switch is not functioning properly, check for continuity through the switch at the red-with-green-tracer wires on both sides of the with the switch in either the **P** or **N** detent.

If the reverse light circuit of the inhibitor switch is not functioning properly, check for continuity through the switch at the red-with-blue-tracer wires on both sides of the switch with the switch in the **R** detent.

Overdrive Switch

In all vehicles, the overdrive switch is functionally identical. To check the switch, check for continuity through the switch while it is in the O/D **ON** position.

NOTE: On Mitsubishi, the yellow wire is connected to the O/D OFF lamp, so check continuity through that terminal with the switch in the O/D OFF position. On Isuzu P'up, the green-with-blue-tracer wire is connected to the O/D OFF lamp, so check continuity through that terminal with the switch in the O/D OFF position.

Overdrive Relay and Solenoid Valve

In all vehicles, the overdrive relay is functionally identical. To check the relay, check for 12V at the wire from the overdrive switch. Also check for ground either to the body on Isuzu or to the thermo switch on Mitsubishi.

In addition, check for 12V at the other 2 terminals when the

tioning properly, check for continuity through the switch at the red and black wires with the switch in the **R** detent.

1987–89 ISUZU IMPULSE

If the starter circuit of the inhibitor switch is not functioning properly, check for continuity through the switch at the white-with-black-tracer and the black-with-blue-tracer wires with the switch in either the **P** or **N** detent.

If the reverse light circuit of the inhibitor switch is not functioning properly, check for continuity through the switch at the red-with-blue-tracer and the red-with-white-tracer wires with the switch in the **R** detent.

relay is energized by the overdrive switch. Finally, inspect the solenoid for movement or a clicking noise when it is energized by the relay. The resistance between the overdrive solenoid body and terminal should be 13 ohms.

If necessary, remove the relay and check continuity through it using an external power source.

Converter Clutch Operation and Diagnosis

TORQUE CONVERTER CLUTCH

The torque converter consists of the pump impeller which is rotated by the engine, the turbine and the lockup clutch, if equipped, which are connected to the transmission input shaft and the stator which is attached to the stator shaft via the one-way clutch.

The rotation of the impeller produces a flow of transmission fluid inside the converter. This flow strikes the turbine and causes it to rotate, thus transmitting torque to the input shaft. The flow of transmission fluid which has hit the turbine rebounds and tries to flow in the direction opposite to the direction of rotation of the pump impeller, but the stator returns the flow to the original direction of rotation. This action forces the fluid to support the pump impeller and increases torque.

Although the stator is immobilized by the one-way clutch, should the one-way clutch become defective, the stator will be rotated by the flow of transmission fluid. In this instance, the flow will not be reversed, torque will not be increased and inadequate acceleration will result.

When the vehicle is driven in 4th gear at speeds of about 45 mph, governor pressure pushes the signal valve up allowing line pressure to be applied to the lockup relay valve. The lockup relay valve then moves upward and converter pressure can act upon the rear of the damper clutch. This causes the damper clutch to engage with the front cover and since there is no engine loss through hydraulic slippage, fuel mileage is increased.

TROUBLESHOOTING THE TORQUE CONVERTER CLUTCH

While driving in 3rd gear with the overdrive switch **OFF**, press the accelerator lightly with the lockup clutch engaged. Take

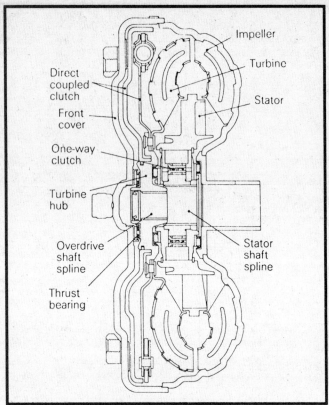

Construction of the torque converter

note of if the engine rpm change is very small. Since driving force is transmitted through the fluid in the torque converter when the damper clutch is not operational, excessive rpm change under these conditions indicates a faulty lockup clutch.

This lockup converter utilizes purely hydraulic means to operate. The control valves in the valve body can be inspected for sticking and clogging of the fluid passages can also prevent operation of the lockup mechanism. If this does not solve the problem, replace the torque converter if it does not function properly.

ON CAR SERVICES

Adjustments

THROTTLE CABLE

1. Depress the accelerator pedal fully and make sure the throttle valve opens fully. If it does not, adjust the accelerator link.
2. Check for a bent throttle lever or throttle cable bracket.
3. Measure the distance between the end of the rubber boot and the stopper on the cable at wide open throttle. The distance should be 0.03–0.06 in. (0.8–1.5mm) on Isuzu, 2.05–2.09 in. (52–53mm) on Mitsubishi Pick-up and 0–0.04 in. (0–1mm) on Mitsubishi Van.
4. If out of specification, loosen the adjusting nuts and bring the distance to the proper value. Adjust the cable by moving the bracket on Mitsubishi Pick-up.
5. Tighten the adjusting nuts or bolts.
6. Recheck the adjustment and road test the vehicle.

SHIFTER LINKAGE

ISUZU VEHICLES

1. Raise the vehicle and support safely. Check that all pivot points are well lubricated and that the indicator functions correctly.
2. Loosen the nut on the shift linkage.
3. Move the manual lever fully rearward and return 2 detents to the **N** position on P'up. Move the lever full forward and return 3 detents to the **N** position on Impulse.
4. Hold the lever lightly toward the **R** detent. Tighten the nut and check for proper operation of the assembly as well as the inhibitor switch.

MITSUBISHI PICK-UP

1. Raise the vehicle and support safely. Check that all pivot points are well lubricated and that the indicator functions correctly.

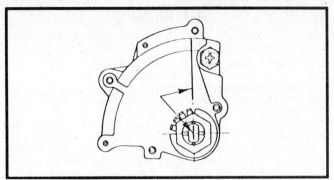

Isuzu inhibitor switch adjustment

2. Position the shifter in the **N** detent.
3. Loosen the nut on the shift linkage.
4. Align the selector lever so the notch points straight down.
5. Tighten the nut and check for proper operation of the assembly as well as the inhibitor switch.

MITSUBISHI VAN

1. Remove the floor console.
2. Shift the selector lever into the **N** detent.
3. Loosen the adjusting bolt.
4. Make sure the lever on the transmission is in the **N** detent. Jiggle the selector rod inside the vehicle to settle the assembly in position.
5. Tighten the adjusting bolt and check for proper operation of the assembly as well as the inhibitor switch.

INHIBITOR SWITCH

1. If the engine starts in any gear except **P** or **R** or does not start in **P** or **N**, check for correct adjustment of the switch.
2. Make sure the shifter linkage is correctly adjusted.
3. Place the selector in the **N** detent.
4. Loosen the mounting bolt(s).
5. On Isuzu, align the groove on the end of the shaft with the neutral basic line on the switch. On Mitsubishi, align the lever with the positioning boss.
6. Hold the position and tighten the bolt(s). Check for proper operation.

Services

FLUID CHANGE

The conditions under which the vehicle is operated is the main consideration in determining how often the transmission fluid should be changed. Different driving conditions result in different fluid temperatures. These temperatures affect change intervals.

If the vehicle is driven under severe conditions, change the transmission fluid every 15,000 miles. If the vehicle is not used under severe conditions, change the fluid and replace the filter every 30,000 miles.

Do not overfill the transmission. It only takes about a pint of Dexron®II to raise the level from one line or notch to the next on the dipstick. Overfilling the unit can cause damage to the internal components of the automatic transmission.

OIL PAN

Removal and Installation

1. Raise the vehicle and support safely. Remove the undercover, if equipped. Position a large drain pan under the drain plug and remove the drain plug.

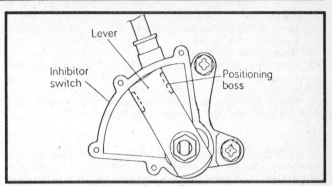

Mitsubishi inhibitor switch adjustment

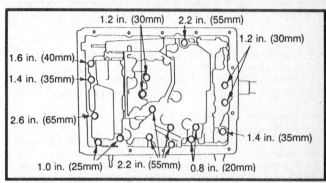

Locations and lengths of valve body mounting bolts

2. After the fluid has drained, reinstall the drain plug.
3. If desired, remove the pan bolts and carefully pull the pan down in order to inspect the strainer and pan for any concentrations of friction material and metal pieces. A small amount of accumulation around the pan magnet or strainer is considered normal, but larger amounts may indicate heavy wear. If metal pieces are present, more serious damage is possible.
4. If removed, clean the pan thoroughly with clean solvent and straighten the mating surface with a block of wood and a mallet if necessary. Pay special attention to the cleanliness of the mating surface.
5. Replace the strainer if necessary.
6. Clean and completely dry all bolts and bolt holes with solvent and compressed air.
7. Glue the new gasket to the pan and hold against the case while installing a few bolts finger tight. Torque the pan bolts to 15 ft. lbs. (20 Nm) in crisscross order.
8. Lower the vehicle. Fill with the proper amount of Dexron®II. Start the engine and allow it to reach operating temperature. Run through the gears.
9. Check the fluid level in **N** and add until at the proper lever on the dipstick. Road test, check for leaks and recheck the fluid level on level surface.

VALVE BODY

Removal and Installation

NOTE: The valve body is a precisely machined part used in the automatic transmission. Handle it with care and do not clamp in a vise. The material is fragile and could distort easily. Keep all parts labeled and in a well-arranged order, since many of them look similar. Cleanliness is of the utmost importance when working with valve bodies; even the most minuscule scratch or piece of dirt can restrict valve movement and impair the transmission's performance.

1. Raise the vehicle and support safely. Drain the transmis-

sion fluid.

2. Remove the oil pan and gasket.
3. Remove the oil pipes.
4. Remove the oil screen.
5. Remove 17 valve body mounting bolts. These bolts are different lengths, so take note of their locations before removing them.
6. Lower the valve body and disconnect the throttle cable from the cam. Remove the valve body from the vehicle.

NOTE: The accumulator pistons and parking mechanism may also be serviced at this point. The accumulator pistons and springs look similar, so do not confuse them. Take careful notes for reference during reassembly if removing the accumulator pistons and springs.

7. Position the valve body into place. Hold the cam down and install the throttle cable end into the slot on the cam.
8. Install the valve body mounting bolts in their correct locations finger tight initially. Torque the mounting bolts to 3.6–4.3 ft. lbs. (5–5.5 Nm).
9. Install the oil strainer.
10. Install the oil tubes.
11. Completely clean and dry the pan. Install the pan with a new gasket.
12. Fill the transmission with the proper amount of Dexron®II and road test the vehicle. Check for leaks and recheck the fluid level.

GOVERNOR

1. Raise the vehicle and safely support. Matchmark and remove the driveshaft.
2. Remove the speedometer driven gear.
3. Remove the extension housing and gasket.
4. Remove the speedometer drive gear
5. Loosen the staked part of the lock plate.
6. Remove the governor body lock bolt.
7. Lift the retaining clip and slide the governor body from the output shaft.
8. If desired, remove the governor strainer plate and strainer.
9. Clean the strainer and install into the case. Install the plate and tighten the screws.
10. Lift the retaining clip and slide the governor body onto the output shaft. Insert the retaining clip into the hole on the shaft.
11. Install the lock plate and bolt and stake the lock plate.
12. Install the speedometer drive gear.
13. Install the extension housing with new gasket.
14. Install the speedometer driven gear.
15. Install the driveshaft.

REAR OIL SEAL

1. Raise the vehicle and safely support. Matchmark and remove the driveshaft.
2. Remove the dust cover.
3. Use a suitable tool and remove the seal.
4. Lubricate the inner lip of the new seal with multi-purpose grease and install using the special tool.
5. Install the dust cover.
6. Install the driveshaft.

REMOVAL AND INSTALLATION

TRANSMISSION REMOVAL

1. Disconnect the negative battery cable. Disconnect the throttle cable from the throttle linkage and remove it with the bracket.
2. Raise the vehicle and safely support.
3. Remove the undercover and transfer case protector, if equipped.
4. Drain the transmission. Drain the transfer case fluid, if equipped.
5. Matchmark and remove the rear driveshaft. Do the same with the front driveshaft if equipped with 4WD.
6. Disconnect the speedometer cable.
7. Disconnect the shifter linkage or cable.
8. Unplug all transmission electrical connectors.
9. Unbolt the exhaust pipe from the manifold and unbolt the bracket from the transmission case.
10. Remove the filler tube with dipstick.
11. Remove the torque converter inspection plate.
12. Remove the torque converter bolts.
13. Remove the starter.
14. Disconnect and plug the oil cooler pipes.
15. Support the transmission safely with the proper equipment.
16. Unbolt the transmission from the rear crossmember.
17. On all vehicles except Mitsubishi Van, remove the rear crossmember from the vehicle.
18. Let the transmission down slightly and unbolt the transfer shifter from the transfer case, if equipped with 4 wheel drive.
19. Remove the bellhousing bolts and brackets.
20. Pull the transmission backwards to clear the dowel pins and remove it from the vehicle.

TRANSMISSION INSTALLATION

1. Install the transmission onto the engine using the dowel pins as guides. Install the bellhousing bolts and torque to specification.
2. Install the bellhousing bolts and brackets. Torque the bolts to specification.
3. Install the transfer shifter with gasket, if equipped with 4WD. Jack the assembly up and install the rear crossmember, if it was removed. Torque the bolts to 30–35 ft. lbs. (40–50 Nm).
4. Bolt the transmission to the rear crossmember. Torque the bolts to specification. Remove the support fixture.
5. Install the oil cooler pipes.
6. Install the starter. Torque the bolts to 18–25 ft. lbs. (25–34 Nm).
7. Apply Loctite® to the threads and install the torque converter bolts. Torque the bolts to specification.
8. Install the torque converter inspection plate.
9. Install the filler tube with a new O-ring and dipstick.
10. Install the exhaust pipe to the manifold and install the bracket.
11. Plug in electrical connectors.
12. Connect the shifter linkage or cable.
13. Connect the speedometer cable.
14. Install the driveshaft(s).
15. Lower the vehicle.
16. Connect the throttle cable.
17. Connect the negative battery cable.
18. Fill the transmission and transfer case with the proper amount of Dexron®II. Start the engine and run through the gears. Add fluid until the transmission is properly filled.
19. Check the operation of the inhibitor switch and make sure the reverse lights come on in the **R** detent. Adjust cables and linkage if necessary, road test, check for leaks and recheck the fluid level.

BENCH OVERHAUL

Before Disassembly

Cleanliness is an important factor in the overhaul of the automatic transmission. Before opening up this unit, the entire outside of the transmission assembly should be cleaned, preferably with a high pressure washer such as a car wash spray unit. Dirt entering the internal parts will negate all the time and effort spent on the overhaul. During inspection and reassembly all parts should be thoroughly cleaned with solvent then dried with compressed air. Wiping cloths and rags should not be used to dry parts since lint will find its way into the valve body passages.

Wheel bearing grease, long used to hold thrust washers and lube parts, should not be used. Lube seals with clean transmission fluid and use ordinary unmedicated petroleum jelly to hold the thrust washers and to ease the assembly of seals, since it will not leave a harmful residue as grease often will. Do not use solvent on neoprene seals, friction plates if they are to be reused, or thrust washers. Be wary of nylon parts if the transmission failure was due to failure of the cooling system. Nylon parts exposed to water or antifreeze solutions can swell and distort and must be replaced.

Before installing bolts into aluminum parts, always dip the threads into clean transmission fluid. Antiseize compound can also be used to prevent bolts from galling the aluminum and

seizing. Always use a torque wrench to keep from stripping the threads. Take care when installing new O-rings, especially the smaller O-rings. The internal snaprings should be expanded and the external rings should be compressed, if they are to be reused. This will help insure proper seating when installed.

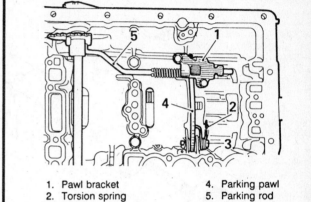

1. Pawl bracket
2. Torsion spring
3. Pivot pin
4. Parking pawl
5. Parking rod

Parking pawl assembly

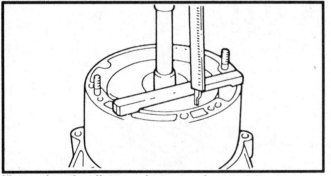

Measuring the distance between the ovrdrive case and the clutch cylinder

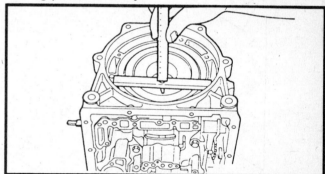

Measuring the distance between the case flange and the forward clutch drum

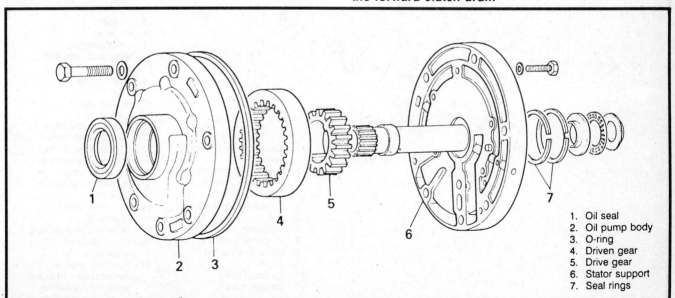

1. Oil seal
2. Oil pump body
3. O-ring
4. Driven gear
5. Drive gear
6. Stator support
7. Seal rings

Exploded view of the oil pump

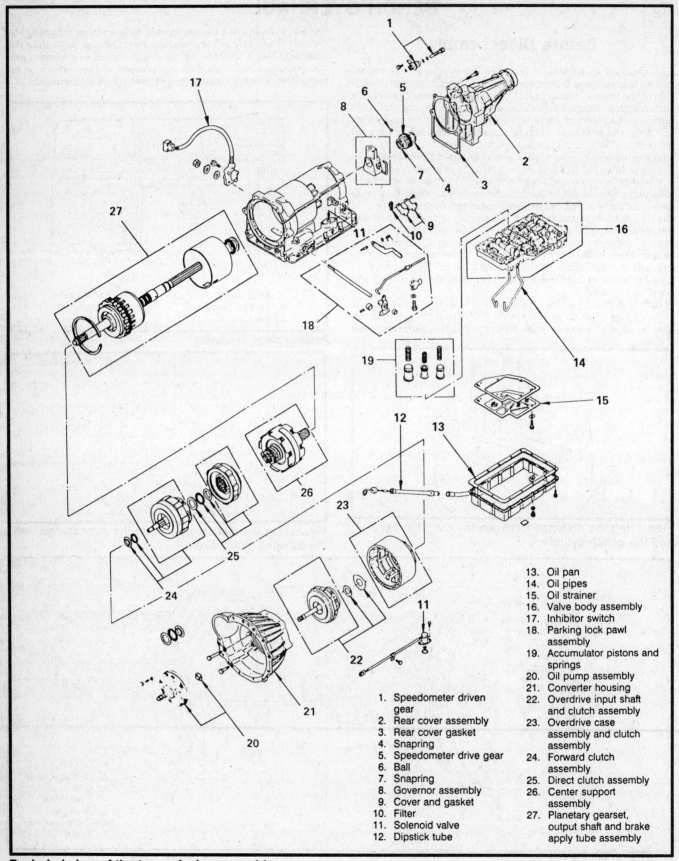

13. Oil pan
14. Oil pipes
15. Oil strainer
16. Valve body assembly
17. Inhibitor switch
18. Parking lock pawl
    assembly
19. Accumulator pistons and
    springs
20. Oil pump assembly
21. Converter housing
22. Overdrive input shaft
    and clutch assembly
23. Overdrive case
    assembly and clutch
    assembly
24. Forward clutch
    assembly
25. Direct clutch assembly
26. Center support
    assembly
27. Planetary gearset,
    output shaft and brake
    apply tube assembly

1. Speedometer driven
   gear
2. Rear cover assembly
3. Rear cover gasket
4. Snapring
5. Speedometer drive gear
6. Ball
7. Snapring
8. Governor assembly
9. Cover and gasket
10. Filter
11. Solenoid valve
12. Dipstick tube

Exploded view of the transmission assembly

Converter Inspection

1. The converter should be replaced if any cracks or external damage of any sort are found.

2. Insert a turning tool into the inner race of the one-way clutch.

3. Install the stopper so it fits in the notch of the converter hub and outer race of the one-way clutch.

4. Position the converter facing up. The clutch should lock when turned counterclockwise and rotate freely and smoothly when turned clockwise. Less than 22 inch lbs. (25 Nm) of turning torque should be required to turn the clutch. Replace the converter if it fails the test.

Transmission Disassembly

1. Remove the transfer case, if equipped. Remove the overdrive solenoid valve.

2. Remove the inhibitor switch.

3. Remove the speedometer driven gear. Position the unit in a suitable holding fixture.

4. Remove the oil pump mounting bolts.

5. Use the special tool to separate the pump from the case. Remove the pump by hand by grasping the stator shaft and pulling it out. Watch for the bearing and race behind the pump.

6. Remove the torque converter housing to case bolts. Hold the input shaft and remove the converter housing.

7. Remove the extension housing and gasket.

8. Remove the speedometer drive gear

9. Loosen the staked part of the lockplate.

10. Remove the governor body lock bolt.

11. Lift the retaining clip and slide the governor body from the output shaft.

12. Remove the governor strainer plate and strainer.

13. Remove the oil pan and gasket.

NOTE: Do not turn the transaxle upside-down when removing the pan as this could contaminate the components inside the case with foreign matter from the pan.

14. Turn the transmission over and remove the oil tubes.

15. Remove the oil strainer.

16. Remove the 17 valve body mounting bolts.

17. Lift the valve body slightly and disconnect the throttle cable from the cam. Remove the valve body.

18. Push the plastic throttle cable retainer out of the transmission case and remove the cable and retainer.

19. Disassemble and remove the parking assembly. Remove the pawl plate, torsion spring, pivot pin, parking pawl and parking rod from the manual valve detent lever.

20. Drive the roll pin from the manual shaft and remove the shaft and manual valve lever. Remove the oil seal from the manual valve shaft.

21. Blow low pressure compressed air into each of the accumulator apply holes and carefully blow the pistons out of their bores into a rag. Remove the springs and keep them in order for reassembly later. Make accurate notes as to the proper order and positioning of the accumulator pistons and springs for reference when assembling.

22. Set the special tool for measuring the distance between the overdrive case and the clutch cylinder on the overdrive case. Record the measurement for reference when assembling. Remove the overdrive input shaft, planetary gear and overdrive clutch assembly from the overdrive case as an assembly. Watch for bearings and races on both sides of the assembly when removing.

23. Remove the overdrive case assembly.

24. Pull the forward clutch assembly out of the case by the shaft.

25. Set the special tool for measuring the distance between the top of the case flange and the forward clutch drum on the case.

Record the measurement for reference when assembling. Remove the direct clutch assembly.

26. Remove the 2 center support bolts.

27. Remove the center support and sun gear assembly together.

28. Remove the flange retaining snapring.

29. Remove the planetary carrier assembly by the intermediate shaft.

30. Remove the brake apply tube and output shaft thrust bearing and race.

31. Remove the rear cover and gasket.

Unit Disassembly and Assembly

OIL PUMP

Disassembly

1. Remove the seal rings from the stator support.

2. Remove the stator support from the oil pump body.

3. Matchmark the drive and driven gear and remove them from the pump body.

4. Remove the O-ring from the pump body.

5. Remove the front seal from the pump body.

Inspection

1. Visually inspect all components for damage of any type, especially ridged wear on the body and drive gear contact surfaces.

2. Measure the clearance between the driven gear and the body. The specification is 0.003–0.012 in. (0.07–0.30mm).

3. Measure the clearance between the driven and drive gear teeth and the crescent. The specification is 0.004–0.012 in. (0.11–0.30mm).

4. Measure the side clearance of the drive and driven gears. The specification is 0.001–0.004 in. (0.02–0.10mm).

Assembly

1. Install a new front seal on the pump body. Set the body on the torque converter.

2. Install the gears in the pump body according to the matchmarks.

3. Install the stator support on the body.

4. Install the bolts with washer fingertight. Install the special tool to align the body and support.

5. Torque the bolts to 5.4 ft. lbs. (7.5 Nm). Remove the tool.

6. Coat the seal rings with Dexron®II and install on the stator support.

7. Coat the new O-ring with Dexron®II and install on the pump body.

OVERDRIVE INPUT SHAFT AND CLUTCH ASSEMBLY

Disassembly

1. Check the operation of the one-way clutch. Hold the over-

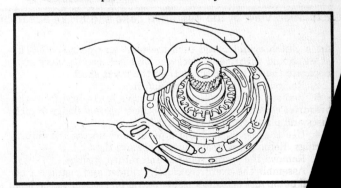

Removing the overdrive clutch piston

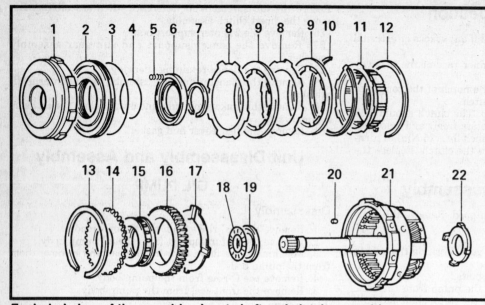

1. Overdrive clutch cylinder
2. Overdrive clutch piston
3. O-ring
4. O-ring
5. Return spring
6. Spring retainer
7. Snapring
8. Clutch plates
9. Clutch discs
10. Snapring
11. Overdrive brake hub
12. Snapring
13. Snapring
14. One-way clutch retainer
15. One-way clutch assembly
16. One-way clutch outer race
17. Thrust washer
18. Thrust bearing
19. Thrust bearing race
20. Pinion shaft plug
21. Overdrive planetary gear
22. Thrust washer

Exploded view of the overdrive input shaft and clutch assembly

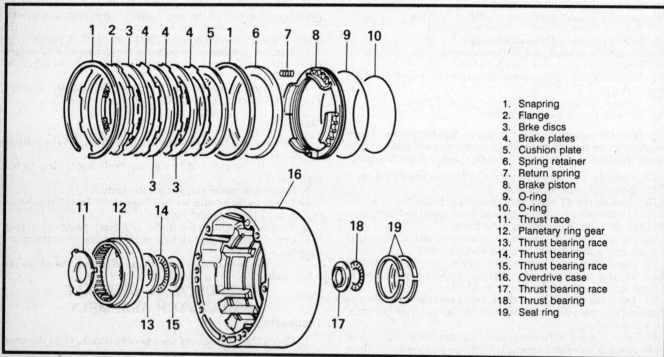

1. Snapring
2. Flange
3. Brke discs
4. Brake plates
5. Cushion plate
6. Spring retainer
7. Return spring
8. Brake piston
9. O-ring
10. O-ring
11. Thrust race
12. Planetary ring gear
13. Thrust bearing race
14. Thrust bearing
15. Thrust bearing race
16. Overdrive case
17. Thrust bearing race
18. Thrust bearing
19. Seal ring

Exploded view of the overdrive case and brake assembly

drive clutch cylinder and turn the planetary gear shaft. The shaft should turn freely clockwise and lock counterclockwise. Separate the clutch assembly from the input shaft.

2. Remove the thrust bearing and race.

Remove the snapring and overdrive brake hub from the ~~drive~~ clutch assembly. Remove the snapring, flange, clutch ~~and~~ plates from the clutch cylinder.

~~Use~~ the special tool and a press to compress the return ~~Remove~~ the snapring and remove the tool.

~~Remove~~ the spring retainer and return springs.

~~Place~~ the overdrive clutch cylinder and piston set on ~~a~~ ~~bench and~~ apply low pressure compressed air to the hole ~~to~~ blow out the piston.

7. Remove the O-rings from the piston.

8. Remove the snapring from the overdrive planetary gear assembly.

9. Remove the one-way clutch retainer (the AW70 transmission has a thrust washer), one-way clutch and outer race from the overdrive planetary gear assembly.

10. Remove the 4 pinion shaft plugs and keep them in a safe place.

11. Remove the one-way clutch from the outer race.

Inspection

1. Inspect the planetary gear for excessive play or wear.
2. Inspect all seal grooves for burrs or cracks.

3. Inspect all snaprings for deformation.

4. Inspect the return springs and retainer for deformation. The free height of the springs should be about 0.60 in. (14.90mm)

5. Inspect the one-way clutch assembly for any damage.

6. Make sure the check ball in the piston is free and that the valve is not leaking.

7. Inspect the thrust bearing, race and washer for wear.

Assembly

1. Install the pinion shaft plugs.

2. Install the thrust bearing race and bearing onto the planetary gear.

3. Install the one-way clutch into the outer race.

4. Install the thrust washer, grooves facing up, on the planetary gear.

5. Install the one-way clutch assembly.

6. Install the retainer or thrust washer. Install the snapring.

7. Coat the new O-rings with Dexron®II and install on the clutch piston. Install the piston in the drum with the cup side up.

8. Install the return springs and position the retainer and snapring on top.

9. Use the special tool and a press to compress the springs and install the snapring. Do not align the snapring ends with the retainer claw.

10. Install the Dexron®II soaked plates and discs.

11. Install the clutch hub and snapring. Install the clutch cylinder onto the oil pump. Measure the piston stroke by applying low pressure compressed air to the apply hole in the pump. The specification is 0.061–0.100 in. (1.56–2.53mm). Remove the snapring and overdrive brake hub.

12. Install the snapring in the clutch cylinder. Do not align the snapring ends with any of the cutouts.

13. Install the overdrive brake hub and snapring. Do not align the snapring ends with any of the cutouts.

14. Assemble the overdrive clutch assembly and overdrive planetary gear assembly together. Check the operation of the one-way clutch.

OVERDRIVE CASE AND BRAKE ASSEMBLY

Disassembly

1. Remove the snapring from the overdrive case.

2. Remove the flange, discs, plates and cushion plate.

3. Remove the planetary ring gear and thrust race.

4. Remove the thrust bearing and races from the overdrive case.

5. Remove the snapring, spring retainer and return springs.

6. Remove the piston by blowing low pressure compressed air through the apply hole in the overdrive case.

7. Remove the seal rings from the case.

8. Remove the O-rings from the piston.

Inspection

1. Inspect the case and piston sliding surfaces for wear or scratches.

2. Inspect the planetary ring gear for damage of any type.

3. Inspect the seal ring grooves for burrs or cracks.

4. Inspect the snaprings for deformation.

5. Inspect the return springs, retainer and seats for deformation. The free height of the springs should be about 0.60 in. (15.90mm).

6. Inspect the thrust bearing and races for wear.

Assembly

1. Coat the seal rings with Dexron®II and install on the overdrive case.

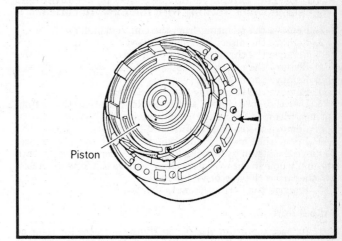

Piston

Forward clutch piston apply hole

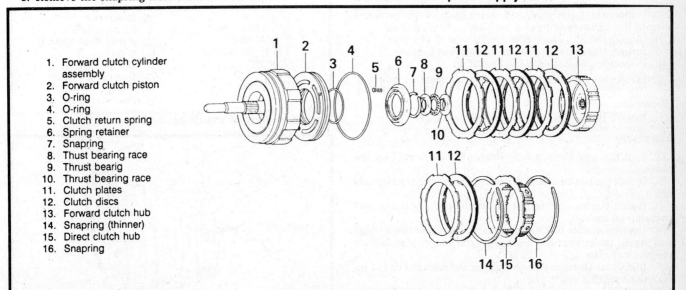

1. Forward clutch cylinder assembly
2. Forward clutch piston
3. O-ring
4. O-ring
5. Clutch return spring
6. Spring retainer
7. Snapring
8. Thust bearing race
9. Thrust bearig
10. Thrust bearing race
11. Clutch plates
12. Clutch discs
13. Forward clutch hub
14. Snapring (thinner)
15. Direct clutch hub
16. Snapring

Exploded view of the forward clutch

2. Coat new O-rings with Dexron®II and install on the piston.

3. Install the brake piston in the overdrive case with the cup side up.

4. Install the return springs, position the spring retainer and install the snapring. Do not align the snapring ends with any of the cutouts.

5. Install the thrust bearing and races in the proper direction to the planetary ring gear and install the ring gear in the overdrive case.

6. Install the cushion plate dished side up, Dexron®II soaked plates, discs and flange in the case.

7. Install the snapring. Do not align the snapring ends with any of the cutouts.

8. Measure the distance between the flange and the snapring to check the brake clearance. The specification for Isuzu and Mitsubishi Pick-up applications is 0.040–0.062 in. (0.35–1.6mm) and 0.026–0.087 in. (0.65–2.21mm) for Mitsubishi Van applications.

9. Install the thrust washer onto the ring gear.

FORWARD CLUTCH

Disassembly

NOTE: The extension housing makes a convenient work stand when working with the forward clutch.

1. Remove the snapring from the clutch cylinder.
2. Remove the direct hub and forward clutch hub.
3. Remove the thrust bearing and races.
4. Remove the clutch plate(s) and disc(s).
5. Remove the snapring.
6. Remove the remaining plates and discs.
7. Use the special tool and press to compress the return springs. Remove the snapring and remove the tool.
8. Remove the spring retainer and the return springs.
9. Install the forward clutch cylinder onto the overdrive case. Remove the piston by blowing low pressure compressed air into the apply hole in the overdrive case. Remove the forward clutch cylinder from the overdrive case.
10. Remove the O-rings from the piston.

Inspection

1. Inspect the drum and piston sliding surfaces for wear or scratches. Make sure the check ball is free and the valve does not leak.

2. Inspect the input shaft and clutch cylinder for excessive wear of the thrust bearing and bushing contact surfaces.

3. Inspect the hub assemblies for damage of any type.

4. Inspect the seal ring grooves for burrs or cracks.

5. Inspect the snaprings for deformation.

6. Inspect the return springs, retainer and seats for deformation. The free height of the springs should be about 0.60 in. (15.90mm).

7. Inspect the thrust bearing and races for wear.

Assembly

1. Coat the new O-rings with Dexron®II and install on the piston.

2. Install the piston into the clutch cylinder with the cup side up.

3. Install the return springs and position the retainer and snapring on top.

4. Use the special tool and a press to compress the springs and install the snapring. Do not align the snapring ends with the retainer claw.

5. Install the Dexron®II soaked plates and discs but do not install the snapring yet.

6. Install the direct clutch hub and snapring. Install the forward clutch cylinder assembly onto the overdrive case. Apply low pressure compressed air to the apply hole and measure the piston stroke. The specification is 0.056–0.115 in. (1.43–2.93mm). Remove the snapring and the direct clutch hub. Remove the forward clutch cylinder from the overdrive case.

7. Install the thinner snapring. Do not align the snapring ends with any of the cutouts.

8. Install the Dexron®II soaked clutch disc(s) and plate(s).

9. Install the thrust bearing and races.

10. Install the forward clutch hub. Make sure the hub meshes with all of the discs and is fully inserted.

11. Install the direct clutch hub and install the snapring. Do not align the snapring ends with any of the cutouts.

DIRECT CLUTCH

Disassembly

1. Remove the snapring from the direct clutch cylinder.
2. Remove the flange, clutch discs and plates.
3. Use the special tool and a press to compress the return springs. Remove the snapring and remove the tool.
4. Remove the spring retainer and the return springs.

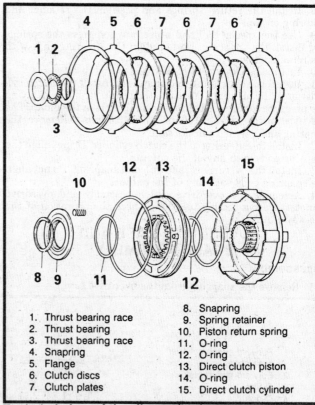

1. Thrust bearing race	8. Snapring
2. Thrust bearing	9. Spring retainer
3. Thrust bearing race	10. Piston return spring
4. Snapring	11. O-ring
5. Flange	12. O-ring
6. Clutch discs	13. Direct clutch piston
7. Clutch plates	14. O-ring
	15. Direct clutch cylinder

Exploded view of the direct clutch

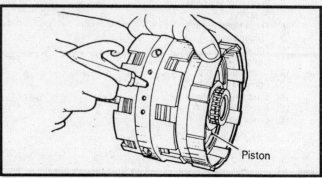

Direct clutch apply hole

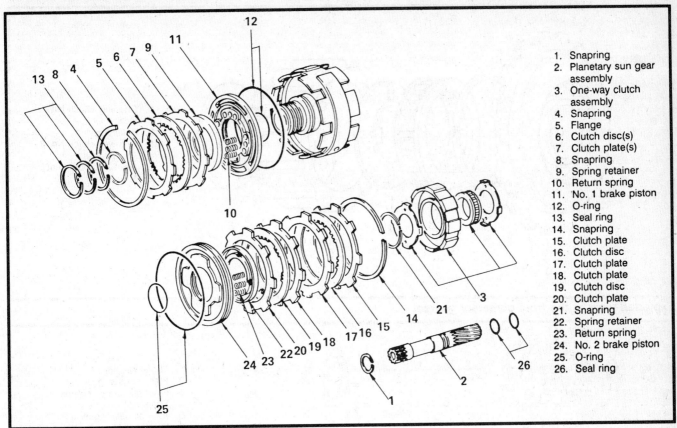

1. Snapring
2. Planetary sun gear assembly
3. One-way clutch assembly
4. Snapring
5. Flange
6. Clutch disc(s)
7. Clutch plate(s)
8. Snapring
9. Spring retainer
10. Return spring
11. No. 1 brake piston
12. O-ring
13. Seal ring
14. Snapring
15. Clutch plate
16. Clutch disc
17. Clutch plate
18. Clutch plate
19. Clutch disc
20. Clutch plate
21. Snapring
22. Spring retainer
23. Return spring
24. No. 2 brake piston
25. O-ring
26. Seal ring

Exploded view of the center support

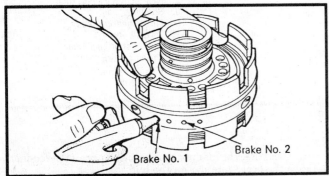

Brake Nos. 1 and 2 apply holes

5. Install the direct clutch cylinder on the center support. Remove the piston by blowing low pressure compressed air into the apply hole in the center support. Remove the direct clutch cylinder from the center support.

6. Remove the O-rings from the piston.

Inspection

1. Inspect the cylinder and piston sliding surfaces for wear or scratches. Make sure the check ball is free and the valve does not leak.

2. Inspect the clutch cylinder for excessive wear of the thrust bearing contact surfaces.

3. Inspect the seal ring grooves for burrs or cracks.

4. Inspect the snaprings for deformation.

5. Inspect the return springs, retainer and seats for deformation. The free height of the springs should be about 0.58 in. (14.70mm), except Isuzu Impulse with 2.3 engine. For that application, the specification is 0.63 in. (16.12mm).

Assembly

1. Coat the new O-rings with Dexron®II and install on the piston.

2. Install the piston into the clutch cylinder with the cup side up.

3. Install the return springs and position the retainer and snapring on top.

4. Use the special tool and a press to compress the springs and install the snapring. Do not align the snapring ends with the retainer claw.

5. Install the Dexron®II soaked plates, discs and flange flat end down and install the snapring.

6. Install the direct clutch onto the center support and blow low pressure compressed air into the apply hole to check the piston stroke. The specification for Isuzu is 0.056–0.092 in. (1.42–2.33mm) and 0.036–0.078 in. (0.91–1.99mm) for Mitsubishi.

CENTER SUPPORT

Disassembly

1. Remove the snapring from the front of the sun gear and remove the sun gear (with the one-way clutch) from the center support. Hold the No. 2 brake hub and check the operation of the one-way clutch. The sun gear should turn freely and smoothly counterclockwise and lock clockwise.

2. Remove the snapring from the center support and remove the clutch flange, disc(s) and plate(s).

3. Use the special tool and a press to compress the return springs. Remove the snapring and remove the tool.

4. Remove the spring retainer and the return springs.

5. Remove the No. 1 brake piston by blowing low pressure compressed air into the apply hole. Remove the O-rings from the piston.

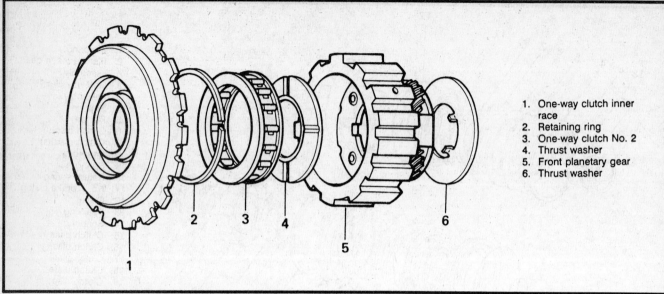

1. One-way clutch inner race
2. Retaining ring
3. One-way clutch No. 2
4. Thrust washer
5. Front planetary gear
6. Thrust washer

Exploded view of the front planetary gearset

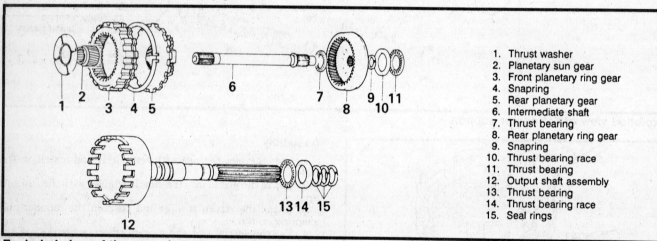

1. Thrust washer
2. Planetary sun gear
3. Front planetary ring gear
4. Snapring
5. Rear planetary gear
6. Intermediate shaft
7. Thrust bearing
8. Rear planetary ring gear
9. Snapring
10. Thrust bearing race
11. Thrust bearing
12. Output shaft assembly
13. Thrust bearing
14. Thrust bearing race
15. Seal rings

Exploded view of the rear planetary gearset and output shaft

6. Remove the seal rings from the center support.

7. Disassemble brake No. 2 on the other side of the center support following the same procedure as for brake No. 1.

8. Remove the one-way clutch assembly and seal rings from the planetary sun gear.

Inspection

1. Inspect the planetary sun gear for excessive wear at the one-way clutch springs contact surface .

2. Inspect all seal grooves for burrs or cracks.

3. Inspect all snaprings for deformation.

4. Inspect the return springs and retainers for deformation. The free height of the springs should be about 0.64 in. (16.12mm).

5. Inspect the one-way clutch assemblies for any damage.

6. Inspect the center support for damage of any type, especially clutch plate slot wear.

7. Inspect the cylinder and piston sliding surfaces for wear or scratches.

Assembly

1. If necessary, replace the one-way clutch:

a. Bend the rear retainer tabs back and pry off the retainer. Leave the other retainer on the hub.

b. Remove the one-way clutch.

c. Install the new one-way clutch into the brake hub facing the spring cage toward the front.

d. Carefully clamp the assembly in a vise and bend the tabs back into position; make sure the retainer is centered.

2. Coat the sun gear seal rings with Dexron®II and install on the sun gear. Install the one-way clutch assembly on the sun gear. Hold the No. 2 brake hub and check the operation of the one-way clutch. The sun gear should turn freely and smoothly counterclockwise and lock clockwise.

3. Coat the brake No. 1 side of the center support seal rings with Dexron®II and install on the center support.

4. Coat the new O-rings with Dexron®II and install on the No. 1 piston. Install the piston into the center support with the cup side up.

5. Install the return springs and position the retainer and snapring on top.

6. Use the special tool and a press to compress the springs and install the snapring. Do not align the snapring ends with the retainer claw.

7. Install the Dexron®II soaked plates, discs and flange chamfered edge down and install the snapring.

8. Check the piston stroke of the No. 1 piston. The specification is 0.032–0.068 in. (0.80–1.73mm).

9. Flip the center support over and assemble brake No. 2 on the other side of the center support following the same procedure as for brake No. 1.

10. Check the piston stroke of the No. 2 piston. The specification is 0.040–0.089 in. (1.01–2.25mm).

11. Mesh the No. 2 brake hub with the discs and install the planetary sun gear assembly to the center support.

12. Install the snapring on the end of the sun gear.

FRONT PLANETARY GEARSET

Disassembly

1. Check the operation of the one-way clutch. Hold the one-way clutch inner race. The planetary carrier should turn freely counterclockwise and lock clockwise.

2. Separate the one-way clutch inner race from the planetary carrier.

3. Remove the snapring from the carrier.

4. Remove the one-way clutch No. 2 assembly and thrust washers.

Inspection

1. Inspect the thrust washer for wear or bending.

2. Inspect the planetary carrier for pinion play, smooth rotation and one-way clutch contact surface wear.

3. Inspect the one-way clutch assembly for damage of any type.

4. Inspect the inner race for excessive wear.

Assembly

1. Install the front thrust washer on the planetary carrier.

2. Install the one-way clutch in the planetary carrier and install the snapring.

3. Install the one-way clutch inner race on the carrier.

4. Recheck the operation of the one-way clutch.

5. Install the rear thrust washer to the planetary carrier.

REAR PLANETARY GEARSET AND OUTPUT SHAFT

Disassembly

1. Loosen the snapring and remove the intermediate shaft with the front planetary ring gear and rear planetary gear from the output shaft assembly.

2. Remove the front planetary ring gear, thrust washer and rear planetary ring gear from the intermediate shaft.

3. Remove the snapring from the rear of the intermediate shaft and remove the rear planetary ring gear and the thrust bearing.

4. Remove the seal rings from the output shaft.

Inspection

1. Inspect the ring gear for damage to the inner and outer teeth.

2. Inspect the intermediate shaft for wear of the bushing seating surfaces and oil hole clogging.

3. Inspect the planetary gear for pinion play and smooth rotation.

4. Inspect the rear ring gear for damage to the teeth or splines.

5. Inspect the output shaft for thrust bearing wear and oil hole clogging.

6. Inspect all seal grooves for burrs and cracks.

Assembly

1. Install the thrust bearing on the intermediate shaft and install the rear planetary ring gear. Install the snapring.

2. Install the thrust bearing and race on the output shaft.

3. Install the intermediate shaft together with the rear planetary ring gear on the output shaft flange.

4. Install the rear planetary carrier and thrust washer.

5. Install the snapring on the front planetary ring gear and install the ring gear on the output flange while compressing the snapring. Align the snapring ends with the wide gap between the teeth.

6. Install the seal rings on the output shaft.

1ST/REVERSE BRAKE

Disassembly

1. Use the special tools to compress the return springs. Do

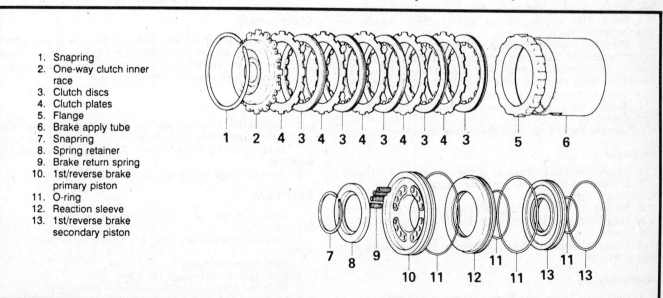

1. Snapring
2. One-way clutch inner race
3. Clutch discs
4. Clutch plates
5. Flange
6. Brake apply tube
7. Snapring
8. Spring retainer
9. Brake return spring
10. 1st/reverse brake primary piston
11. O-ring
12. Reaction sleeve
13. 1st/reverse brake secondary piston

Exploded view of the 1st/reverse brake

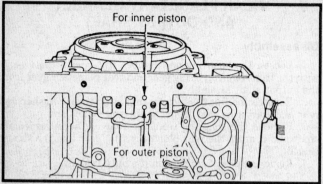

1st/reverse brake pistons apply holes

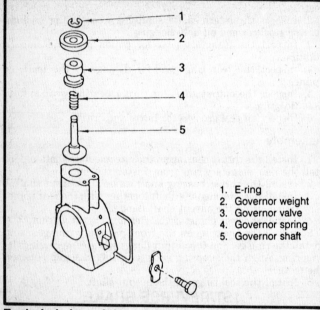

Exploded view of the governor—AW370 transmission

1. E-ring
2. Governor weight
3. Governor valve
4. Governor spring
5. Governor shaft

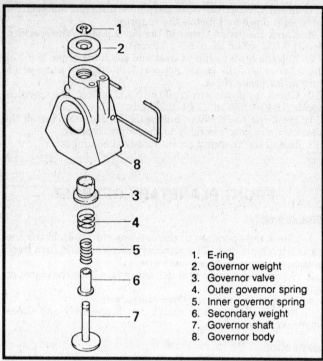

Exploded view of the governor—AW372 and KM148 transmissions

1. E-ring
2. Governor weight
3. Governor valve
4. Outer governor spring
5. Inner governor spring
6. Secondary weight
7. Governor shaft
8. Governor body

not damage the case with the tools.

2. Remove the snapring, the special tools, the spring retainer and the return springs.

3. Place the transmission case with the front end down. Remove the primary and secondary pistons out simultaneously by blowing low pressure compressed air into both apply holes at the same time. Place shop rags below the case to protect the pistons. The reaction sleeve should come out with the pistons.

4. Remove the primary and secondary pistons from the reaction sleeve.

5. Remove the O-rings from the pistons and reaction sleeve.

Inspection

1. Inspect the flange for wear at the tube contact surface.

2. Inspect the apply tube for deformation or damage, especially at the detent lug.

3. Inspect the return springs and snaprings for deformation. The free height of the springs should be about 0.64 in. (16.12mm).

4. Inspect the pistons and sliding surface in the case for wear and scratches.

Assembly

1. Coat new O-rings with Dexron®II and install on the primary and secondary pistons and the reaction sleeve.

2. Install the inner piston into the reaction sleeve and install the outer piston.

3. Slide the pistons and sleeve assembly into the case cylinder.

4. Apply a liberal amount of petroleum jelly to the return springs and install them on the outer piston. Install the spring retainer.

5. Use the special tools to compress the springs and install the snapring. Remove the tools.

GOVERNOR

Disassembly

1. Compress the springs by pushing up on the governor valve shaft and down on the governor weight. Remove the E-ring.

2. Remove the governor shaft, springs, weight and valve.

3. Remove the governor retaining ring.

Inspection

1. Inspect the governor valve for damage and wear and check that it slides smoothly in the body.

2. Inspect the governor body for damage and oil hole clogging.

3. Inspect the governor springs for deformation.

Assembly

1. Install the governor retaining ring by inserting the ends in the holes.

2. Install the secondary weight, if equipped, to the governor shaft.

3. Install the spring(s).

4. Slide the valve through the bore.

5. Slide the spring and shaft assembly through the bore.

6. Compress the springs and install the E-ring on the shaft. Make sure the valve moves smoothly.

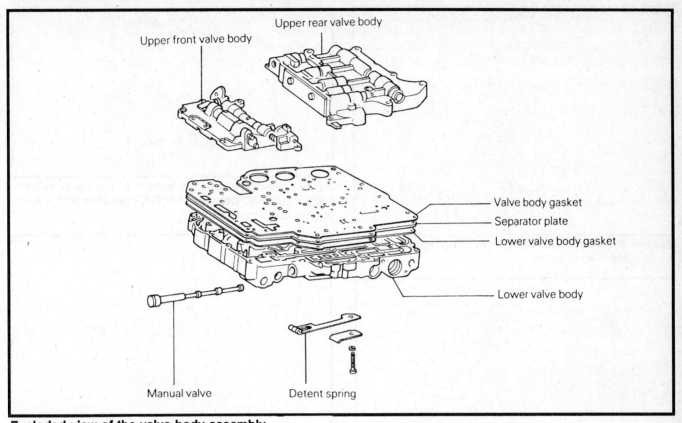

Exploded view of the valve body assembly

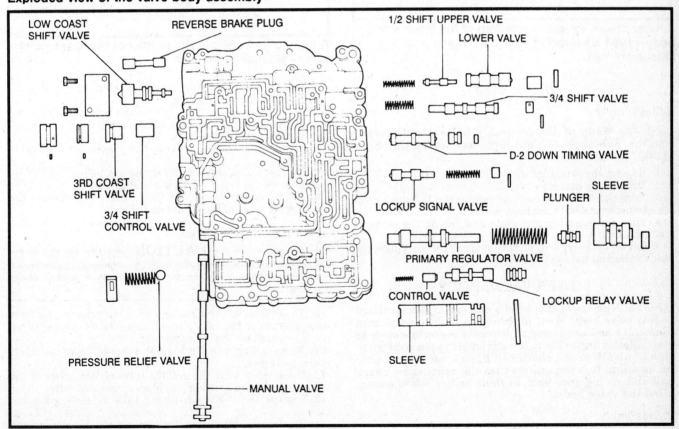

Exploded view of the lower valve body

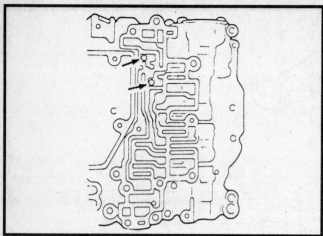

Rubber check balls in the bottom of the lower valve body—1984–85 Impulse

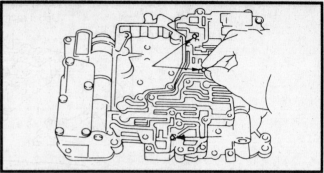

Rubber check balls in the bottom of the lower valve body—1986–87 Impulse, 1988–89 Impulse with 2.0L engine and Isuzu P'up

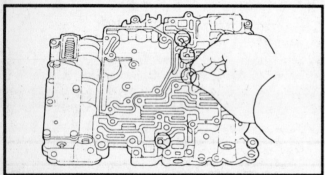

Rubber check balls in the bottom of the lower valve body—1988–89 Impulse with 2.3L engine and Mitsubishi Van

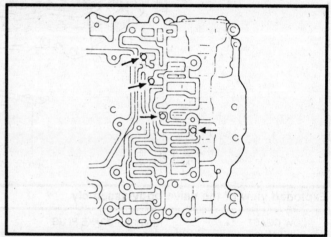

Rubber check balls in the bottom of the lower valve body—Mitsubishi Pick-up

VALVE BODY

Disassembly

NOTE: Many of the assembly bolts are different lengths. Take note of their locations during the disassembly procedure.

1. Remove the detent spring.
2. Remove the manual valve.
3. Turn the valve body over and remove the 10 bolts attaching the upper bodies to the lower body.
4. Turn the assembly over again and remove the set bolts from the lower body.
5. Lift off the lower body and plate together. Do not allow the check valve and balls to fall out.

LOWER VALVE BODY

NOTE: Numerous check balls and springs are utilized in this valve body. Many of the check balls are different diameters and are made of different materials such as steel, plastic and rubber. It it advisable to use a micrometer to identify each check ball upon removal and note its location. It is imperative that the exact same check ball and spring goes back in their orifice when assembling the valve body.

Disassembly

1. Remove the lower body plate and gaskets.

2. Remove the check balls, damping check valve spring, oil cooler bypass valve and spring.
3. Turn the assembly over, remove the remaining bolts and remove the lower body cover, plate and gaskets.
4. Remove the 4 check balls.
5. Remove the retainer from the pressure relief valve assembly.
6. Remove the pressure relief spring and ball.
7. Remove the lower valve plate and gasket.
8. If equipped with the AW372 transmission, remove the lockup relay valve plug retainer and plug.
9. Remove the sleeve with the lockup relay valves, control valve and spring, if equipped.

CAUTION

The primary regulator valve spring is highly compressed. Use the proper precautions when working with this valve assembly or personal injury may occur.

10. To remove the valve retainer from the primary regulator valve, press in on the valve sleeve firmly. The retainer will drop out. Slowly relieve the spring tension.
11. Remove the primary regulator valve sleeve, plunger, spring and valve.
12. If equipped with the AW372 transmission, remove the lockup signal valve locating pin, plug, spring and valve.
13. Remove the D-2 down timing valve retainer, plug and valve.
14. Remove the 3/4 shift valve locating pin, plug, valve and spring.

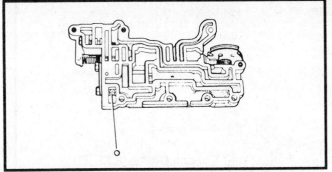

Location of the check ball in the upper front valve body

15. Remove the 1/2 shift valve retainer, plug, valves and spring.
16. Remove the low coast shift valve cover plate.
17. Remove the reverse brake plug.
18. Remove the low coast shift valve.
19. Remove the 3rd coast shift valve locating pins, plugs, valve and 3/4 shift control valve.

Inspection

1. Check the body for damage, wear and cracks.
2. Check the valves, plugs and their bores for damage and burrs. Slight burrs may be sanded out with crocus cloth only.
3. Check for oil passage damage and restrictions.
4. Check for spring fatigue and rust.

Assembly

1. Install the reverse brake plug.
2. Install the low coast shift valve.
3. Install the 3/4 coast shift valve.
4. Install the 3rd coast valve.
5. Install the 3rd coast shift valve inner plug and the locating pin.
6. Install the outer plug and the locating pin.
7. Install the low coast shift valve cover.
8. Install the 1/2 shift spring, upper valve, lower valve, plug and retainer.
9. Install the 3/4 shift spring, plug and locating pin.
10. Install the D-2 down timing valve, plug and retainer.
11. If equipped with the AW372 transmission, install the lock-up signal valve, spring, plug and locating pin.
12. Install the primary regulator valve and spring. The primary valve must fit flush with the valve body.
13. Insert the primary regulator valve plunger into the sleeve fully. The plunger should be recessed inside the sleeve.
14. Install the sleeve and plunger assembly.
15. Install the retainer.
16. If equipped with the AW372 transmission, assemble the lockup relay control valve spring, control valve and relay valves in the sleeve.
17. Install the assembly into the bore in the valve body. Install the sleeve with the smaller hollow on the sleeve top facing up.
18. Install the plug retainer.
19. Install the plate and gasket.
20. Install the pressure relief valve, spring and retainer.
21. Install the check balls.
22. Install the lower body cover upper gasket, plate, lower gasket and cover.
23. Install the cover set bolts.
24. Install the smaller check ball, larger check ball (damping check ball with spring), oil cooler bypass valve and spring and the remaining check balls, if equipped.
25. Install the lower valve body gasket, separator plate and up-

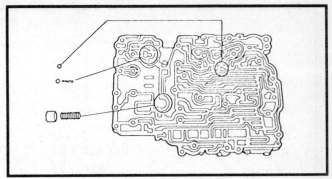

Cooler bypass check valve, check balls and springs in the top of the lower valve body—1984–85 Impulse and all Mitsubishi

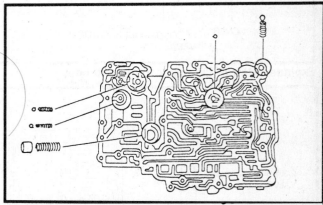

Cooler bypass check valve, check balls and springs in the top of the lower valve body—1986–87 Impulse

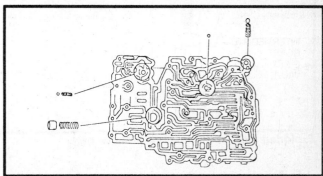

Cooler bypass check valve, check balls and springs in the top of the lower valve body—all 1988–89 Isuzu

per gasket. The gaskets are not interchangeable. Match new ones before installing.
26. Temporarily install 2 short bolts finger tight to compress the plate against the spring loaded check valve.

UPPER FRONT VALVE BODY

Disassembly

1. Remove the cut back valve retainer, plug and valve.
2. Remove the inner secondary regulator valve cover bolt and just loosen the other bolt. Rotate the cover slowly and carefully to relieve the spring tension.
3. Remove the secondary regulator valve and spring.
4. Remove the attached bolt and the cover.

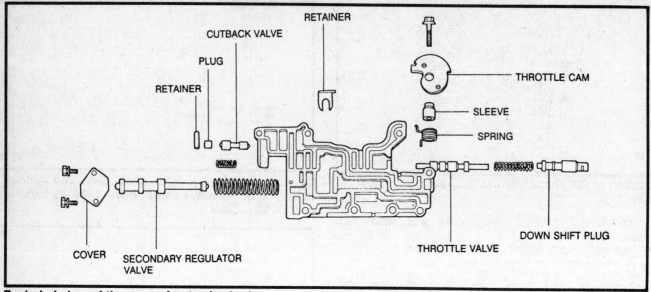

Exploded view of the upper front valve body

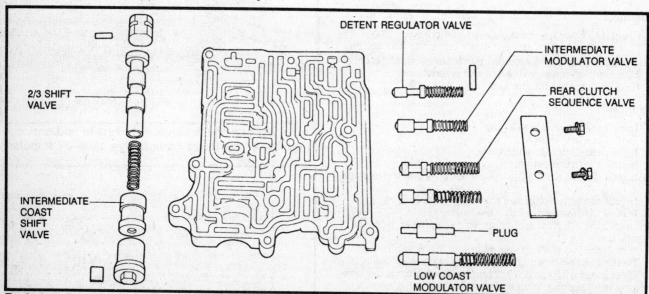

Exploded view of the upper rear valve body

5. While turning the throttle cam, push the down shift plug in and insert the cut back valve retainer to hold the plug in place.

6. Remove the throttle cam spring.

7. Remove the retainer and remove the down shift plug, spring, throttle valve retainer, throttle valve and spring.

Inspection

1. Check the body for damage, wear and cracks.

2. Check the valves, plugs and their bores for damage and burrs. Slight burrs may be sanded out with crocus cloth only.

3. Check for oil passage damage and restrictions.

4. Check for spring fatigue and rust.

Assembly

1. Install the throttle valve in its bore.

2. Coat the throttle valve retainer with petroleum jelly and install.

3. Install the downshift plug, push it in and use the cut back valve plug retainer to hold it in place.

4. Install the spring with its end hooked in the hole in the cam. Insert the sleeve.

5. Install the throttle cam assembly on the valve body. Remove the retainer.

6. Install the secondary regulator valve cover with the outer bolt.

7. Install the secondary regulator valve spring and the valve.

8. Push the valve in and swing the cover into place. Install the other bolt.

9. Install the cut back valve, plug. Coat the retainer with petroleum jelly and install.

UPPER REAR VALVE BODY

Disassembly

1. Remove the check balls.

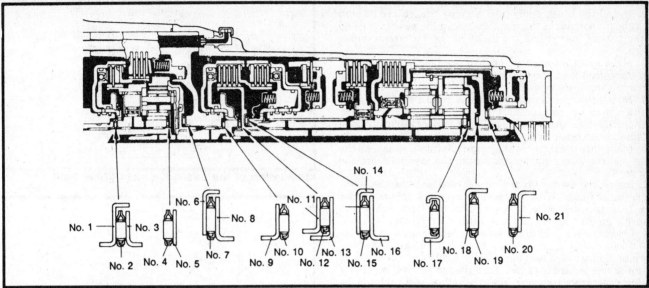

Identifying thrust bearings and races

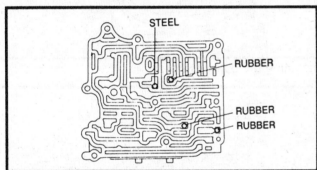

Locations of the check balls in the upper rear valve body

2. Remove the intermediate coast shift valve retainer, plug, valve and spring.

3. Remove the 2/3 shift valve retainer, plug and valve.

4. Remove the bolt nearest to the low coast modulator valve from the rear valve cover.

5. Rotate the cover slightly to expose the low coast modulator valve only. Remove the spring and the valve.

6. Rotate the cover farther and remove the plug.

7. Rotate the cover farther and remove the reverse clutch sequence valve.

8. Remove the valve cover, intermediate modulator valve spring and valve.

9. Remove the detent regulator valve retainer, spring and valve.

Inspection

1. Check the body for damage, wear and cracks.

2. Check the valves, plugs and their bores for damage and burrs. Slight burrs may be sanded out with crocus cloth only.

3. Check for oil passage damage and restrictions.

4. Check for spring fatigue and rust.

Assembly

1. Install the detent regulator valve, spring and retainer. Make sure the retainer fully covers the end of the spring.

2. Insert the intermediate modulator valve and spring.

3. Install the cover using only the bolt nearest the intermediate modulator valve.

4. Install the reverse clutch sequence valve, spring and plug.

5. Install the low coast modulator valve and spring.

6. Swing the cover in place and tighten the bolts.

7. Install the 2/3 shift valve and plug. Push in the plug and install the intermediate coast shift valve retainer.

8. Install the intermediate coast shift valve spring, valve and plug and secure the retainer.

9. Install the check balls.

VALVE BODY

Assembly

1. Position the upper rear valve body upside down on a clean working surface.

2. Match the new gasket with the old one and position it on the upper rear body aligning the lower right corner.

3. Place the lower valve body with place on top of the upper rear body with the right edge aligned.

4. Install and finger tighten the 3 bolts in the lower body that attach the upper rear body to the lower body.

5. Turn the assembly over and recheck the gasket alignment. Install and finger tighten the 5 bolts in the upper rear body that attach the upper rear body to the lower body.

6. Remove the bolts that were temporarily placed in the lower body in the last step of the lower body assembly procedure.

7. Position the upper front valve body upside down and place the lower and upper rear bodies assembly on the upper front body.

8. Install and finger tighten the set bolts in the lower body that attach the upper front body to the lower body.

9. Turn the assembly over. Install and finger tighten the 5 bolts in the upper front body that attach the upper front body to the lower body.

10. Recheck the alignment of the gaskets. Tighten all upper valve body bolts to specification.

11. Tighten all lower valve body bolts to specification.

12. Install the manual valve in the valve body.

13. Install the detent spring and torque the bolts to specification.

Transmission Assembly

1. Install the output shaft thrust bearing race (No. 21) cup

side down and install the thrust bearing (No. 20).

2. Install the brake apply tube aligning the locking tabs on the tube properly with the case. Make sure the pawl at the end of the tube is inserted to the inside of the 1st/reverse brake piston.

3. Make sure the thrust washer is properly seated on the rear planetary gear with the finger on the washer inserted in the notch in the planetary gear.

4. Install the rear planetary gear and output shaft assembly in the case slowly and carefully

5. Install the 1st/reverse brake flange in the case firmly until it contacts the brake apply tube.

6. Make sure the thrust washers are properly installed on the front planetary gear carrier and install the assembly into the ring gear.

7. Install the Dexron®II soaked 1st/reverse brake discs and plates on the flange. With the case in the upright position, make sure that the last plate is lower than the ledge below the snapring groove; do not continue until this condition is met.

8. Insert the sun gear in the one-way clutch inner race and install the assembly in the case with the notched tooth of the one-way clutch inner race toward the valve body side of the case. If the inner race is hard to engage, turn the sun gear while holding the front planetary ring gear. Then, hold the one-way clutch inner race and remove the sun gear. Install the sun gear into the center support and install with that assembly.

9. Install the snapring.

10. Install the center support assembly aligning the oil and bolt holes with those in the case. Check correct seating of the one-way clutch on the center support. The center support will not be installed completely if the one-way clutch is floating.

11. Install the 2 center support bolts with wave washers, if equipped and temporarily finger tighten the bolts.

12. Install the direct clutch assembly turning its hub to mesh with the center support. The splined center of the direct clutch will be flush with the end of the planetary sun gear shaft when the direct clutch is properly installed.

13. Install the thrust bearing race (No. 16) over the splined end of the direct clutch with the lip towards the direct clutch.

14. Coat the the thrust bearing (No. 15) and race (No. 14) liberally with petroleum jelly and attach them to the forward clutch hub, with the race lip facing outward.

15. Install the forward clutch into the case. Make sure the thrust bearing and race do not fall from the forward clutch.

16. Use the special tool to measure the distance between the top of the case flange and the forward clutch drum. The forward clutch has been correctly installed if that distance matches the distance measured in Step 25 of the disassembly procedure. The standard value is approximately 0.06 in. (1.5mm).

17. Install the thrust bearing (No. 10) on the forward clutch.

18. Coat the thrust bearing race (No. 9) liberally with petroleum jelly and install to the overdrive case with the lip toward the overdrive case.

19. Install the special guide tools in the case.

20. Install the overdrive case assembly in the case through the guide pins. Make sure the notch in the bottom of the overdrive case is positioned properly.

21. Coat the thrust washers liberally with petroleum jelly and install to the overdrive planetary gear inserting the lugs in the holes and install the overdrive clutch and planetary gear assembly in the case. Make sure the thrust washers remain intact.

22. Use the special tool to measure the distance between the overdrive case and the clutch cylinder. The overdrive clutch assembly has been correctly installed if that distance matches the distance measured in Step 22 of the disassembly procedure. The standard value is approximately 0.08 in. (2.0mm).

23. Remove the guide pins. Install a new O-ring on the overdrive case and install the converter housing. Torque the bolts to specification.

24. Install the thrust bearing race (No. 3) and the thrust bearing (No. 2) over the overdrive input shaft.

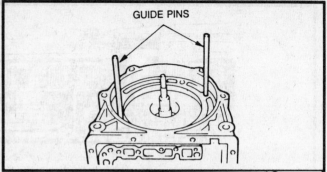
Installation of the overdrive case guide pins

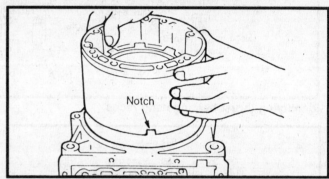
Installing the overdrive case

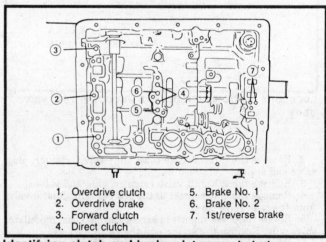

1. Overdrive clutch	5. Brake No. 1
2. Overdrive brake	6. Brake No. 2
3. Forward clutch	7. 1st/reverse brake
4. Direct clutch	

Identifying clutch and brake piston apply holes

25. Coat the thrust thrust bearing race (No. 1) liberally with petroleum jelly and install to the oil pump.

26. Install the special oil pump guide bolts and install the oil pump. Apply sealant to the 5 bolts and finger tighten them. Remove the special guide bolts and replace them with the remaining oil pump bolts with sealant applied. Torque the bolts to specification gradually and evenly.

27. Tighten the center support bolts in 5 ft. lb. (7 Nm) increments until the specified torque is reached. Start the torquing procedure with the accumulator side bolt first.

28. Check the operation of all pistons. Blow low pressure compressed air into each of the apply holes and listen for movement of the corresponding piston. Do not continue until every piston has been checked and is operational.

29. Make sure the input shaft turns smoothly and lightly. Check the input shaft endplay. The specification is 0.012–0.035 in. (0.3–0.9mm).

30. Install the parking rod assembly on the manual valve lever and install the manual valve lever shaft in the case. Drive in the roll pin so it protrudes slightly from the lever.

31. Install the parking pawl and install the pivot pin and spring.

32. Install the cam plate making sure the parking rod assembly protrudes from the plate. Make sure the pawl moves freely.

NOTE: It is easy to install the cam plate too far forward, where it will bind the pawl. Make sure the assembly is properly installed before proceding.

33. Check the operation of the parking pawl. The planetary gear output shaft must lock when the manual valve lever is placed in the **P** detent.

34. Install the throttle cable with a new O-ring.

35. Install the accumulator pistons and all springs in the proper positions, using the notes taken in Step 21 of the disassembly procedure.

36. Align the manual valve with the pin on the manual valve lever and lower the valve body into place. Attach the throttle cable to the cam.

37. Install the valve body bolts and torque the valve body bolts to specification gradually and evenly.

38. Install the detent spring. Make sure the detent spring roller is completely seated in every portion of the detent lever as the gears are shifted.

39. Install a new oil strainer and gasket.

40. Install the oil pipes.

41. Attach the magnet to the pan in a position that it is directly below the strainer. Make sure the magnet does not contact the oil pipes. Install the oil pan with a new gasket.

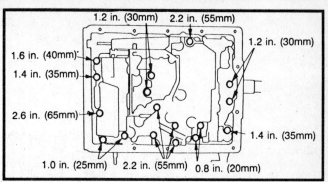

Locations and lengths of valve body mounting bolts

42. Install the governor line strainer in the rear of the transmission case and install the plate with a new gasket.

43. Install the governor assembly onto the output shaft. Install the lock plate and bolt and stake the lock plate.

44. Install the speedometer gear onto the output shaft.

45. Install the extension housing with a new gasket and seal.

46. Install the speedometer driven gear to the shaft sleeve with new O-rings. Install the speedometer driven gear assembly to the extension housing. Install the lock plate and bolt.

47. Install the inhibitor switch and shift lever. Adjust the inhibitor switch.

48. Install the overdrive solenoid with new O-rings. Be sure to replace both the inner and outer O-rings on the solenoid.

49. Install the transfer case with gasket, if equipped.

SPECIFICATIONS

ACCUMULATOR SPRING SPECIFICATIONS
Isuzu

Spring Name	Free Height in. (mm)	Wire Diameter in. (mm)
Forward Clutch	2.55 (64.68)	0.08 (2.00)
Direct Clutch①	2.70 (68.56)	0.08 (2.00)
Direct Clutch②③	1.21 (30.80)	0.06 (1.52)
Direct Clutch②④	1.71 (43.56)	0.07 (1.80)
Brake No. 2⑤	2.63 (66.68)	0.10 (2.54)
Brake No. 2⑥③	1.21 (35.13)	0.05 (1.30)
Brake No. 2⑥③	2.00 (50.70)	0.10 (2.54)

① AW370 transmission
② AW372 transmission
③ Valve body side
④ Transmission case side
⑤ Except 2.3L engine
⑥ With 2.3L engine

ACCUMULATOR SPRING SPECIFICATIONS
Mitsubishi Van

Spring Name	Free Height in. (mm)	Outer Diameter in. (mm)	Number of Coils	Wire Diameter in. (mm)
Forward clutch	2.55 (64.68)	0.70 (17.50)	18.5	0.08 (2.00)
Direct clutch (green)	1.29 (32.73)	0.58 (14.80)	8.25	0.05 (1.30)
Direct clutch (red)	1.70 (43.22)	0.54 (13.84)	10.5	0.08 (2.00)
Brake No. 2	2.63 (66.68)	0.68 (17.34)	14	0.11 (2.80)

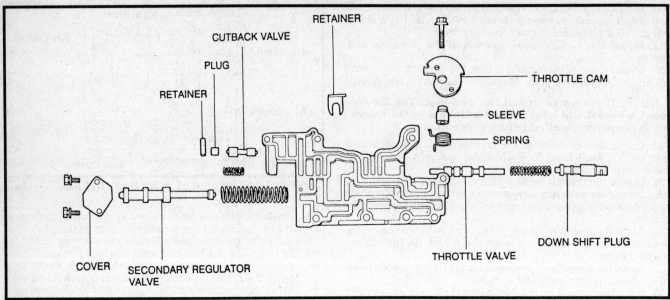

Exploded view of the upper front valve body

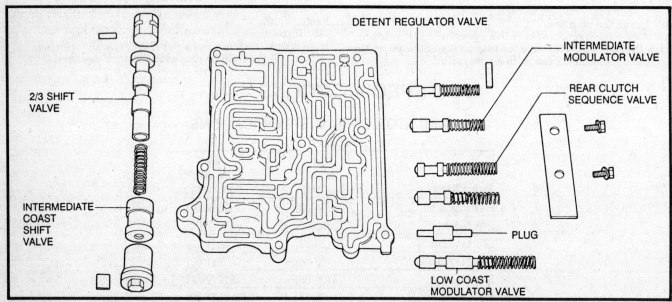

Exploded view of the upper rear valve body

5. While turning the throttle cam, push the down shift plug in and insert the cut back valve retainer to hold the plug in place.

6. Remove the throttle cam spring.

7. Remove the retainer and remove the down shift plug, spring, throttle valve retainer, throttle valve and spring.

Inspection

1. Check the body for damage, wear and cracks.

2. Check the valves, plugs and their bores for damage and burrs. Slight burrs may be sanded out with crocus cloth only.

3. Check for oil passage damage and restrictions.

4. Check for spring fatigue and rust.

Assembly

1. Install the throttle valve in its bore.

2. Coat the throttle valve retainer with petroleum jelly and install.

3. Install the downshift plug, push it in and use the cut back valve plug retainer to hold it in place.

4. Install the spring with its end hooked in the hole in the cam. Insert the sleeve.

5. Install the throttle cam assembly on the valve body. Remove the retainer.

6. Install the secondary regulator valve cover with the outer bolt.

7. Install the secondary regulator valve spring and the valve.

8. Push the valve in and swing the cover into place. Install the other bolt.

9. Install the cut back valve, plug. Coat the retainer with petroleum jelly and install.

UPPER REAR VALVE BODY

Disassembly

1. Remove the check balls.

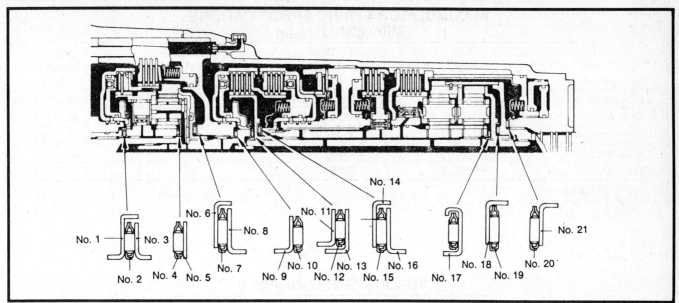

Identifying thrust bearings and races

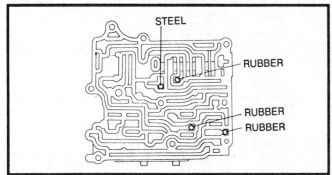

Locations of the check balls in the upper rear valve body

2. Remove the intermediate coast shift valve retainer, plug, valve and spring.
3. Remove the 2/3 shift valve retainer, plug and valve.
4. Remove the bolt nearest to the low coast modulator valve from the rear valve cover.
5. Rotate the cover slightly to expose the low coast modulator valve only. Remove the spring and the valve.
6. Rotate the cover farther and remove the plug.
7. Rotate the cover farther and remove the reverse clutch sequence valve.
8. Remove the valve cover, intermediate modulator valve spring and valve.
9. Remove the detent regulator valve retainer, spring and valve.

Inspection

1. Check the body for damage, wear and cracks.
2. Check the valves, plugs and their bores for damage and burrs. Slight burrs may be sanded out with crocus cloth only.
3. Check for oil passage damage and restrictions.
4. Check for spring fatigue and rust.

Assembly

1. Install the detent regulator valve, spring and retainer. Make sure the retainer fully covers the end of the spring.
2. Insert the intermediate modulator valve and spring.

3. Install the cover using only the bolt nearest the intermediate modulator valve.
4. Install the reverse clutch sequence valve, spring and plug.
5. Install the low coast modulator valve and spring.
6. Swing the cover in place and tighten the bolts.
7. Install the 2/3 shift valve and plug. Push in the plug and install the intermediate coast shift valve retainer.
8. Install the intermediate coast shift valve spring, valve and plug and secure the retainer.
9. Install the check balls.

VALVE BODY

Assembly

1. Position the upper rear valve body upside down on a clean working surface.
2. Match the new gasket with the old one and position it on the upper rear body aligning the lower right corner.
3. Place the lower valve body with place on top of the upper rear body with the right edge aligned.
4. Install and finger tighten the 3 bolts in the lower body that attach the upper rear body to the lower body.
5. Turn the assembly over and recheck the gasket alignment. Install and finger tighten the 5 bolts in the upper rear body that attach the upper rear body to the lower body.
6. Remove the bolts that were temporarily placed in the lower body in the last step of the lower body assembly procedure.
7. Position the upper front valve body upside down and place the lower and upper rear bodies assembly on the upper front body.
8. Install and finger tighten the set bolts in the lower body that attach the upper front body to the lower body.
9. Turn the assembly over. Install and finger tighten the 5 bolts in the upper front body that attach the upper front body to the lower body.
10. Recheck the alignment of the gaskets. Tighten all upper valve body bolts to specification.
11. Tighten all lower valve body bolts to specification.
12. Install the manual valve in the valve body.
13. Install the detent spring and torque the bolts to specification.

Transmission Assembly

1. Install the output shaft thrust bearing race (No. 21) cup

ACCUMULATOR SPRING SPECIFICATIONS
Mitsubishi Pick-up

Spring Name	Free Height in. (mm)	Outer Diameter in. (mm)	Number of Coils	Wire Diameter in. (mm)
Forward clutch	2.55 (64.70)	0.69 (17.50)	18.5	0.08 (2.00)
Direct clutch①	2.41 (61.20)	0.65 (16.45)	NA	0.10 (2.50)
Direct clutch②	2.17 (55.20)	0.65 (16.45)	NA	0.09 (2.30)
Brake No. 2①	2.63 (66.70)	0.71 (17.90)	NA	0.10 (2.60)
Brake No. 2②	2.63 (66.70)	0.68 (17.30)	NA	0.11 (2.80)

NA Not available
① With 2.0L engine
② With 2.6L engine

TORQUE SPECIFICATIONS

Part	ft. lbs.	Nm
Oil pan bolts	3–4	4–5
Transmission to engine bolts	45–50	61–68
Starter bolts	18–25	25–34
Oil pump assembly bolts	4.5–6.5	6–8.5
Oil pump mounting bolts	13–18	18–24
10mm converter housing bolts	20–30	27–41
12mm converter housing bolts	35–49	47–66
Valve body mounting bolts	4.5–6	6–8
Valve body assembly bolts	3.5–4.5	5–5.5
Rear crossmember bolts	30–35	40–50
Parking lock pawl bracket bolts	4.5–6.5	6–8.5
Center support bolts	18–20	24–27
Torque converter bolts①	22–27	30–37
Torque converter bolts②	11–16	15–20
Transmission insulator mount bolt	50–65	70–95
Extension housing bolts	23–27	32–37

① Except Isuzu Impulse
② Isuzu Impulse

SPECIAL TOOLS

Retainer	Stopper
Oil pump puller	Oil pump band
Gauge	Guide
Spring compressor	Bolt
Wrench	Adapter

OIL FLOW CIRCUIT — P RANGE — KM 148 AND AW 372 TRANSMISSIONS

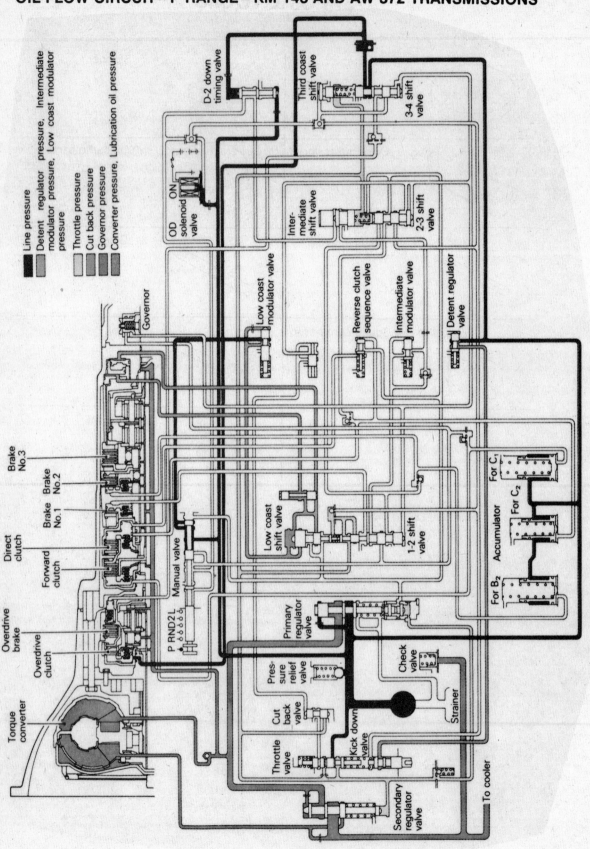

OIL FLOW CIRCUIT – N RANGE – KM 148 AND AW 372 TRANSMISSIONS

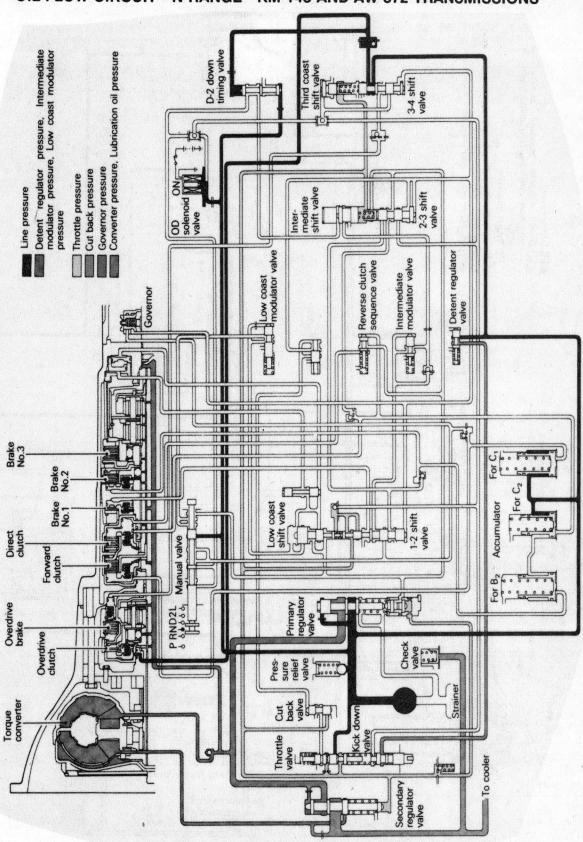

OIL FLOW CIRCUIT – R RANGE – KM 148 AND AW 372 TRANSMISSIONS

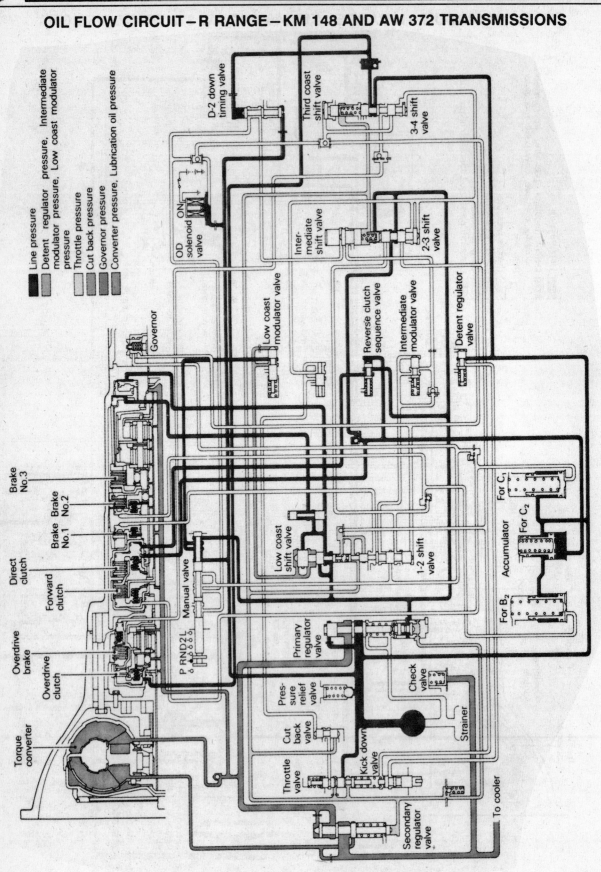

OIL FLOW CIRCUIT — D RANGE FIRST SPEED — KM 148 AND AW 372 TRANSMISSIONS

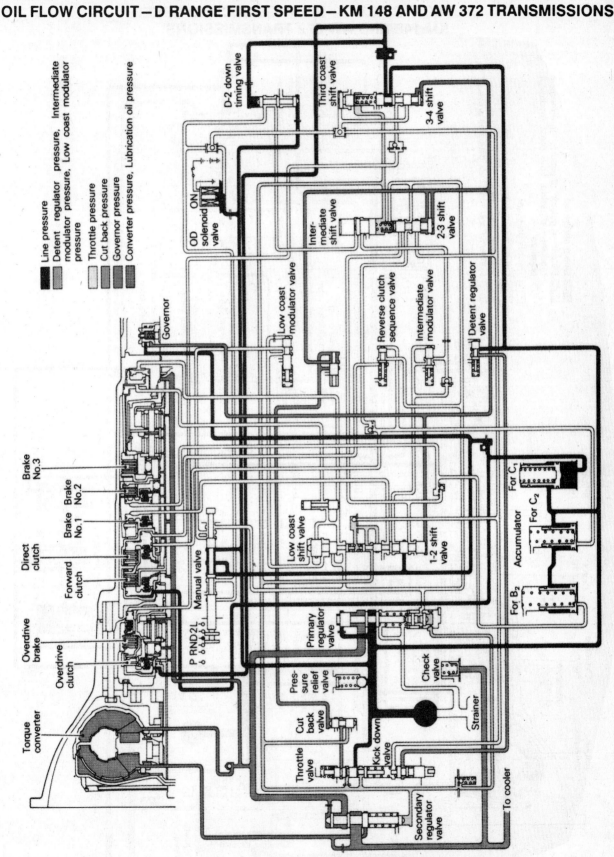

OIL FLOW CIRCUIT—D RANGE SECOND SPEED
KM 148 AND AW 372 TRANSMISSIONS

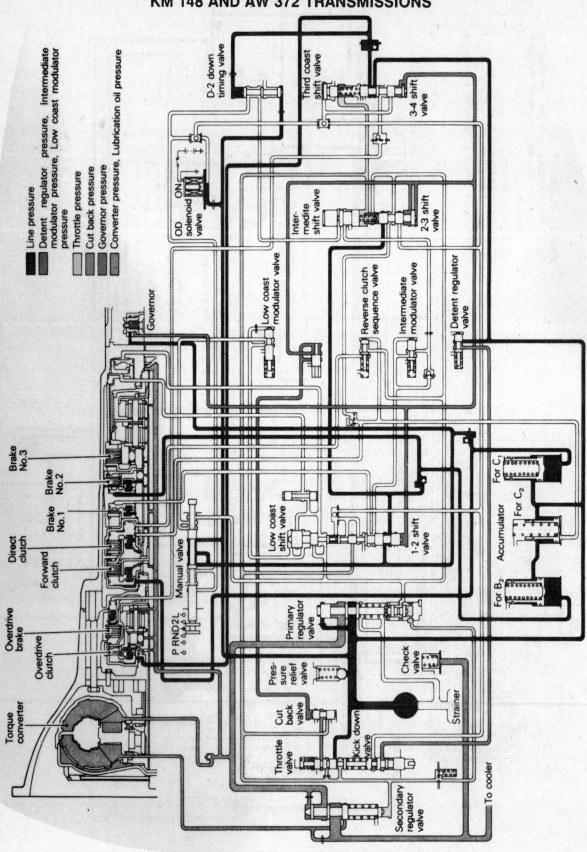

OIL FLOW CIRCUIT – D RANGE THIRD SPEED – KM 148 AND AW 372 TRANSMISSIONS

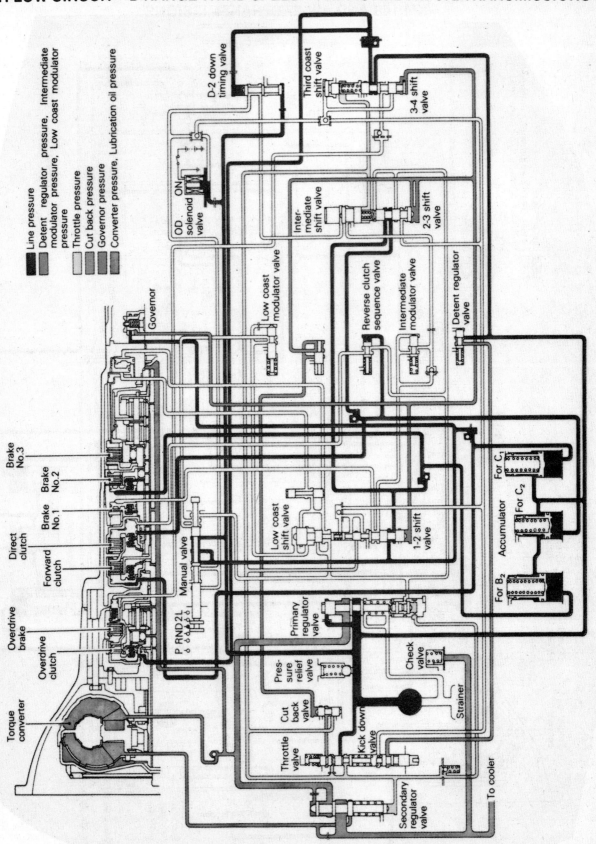

OIL FLOW CIRCUIT – D RANGE FOURTH SPEED
KM 148 AND AW 372 TRANSMISSIONS

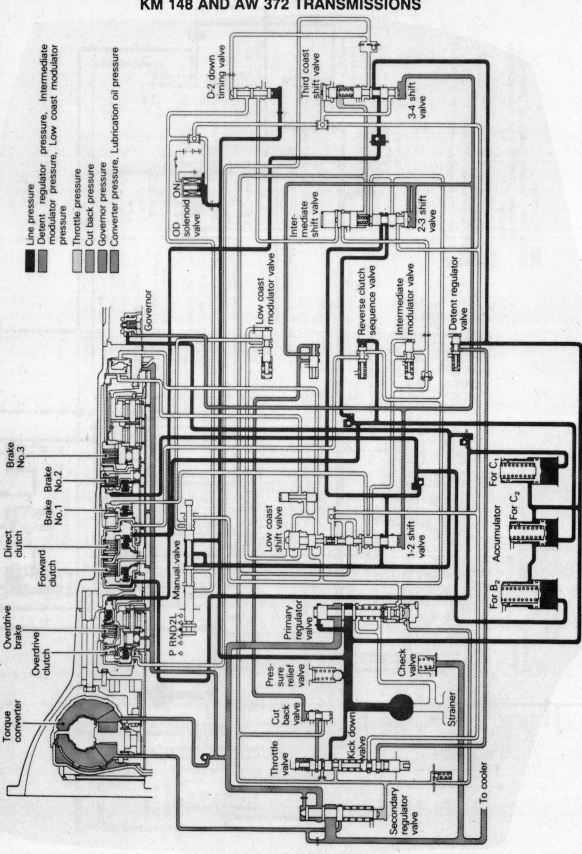

OIL FLOW CIRCUIT—2 RANGE SECOND—KM 148 AND AW372 TRANSMISSIONS

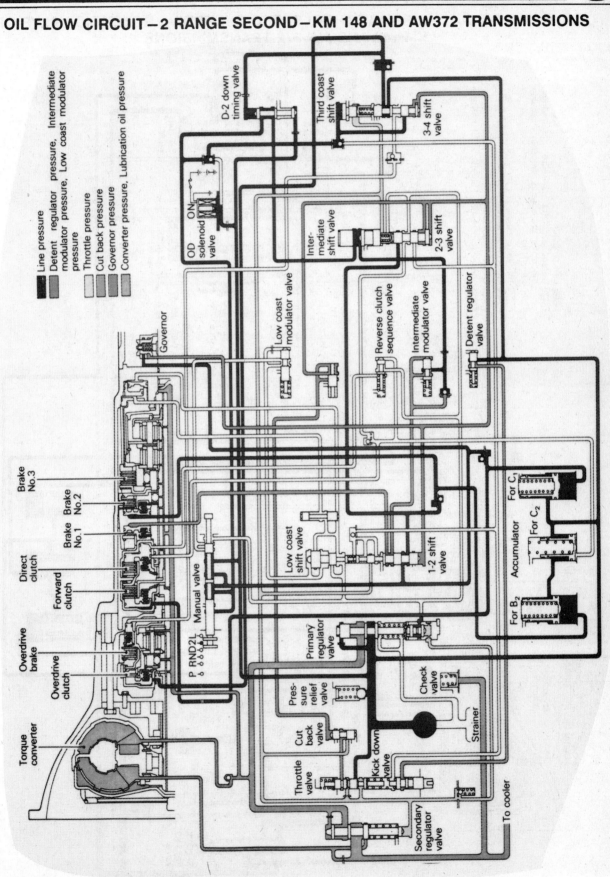

OIL FLOW CIRCUIT – D RANGE THIRD SPEED OVERDRIVE SOLENOID VALVE OFF
KM 148 AND AW 372 TRANSMISSIONS

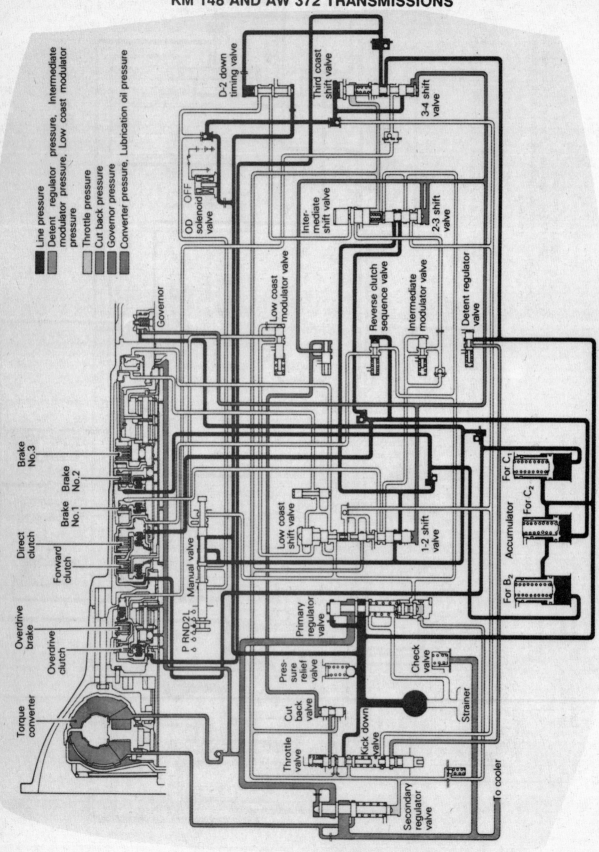

OIL FLOW CIRCUIT – D RANGE KICKDOWN 4TH TO 3RD
KM 148 AND AW 372 TRANSMISSIONS

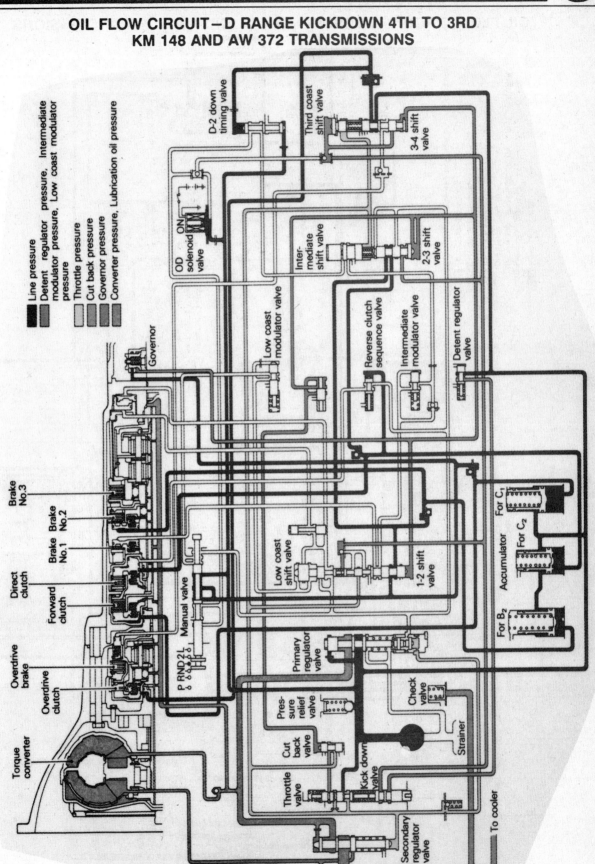

OIL FLOW CIRCUIT—LOCKUP—KM 148 AND AW 372 TRANSMISSIONS

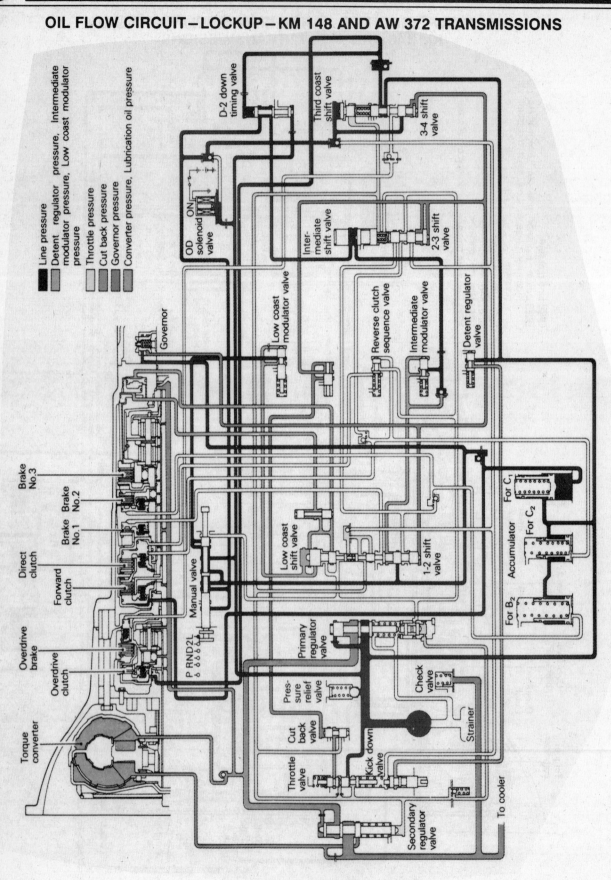

OIL FLOW CIRCUIT—P RANGE—372L TRANSMISSION

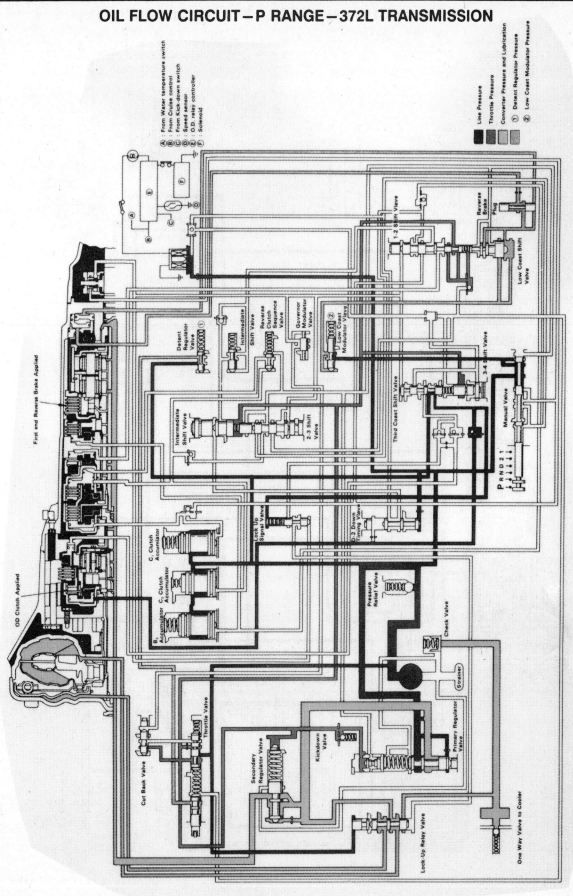

OIL FLOW CIRCUIT—N RANGE—372L TRANSMISSION

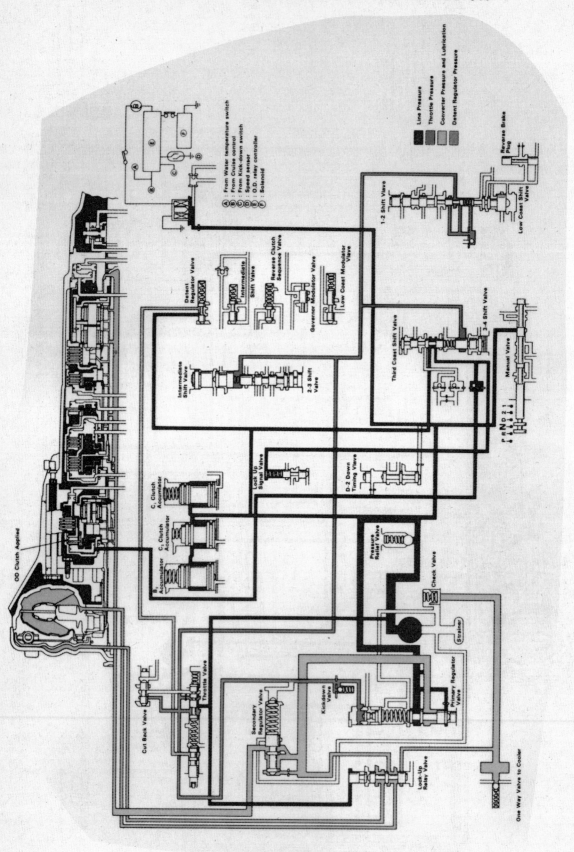

OIL FLOW CIRCUIT—R RANGE—372L TRANSMISSION

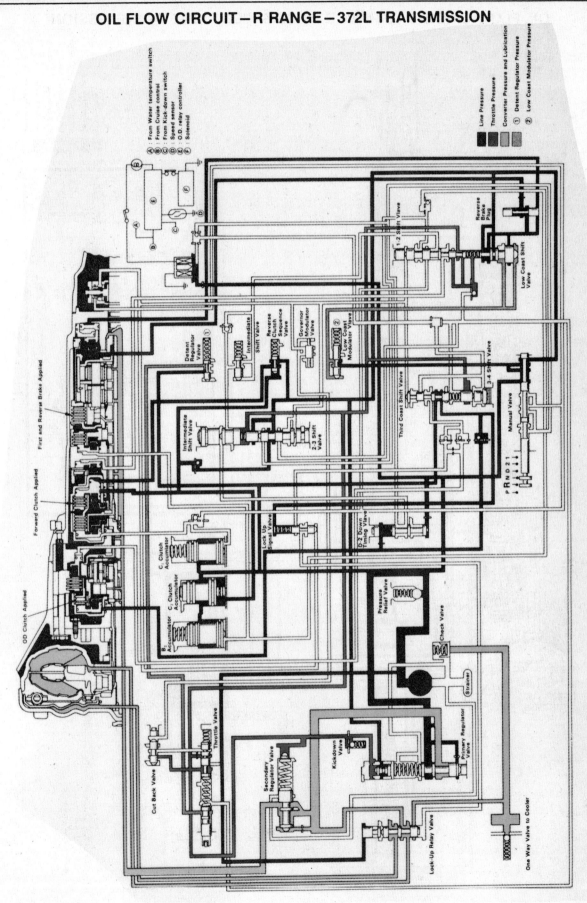

OIL FLOW CIRCUIT—D RANGE FIRST SPEED—372L TRANSMISSION

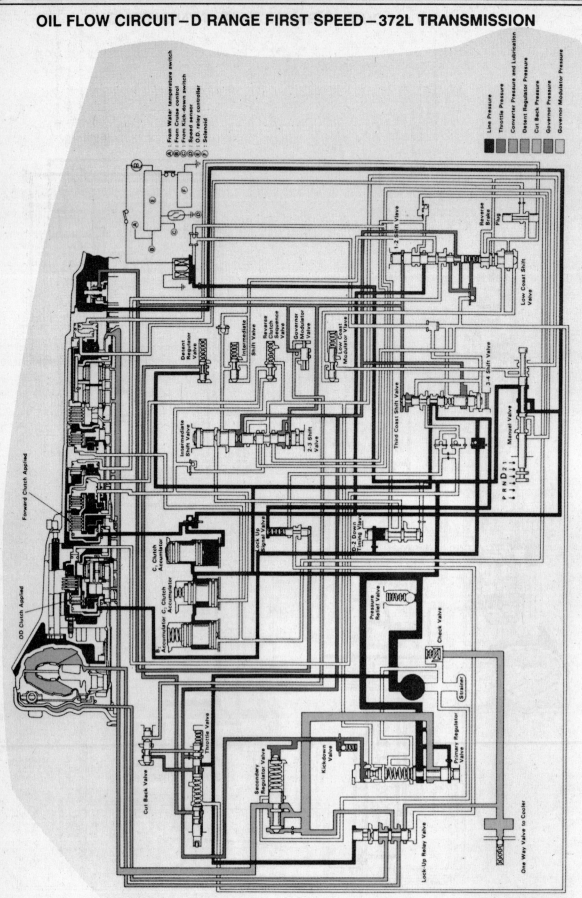

OIL FLOW CIRCUIT – D RANGE SECOND SPEED – 372L TRANSMISSION

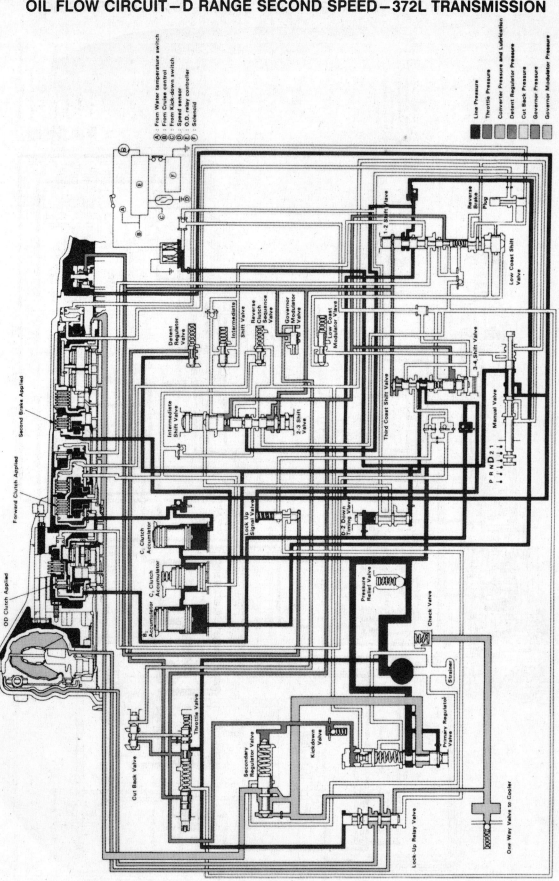

OIL FLOW CIRCUIT – D RANGE THIRD SPEED – 372L TRANSMISSION

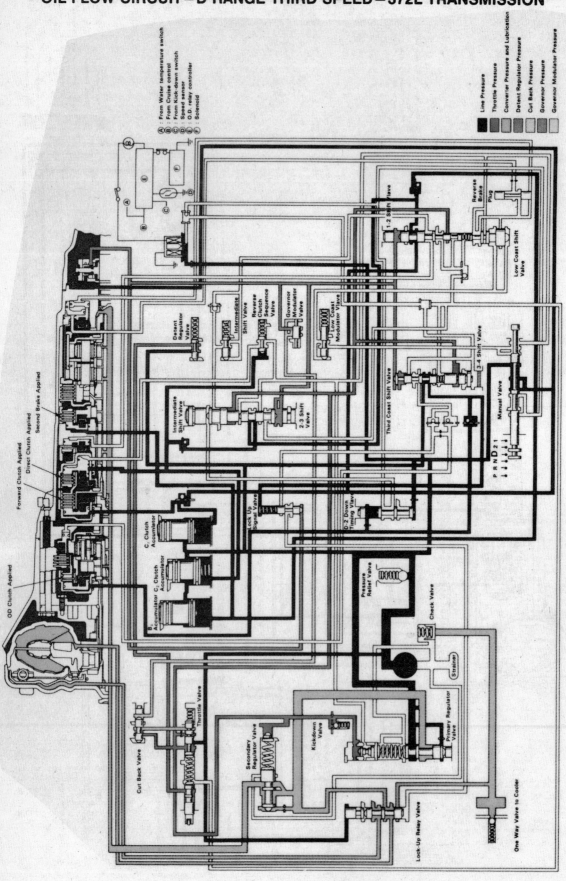

OIL FLOW CIRCUIT – D RANGE KICKDOWN OVERDRIVE THIRD
372L TRANSMISSION

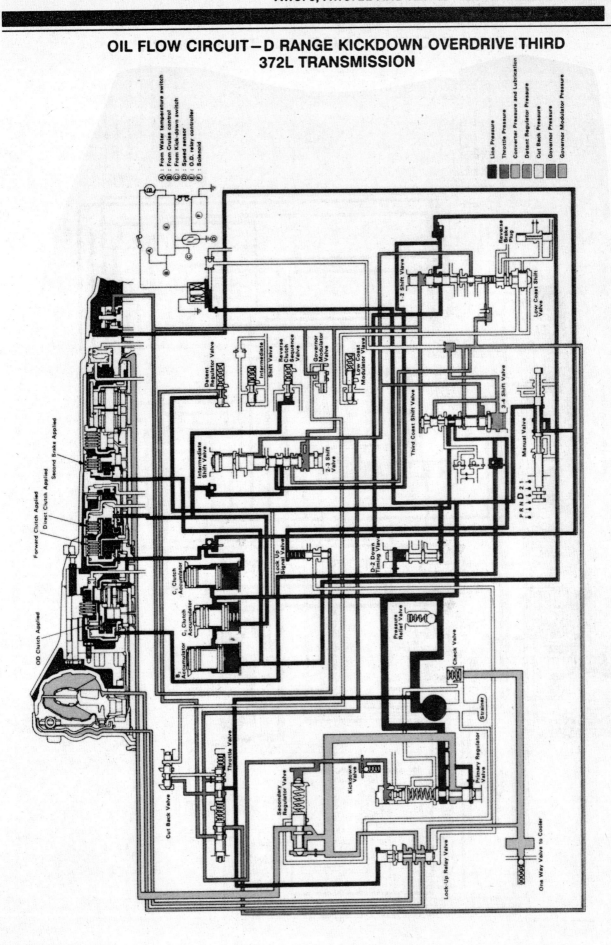

OIL FLOW CIRCUIT—1 RANGE—372L TRANSMISSION

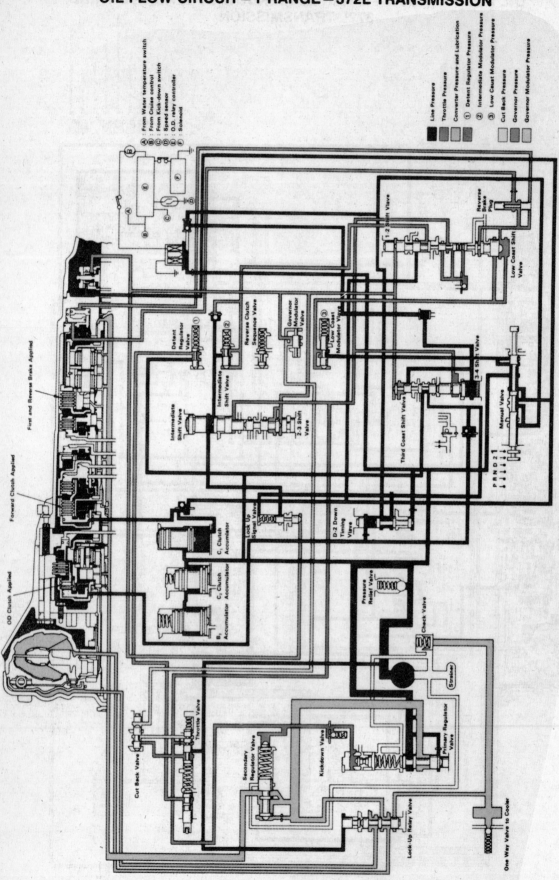

Section 3

AW30–80LE, A340E and A340H Transmissions
Isuzu and Toyota

APPLICATION

ISUZU AW30-80LE,
TOYOTA A340H and H340E TRANSMISSIONS

Year	Vehicle	Engine	Transmission
1986	Toyota 4-Runner	2.3L	A340H
	Toyota Pick-up	2.3L	A340H or A340E
1987	Toyota 4-Runner	2.3L	A340H
	Toyota Pick-up	2.3L	A340H
	Toyota Supra	3.0L	A340E
	Toyota Cressida	3.0L	A340E
1988	Toyota 4-Runner	2.3L	A340H
	Toyota Pick-up	2.3L	A340H
	Toyota Supra	3.0L	A340E
	Toyota Cressida	3.0L	A340E
	Isuzu Trooper II	2.6L	AW30-80LE
	Isuzu Pick-up	2.6L	AW30-80LE
1989	Toyota 4-Runner	2.3DWD-3.0L	A340H
	Toyota Pick-up	2.3DWD-3.0L	A340H or A340E
	Toyota Supra	3.0L	A340E
	Toyota Cressida	3.0L	A340E
	Isuzu Trooper II	2.6L	AW30-80LE
	Isuzu Pick-up	2.6L	AW30-80LE

GENERAL DESCRIPTION

The A340E, A340H and AW30-80LE transmissions are fully automatic 4 speed transmission assemblies that share a common transmission unit and are manufactured by Asian Warner. The A340E consists of 4 clutch packs, 4 brakes, 3 one-way clutches, 3 planetary gearsets and a series of 4 solenoids. The A340H and AW30-80LE are automatic transmission and transfer case combinations consisting of 5 clutch packs, 5 brakes, 3 one-way clutches, 3 planetary gearsets and a series of 4 solenoids. In either case, these components provide 4 forward ratios and 1 reverse in conjunction with dual range 4WD capability in 4WD applications.

Operation is controlled by selecting the appropriate position from a console-mounted selector lever mounted on the passenger compartment floor and a push-button overdrive control switch. A power/economy switch is included to further increase the driveability of the vehicle. The on-board computer determines the shift and lockup points of the transmission as well as the speed change range of the transfer system based upon the input data signals received from various sensors.

Power from the engine is transmitted to the input shaft by the torque converter and is then transmitted to the planetary gears by the operation of the clutches. The power flow depends on the engagement or disengagement of the clutches and brakes.

Each clutch and brake operates by hydraulic pressure which is produced by the rotation of the oil pump. The pressurized fluid is regulated by the valve body. Shift change automatically occurs according to throttle opening, vehicle speed and solenoid activation.

The torque converter provides a fluid coupling between the engine and transmission for optimum power transfer when driving at a constant speed and increased torque when starting, accelerating and climbing an incline. When used, the damper clutch provides a solid coupling for improved fuel mileage when at cruising ranges.

Transmission and Converter Identification

TRANSMISSION

An identification tag is riveted to the right rear side of the transmission case above the oil pan. Included on the tag is the Asian Warner model number and serial number of the unit.

CONVERTER

The torque converter is a 3 element, single stage, 2 phase type with an internal damper clutch. It is a welded 1 piece unit and cannot be disassembled for inspection purposes.

Electronic Controls

ELECTRONIC CONTROL TRANSMISSION (ECT) COMPUTER

The ECT computer is located to the lower left of the instrument panel. It receives information from various sensors and

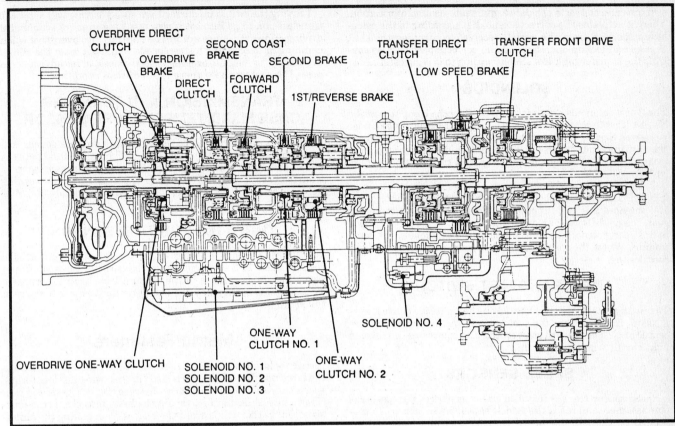

Cross sectional of the AW30-80LE and A340H 4WD transmissions

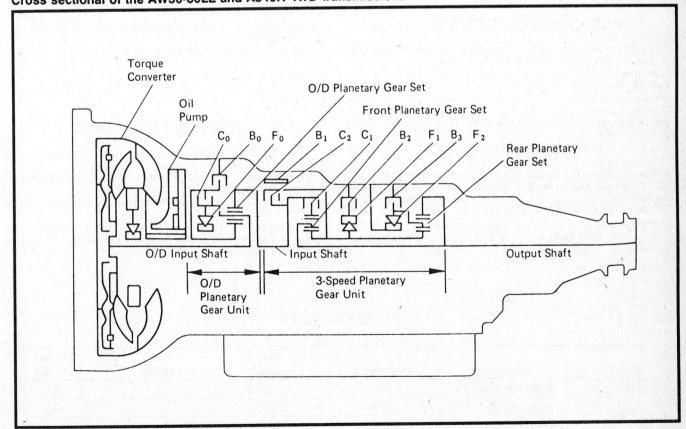

Cross sectional of the A340E transmission

switches and converts the data signals into usable information. Then, it activates the correct solenoid(s) according to the calculations derived from the signals received, controlling the shift change and lockup operations at the correct speed. It also controls the transfer high-low shift according to driving conditions.

SOLENOIDS

The 3 or 4 solenoids are turned on or off by the computer at the correct time to provide the correct shift or transfer range under any given driving circumstances. Solenoids No. 1 and 2 control the shifting from 1st to overdrive. Solenoid No. 3 controls the lockup converter. Solenoid No. 4 controls the transfer system, where applicable.

The relationship of the gears and the solenoid activity is as follows. When the vehicle is in 1st gear, solenoid 1 is functioning and solenoid 2 is not functioning. When the vehicle is in 2nd gear, solenoids 1 and 2 are both functioning. When the vehicle is in 3rd gear, solenoid 1 is not functioning and solenoid 2 is functioning. When the vehicle is in 4th gear, neither solenoid is functioning.

NEUTRAL START SWITCH

The neutral start switch is located on the right side of the transmission. It will prevent the vehicle from starting in any gear except **P** or **N**. The neutral start switch also completes the reverse light circuit when backing up.

SPEED SENSORS

Speed sensor No. 1 is installed either as part of the speedometer assembly and reads the vehicle speed. Speed sensor No. 2 is located on the left side of the transfer case and reads output shaft speed.

PATTERN SELECTION SWITCH

The pattern selection switch is located on the console, near the shifter. The corresponding light on the console will illuminate according to which pattern is selected. In the power mode, the shift points are later than in the normal mode, thus increasing the amount of power the vehicle is able to deliver during acceleration. In the normal mode, the gears will change faster; high gear will be attained sooner, thus achieving better fuel economy.

OVERDRIVE OFF SWITCH

The overdrive OFF switch is mounted on the gear shaft handle. This push-button switch disengages overdrive when depressed. The indicator light will illuminate when the switch is turned **OFF**. Automatic shifting will occur in either case, be it to third or fourth gear, according to the position of the switch. The coolant must be at least 160°F (70°C) for overdrive to be operational.

Leaving the switch up during high speed driving will allow the transmission to go into overdrive resulting in more economical driving. However, since automatic shifting into overdrive when climbing or descending a steep grade would decrease the climbing ability or engine braking effectiveness, it is advisable to press the switch under these types of road conditions.

TRANSMISSION AND TRANSFER CASE FLUID TEMPERATURE SENSOR

Located on the right side of the transmission, this sensor will cause the warning light on the dash to light if the fluid gets too hot so the driver can be forwarned of possible transmission or transfer case damage. The switch is set to turn the warning light on at about 280°F (140°C) and back off at about 250°F (120°C).

THROTTLE POSITION SENSOR

The Throttle Position Sensor (TPS) is a rotating type variable resistor. The TPS is connected to the throttle valve shaft and provides signals relative to the amount the throttle is opened. These signals are read by the computer so it knows how much the engine is being accelerated.

Metric Fasteners

Metric tools will be required to service this transmission. Due to the large number of alloy parts used in this transmission, torque specifications should be strictly observed. Before installing capscrews into aluminum parts, dip the bolts into clean transmission fluid as this will prevent the screws from galling the aluminum threads, thus causing damage.

Metric fastener dimensions are very close to the dimensions of the familiar inch system fasteners. For this reason replacement fasteners must have the same measurement and strength as the original fastener.

Do not attempt to interchange metric fasteners for inch system fasteners. Mismatched or incorrect fasteners can cause damage to the automatic transmission unit and possible personal injury. Care should be taken to reuse fasteners in their original locations.

Checking Fluid Level

1. Run the engine until at operating temperature.
2. Move the gear selector through all ranges.
3. Park the vehicle on level surface and check the fluid level with the gear selector in **P**.
4. The fluid level is sufficient when it is between the holes or dimples in the **HOT** range of the dipstick.
5. To check the fluid level in the chain case, remove the filler plug. The fluid is at the proper level when it is even with bottom of the filler hole.

FLUID CAPACITY
All capacities given in quarts

Year	Vehicle	Transmission	Fluid Type	Pan Capacity	Overhaul Capacity
1986	Toyota 4-Runner	A340H	Dexon® II	4.8	10.9
	Toyota Pick-up	A340H	Dexon® II	4.8	10.9
	Toyota Pick-up	A340E	Dexon® II	1.7	7.3

FLUID CAPACITY

All capacities given in quarts

Year	Vehicle	Transmission	Fluid Type	Pan Capacity	Overhaul Capacity
1987	Toyota 4-Runner	A340H	Dexon® II	4.8	10.9
	Toyota Pick-up	A340H	Dexon® II	4.8	10.9
	Toyota Supra	A340E	Dexon® II	1.7	7.6
	Toyota Cressida	A340E	Dexon® II	1.7	7.3
1988	Toyota 4-Runner	A340H	Dexon® II	4.8	10.9
	Toyota Pick-up	A340H	Dexon® II	4.8	10.9
	Toyota Supra	A340E	Dexon® II	1.7	7.6
	Toyota Cressida	A340E	Dexon® II	1.7	7.3
	Isuzu Trooper II	AW30–80LE	Dexon® II	4.8	12.1
	Isuzu Pick-up	AW30–80LE	Dexon® II	4.8	12.1
1989	Toyota 4-Runner	A340H	Dexon® II	4.8	10.9
	Toyota Pick-up	A340H	Dexon® II	4.8	10.9
	Toyota Pick-up	A340E	Dexon® II	1.7	7.6
	Toyota Supra	A340E	Dexon® II	1.7	7.6
	Toyota Cressida	A340E	Dexon® II	1.7	7.6
	Isuzu Trooper II	AW30–80LE	Dexon® II	4.8	12.1
	Isuzu Pick-up	AW30–80LE	Dexon® II	4.8	12.1

TRANSMISSION MODIFICATIONS

No modifications are available at the time of publication.

TROUBLE DIAGNOSIS

CLUTCH AND BRAKE APPLICATION CHART

Shift-Lever Position	Gear Position	Overdrive Direct Clutch	Forward Clutch	Direct Clutch	Overdrive Brake	Second Coast Brake	Second Brake	1st/reverse Brake	Overdrive One-way Clutch	One-way Clutch No. 1	One-way Clutch No. 2
P	Parking	Applied	—	—	—	—	—	—	—	—	—
R	Reverse	Applied	—	Applied	—	—	—	Applied	Applied	—	—
N	Neutral	Applied	—	—	—	—	—	—	—	—	—
D	1st	Applied	Applied	—	—	—	—	—	Applied	—	Applied
	2nd	Applied	Applied	—	—	—	Applied	—	Applied	Applied	—
	3rd	Applied	Applied	Applied	—	—	Applied	—	Applied	—	—
	OD	—	Applied	Applied	Applied	—	Applied	—	—	—	—
2	1st	Applied	Applied	—	—	—	—	—	Applied	—	Applied
	2nd	Applied	Applied	—	—	Applied	Applied	—	Applied	Applied	—
	3rd	Applied	Applied	Applied	—	—	Applied	—	Applied	—	—
L	1st	Applied	Applied	—	—	—	—	Applied	Applied	—	Applied
	2nd	Applied	Applied	—	—	Applied	Applied	—	Applied	Applied	—

CHILTON'S THREE C's TRANSMISSION DIAGNOSIS

Condition	Cause	Correction
Fluid discolored or smells burnt	a) Fluid contaiminated b) Torque converter faulty c) Transmission faulty	a) Replace fluid b) Replace torque converter c) Disassemble and inspect transmission
Vehicle does not move in any forward range or reverse	a) Manual linkage out of adjustment b) Valve body or primary regulator faulty c) Parking lock pawl faulty d) Torque converter faulty e) Converter drive plate broken f) Oil pump intake screen blocked g) Transmission faulty	a) Adjust linkage b) Inspect valve body c) Inspect parking lock pawl d) Replace torque converter e) Replace drive plate f) Clear or replace screen g) Disassemble and inspect transmission
Shift lever position incorrect	a) Manual linkage out of adjustment b) Manual valve and lever faulty c) Transmission faulty	a) Adjust linkage b) Inspect valve body c) Disassemble and inspect transmission
Harsh engagement into any drive range	a) Throttle cable out of adjustment b) Valve body or primary regulator faulty c) Accumulator pistons faulty d) Transmission faulty	a) Adjust throttle cable b) Inspect valve body c) Inspect accumulator pistons d) Disassemble and inspect transmission
Delayed 1/2, 2/3 or 3/4 up-shift, or down-shifts from 4/3 or 3/2 and shifts back to 4th or 3rd	a) Electronic control faulty b) Valve body faulty c) Solenoid valve faulty	a) Inspect electronic control b) Inspect valve body c) Inspect solenoid valve
Slips on 1/2, 2/3 or 3/4 up-shift, or slips or shudders on acceleration	a) Manual linkage out of adjustment b) Throttle cable out of adjustment c) Valve body faulty d) Solenoid valve faulty e) Transmission faulty	a) Adjust linkage b) Adjust throttle cable c) Inspect valve body d) Inspect solenoid valve e) Disassemble and inspect transmission
Drag, binding or tie-up on 1/2, 2/3 or 3/4 up-shift	a) Manual linkage out of adjustment b) Valve body faulty c) Transmission faulty	a) Adjust linkage b) Inspect valve body c) Disassemble and inspect transmission
No lockup in 2nd, 3rd or 4th	a) Electronic control faulty b) Valve body faulty c) Solenoid valve faulty d) Transmission faulty	a) Inspect electronic control b) Inspect valve body c) Inspect solenoid valve d) Disassemble and inspect transmission
Harsh down shift	a) Throttle cable out of adjustment b) Throttle cable and cam faulty c) Accumulator pistons faulty d) Valve body faulty e) Transmission faulty	a) Adjust throttle cable b) Inspect throttle cable and cam c) Inspect accumulator pistons d) Inspect valve body e) Disassemble and inspect transmission
No down shift when coasting	a) Valve body faulty b) Solenoid valve faulty c) Electronic control faulty	a) Inspect valve body b) Inspect solenoid valve c) Inspect electronic control
Down shift occurs too quickly or too late while coasting	a) Throttle cable faulty b) Valve body faulty c) Transmission faulty d) Solenoid valve faulty e) Electronic control faulty	a) Inspect throttle cable b) Inspect valve body c) Disassemble and inspect transmission d) Inspect solenoid valve e) Inspect electronic control
No 4/3, 3-2 or 2-1 kickdown	a) Solenoid valve faulty b) Electronic control faulty c) Valve body faulty	a) Inspect solenoid valve b) Inspect electronic control c) Inspect valve body
No engine braking in 2 or L range	a) Solenoid valve faulty b) Electronic control faulty c) Valve body faulty d) Transmission faulty	a) Inspect solenoid valve b) Inspect electronic control c) Inspect valve body d) Disassemble and inspect transmission
Vehicle does not hold in P	a) Manual linkage out of adjustment b) Parking lock pawl cam and spring faulty	a) Adjust linkage b) Inspect cam and spring

CHILTON'S THREE C's TRANSMISSION DIAGNOSIS

Condition	Cause	Correction
No H2/H4, H4/L4, L4/H4 or H4/H2 change gear position of transfer	a) Transfer linkage out of adjustment b) Electronic control faulty c) Transfer valve body faulty d) Transfer faulty	a) Adjust linkage b) Inspect electronic control c) Inspect valve body d) Disassemble and inspect transfer

Hydraulic Control System

HYDRAULIC OPERATION

The hydraulic control system is comprised of the oil pump, valve body, solenoid valves, clutch and brakes and all the fluid passages that connect all of the hydraulic components. Based on the pressure created by the oil pump, the hydraulic control system governs the pressure acting on the torque converter, clutches and brakes in accordance with the vehicles driving conditions.

There are 3 solenoids on the transmission valve body and 1 on the transfer case valve body on 4 wheel drive units. These solenoid valve are turned **ON** and **OFF** by signals from the computer to operate the shift valves in the valve body. The shift valves then switch the fluid passages so that fluid goes to the torque converter and appropriate planetary gear units. Except for the solenoid valves, the hydraulic control system of this transmission is the same as that of a fully hydraulic transmission.

LINE PRESSURE

The line pressure, regulated by the primary regulator valve, is used to operate all of the clutches and brakes in the transmission. If the primary regulator valve does not operate correctly, line pressure will be inaccurate. Line pressure that is too high will lead to shifting shock. Too low of a line pressure will cause slippage.

THROTTLE PRESSURE

Throttle pressure is relative to the throttle opening since the throttle pressure valve is directly connected to the engine throttle valve by a cable. In contrast to a fully hydraulic transmission, the throttle pressure is only used for regulating the line pressure. Consequently, improper adjustment of the throttle cable may result in improper line pressure.

MANUAL VALVE

The manual valve is connected by linkage to the selector lever inside the vehicle. It opens or closes oil passages to start hydraulic pressure movement according to the range selected.

VALVE BODY

The valve body delivers the hydraulic pressure sent from the oil pump to its components. It also regulates the pressure according to throttle valve opening and vehicle speed to provide automatic gearshifting.

ACCUMULATOR

Accumulators are provided for the forward clutch, direct clutch and brake No. 2. Their function is to dampen the shock when each is actuated.

When the circuit to the pressure receiving side opens causing the line pressure to be applied to the piston, the piston is slowly pushed downward, thus dampening the shift shock.

Diagnosis Tests

STALL SPEED TEST

CAUTION

Never allow anyone to stand near — especially in front of or behind — the vehicle when performing a stall test

---

1. Check the fluid level and condition. Perform the test at normal operating temperature.
2. Block the wheels securely and firmly set the parking brake.
3. Connect a tachometer to the engine.
4. Push down the brake pedal firmly and shift the gear selector to the **D** detent.
5. Gradually depress the accelerator pedal. Do not perform this step for more than 5 seconds.

STALL SPEED SPECIFICATIONS

Year	Vehicle	Stall Speed (rpm)
1986	Toyota 4-Runner	1850–2150 ① 2100–2400 ②
	Toyota Pick-up	1850–2150 ① 2100–2400 ②
1987	Toyota 4-Runner	1850–2150 ① 2100–2400 ②
	Toyota Pick-up	1850–2150 ① 2100–2400 ②
	Toyota Cressida	1950–2250
	Toyota Supra	2050–2350 ③ 2150–2450 ④
1988	Toyota 4-Runner	2050–2350
	Toyota Pick-up	2050–2350
	Toyota Cressida	1950–2250
	Toyota Supra	2050–2350 ③ 2150–2450 ④
	Isuzu Trooper II	2250–2550
	Isuzu Pick-up	2250–2550
1989	Toyota 4-Runner	2050–2350
	Toyota Pick-up	2050–2350
	Toyota Cressida	2050–2350
	Toyota Supra	2050–2350 ③ 2350–2650 ④

① with 22R-E engine
② with 22R-TE engine
③ with 7M-GE engine
④ with 7M-GTE engine

6. When the engine has stopped increasing in speed, read the tachometer and immediately release the accelerator pedal.

7. Shift into the **N** detent. Allow the engine to idle for 1 minute so the fluid can cool and to prevent the possibility of overheating.

8. Perform the stall test in **R** range.

9. If the stall speed is lower than specification in **D** and **R**, then either the engine output is too low or the stator one-way clutch is faulty.

10. If the stall speed is higher than specification in **D**, then either the overdrive one-way clutch is faulty, the forward clutch is slipping, one-way clutch No. 2 is faulty or the line pressure is low.

11. If the stall speed is higher than specification in **R**, then either the overdrive one-way clutch is faulty, the direct clutch is slipping, the 1st/reverse brake is slipping or the line pressure is low.

12. If the stall speed is higher than specification in **D** and **R**, then either the fluid or line pressure is low or the overdrive one-way clutch is faulty.

LINE PRESSURE TEST

1. Check the fluid level and condition. Perform the test at normal operating temperature.

2. Raise the vehicle and support safely. Connect an oil pressure gauge to the proper fitting. Lower the vehicle. Connect a tachometer to the engine.

3. Block the wheels securely and firmly set the parking brake.

4. Shift the gear selector to **D** and read the line pressure at idle.

5. Repeat the test and read the pressure at the stall speed. Allow 1 minute cooling time.

6. Repeat Steps 4 and 5 in **R**.

7. If the pressures are not at the specified values, check the throttle cable adjustment and repeat the test.

8. If the line pressure is higher than specification in all ranges, then either the regulator valve is faulty, the throttle valve is faulty or the throttle control cable is incorrectly adjusted.

9. If the line pressure is lower than specification in all ranges, then either the regulator valve is faulty, the throttle valve is faulty, the oil pump is faulty, the overdrive direct clutch is faulty or the throttle control cable is incorrectly adjusted.

10. If the line pressure is lower than specification in **D**, then either the forward clutch is faulty or there is a fluid leak in the **D** range hydraulic circuit.

11. If the line pressure is lower than specification in **R**, then either the direct clutch is faulty, the 1st/reverse brake is faulty or there is a fluid leak in the **R** range hydraulic circuit.

Line Pressure Specifications

Year	Vehicle	Drive Range		Reverse Range	
		Idle Speed psi (kpa)	Stall Speed psi (kpa)	Idle Speed psi (kpa)	Stall Speed psi (kpa)
1986	Toyota 4-Runner	53-61 (363-422)	134-169 (922-1167)	73-87 (500-598)	186-236 (1285-1628)
	Toyota Pick-up ①	53-61 (363-422)	134-169 (922-1167)	73-87 (500-598)	186-236 (1285-1628)
	Toyota Pick-up ②	53-61 (363-422)	161-196 (1108-1355)	73-87 (500-598)	223-273 (1540-1883)
1987	Toyota 4-Runner	53-61 (363-422)	135-171 (932-1177)	73-87 (500-598)	188-238 (1294-1638)
	Toyota Pick-up	53-61 (363-422)	135-171 (932-1177)	73-87 (500-598)	188-238 (1294-1638)
	Toyota Cressida	53-61 (363-422)	161-196 (1108-1353)	73-87 (500-598)	223-273 (1540-1883)
	Toyota Supra	50-61 (343-422)	158-196 (1089-1353)	70-87 (481-598)	220-273 (1520-1883)
1988	Toyota 4 Runner	53-61 (363-422)	135-171 (932-1177)	73-87 (500-598)	188-238 (1294-1638)
	Toyota Pick-up	53-61 (363-422)	135-171 (932-1177)	73-87 (500-598)	188-238 (1294-1638)
	Toyota Cressida	53-61 (363-422)	161-196 (1108-1353)	73-87 (500-598)	223-273 (1540-1883)
	Toyota Supra	50-61 (343-422)	158-196 (1089-1353)	70-87 (481-598)	220-273 (1520-1883)
	Isuzu Trooper II	53-61 (363-422)	132-168 (910-1158)	73-87 (500-598)	185-235 (1275-1619)
	Isuzu Pick-up	53-61 (363-422)	132-168 (910-1158)	73-87 (500-598)	185-235 (1275-1619)
1989	Toyota 4-Runner ③	53-61 (363-422)	132-168 (910-1158)	73-87 (500-598)	185-235 (1275-1619)
	Toyota 4-Runner ④	61-70 (427-481)	164-199 (1128-1373)	74-88 (510-608)	201-250 (1383-1726)
	Toyota Pick-up ③	53-61 (363-422)	132-168 (910-1158)	73-87 (500-598)	185-235 (1275-1619)
	Toyota Pick-up ④	61-70 (427-481)	164-199 (1128-1373)	74-88 (510-608)	201-250 (1383-1726)
	Toyota Cressida	53-61 (363-422)	135-171 (932-1177)	73-87 (500-598)	188-238 (1294-1638)
	Toyota Supra ⑤	50-61 (343-422)	125-164 (863-1128)	70-87 (481-598)	174-226 (1196-1559)
	Toyota Supra ⑥	58-70 (402-481)	175-213 (1206-1471)	71-88 (490-608)	215-267 (1481-1844)
	Isuzu Trooper II	53-61 (363-422)	132-168 (910-1158)	73-87 (500-598)	185-235 (1275-1619)
	Isuzu Pick-up	53-61 (363-422)	132-168 (910-1158)	73-87 (500-598)	185-235 (1275-1619)

① with A340H transmission
② with A340E transmission
③ with 2.3L engine
④ with 3.0L engine
⑤ with 7M-GE engine
⑥ with 7M-GTE engine

TIME LAG TEST

1. Check the fluid level and condition. Perform the test at normal operating temperature.

2. Block the wheels securely and firmly set the parking brake.

3. Shift from **N** to **D** and measure the time it takes from shifting the lever until the shift is felt.

4. Repeat the test twice allowing 1 minute between tests and average the results. The average time lag should be less than 1.2 seconds.

5. Repeat the entire procedure shifting from **N** to **R**. The average time lag should be less than 1.5 seconds.

6. If the **N** to **D** time lag is longer than specification, then either the line pressure is too low, the forward clutch is worn or the overdrive one-way clutch is faulty.

7. If the **N** to **D** time lag is longer than specification, then the line pressure is too low, the direct clutch or the 1st/reverse brake is worn or the overdrive one-way clutch is faulty.

ROAD TEST

This test is designed to check if upshift and downshift occurs at the correct speeds and if slippage or excessive shock is detected while actually driving the vehicle. The test should be performed on a long level road, with little or no traffic so that speeds can be chosen and maintained and not forced or altered by others on the road.

1. Run the engine until at operating temperature and check the fluid level. Place the pattern select switch in the CF35"NORM" mode.

2. Shift into **D** and start off with the pedal about half way down. Check all shift points and any clutch slippage when the transmission shifts gears. Shifting from 1st to 2nd should occur at 20–25 mph. Shifting from 2nd to 3rd should occur at 35–45 mph. Shifting from 3rd to 4th should occur at 50–60 mph, providing the overdrive switch is **ON**. In addition, check the operation of the lockup torque converter. The damper clutch should engage at about 45 while in 4th gear.

NOTE: There is no overdrive or lockup when the vehicle is in 4L, when the coolant temperature is below 160°F (70°C) or if there is at least a 6 mph difference between the set cruise control speed and the actual road speed.

3. Come to a gradual stop. Automatic downshifting through the gears should occur at 10–15 mph less than the corresponding upshift.

4. Repeat Steps 2 and 3 in the power mode. Everything that occurred in the norm mode should occur in the power mode, but 5–15 mph later. Come to a complete stop.

5. Start up again. While in 2nd, 3rd and 4th gears, check the kickdown mechanism by fully depressing the accelerator pedal. The transmission should automatically downshift through the gears.

6. While in 3rd or 4th gear, release the accelerator and shift into **L**. Engine braking should be felt. Also automatic shifting from 3rd to 2nd or 4th to 3rd to 2nd should occur immediately and shifting from 2nd to 1st should occur at 20–30 mph. Accelerate back up to 3rd gear and shift into **2**. Engine braking should be felt. Come to a complete stop.

7. Start off in **2** with the pedal depressed about half way down. Shifting from 1st to 2nd should occur at 15–20 mph and kickdown to 1st should operate. Come to a complete stop.

8. Start off in **L** and check that no upshift occurs. Release the accelerator pedal. Engine braking should occur. Come to a complete stop.

9. Shift into **R**. Check for clutch slippage by cautiously making full throttle starts. If possible, check for clutch slippage by depressing the accelerator pedal lightly while in motion. Come to a complete stop.

10. Shift into **P** and check the operation of the parking pawl while on a slope.

11. If any abnormal behavior or loud noise is noticed during the road test, compare the findings with the Chilton Three C's Transmission Diagnosis Chart.

Electronic Control System

SELF-DIAGNOSIS SYSTEM

Description

A self-diagnosis function is built into the electrical control system of vehicles equipped with the A340E, A340H or AW30-80LE transmission. Warning and diagnostic codes can be read only when the overdrive OFF switch is in **ON**. If left in the **OFF** position, the indicator light will be lit continuously and will not blink.

NOTE: Low battery voltage will cause faulty operation of the diagnosis system; always check the condition of the battery before relying on the codes generated by the system.

If a malfunction occurs within the speed sensors or solenoids, the overdrive OFF light will blink to warn the driver of a problem. There is, however, no warning of a malfunction with the lockup solenoid, brake signal or throttle position sensor. These items can be checked separately. To find out if the system is retaining fault codes:

1. Turn the ignition switch **ON**.

2. The overdrive OFF light should come on when the switch is turned **OFF**.

3. When the overdrive OFF switch is turned **ON**, the overdrive OFF light should go out. If the overdrive OFF light flashes when the overdrive OFF switch is **ON**, the electronic control system is faulty.

The diagnostic code is retained in the memory of the computer and due to back-up voltage, is not cancelled out when the engine is turned off. Therefore, after repairs have been completed, it is necessary to disconnect the computer connector or remove the appropriate fuse with the ignition **OFF** according to the following list for at least 10 seconds in order to cancel the codes:

1986–88 Toyota 4 Runner and Pick-up—STOP fuse (15A)
1989 Toyota 4 Runner and Pick-up—EFI fuse (15A)
1987–89 Toyota Supra—RAD No. 1 fuse (15A)
1987–88 Toyota Cressida—DOME fuse (7.5A)
1989 Toyota Cressida—EFI fuse (20A)
1988–89 Isuzu Trooper II and Pick-up—fuse No. 6 ECT CLOCK (10A)

NOTE: The lower the ambient temperature, the longer the fuse must be left out. It is not recommended that the battery be disconnected for the purpose of cancelling out transmission fault codes, or other memories throughout the vehicles will be unnecessarily cancelled.

Fault Code Data

OBTAINING CODES

WITHOUT SUPER MONITOR DISPLAY

1. Turn the ignition switch and overdrive OFF switch to their **ON** positions.

2. Connect the appropriate terminal(s) of the service connector with a jumper wire or to ground.

    a. On 1986–88 Toyota 4-Runner and Pick-up, connect the diagnostic connector to ground.

    b. On 1989 Toyota 4-Runner, Pick-up and Cressida, connect the TE1 and E1 terminals. The connector is located on the right side of the engine compartment on trucks. On Cres-

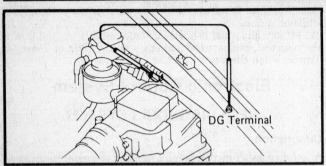

1986–88 Toyota 4-Runner and Pick-up diagnostic connector

sida, look for the square connector on the left side of the engine compartment. If the connector is not there, look for a round connector to the left of the steering column.

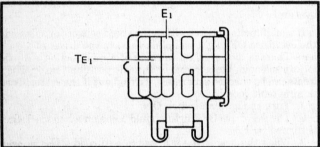

1989 Toyota 4-Runner, Pick-up and Cressida square diagnostic connector

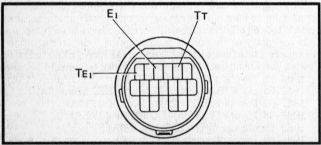

1989 Toyota Cressida round diagnostic connector.

c. On Toyota Celica and 1987–88 Cressida, connect the E1 and ECT or Tt wires. The connector is located on the left side of the engine compartment.

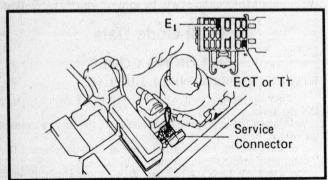

Toyota Celica and 1987–88 Cressida diagnostic connector

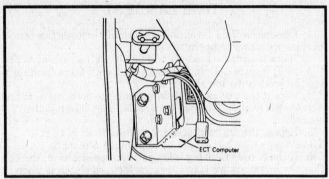

Isuzu diagnostic connector

d. On Izusu, connect the yellow-with-black-tracer wire to ground. The connector is located to the left of the steering column near the ECT computer.

3. Read the fault codes as indicated by the number of times the overdrive OFF light flashes.

4. If the system is operating normally, the light will blink twice per second continuously.

5. In the event of a malfunction, the light will blink once every ½ second, pause for 1½ seconds, then blink again once every ½ second. The first group of blinks is the first digit of the code and the second group is the second digit. If there are 2 or more codes, there will be a 2½ second pause between codes and they will appear from the smallest numerically to the largest. The entire process will repeat itself after a 4½ second pause.

WITH SUPER MONITOR DISPLAY

NOTE: Do not depress the accelerator pedal while the super monitor display diagnostic code is displayed. This will cancel the display.

1. Turn the ignition **ON**. There is no need to use a diagnostic connector.

2. Simultaneously push and hold the "SELECT" and "INPUT M" keys for at least 3 seconds. The letters "DIAG" will appear on the screen.

3. After a short pause, push and hold the "SET" button for at least 3 seconds.

4. If the system is operating normally, "ECT OK" will appear on the screen.

5. In the event of a malfunction, "ECT" followed by a code number will appear on the screen. If there are 2 or more codes, they will appear in 5 second intervals.

6. To get the time back on screen, either turn the ignition switch **OFF** or push the "SELECT" button until the time appears.

DIAGNOSING CODES

Code 42 (Toyota) or Code 21 (Isuzu) — No. 1 Speed Sensor

SYSTEM CHECK

1. Check for continuity between the suspect speed sensor terminal at the computer (SP1 or SP2) and ground. If continuity exists, try a known good computer.

2. If the circuit is open, inspect the speed sensor.

3. If the speed sensor is functioning properly, check the wiring between the computer and the speed sensor.

SPEED SENSOR NO. 1 CHECK

1986–88 Toyota 4-Runner and Pick-up

1. Remove the combination meter assembly.

2. Connect an ohmmeter between the SPD and GND terminals.

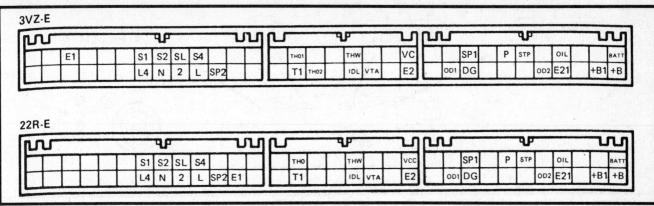

Computer connector terminals – 1989 Toyota 4- Runner and Pick-up

					THW		VC		SP1 SP2	TT		M.REL	P	IG SW	BATT
	S1	S2	SL		E1	STP	IDL	VTA	E2	N	OD1 OD2			L		S	+B	+B1

Computer connector terminals – 1989 Toyota Cressida

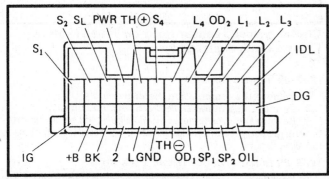

Computer connector terminals, except 1989 Toyota trucks and Cressida

3. Revolve the speedometer shaft. The speed sensor is functioning properly if the needle repeatedly deflects from 0 ohms to infinate ohms.

1989 Toyota 4-Runner and Pick-up

1. Remove the combination meter assembly.
2. Connect an ohmmeter between terminals A and B.
3. The speed sensor is functioning properly if there is continuity 4 times per each revolution of the speedometer shaft.
4. If incorrect, replace the speedometer.

1987–88 Toyota Cressida

1. If the vehicle is equipped with analog gauges, remove the combination meter assembly.
2. Connect an ohmmeter between the STD(+) and SPD(-) terminals.
3. Revolve the speedometer shaft. The speed sensor is functioning properly if the needle repeatedly deflects from 0 ohms to infinate ohms.
4. If the vehicle is equipped with digital gauges, remove the combination meter assembly, but leave the wire harness connected.

5. Connect a voltmeter between the SP and GND terminals.
6. Turn the ignition switch **ON**.
7. Revolve the speedometer shaft. The speed sensor is functioning properly if the needle repeatedly deflects from 0V to 2V.

1989 Toyota Cressida

1. If the vehicle is equipped with analog gauges, remove the combination meter assembly.
2. Connect an ohmmeter between terminals A and B.
3. The speed sensor is functioning properly if there is continuity 4 times per each revolution of the speedometer shaft.
4. If incorrect, replace the speedometer.
5. If the vehicle is equipped with digital gauges, remove the combination meter assembly and remove the total counter (speedometer) with speed sensor.
6. Connect a series of three 1.5volts dry cell batteries.
7. Connect the positive lead from the batteries to terminal 1 and the negative lead to terminal 3.
8. Connect the positive lead from the batteries to terminal 2 through a 3.4 watts known good bulb.
9. The speed sensor is functioning properly if the test bulb lights 20 times per each revolution of the total counter shaft. If incorrect, replace the total counter with speed sensor.

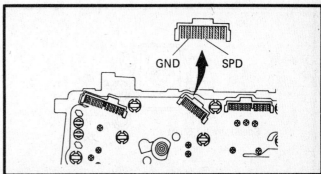

Speed sensor No. 1 terminals behind the dash – 1986–88 Toyota 4-Runner and Pick-up

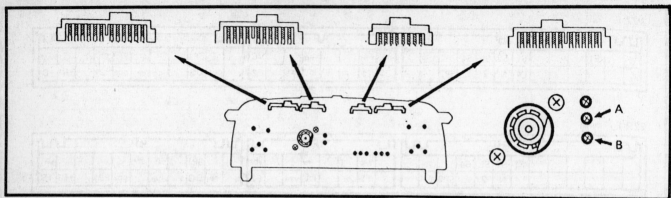

Speed sensor No. 1 terminals behind the dash – 1989 Toyota 4-Runner and Pick-up

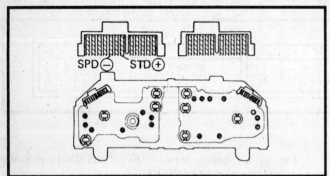

Speed sensor No. 1 terminals behind the dash – 1987–88 Toyota Cressida with analog gauges

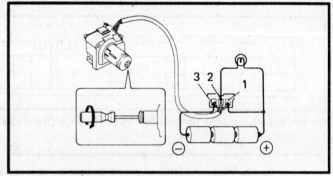

Checking speed sensor No. 1 on 1989 Toyota Cressida with digital gauges

1987–89 Toyota Supra

1. Remove the combination meter assembly.
2. Connect an ohmmeter between terminals A and B.
3. Revolve the speedometer shaft. The speed sensor is functioning properly if the needle repeatedly deflects from 0 ohms to infinate ohms.

1988–89 Isuzu Trooper II and Pick-up

1. Remove the combination meter assembly and remove the speedometer with speed sensor.
2. Connect an ohmmeter between the 2 small bolts in the speed sensor.
3. The speed sensor is functioning properly if there is continuity between the bolts 4 times per each revolution of the speedometer shaft.
4. If incorrect, replace the speedometer.

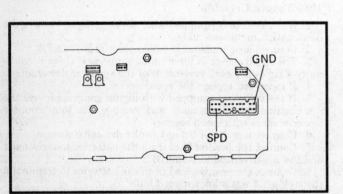

Speed sensor No. 1 terminals behind the dash – 1987–88 Toyota Cressida with gauges

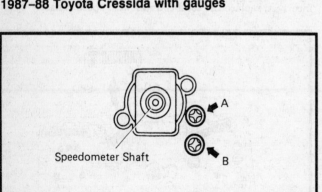

Speed sensor No. 1 terminals – 1989 Toyota Cressida with analog gauges

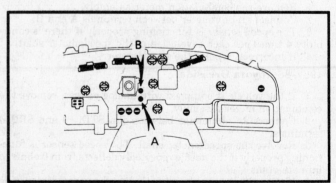

Speed sensor No. 1 terminals behind the dash – 1987–89 Toyota Supra

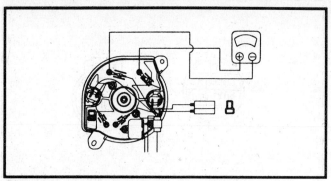

Checking speed sensor No. 1 on 1988–89 Isuzu Trooper II and Pick-up

Code 61 (Toyota) or Code 22 (Isuzu) – No. 2 Speed Sensor

SYSTEM CHECK

1. Check for continuity between the suspect speed sensor terminal at the computer (SP1 or SP2) and ground. If continuity exists, try a known good computer.
2. If the circuit is open, inspect the speed sensor.
3. If the speed sensor is functioning properly, check the wiring between the computer and the speed sensor.

SPEED SENSOR NO. 2 CHECK

Removed From Vehicle

NOTE: Do not perform this test on vehicles with ABS.

1. Raise the vehicle and support safely. Remove the speed sensor from the transmission.
2. Connect an ohmmeter between the terminals in the connector.
3. Bring a magnet close to and away from the sensor tip. The speed sensor is functioning properly if the needle deflects from 0 ohms to infinate ohms.

Installed in Vehicle

1. If the vehicle is not equipped with ABS, raise and safely support 1 of the rear wheels.
2. Connect an ohmmeter between the terminals in the connector.
3. Spin the wheel. The speed sensor is functioning properly if the needle deflects from 0 ohms to infinate ohms.
4. If the vehicle is equipped with ABS, raise the vehicle and support safely. Disconnect the speed sensor connector.
5. Check for continuity between each terminal and the sensor body.
6. Replace the speed sensor if there is continuity in any of the checks.

Codes 62, 63, 64 and 65 (Toyota)
Codes 31, 32, 33 and 34 (Isuzu) –
Solenoid Valve Nos. 1–4, Respectively

SYSTEM CHECK

NOTE: If any of the above codes appear, there is an electronic malfunction with the solenoid(s), computer or wiring. Causes due to mechanical problems such as sticking valves, will not generate a fault code.

1. Disconnect the connector from the computer.
2. Measure the resistance between the suspect solenoid terminal – S1, S2, S3 and S4 (4WD only) – and ground. The specification is 11–15 ohms.

3. If the resistance is within specification, try a known good computer.
4. If the resistance is not within specification, remove the oil pan (solenoid valves 1–3) or transfer case pan (solenoid valve 4) and measure the resistance between the suspect solenoid valve connector and ground. The specification is 11–15 ohms.
5. If the resistance in Step 4 was within specification, but the resistance in Step 2 was not, check the wiring between the solenoid valve and the computer.
6. If the resistance in Step 4 was not within specification, replace the solenoid valve.

SOLENOID VALVES CHECK

1. Remove the solenoid valve from the transmission and measure the resistance between the terminal on the solenoid body and the body itself. The specification is 11–15 ohms.
2. Confirm operation of the solenoid by grounding the body to the negative terminal of a battery and connecting the terminal on the solenoid to the positive terminal of the battery.

NOTE: If there is foreign material in the solenoid valve, there will be no fluid control even though the solenoid is operational.

3. Solenoid valve Nos. 1, 2 and 4 (4WD only) should not leak any air when low pressure compressed air is applied and it is not energized. The valve should open when energized, allowing the compressed air to flow through it. Replace any solenoid valve that is defective or leaky.
4. Solenoid valve No. 3 (for lockup) should be open when NOT energized. Energize the solenoid and apply low pressure compressed air; it should not leak the air. Replace the solenoid valve if it is defective or leaky.

Various Components

THROTTLE POSITION SENSOR (TPS)

TOYOTA

1. Unplug the TPS conector.
2. Check the resistance between the IDL and E2 terminals. With the throttle valve fully closed, the resistance should be less than 2.3 kilo ohms. With the throttle valve fully open, the circuit should be open.
3. Check the resistance between the VC and E2 terminals. The resistance should be 4–9 kilo ohms regardless of throttle position.
4. Check the resistance between the VTA and E2 terminals. With the throttle valve fully closed, the resistance should be 0.2–0.8 kilo ohms. With the throttle valve fully open, the resistance should be 3.3–10.0 kilo ohms.

ISUZU

1. Turn the ignition switch to the **ON** position.
2. Remove the water shield. Do not remove the connector.

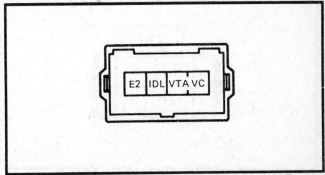

Throttle Position Sensor connector terminals – Toyota

3. Place the positive lead of a voltmeter in the red wire cavity (5 volt source) and the negative lead in the black wire cavity (ground). Confirm that 4.5–5.5 volts are present at the red wire.

4. Switch the positive lead of the voltmeter to the white wire cavity (output). With the throttle valve closed, the voltage should be more than 4 volts. With the throttle valve fully open, the voltage should be less than 2 volts. Also, the difference between the 2 voltage readings should be 2.6–4.6 volts.

NEUTRAL START SWITCH

EXCEPT ISUZU AND 1989 TOYOTA

1. Raise the vehicle and support safely.
2. Unplug the neutral start switch, located on the left side of the transmission.
3. Place the shifter in the **N** detent. There should be continuity between the N and C terminals of the switch.
4. Place the shifter in the **2** detent. There should be continuity between the 2 and C terminals of the switch.
5. Place the shifter in the **L** detent. There should be continuity between the L and C terminals of the switch.

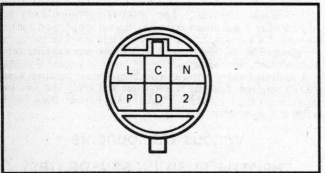

Neutral start switch terminals—except Isuzu and 1989 Toyota

1989 TOYOTA

1. Raise the vehicle and support safely.
2. Unplug the neutral start switch, located on the right side of the transmission.
3. Place the shifter in the **P** detent. There should be continuity between the B and N terminals and the PL or PB and C terminals of the switch.
4. Place the shifter in the **R** detent. There should be continuity between the RL or RB and C terminals of the switch.
5. Place the shifter in the **N** detent. There should be continuity between the B and N terminals and the NL or NB and C terminals of the switch.

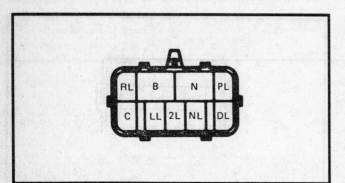

Neutral start switch terminals—1989 Toyota Trucks

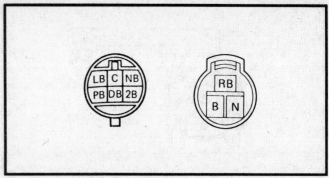

Neutral start switch terminals—1989 Toyota Cressida and Supra

6. Place the shifter in the **D** detent. There should be continuity between the DL or DB and C terminals of the switch.
7. Place the shifter in the **2** detent. There should be continuity between the 2L or 2B and C terminals of the switch.
8. Place the shifter in the **L** detent. There should be continuity between the LL or LB and C terminals of the switch.

ISUZU TROOPER II AND PICK-UP

1. Raise the vehicle and support safely.
2. Unplug the neutral start switch, located on the right side of the transmission.
3. Place the shifter in the **P** detent. There should be continuity between the B and N terminals of the switch.
4. Place the shifter in the **R** detent. There should be continuity between the E and RB terminals of the switch.
5. Place the shifter in the **N** detent. There should be continuity between the B and N terminals of the switch.
6. Place the shifter in the **D** detent. There should be continuity between the E and DB terminals of the switch.

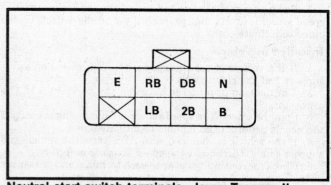

Neutral start switch terminals—Isuzu Trooper II

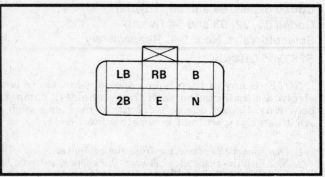

Neutral start switch terminals—Isuzu Pick-up

7. Place the shifter in the **2** detent. There should be continuity between the E and 2B terminals of the switch.

8. Place the shifter in the **L** detent. There should be continuity between the E and LB terminals of the switch.

PATTERN SELECTION SWITCH

TOYOTA EXCEPT 1989 SUPRA AND CRESSIDA

NOTE: As there are diodes in the switch, be careful of the tester probe polarity.

1. Unplug the pattern selection switch.
2. Place the switch in the **NORM** mode. There should be continuity between the 4 and 5 terminals of the switch on 1986–88 trucks and open on 1989 trucks.
3. Place the switch in the **PWR** mode. There should be continuity between the 3 and 5 terminals of the switch.

1989 TOYOTA CRESSIDA AND SUPRA

1. Unplug the pattern selection switch.
2. Place the switch in the **NORM** mode. There should be continuity between the 2 and 4 terminals of the switch.
3. Place the switch in the **PWR** mode. There should be continuity between the 2 and 3 terminals of the switch.

ISUZU TROOPER II AND PICK-UP

1. Unplug the pattern selection switch.
2. Place the switch in the **NORM** mode. There should be continuity between the 1 and 3 terminals of the switch.
3. Place the switch in the **PWR** mode. There should be continuity between the 1 and 2 terminals of the switch.

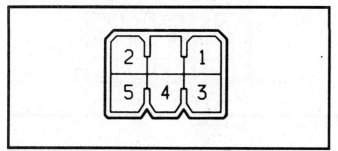

Pattern selection switch terminals — Toyota

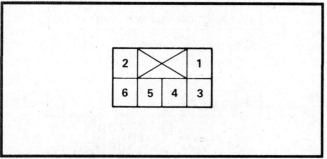

Pattern selection switch terminals — Isuzu

OVERDRIVE OFF SWITCH

TOYOTA

1. Unplug the switch.
2. With the switch in the **ON** position (depressed), there should not be continuity between any terminals.
3. With the switch in the **OFF** position (left up), there should be continuity between terminals 1 and 3 of the switch.

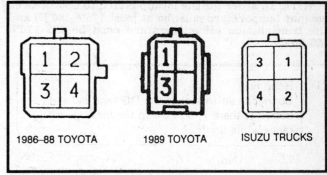

1986–88 TOYOTA   1989 TOYOTA   ISUZU TRUCKS

Overdrive OFF switch terminals

ISUZU

1. Unplug the switch.
2. With the switch in the **ON** position (depressed), there should be continuity between terminals 1 and 2 of the switch.
3. With the switch in the **OFF** position (left up), there should not be continuity between any terminals.

OIL TEMPERATURE SENSOR

1. Remove the sensor from the transmission and heat it in an oil bath.
2. The temperature-to-resistance relationship is as follows:
68°F (20°C) — 5–20 kilo ohms
248°F (120°C) — 540–690 kilo ohms
302°F (150°C) — 300–340 kilo ohms

Converter Clutch Operation and Diagnosis

TORQUE CONVERTER CLUTCH

A lockup clutch operation pattern for each driving mode is programmed in the memory of the transmission computer. Based on this lockup pattern, the lockup solenoid is turned on or off according to signals generated by the vehicle speed sensor and throttle position sensor. The lockup relay valve changes the fluid passages for the converter pressure acting on the torque converter to engage or disengage the lockup clutch.

The lockup solenoid valve will automatically be turned off by the computer every time the brake light switch comes on or when the throttle valve closes. The purpose of these cancellations is so that the engine will not stall if the rear wheels lock.

The lockup solenoid will also be turned off if the vehicle speed drops 2 mph below the set speed of the cruise control system when in use. If the clutch was not to disengage, torque multiplication would be lost and smooth acceleration back to the set speed would be difficult.

The lockup converter does not operate when the coolant or transmission oil temperature is below normal operating temperature. The purpose of this is to improve general cold driveability and to speed up transmission warm up time. Also, the lockup mechanisms temporarily disengeged during upshifts or downshifts to decrease shifting shock.

TROUBLESHOOTING THE TORQUE CONVERTER CLUTCH

1. Warm up and road test the vehicle to confirm that the lockup torque converter does not engage correctly.

NOTE: In order for the lockup clutch to operate, the coolant temperature must be at least 176°F (80°C) and the transmission oil temperature must be 122–176°F (50–80°C).

2. If the lockup torque converter is malfunctioning, follow the appropriate flow chart according to the vehicle being worked on. Check all connectors for corrosion and looseness during the operations

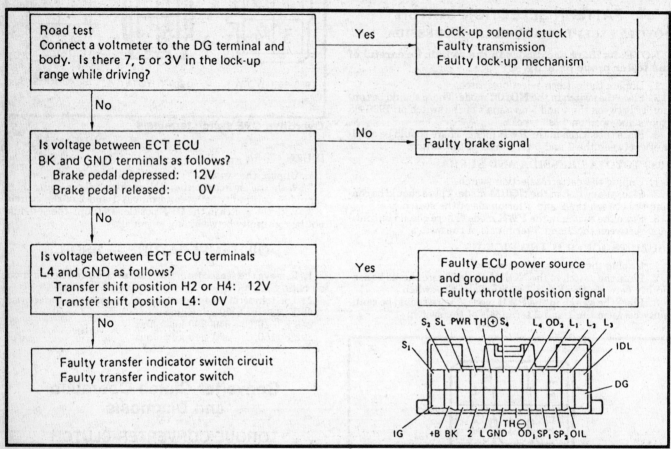

Road test
Connect a voltmeter to the DG terminal and body. Is there 7, 5 or 3V in the lock-up range while driving?

— Yes → Lock-up solenoid stuck / Faulty transmission / Faulty lock-up mechanism

No ↓

Is voltage between ECT ECU BK and GND terminals as follows?
Brake pedal depressed: 12V
Brake pedal released: 0V

— No → Faulty brake signal

No ↓

Is voltage between ECT ECU terminals L4 and GND as follows?
Transfer shift position H2 or H4: 12V
Transfer shift position L4: 0V

— Yes → Faulty ECU power source and ground / Faulty throttle position signal

No ↓

Faulty transfer indicator switch circuit
Faulty transfer indicator switch

Diagnosing the lockup clutch – 1986–88 Toyota Trucks and 1988–89 Isuzu Trucks

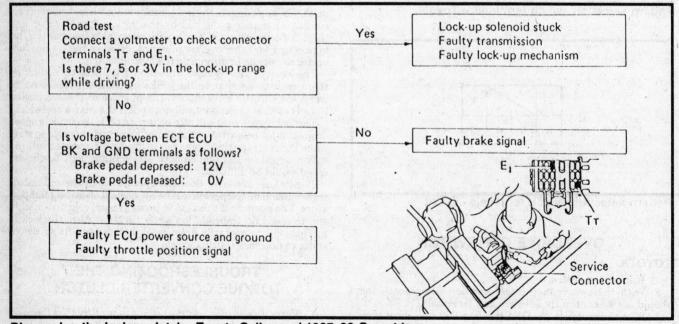

Road test
Connect a voltmeter to check connector terminals Tт and E₁.
Is there 7, 5 or 3V in the lock-up range while driving?

— Yes → Lock-up solenoid stuck / Faulty transmission / Faulty lock-up mechanism

No ↓

Is voltage between ECT ECU BK and GND terminals as follows?
Brake pedal depressed: 12V
Brake pedal released: 0V

— No → Faulty brake signal

Yes ↓

Faulty ECU power source and ground
Faulty throttle position signal

Service Connector

Diagnosing the lockup clutch – Toyota Celica and 1987–88 Cressida

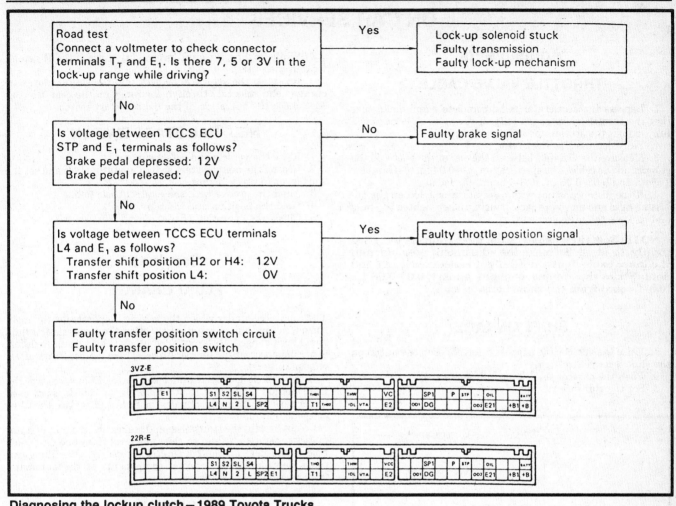

Diagnosing the lockup clutch – 1989 Toyota Trucks

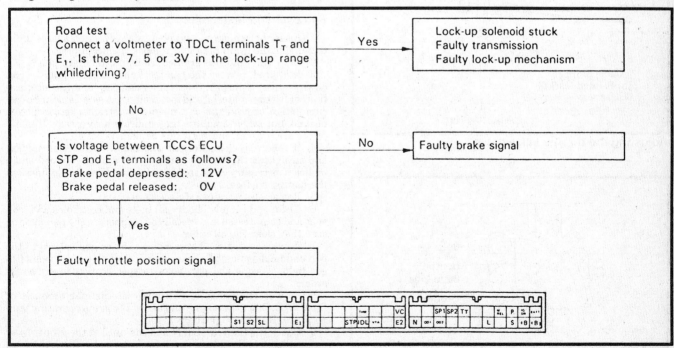

Diagnosing the lockup clutch – 1989 Toyota Cressida

ON CAR SERVICES

Adjustments

THROTTLE VALVE CABLE

1. Depress the accelerator pedal completely and make sure that the throttle valve opens fully. If the valve does not open fully, adjust the accelerator linkage as required.
2. Fully depress the accelerator.
3. Measure the distance between the end of the boot and the stopper on the cable. The specification is 0–0.04 in. (0–1mm) for Toyota and 0.03–0.06 in. (0.8–1.5mm) for Isuzu.
4. If the distance is not within specifications, loosen the adjusting nuts and move the cable housing. Then tighten the nuts and recheck the measurement.

NOTE: Some new cables do not have stoppers installed tightly, or at all. To make the adjustment possible, pull the inner cable lightly until slight resistance is felt and hold. Stake the stopper or paint a mark 0.09–0.06 in. (0.8–1.5mm) from the cable housing end.

SHIFT LINKAGE

1. Raise the vehicle and support safely. Loosen the nut(s) on the shift lever control rod.
2. Push the control shaft lever fully rearward.
3. Set the shift lever to the **N** detent.

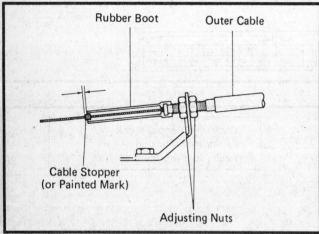

Adjusting the throttle valve cable

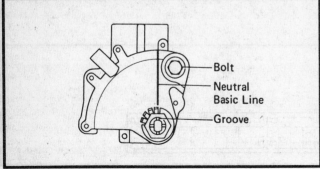

Adjusting the neutral start switch

4. While holding the shift lever lightly toward the **R** detent, tighten the nut(s).
5. Road test the vehicle and check that the shifter moves accurately and smoothly through the range on the gear selector. Also check the operation of the neutral start switch.

NEUTRAL START SWITCH

1. Raise the vehicle and safely support.
2. Loosen the neutral start switch mounting bolt and set the shift lever to the **V** detent.
3. Align the groove with the neutral basic line.
4. Hold the position and tighten the bolt.
5. Check the operation of the neutral start switch.

Services

FLUID CHANGE

The conditions under which the vehicle is operated is the main consideration in determining how often the transmission fluid should be changed. Different driving conditions result in different transmission fluid temperatures. These temperatures affect change intervals.

If the vehicle is driven under severe conditions, change the transmission fluid every 15,000 miles. If the vehicle is not used under severe conditions, change the fluid and replace the filter every 30,000 miles.

Do not overfill the transmission. It takes about a pint of automatic transmission fluid to raise the level from one dimple or hole to the next on the transmission dipstick. Overfilling can cause damage to the internal components of the automatic transmission.

OIL PAN

Removal and Installation

1. Raise the vehicle and support safely. Position a large drain pan under the drain plug and remove the drain plug.
2. After the fluid has drained, reinstall the drain plug.
3. If desired, remove the pan bolts and carefully pull the pan down in order to inspect the strainer and pan for any concentrations of friction material and metal pieces. A small amount of accumulation around the pan magnet or strainer is considered normal, but larger amounts may indicate heavy wear. If metal pieces are present, more serious damage is possible.
4. If removed, clean the pan thoroughly with clean solvent and straighten the mating surface with a block of wood and a mallet if necessary. Pay special attention to the cleanliness of the mating surface.
5. Replace the strainer if necessary.
6. Clean and completely dry all bolts and bolt holes with solvent and compressed air. Install the magnets in the pan making sure they clear the oil tubes.
7. Apply new sealer (Three Bond 1281 or equivalent) to the pan and hold against the case while installing the few bolts finger tight. Torque the pan bolts to specification in crisscross order.
8. Lower the vehicle. Fill with the proper amount of Dexron®II. Start the engine and allow it to get to operating temperature. Run through the gears.
9. Check the fluid level in **N** and add until at the proper lever on the dipstick. Road test, check for leaks and recheck the fluid level on level surface.

VALVE BODY

Removal and Installation

NOTE: The valve body is a precisely machined part used in the automatic transmission. Handle it with care and do not clamp in a vise. The material is fragile and could distort easily. Keep all parts labeled and in a well-arranged order, since many of them look similar. Cleanliness is of the utmost importance when working with valve bodies; even the most minuscule scratch or piece of dirt can restrict valve movement and impair the transmission's performance.

1. Raise the vehicle and support safely. Drain the transmission fluid.
2. Remove the oil pan.
3. Remove the oil strainer and gaskets. Remove the oil strainer case and gaskets, if equipped.
4. Remove the oil tubes carefully.
5. Disconnect the 3 connectors from the solenoids.

NOTE: It is difficult to do Steps 6 and 7 without the aid of a helper. The check ball body and spring along with various accumulator springs and spacers will come out with the valve body. Do not drop or misplace any of the components that are on top of the valve body once it is removed.

6. Remove the valve body mounting bolts (4WD have 16; 2WD have 17). Watch for accumulator spring tension above the valve body.
7. Disconnect the throttle cable from the cam and remove the valve body from the vehicle.
8. Label every spring, spacer and check ball for accurate installation.
9. The accumulators may be serviced by applying low pressure compressed air to the appropriate oil hole and removing the accumulator and corresponding spring(s).

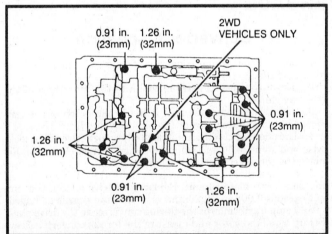

Valve body bolts. The indicated bolt is not installed on 4WD vehicles.

10. To install the valve body, position the check ball body and spring and each accumulator spring and pin in their proper locations on the valve body.
11. Align the groove of the manual valve to the pin on the lever. Lift the body into position and connect the throttle cable to the cam.
12. Install the mounting bolts and torque to 7 ft. lbs. (10 Nm).
13. Connect the solenoids.
14. Install the oil tubes.
15. Install the oil strainer case and gaskets, if equipped. Install the oil strainer and gaskets. Torque all bolts to 7 ft. lbs. (10 Nm). Clamp the solenoid wire.
16. Install the magnets in the pan making sure they clear the oil tubes.
17. Apply new sealer (Three Bond 1281 or equivalent) to the pan and hold against the case while installing the few bolts finger tight. Torque the pan bolts to specification in crisscross order.
18. Lower the vehicle. Fill with the proper amount of Dexron®II. Start the engine and allow it to get to operating temperature. Run through the gears.
19. Check the fluid level in N and add until at the proper lever on the dipstick. Road test, check for leaks and recheck the fluid level on level surface.

PARKING LOCK PAWL

Removal and Installation

1. Raise the vehicle and support safely. Drain the transmission fluid if 2WD or the transfer case fluid if 4WD.
2. Remove the transmission valve body if 2WD or the transfer case valve body if 4WD.
3. Remove the parking lock pawl bracket.
4. Note its positioning and remove the spring from the parking pawl pivot pin.
5. Remove the parking lock pawl pivot and pin.
6. Install the parking lock pawl and parking pawl pivot pin.
7. Install the pivot spring in the correct position.
8. Push the lock rod fully forward.
9. Install the bolts fingertight.
10. Make sure the parking lock pawl operates smoothly and tighten the bolts.
11. Install the valve body and oil pan. Fill the transmission with the proper amount of Dexron®II.

REAR OIL SEAL

Removal and Installation

1. Raise the vehicle and support safely. Position a drain pan to catch fluid that may drip from the extension housing.
2. Remove the driveshaft and center bearing, if equipped.
3. Clean the extension housing before removing the oil seal
4. Remove the defective seal using the special seal puller.
5. Clean the mounting surface and install the new seal using the special installer. Drive in the seal as far as it will go.
6. Install the driveshaft.
7. Lower the vehicle and check the fluid level. Add fluid if necessary.

REMOVAL AND INSTALLATION

TRANSMISSION REMOVAL

1. Remove the negative battery cable.
2. Remove the air intake connector and disconnect the throttle cable from the throttle linkage. Instead of loosing the nuts, unbolt the bracket, if possible. If the nuts are loosened, mark the threads for accurate installation.
3. Disconnect all transmission wiring harnesses, located either near the starter or under the air intake chamber.
4. Remove the upper starter mounting bolt.

5. Raise the vehicle and support safely.

6. Remove the under cover(s), if equipped. Drain the transmission fluid and the transfer case fluid if 4WD.

7. Remove the U-joint cover, if equipped. Matchmark the driveshaft(s) to their flange(s) and remove with center bearing, if equipped.

8. Remove the front exhaust pipe, bracket and hanger.

9. Disconnect the oil cooler pipes from the transmission fittings and transfer case fittings, if 4WD.

10. Disconnect the manual shift linkage. Disconnect the transfer shift linkage and remove the cross shaft from the body, if 4WD.

11. Remove the oil filler tube. The filler tube may be left installed on trucks, if desired.

12. Disconnect the speedometer cable.

13. Remove the stiffener plates, if equipped. Remove the torque converter inspection cover.

14. Remove the torque converter bolts.

15. Using the proper equipment, support the transmission assembly securely and safely. Lift the assembly up slightly to relieve the weight from the rear support member.

16. Remove the rear support member.

17. Remove the starter.

18. Remove the converter housing to engine bolts.

19. Carefully remove the transmission from the vehicle.

TRANSMISSION INSTALLATION

1. Install the filler tube with new O-ring.

2. Apply grease to the center hub of the torque converter and pilot hole in the crankshaft.

3. Using the proper equipment, jack the transmission into place and mount the transmission to the block using the pins as guides.

4. Install the converter housing to engine bolts. If both starter bolts can be installed, do so. If the upper bolt cannot be installed from underneath, install the lower starter bolt just tight enough to hold the starter in place.

5. Install the torque converter bolts and torque gradually to specification.

6. Install the torque converter inspection plate and stiffener plates, if equipped.

7. Jack the assembly up and install the rear support member. Remove the transmission jack.

8. Install the transfer case oil cooler pipes and bracket, if 4WD.

9. Install the speedometer cable.

10. Connect the manual shift linkage.

11. If the cross shaft was removed, apply grease to the joint and install to the body. Connect the transfer case shift linkage.

12. Connect the transmission oil cooler pipes and clamp.

13. Install the exhaust pipe with new gasket, bracket and hanger.

14. Install the driveshaft(s) with center bearing, if equipped. Install the U-joint cover, if equipped. Lower the vehicle.

15. Install the upper starter mount bolt if it was not installed in Step 4. Raise the vehicle back up and properly tighten the lower bolt. Lower the vehicle.

16. Connect the transmission wiring harnesses.

17. Connect the throttle cable to the throttle linkage. Install the bracket, if it was removed. Adjust the cable as required.

18. Install the air intake connector.

19. Connect the negative battery cable.

20. Fill the transmission with the proper amount of Dexron®II.

21. Start the engine and run through the gears.

22. Road test the vehicle, check for leaks and recheck the fluid level.

BENCH OVERHAUL

Before Disassembly

Cleanliness is an important factor in the overhaul of this automatic transmission. Before opening up this unit, the entire outside of the transmission assembly should be cleaned, preferably with a high pressure washer such as a car wash spray unit. Dirt entering the transmission internal parts will negate all the time and effort spent on the overhaul. During inspection and reassembly all parts should be thoroughly cleaned with solvent, then dried with compressed air. Wiping cloths and rags should not be used to dry parts since lint will find its way into the valve body passages.

Wheel bearing grease, long used to hold thrust washers and lubricate parts, should not be used. Lubricate seals with clean transmission fluid and use ordinary unmedicated petroleum jelly to hold thrust washers in place and to ease the assembly of seals, since it will not leave a harmful residue as grease often will. Do not use solvent on neoprene seals, friction plates if they are to be reused, or thrust washers. Be wary of nylon parts if the transmission failure was due to failure of the cooling system. Nylon parts exposed to water or antifreeze solutions can swell and distort and must be replaced.

Before installing bolts into aluminum parts, always dip the threads into clean transmission fluid. Antiseize compound can also be used to prevent bolts from galling the aluminum and seizing. Always use a torque wrench to keep from stripping the threads. Take care when installing new O-rings, especially smaller O-rings. The internal snaprings should be expanded and the external rings should be compressed, if they are to be reused. This will help ensure proper seating when installed.

Converter Inspection

1. Replace the torque converter if external damage of any kind is found.

2. Install the special turning tool into the inner race of the one-way clutch.

3. Install the stopper so that it fits in the notch of the converter hub and outer race of the one-way clutch.

4. The one-way clutch should lock when turned counterclockwise and spin freely and smoothly when turned clockwise. Replace the torque converter if it fails the test.

5. Set up a dial indicator on the rear of the engine block and measure drive plate runout. Replace the drive plate if the runout exceeds 0.008 in. (0.20mm) or if the ring gear is damaged.

6. Temporarily mount the torque converter to the drive plate. Set up a dial indicator and measure the torque converter sleeve runout. If runout exceeds 0.002 in. (0.30mm), try to remount the converter and measure runout again. If excessive runout cannot be corrected, replace the converter.

Transmission Disassembly

2WD VEHICLES

1. Mount the transmission in a suitable holding fixture. Remove the wire harness and throttle cable clamps.

2. Remove the control shaft lever.

3. Remove the neutral start switch, lock washer and grommet.

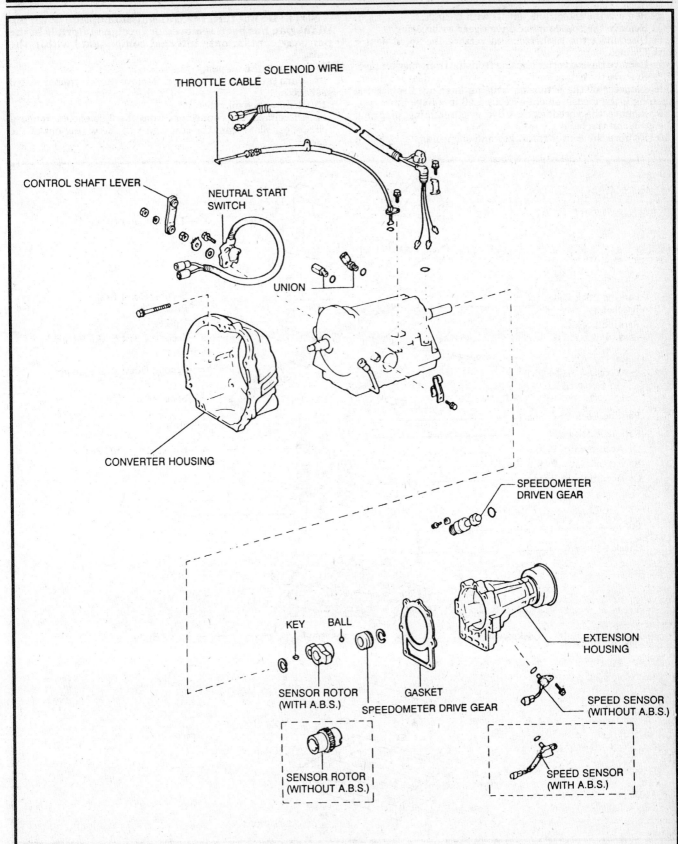

Exploded view of the transmission case and related components

4. Remove the cooler line unions with O-rings.

5. Remove the speedometer driven gear with O-ring.

6. Disconnect the connector and remove the speed sensor with O-ring.

7. Remove the converter housing from the transmission case.

8. Remove the extension housing and gasket. Measure the inside diameter of the extension housing bushing. Replace the bushing if the measurement exceeds 1.58 in. (40.09mm).

9. Remove the speedometer drive gear retaining snapring, the gear and the ball.

10. Remove the sensor rotor, key and snapring.

NOTE: Do not turn the transmission upside down until the pan has been removed or foreign materials in the pan may contaminate internal components within the unit.

11. Remove the oil pan.

12. Turn the transmission over. Remove the oil strainer with 2 gaskets.

13. Remove the oil tubes.

14. Disconnect the connectors from the 3 solenoids. Remove the stopper plate from the case and pull the wiring out of the case.

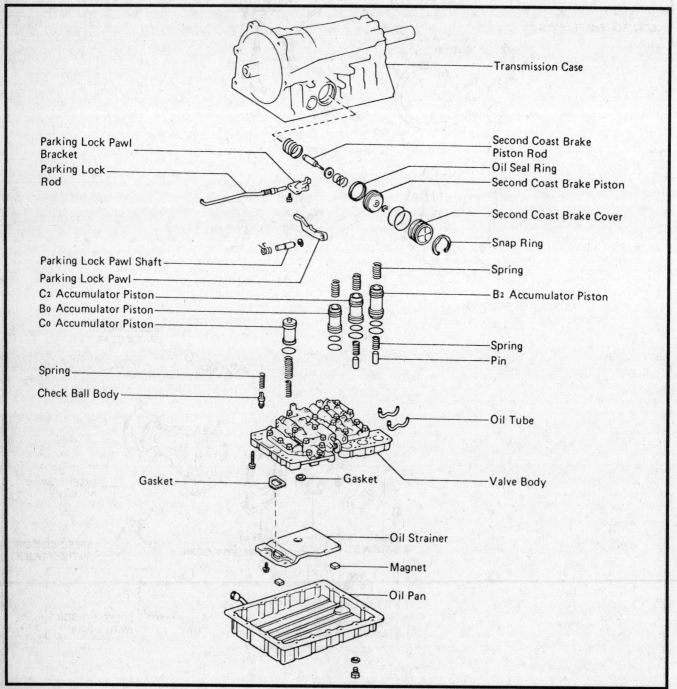

Exploded view of the hydraulic control system. Note that accumulator spring arrangement varies between applications

15. Disconnect the throttle cable from the cam. Remove the 17 valve body bolts and remove the valve body. Remove the check ball body and spring.

16. Label every accumulator spring and pin for accurate reassembly and remove.

17. Apply low pressure compressed air to the corresponding oil holes and remove the 4 accumulators with springs. Keep the parts together and in order.

18. Remove the throttle cable with O-ring.

19. Unbolt the oil pump from the case. Use the special puller to remove the oil pump from the case. Remove the race from the oil pump.

20. Remove the overdrive planetary gear with the overdrive direct clutch and one-way clutch from the case. Remove the race from the bottom of the assembly and the assembled bearing and race from the top.

21. Remove the bearing and race from the top of the overdrive planetary ring gear and remove the ring gear.

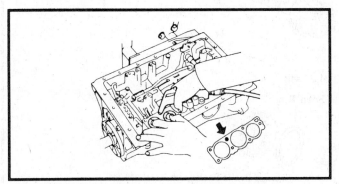

Removing the second brake and direct clutch accumulator pistons

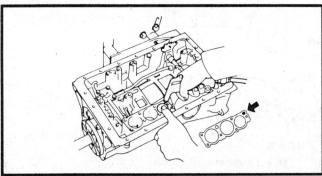

Removing the overdrive brake accumulator piston

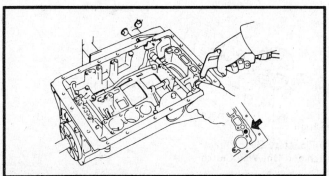

Removing the overdrive direct clutch accumulator piston

22. Remove the overdrive clutches retaining snapring, flanges, plates and discs.

23. Place a mark on the second coast brake piston rod in order to measure the piston stroke. Apply low pressure compressed air to the oil hole and measure the stroke with a drill gauge. The specification is 0.06–0.12 in. (1.5–3.0mm). If the stroke is not within specifications, inspect the band or try a different rod. They are available in 2.81 in. (71.4mm) and 2.87 in. (72.9mm) sizes.

24. Remove the second coast brake pison cover retaining snapring. Apply low pressure compressed air to the apply hole and remove the cover, piston assembly and spring.

25. Remove the thrust bearing and race(s) from the top of the overdrive support assembly.

26. Remove the 2 overdrive support retaining bolts from the bottom of the case. Remove the large snapring.

27. Using the special puller, remove the overdrive support assembly from the case. Remove the race.

28. Remove the direct clutch and forward clutch together from the case. Remove the bearing(s) and race.

29. Remove the E-ring from the brake band pin and remove the pin from the band. Remove the brake band from the case.

30. Remove the race from the top of the front planetary ring gear and remove the ring gear from the case. Remove the bearing and race from the ring gear.

31. Remove the race from the top of the front planetary gear.

32. Stand the transmission on the output shaft, supported with wooden blocks.

33. Remove the snapring and remove the front planetary gear from the case. Remove the bearing and race from inside the planetary gear.

34. Remove the sun gear input drum with one-way clutch.

35. Remove the second brake clutch retaining snapring, flange, plates and discs.

36. Remove the parking lock pawl bracket. Remove the parking lock rod from the manaul valve lever.

37. Remove the spring, parking lock pawl and shaft and remove the E-ring from the shaft.

38. Remove the second brake piston sleeve.

39. Remove the output shaft assembly retaining snapring. Remove the rear planetary gear with second brake drum, 1st/reverse brake pack and output shaft as an assembly. Remove the second brake drum, flange, plates and discs from the assembly.

40. Remove the assembled thrust bearing and race from the case.

41. Remove the brake drum gasket.

42. Apply and release low pressure compressed air to the 1st/reverse brake pistons apply port to ensure smooth piston movement.

43. Set the No. 3 piston spring compressor tool on the spring retainer and compress the return spring. Remove the snapring, the tool and the return spring.

44. Hold the No. 2 first/reverse brake piston by hand, apply low pressure compressed air to the apply port and remove the piston.

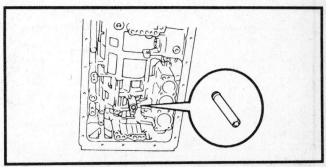

Location of the brake drum gasket

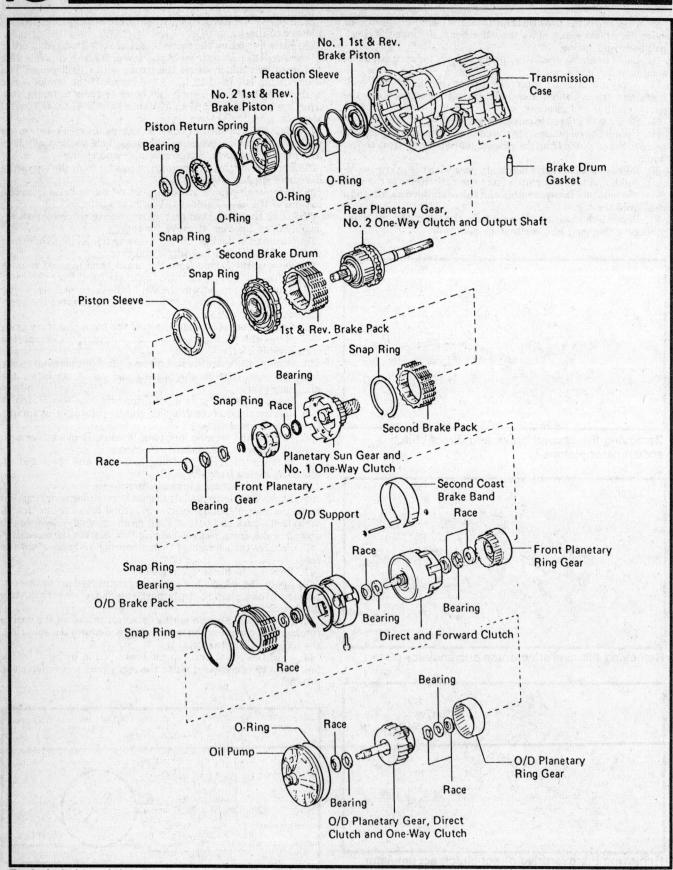

Exploded view of the clutches, brakes and related components

45. Insert the reaction sleeve behind the reaction sleeve and lift it out of the case.

46. Insert the No. 1 brake piston puller behind the No. 1 brake piston and lift it out of the case.

4WD VEHICLES

1. Remove the transmission control shaft lever from the neutral start switch.

2. Remove the neutral start switch

3. Remove the transmission cooling tube unions with O-rings.

4. Remove the oil temperature sensor(s) with O-rings.

5. Remove the transfer case oil cooler tubes, brackets and unions with O-rings. Install a suitable holding fixture to the case.

6. Remove the transfer control shaft lever, transfer position switch, lock washer and grommet.

7. Remove the speedometer driven gear lock plate bolt and lock plate. Pull out the sleeve, remove the clip and remove the driven gear from the sleeve.

8. Remove the speed sensor.

9. Remove the converter housing.

NOTE: Do not turn the transmission upside down until the pan has been removed or foreign materials in the pan may contaminate internal components within the unit.

10. Remove the transmission and transfer case oil pans.

11. Disconnect the No. 4 solenoid and transfer case pressure switch, if equipped, in the transfer case. Remove the solenoid wiring stopper plate and remove the wires from the transfer case.

12. Remove the 6 valve body bolts and remove the transfer case valve body.

13. Remove the parking lock pawl bracket.

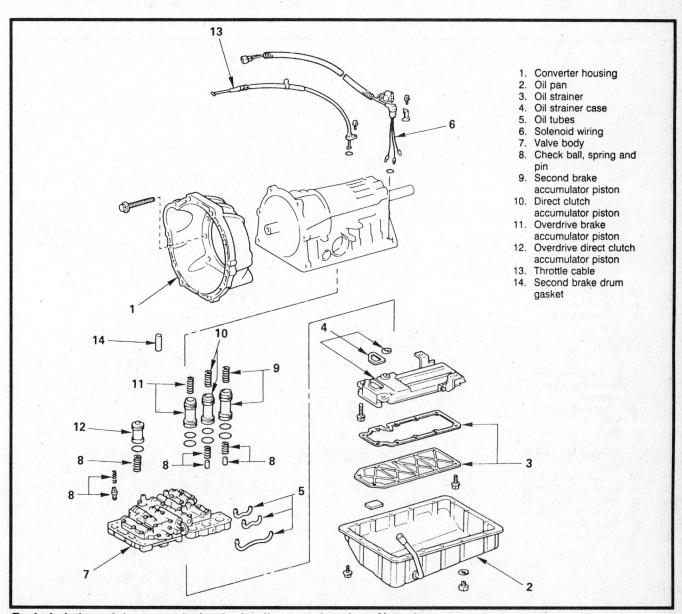

1. Converter housing
2. Oil pan
3. Oil strainer
4. Oil strainer case
5. Oil tubes
6. Solenoid wiring
7. Valve body
8. Check ball, spring and pin
9. Second brake accumulator piston
10. Direct clutch accumulator piston
11. Overdrive brake accumulator piston
12. Overdrive direct clutch accumulator piston
13. Throttle cable
14. Second brake drum gasket

Exploded view of the transmission hydraulic control system. Note that accumulator spring arrangement varies between applications

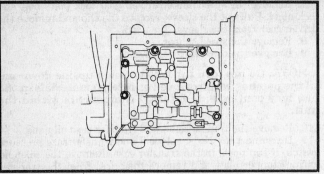

Transfer case valve body mounting bolts

14. Remove the transmission oil strainer and gasket from the oil strainer case. Remove the oil strainer case with 2 gaskets.
15. Remove the oil tubes.

16. Disconnect the 3 solenoid connectors. Remove the stopper plate from the case and pull the wires from the case.
17. Disconnect the throttle cable from the cam. Remove the 16 valve body bolts and remove the valve body. Remove the check ball body and spring.
18. Label every accumulator spring and pin for accurate reassembly and remove.
19. Apply low pressure compressed air to the corresponding oil holes and remove the 4 accumulators with springs. Keep the parts together and in order.
20. Remove the throttle cable with O-ring.
21. Unstake the rear companion flange retaining nut. Using the special holding tool to hold the flange, remove the nut and washer and remove the companion flange.
22. Remove the front companion flange using the same procedure.
23. Remove the transfer case extension housing. Remove the speedometer drive gear.
24. Remove the transfer chain case cover.

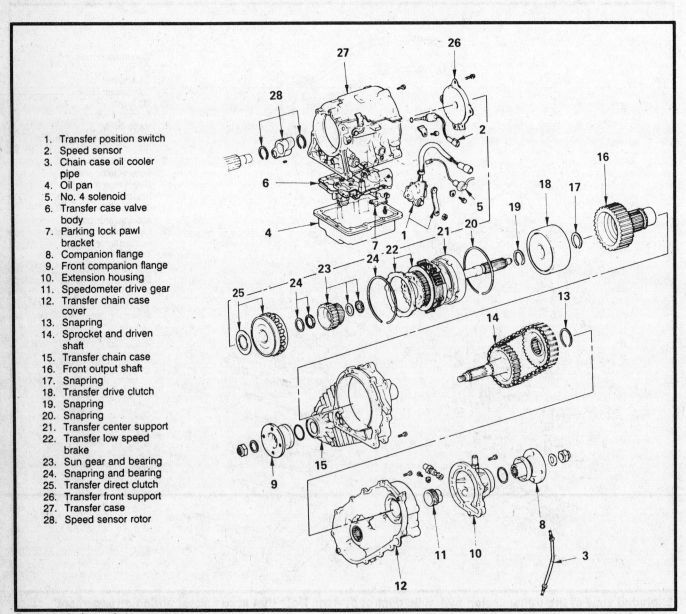

1. Transfer position switch
2. Speed sensor
3. Chain case oil cooler pipe
4. Oil pan
5. No. 4 solenoid
6. Transfer case valve body
7. Parking lock pawl bracket
8. Companion flange
9. Front companion flange
10. Extension housing
11. Speedometer drive gear
12. Transfer chain case cover
13. Snapring
14. Sprocket and driven shaft
15. Transfer chain case
16. Front output shaft
17. Snapring
18. Transfer drive clutch
19. Snapring
20. Snapring
21. Transfer center support
22. Transfer low speed brake
23. Sun gear and bearing
24. Snapring and bearing
25. Transfer direct clutch
26. Transfer front support
27. Transfer case
28. Speed sensor rotor

Exploded view of the transfer system

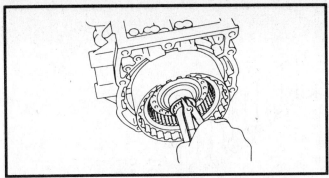

Removing the transfer front drive clutch snapring

25. Remove the snapring from the driven shaft. Remove the drive chain with the drive sprocket and driven shaft.

26. Remove the transfer chain case and front output shaft.

27. Remove the transfer front drive clutch snapring, the clutch assembly and the output shaft snapring.

28. Push the transfer center support forward slightly and remove the large snapring. Grasp the shaft and pull out the center support with the transfer low speed brake assembly. Remove the flange from inside the transfer case and the race and assembled bearing and race from the top of the sun gear.

29. Pull out the sun gear. Remove the race and assembled bearing and race from the transfer direct clutch.

30. Remove the large transfer direct clutch retaining snapring and the clutch assembly from the transfer case.

31. Remove the front support. Remove the assembled bearing and race from the support.

32. Remove the transfer case from the transmission case.

33. Remove the snapring, speed sensor rotor and key and the front snapring.

34. Unbolt the oil pump from the case. Use the special oil pump puller to remove the oil pump from the case. Remove the race from the oil pump.

35. Remove the overdrive planetary gear with the overdrive direct clutch and one-way clutch from the case. Remove the race from the bottom of the assembly and the assembled bearing and race from the top.

36. Remove the bearing and race from the top of the overdrive planetary ring gear and remove the ring gear.

37. Remove the overdrive clutches retaining snapring, flanges, plates and discs.

38. Place a mark on the second coast brake piston rod in order to measure the piston stroke. Apply low pressure compressed air to the oil hole and measure the stroke with a drill gauge. The specification is 0.06–0.12 in. (1.5–3.0mm). If the stroke is not within specifications, inspect the band or try a different rod. They are available in 2.81 in. (71.4mm) and 2.87 in. (72.9mm) sizes.

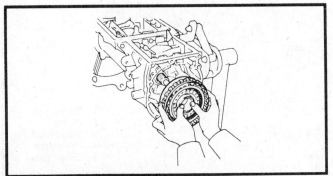

Removing the transfer direct drive

39. Remove the second coast brake piston cover retaining snapring. Apply low pressure compressed air to the apply hole and remove the cover, piston assembly and spring.

40. Remove the thrust bearing and race(s) from the top of the overdrive support assembly.

41. Remove the 2 overdrive support retaining bolts from the bottom of the case. Remove the large snapring.

42. Using the overdrive support puller, remove the overdrive support assembly from the case. Remove the race.

43. Remove the direct clutch and forward clutch together from the case. Remove the bearing(s) and race.

44. Remove the E-ring from the brake band pin and remove the pin from the band. Remove the brake band from the case.

45. Remove the race from the top of the front planetary ring gear and remove the ring gear from the case. Remove the bearing and race from the ring gear. Measure the inside diameter of the front planetary ring gear bushing. The specification is 0.95 in. (24.08mm). If beyond specification, replace the ring gear.

46. Remove the race from the top of the front planetary gear.

47. Stand the transmission on the output shaft, supported with wooden blocks.

48. Remove the snapring and remove the front planetary gear from the case. Remove the bearing and race from inside the planetary gear. Measure the planeary pinion gear clearance. The specification is 0.008–0.040 in. (0.20–1.00mm). If beyond specification, replace the planetary gear assembly.

49. Remove the sun gear input drum with one-way clutch.

50. Remove the second brake clutch retaining snapring, flange, plates and discs.

51. Remove the parking lock pawl bracket. Remove the parking lock rod from the manaul valve lever.

52. Remove the spring, parking lock pawl and shaft and remove the E-ring from the shaft.

53. Remove the second brake piston sleeve.

54. Remove the output shaft assembly retaining snapring. Remove the rear planetary gear with second brake drum, 1st/reverse brake pack and output shaft as an assembly. Remove the second brake drum, flange, plates and discs from the assembly.

55. Remove the assembled thrust bearing and race from the case.

56. Remove the brake drum gasket.

57. Apply and release low pressure compressed air to the 1st/reverse brake pistons apply port to ensure smooth piston movement.

58. Set the No. 3 piston spring compressor tool the spring retainer and compress the return spring. Remove the snapring, the tool and the return spring.

59. Hold the No. 2 first/reverse brake piston by hand, apply low pressure compressed air to the apply port and remove the piston.

60. Insert the reaction sleeve puller behind the reaction sleeve and lift it out of the case.

61. Insert the special puller behind the No. 1 brake piston and lift it out of the case.

Unit Disassembly and Assembly

OIL PUMP

Disassembly

1. Remove the oil seal rings.

2. Remove 13 bolts and remove the stator shaft from the oil pump body.

3. Remove the drive and driven gears from the body.

4. Remove the O-ring from the outside of the pump body.

5. Remove the oil seal from the front of the body.

Inspection

1. Measure the inside diameter of the oil pump body bushing.

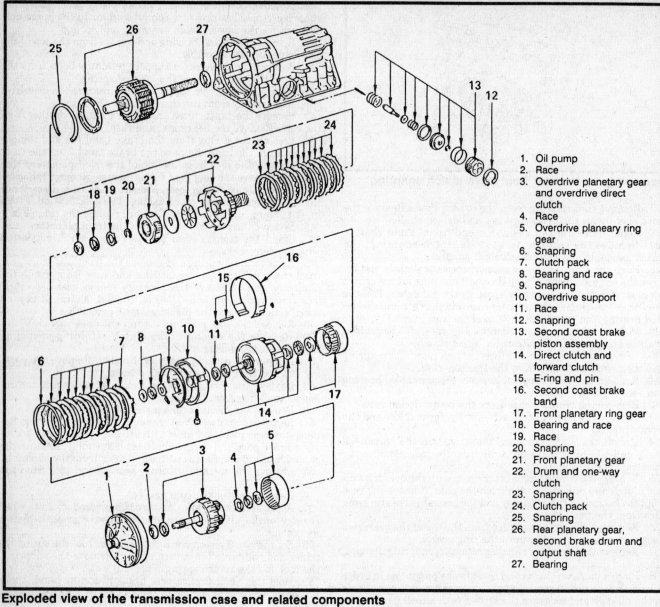

1. Oil pump
2. Race
3. Overdrive planetary gear and overdrive direct clutch
4. Race
5. Overdrive planeary ring gear
6. Snapring
7. Clutch pack
8. Bearing and race
9. Snapring
10. Overdrive support
11. Race
12. Snapring
13. Second coast brake piston assembly
14. Direct clutch and forward clutch
15. E-ring and pin
16. Second coast brake band
17. Front planetary ring gear
18. Bearing and race
19. Race
20. Snapring
21. Front planetary gear
22. Drum and one-way clutch
23. Snapring
24. Clutch pack
25. Snapring
26. Rear planetary gear, second brake drum and output shaft
27. Bearing

Exploded view of the transmission case and related components

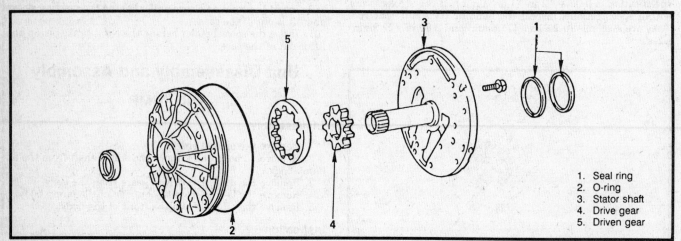

1. Seal ring
2. O-ring
3. Stator shaft
4. Drive gear
5. Driven gear

Exploded view of the oil pump

The maximum inside diameter of the bushing is 1.50 in. (38.19mm). If beyond specification, replace the oil pump body.

2. Measure the inside diameter of the stator shaft bushing. The maximum inside diameter of the front side is 0.85 in. (21.58mm). The maximum inside diameter of the rear side is 1.07 in. (27.08mm). If either is beyond specification, replace the stator shaft.

3. Measure the driven gear body clearance. Push the driven gear to one side of the body. Measure the clearance between the other side of the gear and the body. The specification is 0.003–0.012 in. (0.07–0.30mm). If beyond specification, replace both gears and the body.

4. Measure the driven gear tip clearance. Measure the clearance between the driven gear teeth and the outer edge of the crescent. The specification is 0.004–0.012 in. (0.11–0.30mm). If beyond specification, replace both gears and the body.

5. Using a straight edge and feeler gauge, measure the side clearance of both gears. The specification is 0.001–0.004 in. (0.02–0.10mm). If beyond specification, replace both gears and the body.

Assembly

1. Install a new front seal using the seal installer.
2. Place the pump body in the torque converter. Coat the driven and drive gears with Dexron®II and install in the pump body.
3. Align the stator shaft bolts holes with those in the body and install. Torque the 13 bolts to 7 ft. lbs. (10 Nm).
4. Coat the oil seal rings with Dexron®II and install to the stator shaft. Check the rings for smooth rotation.
5. Make sure the pump drive gear rotates smoothly.
6. Coat the new body O-ring with Dexron®II and install to the groove in the body.

OVERDRIVE PLANETARY GEAR AND OVERDRIVE DIRECT CLUTCH ASSEMBLY

Disassembly

1. Before disassembling, inspect the operation of the one-way

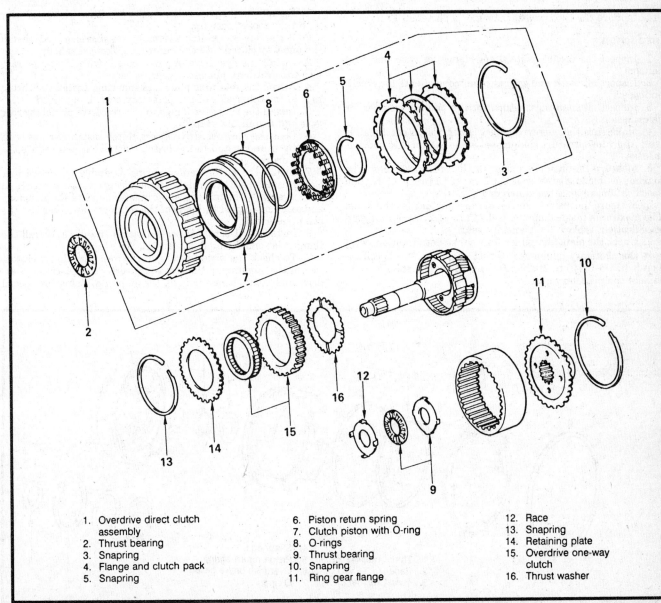

1. Overdrive direct clutch assembly
2. Thrust bearing
3. Snapring
4. Flange and clutch pack
5. Snapring
6. Piston return spring
7. Clutch piston with O-ring
8. O-rings
9. Thrust bearing
10. Snapring
11. Ring gear flange
12. Race
13. Snapring
14. Retaining plate
15. Overdrive one-way clutch
16. Thrust washer

Exploded view of the overdrive planetary gear and overdrive direct clutch assembly

clutch. Hold the direct clutch drum. The input shaft should turn freely and smoothly clockwise and lock counterclockwise.

2. Remove the overdrive direct clutch assembly from the overdrive planetary gear. Remove the thrust race from the other side of the planetary gear, if equipped.

3. Remove the snapring from the overdrive direct clutch drum. Remove the flange, plate(s) and disc(s).

4. Place the spring compressor on the spring retainer and compress the return spring with a shop press. Remove the snapring, the compressor and the piston return spring.

5. Install the oil pump to the torque converter and then place the overdrive direct clutch on the oil pump.

6. Apply low pressure compressed air to the apply port on the oil pump and remove the overdrive direct clutch piston. Remove the O-rings from the piston.

7. Remove the ring gear flange snapring and the flange.

8. Remove the retaining plate snapring and the retaining plate.

9. Remove the overdrive one-way clutch with outer race.

10. If damaged, remove the one-way clutch from the inner race.

11. Remove the thrust washer from the planetary gear.

Inspection

1. Inspect the disc(s), plate(s) and flange for wear and heat damage.

2. Inspect all teeth and splines of all components for cracks and wear.

3. Inspect all snaprings, return springs and the retainer for deformation.

4. Make sure the overdrive direct clutch piston check ball is free. Apply low pressure compressed air to the valve to check is it leaks.

5. Measure the inside diameter of the drum bushings. The maximum inside diameter is 1.07 in. (27.11mm). If beyond specification, replace the clutch drum.

6. Measure the inside diameter of the planetary gear bushing. The maximum inside diameter is 0.44 in. (11.27mm). If beyond specification, replace the planetary gear.

7. Check the planetary pinion for wear smooth rotation. Measure the planetary pinion gear thrust clearance. The specification is 0.008–0.040 in. (0.20–1.00mm). If beyond specification, replace the planetary gear.

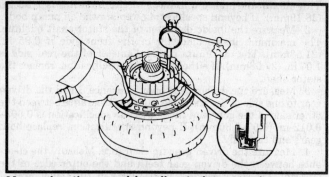

Measuring the overdrive direct piston stroke

8. Inspect the one-way clutch components if the one-way clutch does not function properly. Replace all faulty parts.

Assembly

1. Install the thrust washer to the overdrive planetary gear with the grooved face up.

2. If the one-way clutch assembly was disassembled, install the one-way clutch into the outer race, flanged side up.

3. Install the overdrive one-way clutch with the outer race into the overdrive planetary gear.

4. Install the retaining plate and snapring. Install the thrust race to the other side of the planetary gear, if equipped.

5. Install the ring gear flange to the overdrive planetary ring gear and install the snapring.

6. Coat the new overdrive direct clutch piston O-rings with Dexron®II and install to the piston. Install the piston into the clutch drum.

7. Install the piston return spring assembly on the piston. Compress the return spring with the spring compressor tool and shop press and install the snapring. Make sure the snapring ends are not aligned with any of the retainer claws. Remove the compressor tool.

8. Install the Dexron®II soaked plates and discs. Install the flange, flat end facing down. Install the snapring.

9. To check the piston stroke of the overdrive direct clutch, mount the oil pump in the torque converter and place the overdrive direct clutch assembly on the oil pump. Using the special

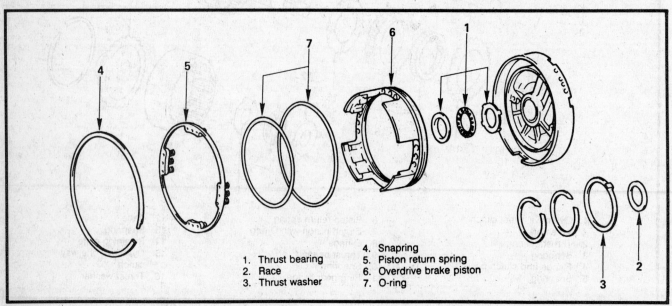

1. Thrust bearing
2. Race
3. Thrust washer
4. Snapring
5. Piston return spring
6. Overdrive brake piston
7. O-ring

Exploded view of the overdrive support assembly

No. 2 measuring terminal tool and a dial indicator, measure the piston stroke by applying low pressure compressed air to the apply port in the oil pump. The specification is 0.07–0.08 in. (1.8–2.1mm). If the stroke is not within limits, check for incorrect assembly. If nothing is found, use a different flange. Selective flanges are available in the following thicknesses:

No. 16 – 0.142 in. (3.6mm)
No. 17 – 0.138 in. (3.5mm)
No. 18 – 0.134 in. (3.4mm)
No. 19 – 0.130 in. (3.3mm)
No. 20 – 0.126 in. (3.2mm)
No. 21 – 0.122 in. (3.1mm)

10. Install the direct clutch assembly onto the overdrive planetary gear.
11. Check the operation of the one-way clutch.

OVERDRIVE SUPPORT ASSEMBLY

Disassembly

1. Remove the clutch drum thrust washer from the overdrive support.
2. Place the special spring compressor on the spring retainer and compress the spring using a shop press. Remove the snapring and the compressor. Remove the return spring.
3. Place the overdrive support on the direct clutch assembly. Hold the overdrive brake piston so it does not slant inside the support.
4. Apply low pressure compressed air to the proper oil hole in the support and remove the brake piston.
5. Remove the O-rings from the piston.
6. Remove the oil seal rings from the overdrive support.

Inspection

1. Inspect the support for damage of any type.
2. Inspect the piston for cracks or scrapes.
3. Inspect the bearing and races for wear and roughness.
4. Inspect the seal grooves for burrs.
5. Inspect all snaprings, return springs and the retainer for deformation.

Assembly

1. Coat the new oil seal rings with Dexron®II and install to the overdrive support. Make sure the rings rotate smoothly.

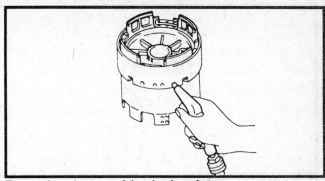

Removing the overdrive brake piston

2. Coat the new piston O-rings with Dexron®II and install to the piston. Install the piston into the support.
3. Place the piston return spring on the piston making sure the springs fit into the holes properly.
4. Place the special compressor on the spring and compress with a shop press. Install the snapring. Make sure the snapring ends are not aligned with the cutouts of the overdrive support. Remove the compressor.
5. Coat the thrust washer with petroleum jelly and install to the support. make sure the lug on the thrust washer fits into the hole in the support.
6. Place the overdrive support assembly on the direct clutch assembly. Apply and release low pressure compressed air to the apply hole to ensure smooth piston movement.

DIRECT CLUTCH ASSEMBLY

Disassembly

1. Remove the direct clutch assembly from the forward clutch assembly.
2. Remove the clutch drum thrust washer.
3. Remove ths snapring from inside the drum.
4. Remove the flange, plates and discs.
5. Place the spring compressor on the spring retainer and compress the return spring with a shop press. Remove the snapring, the compressor and the return spring.

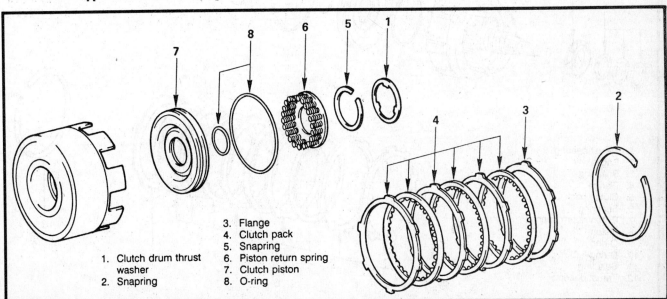

1. Clutch drum thrust washer
2. Snapring
3. Flange
4. Clutch pack
5. Snapring
6. Piston return spring
7. Clutch piston
8. O-ring

Exploded view of the direct clutch assembly

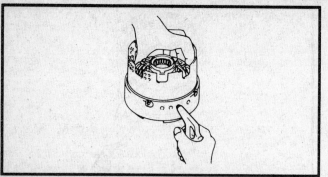

Removing the direct clutch piston

6. Place the direct clutch drum on the overdrive support. Apply low pressure compressed air to the proper oil hole in the support and remove the piston. Remove the O-rings from the piston.

Inspection

1. Inspect the discs, plates and flange for wear and heat damage.
2. Inspect all snaprings, return springs and the retainer for deformation.
3. Make sure the direct direct clutch piston check ball is free. Apply low pressure compressed air to the valve to check is it leaks.
4. Measure the inside diameter of the direct clutch drum bushings. The maximum inside diameter is 2.12 in. (54.00mm). If beyond specification, replace the clutch drum.

Assembly

1. Coat the new piston O-rings with Dexron®II and install to the piston. Install the piston into the drum.
2. Place the return spring on the piston. Place the spring compressor on the spring retainer and compress the spring with a shop press. Install the snapring, making sure the snapring ends are not aligned with any of the retainer claws. Remove the compressor.
3. Install the Dexron®II soaked plates and discs. Install the flange, flat end facing down.
4. Install the snapring making sure the snapring ends are not aligned with the cutouts of the direct clutch drum.
5. To check the direct clutch piston stroke, place the direct clutch assembly on the overdrive support assembly. Using the special No. 2 measuring terminal tool and a dial indicator, measure the piston stroke by applying low pressure compressed air to the apply port in the support. The specification is 0.05–0.07 in. (1.37–1.64mm) for all applications except Toyota trucks with 22R-E engine and Isuzu. The specifications for the above is 0.04–0.05 in. (1.03–1.33mm). If the stroke is not within limits, check for incorrect assembly. If nothing is found, use a different flange. Selective flanges are available in the following thicknesses:

No. 33 — 0.118 in. (3.0mm)
No. 32 — 0.122 in. (3.1mm)
No. 31 — 0.126 in. (3.2mm)
No. 30 — 0.130 in. (3.3mm)
No. 29 — 0.134 in. (3.4mm)
No. 28 — 0.138 in. (3.5mm)
No. 27 — 0.142 in. (3.6mm)
No. 34 — 0.146 in. (3.7mm)

6. Coat the thrust washer with petroleum jelly and install to

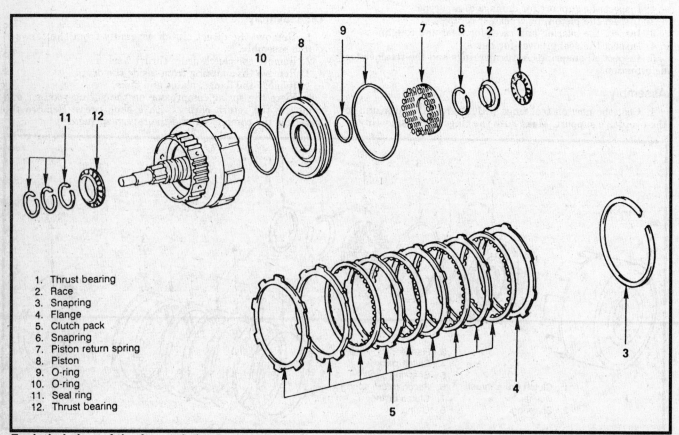

1. Thrust bearing
2. Race
3. Snapring
4. Flange
5. Clutch pack
6. Snapring
7. Piston return spring
8. Piston
9. O-ring
10. O-ring
11. Seal ring
12. Thrust bearing

Exploded view of the forward clutch assembly

the support. make sure the lug on the thrust washer fits into the hole in the support.

FORWARD CLUTCH ASSEMBLY

Disassembly

1. Place wooden blocks under the overdrive support to prevent the forward clutch shaft from touching the work surface and place the forward clutch on the overdrive support.
2. Remove the snapring from the forward clutch drum. Remove the flange, plates and discs.
3. Remove the cushion plate.
4. Place the spring compressor on the spring retainer and compress the return spring with a shop press. Remove the snapring, the compressor and the return spring.
5. Place the forward clutch drum on the overdrive support.

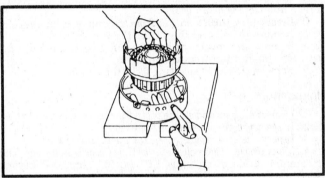

Removing the forward clutch piston

Apply low pressure compressed air to the proper oil hole in the support and remove the piston. Remove the O-rings from the piston.

6. Remove the O-ring from the forward clutch drum.
7. Remove the oil seal rings from the forward clutch shaft.

Inspection

1. Inspect the discs, plates and flange for wear and heat damage.
2. Inspect all snaprings, return springs and the retainer for deformation.
3. Make sure the forward clutch piston and clutch drum check balls are free. Apply low pressure compressed air to the piston valve to check is it leaks.
4. Measure the inside diameter of the direct clutch drum bushings. The maximum inside diameter is 0.95 in. (24.08mm). If beyond specification, replace the clutch drum.

Assembly

1. Install the assembled bearing and race to the drum. Coat the new forward clutch shaft oil seal rings with Dexron®II and install to the shaft. Make sure the rings rotate smoothly. Place the forward clutch drum in the overdrive support using the set-up with the wooden blocks.
2. Coat the new forward clutch drum O-ring with Dexron®II and install to the drum.
3. Coat the new piston O-rings with Dexron®II and install to the piston. Install the piston into the drum.
4. Place the return spring on the piston. Place the spring compressor on the spring retainer and compress the spring with a shop press. Install the snapring, making sure the snapring ends are not aligned with any of the retainer claws. Remove the compressor.

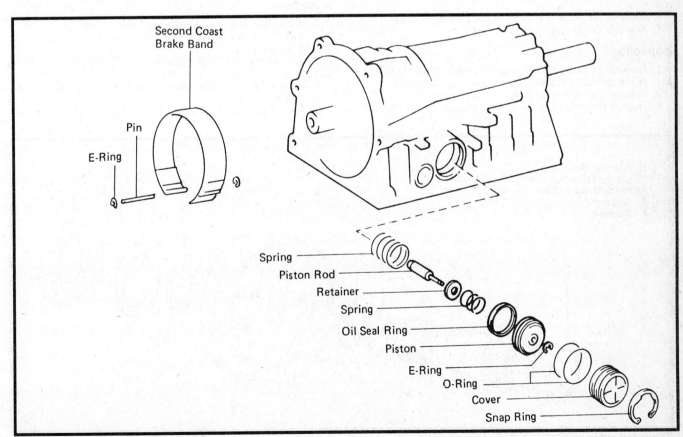

Second coast brake components

5. Install the cushion plate with the rounded side facing down.

6. Install the Dexron®II soaked plates and discs into the drum. Install the flange, rounded side facing down.

7. To check the forward clutch piston stroke, place the forward clutch assembly on the overdrive support assembly. Using the special No. 2 measuring terminal tool and a dial indicator, measure the piston stroke by applying low pressure compressed air to the apply port in the support. The specifications are:
1986–87 Toyota Trucks – 0.11–0.15 in. (2.75–3.88mm)
1988–89 Toyota Trucks with 22R-E engine and Isuzu – 0.12–0.15 in. (3.11–3.88mm)
1989 Toyota Trucks with 3VZ-E engine – 0.13–0.17 in. (3.42–4.24mm)
Cressida and Supra with 7M-GE engine – 0.13–0.17 in. (3.42–4.24mm)
Supra with 7M-GTE engine – 0.15–0.18 in. (3.73–4.59mm)
If the stroke is not within limits, check for incorrect assembly.

8. Coat the race and bearing with petroleum jelly and install to the drum.

9. Install the direct clutch assembly to the forward clutch assembly.

10. Check that the distance from the direct clutch end to the end of the forward clutch shaft is 2.80 in. (71.2mm). If the distance is not correct, something has been incorrectly installed; do not continue until the cause has been resolved.

SECOND COAST BRAKE

Disassembly

1. Remove the E-ring from the end of the piston rod.
2. Remove the piston, spring and retainer from the piston rod.
3. Remove the oil seal ring from the piston.
4. Remove the O-rings from the cover.

Inspection

1. Inspect the brake band lining for peeling or glazing. If any part of the printed numbers are defaced, replace the band.
2. Inspect the piston for scrapes and pitting.
3. Inspect the snapring, E-ring and springs for deformation.

Assembly

1. Coat the oil seal ring with Dexron®II and install to the second coast brake piston
2. Install the retainer, spring and piston to the piston rod.
3. Secure the assemble with the E-ring.
4. Coat the new O-rings with Dexron®II and install to the cover.

PLANETARY SUN GEAR AND NO. 1 ONE-WAY CLUTCH

Disassembly

1. Before disassembling, check the operation of the one-way clutch. Hold the planetary sun gear and turn the second brake hub. The hub should turn freely and smoothly clockwise and lock counterclockwise.
2. Remove the assembled No. 1 one-way clutch and second brake hub from the sun gear.
3. Remove the thrust washer from the sun gear input drum.
4. Remove the oil seal rings from the sun gear.
5. Remove the snapring from the sun gear and remove the sun gear input drum from the sun gear.
6. Remove the other snapring from the sun gear.

Inspection

1. Inspect all gear and spline teeth for cracks, chips and wear.
2. Inspect the thrust washer for wear.
3. Inpect the seal ring grooves for burrs and cracks.
4. Measure the inside diameter of the sun gear bushings. The maximum inside diameter is 1.07 in. (27.08mm). If beyond specification, replace the sun gear.

Assembly

1. Install the snapring on the sun gear.
2. Install the sun gear input drum to the planetary sun gear. Install the snapring.
3. Coat the new oil seal rings with Dexron®II and install to the sun gear. Make sure the rings rotate freely.
4. Install the thrust washer, making sure the lugs fit into the holes in the input drum.
5. Install the assembled No. 1 one-way clutch and second

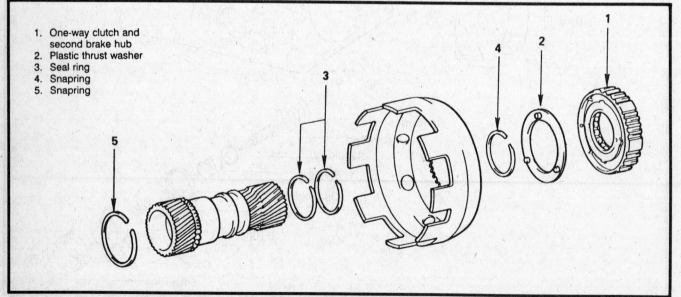

1. One-way clutch and second brake hub
2. Plastic thrust washer
3. Seal ring
4. Snapring
5. Snapring

Exploded view of the planetary sun gear and No. 1 one-way clutch

brake hub on the planetary sun gear with the taller edge of the hub facing up.

6. Recheck the operation of the one-way clutch.

SECOND BRAKE ASSEMBLY

Disassembly

1. Remove the thrust washer from the second brake drum.
2. Place the spring compressor on the spring retainer and compress the return spring with a shop press. Remove the snapring, the compressor, the retainer and the return spring.
3. Apply low pressure compressed air to the apply hole in the brake drum to remove the second brake piston. Remove the O-rings from the piston.

Inspection

1. Inspect the piston and drum for scrapes and cracks.
2. Inspect the O-ring grooves for burrs.
3. Inspect the bushings for wear.
4. Inspect the snaprings and springs for deformation.

Assembly

1. Coat the new O-rings with Dexron®II and install to the piston.
2. Install the piston into the drum.
3. Install the return spring and retainer. Place the compressor on the retainer and compress the spring with a press. Install the snapring.
4. Check for piston movement by applying and releasing low pressure compressed air to the oil hole on the outside of the drum.
5. Coat the thrust washer with petroleum jelly and install to

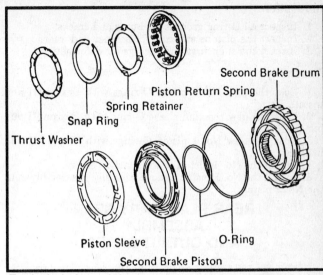

Exploded view of the second brake assembly

the drum. Make sure the cutouts of the thrust washer match the teeth in the spring retainer.

1ST/REVERSE BRAKE

Disassembly

1. Remove the O-ring from the No. 2 piston.
2. Remove the O-ring from the reaction sleeve.
3. Remove the O-rings from the No. 1 piston.

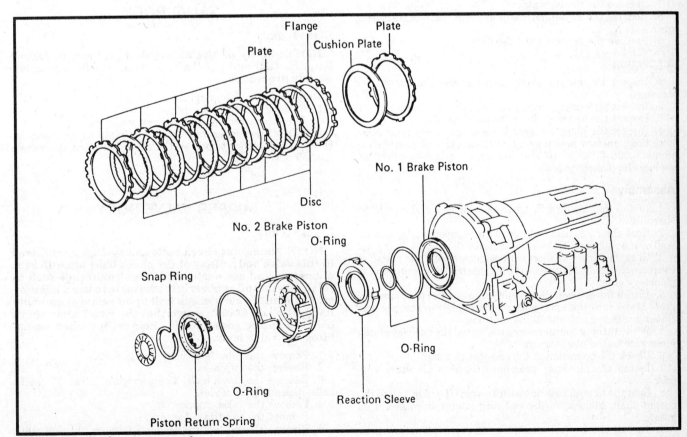

1st/reverse brake components

Inspection

1. Inspect all O-ring grooves for burrs and cracks.
2. Inspect the pistons and case for scrapes and wear.
3. Inspect the snaprings and springs for deformation.

Assembly

1. Coat the new No. 1 piston O-rings with Dexron®II and install.
2. Coat the new reaction sleeve O-ring with Dexron®II and install.
3. Coat the new No. 1 piston O-rings with Dexron®II and install.
4. Install the No. 1 piston to the reaction sleeve.
5. Install the No. 1 piston and reaction sleeve assembly onto the No. 2 piston.

REAR PLANETARY GEAR ASSEMBLY AND OUTPUT SHAFT

1. Remove the output shaft from the rear planetary gear assembly.
2. Remove the oil seal ring from the output shaft.
3. Remove the rear planetary gear from the rear planetary ring gear.
4. To check the operation of the No. 2 one-way clutch, hold the planetary gear and turn the one-way clutch inner race. The inner race should turn freely and smoothly counterclockwise and lock clockwise.
5. Remove the one-way clutch inner race from the planetary gear.
6. Remove the snapirng and the one-way clutch with retainers from the planetary gear.
7. Remove the thrust washers.
8. Remove the races and bearings from the planetary ring gear.
9. Remove the snapring and the flange.

Inspection

1. Inspect the output shaft for wear and the splines for damage.
2. Inspect all bearings, races and washers for wear.
3. Inspect the one-way clutch for any damage.
4. Inspect the planetary gear for damage of any type. Measure the planetary pinion gear thrust clearance. The specification is 0.008–0.039 in. (0.60–1.00mm). If beyond specification, replace the planetary gear.

Assembly

1. Install the ring gear flange in the ring gear and install the snapring.
2. Coat the races and bearings with petroleum jelly and install to the ring gear. Make sure both race flanges are facing up.
3. Coat the thrust washers with petroleum jelly and install to the planetary gear. Make sure the lugs match the cutouts on the planetary gear.
4. Install the one-way clutch and retainers into the planetary gear. Make sure the open ends of the guides on the one-way clutch are facing up. Install the snapring.
5. While turning counterclockwise, install the one-way clutch inner race to the planetary gear.
6. Check the operation of the one-way clutch.
7. Install the planetary gear onto the rear planetary ring gear.
8. Coat the new oil seal ring with Dexron®II and install to the output shaft. Make sure the seal ring rotates smoothly in its groove.
9. Install the output shaft into the rear planetary gear assembly.

MANUAL VALVE LEVER SHAFT AND CASE BUSHING

Disassembly

NOTE: It is not necessary to disassemble the manual valve lever mechanism unless it is damaged and needs replacing.

1. Cut off the spacer and remove it from the shaft.
2. Drive out the roll pin.
3. Pull the manual valve lever shaft out through the case and remove the lever.
4. Remove the oil seals.

Inspection

1. Inspect the manual valve lever components for damage and replace faulty parts.
2. Measure the inside diameter of the transmission case rear bushing. The maximum inside diameter is 1.50 in. (38.19mm). If beyond specification, replace the bushing if available; otherwise replace the case.

Assembly

1. Install the new oil seals.
2. Assembly the new spacer to the manual shaft lever.
3. Install the manual valve lever shaft to the case through the manual valve lever.
4. Drive the roll pin into the shaft.
5. Match the spacer hole to the lever calking hollow and calk the spacer to the lever.
6. Make sure the manual valve shaft turns smoothly.

VALVE BODY

Disassembly

NOTE: Many of the assembly bolts are different lengths. Take note of their locations during the disassembly procedure.

1. Remove the detent spring.
2. Remove the manual valve.
3. Turn the assembly over and remove 25 bolts.
4. Lift off the upper valve body and plate as an assembly. Hold them together tightly so the check balls and strainer do not fall out.

UPPER VALVE BODY

Disassembly

NOTE: Numerous check balls and springs are utilized in this valve body. Many of the check balls are different diameters and are made of different materials such as steel, plastic and rubber. It it advisable to use a micrometer to identify each check ball upon removal and note its location. It is imperative that the exact same check ball and spring goes back in their orifice when assembling the valve body.

1. Remove the valve body plate and gaskets.
2. Remove the strainer.
3. Remove the check balls. There may be 8, 9 or 10 checks balls, depending on model.
4. Remove the valve stopper.
5. Remove the throttle valve cam.
6. Remove the pin with a magnet. Remove the downshift plug, spring and throttle valve.

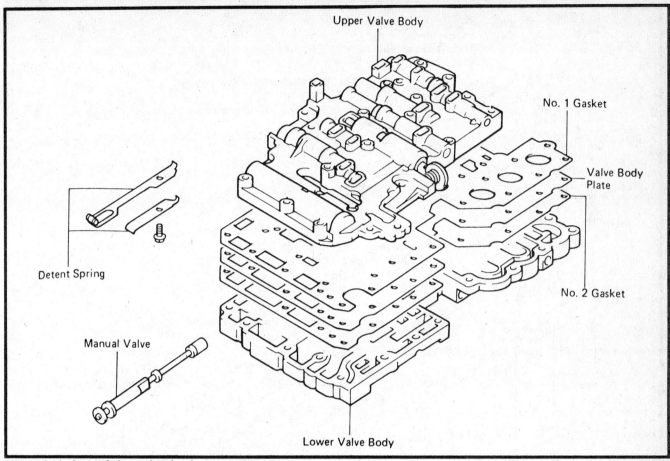

Exploded view of the valve body assembly

NOTE: The throttle pressure is changed according to the number of throttle rings used. Count the number of rings before removing so that the throttle pressure is not changed. Some units do not have any rings.

7. Turn the assembly over and remove the spring and adjusting rings.

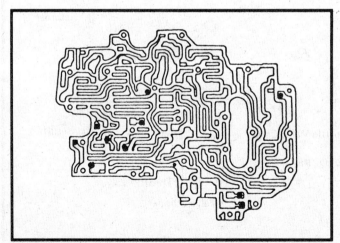

Locations of check balls in the upper valve body. The number of check balls varies according to application

8. Remove the 3/4 shift valve retainer, plug, valve and spring.
9. Remove the second coast modulator valve retainer, plug, valve and spring.
10. Remove the lockup relay valve retainer, sleeve with plunger, spring and valve. Remove the relay valve, spring and plunger from the sleeve.
11. Remove the secondary regulator valve retainer, plug, valve and spring.
12. Remove the cutback valve retainer, plug, valve and spring.
13. Remove the 2/3 shift valve retainer, plug, spring and valve.
14. Remove the low coast modulator valve retainer, plug, spring and valve.

Inspection

1. Check the body for damage, wear and cracks.
2. Check the valves, plugs and their bores for damage and burrs. Slight burrs may be sanded out with crocus cloth only.
3. Check for oil passage damage and restrictions.
4. Check for spring fatigue and rust.
5. Inspect the strainer for clogging and damage. Clean or replace as necessary.

Assembly

1. Install the low coast modulator valve, spring, plug and retainer.
2. Install the 2/3 shift valve, spring, plug and retainer.
3. Install the cutback valve spring, valve, plug and retainer.
4. Install the secondary regulator valve spring, valve, plug and retainer.
5. Install the plunger 'rand spring into the sleeve. Install the

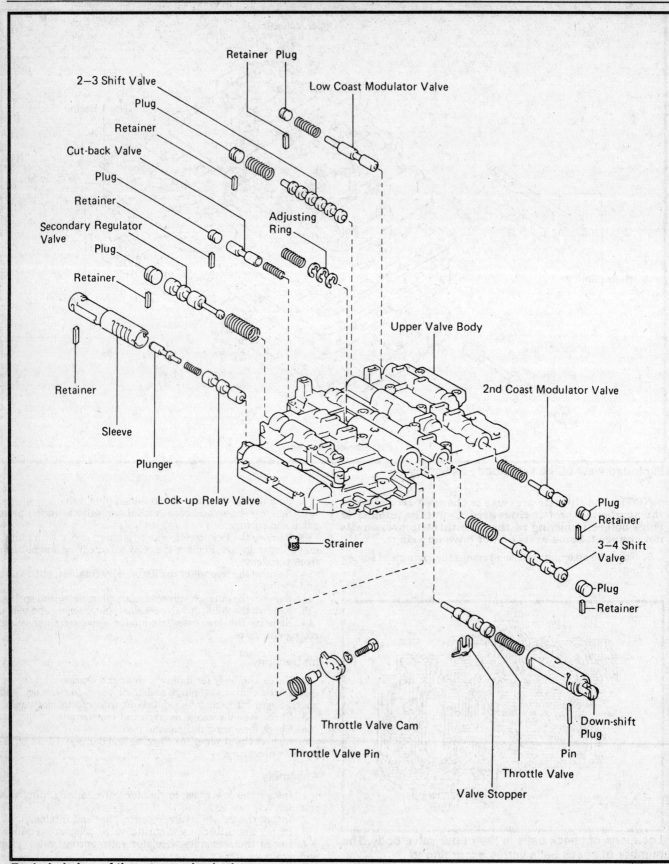

Retainer   Plug

Low Coast Modulator Valve

2—3 Shift Valve

Plug

Retainer

Cut-back Valve

Plug

Retainer

Secondary Regulator Valve

Plug

Retainer

Retainer

Sleeve

Plunger

Lock-up Relay Valve

Adjusting Ring

Upper Valve Body

2nd Coast Modulator Valve

Strainer

Plug

Retainer

3—4 Shift Valve

Plug

Retainer

Throttle Valve Cam

Throttle Valve Pin

Down-shift Plug

Pin

Throttle Valve

Valve Stopper

Exploded view of the upper valve body

lockup relay valve into the sleeve. Install the sleeve with plunger, spring and relay valve into the bore and install the retainer.

6. Install the second coast modulator valve spring, valve, plug and retainer.

7. Install the 3/4 shift valve spring, valve, plug and retainer.

8. Install the throttle valve and stopper. Turn the valve body over and install the same number of adjusting rings as was removed during the disassembly procedure. Install the spring on the end of the valve shaft.

9. Install the downshift plug spring, plug and retainer.

10. Insert the sleeve through one side of the cam. Install the spring to the cam. Install the cam on the upper valve body. Make sure the spring end engages with the body. Torque the mounting bolt to 7 ft. lbs. (10 Nm).

11. Make sure the pin, valve stopper and 7 retainers are installed properly.

12. Install the check balls and hold each in place with petroleum jelly.

13. Install the strainer.

LOWER VALVE BODY

Disassembly

1. Remove the check valve, pressure relief valve and springs.

2. Remove the 3 strainers.

3. Remove the check valve with steel ball and other check balls, if equipped.

4. Remove the 3 solenoids and remove their O-rings

5. Remove the release control valve retainer, plug and valve.

6. Remove the 1/2 shift valve retainer, plug, spring and valve.

> **CAUTION**
>
> *There is a highly compressed spring behind the primary regulator valve. Exercise caution when removing the valve or personal injury may result.*

7. Matchmark the bevel to the primary valve retainer so that the pieces can be realigned when assembling.

8. Remove the retainer, sleeve with plunger, spring and washer. Remove the primary regulator valve. Remove the plunger from the sleeve.

9. Remove the pressure reducing plug retaining clip and plug.

10. Remove the accumulator control valve retainer, sleeve with control valve and spring. Remove the valve and sprig from the sleeve.

Inspection

1. Check the body for damage, wear and cracks.

2. Check the valves, plugs and their bores for damage and burrs. Slight burrs may be sanded out with crocus cloth only.

3. Check for oil passage damage and restrictions.

4. Check for spring fatigue and rust.

5. Inspect the strainers for clogging and damage. Clean or replace them as necessary.

Assembly

1. Install the accumulator valve and spring into the sleeve. Install the assembled sleeve into the bore and install the retainer.

2. Install the pressure reducing plug and install the clip into the groove in the plug.

3. Install the washer onto the primary regulator valve. Install the primary regulator valve with washer into the valve body. Install the plunger into the sleeve and install the assembled sleeve

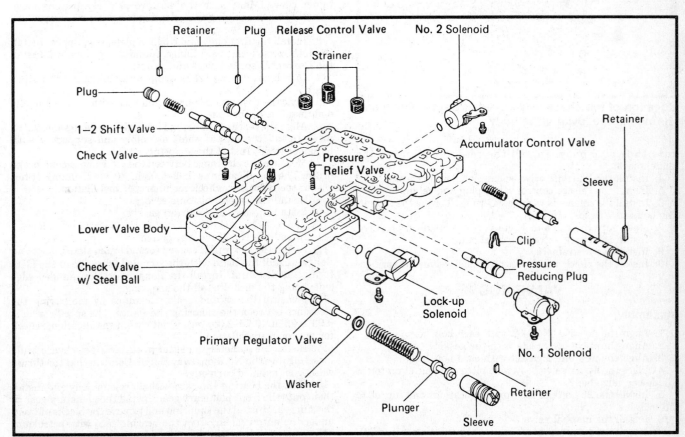

Exploded view of the lower valve body

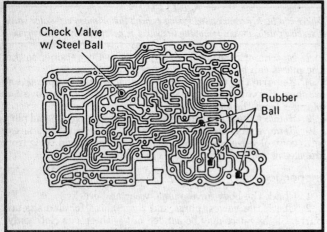

Locations of check balls in the lower valve body. Valve bodies may have 0, 1 or 3 rubber balls

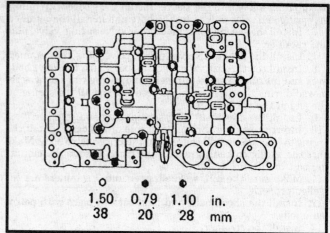

Valve body bolt lengths

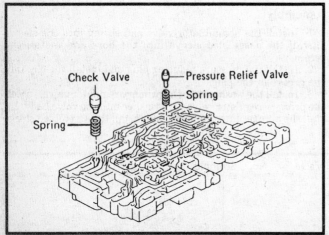

Location of the check valve, pressure relief valve and springs in the lower valve body

into the valve body. Install the retainer aligning the matchmarks.

4. Install the 1/2 shift valve, spring, plug and retainer.
5. Install the release control valve, plug and retainer.
6. Install the solenoids with new O-rings. Torque the mounting bolts to 7 ft. lbs. (10 Nm).
7. Make sure the clip and 4 retainers are installed properly.
8. Install the check valve with steel ball.
9. Install the 3 strainers.
10. Install the check valve, pressure relief valve and springs.

VALVE BODY

Assembly

1. Align the new No. 1 gasket with each bolt hole.
2. Align the valve body plate with the gasket.
3. Align the new No. 2 gasket with each bolt hole.
4. Place the upper valve body with plate and gasket on top of the lower valve body.
5. Install the 25 bolts in their proper locations and torque to 56 inch lbs. (6.4 Nm).
6. Install the manual valve.
7. Install the detent spring. Torque the mounting bolt to 7 ft. lbs. (10 Nm).

Transmission Assembly

4WD VEHICLES

1. Align the teeth of the No. 2 first/reverse brake piston into the proper grooves and install the Nos. 1 and 2 pistons into the case.
2. Place the return spring on the No. 2 piston. Compress the spring with the spring compressor and install the snapring. Make sure the snapring ends are not aligned with any of the retainer claws. Make sure the 1st/reverse brake pistons move smoothly when applying and releasing low pressure compressed air to the hole in the case.
3. Install the first plate and cushion plate, if equipped. Install the 1st/reverse brake pack flange, rounded edge forward. Install the Dexron®II soaked discs and plates.
4. Install the second brake drum assembly onto the output shaft.
5. Coat the assembled bearing and race with petroleum jelly and install it to the case.
6. Align the teeth of the second brake drum, flange and clutch pack. Install the output shaft assembly and support it with blocks of wood. Install the snapring.
7. Measure the clearance between the plate and second brake drum. The specification is 0.02–0.08 in. (0.51–2.10mm). If not within specifications, check for improper installation.
8. Install the second piston sleeve.
9. Install the new brake drum gasket.
10. Connect the parking lock rod to the manual valve lever.
11. Install the No. 1 one-way clutch.
12. Install the Dexron®II soaked second brake plates, discs and flange. Install the plate with the rounded edge side of the plate facing the disc first. Install the flange with the rounded edge side facing the disc. Install the snapring.
13. Measure the second brake clearance by measuring the clearance between the snapring and flange. The specification is 0.03–0.08 in. (0.76–2.05mm). If not within specifications, check for improper installation.
14. Install the planetary sun gear by turning it clockwise while inserting into the No. 1 one-way clutch. Confirm that the thrust washer is installed correctly.
15. Coat the bearing and race with petroleum jelly and install them onto the front planetary gear. Install the planetary gear to the sun gear. Install the snapring and remove the blocks of wood under the output shaft. Coat the bearing race with petroleum jelly and install it to the planetary gear fitting the lugs into the holes.

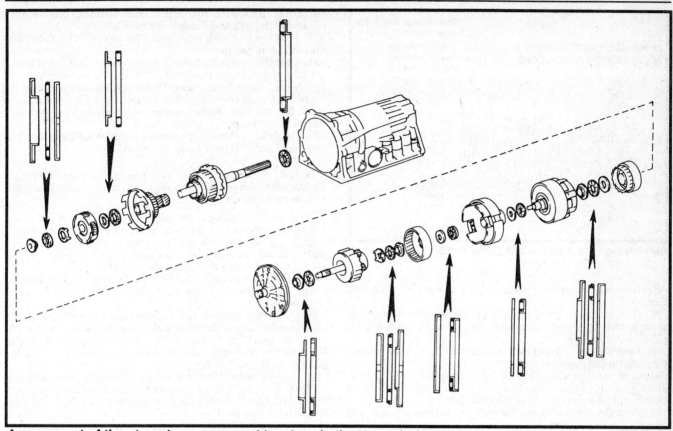

Arrangement of thrust washers, races and bearings in the transmission

16. Install the second coast brake band into the case. Install the pin through the band and install the E-ring to the pin.

17. Coat the bearing and race with petroleum jelly and install them onto the forward clutch.

18. Coat the race with petroleum jelly and install it to the front planetary ring gear. Install the front planetary ring gear to the forward clutch.

19. Coat the bearing and race with petroleum jelly and install them to the ring gear. Install the assembled direct clutch, forward clutch and front planetary ring gear into the transmission case.

20. Measure the distance between the sun gear input drum and the direct clutch drum. The specification is 0.386–0.465 in. (9.80–11.80mm). If not within specifications, check for improper installation. Do not continue until the specification is met.

21. Coat the assembled bearing and race with petroleum jelly and install it to the forward clutch.

22. Install the second coast brake spring, piston assembly and cover with new O-rings to the case. Install the snapring.

23. Remeasure the piston stroke. Apply low pressure compressed air to the oil hole and measure the stroke with a drill gauge. The specification is 0.06–0.12 in. (1.5–3.0mm). If the stroke is not within specifications, reinspect the band or try a different rod. Piston rods are available in 2.81 in. (71.4mm) and 2.87 in. (72.9mm) sizes.

24. Coat the race with petroleum jelly and install it to the bottom of the overdrive support assembly

25. Using 2 bolts of the oil pump puller tool assembly, install the overdrive support with the bolt holes and oil hole in line with those on the valve body side of the transmission case and install the snapring. Install the 2 bolt and torque to 19 ft. lbs. (25 Nm).

26. Measure the output shaft endplay. The specification is 0.01–0.03 in. (0.27–0.86mm). If not within specifications, check

Checking the overdrive brake piston stroke

for improper installation. Do not continue until the specification is met. Make sure the output shaft rotates smoothly.

27. Install the flat 0.157 in. (4.0mm) thick overdrive brake flange with the rounded edge facing the disc. Install the Dexron®II soaked discs and plates. Install the stepped flange with the flat side facing the disc. Install the snapring.

28. To check the piston stroke of the overdrive brake, use the special No. 2 measuring terminal tool and a dial indicator and measure the piston stroke by applying low pressure compressed air to the apply port in the case. The specification is 0.05–0.07 in. (1.30–1.80mm). If the stroke is not within limits, check for incorrect assembly. If nothing is found, use a different flange. Selective flanges are available in the following thicknesses:

No. 26 – 0.130 in. (3.3mm)
No. 25 – 0.138 in. (3.5mm)
No. 12 – 0.142 in. (3.6mm)
No. 24 – 0.146 in. (3.7mm)
No. 11 – 0.150 in. (3.8mm)
No. 23 – 0.154 in. (3.9mm)
None – 0.157 in. (4.0mm)

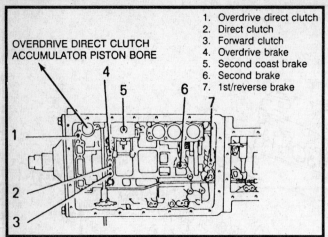

OVERDRIVE DIRECT CLUTCH
ACCUMULATOR PISTON BORE

1. Overdrive direct clutch
2. Direct clutch
3. Forward clutch
4. Overdrive brake
5. Second coast brake
6. Second brake
7. 1st/reverse brake

Identifying oil holes for checking piston movement

After the specification is met, remove the clutch pack and flanges.

29. Coat the bearing and race with petroleum jelly and install them to the top of the overdrive support. Install the overdrive planetary ring gear.

30. Coat the bearing and race with petroleum jelly and install them to the ring gear.

31. Coat the race with petroleum jelly and install it to the planetary gear. Install the planetary gear with the overdrive direct clutch and one-way clutch. to the ring gear.

32. Coat the assembled bearing and race with petroleum jelly and install to the overdrive direct clutch. Reinstall the overdrive brake clutch pack and flanges in order.

33. Coat the race with petroleum jelly and install it to the bottom of the oil pump.

34. Coat the new pump body O-ring with Dexron®II and install the oil pump through the input shaft. Hold the input shaft and lightly press the oil pump body to slide the oil seal rings into the overdrive clutch drum. Install the attaching bolts and torque to 16 ft. lbs. (22 Nm). Make sure the input shaft turns smoothly before continuing.

35. Apply and release low pressure compressed air to each piston apply port to check their operation.

NOTE: When checking the overdrive direct clutch, check with the overdrive direct clutch accumulator piston bore blocked.

If there is no operating noise from any of the pistons, disassemble as necessary and correct the problem before continuing.

36. Install the snapring and speed sensor rotor key on the output shaft. Align the groove of the sensor rotor with the key and install the sensor rotor. Install the snapring.

37. Clean the mating surfaces of the transmission and transfer cases. Apply sealer (Three Bond 1281 or equivalent) to the transfer case.

38. Confirm that the 2 apply gaskets are correctly installed.

39. Install the transfer case; make sure the parking lock rod is above the pawl. The 3 lower bolts are equal length and shorter than the 4 middle bolts, which are also equal length. Torque the bolts to 25 ft. lbs. (34 Nm).

40. Coat the assembled bearing and race with petroleum jelly and install it to the front support. Confirm the apply gasket is installed correctly. Install the front support and torque the bolts to 25 ft. lbs. (34 Nm).

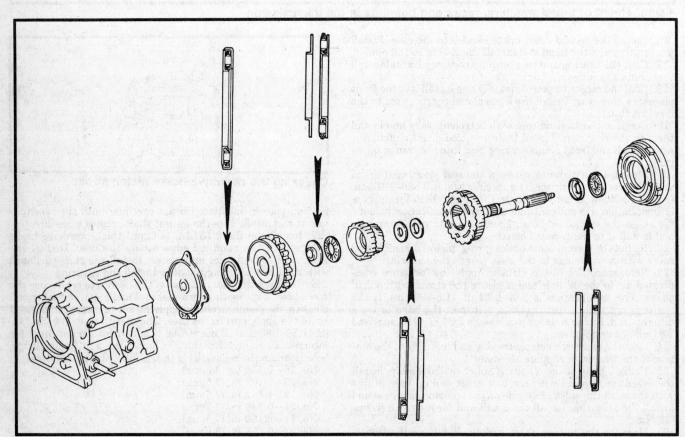

Arrangement of thrust washers, races and bearings in the transfer case assembly

41. Coat the race with petroleum jelly and install it onto the front support.

42. Coat the assembled bearing and race with petroleum jelly and install it to the sun gear. Install the sun gear to the transfer direct clutch.

43. Install the transfer direct clutch with the sun gear. Shift the manual valve lever to the **P** detent and confirm that the transfer direct clutch drum is correctly engaged by the pawl.

44. Coat the assembled bearing and race with petroleum jelly and install to the sun gear. Install the snapring.

45. Coat the races with petroleum jelly and install them onto the planetary gear and planetary ring gear. Install the output shaft with the planetary ring gear.

46. Install the front transfer low speed bake flange. Install the plates, discs, rear flange and cushion plate, rounded end facing rearward.

47. Install the transfer low speed brake piston return spring.

48. Coat the assembled bearing and race with petroleum jelly and install it onto the center support. Install the center support to the case, aligning the oil holes and bolt hole. Push the center support forward and install the snapring.

49. Install the snapring to the output shaft. Install the front drive clutch and install the snapring.

50. Install the front output shaft into the transfer front drive clutch.

51. Clean the mating surfaces of the transfer chain front case and transfer case. Apply sealer (Three Bond 1281 or eqivalent) to the transfer case.

52. Install the transfer chain front case to the transfer case. Apply sealant (Three Bond 1324 or equivalent) to the bolt threads and torque the bolts to 25 ft. lbs. (34 Nm).

53. Install the transfer chain oil receiver to the transfer chain front case. Apply sealant (Three Bond 1324 or equivalent) to the bolt threads and torque to 7 ft. lbs. (10 Nm).

54. Install the drive chain together with the drive sprocket and driven shaft and install the snapring.

55. Clean the mating surfaces of the transfer chain front and rear cases. Apply sealer (Three Bond 1281 or equivalent) to the chain rear case and install to the front case. The 2 end bolts are longer than the rest, which are equal length. Torque the bolts to 25 ft. lbs. (34 Nm).

56. Clean the mating surfaces of the transfer oil pump and the transfer chain rear case. Apply sealer (Three Bond 1281 or equivalent) to the chain case. Install the oil pump and torque the bolts to 12 ft. lbs. (16 Nm).

57. Install the speedometer drive gear.

58. Clean the mating surfaces of the extension housing and chain case. Apply sealer (Three Bond 1131 or equivalent) to the extension housing and install. The 2 top bolts are longer than the other 4, which are equal length. Torque the bolts to 25 ft. lbs. (34 Nm).

59. Coat the new O-ring with Dexron®II and install to the inside of the rear companion flange. Install the companion flange and washer to the shaft. Using the special holding tool to hold the flange, torque the nut to 90 ft. lbs. (123 Nm). Stake the nut.

60. Install the front companion flange following the same procedure as for the rear.

61. Check for an operating noise while applying and releasing low pressure compressed air to each of the apply holes. If there is no noise in any of the pistons, disassemble as necessary t resolve the problem.

62. Coat the new throttle cable O-ring with Dexron®II and install to the cable. Install the cable in the case.

63. Coat the new accumulator piston O-rings with Dexron®II and install them in their bores with all springs and pins in the exact same positions as when removed.

64. Install the check ball body and spring.

65. Align the groove of the manual valve with the pin of the lever. Connect the throttle lever to the cam and install the transmission valve body. Make sure the accumulator springs are still in position when the valve body is installed. Torque the bolts to 7 ft. lbs. (10 Nm).

66. Coat the new O-ring with Dexron®II and install to the transmission wire harness grommet. Install the wiring harness to the case and install the stopper plate. Connect the solenoid connectors.

67. Install the oil tubes.

68. Install 2 new gaskets to the oil strainer case. Install the case and torque the bolts to 7 ft. lbs. (10 Nm).

69. Install a new gasket to the oil strainer case and install the strainer. Torque the bolts to 61 inch lbs. (6.9 Nm).

70. Install the parking lock pawl bracket. Torque the bolts to 61 inch lbs. (6.9 Nm).

71. Coat the new O-ring with Dexron®II and install to the transfer case wire harness grommet. Install the wiring harness to the case and install the stopper plate.

72. Align the groove of the manual valve with the pin of the lever and install the transfer case valve body. Torque the 6 bolts to 7 ft. lbs. (10 Nm). Connect the solenoid connectors and clamp the wiring.

73. Clean the mating surfaces of the 2 pans and respective cases and install the magnets in such positions so that they will not interfere with the oil tubes. Apply sealer (Three Bond 1281 or equivalent) to the pans and install. Torque the bolts to 65 inch lbs. (7.4 Nm).

74. Install the converter housing. Torque the 10mm bolts to 25 ft. lbs. (34 nM0. Torque the 12mm bolts to 42 ft. lbs. (57 Nm).

75. Coat the new O-ring with Dexron®II and install to the speed sensor. Install the speed sensor and stopper plate and connect the connector.

76. Install the transfer position switch and loosely install the adjusting bolt. Install the grommet, new lock washer and nut and torque to 35 inch lbs. (3.9 Nm).

77. Place the lever into the **4H** position and align the basic line with the switch groove. Torque the bolt to 9 ft. lbs. (13 Nm) and bend at least 2 tabs of the lock washer over.

78. Install the transfer control shaft lever.

79. Coat the new O-ring with Dexron®II and install and install to the speedometer driven gear sleeve. Insert the driven gear into the sleeve and install the clip. Install the sleeve into the extension housing. Install the lockplate and torque the bolt to 12 ft. lbs. (16 Nm).

80. Install the transfer case side unions with new O-rings.

81. Install the transfer case oil cooler tubes and secure with the clamp brackets.

82. Install the transmission and transfer case fluid temperature sensors with new O-rings.

83. Install the transmission cooler tube unions with new O-rings.

84. Install the neutral start switch onto the manual valve lever shaft and loosely install the adjusting bolt. Install the grommet and new lock washer. Torque the nut to 61 inch lbs. (6.9 Nm).

85. Using the control shaft lever, turn the manual lever shaft fully backwards and return 2 notches to the **N** detent. Align the neutral basic line with the switch groove. Torque the bolt to 9 ft. lbs. (13 Nm) and bend at least 2 tabs of the lock washer over.

86. Install the transmission control shaft lever.

87. Install the wire harness clamps.

2WD VEHICLES

1. Align the teeth of the No. 2 first/reverse brake piston into the proper grooves and install the Nos. 1 and 2 pistons into the case.

2. Place the return spring on the No. 2 piston. Compress the spring with the spring compressor and install the snapring. Make sure the snapring ends are not aligned with any of the retainer claws. Make sure the 1st/reverse brake pistons move smoothly when applying and releasing low pressure compressed

air to the hole in the case.

3. Install the 1st/reverse brake pack flange, rounded edge forward. Install the Dexron®II soaked discs and plates.

4. Install the second brake drum assembly onto the output shaft.

5. Coat the assembled bearing and race with petroleum jelly and install it to the case.

6. Align the teeth of the second brake drum, flange and clutch pack. Install the output shaft assembly and support it with blocks of wood. Install the snapring.

7. Measure the clearance between the plate and second brake drum. The specification is 0.02–0.08 in. (0.51–2.10mm). If not within specifications, check for improper installation.

8. Install the second piston sleeve.

9. Install the new brake drum gasket.

10. Install the E-ring to the parking pawl sgaft. Install the parking lock pawl, shaft and spring.

11. Connect the parking lock rod to the manual valve lever. Install the bracket. Shift the manual valve lever into the **P** detent and confirm that the lock pawl engeages the planetary ring gear correctly.

12. Install the No. 1 one-way clutch.

13. Install the Dexron®II soaked second brake plates, discs and flange. Install the plate with the rounded edge side of the plate facing the disc first. Install the flange with the rounded edge side facing the disc. Install the snapring.

14. Measure the second brake clearance by measuring the clearance between the snapring and flange. The specification is 0.03–0.08 in. (0.76–2.05mm). If not within specifications, check for improper installation.

15. Install the planetary sun gear by turning it clockwise while inserting into the No. 1 one-way clutch. Confirm that the thrust washer is installed correctly.

16. Coat the bearing and race with petroleum jelly and install them onto the front planetary gear. Install the planetary gear to the sun gear. Install the snapring and remove the blocks of wood under the output shaft. Coat the bearing race with petroleum jelly and install it to the planetary gear fitting the lugs into the holes.

17. Install the second coast brake band into the case. Install the pin through the band and install the E-ring to the pin.

18. Coat the bearing and race with petroleum jelly and install them onto the forward clutch.

19. Coat the race with petroleum jelly and install it to the front planetary ring gear. Install the front planetary ring gear to the forward clutch.

20. Coat the bearing and race with petroleum jelly and install them to the ring gear. Install the assembled direct clutch, forward clutch and front planetary ring gear into the transmission case.

21. Measure the distance between the sun gear input drum and the direct clutch drum. The specification is 0.386–0.465 in. (9.80–11.80mm). If not within specifications, check for improper installation. Do not continue until the specification is met.

22. Coat the assembled bearing and race with petroleum jelly and install it to the forward clutch.

23. Install the second coast brake spring, piston assembly and cover with new O-rings to the case. Install the snapring. Remeasure the piston stroke. Apply low pressure compressed air to the oil hole and measure the stroke with a drill gauge. The specification is 0.06–0.12 in. (1.5–3.0mm). If the stroke is not within specifications, reinspect the band or try a different rod. Piston rods are available in 2.81 in. (71.4mm) and 2.87 in. (72.9mm) sizes.

24. Coat the race with petroleum jelly and install it to the bottom of the overdrive support assembly

25. Using 2 bolts of the oil pump puller tool assembly, install the overdrive support with the bolt holes and oil hole in line with those on the valve body side of the transmission case and install the snapring. Install the 2 bolt and torque to 19 ft. lbs. (25 Nm).

26. Measure the output shaft endplay. The specification is 0.01–0.03 in. (0.27–0.86mm). If not within specifications, check for improper installation. Do not continue until the specification is met. Make sure the output shaft rotates smoothly.

27. Install the flat 0.157 in. (4.0mm) thick overdrive brake flange with the rounded edge facing the disc. Install the Dexron®II soaked discs and plates. Install the stepped flange with the flat side facing the disc. Install the snapring.

28. To check the piston stroke of the overdrive brake, use the special No. 2 measuring terminal tool and a dial indicator and measure the piston stroke by applying low pressure compressed air to the apply port in the case. The specification except for Supra with 7M-GTE engine is 0.05–0.07 in. (1.30–1.80mm). The specification for Supra with 7M-GTE engine is 0.07–0.08 in. (1.75–2.05mm). If the stroke is not within limits, check for incorrect assembly. If nothing is found, use a different flange. Selective flanges are available in the following thicknesses:

No. 26 — 0.130 in. (3.3mm)
No. 25 — 0.138 in. (3.5mm)
No. 12 — 0.142 in. (3.6mm)
No. 24 — 0.146 in. (3.7mm)
No. 11 — 0.150 in. (3.8mm)
No. 23 — 0.154 in. (3.9mm)
None — — — 0.157 in. (4.0mm)

After the specification is met, remove the clutch pack and flanges.

29. Coat the bearing and race with petroleum jelly and install them to the top of the overdrive support. Install the overdrive planetary ring gear.

30. Coat the bearing and race with petroleum jelly and install them to the ring gear.

31. Coat the race with petroleum jelly and install it to the planetary gear. Install the planetary gear with the overdrive direct clutch and one-way clutch. to the ring gear.

32. Coat the assembled bearing and race with petroleum jelly and install to the overdrive direct clutch. Reinstall the overdrive brake clutch pack and flanges in order.

33. Coat the race with petroleum jelly and install it to the bottom of the oil pump.

34. Coat the new pump body O-ring with Dexron®II and install the oil pump through the input shaft. Hold the input shaft and lightly press the oil pump body to slide the oil seal rings into the overdrive clutch drum. Install the attaching bolts and torque to 16 ft. lbs. (22 Nm). Make sure the input shaft turns smoothly before continuing.

35. Apply and release low pressure compressed air to each piston apply port to check their operation.

NOTE: When checking the overdrive direct clutch, check with the overdrive direct clutch accumulator piston bore blocked.

If there is no operating noise from any of the pistons, disassemble as necessary and correct the problem before continuing.

36. Coat the new O-ring with Dexron®II and install to the throttle cable. Install the cable to the case.

37. Coat the new accumulator piston O-rings with Dexron®II and install them in their bores with all springs and pins in the exact same positions as when removed.

38. Install the check ball body and spring.

39. Align the groove of the manual valve with the pin of the lever. Connect the throttle lever to the cam and install the valve body. Make sure the accumulator springs are still in position when the valve body is installed. Torque the bolts to 7 ft. lbs. (10 Nm).

40. Coat the new O-ring with Dexron®II and install to the transmission wire harness grommet. Install the wiring harness to the case and install the stopper plate. Connect the solenoid connectors.

41. Install the oil tubes.

42. Install 2 new gaskets to the oil strainer. Install the stainer and torque the bolts to 7 ft. lbs. (10 Nm). Clamp the solenoid wire.

43. Install the magnets in the indentations of the oil pan. Clean the mating suraces of the pan and case. Apply sealer (Three Bond 1281 or equivalent) to the pan and install.

44. Install the snapring on the output shaft and install the key. Align the groove of the sensor rotor with the key and install the sensor rotor.

45. Install the lockball on the output shaft. Align the groove of the drive gear with the ball and install the drive gear. Install the snapring.

46. Install the extension housing with a new gasket. The 2 lower bolts are shorter than the rest, which are equal length. Torque the bolts to 27 ft. lbs. (36 Nm).

47. Install the converter housing. Torque the 10mm bolts to 25 ft. lbs. (34 Nm) and torque 12mm bolts to 42 ft. lbs. (57 Nm).

48. Coat the new O-ring with Dexron®II and install to the speed sensor. Install the speed sensor and connect the connector.

49. Coat the new O-ring with Dexron®II and install to the speedometer driven gear and install the gear.

50. Install the cooler tube unions with new O-rings.

51. Install the neutral start switch onto the manual valve lever shaft and loosely install the adjusting bolt. Install the grommet and new lock washer. Torque the nut to 61 inch lbs. (6.9 Nm).

52. Using the control shaft lever, turn the manual lever shaft fully backwards and return 2 notches to the **N** detent. Align the neutral basic line with the switch groove. Torque the bolt to 9 ft. lbs. (13 Nm) and bend at least 2 tabs of the lock washer over.

53. Install the transmission control shaft lever.

54. Install the wire harness clamps.

SPECIFICATIONS

Valve Body Spring Specifications

Body	Spring Name	Free Height in. (mm)	Outer Diameter in. (mm)	Number Of Coils	Color
Upper	Downshift Plug	1.075 (27.3)	0.343 (8.4)	12.5	Yellow
	Throttle Valve	0.811 (20.6)	0.362 (9.2)	9.5	Blue
	or	0.917 (23.3)	0.362 (9.2)	9.5	White
	3/4 Shift Valve	1.213 (30.8)	0.382 (9.7)	10.5	Purple
	Second Coast Modulator Valve ①	0.996 (25.3)	0.339 (8.6)	11.5	Orange
	Second Coast Modulator Valve ②	1.165 (29.6)	0.327 (8.3)	12.5	Red
	Second Coast Modulator Valve ③	0.963 (24.6)	6.327 (8.3)	9.0	Blue
	Lockup Relay Valve	0.843 (21.4)	0.217 (5.5)	7.5	Lt. Gray
	Secondary Regulator Valve	1.217 (30.9)	0.441 (11.2)	10.5	Blue
	Cutback Valve	0.858 (21.8)	0.236 (6.0)	13.5	None
	2/3 Shift Valve	1.213 (30.8)	6.382 (9.7)	10.5	Purple
	Low Coast Modulator Valve ④	1.094 (27.8)	0.327 (8.3)	10.5	Pink
	Low Coast Modulator Valve ⑤	1.197 (30.4)	0.327 (8.3)	10.5	Lt. Green
	Low Coast Modulator Valve ⑥	1.039 (26.4)	0.327 (8.3)	10.5	Yellow
Lower	Check Valve	0.795 (20.2)	0.476 (12.2)	6.5	None
	Pressure Relief Valve	0.441 (11.2)	0.252 (6.4)	7.5	None
	1/2 Shift Valve	1.213 (30.8)	6.382 (9.7)	10.5	Purple
	Primary Regulator Valve ⑦	2.626 (66.7)	0.732 (18.6)	12.5	None
	Primary Regulator Valve ⑧	2.453 (62.3)	6.732 (18.6)	12.5	None
	Accumulator Control Valve ⑨	1.335 (33.9)	6.346 (8.8)	12.0	Pink
	Accumulator Control Valve ⑩	1.406 (35.7)	N/A	N/A	N/A
	Accumulator Control Valve ⑪	1.421 (36.1)	0.350 (8.9)	14.0	White
	Accumulator Control Valve ⑫	1.362 (34.6)	0.346 (8.8)	18.0	Yellow

① Except 1987–89 Toyota Supra with 7M-GTE engine and 1989 Toyota Cressida
② 1987–89 Toyota Supra with 7M-GTE engine
③ 1989 Toyota Cressida
④ Except Pick-up and 1989 Toyota Cressida
⑤ Pick-up
⑥ 1989 Toyota Cressida
⑦ Except 1989 Toyota Trucks
⑧ 1989 Toyota Trucks
⑨ 1986–89 Toyota Trucks
⑩ 1988–89 Isuzu Trucks
⑪ 1987–89 Toyota Supra with 7M-GE engine and 1987–88 Cressida
⑫ 1987–89 Toyota Supra with 7M-GTE engine and 1989 Cressida

Selective Flange Thicknesses

Item	Flange	in.	mm
Overdrive Direct Clutch	No. 21	0.122	3.1
	No. 20	0.126	3.2
	No. 19	0.130	3.3
	No. 18	0.134	3.4
	No. 17	0.138	3.5
	No. 16	0.142	3.6
Direct Clutch	No. 33	0.118	3.0
	No. 32	0.122	3.1
	No. 31	0.126	3.2
	No. 30	0.130	3.3
	No. 29	0.134	3.4
	No. 28	0.138	3.5
	No. 27	0.142	3.6
	No. 34	0.146	3.7
Overdrive Brake	No. 26	0.130	3.3
	No. 25	0.138	3.5
	No. 12	0.142	3.6
	No. 24	0.146	3.7
	No. 11	0.150	3.8
	No. 23	0.154	3.9
	None	0.157	4.0

Torque Specifications

Part	ft. lbs.	Nm
Oil pan bolts	65 ①	7.4
Transmission to engine bolt	50	65
Oil pump assembly bolts	7	10
Oil pump mounting bolts	16	22
10mm Converter housing to case bolts	25	34
12mm Converter housing to case bolts	42	57
Valve body assembly bolts	56 ①	6.4
Valve body mounting bolts	7	10
Rear mount bolts 2WD vehicles	18	25
Rear support member 4WD vehicles	70	90
Parking lock pawl bracket	65 ①	7.4
Overdrive support bolts	19	25
Torque converter bolts 1986–88	20	27
Torque converter bolts 1989	30	41
Extension housing bolts	27	36
Oil strainer bolts	7	10
Neutral start switch bolt	9	13
Neutral start switch nut	61 ①	6.9
Solenoid mounting bolt	7	19
Control shaft lever bolt	12	16
Speedometer driven gear lock plate	12	16

① Inch. lbs.

Maximum Bushing Bore Specifications

Item	in.	mm
Oil pump body	1.5035	38.19
Stator shaft (front)	0.8496	21.58
Overdrive (gear)	1.0661	27.08
Overdrive direct clutch drum	1.0673	27.11
Overdrive planetary gear	0.4437	11.27
Direct clutch drum	2.1256	53.99
Forward clutch drum	0.9480	24.08
Front planetary ring gear	0.9480	24.08
Planetary sun gear	1.0661	27.08
Transmission case	1.5035	38.19
Extension housing	1.5783	40.09

SPECIAL TOOLS

	Oil pump puller		Small Spring compressor
	One-way clutch testing tool: Torque converter		Holding fixture base
	OD brake piston spring compressor		Manual valve shaft oil seal remover
	Spring compressor		Manual valve shaft oil seal installer
	1st/reverse brake reaction sleeve puller		Pressure gauge
	1st/reverse brake piston puller		O/D case guide bolt
	Front companion flange oil seal installer / Extension housing oil seal installer		Holding fixture
	Chain case oil seal installer		No. 3 Piston Spring Compressor
	Front driveshaft bearing remover and installer		Companion flange Holding wrench
	Oil pump oil seal installer		

OIL FLOW CIRCUIT – R RANGE – A 340E TRANSMISSION

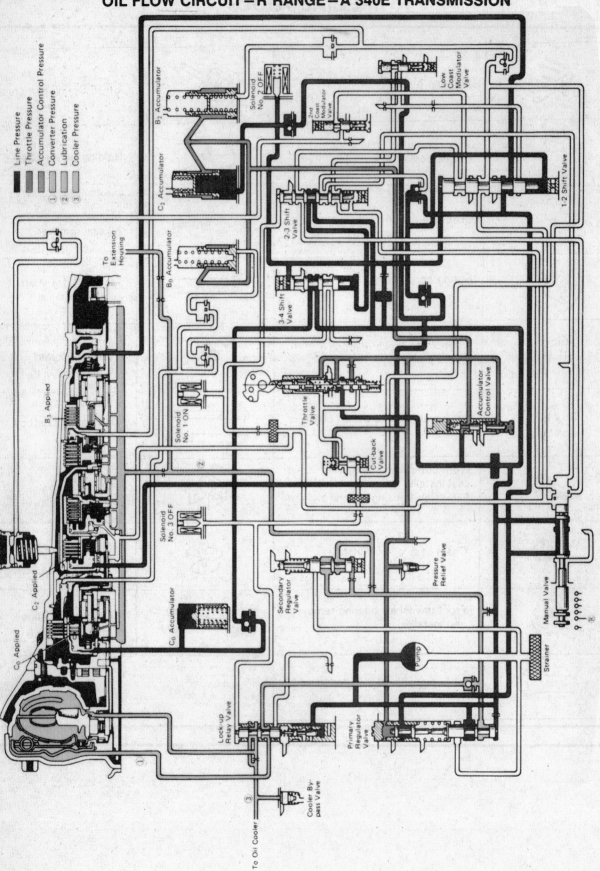

OIL FLOW CIRCUIT – D RANGE FIRST SPEED – A 340E TRANSMISSION

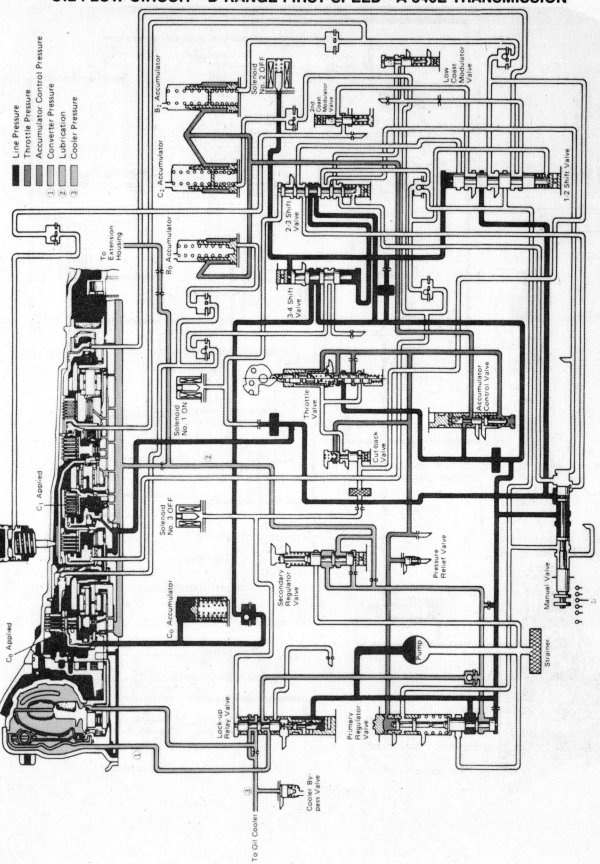

OIL FLOW CIRCUIT – D RANGE SECOND SPEED – A 340E TRANSMISSION

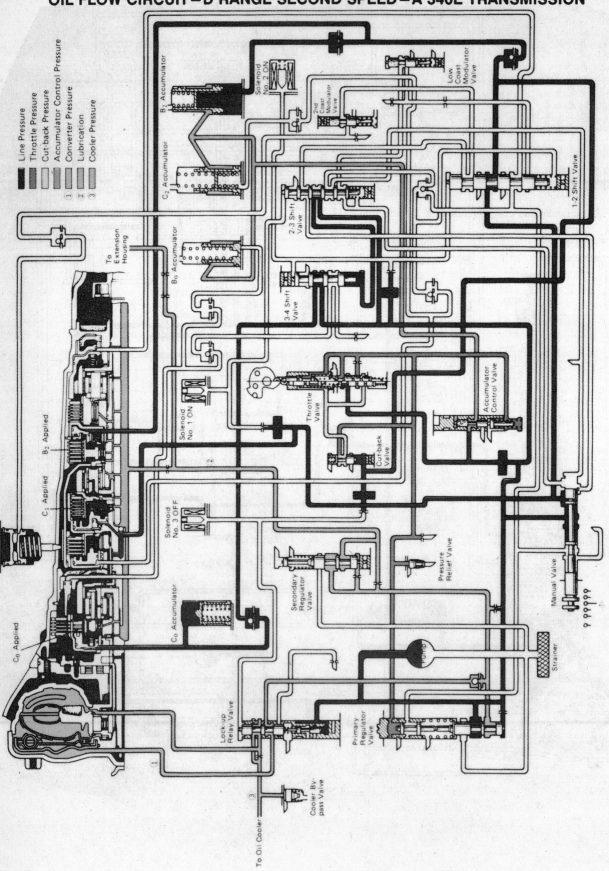

OIL FLOW CIRCUIT—D RANGE THIRD SPEED—A 340E TRANSMISSION

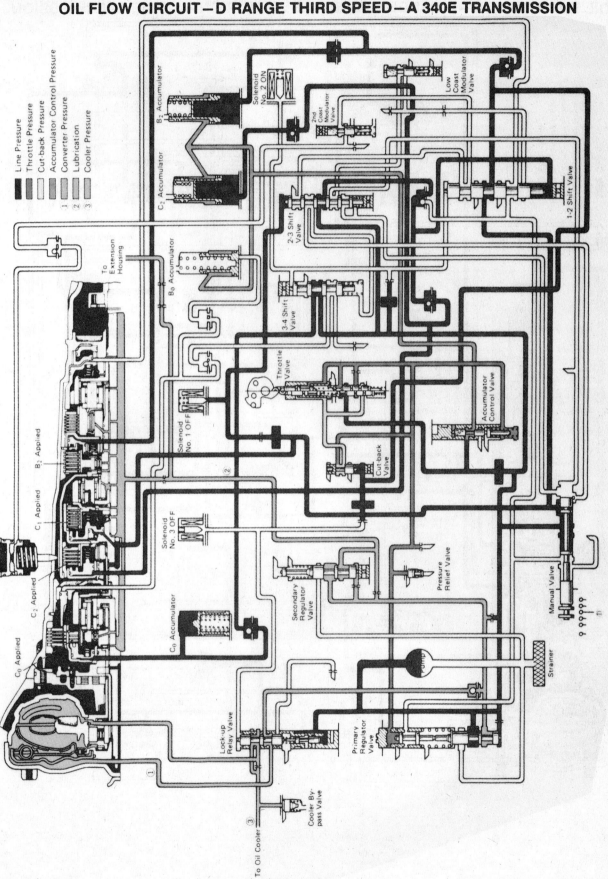

OIL FLOW CIRCUIT – D RANGE OVERDRIVE LOCKUP ON – A 340E TRANSMISSION

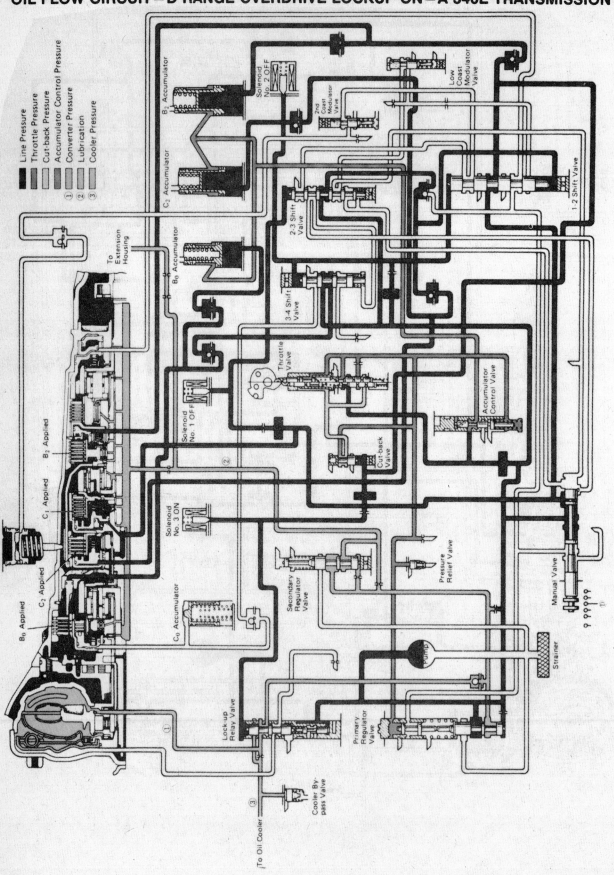

OIL FLOW CIRCUIT — 2 RANGE FIRST SPEED — A 340E TRANSMISSION

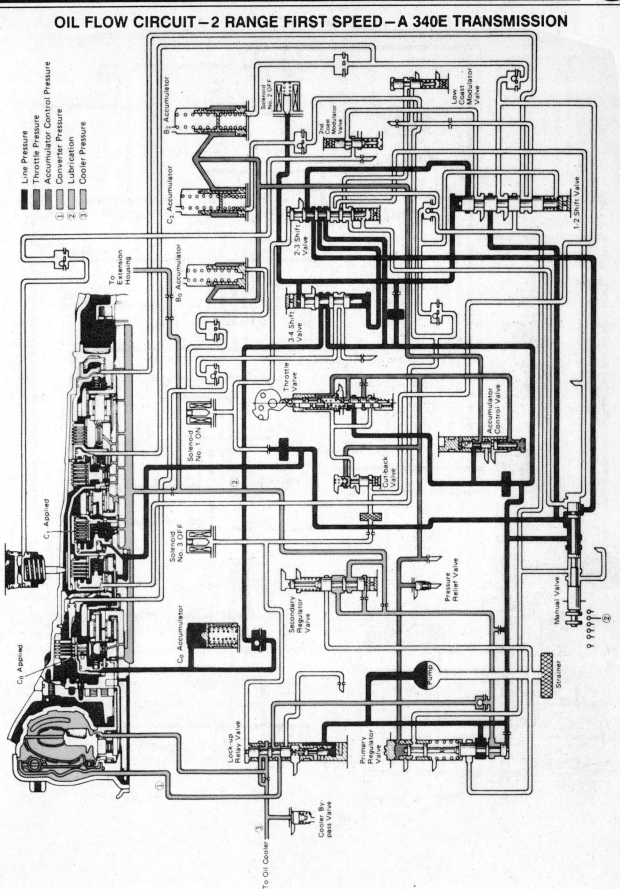

AUTOMATIC TRANSMISSIONS
AW30-80LE, A340E AND A340H—ISUZU

OIL FLOW CIRCUIT—2 RANGE SECOND SPEED—A 340E TRANSMISSION

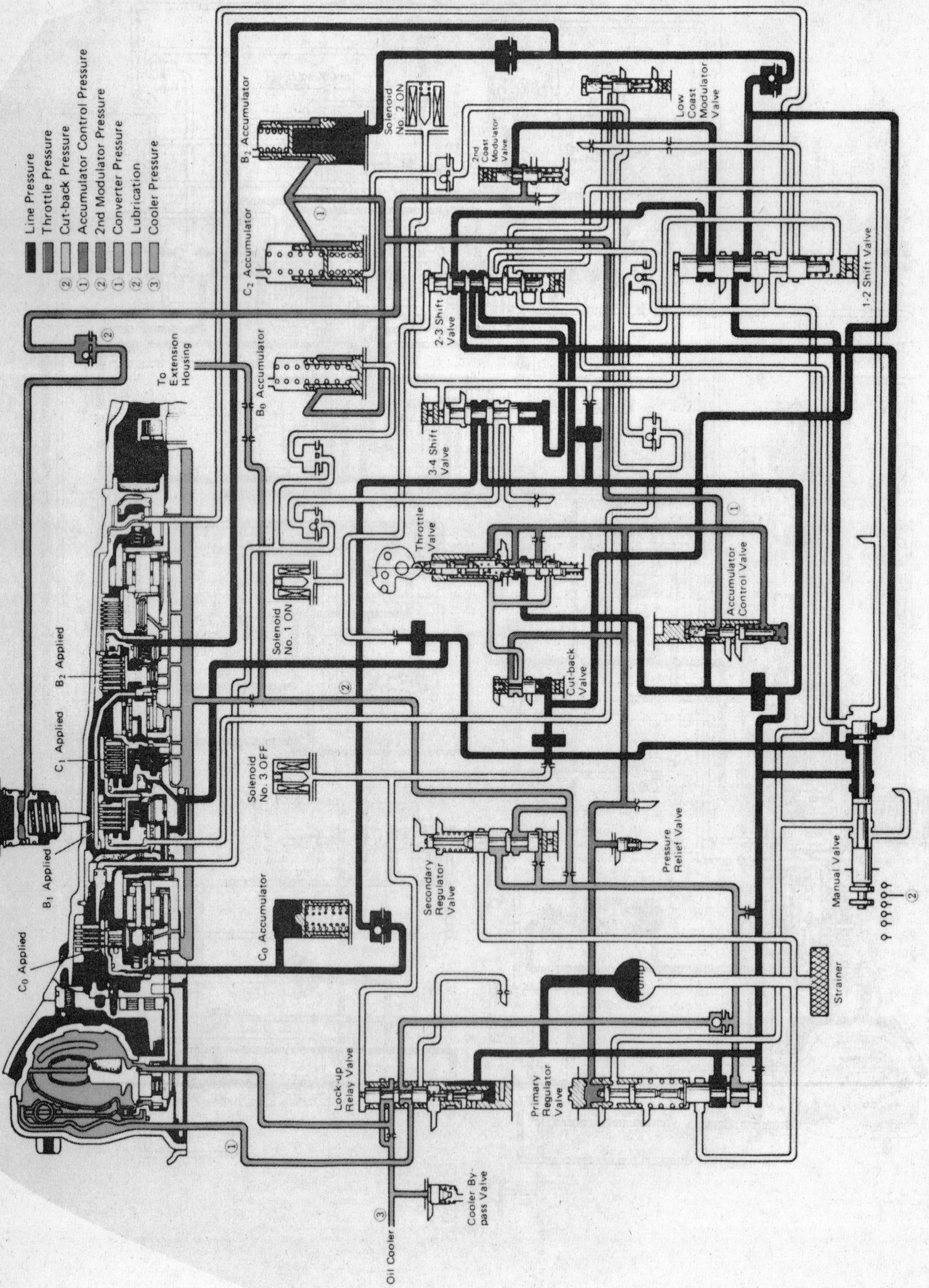

Line Pressure
Throttle Pressure
Cut-back Pressure
Accumulator Control Pressure
2nd Modulator Pressure
Converter Pressure
Lubrication
Cooler Pressure

B2 Accumulator
C2 Accumulator
B0 Accumulator
C0 Accumulator
C0 Accumulator

Solenoid No. 2 ON
Solenoid No. 1 ON
Solenoid No. 3 OFF

2nd Coast Modulator Valve
Low Coast Modulator Valve
1-2 Shift Valve
2-3 Shift Valve
3-4 Shift Valve
Throttle Valve
Accumulator Control Valve
Cut-back Valve
Pressure Relief Valve
Manual Valve
Secondary Regulator Valve
Lock-up Relay Valve
Primary Regulator Valve
Strainer
Cooler By-pass Valve

To Extension Housing
To Oil Cooler

B2 Applied
C1 Applied
B1 Applied
C0 Applied

OIL FLOW CIRCUIT – 2 RANGE THIRD SPEED – A 340E TRANSMISSION

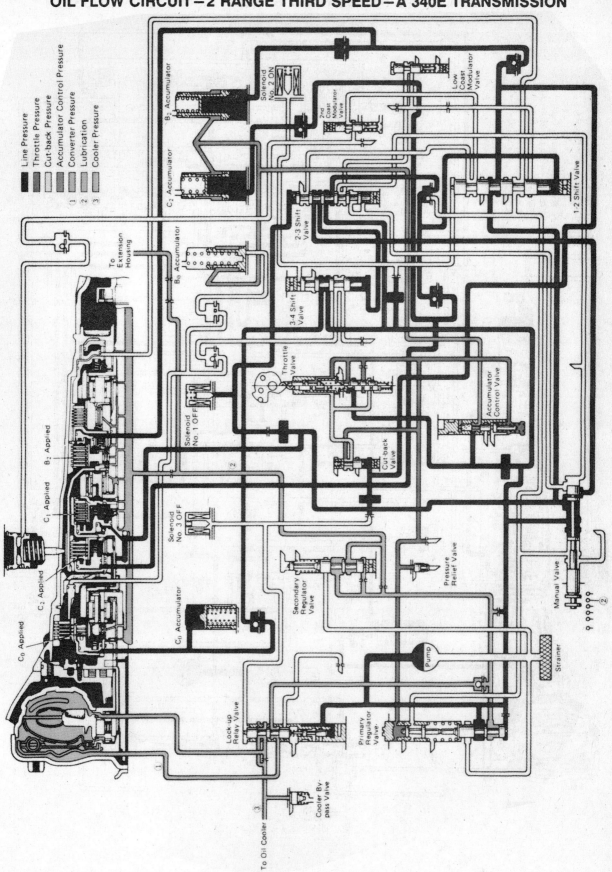

OIL FLOW CIRCUIT – L RANGE FIRST SPEED – A 340E TRANSMISSION

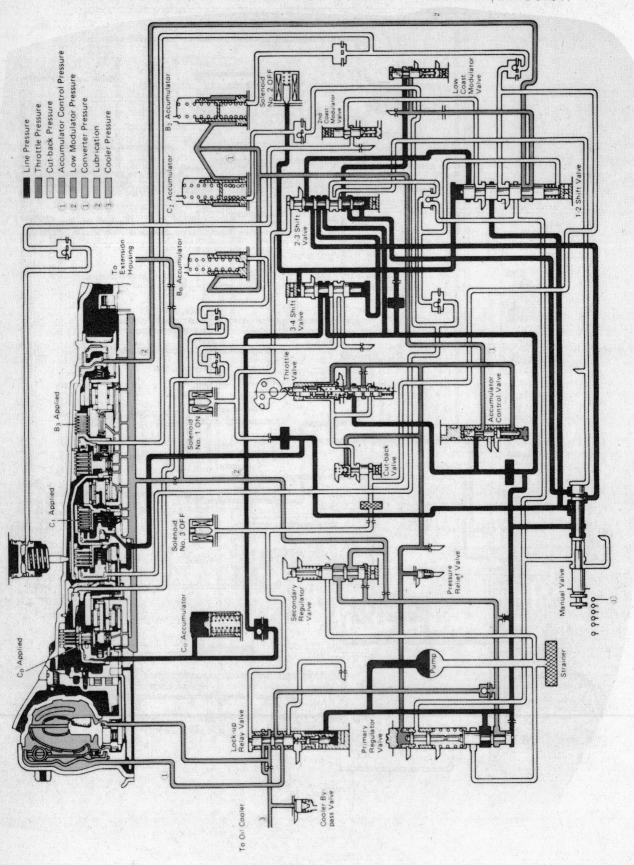

OIL FLOW CIRCUIT – R RANGE – A 340H TRANSMISSION

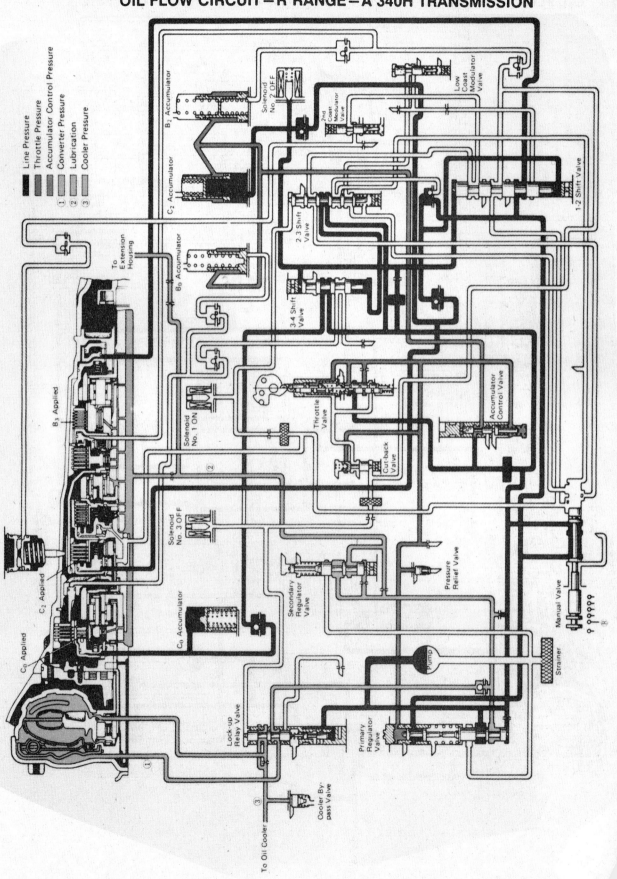

OIL FLOW CIRCUIT – D RANGE FIRST SPEED – A 340H TRANSMISSION

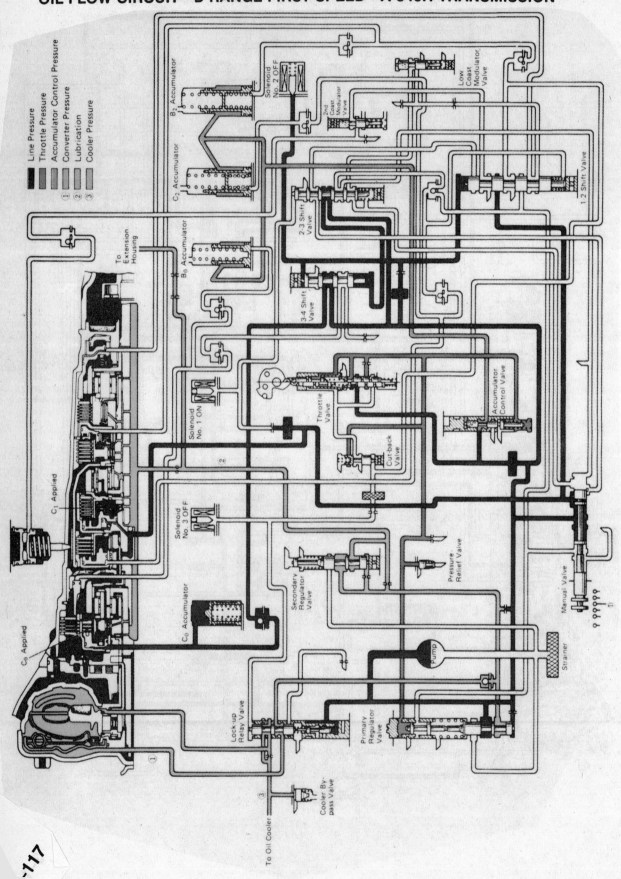

OIL FLOW CIRCUIT – D RANGE SECOND SPEED – A 340H TRANSMISSION

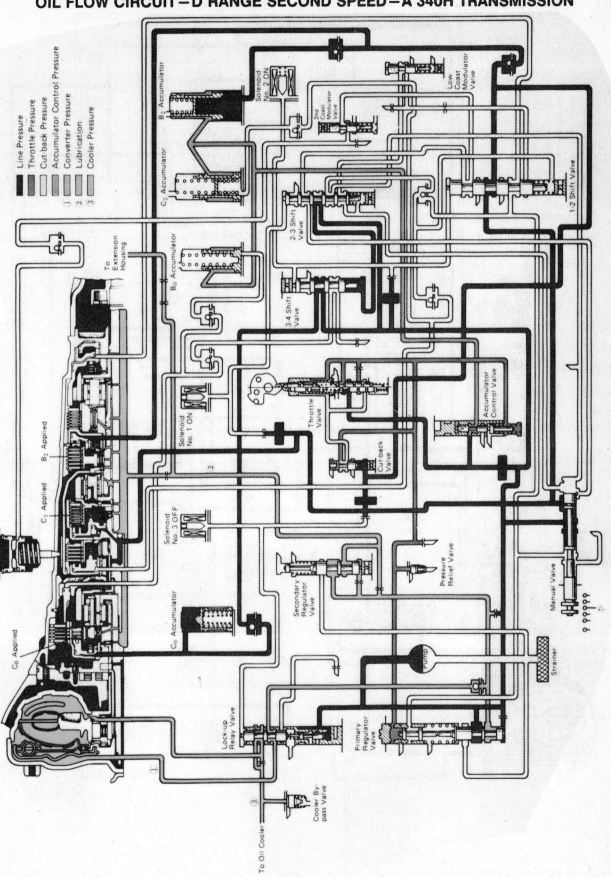

OIL FLOW CIRCUIT – D RANGE THIRD SPEED – A 340H TRANSMISSION

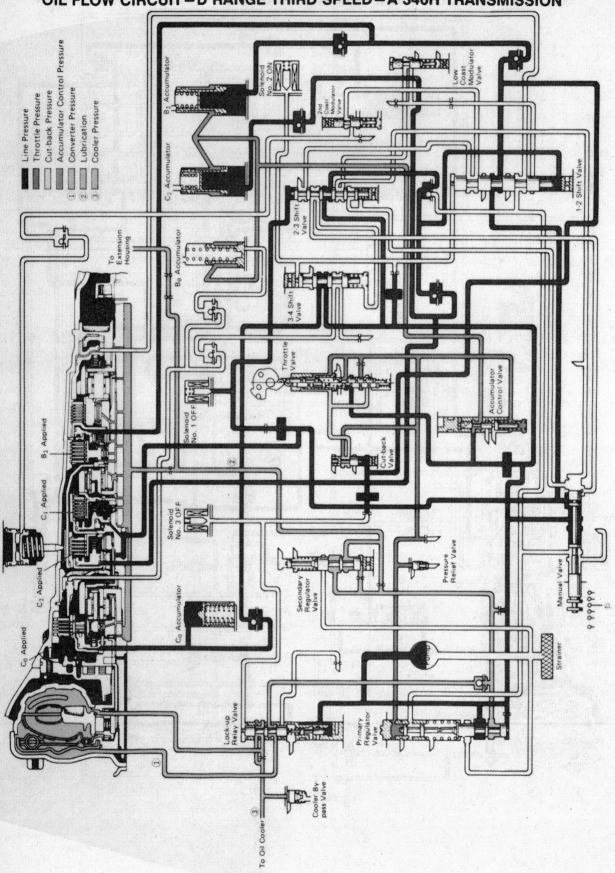

OIL FLOW CIRCUIT — D RANGE OVERDRIVE LOCKUP ON — A 340H TRANSMISSION

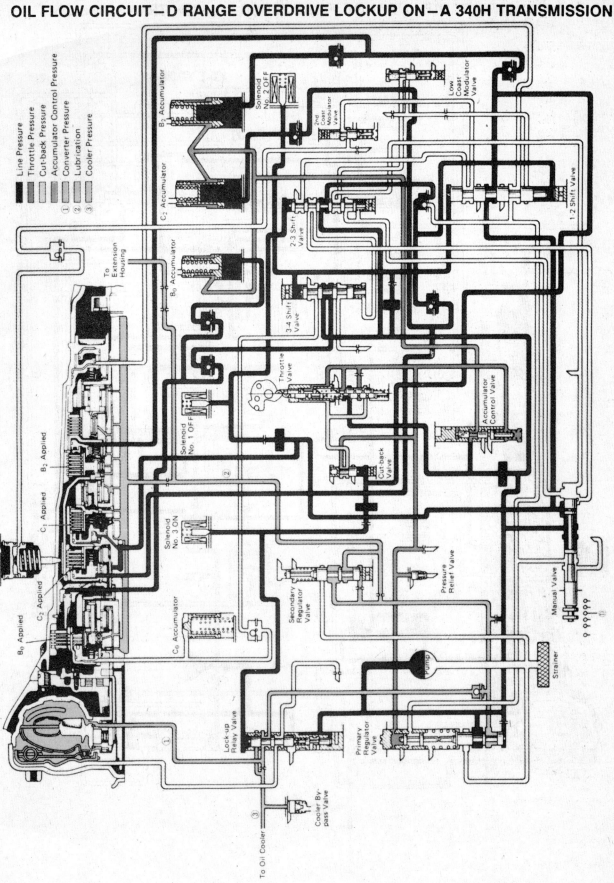

OIL FLOW CIRCUIT – 2 RANGE FIRST SPEED – A 340H TRANSMISSION

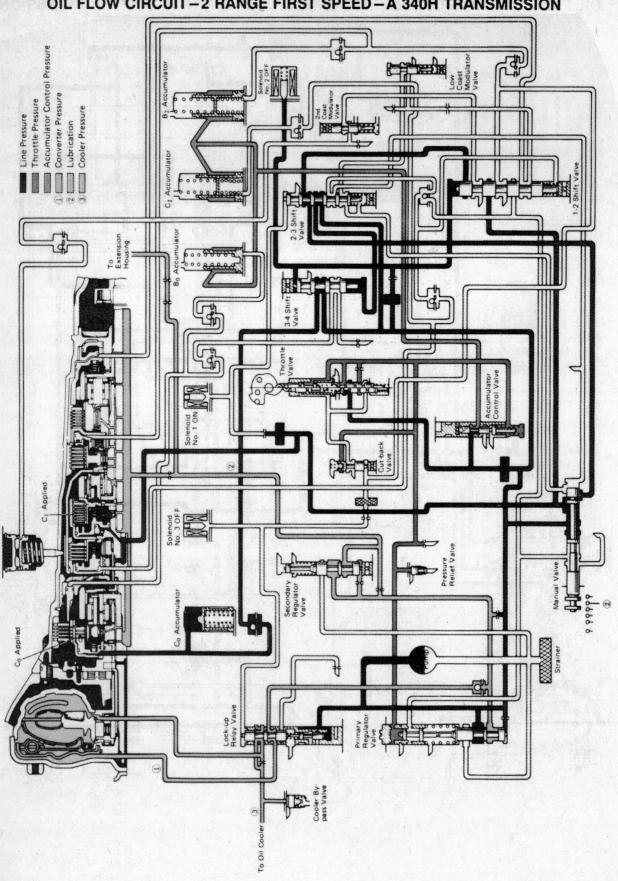

OIL FLOW CIRCUIT — 2 RANGE SECOND SPEED — A 340H TRANSMISSION

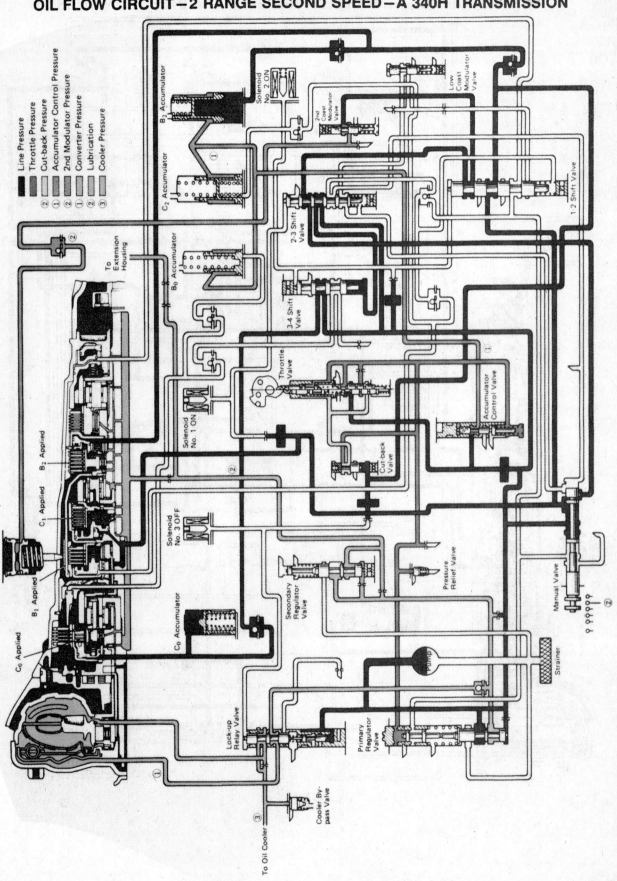

OIL FLOW CIRCUIT – 2 RANGE THIRD SPEED – A 340H TRANSMISSION

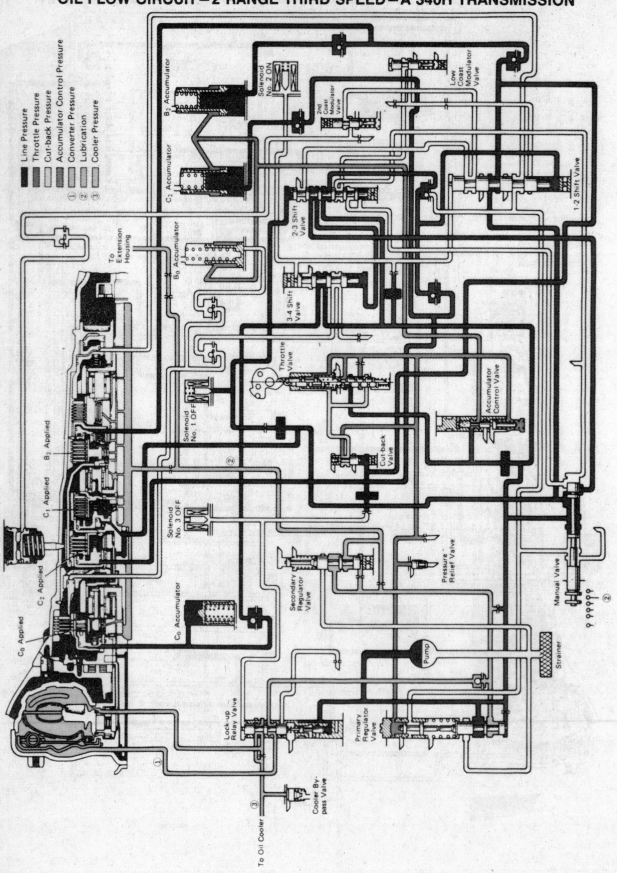

OIL FLOW CIRCUIT – L RANGE FIRST SPEED – A 340H TRANSMISSION

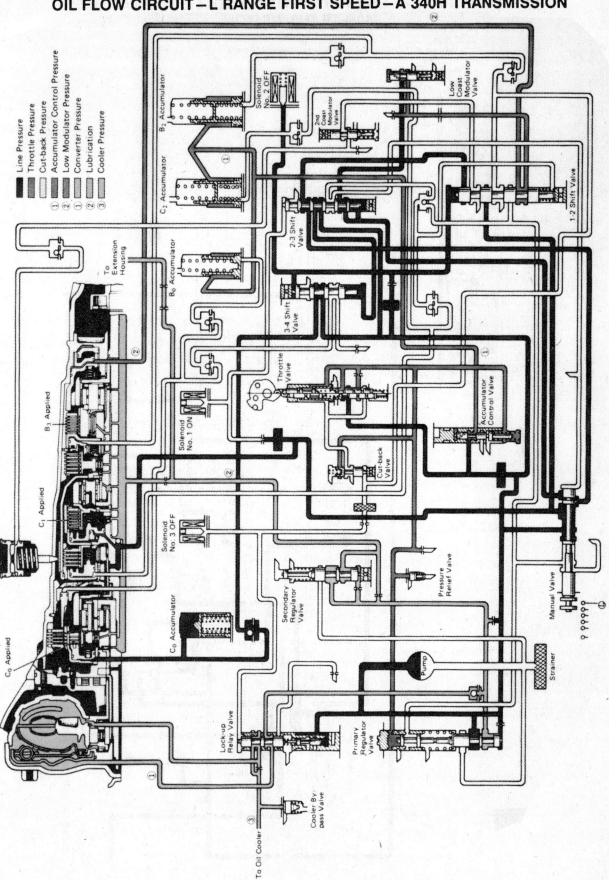

OIL FLOW CIRCUIT – SHIFT POSITION H2 NO. 4 SOLENOID OFF
A 340H TRANSMISSION

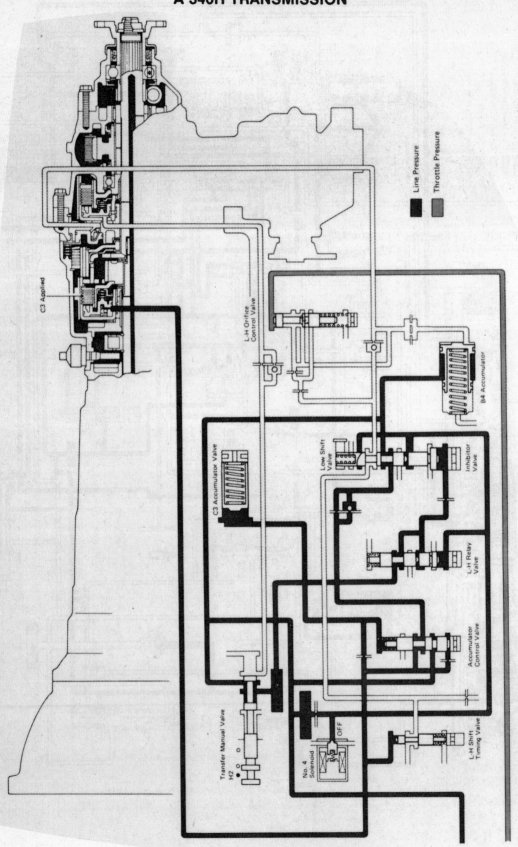

OIL FLOW CIRCUIT – SHIFT POSITION H4 NO. 4 SOLENOID OFF
A 340H TRANSMISSION

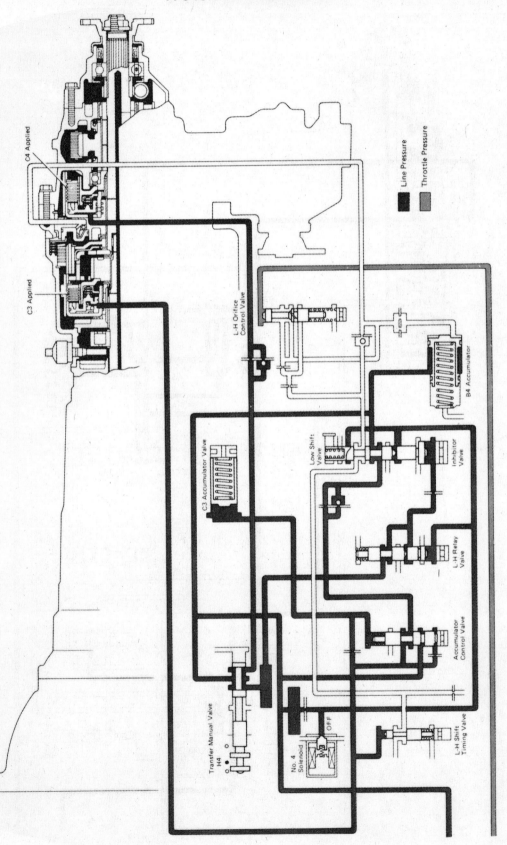

OIL FLOW CIRCUIT–SHIFT POSITION L4 NO. 4 SOLENOID ON A 340H TRANSMISSION

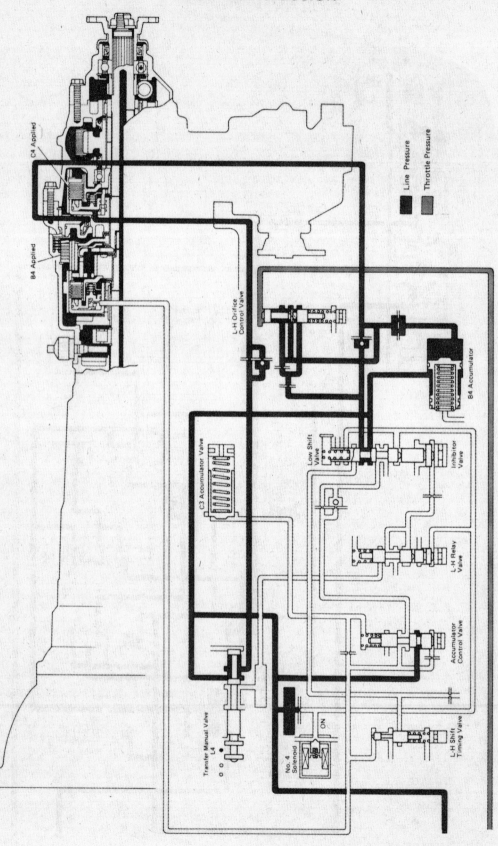

OIL FLOW CIRCUIT – SHIFT POSITION H4 TO L4 NO. 4 SOLENOID OFF
A 340H TRANSMISSION

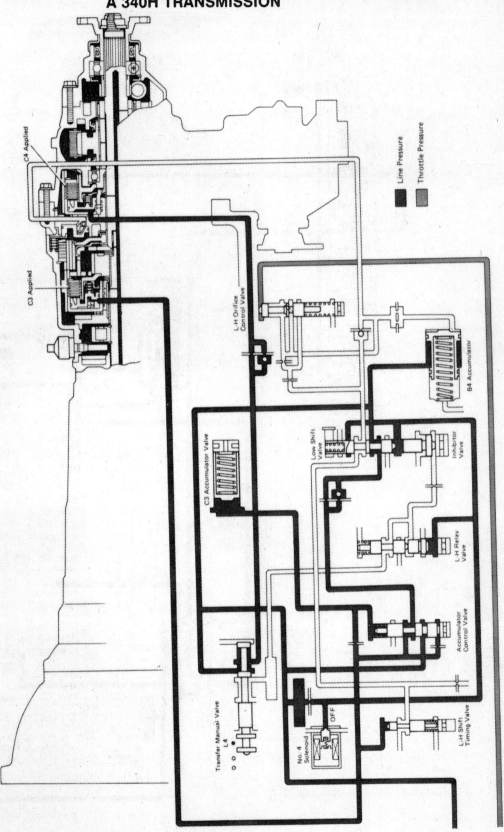

OIL FLOW CIRCUIT – SHIFT POSITION L4 TO H4 NO. 4 SOLENOID ON A 340H TRANSMISSION

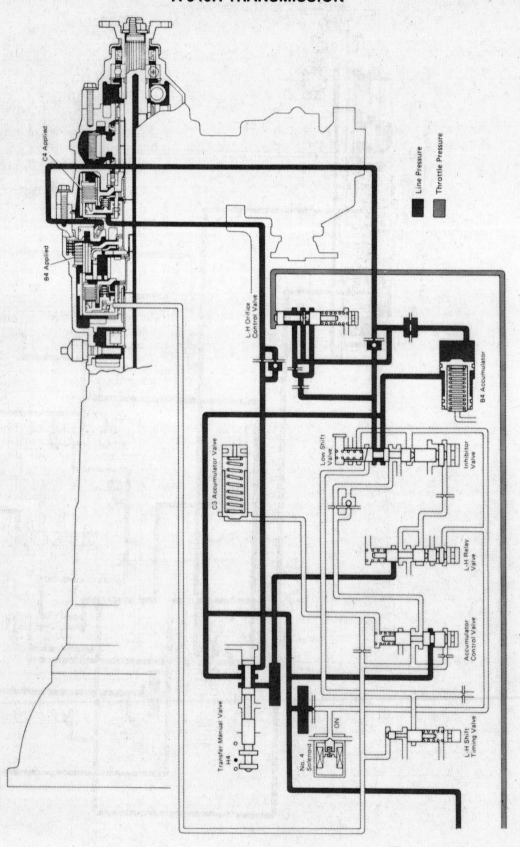

OIL FLOW CIRCUIT – R RANGE – 30-80LE TRANSMISSION

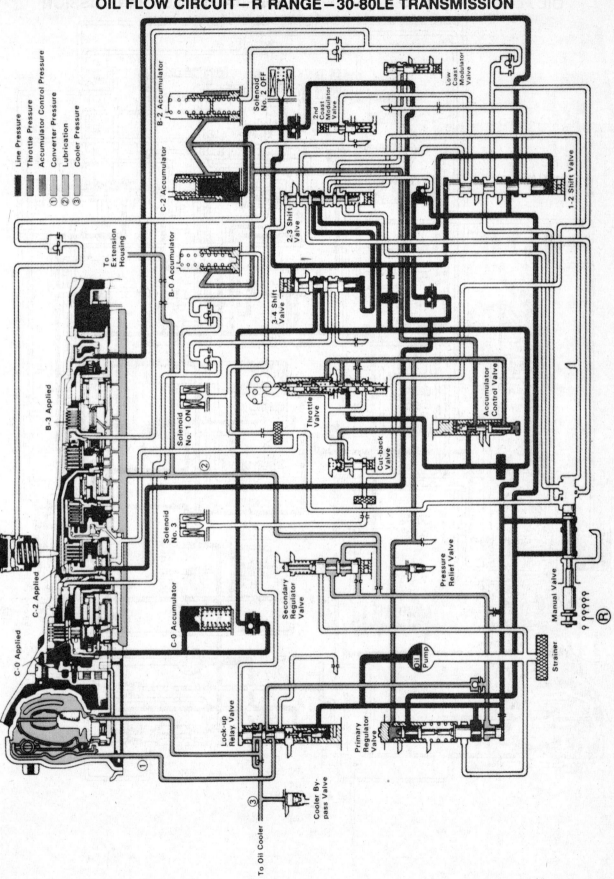

OIL FLOW CIRCUIT – D RANGE FIRST SPEED – 30-80LE TRANSMISSION

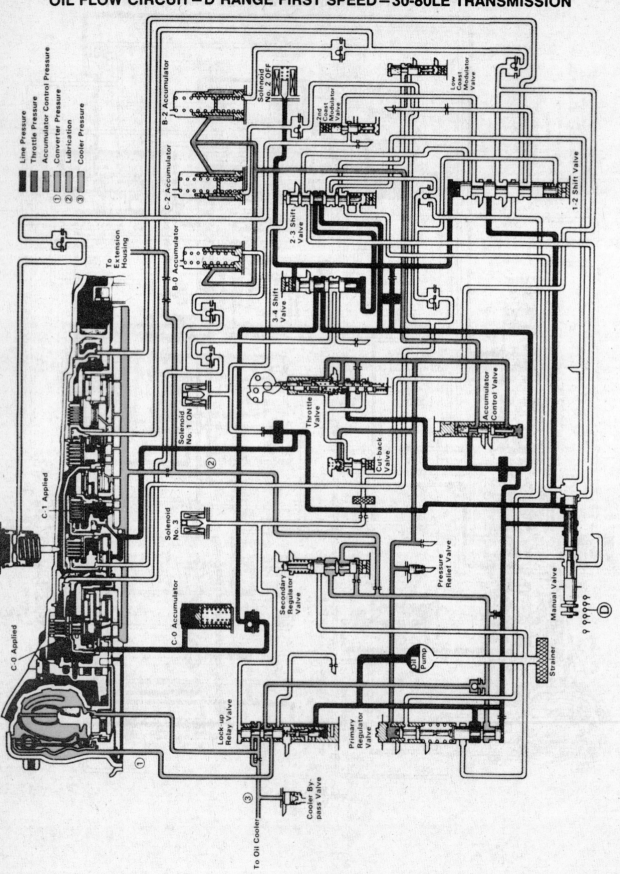

OIL FLOW CIRCUIT — D RANGE SECOND SPEED — 30-80LE TRANSMISSION

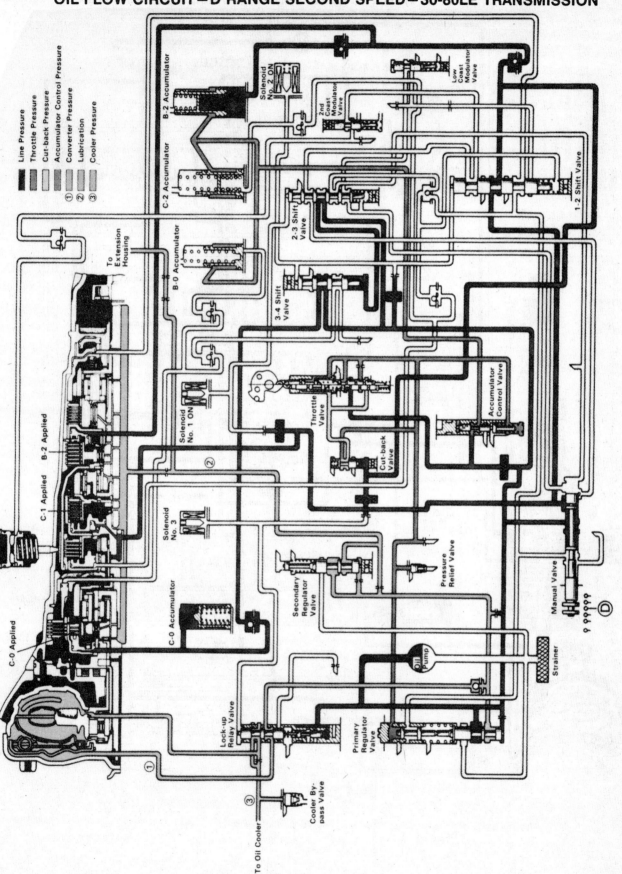

OIL FLOW CIRCUIT – D RANGE THIRD SPEED – 30-80LE TRANSMISSION

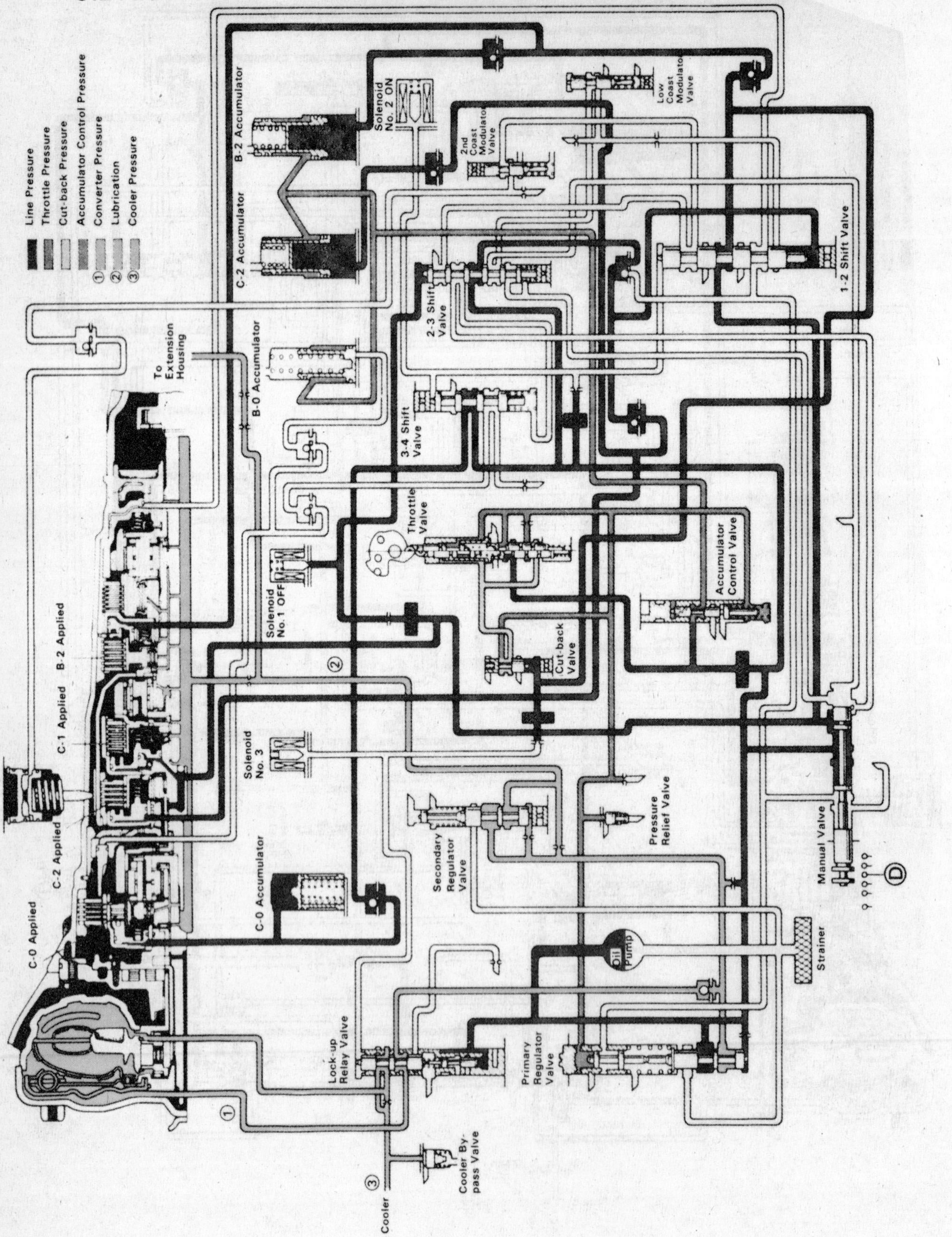

Line Pressure
Throttle Pressure
Cut-back Pressure
Accumulator Control Pressure
Converter Pressure
Lubrication
Cooler Pressure
① ② ③

To Extension Housing

B-2 Accumulator
C-2 Accumulator
B-0 Accumulator

Solenoid No. 2 ON

2nd Coast Modulator Valve

Low Coast Modulator Valve

1-2 Shift Valve

2-3 Shift Valve

3-4 Shift Valve

Throttle Valve

Accumulator Control Valve

Solenoid No. 1 OFF

Cut-back Valve

②

Solenoid No. 3

Secondary Regulator Valve

Pressure Relief Valve

Manual Valve

C-1 Applied
B-2 Applied
C-2 Applied

C-0 Applied

C-0 Accumulator

Oil Pump

Strainer

Lock-up Relay Valve

Primary Regulator Valve

①

Cooler By-pass Valve

③

To Oil Cooler

D

OIL FLOW CIRCUIT – 2 RANGE FIRST SPEED – 30-80LE TRANSMISSION

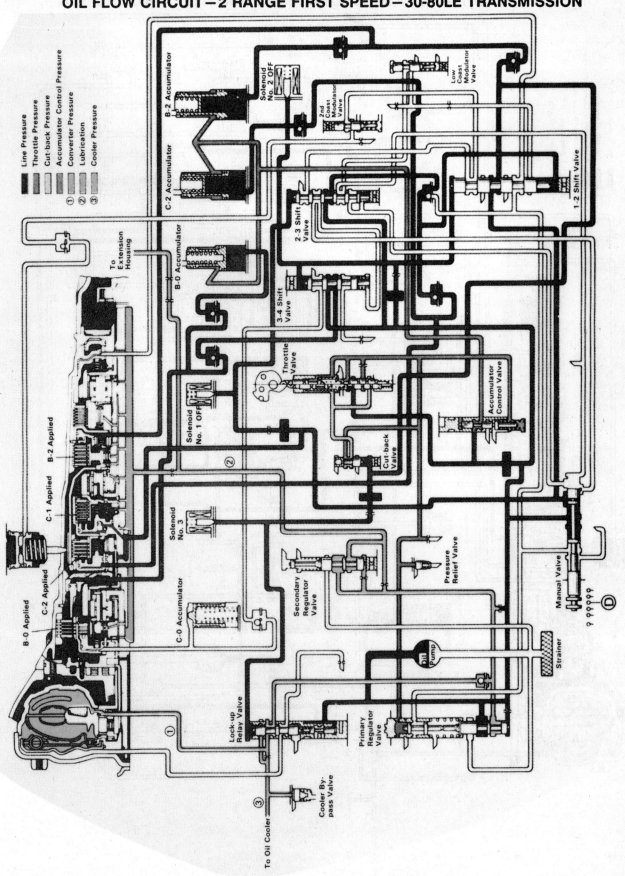

OIL FLOW CIRCUIT – 2 RANGE SECOND SPEED – 30-80LE TRANSMISSION

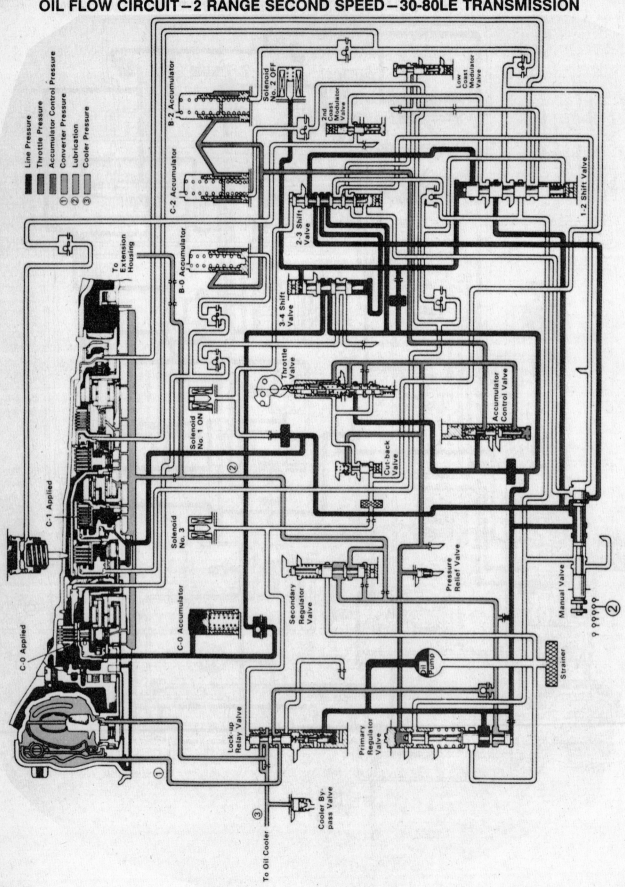

OIL FLOW CIRCUIT — 2 RANGE THIRD SPEED — 30-80LE TRANSMISSION

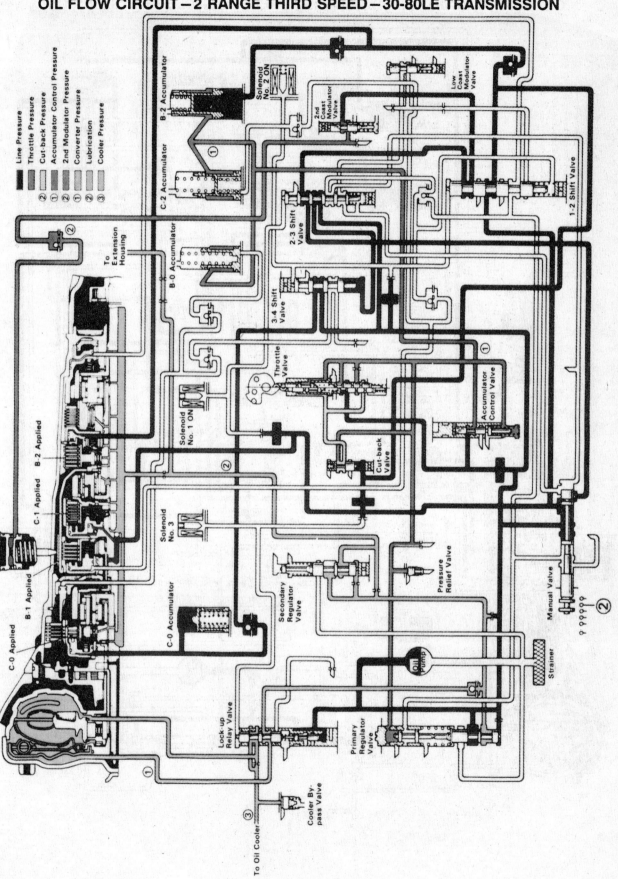

OIL FLOW CIRCUIT — L RANGE FIRST SPEED — 30-80LE TRANSMISSION

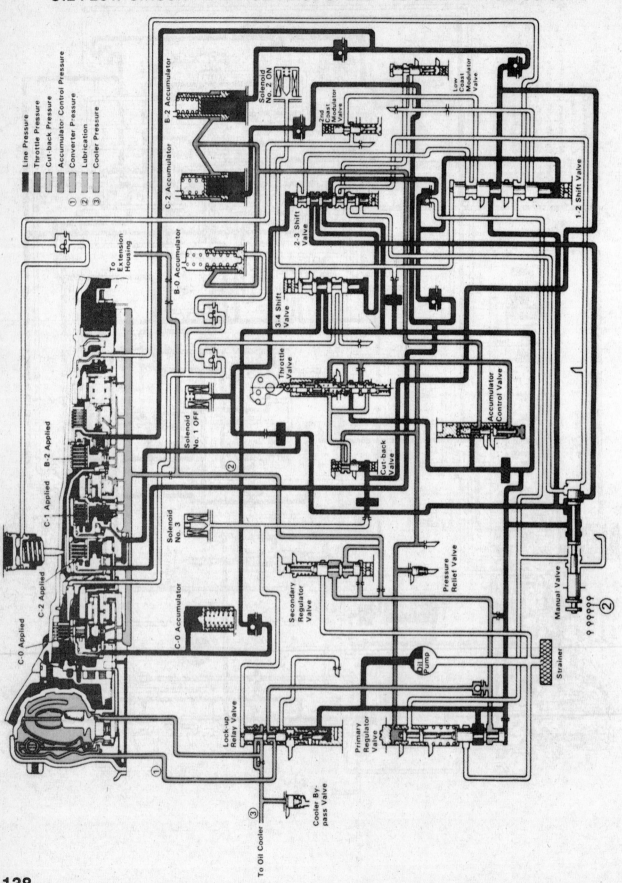

OIL FLOW CIRCUIT – D RANGE OVERDRIVE LOCKUP ON – 30-80LE TRANSMISSION

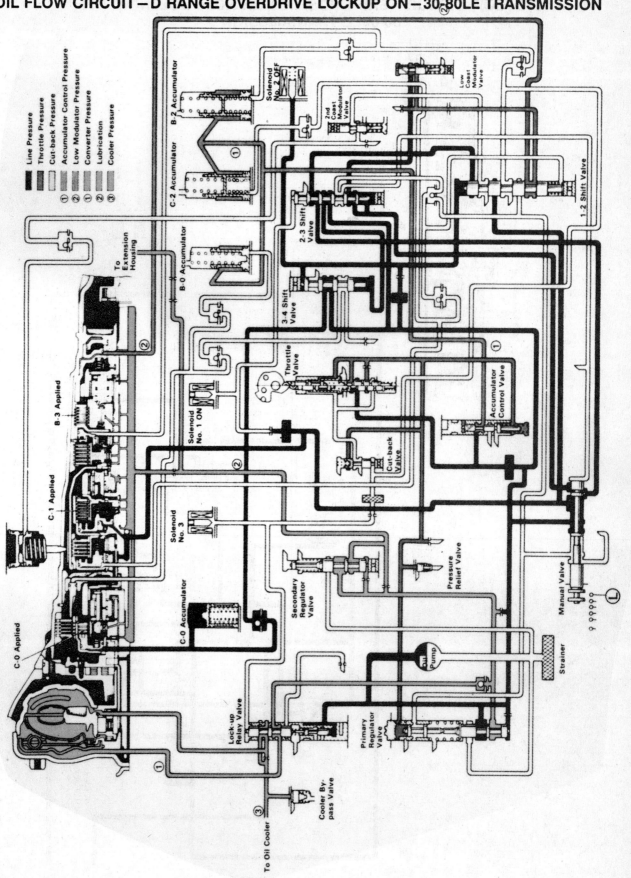

OIL FLOW CIRCUIT – SHIFT POSITION 2H NO. 4 SOLENOID OFF
30-80LE TRANSMISSION

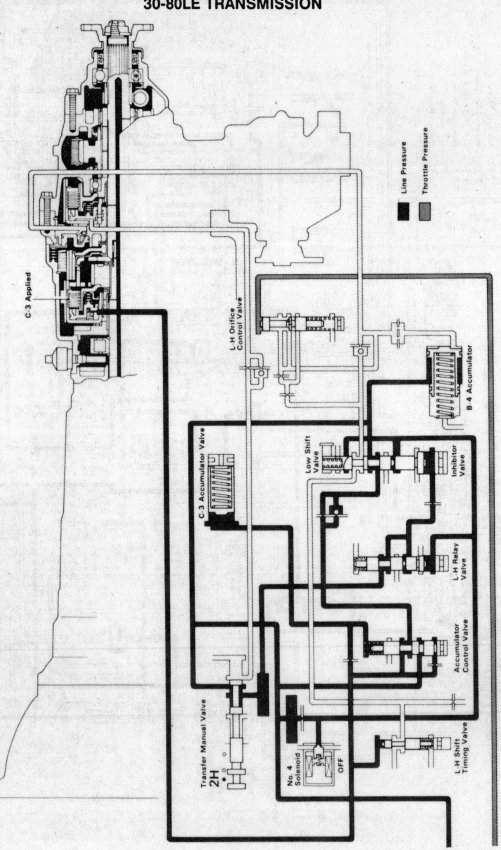

OIL FLOW CIRCUIT – SHIFT POSITION 4H NO. 4 SOLENOID OFF
30-80LE TRANSMISSION

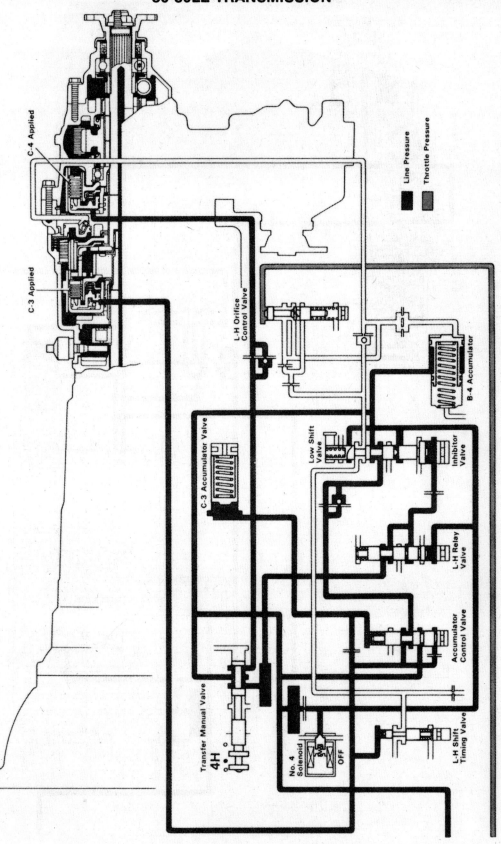

OIL FLOW CIRCUIT — SHIFT POSITION 4L NO. 4 SOLENOID ON
30-80LE TRANSMISSION

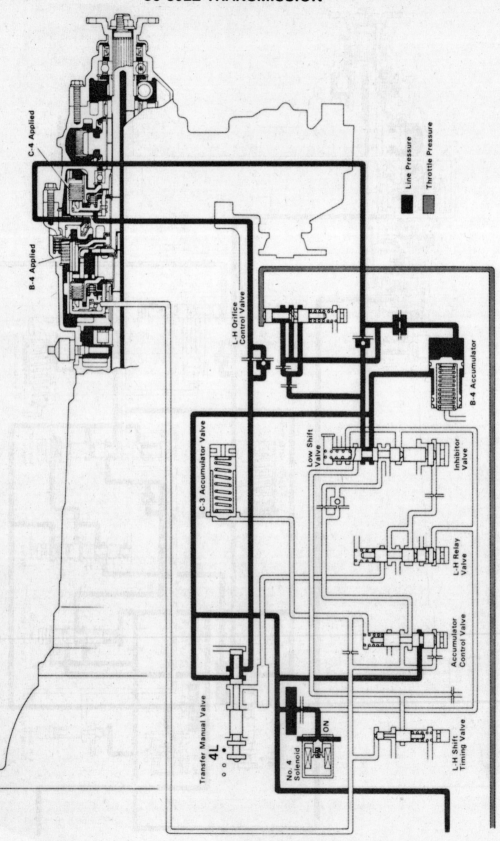

OIL FLOW CIRCUIT – SHIFT POSITION 4H TO 4L NO. 4 SOLENOID OFF TO OFF
30-80LE TRANSMISSION

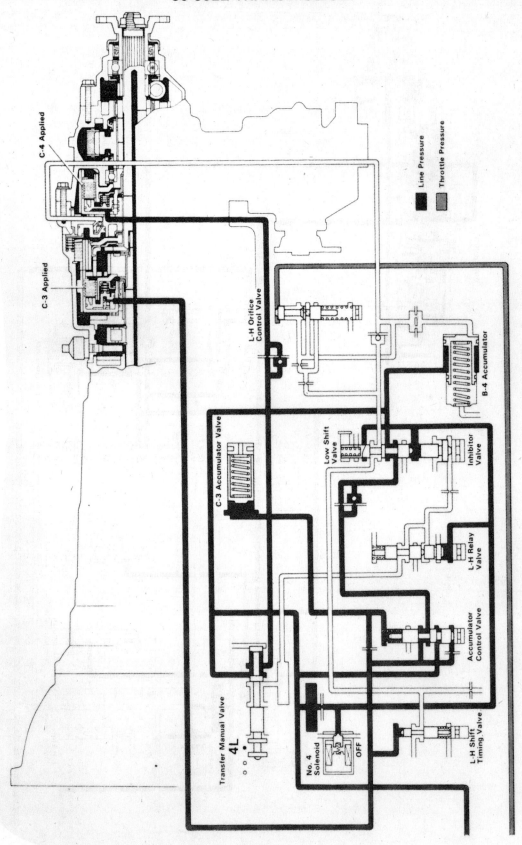

OIL FLOW CIRCUIT – SHIFT POSITION 4L TO 4H NO. 4 SOLENOID ON TO ON
30-80LE TRANSMISSION

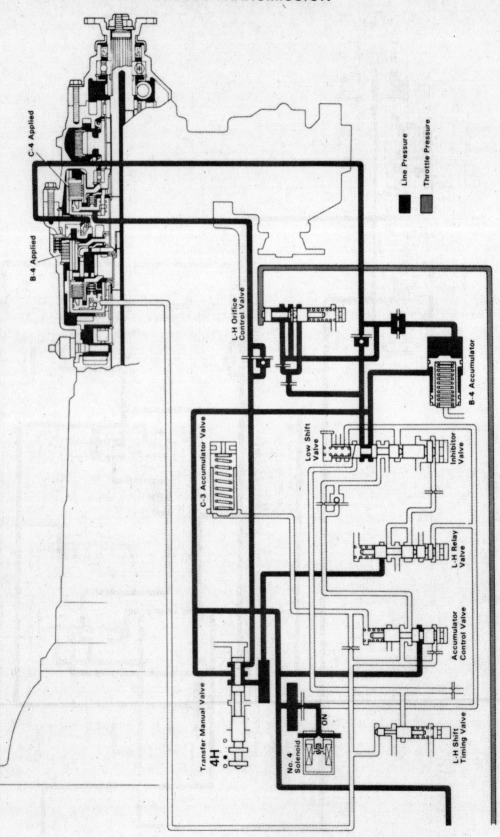

Section 3
AW03-55 and AW03-75 Transmissions
Isuzu

APPLICATION

AW03-55 AND AW03-75

Year	Vehicle	Engine	Transaxle
1984-85	I-Mark	1.5L	AW03-55
1984-85	I-Mark	1.8L	AW03-55
1984-85	P'UP	1.8L	AW03-55
1985-87	P'UP	2.3L	AW03-55
1986-87	P'UP	2.2L	AW03-75

General Description

The transmission AW03-55 and AW03-75 are fully automatic units consisting of 3 element hydraulic torque converter, 5 multi-disc clutches, 2 one-way clutches, 3 piece type control valve body, oil pump and compound planetary gear set. The planetary gear set provides 3 forward speeds and 1 reverse.

The AW03-75 automatic transmission is used with the 2.2L diesel powered P'UP. It is a modified version of the AW03-55, all basic functions and components are the same on both transmissions.

TRANSMISSION AND CONVERTER IDENTIFICATION

An identification plate is located on the side of the automatic transmission that includes the model and serial number.

CONVERTER

The torque converter is composed of the pump impeller which is rotated by the engine, the turbine runner which is fixed to the automatic transmission input shaft and the stator which is attached the the stator shaft. The torque converter is not serviceable, if defective it must be replaced.

Metric Fasteners

Metric tools will be required to service this transmission. Due to the large number of alloy parts used in this transmission, torque specifications should be strictly observed. Before installing capscrews into aluminum parts, dip the bolts into clean transmission fluid as this will prevent the screws from galling the aluminum threads, thus causing damage.

Metric fastener dimensions are very close to the dimensions of the familiar inch system fasteners. For this reason replacement fasteners must have the same measurement and strength as the original fastener.

Do not attempt to interchange metric fasteners for inch system fasteners. Mismatched or incorrect fasteners can cause damage to the automatic transmission unit and possible personal injury. Care should be taken to reuse fasteners in their original locations.

Capacities

The I-Mark requires 13.4 pts. (6.3L) the P'UP with the AW03-55 requires 12.6 pts. (6.0L) and the P'UP with the AW03-75 requires 13.4 pts. (6.3L). Both transmission use Dexron®II automatic transmission fluid.

Checking Fluid Level

The engine and transmission must be at normal operating temperature.
1. Park the vehicle on a level surface.
2. Set the parking brake.
3. With the engine idling, move the selector from **P** to **L** and back to **P**.
4. Pull out the transmission dipstick and wipe it clean.
5. Push the dipstick fully back into the tube.
6. Pull it out and check that the level in the **HOT** range and between the top notches.
7. Add Dexron®II fluid as needed. Do not overfill.

TROUBLE DIAGNOSIS

Hydraulic Control System

The hydraulic control systems consists of an oil pump, which generates hydraulic pressure, the governor which detects vehicle speed and the valve body assembly which controls the operation of the clutches and brakes.

Before the transmission can transfer the engine power to the rear wheels, the hydraulic pressures must be developed and routed to the varied components to cause them to operate, through internal systems and passages.

OIL PUMP

The oil pump is in operation whenever the engine is running, delivering more fluid than the transmission needs. The excess is bled off by the pressure regulator valve and return to the transmission pan. The oil pump is driven by a shaft which is splined into the torque converter cover and through a drive gear insert. The gears are installed in a body, which is bolted to the pump support.

GOVERNOR

The governor assembly reacts to the vehicle speed and provides a pressure signal to control the valves. This pressure signal causes the automatic upshifts to occur as the road speed increases and permits downshifts as road speed decreases. The governor has hydraulic passages used for line pressure in, controlled pressure out and an exhaust pressure dumped back to the transmission pan. Pressure sent to the valve body by the governor is controlled by springs and weights position determined by centrifugal force as the governor rotates.

THROTTLE VALVE

The throttle valve controls the throttle pressure based on the power demand of the driver. When the accelerator pedal is pushed, the throttle cable is pulled. This moves the throttle valve which opens a line pressure passage. The throttle pressure works against the governor pressure to determine proper up and down shifts, based on vehicle speed and engine load as seen by the throttle valve position.

Diagnosis Tests

— CAUTION —
Make certain all pressure testing is performed with the parking brake applied and all wheels chocked. Do not run tests longer than 5 seconds at a time. Never make range shifts when the throttle is wide open.

LINE PRESSURE TEST

1. Remove the line pressure outlet plug on the left side of the transmission case and install a pressure gauge.
2. Attach a tachometer to the engine and start engine.
3. With the transmission in **D**, and with brake depressed, check the line pressure when 1000 rpm is reached and again when stall speed is reached.
4. Repeat Step 3 in **R** range.
5. If the pressure is not in the correct range, check the throttle valve control cable for proper adjustment and retest.

Evaluation

HIGH IN D AND R RANGES
1. Throttle cable out of adjustment.
2. Throttle valve defective.
3. Regulator valve defective.

LOW IN D AND R RANGES
1. Throttle cable out of adjustment.
2. Throttle valve defective.

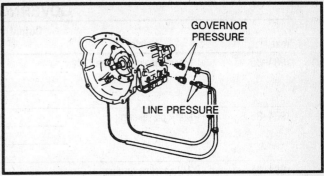

Oil pressure testing

3. Regulator valve defective.
4. Oil pump defective.

LOW IN D RANGE ONLY
1. Fluid leakage in the **D** range circuit.
2. Forward clutch defective.

LOW IN R RANGE ONLY
1. Fluid leakage in the **R** range circuit.
2. Direct clutch defective.
3. First and reverse brake defective.

GOVERNOR PRESSURE

1. Remove the governor pressure outlet plug on left side of the transmission and install a pressure gauge.
2. Bring the transmission up to normal operation temperature.
3. Measure governor pressure at appropriate vehicle speed.
4. If governor pressure is not within specifications, make certain line pressure is correct.
5. If line pressure is correct, either the governor is defective or the governor circuit is leaking.

STALL SPEED TEST

1. Warm engine and transmission to normal operating temperature.
2. Connect a tachometer to the engine.
3. Fully apply the parking brake.
4. Start engine and check for proper idle.
5. Apply the service brake and shift automatic transmission into **D**.

LINE PRESSURE SPECIFICATIONS

Year	Vehicle	rpm	D Range	R Range
			psi (kg/cm²)	psi(kg/cm²)
1984–85	I-Mark and P'up	1000	56.9–64 (4.0–4.5)	82.5–96.7 (5.8–6.8)
		Stall speed	135.1–170.7 (9.5–12)	1991–241.8 (14–17)
1986–87	P'up Gasoline engine	1000	65.4–76.8 (4.6–5.4)	99.5–120.9 (7.–8.5)
		Stall speed	142.2–170.7 (10–12)	213.3–270.2 (15–19)
1986–87	P'up Diesel engine	1000	56.9–64 (4–4.5)	82.5–96.7 (5.8–6.8)
		Stall speed	135.1–170.7 (9.5–12)	199.1–241.8 (14–17)

GOVERNOR PRESSURE

Year	Vehicle	Output shaft speed rpm	Vehicle speed mph (km/h)	Governor Pressure psi (kg/cm²)
1984–85	I-Mark gasoline engine	1000	19 (31)	12.8–21.3 (0.9–1.5)
		2000	39 (63)	22.8–32.7 (1.6–2.3)
		3500	68 (110)	58.3–75.4 (4.1–5.3)
1984–85	I-Mark diesel engine	1000	18 (29)	14.2–22.8 (1.0–1.6)
		2000	37 (59)	32.7–42.7 (2.3–3.0)
		3000	64 (103)	64.0–81.1 (4.5–5.7)
1984–85	P'UP gasoline engine	1000	17 (28)	12.8–21.3 (0.9–1.5)
		2000	35 (56)	24.1–35.6 (1.7–2.5)
		3500	61 (99)	64.0–82.5 (4.5–5.8)
1984–85	P'UP diesel engine	1000	17 (28)	17.1–25.6 (1.2–1.8)
		2000	35 (56)	37.0–46.9 (2.6–3.3)
		3000	61 (99)	66.8–83.9 (4.7–5.9)
1986–87	P'UP gasoline engine	1000	20 (32)	12.8–21.3 (0.9–1.5)
		2000	40 (64)	24.1–35.6 (1.7–2.5)
		3500	71 (113)	64.0–82.5 (4.5–5.8)
1986–87	P'UP diesel engine	1000	17 (28)	17.1–25.6 (1.2–1.8)
		2000	35 (56)	37.0–46.9 (2.6–3.3)
		3000	61 (99)	66.8–83.9 (4.7–5.9)

STALL SPEED

Year	Vehicle	Engine	rpm
1984–85	I-Mark	Gasoline	1700–2000
		Diesel	1900–2200
1984–85	P'UP	Gasoline	1950–2250
		Diesel	1900–2200
1986–87	P'UP	Gasoline	2150–2450
		Diesel	1900–2200

6. Press accelerator pedal all the way down. Quickly read the highest engine rpm obtained, which is the stall speed, and release the pedal.

7. Perform Steps 5 and 6 again with shifter in **R**.

Evaluation

LOW BOTH RANGES

1. Engine output may be insufficient.
2. Stator one-way clutch is not operating properly.
3. If very low — Defective torque converter.

HIGH IN D RANGE

1. Line pressure too low.
2. Forward clutch slipping.
3. Rear one-way clutch not operating properly.

HIGH IN R RANGE

1. Line pressure too low.
2. Direct clutch slipping.
3. First and reverse clutch slipping.

TIME LAG TEST

1. Warm engine and transmission to normal operating temperature.
2. Fully apply parking brake and block all the wheels.
3. Start engine and allow to idle.
4. Apply the service brake and shift automatic transmission from **N** to **D**.
5. Measure the time, using a stop watch, that it takes from shifting the lever until the shock is felt. Repeat this test 3 times and take the average, allow at least 1 minute between tests.
6. Time lag should be 1.2 seconds or less.
7. Apply the service brake and shift automatic transmission from **N** to **R**.
8. Measure the time, using a stop watch, that it takes from shifting the lever until the shock is felt. Repeat this test 3 times and take the average allow at least 1 minute between tests.
9. Time lag should be 1.5 seconds or less.

Evaluation

N TO D TOO LONG

1. Line pressure too low.
2. Forward clutch worn.

N TO R TOO LONG

1. Line pressure too low.
2. Direct clutch worn.
3. First and reverse brake clutch worn.

ROAD TEST

D Range Test

1. Warm engine and transmission to normal operating temperature.

UPSHIFT POINTS

Year	Vehicle	Engine	Upshift operation	Upshift point ① Upshift operation	Vehicle Speed mph (km/h)
1984–85	I-Mark	Gasoline	1 → 2	1850–2200	36–43 (58–69)
			2 → 3	3400–3750	67–73 (107–117)
		Diesel	1 → 2	1600–1900	29–35 (47–56)
			2 → 3	2900–3200	53–58 (85–94)
1984–87	P'UP	Gasoline	1 → 2	1750–2100	35–43 (50–68)
			2 → 3	3300–3650	66–74 (106–118)
		Diesel	1 → 2	1300–1650	23–29 (37–47)
			2 → 3	2650–3000	46–53 (75–85)

① At full throttle valve opening

KICKDOWN POINTS

Year	Vehicle	Engine	Kickdown Shift Operation	Kickdown shift point ① Output Shaft Speed rpm	Vehicle Speed mph (km/h)
1984–85	I-Mark	Gasoline	3 → 1 or 2 → 1	1150–1450	22–29 (36–46)
			3 → 2	3050–3400	60–67 (96–107)
		Diesel	3 → 1 or 2 → 1	1100–1400	20–25 (32–41)
			3 → 2	2700–3000	49–55 (79–88)
1984–85	P'UP	Gasoline	3 → 1 or 2 → 1	1350–1700	24–30 (38–48)
			3 → 2	3100–3450	55–61 (87–98)
1984–87	P'UP	Diesel	3 → 1 or 2 → 1	900–1300	16–23 (25–37)
			3 → 2	2300–2650	40–46 (65–75)
1986–87	P'UP	Gasoline	3 → 1 or 2 → 1	1150–1500	23–31 (37–49)
			3 → 2	3000–3350	60–68 (96–108)

① At full throttle valve opening

2. Shift transmission into **D** and hold accelerator pedal constant at full throttle.

3. Check that all upshifts take place at the correct speeds.

4. While driving with the transmission in 2nd or 3rd gear, fully depress the accelerator.

5. Check to see if the maximum vehicle speed at which kickdown from 2nd to 1st, 3rd to 1st and 3rd to 2nd take place within the proper range.

6. If no 1st to 2nd upshift, inspect the governor and the 1-2 shift valve.

7. If no 2nd to 3rd upshift, inspect the 2-3 shift valve.

2ND TO 1ST DOWNSHIFT POINTS

Year	Vehicle	Engine	2 → 1 downshift point in "1" range Output shaft speed rpm	Vehicle speed mph (km/h)
1984–85	I-Mark	Gasoline	1600–2000	31–40 (50–63)
		Diesel	1200–1500	22–27 (35–44)
1984–87	P'UP	Gasoline	1350–1800	24–32 (38–51)
		Diesel	900–1400	16–25 (25–39)

8. If shift points are incorrect, adjust throttle cable and retest. If still incorrect inspect the throttle valve, 1-2 shift valve or 2-3 shift valve.

9. If there is excessive shift shock during operation, possible defective accumulator, check ball or excessive line pressure.

2nd Range Test

1. Shift into the **2** range and while driving with the accelerator pedal held constantly at full throttle, check for proper 1-2 up shift.

2. Check for proper 2nd to 1st kick-down points.

3. Check that engine braking is obtained when downshift is made from **D** to **2**. If engine braking is not obtained, inspect for a possible defective second coast brake.

4. Check for abnormal noise at acceleration and deceleration, and for excessive shift shock.

1st Range Test

1. Shift into the **1** range and while driving, check that there is no up shift.

2. Road test vehicle at a speed greater than 37mph (60km/h) in **D** and shift into **1**. Check for proper down shift ranges.

3. If there is no engine braking when down shift is made to **1** from **D** or **2**, inspect for a possible defective 1st/Reverse brake.

4. Check for abnormal noise at acceleration and deceleration, and for excessive shift shock.

R Range Test

1. Shift into the **R** range and check for slippage with accelerator slighly depressed.
2. Check for slippage while starting at full throttle.
3. Check for abnormal noises.

P Range Test

1. Stop the vehicle on a gradient of at least 5 degrees.
2. Shift into **P**.
3. Release the parking brake.
4. Check that the parking pawl holds the vehicle.

Converter Clutch Operation and Diagnosis

The torque converter provides the coupling for transmitting the engine torque smoothly to the transmission. Increase torque is provided for starting and accelerating. The torque converter used with this transmission is not a lock-up type torque converter. This torque converter is a sealed unit and if defective must be replaced.

TROUBLESHOOTING THE TORQUE CONVERTER CLUTCH

1. Check the torque converter for any signs of leakage.
2. Check the surface of the converter hub for wear and scoring.
3. With torque converter removed from vehicle, measure the stator endplay.
4. If the stator endplay is greater than 0.059 in. (1.5mm) the torque converter should be replaced.
5. Insert a turning tool J–33953 or equivalent, through the sleeve in the converter and set it to cutaway portion of the stator thrush washer.
6. Insert the stopper so that it fits in the notch of the converter hub outer race and outer race of the one-way clutch.
7. The one-way clutch should lock when turned counterclockwise and rotate freely when turned clockwise.

ON CAR SERVICES

Adjustments

THROTTLE CABLE

GASOLINE ENGINE

1. Loosen the throttle valve control cable adjusting nuts.
2. Check that the carburetor throttle adjusting screw is in contact with the normal idle stop. Make certain the choke is in the full open position and the fast idle mechanism is not working.
3. Adjust the setting of the outer cable with the adjusting nuts, so that the distance between the upper face of the rubber boot on the end of the outer cable and cable stopper on the inner cable is adjusted to 0.032–0.059 in. (0.8–1.5mm).
4. Tighten the adjusting nuts.
5. When adjustment is complete, check that the stroke of the inner cable from the closed position of throttle valve to wide open position is adjusted to 1.30–1.36 in. (32.9–33.9mm).

DIESEL ENGINE

1. Loosen the throttle valve control cable adjusting nuts.
2. With the accelerator pedal fully depressed, check that the injection pump lever is in contact with the maximum speed adjust screw and hold the lever in that position. If it is not in contact it will be necessary to adjust the accelerator linkage.
3. Adjust setting of the outer cable with the adjusting nuts, so that the distance between the end of the rubber boot on the end of the outer cable and cable stopper on the inner cable is 0–0.04 in. (0–1mm).
4. When the adjustment is complete, check the stroke of the inner cable form the normal idling position to maximum speed position is adjusted to 1.30–1.36 in. (32.9–33.9mm).

SHIFT LINKAGE

1. Loosen the shift control rod adjusting nuts.
2. Turn the manual shaft fully in a clockwise direction, as viewed from the right side of the transmission. Then back off to the 3rd stop and set the shaft in neutral position.
3. Hold the manual shaft in that position and place the shift lever in **N**.
4. To remove any play, tighten the adjusting nuts with the lower control shaft lever on the shift lever pushed rearward together with the shift control lever.
5. Road test the vehicle to make certain the shift lever moves properly and the transmission shifts smoothly in each range.

NEUTRAL SAFETY SWITCH

1. Loosen the 2 switch screws and set the shift lever in **N**.
2. Adjust switch to bring the center of the switch slide bar into alignment with the line on the steel case of the switch indication neutral position.
3. When adjustment is complete, check switch for proper operation in each lever position.

Services

FLUID CHANGE

The conditions under which the vehicle is operated is the main consideration in determining how often the transmission fluid should be changed. Different driving conditions result in different transmission fluid temperatures. These temperatures affect change intervals.

If the vehicle is driven under severe conditions, change the transmission fluid every 15,000 miles. If the vehicle is not used under severe conditions, change the fluid and replace the filter every 30,000 miles.

Do not overfill the transmission. Overfilling the unit can cause damage to the internal components of the automatic transmission.

OIL PAN

Removal and Installation

1. Raise and safely support vehicle.
2. Remove the drain plug and drain the transmission fluid.
3. Replace the drain plug and remove the 14 transmission pan bolts.
4. Remove and clean oil pan and magnet, if equipped.

5. Examine the pan for metal particles, which are a sign of bearing, gear or plate wear.

6. Remove the 5 oil screen bolts and the oil screen.

7. Clean all old gasket material from mating surfaces.

8. Install new oil screen and torque the bolts to 3.6–4.3 ft. lbs. (5–6 Nm).

9. Replace magnet and install oil pan with a new gasket.

10. Torque pan bolts to 2.9–3.6 ft. lbs. (0.4–0.5 Nm).

11. Lower the vehicle and fill the transmission with correct amount of Dexron®II transmission fluid.

12. Bring engine and transmission to normal operating temperature, check transmission for proper fluid level and leaks.

VALVE BODY

Removal and Installation

NOTE: The valve body bolt lengths are different, note the locations and lengths of each bolt as removed to use for reference during reassembly.

1. Raise and safely support vehicle. Clean all external parts.

2. Remove the drain plug and drain the transmission fluid.

3. Replace the drain plug and remove transmission pan.

4. To prevent the accidental removal of the accumulator pistons while the valve body assembly is removed, it is advisable to make a holding plate.

5. Remove the 17 valve body bolts, note the locations and length of each bolt for reference during assembly.

6. Raise the valve body slightly and install the prefabricated holding plate, using the oil pan bolts.

7. Disconnect the throttle valve control cable from the throttle cam and remove the valve body from the transmission.

8. When installing the valve body, hold the throttle cam in fully raised position and connect the end of the throttle valve cable to the slot in the throttle cam.

9. Install the valve body by aligning the manual valve shift lever pin with the manual valve.

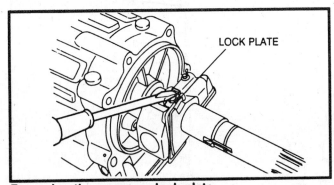

Removing the governor lock plate

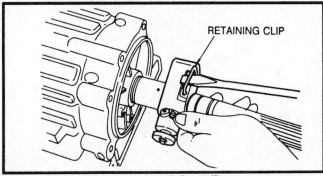

Removing the governor retaining clip

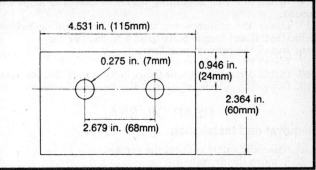

Accumulator holding plate dimensions

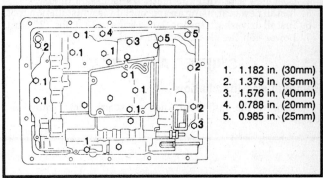

Valve body bolt locations and lengths

1. 1.182 in. (30mm)
2. 1.379 in. (35mm)
3. 1.576 in. (40mm)
4. 0.788 in. (20mm)
5. 0.985 in. (25mm)

10. Install and hand tighten 4 bolts, then remove the accumulator piston holding plate.

11. Install all the valve body bolts in the correct locations and torque to 5.8–8.7 ft. lbs. (8.0–12.0 Nm).

12. Install new oil screen and torque the bolts to 3.6–4.3 ft. lbs. (5–6 Nm).

13. Install oil pan with a new gasket.

14. Torque pan bolts to 2.9–3.6 ft. lbs. (0.4–0.5 Nm).

15. Lower the vehicle and fill the transmission with correct amount of Dexron®II transmission fluid.

16. Bring engine and transmission to normal operating temperature, check transmission for proper fluid level and leaks and operation.

GOVERNOR

Removal and Installation

1. Raise and safely support the vehicle.

2. Remove the driveshaft.

3. Disconnect the speedometer cable.

4. Remove the mounting rubber bolt on the center part of the rear mounting frame.

5. Remove the exhaust pipe bracket.

6. Remove the 4 bolts and bracket from the rear mounting frame.

7. Remove the 6 bolts, rear cover and gasket.

8. Remove the snapring, pull out the speedometer drive gear and then the next snapring.

9. Raise the governor retaining clip and remove the governor assembly from the output shaft.

10. Install the governor assembly onto the output shaft while raising the retaining clip.

11. Insert the end of the retaining clip into the hole in the output shaft and check that it is fitted properly.

12. Install the snapring, speedometer gear and next snapring onto the output shaft.

13. Install a new rear cover seal and gasket and torque the cover bolts to 19.5–30.4 ft. lbs. (27–42 Nm).

14. Install the rear mounting frame bracket and align the mount.
15. Lower the transmission to align the mounting rubber bolts. Install and torque bolts to 32.5 ft. lbs. (45 Nm).
16. Install the exhaust pipe bracket.
17. Install the speedometer cable.
18. Install driveshaft, torque flange bolts to 18 ft. lbs. (25 Nm).
19. Lower the vehicle, check and add fluid as needed.

REAR OIL SEAL

Removal and Installation

1. Raise and safely support the vehicle.
2. Remove the driveshaft.
3. Pry seal from case, using an appropriate tool.
4. Coat new seal with automatic transmission fluid.
5. Install new seal, using an appropriate seal installation tool.
6. Install driveshaft, torque flange bolts to 18 ft. lbs. (25 Nm).
7. Lower vehicle, check and add fluid as needed.

SHIFTER ASSEMBLY

Removal and Installation

1. Remove the shift lever knob set screw, then remove the knob.

2. Remove the 4 screws to upper cover and remove upper cover, with light.
3. Remove the neutral safety switch.
4. Remove the rubber boot from the shift bracket.
5. Remove the nut and spring washer, control shaft and shift lever. Then remove the control shaft and shift lever from its bracket.

NOTE: The shift lever is pressed to the control shaft and must be replace with new when removed.

6. Disconnect the shift lever rod by turning it counterclockwise, then remove the rod from the opening at the upper side of the shift lever.
7. Compress the shift lever rod return spring and remove the selector pin from the slot in the lower part of the shift lever by turning it 90 degrees. Then remove the spring.
8. Inspect the shifter assembly for wear and damage.
9. Install the shift lever rod return spring into position through the upper opening in the shift lever.
10. Apply a thin coat of grease to the selector pin.
11. Install the selector pin to the shift lever by compressing the return spring. The longer end should be turned to the shift lever bracket.
12. Insert the shift lever rod into the shift lever, then screw it onto the selector pin.

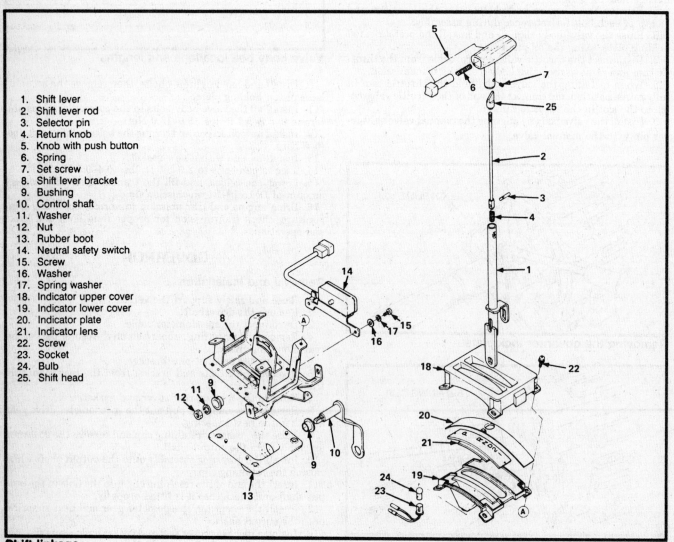

1. Shift lever
2. Shift lever rod
3. Selector pin
4. Return knob
5. Knob with push button
6. Spring
7. Set screw
8. Shift lever bracket
9. Bushing
10. Control shaft
11. Washer
12. Nut
13. Rubber boot
14. Neutral safety switch
15. Screw
16. Washer
17. Spring washer
18. Indicator upper cover
19. Indicator lower cover
20. Indicator plate
21. Indicator lens
22. Screw
23. Socket
24. Bulb
25. Shift head

Shift linkage

13. Adjustment the shift lever rod to projection beyond the upper face of the shift lever approximately 1.8 in. (46mm) when the tapper face at the end of the rod is turned to the push button.

14. Install the 2 bushings to the shift lever bracket.

15. Apply a thin coat of grease to the bushings and then install the control shaft to the bracket.

16. Press the the shift lever to the control shaft. Install a washer and nut, torque the nut to 21.7 ft. lbs. (30 Nm).

17. Remove the nut and washer, reinstall the nut and spring washer and torque nut to 21.7 ft. lbs. (30 Nm).

18. Install the rubber boot on the shift bracket.

19. Install and adjust the neutral safety switch.

20. Install the indicator light on the lower cover and install to bracket with slider and upper cover.

21. Adjust the setting position of the upper cover, so that the red mark on the slider lines up with the indicator plate when the shift lever is moved through each position.

22. Apply a thin coat of grease to the cutaway portion of the push button contact with the shift lever rod end, then install the push button with the grease face down on the knob together with the spring.

23. Install the knob assembly on the shift lever by depressing the push button, then attaching the knob with a new setscrew.

24. Move the shift lever into position of **N** or **P** and check that the push button freeplay is 0.008–0.047 in. (0.2–1.2mm). If out of range repeat adjustment in Step 13.

25. Check shifter for proper operation.

REMOVAL AND INSTALLATION

TRANSMISSION REMOVAL

NOTE: Note the location and length of each bolt, to use as reference during reassembly.

1. Disconnect the negative battery cable.
2. Disconnect the throttle valve control cable.
3. Remove the transmission dipstick.
4. Raise and safely support vehicle.
5. Drain the transmission.
6. Remove the starter bolts, move starter to the front of the vehicle and support.
7. Disconnect the driveshaft.
8. Disconnect the shifter control rod.
9. Disconnect the speedometer cable.
10. Remove the exhaust pipe bracket.
11. Disconnect the transmission cooler lines.
12. Remove the torque converter housing cover.
13. Remove the torque converter to engine bolts.
14. Remove the bolt on the center part of the rear mounting frame.
15. Raise the engine and transmission and support the rear of the engine to hold in in position when the transmission is removed.
16. Support transmission with transmission jack.
17. Remove the rear mounting bolts or nuts and remove bracket.
18. Lower the engine and transmission slightly, remove remaining bolts and nuts.
19. Carefully lower transmission toward rear of the vehicle, taking care so the torque converter does not fall out.

TRANSMISSION INSTALLATION

NOTE: If the distance between the torque converter housing to the front face of the converter is not approximately 1.3779 in. (35mm), reinstall the torque converter, before installing the transmission to engine.

1. Install the transmission to the engine, then install the converter housing bolts and nuts. Torque the bolts and nuts to 29 ft. lbs. (40 Nm).
2. Install the rear mounting frame bracket and align the mount.
3. Lower the transmission to align the mounting rubber bolts. Install and torque bolts to 32.5 ft. lbs. (45 Nm).
4. Install the converter to drive plate bolts and torque to 13.7 ft. lbs. (19 Nm).
5. Install the under cover on the converter housing.
6. Install the under cover on the front part of the engine.
7. Connect the oil cooler lines to the transmission side joints and tighten the joint nuts to 14.5 ft. lbs. (20 Nm).
8. Install the exhaust pipe bracket and connect the speedometer cable.
9. Connect the shift lever control rod to the shift lever.
10. If the joint pin hole in the shift lever is not in alignment with that in the control rod when the transmission and shift lever are in neutral, the length of the control rod should be adjusted.
11. Connect the driveshaft and torque the flange bolts to 18 ft. lbs. (25 Nm).
12. Install the starter and torque the bolts to 28.9 ft. lbs. (40 Nm).
13. Lower the vehicle and install the dipstick tube.
14. Connect the throttle cable valve control cable and adjust the setting of the cable.
15. Connect the negative battery cable.
16. Refill the transmission to the proper level with Dexron®II transmission fluid.

BENCH OVERHAUL

Before Disassembly

Cleanliness is an important factor in the overhaul of the automatic transmission. Before opening up this unit, the entire outside of the transmission assembly should be cleaned, preferable with a high pressure washer such as a car wash spray unit. Dirt entering the transmission internal parts will negate all the time and effort spent on the overhaul. During inspection and reassembly all parts should be thoroughly cleaned with solvent then dried with compressed air. Wiping cloths and rags should not be used to dry parts since lint will find its way into the valve body passages.

Wheel bearing grease, long used to hold thrust washers and lube parts, should not be used. Lube seals with clean transmission fluid and use ordinary petroleum jelly to hold the thrust washers and to ease the assembly of seals, since it will not leave a harmful residue as grease often will. Do not use solvent on neoprene seals, friction plates if they are to be reused, or thrust washers. Be wary of nylon parts if the transmission failure was due to failure of the cooling system. Nylon parts exposed to water or antifreeze solutions can swell and distort and must be replaced.

Before installing bolts into aluminum parts, always dip the threads into clean transmission fluid. Antiseize compound can also be used to prevent bolts from galling the aluminum and seizing. Always use a torque wrench to keep from stripping the threads. Take care when installing new O-rings, especially the smaller O-rings. The internal snaprings should be expanded and the external rings should be compressed, if they are to be re-used. This will help insure proper seating when installed.

Converter Inspection

1. Remove the torque converter from the transmission.
2. Drain and inspect the fluid from the converter.
3. If the converter fluid is discolored but does not contain any metal particles, the converter is probably not damaged. Color is not an indicator of torque converter damage.
4. If the converter fluid contains metal particles, the converter is damaged internally and must be replaced.

5. Check the surface of the converter hub for wear and scoring.
6. Measure the stator endplay, if the stator endplay is greater than 0.059 in. (1.5mm), the torque converter should be replaced.
6. Insert a turning tool J–33953 or equivalent, through the sleeve in the converter and set it to cutaway portion of the stator thrush washer.
7. Insert the stopper so that it fits in the notch of the convert-er hub outer race and outer race of the one-way clutch.
8. The one-way clutch should lock when turned counterclock-wise and rotate freely when turned clockwise.
9. If the clutch does not pass these test, the torque converter must be replaced.

Transmission Disassembly

NOTE: The valve body and other components use bolts of different lengths. Note the locations and lengths of each bolt as removed to use for reference during reassembly.

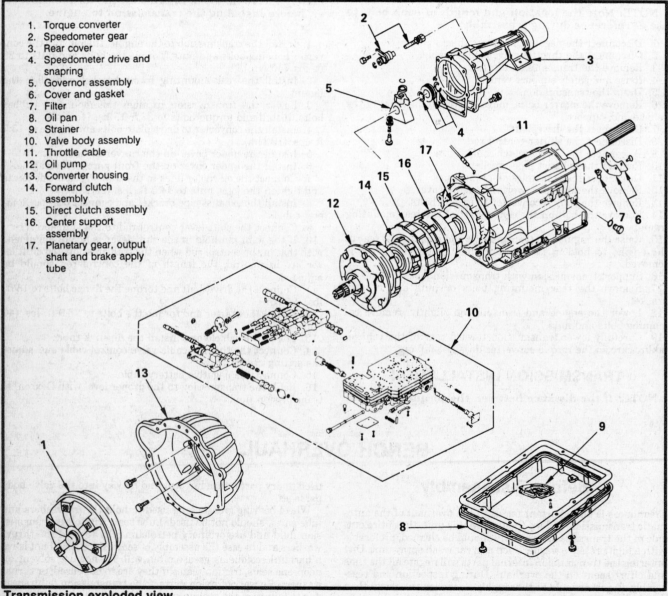

1. Torque converter
2. Speedometer gear
3. Rear cover
4. Speedometer drive and snapring
5. Governor assembly
6. Cover and gasket
7. Filter
8. Oil pan
9. Strainer
10. Valve body assembly
11. Throttle cable
12. Oil pump
13. Converter housing
14. Forward clutch assembly
15. Direct clutch assembly
16. Center support assembly
17. Planetary gear, output shaft and brake apply tube

Transmission exploded view

1. Make certain the transmission is properly secured on a transmission stand.

2. Remove the rear cover, taking care not to damage oil seal.

3. Flatten out the lock plate and remove bolt at governor.

4. Remove the governor valve assembly by releasing the retaining spring.

5. Remove the oil pan with the transmission positioned so the oil pan side is down.

6. Remove the valve body mounting bolts and valve body, note the locations and lengths of bolts as removed.

7. Disengage the throttle control cable from the cam and remove the valve body.

8. Remove the accumulator pistons, by blowing compressed air into the valve body from the opening.

CAUTION

Wear eye protection when using compressed air. This procedure with force fluid out with the accumulator pistons.

---

9. Remove the parking lock pawl bracket, torsion spring, lock pawl shaft and lock pawl.

10. Remove the slotted spring pin, by drilling out the staked portion.

11. Remove the manual shaft, manual valve lever and parking lock rod.

12. Using an appropriate puller, remove oil pump assembly.

13. Remove the forward clutch assembly.

14. Remove the direct clutch assembly.

15. Remove the center support assembly retaining bolts on the valve body side.

16. Remove the center support assembly and sun gear assembly together.

17. Remove the retaining snapring, planetary gear, output shaft and brake apply tube. If the brake apply tube and thrust washer are stuck together and will not come out, remove then from the case.

Unit Disassembly and Assembly
FORWARD CLUTCH ASSEMBLY

Disassembly

1. Remove the snapring, then remove the direct clutch hub, forward clutch hub, clutch plates and discs.

2. Remove the thrust bearing and bearing races fitted between the input shaft and clutch hub.

3. Remove the inner snapring, then remove the clutch plates

and discs. Fasten these parts together to maintain the original combination.

4. Compress the spring retainer and return springs, using an appropriate spring compressor.

5. Remove the snapring, then remove the spring compressor.

6. Remove the spring retainer and return springs.

7. Temporarily install the forward clutch to the oil pump, and apply compressed air to oil passage in pump to remove piston.

8. Remove forward clutch from oil pump.

9. Remove the O-rings from the inner and outer circumferences of the forward clutch piston. Take care not to damage surfaces with metal tools.

Inspection

1. Inspect piston assembly components for any signs of wear.

2. Shake the piston to see that the check ball moves freely.

3. Check for leaks in piston, by using compressed air.

4. Check sealing faces, splines and thrust bearing face for wear.

5. Check the direct clutch hub lugs and face for wear.

6. Check that the return spring free height is 1.312 in. (33.3mm) for the I-Mark and 0.635 in. (16.12mm) for the P'UP.

7. Check springs for distortion.

8. Check that the disc thickness is at least 0.082 in. (2.1mm).

9. Inspect bearing surfaces for wear.

Assembly

1. Install new O-rings onto piston.

2. Apply transmission fluid to piston and O-rings and install piston, with check ball side toward the forward clutch.

3. Install the return spring and retainer.

4. Compress the return springs and spring retainer and install the snapring.

5. Temporarily install the clutch assembly to the case with the inner snapring and then install the outer snapring.

7. Temporarily install the forward clutch to the oil pump.

8. Using a dial indicator, measure the piston stroke by applying 57–114 psi (4–8 kg/cm^2) of compressed air to oil passage in pump.

9. If the piston stroke is beyond 0.060–0.092 in. (1.42–2.33mm), the clutch pack must be inspected for wear, distortion or excessive fluid on discs.

10. Remove the outer snapring ring, direct clutch hub and a single clutch plate and disc.

11. Install the thin inner snapring into the ring groove in the lower side of the drum. The snapring ends should not be positioned near the groove into which the clutch plate lug is fitted.

12. Install the disc and plate.

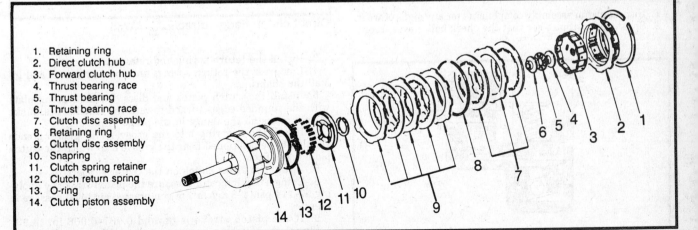

1. Retaining ring
2. Direct clutch hub
3. Forward clutch hub
4. Thrust bearing race
5. Thrust bearing
6. Thrust bearing race
7. Clutch disc assembly
8. Retaining ring
9. Clutch disc assembly
10. Snapring
11. Clutch spring retainer
12. Clutch return spring
13. O-ring
14. Clutch piston assembly

Forward clutch assembly

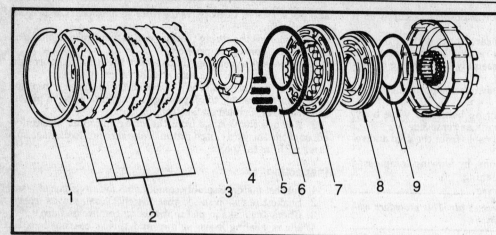

1. Retaining ring
2. Clutch disc assembly
3. Snapring
4. Clutch return spring retainer
5. Clutch return springs
6. O-rings
7. Clutch piston assembly
8. Direct clutch and brake piston
9. O-rings

Direct clutch assembly

13. Install the thrust bearing and race fitted between the input shaft and clutch hub, to the input shaft using petroleum jelly.
14. Install the forward clutch hub fully into position by aligning the lugs on the forward clutch discs with the grooves in the forward clutch hub.
15. Install the direct clutch hub outer snapring into the forward clutch drum. The snapring ends should not be positioned near the groove into which the clutch plate lug is fitted.
16. Secure the thrust bearing and bearing race to the forward clutch hub, using petroleum jelly.

DIRECT CLUTCH

Disassembly

1. Remove the snapring, then remove the clutch backing plate, discs and plates from the direct clutch drum.
2. Compress the return spring and spring retainer using an appropriate spring compressor.
3. Remove the snapring and spring compressing tool.
4. Remove the return spring and spring retainer.
5. Temporarily assembly the direct clutch to the center support and using extreme care apply compressed air to oil passage to remove piston. Protect piston from impact damage by placing a rag on work bench.
6. Remove the direct clutch from the center support.
7. Remove O-rings from the inner and outer pistons.

Inspection

1. Inspect piston assembly components for any signs of wear.
2. Shake the piston to see that the check ball moves freely.

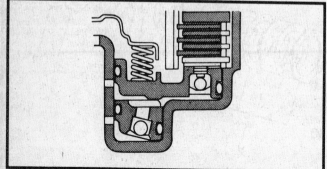

Direct clutch flange direction—AW75

3. Check for leaks in piston, by using compressed air.
4. Check sealing faces, splines and thrust bearing face for wear.
5. Check the direct clutch hub lugs and face for wear.
6. Check that the return spring free height is 1.312 in. (33.3mm) for the I-Mark and 0.635 in. (16.12mm) for the P'UP.
7. Check springs for distortion.
8. Check that the disc thickness is at least 0.082 in. (2.1mm).
9. Inspect bearing surfaces for wear.

Assembly

1. Install new O-rings onto piston.
2. Apply transmission fluid to piston and O-rings and install piston, with check ball side toward the forward clutch.

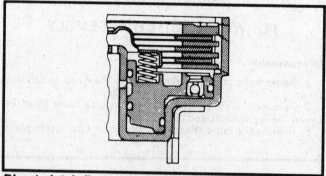

Direct clutch flange direction—AW55

3. Install the return spring and retainer.
4. Compress the return springs and spring retainer and install the snapring.
5. Install the clutch plates and discs. Install backing plate with the rounded edges turned toward the clutch discs. Make certain to install the flange in the proper direction.
6. Install the snapring into the groove. The snapring ends should not be positioned near the groove into which the clutch plate lug is fitted.
7. Install the direct clutch on the center support.
8. Using a dial indicator measure the piston stroke by applying 57–114 psi (4–8 kg/cm²) of compressed air to oil passage in pump.
9. If the piston stroke is beyond 0.037–0.068 in. (0.93–1.72mm), the clutch pack must be inspected for wear, distortion or excessive fluid on discs.

CENTER SUPPORT

Disassembly

1. Remove the snapring at the end of the sun gear at the front side of the center support assembly.
2. Remove the rear brake hub assembly and sun gear from the center support.
3. Remove the snapring from the front brake side of the center support and remove the clutch backing plate, disc and plate.
4. Compress the return spring and spring retainer using an appropriate spring compressor.
5. Remove the snapring, then remove the compressor.
6. Remove the spring retaining and return springs.
7. Position the center support on the work bench with the front brake side down, then remove the piston by applying compressed air into the front brake piston oil passage in the center support. Protect piston from impact damage by placing a rag on work bench.
8. Remove the O-rings from the piston. Take care not to damage grooves with metal tools.
9. Invert the center support and remove snapring for rear side piston.
10. Remove the clutch backing plate, discs and plates from the center support. Fasten plates together in order of removal to maintain original combinations.
11. Compress the spring retainer and return spring, using an appropriate spring compressor.
12. Remove the snapring and spring compressor.
13. Remove the spring retainer and the return springs.
14. Position the center support assembly on work bench with rear brake side down and remove the rear piston by applying compressed air pressure to the oil passage in the center support.

Protect piston from impact damage by placing a rag on work bench.
15. Remove O-rings from the pistons.

Inspection

1. Inspect piston assembly components for any signs of wear.
2. Shake the piston to see that the check ball moves freely.
3. Check for leaks in piston, by using compressed air.
4. Check sealing faces, splines and thrust bearing face for wear.
5. Check the gear teeth, splines and inner race for damage or wear.
6. Check that the return spring free height is 0.635 in. (16.12mm).
7. Check springs for distortion.
8. Check that the disc thickness is at least 0.082 in. (2.1mm).
9. Inspect bearing surfaces for wear.
10. Check the hub and lugs for damage or wear.
11. Check all snapring and sealing ring grooves for wear.

Assembly

1. Insert new seal rings on the center support and the sun gear ring grooves, fasten the ring ends together, then apply transmission fluid to the rings.
2. Install the new O-rings on the front and rear brake pistons.
3. Apply transmission fluid to the front brake piston. Install the piston on the seal ring side of the center support, so that the spring seat hole is turned outward.
4. Install the return springs into the seat holes in the front brake piston and install the spring retainer over the springs.
5. Compress the springs and retainer using an appropriate spring compressor and install the snapring.

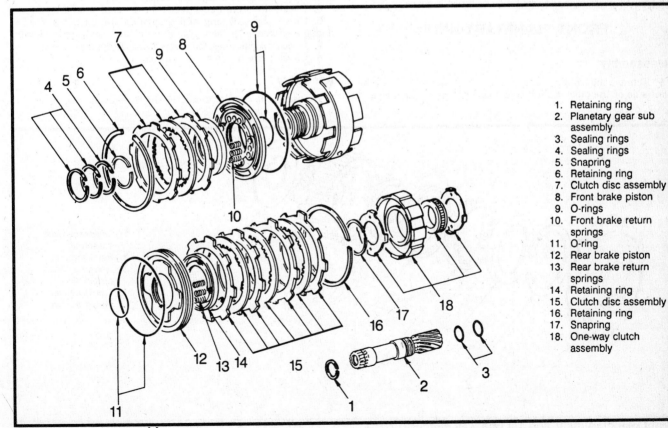

1. Retaining ring
2. Planetary gear sub assembly
3. Sealing rings
4. Sealing rings
5. Snapring
6. Retaining ring
7. Clutch disc assembly
8. Front brake piston
9. O-rings
10. Front brake return springs
11. O-ring
12. Rear brake piston
13. Rear brake return springs
14. Retaining ring
15. Clutch disc assembly
16. Retaining ring
17. Snapring
18. One-way clutch assembly

Center support assembly

6. Remove the spring compressor.

7. Apply transmission fluid to the rear brake piston. Install the piston on the center support.

8. Install the return springs into the seat holes in the rear brake piston and install the spring retainer over the springs.

9. Compress the springs and retainer using an appropriate spring compressor and install the snapring.

10. Remove the spring compressor.

11. Invert the center support and install the front brake clutch plate, disc and backing plate. The backing plate should be installed so the rounded edges are facing the disc.

12. Install the snapring, making certain the ends are not positioned near the clutch plate lug fitting groove.

13. Invert the center support to bring the rear side up. Install the rear brake plates, discs and backing plate. The face of the backing plate with the rounded edges should face the clutch disc.

14. Install the snapring and make certain that it fits properly into the groove.

15. Using a dial indicator measure the piston stroke by applying 57–114 psi (4–8 kg/cm^2) of compressed air to the front and rear brake oil passage intermittently.

16. If the piston stroke is beyond 0.026–0.051 in. (0.65–1.30mm) for the front brake and 0.037–0.068 in. (0.93–1.72mm) for the AW55 or 0.040–0.089 in. (1.01–2.25mm) for the AW75 rear brake, the clutch pack must be inspected for wear, distortion or excessive fluid on discs.

17. Install the brake hub assembly to the sun gear with the cupped side turned to the sun gear splines.

18. Hold the rear brake hub and check that the sun gear can be rotated freely in the counterclockwise direction and is locked in the clockwise direction. If not replace the rear brake hub.

19. Install the sun gear on the center support and push it fully into position by aligning the grooves in the outer circumference of the brake hub with lugs on the discs. Install the snapring in the splined portion at the front side of the sun gear.

FRONT PLANETARY UNIT

Disassembly

1. Remove the front planetary gear carrier assembly from the front side of the output shaft together with the brake disc and clutch plates. If the thrust washers were not removed, remove them now.

2. Remove the thrust plate from the front planetary gear carrier.

3. Remove the brake disc and clutch plates from the planetary gear carrier. Fasten plates together in order of removal to maintain original combinations.

4. Remove the reaction plate from the planetary gear carrier.

5. Remove the snapring from the gear carrier and remove the one-way clutch and nylon thrust washer.

6. Remove the backing plate from the output shaft and remove the brake apply tube, if not already removed.

7. Compress the snapring retaining the front planetary ring gear on the output shaft drum and remove the front planetary ring gear from the output shaft.

8. Remove the intermediate shaft assembly and rear planetary gear from the output shaft.

9. Remove the thrust bearing and bearing race from the output shaft. This thrust washer requires only a single bearing race.

10. Remove the nylon thrust washer and rear planetary gear carrier assembly from the intermediate shaft.

11. Remove the thrust bearing and bearing race fitted in position between the rear planetary gear carrier and ring gear.

12. Invert the intermediate shaft assembly and remove the ring retaining the rear planetary ring gear on the shaft, then remove the ring gear and thrust bearing race from the intermediate shaft.

Inspection

1. Check bearings and races for any signs of damage or wear.

2. Check the one-way clutch sprags for wear or damage.

3. Check the one-way clutch races for damage or wear.

4. Check the reaction plate lugs, face contact with the disc, and inner race for damage or wear.

5. Check the pinion gear teeth for damage or wear.

6. Check the seal ring and groove on the output shaft for damage or wear. The seal ring must rotate freely on the shaft.

7. Check oil passages for restrictions or damage.

8. Check plate and washer surfaces for wear.

Assembly

1. Install the smaller diameter thrust bearing race on the in-

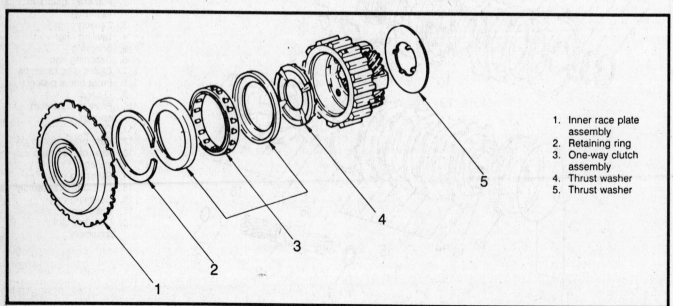

1. Inner race plate assembly
2. Retaining ring
3. One-way clutch assembly
4. Thrust washer
5. Thrust washer

Front planetary gear and 1st one-way clutch

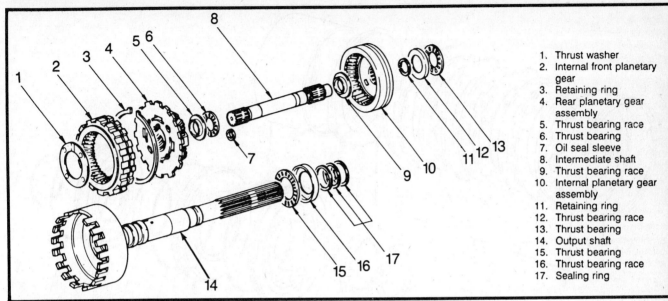

1. Thrust washer
2. Internal front planetary gear
3. Retaining ring
4. Rear planetary gear assembly
5. Thrust bearing race
6. Thrust bearing
7. Oil seal sleeve
8. Intermediate shaft
9. Thrust bearing race
10. Internal planetary gear assembly
11. Retaining ring
12. Thrust bearing race
13. Thrust bearing
14. Output shaft
15. Thrust bearing
16. Thrust bearing race
17. Sealing ring

Rear planetary gear and output shaft

termediate shaft in position between the rear planetary ring gear and the carrier.

2. Install the rear planetary ring gear and carrier, with the spline boss turned outward, then install the retaining ring and check that it is properly seated in position.

3. Invert the intermediate shaft assembly and install the thrust bearing and race.

4. Install the rear planetary gear carrier assembly by meshing the gear with the ring gear.

5. Install the new nylon thrust washer by aligning its tangs with the fitting grooves in the rear planetary gear carrier.

6. Install new seal rings into the seal ring grooves in the output shaft and fasten the ring ends together. Apply transmission fluid to the rings.

7. Install the thrust bearing and race in position between the output shaft and rear planetary gear.

NOTE: The bearing race is not installed on the output shaft side.

8. Install the intermediate shaft assembly on the output shaft.

9. Turn the front planetary ring gear to bring the snapring to the output shaft rear side.

10. The snapring end should be positioned within a large groove between the lugs on the output shaft.

11. Compress the snapring and depress the ring gear to force the snapring into the groove.

12. Check that the snapring is installed correctly into the groove.

13. Install the thrust bearing in position between the output shaft and case.

14. Set the bearing race to the transmission case using petroleum jelly.

FIRST AND REVERSE BRAKE

Disassembly

1. Remove the brake apply tube if not already removed.

2. Compress the spring retainer and return springs, using and appropriate spring compressor.

3. Remove the snapring, then remove the spring compressor, spring retainer and return springs.

4. Invert the transmission on the stand to bring the front side down.

5. Remove the inner and outer piston and reaction sleeve from the cylinder by applying compressed air into the inner and outer piston oil passages in the case. Place a clean cloth over the work bench to protect the piston against damage.

Inspection

1. Inspect piston assembly components for any signs of wear.

2. Inspect the transmission case for cracks.

2. Check the gasket fitting faces of the case for scores or distortion.

3. Check the clutch lugs, piston bores, O-rings or seal ring fitting faces, output shaft bushing and snapring grooves for damage or wear.

4. Check that the return spring free height is 0.635 in. (16.12mm). The wear limit is 0.619 in. (15.7mm).

5. Check springs for distortion.

Assembly

1. Install new O-rings onto piston. The thin O-ring is fitted to the outer circumference of the reaction sleeve.

2. Apply transmission fluid to the O-rings.

3. Install the O-rings on the inner piston and cupped side of the reaction sleeve, then install the outer piston into the other side of the reaction sleeve.

4. Set the transmission case with the front side up.

5. Install the return springs on the seating face of the outer piston, then position the spring retainer over the springs.

6. Using a spring compressor, compress the return springs and spring retainer, then install the snapring. Remove the spring compressor.

OIL PUMP

Disassembly

1. To gain stability, install the oil pump onto the torque converter.

2. Remove the bolts holding the cover and remove the pump cover.

3. Remove the O-rings and seal rings from the pump.

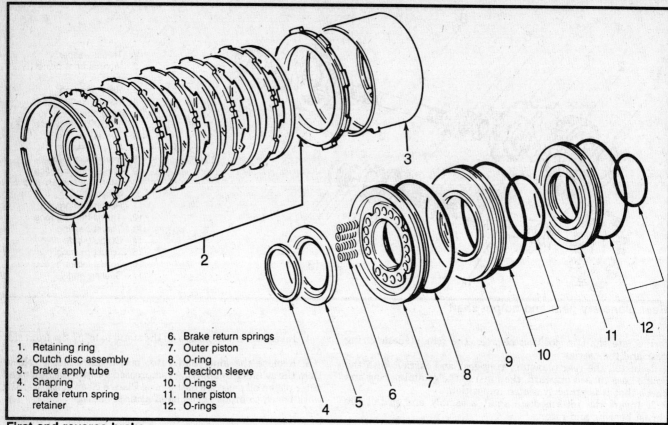

1. Retaining ring
2. Clutch disc assembly
3. Brake apply tube
4. Snapring
5. Brake return spring retainer
6. Brake return springs
7. Outer piston
8. O-ring
9. Reaction sleeve
10. O-rings
11. Inner piston
12. O-rings

First and reverse brake

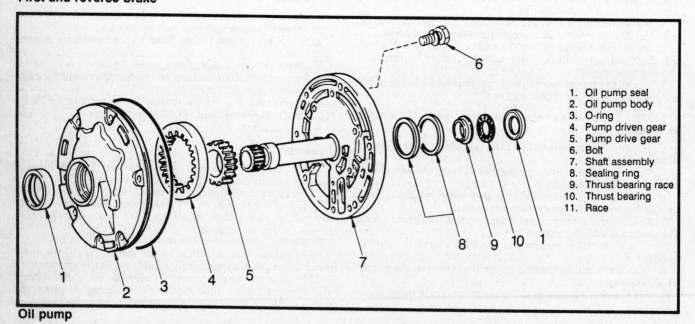

1. Oil pump seal
2. Oil pump body
3. O-ring
4. Pump driven gear
5. Pump drive gear
6. Bolt
7. Shaft assembly
8. Sealing ring
9. Thrust bearing race
10. Thrust bearing
11. Race

Oil pump

4. Remove the pump body from the torque converter, then remove the oil pump drive gear and driven gear.

Inspection

1. Check the sliding faces of the pump gears for wear, scores or damage.
2. Install the drive gear and driven gear into the pump body.

3. Check that the clearance between the driven gear and body is 0.0028–0.0059 in. (0.07–0.15mm).
4. Check that the clearance between the tip of the driven gear teeth and the crescent is 0.0043–0.0055 in. (0.11–0.14mm).
5. Using a feeler gauge and straight edge, check that the clearance between the gear face and body face is 0.0008–0.0020 in. (0.02–0.05mm)..

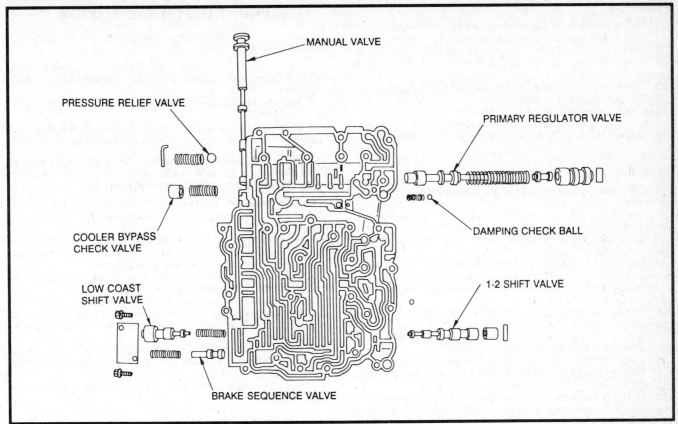

Lower valve body

6. Check the joint faces for cracks, scores, damage and flatness.
7. Check the oil seal for damage and lipped portion for deterioration. Check the seal ring groove for damage.
8. Check the bushings for scores or damage.
9. Check the splines on the stator shaft for damage.
10. Check the oil passages for restrictions.

Assembly

1. Install new seal rings into the seal ring grooves in the pump cover and fasten the ring ends together. Apply transmission fluid to the rings.
2. Install a new oil seal, using an appropriate seal tool.
3. Install the driven gear and drive gear, into the pump body.
4. Assemble the pump body to the torque converter.
5. Install the pump cover on the pump body and finger tighten the bolts.
6. Install the pump alignment tool J-25280, or equivalent over the pump body and cover.
7. Torque the pump cover bolts to 4.3–6.5 ft. lbs. (6–9 Nm).
8. Remove the pump alignment tool.
9. Install a new O-ring on the outer circumference of the pump body and remove the pump from the torque converter.

LOWER VALVE BODY

Disassembly

NOTE: The valve body bolt lengths are different. Note the locations and lengths of each bolt as removed to use for reference during reassembly.

1. Remove the bolts holding the upper valve body side.

2. Invert the valve body assembly. Remove the shift lever detent spring after removing the single bolt. Then remove the manual valve from the lower valve body.
3. Remove bolts from the lower valve body side, then remove the small valve body cover.
4. Raise and invert the lower valve body together with the plate. When inverting the lower valve body, take care not to lose the check ball. Keep the separated valve bodies in a safe place to prevent losing the check balls.
5. Remove the separator plate and gaskets from the lower valve body. Keep the gasket until inspection is complete.
6. Carefully note the locations of the check ball and valves.
7. Remove the cooler bypass check valve and spring, then remove the regulator valve damping check ball and spring and second brake ball.
8. Depress the 1-2 shift valve inward and remove the 1-2 shift valve retainer, plug, valve and spring. Keep spring with valve for reassembly.
9. Remove the bolts holding the low coast shift valve cover plate by loosening them gradually. They are under spring pressure.

NOTE: Some valves are under heavy spring pressure. Care should be exercised after the removal of retainers to not allow parts to jump out of position.

10. Shake out the brake sequence valve, spring and low coast valve carefully.
11. Remove the primary regulator valve retainer by depressing the valve sleeve inward, then shake out the sleeve, plunger, spring and primary regulator valve.
12. Remove the pressure relief valve spring retainer, while holding the spring. Keep the ball and spring together for reassembly.

Inspection

1. Check valves for wear, scoring, cracks or damage.
2. Check that each valve moves freely.
3. Check the valve body for cracks or damage.
4. Check valve bores and gasket faces for wear, scores or damage.
5. Check the separator plate for warpage or damage.
6. Check the ports for restrictions.
7. Check valve springs for distortion.
8. Measure the free length of the springs.
9. Inspect check balls for wear, damage and roundness.

Assembly

1. Install the pressure relief ball, spring retainer into the valve body.
2. Install the primary regulator valve and spring into the valve body.
3. Insert the plunger into the sleeve, then install parts into the valve body.
4. Depress the sleeve inward until the regulator valve retainer fitting hole is exposed, then install the retainer.
5. Install the low coast shift valve, brake sequence valve and spring into the valve bores.
6. Install the cover plate with the machined face turned inward.
7. Install the bolts while depressing the cover plate and torque to 3.6–4.3 ft. lbs. (5–6 Nm).
8. Install the 1-2 shift valve spring, valve and plug.
9. Depress the plug inward until the retainer fitting hole is exposed, then install the retainer.
10. Install the new second brake check ball – smaller ball, new regulator valve damping check ball – larger ball, springs, cooler bypass check valve and springs.
11. Install the new lower valve body gasket.

NOTE: The lower valve body gasket differs from the upper valve body gasket.

12. Check that the new gaskets match the old gaskets.
13. Install the separator plate on the valve body.
14. Temporarily install a shorter bolt against the check valve spring tension, so that the plate is compressed.

FRONT UPPER VALVE BODY

Disassembly

1. Invert the valve body while holding the throttle valve retainer in place and remove the check ball and cut-back valve retainer.
2. Remove the cut-back valve plug and valve by tilting the valve body.
3. Remove the fixing bolts while depressing the secondary regulator valve cover plate inward, then remove the cover plate.

NOTE: The internal parts are under spring pressure. Care should be exercised after the removal of retainers to not allow parts to jump out of position.

4. Remove the secondary regulator valve and spring by tilting the valve body. Keep the valve and spring together for reassembly.
5. Depress the kick-down valve inward by turning the throttle cam and hold the valve in that position by setting the cut-back valve retainer temporarily in position.
6. Hold the throttle cam securely by hand and remove the bolt, washers, cam, sleeve and spring.
7. Depress the kick-down valve fully inward and remove the throttle valve retainer and kick-down valve retainer, then remove the kick-down valve, valve spring and throttle valve by tilting the valve body.
8. Remove the throttle valve and spring shims from the opposite side of the body. Kepp the spring and throttle valve together for reassembly.
9. Note the number of shims used and keep them together for reassembly.

Inspection

1. Check valves for wear, scoring, cracks or damage.
2. Check that each valve moves freely.
3. Check the valve body for cracks or damage.
4. Check valve bores and gasket faces for wear, scores or damage.
5. Check the gasket for traces of fluid leakage.
6. Check the ports for restrictions.
7. Check valve springs for distortion.

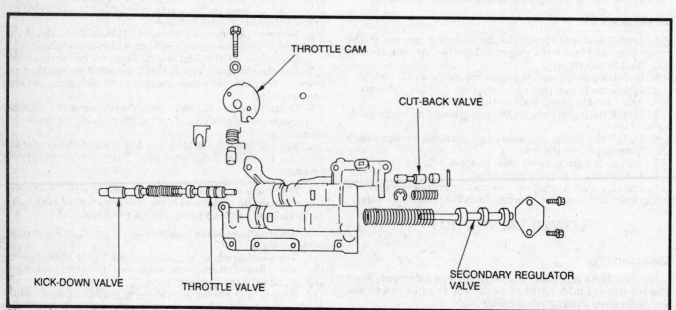

Upper front valve body

8. Measure the free length of the springs.

9. Check the throttle cam face and the hole in the rotary shaft for wear or damage.

Assembly

1. Push the throttle valve fully into the bore.

2. Install the throttle valve retainer, so that its finger is turned to kick-down valve side.

3. Install the throttle valve spring shims and spring on the end of the throttle valve shaft.

4. Install the kick-down valve spring and valve.

5. Depress the kick-down valve and hold it in position temporarily with the cut-back valve retainer.

6. Install the throttle cam sleeve, spring and bolt, by fitting them to the throttle cam.

7. Depress the kick-down valve by turning the throttle cam and remove the temporarily installed retainer.

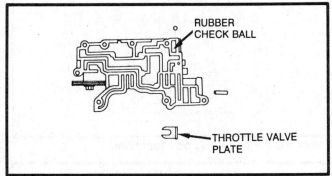

Rubber check ball location

8. Check that the throttle cam returns smoothly to original position when released.

9. Install the secondary regulator valve spring and valve.

10. Install the cover plate with the machined face turned inward. Depress the cover plate and torque the bolts to 3.6–4.3 ft. lbs. (5–6 Nm). Check that the cover plate is not in contact with the throttle valve spring shims.

11. Install the cut-back valve and plug, then install the retainer.

12. Install the new check ball into the correct position.

REAR UPPER VALVE BODY

Disassembly

1. Carefully note the location of the 3 rubber check balls and single steel ball.

2. Remove the check balls. The rubber check balls are not interchangeable with each other.

3. Depress the intermediate shift valve and remove the valve retainer, then remove the intermediate valve plug, valve, 2-3 shift valve and spring. Keep the valve and spring together for reassembly.

4. Depress the 2-3 shift valve body plug and remove the valve retainer, then remove the 2-3 shift valve plug and valve.

5. Remove the bolts on the front side face, while depressing the cover plate and remove the cover plate.

NOTE: Remove cover slowly, it is under pressure from 4 different springs. Take note of the springs locations.

6. Remove the low coast modulator valve, governor modulator valve, clutch sequence valve, intermediate coast modulator valve and the valve springs from their bores. Keep each valve together with its spring for reassembly.

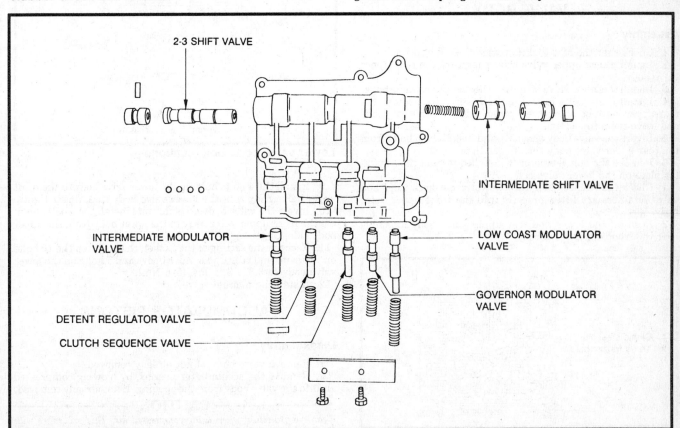

Upper rear valve body

7. Carefully remove the detent regulator valve retainer, then remove the dent regulator valve spring and valve. Keep the valve and spring together for reassembly.

Inspection

1. Check valves for wear, scoring, cracks or damage.
2. Check that each valve moves freely.
3. Check the valve body for cracks or damage.
4. Check valve bores and gasket faces for wear, scores or damage.
5. Check the gasket for traces of fluid leakage.
6. Check the ports for restrictions.
7. Check valve springs for distortion.
8. Measure the free length of the springs.
9. Inspect check balls for wear, damage and roundness.

Assembly

1. Install the detent regulator valve and spring. Depress the valve spring, using a suitable tool that fits into the diameter of the spring coil, then install the retainer.
2. From the detent regulator valve fitting side, install the intermediate modulator valve, sequence valve, governor modulator valve, low modulator valve and valve springs. Install the cover plate with the machined surface turned inward.
3. While holding the cover, install and torque the bolts to 3.6–4.3 ft. lbs. (5–6 Nm).
4. Install the 2-3 shift valve and plug into its bore. Depress the plug and install the retainer.
5. From the opposite side of the bore into which the 2-3 shift valve is, install the 2-3 shift valve spring, intermediate shift valve and plug. Depress the plug and install the retainer.
6. Install the 4 check ball into the correct locations. The rubber balls must be replaced with new.

VALVE BODY

Assembly

1. Check that the new gaskets match the old gaskets.
2. Install a new upper valve body gasket on the rear upper valve body.
3. Install the lower valve body over the rear upper valve body.
4. Install the 3 bolts fastening the lower valve body to the rear upper valve body together from the lower valve body side and leave them finger tight.
5. Invert the valve body assembly and install the 5 bolts from the rear upper valve body side, finger tight.
6. Remove the bolt temporarily installed to hold the separator plate on the lower valve body.
7. Check that a check ball, throttle valve, cut-back valve and valve retainers are fitted properly into the front upper valve body.
8. Position the lower and rear upper valve body assembly over the front upper valve body.

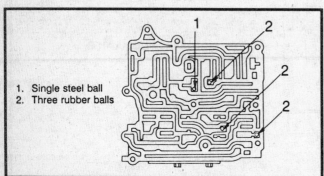

1. Single steel ball
2. Three rubber balls

Check ball locations

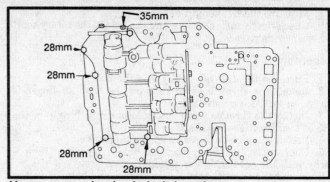

Upper rear valve body bolt locations

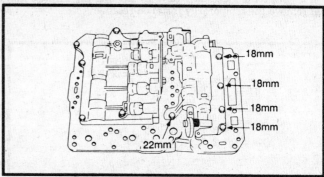

Upper front valve body bolt locations

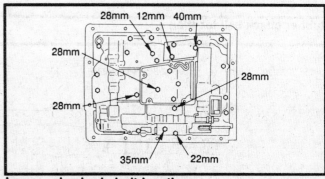

Lower valve body bolt locations

9. Install the 4 bolts holding the lower valve body to the front upper valve body fron the lower valve body side, finger tight.
10. Invert the valve body assembly and install the 5 bolts holding the front upper valve body to the lower body from the upper body side, finger tight.
11. Recheck the setting of the gasket, then tighten the 10 bolts on the front and rear upper valve bodys and 7 bolts on the lower valve body to 3.6–4.3 ft. lbs. (5–6 Nm).
12. Install the manual valve.

ACCUMULATOR PISTONS

Disassembly

1. Remove valve body, if not already removed.
2. Remove the accumulator pistons, by blowing compressed air into the valve body from the opening. If not already removed.

— CAUTION —

Wear eye protection when using compressed air. This procedure with force fluid out with the accumulator pistons.

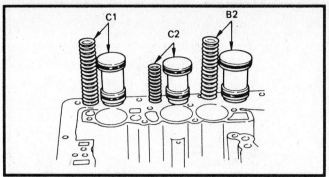

Accumulator pistons

Inspection

1. Inspect piston assembly components for any signs of wear.
2. Check that the spring free height is correct for each spring.
3. Check springs for distortion.

Assembly

1. Install new O-rings onto piston.
2. Install the acculumator pistons and springs into the correct bores.

GOVERNOR

Disassembly

1. Insert finger into bore in the valve body and raise the valve. Remove the retaining ring on the end of the valve shaft, then remove the governor weight.
2. Remove the governor valve shaft, spring and governor valve from the valve bore side of the body.

Inspection

1. Check the valve bore for wear, scoring or damage.
2. Check that the valve moves freely.
3. Check the body for cracks or damage.
4. Check the oil passages for restrictions.
5. Check that the projection of the retaining clip in the valve body bore is more than 0.16 in. (4mm).
6. Check that weight moves freely.
7. Check the spring for distortion.
8. Check that spring free length is 0.813 in. (20.63mm) for gasoline engines or 0.699 in. (17.75mm) for diesel engines.

Assembly

1. Install the governor valve, spring and shaft into body from the valve bore side.
2. Depress the shaft from the bore side and install the weight and retaining ring, then check that the ring is fitted properly into the groove.

Transmission Assembly

1. Position transmission case with front side facing up.
2. Install the thrust bearings and races, taking care that races are facing in the correct direction.
3. Install brake apply tube, so the the cut-out portion of tube is aligned with opening on valve body side of the transmission case. Each finger at the end must be fitted inside the piston properly.
4. Install the planetary carrier assembly.
5. Engage clutch pressure plates with the apply tube.
6. Install the front planetary carrier assembly. Install the thrust bearing in front of the behind carrier.

ACCUMULATOR SPRINGS

Engine		Position Diameter	Spring Free Length	Spring Wire Diameter
Gasoline	C$_1$	1.2529—1.2549 (31.80—31.85)	2.7013 (68.56)	0.0800 (2.03)
	C$_2$	1.2529—1.2549 (31.80—31.85)	2.1729 (55.15)	0.0790 (2.00)
	B$_2$	1.3711—1.3731 (34.80—34.85)	2.6201 (66.50)	0.1024 (2.60)
Diesel	C$_1$	1.2629—1.2549 (31.80—31.85)	2.7013 (68.56)	0.0800 (2.03)
	C$_2$	1.2529—1.2549 (31.80—31.85)	1.5137 (38.42)	0.0800 (2.03)
	B$_2$	1.3711—1.3731 (34.80—34.85)	2.6930 (68.35)	10.1024 (2.60)

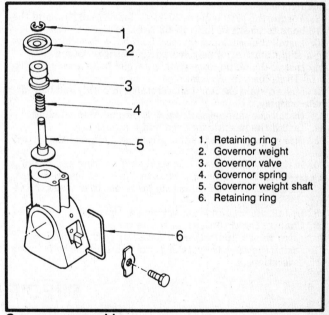

1. Retaining ring
2. Governor weight
3. Governor valve
4. Governor spring
5. Governor weight shaft
6. Retaining ring

Governor assembly

7. Install the clutch discs and plates.
8. Measure the clearance between the clutch plate and case. If the clearance is not 0.028–0.099 in. (0.75–2.5mm), replace the disc or plates.
9. Install the cutaway portion of the inner race plate assembly in the correct location at the valve side of the transmission case. The plate is correctly installed when the snapring groove can be seen.
10. Install the retaining ring.
11. Install the center support assembly and check the operation of the one-way clutch. The sun gear should turn freely counterclockwise and be locked in the clockwise direction.
12. Make certain the oil port in the case is in alignment with that in the center support and install the bolts. Torque the bolts in steps alternately to 17–20 ft. lbs. (24–28 Nm).
13. Install the direct clutch assembly. When properly installed, the end of the sun gear splines coincides with that of the direct clutch splines.
14. Install the races to the direct clutch. Making certain the races are facing in the correct direction.

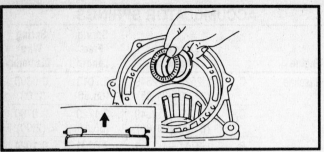

Output shaft thrust bearing direction

15. Install the forward clutch assembly, keep fingers of the direct clutch discs aligned.

16. Check the setting height with a straight edge to see that parts are in proper alignment. The measured valve minus the thickness of the gauge should be approximately 0.06 in. (1.5mm).

17. Install the bearing to the forward clutch. Install the races after applying a slight amount of petroleum jelly to the case.

18. Install the housing O-ring and install the conventer housing.

19. Torque the M10 bolts to 20–30 ft. lbs. (27–42 Nm) and the M12 bolts to 35–49 ft. lbs. (48–68 Nm).

20. Install the bearing and races. Install the races after applying a slight amount of petroleum jelly to the oil pump.

21. Install the oil pump assembly, torque bolts evenly in step to 13–18 ft. lbs. (18–25 Nm).

22. Make certain the input shaft rotates smoothly and has adequate endplay.

23. Install the manual shift valve lever and manual shaft.

24. Install the parking lock rod and a new sleeve.

25. Stake the sleeve in position after installation of the slotted pin.

26. Install the lock pawl, lock pawl shaft, spring and parking lock pawl bracket. Torque the bolts to 4.3–6.5 ft. lbs. (6–9 Nm).

27. Install the throttle cable using care not to damage the O-ring.

28. Install the accumulator pistons and springs.

29. Connect the throttle cable to the cam.

30. Align the manual valve with the pin on the valve lever.

31. Install the valve body, taking care to install the bolts in the correct locations.

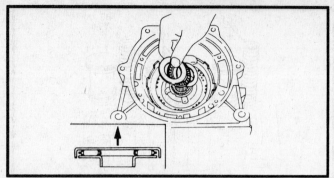

Direct clutch thrust bearing direction

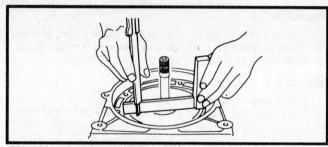

Checking setting height with a straight edge

32. Torque the valve body bolts to 5.8–8.7 ft. lbs. (8.0–12.0 Nm).

33. Install new oil screen and torque the bolts to 3.6–4.3 ft. lbs. (5–6 Nm).

34. Install oil pan with a new gasket.

35. Torque pan bolts to 2.9–3.6 ft. lbs. (0.4–0.5 Nm).

36. Install the filter at the governor.

37. Install the governor assembly onto the output shaft while raising the retaining clip.

38. Insert the end of the retaining clip into the hole in the output shaft and check that it is fitted properly.

39. Install the snapring, speedometer gear and next snapring onto the output shaft.

40. Install a new rear cover seal and gasket and torque the cover bolts to 19.5–30.4 ft. lbs. (27–42 Nm).

SPECIFICATIONS

TORQUE SPECIFICATIONS

	ft. lbs.	kg-m
Converter housing to case (10 mm diameter bolts)	19.5—30.4	2.7—4.2
(12 mm diameter bolts)	34.7—49.2	4.8—6.8
Converter housing to engine	28.9	4.0
Torque converter to drive plate	13.7	1.9
Oil pump to case	13.0—18.1	1.8—2.5
Oil pump cover to pump body	4.3—6.5	0.6—0.9
Drain plug	10.8—14.5	1.5—2.0
Oil pan to case	2.9—3.6	0.4—0.5
Oil screen to valve body	3.6—4.3	0.5—0.6
Valve body to case	5.8—8.7	0.8—1.2

TORQUE SPECIFICATIONS

	ft. lbs.	kg-m
Upper valve body to lower valve body	3.6—4.3	0.5—0.6
Cover plate to valve body	3.6—4.3	0.5—0.6
Throttle cam to valve body	4.3—6.5	0.6—0.9
Parking pawl bracket case	4.3—6.5	0.6—0.9
Center support to case	17.4—20.3	2.4—2.8
Cooler pipe connector to case	14.5—21.7	2.0—3.0
Cooler pipe to connector	14.5	2.0
Rear cover to case	19.5—30.4	2.7—4.2
Rear mounting rubber fixing bolt	32.5	4.5
Rear mounting frame bracket to frame	28.9	4.0
Shift lever to control shaft	21.7	3.0

SPECIAL TOOLS

	J-33950 Pilot sleeve remover		**J-25048** Spring compressor
	J-23907 Pilot bearing remover		**J-25280** Pump alignment tool
	J-26516-A Pilot bearing installer		**J-26508** Oil seal installer ; Rear cover
	J-25041 Holding fixture		**J-29770** Pressure gauge
	J-25042 Oil pump assembly remover		**J-33951** Oil seal installer ; Manual shift valve
	J-25045 Oil seal installer ; Oil pump		**J-33953** Torque converter One-way clutch testing tool kit

OIL FLOW CIRCUIT—P RANGE—AW 55 AND AW 75 TRANSMISSIONS

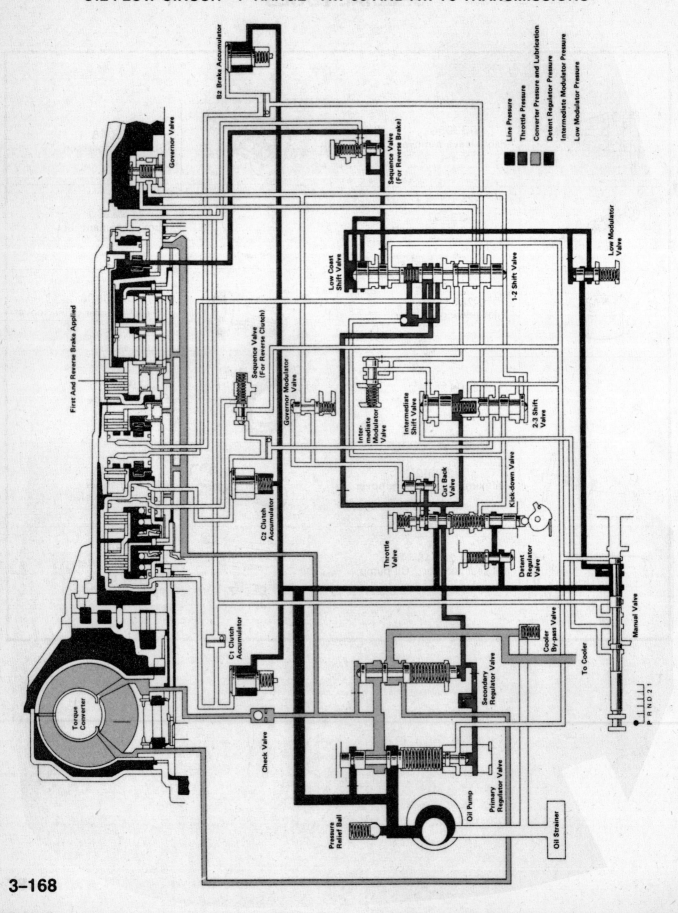

OIL FLOW CIRCUIT — N RANGE — AW 55 AND AW 75 TRANSMISSIONS

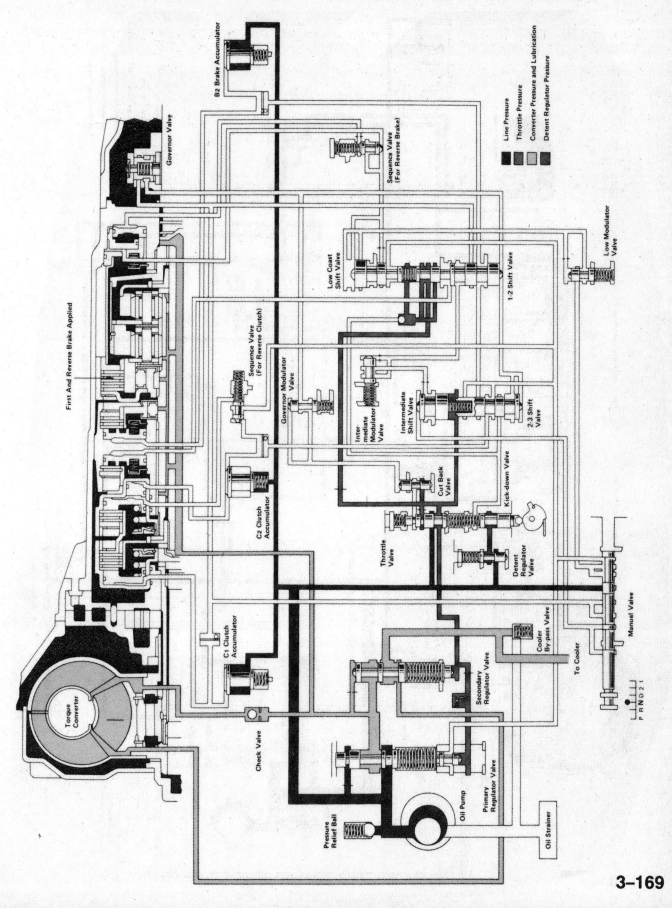

OIL FLOW CIRCUIT – R RANGE – AW 55 AND AW 75 TRANSMISSIONS

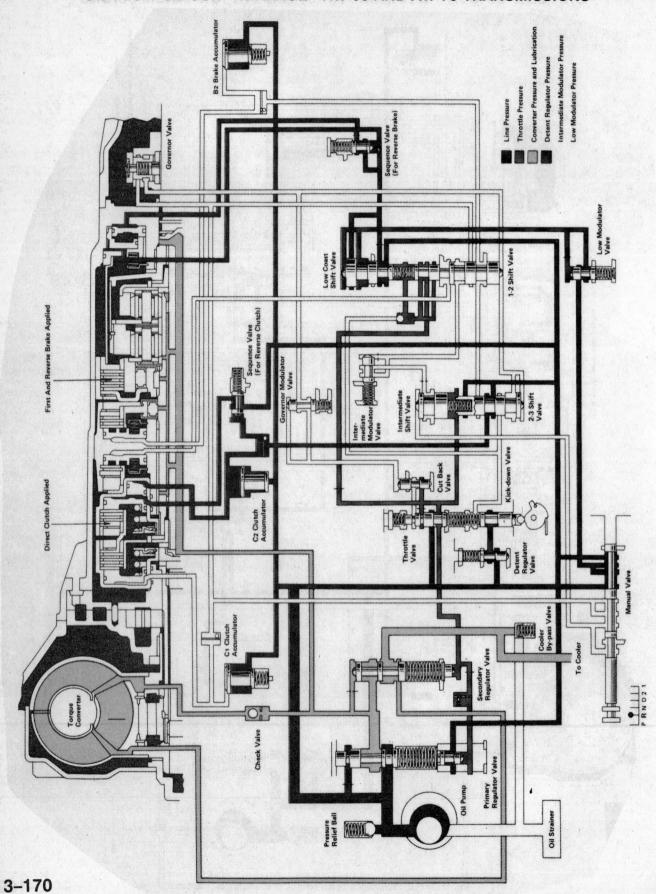

OIL FLOW CIRCUIT — D RANGE FIRST SPEED — AW 55 AND AW 75 TRANSMISSIONS

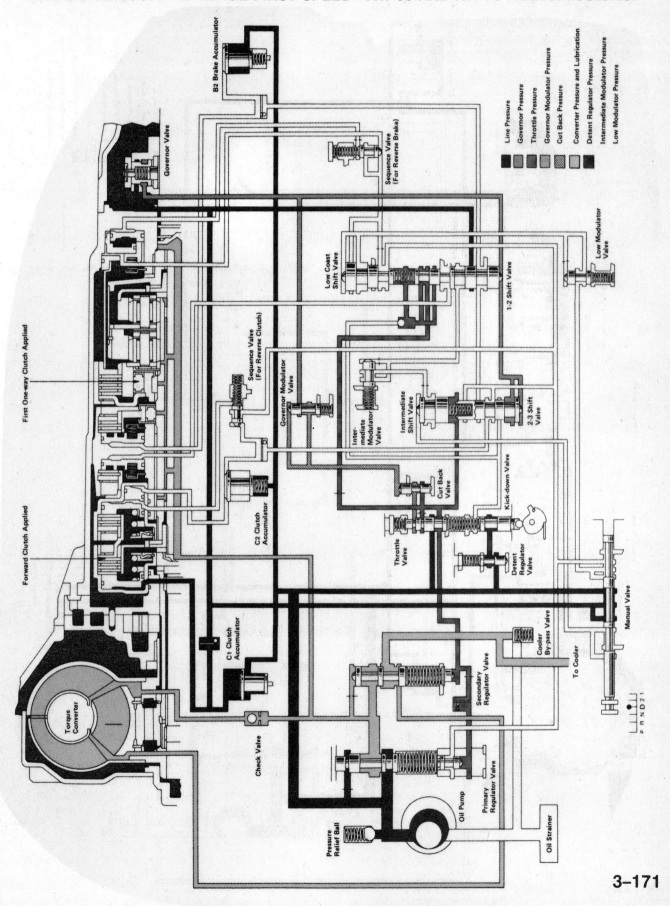

Line Pressure
Governor Pressure
Throttle Pressure
Governor Modulator Pressure
Cut Back Pressure
Converter Pressure and Lubrication
Detent Regulator Pressure
Intermediate Modulator Pressure
Low Modulator Pressure

OIL FLOW CIRCUIT – D RANGE SECOND SPEED – AW 55 AND AW 75 TRANSMISSIONS

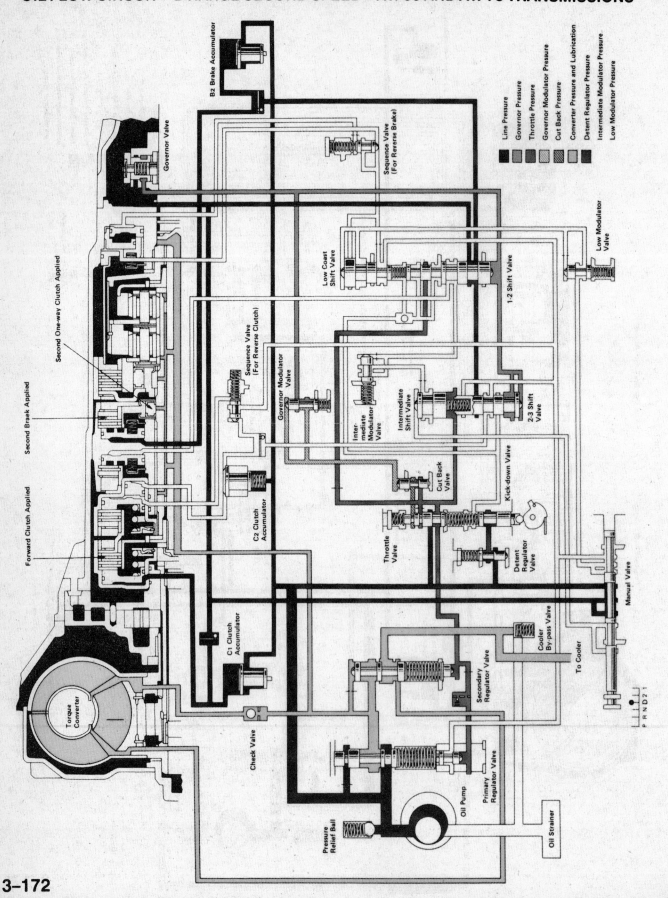

OIL FLOW CIRCUIT – D RANGE THIRD SPEED – AW 55 AND AW 75 TRANSMISSIONS

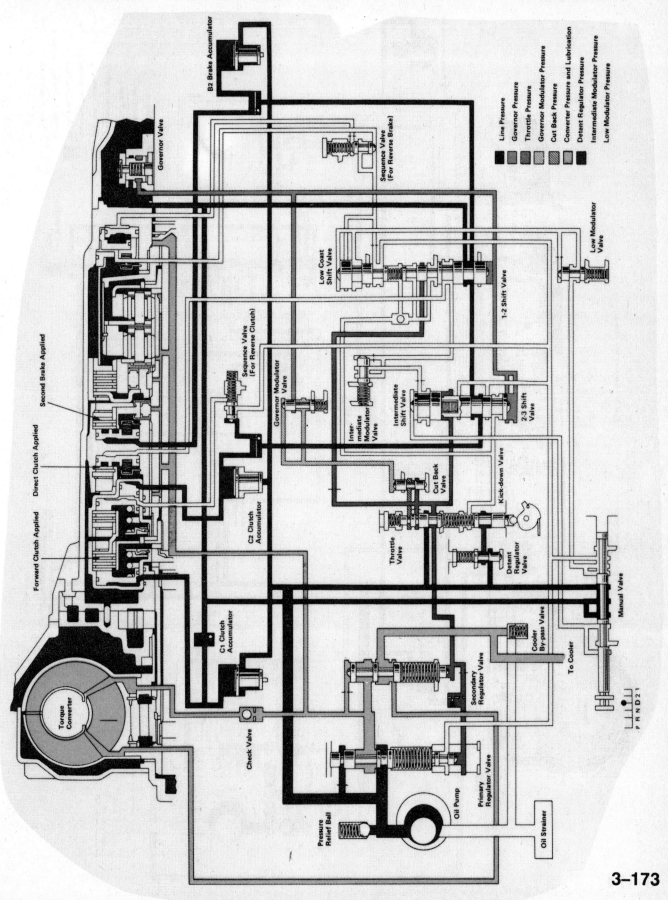

OIL FLOW CIRCUIT – 1 RANGE – AW 55 AND AW 75 TRANSMISSIONS

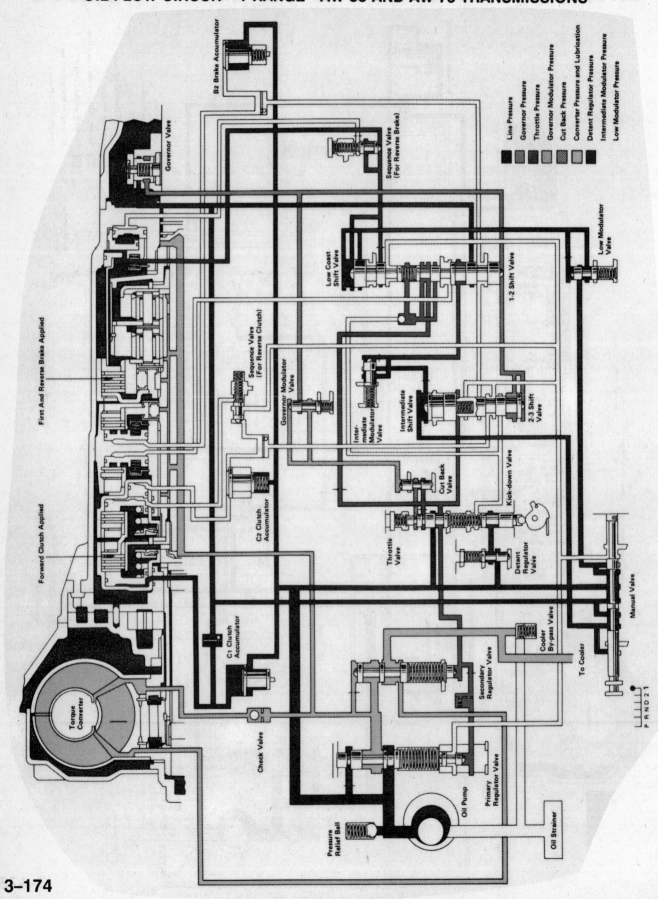

OIL FLOW CIRCUIT — 2 RANGE SECOND SPEED — AW 55 AND AW 75 TRANSMISSIONS

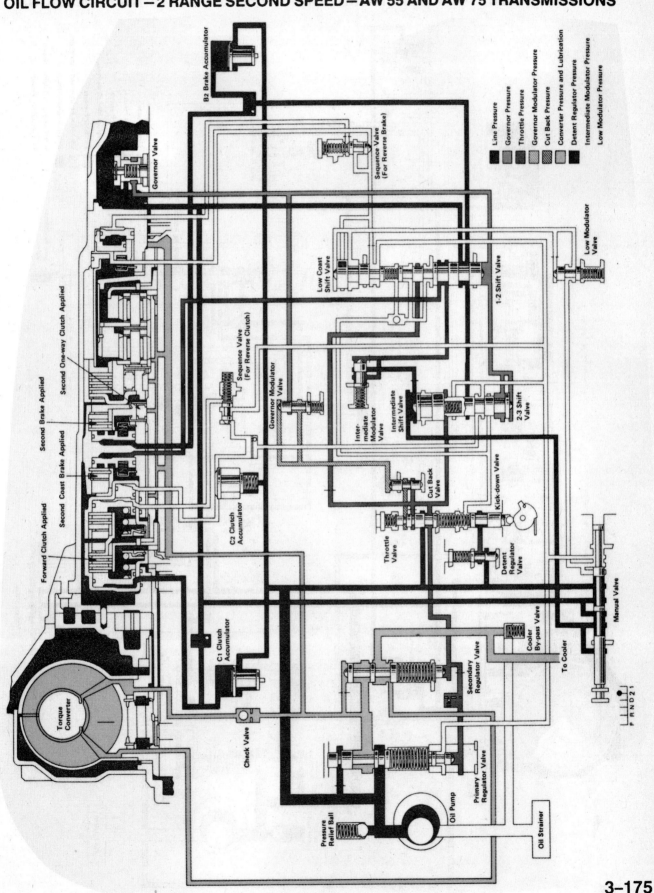

OIL FLOW CIRCUIT — D RANGE KICKDOWN — AW 55 AND AW 75 TRANSMISSIONS

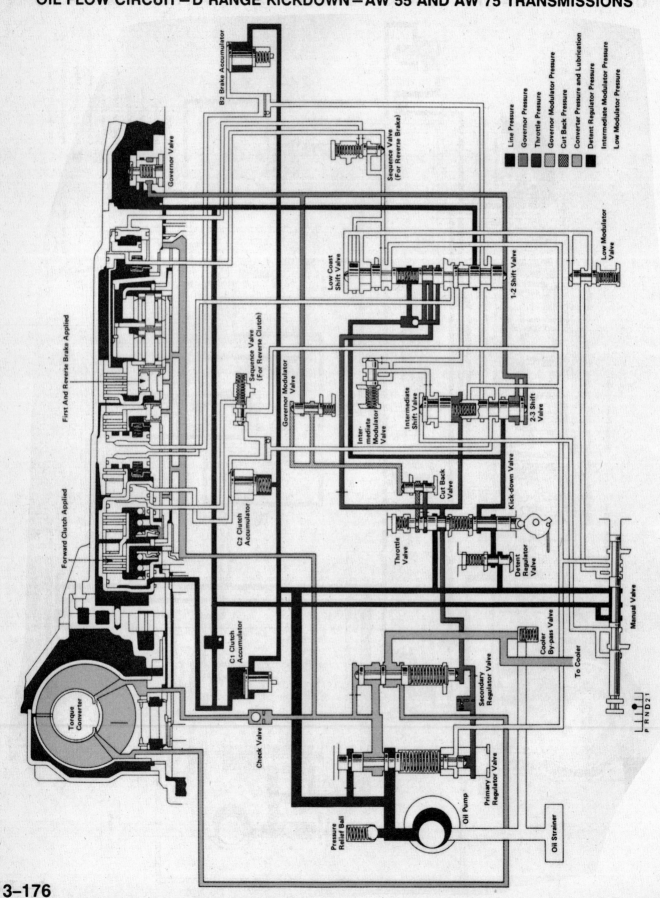

Section 3

N4AEL Transmissions
Mazda

APPLICATION

1988–89 Mazda 929

GENERAL DESCRIPTION

The N4A-EL automatic transmission is a 4 speed, electronically controlled transmission. This transmission consists of a torque converter, oil pump, 3 clutches, 3 brakes, 2 one-way clutches, 2 planetary gears, sensing rotor and a turbine sensor. The power train provides, 1st, 2nd, 3rd, 3rd (lockup:ON), overdrive, overdrive (lockup:ON), neutral and reverse gears.

The electronic system is based on 10 input signals which controls shifting, line pressure and 3rd/4th downshift. Input data is provided by 3 sensors and 5 switches. The output components consists of the EC-AT tester, the hold indicator and 5 solenoid valves within the hydraulic system. This system also includes self-diagnosis malfunctions of the major input and output components. Each malfunction is indicated by a code number and buzzer. These code number are as follow:

06 — Speed sensor or circuit
12 — Throttle sensor or circuit
55 — Turbine sensor or circuit
60 — 1/2 shift solenoid valve or circuit
61 — 2/3 shift solenoid valve or circuit
62 — 3/4 shift solenoid valve or circuit
63 — Lockup control solenoid valve or circuit
64 — 3/2 control solenoid valve or circuit

The hydraulic system consists of 3 shift valves, 5 switches, 6 pressure regulating valves and 3 accumulators. The system controls operation of the power train through a manual valve, 5 solenoid valves controlled by the electronic system and the intake manifold vacuum.

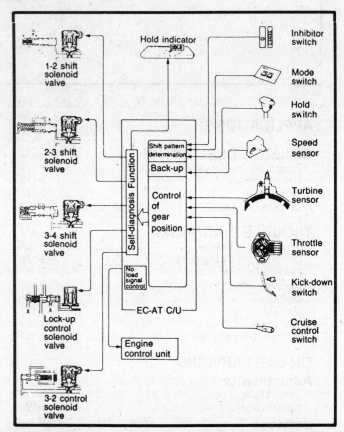

N4A-EL automatic transmission electronic system

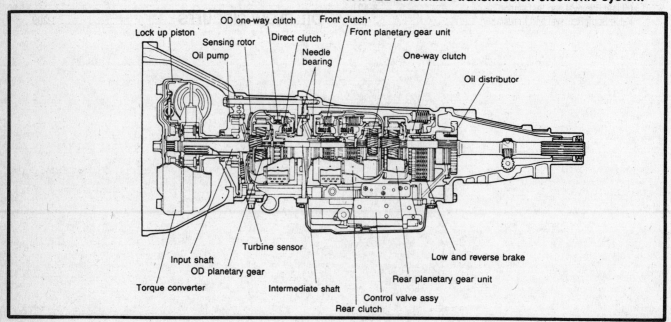

N4A-EL automatic transmission — exploded view

Transmission and Converter Identification

TRANSMISSION

The N4A-EL automatic transmission identification plate is attached to the right hand side of the transmission, adjacent to the inhibitor switch. This data plate provides the transmission model and serial number.

CONVERTER

The N4A-EL automatic transmission use a lockup converter. The torque converter consists of a pump, a turbine and a stator. The converter housing is filled with oil and is attached to the engine crankshaft by a flex plate and always rotates at engine speed.

Metric Fasteners

Metric tools will be required to service this transmission. Due to the large number of alloy parts used in this transmission, torque specifications should be strictly observed. Before installing capscrews into aluminum parts, dip the bolts into clean transmission fluid as this will prevent the screws from galling the aluminum threads, thus causing damage.

Metric fastener dimensions are very close to the dimensions of the familiar inch system fasteners. For this reason replacement fasteners must have the same measurement and strength as the original fastener.

Do not attempt to interchange metric fasteners for inch system fasteners. Mismatched or incorrect fasteners can cause damage to the automatic transmission unit and possible personal injury. Care should be taken to reuse fasteners in their original locations.

Capacity

The dry refill capacity of the N4A-EL automatic transmission is 7.7 qts. (7.3 liters).

Checking Fluid Level

1. Start the engine and allow to run until normal operating temperature is reached.
2. Place the vehicle on a flat level surface. Apply the parking brake and block the drive wheels.
3. With the engine idling, shift the selector lever from **P** to **L** and back again.
4. Check that the fluid level is between the **F** and **L** marks on the oil indicator gauge. If necessary, adjust the fluid level.

TROUBLE DIAGNOSIS

CHILTON'S THREE C's TRANSMISSION DIAGNOSIS

Condition	Cause	Correction
Vehicle does not move in D, S, L, or R range	a) Transmission fluid level	a) Adjust the fluid level
	b) Selector lever	b) Adjust the selector lever
	c) Control valves	c) Repair or replace the control valve body assembly
	d) Oil pump	d) Repair or replace the oil pump assembly
	e) Torque converter	e) Replace the torque converter
	f) Direct clutch	f) Repair or replace the direct clutch assembly
	g) Front clutch	g) Repair the front clutch assembly
	h) Rear clutch	h) Repair the rear clutch assembly
	i) Low/reverse brake	i) Repair the low/reverse brake assembly
	j) One-way clutch	j) Repair the one-way clutch assembly
Vehicle moves in N range	a) Selector lever	a) Adjust the selector lever
	b) Control valves	b) Repair or replace the control valve body assembly
Excessive creep	a) Idle speed of ignition timing	a) Adjust idle speed and ignition timing
	b) Torque converter	b) Replace the torque converter
No creep at all	a) Transmission fluid level	a) Adjust the fluid level
	b) Idle speed and ignition timing	b) Adjust the idle speed and ignition timing
	c) Control valves	c) Repair or replace the control valve body assembly
	d) Oil pump	d) Repair or replace the oil pump

CHILTON'S THREE C's TRANSMISSION DIAGNOSIS

Condition	Cause	Correction
No shift	a) Inhibitor switch	a) Adjust or replace the inhibitor switch
	b) Hold switch	b) Replace the hold switch
	c) Shift solenoid and 3/2 control solenoid	c) Replace the shift solenoid or 3/2 control solenoid
	d) Selector lever	d) Adjust the selector lever
	e) Control valves	e) Repair or replace the control valve body assembly
	f) Oil pump	f) Repair or replace the oil pump
Abnormal shift sequence	a) Inhibitor switch	a) Adjust or replace the inhibitor switch
	b) Hold switch	b) Replace the hold switch
	c) Cruise control switch or cruise control unit	c) Repair or replace the cruise control switch or cruise control unit
	d) Throttle sensor	d) Replace the throttle sensor
	e) Shift solenoid and 3/2 control solenoid	e) Replace the shift solenoid or 3/2 control solenoid
	f) Turbine sensor	f) Replace the turbine sensor
	g) Transmission fluid level	g) Adjust the fluid level
	h) Selector lever	h) Adjust the selector lever
	i) Control valves	i) Repair or replace the control valve body assembly
	j) Overdrive brake band	j) Repair the overdrive brake band assembly
	k) Front clutch	k) Repair the front clutch assembly
	l) 2nd brake band	l) Repair the 2nd brake band assembly
	m) Overdrive band servo	m) Repair or replace the overdrive band servo
	n) 2nd band servo	n) Repair or replace the 2nd band servo
Frequent shifting	a) Kick down switch	a) Adjust or replace the kick down switch
	b) Inhibitor switch	b) Adjust or replace the inhibitor switch
	c) Mode switch	c) Replace the mode switch
	d) Cruise control switch Cruise control unit	d) Repair or replace the cruise control switch or cruise control unit
	e) Throttle sensor	e) Replace the throttle sensor
	f) Turbine sensor	f) Replace the turbine sensor
	g) Control valves	g) Repair or replace the control valve body assembly
Excessively high or low shift point	a) Inhibitor switch	a) Adjust or replace the inhibitor switch
	b) Mode switch	b) Replace the mode switch
	c) Hold switch	c) Replace the hold switch
	d) Idle switch	d) Adjust or replace the idle switch
	e) Throttle sensor	e) Replace the throttle sensor
	f) Shift solenoid and 3/2 control solenoid	f) Replace the shift solenoid or 3/2 control solenoid
	g) Turbine sensor	g) Replace the turbine sensor
	h) Selector lever	h) Adjust the selector lever
	i) Control valves	i) Repair or replace the control valve body assembly
No lock-up	a) Cruise control switch or cruise control unit	a) Repair or replace the cruise control switch or cruise control unit
	b) Throttle sensor	b) Replace the throttle sensor
	c) Shift solenoid or 3/2 control solenoid	c) Replace the shift solenoid or 3/2 control solenoid
	d) Turbine sensor	d) Replace the turbine sensor
	e) Lock-up control solenoid	e) Replace the lock-up control solenoid
	f) Selector lever	f) Adjust the selector lever
	g) Control valves	g) Repair or replace the control valve body assembly
	h) Torque convertor	h) Replace the torque converter

CHILTON'S THREE C's TRANSMISSION DIAGNOSIS

Condition	Cause	Correction
No kick-down	a) Kick down switch b) Inhibitor switch c) Hold switch d) Selector lever	a) Adjust or replace the kick down switch b) Adjust or replace the inhibitor switch c) Replace the hold switch d) Replace the selector lever
Engine run away or slip when starting vehicle	a) Inhibitor switch b) Transmission fluid level c) Vacuum diaphragm and rod d) Control valves e) Oil pump f) Direct clutch g) 2nd brake band h) Rear clutch i) Low/reverse brake j) One-way clutch k) 2nd band servo	a) Adjust or replace the inhibitor switch b) Adjust the transmission fluid level c) Adjust or replace the vacuum diaphragm and rod d) Repair or replace the control valve body assembly e) Repair or replace the oil pump f) Repair or replace the direct clutch assembly g) Repair or replace the 2nd brake band h) Repair or replace the rear clutch assembly i) Repair or replace the low/reverse brake j) Repair or replace the one-way clutch k) Repair or replace the 2nd band servo
Engine run away or slip when up- or down-shifting	a) Transmission fluid level b) Control valves c) Oil pump d) Direct clutch e) Overdrive brake band f) Overdrive one-way clutch g) Front clutch h) 2nd brake band i) Rear clutch j) Overdrive band servo k) 2nd band servo	a) Adjust the transmission fluid level b) Repair or replace c) Repair or replace the oil pump d) Repair or replace the direct clutch assembly e) Repair or replace the overdrive brake band assembly f) Repair or replace the one-way clutch assembly g) Repair or replace the front clutch assembly h) Repair or replace the 2nd brake band assembly i) Repair or replace the rear clutch assembly j) Repair or replace the overdrive band servo assembly k) Repair or replace the 2nd band servo assembly
Excessive N to D or N to R shift shock	a) Inhibitor switch b) Speed sensor c) Turbine sensor d) Idle speed and ignition timing e) Vacuum diaphragm and rod f) Control valves g) Accumulator(s)	a) Adjust or replace the inhibitor switch b) Replace the speed sensor c) Replace the turbine sensor d) Adjust the idle speed and ignition timing e) Adjust or replace the vacuum diaphragm and rod f) Repair or replace the control valve body assembly g) Repair or replace the accumulator(s)
Excessive shift shock when upshifting or downshifting	a) Vacuum diaphragm and rod b) Control valves c) Accumulator(s) d) Overdrive brake band e) Overdrive band servo	a) Adjust or replace the vacuum diaphragm and rod b) Repair or replace the control valve body assembly c) Repair or replace the accumulator(s) d) Repair or replace the overdrive brake band assembly e) Repair or replace the overdrive band servo assembly

CHILTON'S THREE C's TRANSMISSION DIAGNOSIS

Condition	Cause	Correction
Excessive shift shake when changing range	f) 2nd brake band	f) Repair or replace the 2nd brake band assembly
	g) 2nd band servo	g) Repair or replace the 2nd band servo assembly
Excessive shift shake when changing range	a) Inhibitor switch	a) Adjust or replace the inhibitor switch
	b) Selector lever	b) Adjust the selector lever
	c) Control valves	c) Repair or replace the control valve body assembly
	d) 2nd band servo	d) Repair or replace the 2nd band servo
Transmission noisy in N or P range	a) Transmission fluid level	a) Adjust the transmission fluid level
	b) Vacuum diaphragm and rod	b) Adjust or replace vacuum diaphragm and rod
	c) Control valves	c) Repair or replace control valve body assembly
	d) Direct clutch	d) Repair or replace the direct clutch
Transmission noisy in D, S, L, or R range	a) Vacuum diaphragm and rod	a) Adjust or replace vacuum diaphragm and rod
	b) Torque converter	b) Replace the torque converter
No engine braking	a) Shift solenoid and 3/2 control solenoid	a) Replace the shift solenoid or 3/2 control solenoid
	b) Transmission fluid level	b) Adjust the transmission fluid level
	c) Selector lever	c) Adjust the selector lever
	d) Control valves	d) Repair or replace the control valve assembly
	e) Oil pump	e) Repair or replace the oil pump
	f) Torque converter	f) Replace the torque converter
	g) Direct clutch	g) Repair or replace the direct clutch assembly
	h) Front clutch	h) Repair or replace the front clutch assembly
	i) 2nd brake band	i) Repair or replace the 2nd brake band assembly
	j) Rear clutch	j) Repair or replace the rear clutch assembly
	k) Low/reverse brake	k) Repair or replace the low/reverse brake assembly
	l) Overdrive band servo	l) Repair or replace the overdrive band servo assembly
	m) 2nd band servo	m) Repair or replace the 2nd band servo assembly
No mode change	a) Inhibitor switch	a) Adjust or replace the inhibitor switch
	b) Mode switch	b) Replace the mode switch
	c) Hold switch	c) Replace the hold switch
	d) Throttle sensor	d) Replace the throttle sensor
	e) Shift solenoid and 3/2 control solenoid	e) Replace the shift solenoid and 3/2 control solenoid
	f) Turbine sensor	f) Replace the turbine sensor
Transmission overheats	a) Lock up control solenoid	a) Replace the lock up control solenoid
	b) Transmission fluid level	b) Adjust the transmission fluid level
	c) Control valves	c) Repair or replace the control valve body assembly
	d) Oil pump	d) Repair or replace the oil pump
	e) Torque converter	e) Replace the torque converter

CHILTON'S THREE C's TRANSMISSION DIAGNOSIS

Condition	Cause	Correction
White smoke discharged from exhaust	a) Transmission fluid level b) Vacuum diaphragm and rod c) Control valves	a) Adjust the transmission fluid level b) Repair or replace the vacuum diaphragm and rod c) Repair or replace the control valve body assembly
Hold indicator flashes	a) Speed sensor b) Throttle sensor c) Shift solenoid and 3/2 control solenoid d) Turbine sensor e) Lock up control solenoid	a) Replace the speed sensor b) Replace the throttle sensor c) Replace the shift solenoid or 3/2 control solenoid d) Replace the turbine sensor e) Replace the lock up control solenoid
Engine will not start	a) Inhibitor switch b) Selector lever	a) Adjust or replace the inhibitor switch b) Adjust the selector lever

CLUTCH AND BRAKE APPLICATION CHART

Range	Gear Position	Direct Clutch	Overdrive Brake	Overdrive One-way Clutch	Reverse Clutch	Forward Clutch	2nd Brake	Low/Reverse Brake	One-way Clutch	Solenoid Valves 1/2	2/3	3/4
P	—	Applied	Released ①	—	—	—	—	Applied	—	Energized	Energized	Energized
R	—	Applied	Released ①	Holding	—	Applied	Released ①	Applied	—	—	—	Energized
N	Below 9 mph (15 km/H)	Applied	Released ①	—	—	—	—	—	—	Energized	Energized	Energized
	Above 11 mph (17 km/h)	Applied	Released ①	—	—	—	—	—	—	—	—	Energized
D	1st	Applied	Released ①	Holding	Applied	—	—	—	Holding	Energized	Energized	Energized
	2nd	Applied	Released ①	Holding	Applied	—	—	—	—	—	Energized	Energized
	3rd	Applied	Released ①	Holding	Applied	Applied	Released ①	—	—	—	—	Energized
	Overdrive	—	Applied	—	Applied	Applied	Released ①	—	—	—	—	—
S	1st	Applied	Released ①	Holding	Applied	—	—	—	Holding	Energized	Energized	Energized
	2nd	Applied	Released ①	Holding	Applied	—	—	—	—	—	Energized	Energized
										—	Energized	—
	3rd	Applied	Released ①	Holding	Applied	Applied	Released ①	—	—	—	—	Energized
L	1st	Applied	Released ①	Holding	Applied	—	—	Applied	—	Energized	Energized	Energized
	2nd	Applied	Released ①	Holding	Applied	—	—	—	—	—	Energized	Energized
										—	Energized	—

NOTE: The lockup control solenoid valve operates only during lockup. The 3/2 control solenoid valve operates momentarily during 3/2 downshift. The Overdrive one-way clutch operated momentarily during Overdrive-3 downshift
① Oil pressure is directed toward the release side of the overdrive brake although the band servo remain deactivated due to the large area of the release pressure side

DIAGNOSTIC TRANSMISSION CODE DATA

Inspection Procedure
No. 06 Code Display (Speed Sensor)

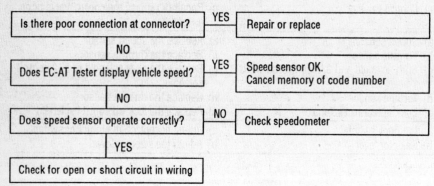

Is there poor connection at connector?	YES →	Repair or replace
↓ NO		
Does EC-AT Tester display vehicle speed?	YES →	Speed sensor OK. Cancel memory of code number
↓ NO		
Does speed sensor operate correctly?	NO →	Check speedometer
↓ YES		
Check for open or short circuit in wiring		

No. 12 Code Display (Throttle Sensor)

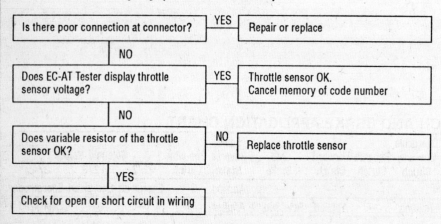

Is there poor connection at connector?	YES →	Repair or replace
↓ NO		
Does EC-AT Tester display throttle sensor voltage?	YES →	Throttle sensor OK. Cancel memory of code number
↓ NO		
Does variable resistor of the throttle sensor OK?	NO →	Replace throttle sensor
↓ YES		
Check for open or short circuit in wiring		

No. 55 Code Display (Turbine Sensor)

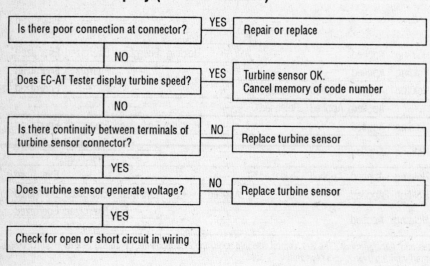

Is there poor connection at connector?	YES →	Repair or replace
↓ NO		
Does EC-AT Tester display turbine speed?	YES →	Turbine sensor OK. Cancel memory of code number
↓ NO		
Is there continuity between terminals of turbine sensor connector?	NO →	Replace turbine sensor
↓ YES		
Does turbine sensor generate voltage?	NO →	Replace turbine sensor
↓ YES		
Check for open or short circuit in wiring		

DIAGNOSTIC TRANSMISSION CODE DATA

Inspection Procedure
No. 60, 61, 62, or 64 Code Display (1-2 Shift, 2-3 Shift, 3-4 Shift, or 3-2 Control Solenoid Valve)

Is there poor connection at connector? — YES → Repair or replace

NO ↓

Is there continuity in each transistor in EC-AT control unit? — NO → Replace EC-AT control unit then continue with next step → Check for short circuit in wiring

Is there 13-27 ohms between terminals of solenoid valve connector and ground? — NO → Is there poor connection at connector in transmission? — NO → Replace solenoid valve

YES ↓ Repair or replace connector

YES ↓

Is there continuity between terminals of the EC-AT control unit connector and ground? — NO → Open circuit in wiring

YES ↓

Solenoid valve and circuit OK. Cancel memory of code number

No. 63 Code Display (Lockup Control Solenoid Valve)

Is there poor connection at connector? — YES → Repair or replace

NO ↓

Is there continuity in transistor in EC-AT control unit? — NO → Replace EC-AT control unit then continue with next step → Check for short circuit in wiring

YES ↓

Is there 13-25 ohms between terminals of lock-up control solenoid valve? — NO → Is there poor connection at connector in transmission? — NO → Replace solenoid valve

YES ↓ Repair or replace connector

YES ↓

Is there continuity between the 2N terminal of EC-AT control unit connector and ground? — NO → Open circuit in wiring

YES ↓

Solenoid valve and circuit OK. Cancel memory of code number

CODE RETRIEVAL

Procedure

Code retrieval is performed using the EC-AT tester.

1. Locate the check connector and connect the EC-AT tester. The check connector is a blue-colored 6 pin connector.
2. Ground the ground connector of the EC-AT tester.
3. Connect the 6 pin connector of the EC-AT tester to the check connector.
4. Ground the 1 pin check connector. This service connector is a blue-colored 1 pin connector.
5. Turn the ignition switch **ON** and check that the number 88 flashes on the digital display and the buzzer sounds for 3 seconds. If the 88 does not flash, check the service connector wiring.
6. If the 88 flashes and the buzzer sonds continuously for more than 20 seconds, check the wiring to 2M terminal of the EC-AT control unit for short circuit then replace the EC-AT control unit and repeat Steps 3 and 4.
7. Note the code numbers and check the cause by referring to the code number diagnosis chart.
8. After repairs are made, cancel the memory of malfunctions by disconnecting the negative battery cable for at least 5 seconds, then reconnect it.
9. Remove the EC-AT tester and drive the vehicle at 31 mph (50 km/h); then, depress the accelerator pedal fully to activate the kickdown. Stop the vehicle gradually.
10. Reconnect the EC-AT tester to the check connector and ground the EC-AT check connector with a jumper wire.
11. Turn the ignition switch **ON** and check that no code numbers are displayed.

Hydraulic Control System

Diagnosis Tests

OIL PRESSURE

1. Check the engine coolant, engine oil and transmission fluid levels.
2. Warm the engine until the transmission fluid temperature is within 122–176°F (50–80°C).
3. Apply the parking brake and block the drive wheels.
4. Connect a tachometer to the engine. Connect oil pressure adaptor tool 49H019002 or equivalent to the line pressure inspection hole.

NOTE: The left side hole is for R range. The right side hole is for D, S, L ranges. The R range should be performed before D, S, L range tests.

5. Start the engine and check that the idle speed is 630–670 rpm.
6. Shift the selector lever to the **R** range and read the oil pressure at idle.
7. Depress the brake pedal firmly and gradually depress the accelerator. Read the oil pressure as soon as the engine speed becomes constant, then release the accelerator pedal.

NOTE: Step 7 must be performed within 5 seconds.

8. Shift the selector lever to the **N** range and run the engine at idle for at least 1 minute. This 1 minute period is performed to cool the transmission fluid and prevent oil degeneration.
9. Read the line pressure at idle and engine stall speeds for each range in the same manner.
10. Cool the transmission and reconnect the oil pressure adaptor tool 49H019002 or equivalent to the right side inspection hole.

11. Disconnect the vacuum hose from the surge tank and connect a vacuum pump to the hose.
12. Shift the selector lever to the **N** range and read the line pressure at idle.

SPECIFIED LINE PRESSURE

Range		Pressure (psi) kPa	
		Idle	Stall
D range	Economy mode	43–57 (290–390)	128–156 (880–1080)
S range	Economy mode	43–57 (290–390)	128–156 (880–1080)
	Hold mode	43–57 (290–390)	128–156 (880–1080)
L range		43–57 (290–390)	128–156 (880–1080)
R range		78–92 (540–640)	213–242 (1470–1670)

LINE PRESSURE—VACUUM APPLIED

Vacuum in Hg (mm Hg)	Line pressure (psi) kPa
Atmospheric pressure	128–156 (880–1080)
7.87 (200)	100–114 (690–780)
15.7 (400)	57–71 (390–490)

STALL LINE PRESSURE EVALUATION

Condition		Cause
Below specification	In all ranges	Worn oil pump Fluid leakage from the oil pump, control valve body, and/or transmission case Stuck pressure regulator valve Fluid leakage from the direct clutch and/or OD band servo release side hydraulic circuit
	In D (Eco.), S (Eco.), and L ranges	Fluid leakage from the rear clutch hydraulic circuit Stuck pressure modifier valve
	In S (Eco. & Hold) and L ranges	Fluid leakage from the throttle back-up valve hydraulic circuit
	In L and R ranges	Fluid leakage from the low/reverse hydraulic circuit
	In R range only	Fluid leakage from the front clutch and/or 2nd band servo release side hydraulic circuit
	In S range (Hold)	Stuck throttle back-up valve Stuck back-up control valve Back-up control function (electronic) not operating properly
Excessive line pressure		Stuck pressure modifier valve Stuck back-up control valve

STALL TEST

1. Check the engine coolant, engine oil and ATF levels.
2. Warm the engine until the transmission fluid temperature is within 122–176°F (50–80°C).
3. Apply the parking brake and block the drive wheels.
4. Connect a tachometer to the engine.
5. Shift the selector lever to the **D** range (Economy). Depress the brake pedal firmly and gradually depress the accelerator. Read and note the engine speed as soon as the engine speed becomes constant, then release the accelerator pedal.

NOTE: Step 5 must be performed within 5 seconds.

6. Shift the selector lever to the **N** range and run the engine at idle for at least 1 minute. This 1 minute period is performed to cool the transmission fluid and prevent oil degeneration.
7. Perform the stall tests in the same manner for **L** and **R** ranges.

NOTE: Be certain to provide adequate cooling time between individual range stall tests.

8. The standard stall speed is 2100–2500 rpm.

TIME LAG TEST

If the selector lever is shifted while the engine is idling, there will be a certain time lapse or time lag before shock is felt. This

STALL TEST EVALUATION

Condition			Cause
Above specification	In all ranges	Insufficient line pressure	Worn oil pump
			Oil leakage from oil pump, control valve, and/or transmission case
			Stuck pressure regulator valve
			Direct clutch and overdrive one-way clutch slipping
	In D (Economy), and L ranges	Rear clutch slipping	
	In D (Economy) range only	One-way clutch slipping	
	In R range only	Low/reverse brake slipping	
		Front clutch slipping	
		Perform the road test, to determine if this is caused by the low/reverse brake or the front clutch, as follows: a) Effective engine braking in L range, front clutch b) No engine braking in L range Low/reverse brake	
Within specification		All shift control elements within transmission are functioning normally	
Below specification		Engine out of tune	
		One-way clutch slipping within torque converter	

STALL TEST SPECIFICATION CHART

Condition	rpm	Vehicle Speed mph (Km/h)
1st gear, L range, hold mode	1000	7 (11)
	2000	13 (21)
	3000	19 (31)
	4000	25 (41)
1st gear, D range, economy mode	1000	7 (11)
	2000	13 (21)
	3000	19 (31)
	4000	25 (41)
2nd gear, 5 range, hold mode	1000	12 (19)
	2000	24 (38)
	3000	35 (57)
	4000	16 (26)
3rd gear, D range hold mode	1000	19 (31)
	2000	37 (59)
	3000	55 (88)
	4000	73 (118)
OD gear, D range, economy mode	1000	25 (41)
	2000	51 (82)
	3000	76 (123)
	4000	102 (164)

step checks this time lag for checking condition of the 1/2, N–R/2–3 and N/D accumulators, front, rear and one-way clutches, 2nd brake band, and low/reverse brake.

1. Check the engine coolant, engine oil and transmission fluid levels.
2. Warm the engine until the transmission fluid temperature is within 122–176°F (50–80°C).

TIME LAG TEST EVALUATION

Condition		Cause
N → D (Economy) shifting	More than specification	Insufficient line pressure
		Rear clutch slipping
		One-way clutch slipping
	Less than specification	N/D accumulator not operating properly
		Excessive line pressure
N → D (Hold) shifting	More than specification	Insufficient line pressure
		Rear clutch slipping
		2nd brake band slipping
	Less than specification	1/2 accumulator not operating properly
		Excessive line pressure
N → R shifting	More than specification	Insufficient line pressure
		Low/reverse brake slipping
		Front clutch slipping
	Less than specification	N-R/2-3 accumulator not operating properly
		Excessive line pressure

3. Apply the parking brake and block the drive wheels.

4. Connect a tachometer to the engine.

5. Start the engine and check that the idle speed is 630–670 rpm.

6. Shift the selector lever from **N** to **D** range (economy mode).

7. With the use of a stop watch, measure the time it takes from shifting until shock is felt.

8. Shift the selector lever to **N** range and run the engine at idle speed for at least 1 minute.

9. Perform the test in the same manner for **D** and **R** ranges.

NOTE: Make 3 measurements for each test and take the average value.

The specified time lag is as follow:
N to D range (Economy mode)–0.4–0.8 seconds
N to D range (Hold mode)–0.4–0.8 seconds
N to R range–0.6–1.0 seconds

SLIPPAGE TEST

1. Check the engine coolant, engine oil and transmission fluid levels.

2. Warm the engine until the transmission fluid temperature is within 122–176°F (50–80°C).

3. Apply the parking brake and block the drive wheels.

4. Connect a tachometer to the engine. Connect the EC-AT tester between the EC-AT control unit and wiring harness.

5. Drive the vehicle in each gears indicated in the slippage test chart and check that the vehicle speed or engine speed is excessively above or below specification indicated by turbine speed.

Electronic Control System

MODE SWITCH

Testing

1. Disconnect the negative battery cable.

2. Remove the upper plate and disconnect the mode switch connector.

3. Check for continuity between terminal **A** and **C** in the power mode.

4. Check for continuity between terminal **A** and **B** in the economy mode.

5. If not correct, replace the mode switch.

6. If correct, check the terminal voltage.

7. Reconnect the mode switch connector. Turn the ignition **ON**.

8. Check the voltage between each terminal A and ground. The voltage should be as follow:
Power Mode–Below 1.5 volts
Economy mode–Below 1.5 volts
Hold mode–Approximately 12 volts

9. If not correct at the power or economy mode, check the wiring harness.

10. If not correct at the hold mode, check the 1A terminal (mode indicator) of the EC-AT control unit and the hold switch.

HOLD SWITCH

Testing

1. Disconnect the negative battery cable.

2. Remove the upper plate and disconnect the hold switch connector.

3. Check for continuity between the terminals while depressig the switch.

4. With the switch released, there should be continuity.

5. With the switch depressed, there should be no continuity.

6. If not correct, replace the hold switch.

SLIPPAGE TEST EVALUATION

Driving Conditions Below Specification	Cause
No. 1 condition only	Low/reverse brake
No. 2 condition only	One-way clutch
No. 3 condition only	2nd brake band
No. 4 condition only	Front clutch
No. 5 condition only	Overdrive brake band
No. 1, 2, 3, and 4 conditions	Direct clutch
No. 6 condition only	Lock up piston
All conditions	Rear clutch

7. If correct, check the terminal voltage.

8. Reconnect the hold switch connector. Turn the ignition **ON**.

9. Check the voltage between terminal **LY** and ground while depressing the switch.

10. With the switch depressed, there should be approximately 12 volts. With the switch released, the voltage should be below 1.5 volts.

INHIBITOR SWITCH

Testing

1. Disconnect the negative battery cable.

2. Disconnect the inhibitor switch connector.

3. Check for continuity at the following terminals in each gear positions as follow:
P – terminal A to B and terminal C to D
R – terminal C to E
N – terminal A to B and terminal C to F
D – terminal C to G
S – terminal C to H
L – terminal C to I

4. If not correct, replace the inhibitor switch.

Adjustment

1. Shift the selector lever to **N** range.

2. Loosen the inhibitor switch mounting bolts.

3. Remove the screw and move the inhibitor switch so that the small hole is aligned with the screw hole. Insert a 0.079 in. (2.0mm) diameter pin through the hole.

4. Loosely tighten the switch mounting bolt, remove the alignment pin and replace the screw. Tighten the switch mounting bolts 43–61 inch lbs. (4.9–6.9 Nm).

KICKDOWN SWITCH

Testing

1. Turn the ignition switch **ON**.

2. Check the voltage at terminal V with a voltmeter.

3. With the pedal depressed to a full stroke, there should be approximately 12 volts.

4. With the pedal depressed below a full stroke, the voltage should be below 1.5 volts.

5. If the voltage is not correct, check the wiring harness, switch or adjustment.

6. Disconect the kickdown switch connector. Check for continuity between the switch terminals.

7. With the switch depressed, there should be continuity.

8. With the switch released, there should be no continuity.

9. If not correct, replace the kickdown switch.

Adjustment

Loosen the kickdown switch locknut and turn the switch counterclockwise ½ revolution; then, secure the switch with the locknut.

TURBINE SENSOR

Testing

1. Disconnect the turbine sensor connector and check the resistance at the terminals. The resistance should be approximately 245 ohms.
2. If not correct, check the voltage generation of the sensor.
3. Remove the sensor and connect a voltmeter (0.1 volt range) to the terminals.
4. Wave the tip of the turbine sensor approximately 0.197 in. (5mm) away from a magnet and check that the sensor generates voltage. If not, replace the turbine sensor.

SPEED SENSOR

Testing

1. Disconnect the 16 pin connector from the EC-AT control unit.
2. Connect a voltmeter between the 1P terminal and ground. Turn the ignition switch **ON**.
3. Remove the speedometer cable from the transmission and slowly turn the speedometer cable 1 turn.
4. Check that approximately 7 volts is shown 4 times.
5. If not correct, check the combination meter.

SOLENOID VALVE

Testing

1/2 SHIFT, 2/3 SHIFT, 3/4 SHIFT AND 3/2 CONTROL

1. Disconnect the solenoid valve connector and check the re-sistance between each terminal and ground. The resistance should be 13–27 ohms.
2. If not correct, check the wiring harness for an open or short circuit. Replace the solenoid valve if necessary.
3. To check for continuity, disconnect the 20 pin connector from the EC-AT control unit. Remove the plug from the connector.
4. Check for continuity between terminals 2K, 2M, 2O and 2P to ground.
5. If not correct, check the wiring harness for an open circuit.

LOCKUP CONTROL

1. Disconnect the solenoid valve connector and check the re-sistance between the terminal. The resistance should be 13–25 ohms.
2. If not correct, replace the solenoid valve.
3. To check for continuity, disconnect the 20 pin connector from the EC-AT control unit. Remove the plug from the connector.
4. Check for continuity between terminals 2N and ground.
5. If not correct, check the wiring harness for an open circuit.

EC-AT CONTROL UNIT

Testing

1. Disconnect the connectors from the EC-AT control unit.
2. Check for continuity between terminals 2K, 2M, 2N, 2O and 2P to terminal 2S.
3. If there is no continuity at any terminal, replace the EC-AT control unit.

EC-AT TERMINAL VOLTAGE

Terminal	Connected To	Voltage	Condition
1A (Output)	Mode indicator	Approx. 12V	Hold mode
		Below 1.5V	Power or economy mode
1B (Output)	Hold indicator	Below 1.5V	Hold mode
		Approx. 12V	Other modes
1C (Output)	EC-AT Tester (malfunction code)	Approx. 12V	Normal
		Below 1.5V or approx. 12V (fluctuating)	If malfunction present
		Code signal	Self-diagnosis check connector grounded
1E (Input)	EC-AT check connector	Approx. 12V	—
1G (Input)	Kick down switch	Approx. 12V	Accelerator pedal fully depressed
		Below 1.5V	Accelerator pedal less than 7/8 of full stroke
1H (Input)	Hold switch	Approx. 12V	Switch depressed
		Below 1.5V	Switch released
1I (Input)	Mode switch (Economy side)	Below 1.5V	Economy switch depressed (Economy mode)
		Approx. 12V	Power switch depressed or hold mode
1J (Ground)	Engine ground	Below 1.5V	—
1M (Input)	Cruise control unit	Below 1.5V	SET or RESUME switch ON or vehicle speed 2 mph (3 km/h) lower than pre-set speed (Driving vehicle; cruise control ON)
		Approx. 12V	Other (normal) conditions

EC-AT TERMINAL VOLTAGE

Terminal	Connected To	Voltage	Condition
1N (Input)	EGI control unit (IU terminal)	Below 1.5V	Coolant temperature below 131°F (55°C)
		Approx. 12V	Coolant temperature above 131°F (55°C)
10 (Input)	Idle switch (in throttle sensor)	Below 1.5V	Throttle valve closed fully
		Approx. 12V	Throttle valve opened
1P (Input)	Speed sensor	Approx. 4V	During driving
		Approx. 7–9V or below 1.5V	Vehicle stopped
2A (Input)	Inhibitor switch (D range)	Approx. 12V	D range
		Below 1.5V	Other ranges
2B (Input)	Inhibitor switch (N and P range)	Below 1.5V	N or P range
		Approx. 12V	Other ranges
2C (Input)	Inhibitor switch (L range)	Approx. 12V	L range
		Below 1.5V	Other ranges
2D (Input)	Inhibitor switch (S range)	Approx. 12V	S range
		Below 1.5V	Other ranges
2E (Input)	Turbine sensor	0.05–0.1	Engine running
		Approx. 0.05V	Engine stopped
2F (Ground)	Turbine sensor	Below 1.5V	—
2G (Input)	Throttle sensor	0.4–4.4V	Ignition switch ON
2I (Input)	Throttle sensor	4.5–5.5V	Ignition switch ON
2K (Output)	3/2 control solenoid valve	Approx. 12V	3/2 or 4/2 downshift
		Below 1.5V	Other conditions
2L (Memory power)	Battery	Approx. 12V	—
2M (Output)	2/3 shift solenoid valve	Approx. 12V	1st or 2nd gear position
		Below 1.5V	3rd or OD gear position
2N (Output)	Lock up control solenoid valve	Approx. 12V	Lock-up
		Below 1.5V	Other
2O (Output)	1/2 shift solenoid valve	Approx. 12V	1st gear position
		Below 1.5V	2nd, 3rd and OD gear position
2P (Output)	3/4 shift solenoid valve	Approx. 12V	1st, 2nd, and 3rd gear position
		Below 1.5V	OD position
2Q (Battery power)	Battery	Approx. 12V	—
2R (Ground)	Engine ground	Below 1.5V	—
2S (Battery power)	Battery	Approx. 12V	—
2T (Output)	EC-AT indicator	Below 1.5V	—

ON CAR SERVICES

Adjustments

SELECTOR LEVER

1. Shift the selector lever into **P** range.
2. Loosen the locknuts at the adjuster lever.
3. Shift the transmission into **P** range by moving the transmission manual shaft.
4. With the bolt at 90 degrees to the lever, adjust the clearance between the adjuster lever and locknut to 0.039 in. (1mm). Then, tighten the outer locknut.
5. Measure the clearance between the guide plate and the guide pin in **P** range.
Clearance:
   Front side – Approximately 0.039 in. (1mm)
   Rear side – Approximately 0.020 in. (0.5mm)
6. Move the selector lever to **N** and **D** ranges and check that there is the same clearance between the guide plate bracket and the guide pin.

7. If there is no clearance, readjust the locknuts and check that the selector lever operate in the following manner.

a. Check that the positions of the selector lever and the indicator are aligned.

b. Check that the button returns smoothly when used to shift.

c. Make sure there is a click at each range when shifted from **P** to **L** range.

VACUUM DIAPHRAGM

1. Disconnect the negative battery cable. Raise and support the vehicle safely.

2. Place a drain pan under the transmission oil pan. Remove the vacuum diaphragm, rod and O-ring from the transmission body.

3. Measure the **N** dimension indicated with special tool 49G032355 or equivalent and a scale.

4. Select the proper diaphragm rod from the application chart.

5. Lubricate a new O-ring and install it on the vacuum diaphragm. Install the diaphragm rod and vacuum diaphragm into the transmission case.

6. Lower the vehicle, adjust the transmission fluid level, reconnect the negative battery cable and check the vehicle operation.

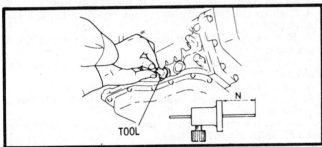

Checking vacuum diaphragm rod dimension

Services

FLUID CHANGE

The conditions under which the vehicle is operated is the main consideration in determining how often the transmission fluid should be changed. Different driving conditions result in different transmission fluid temperatures. These temperatures affect change intervals.

If the vehicle is driven under severe conditions, change the transmission fluid every 15,000 miles. If the vehicle is not used under severe conditions, change the fluid and replace the filter every 30,000 miles.

Do not overfill the transmission. It takes about a pint of automatic transmission fluid to raise the level from the **ADD** to the **FULL** mark on the transmission indicator dipstick. Overfilling the unit can cause damage to the internal components of the automatic transmission.

OIL PAN

Removal and Installation

1. Raise and support the vehicle safely.

2. Place a drain pan under the transmission oil pan. Clean the area arount the oil pan to prevent entry of dust into the unit. Remove the oil pan attaching bolts from the front and side of the pan.

3. Loosen the rear pan attaching bolts approximately 4 turns.

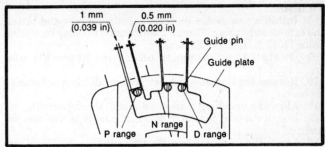

Checking guide plate to guide pin clearance

4. Carefully pry the transmission oil pan loose and allow the fluid to drain.

5. Remove the remaining bolts. Remove the oil pan, gasket and magnet. If required, remove the filter.

6. Thoroughly clean the oil pan and transmission gasket surfaces. Dry with compressed air.

7. Install the magnet into the oil pan. Install the oil pan using a new gasket and alternately tighten the retaining bolts to 52–69 inch lbs. (5.9–7.8 Nm).

8. Lower the vehicle and add the proper amount of Dextron® II transmission fluid.

VALVE BODY

Removal and Installation

1. Disconnect the negative battery cable. Raise and support the vehicle safely.

2. Drain the transmission fluid. Remove the bracket, oil pan and gasket.

3. Remove the vacuum diaphragm and rod.

4. Disconnect the solenoid valve and remove the electrical harness from the bracket.

5. Remove the valve body mounting bolts and remove the valve body assembly.

To install:

6. Position the valve body in the transmission. Make certain the manual plate is in the correct position of the manual valve. Install the mounting bolts and torque them 95–130 inch lbs. (11–15 Nm).

7. Connect the solenoid valve connector and install the electrical harness to the bracket.

8. Install the vacuum diaphragm and rod. Adjust the vacuum diaphragm.

9. Install the oil pan using a new gasket. Install the bracket and retaining bolts. Torque the retaining bolts 52–69 inch lbs. (5.9–7.8 Nm).

10. Connect the vacuum diaphragm hose.

11. Lower the vehicle, adjust the transmission fluid level, reconnect the negative battery cable and check the vehicle operation.

EXTENSION HOUSING

Removal and Installation

1. Disconnect the negative battery cable. Raise and support the vehicle safely.

2. Drain the transmission fluid.

3. Remove the silencer hanger, front exhaust pipes and heat insulator.

4. Mark the driveshaft flanges and remove the driveshaft.

5. Remove the speedometer cable.

6. Support the transmission with a transmission jack. Remove the crossmember and transmission mount assembly.

7. Remove the extension housing mounting bolts. Remove the extension housing and gasket.

To install:

8. Install a new gasket on the transmission case and install the extension housing. Torque the extension housing mounting bolts 14–18 ft. lbs. (20–25 Nm).

9. Install the transmission mount assembly and crossmember.

10. Remove the transmission jack and install the speedometer cable.

11. Align the matching marks and install the driveshaft.

12. Install the heat insulator, front exhaust pipe and silencer hanger.

13. Lower the vehicle, adjust the transmission fluid level, reconnect the negative battery cable and check the vehicle operation.

REAR OIL SEAL

Removal and Installation

1. Disconnect the negative battery cable. Raise and support the vehicle safely.

2. Match mark the driveshaft and flange; then, remove the driveshaft.

3. Pry the extension housing seal from the extension housing.

To install:

4. Lubricate the new extension housing seal lip and tap it into place using a plastic mallet.

5. Install the driveshaft while aligning the match marks.

6. Lower the vehicle and reconnect the negative battery cable. Check the transmission fluid level.

REMOVAL AND INSTALLATION

TRANSMISSION REMOVAL

1. Disconnect the negative battery cable. Raise and support the vehicle safely.

2. Remove the transmission filler tube retaining bolt and remove the filler tube.

3. Remove the shift rod.

4. Remove the front exhaust pipe and heat insulator.

5. Mark the driveshaft flanges to aid during reassemble. Remove the driveshaft and install tool 49S120440 or equivalent to prevent oil leakage. Remove the speedometer cable.

6. Remove the starter motor.

7. Disconnect and tag all electrical connectors.

8. Disconnect and plug the cooler lines at the transmission.

9. Disconnect the transmission vacuum pipe.

10. Remove the transmission under cover.

11. Remove the converter to flexplate retaining bolts.

12. Remove the transmission housing to engine mounting bolts. Remove the transmission mount retaining bolts.

13. Remove the transmission and mount assembly.

TRANSMISSION INSTALLATION

1. Install the transmission mount on the transmission and loosely tighten the retaining bolts.

2. Position the transmission on the transmission jack. Raise the transmission into place and install the mounting bolts. Torque the mounting bolts 27–38 ft. lbs. (37–52 Nm).

3. Install the torque converter to flex plate retaining bolts. Torque the retaining bolts 25–36 ft. lbs. (34–49 Nm).

4. Tighten the transmission mount retaining bolts. Install the undercover.

5. Remove the plugs from the oil hoses and connect the oil pipes vacuum pipe.

6. Install the brackets on the transmission and connect all electrical connectors.

7. Install the starter motor and speedometer cable.

8. Align the mating marks and install the driveshaft. Torque the retaining bolts 36–43 ft. lbs. (49–59 Nm).

9. Install the center bearing assembly. Torque the retaining bolts 27–38 ft. lbs. (37–52 Nm).

10. Install the front exhaust pipes.

11. Install the shift rod and a new spring clip. Install filler tube and retaining bolt.

12. Lower the vehicle, adjust the transmission fluid level, reconnect the negative battery cable and check the vehicle operation.

BENCH OVERHAUL

Before Disassembly

Cleanliness is an important factor in the overhaul of the transmission unit. Before opening up this unit, the entire outside of the transmission assembly should be cleaned, preferable with a high pressure washer such as a car wash spray unit. Dirt entering the transmission internal parts will negate all the time and effort spent on the overhaul. During inspection and reassembly all parts should be thoroughly cleaned with solvent then dried with compressed air. Wiping cloths and rags should not be used to dry parts since lint will find its way into the valve body passages.

Wheel bearing grease, long used to hold thrust washers and lube parts, should not be used. Lube seals with clean transmission fluid and use ordinary unmedicated petroleum jelly to hold the thrust washers and to ease the assembly of seals, since it will not leave a harmful residue as grease often will. Do not use solvent on neoprene seals, friction plates if they are to be reused, or thrust washers. Be wary of nylon parts if the transmission failure was due to failure of the cooling system. Nylon parts exposed to water or antifreeze solutions can swell and distort and must be replaced.

Before installing bolts into aluminum parts, always dip the threads into clean transmission fluid. Antiseize compound can also be used to prevent bolts from galling the aluminum and seizing. Always use a torque wrench to keep from stripping the threads. Take care when installing new O-rings, especially the smaller O-rings. The internal snaprings should be expanded and the external rings should be compressed, if they are to be reused. This will help insure proper seating when installed.

Converter Inspection

Check the outer part of the converter for damage and cracks. Replace it if there is any problem. Also, check for rust on the pilot and base. If there is any, remove it completely.

Transmission Disassembly

1. Properly support the transmission in a holding fixture. Drain the transmission oil and remove the torque converter.

2. Remove vacuum diaphragm, diaphragm rod, lockup con-

trol solenoid, turbine sensor and O-rings.

3. Remove the nut and remove the inhibitor switch by rotating the manual shaft fully forward, then return it 2 notches to the **N** position. Remove the bolt and bracket.

4. Remove the oil pan, gasket and magnet.

5. Disconnect the solenoid valve connectors and remove the harnesses from the bracket.

6. Remove the valve body.

7. Remove the solenoid valve connector from the transmission case.

8. Put marks on the converter housing, overdrive case and the transmission case for proper reassembly. Remove the converter housing.

9. Remove the overdrive band servo cover and gasket.

10. Loosen the overdrive band servo locknut and tighten the piston stem.

11. Put marks on the overdrive case and oil pump for proper reassembly.

12. Screw oil pump removal tool 490378390 or equivalent into the oil pump and remove the pump and gasket.

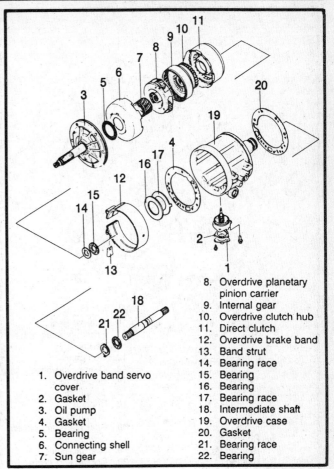

1. Overdrive band servo cover	8. Overdrive planetary pinion carrier
2. Gasket	9. Internal gear
3. Oil pump	10. Overdrive clutch hub
4. Gasket	11. Direct clutch
5. Bearing	12. Overdrive brake band
6. Connecting shell	13. Band strut
7. Sun gear	14. Bearing race
	15. Bearing
	16. Bearing
	17. Bearing race
	18. Intermediate shaft
	19. Overdrive case
	20. Gasket
	21. Bearing race
	22. Bearing

Components exploded view

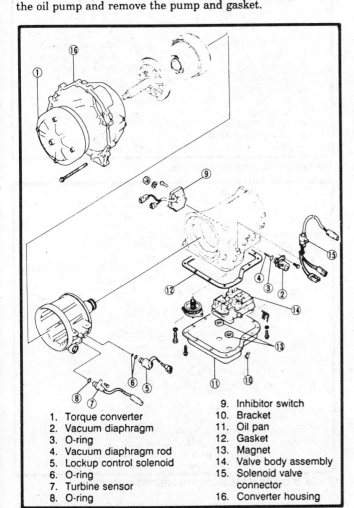

1. Torque converter	9. Inhibitor switch
2. Vacuum diaphragm	10. Bracket
3. O-ring	11. Oil pan
4. Vacuum diaphragm rod	12. Gasket
5. Lockup control solenoid	13. Magnet
6. O-ring	14. Valve body assembly
7. Turbine sensor	15. Solenoid valve connector
8. O-ring	16. Converter housing

Components exploded view

NOTE: Gently remove the oil pump to prevent the overdrive connecting shell sun gear and planetary pinion carrier from falling out.

13. Loosen the piston stem of the overdrive band servo. Remove the bearings and direct clutch assemby.

14. Remove the overdrive brake band and band strut. Secure the brake band ends with a wire clip to prevent the brake lining from cracking or peeling due to overstretching.

15. Remove the bearing races and bearing. Remove the intermediate shaft.

16. Loosen the 2nd band servo locknut and tighten the piston stem.

17. Separate the overdrive case from the transmission case by tapping it lightly with a plastic hammer. Remove the gasket.

18. Remove the bearing race and bearings.

19. Loosen the piston stem of the 2nd band servo. Remove the 2nd brake band and band strut. Secure the brake band ends with a wire clip to prevent the brake lining from cracking or peeling due to overstretching.

20. Remove the front clutch, rear clutch, rear clutch hub, front planetary pinion carrier, connecting shell, internal gear, bearing races, bearing and sun gear as a unit.

21. Remove the snapring from the output shaft.

22. Remove the connecting drum, rear planetary pinion carrier, internal gear and bearings as a unit.

23. Remove the rear extension housing and gasket. Pull out the output shaft and remove the oil distributor.

24. Remove the bearing race and bearing.

25. Remove the snapring from the low/reverse brake. Remove the retaining plate, drive plates and driven plates.

26. Using tool 490378346 or equivalent, remove the hexagonal head bolt from the rear of the transmission case.

27. Remove the oneway clutch inner race, thrust washer and piston return spring.

28. Apply compressed air to the oil passage and remove the low/reverse brake piston.

29. Remove the O-ring trand piston seal.

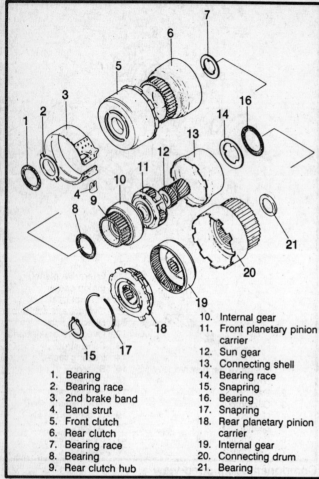

10. Internal gear
11. Front planetary pinion carrier
12. Sun gear
13. Connecting shell
14. Bearing race
15. Snapring
16. Bearing
17. Snapring
18. Rear planetary pinion carrier
19. Internal gear
20. Connecting drum
21. Bearing

1. Bearing
2. Bearing race
3. 2nd brake band
4. Band strut
5. Front clutch
6. Rear clutch
7. Bearing race
8. Bearing
9. Rear clutch hub

Components exploded view

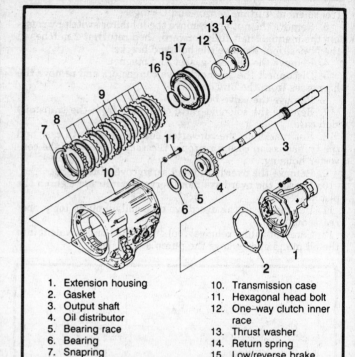

1. Extension housing
2. Gasket
3. Output shaft
4. Oil distributor
5. Bearing race
6. Bearing
7. Snapring
8. Retaining plate
9. Drive plates and driven plates
10. Transmission case
11. Hexagonal head bolt
12. One-way clutch inner race
13. Thrust washer
14. Return spring
15. Low/reverse brake piston
16. O-ring
17. Piston seal

Components exploded view

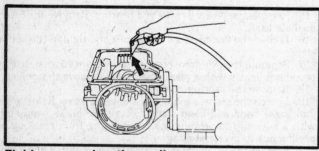

Fluid passage location—oil pump

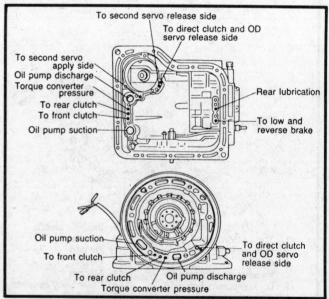

To second servo release side
To direct clutch and OD servo release side
To second servo apply side
Oil pump discharge
Torque converter pressure
To rear clutch
To front clutch
Oil pump suction
Rear lubrication
To low and reverse brake

Oil pump suction
To front clutch
To rear clutch
Oil pump discharge
Torque converter pressure
To direct clutch and OD servo release side

Fluid passage location—transmission case

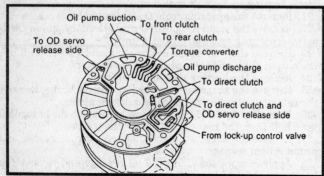

Oil pump suction
To front clutch
To rear clutch
To OD servo release side
Torque converter
Oil pump discharge
To direct clutch
To direct clutch and OD servo release side
From lock-up control valve

Fluid passage location—overdrive case

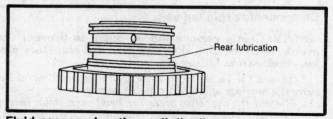

Rear lubrication

Fluid passage location—oil distributor

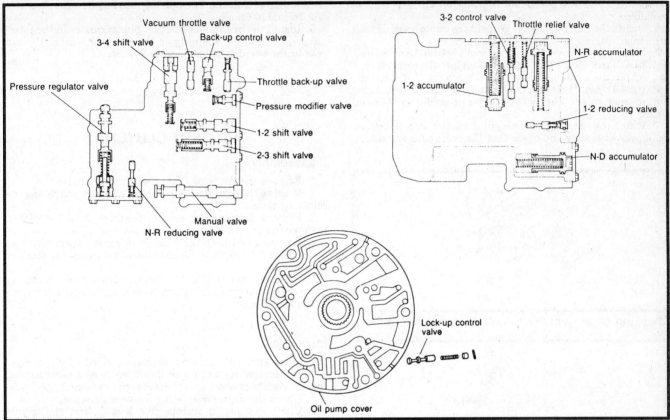

Fluid passage location – control valve

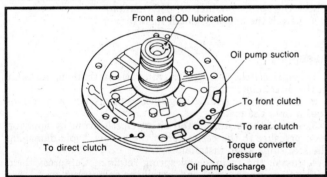

Fluid passage location – drum support

Unit Disassembly and Assembly
OIL PUMP

Disassembly

1. Remove the oil pump cover retaining bolts and remove the pump cover from the housing.
2. Before remove the pump gears, mark on the inner and outer gear position; then, remove the gears from the housing. Do not use a punch to mark the gears.
3. Tap the lockup control valve roll pin from the pump cover. Remove the lockup control valve, spring and plug.

Inspection

Clean each part with cleaning solvent, clean out all oil passages with compressed air and check that there are no obstructions. Inspect each part and check all clearances, replace if necessary.

1. Check the pump cover to gears end clearance. The standard clearance should be 0.0008–0.0016 in. (0.02–0.04mm). The maximum clearance should not exceed 0.0031 in. (0.08mm).
2. Check the outer gear teeth tip to cresent clearance. The standard clearance should be 0.0055–0.0083 in. (0.14–0.21mm). The maximum clearance should not exceed 0.0098 in. (0.25mm).
3. Check the outer gear to housing side clearance. The standard clearance should be 0.0020–0.0079 in. (0.05–0.20mm). The maximum clearance should not exceed 0.0098 in. (0.25mm).
4. Check the lockup control valve for damage and the control valve spring tension. The spring free length should be 1.01 in. (25.7mm).

Assembly

1. Position the lockup control valve, spring and plug into the pump cover. Tap the roll pin into place.
2. Using tool 49G030795 or equivalent, install a new oil seal.
3. Assembly tools 49S019001, 49S019002, 49S019003 or their equivalent and secure in a vise. Place a new O-ring in the

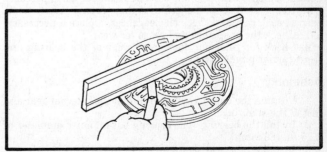

Checking pump cover to gears end clearance

pump cover and set the pump housing on the special tool assembled.

4. Install the inner and outer gears in the pump housing with their matching marks toward the pump cover.

5. Set the pump cover on holding tool 49S0190A0 or equivalent. Install tool 49S019004 or equivalent into the cover. Install and tighten the retaining bolts to 52–69 inch lbs. (5.9–7.8 Nm).

6. Install a new O-ring on the input shaft. Install the bearing and sensing rotor. The bearing outer diameter is 2.75 in. (69.9mm).

7. Install the snapring on the input shaft. Set the oil pump on the torque converter and check that the gears turn smoothly.

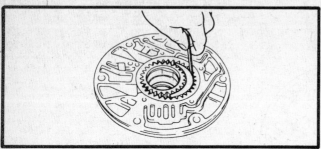

Checking outer gear teeth tip to crescent clearance

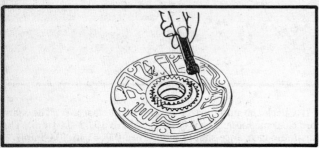

Checking outer gear to housing side clearance

OVERDRIVE PLANETARY GEAR UNIT

Disassembly

1. Remove the snapring from the sun gear. Pay close attention to the front and rear direction of the sun gear. The front side is equipped with a groove.

2. Remove the sun gear, overdrive planetary pinion carrier, bearing race, seal sleeve and bearing.

3. Remove the rear snapring. Remove the overdrive clutch hub and internal gear.

Inspection

Clean each part with cleaning solvent, clean out all oil passages with compressed air and check that there are no obstructions. Inspect each part and check all clearances, replace if necessary.

1. Check the snaprings and gears for wear.

2. Check for rotation, damage or wear of the bearing and front carrier pinion gear.

Assembly

1. Position the overdrive clutch hub in the internal gear and install the snapring.

2. Install the bearing. The bearing has an outer diameter of 2.75 in. (69.9mm).

3. Install a new seal sleeve in the overdrive clutch hub.

4. Install the bearing race in the overdrive planetary pinion.

Retain with petroleum. The bearing race has an outer diameter of 2.76 in. (70.0mm).

5. Install the overdrive planetary pinion carrier in the internal gear. Install the snapring on the sun gear. Install the sun gear in the overdrive planetary pinion carrier.

DIRECT CLUTCH

Disassembly

1. Remove the snapring from the direct clutch unit.

2. Remove the side plate, outer race, one-way clutch and the retaining plate.

3. Remove the snapring retaining the drive and driven plates. Remove the drive and driven clutch plates.

4. Compressed the spring retainer using an appropriate tool and remove the snapring. Remove the snapring, spring retainer and springs.

5. Set the direct clutch drum on the drum support and remove the piston by applying compressed air (57 psi maximum) to the oil passage.

Inspection

Clean each part with cleaning solvent, clean out all oil passages with compressed air and check that there are no obstructions. Inspect each part and check all clearances, replace if necessary.

1. Check the drive plate facing for wear or damage.

2. Check the piston springs free length. The spring free length should be 1.20 in. (30.5mm).

3. Check that the piston ball if free by shaking the piston. Check the spring retainer for deformation.

4. Check the one-way clutch for wear.

Assembly

1. Lubricate the O-ring with transmission fluid and install it in the direct clutch drum.

2. Lubricate the sealing ring with transmission fluid and install it onto the piston.

3. Install the piston in the direct clutch drum by applying even pressure to the perimeter of the piston. Avoid damaging the seal rings when installing.

4. Install the springs and spring retainer. Compress them with an appropriate tool and install the snapring.

5. Install the driven and drive plates starting with a driven plate; then, install a drive plate. Install the snapring.

6. Install the retaining plate, one-way clutch, outer race and side plate. Check that the spring cage of the one-way clutch faces toward the direct clutch drum. Also, align the flats of the retaining plate and the outer race with the lubrication holes of the clutch drum, then set them in the drum. Install the snapring.

7. Measure the clearance between the side plate and the snapring. Adjust the clearance by installing the correct side plate. The side plate clearance should be 0.008 in. (0.2mm) maximum.

8. Insert the direct clutch hub on the top of the direct clutch. Check that the one-way clutch hub turns clockwise only. If it turns counterclockwise, the one-way clutch is reversely installed.

9. Set the direct clutch on the drum support. Apply compressed air (57 psi maximum) to the oil passage, and check the clutch operation. Do not apply compressed air for longer than 3 seconds.

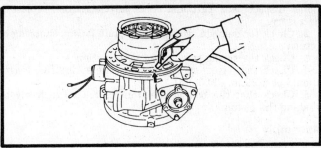

Removing the direct clutch and front clutch piston

OVERDRIVE AND 2ND BAND SERVO

Disassembly

1. Remove the overdrive servo cover retaining bolts and remove the servo cover.
2. Remove the return spring, nut, washer, piston stem.
3. Remove the piston assembly by applying compressed air to the oil passage hole. Remove the piston seal and O-rings.

Inspection

1. Clean each part with cleaning solvent, clean out all oil passages with compressed air and check that there are no obstructions. Inspect each part and check all clearances, replace if necessary.
2. Check the piston stem, piston assembly and body for damage or wear.
3. Check the servo return spring free length. The overdrive spring free length should be 1.89 in. (48.0mm) and 2nd 1.38 in. (35.0mm).
4. Check for cracking or pealing of the brake band facing.

Assembly

1. Lubricate the O-rings with transmission fluid and install them onto the piston body and piston assembly.
2. Install the piston assembly in the body by applying even pressure to the perimeter of the piston. Avoid damaging the seal rings when installing.
3. Install the piston stem and washer. Loosely install the nut.
4. Install the return spring, piston assembly and body. Apply even pressure to the perimeter of the body to avoid damaging the O-rings when installing.
5. Install the retaining bolts. Torque the overdrive band servo to 87–130 inch lbs. (10–15 Nm) and the 2nd band servo to 61–78 inch lbs. (6.9–8.8 Nm).

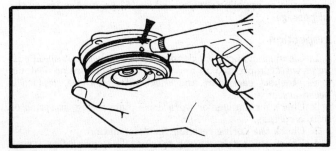

Removing the 2nd band servo piston

DRUM SUPPORT, ACCUMULATOR AND OVERDRIVE CASE

Disassembly

1. Make matching marks on the overdrive case and the drum support for proper reassembly. Then, remove the drum support, gasket and overdrive case.
2. Remove the case sealing ring, one-way check valve, steel ball and plug.
3. Remove the roll pin, plug and sealing rings from the drum support.
4. Remove the accumulator snapring. Remove the accumulator plug, piston, spring, seal ring and O-ring.

Inspection

1. Clean each part with cleaning solvent, clean out all oil passages with compressed air and check that there are no obstructions. Inspect each part and check all clearances, replace if necessary.

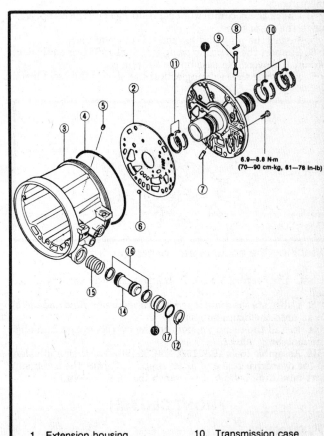

1. Extension housing
2. Gasket
3. Output shaft
4. Oil distributor
5. Bearing race
6. Bearing
7. Snapring
8. Retaining plate
9. Drive plates and driven plates
10. Transmission case
11. Hexagonal head bolt
12. One–way clutch inner race
13. Thrust washer
14. Return spring
15. Low/reverse brake piston
16. O-ring
17. Piston seal

Drum support, accumulator and overdrive case exploded view

2. Check the drum support and case for cracks.

3. Check the oil passage, gasket and plug for damage.

4. Check that the ball in the overdrive case move freely by shaking the overdrive case. Check the drum support sealing rings for wear or damage.

5. Check the clearance between the seal ring and seal ring groove. The standard clearance should be 0.0016–0.0063 in. (0.04–0.16mm). The maximum clearance should not exceed 0.0157 in. (0.40mm).

6. Check the accumulator piston, snapring and seal rings for wear or damage. Check the return spring free length. The spring free length should be 1.59 in. (40.4mm).

Assembly

1. Lubricate the seal rings with transmission fluid and install them onto the accumulator piston.

2. Install the accumulator spring and piston by applying even pressure to the perimeter of the piston. Avoid damaging the seal rings when installing.

3. Lubricate the O-ring with transmission fluid and install it onto the accumulator plug. Install the accumulator plug and snapring.

4. Check the accumulator operation by applying compressed air to the oil passage.

5. Install the plug and tap the roll pin into place.

6. Support the oil pump using tool 49S0190A0 or equivalent. Mount the overdrive case on the oil pump.

7. Lubricate the seal-ring with transmission fluid and install

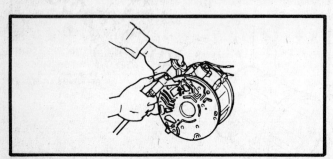

Checking the accumulator operation

it onto the overdrive case. Install the one-way valve and steel ball.

8. Lubricate the seal-rings with transmission fluid and install them onto the drum support.

9. Install the drum support on the overdrive case and align the matching marks.

10. Assemble tools 49S019004, 49S0190A0 or their equivalent to the overdrive case and drum support. Torque the drum support mounting bolts to 61–78 inch lbs. (6.9–8.8 Nm).

FRONT CLUTCH

Disassembly

1. Remove the snapring from the front clutch unit.

2. Remove the retaining plate, drive plates and driven plates, and dished plate.

3. Compressed the spring retainer using an appropriate tool and remove the snapring. Remove the spring retainer and springs.

4. Position the front clutch drum on the drum support. Remove the piston by applying compressed air (57 psi maximum) to the oil passage.

Inspection

1. Clean each part with cleaning solvent, clean out all oil passages with compressed air and check that there are no obstruc-

tions. Inspect each part and check all clearances, replace if necessary.

2. Check for damage or worn drive plate facing, snapring or return springs.

3. Check the spring retainer for deformation.

4. Check the return spring tension. The spring free length should be 1.20 in. (30.5mm).

5. Check that the ball in the front clutch move freely by shaking the piston.

Assembly

1. Lubricate the O-ring with transmission fluid and install it in the front clutch drum.

2. Lubricate the seal-ring with transmission fluid and install it onto the piston.

3. Install the piston in the front clutch drum. Apply even pressure to the perimeter of the piston to avoid damaging the seal-rings when installing.

4. Install the springs and spring retainer. Compress the spring retainer using an appropriate tool and install the snapring.

5. Install the dished plate, then install the driven plates and drive plates. Start with a driven plate, then alternate drive-driven-drive-driven.

6. Install the retaining plate with the step facing upward, then install the snapring.

7. Measure the clearance between the retaining plate and the snapring. Adjust the clearance by installing the correct retaining plate. The clearance should be 0.035–0.043 in. (0.9–1.1mm).

8. Set the front clutch on the drum support. Apply compressed air (57 psi maximum) for no more than 3 seconds to the oil passage and check the clutch operation.

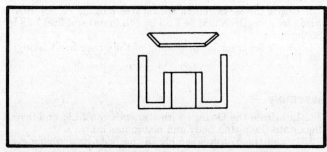

Proper installation of the front clutch dished plate

REAR CLUTCH

Disassembly

1. Remove the rear clutch snapring, retaining plate, drive and driven plates and dished plate.

2. Compressed the spring retainer using an appropriate tool and remove the snapring. Remove the spring retainer and springs.

3. Set the rear clutch drum on the drum support and remove the piston by applying compressed air (57 psi maximum) to the oil passage.

Inspection

1. Clean each part with cleaning solvent, clean out all oil passages with compressed air and check that there are no obstructions. Inspect each part and check all clearances, replace if necessary.

2. Check for damage or worn drive plate facing, snapring or return springs.

3. Check the spring retainer for deformation.

4. Check the return spring tension. The spring free length should be 1.20 in. (30.5mm).

5. Check that the ball in the rear clutch move freely by shaking the piston.

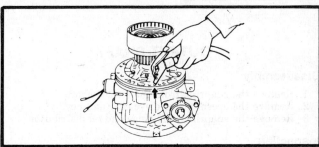

Removing the rear clutch

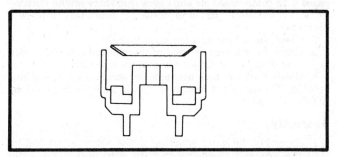

Proper installation of the rear clutch dished plate

Assembly

1. Lubricate the O-ring with transmission fluid and install it in the rear clutch drum.
2. Lubricate the seal-ring with transmission fluid and install it onto the piston.
3. Install the piston in the rear clutch drum. Apply even pressure to the perimeter of the piston to avoid damaging the seal-rings when installing.
4. Install the springs and spring retainer. Compress the spring retainer using an appropriate tool and install the snapring.
5. Install the dished plate, then install the driven plates and drive plates. Start with a driven plate, then alternate drive-driven-drive-driven.
6. Install the retaining plate with the step facing upward, then install the snapring.
7. Measure and adjust the rear clutch clearance. Replace all drive and driven plates if the clearance exceeds specification. The clearance should be 0.031–0.039 in. (0.8–0.1mm).
8. Set the rear clutch on the drum support. Apply compressed air (57 psi maximum) for no more than 3 seconds to the oil passage and check the clutch operation.

FRONT PLANETARY GEAR UNIT

Disassembly

1. Remove the snapring from the sun gear.
2. Remove the sun gear, front planetary pinion carrier, bearing race and bearing. Pay close attention to the direction of the sun gear. The grooved side is the front.
3. Remove the snapring from the rear clutch hub. Remove the rear clutch hub and internal gear.

Inspection

1. Clean each part with cleaning solvent, clean out all oil passages with compressed air and check that there are no obstructions. Inspect each part and check all clearances, replace if necessary.

2. Check the snaprings and gears for wear.
3. Check for rotation, damage or wear of the bearing and front carrier pinion gear.
4. Check the clearance between the pinion washer and planetary pinion carrier. The standard clearance should be 0.008–0.028 in. (0.2–0.7mm). The maximum clearance should not exceed 0.031 in. (0.8mm).

Assembly

1. Position the rear clutch hub in the internal gear and install the snapring.
2. Install the bearing. The bearing has an outer diameter of 2.75 in. (69.9mm).
3. Install the bearing race on the front planetary pinion carrier. Retain with petroleum. The bearing race has an outer diameter of 2.76 in. (70.0mm).
4. Install the front planetary pinion carrier in the internal gear. Install the snapring on the sun gear. Install the sun gear in the front planetary pinion carrier.

REAR PLANETARY GEAR UNIT

Disassembly

1. Remove the snapring from the connecting drum. Remove the rear planetary pinion carrier, bearing race and bearing from the connecting drum.
2. Remove the snapring from the drive flange. Remove the drive flange from the internal gear.
3. Remove the snapring retaining the one-way clutch assembly. Remove the one-way clutch assembly and connecting drum snapring.

Inspection

1. Clean each part with cleaning solvent, clean out all oil passages with compressed air and check that there are no obstructions. Inspect each part and check all clearances, replace if necessary.
2. Check the snaprings and gears for wear.
3. Check for rotation, damage or wear of the individual gears.
4. Check the one-way clutch for wear or damage. Check the clearance between the pinion washer and planetary pinion carrier. The standard clearance should be 0.008–0.028 in. (0.2–0.7mm). The maximum clearance should not exceed 0.031 in. (0.8mm).

Assembly

1. Install the snapring into the connecting drum.
2. Install the one-way clutch unit. Position the one-way clutch into the one-way clutch outer race as shown, with the arrow toward the front when inserted.
3. Install the one-way clutch retaining snapring.
4. Install the drive flange in the internal gear and install the snapring.
5. Install the internal gear and drive flange in the connecting drum.
6. Install the bearing. The bearing has an outer diameter of 2.75 in. (69.9mm).
7. Install the bearing race on the rear planetary pinion carrier. Retain with petroleum. The bearing race has an outer diameter of 2.76 in. (70.0mm).
8. Install the rear planetary pinion carrier in the connecting drum. Install the snapring.

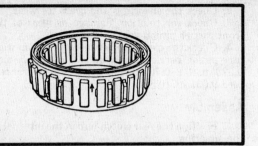

Proper installation of the one-way clutch to one-way clutch outer race

LOW AND REVERSE BRAKE

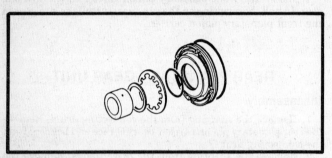

Checking low/reverse brake return spring length

Disassembly

1. Remove the snapring from the low/reverse brake. Remove the retaining plate, drive plates and driven plates.
2. Using an appropriate tool, remove the hexagonal head bolt from the rear of the transmission case.
3. Remove the one-way clutch inner race, thrust washer and piston return spring.
4. Apply compressed air to the oil passage and remove the low/reverse brake piston, O-ring and seal ring.

Inspection

1. Clean each part with cleaning solvent, clean out all oil passages with compressed air and check that there are no obstructions. Inspect each part and check all clearances, replace if necessary.
2. Check the snapring, driven plates and the one-way clutch inner race for wear.
3. Check the drive plates for worn or damage facing.
4. Check for damage to the thrust washer.
5. Check for damage or wear of the low/reverse brake piston or seal rings.
6. Check for a weakening return spring. The spring free length should be 0.209–0.244 in. (5.3–6.2mm).

Assembly

1. Lubricate the O-ring and seal ring with transmission fluid and install them on the low/reverse brake piston. Carefully install the piston while applying even pressure to the perimeter of the piston.
2. Install the piston return spring, thrust washer and one-way clutch inner race.
3. Check that the return spring, thrust washer and rings are properly positioned; then, install the hexagonal head bolt in the rear of the transmission case.
4. Install and torque the inner race mounting bolts to 113–156 inch lbs. (13–18 Nm).

5. Install the drive and driven plates. Start with a driven plate, then alternate drive-driven-drive-driven. Install the retaining plate and snapring.

OUTPUT SHAFT

Disassembly

1. Remove the snapring from the output shaft.
2. Remove the speedometer drive gear and key.
3. Remove the snapring, seal rings and oil distributor.

Inspection

1. Clean each part with cleaning solvent, clean out all oil passages with compressed air and check that there are no obstructions. Inspect each part and check all clearances, replace if necessary.
2. Check for a bent or worn output shaft.
3. Check for damage or wear of the speedometer drive gear, key or oil distributor. Check for damage seal rings.
4. Check the clearance between the seal rings and seal ring grooves. The standard clearance should be 0.0016–0.0063 in. (0.04–0.16mm).

Assembly

1. Assembly the inner snapring to the output shaft and install the key and speedometer drive gear. Install the outer snapring.
2. Lubricate the seal rings with transmission fluid and install them onto the oil distributor.

EXTENSION HOUSING

Disassembly

1. Remove the dowel spacer, return spring, parking pawl and pawl shaft.
2. Remove the actuator support retaining plate. Slowly remove the actuator support being aware of the steel balls popping out.
3. Remove the steel balls, retainer and springs.
4. Remove the oil seal from the extension housing.

Inspection

1. Clean each part with cleaning solvent, clean out all oil passages with compressed air and check that there are no obstructions. Inspect each part and check all clearances, replace if necessary.
2. Check for a damage or worn parking pawl, pawl shaft or actuator support.
3. Check the steel balls for damage.
4. Check the springs tension. The spring free length should be 1.26 in. (32.0mm).

Assembly

1. Install a new oil seal in the extension housing.
2. Install the spring and retainer. Install the steel balls, actuator support and retaining plate. Tighten and torque the retaining plate attaching bolts to 69–95 inch lbs. (7.8–10.8 Nm).
3. Install the pawl shaft, parking pawl and return spring. Install the dowel spacer.

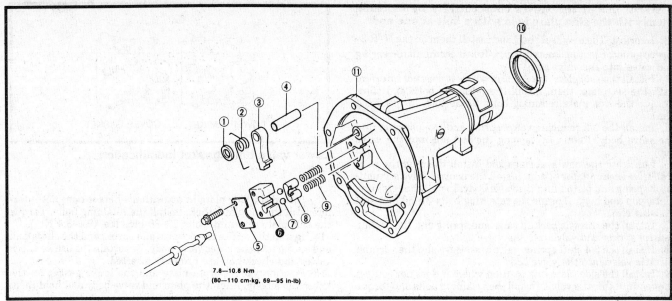

7.8—10.8 N·m
(80—110 cm-kg, 69—95 in-lb)

Extension housing exploded view

TRANSMISSION CASE

Disassembly

1. Remove the retaining ring from the manual shaft. Remove the manual plate, parking rod, spacer and manual shaft.
2. Remove the O-ring from the manual shaft.

Inspection

1. Clean each part with cleaning solvent. Dry using compressed air. Inspect each and replace if necessary.
2. Check for a damage or worn parking rod, manual plate or manual rod.

Assembly

1. Lubricate the O-ring with transmission fluid and install in onto the manual shaft.
2. Install the manual shaft and spacer.
3. Install the manual plate on the manual shaft.
4. Install the locknut and torque to 22–29 ft. lbs. (29–39 Nm). Check the parking mechanism operation.

VALVE BODY

Disassmbly

NOTE: Pay close attention when handling the control valve because it consists of the most precise and delicate parts of the transmission. Neatly arrange the parts in order to avoid mixing up similar parts.

1. Remove the manual valve from the control valve body.
2. Remove the 3/2 control solenoid valve, strainer and O-ring.
3. Remove 1/2 shift solenoid valve, strainer and O-ring.
4. Remove 2/3 shift solenoid valve, strainer and O-ring.
5. Remove 3/4 shift solenoid valve, strainer and O-ring.
6. Remove the upper valve body retaining bolts. Remove the upper valve body and gasket. Carefully remove the separate plate and lower gasket to avoid losing the orifice check valves, springs and balls.
7. Remove the orifice check valve and spring. Remove the throttle relief ball and spring.
8. Remove the valve body cover retaining bolts and remove the valve body cover.

9. Remove the inner strainer and cover gasket. Carefully remove the separate plate and lower gasket to avoid losing the orifice check valves, springs and balls.
10. Remove the orifice check valve and spring.
11. Remove the lower valve body and side plate.
12. Remove the neutral/reverse reducing spring and reducing valve.
13. Remove the pressure regulator sleeve, regulator plug, spring seat, spring and regulator valve.
14. Remove the side plate. Remove the pressure modifier valve, modifier spring.
15. Remove the 1/2 shift valve and spring.
16. Remove the 2/3 shift valve and spring.
17. Remove the side plate. Remove the vacuum throttle valve.
18. Remove the 3/4 shift sleeve, shift valve and spring.
19. Remove the back-up control valve and spring.
20. Remove the throttle back-up spring and valve.
21. Remove the retaining clip and side plate. Remove N/D accumulator piston, spring and seal ring.
22. Remove the retaining roll pin from the 1/2 reducing valve. Remove the stopper, 1/2 reducing spring and valve.
23. Remove the retaining clip and side plate. Remove 1/2 accumulator spring, piston and seal ring.
24. Remove the 3/2 control spring and control valve.
25. Remove the throttle relief spring and throttle relief valve.
26. Remove the N–R/2–3 accumulator piston, spring and seal ring.

Inspection

1. Check each individual valve for damage or wear.
2. Check the operation of each valve.
3. Check for damage oil passage
4. Check the valve body for cracks or damage.
5. Check the side plates for damage or wear.
6. Check the oil strainer for damage.

Assembly

1. Lubricate the new seal rings and install them onto the 1/2 accumulator piston. Install the 1/2 accumulator piston and spring into the valve body.
2. Install the 3/2 control valve and spring and the throttle relief valve and spring into the valve body.

NOTE: Install the valves consecutively by blocking them with the side plate held with a bolt at one end.

3. Lubricate the new seal rings and install them on the N–R/2–3 accumulator piston. Install the N–R/2–3 accumulator spring and valve into the valve body.

4. Install the side plate in a position where it does not interfere with the set plate; then, install the retaining bolts and clips. Torque the side plate retaining bolts 22–30 inch lbs. (2.5–3.4 Nm).

5. Install the 1/2 reducing valve, spring and stopper plug into the valve body. Retain by tapping the roll pin into the valve body.

6. Lubricate the new seal rings and install them on the neutral/drive accumulator piston. Install the neutral/drive accumulator spring and piston into the valve body. Install the retaining plate, clip and bolts. Torque the retaining bolts 22–30 inch lbs. (2.5–3.4 Nm).

7. Install the throttle backup valve and spring and the backup control spring and valve into the valve body.

8. Install the 3/4 shift spring, valve and sleeve and the vacuum throttle valve into the valve body.

9. Install the side plate in a position where it does not contact the vacuum throttle valve. Install the retaining bolts and torque them 22–30 inch lbs. (2.5–3.4 Nm).

10. Install the 2/3 shift spring and valve, the 1/2 shift spring and valve and the pressure modifier spring and valve into the valve body.

11. Install the side plate in a position where it does not interfere with the set plate; then, install the retaining bolts. Torque the side plate retaining bolts 22–30 inch lbs. (2.5–3.4 Nm).

12. Install the pressure regulator valve, spring, spring seat, plug and sleeve and the neutral/reverse reducing valve and spring into the valve body.

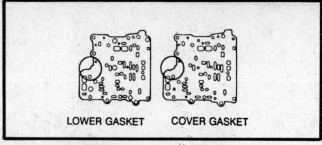

LOWER GASKET   COVER GASKET

Lower valve body gasket indetification

13. Install the side plate in a position where it does not interfere with the set plate; then, install the retaining bolts. Torque the side plate retaining bolts 22–30 inch lbs. (2.5–3.4 Nm).

14. Install the orifice check valve and spring and the check ball and spring into the lower valve body. Be certain the orifice check valves and check ball are properly inserted.

15. Position the separate plate and the lower gasket on the lower valve body. Align the plate and valve body and hold them together with large clips.

16. Install the upper gasket and upper valve body on the separate plate; then, install the retaining bolts. Be certain the retaining bolts are in their correct locations. Torque the retaining bolts 57–69 inch lbs. (6.5–7.8 Nm).

17. Turn the valve body assembly over and install the orifice check valves and springs in the lower valve body. Be certain the orifice check valves are properly inserted.

18. Install the lower gasket, separate plate and cover gasket on the valve body.

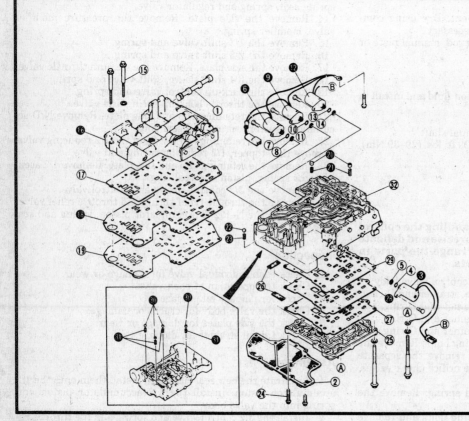

1. Manual valve
2. Oil strainer
3. 3/2 control solenoid valve
4. O-ring
5. Oil strainer
6. 1/2 shift solenoid valve
7. O-ring
8. Oil strainer
9. 2/3 shift solenoid valve
10. O-ring
11. Oil strainer
12. 3/4 shift solenoid valve
13. O-ring
14. Oil strainer
15. Bolt
16. Upper valve body
17. Upper gasket
18. Separate plate
19. Lower gasket
20. Orifice check valve
21. Spring
22. Throttle relief ball
23. Spring
24. Bolt
25. Valve body cover
26. Inner strainer
27. Cover gasket
28. Separate plate
29. Lower gasket
30. Orifice check valve
31. Spring
32. Lower valve body

Control valve exploded view

19. Install the inner strainer in the valve body; then, install the valve body cover on the cover gasket. Install the retaining bolts making certain they are in their correct locations. Torque the retaining bolts 57–69 inch lbs. (6.5–7.8 Nm).

20. Lubricate the new O-rings and install them on each solenoid valve.

21. Install the 3/2 control solenoid valve, 3/4 shift solenoid valve, 2/3 shift solenoid valve, 1/2 shift solenoid valve to the valve body. Install the solenoid retaining bolts and torque 22–30 inch lbs. (2.5–3.4 Nm).

22. Install the manual valve into the valve body.

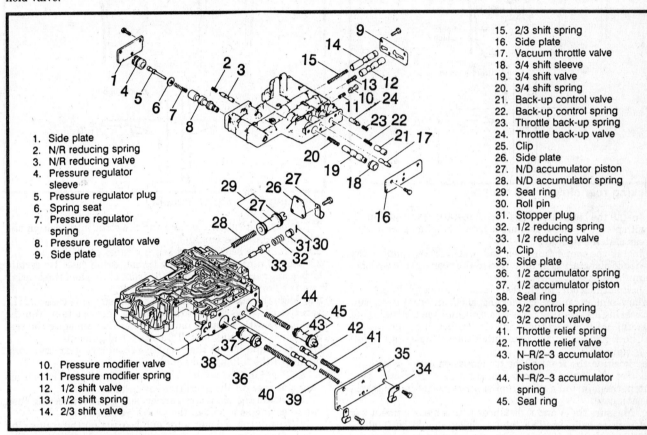

1. Side plate
2. N/R reducing spring
3. N/R reducing valve
4. Pressure regulator sleeve
5. Pressure regulator plug
6. Spring seat
7. Pressure regulator spring
8. Pressure regulator valve
9. Side plate
10. Pressure modifier valve
11. Pressure modifier spring
12. 1/2 shift valve
13. 1/2 shift spring
14. 2/3 shift valve
15. 2/3 shift spring
16. Side plate
17. Vacuum throttle valve
18. 3/4 shift sleeve
19. 3/4 shift valve
20. 3/4 shift spring
21. Back-up control valve
22. Back-up control spring
23. Throttle back-up spring
24. Throttle back-up valve
25. Clip
26. Side plate
27. N/D accumulator piston
28. N/D accumulator spring
29. Seal ring
30. Roll pin
31. Stopper plug
32. 1/2 reducing spring
33. 1/2 reducing valve
34. Clip
35. Side plate
36. 1/2 accumulator spring
37. 1/2 accumulator piston
38. Seal ring
39. 3/2 control spring
40. 3/2 control valve
41. Throttle relief spring
42. Throttle relief valve
43. N–R/2–3 accumulator piston
44. N–R/2–3 accumulator spring
45. Seal ring

Control valve exploded view

Transmission Assembly

1. Mount the transmission in a suitable holding fixture.

2. Lubricate the O-ring and seal ring with transmission fluid and install them on the low/reverse brake piston. Carefully install the piston while applying even pressure to the perimeter of the piston.

3. Install the piston return spring, thrust washer and one-way clutch inner race.

4. Check that the return spring, thrust washer and rings are properly positioned; then, install the hexagonal head bolt in the rear of the transmission case.

5. Install and torque the inner race mounting bolts to 113–156 inch lbs. (13–18 Nm).

6. Install the drive and driven plates. Start with a driven plate, then alternate drive-driven-drive-driven. Install the retaining plate and snapring.

7. Measure the clearance between the snapring and the retaining plate. If the clearance exceed 0.031–0.041 in. (0.8–1.05mm), install the proper retaining plate.

8. Check the operation of the piston by applying compressed air (57 psi maximum) for no more than 3 seconds to the oil passage of the low/reverse brake.

9. Install the bearing in the rear of the transmission case and retain with petroleum jelly.

10. Install the bearing race on the oil distributor and install in the transmission case.

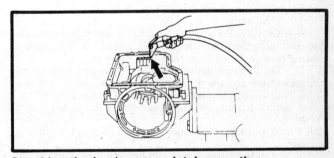

Checking the low/reverse clutch operation

11. Install the output shaft.

12. Install the bearings on the rear and front side of the planetary gear unit and retain with petroleum jelly. Install the rear planetary gear unit in the low/reverse brake side and install the snap ring on the front side of the output shaft.

13. Install a new gasket on the transmission case; then, install the rear extension housing. Torque the retaining bolts 14–18 ft. lbs. (20–25 Nm).

14. Check the manual lever and output shaft operation. The output shaft should locked with the manual lever in the **P** range.

15. Set the rear clutch assembly on the top of the front clutch assembly and install the bearing race on the rear clutch.

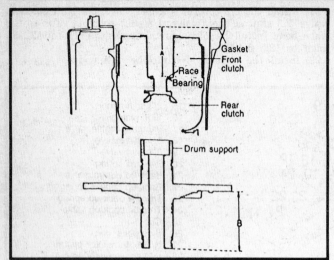

Checking rear clutch total endplay

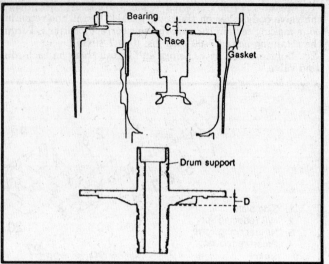

Checking front clutch endplay

16. Install the bearing on the front planetary gear unit and retain with petroleum jelly. Install the front planetary gear unit in the rear clutch assembly.

17. Install the connecting shell and bearing race from the top of the front planetary gear unit. Retain the bearing race with petroleum jelly.

18. Install the front clutch, rear clutch, rear clutch hub, front planetary pinion carrier, connecting shell, internal gear, sun gear, bearing and bearing races as a unit into the transmission. Be careful not to mixed the many similar bearings and races.

19. Check and adjust the rear clutch total endplay in the following manner:

    a. Position the front of the transmission case upward.

    b. Set the drum support bearing and race on the rear clutch; then, install a new drum support gasket in the transmission case.

    c. Measure the A and B distances with a measurement bar and vernier calipers. The total endplay should be 0.0098–0.0197 in. (0.25–0.50mm). Calculate the total endplay using the formula below.

    Formula: $T = A - B - 0.0039$ in. (0.1mm)

    T: – Total endplay

    A: – The distance between the drum support mounting surface (including the drum support gasket) and the drum support bearing race surface on the rear clutch assembly.

    B: – The distance between the drum support bearing race contact surface and the drum support gasket contact surface.

    0.0039: – The compression amount of a new gasket.

    d. Adjust the total endplay by selecting the proper bearing race.

20. Check and adjust the front clutch endplay in the following manner:

    a. Install the bearing race and bearing in position and retain with petroleum jelly.

    b. Measure the C and D distances with a measurement bar and vernier calipers. The front clutch endplay should be 0.020–0.031 in. (0.5–0.8mm). Calculate the total endplay using the formula below.

    Formula: $T = C - D - 0.0039$ in. (0.1mm)

    T: – Total endplay

    C: – The distance between the drum support mounting surface (including the drum support gasket) of the transmission case and the bearing surface on the front clutch assembly.

    D: – The distance between the sliding surface of the bearing and the drum support gasket contact surface.

    0.0039: – The compression amount of a new gasket.

    c. Adjust the front clutch endplay by selecting the proper bearing race.

21. Install the 2nd brake band and the strut into position and tighten the piston stem lightly.

22. Install the bearings and bearing races position.

23. Install a new gasket in the transmission case. Be certain the bearing race is no the top of the front clutch and the bearing is on the bottom of the front clutch hole.

24. Align the matching marks of the transmission case and the overdrive case and set the overdrive case into position. Tap the unit lightly with a plastic hammer to avoid damaging the seal rings when installing. Install 2 bolts for alignment.

25. Check and adjust the overdrive planetary gear unit total endplay in the following manner:

    a. Position the overdrive case upright and install the bearing and race on the overdrive case.

    b. Install the planetary carrier, sun gear, connecting shell and bearing as a unit in the overdrive case.

    c. Install the sensing rotor and bearing on the connecting shell. Do not install the direct clutch drum at this time. The sensing rotor and the bearing are part of the oil pump assembly.

    d. Install a new oil pump gasket in the overdrive case and measure the E and H distances with a measurement bar and a vernier calipers. The overdrive total endplay should be

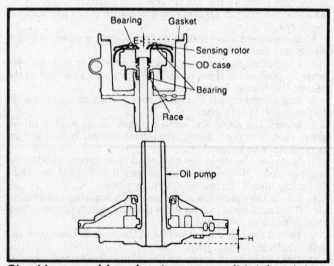

Checking overdrive planetary gear unit total endplay

0.0098–0.0197 in. (0.25–0.50mm). Calculate the total endplay using the formula below.

Formula: T = E - H - 0.0039 in. (0.1mm)

T: – Total endplay

E: – The distance between the oil pump mounting surface (including the oil pump gasket) and the sensing rotor bearing surface.

H: – The distance between the oil pump side sensing rotor bearing contact surface and the oil pump gasket contact surface.

0.0039: – The compression amount of a new gasket.

e. Adjust the endplay by selecting the proper bearing race.

26. Check and adjust the direct clutch endplay in the following manner:

a. Install the bearing race in the overdrive case.

b. Install the direct clutch, sun gear, connecting shell and bearings in the overdrive case.

c. Install the sensing rotor and bearing on the connecting shell. Do not install the planetary pinion carrier at this time. The sensing rotor and the bearing are part of the oil pump assembly.

d. Measure the G and H distances with a measurement bar and vernier calipers. The total endplay should be 0.020–0.031 in. (0.5–0.8mm). Calculate the direct clutch endplay using the formula below.

Formula: T = G - H - 0.0039 in. (0.1mm)

T: – Total endplay

G: – The distance between the oil pump mounting surface (including the oil pump gasket) and the sensing rotor bearing surface.

H: – The distance between the oil pump side sensing rotor bearing contact surface and the oil pump gasket contact surface.

0.0039: – The compression amount of a new gasket.

e. Adjust the direct clutch endplay by selecting the proper bearing race.

27. Insert the intermediate shaft. The end with the long spline is the front.

28. Install the large bearing race and retain with petroleum jelly.

29. Install the small bearing, then the small bearing race.

30. Install the overdrive brake band and band strut, then install the overdrive planetary gear unit on the direct clutch.

31. Install the overdrive connecting shell on the overdrive planetary gear unit.

32. Install the bearing on the direct clutch assembly and retain with petroleum jelly. Install the direct clutch assembly.

33. Install the bearing on the overdrive connecting shell and retain with petroleum jelly.

34. Install a new gasket in the overdrive case. Install the oil pump, input shaft, bearing and sensing rotor as a unit. Align the pump with 2 bolts and carefully tap into place using a plastic mallet.

35. Apply sealant to the bolt flanges and converter housing contact surface, then install the converter housing. Torque the mounting bolts 43–51 ft. lbs. (59–69 Nm).

36. Lubricate the piston stem with transmission fluid and adjust the 2nd brake band as followed:

a. Loosen the locknut and tighten the piston stem 109–126 inch lbs. (12–14 Nm).

b. Loosen the stem 2½ turns, then tighten the locknut 11–29 ft. lbs. (15–39 Nm).

37. Check the servo piston operation by applying compressed air (57 psi maximum) for no more than 3 seconds to the oil passage of the 2nd band servo.

38. Lubricate the piston stem with transmission fluid and adjust the overdrive brake band as followed:

a. Loosen the locknut and tighten the piston stem 104–130 inch lbs. (12–15 Nm).

b. Loosen the stem 2 turns, then tighten the locknut 11–29 ft. lbs. (15–39 Nm).

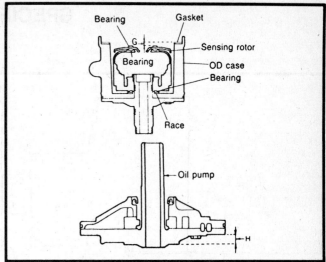

Checking the direct clutch endplay

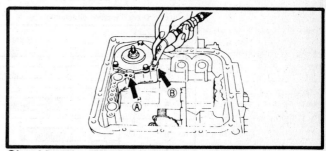

Checking the 2nd band servo operation

39. Check the servo piston operation by applying compressed air (57 psi maximum) for no more than 3 seconds to the oil passage of the overdrive band servo.

40. Install a new gasket on the overdrive band servo, then install the overdrive band servo cover. Tighten the retaining bolts 43–61 inch lbs. (4.9–6.9 Nm).

41. Lubricate the O-ring with transmission fluid and install it on the solenoid valve connector. Install the solenoid valve connector in the transmission case.

42. Install the valve body. Remember to place the manual plate in the correct position of the manual valve. Install the retaining bolts and torque to 95–130 inch lbs. (11–15 Nm).

43. Connect the solenoid valve connectors and install the harnesses.

44. Lubricate the O-ring with transmission fluid and install it on the vacuum diaphragm. Select the proper diaphragm rod using the vacuum diaphragm rod application chart.

45. Install the magnet into the oil pan. Set the oil pan in place using a new gasket. Install the bracket and bolts and torque the retaining bolts 52–69 inch lbs. (5.9–7.8 Nm).

46. Lubricate the O-ring with transmission fluid and install it on the turbine sensor. Apply locking compound to the bolt threads; then, install the turbine sensor. Tighten the retaining bolt 69–95 inch lbs. (7.8–10.8 Nm).

47. Lubricate the O-rings with transmission fluid and install them on the transmission case. Install the lockup control solenoid.

48. Install and adjust the inhibitor switch.

49. Install the torque converter. Be certain the torque converter is installed correctly by measuring the clearance between the end of the torque converter and the end of the converter housing. The clearance should be 1.26 in. (32mm) minimum.

SPECIFICATIONS

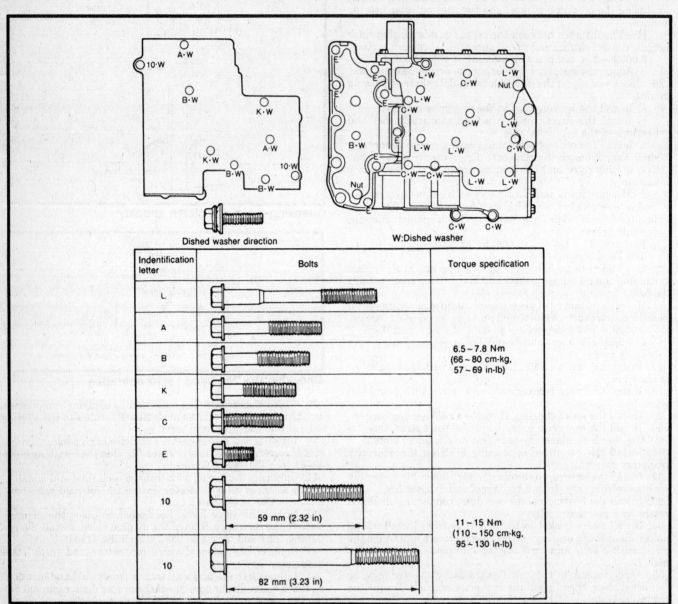

Dished washer direction

W:Dished washer

Indentification letter	Bolts	Torque specification
L		6.5~7.8 N·m (66~80 cm-kg, 57~69 in-lb)
A		
B		
K		
C		
E		
10	59 mm (2.32 in)	11~15 N·m (110~150 cm-kg, 95~130 in-lb)
10	82 mm (3.23 in)	

Control valve bolts location

VACUUM DIAPHRAGM ROD APPLICATION

Dimension N		Rod Length	
in.	mm	in.	mm
Below 1.0748	Below 27.30	1.14	29.0
1.0748–1.0945	27.30–27.80	1.16	29.5
1.0945–1.1142	27.80–28.30	1.18	30.0
1.1142–1.1339	28.30–28.80	1.20	30.5
1.1339 or over	28.80 or over	1.22	31.0

FRONT CLUTCH RETAINING PLATE SIZES

in.	mm
0.197	5.0
0.205	5.2
0.213	5.4
0.220	5.6
0.228	5.8
0.236	6.0
0.244	6.2

OVERDRIVE SELECTIVE BEARING RACE SIZES

in.	mm
0.047	1.2
0.055	1.4
0.063	1.6
0.071	1.8
0.079	2.0
0.087	2.2

LOW/REVERSE CLUTCH RETAINING PLATE SIZES

in.	mm
0.465	11.8
0.472	12.0
0.480	12.2
0.488	12.4
0.496	12.6
0.503	12.8

REAR CLUTCH SELECTIVE BEARING RACE SIZES

in.	mm
0.047	1.2
0.055	1.4
0.063	1.6
0.071	1.8
0.079	2.0
0.087	2.2

FRONT CLUTCH SELECTIVE BEARING RACE SIZES

in.	mm
0.031	0.8
0.039	1.0
0.047	1.2
0.055	1.4
0.063	1.6
0.071	1.8
0.079	2.0
0.087	2.2

DIRECT CLUTCH SELECTIVE BEARING RACE SIZES

in.	mm
0.031	0.8
0.039	1.0
0.047	1.2
0.055	1.4
0.063	1.6
0.071	1.8

DIRECT CLUTCH SIDE PLATE SIZES

in.	mm
0.016	0.4
0.024	0.6
0.031	0.8
0.039	1.0
0.047	1.2

BEARING AND RACE OUTER DIAMETER

Item	Bearing in.	(mm)	Race in.	(mm)
1	2.75	(69.9)	—	—
2	2.75	(69.9)	—	—
3	2.75	(69.9)	2.76	(70.0)
4	1.37	(34.9)	1.30	(33.0)
5	2.75	(69.9)	2.76	(70.0)
6	2.75	(69.9)	2.99	(76.0)
7	1.37	(34.9)	1.30	(33.0)
8	2.08	(52.9)	2.03	(51.5)
9	2.75	(69.9)	2.76	(70.0)
10	2.75	(69.9)	2.76	(70.0)
11	2.75	(69.9)	2.76	(70.0)
12	1.85	(46.9)	—	—
13	2.08	(52.9)	2.03	(51.5)

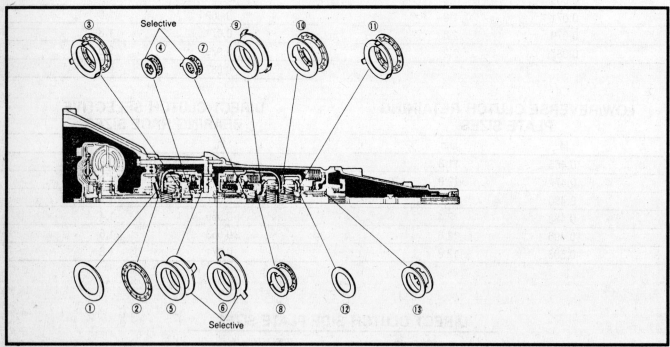

Thrust washer, bearing and race location

PARK RANGE

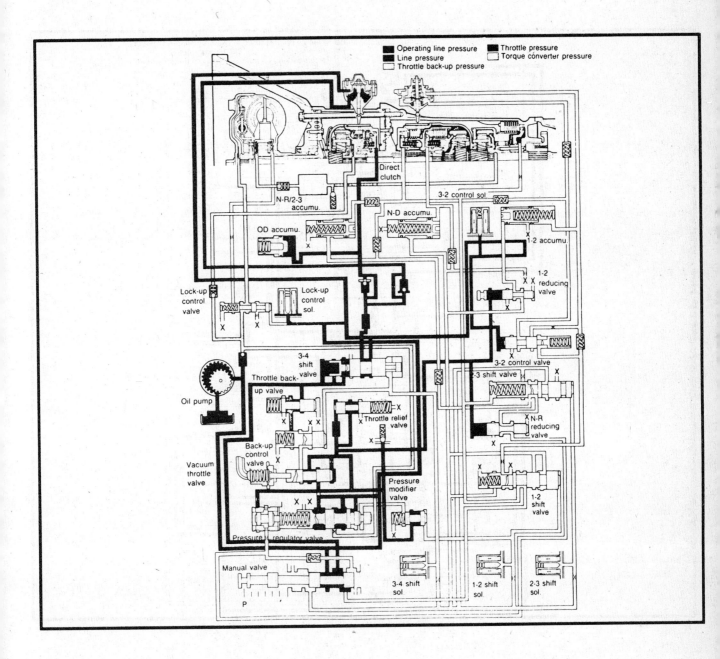

REVERSE RANGE

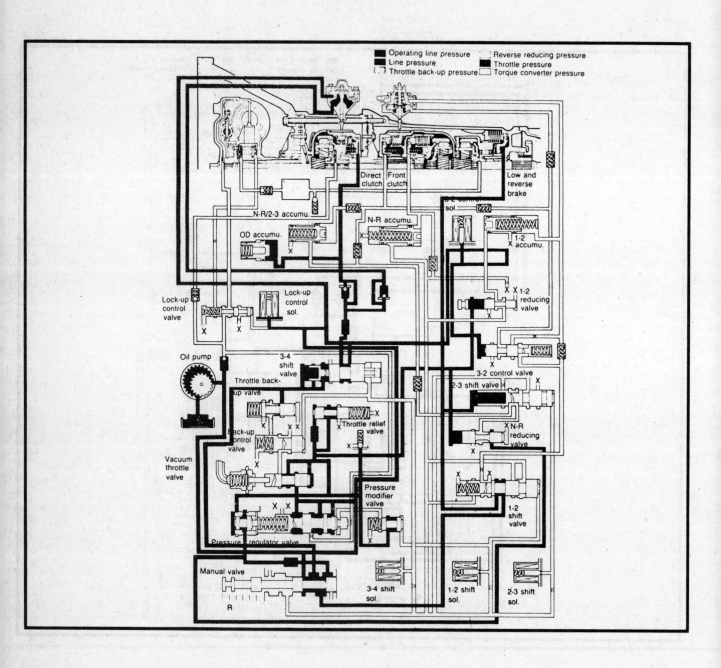

NEUTRAL RANGE — BELOW 9 mph (15 km/h)

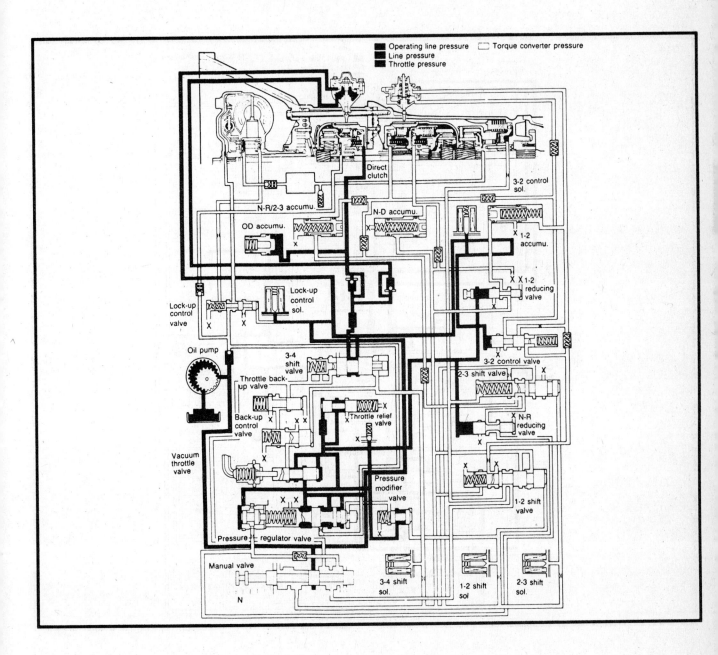

NEUTRAL RANGE – ABOVE 11 mph (17 km/h)

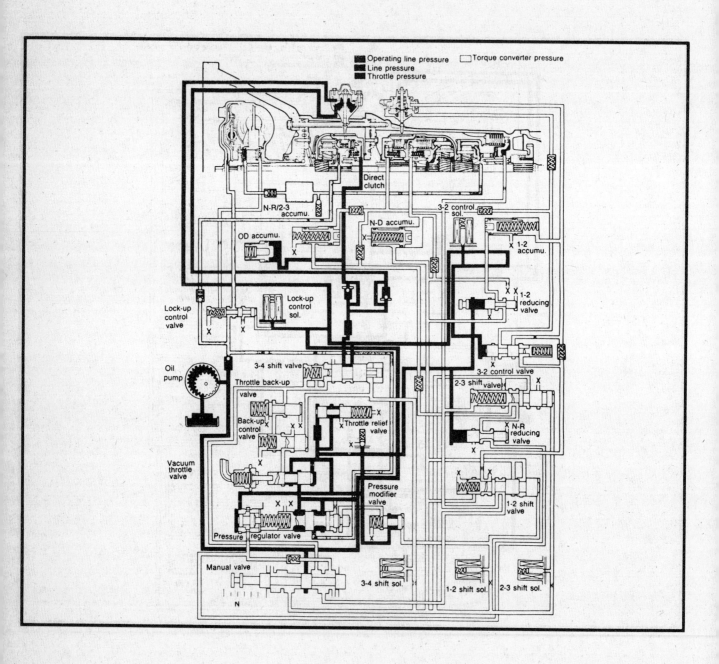

DRIVE RANGE—1ST GEAR

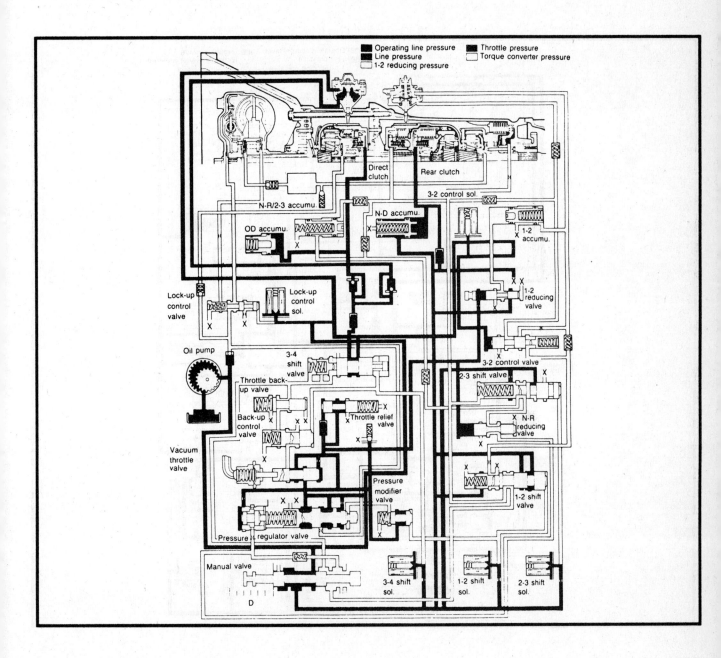

DRIVE RANGE—2ND GEAR

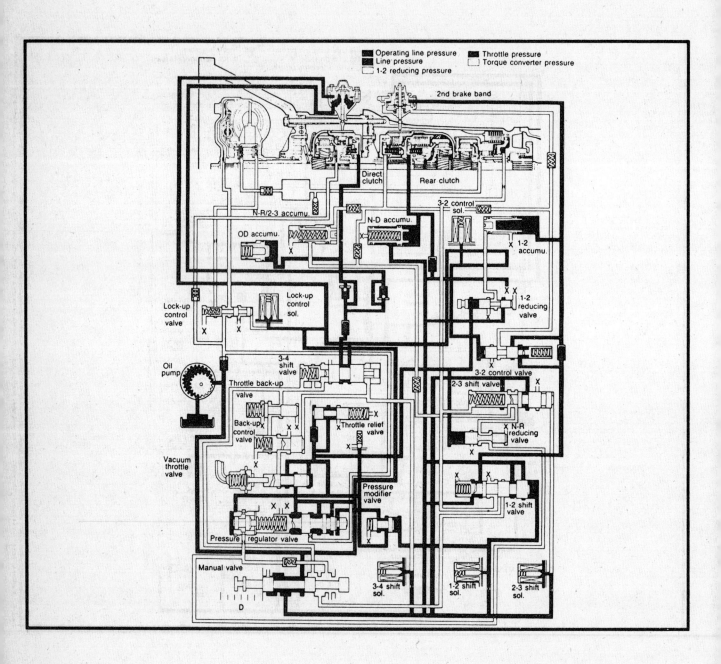

DRIVE RANGE—3RD GEAR

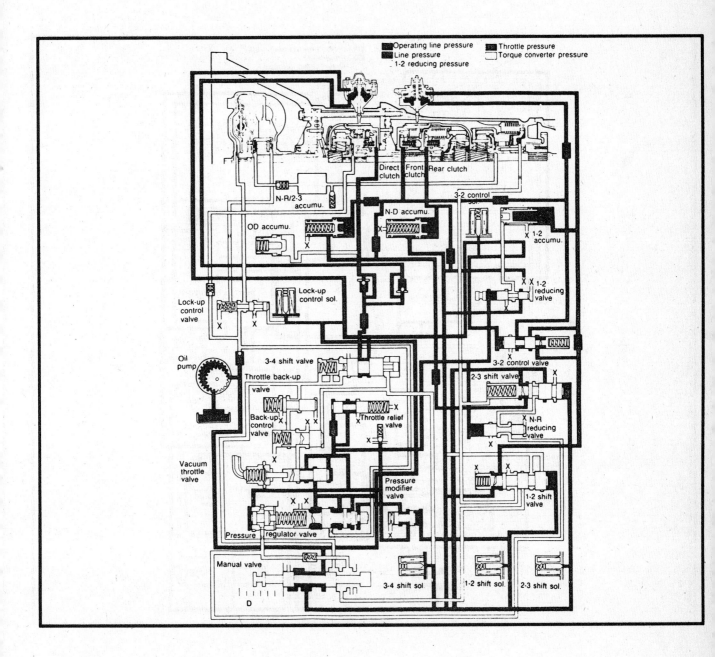

AUTOMATIC TRANSMISSIONS
N4AEL—MAZDA

DRIVE RANGE—OVERDRIVE, LOCKUP ON

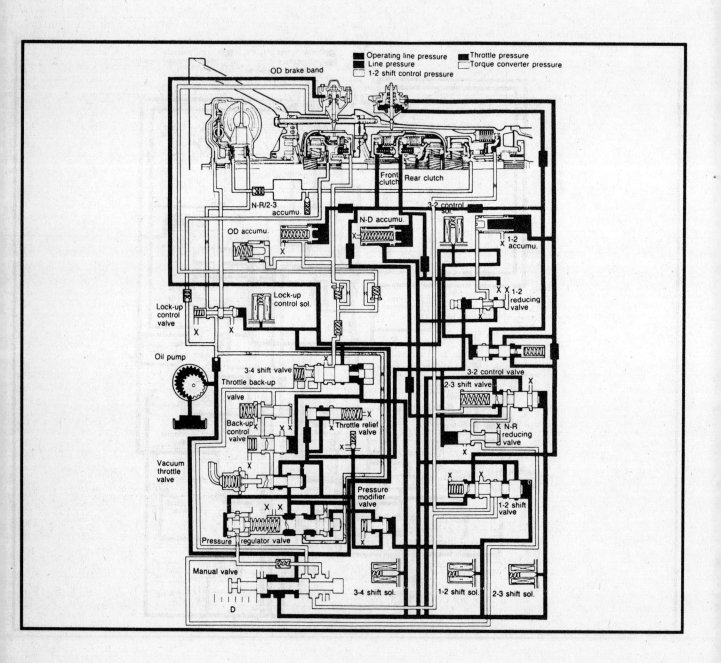

SECOND RANGE—1ST GEAR

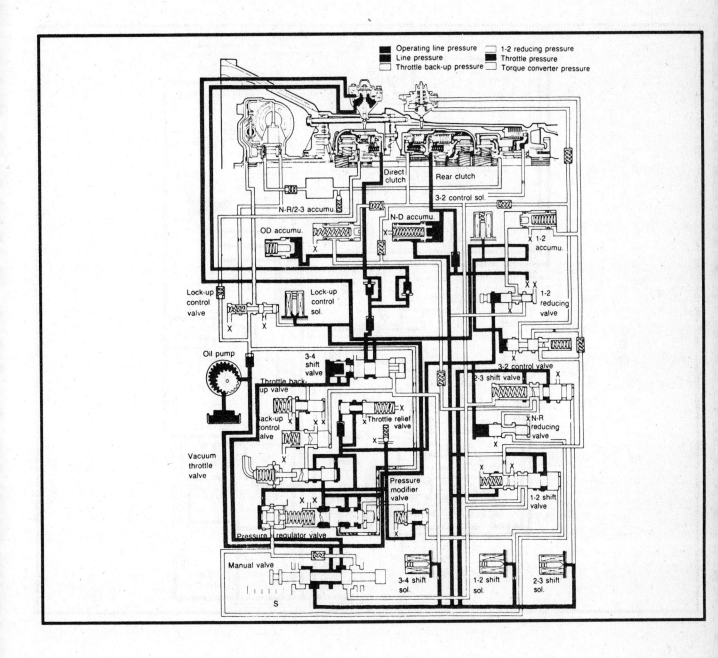

SECOND RANGE—2ND GEAR

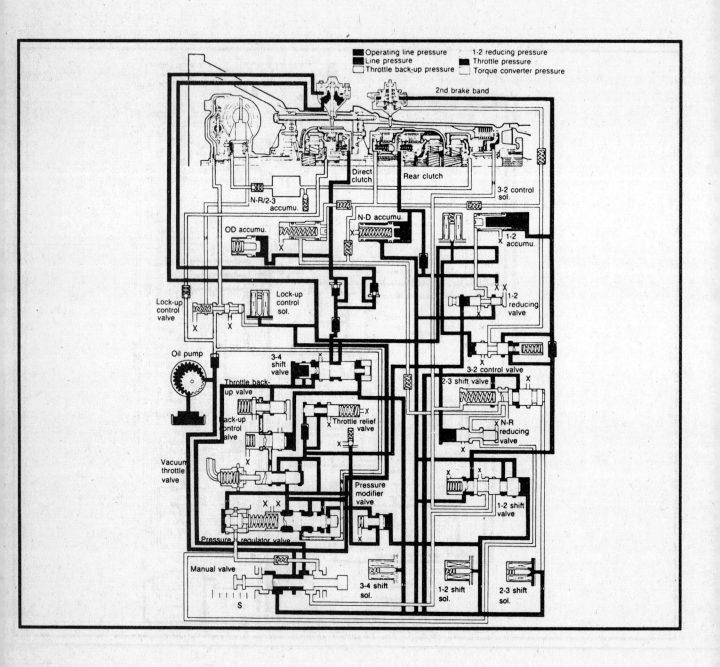

■ Operating line pressure	■ 1-2 reducing pressure
■ Line pressure	■ Throttle pressure
□ Throttle back-up pressure	□ Torque converter pressure

SECOND RANGE – 3RD GEAR

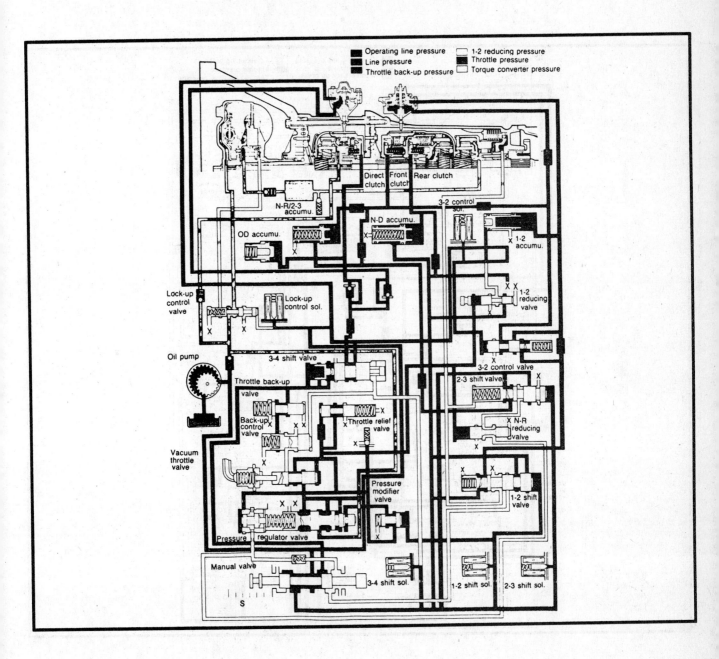

Operating line pressure 1-2 reducing pressure
Line pressure Throttle pressure
Throttle back-up pressure Torque converter pressure

LOW RANGE—1ST GEAR

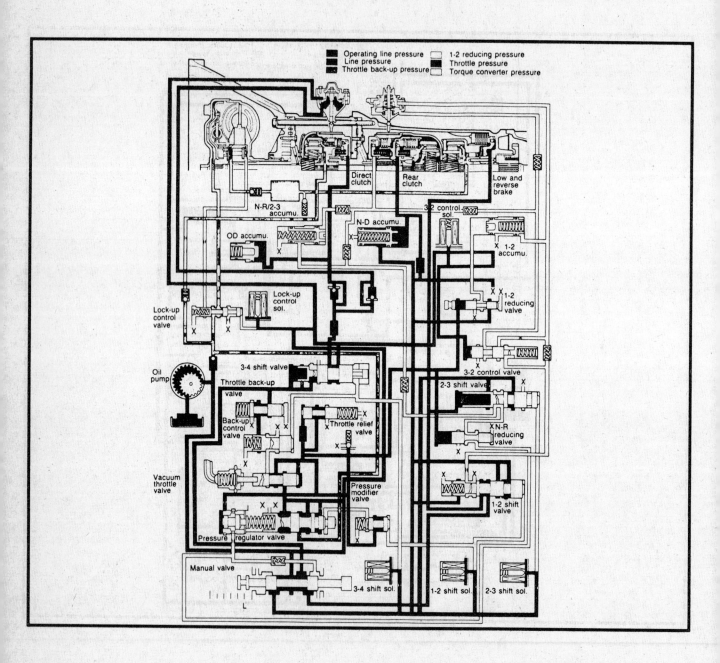

R4AEL Transmission
Mazda

APPLICATION

1989 Mazda MPV

GENERAL DESCRIPTION

The R4A-EL automatic transmission is a 4 speed, electronically controlled transmission. This transmission consists of a torque converter, oil pump, 5 clutches, 2 brakes, 2 one-way clutches, 2 planetary gears and an electronic control system.

The electronic system is based on 8 input signals which controls shifting and line pressure. This system also includes self-diagnosis malfunctions of the major input and output components. Each malfunction is indicated by a code number and buzzer. These code number are as follow:

- 01—Engine rpm sensor
- 06— Speed sensor 1
- 07—Speed sensor 2 (in speedmeter)
- 12—Throttle sensor
- 56—Automatic transmission fluid thermosensor
- 60—Shift solenoid A
- 61—Shift solenoid B
- 62—Overrunning clutch solenoid
- 63—Lockup solenoid
- 64—Line pressure solenoid

Transmission and Converter Identification

TRANSMISSION

The R4A-EL automatic transmission identification plate is attached to the right hand side of the transmission, adjacent to the solenoids electrical harness. This data plate provides the transmission model and serial number.

CONVERTER

The R4A-EL automatic transmission use a lockup converter. The torque converter consists of a pump, a turbine and a stator. The converter housing is filled with oil and is attached to the engine crankshaft by a flex plate and always rotates at engine speed.

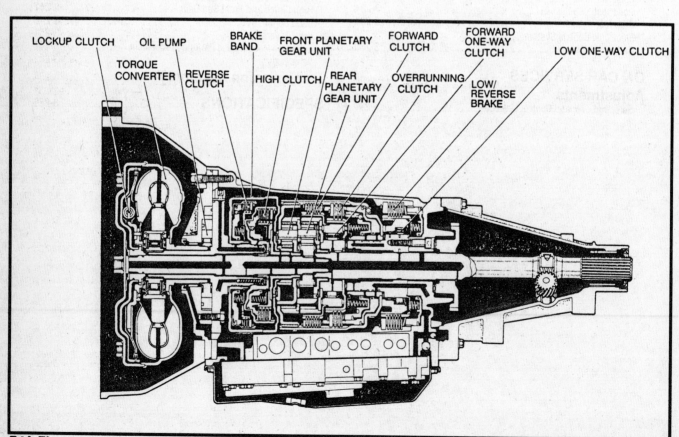

R4A-EL automatic transmission

Electronic Controls

The R4A-EL automatic transmission consists of the following electronic components:
  Mode switch
  Hold switch
  Inhibitor switch
  Automatic transmission fluid thermosensor
  Speed sensor
  Solenoid valves assembly
  Dropping resistor
  EC-AT control unit

Metric Fasteners

Metric tools will be required to service this transmission. Due to the large number of alloy parts used in this transmission, torque specifications should be strictly observed. Before installing capscrews into aluminum parts, dip the bolts into clean transmission fluid as this will prevent the screws from galling the aluminum threads, thus causing damage.

Metric fastener dimensions are very close to the dimensions of the familiar inch system fasteners. For this reason replacement fasteners must have the same measurement and strength as the original fastener.

Do not attempt to interchange metric fasteners for inch system fasteners. Mismatched or incorrect fasteners can cause damage to the automatic transmission unit and possible personal injury. Care should be taken to reuse fasteners in their original locations.

Capacity

The R4A-EL automatic transmission has a capacity of 9.1 qts. (8.6L).

Checking Fluid Level

1. Place the vehicle on a flat level surface. Apply the parking brake and block the drive wheels.
2. Start the engine and allow to run until normal operating temperature is reached.
3. With the engine idling, shift the selector lever from **P** to **L** and back again.
4. Check that the transmission fluid level is between the notches on the oil indicator gauge. If necessary, adjust the fluid level.

TROUBLE DIAGNOSIS

CLUTCH AND BAND APPLICATION

Mode	Range	Gear	Reverse Clutch	High Clutch	Forward Clutch	Overrunning Clutch	Brake Band 2nd Applied	Brake Band 3rd Released	Brake Band Overdrive Applied	Forward One-Way Clutch	Low One-Way Clutch	Low/Reverse Brake
Hold	P	—	—	—	—	—	—	—	—	—	—	—
	R	Reverse	Applied	—	—	—	—	—	—	—	—	Applied
	N	—	—	—	—	—	—	—	—	—	—	—
	D	1st	—	—	Applied	②	—	—	—	Applied ⑥	Applied ⑥	—
		2nd	—	—	Applied	③	Applied	—	—	Applied ⑥	—	—
		3rd	—	Applied	Applied	③	⑦	①	—	Applied ⑥	—	—
		Overdrive	—	Applied	①	—	⑦	①	Applied	—	—	—
	S	1st	—	—	Applied	⑤	—	—	—	Applied ⑥	Applied ⑥	—
		2nd	—	—	Applied	⑤	Applied	—	—	Applied ⑥	—	—
		3rd	—	Applied	Applied	⑤	⑦	①	—	Applied ⑥	—	—
	L	1st	—	—	Applied	Applied	—	—	—	Applied ⑥	—	Applied
		2nd	—	—	Applied	Applied	Applied	—	—	Applied ⑥	—	—
Economy/ Power	D	2nd	—	—	Applied	⑤	Applied	—	—	Applied ⑥	—	—
		3rd	—	Applied	Applied	⑤	⑦	①	—	Applied ⑥	—	—
	S	2nd	—	—	Applied	⑤	Applied	—	—	Applied ⑥	—	—
	L	1st	—	—	Applied	Applied	—	—	—	Applied ⑥	—	Applied

① Operates but does not transmit power.
② Operates when the EC-AT control unit receives OD inhibit signal from the cruise control unit and throttle opening less than 1/8. Engine braking effect not available.
③ Operates when the EC-AT control unit receives OD inhibit signal from the cruise control unit and throttle opening less than 1/8. Engine braking effect available.
④ Operates when throttle opening is less than 1/8. Engine braking effect not available.
⑤ Operates when throttle opening is less than 1/8. Engine braking effect available.
⑥ Operates during acceleration and cruising.
⑦ A. Operates but does not transmit power.
  B. Hydraulic pressure is applied to both 2nd applied side and 3rd released side of band servo piston. However, because the area of the 3rd released side is larger than the 2nd applied side, the brake band does not operate.
  C. Hydraulic pressure is applied to OD applied side, plus condition above. Brake band is applied. Operates.

CHILTON'S THREE C's TRANSMISSION DIAGNOSIS

Condition	Cause	Correction
Engine does not start in N and/or P range	a) Ignition switch or starter	a) Repair or replace the ignition switch or starter
	b) Selector lever or control linkage	b) Adjust the selector lever or control linkage
	c) Inhibitor switch	c) Adjust or replace the inhibitor switch
Engine starts in ranges other than N and P range	a) Selector lever or control	a) Adjust the selector lever or control linkage
	b) Inhibitor switch	b) Adjust or replace the inhibitor switch
Vehicle does not move in D range (moves in L, S, and R ranges)	a) Selector lever or control linkage	a) Adjust the selector lever or control linkage
	b) Low one way clutch	b) Repair or replace the low oneway clutch
Vehicle does not move in forward ranges (moves in R range) Extremely poor acceleration	a) Transmission fluid level	a) Adjust the transmission fluid level
	b) Line pressure incorrect	b) Perform line pressure test
	c) Line pressure solenoid	c) Replace the line pressure solenoid
	d) Control valve body	d) Repair or replace the control valve body ASM.
	e) Neutral/drive accumulator	e) Repair or replace the neutral/drive accumulator
	f) Reverse clutch	f) Repair or replace the reverse clutch
	g) High clutch	g) Repair or replace the high clutch
	h) Forward clutch	h) Repair or replace the forward clutch
	i) Forward oneway clutch	i) Repair or replace the forward oneway clutch
	j) Low oneway clutch	j) Repair or replace the low oneway clutch
Vehicle does not move in R range (moves in forward ranges) Extremely poor acceleration	a) Selector lever or control linkage	a) Adjust the selector lever or control linkage
	b) Line pressure incorrect	b) Perform line pressure test
	c) Line pressure solenoid	c) Repair or replace the line pressure solenoid
	d) Control valve body	d) Repair or replace the control valve body ASM
	e) Reverse clutch	e) Repair or replace the reverse clutch
	f) High clutch	f) Repair or replace the high clutch
	g) Forward clutch	g) Repair or replace the forward clutch
	h) Overrunning clutch	h) Repair or replace the overrunning clutch
	i) Low/reverse brake	i) Repair or replace the low/reverse brake
Vehicle does not move in any range	a) Transmission fluid level	a) Adjust the transmission fluid level
	b) Selector lever or control linkage	b) Adjust the selector lever or control linkage
	c) Line pressure incorrect	c) Perform line pressure test
	d) Line pressure solenoid	d) Replace the line pressure solenoid
	e) Oil pump	e) Repair or replace the oil pump
	f) High clutch	f) Repair or replace the high clutch
	g) Brake band and band servo	g) Adjust or repair the brake band and band servo
	h) Low/reverse brake	h) Repair or replace the low/reverse brake
	i) Torque converter	i) Replace the torque converter
	j) Parking mechanism	j) Repair the parking mechanism
Slippage felt when accelerating	a) Transmission fluid level	a) Adjust the transmission fluid level
	b) Selector lever or control linkage	b) Adjust the selector lever or control linkage
	c) Throttle sensor	c) Adjust or replace the throttle sensor
	d) Line pressure incorrect	d) Perform line pressure test
	e) Line pressure solenoid	e) Replace the line pressure solenoid
	f) Control valve body	f) Repair or replace the control valve body ASM

CHILTON'S THREE C's TRANSMISSION DIAGNOSIS

Condition	Cause	Correction
Slippage felt when accelerating	g) N/D accumulator	g) Repair or replace the N/D accumulator
	h) 3-4/N-R accumulator	h) Repair or replace the 3-4/N-R accumulator
	i) Forward clutch	i) Repair or replace the forward clutch
	j) Reverse clutch	j) Repair or replace the reverse clutch
	k) Low/reverse brake	k) Repair or replace the low/reverse brake
	l) Oil pump	l) Repair or replace the oil pump
	m) Torque converter	m) Replace the torque converter
Vehicle moves in N range	a) Selector lever or control linkage	a) Adjust the selector lever or control linkage
	b) Forward clutch	b) Repair or replace the forward clutch
	c) Reverse clutch	c) Repair or replace the reverse clutch
	d) 3-4/N-R accumulator	d) Repair or replace the 3-4/N-R accumulator
	e) Overrunning clutch	e) Repair or replace the overrunning clutch
Excessive creep	a) Idle speed	a) Adjust the idle speed
No creep	a) Transmission fluid level	a) Adjust the transmission fluid level
	b) Line pressure	b) Perform line pressure test
	c) Control valve body	c) Repair or replace the control valve body
	d) Forward clutch	d) Repair or replace the forward clutch
	e) Oil pump	e) Repair or replace the oil pump
	f) Torque converter	f) Replace the torque converter
Low maximum speed and poor acceleration	a) Transmission fluid level	a) Adjust the transmission fluid level
	b) Inhibitor switch	b) Adjust or replace the inhibitor switch
	c) Shift solenoid A	c) Replace the shift solenoid A
	d) Shift solenoid B	d) Replace the shift solenoid B
	e) Control valve body	e) Repair or replace the control valve body
	f) Reverse clutch	f) Repair or replace the reverse clutch
	g) High clutch	g) Repair or replace the high clutch
	h) Brake band and band servo	h) Adjust or repair the brake band and band servo
	i) Low/reverse brake	i) Repair or replace the low/reverse brake
	j) Oil pump	j) Repair or replace the oil pump
	k) Torque converter	k) Replace the torque converter
Does not shift from 1st to 2nd	a) Hold switch	a) Replace the hold switch
	b) Inhibitor switch	b) Adjust or replace the inhibitor switch
	c) Selector lever and control linkage	c) Adjust the selector lever or control linkage
	d) Shift solenoid A	d) Replace the shift solenoid A
	e) Control valve body	e) Repair or replace the control valve body
	f) Speed sensor 1	f) Replace the speed sensor 1
	g) Brake band or band servo	g) Adjust or repair the brake band or band servo
Does not shift from 2nd to 3rd	a) Hold switch	a) Replace the hold switch
	b) Inhibitor switch	b) Adjust or replace the inhibitor switch
	c) Selector lever or control linkage	c) Adjust the selector lever or control linkage
	d) Shift solenoid B	d) Replace the shift solenoid B
	e) Control valve body	e) Repair or replace the control valve body
	f) Speed sensor 1	f) Replace the speed sensor 1
	g) High clutch	g) Repair or replace the high clutch
	h) Brake band and band servo	h) Adjust or repair the brake band and band servo

CHILTON'S THREE C's TRANSMISSION DIAGNOSIS

Condition	Cause	Correction
Does not shift from 3rd to OD	a) Hold switch	a) Replace the hold switch
	b) Cruise control switch	b) Repair or replace the cruise control switch
	c) Inhibitor switch	c) Adjust or replace the inhibitor switch
	d) Selector lever or control linkage	d) Adjust the selector lever or control linkage
	e) Shift solenoid A	e) Replace the shift solenoid A
	f) Speed sensor 1	f) Replace the speed sensor 1
	g) ATF thermosensor	g) Replace the thermosensor
	h) Brake band and band servo	h) Adjust or repair the brake band and band servo
Lockup does not occur	a) Idle switch	a) Adjust or replace the idle switch
	b) Throttle sensor	b) Adjust or replace the throttle sensor
	c) Speed sensor 1	c) Replace the speed sensor 1
	d) Inhibitor switch	d) Adjust or replace the inhibitor switch
	e) Engine rpm sensor	e) Replace the rpm sensor
	f) Line pressure	f) Perform the line pressure test
	g) ATF thermosensor	g) Replace the ATF thermosensor
	h) Lockup solenoid	h) Replace the lockup solenoid
	i) Control valve body	i) Repair or replace the control valve body
	j) Torque converter	j) Replace the torque converter
Does not shift from OD to 3rd	a) Transmission fluid level	a) Adjust the transmission fluid level
	b) Throttle sensor	b) Adjust or replace the throttle sensor
	c) Overrunning clutch solenoid	c) Replace the overrunning clutch solenoid
	d) Shift solenoid A	d) Replace the shift solenoid A
	e) Line pressure solenoid	e) Replace the line pressure solenoid
	f) Control valve body	f) Repair or replace the control valve body
	g) Low/reverse brake	g) Repair or replace the low/reverse brake
	h) Overrunning clutch	h) Repair or replace the overrunning clutch
Does not shift from 3rd to 2nd, or from OD to 2nd	a) Transmission fluid level	a) Adjust the transmission fluid level
	b) Throttle sensor	b) Adjust or replace the throttle sensor
	c) Shift solenoid A	c) Replace the shift solenoid A
	d) Shift solenoid B	d) Replace the shift solenoid B
	e) Control valve body	e) Repair or replace the control valve body
	f) High clutch	f) Repair or replace the high clutch
	g) Brake band or band servo	g) Adjust or repair the brake band and band servo
Does not shift from 2nd to 1st or from 3rd to 1st	a) Transmission fluid level	a) Adjust the transmission fluid level
	b) Throttle sensor	b) Adjust or replace the throttle sensor
	c) Hold switch	c) Replace the hold switch
	d) Shift solenoid A	d) Replace the shift solenoid A
	e) Shift solenoid B	e) Replace the shift solenoid B
	f) Control valve body	f) Repair or replace the control valve body
	g) Low one-way clutch	g) Replace the low one-way clutch
	h) High clutch	h) Repair or replace the high clutch
	i) Brake band and band servo	i) Adjust or repair the brake band and band servo
Does not kickdown when accelerator is depressed in OD within kickdown range	a) Throttle sensor	a) Adjust or replace the throttle sensor
	b) Speed sensor 1	b) Replace the speed sensor 1
	c) Shift solenoid A	c) Replace the shift solenoid A
	d) Shift solenoid B	d) Replace the shift solenoid B
Excessive engine speed when accelerated in OD due to delayed kickdown	a) Speed sensor 1	a) Replace the speed sensor 1
	b) Throttle sensor	b) Adjust or replace the throttle sensor
	c) Shift solenoid A	c) Replace the shift solenoid A
	d) Shift solenoid B	d) Replace the shift solenoid B

CHILTON'S THREE C's TRANSMISSION DIAGNOSIS

Condition	Cause	Correction
Does not shift from 2nd to 1st in L range	a) Inhibitor switch b) Speed sensor 1 c) Shift solenoid A d) Control valve body e) Overrunning clutch solenoid f) Overrunning clutch g) Low/reverse brake	a) Adjust or replace the inhibitor switch b) Replace the speed sensor c) Replace the shift solenoid A d) Repair or replace the control valve body e) Replace the overrunning clutch solenoid f) Repair or replace the overrunning clutch g) Repair or replace the low/reverse brake
Excessive N to D range shift shock	a) Idle speed b) Throttle sensor c) Line pressure d) ATF thermosensor e) Atmospheric pressure sensor f) Dropping resistor g) Engine rpm sensor h) Line pressure solenoid i) Control valve body j) N/D accumulator k) Forward clutch	a) Adjust the engine idle speed b) Adjust or replace the throttle sensor c) Perform the line pressure test d) Replace the ATF thermosensor e) Replace the atmospheric pressure sensor f) Replace the dropping resistor g) Replace the engine rpm sensor h) Replace the line pressure solenoid i) Repair or replace the control valve body j) Repair or replace the N/D accumulator k) Repair or replace the forward clutch
Excessive 1st to 2nd shift shock	a) Throttle sensor b) Line pressure c) 1/2 accumulator d) Control valve body e) ATF thermosensor f) Atmospheric pressure sensor g) Dropping resistor h) Brake band and band servo	a) Adjust or replace the throttle sensor b) Perform the line pressure test c) Repair or replace the 1/2 accumulator d) Repair or replace the control valve body e) Replace the ATF thermosensor f) Replace the atmospheric pressure sensor g) Replace the dropping resistor h) Adjust or repair the brake band and band servo
Excessive 2nd to 3rd shift shock	a) Throttle sensor b) Line pressure c) 2/3 accumulator d) Control valve body e) ATF thermosensor f) Atmospheric pressure sensor g) Dropping resistor h) High clutch	a) Adjust or replace the throttle sensor b) Perform the line pressure test c) Repair or replace the 2/3 accumulator d) Repair or replace the control valve body e) Replace the thermosensor f) Replace the atmospheric pressure sensor g) Replace the dropping resistor h) Repair or replace the high clutch
Excessive 3rd to OD shift shock	a) Throttle sensor b) Line pressure c) 3-4/N-R accumulator d) Control valve body e) Atmospheric pressure sensor f) Dropping resistor g) Brake band and band servo h) Overrunning clutch	a) Adjust or replace the throttle sensor b) Perform the line pressure test c) Repair or replace the 3-4/N-R accumulator d) Repair or replace the control valve body e) Replace the atmospheric pressure sensor f) Replace the dropping resistor g) Adjust or repair the brake band and band servo h) Repair or replace the overrunning clutch
Vehicle brakes when shifted from 1st to 2nd	a) Transmission fluid level b) Reverse clutch c) Low/reverse brake d) High clutch e) Low one-way clutch	a) Adjust the transmission fluid level b) Repair or replace the reverse clutch c) Repair or replace the low/reverse brake d) Repair or replace the high clutch e) Replace the low one-way clutch

CHILTON'S THREE C's TRANSMISSION DIAGNOSIS

Condition	Cause	Correction
Vehicle brakes when shifted from 2nd to 3rd	a) Transmission fluid level b) Brake band and band servo	a) Adjust the transmission fluid level b) Adjust or repair the brake band and band servo
Vehicle brakes when shifted from 3rd to OD	a) Transmission fluid level b) Overrunning clutch c) Forward one-way clutch d) Reverse clutch	a) Adjust the transmission fluid level b) Repair or replace the overrunning clutch c) Replace the forward one-way clutch d) Repair or replace the reverse clutch
Shift shock felt when accelerator released and deceleration occurs	a) Throttle sensor b) Line pressure c) Atmospheric pressure sensor d) Dropping resistor e) Overrunning clutch solenoid f) Control valve body	a) Adjust or replace the throttle sensor b) Perform the line pressure test c) Replace the atmospheric pressure sensor d) Replace the dropping resistor e) Replace the overrunning clutch solenoid f) Repair or replace the control valve body
Excessively large 2nd to 1st shift shock in L range	a) Control valve body b) Low/reverse brake	a) Repair or replace the control valve body b) Repair or replace the low/reverse brake
Engine overruns or slips when shifting OD to 3rd	a) Transmission fluid level b) Throttle sensor c) Line pressure d) Line pressure solenoid e) Control valve body f) High clutch g) Forward clutch	a) Adjust the transmission fluid level b) Adjust or replace the throttle sensor c) Perform the line pressure test d) Replace the line pressure solenoid e) Repair or replace the control valve body f) Repair or replace the high clutch g) Repair or replace the forward clutch
Engine overruns or slips when shifting OD to 2nd	a) Transmission fluid level b) Throttle sensor c) Line pressure d) Line pressure solenoid e) Shift solenoid A f) Control valve body g) Brake band and band servo h) Forward clutch	a) Adjust the transmission fluid level b) Adjust or replace the throttle sensor c) Perform the line pressure test d) Replace the line pressure solenoid e) Replace the shift solenoid A f) Repair or replace the control valve body g) Adjust or repair the brake band and band servo h) Repair or replace the forward clutch
Engine overruns or slips when shifting 3rd to 2nd	a) Transmission fluid level b) Throttle sensor c) Line pressure d) Line pressure solenoid e) Control valve body f) Brake band or band servo g) Forward clutch h) Overrunning clutch solenoid i) High clutch j) ²/₃ accumulator	a) Adjust the transmission fluid level b) Adjust or replace the throttle sensor c) Perform the line pressure test d) Replace the line pressure solenoid e) Repair or replace the control valve body f) Adjust or repair the brake band and band servo g) Repair or replace the forward clutch h) Repair or replace the overrunning clutch solenoid i) Repair or replace the high clutch j) Repair or replace the ²/₃ accumulator

CODE RETRIEVAL

Procedure

Code retrieval is performed using the EC-AT tester.

1. Locate the check connector and test connector at the EC-AT control unit. The EC-AT control unit is located behind the instrument panel, left of the steering wheel.

2. Connect the EC-AT tester to the check connector. The check connector is a blue-colored 6 pin connector and the test connector is a blue-colored 1 pin connector.

3. Ground the ground connector of the EC-AT tester.

4. Ground the 1 pin test connector.

5. Turn the ignition switch **ON** and check that the 88 flashes on the digital display and the buzzer sounds for 3 seconds. If the 88 does not flash, check the service connector wiring.

6. If the 88 flashes and the buzzer sounds continuously for more than 20 seconds, check the wiring to terminal **2N** of the EC-AT control unit for short circuit then replace the EC-AT control unit and repeat Steps 2 through 5.

7. Note the code numbers and check the cause by referring to the code number diagnosis chart.

8. After repairs are made, cancel the memory of malfunctions by disconnecting the negative battery cable for at lease 5 seconds with the brake pedal depressed, then reconnect it.

9. Remove the EC-AT tester and drive the vehicle at 31 mph (50 km/h); then, depress the accelerator pedal fully to activate the kickdown. Stop the vehicle gradually.

10. Reconnect the EC-AT tester to the test connector (blue 6 pin) and ground the EC-AT ground connector.

11. Ground the check connector (blue 1 pin).

12. Turn the ignition switch **ON** and check that no code numbers are displayed.

Hydraulic Control System Diagnosis Tests

OIL PRESSURE

1. Check the engine coolant, engine oil and transmission fluid levels.

2. Warm the engine until the transmission fluid temperature is within 122–176°F (50–80°C).

3. Apply the parking brake and block the drive wheels.

4. Connect a tachometer to the engine. Connect oil pressure adaptor tool 49H019002 or equivalent to the line pressure inspection hole.

5. Start the engine and check that the idle speed is 780–820 rpm.

6. Shift the selector lever to the **D** range and read the oil pressure at idle.

NOTE: Step 7 must be performed within 5 seconds.

7. Depress the brake pedal firmly and gradually depress the accelerator. Read the oil pressure as soon as the engine speed becomes constant, then release the accelerator pedal.

8. Shift the selector lever to the **N** range and run the engine at idle for at least 1 minute. This 1 minute period is performed to cool the transmission fluid and prevent oil degeneration.

9. Read the line pressure at idle and engine stall speeds for each range in the same manner.

LINE PRESSURE RANGE

Range	Line Pressure psi (kPa)	
	Idle	Specification
D, S, L	68—74 (471—510)	175—186 (1,207—1,285)
R	88—94 (608—647)	219—230 (1,511—1,589)

LINE PRESSURE EVALUATION

Condition		Possible Cause
When idling	Low pressure in every range	Worn oil pump
		Damaged control piston (in oil pump)
		Pressure regulator valve or plug sticking
		Damage pressure regulator valve spring
		Fluid leaking between oil strainer and pressure regulator valve
	Low pressure in forward ranges	Fluid leaking from hydraulic circuit of forward clutch
	Low pressure in D and S ranges (Hold mode only)	Fluid leaking from hydraulic circuit of band servo 2nd apply side
	Low pressure in R ranges only	Fluid leaking from hydraulic circuit of reverse clutch
	Low pressure in R and L ranges only	Fluid leaking from hydraulic circuit of low and reverse brake
	Higher than specification	Throttle sensor out of adjustment
		Damaged fluid thermosensor
		Line pressure solenoid sticking
		Short circuit of line pressure solenoid circuit
		Pressure modifier valve sticking
		Pressure regulator valve or plug sticking
At stall speed	Low pressure	Throttle sensor out of adjustment
		Damaged control piston (in oil pump)
		Line pressure solenoid sticking
		Short circuit of line pressure solenoid circuit
		Pressure regulator valve or plug sticking
		Pressure modifier valve sticking
		Pilot valve sticking

NO. 01 CODE DISPLAY (ENGINE RPM SENSOR)

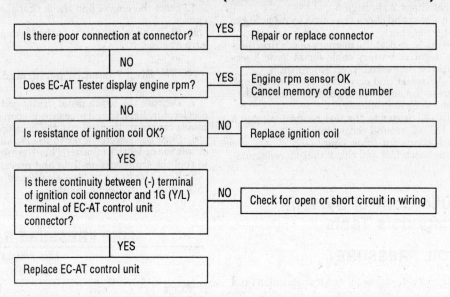

Is there poor connection at connector?	YES →	Repair or replace connector
↓ NO		
Does EC-AT Tester display engine rpm?	YES →	Engine rpm sensor OK Cancel memory of code number
↓ NO		
Is resistance of ignition coil OK?	NO →	Replace ignition coil
↓ YES		
Is there continuity between (-) terminal of ignition coil connector and 1G (Y/L) terminal of EC-AT control unit connector?	NO →	Check for open or short circuit in wiring
↓ YES		
Replace EC-AT control unit		

NO. 06 CODE DISPLAY (SPEED SENSOR 1)

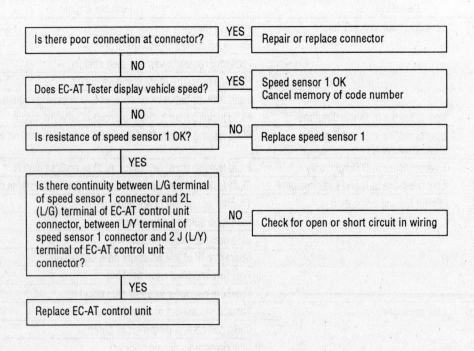

Is there poor connection at connector?	YES →	Repair or replace connector
↓ NO		
Does EC-AT Tester display vehicle speed?	YES →	Speed sensor 1 OK Cancel memory of code number
↓ NO		
Is resistance of speed sensor 1 OK?	NO →	Replace speed sensor 1
↓ YES		
Is there continuity between L/G terminal of speed sensor 1 connector and 2L (L/G) terminal of EC-AT control unit connector, between L/Y terminal of speed sensor 1 connector and 2 J (L/Y) terminal of EC-AT control unit connector?	NO →	Check for open or short circuit in wiring
↓ YES		
Replace EC-AT control unit		

NO. 07 CODE DISPLAY (SPEED SENSOR 2)

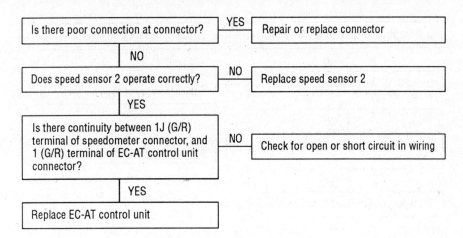

Is there poor connection at connector? — YES → Repair or replace connector

NO

Does speed sensor 2 operate correctly? — NO → Replace speed sensor 2

YES

Is there continuity between 1J (G/R) terminal of speedometer connector, and 1 (G/R) terminal of EC-AT control unit connector? — NO → Check for open or short circuit in wiring

YES

Replace EC-AT control unit

NO. 56 CODE DISPLAY (ATF THERMOSENSOR)

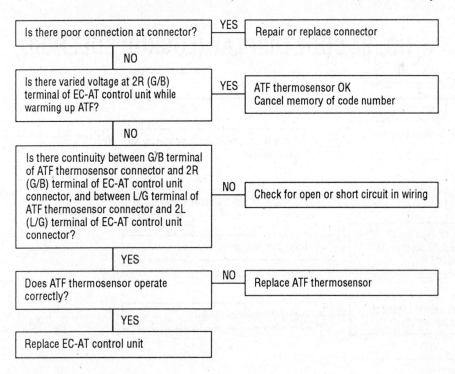

Is there poor connection at connector? — YES → Repair or replace connector

NO

Is there varied voltage at 2R (G/B) terminal of EC-AT control unit while warming up ATF? — YES → ATF thermosensor OK
Cancel memory of code number

NO

Is there continuity between G/B terminal of ATF thermosensor connector and 2R (G/B) terminal of EC-AT control unit connector, and between L/G terminal of ATF thermosensor connector and 2L (L/G) terminal of EC-AT control unit connector? — NO → Check for open or short circuit in wiring

YES

Does ATF thermosensor operate correctly? — NO → Replace ATF thermosensor

YES

Replace EC-AT control unit

NO. 12 CODE DISPLAY (THROTTLE SENSOR)

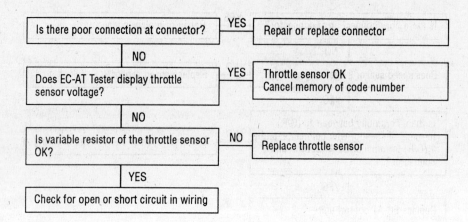

Is there poor connection at connector?	—YES→ Repair or replace connector
↓ NO	
Does EC-AT Tester display throttle sensor voltage?	—YES→ Throttle sensor OK / Cancel memory of code number
↓ NO	
Is variable resistor of the throttle sensor OK?	—NO→ Replace throttle sensor
↓ YES	
Check for open or short circuit in wiring	

NO. 64 CODE DISPLAY (LOCKUP SOLENOID)

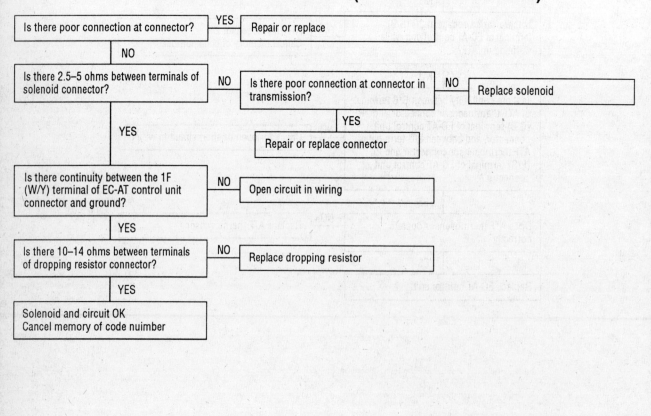

Is there poor connection at connector?	—YES→ Repair or replace
↓ NO	
Is there 2.5–5 ohms between terminals of solenoid connector?	—NO→ Is there poor connection at connector in transmission? —NO→ Replace solenoid
	—YES→ Repair or replace connector
↓ YES	
Is there continuity between the 1F (W/Y) terminal of EC-AT control unit connector and ground?	—NO→ Open circuit in wiring
↓ YES	
Is there 10–14 ohms between terminals of dropping resistor connector?	—NO→ Replace dropping resistor
↓ YES	
Solenoid and circuit OK / Cancel memory of code nuimber	

NO. 63 CODE DISPLAY (LINE PRESSURE SOLENOID)

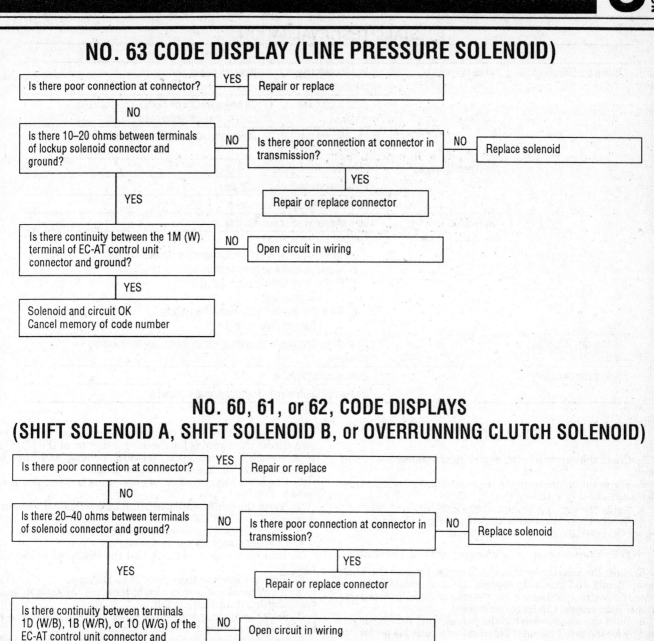

Is there poor connection at connector? — YES → Repair or replace

NO

Is there 10–20 ohms between terminals of lockup solenoid connector and ground? — NO → Is there poor connection at connector in transmission? — NO → Replace solenoid

YES (from transmission question) → Repair or replace connector

YES

Is there continuity between the 1M (W) terminal of EC-AT control unit connector and ground? — NO → Open circuit in wiring

YES

Solenoid and circuit OK
Cancel memory of code number

NO. 60, 61, or 62, CODE DISPLAYS
(SHIFT SOLENOID A, SHIFT SOLENOID B, or OVERRUNNING CLUTCH SOLENOID)

Is there poor connection at connector? — YES → Repair or replace

NO

Is there 20–40 ohms between terminals of solenoid connector and ground? — NO → Is there poor connection at connector in transmission? — NO → Replace solenoid

YES (from transmission question) → Repair or replace connector

YES

Is there continuity between terminals 1D (W/B), 1B (W/R), or 10 (W/G) of the EC-AT control unit connector and ground? — NO → Open circuit in wiring

YES

Solenoid and circuit OK
Cancel memory of code nuimber

STALL TEST EVALUATION

Condition		Cause	
Above specification	In all ranges	Insufficient line pressure	Worn oil pump
		Insufficient line pressure	Oil leakage from oil pump, control valve, and/or transmission case
		Insufficient line pressure	Stuck pressure regulator valve
	In D and S ranges	Forward clutch slipping	
		Forward one-way clutch slipping	
		Low one-way clutch slipping	
	In R range	Low and reverse brake slipping	

		Reverse clutch slipping
		  Perform road test to determine whether problem is low and reverse brake or reverse clutch
		  a) Engine brake applied in L range 1st
		    . . . Reverse clutch
		  b) Engine brake not applied in L range 1st
		    . . . Low and reverse brake	

Within specification		All shift control elements within transmission are functioning normally	
Below specification		Engine out of tune	
		One-way clutch slipping within torque converter	

STALL TEST

1. Check the engine coolant, engine oil and transmission fluid levels.

2. Warm the engine until the transmission fluid temperature is within 122–176°F (50–80°C).

3. Apply the parking brake and block the drive wheels.

4. Connect a tachometer to the engine. Start the engine and check that the idle speed is 780–820 rpm.

NOTE: Step 5 must be performed within 5 seconds.

5. Shift the selector lever to the R range. Depress the brake pedal firmly and gradually depress the accelerator. Read and note the engine speed as soon as the engine speed becomes constant, then release the accelerator pedal.

6. Shift the selector lever to the N range and run the engine at idle for at least 1 minute. This 1 minute period is performed to cool the transmission fluid and prevent oil degeneration.

7. Perform the stall tests in the same manner for D and S and L ranges.

NOTE: Be certain to provide adequate cooling time between individual range stall tests.

TIME LAG TEST

If the selector lever is shifted while the engine is idling, there will be a certain time lapse or time lag before shock is felt. This step checks this time lag for checking condition of the 1/2, 3–4/ N–R and N/D accumulators, forward, reverse, and one-way clutches; brake band and low/reverse brake.

1. Check the engine coolant, engine oil and transmission fluid levels.

2. Warm the engine until the transmission fluid temperature is within 122–176°F (50–80°C).

3. Apply the parking brake and block the drive wheels.

4. Connect a tachometer to the engine.

5. Start the engine and check that the idle speed is 780–820 rpm.

6. Shift the selector lever from N to D range.

7. With the use of a stop watch, measure the time it takes from shifting until shock is felt.

8. Shift the selector lever to N range and run the engine at idle speed for at least 1 minute.

9. Perform the test in the same manner for N to D, N to D **(Hold Mode)** and N to R ranges.

NOTE: Make 3 measurements for each test and take the average value.

The specified time lag is as follow:
  N to D range—less than 1.0 second
  N to R range—less than 1.2 seconds

Road Test Evaluation Chart

Mode	Range	Throttle Condition (Throttle Sensor Voltage)	Shift	Vehicle Speed mph (km/h)
Power	D	Fully opened (4.3 volt)	$D_1 \rightarrow D_2$	31—33 (50—54)
			$D_2 \rightarrow D_3$	61—66 (99—107)
			$D_3 \rightarrow OD$	97—104 (157—167)

ROAD TEST EVALUATION

Mode	Range	Throttle Condition (Throttle Sensor Voltage)	Shift	Vehicle Speed mph (km/h)
Power	D	Fully opened (4.3 volt)	$D_1 \rightarrow D_2$	31—33 (50—54)
			$D_2 \rightarrow D_3$	61—66 (99—107)
			$D_3 \rightarrow OD$	97—104 (157—167)
		Half throttle (1.6—2.2 volt)	$D_1 \rightarrow D_2$	26—29 (42—46)
			$D_2 \rightarrow D_3$	41—45 (66—72)
			Lockup on (D_3)	60—64 (96—104)
			$D_3 \rightarrow OD$	70—75 (113—121)
			Lockup on (OD)	84—89 (136—144)
			Lockup off (OD)	78—83 (126—134)
			$OD \rightarrow D_3$	49—54 (79—87)
			Lockup off (D_3)	53—58 (86—94)
			$D_3 \rightarrow D_2$	27—30 (43—49)
		Kickdown	$OD \rightarrow D_3$	92—99 (149—159)
			$OD \rightarrow D_2$	54—59 (87—95)
			$OD \rightarrow D_1$	27—29 (43—47)
			$D_3 \rightarrow D_2$	54—59 (87—95)
			$D_3 \rightarrow D_1$	27—29 (43—47)
			$D_2 \rightarrow D_1$	27—29 (43—47)
Economy		Fully opened (4.3 volt)	$D_1 \rightarrow D_2$	31—33 (50—54)
			$D_2 \rightarrow D_3$	61—66 (99—107)
			$D_3 \rightarrow OD$	97—104 (157—167)
		Half throttle (1.6—2.2 volt)	$D_1 \rightarrow D_2$	19—22 (31—35)
			$D_2 \rightarrow D_3$	35—38 (56—62)
			$D_3 \rightarrow OD$	49—54 (79—87)
			Lockup on (OD)	49—54 (79—87)
			Lockup off (OD)	46—51 (74—82)
			$OD \rightarrow D_3$	31—36 (50—58)
			$D_3 \rightarrow D_2$	14—17 (22—28)
		Kickdown	$OD \rightarrow D_3$	78—84 (126—136)
			$OD \rightarrow D_2$	50—55 (81—89)
			$OD \rightarrow D_1$	27—29 (43—47)
			$D_3 \rightarrow D_2$	50—55 (81—89)
			$D_3 \rightarrow D_1$	27—29 (43—47)
			$D_2 \rightarrow D_1$	27—29 (43—47)
Economy/Power	S	Fully opened (4.3 volt)	$S_1 \rightarrow S_2$	30—33 (49—53)
			$S_2 \rightarrow S_3$	59—64 (95—103)
			$S_3 \rightarrow S_2$	55—58 (88—94)
			$S_2 \rightarrow S_1$	27—29 (43—47)
		Half throttle (1.6—2.2 volt)	$S_1 \rightarrow S_2$	26—29 (42—46)
			$S_2 \rightarrow S_3$	42—46 (68—74)
			$S_3 \rightarrow S_2$	27—30 (43—49)
Economy/Power	L	Fully opened (4.3 volt)	$L_1 \rightarrow L_2$	30—33 (49—53)
			$L_2 \rightarrow L_1$	27—29 (43—47)
		Half throttle (1.6—2.2 volt)	$L_1 \rightarrow L_2$	26—29 (42—46)

ROAD TEST EVALUATION

Mode	Range	Throttle Condition (Throttle Sensor Voltage)	Shift	Vehicle Speed mph (km/h)
Hold	D	—	$D_2 \rightarrow D_3$	11—14 (18—22)
			$D_3 \rightarrow D_2$	4—8 (7—13)
	S	Fully closed (0.5 volt)	$OD \rightarrow D_3$	97—104 (157—167)
			$S_3 \rightarrow S_2$	61—66 (99—107)
	L		$L_2 \rightarrow L_1$	27—30 (44—48)

TIME LAG TEST EVALUATION

Condition	Possible Cause
N→D and N→D (Hold) shift	Insufficient line pressure
	Forward clutch slipping
	Forward one-way clutch slipping
N→D shift	Insufficient line pressure
	Low one-way clutch slipping
	N-D accumulator not operating properly
N→D (Hold) shift	Insufficient line pressure
	Brake band slipping
	1-2 accumulator not operating properly
N→R shift	Insufficient line pressure
	Reverse clutch slipping
	Low and reverse brake slipping
	3-4/N-R accumulator not operating properly

Electronic Control System

MODE SWITCH

Testing

1. Remove the instrument panel at the steering column and locate the mode switch.
2. Turn the ignition **ON**.
3. Check the voltage from the gray/yellow terminal wire to ground. With the switch released, there should be approximately 12 volts. With the switch depressed (held to the left), there should be less than 1.5 volts.
4. If the voltage is not correct, remove the electrical connector.
5. Disconnect the negative battery cable.
6. Check for continuity between terminal A and **B**. With the switch released, there should be no continuity. With the switch depressed (held to the left), there should be continuity.
7. If not correct, replace the change knob as an assembly.

HOLD SWITCH

Testing

1. Remove the instrument panel at the steering column and locate the hold switch.
2. Turn the ignition **ON**.
3. Check the voltage from the green/yellow terminal wire to ground. With the switch released, there should be approximate-ly 12 volts. With the switch depressed, there should be less than 1.5 volts.
4. If the voltage is not correct, remove the electrical connector.
5. Disconnect the negative battery cable.
6. Check for continuity between terminal B and C. With the switch depressed there should be no continuity. With the switch released, there should be continuity.
7. If not correct, replace the change knob as an assembly.

INHIBITOR SWITCH

Testing

1. Disconnect the negative battery cable.
2. Raise the vehicle and support it safely.
3. Disconnect the control linkage from the manual shaft.
4. Disconnect the inhibitor switch connector.

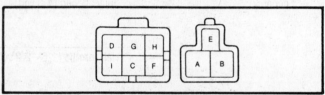

Inhibitor switch terminals identification

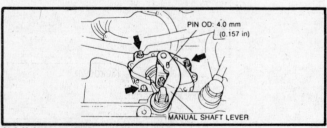

Inhibitor switch adjustment

5. Check for continuity at the following terminals in each gear positions as follow:
P – terminal A to B and terminal C to D
R – terminal C to E
N – terminal A to B and terminal C to F
D – terminal C to G
S – terminal C to H
L – terminal C to I
6. If not correct, adjust the inhibitor switch.
7. If correct, check or adjust the selector lever and control linkage.

Adjustment

1. Shift the selector lever to **N** range.
2. Loosen the inhibitor switch mounting bolts.
3. Align the holes of the inhibitor switch and the manual shaft lever by inserting a pin with an approximate diameter of 0.157 inch (4.0mm) through the holes.

4. Loosely tighten the switch mounting bolt, remove the alignment pin and replace the screw. Tighten the switch mounting bolts 17–23 inch lbs. (2.0–2.6 Nm).

5. Recheck the switch for continuity. If not correct, replace the inhibitor switch.

6. After the inhibitor switch has been adjusted, check for the following:

  a. Check that the starter operates in the **START** position with the selector lever in **P** or **N** only.

  b. Check that the back-up lights illuminate when shifted into **R** range with the ignition switch in the **ON** position.

AUTOMATIC TRANSMISSION FLUID THERMOSENSOR

Testing

1. Disconnect the negative battery cable.

2. Raise the vehicle and support it safely.

3. Loosen the oil pan retaining bolts and drain the transmission fluid. Remove the oil pan.

4. Disconnect the transmission fluid thermosensor electrical connector and remove the thermosensor.

5. Place the transmission fluid thermosensor in a container of water. Place a thermometer inside the container.

6. Measure the resistance between the thermosensor terminals with the water temperature at 68°F (20°C). The resistance should be approximately 2.5k ohms.

7. Measure the resistance between the thermosensor terminals with the water temperature at 176°F (80°C). The resistance should be approximately 0.3k ohms.

8. If correct, install the thermosensor and the oil pan. Lower the vehicle.

9. Refill the transmission with the proper fluid, reconnect the negative battery cable, start the engine and check for leaks.

SPEED SENSOR

Testing

1. Disconnect the negative battery cable.

2. Raise the vehicle and support it safely.

3. Disconnect the speed sensor electrical connector and measure the resistance between the following connectors:

  a. Terminal A to B — 504–616 ohms

  b. Terminal B to C — infinite

  c. Terminal A to C — infinite

4. If not correct, replace the speed sensor.

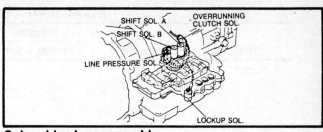

Solenoid valves assembly

SOLENOID VALVES

Testing

1. Disconnect the negative battery cable.

2. Raise the vehicle and support it safely.

3. Disconnect the solenoid valves electrical connector and measure the resistance between the following connectors:

  a. Terminal D to shift solenoid A — 20–40 ohms

  b. Terminal B to shift solenoid B — 20–40 ohms

  c. Terminal E to the overrunning clutch solenoid — 20–40 ohms

  d. Terminal C to the line pressure solenoid — 2.5–5.0 ohms

  E. Terminal F to the lockup solenoid — 10–20 ohms

4. If any solenoid measurement is incorrect, replace as an assembly.

DROPPING RESISTOR

Testing

1. Disconnect the negative battery cable.

2. Disconnect the dropping resistor electrical connector and measure the resistance of the terminals.

3. The resistance should be 10–14 ohms.

4. If the resistance measurement is incorrect, replace the dropping resistor.

EC-AT CONTROL UNIT

Testing

1. Turn the ignition switch **ON**. Check the EC-AT control unit terminal voltage to ground with a high impedance voltmeter. Each terminal voltage should be as specified in the EC-AT unit terminal voltage chart.

2. If the voltage is incorrect, check or replace the component(s), wiring and/or the EC-AT control unit.

EC-AT UNIT TERMINAL VOLTAGE

Terminal	Connected to	Voltmeter + terminal	Voltmeter − terminal	Voltage	Condition
1A (Memory power)	Battery	1A	Ground	Approx. 12 V	Constant
1B (Output)	Shift solenoid B	1B		Approx. 12 V	Solenoid ON in following condition: 1st and 2nd gear positions
				Below 1.5 V	Solenoid OFF in following condition: 3rd and OD gear positions
1C	—	—	—	—	—
1D (Output)	Shift solenoid A	1D	Ground	Approx. 12 V	Solenoid ON in following condition: 1st and OD gear positions
				Below 1.5 V	Solenoid OFF in following condition 2nd and 3rd gear positions
1E (Input)	Inhibitor switch (R range)	1E		Approx. 12 V	R range
				Below 1.5 V	Other ranges

EC-AT UNIT TERMINAL VOLTAGE

Terminal	Connected to	Voltmeter + terminal	Voltmeter – terminal	Voltage	Condition
1F (Output)	Line pressure solenoid	1F		1.7—4.5 V	Accelerator pedal depressed (After ATF warm, engine stopped)
				Below 1.5 V	Accelerator pedal fully released (After ATF warm, engine stopped)
1G (Input)	Engine rpm sensor ①	1G		Above 1 V (AC)	Engine running
				Below 0.5 V (AC)	Engine stopped
1H (Output)	Dropping resistor	1H		Approx. 12 V	Accelerator pedal fully released (After ATF warm, engine stopped)
				Below 1.5 V	Accelerator pedal depressed (After ATF warm, engine stopped)
1I (Input)	Speed sensor 2	1I	Ground	Approx. 1—6 ± 1 V	While driving
				Approx. 5—7 V or below 1.5 V	Vehicle stopped
1J (Ground)	—	1J		Below 1.5 V	—
1K (Output)	Hold indicator	1K		Approx. 12 V	Power or Economy mode
				Below 1.5 V	Hold mode
1L (Ground)	—	1L		Below 1.5 V	—
1M (Output)	Lockup solenoid	1M		Approx. 12 V	Solenoid ON, Lockup
				Below 1.5 V	Solenoid OFF, Non-lockup
1N (Battery power)	Battery	1N		Approx. 12 V	Ignition switch ON
				Below 1.5 V	Ignition switch OFF
1O (Output)	Overrunning clutch solenoid	1O		Approx. 12 V	Solenoid ON in following condition: D range (Engine stopped)
				Below 1.5 V	Solenoid OFF in following condition: Except D range (Engine stopped)
1P (Battery power)	Battery	1P		Approx. 12 V	Ignition switch ON
				Below 1.5 V	Ignition switch OFF
2A (Input)	Throttle sensor	2A	2L	Approx. 5 V	Ignition switch ON
				Below 1.5 V	Ignition switch OFF
2B (Input)	Inhibitor switch (D range)	2B	Ground	Approx. 12 V	D range
				Below 1.5 V	Other ranges
2C (Input)	Mode switch	2C		Above 6 V	Switch released (Right position)
				Below 1.5 V	Switch held to left
2D (Input)	Inhibitor switch (N and P ranges)	2D		Approx. 12 V	N or P range
				Below 1.5 V	Other range
2E (Input)	Cruise control unit	2E		Above 6 V	Normal conditions
				Below 1.5 V	Set or Resume switch ON or vehicle speed 8 km/h (5 mph) lower than preset speed (Driving vehicle cruise control operation)
2F (Output)	Mode indicator	2F		Approx. 12 V	Hold or Economy mode
				Below 1.5 V	Power mode
2G (Input)	Engine control unit	2G		Above 6 V	Normal condition
				Below 1.5 V	Atmospheric pressure below 672 mmHg (26.46 inHg) which is approximately at 1,500 m (4,921 ft)

EC-AT UNIT TERMINAL VOLTAGE

Terminal	Connected to	Voltmeter + terminal	Voltmeter − terminal	Voltage	Condition
2H	—	—	—	—	—
2I (Input)	Hold switch	2I	Ground	Above 6 V	Switch released
				Below 1.5 V	Switch depressed
2J (Input)	Speed sensor 1 ①	2J		Above 1 V (AC)	Vehicle speed above 25 km/h (16 mph)
				Approx. 0 V (AC)	Vehicle stopped
2K (Input)	EC-AT check connector	2K		Above 6 V	Normal
				Below 1.5 V	Check connector grounded
2L (Ground)	Ground (For sensors)	2L		Below 1.5 V	—
2M (Input)	Idle switch	2M		Approx. 12 V	Idle switch OFF (Throttle valve open)
				Below 1.5 V	Idle switch ON (Throttle valve fully closed)
2N (Output)	EC-AT Tester (Malfunction code)	2N		Approx. 12 V	Normal (With EC-AT tester)
				Below 1.5 V	If malfunction present (With EC-AT tester)
				Code signal	EC-AT check connector grounded (With EC-AT tester)
2O	—	—	—	—	—
2P	—	—	—	—	—
2Q (Input)	Inhibitor switch (L range)	2Q	Ground	Approx. 12 V	L range
				Below 1.5 V	Other ranges
2R (Input)	ATF thermosensor	2R	2L	Approx. 2.4—0.4 V	While warming up ATF Note Approx. 1.8 V: ATF temp. 10°C (50°F) Approx. 1.1 V: ATF temp. 40°C (104°F)
2S (Input)	Inhibitor switch (S range)	2S	Ground	Approx. 12 V	S range
				Below 1.5 V	Other ranges
2T (Input)	Throttle sensor	2T	2L	Approx. 0.4—4.4 V	Throttle valve fully closed to fully open

① Checked in AC Range

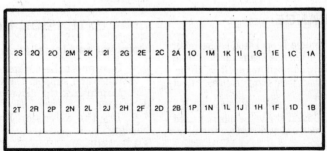

EC-AT unit terminals identification

ON CAR SERVICES

Adjustments

SELECTOR LEVER AND CONTROL LINKAGE

1. Shift the selector lever into **P** range.
2. Remove the steering column covers. Pull the selector lever reward and insert an alignment pin with an approximate outer diameter of 0.197 inch (5.0mm). into the gear shift rod assembly.
3. Remove the air intake pipe. Loosen the shift lever and top lever mounting bolts.
4. Shift the manual shaft to **P** range. Adjust the clearance between the lower bracket and the shift lever bushing by sliding the shift lever assembly. The specified clearance should be 0 inch (0mm).
5. Tighten and torque the shift lever mounting bolts 12–17 ft. lbs. (16–23 Nm).
6. Verify the the detent ball is positioned in the center of the **P** range detent. If not, loosen the mounting bolts and turn the bracket to adjust the position; then, retighten the bolts.
7. Adjust the clearance between the lower bracket and the shift lever bushing by turning the top lever. The specified clearance should be 0 inch (0mm).
8. Tighten the top lever mounting bolt then tighten the retaining bolts 12–17 ft. lbs. (16–23 Nm).
9. Remove the alignment pin from the gear shift rod assembly.
10. If it is necessary to adjust the axial play (thrust play), measure the clearence between the bracket of the steering shaft and the adjustment washer. The clearance should be 0.012 inch (0.3mm) maximum. The adjustment washer sizes are 0.039 inch (1.0mm), 0.047 inch (1.2mm) and 0.055 inch (1.4mm).
11. Check the selector lever operation as followed:
   a. Check that the selector lever move smoothly and can only be shifted from **D, S** and **L** ranges when the selector lever is pulled rearward.
   b. The selector lever and the indicator should be aligned.
   c. The should be a click when the selector is shifted from **P** to **L** range.
12. Install the column covers.

Services

FLUID CHANGE

The conditions under which the vehicle is operated is the main consideration in determining how often the transmission fluid should be changed. Different driving conditions result in different transmission fluid temperatures. These temperatures affect change intervals.

If the vehicle is driven under severe conditions, change the transmission fluid every 15,000 miles. If the vehicle is not used under severe conditions, change the fluid and replace the filter every 30,000 miles.

Do not overfill the transmission. It takes about a pint of automatic transmission fluid to raise the level from the **ADD** to the **FULL** mark on the transmission indicator dipstick. Overfilling the unit can cause damage to the internal components of the automatic transmission.

OIL PAN

Removal and Installation

1. Raise and support the vehicle safely.

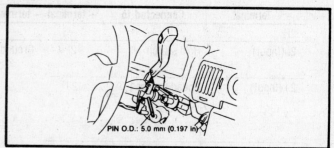

PIN O.D.: 5.0 mm (0.197 in)

Selector lever adjustment

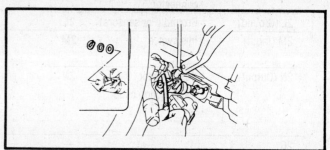

Adjustment washer location – selector lever

2. Place a drain pan under the transmission oil pan. Clean the area around the oil pan to prevent entry of dust into the unit. Remove the oil pan attaching bolts from the front and side of the pan.
3. Loosen the rear pan attaching bolts approximately 4 turns.
4. Carefully pry the transmission oil pan loose and allow the fluid to drain.
5. Remove the remaining bolts. Remove the oil pan, gasket and magnet. If required, remove the filter.
6. Thoroughly clean the oil pan and transmission gasket surfaces. Dry with compressed air.
7. Install the magnet into the oil pan. Install the oil pan using a new gasket and alternately tighten the retaining bolts to 52–69 inch lbs. (5.9–7.8 Nm).
8. Lower the vehicle and add the proper amount of transmission fluid.

EXTENSION HOUSING OIL SEAL

Removal and Installation

1. Disconnect the negative battery cable.
2. Raise and support the vehicle safely.
3. Matchmark the driveshaft and flange; then, remove the driveshaft.
4. Pry the extension housing seal from the extension housing.
To install:
5. Lubricate the new extension housing seal lip and tap it into place using a plastic mallet.
6. Install the driveshaft while aligning the matchmarks.
7. Lower the vehicle and reconnect the negative battery cable.

MANUAL SHAFT SEAL

Removal and Installation

1. Disconnect the negative battery cable.
2. Raise and support the vehicle safely.

3. Drain the transmission fluid and remove the transmission oil pan.

4. Remove the manual shaft retaining roll pin, detent spring, locknuts and manual plate.

5. Remove manual shaft and pry the seal from the transmission case.

To install:

6. Lubricate the new manual shaft seal lip and tap it into place using a plastic mallet.

7. Install the manual shaft, manual plate, parking rod and locknuts.

8. Install the manual shaft retaining pin and detent spring. Install the transmission pan using a new gasket.

9. Lower the vehicle and reconnect the negative battery cable. Fill the transmission with the proper fluid, start the engine and check for leaks.

CONTROL VALVE BODY

Removal and Installation

1. Disconnect the negative battery cable. Raise and support the vehicle safely.

2. Loosen the oil pan retaining bolts and drain the transmission fluid.

3. Remove the oil pan and gasket. Remove the magnet from the oil pan.

4. Separate the solenoid connector clips. Disconnect the lockup solenoid connector and automatic transmission fluid thermosensor connector. Remove the thermosensor.

5. Remove the oil strainer and O-ring.

6. Remove the valve body retaining bolts and solenoid connector harness clips.

7. Carefully remove the control valve body assembly and accumulator springs. Be careful not to damage the oil pipes or drop the springs while removing.

8. If necessary, remove the solenoid connector from the transmission case.

To install:

9. If removed, install the solenoid connector into the transmission case.

10. Connect the solenoid connector to the solenoid and install the clip.

11. Position the accumulator springs into the control valve body.

12. Position the control valve against the transmission case and install the mounting bolts and brackets. Tighten the bolts to the torque value listed in the bolts and nuts specifications chart.

13. Lubricate the oil strainer O-ring and install it on the oil strainer. Install the oil strainer.

14. Mount the harness of the solenoid connectors with the harness clips.

15. Install the automatic transmission fluid thermosensor.

16. Connect the lockup solenoid and automatic transmission fluid thermosensor connectors and install the clip.

17. Place the magnet into the oil pan. Install the oil pan using a new gasket. Torque the oil pan retaining bolts 43–69 inch lbs. (4.9–7.8 Nm).

18. Lower the vehicle and add approximately 4.2 qts. (4.0 liters) of automatic transmission fluid.

19. Reconnect the negative battery cable, start the engine and check for leaks. Check the transmission fluid level.

REMOVAL AND INSTALLATION

TRANSMISSION REMOVAL

1. Disconnect the negative battery cable. Raise and support the vehicle safely.

2. Drain the transmission fluid into a suitable container.

3. Disconnect and tag all electrical connectors. Remove the speedometer cable.

4. Remove the front exhaust pipe and heat insulator.

5. Mark the driveshaft flanges to aid during reassemble. Remove the driveshaft and install tool 49S120440 or equivalent to prevent oil leakage.

6. Remove the transmission filler tube.

7. Remove the torque convertor inspection cover. Remove the converter to flexplate retaining bolts.

8. Remove the starter motor and exhaust pipe bracket from the transmission.

9. Support the transmission with a transmission jack and remove the transmission mount bolts; then, lean the transmission downward.

10. Remove the transmission cooler oil pipes and gusset plates from the lower converter housing.

11. Remove the transmission lower and upper mounts. Remove the transmission assembly and mount in a suitable holding fixture.

TRANSMISSION INSTALLATION

1. Position the transmission mounts on the transmission and loosely tighten the retaining bolts.

2. Set the transmission on the transmission jack and install the exhaust pipe brackets.

3. Raise the transmission into place and install the mounting bolts. Torque the mounting bolts 27–38 ft. lbs. (37–52 Nm).

4. Connect the oil cooler pipes. Torque the transmission mounts retaining bolts 32–45 ft. lbs. (43–61 Nm).

5. Install the torque converter to flex plate retaining bolts. Torque the retaining bolts 27–40 ft. lbs. (36–54 Nm).

6. Install the undercover. Install the starter motor and brackets. Torque the mounting bolts 27–38 ft. lbs. (37–52 Nm).

7. Install the filler tube and all retaining brackets.

8. Reconnect all electrical connectors and the speedometer.

9. Install the insulator and exhaust pipe.

10. Align the mating marks and install the driveshaft. Torque the retaining bolts 36–43 ft. lbs. (49–59 Nm).

11. Install the center bearing support assembly and change counter assembly.

12. Lower the vehicle and connect the negative battery cable.

13. Fill the transmission with the proper fluid. Start the engine and check for leaks. Recheck the fluid level.

BENCH OVERHAUL

Before Disassembly

Cleanliness is an important factor in the overhaul of the transmission unit. Before opening up this unit, the entire outside of the transmission assembly should be cleaned, preferable with a high pressure washer such as a car wash spray unit. Dirt entering the transmission internal parts will negate all the time and effort spent on the overhaul. During inspection and reassembly all parts should be thoroughly cleaned with solvent then dried with compressed air. Wiping cloths and rags should not be used to dry parts since lint will find its way into the valve body passages.

Wheel bearing grease, long used to hold thrust washers and lube parts, should not be used. Lube seals with clean transmission fluid and use ordinary unmedicated petroleum jelly to hold the thrust washers and to ease the assembly of seals, since it will not leave a harmful residue as grease often will. Do not use solvent on neoprene seals, friction plates if they are to be reused, or thrust washers. Be wary of nylon parts if the transmission failure was due to failure of the cooling system. Nylon parts exposed to water or antifreeze solutions can swell and distort and must be replaced.

Before installing bolts into aluminum parts, always dip the threads into clean transmission fluid. Antiseize compound can also be used to prevent bolts from galling the aluminum and seizing. Always use a torque wrench to keep from stripping the threads. Take care when installing new O-rings, especially the smaller O-rings. The internal snaprings should be expanded and the external rings should be compressed, if they are to be reused. This will help insure proper seating when installed.

Converter Inspection

Check the outer part of the converter for damage and cracks. Replace it if there is any problem. Also, check for rust on the pilot and base. If there is any, remove it completely.

1. Completely drain all transmission fluid from the converter.

2. Pour approximately ½ qt. of solvent into the converter. Shake the converter to clean the inside; then, drain the solvent from the converter.

3. Clean the inside of the converter with compressed air so that the inside is perfectly empty. Rinse the converter with clean automatic transmission fluid.

Transmission Disassembly

1. Properly support the transmission in a holding fixture in an upright position. Remove the oil pan and gasket.

2. Examine any material found in the pan or on the magnet to determine the condition of the transmission. If large amounts of material are found, replace the torque converter and carefully check the transmission for the cause.

3. Remove the torque converter.

4. Remove the connector brackets and the inhibitor switch from the transmission.

5. Remove the speedometer driven gear from the transmission. Be careful not to damage the speed sensor.

6. Remove the speed sensor 1, extension housing and gasket. Mark the extension housing retaining bolts so they can be reinstalled in their proper locations. The retaining bolts are different sizes.

7. Disconnect the lockup solenoid and transmission fluid thermosensor connectors. Be careful not to damage the harness connectors.

8. Remove the transmission fluid thermosensor. Mark the transmission fluid thermosensor retaining bolts so they can be

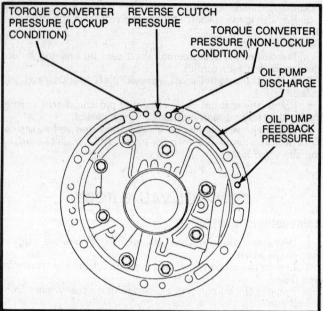

Fluid passage location—oil pump

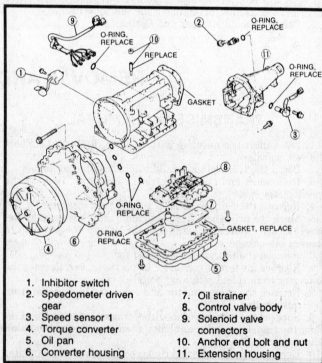

1. Inhibitor switch
2. Speedometer driven gear
3. Speed sensor 1
4. Torque converter
5. Oil pan
6. Converter housing
7. Oil strainer
8. Control valve body
9. Solenoid valve connectors
10. Anchor end bolt and nut
11. Extension housing

Transmission disassembly—components exploded view

reinstalled in their proper locations. The retaining bolts are different sizes.

9. Remove the oil strainer and separate the solenoid harness from the harness clips. Mark the retaining bolts so they can be reinstalled in their proper locations. The retaining bolts are different sizes.

10. Disconnect the solenoid connectors and remove the control valve body oil pipes. Remove the control valve body.

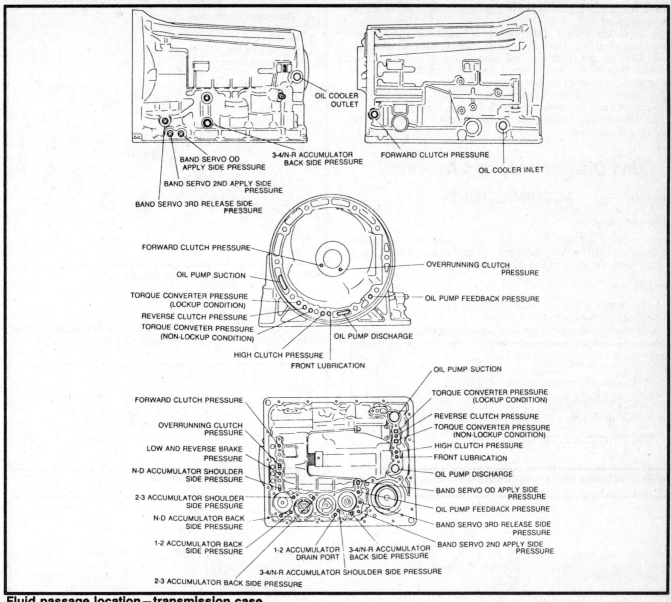

Fluid passage location—transmission case

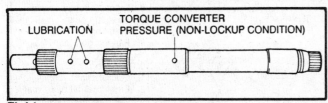

Fluid passage location—input shaft

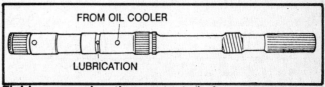

Fluid passage location—output shaft

11. Remove the solenoid connectors from the transmission case. Remove the converter housing and O-rings. Be careful not to damage the housing.

12. Remove the O-ring from the input shaft. Install a suitable oil pump puller 180 degrees apart and remove the oil pump. Be careful not to scratch the pump housing. Remove the oil pump gasket.

13. Pull out the input shaft while holding the reverse clutch drum.

14. Hold the anchor end bolt and loosen the locknut. Remove the locknut from the anchor end bolt and remove the anchor end bolt. Do not reuse the anchor end bolt.

15. Remove the brake band and the band strut. Secure the brake band ends with a wire clip to prevent the brake lining from cracking or peeling due to over-stretching.

16. Remove the reverse clutch, high clutch and the front sun gear.

17. Remove the front planetary carrier, bearings and the rear sun gear. Remove the rear snap ring and the speedometer drive gear. Remove the key and the front snapring.

18. Remove the rear snapring from the output shaft and re-

move the parking gear. Remove the bearing behind the transmission case.

19. Push the output shaft slightly forward and remove the front snapring from the output shaft. Remove the output shaft.

20. Remove the front internal gear with the rear planetary carrier. Remove the rear internal gear, forward clutch hub and overrunning clutch hub as an assembly.

21. Remove the forward clutch drum, forward clutch, overrunning clutch and low one–way clutch as as assembly.

22. Remove the low/reverse brake, extension housing and parking mechanism.

Unit Disassembly and Assembly

ACCUMULATORS

Disassembly

Remove the 3–4/N–R accumulator, 1/2 accumulator, 2/3 accumulator and N/D accumulator springs and pistons by applying compressed air through the oil passages.

Inspection

1. Remove the O-rings from the pistons.
2. Measure the springs free length.
3. If not within specification, replace the spring.

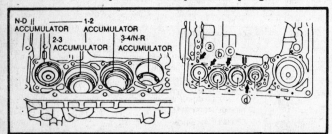

Accumulators – apply compressed air to a, b, c and d

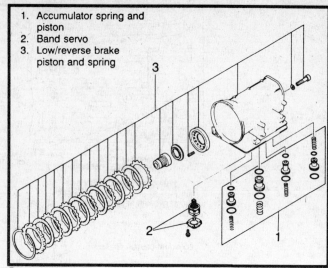

1. Accumulator spring and piston
2. Band servo
3. Low/reverse brake piston and spring

Components exploded view continued

Assembly

1. Lubricate the new O-rings with clean transmission fluid and install them on the accumulator pistons.

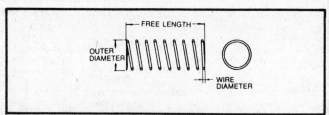

Accumulator spring measurement

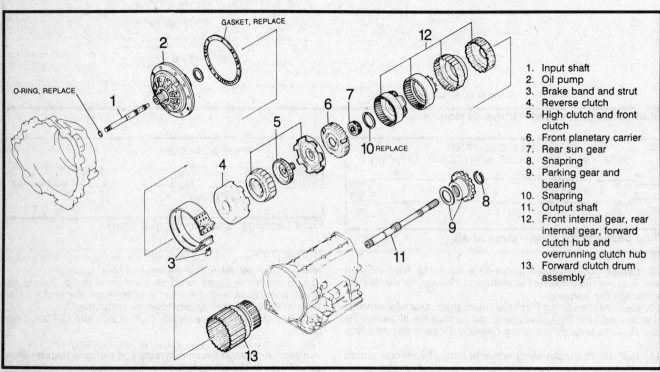

1. Input shaft
2. Oil pump
3. Brake band and strut
4. Reverse clutch
5. High clutch and front clutch
6. Front planetary carrier
7. Rear sun gear
8. Snapring
9. Parking gear and bearing
10. Snapring
11. Output shaft
12. Front internal gear, rear internal gear, forward clutch hub and overrunning clutch hub
13. Forward clutch drum assembly

Components exploded view continued

2. Install the accumulator pistons and springs in the following order:
1st – N/D accumulator
2nd – 2/3 accumulator
3rd – 1/2 accumulator
4th – 3–4/N–R accumulator

3. Apply even pressure to the perimeter of the accumulator pistons to avoid damaging the O-rings when installing.

OIL PUMP

Disassembly

1. Loosen the oil pump cover retaining bolts evenly in the proper sequence. Remove the oil pump cover from the oil pump housing.

2. Mark the rotor and cam ring; then, separate the rotor and vanes from the cam ring.

3. Tape the areas around the cam ring and pivot pin and carefully push on the cam ring; then, remove the pivot pin. Be careful not to scratch the oil pump housing. Hold the cam ring spring to prevent it from popping out and remove the cam ring and spring.

Inspection

1. Measure the clearance between the seal ring and the ring groove of the oil pump cover. The standard clearance is 0.0039–0.0098 inch (0.10–0.25mm). The maximum clearance should not exceed 0.0098 inch (0.25mm).

2. In the clearance is not within specification, replace the oil pump as an assembly.

3. Install the cam ring vanes, rotor and control piston. Do not install the friction ring O-ring, control piston side seals or the cam ring spring.

4. Measure the clearance between the end of the oil pump housing and the cam ring, rotor, vanes and control piston in at least 4 places along their circumferences.

5. The standard clearance between the cam ring is 0.0004–0.009 (0.010–0.024mm). The maximum clearance should not exceed 0.0012 inch (0.030mm).

6. The standard clearance between the rotor, vane and control piston is 0.0012–0.0017 (0.030–0.044mm). The maximum clearance should not exceed 0.0020 inch (0.050mm). If not within specification, replace the oil pump as an assembly.

7. Measure the cam ring spring and compare with the following specifications:
    a. Coil outer diameter – 0.539 inch (13.7mm)
    b. Free length – 1.567 inch (39.8mm)
    c. Coil thickness – 0.091 inch (2.3mm)
    d. No. of coil – 7.8

8. If the cam ring spring is not within specification, replace the spring.

Assembly

1. Lubricate the new front pump seal with clean automatic transmission fluid and install the seal using an appropriate seal installer.

2. Lubricate the new side seal with clean automatic transmission fluid and install them on the control piston with the black surface facing toward the control piston; then, install the control piston and pivot pin.

3. Apply petroleum jelly to the cam ring groove and install a new O-ring and friction ring into the cam ring.

4. Install the cam ring and spring while compressing the spring against the oil pump housing.

5. Tape the areas around the cam ring and pivot pin and carefully push on the cam ring; then, install the pivot pin. Be careful not to scratch the oil pump housing.

6. Locate the marks and install the rotor, vanes and vane rings.

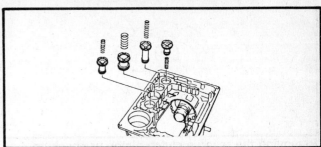

Installing the accumulators

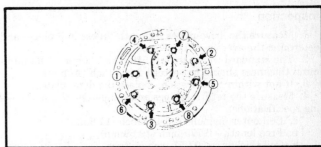

Oil pump cover removal and installation retaining bolts torque sequence

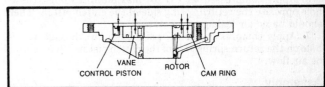

Oil pump housing, cam ring, rotor, vane and control piston measurement

7. Install the oil pump cover onto the oil pump housing. Be careful not to damage the oil seal with the splines of the oil pump cover when installing.

8. Tighten the bolts evenly and gradually in the proper sequence. Torque the retaining bolts 12–15 ft. lbs. (16–21 Nm).

9. Put petroleum jelly into the ring grooves. Lubricate the new seal rings with clean transmission fluid and install them on the oil pump. Do not overexpand the seal rings when installing. Press the seal rings down into the petroleum jelly to secure them.

NOTE: The seal rings come in 2 different diameters. Small diameter seal ring has no marks. Large diameter seal ring can be identified with a yellow mark.

10. Install the bearing on the oil pump and retain it with petroleum.

REVERSE CLUTCH

Disassembly

1. Remove the snapring from the reverse clutch drum.

2. Remove the selective retaining ring. Remove the drive plates, driven plates and the dish plate.

3. Using an appropriate spring compressor, depress the piston spring retainer only enough to remove the snapring; then, remove the snapring.

4. Remove the spring retainer and springs.

5. Install the reverse clutch onto the oil pump along with the seal rings and remove the piston by applying compressed air (57 psi maximum) to the oil passage.

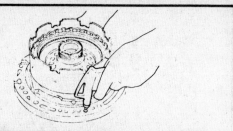

Removing the reverse clutch piston or checking piston operation

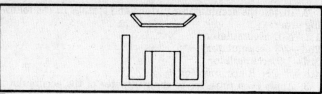

Reverse clutch and high clutch dish plate positioning

Inspection

1. Measure the drive plates facing thickness in 3 places and determine the average of the 3 reading.
2. The standard thickness is 0.079 inch (2.0mm). The minimum thickness should not exceed 0.071 inch (1.8mm).
3. If not within specification, replace the drive plates.
4. Measure the return springs and compare with the following specifications:
   a. Coil outer diameter – 0.457 inch (11.6mm)
   b. Free length – 0.775 inch (19.69mm)
   c. Coil thickness – 0.051 inch (1.3mm)
   d. No. of coil – 4.0
5. If not within specification, replace the return spring.
6. Apply compressed air (57 psi maximum) through the oil hole opposite the return spring side of the clutch piston. There should be no air leakage.
7. Apply compressed air (57 psi maximum) through the oil hole on the return spring side of the clutch piston. There should be air flow.

Assembly

1. Lubricate the new D-ring and seal ring with clean transmission fluid and install them onto the clutch piston.

2. Lubricate the inner surface of the reverse clutch drum.
3. Install the clutch piston in the reverse clutch drum by apply pressure to the perimeter of the piston. Turn the piston evenly and gradually to avoid damaging the seal ring and D-ring when installing.
4. Install the return springs and spring retainer.

NOTE: Depress the spring retainer only enough to install the snapring. Do not over expand the snapring. Do not align the snapring end gap with the spring retainer stop.

5. Install the snapring. Install the dish plate.
6. Lubricate the drive and driven plates with clean transmission fluid and install them into the reverse clutch drum.
7. Install the retaining plate and snapring.
8. Measure the clearance between the retaining plate and the snapring. The standard clearance is 0.020–0.047 inch (0.50–1.20mm).
9. If not within specification, correct the clearance by replacing the selective retaining plate. If the clearance cannot be brought within specification after installing the thickest retaining plate, replace the dished plate, driven plates and drive plate.
10. After the reverse clutch is completely assembled, apply compressed air (57 psi maximum) for no more than 3 seconds to the oil passage and check the clutch operation.
11. Verify that the retaining plate moves to the snapring. In not, the D-ring or the oil seal may be damaged or fluid may be leaking at the piston check ball.

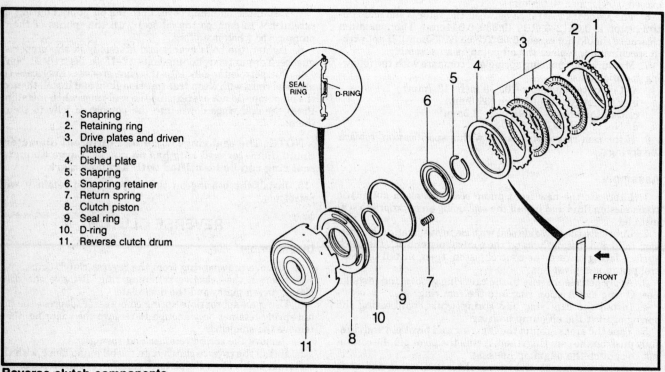

1. Snapring
2. Retaining ring
3. Drive plates and driven plates
4. Dished plate
5. Snapring
6. Snapring retainer
7. Return spring
8. Clutch piston
9. Seal ring
10. D-ring
11. Reverse clutch drum

Reverse clutch components

HIGH CLUTCH AND FRONT SUN GEAR

Disassembly

1. Remove the front sun gear assembly (sun gear, high clutch hub, bearing and races).
2. Remove the snapring and retaining plate from the high clutch drum.
3. Remove the drive and driven plates. Remove the dish plate.
4. Using an appropriate spring compressor, depress the piston spring retainer only enough to remove the snapring; then, remove the snapring.
4. Remove the spring retainer and springs.
5. Install the high clutch onto the oil pump along with the seal rings and remove the piston by applying compressed air (57 psi maximum) to the oil passage.

Inspection

1. Measure the drive plates facing thickness in 3 places and determine the average of the 3 reading.
2. The standard thickness is 0.063 inch (1.6mm). The minimum thickness should not exceed 0.055 inch (1.4mm).
3. If not within specification, replace the drive plates.
4. Measure the return springs and compare with the following specifications:
   a. Coil outer diameter—0.457 inch (11.6mm)
   b. Free length—0.869 inch (22.06mm)
   c. Coil thickness—0.051 inch (1.3mm)
   d. No. of coil—6.0
5. If not within specification, replace the return spring.
6. Apply compressed air (57 psi maximum) through the oil hole opposite the return spring side of the clutch piston. There should be no air leakage.
7. Apply compressed air (57 psi maximum) through the oil hole on the return spring side of the clutch piston. There should be air flow.

Assembly

1. Lubricate the new D-rings with clean transmission fluid and install them onto the clutch piston.
2. Lubricate the inner surface of the high clutch drum.
3. Install the clutch piston in the high clutch drum by apply

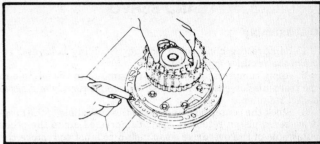

Removing the high clutch piston or checking piston operation

pressure to the perimeter of the piston. Turn the piston evenly and gradually to avoid damaging the D-rings when installing.
4. Install the return springs and spring retainer.

NOTE: Depress the spring retainer only enough to install the snapring. Do not over expand the snapring. Do not align the snapring end gap with the spring retainer stop.

5. Install the snapring. Install the dish plate.
6. Lubricate the drive and driven plates with clean transmission fluid and install them into the reverse clutch drum. Start with a driven plate, then alternate drive-driven-drive-driven.
7. Install the retaining plate and snapring.
8. Measure the clearance between the retaining plate and the snapring. The standard clearance is 0.071–0.118 inch (1.8–3.0mm).
9. If not within specification, correct the clearance by replacing the selective retaining plate. If the clearance cannot be brought within specification after installing the thichest retaining plate, replace the dished plate, driven plates and drive plate.
10. After the high clutch is completely assembled, apply compressed air (57 psi maximum) for no more than 3 seconds to the oil passage and check the clutch operation.
11. Install the bearing races and bearing into the high clutch and retain them with petroleum.
12. Lubricate the high clutch hub with clean transmission fluid and install it into the high clutch.
13. Install the bearing races and bearing to the front sun gear.

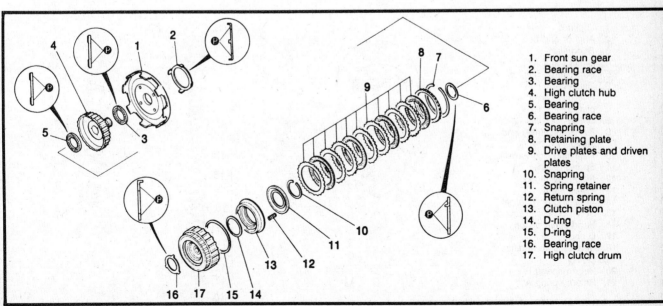

1. Front sun gear
2. Bearing race
3. Bearing
4. High clutch hub
5. Bearing
6. Bearing race
7. Snapring
8. Retaining plate
9. Drive plates and driven plates
10. Snapring
11. Spring retainer
12. Return spring
13. Clutch piston
14. D-ring
15. D-ring
16. Bearing race
17. High clutch drum

High clutch and front sun gear components

BAND SERVO

Disassembly

1. Remove the band servo retainer retaining bolts and remove the retainer and gasket.
2. Apply compressed air (57 psi maximum) to the oil hole in the transmission case to remove the piston assembly and servo piston retainer.
3. Block the center hole and one of the outer hole of the overdrive servo piston retainer. Apply compressed air to the other outer hole of the overdrive servo piston retainer to remove the overdrive band servo piston.
4. Remove the D-ring from the overdrive band servo piston.

Inspection

1. Check the D-ring and seals for damage.
2. Inspect the piston stem.
3. Measure the return springs and compare with the return spring specification chart.

Assembly

1. Lubricate the new O-rings with clean transmission fluid and install them onto the servo piston retainer.
2. Lubricate the new D-rings and install them onto the band servo piston.
3. Lubricate the servo cushion spring retainer and retaining ring and assemble them in the band servo piston.
4. Lubricate the servo piston and install it on the servo piston retainer.

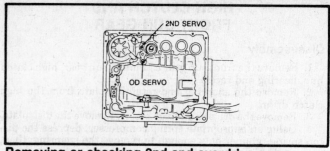

Removing or checking 2nd and overdrive servo piston operation

5. Lubricate the piston stem return spring and spring retainer and assemble them in the band servo piston. Install the retaining ring.
6. Lubricate the D-ring and install it on the overdrive band servo piston.
7. Lubricate the overdrive band servo piston and install it on the band servo retainer. Install return spring A and B.
8. Lubricate the piston assembly and install it into the transmission case.
9. Lubricate the band servo retainer and new gasket and install them on the transmission case. Tighten and torque the servo retainer retaining bolts 61–78 inch lbs. (6.9–8.8 Nm).
10. After the band servo is completely assembled, apply compressed air (57 psi maximum) for no more than 3 seconds through the oil holes and check the servo piston operation.

FRONT INTERNAL GEAR
REAR INTERNAL GEAR
FORWARD CLUTCH HUB
AND OVERRUNNING CLUTCH HUB

Disassembly

1. Remove the front internal gear, bearing race and bearing.
2. Remove the rear internal gear, thrust washer and bearing.
3. Remove the overrunning clutch hub and thrust washer.
4. Disassembly the forward one-way clutch by removing both snaprings.

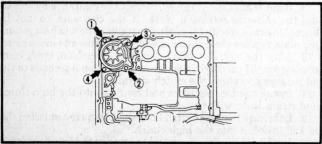

Band servo retainer torque sequence

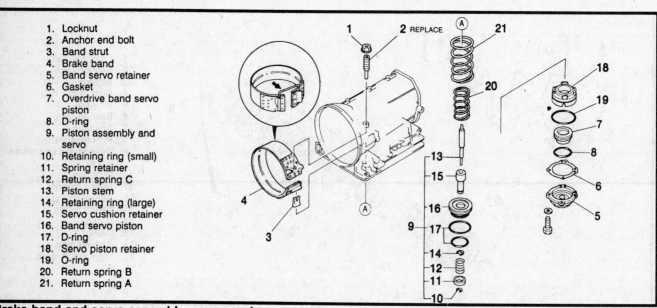

1. Locknut
2. Anchor end bolt
3. Band strut
4. Brake band
5. Band servo retainer
6. Gasket
7. Overdrive band servo piston
8. D-ring
9. Piston assembly and servo
10. Retaining ring (small)
11. Spring retainer
12. Return spring C
13. Piston stem
14. Retaining ring (large)
15. Servo cushion retainer
16. Band servo piston
17. D-ring
18. Servo piston retainer
19. O-ring
20. Return spring B
21. Return spring A

Brake band and servo assembly components

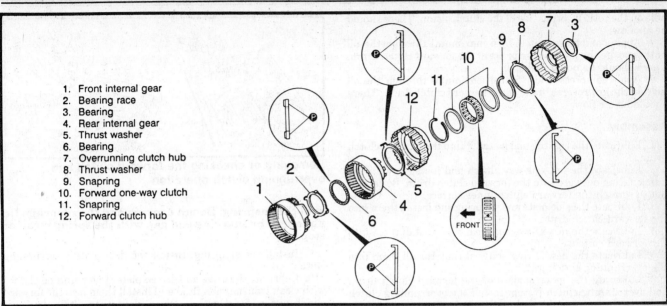

Front internal gear, Rear internal gear Forward clutch hub and overrunning clutch hub

1. Front internal gear
2. Bearing race
3. Bearing
4. Rear internal gear
5. Thrust washer
6. Bearing
7. Overrunning clutch hub
8. Thrust washer
9. Snapring
10. Forward one-way clutch
11. Snapring
12. Forward clutch hub

Inspection

1. Inspect the individual gear teeth for damage, wear, cracks or rotation of the pinion gears.
2. Inspect the bearing surfaces for scoring, scratches or rough rotation.

Assembly

1. Install the snapring into the forward clutch hub.
2. Install the forward one-way clutch with the side indicated by the arrow toward the front when installing the one-way clutch into the one-way clutch outer race.
3. Lubricate the forward one-way clutch and install it in the forward clutch hub and the snapring.
4. Apply petroleum jelly to the thrust washer and set it on the rear internal gear. Be sure the locating tabs of the thrust washer are set into the holes in the rear internal gear.
5. Lubricate the internal gear and install it in the forward clutch hub by turning it evenly and gradually. If it turns counterclockwise, the one-way clutch is installed upside down.

NOTE: Hold the forward clutch hub and check that the forward one-way clutch operation by turning right and left. It should turn clockwise only and locked counterclockwise.

6. Apply petroleum jelly to the bearing and set it on the rear internal gear.
7. Apply petroleum jelly to the thrust washer and set it in the overrunning clutch hub. Be sure the locating tabs of the thrust washer are set into the holes in the overrunning clutch hub.
8. Set the overrunning clutch hub on the rear internal gear.
9. Apply petroleum jelly to the bearing and set it on the overrunning clutch hub.

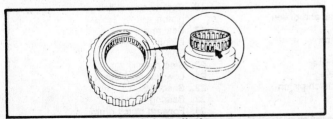

Forward one-way clutch installation

10. Apply petroleum jelly to the bearing race and set it on the front internal gear.

FORWARD CLUTCH DRUM (FORWARD CLUTCH OVERRUNNING CLUTCH LOW ONE—WAY CLUTCH)

Disassembly

1. Remove the snaprings, retaining plate, drive and driven plates and dish plate (forward clutch).
2. Remove the retaining plate, drive and driven plates and dish plate (overrunning clutch).
3. Using an appropriate spring compressor, depress the spring retainer and remove the snapring. Remove the spring retainer and springs.
4. Set the forward clutch drum in the transmission case and remove the piston by applying compressed air (57 psi maximum) through the oil passage.
5. Remove the seal rings, D-rings, snapring rings and side plate.
6. Remove the low one-way clutch, bearing and forward clutch drum.

Inspection

1. Measure the drive plates in 3 places and determine the average of the 3 readings. The standard reading is 0.079 inch (2.0mm). The minimum thickness should not exceed 0.071 inch (1.8mm).
2. Inspect the drive and driven plates for wear or burning.
3. Measure the return springs and compare with the following specifications:
   a. Coil outer diameter—0.382 inch (9.7mm)
   b. Free length—1.409 inch (35.8mm)
   c. Coil thickness—0.051 inch (1.3mm)
   d. No. of coil—10.3
4. If not within specification, replace the return spring.
5. Apply compressed air (57 psi maximum) through the oil hole opposite the return spring side of the clutch piston. There should be no air leakage.
6. Apply compressed air (57 psi maximum) through the oil

hole on the return spring side of the clutch piston. There should be air flow.

7. Apply compressed air (57 psi maximum) through the oil hole opposite the low/reverse brake of the forward clutch drum. There should be no air leakage.

8. Apply compressed air (57 psi maximum) through the oil hole on the low/reverse brake of the forward clutch drum. There should be air flow.

Assembly

1. Lubricate the bearing and install it into the forward clutch drum.

2. Lubricate the low one-way clutch and install it with the flange facing outward into the forward clutch drum. Be careful not to scratch the forward clutch inner surface.

3. Lubricate the side plate and snapring and install them into the forward clutch drum.

4. Lubricate the new D-ring and seal ring. Install them into the forward clutch.

5. Lubricate the new D-ring and seal ring. Install them into the overrunning clutch piston.

6. Lubricate the inner surface of the forward clutch drum and overrunning clutch piston. Install the overrunning clutch piston in the forward clutch drum by gradually turning it in an even manner. Align the notches with the grooves with the forward clutch drum.

7. Lubricate the inner surface of the forward clutch piston and overrunning clutch piston. Install the overrunning clutch piston in the forward clutch piston by gradually turning it while applying pressure to the perimeter of the piston. Avoid damaging the D-ring and the seal ring when installing.

8. Install the return springs and spring retainer.

NOTE: Depress the spring retainer only enough to in-

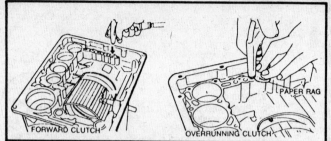

Removing or checking the forward clutch and overrunning clutch operation

stall the snapring. Do not over expand the snapring. Do not align the snapring end gap with the spring retainer stop.

9. Install the snapring. Install the dish plate (overrunning clutch).

10. Lubricate the drive and driven plates (overrunning clutch) with clean transmission fluid and install them into the forward clutch piston. Start with a driven plate, then alternate drive-driven-drive-driven.

11. Install the retaining plate and snapring.

12. Measure the clearance between the retaining plate and the snapring. The standard clearance is 0.039–0.079 inch (1.0–2.0mm).

13. If not within specification, correct the clearance by replacing the selective retaining plate. If the clearance cannot be brought within specification after installing the thickest retaining plate, replace the dished plate, driven plates and drive plate.

14. Install the dish plate (forward clutch).

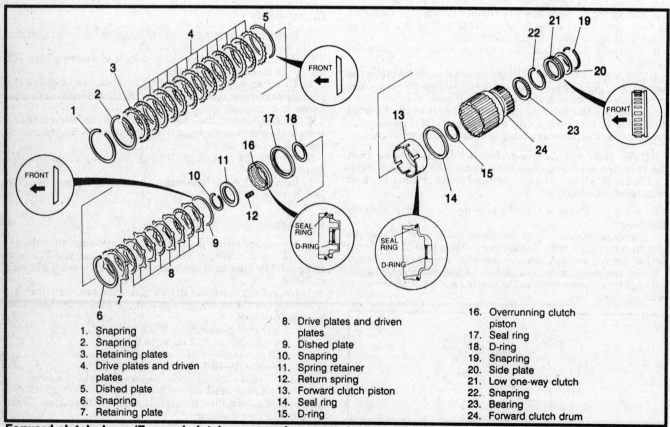

1. Snapring
2. Snapring
3. Retaining plates
4. Drive plates and driven plates
5. Dished plate
6. Snapring
7. Retaining plate
8. Drive plates and driven plates
9. Dished plate
10. Snapring
11. Spring retainer
12. Return spring
13. Forward clutch piston
14. Seal ring
15. D-ring
16. Overrunning clutch piston
17. Seal ring
18. D-ring
19. Snapring
20. Side plate
21. Low one-way clutch
22. Snapring
23. Bearing
24. Forward clutch drum

Forward clutch drum (Forward clutch, overrunning clutch low one-way clutch) components

15. Lubricate the drive and driven plates (forward clutch) with clean transmission fluid and install them into the forward clutch piston. Start with a driven plate, then alternate drive-driven-drive-driven.

16. Install the retaining plate and snapring.

17. Measure the clearance between the retaining plate and the snapring. The standard clearance is 0.018–0.081 inch (0.45–2.05mm).

18. If not within specification, correct the clearance by replacing the selective retaining plate. If the clearance cannot be brought within specification after installing the thickest retaining plate, replace the dished plate, driven plates and drive plate.

19. Install the snapring.

20. After the high clutch is completely assembled, set the forward clutch drum in the transmission. Apply compressed air (57 psi maximum) for no more than 3 seconds to the oil passages and check the forward clutch and overrunning clutch operation.

21. Check the low one-way clutch operation by turning right and left. It should turn clockwise only and locked counterclockwise.

LOW/REVERSE BRAKE

Disassembly

1. Remove the snapring, retaining plate, drive plates and driven plates.

2. Remove the Allen head bolts holding the low one-way clutch inner race and spring retainer. Remove the low one-way clutch inner race, spring retainer and springs.

3. Remove the low/reverse brake piston by applying compressed air (57 psi maximum) through the oil passage.

4. Remove the D-ring and seal ring.

Inspection

1. Measure the drive plates in 3 places and determine the average of the 3 readings. The standard reading is 0.079 inch (2.0mm). The minimum thickness should not exceed 0.071 inch (1.8mm).

2. Inspect the drive and driven plates for wear or burning.

3. Measure the return springs and compare with the following specifications:
   a. Coil outer diameter—0.457 inch (11.6mm)
   b. Free length—0.933 inch (23.7mm)
   c. Coil thickness—0.043 inch (11.0mm)
   d. No. of coil—5.0

4. If not within specification, replace the return spring.

5. Apply compressed air (57 psi maximum) through the oil hole opposite the return spring side of the clutch piston. There should be no air leakage.

6. Apply compressed air (57 psi maximum) through the oil hole on the return spring side of the clutch piston. There should be air flow.

7. Apply petroleum jelly to a new seal ring and install it on the low one-way clutch inner race. Measure the clearance between the seal ring and the ring groove. The standard clearance is 0.0039–0.0098 inch (0.10–0.25mm). The maximum clearance should not exceed 0.0098 inch (0.25mm).

8. If not within specification, replace the low one-way clutch inner race.

9. Inspect the low/reverse brake piston ball for sticking by shaking the low/reverse brake piston.

Assembly

1. Lubricate the new D-ring and seal ring and install them on the low/reverse brake piston.

2. Lubricate the inner surface of the transmission case and install the low/reverse brake piston by turning it evenly while applying even pressure to the perimeter of the piston.

3. Apply petroleum jelly to the bearing and install it on the low one-way clutch inner race.

4. Properly assemble the return springs, spring retainer and low one-way clutch inner race to the low/reverse brake piston; then, secure them with the Allen head bolts. Tighten and torque the Allen head bolts in sequence to 15–20 ft. lbs. (21–26 Nm).

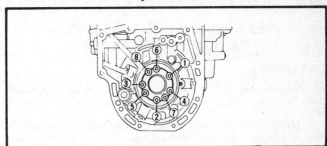

Low/reverse brake assembly—torque sequence

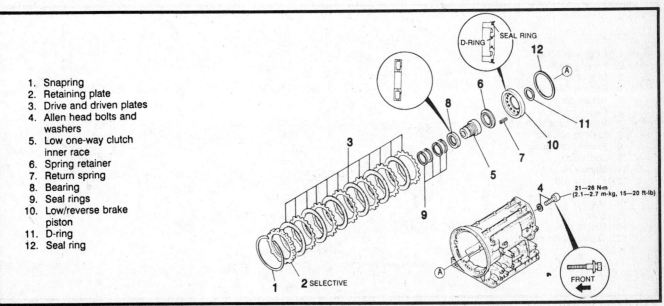

1. Snapring
2. Retaining plate
3. Drive and driven plates
4. Allen head bolts and washers
5. Low one-way clutch inner race
6. Spring retainer
7. Return spring
8. Bearing
9. Seal rings
10. Low/reverse brake piston
11. D-ring
12. Seal ring

Low/reverse brake components

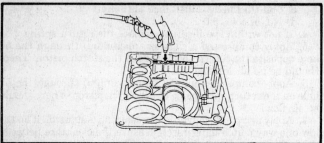

Removing or checking the low/reverse brake operation

5. Lubricate the drive and driven plates with clean transmission fluid and install them into the transmission case. Start with a driven plate, then alternate drive-driven-drive-driven.

6. Install the retaining plate and snapring.

7. Measure the clearance between the retaining plate and the snapring. The standard clearance is 0.043–0.106 inch (1.1–2.7mm).

8. If not within specification, correct the clearance by replacing the selective retaining plate. If the clearance cannot be brought within specification after installing the thickest retaining plate, replace the dished plate, driven plates and drive plate.

9. Install the snapring.

10. Check the operation of the clutch by applying compressed air (57 psi maximum) for no more than 3 seconds to the oil passage of the low/reverse brake.

11. Apply petroleum jelly to the seal rings and install them onto the low one-way clutch inner race.

EXTENSION HOUSING AND PARKING MECHANISM

Disassembly

1. Remove the detent spring and spacer, locknut, manual plate, parking rod, manual shaft retaining pin and manual shaft.

2. Mark the extension housing retaining bolts as they are removed. The bolts are of different length. Remove the extension housing and gasket.

3. Remove the output shaft and parking gear

4. Remove the parking pawl spacer, return spring, parking pawl and parking pawl shaft.

5. Remove the parking actuator and parking rod guide.

6. Remove the extension housing seal and manual shaft seal.

Inspection

1. Check the parking gear teeth for damage or wear and rough rotation of the bearing.

2. Inspect the output shaft splines for damage or wear.

3. Inspect the detent spring for fracture or wear.

4. Inspect the transmission case for damage at the oil seal surfaces.

5. Inspect the transmission case inner bearing for damage or rough rotation.

Assembly

1. Lubricate the seal lip of the new extension housing seal and install it into the extension housing.

2. Lubricate the parking rod guide and parking actuator and install them on the extension housing.

3. Lubricate the parking pawl shaft, parking pawl, return spring and spacer. Install them in the extension housing.

4. Wrap the threads of the manual shaft with tape. Lubricate the seal lip of the new manual shaft seal and install it onto the manual shaft.

5. Lubricate the bearing in the transmission case. Install the manual shaft by pushing it squarely into the transmission case; then, remove the tape.

6. Align the groove in the manual shaft with the roll pin hole and tap the roll pin into the case.

7. Install the detent spring, spacer, manual plate and parking rod.

8. Install the locknut and check the parking mechanism operation.

VALVE BODY

Disassembly

NOTE: Pay close attention when handling the control valve because it consists of the most precise and delicate parts of the transmission. Neatly arrange the parts in order to avoid mixing up similar parts.

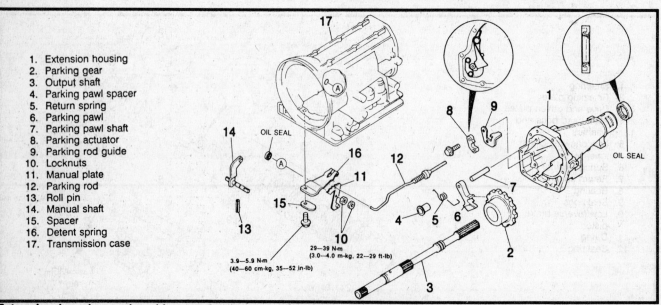

1. Extension housing
2. Parking gear
3. Output shaft
4. Parking pawl spacer
5. Return spring
6. Parking pawl
7. Parking pawl shaft
8. Parking actuator
9. Parking rod guide
10. Locknuts
11. Manual plate
12. Parking rod
13. Roll pin
14. Manual shaft
15. Spacer
16. Detent spring
17. Transmission case

OIL SEAL

29–39 N·m
(3.0–4.0 m·kg, 22–29 ft-lb)

3.9–5.9 N·m
(40–60 cm·kg, 35–52 in·lb)

OIL SEAL

Extension housing and parking mechanism – components exploded view

UPPER BODY

1. Place a finger over the torque converter relief valve bore to prevent the valve from popping out; then, remove the torque converter relief valve retainer, spring and valve.

2. Place a finger over the pressure regulator valve bore to prevent the valve from popping out; then, remove the pressure regulator valve stopper pin, sleeve, spring, regulator plug and valve.

3. Place a finger over the pressure modifier valve bore to prevent the valve from popping out; then, remove the pressure modifier valve stopper pin, plug, spring and valve.

4. Place a finger over the accumulator control valve bore to prevent the valve from popping out; then, remove the accumulator control valve stopper pin, plug, spring, valve and sleeve.

5. Place a finger over the shuttle shift valve D bore to prevent the valve from popping out; then, remove the shuttle shift valve D stopper pin, plug, valve and spring.

6. Place a finger over the shift valve **B** bore to prevent the valve from popping out; then, remove the shift valve **B** retainer, spring and valve.

7. Place a finger over the 4/2 sequence valve bore to prevent the valve from popping out; then, remove the 4/2 sequence valve stopper pin, valve and spring.

8. Place a finger over the shift valve **A** bore to prevent the valve from popping out; then, remove the shift valve **A** retainer, spring and valve.

9. Place a finger over the 4/2 relay valve bore to prevent the valve from popping out; then, remove the 4/2 relay valve stopper pin, plug, valve and spring.

10. Place a finger over the overrunning clutch control valve bore to prevent the valve from popping out; then, remove the overrunning clutch control valve stopper pin, plug, spring and valve.

11. Place a finger over the overrunning clutch reducing valve bore to prevent the valve from popping out; then, remove the overrunning clutch reducing valve stopper pin, plug, valve and spring.

12. Place a finger over the shuttle shift valve S bore to prevent the valve from popping out; then, remove the shuttle shift valve **S** stopper pin, plug, spring and valve.

13. Place a finger over the pilot valve bore to prevent the valve from popping out; then, remove the pilot valve retainer, spring and valve.

14. Place a finger over the lockup clutch control valve bore to prevent the valve from popping out; then, remove the lockup clutch control valve stopper pin, sleeve, plug, valve and spring.

LOWER BODY

1. Place a finger over the modifier accumulator valve bore to prevent the valve from popping out; then, remove the modifier accumulator valve stopper pin, plug, spring and valve.

2. Place a finger over the 1st reducing valve bore to prevent the valve from popping out; then, remove the 1st reducing valve retainer, spring and valve.

3. Place a finger over the 3/2 timing valve bore to prevent the valve from popping out; then, remove the 3/2 timing valve retainer, spring and valve.

4. Place a finger over the servo charger valve bore to prevent the valve from popping out; then, remove the servo charger valve stopper pin, plug, valve and spring.

Inspection

1. Inspect all valves and sleeves for sticking, scoring or scratches.

2. Inspect the valve body for damage or scoring.

3. Check all springs free length, coil outer diameter, coil thickness and No. of coils. Compare the springs with the specification chart.

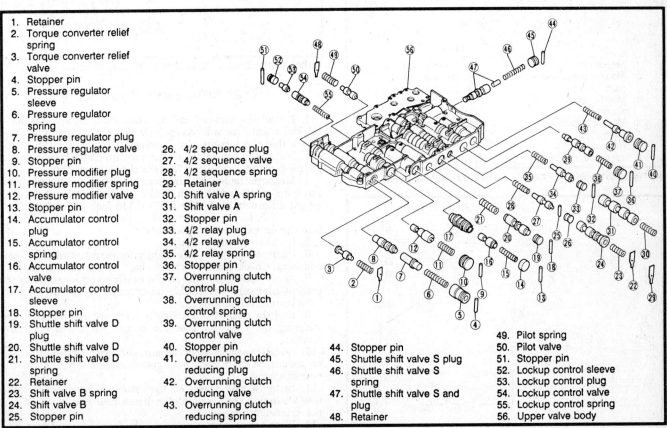

1. Retainer
2. Torque converter relief spring
3. Torque converter relief valve
4. Stopper pin
5. Pressure regulator sleeve
6. Pressure regulator spring
7. Pressure regulator plug
8. Pressure regulator valve
9. Stopper pin
10. Pressure modifier plug
11. Pressure modifier spring
12. Pressure modifier valve
13. Stopper pin
14. Accumulator control plug
15. Accumulator control spring
16. Accumulator control valve
17. Accumulator control sleeve
18. Stopper pin
19. Shuttle shift valve D plug
20. Shuttle shift valve D
21. Shuttle shift valve D spring
22. Retainer
23. Shift valve B spring
24. Shift valve B
25. Stopper pin
26. 4/2 sequence plug
27. 4/2 sequence valve
28. 4/2 sequence spring
29. Retainer
30. Shift valve A spring
31. Shift valve A
32. Stopper pin
33. 4/2 relay plug
34. 4/2 relay valve
35. 4/2 relay spring
36. Stopper pin
37. Overrunning clutch control plug
38. Overrunning clutch control spring
39. Overrunning clutch control valve
40. Stopper pin
41. Overrunning clutch reducing plug
42. Overrunning clutch reducing valve
43. Overrunning clutch reducing spring
44. Stopper pin
45. Shuttle shift valve S plug
46. Shuttle shift valve S spring
47. Shuttle shift valve S and plug
48. Retainer
49. Pilot spring
50. Pilot valve
51. Stopper pin
52. Lockup control sleeve
53. Lockup control plug
54. Lockup control valve
55. Lockup control spring
56. Upper valve body

Upper valve body—components exploded view

4. Do not reuse any parts that have been dropped.

Assembly

UPPER BODY

1. Install the torque converter relief valve and spring into the valve body; then, install the spring retainer.
2. Install the pressure regulator valve, plug, spring, sleeve and stopper pin.
3. Install the pressure modifier valve, spring, plug and stopper pin.
4. Install the accumulator control valve, sleeve, plug and stopper pin.
5. Install the shuttle valve **D**, spring, plug and stopper pin.
6. Install the 4/2 sequence valve, spring, plug and stopper pin.

7. Install the shift valve **B**, spring and retainer.
8. Install the 4/2 relay valve, spring, plug and stopper pin.
9. Install the shift valve **A**, spring and retainer.
10. Install the overrunning clutch control valve, spring, plug and stopper pin.
11. Install the overrunning clutch reducing valve, spring plug and stopper pin.
12. Install the shuttle shift valve **S**, plug, spring, and stopper pin.
13. Install the lockup control valve, spring, plug, sleeve and stopper pin.
14. Install the pilot valve, spring and retainer.

LOWER BODY

1. Install the servo charger valve spring and plug into the valve body. Install the stopper pin while pushing the plug.
2. Install the 3/2 timing valve, spring and retainer.
3. Install the 1st reducing valve, spring and retainer.
4. Install the modifier accumulator valve, spring, plug and stopper pin.

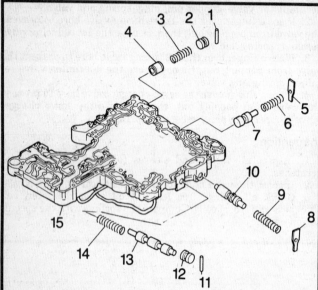

1. Stopper pin	7. 1st reducing valve
2. Modifier accumulator plug	8. Retainer
3. Modifier accumulator spring	9. 3/2 timing spring
	10. 3/2 timing valve
4. Modifier accumulator valve	11. Stopper pin
	12. Servo charger plug
5. Retainer	13. Servo charger valve
6. 1st reducing spring	14. Servo charger spring
	15. Lower valve body

Lower valve body—components exploded view

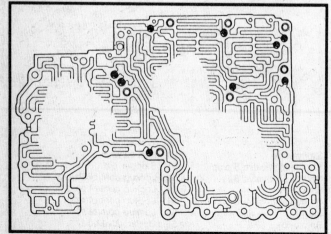

Check ball installation positions

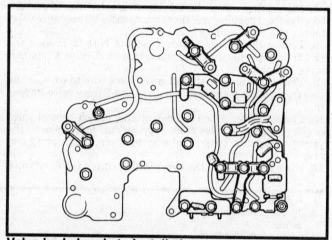

Valve body brackets installation positions

Transmission Assembly

1. Install the forward clutch drum while slowly turning it clockwise until its hub passes fully over the clutch inner race. Check that the forward clutch assembly turns only clockwise.
2. Install the rear internal gear, forward clutch hub and overrunning clutch hub in the forward clutch assembly.
3. Measure the height difference between the forward clutch retaining plate and the top of the forward clutch drum. The height difference should be 0.079–0.118 inch (2.0–3.0mm).
4. Install the front internal gear and rear planetary carrier into the forward clutch assembly.
5. Install the output shaft.
6. Push the output shaft slightly forward and install a new snapring. Check that the output shaft cannot be removed.
7. Apply petroleum jelly to the bearing and install it to the transmission case with the black surface facing toward the rear.
8. Install the parking gear.
9. Pull the output shaft slightly rearward and install a new snapring on it. Check that the output shaft will not move forward.
10. Install the front snapring, key, and speedometer drive gear on the output shaft. Secure the speedometer drive gear with the rear snapring.
11. Install a new gasket on the extension housing. Install a new O-ring on the speedometer driven gear and install it into the extension housing.
12. Install the rear sun gear into the front internal gear. The oil grooves in the rear sun gear must face forward.

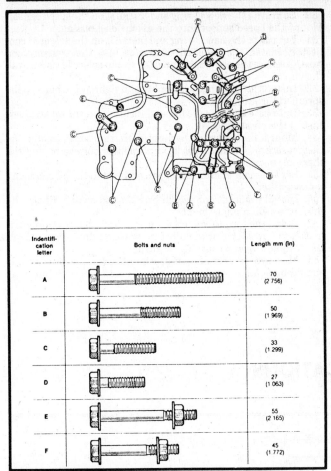

Indentifi-cation letter	Bolts and nuts	Length mm (In)
A		70 (2 756)
B		50 (1 969)
C		33 (1 299)
D		27 (1 063)
E		55 (2 165)
F		45 (1 772)

Valve body bolts and nuts installation positions and specifications

13. Check that the bearing and bearing race are installed correctly.
14. Install the front planetary carrier into the forward clutch assembly while rotating the forward clutch drum clockwise.
15. Install the reverse clutch, high clutch and front sun gear as an assembly into the transmission case.
16. Adjust the total endplay.
17. Measure height A and B using a vernier caliper and a straight edge; then, install the needle bearing on the oil pump and measure height C. Calculate the total endplay using the formular below.

Formular: $T1 = A-B-C-0.0039$ inch (.01mm)

$T1$: – Oil pump endplay

A: – Distance between the bearing race of the front side of the transmission case and the reverse clutch.

B: – Distance between the front side of the transmission case and the oil pump gasket.

C: – Distance between the upper surface of the needle bearing of the oil pump and the oil pump gasket contact surface.

0.1: – Amount the new oil pump gasket is compressed.

18. If the total endplay is not within specification, adjust by selecting and installing the proper bering race.
19. Adjust the reverse clutch endpaly. Install the thrust washer on the reverse clutch and measure height E, B and F using a vernier caliper and a straight edge. Calculate the reverse clutch endplay using the formula below.

Formular: $T2 = E-B-F-0.0039$ inch (.01mm)

$T2$: – Reverse clutch endplay

B: – Distance between the front side of the transmission case and the oil pump gasket.

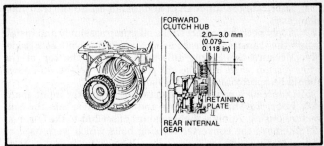

Checking forward clutch drum to forward clutch retaining plate height

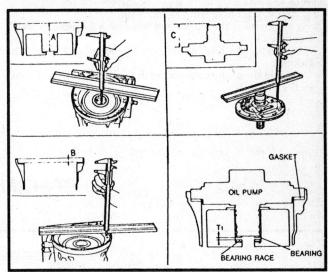

Checking total endplay

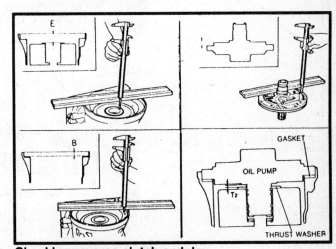

Checking reverse clutch endplay

E: – Distance between the thrust washer of front side of transmission case and the reverse clutch.

F: – Distance between the reverse clutch thrust washer contact surface of oil pump and the oil pump gasket contact surface.

0.1: – Amount the new oil pump gasket is compressed.

20. If the reverse clutch endplay is not within specification, adjust by selecting and installing the proper reverse clutch thrust washer.
21. Lubricate the brake band and band strut and install them into the transmission. Install a new anchor end bolt.

3–255

22. Lubricate the input shaft and install it into the transmission case.

23. Apply petroleum jelly to the oil pump assembly and install it into the transmission case using 2 convertor bolts as a guide.

24. Measure the height difference between the top of the transmission case and the oil pump. The height difference should be approximately 0.039 inch (1.0mm).

25. Lubricate a new O-ring and install it onto the input shaft.

26. Lubricate the new O-rings and install them into the converter housing. Apply a slight amount of sealant to the O-rings.

27. Remove the converter housing bolts which were used as the oil pump guide.

28. Install the converter housing onto the transmission case and tighten the retaining bolts evenly in a crisscross pattern. Torque the retaining bolts 45–47 ft. lbs. (61–64 Nm).

29. Adjust the brake band as followed:

   a. Tightening the anchor end bolt with a hex wrench 35–52 inch lbs. (3.9–5.9 Nm).

   b. Loosen the anchor end bolt 2.5 turns and install the locknut.

   c. Hold the anchor end bolt with the hex wrench and tighten the locknut.

30. Lubricate the new O-ring and install it on the speed sensor. Mount the speed sensor into the extension housing.

31. Lubricate the new O-ring and install it on the solenoid connector. Install the solenoid connector into the transmission case. Connect the solenoid connector to the solenoid and install the clip.

32. Install the valve body assembly and tighten the bolts to the specified torque value.

33. Lubricate the new O-ring and install it on the oil strainer. Install the oil strainer.

34. Mount the solenoid harness with the clips. Install the thermosensor. Connect the lockup solenoid connector and the thermosensor connector.

35. Set the magnet into the oil pan and install the oil pan using a new gasket.

36. Install the inhibitor switch bracket and switch. Check the inhibitor switch adjustment.

37. Stand the torque converter upright and fill it with approximately 2.1 qt. (2L) of automatic transmission fluid; then, install the torque converter into the transmission.

38. Measure the installation depth of the torque converter. It should have an approximate depth of 0.925 inch (23.5mm).

SPECIFICATIONS

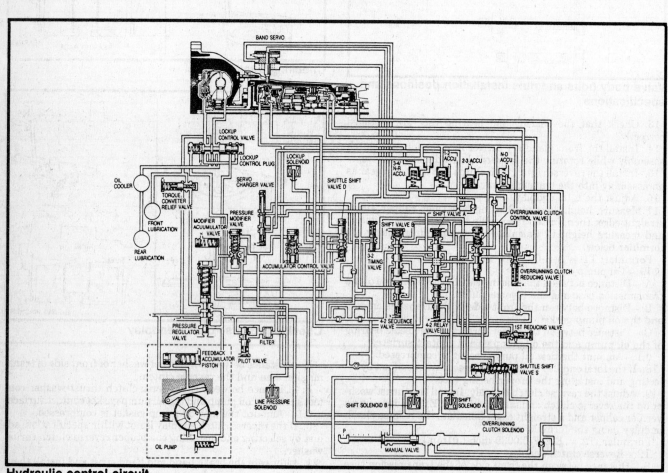

Hydraulic control circuit

TOTAL ENDPLAY SELECTIVE BEARING RACE SIZES

in.	mm
0.031	0.8
0.039	1.0
0.047	1.2
0.055	1.4
0.063	1.6
0.071	1.8
0.079	2.0

REVERSE CLUTCH RETAINING PLATE SIZES

in.	mm
0.185	4.6
0.189	4.8
0.197	5.0
0.205	5.2
0.213	5.4
0.220	5.6
0.228	5.8

LOW/REVERSE BRAKE RETAINING PLATE SIZES

in.	mm
0.339	8.6
0.346	8.8
0.354	9.0
0.362	9.2
0.370	9.4
0.378	9.6

BAND SERVO RETURN SPRING SPECIFICATION

	Outer Dia. in (mm)	Free Length in (mm)	No. of Coils	Wire Dia. in (mm)
Return spring A	1.350 (34.3)	1.795 (45.6)	3.0	0.091 (2.3)
Return spring B	1.587 (40.3)	2.118 (53.8)	3.0	0.091 (2.3)
Return spring C	1.087 (27.6)	1.169 (29.7)	3.2	0.102 (2.6)

HIGH CLUTCH RETAINING PLATE SIZES

in.	mm
0.118	3.0
0.126	3.2
0.134	3.4
0.142	3.6
0.150	3.8
0.157	4.0
0.165	4.2
0.173	4.4

FORWARD CLUTCH AND OVERRUNNING CLUTCH RETAINING PLATE SIZES

in.	mm
0.157	4.0
0.165	4.2
0.173	4.4
0.181	4.6
0.189	4.8
0.197	5.0
0.205	5.2

GENERAL SPECIFICATIONS

Item		Specifications
Torque converter stall torque ratio		2.000 : 1
Gear ratio	1st	3.027
	2nd	1.619
	3rd	1.000
	OD (4th)	0.694
	Reverse	2.272
Number of drive/ driven plates	Reverse clutch	2/2
	High clutch	4/7
	Forward clutch	6/6
	Overrunning clutch	3/5
	Low and reverse brake	6/6

ACCUMULATOR SPRING MEASUREMENT SPECIFICATIONS

	Outer Diameter in (mm)	Free Length in (mm)	No. of Coils	Wire Diameter in (mm)
N/D accumulator piston	0.681 (17.3)	1.772 (45.0)	9.0	0.091 (2.3)
1/2 accumulator piston	1.154 (29.3)	1.772 (45.0)	3.6	0.157 (4.0)
2/3 accumulator piston	0.787 (20.0)	2.598 (66.0)	11.4	0.138 (3.5)
3-4/N-R accumulator piston	0.681 (17.3)	2.299 (58.4)	12.3	0.091 (2.3)

UPPER VALVE BODY—SPRINGS SPECIFICATION

Spring	Outer Diameter in. (mm)	Free Length in. (mm)	No. of Coils	Wire Diameter in. (mm)
Shift valve B	0.276 (7.0)	0.984(25.0)	9.5	0.026 (0.65)
4-2 relay valve	0.274 (6.95)	1.146(29.1)	11.0	0.022 (0.55)
Shift valve A	0.276 (7.0)	0.984(25.0)	9.5	0.026 (0.65)
Overrunning clutch control valve	0.276 (7.0)	0.929(23.6)	7.9	0.024 (0.6)
Overrunning clutch reducing valve	0.276 (7.0)	1.383(35.14)	14.71	0.037 (0.95)
Shuttle shift valve S	0.236 (6.0)	1.051(26.7)	14.1	0.035 (0.9)
Pilot valve	0.358 (9.1)	1.012(25.7)	8.3	0.043 (1.1)
Lockup control valve	0.512 (13.0)	0.728(18.5)	3.5	0.030 (0.75)
Torque converter relief valve	0.354 (9.0)	1.272(32.3)	11.5	0.055 (1.4)
Pressure regulator valve	0.350 (8.9)	2.028(51.5)	18.7	0.055 (1.4)
Pressure modifier valve	0.268 (6.8)	1.258(31.95)	10.0	0.031 (0.8)
Accumulator control plug	0.413 (10.5)	0.669(17.0)	4.3	0.020 (0.5)
Shuttle shift valve D	0.236 (6.0)	1.043(26.5)	12.0	0.028 (0.7)
4-2 sequence valve	0.274 (6.95)	1.146(29.1)	11.0	0.022 (0.55)

LOWER VALVE BODY—SPRINGS SPECIFICATION

Spring	Outer Diameter in. (mm)	Free Length in. (mm)	No. of Coils	Wire Diameter in. (mm)
Modifier accumulator piston	0.386 (9.8)	1.201 (30.5)	8.8	0.051 (1.3)
1st reducing valve	0.266 (6.75)	1.0 (25.4)	12.5	0.030 (0.75)
3-2 timing	0.266 (6.75)	0.809 (20.55)	7.5	0.030 (0.75)
Servo charger valve	0.264 (6.7)	0.906 (23.0)	9.0	0.028 (0.7)

REVERSE CLUTCH ENDPLAY SELECTIVE THRUST WASHER SIZES

in.	mm
0.028	0.7
0.035	0.9
0.043	1.1
0.051	1.3
0.059	1.5
0.067	1.7
0.075	1.9

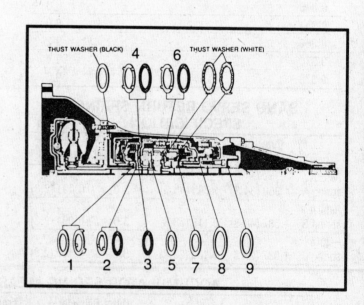

BEARING AND RACE OUTER DIAMETER SPECIFICATION
in. (mm)

	1	2	3	4	5	6	7	8	9
Bearing	1.850 (47.0)	2.087 (53.0)	2.087 (53.0)	3.071 (78.0)	2.087 (53.0)	3.071 (78.0)	2.323 (59.0)	3.075 (78.1)	2.520 (64.0)
Race	1.713 (43.5)	2.028 (51.5)	—	2.953 (75.0)	—	2.953 (75.0)	—	—	—

Section 3

N4AHL Transmission
Mazda

APPLICATION

1989 Mazda MPV

GENERAL DESCRIPTION

The N4A-HL automatic transmission is a 4 speed, hydraulically controlled transmission. This transmission consists of a torque converter, oil pump, 4 clutches, 2 brakes, 1 one-way clutches, 3 planetary gears and an electronic control system.

Transmission and Converter Identification

TRANSMISSION

The N4A-HL automatic transmission identification plate is attached to the right hand side of the transmission, adjacent to the solenoids electrical harness. This data plate provides the transmission model and serial number.

CONVERTER

The N4A-HL automatic transmission use a lockup converter. The torque converter consists of a pump, a turbine and a stator. The converter housing is filled with oil and is attached to the engine crankshaft by a flex plate and always rotates at engine speed.

Electronic Controls

The N4A-HL automatic transmission consists of the following electronic components:
- Overdrive off switch
- Kickdown and 4/3 switch
- Inhibitor switch
- Kickdown solenoid
- Overdrive cancel solenoid
- Lockup solenoid
- Oil pressure switch
- Kickdown relay
- 4AT control unit

Metric Fasteners

Metric tools are required to service this transmission. Due to the large number of alloy parts used in this transmission, torque specifications should be strictly observed. Before installing capscrews into aluminum parts, dip the bolts into clean transmission fluid as this will prevent the screws from galling the aluminum threads, thus causing damage.

Metric fastener dimensions are very close to the dimensions of the familiar inch system fasteners. For this reason replacement fasteners must have the same measurement and strength as the original fastener.

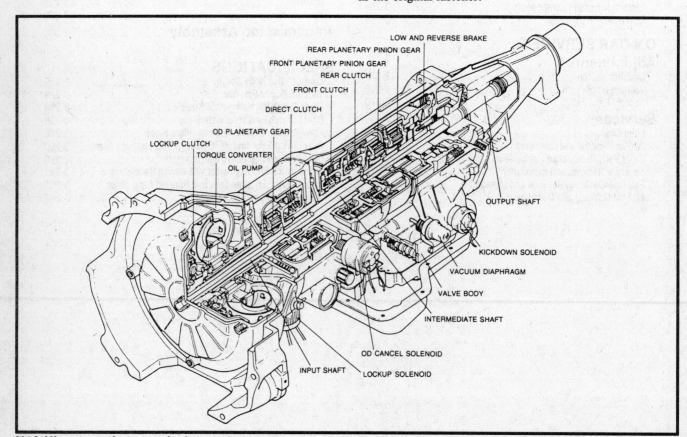

N4A-HL automatic transmission exploded view

Do not attempt to interchange metric fasteners for inch system fasteners. Mismatched or incorrect fasteners can cause damage to the automatic transmission unit and possible personal injury. Care should be taken to reuse fasteners in their original locations.

Capacity

The N4A-HL automatic transmission has a capacity of 7.9 qts. (7.5 liters).

Checking Fluid Level

1. Place the vehicle on a flat level surface. Apply the parking brake and block the drive wheels.
2. Start the engine and allow to run until normal operating temperature is reached.
3. With the engine idling, shift the selector lever from **P** to **L** and back again.
4. Check that the transmission fluid level is between the notches on the oil indicator gauge. If necessary, adjust the fluid level.

TROUBLE DIAGNOSIS

CHILTON'S THREE C's TRANSMISSION DIAGNOSIS

Condition	Cause	Correction
Engine does not start in N or P range	a) Selector lever and linkage b) Ignition switch and starter c) Inhibitor switch	a) Adjust the selector lever and linkage b) Repair or replace the ignition switch or starter c) Adjust or replace the inhibitor switch
Engine starts in ranges other than N, and P ranges	a) Selector lever and linkage b) Inhibitor switch	a) Adjust the selector lever and linkage b) Adjust or replace the inhibitor switch
Vehicle does not move in D range (moves in 1, 2 and R ranges)	a) Selector lever and linkage b) Line and governor pressure c) Control valve body d) One-way clutch	a) Adjust the selector lever and linkage b) Perform the line and governor pressure test c) Repair or replace the control valve body d) Replace the one-way clutch
Vehicle does not move in any range	a) Transmission fluid level b) Selector lever and linkage c) Line and governor pressure d) Control valve body e) Oil pump f) Direct clutch g) Parking gear	a) Adjust the transmission fluid level b) Adjust the selector lever and linkage c) Perform the line and governor pressure test d) Repair or replace the control valve body e) Repair or replace the oil pump f) Repair or replace the direct clutch g) Replace the parking gear
Slippage felt when accelerating	a) Transmission fluid level b) Selector lever and linkage c) Line and governor pressure d) Control valve body e) Oil pump	a) Adjust the transmission fluid level b) Adjust the selector lever and linkage c) Perform the line and governor pressure test d) Repair or replace the control valve body e) Repair or replace the oil pump
Vehicle moves in N range	a) Selector lever and linkage b) Control valve body c) Rear clutch	a) Adjust the selector lever and linkage b) Repair or replace the control valve body c) Repair or replace the rear clutch
Excessive creep	a) Engine idle speed or condition	a) Correct the engine idle speed or condition
Low maximum speed and poor acceleration	a) Transmission fluid level b) Selector lever and linkage c) Engine stall speed d) Line and governor pressure e) Control valve body f) Engine idle speed or condition g) 2nd brake band h) Low/reverse brake	a) Adjust the transmission fluid level b) Adjust the selector lever and linkage c) Correct the engine stall speed d) Perform the line and governor pressure test e) Repair or replace the control valve body f) Correct the engine idle speed or condition g) Replace the 2nd brake band h) Repair or replace the lower/reverse brake

CHILTON'S THREE C's TRANSMISSION DIAGNOSIS

Condition	Cause	Correction
Low maximum speed and poor acceleration	i) Direct clutch j) Front clutch k) Rear clutch	i) Repair or replace the direct clutch j) Repair or replace the front clutch k) Repair or replace the rear clutch
Does not shift from 1st to 2nd	a) Selector lever and linkage b) Vacuum diaphragm c) Kickdown switch or solenoid d) Control valve body e) Governor valve f) 2nd band servo g) Rear clutch h) 2nd brake band	a) Adjust the selector lever and linkage b) Adjust or replace the vacuum diaphragm c) Replace the kickdown switch or solenoid d) Repair or replace the control valve body e) Replace the governor valve f) Repair or replace the 2nd band servo g) Repair or replace the rear clutch h) Replace the 2nd brake band
Does not shift from 2nd to 3rd	a) Selector lever and linkage b) Vacuum diaphragm c) Kickdown switch or solenoid d) Control valve body e) Governor valve f) 2nd band servo g) Front clutch h) Hydraulic circuit	a) Adjust the selector lever and linkage b) Adjust or replace the vacuum diaphragm c) Replace the kickdown switch or solenoid d) Repair or replace the control valve body e) Replace the governor valve f) Repair or replace the 2nd band servo g) Repair or replace the front clutch h) Perform the line pressure test
Does not shift from 3rd to OD	a) Selector lever and linkage b) Vacuum diaphragm c) Kickdown switch or solenoid d) Control valve body e) Governor valve f) Overdrive band servo g) Overdrive off switch h) Overdrive cancel solenoid i) Direct clutch j) Overdrive brake band k) Overdrive cancel valve	a) Adjust the selector lever and linkage b) Adjust or replace the vacuum diaphragm c) Replace the kickdown switch or solenoid d) Repair or replace the control valve body e) Replace the governor valve f) Repair or replace the overdrive band servo g) Replace the overdrive switch h) Replace the overdrive cancel solenoid i) Repair or replace the direct clutch j) Replace the overdrive brake band k) Replace the overdrive cancel valve
Lockup does not occur in OD	a) Governor valve b) Overdrive band servo c) Lockup solenoid d) Overdrive brake band e) Lockup control valve	a) Replace the governor valve b) Repair or replace the overdrive band servo c) Replace the lockup solenoid d) Replace the overdrive brake band e) Replace the lockup control valve
Does not shift from OD to 3rd	a) Transmission fluid level b) Vacuum diaphragm c) Control valve body d) Governor valve e) Overdrive off switch f) Overdrive cancel solenoid g) Direct clutch h) Front clutch i) Overdrive brake band	a) Adjust the transmission fluid level b) Adjust or replace the vacuum diaphragm c) Repair or replace the control valve body d) Replace the governor valve e) Replace the overdrive off switch f) Replace the overdrive cancel solenoid g) Repair or replace the direct clutch h) Repair or replace the front clutch i) Replace the overdrive brake band
Does not shift from 3rd to 2nd or from OD to 2nd	a) Transmission fluid level b) Vacuum diaphragm	a) Adjust the transmission fluid level b) Adjust or replace the vacuum diaphragm

CHILTON'S THREE C's TRANSMISSION DIAGNOSIS

Condition	Cause	Correction
Does not shift from 3rd to 2nd or from OD to 2nd	c) Control valve body d) Governor valve e) 2nd band servo f) Front clutch g) Overdrive brake band h) 2nd brake band	c) Repair or replace the control valve body d) Replace the governor valve e) Repair or replace the 2nd band servo f) Repair or replace the front clutch g) Replace the overdrive brake band h) Replace the 2nd brake band
Does not shift from 2nd to 1st or from 3rd to 1st	a) Transmission fluid level b) Vacuum diaphragm c) Control valve body d) Governor valve e) 2nd band servo f) 2nd brake band g) One-way clutch	a) Adjust the transmission fluid level b) Adjust or replace the vacuum diaphragm c) Repair or replace the control valve body d) Replace the governor valve e) Repair or replace the 2nd band servo f) Replace the 2nd brake band g) Replace the one-way clutch
Does not kickdown when accelerator depressed in 3rd within kickdown range	a) Transmission fluid level b) Kickdown switch or solenoid c) Vacuum diaphragm d) Control valve body e) Governor valve f) 2nd brake band g) Hydraulic circuit	a) Adjust the transmission fluid level b) Replace the kickdown switch or solenoid c) Adjust or replace the vacuum diaphragm d) Repair or replace the control valve body e) Replace the governor valve f) Replace the 2nd brake band g) Perform the line pressure test
Does not kickdown when accelerator depressed in OD within kickdown range	a) Transmission fluid level b) Kickdown switch or solenoid c) Vacuum diaphragm d) Control valve body e) Governor valve f) Direct clutch g) Hydraulic circuit	a) Adjust the transmission fluid level b) Replace the kickdown switch or solenoid c) Adjust or replace the vacuum diaphragm d) Repair or replace the control valve body e) Replace the governor valve f) Repair or replace the direct clutch g) Perform the line pressure test
Excessive engine speed when accelerated in 3rd due to delayed kickdown	a) Transmission fluid level b) Selector lever and linkage c) Line and governor pressure d) Control valve body e) Governor valve f) Front clutch	a) Adjust the transmission fluid level b) Adjust the selector lever and linkage c) Perform the line or governor pressure test d) Repair or replace the control valve body e) Replace the governor valve f) Repair or replace the front clutch
Excessive engine speed when accelerated in OD due to delayed kickdown	a) Transmission fluid level b) Selector lever and linkage c) Line and governor pressure d) Control valve body e) Governor valve f) Overdrive brake band	a) Adjust the transmission fluid level b) Adjust the selector lever and linkage c) Perform the line or governor pressure test d) Repair or replace the control valve body e) Replace the governor valve f) Replace the overdrive brake band
Does not shift from 3rd to 2nd on D range to 2-range shift	a) Transmission fluid level b) Selector lever and linkage c) Control valve body d) Governor valve e) 2nd band servo f) Front clutch g) 2nd brake band h) Hydraulic circuit	a) Adjust the transmission fluid level b) Adjust the selector lever and linkage c) Repair or replace the control valve body d) Replace the governor valve e) Repair or replace the 2nd band servo f) Repair or replace the front clutch g) Replace the 2nd brake band h) Perform the line pressure test
Does not shift from 3rd to 1st on D range to 1-range shift	a) Transmission fluid level b) Selector lever and linkage	a) Adjust the transmission fluid level b) Adjust the selector lever and linkage

CHILTON'S THREE C's TRANSMISSION DIAGNOSIS

Condition	Cause	Correction
Does not shift from 3rd to 1st on D range to 1-range shift	c) Line and governor pressure	c) Perform the line and governor pressure test
	d) Control valve body	d) Repair or replace the control valve body
	e) Governor valve	e) Replace the governor valve
	f) 2nd band servo	f) Repair or replace the 2nd band servo
	g) Front clutch	g) Repair or replace the front clutch
	h) 2nd brake band	h) Replace the 2nd brake band
Shifts directly from 1st to 3rd	a) Transmission fluid level	a) Adjust the transmission fluid level
	b) Control valve body	b) Repair or replace the control valve body
	c) Governor valve	c) Replace the governor valve
	d) Overdrive brake band	d) Replace the overdrive brake band
	e) Hydraulic circuit	e) Perform the line pressure test
Shifts directly from 2nd to OD	a) Transmission fluid level	a) Adjust the transmission fluid level
	b) Control valve body	b) Repair or replace the control valve body
	c) Governor valve	c) Replace the governor valve
	d) Front clutch	d) Repair or replace the front clutch
	e) Hydraulic circuit	e) Perform the line pressure test
Shifts from 2nd to 1st, or 2nd to 3rd in 2 range	a) Selector lever and linkage	a) Adjust the selector lever and linkage
	b) Line pressure and governor	b) Perform the line and governor pressure test
	c) Control valve body	c) Repair or replace the control valve body
Shifts from 1st to 2nd, or 2nd to 3rd in 1 range	a) Selector lever and linkage	a) Adjust the selector lever and linkage
	b) Line pressure and governor	b) Perform the line and governor pressure test
	c) Hydraulic circuit	c) Perform the line pressure test
Transmission shifts to OD even when OD OFF switch depressed	a) Overdrive off switch	a) Replace the overdrive off switch
	b) Overdrive cancel solenoid	b) Replace the overdrive cancel solenoid
	c) Overdrive cancel valve	c) Replace the overdrive cancel valve
Vehicle surges in OD	a) Lockup solenoid	a) Replace the lockup solenoid
Little shift shock or excessive slippage while 1st to 2nd shifting	a) Transmission fluid level	a) Adjust the transmission fluid level
	b) Selector lever and linkage	b) Adjust the selector lever and linkage
	c) Vacuum diaphragm	c) Adjust or replace the vacuum diaphragm
	d) Line and governor pressure	d) Perform the line or governor pressure test
	e) Control valve body	e) Repair or replace the control valve body
	f) Overdrive band servo	f) Repair or replace the overdrive band servo
	g) 2nd brake band	g) Replace the 2nd brake band
Little shift shock or excessive slippage while 2nd to 3rd shifting	a) Transmission fluid level	a) Adjust the transmission fluid level
	b) Selector lever and linkage	b) Adjust the selector lever and linkage
	c) Vacuum diaphragm	c) Adjust or replace the vacuum diaphragm
	d) Line and governor pressure	d) Perform the line or governor pressure test
	e) Control valve body	e) Repair or replace the control valve body
	f) Overdrive band servo	f) Repair or replace the overdrive band servo
	g) Front clutch	g) Repair or replace the front clutch
Shift shock or excessive slippage while 3rd to OD shifting	a) Transmission fluid level	a) Adjust the transmission fluid level
	b) Selector lever and linkage	b) Adjust the selector lever and linkage
	c) Vacuum diaphragm	c) Adjust or replace the vacuum diaphragm
	d) Line and governor pressure	d) Perform the line or governor pressure test

CHILTON'S THREE C's TRANSMISSION DIAGNOSIS

Condition	Cause	Correction
Shift shock or excessive slippage while 3rd to OD shifting	e) Control valve body	e) Repair or replace the control valve body
	f) Overdrive band servo	f) Repair or replace the overdrive band servo
	g) Overdrive brake band	g) Replace the overdrive brake band
No shift shock or engine overruns when shifting 1st to 2nd	a) Transmission fluid level	a) Adjust the transmission fluid level
	b) Selector lever and linkage	b) Adjust the selector lever and linkage
	c) Vacuum diaphragm	c) Adjust or replace the vacuum diaphragm
	d) Engine idle speed or condition	d) Correct the engine idle speed or condition
	e) Engine stall speed	e) Correct the engine stall speed
	f) Control valve body	f) Repair or replace the control valve body
	g) 2nd brake band	g) Replace the 2nd brake band
	h) Oil pump	h) Repair or replace the oil pump
Engine overruns or slips when shifting OD to 3rd	a) Transmission fluid level	a) Adjust the transmission fluid level
	b) Vacuum diaphragm	b) Adjust or replace the vacuum diaphragm
	c) Line and governor pressure	c) Perform the line or governor pressure test
	d) Control valve body	d) Repair or replace the the control valve body
	e) 2nd band servo	e) Repair or replace the 2nd band servo
	f) Direct clutch	f) Repair or replace the direct clutch
	g) Front clutch	g) Repair or replace the front clutch
	h) Overdrive brake band	h) Replace the overdrive brake band
Excessive N range to D range shift shock	a) Engine idle speed or condition	a) Correct the engine idle speed or condition
	b) Vacuum diaphragm	b) Adjust or replace the vacuum diaphragm
	c) Line or governor pressure	c) Perform the line or governor pressure test
	d) Control valve body	d) Repair or replace the control valve body
	e) Rear clutch	e) Repair or replace the rear clutch
Excessive 1st to 2nd shift shock	a) Transmission fluid level	a) Adjust the transmission fluid level
	b) Vacuum diaphragm	b) Adjust or replace the vacuum diaphragm
	c) Engine stall speed	c) Correct the engine stall speed
	d) 2nd band servo	d) Repair or replace the 2nd band servo
	e) 2nd brake band	e) Replace the 2nd brake band
	f) Lockup control valve	f) Replace the lockup control valve
Excessive 2nd to 3rd shift shock	a) Vacuum diaphragm	a) Adjust or replace the vacuum diaphragm
	b) Line and governor pressure	b) Perform the line and governor pressure test
	c) Control valve body	c) Repair or replace the control valve body
	d) 2nd band servo	d) Repair or replace the 2nd band servo
	e) 2nd brake band	e) Replace the 2nd brake band
	f) Lockup control valve	f) Replace the lockup control valve
Excessive 3rd to OD shift shock	a) Vacuum diaphragm	a) Adjust or replace the vacuum diaphragm
	b) Line and governor pressure	b) Perform the line and governor pressure test
	c) Control valve body	c) Repair or replace the control valve body
	d) Overdrive brake band	d) Replace the overdrive brake band
	e) Overdrive cancel valve	e) Replace the overdrive cancel valve

CHILTON'S 3 C's TRANSMISSION DIAGNOSIS

Problem	Possible cause	Remedy
Transmission noisy in P and N ranges	a) Transmission fluid level b) Line and governor pressure c) Oil pump	a) Adjust the transmission fluid level b) Perform the line and governor pressure test c) Repair or replace the oil pump
Transmission noisy in D, 2, 1, and R ranges	a) Transmission fluid level b) Line and governor pressure c) Rear clutch d) Oil pump e) One-way clutch f) Planetary gear	a) Adjust the transmission fluid level b) Perform the line and governor pressure test c) Repair or replace the rear clutch d) Repair or replace the oil pump e) Replace the one-way clutch f) Replace the planetary gear

CLUTCH AND BRAKE APPLICATION

Range	Gear	Direct Clutch	Overdrive Band Servo	Front Clutch	Rear Clutch	2nd Band Servo	Low/Reverse Brake	One-way Clutch
P	—	Applied	Released ①	—	—	—	Applied	—
R	Reverse	Applied	Released ①	Applied	—	Released	Applied	—
N	—	Applied	Released ①	—	—	—	—	—
D	1st	Applied	Released ①	—	Applied	—	—	Applied
	2nd	Applied	Released ①	—	Applied	Applied	—	—
	3rd	Applied	Released ①	Applied	Applied	Released ①	—	—
	Overdrive	—	Applied	Applied	Applied	Released ①	—	—
2	—	Applied	Released ①	—	Applied	Applied	—	—
1	2nd	Applied	Released ①	—	Applied	Applied	—	—
	1st	Applied	Released ①	—	Applied	—	Applied	—

① Operates although the band servos remain deactivated because of the larger release pressure side area.
  Brake band does not operate.

STALL TEST EVALUATION

Condition		Possible cause
Above specification	In all ranges	Insufficient line pressure—Worn oil pump
		Insufficient line pressure—Oil leakage from oil pump, control valve, and/or transmission case
		Insufficient line pressure—Stuck pressure regulator valve
		Insufficient line pressure—Direct clutch slipping
	In D, 2, and 1 ranges	Rear clutch slipping
	In D range only	One-way clutch slipping
	In 2 range only	Brake band slippping
	In R range only	Low and reverse brake slipping
		Front clutch slipping
		Perform road test to determine if this is caused by low and reverse brake or front clutch, as follows: a) Effective engine braking in 1 range . . . . . Front clutch b) No engine braking in 1 range . . . . . Low and reverse brake
Within specification		All shift control elements within transmission are functioning normally
Below specification		Engine out of tune
		One-way clutch slipping within torque converter

LAG TEST EVALUATION

Condition		Possible Cause
N → D shift	More than specification	Insufficient line pressure
		Rear clutch slipping
		One-way clutch slipping
	Less than specification	Excessive line pressure
N → R shift	More than specification	Insufficient line pressure
		Low and reverse brake slipping
		Front clutch slipping
	Less than specification	Stuck orifice check valve
		Excessive line pressure

SPECIFIED LINE PRESSURE

Range	Pressure psi (kPa)	
	Idle	Stall
D, 1	43–57 (294–392)	164–192 (1,128–1,324)
2	164–192 (1,128–1,324)	164–192 (1,128–1,324)
R	68–111 (471–765)	314–357 (2,168–2,462)

Hydraulic Control System
Diagnosis Tests

STALL TEST

1. Check the engine coolant, engine oil and transmission fluid levels.
2. Warm the engine until the transmission fluid temperature is within 122–176°F (50–80°C).
3. Apply the parking brake and block the drive wheels.
4. Connect a tachometer to the engine. Start the engine and check that the idle speed is 750–790 rpm.

NOTE: Step 5 must be performed within 5 seconds.

5. Shift the selector lever to the **R** range. Depress the brake pedal firmly and gradually depress the accelerator. Read and note the engine speed as soon as the engine speed becomes constant, then release the accelerator pedal.
6. Shift the selector lever to the **N** range and run the engine at idle for at least 1 minute. This 1 minute period is performed to cool the transmission fluid and prevent oil degeneration.
7. Perform the stall tests in the same manner for **D** and **2** and **1** ranges.

NOTE: Be certain to provide adequate cooling time between individual range stall tests.

8. The standard stall speed is 1800–2200 rpm.

TIME LAG TEST

If the selector lever is shifted while the engine is idling, there will be a certain time lapse or time lag before shock is felt. The following steps measure this time lag for checking condition of the front, rear and one-way clutches; low/reverse brake and orifice check valve.

1. Check the engine coolant, engine oil and transmission fluid levels.
2. Warm the engine until the transmission fluid temperature is within 122–176°F (50–80°C).
3. Apply the parking brake and block the drive wheels.
4. Connect a tachometer to the engine.
5. Start the engine and check that the idle speed is 750–790 rpm.
6. Shift the selector lever from **N** to **D** range.
7. With the use of a stop watch, measure the time it takes from shifting until shock is felt.
8. Shift the selector lever to **N** range and run the engine at idle speed for at least 1 minute.
9. Perform the test in the same manner for **N** to **R**.

NOTE: Make 3 measurements for each test and take the average value.

The specified time lag is as follow:
N to D range — 0.5–1.0 second
N to R range — 0.5–1.0 seconds

OIL PRESSURE

1. Check the engine coolant, engine oil and transmission fluid levels.
2. Warm the engine until the transmission fluid temperature is within 122–176°F (50–80°C).
3. Apply the parking brake and block the drive wheels.
4. Connect a tachometer to the engine. Connect oil pressure adaptor tool 49H019002 or equivalent to the line pressure inspection hole.
5. Start the engine and check that the idle speed is 750–790 rpm.
6. Shift the selector lever to the **D** range and read the oil pressure at idle.

NOTE: Step 7 must be performed within 5 seconds.

7. Depress the brake pedal firmly and gradually depress the

LINE PRESSURE TEST EVALUATION

Condition		Possible Cause
Below standard	In all ranges	Worn oil pump
		Fluid leakage from the oil pump, control valve, or transmission case
		Stuck pressure regulator valve
		Fluid leakage from the direct clutch and/or OD band servo release side
	In D, 1, and 2 ranges	Fluid leakage from the rear clutch or governor hydraulic circuit, or both
	In R range only	Fluid leakage from the low and reverse brake hydraulic circuit
Excessive line pressure at idle		Leaking or disconnected vacuum hose
		Leaking vacuum diaphragm

VEHICLE SHIFT POINT SPECIFICATIONS

Range	Throttle Condition (Manifold Vacuum)	Shifting	Vehicle speed mph (km/h)
D	Full throttle	$D_1 \rightarrow D_2$	30–34 (49– 55)
		$D_2 \rightarrow D_3$	56–60 (91– 97)
		$D_3 \rightarrow OD$	65–69 (105–111)
		$OD \rightarrow D_3$	33–37 (53– 59)
		$D_3 \rightarrow D_2$	53–56 (85– 91)
		$D_2 \rightarrow D_1$	23–27 (37– 43)
	Half throttle 7.87 inHg (200 mmHg)	$D_1 \rightarrow D_2$	15–19 (24– 30)
		$D_2 \rightarrow D_3$	24–28 (39– 45)
		$D_3 \rightarrow OD$	40–44 (65– 71)
		Lockup ON (OD)	43–47 (70– 76)
		Lockup OFF (OD)	42–45 (67–73)
		$OD \rightarrow D_3$	18–22 (29– 35)
		$D_3 \rightarrow D_2$	11–15 (18– 24)
		$D_2 \rightarrow D_1$	6– 9 (9– 15)
	Closed throttle	$D_1 \rightarrow D_2$	7–11 (11– 17)
		$D_2 \rightarrow D_3$	16–20 (26– 32)
		$D_3 \rightarrow OD$	23–27 (37– 43)
		$OD \rightarrow D_3$	13–17 (21– 27)
		$D_3 \rightarrow D_2$	7–11 (11– 17)
		$D_2 \rightarrow D_1$	7–11 (11– 17)
1	—	$1_2 \rightarrow 1_1$	24–28 (39– 45)

accelerator. Read the oil pressure as soon as the engine speed becomes constant, then release the accelerator pedal.

8. Shift the selector lever to the **N** range and run the engine at idle for at least 1 minute. This 1 minute period is performed to cool the transmission fluid and prevent oil degeneration.

9. Read the line pressure at idle and engine stall speeds for each range in the same manner.

GOVERNOR PRESSURE TEST

1. Check the engine coolant, engine oil and transmission fluid levels.

2. Warm the engine until the transmission fluid temperature is within 122–176°F (50–80°C).

3. Connect oil pressure adaptor tool 49H075406 or equivalent to the governor pressure output hole. Route the pressure gauge inside the vehicle.

4. Road test the vehicle in **D** range and read the governor pressure at the speeds listed below.

19 mph (30 km/h) – 13–21 psi (88–147 kpa)
34 mph (55 km/h) – 26–37 psi (177–255 kpa)
53 mph (85 km/h) – 54–68 psi (373–471 kpa)

5. If not within specification, check the following:
   a. Fluid leakage from the line pressure hydraulic circuit
   b. Fluid leakage from the governor pressure hydraulic circuit
   c. Defective or stuck governor valve

LINE PRESSURE CUTBACK POINT TEST

1. Check the engine coolant, engine oil and transmission fluid levels.

2. Warm the engine until the transmission fluid temperature is within 122–176°F (50–80°C).

3. Connect an oil pressure adaptor tool 49H075406 or equivalent to the governor pressure output hole and the line pressure output hole. Route the pressure gauges inside the vehicle.

4. Disconnect and plug the vacuum hose to the vacuum diaphragm. Connect a vacuum pump to the vacuum diaphragm and route inside the vehicle.

5. Start the engine and check that the idle speed is 750–790 rpm.

6. Gradually accelerate the vehicle in **D** range; then, read the governor pressure at the point where the line pressure drops. The governor pressure should be 18–27 psi (128–186 kpa).

7. Apply 7.87 in. Hg. and repeat Step 6. The governor pressure should be 11–20 psi (78–137 kpa).

8. If the cutback point test is not within specification, the cause may be due to a missing diaphragm rod, rod length incorrect or a stuck valve in the control valve.

ROAD TEST

1. Road test the vehicle in **D** range and release the overdrive OFF switch.

2. Accelerate the vehicle with half and full throttle opening.

3. Check that 1/2, 2/3 and 3/overdrive upshifts, downshifts and lockup are obtained. The shift points must correspond with the vehicle shiftpoint specifications chart.

Electronic System Components

OVERDRIVE OFF SWITCH

Testing

1. Remove the steering column cover.

4AT CONTROL UNIT—TERMINAL VOLTAGE

Terminal	Connected to	Voltage	Condition
1A (Output)	OD cancel solenoid	Approx. 12 V	Solenoid Off; OD gear position
		Below 1.5V	Solenoid on; 1st, 2nd, and 3rd gear positions in forward ranges; P, R, and N ranges
1B (Ground)	—	Below 1.5V	—
1C (Input)	Kickdown relay	Approx. 12V	Kickdown relay off; other than conditions below
		Below 1.5V	Kickdown relay on; kickdown switch on (throttle opening more than 7/8)
1D (Output)	Lockup solenoid	Approx. 12V	Solenoid off; Non-lockup
		Below 1.5V	Solenoid on; Lockup
1E (Input)	OD off switch	Approx. 12V	OD off switch depressed (on): OD not available
		Below 1.5V	OD off switch released (off): OD available
1F (Input)	Cruise control unit	Approx. 12V	Normal conditions
		Below 1.5V	Set or Resume switch on, or vehicle speed 8 km/h (5 mph) lower than preset speed (Driving vehicle: cruise control operation)
1G	—	—	—
1H (Battery power)	Battery	Approx. 12V	Ignition switch on
		Below 1.5V	Ignition switch off
1I (Input)	Speed sensor	1.5–7V	During driving
		Approx. 7V or below 1.5V	vehicle stopped
1J (Input)	Oil pressure switch	Approx. 12V	Switch off: 1st, 2nd, and 3rd gear positions in forward ranges; P, R, and N ranges
		Below 1.5V	Switch on: OD gear position
1K (Input)	4–3 switch	Approx. 12V	Switch on: throttle opening 6/8–8/8
		Below 1.5V	Switch off: other than conditions above
1L (Input)	Engine control unit	Approx. 12V	20 terminal of engine control unit voltage approx. 12V; normal condition
		Below 1.5V	20 terminal of engine control unit voltage below 1.5V; throttle fully-open position

2. Turn the ignition switch **ON**.

3. Check the voltate at the terminals. With the switch depressed there should be approximately 12 volts.

4. With the switch released there should be approximately 1.5 volts.

INHIBITOR SWITCH

Testing

1. Disconnect the negative battery cable.
2. Raise the vehicle and support it safely.
3. Disconnect the control linkage from the manual shaft.
4. Disconnect the inhibitor switch connector.
5. Check for continuity at the following terminals in each gear positions as follow:

P – terminal C to D.
R – terminal A to B.
N – terminal C to D.

6. If not correct, adjust the inhibitor switch.
7. If correct, check or adjust the selector lever and control linkage.

KICKDOWN AND 4/3 SWITCH

Testing

1. Turn the ignition switch **ON**.
2. Check the kickdown switch voltage from terminal **C** to ground.
3. With the accelerator pedal fully depressed, there should be approximately 12 volts.
4. With the accelerator pedal depressed up to $7/8$ of the way, the voltage should be below 1.5 volts.
5. If not correct, disconnect the kickdown switch connector. Check for continuity between terminals **C** and **D** with the tip of the switch depressed 0.236–0.256 in. (6.0–6.5mm).
6. If not correct, replace the switch. If correct, adjust the switch.
7. Check the 4/3 switch for continuity between terminals **A** and **B** when the tip of the switch is depressed 0.14–0.18 in. (3.5–4.5mm).
8. If not correct, replace the switch. If correct, adjust the switch.

Adjustment

1. Disconnect the connector. Loosen the locknut and back the

switch out fully.

2. Depress the accelerator pedal fully and hold it.

3. With the accelerator pedal fully down, turn the kickdown switch clockwise until it turns **ON** (clicking sound is heard). Then, turn the switch ¼ turn further clockwise.

4. Tighten the locknut and release the accelerator pedal.

KICKDOWN SOLENOID

Testing

1. Raise and support the vehicle safely.

2. Drain approximately 1.1 qts. (1.0L) of transmission fluid from the transmission.

3. Remove the kickdown solenoid. Check that the kickdown solenoid clicks when 12 volts is applied to it.

4. If not, replace the kickdown solenoid.

5. Lubricate the seal and install the kickdown solenoid.

6. Lower the vehicle and adjust the transmission fluid level.

OVERDRIVE CANCEL SOLENOID

Testing

1. Raise the vehicle and support it safely.

2. Drain the transmission fluid and remove the overdrive cancel solenoid.

3. Check that the solenoid closes when 12 volts is applied to it and opens when it is cut off.

4. If not, replace the overdrive cancel solenoid.

5. Lubricate the seal and install the solenoid.

6. Lower the vehicle and adjust the transmission fluid level.

LOCKUP SOLENOID

Testing

1. Raise the vehicle and support it safely.

2. Drain the transmission fluid and remove the lockup solenoid.

3. Check that the solenoid closes when 12 volts is applied to it and opens when it is cut off.

4. If not, replace the lockup solenoid.

5. Lubricate the seal and install the solenoid.

6. Lower the vehicle and adjust the transmission fluid level.

OIL PRESSURE SWITCH

Testing

1. Raise the vehicle and support it safely.

2. Drain the transmission fluid and remove the oil pressure switch.

3. Check the switch for continuity by applying air pressure (less than 7.1 psi) to the switch opening. Continuity should be indicated.

4. With more that 42.7 psi of air pressure, there should be no continuity.

5. If not, replace the lockup solenoid.

6. Lubricate the seal and install the switch.

7. Lower the vehicle and adjust the transmission fluid level.

4AT CONTROL UNIT

Testing

1. Turn the ignition switch **ON**.

2. Check the 4AT control unit terminal voltage and compare with the terminal voltage chart.

3. If the voltages are not correct, replace the component(s), wiring and/or the 4AT control unit.

ON CAR SERVICES

Adjustments

INHIBITOR SWITCH

1. Shift the selector lever to **N** range.

2. Loosen the inhibitor switch mounting bolts.

3. Remove the screw on the switch body and move the inhibitor switch so that the screw hole is aligned with the small hole inside the switch. Check the alignment by inserting a pin with an approximate diameter of 0.079 in. (2.0mm) through the holes.

4. Tighten the switch mounting bolt, remove the alignment pin and install the screw in the switch body.

VACUUM DIAPHRAGM

1. Remove the vacuum diaphragm, rod and O-ring from the transmission case.

2. Measure the dimension N indicated with tool 49G032355 or equivalent and select the proper diaphragm rod from the specification chart.

3. Install the correct vacuum diaphragm rod, O-ring and vacuum diaphragm.

OVERDRIVE BAND SERVO

1. Remove the overdrive band servo cover and gasket.

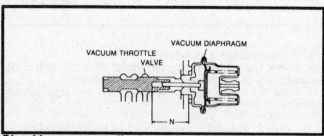

Checking vacuum diaphragm rod length

2 Loosen the locknut and torque the piston stem 104–130 inch lbs. (12–15 Nm).

3. Loosen the stem 2 turns; then, tighten the locknut 11–30 ft. lbs. (15–40 Nm).

4. Install the overdrive band servo cover using a new gasket. Tighten the retaining bolts 43–61 inch lbs. (4.9–6.9 Nm).

2ND BAND SERVO

1. Remove the valve body assembly.

2. Loosen the locknut and tighten the piston stem 109–126 inch lbs. (12–14 Nm).

3. Loosen the stem 3 turns; then, hold the stem and tighten the locknut 11–29 ft. lbs. (15–39 Nm).

4. Install the valve body assembly.

Services

FLUID CHANGE

The conditions under which the vehicle is operated is the main consideration in determining how often the transmission fluid should be changed. Different driving conditions result in different transmission fluid temperatures. These temperatures affect change intervals.

If the vehicle is driven under severe conditions, change the transmission fluid every 15,000 miles. If the vehicle is not used under severe conditions, change the fluid and replace the filter every 30,000 miles.

Do not overfill the transmission. It takes about a pint of automatic transmission fluid to raise the level from the **ADD** to the **FULL** mark on the transmission indicator dipstick. Overfilling the unit can cause damage to the internal components of the automatic transmission.

OIL PAN

Removal and Installation

1. Raise and support the vehicle safely.
2. Place a drain pan under the transmission oil pan. Clean the area around the oil pan to prevent entry of dust into the unit. Remove the oil pan attaching bolts from the front and side of the pan.
3. Loosen the rear pan attaching bolts approximately 4 turns.
4. Carefully pry the transmission oil pan loose and allow the fluid to drain.
5. Remove the remaining bolts. Remove the oil pan, gasket and magnet. If required, remove the filter.
6. Thoroughly clean the oil pan and transmission gasket surfaces. Dry with compress air.
7. Install the magnet into the oil pan. Install the oil pan using a new gasket and alternately tighten the retaining bolts to 52–69 inch lbs. (5.9–7.8 Nm).
8. Lower the vehicle and add the proper amount of transmission fluid.

VACUUM DIAPHRAGM

Removal and Installation

1. Disconnect the negative battery cable. Raise and support the vehicle safely.
2. Loosen the oil pan retaining bolts and drain approximately 1.1 qts. (1.0L) of the transmission fluid.
3. Disconnect the vacuum hose and remove the vacuum diaphragm, O-ring and vacuum diaphragm rod.
4. Check that the vacuum diaphragm rod moves when vacuum is applied to the diaphragm. If not, replace the vacuum diaphragm.
5. Lubricate the new O-ring and install it on the vacuum diaphragm. Lubricate the diaphragm rod and vacuum diaphragm. Install them into the transmission case. Connect the vacuum hose.
6. Lower the vehicle and connect the negative battery cable. Add the proper amount of transmission fluid.

EXTENSION HOUSING AND PARKING MECHANISM

Removal and Installation

1. Disconnect the negative battery cable. Raise and support the vehicle safely. Drain the transmission fluid.
2. Mark the propeller shaft flanges for correct reassembly. Push a rag into the double offset joint to hold the propeller shaft straight and prevent damaging the boot. Remove the propeller shaft.
3. Install tool 49S120440 or equivalent into the extension housing to prevent oil leakage.
4. Disconnect the speedometer cable.
5. Support the transmission with a transmission jack and remove the upper and lower mounts.
6. Remove the extension housing and gasket.

To install:

7. Install a new gasket on the transmission case and install the extension housing. Tighten and torque the retaining bolts 14–18 ft. lbs. (20–25 Nm).
8. Install the transmission upper and lower mounts.
9. Remove the transmission jack. Install the speedometer cable and propeller shaft. Align the marks on the propeller shaft flanges.
10. Lower the vehicle and connect the negative battery cable. Add the proper amount of transmission fluid.

GOVERNOR

Removal and Installation

1. Disconnect the negative battery cable. Raise and support the vehicle safely.
2. Loosen the oil pan retaining bolts and drain the transmission fluid.
3. Remove the extension housing and speedometer drive gear.
4. Remove the snapring. Remove the governor and parking gear assembly from the output shaft; then, separate the governor from the parking gear.

To install:

5. Assemble the governor to the parking gear; then, install it to the output shaft. Secure it using a new snapring.
6. Install the speedometer drive gear and extension housing.

OIL SEAL

Removal and Installation

1. Disconnect the negative battery cable. Raise and support the vehicle safely.
2. Mark the propeller shaft flanges for correct reassembly; then, remove the propeller shaft.
3. Pry the oil seal from the extension housing.

To install:

4. Lubricate the new oil seal lip and install the seal squarely into the extension housing using a plastic mallet.
5. Install the propeller shaft. Align the marks on the propeller shaft flanges.
6. Lower the vehicle and connect the negative battery cable. Check and adjust the transmission fluid level.

CONTROL VALVE BODY

Removal and Installation

1. Disconnect the negative battery cable. Raise and support the vehicle safely.
2. Loosen the oil pan retaining bolts and drain the transmission fluid.
3. Disconnect the vacuum hose and remove the vacuum diaphragm, O-ring and vacuum diaphragm rod.
4. Remove the kickdown solenoid, oil pan and gasket.
5. Remove the oil strainer and O-ring.
6. Remove the valve body retaining bolts and carefully remove the control valve body assembly.

To install:

7. Position the control valve in the transmission and install the mounting bolts. Check that the manual valve and manual valve shaft are assembled correctly. Torque the mounting bolts

8–11 ft. lbs. (11–15 Nm).

8. Lubricate the oil strainer O-ring and install it on the oil strainer. Install the oil strainer.

9. Install the oil pan using a new gasket. Torque the oil pan retaining bolts 52–69 inch lbs. (5.9–7.8 Nm).

10. Lubricate the new O-rings and install them to the kickdown solenoid and vacuum diaphragm. Install the kickdown solenoid and vacuum diaphragm into the transmission case and connect the vacuum hose.

11. Lower the vehicle and adjust the fluid level.

12. Reconnect the negative battery cable, start the engine and check for leaks. Check the transmission fluid level.

REMOVAL AND INSTALLATION

TRANSMISSION REMOVAL

1. Disconnect the negative battery cable. Raise and support the vehicle safely.

2. Drain the transmission fluid into a suitable container.

3. Disconnect and tag all electrical connectors. Remove the speedometer cable.

4. Remove the front exhaust pipe and heat insulator.

5. Mark the propeller shaft flanges to aid during reassemble. Remove the propeller shaft and install tool 49S120440 or equivalent to prevent oil leakage.

6. Remove the transmission filler tube and change counter assembly.

7. Remove the torque convertor inspection cover. Remove the converter to flexplate retaining bolts.

8. Remove the starter motor and exhaust pipe bracket from the transmission.

9. Remove the transmission cooler oil pipes and gusset plates from the lower converter housing.

10. Support the transmission with a transmission jack and remove the transmission mounting bolts.

11. Remove the transmission lower and upper mounts and let it drop downward. Disconnect the vacuum pipe.

12. Remove the transmission assembly and mount in a suitable holding fixture.

TRANSMISSION INSTALLATION

1. Set the transmission on the transmission jack and install the exhaust pipe brackets.

2. Raise the transmission into place and install the mounting bolts. Torque the mounting bolts to the proper specifications.

3. Connect the oil cooler pipes. Install the transmission mount crossmember.

4. Install the torque converter to flex plate retaining bolts. Torque the retaining bolts 27–40 ft. lbs. (36–54 Nm).

5. Install the undercover. Install the starter motor and brackets. Torque the mounting bolts 27–38 ft. lbs. (37–52 Nm).

6. Install the filler tube, vacuum pipe and brackets to the transmission.

7. Connect the inhibitor switch, kickdown solenoid, oil pressure switch, overdrive cancel solenoid and lockup solenoid connectors. Connect the speedometer cable.

8. Install the insulator and exhaust pipe.

9. Align the mating marks and install the propeller shaft. Torque the retaining bolts 36–43 ft. lbs. (49–59 Nm).

10. Install and tighten the center bearing support assembly. Install the change counter assembly.

11. Lower the vehicle and connect the negative battery cable.

12. Fill the transmission with the proper fluid. Start the engine and check for leaks. Recheck the fluid level.

BENCH OVERHAUL

Before Disassembly

Cleanliness is an important factor in the overhaul of the transmission unit. Before opening up this unit, the entire outside of the transmission assembly should be cleaned, preferable with a high pressure washer such as a car wash spray unit. Dirt entering the transmission internal parts will negate all the time and effort spent on the overhaul. During inspection and reassembly all parts should be thoroughly cleaned with solvent then dried with compress air. Wiping cloths and rags should not be used to dry parts since lint will find its way into the valve body passages.

Wheel bearing grease, long used to hold thrust washers and lube parts, should not be used. Lube seals with clean transmission fluid and use ordinary unmedicated petroleum jelly to hold the thrust washers and to ease the assembly of seals, since it will not leave a harmful residue as grease often will. Do not use solvent on neoprene seals, friction plates if they are to be reused, or thrust washers. Be wary of nylon parts if the transmission failure was due to failure of the cooling system. Nylon parts exposed to water or antifreeze solutions can swell and distort and must be replaced.

Before installing bolts into aluminum parts, always dip the threads into clean transmission fluid. Antiseize compound can also be used to prevent bolts from galling the aluminum and seizing. Always use a torque wrench to keep from stripping the threads. Take care when installing new O-rings, especially the smaller O-rings. The internal snaprings should be expanded and the external rings should be compressed, if they are to be reused. This will help insure proper seating when installed.

Converter Inspection

Check the outer part of the converter for damage and cracks. Replace it if there is any problem. Also, check for rust on the pilot and base. If there is any, remove it completely.

1. Completely drain all transmission fluid from the converter.

2. Pour approximately ½ qt. of solvent into the converter. Shake the converter to clean the inside; then, drain the solvent from the converter.

3. Clean the inside of the converter with compress air so that the inside is perfectly empty. Rinse the converter with clean automatic transmission fluid.

Transmission Disassembly

1. Properly support the transmission in a holding fixture in an upright position. Remove the oil pan and gasket.

2. Examine any material found in the pan or on the magnet to determine the condition of the transmission. If large amounts of material are found, replace the torque converter and carefully check the transmission for the cause.

3. Remove the governor pressure pipe, kickdown solenoid, vacuum diaphragm, oil pressure switch, overdrive cancel solenoid and lockup solenoid.

4. Remove the inhibitor switch and speedometer driven gear. Remove the torque converter.

5. Remove the control valve body retaining bolts. Mark the

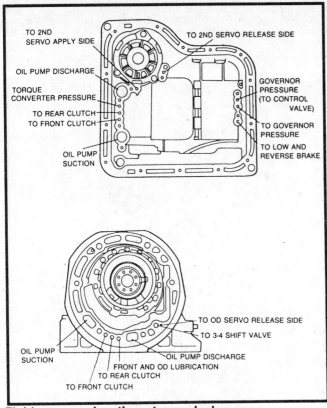

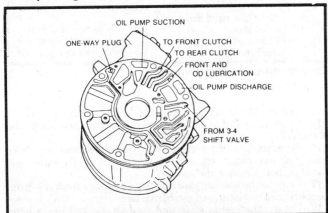

Fluid passage location – transmission case

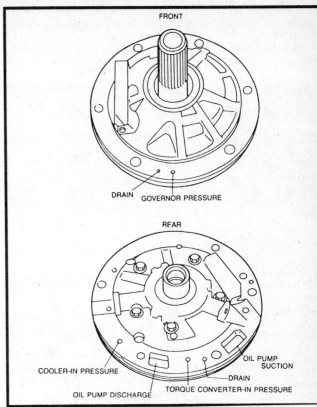

Fluid passage location – oil pump

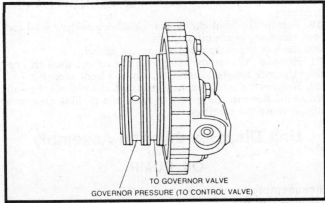

Fluid passage location – overdrive case

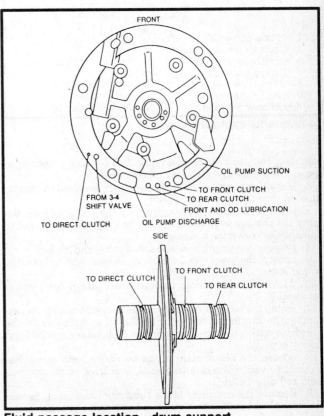

Fluid passage location – drum support

Fluid passage location – parking gear (oil distributor)

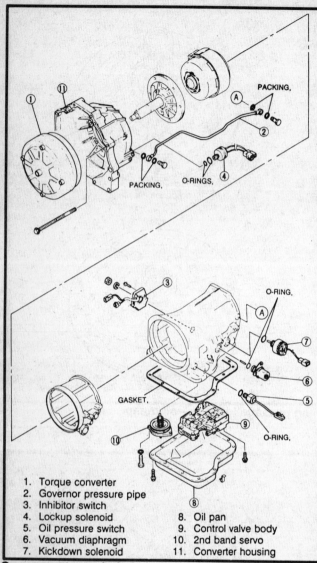

1. Torque converter
2. Governor pressure pipe
3. Inhibitor switch
4. Lockup solenoid
5. Oil pressure switch
6. Vacuum diaphragm
7. Kickdown solenoid
8. Oil pan
9. Control valve body
10. 2nd band servo
11. Converter housing

Components exploded view

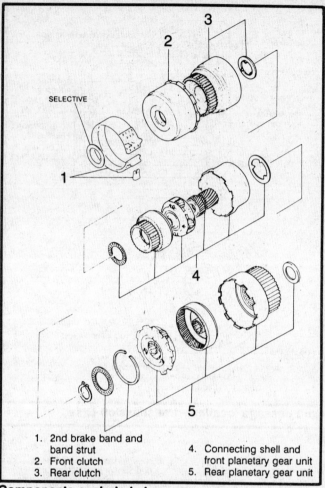

1. 2nd brake band and band strut
2. Front clutch
3. Rear clutch
4. Connecting shell and front planetary gear unit
5. Rear planetary gear unit

Components exploded view

retaining bolts so they can be reinstalled in their proper locations. The retaining bolts are different sizes.

6. Mark the converter housing, overdrive case and the transmission case for proper reassembly.

7. Remove the converter housing from the overdrive case. Remove the O-rings from the converter housing. Be careful not to damage the converter housing.

8. Remove the overdrive band servo cover and gasket.

9. Loosen the overdrive band servo locknut and tighten the piston stem.

10. Mark the overdrive case and oil pump for proper reassembly.

11. Install the oil pump puller tool and remove the oil pump assembly. Be careful when removing the oil pump to avoid the overdrive connection shell, sun gear and planetary carrier from falling out.

12. Loosen the piston stem of the overdrive band servo. Remove the overdrive connecting shell, overdrive planetary gear unit and direct clutch.

13. Remove the overdrive brake band and band strut. Secure the brake band ends with a wire clip to prevent the brake lining from cracking or peeling due to over-stretching.

14. Remove the bearing races, bearing and thrust washer.

15. Loosen the 2nd band servo locknut and tighten the piston stem.

16. Separate the drum support, accumulator and overdrive case from the transmission case by tapping it lightly with a soft faced mallet. Remove the gasket.

17. Remove the bearing race and thrust washer from the drum support, accumulator and overdrive case.

18. Loosen the piston stem and remove the 2nd brake band and band strut. Secure the brake band ends with a wire clip to prevent the brake lining from cracking or peeling due to over-stretching.

19. Remove the front clutch, rear clutch, connecting shell and front planetary gear unit as a unit.

20. Remove the extension housing and gasket.

21. Remove the rear snapring from the output shaft and remove the speedometer drive gear, key and front snapring.

22. Remove the rear planetary gear unit and pull out the output shaft. Remove the governor valve and parking gear as a unit. Remove the bearings.

Unit Disassembly and Assembly

OIL PUMP

Disassembly

1. Loosen the oil pump cover mounting bolts evenly and re-

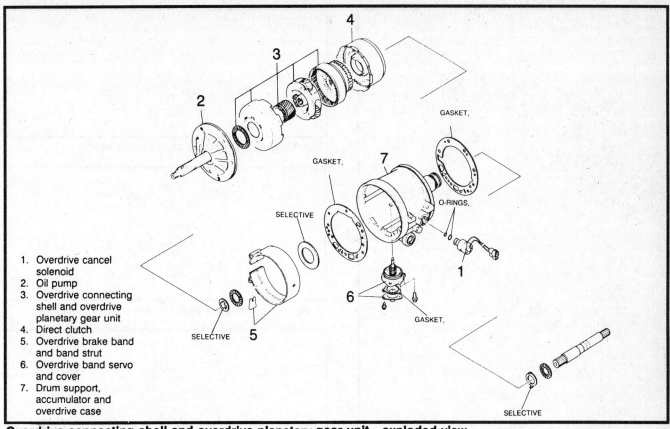

1. Overdrive cancel solenoid
2. Oil pump
3. Overdrive connecting shell and overdrive planetary gear unit
4. Direct clutch
5. Overdrive brake band and band strut
6. Overdrive band servo and cover
7. Drum support, accumulator and overdrive case

Overdrive connecting shell and overdrive planetary gear unit – exploded view

move the oil pump cover from the oil pump housing.

2. Mark the inner and outer gear positions. Remove the gears from the housing.

Inspection

1. Measure the clearance between the outer gear teeth tip and the cresent. The standard clearance is 0.0055–0.0083 (0.14–0.21mm). The maximum clearance should not exceed 0.0098 (0.25mm).

2. Measure the clearance between the gears and the pump cover. The standard clearance is 0.0008–0.0016 (0.02–0.04mm). The maximum clearance should not exceed 0.0031 (0.08mm).

3. Measure the clearance between the outer gear and the housing. The standard clearance is 0.0020–0.0079 (0.05–0.20mm). The maximum clearance should not exceed 0.0098 (0.25mm).

4. If any measurement is not within specification, replace the oil pump assembly.

5. Measure the control valve spring and compare with the following specifications:
   a. Coil Outer diameter – 0.217 in. (5.5mm)
   b. Free length – 1.012 in. (25.7mm)
   c. Coil thickness – 0.028 in. (0.7mm)
   d. No. of coil – 16.5

6. If the control valve spring is not within specification, replace the spring.

Assembly

1. Lubricate the control valve, spring and plug and install them into the oil pump housing. Tap in a new roll pin.

2. Lubricate the new seal and install it into the oil pump housing.

3. Assemble tools 49SO19001, 49SO19002 and 49SO19003 or their equivalent in a vise.

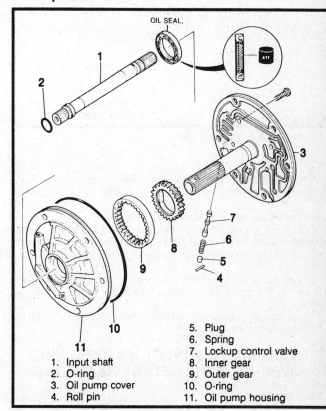

1. Input shaft
2. O-ring
3. Oil pump cover
4. Roll pin
5. Plug
6. Spring
7. Lockup control valve
8. Inner gear
9. Outer gear
10. O-ring
11. Oil pump housing

Oil pump exploded view

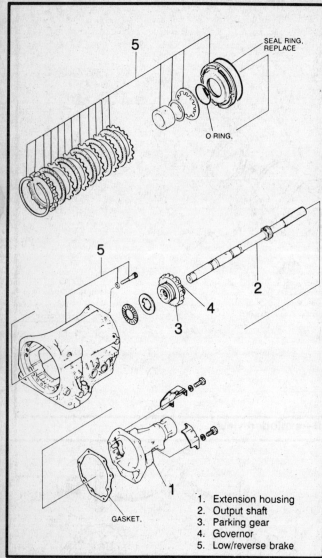

Components exploded view

1. Extension housing
2. Output shaft
3. Parking gear
4. Governor
5. Low/reverse brake

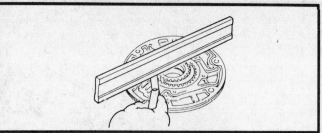

Checking gear to pump cover clearance

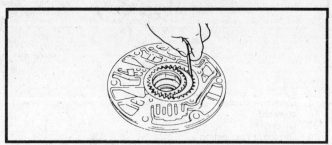

Checking outer gear teeth to crescent clearance

Checking outer gear to housing clearance

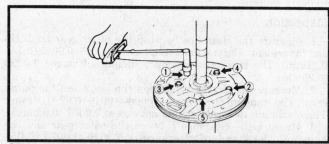

Oil pump mounting bolts torque sequence

4. Lubricate the new O-ring and place it on the pump cover. Set the pump housing on the assembled tools. Lubricate the inner and outer gears and install them in the pump housing with their matching marks toward the pump cover.

5. Set the pump cover on the assembled tools and install alignment pins (tool 49SO19004 or equivalent). Install the retaining bolts and torque in sequence to 52–69 inch lbs. (5.9–7.8 Nm).

6. Lubricate the input shaft and a new O-ring and install the O-ring on the input shaft. Install the input shaft into the oil pump.

7. Set the oil pump on the torque converter and check that the pump turns smoothly.

OVERDRIVE CONNECTING SHELL AND OVERDRIVE PLANETARY GEAR UNIT

Disassembly

1. Remove the bearing, overdrive connecting shell, sun gear and planetary carrier.

2. Remove the bearing race, bearing, internal gear and overdrive clutch hub.

Inspection

1. Measure the clearance between the pinion washer and the overdrive planetary pinion carrier. The standard clearance is 0.008–0.028 in. (0.2–0.7mm). The maximum clearance should not exceed 0.031 in. (0.8mm).

2. If the clearance is not within specification, replace the planetary pinion carrier.

3. Inspect the bearing and race for scoring, scratches, damage or rough rotation.

4. Inspect the individual gear teeth for damage, wear, or cracks.

Assembly

1. Lubricate the overdrive clutch hub and the internal gear and assemble them with the snapring.
2. Apply petroleum jelly to the bearing and install it into the overdrive clutch hub.
3. Apply petroleum jelly to the bearing race and install it into the overdrive planetary pinion carrier.
4. Lubricate the overdrive planetary pinion carrier and install it into the internal gear.
5. Install the snapring onto the sun gear. The grooved side of the sun gear is the front.
6. Lubricate the sun gear and install it into the overdrive planetary pinion carrier.

DIRECT CLUTCH

Disassembly

1. Remove the direct clutch snapring, selective retaining plate, drive and driven plates and dish plate.
2. Using an appropriate spring compressor, depress the piston spring retainer only enough to remove the snapring; then, remove the snapring.
3. Remove the spring retainer and springs.
4. Install the direct clutch drum onto the drum support along with the seal rings and remove the piston by applying compress air (57 psi maximum) to the oil passage.

Inspection

1. Measure the drive plates facing thickness in 3 places and determine the average of the 3 reading.
2. The standard thickness is 0.063 in. (1.6mm). The minimum thickness should not exceed 0.055 in. (1.4mm).
3. If not within specification, replace the drive plates.
4. Measure the return springs and compare with the following specifications:
   a. Coil Outer diameter—0.315 in. (8.0mm)
   b. Free length—1.201 in. (30.5mm)
   c. Coil thickness—0.051 in. (1.3mm)
   d. No. of coil—14.5
5. If not within specification, replace the return spring.
6. Apply compress air (57 psi maximum) through the oil hole opposite the return spring side of the clutch piston. There should be no air leakage.

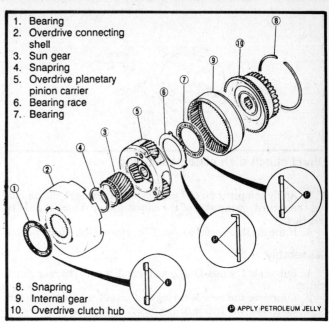

1. Bearing
2. Overdrive connecting shell
3. Sun gear
4. Snapring
5. Overdrive planetary pinion carrier
6. Bearing race
7. Bearing
8. Snapring
9. Internal gear
10. Overdrive clutch hub

Ⓟ APPLY PETROLEUM JELLY

Overdrive connecting shell and overdrive planetary gear unit—exploded view

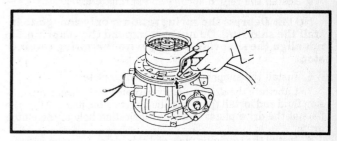

Removing the direct clutch piston or checking piston operation

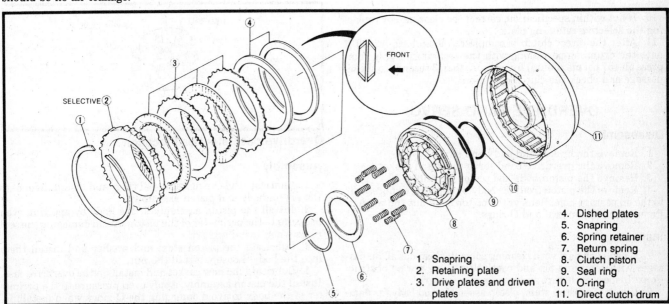

1. Snapring
2. Retaining plate
3. Drive plates and driven plates
4. Dished plates
5. Snapring
6. Spring retainer
7. Return spring
8. Clutch piston
9. Seal ring
10. O-ring
11. Direct clutch drum

Direct clutch—exploded view

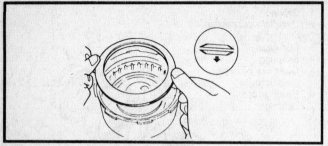

Direct clutch dish plate positioning

7. Apply compress air (57 psi maximum) through the oil hole on the return spring side of the clutch piston. There should be air flow.

8. If the air flow is not as specified, replace the clutch piston.

Assembly

1. Lubricate the new O-ring and install it onto the rear clutch drum.

2. Lubricate the new seal ring and install it onto the piston.

3. Lubricate the inside of the direct clutch drum.

4. Install the clutch piston in the direct clutch drum by apply pressure to the perimeter of the piston. Turn the piston evenly and gradually to avoid damaging the seal rings when installing.

5. Install the return springs and spring retainer.

NOTE: Depress the spring retainer only enough to install the snapring. Do not over expand the snapring. Do not align the snapring end gap with the spring retainer stop.

6. Install the snapring. Install the dish plate.

7. Lubricate the drive and driven plates with clean transmission fluid and install them into the direct clutch drum. Align the flats of the drive plates with the lubrication hole of the clutch drum.

8. Install the retaining plate and side plate. Align the flat portion of the retaining plate with the lubrication hole of the clutch drum. Install the snapring.

9. Measure the clearance between the retaining plate and the snapring. The standard clearance is 0.063–0.071 in. (1.6–1.8mm).

10. If not within specification, correct the clearance by replacing the selective retaining plate.

11. After the direct clutch is completely assembled, install it onto the drum support along with the seal rings. Apply compress air (57 psi maximum) for no more than 3 seconds to the oil passage and check the clutch operation.

OVERDRIVE BAND SERVO

Disassembly

1. Remove the brake band and band strut.
2. Remove the overdrive band servo cover and gasket.
3. Remove the piston body and piston assembly.
4. Remove the piston from the body by applying compress air to the oil passage hole. Remove the piston stem nut and washer. Remove the piston seal and O-rings.

Inspection

1. Clean each part with cleaning solvent, clean out all oil passages with compress air and check that there are no obstructions. Inspect each part and replace if necessary.
2. Check the piston stem, piston assembly and body for damage or wear.
3. Check for cracking or pealing of the brake band facing.

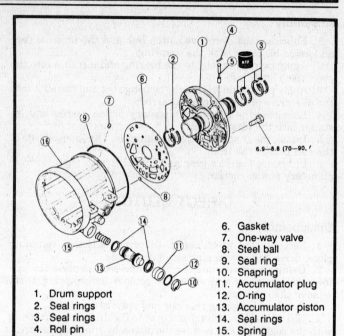

6.9—8.8 (70—90, '

1. Drum support	6. Gasket
2. Seal rings	7. One-way valve
3. Seal rings	8. Steel ball
4. Roll pin	9. Seal ring
5. Overdrive cancel valve	10. Snapring
	11. Accumulator plug
	12. O-ring
	13. Accumulator piston
	14. Seal rings
	15. Spring
	16. Overdrive case

Drum support, accumulator and overdrive case—exploded view

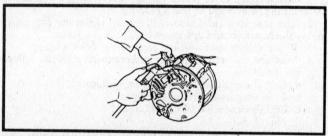

Removing the accumulator piston assembly or checking the piston operation

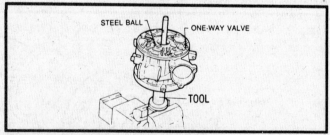

STEEL BALL   ONE-WAY VALVE

TOOL

Overdrive case steel ball location

Assembly

1. Lubricate the O-rings and seal rings and install them onto the piston body and piston assembly.

2. Install the piston assembly in the body by applying even pressure to the perimeter of the piston. Avoid damaging the seal rings when installing.

3. Lubricate the piston stem and washer and install them into the body. Loosely install the nut.

4. Lubricate the new gasket and install on the overdrive case. Install the piston assembly. Apply even pressure to the perimeter of the body to avoid damaging the O-rings when installing.

5. Apply compress air through the oil passage and check that the piston stem moves toward the brake band.

DRUM SUPPORT, ACCUMULATOR AND OVERDRIVE CASE

Disassembly

1. Make matching marks on the overdrive case and the drum support for proper reassembly. Remove the drum support. Remove the sealing rings from the drum support.
2. Remove the overdrive cancel valve roll pin and remove the valve.
3. Remove the drum support gasket. Remove the one-way valve from the overdrive case.
4. Remove the accumulator piston snapring and O-ring. Place a finger over the accumulator piston bore and remove the accumulator plug, seal rings and spring by applying compress air through the oil passage.

Inspection

1. Clean each part with cleaning solvent, clean out all oil passages with compress air and check that there are no obstructions. Inspect each part and check all clearances, replace if necessary.
2. Check the drum support and case for cracks.
3. Check the oil passage, gasket and plug for damage.
4. Measure the clearance between the seal ring and seal ring groove of the drum support. The standard clearance should be 0.0016–0.0063 in. (0.04–0.16mm). The maximum clearance should not exceed 0.016 in. (0.40mm).
5. If the clearance is not within specification, replace the drum support.
6. Measure the return spring and compare with the following specifications:
   a. Coil Outer diameter—0.585 in. (14.85mm)
   b. Free length—1.563 in. (39.7mm)
   c. Coil thickness—0.071 in. (1.8mm)
   d. No. of coil—9.3
7. If not within specification, replace the return spring.

Assembly

1. Lubricate the seal rings and install them onto the accumulator piston.
2. Lubricate the spring and accumulator piston and install them into the overdrive case.
3. Lubricate the new O-ring and install it on the accumulator plug. Install the plug and snapring.
4. Apply compress air (57 psi maximum) for no more than 3 seconds to the oil passage and check the accumulator operation.
5. Lubricate the overdrive cancel valve and install it into the drum support. Then, tap a new roll pin into place.
6. Lubricate the new seal ring and install it on the drum support.
7. Mount holding tool 49S0190A0 or equivalent into a vise and set the oil pump on it.
8. Lubricate the overdrive case and mount it on the oil pump. Install the steel ball and the one-way valve. Lubricate the new seal rings and install them on the drum support.
9. Lubricate the drum support and install it, using a new gasket, on the overdrive case. Align the matching marks. Install the alignment pins 49S019004 or equivalent; then, tighten the drum support mounting bolts 61–71 inch lbs. (6.9–8.8 Nm).

2ND BAND SERVO

Disassembly

1. Remove the piston assembly mounting bolts.
2. Remove the piston assembly by applying compress air through the oil passage.
3. Remove the piston stem nut and washer. Remove the piston assembly from the body. Remove the seals and O-rings.

Inspection

1. Clean each part with cleaning solvent, clean out all oil passages with compress air and check that there are no obstructions. Inspect each part and replace if necessary.
2. Check the piston stem, piston assembly and body for damage or wear.
3. Measure the return spring and compare with the following specifications:
   a. Coil thickness—0.138 in. (3.5mm)
   b. Free length—1.524 in. (38.7mm)
4. Check for cracking or pealing of the brake band facing.

Assembly

1. Lubricate the new O-ring and seal rings and install them onto the piston assembly.
2. Lubricate the piston assembly and body and press the assembly into the body. Apply even pressure to the perimeter of the body to avoid damaging the O-rings when installing.
3. Lubricate the piston stem and washer and install them into the body. Loosely tighten the nut.
4. Lubricate the return spring and install it into the transmission case. Install the piston assembly. Apply even pressure to the perimeter of the body to avoid damaging the O-rings when installing.
5. Install the piston assembly mounting bolts and torque 61–78 inch lbs. (6.9–8.8 Nm).

FRONT CLUTCH

Disassembly

1. Remove the snapring from the front clutch unit.
2. Remove the retaining plate, drive and driven plates and dished plates.
3. Compress the spring retainer using an appropriate tool and remove the snapring. Remove the spring retainer and springs.
4. Position the front clutch drum on the drum support along with the seal rings. Remove the piston by applying compress air (57 psi maximum) to the oil passage.

Inspection

1. Check the spring retainer for deformation.
2. Check for damage or worn drive plate facing, snapring or return springs.
3. Measure the drive plates facing thickness in 3 places and determine the average of the 3 reading.
4. The standard thickness is 0.063 in. (1.6mm). The minimum thickness should not exceed 0.055 in. (1.4mm).
5. If not within specification, replace the drive plates.
6. Measure the return springs and compare with the following specifications:
   a. Coil Outer diameter—0.315 in. (8.0mm)
   b. Free length—1.201 in. (30.5mm)
   c. Coil thickness—0.051 in. (1.3mm)
   d. No. of coil—14.5
7. If not within specification, replace the return spring.
8. Apply compress air (57 psi maximum) through the oil hole opposite the return spring side of the clutch piston. There should be no air leakage.
9. Apply compress air (57 psi maximum) through the oil hole on the return spring side of the clutch piston. There should be air flow.
10. If the air flow is not as specified, replace the clutch piston.

Assembly

1. Lubricate the new O-ring and install it onto the front clutch drum.
2. Lubricate the new seal ring and install it onto the piston.
3. Lubricate the inside of the front clutch drum.

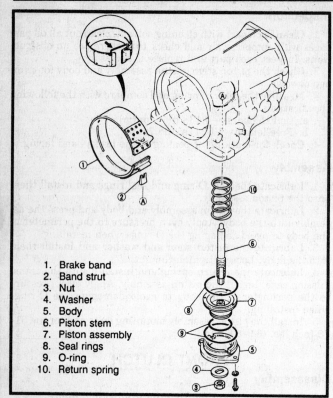

1. Brake band
2. Band strut
3. Nut
4. Washer
5. Body
6. Piston stem
7. Piston assembly
8. Seal rings
9. O-ring
10. Return spring

2nd band servo — exploded view

4. Install the clutch piston in the front clutch drum by apply pressure to the perimeter of the piston. Turn the piston evenly and gradually to avoid damaging the seal rings when installing.

5. Install the return springs and spring retainer.

NOTE: Depress the spring retainer only enough to install the snapring. Do not over expand the snapring. Do not align the snapring end gap with the spring retainer stop.

6. Install the snapring. Install the dish plates; then, install the driven plates and drive plates. Start with a driven plate, then alternate drive-driven-drive-driven. Align the flats of the drive plates with the lubrication hole of the clutch drum.

7. Install the retaining plate with the step facing upward. Align the flat portion of the retaining plate with the lubrication hole of the clutch drum. Install the snapring.

8. Measure the clearance between the retaining plate and the snapring. The standard clearance is 0.063–0.071 in. (1.6–1.8mm).

9. If not within specification, correct the clearance by replacing the selective retaining plate.

10. After the front clutch is completely assembled, install it onto the drum support along with the seal rings. Apply compress air (57 psi maximum) for no more than 3 seconds to the oil passage and check the clutch operation.

REAR CLUTCH

Disassembly

1. Remove the bearing race from the rear clutch drum. Remove the rear clutch snapring, retaining plate, drive and driven plates and dished plate.

2. Compress the spring retainer using an appropriate tool and remove the snapring. Remove the spring retainer and springs.

3. Set the rear clutch drum on the drum support along with

the seal rings and remove the piston by applying compress air (57 psi maximum) to the oil passage.

Inspection

1. Check the spring retainer for deformation.

2. Check for damage or worn drive plate facing, snapring or return springs.

3. Measure the drive plates facing thickness in 3 places and determine the average of the 3 reading.

4. The standard thickness is 0.063 in. (1.6mm). The minimum thickness should not exceed 0.055 in. (1.4mm).

5. If not within specification, replace the drive plates.

6. Measure the return springs and compare with the following specifications:
    a. Coil Outer diameter — 0.315 in. (8.0mm)
    b. Free length — 1.201 in. (30.5mm)
    c. Coil thickness — 0.051 in. (1.3mm)
    d. No. of coil — 14.5

7. If not within specification, replace the return spring.

8. Apply compress air (57 psi maximum) through the oil hole opposite the return spring side of the clutch piston. There should be no air leakage.

9. Apply compress air (57 psi maximum) through the oil hole on the return spring side of the clutch piston. There should be air flow.

10. If the air flow is not as specified, replace the clutch piston.

Assembly

1. Lubricate the O-ring and install it in the rear clutch drum.

2. Lubricate the seal-ring and install it onto the piston.

3. Lubricate the inside of the rear clutch drum and install the piston. Apply even pressure to the perimeter of the piston to avoid damaging the seal-rings when installing.

4. Install the springs and spring retainer.

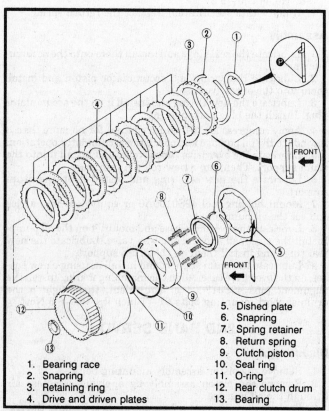

1. Bearing race
2. Snapring
3. Retaining ring
4. Drive and driven plates
5. Dished plate
6. Snapring
7. Spring retainer
8. Return spring
9. Clutch piston
10. Seal ring
11. O-ring
12. Rear clutch drum
13. Bearing

Rear clutch — exploded view

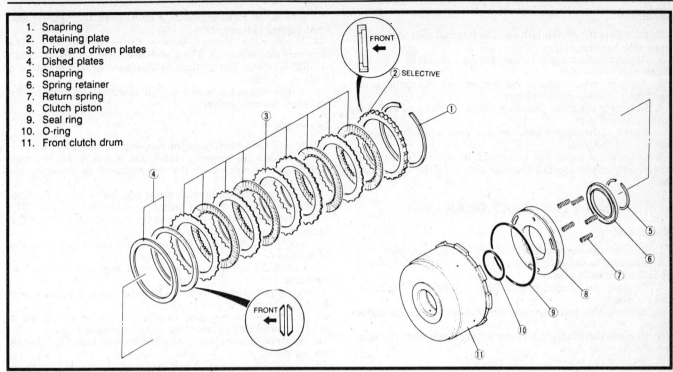

1. Snapring
2. Retaining plate
3. Drive and driven plates
4. Dished plates
5. Snapring
6. Spring retainer
7. Return spring
8. Clutch piston
9. Seal ring
10. O-ring
11. Front clutch drum

FRONT
② SELECTIVE

FRONT

Front clutch — exploded view

NOTE: Depress the spring retainer only enough to install the snapring. Do not over expand the snapring. Do not align the snapring end gap with the spring retainer stop.

5. Install the snapring. Install the dish plates; then, install the driven plates and drive plates. Start with a driven plate, then alternate drive-driven-drive-driven. Align the flats of the drive plates with the lubrication hole of the clutch drum.

6. Install the retaining plate with the step facing upward. Align the flat portion of the retaining plate with the lubrication hole of the clutch drum. Install the snapring.

7. Measure the clearance between the retaining plate and the snapring. The standard clearance is 0.031–0.059 in. (0.8–1.5mm).

8. If the clearance is not within specification, replace the dished plate, drive and driven plates and retaining plate.

9. Set the rear clutch on the drum support along with the seal rings. Apply compress air (57 psi maximum) for no more than 3 seconds to the oil passage and check the clutch operation.

10. Apply petroleum jelly to the bearing race and install it on the rear clutch drum.

CONNECTING SHELL AND FRONT PLANETARY GEAR UNIT

Disassembly

1. Remove the bearing race from the rear clutch hub.
2. Disassemble the rear clutch hub from the internal gear by removing the snapring.
3. Remove the bearing and race from the front planetary carrier.
4. Remove the snapring from the sun gear. Pay close attention to the front and rear directions of the sun gear.

Inspection

1. Check the snaprings for wear.

1. Bearing race
2. Connecting shell
3. Front sun gear
4. Snapring
5. Front planetary pinion carrier
6. Bearing race
7. Bearing
8. Bearing
9. Snapring
10. Rear clutch hub
11. Internal gear

Ⓟ APPLY PETROLEUM JELLY

Connecting shell and front planetary gear unit — exploded view

2. Check the individual gear teeth for damage, wear or cracks.

3. Check for rotation, damage or wear of the bearing and front carrier pinion gear.

4. Measure the clearance between the pinion washer and the planetary pinion carrier. The standard clearance is 0.008–0.028 in. (0.2–0.7mm). The maximum clearance should not exceed 0.031 in. (0.8mm).

5. If the clearance is not within specification, replace the planetary pinion carrier.

Assembly

1. Lubricate the clutch hub and the internal gear. Assemble them with the snapring.
2. Apply petroleum jelly to the bearing and install it on the clutch hub.
3. Apply petroleum jelly to the bearing race and install it on the front planetary pinion carrier.
4. Lubricate the front planetary pinion carrier and install it in the internal gear.
5. Install the snapring onto the sun gear with the grooved side toward the front.
6. Lubricate the sun gear and install it into the front planetary pinion carrier. Install the assemble into the connecting shell.

REAR PLANETARY GEAR UNIT

Disassembly

1. Remove the bearing from the rear planetary carrier.
2. Remove the snapring and the rear planetary pinion carrier from the connecting drum.
3. Remove the internal gear and drive flange from the connecting drum.
4. Remove the bearing race and bearing from the drive flange.
5. Remove the snapring and connecting drum from the one-way clutch outer race.
6. Remove the one-way clutch assembly.

Inspection

1. Check the snaprings for wear.
2. Check the individual gear teeth for damage, wear or cracks.

3. Check for rotation, damage or wear of the bearing and front carrier pinion gear.
4. Measure the clearance between the pinion washer and the planetary pinion carrier. The standard clearance is 0.008–0.028 in. (0.2–0.7mm). The maximum clearance should not exceed 0.031 in. (0.8mm).
5. If the clearance is not within specification, replace the planetary pinion carrier.

Assembly

1. Install the snapring in the one-way clutch outer race.
2. Lubricate the one-way clutch and install it into the one-way clutch outer race with the side indicated by the arrow toward the front.
3. Lubricate the connecting drum and install it into the one-way clutch outer race; then, install the snapring.
4. Lubricate the drive flange and the internal gear. Install the flange into the internal gear. Install the snapring.
5. Apply petroleum jelly to the bearing and install it on the drive flange.
6. Install the internal gear and drive flange into the connecting drum.
7. Apply petroleum jelly to the bearing race and install it into the rear planetary pinion carrier.
8. Lubricate the rear planetary pinion carrier and install it into the connecting drum; then, install the snapring.
9. Apply petroleum jelly to the bearing and install it into the bearing race.
10. Check the one-way clutch operation. It should freewheel clockwise only and lockup counterclockwise.

LOW/REVERSE BRAKE

Disassembly

1. Remove the snapring from the low/reverse brake. Remove

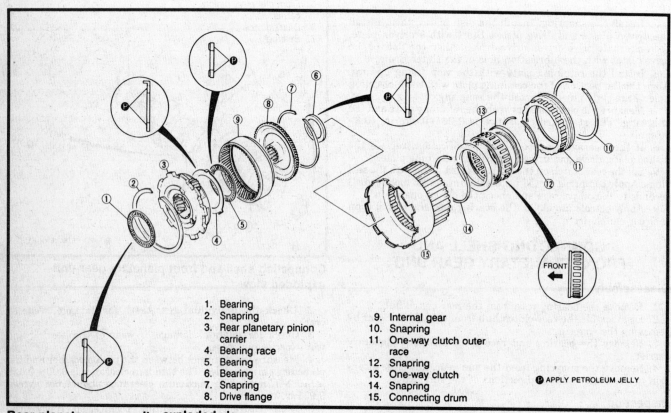

1. Bearing
2. Snapring
3. Rear planetary pinion carrier
4. Bearing race
5. Bearing
6. Bearing
7. Snapring
8. Drive flange
9. Internal gear
10. Snapring
11. One-way clutch outer race
12. Snapring
13. One-way clutch
14. Snapring
15. Connecting drum

Ⓟ APPLY PETROLEUM JELLY

Rear planetary gear unit – exploded view

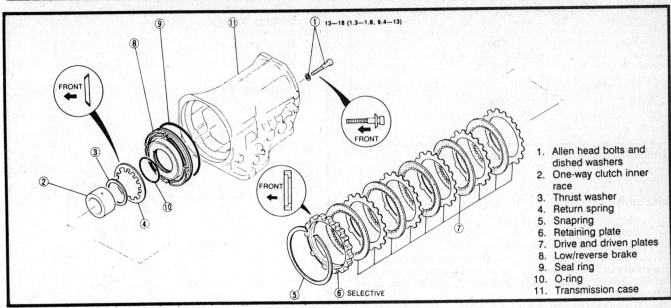

1. Allen head bolts and dished washers
2. One-way clutch inner race
3. Thrust washer
4. Return spring
5. Snapring
6. Retaining plate
7. Drive and driven plates
8. Low/reverse brake
9. Seal ring
10. O-ring
11. Transmission case

Low/reverse brake – exploded view

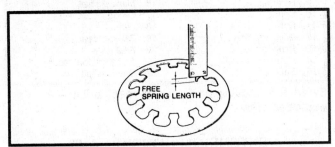

Checking low/reverse brake return spring free length

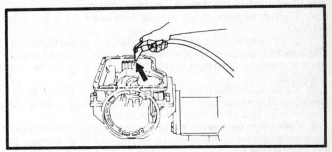

Checking piston operation – low/reverse brake

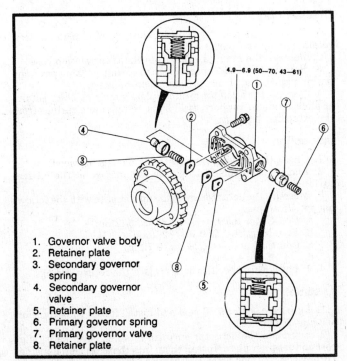

1. Governor valve body
2. Retainer plate
3. Secondary governor spring
4. Secondary governor valve
5. Retainer plate
6. Primary governor spring
7. Primary governor valve
8. Retainer plate

Governor assembly – exploded view

the retaining plate, drive plates and driven plates.

2. Remove the Allen head bolts and dished washers from the rear of the transmission case.

3. Remove the one-way clutch inner race, thrust washer and piston return spring.

4. Apply compress air to the oil passage and remove the low/reverse brake piston.

Inspection

1. Check the snapring, driven plates and the one-way clutch inner race for wear.

2. Measure the drive plates facing thickness in 3 places and determine the average of the 3 reading.

3. The standard thickness is 0.063 in. (1.6mm). The minimum thickness should not exceed 0.055 in. (1.4mm).

4. If not within specification, replace the drive plates.

5. Measure the return spring free length. The spring free length should be 0.209–0.244 in. (5.3–6.2mm).

6. If the spring free length is not within specification, replace the return spring.

7. Apply compress air (57 psi maximum) through the oil hole opposite the return spring side of the clutch piston. There should be no air leakage.

8. Apply compress air (57 psi maximum) through the oil hole on the return spring side of the clutch piston. There should be air flow.

9. If the air flow is not as specified, replace the clutch piston.

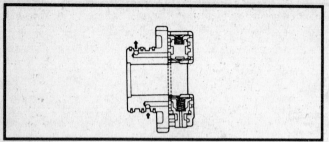

Checking the governor valve operation

Assembly

1. Lubricate the O-ring and seal ring and install them on the low/reverse brake piston. Carefully install the piston while applying even pressure to the perimeter of the piston.
2. Lubricate the one-way clutch inner race, thrust washer and return spring. Assembly the one-way clutch inner race, thrust washer and return spring and install them into the transmission case.
3. Check that the return spring, thrust washer and rings are properly positioned; then, install the Allen head bolts and dished washers in the rear of the transmission case.
4. Torque the inner race mounting bolts to 9.4–13 ft. lbs. (13–18 Nm).
5. Lubricate the drive and driven plates and install them into the transmission case. Start with a driven plate, then alternate drive-driven-drive-driven. Install the retaining plate and snapring.
6. Measure the clearance between the retaining plate and the snapring. If the clearance is not within specification, adjust the clearance by installing the proper retaining plate.
7. Check the operation of the piston by apply compress air (57 psi maximum) for no more than 3 seconds to the oil passage of the low/reverse brake.

GOVERNOR

Disassembly

1. Remove the governor assembly from the parking gear.
2. Remove the secondary governor valve retainer plate, spring and valve from the valve body.
3. Remove the primary governor valve retainer plate, spring and valve from the valve body.
4. Remove the inner retainer plate.

Inspection

1. Inspect the governor valve body for damage or scoring.
2. Inspect the valve for sticking, scoring or scratches.
3. Measure the governor valve springs and compare with the specification chart. If the spring is not within specification, replace the spring.

Assembly

1. Lubricate the primary governor valve, spring and retainer plate and install them into the governor body.
2. Lubricate the secondary governor valve, spring and retainer plate and install them into the governor body.
3. Install the governor assembly to the parking gear. Torque the retaining bolts 43–61 inch lbs. (4.9–6.9 Nm).
4. Check that the governor valves move slightly and that as vibration sound is heard when compress air (71 psi maximum) for no more than 5 seconds is applied.

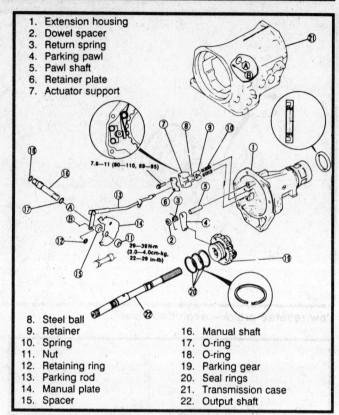

1. Extension housing
2. Dowel spacer
3. Return spring
4. Parking pawl
5. Pawl shaft
6. Retainer plate
7. Actuator support

8. Steel ball	16. Manual shaft
9. Retainer	17. O-ring
10. Spring	18. O-ring
11. Nut	19. Parking gear
12. Retaining ring	20. Seal rings
13. Parking rod	21. Transmission case
14. Manual plate	22. Output shaft
15. Spacer	

Extension housing and parking mechanism— exploded view

EXTENSION HOUSING AND PARKING MECHANISM

Disassembly

1. Remove the manual plate locknut, manual plate, spacer, retaining ring and parking rod.
2. Remove the manual shaft from the transmission case.
3. Remove the dowel spacer, return spring, parking pawl and parking pawl shaft from the extension housing.
4. Remove the actuator retainer plate mounting bolts, retainer plate, actuator support, steel balls, retainer and springs from the extension housing.

Inspection

1. Check the parking gear teeth for damage or wear.
2. Inspect the transmission case for damage at the oil seal surfaces.
3. Measure the actuator springs and compare with the following specifications:
   a. Coil Outer diameter—0.283 in. (7.2mm)
   b. Free length—1.260 in. (32.0mm)
   c. Coil thickness—0.028 in. (0.7mm)
   d. No. of coil—14.0
4. If not within specification, replace the return springs.

Assembly

1. Lubricate the new oil seal and install it into the extension housing, if removed.
2. Lubricate the actuator springs, retainer, steel balls, support and retainer plate. Install them into the extension housing. Torque the retainer plate mounting bolts 69–95 inch lbs. (7.8–11 Nm).

3. Lubricate the parking pawl shaft, parking pawl, return spring and dowel spacer. Install them into the extension housing.

4. Lubricate the new O-ring and install it on the manual shaft.

5. Lubricate the manual shaft and spacer. Install them into the transmission case.

6. Install the parking rod and retaining ring. Lubricate the manual plate and install it on the manual shaft; then, install the locknut. Torque the locknut 22–29 ft. lbs. (29–39 Nm).

7. Check the parking mechanism operation.

8. Lubricate the new seal rings and install them on the parking gear.

CONTROL VALVE BODY

Disassembly

NOTE: Pay close attention when handling the control

valve because it consists of the most precise and delicate parts of the transmission. Neatly arrange the parts in order to avoid mixing up similar parts.

LOWER VALVE BODY

1. Remove the manual valve.

2. Hold the lower valve body and separate plate together with large clips.

3. Remove the retaining bolts and remove the lower valve body.

4. Remove the orifice check valve and spring from the upper valve body; then remove the holding clip.

5. Carefully remove the separate plate to avoid losing the orifice check valves and springs and the throttle relief ball and spring in the valve body.

6. Tag the orifice check valves for proper reassembly; then remove the orifice check valves, throttle relief ball and springs.

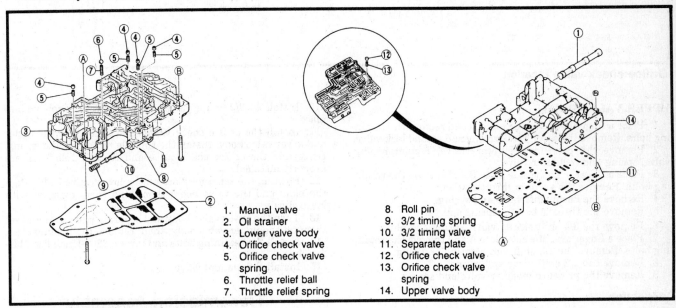

1. Manual valve
2. Oil strainer
3. Lower valve body
4. Orifice check valve
5. Orifice check valve spring
6. Throttle relief ball
7. Throttle relief spring
8. Roll pin
9. 3/2 timing spring
10. 3/2 timing valve
11. Separate plate
12. Orifice check valve
13. Orifice check valve spring
14. Upper valve body

Control valve body— exploded view

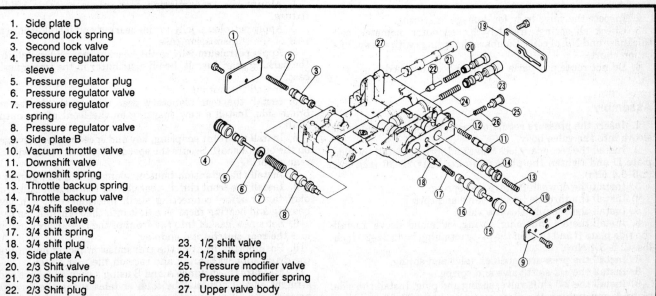

1. Side plate D
2. Second lock spring
3. Second lock valve
4. Pressure regulator sleeve
5. Pressure regulator plug
6. Pressure regulator valve
7. Pressure regulator spring
8. Pressure regulator valve
9. Side plate B
10. Vacuum throttle valve
11. Downshift valve
12. Downshift spring
13. Throttle backup spring
14. Throttle backup valve
15. 3/4 shift sleeve
16. 3/4 shift valve
17. 3/4 shift spring
18. 3/4 shift plug
19. Side plate A
20. 2/3 Shift valve
21. 2/3 Shift spring
22. 2/3 Shift plug
23. 1/2 shift valve
24. 1/2 shift spring
25. Pressure modifier valve
26. Pressure modifier spring
27. Upper valve body

Upper valve body— exploded view

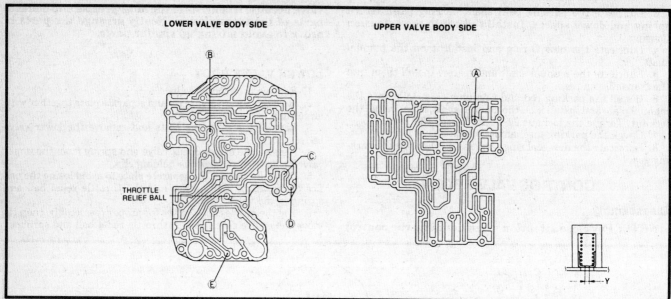

LOWER VALVE BODY SIDE   UPPER VALVE BODY SIDE

THROTTLE RELIEF BALL

Orifice check valve location

UPPER VALVE BODY

1. Place a finger over the side plate D and remove the retaining bolts. Remove the second lock spring and second lock valve.
2. Remove the pressure regulator sleeve, regulator plug, valve, spring and regulator valve.
3. Place a finger over the side plate B and remove the retaining bolts. Remove the vacuum throttle valve.
4. Remove the down shift valve and spring.
5. Remove the throttle backup spring and valve.
6. Remove the 3/4 shift sleeve, valve, spring and plug.
7. Place a finger over the side plate A and remove the retaining bolts. Remove the 2/3 shift valve, spring and plug.
8. Remove the 1/2 shift valve and spring.
9. Remove the pressure modifier valve and spring.

Inspection

1. Inspect all valves and sleeves for sticking, scoring or scratches.
2. Inspect the valve body for damage or scoring.
3. Check all springs free length, coil outer diameter, coil thickness and No. of coils. Compare the springs with the specification chart.
4. Do not reuse any parts that have been dropped.

Assembly

1. Insert the pressure regulator valve, spring, seat, plug and sleeve into the valve body.
2. Install the secondary lock valve and spring. Install the side plate D and tighten the plate retaining bolts 22–30 inch lbs. (2.5–3.4 Nm).
3. Install the downshift valve and spring.
4. Install the throttle backup valve and spring.
5. Install the vacuum throttle valve.
6. Install the 3/4 shift plug, spring, valve and sleeve. Install the side plate B and tighten the plate retaining bolts 22–30 inch lbs. (2.5–3.4 Nm).
7. Install the pressure modifier valve and spring.
8. Install the 1/2 shift valve and spring.
9. Install the 2/3 shift valve, spring and plug. Install the side plate A and tighten the plate retaining bolts 22–30 inch lbs. (2.5–3.4 Nm).

10. Install the 3/2 timing valve and spring. Tap the roll pin into place.
11. Install the orifice check valves and springs to the upper and lower valve body. Install the throttle relief ball and spring. Be certain the orifice check valve and throttle relief ball are properly installed.
12. Position the separate plate on the lower valve body. Align the plate and the valve body; then, hold them together with large clips.
13. Turn the lower valve body and separate plate over and set them on the upper valve body; then, remove the holding clips.
14. Install the retaining bolts and torque 22–30 inch lbs. (2.5–3.4 Nm).
15. Install the manual valve.

Transmission Assembly

1. Mount the transmission case into a suitable holding fixture.
2. Apply petroleum jelly to the bearing and install it into the rear of the transmission case.
3. Apply petroleum jelly to the bearing race and install it on the parking gear. Install the oil distributor in the transmission case.
4. Install the output shaft.
5. Install the rear planetary gear unit in the low/reverse brake side. Install a new snapring on the front of the output shaft.
6. Install the front snapring, key and speedometer drive gear on the output shaft. Secure the speedometer drive gear with the rear snapring.
7. Install the extension housing along with a new gasket.
8. Install the front clutch, rear clutch, rear clutch hub, front planetary carrier, connecting shell, internal gear, sun gear, bearing and bearing races as a unit into the transmission case.
9. Set a new gasket into the front of the case. Check and adjust the rear clutch total endplay.
10. Position the front of the transmission facing upward, set the drum support bearing and race on the rear clutch.
11. Measure the distance A and B using a vernier caliper and a straight edge. Calculate the total endplay using the formular below.

Formular: $T = A - B - 0.0039$ in. (.01mm)

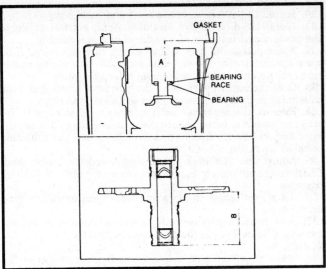

Checking total endplay—rear clutch

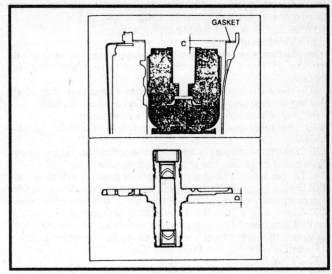

Checking front clutch endplay

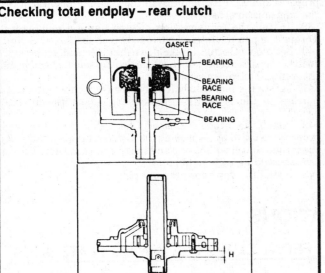

Checking total endplay—OD planetary gear unit

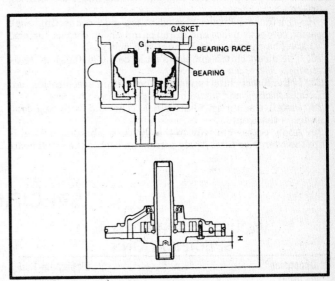

Checking direct clutch endplay

T:—Total endplay

A:—Distance between the drum support mounting surface (including the drum support gasket) and the drum support bearing race surface on the rear clutch assembly.

B:—Distance between the drum support bearing race contact surface and the drum support gasket contact surface.

0.1:—The compression amount of a new gasket.

12. The total endplay should be 0.010–0.020 in. (0.25–0.50mm).

13. If the total endplay is not within specification, adjust by selecting and installing the proper bearing race.

14. Measure the distance C and D using a vernier caliper and a straight edge. Calculate the front clutch endplay using the formular below.

Formular: T = C-D-0.0039 in. (.01mm)

T:—Front clutch endplay

C:—Distance between the drum support mounting surface (including the drum support gasket) and the bearing surface on the front clutch assembly.

D:—Distance between the sliding surface of the bearing and

the drum support gasket contact surface.

0.1:—The compression amount of a new gasket.

15. The front clutch endplay should be 0.020–0.031 in. (0.5–0.8mm).

16. If the front clutch endplay is not within specification, adjust by selecting and installing the proper bearing race.

17. Place the 2nd brake band and strut in position and tighten the piston stem lightly.

18. Apply petroleum jelly to the bearing race and thrust washer and install them. Check that the bearing race is on top the front clutch and that the bearing is on the bottom of the front clutch hole, then mount the overdrive case.

19. Set a new gasket in place. Do not install the direct clutch drum at this time.

20. Position the overdrive case upright and install the bearing and race on the overdrive case. Install the planetary carrier, sun gear, connecting shell and bearing as a unit in the overdrive case.

21. Check and adjust the overdrive planetary gear unit total endplay by measuring the distance E and H using a vernier cali-

per and a straight edge. Calculate the overdrive planetary gear unit total endplay using the formular below.

Formular: T = E-H-0.0039 in. (.01mm)

T:—Total endplay

E:—Distance between the oil pump mounting surface (including the oil pump gasket) and the connecting shell bearing surface.

H:—Distance between the oil pump side connecting shell bearing surface and the oil pump gasket contact surface.

0.1:—The compression amount of a new gasket.

22. The total endplay should be 0.010–0.020 in. (0.25–0.50mm).

23. If the total endplay is not within specification, adjust by selecting and installing the proper bearing race.

24. Do not install the planetary pinion carrier at this time. Install the bearing race in the overdrive case and the direct clutch, sun gear, connecting shell and bearings in the overdrive case.

25. Check and adjust the direct clutch endplay by measuring the distance G and H using a vernier caliper and a straight edge. Calculate the direct clutch endplay using the formular below.

Formular: T = G-H-0.0039 in. (.01mm)

T:—Total endplay

G:—Distance between the oil pump mounting surface (including the oil pump gasket) and the connecting shell bearing surface.

H:—Distance between the oil pump side connecting shell bearing contact surface and the oil pump gasket contact surface.

0.1:—The compression amount of a new gasket.

26. The direct clutch endplay should be 0.020–0.031 in. (0.5–0.8mm).

27. If the direct clutch endplay is not within specification, adjust by selecting and installing the proper bearing race.

28. Install the intermediate shaft. The end with the long splines is the front.

29. Apply petroleum jelly to the thrust washer and install it into the overdrive case. Apply petroleum jelly to the small bearing and race and install them.

30. Install the overdrive brake band and band strut.

31. Install the direct clutch assembly. Apply petroleum jelly to the bearing and install it on the direct clutch assembly.

32. Apply petroleum jelly to the bearing race and install it on the oil pump. Install the oil pump assembly into the transmission case using 2 converter housing bolts as a guide.

33. Coat the contact surfaces of the converter housing and the transmission case with sealant and install new O-rings.

34. Remove the converter housing bolts used as a guide. Install the converter housing onto the transmission case. Coat the mounting bolts with sealant and install. Torque the mounting bolts 43–51 ft. lbs. (59–69 Nm).

35. Adjust the 2nd brake band and overdrive brake band. Check their operation by applying compress air through their oil passages.

36. Set a new gasket in place and install the overdrive band servo cover.

37. Set the valve body assembly into position and install the mounting bolts. Torque the mounting bolts 8.0–11 ft. lbs. (11–15 Nm).

38. Set a new O-ring on the vacuum diaphragm. Select the proper diaphragm rod and install the vacuum diaphragm into the transmission case.

39. Install the transmission oil pan using a new gasket. Torque the pan mounting bolts 52–69 inch lbs. (5.9–7.8 Nm).

40. Set a new O-rings on the downshift solenoid, oil pressure switch, overdrive cancel solenoid and lockup solenoid and install them into the transmission case.

41. Rotate the manual shaft fully rearward; then, return it 2 notches to the **N** position. Install and adjust the inhibitor switch.

42. Install the torque converter. Check that the converter is properly installed by measuring the distance between the end of the torque converter housing and the torque converter. The distance should be 1.26 in. (32mm).

43. Install the governor pressure pipe.

SPECIFICATIONS

VACUUM DIAPHRAGM ROD SPECIFICATIONS

N-Dimension in. (mm)	Diaphragm Rod in. (mm)
Below 1.0099 (25.65)	1.4 (29.0)
1.0099–1.0295 (25.65–26.15)	1.16 (29.5)
1.0295–1.0492 (26.15–26.65)	1.18 (30.0)
1.0492–1.0650 (26.65–27.15)	1.20 (30.5)
1.650 or over (27.15 or over)	1.22 (31.0)

DIRECT CLUTCH RETAINING PLATE SIZES

in.	mm
0.220	5.6
0.228	5.8
0.236	6.0
0.244	6.2
0.252	6.4
0.260	6.6
0.268	6.8
0.276	7.0

FRONT CLUTCH RETAINING PLATE SIZES

in.	mm
0.197	5.0
0.205	5.2
0.213	5.4
0.220	5.6
0.228	5.8
0.236	6.0
0.244	6.2

LOW/REVERSE BRAKE RETAINING PLATE SIZES

in.	mm
0.307	7.8
0.315	8.0
0.323	8.2
0.331	8.4
0.339	8.6
0.346	8.8

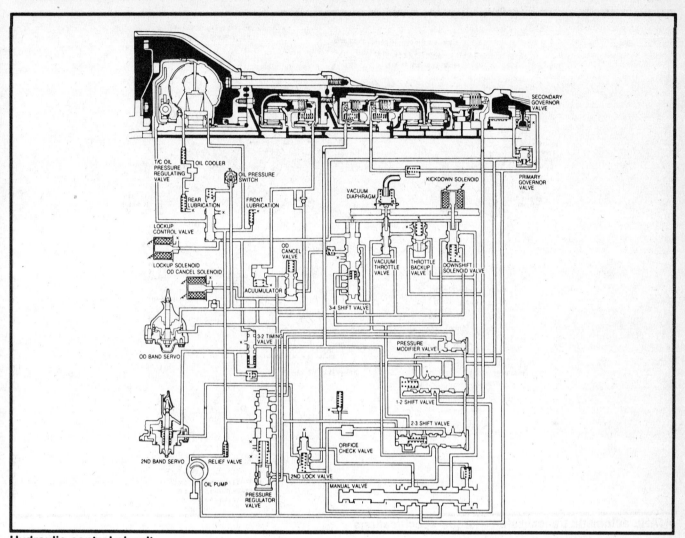

Hydraulic control circuit

CONTROL VALVE BODY—SPRING SPECIFICATIONS

Spring	Outer Diameter		Free Length		No. of Coils	Wire Diameter	
	in.	mm	in.	mm		in.	mm
Second lock	0.219	5.55	1.319	33.5	18.0	0.022	0.55
Pressure regulator	0.461	11.7	1.692	43.0	15.0	0.047	5.2
Downshift	0.219	55.5	0.862	21.9	14.0	0.022	0.55
Throttle backup	0.287	7.3	1.252	31.8	15.5	0.031	0.8
3-4 shift	0.260	6.6	1.193	30.3	14.6	0.031	0.8
2-3 shift	0.321	8.15	1.177	29.9	11.6	0.033	0.85
1-2 shift	0.260	6.6	1.102	28.0	16.0	0.026	0.65
Pressure modifier	0.339	8.6	0.610	15.5	7.5	0.024	0.6
Orifice check	0.197	5.0	0.610	15.5	12.0	0.009	0.23
Throttle relief	0.256	6.5	1.055	26.8	16.0	0.035	0.9
3-2 timing	0.291	7.4	0.815	20.7	11.0	0.035	0.9

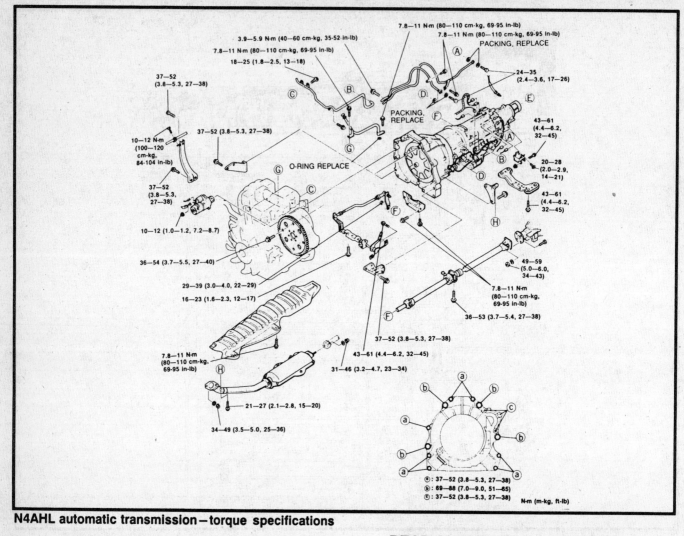

N4AHL automatic transmission–torque specifications

GOVERNOR SPRING SPECIFICATION

	Outer Diameter		Free Length			Wire Diameter	
	in.	mm	in.	mm	No. of coils	in.	mm
Secondary	0.362	9.2	0.992	25.2	7.5	0.028	0.7
Primary	0.344	8.75	0.858	21.8	7.0	0.018	0.45

ORIFICE CHECK VALVE SPECIFICATIONS

Check Valve	y Diameter	
	in.	mm
A	0.079	2.0
B	0.059	1.5
C	0.067	1.7
D	0.087	2.2
E	0.079	2.0

REAR CLUTCH TOTAL ENDPLAY— SELECTIVE BEARING RACE SIZES

In.	mm
0.047	1.2
0.055	1.4
0.063	1.6
0.071	1.8
0.079	2.0
0.087	2.2

OVERDRIVE UNIT—SELECTIVE BEARING RACE SIZES

In.	mm
0.047	1.2
0.055	1.4
0.063	1.6
0.071	1.8
0.079	2.0
0.087	2.2

GENERAL SPECIFICATIONS

Item		Specifications
Torque converter stall torque ratio	—	1.900:1
Gear ratio	1st	2.841
	2nd	1.541
	3rd	1.000
	OD (4th)	0.720
	Reverse	2.400
Number of drive/driven plates	Direct clutch	2/2
	Front clutch	4/5
	Rear clutch	5/5
	Low and reverse brake	5/5
Servo diameter (Piston outer diameter/retainer inner diameter) in. (mm)	OD band servo	2.362/1.417 (60/36)
	2nd band servo	3.150/2.205 (80/56)

FRONT CLUTCH ENDPLAY—SELECTIVE BEARING RACE SIZES

In.	mm
0.051	1.3
0.059	1.5
0.067	1.7
0.075	1.9
0.083	2.1
0.091	2.3
0.098	2.5
0.106	2.7

DIRECT CLUTCH ENDPLAY—SELECTIVE BEARING RACE SIZES

in.	mm
0.051	1.3
0.059	1.5
0.067	1.7
0.075	1.9
0.083	2.1
0.091	2.3
0.098	2.5
0.106	2.7

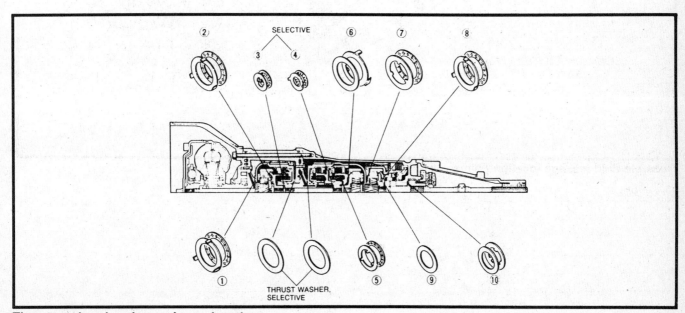

Thrust washer, bearing and race locations

BEARING AND RACE OUTER DIAMETER SPECIFICATIONS

	in.	mm	in.	mm	in.	mm	in.	mm	in.	mm	in.	mm
	1		**2**		**3**		**4**		**5**		**6**	
Bearing	2.756	70.0	2.756	70.0	1.378	35.0	1.378	35.0	2.087	53.0	2.756	70.0
Race	2.756	70.0	2.756	70.0	1.299	33.0	1.299	33.0	2.028	51.5	2.756	70.0
	7		**8**		**9**		**10**					
Bearing	2.756	70.0	2.756	70.0	1.850	47.0	2.087	53.0				
Race	2.756	70.0	2.756	70.0	—	—	2.028	51.5				

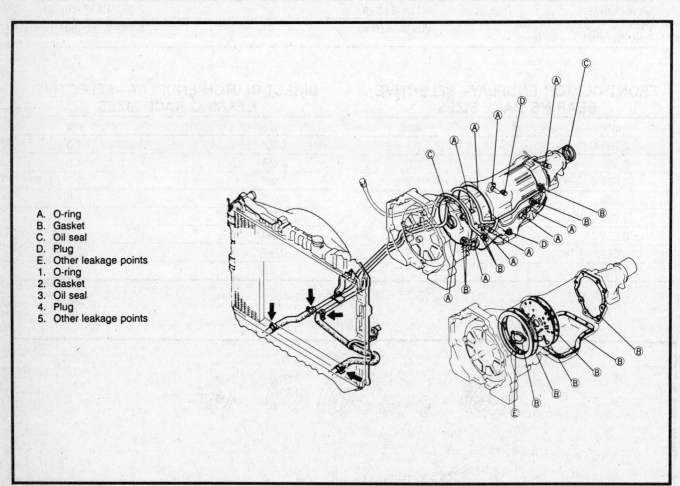

A. O-ring
B. Gasket
C. Oil seal
D. Plug
E. Other leakage points
1. O-ring
2. Gasket
3. Oil seal
4. Plug
5. Other leakage points

Possible fluid leakage location points

Section 3

RE4R01A Transmission
Nissan

APPLICATION

Year	Vehicle	Engine
1987	Pick-Up	VG 30i
	Pathfinder	VG 30i
1988	Pick-Up	VG 30i
	Pathfinder	VG 30i
1989–90	240 SX	KA 24 E
	Pickup	VG 30i
	Pathfinder	VG 30i

GENERAL DESCRIPTION

The RE4R01A transmission is a fully automatic 3 speed, with overdrive, assembly. The assembly consists of: 5 clutch packs, a brake, 2 one-way clutch, a planetary gearset and a series of 5 solenoids. The transmission provides 4 forward ratios and 1 reverse.

When used in a 4WD application, the rear extension housing is replaced with an adapter case that will mount directly to a transfer case.

The on-board computer determines the shift and lockup points of the transmission as well as the speed change range of the transfer system based upon the input data signals received from various sensors.

Engine power is transmitted to the input shaft by the torque converter and is then transmitted to the planetary gears by the operation of the clutches. The power flow depends on the engagement or disengagement of the clutches and brakes.

Each clutch and brake operates by hydraulic pressure which is produced by the rotation of the oil pump. The pressurized fluid is regulated by the valve body and shift change automatically occurs according to throttle opening, vehicle speed and solenoid activation.

The torque converter provides a fluid coupling between the engine and transmission for optimum power transfer when driving at a constant speed and increased torque when starting, accelerating and climbing an incline. When used, the damper clutch provides a solid coupling for improved fuel mileage when at cruising ranges.

Transmission and Converter Identification

TRANSMISSION

An identification number is stamped on a metal tag which is attached to the right rear side of the transmission case.

CONVERTER

The torque converter is a lockup type, with a one-way clutch, welded 1-piece unit and cannot be disassembled.

Electronic Controls

This transmission is controlled by various sensors, switches and a transmission control unit.

THROTTLE SENSOR AND THROTTLE VALVE SWITCH

The throttle sensor and throttle valve switch assembly is mounted on the throttle body. The throttle sensor is a potentiometer which transforms the throttle valve position into output voltage and sends a voltage signal to the ECU. The signal is used to control the engine operation by cutting the fuel flow.

INHIBITOR SWITCH

The inhibitor switch is mounted on the right side of the transmission in conjunction with the manual shaft. It's purpose is to allow the engine to be started in only N or P.

REVOLUTION SENSOR

The revolution sensor is located on the front left side of the extension housing (240SX) or on the front top of the extension housing (4WD Truck and 4WD Pathfinder). It's purpose is to provide speed information to the ECU.

SHIFT SOLENOIDS A AND B

The shift solenoids A and B are located on the upper half of the control valve assembly. They are used to operate the various clutch packs within the transmission.

OVERRUN CLUTCH SOLENOID

The overrun clutch solenoid is located on the upper half of the control valve assembly. It's purposes it to control the overdrive clutch pack.

FLUID TEMPERATURE SENSOR

The fluid temperature sensor is located on the lower half of the control valve assembly. It's purpose it to provide transmission fluid temperature information to the ECU.

LOCKUP SOLENOID

The lockup solenoid is located on the lower half of the control valve assembly. It purpose it to lock the torque converter.

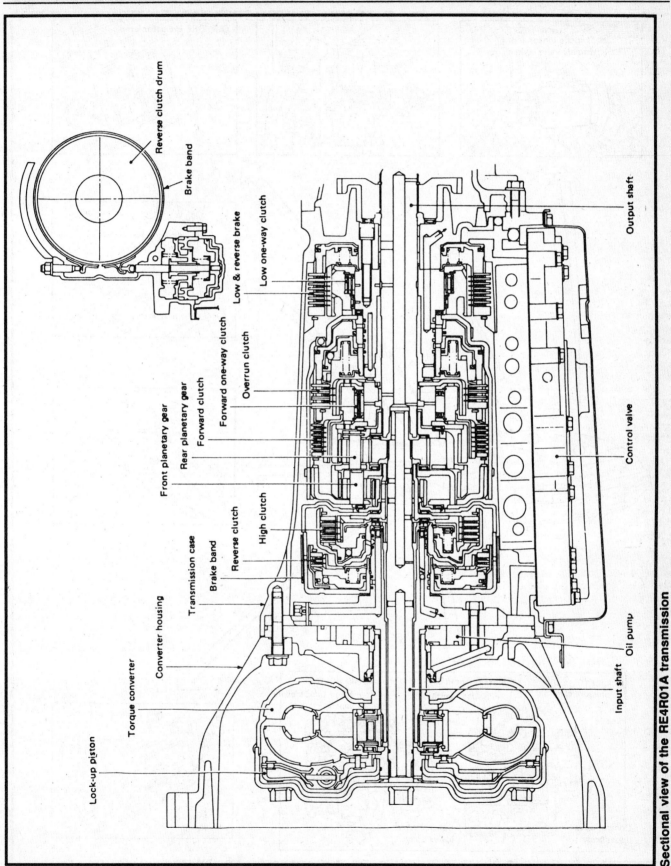

Reverse clutch drum

Brake band

Low & reverse brake

Low one-way clutch

Output shaft

Overrun clutch

Forward one-way clutch

Forward clutch

Rear planetary gear

Front planetary gear

High clutch

Reverse clutch

Brake band

Control valve

Transmission case

Converter housing

Oil pump

Torque converter

Input shaft

Lock-up piston

Sectional view of the RE4R01A transmission

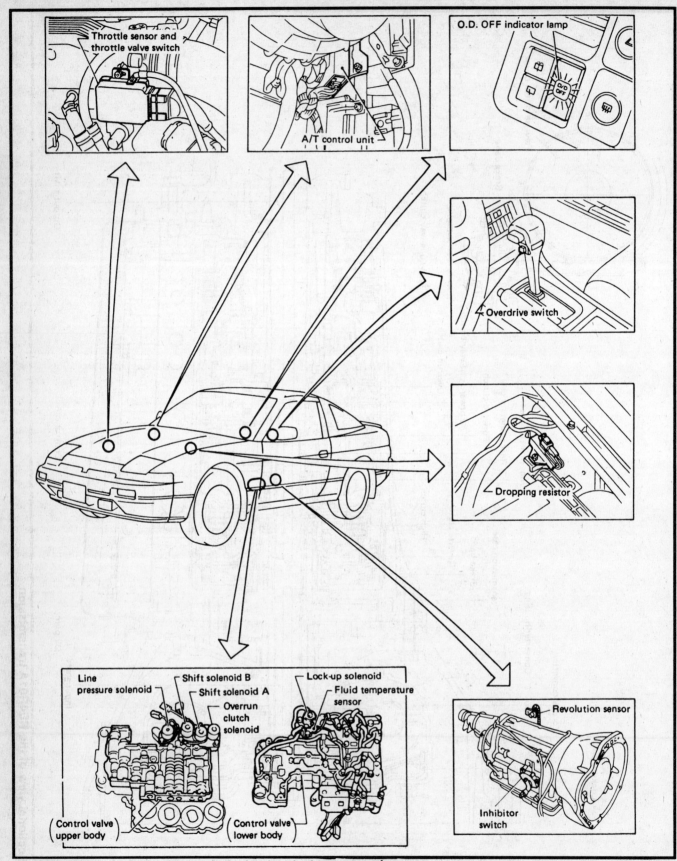

Throttle sensor and throttle valve switch

A/T control unit

O.D. OFF indicator lamp

Overdrive switch

Dropping resistor

Line pressure solenoid

Shift solenoid B

Shift solenoid A

Overrun clutch solenoid

Lock-up solenoid

Fluid temperature sensor

Control valve upper body

Control valve lower body

Revolution sensor

Inhibitor switch

Location of the automatic transmission's electrical components

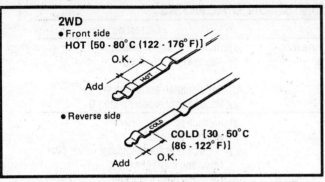

Inspecting the fluid level using the dipstick—2WD

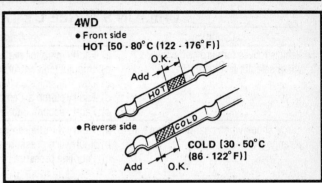

Inspecting the fluid level using the dipstick—4WD

LINE PRESSURE SOLENOID

The line pressure solenoid is located on the upper half of the control valve assembly.

OVERDRIVE SWITCH

The overdrive switch is located on the shift selector handle and is used to turn overdrive **ON** or **OFF**.

ELECTRONIC CONTROL UNIT

The electronic control unit is mounted under the right side of the dash next to the door pillar. It purpose it absorb sensor information and issue commands to control the engine and transmission operation.

OVERDRIVE INDICATOR LAMP

The overdrive indicator lamp is mounted on the lower left side of the instrument panel. It temporarily indicates when the overdrive unit is turned **OFF**.

DROPPING RESISTOR

The dropping resistor is located under the center of the dash and is used in conjunction with control signals sent to the transmission.

Metric Fasteners

Metric tools will be required to service this transmission. Due to the large number of alloy parts used in this transmission, torque specifications should be strictly observed. Before installing cap screws into aluminum parts, dip the bolts into clean transmission fluid as this will prevent the screws from galling the aluminum threads, thus causing damage.

Metric fastener dimensions are very close to the dimensions of the familiar inch system fasteners. For this reason replacement fasteners must have the same measurement and strength as the original fastener.

Do not attempt to interchange metric fasteners for inch system fasteners. Mismatched or incorrect fasteners can cause damage to the automatic transmission unit and possible personal injury. Care should be taken to reuse fasteners in their original locations.

Capacities

The refill capacity is 8.75 quarts (8.3L) of transmission fluid including the torque converter or 6.5 quarts (6.3L) of transmission fluid without the torque converter.

Checking Fluid Level

1. Drive the vehicle for 5–10 minutes in an urban area until the engine is warmed and the transmission fluid is hot.
2. Park the vehicle on a flat surface and firmly set the parking brake.
3. Start the engine and move the shift selector through each gear range, ending in **P**.
4. With the engine idling, check the transmission fluid level.
5. Using a lint free cloth, wipe the dipstick.
6. Insert the dipstick into the dipstick tube, as far as possible, remove it and check the fluid level; it must be in the hot range.
7. If the fluid is low, add fluid to bring it up to the full level.

TROUBLE DIAGNOSIS

CHILTON'S THREE C's TRANSMISSION DIAGNOSIS

Condition	Cause	Correction
Engine cannot be started with selector lever in P or N but can be started in D, 2, 1 or R ranges	a) Faulty inhibitor switch b) Dirty inhibitor switch electrical connectors c) Unadjusted inhibitor switch	a) Replace switch b) Clean connectors c) Adjust inhibitor switch
Vehicle moves when pushed forward or backward with selector lever in P	a) Faulty parking components	a) Repair or replace parking pawl, gear or etc.

CHILTON'S THREE C's TRANSMISSION DIAGNOSIS

Condition	Cause	Correction
Vehicle moves forward or backward when selector lever is in N	a) Faulty inhibitor switch or circuit b) Unadjusted control linkage c) Low transmission fluid d) Faulty clutch assembly(s) e) Faulty accumulator piston D	a) Replace or adjust switch b) Adjust control linkage c) Refill transmission d) Repair clutch assembly(s) e) Rebuild accumulator piston D
Large shock when changing from N to R range	a) Faulty throttle sensor b) Faulty line pressure solenoid c) Poor line pressure d) Dirty electrical harness connector terminals	a) Replace throttle sensor b) Replace solenoid c) Replace pressure regulator valve, pilot valve and pilot filter d) Clean harness terminals
Vehicle does not creep backwards when selector lever is in R	a) Low transmission fluid b) Faulty line pressure c) Dirty electrical harness connector terminals	a) Refill transmission b) Replace or rebuild oil pump, torque converter, clutch assembly(s), pressure regulator, pilot valve and pilot filter c) Clean harness terminals
Vehicle does not creep forward in D, 2 or 1 ranges	a) Low fluid level b) Poor line pressure in D or dirty fluid	a) Refill transmission b) Replace or rebuild oil pump, torque converter, clutch assembly(s), pressure regulator, pilot valve and pilot filter
Vehicle cannot be started from D_1, on cruise test	a) Damaged revolution sensor, speed sensor, shift solenoid A or B b) Faulty throttle sensor c) Faulty line pressure with shift selector in D d) Dirty electrical harness connector terminals	a) Check and replace revolution sensor, speed sensor, shift solenoid A or B b) Replace throttle sensor c) Replace shift valve A, shift valve B, shift solenoid A, shift solenoid B, pilot valve, clutch assembly(s), torque converter or oil pump assembly d) Clean harness terminals
Poor shifting from D_1-D_2 and from D_4-D_2 at full throttle	a) Faulty inhibitor switch b) Faulty revolution sensor or speed sensor c) Faulty throttle sensor d) Dirty fluid e) Dirty electrical harness connector terminals	a) Replace switch or clean terminals b) Replace sensor(s) or clean terminals c) Replace sensor or clean terminals d) Clean or replace shift valve A, solenoid A, pilot valve, pilot filter, servo piston assembly, brake band or oil pump assembly e) Clean terminals
Poor shifting from D_2-D_3 at specified speed	a) Faulty inhibitor switch b) Faulty throttle sensor c) Dirty fluid d) Dirty electrical harness connector terminals	a) Replace switch or clean terminals b) Replace sensor or clean terminals c) Clean or replace shift valve B, solenoid B, pilot valve, pilot filter, servo piston assembly, high clutch assembly or oil pump d) Clean terminals
Poor shifting from D_3-D_4 at specified speed	a) Faulty throttle sensor b) Damaged inhibitor switch, overdrive switch, solenoid A, solenoid B, revolution sensor, speed sensor or fluid temperature switch	a) Replace throttle sensor b) Replace sensor(s) or switch(s); also, clean terminals

CHILTON'S THREE C's TRANSMISSION DIAGNOSIS

Condition	Cause	Correction
Poor shifting from D_3-D_4 at specified speed	c) Dirty fluid	c) Clean or replace shift valve B, overrun clutch control valve, solenoid B, pilot valve, pilot filter, servo piston assembly, brake band, torque converter or oil pump
	d) Dirty electrical harness connector terminals	d) Clean terminals
No lock up at specified speed	a) Faulty lock up solenoid	a) Replace solenoid or clean terminals
	b) Faulty throttle sensor	b) Replace throttle sensor
	c) Defective control valve assembly	c) Clean or replace lock up control valve, shuttle shift valve D, torque converter relief valve, lock up solenoid, pilot valve or pilot filter
	d) Dirty electrical harness connector terminals	d) Clean terminals
Lock up condition does not hold for more than 30 sec.	a) Faulty revolution sensor	a) Replace sensor or clean terminals
	b) Dirty or burnt fluid	b) Clean or replace lock up control valve, pilot valve, pilot filter, torque converter or oil pump
	c) Dirty electrical harness connector terminals	c) Clean terminals
Lock up releases when accelerator is depressed	a) Faulty idle switch	a) Replace switch or clean terminals
	b) Dirty electrical harness connector terminals	b) Clean terminals
Unsmooth idle when shifted from D_4-D_3 with acceleration released. Vehicle does not decelerate by engine brake when turning overdrive switch OFF and accelerator pedal released. Vehicle does not decelerate by engine brake when changing selector lever from D-2 range with accelerator released	a) Faulty overrun clutch solenoid	a) Replace solenoid or clean terminal
	b) Faulty throttle sensor	b) Replace sensor or clean terminals
	c) Dirty or burnt fluid	c) Replace or clean the overrun control valve, overrun clutch reducing valve, overrun clutch solenoid, overrun clutch assembly or oil pump
	d) Dirty electrical harness connector terminals	d) Clean terminals
Vehicle does not start after shifting from D_1	a) Faulty revolution sensor, speed sensor, shift solenoid A or shift solenoid B	a) Replace sensor(s) or solenoid(s); also, clean terminals
	b) Dirty electrical harness connector terminals	b) Clean terminals
No shifting from D_4-D_3 when turning overdrive switch OFF	a) Faulty overdrive switch	a) Replace switch or clean terminals
No shifting from D_3-D_2 when moving shift selector from D-2 range	a) Faulty inhibitor switch	a) Replace switch or clean terminals
No shifting from 2_2-1_1 when moving selector from 2-1 range	a) Faulty inhibitor switch	a) Replace switch or clean terminals
	b) Dirty electrical harness connector terminals	b) Clean terminals

CLUTCH AND BAND APPLICATION

Shift position		Reverse clutch	High clutch	Forward clutch	Overrun clutch	Band servo			Forward one-way clutch	Low one-way clutch	Low reverse brake	Lockup
						2nd apply	3rd release	4th apply				
P		—	—	—	—	—	—	—	—	—	—	—
R		①	—	—	—	—	—	—	—	—	①	—
N		—	—	—	—	—	—	—	—	—	—	—
⑨ D	1st	—	—	①	⑤	—	—	—	③	③	—	—
	2nd	—	—	①	⑥②	①	—	—	③	—	—	—
	3rd	—	①	①	②	⑦④	④	—	③	—	—	—
	4th	—	①	④	—	⑧④	④	①	③	—	—	①
2	1st	—	—	①	⑤	—	—	—	③	③	—	—
	2nd	—	—	①	②	①	—	—	③	—	—	—
1	1st	—	—	①	⑤	—	—	—	③	—	①	—
	2nd	—	—	①	①	①	—	—	③	—	—	—

① Applied.
② Applied when throttle opening is less than 1/16. Engine brake activates.
③ Applied during "progressive" acceleration.
④ Applied but does not affect power transmission.
⑤ Applied when throttle opening is less than 1/16 but does not affect engine brake.
⑥ Applied when overdrive switch is set to "OFF".
⑦ Oil pressure is applied to both 2nd "apply" side and 3rd "release" side of band servo piston. However, because oil pressure area on the "release" side is greater than that on the "apply" side, brake band does not contract.
⑧ Oil pressure is applied to 4th "apply" side in condition ⑦ above, and brake band contracts.
⑨ A/T will not shift to 4th when overdrive switch is set to "OFF" position.

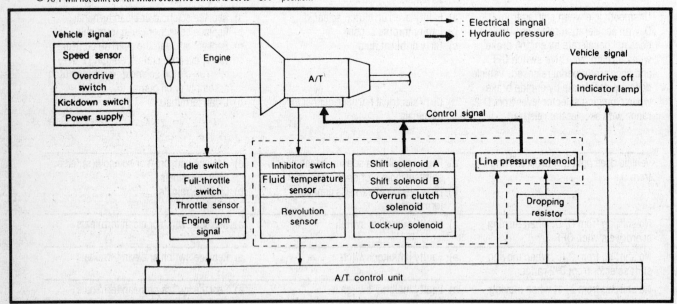

Hydraulic Control System

Diagnosis Tests

LINE PRESSURE TEST

1. Be sure the transmission fluid level is correct.
2. Warm the engine and drive the vehicle for approximately 10 minutes to warm the transmission fluid to 122°F–176°F (50°C–80°C).
3. Set the parking brake and block the wheels.
4. Install a tachometer so it can be seen while driving the vehicle.

NOTE: For easy readability, mark the specified engine rpm on the tachometer.

5. At the lower, right rear side of the transmission case, remove the hexagon bolt and install the oil pressure gauge set tool to the port.
6. Start the engine, move the shift selector into **D** and measure the line pressure at idle; it should be 68–74 psi (471–510 kpa).
7. Move the shift selector into **2** and **1**, respectively, and measure the line pressure at idle; it should be 68–74 psi (471–510 kpa), respectively.

LINE PRESSURE TEST DIAGNOSIS

Problem	Cause
Line pressure is low in all ranges, at idle	a) Oil pump wear b) Control piston damage c) Pressure regulator valve or plug sticking d) Spring for pressure regulator valve damaged e) Fluid pressure leakage between oil strainer and pressure regulator valve
Line pressure is low in particular range, at idle	a) Fluid pressure leakage between manual valve and particular clutch. b) For example: If line pressure is low in "R" and "1" ranges but is normal in "D" and "2" range, fluid leakage exists at or around low & reverse brake circuit.
Line pressure is high, at idle	a) Mal-adjustment of throttle sensor b) Fluid temperature sensor damaged c) Line pressure solenoid sticking d) Short circuit of line pressure solenoid circuit e) Pressure modifier valve sticking f) Pressure regulator valve or plug sticking
Line pressure is low, at stall speed	a) Mal-adjustment of throttle sensor b) Control piston damaged c) Line pressure solenoid sticking d) Short circuit of line pressure solenoid circuit e) Pressure regulator valve or plug sticking f) Pressure modifier valve sticking g) Pilot valve sticking

8. Move the shift selector into **D**. Gradually, accelerate the engine to stall speed and measure the line pressure; it should be 148–159 psi (1020–1098 kpa).

NOTE: Between each stall speed test, move the shift selector lever to N and allow the engine to idle for at least a minute.

9. Move the shift selector into **2** and **1**, respectively. Gradually, accelerate the engine to stall speed and measure the line pressure; it should be 148–159 psi (1020–1098 kpa), respectively.
10. Remove the oil pressure gauge set tool and install a new hexagon pressure plug.
11. At the lower, left front side of the transmission case, remove the hexagon bolt and install the oil pressure gauge set tool to the port.
12. Start the engine, move the shift selector into **R** and measure the line pressure at idle; it should be 95–101 psi (657–696 kpa).
13. Gradually, accelerate the engine to stall speed and measure the line pressure; it should be 206–218 psi (1422–1500 kpa).
14. Move the shift selector lever to **N** and allow the engine to idle for at least a minute.
15. Turn the engine **OFF**. Remove the oil pressure gauge set tool and install a new hexagon pressure plug.

STALL SPEED TEST

1. Make sure the engine and transmission fluid levels are at their proper levels.
2. Warm the engine and drive the vehicle for approximately 10 minutes to warm the transmission fluid to 122°F–176°F (50°C–80°C).
3. Set the parking brake and block the wheels.
4. Install a tachometer so it can be seen while driving the vehicle.

NOTE: For easy readability, mark the specified engine rpm on the tachometer.

5. Start the engine, firmly depress the brake pedal and place the selector lever in **D**.
6. Gradually, accelerate to wide open throttle, note the engine stall speed and release the throttle; the stall speed should be 2050–2250 rpm.

NOTE: Never hold the throttle wide open for more than 5 seconds

7. Move the shift selector lever to **N** and allow the engine to idle for at least a minute.
8. Repeat this test by positioning the shift selector lever in **2**, **1** and **R**, respectively; the stall speed should be 2050–2250 rpm, respectively.

ROAD TEST

TEST I

1. Make sure the engine and transmission fluid levels are at their proper levels.
2. Warm the engine and drive the vehicle for approximately 10 minutes to warm the transmission fluid to 122°F–176°F (50°C–80°C).
3. Turn the overdrive switch **ON**.
4. Move the shift selector to **D**, depress the accelerator ½ way and drive the vehicle; the transmission should shift at the following speeds:
   a. D_1 to D_2 — 24–26 mph (38–42 km/h)
   b. D_2 to D_3 — 45–48 mph (72–78 km/h)
   c. D_3 to D_4 — 69–75 mph (111–121 km/h)
5. The transmission should perform lockup at 70–75 mph (112–120 km/h) in D_4.
6. Release the accelerator pedal; the lockup should release.
7. Apply the brake pedal; the engine speed should return to a smooth idle when the transmission downshifts from D_4 to D_3.

VEHICLE SPEED WHEN SHIFTING GEARS

Throttle Position	$D_1 \to D_2$	$D_2 \to D_3$	$D_3 \to D_4$	Vehicle Speed mph (km/h) $D_4 \to D_3$	$D_3 \to D_2$	$D_2 \to D_1$	$1_2 \to 1_1$
Full throttle	32–35 (52–56)	59–63 (95–101)	91–97 (146–156)	87–93 (140–150)	55–59 (89–95)	25–27 (40–44)	33–35 (53–57)
Half throttle	24–26 (38–42)	45–48 (72–78)	69–75 (111–121)	34–40 (55–65)	21–24 (33–39)	6–9 (10–14)	33–35 (53–57)

VEHICLE SPEED WHEN PERFORMING AND RELEASING LOCKUP

Throttle position	O.D. switch (Shift range)	Vehicle Speed mph (km/h) Lock up On	Lock up Off
Full throttle	On (D₄)	91–97 (146–156)	87–93 (140–150)
	Off (D₃)	59–63 (95–101)	55–59 (89–95)
Half throttle	On (D₄)	70–75 (112–120)	63–68 (102–110)
	Off (D₃)	47–52 (76–84)	44–49 (71–79)

8. Stop the vehicle.
9. Perform road test II.

TEST II

1. Make sure the engine and transmission fluid levels are at their proper levels.
2. Warm the engine and drive the vehicle for approximately 10 minutes to warm the transmission fluid to 122°F–176°F (50°C–80°C).
3. Turn the overdrive switch ON.
4. Move the shift selector to D, depress the accelerator ½ way, accelerate to 6 mph (10 km/h), release the accelerator and fully depress it; the transmission should shift from D_4 to D_2 as soon as the accelerator is fully depressed.
5. With the accelerator fully depressed, the transmission should shift from D_2 to D_3 at 59–63 mph (95–101 km/h).
6. After the transmission shifts from D_2 to D_3, release the accelerator pedal; the transmission should shift from D_3 to D_4, then, decelerate by the engine brake.
7. Stop the vehicle.
8. Perform road test III.

TEST III

1. Make sure the engine and transmission fluid levels are at their proper levels.
2. Warm the engine and drive the vehicle for approximately 10 minutes to warm the transmission fluid to 122°F–176°F (50°C–80°C).
3. Turn the overdrive switch ON.
4. Move the shift selector to D, depress the accelerator ½ way, accelerate until the transmission shifts to D_4 and release the accelerator.
5. While driving in the D_4 range, turn the overdrive switch OFF; the transmission should shift from D_4 to D_3 and the vehicle should decelerate by engine braking.
6. While driving in the D_3 range, move the selector lever from D to 2; the transmission should shift from D_3 to 2_2 and the vehicle should decelerate by the engine braking.
7. While driving in the 2_2 range, move the selector lever from 2_2 to 1_1 range; the vehicle should decelerate by the engine braking.
8. Stop the vehicle.

Electronic Control System

THROTTLE SENSOR AND THROTTLE VALVE SWITCH

Testing

1. Disconnect the throttle sensor harness connector.
2. Turn the ignition switch ON.
3. Using a voltmeter, connect the positive probe to the d terminal and the negative probe to ground; the voltage should be approximately 5.0V.

NOTE: If the voltage is less than 5.0V, disconnect the electrical connector from the ECU and check the harness or connector for a break or ground.

4. At the throttle sensor, connect the voltmeter's positive probe to terminal e. Depress the accelerator and measure the voltage; the voltage should change 0.5–4.0V.
5. Turn the ignition switch OFF, disconnect the electrical connector from the ECU. Using an ohmmeter, check for continuity between terminals f (throttle sensor side) and the 21 and 29 (ECU side) of the electrical harness; continuity should exist.
6. Using an ohmmeter, connect it to terminals e and f of the throttle sensor. Manually, operate the throttle valve and check for changing resistance; if not change is noted, replace the throttle sensor.
7. Reconnect the throttle sensor electrical connector and disconnect the electrical connector from the throttle valve switch.
8. Start the engine and warm the engine.
9. Using a circuit tester, check the throttle valve's ON/OFF speed operation by manually closing the throttle valve; the speed ON/OFF should be 850–1150 rpm. If the setting is not correct, loosen the throttle sensor-to-throttle body screws, turn the sensor to the correct value and retighten the screws.
10. Erase the ECU memory and drive test the vehicle.

INHIBITOR SWITCH

Testing

1. At the right side of the engine compartment, disconnect the electrical connector from the inhibitor switch.
2. Place the transmission into P.
3. Using an ohmmeter, connect it's probes to terminals a and b; there should be continuity.
4. Using an ohmmeter, connect it's probes to terminals a and f; there should not be continuity.
5. Move the shift selector lever to N.
6. Using an ohmmeter, connect it's probes to terminals a and b; there should not be continuity.
7. Using an ohmmeter, connect it's probes to terminals a and f; there should be continuity.

8. Move the shift selector lever to any position, other than N or P, respectively.

9. Using an ohmmeter, connect it's probes to terminals **a** and **b**; there should not be continuity.

10. Using an ohmmeter, connect it's probes to terminals **a** and **f**; there should not be continuity.

11. If the switch does not meet the testing standard, replace it.

REVOLUTION SENSOR

Testing

1. Using a voltmeter, connect the positive probe to terminal **16** of the ECU and the negative probe to ground.

2. Drive the vehicle and record the voltages at different speeds; 0–1V at 0–19 mph (0–30 km/h) and greater than 1V at over 19 mph (over 30 km/h).

3. If the sensor does not meet specifications, replace the sensor.

SHIFT SOLENOID A

Testing

1. At the right side of the engine compartment, disconnect the solenoid electrical harness connector.

2. Using an ohmmeter, check the resistance between terminal **35** and ground; it should be 20–30 ohms.

3. If the resistance is other than 20–30 ohms, replace the shift solenoid A.

SHIFT SOLENOID B

Testing

1. At the right side of the engine compartment, disconnect the solenoid electrical harness connector.

2. Using an ohmmeter, check the resistance between terminal **36** and ground; it should be 20–30 ohms.

3. If the resistance is other than 20–30 ohms, replace the shift solenoid B.

OVERRUN CLUTCH SOLENOID

Testing

1. At the right side of the engine compartment, disconnect the solenoid electrical harness connector.

2. Using an ohmmeter, check the resistance between terminal **21** and ground; it should be 20–30 ohms.

3. If the resistance is other than 20–30 ohms, replace the overrun clutch solenoid.

LOCKUP SOLENOID

Testing

1. At the right side of the engine compartment, disconnect the solenoid electrical harness connector.

2. Using an ohmmeter, check the resistance between terminal **22** and ground; it should be 2.5–5.0 ohms.

3. If the resistance is other than 2.5–5.0 ohms, replace the lockup solenoid.

FLUID TEMPERATURE SENSOR

Testing

1. At the right side of the engine compartment, disconnect the solenoid electrical harness connector.

2. Using an ohmmeter, check the resistance between terminals **12** and **15**; it should be approximately 2.5k ohms at 68°F (20°C).

3. If the resistance is other than 2.5k ohms at 68°F (20°C), replace the fluid temperature sensor.

LINE PRESSURE SOLENOID

Testing

1. At the right side of the engine compartment, disconnect the solenoid electrical harness connector.

2. Using an ohmmeter, check the resistance between terminal **34** and ground; it should be 2.5–5.0 ohms.

3. If the resistance is other than 2.5–5.0 ohms, replace the line pressure solenoid.

OVERDRIVE SWITCH

Testing

1. Turn the ignition switch **ON**.

2. Using a voltmeter, connect the positive probe to terminal **9** of the ECU electrical connector and the negative probe to ground.

3. With the overdrive switch turned **OFF**, the voltage should be 0–1V.

4. Turn the overdrive switch **ON**; the voltage should be 12V.

5. If the switch does not operate according to specifications, replace it.

DROPPING RESISTOR

Testing

1. Disconnect the electrical connector from the dropping resistor.

2. Using an ohmmeter, connect it between both terminals; the resistance should be 11.2–12.8 ohms.

3. If the resistance is not 11.2–12.8 ohms, replace the resistor.

Converter Clutch Operation and Diagnosis

TORQUE CONVERTER CLUTCH

The torque converter is equipped with a lockup clutch assembly, which, when locked up, reacts similar to a manual transmission clutch. As a result, loss or slippage in the medium and high speed ranges is virtually eliminated, thus improving fuel consumption.

The lockup mechanism is installed within the converter's hub and is operated by the control valve assembly.

TROUBLESHOOTING THE TORQUE CONVERTER CLUTCH

Perform the stall speed test to determine if the trouble is in the converter or transmission. If the stall speed in **D** or **R** is equal to each other but lower than nominal value, a faulty converter is suspected.

Schematic of the automatic transmission electrical system

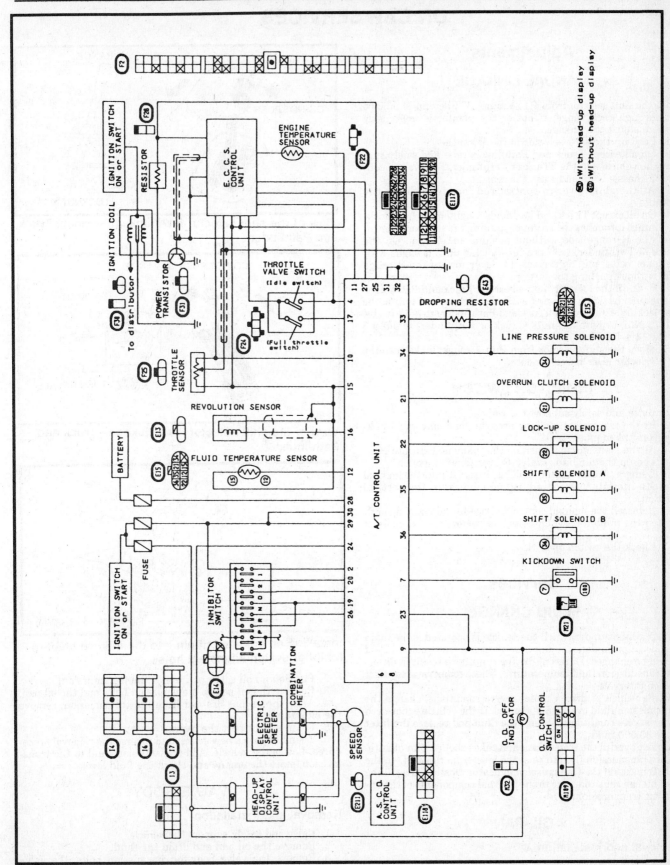

Circuit diagram for quick pin point check

ON CAR SERVICES

Adjustments

MANUAL LINKAGE

Move the shift selector from **P** to **1** range. The detents should be felt through each range; if not or the pointer is improperly aligned, adjust the linkage.

1. Position the shift selector in the **P** range.
2. On all except Truck and Pathfinder, raise and safely support the vehicle. On the Truck or Pathfinder, remove the console-to-chassis bolts and raise the console.
3. At the shift lever-to-control rod location, loosen the locknuts.
4. On all except Truck and Pathfinder, tighten the front locknut **X** until it touches the trunnion, pulling the selector lever toward the **R** range side, without pushing the button. On the Truck or Pathfinder, turn the turn buckle until it aligns with the inner cable, pulling the selector lever toward the **R** range side, without pushing the button.
5. Back off the locknut **X** on all except Truck and Pathfinder or the turn buckle (truck or Pathfinder) 1 turn and torque the rear locknut **Y** (all except Truck and Pathfinder) to 8–11 ft. lbs. (11–15 Nm) or both locknuts (Truck or Pathfinder) to 3.3–4.3 ft. lbs. (4.4–5.9 Nm).
6. Move the shift selector from **P** to **1** range; make sure the shift selector lever moves smoothly.

INHIBITOR SWITCH

1. Raise and safely support the vehicle.
2. At the transmission, disconnect the manual control linkage from the manual shaft.
3. At the transmission, position the manual shaft into **N**.
4. Loosen the inhibitor switch-to-transmission bolts.
5. Using a 0.16 in. (4mm) drill bit, insert it into the manual shaft-to-inhibitor switch adjustment holes, in the vertical position.
6. Reinstall the manual control linkage to the manual shaft, tighten the inhibitor switch bolts and remove the adjustment pin.
7. Check the switch operation.

Services

FLUID CHANGE

The conditions under which the vehicle is operated is the main consideration in determining how often the transmission fluid should be changed. Different driving conditions result in different transmission fluid temperatures. These temperatures affect change intervals.

If the vehicle is driven under severe conditions, change the transmission fluid every 15,000 miles. If the vehicle is not used under severe conditions, change the fluid and replace the filter every 30,000 miles.

Do not overfill the transmission. It takes about a pint of automatic transmission fluid to raise the level from the **ADD** to the **FULL** mark on the transmission indicator dipstick. Overfilling the unit can cause damage to the internal components of the automatic transmission.

OIL PAN

Removal and Installation

1. Raise and safely support the vehicle.

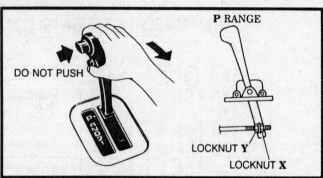

View of the shift selector lever linkage – except Truck and Pathfinder

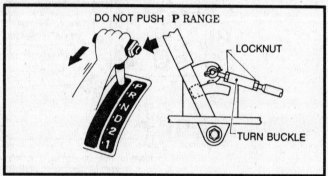

View of the shift selector lever linkage – Truck and Pathfinder

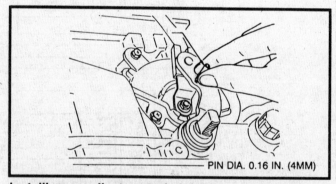

Installing an adjustment pin into the manual shaft-to-inhibitor switch alignment holes

2. Position an oil catch pan under the transmission.
3. Remove the oil pan-to-transmission bolts and the oil pan.
4. After the oil has drained from the transmission, remove the oil strainer.
5. Clean and inspect the parts.
6. To install, use a new gasket and reverse the removal procedures. Lower the vehicle. Add transmission fluid to the transmission, start the engine and check the fluid level.

VALVE BODY

Removal and Installation

1. Raise and safely support the vehicle.
2. Remove the oil pan and drain the fluid.
3. Remove the valve body-to-transmission bolts, the valve body and disconnect the electrical connector.

4. Clean and inspect the parts.

5. To install, use a new gasket and reverse the removal procedures.

6. Lower the vehicle. Add transmission fluid to the transmission, start the engine and check the fluid level.

ACCUMULATORS

Removal and Installation

1. Raise and safely support the vehicle.

2. Drain the fluid and remove the oil pan.

3. Remove the control valve assembly.

4. Using compressed air, support each accumulator with a clean rag and force them from the transmission.

5. To install, use new sealing parts, lubricate them with transmission fluid and reinstall them.

6. To complete the installation, reverse the removal procedures. Refill the transmission.

REVOLUTION SENSOR

Removal and Installation

1. Raise and safely support the vehicle.

2. Using a floor jack and a block of wood, support the rear of the transmission.

3. Remove the transmission-to-crossmember bolts, the crossmember-to-chassis bolts and the crossmember.

4. Lower the transmission as much as possible.

NOTE: On all except Truck and Pathfinder, the revolution sensor is located on the front left side of the extension housing. On the Truck and Pathfinder, the revolution sensor is located on front top of the extension housing.

5. Disconnect the electrical connector from the sensor.

6. Remove the sensor from the transmission.

7. To install, use new seals and reverse the removal procedures.

REAR OIL SEAL

Removal and Installation

1. Raise and safely support the vehicle.

2. Remove the driveshaft on all except Truck and Pathfinder.

3. On 4WD vehicles, perform the following procedures:

a. Drain the oil from the transmission and transfer case.

b. Remove both the front and rear driveshafts; insert a plug into the transfer case's rear oil seal.

c. Remove the torsion bar spring and the 2nd crossmember.

d. Remove the transfer shift control lever from the transfer outer shift lever.

e. Remove the transfer case-to-transmission bolts and the transfer case.

4. Using a small pry bar, remove the oil seal; be careful not to damage the seal surface or scratch the output shaft.

5. Using a new oil seal and an oil seal driver tool, lubricate the seal with automatic transmission fluid and drive it into the extension housing until it is flush with the housing.

6. On 4WD vehicles, perform the following procedures:

a. Using a new gasket, install and torque the transfer case-to-transmission bolts to 23–30 ft. lbs. (31–41 Nm).

b. Install the transfer shift control lever to the transfer outer shift lever.

c. Install the 2nd crossmember and the torsion bar spring.

d. Remove the oil seal plug and reinstall both driveshafts.

e. Refill the transmission and transfer cases with clean fluid.

7. On 2WD vehicles, install the driveshaft and lower the vehicle.

REMOVAL AND INSTALLATION

TRANSMISSION REMOVAL

1. Raise and safely support the vehicle.

2. Scribe alignment matchmarks on the driveshaft-to-final drive flanges and/or on the driveshaft-to-center bearing flanges for a 2-piece driveshaft. If equipped with 4WD, scribe alignment matchmarks on the front driveshaft-to-front final drive flanges and the front driveshaft-to-transfer case flange.

3. If equipped with a 1-piece driveshaft, remove the driveshaft-to-final drive flange bolts and pull the driveshaft from the transmission. If equipped with a 2-piece driveshaft, remove the driveshaft-to-final drive bolts, the driveshaft-to-center bearing flanges bolts and the driveshaft. If equipped with 4WD, remove the front driveshaft-to-front final drive flange bolts, the front driveshaft-to-transfer case flange bolts and the driveshaft.

4. If equipped with a 2-piece driveshaft, remove the center bearing-to-chassis bolts, the retainer and pull the driveshaft from the transmission.

NOTE: After removing the driveshaft(s), be sure to plug the transmission or transfer case opening(s).

5. If necessary, remove the front exhaust pipe.

6. Disconnect the shift lever from the transmission.

7. Disconnect and plug the oil cooler tubes from the transmission. Drain the fluid from the transmission.

8. Label and disconnect any electrical connectors from the transmission.

9. Using a floor jack and wooden blocks, support the engine.

10. Remove the torque converter-to-drive plate cover.

11. Matchmark the torque converter-to-drive plate location.

Remove the torque converter-to-drive plate bolts; it will be necessary to rotate the crankshaft to expose the other bolts. Push the torque converter back into the transmission housing.

12. Remove the dipstick/filler tube from the transmission.

13. Using a transmission jack, connect it to and support the transmission.

14. Remove the transmission-to-crossmember bolts, the crossmember-to-chassis bolts and the support.

15. Remove the transmission-to-engine bolts. Move the transmission rearward and lower it from the vehicle.

TRANSMISSION INSTALLATION

1. Raise the transmission and move it forward to engage the engine.

2. Install the transmission-to-engine bolts and torque to 45–47 ft. lbs. (61–64 Nm).

3. Align the torque converter-to-drive plate matchmark, install the bolts and torque to 29–36 ft. lbs. (39–49 Nm). After installation, rotate the crankshaft to make sure the transmission is not binding and rotates freely.

4. Install the crossmember-to-transmission bolts and the crossmember-to-chassis bolts. Remove the transmission jack.

5. Install the dipstick/filler tube to the transmission. Reconnect the shift lever to the transmission

6. Install the torque converter cover plate and remove the engine support jack.

7. Unplug and reconnect the oil cooler tubes to the transmission.

8. Connect any electrical connectors to the transmission.

9. If the exhaust pipe was removed, install it.

10. If installing a 1-piece driveshaft, slide the front end into the transmission, align the driveshaft flange-to-final drive flange matchmarks and torque the bolts to 29–33 ft. lbs. (39–44 Nm).

11. In installing a 2-piece driveshaft, perform the following procedures:

    a. Install the front section into the transmission and raise the center bearing into the retainer.

    b. Install the center bearing retainer and torque the retainer-to-chassis nuts to 19–29 ft. lbs. (25–39 Nm).

    c. Align the rear section flanges with the matchmarks of the center bearing flange and the final drive flanges.

    d. Install the bolts and torque the driveshaft-to-final drive bolt to 29–33 ft. lbs. (39–44 Nm) and the driveshaft-to-center bearing flange bolts to 25–33 ft. lbs. (34–44 Nm).

12. If equipped with 4WD, align the front driveshaft-to-front final drive flange and the front driveshaft flange-to-transfer case flange matchmarks. Install the bolts and torque to 29–33 ft. lbs. (39–44 Nm).

13. Lower the vehicle. Add transmission fluid to the transmission, start the engine and check the fluid level.

BENCH OVERHAUL

Before Disassembly

Cleanliness is an important factor in the overhaul of the automatic transmission Before opening up this unit, the entire outside of the transmission assembly should be cleaned, preferable with a high pressure washer such as a car wash spray unit. Dirt entering the transmission internal parts will negate all the time and effort spent on the overhaul. During inspection and reassembly all parts should be thoroughly cleaned with solvent then dried with compressed air. Wiping cloths and rags should not be used to dry parts since lint will find its way into the valve body passages.

Wheel bearing grease, long used to hold thrust washers and lube parts, should not be used. Lube seals with clean transmission fluid and use ordinary unmedicated petroleum jelly to hold the thrust washers and to ease the assembly of seals, since it will not leave a harmful residue as grease often will. Do not use solvent on neoprene seals, friction plates if they are to be reused, or thrust washers. Be wary of nylon parts if the transmission failure was due to failure of the cooling system. Nylon parts exposed to water or antifreeze solutions can swell and distort and must be replaced.

Before installing bolts into aluminum parts, always dip the threads into clean transmission fluid. Antiseize compound can also be used to prevent bolts from galling the aluminum and seizing. Always use a torque wrench to keep from stripping the threads. Take care when installing new O-rings, especially the smaller O-rings. The internal snaprings should be expanded and the external rings should be compressed, if they are to be reused. This will help insure proper seating when installed.

Converter Inspection

1. Remove the torque converter from the transmission.

2. Insert a torque converter one-way clutch check tool into the spline of the one-way clutch inner race.

3. Using a wire, hook the one-way clutch outer race bearing support.

4. While holding the bearing support with the wire, turn the check tool to make sure the one-way clutch inner race rotates in the clockwise direction only.

5. If necessary, clean the converter and retest the clutch. Replace the converter if it fails the test.

Transmission Disassembly

1. While holding the torque converter firmly, turn it and pull it straight out.

2. Check the torque converter's one-way clutch.

3. Remove the inhibitor switch-to-transmission bolts and the switch.

4. Remove the oil pan by performing the following procedures:

    a. Drain the transmission fluid from the adapter case.

    b. Using 2 wooden blocks, position them under the adapter case and the converter housing.

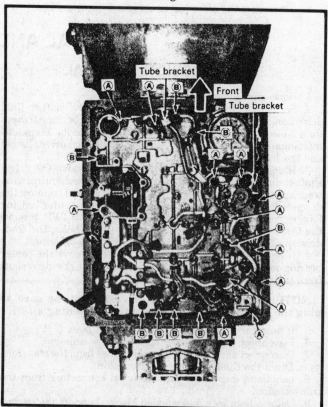

View of the control valve assembly-to-transmission bolts

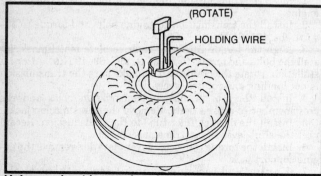

Using a checking tool and a wire to inspect the torque converter's one-way clutch

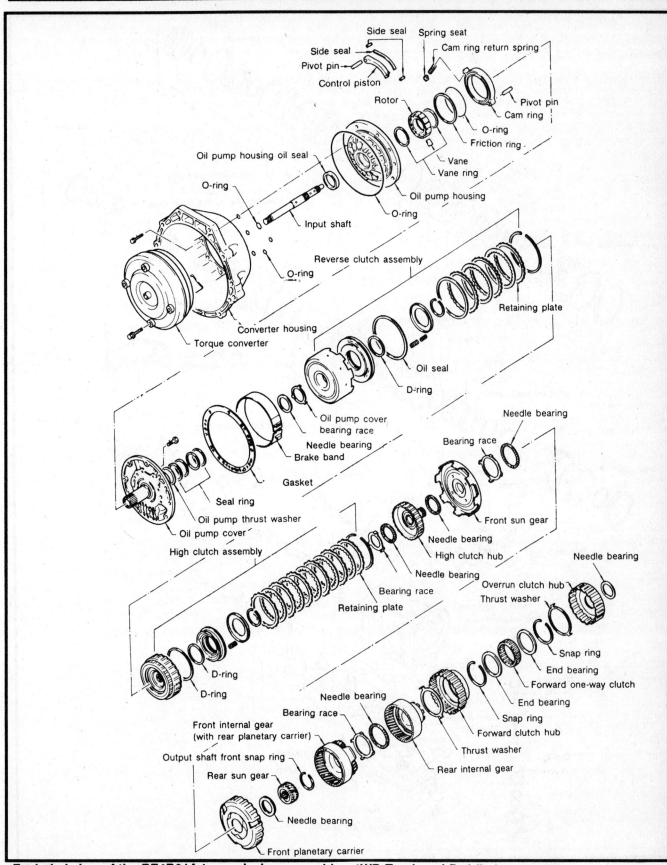

Exploded view of the RE4R01A transmission assembly—4WD Truck and Pathfinder—240SX transmission is similar

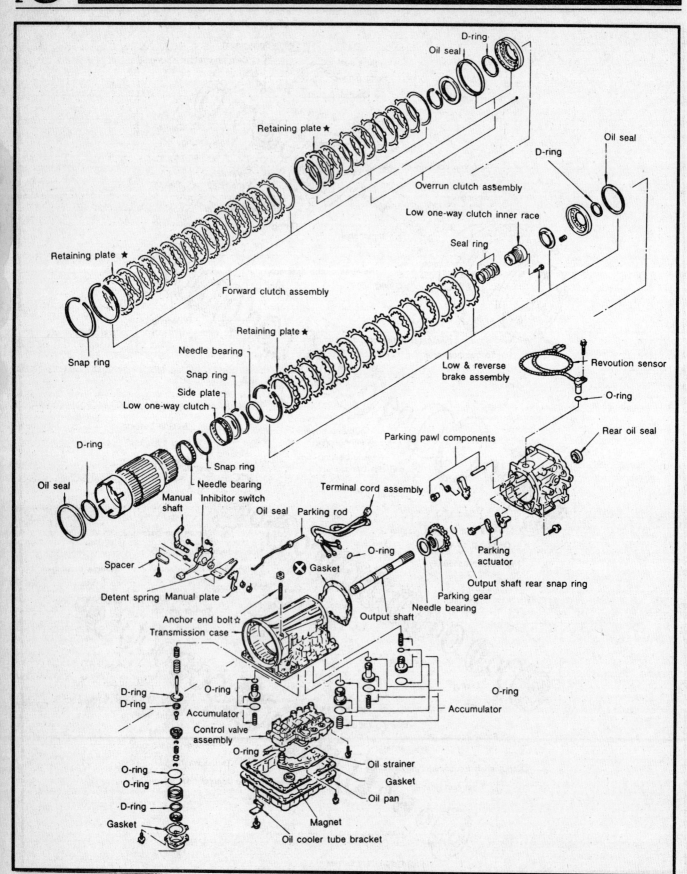

Location of the automatic transmission's components

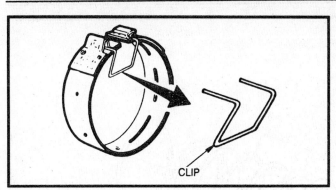

Using a clip to secure the brake band in a circular shape

c. Remove the oil pan-to-transmission bolts. Remove the oil pan from the transmission.

NOTE: The oil pan must be removed in this fashion to retain the sludge in the pan.

5. Inspect the oil pan and strainer for signs of transmission break down:

   a. Pieces of clutch material indicate the clutch plates may be worn.

   b. Metal filings indicate the clutch plates, brake bands or etc. may be worn.

   c. Aluminum filings indicate the bushings or aluminum castings may be worn.

6. Using a transmission stand tool, secure it to and invert the transmission so the control valve is facing upward.

7. Using a small pry bar, separate and disconnect the lockup solenoid and temperature senor connectors; be careful not to damage the connectors.

8. Remove the oil strainer-to-valve body bolts, the oil stainer and the O-ring from the strainer; check the screen for damage.

9. Remove the control valve assembly by performing the following procedures:

   a. At the terminal cords, straighten the clips, remove the cords and the terminal clips.

   b. Remove the control valve-to-transmission **A** and **B** bolts and the control valve assembly.

   c. Using a small pry bar, disconnect the solenoid connector; be careful not to damage the connector.

   d. Remove the manual valve from the control valve assembly.

10. From the transmission case, push on the stopper and remove the terminal cord assembly; be careful not to damage the cord and do not remove the cord unless it is damaged.

11. From inside the converter housing, remove the converter housing-to-transmission bolts, the housing, the O-rings and sealant; be careful not to scratch the converter housing.

12. From the output shaft, remove the O-ring.

13. Remove the oil pump by performing the following procedures:

   a. Using 2–sliding hammer tools, attach them to the oil pump assembly and extract the oil pump evenly from the transmission case.

   b. Remove the sealant and the large O-ring from the outer edge of the oil pump assembly; be careful not to damage the pump housing.

   c. Remove the needle bearing and the thrust washer from the assembly.

14. Remove the input shaft and oil pump gasket.

15. Remove the brake band and band strut by performing the following procedures:

   a. Using an Allen wrench, remove the locknut and the band servo anchor end pin from the transmission case.

b. From inside the case, remove the brake band and band strut.

   c. Using a clip, secure the brake band in a circular shape.

16. Remove the front side clutch and gear components by performing the following procedures:

   a. From the front of the transmission, remove the clutch pack which consists of a reverse clutch, a high clutch and a front sun gear.

   b. From the clutch pack, remove the front bearing race and the rear bearing race.

   c. Remove the front planetary carrier.

   d. From the front planetary carrier, remove the front needle bearing and the rear bearing.

   e. Remove the sun gear.

17. Remove the extension housing (2WD) or the adapter case (4WD) by performing the following procedures:

   a. Remove the housing/case-to-transmission bolts, the housing/case and gasket.

   b. From the rear of the housing/case, remove the oil seal with a pry bar; do not remove the oil seal unless it is to be replaced.

   c. Remove the revolution sensor-to-housing/case bolt, the sensor and the O-ring from the sensor.

18. Remove the output shaft and parking gear by performing the following procedures:

   a. From the output shaft, remove the rear snapring.

   b. Slowly, push the output shaft fully forward; do not use excessive force.

   c. From inside the transmission, remove the output shaft front snapring.

   d. Remove the output shaft and parking gear from the transmission case as a unit and the parking gear from the output shaft.

   e. From the transmission case, remove the needle bearing.

19. Remove the side clutch and gear components by performing the following procedures:

   a. From the front of the transmission, remove the front internal gear and the bearing race from the front internal gear.

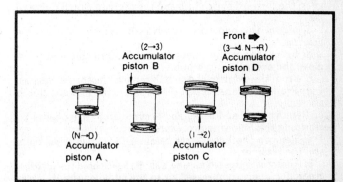

View of the accumulator pistons

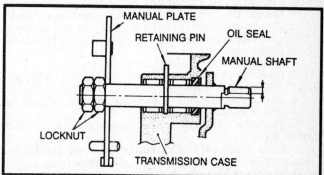

Sectional view of the manual shaft

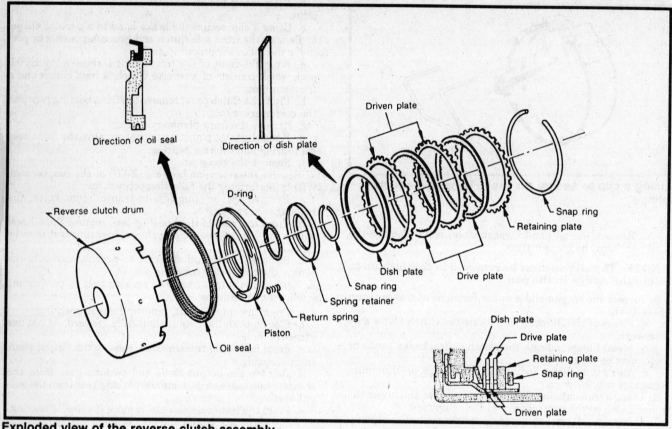

Exploded view of the reverse clutch assembly

b. From the rear internal gear, remove the needle bearing.

c. From the transmission case, remove the rear internal gear, the forward clutch hub and the overrun clutch hub as a set.

d. From the overrun clutch hub, remove the needle bearing.

e. From the rear internal gear and forward clutch hub, remove the overrun clutch hub.

f. From the overrun clutch hub remove the thrust washer.

g. From the transmission case, remove the forward clutch assembly.

20. Remove the band servo and accumulator components by performing the following procedures:

a. Remove the band servo retainer-to-transmission bolts and the retainer.

b. Using compressed air and a shop rag (to hold the piston), gradually, apply compressed air to the oil hole, until the piston comes out.

c. Remove the return spring.

d. Remove the springs from the other accumulator pistons.

e. Using compressed air and a shop rag (to hold each piston), gradually, apply compressed air to each oil hole, until each piston comes out.

f. Remove the O-ring from each piston.

21. If necessary to remove the manual shaft components, perform the following procedures:

a. Secure the shaft flats (outside the transmission) and remove the locknuts (on the inside).

b. From the transmission case, remove the manual shaft retaining.

c. While pushing the detent spring downward, remove the manual plate and parking rod from the transmission case.

d. Remove the manual shaft, the spacer, the detent spring and the oil seal from the transmission case.

Unit Disassembly and Assembly

REVERSE CLUTCH

Disassembly

1. Remove the reverse clutch assembly from the clutch pack.

2. Check the reverse clutch operation by perform the following procedures:

a. Install the seal ring and the reverse clutch onto the oil pump cover.

b. Lightly, apply compressed air into the oil hole; the retaining plate should move to the snapring.

c. If the retaining plate does not move to the snapring, the D-ring or oil seal may be damaged or fluid may be leaking at the piston check ball.

3. Remove the snapring, the retaining plate, the drive plates and the dish plate.

4. Using a clutch spring compressor tool, attach it to the reverse clutch drum and compress the clutch springs. While compressing the clutch springs, remove the snapring from the clutch drum; do not expand the snapring excessively.

5. Remove the spring retainer and return spring.

6. Install the seal ring and the reverse clutch drum onto the oil pump cover. While supporting the piston, gradually, apply compressed air into the oil hole and remove the piston.

─── **CAUTION** ───

Do not, abruptly, apply compressed air to the oil hole, for bodily damage may occur.

7. Remove the D-ring and oil seal from the piston.

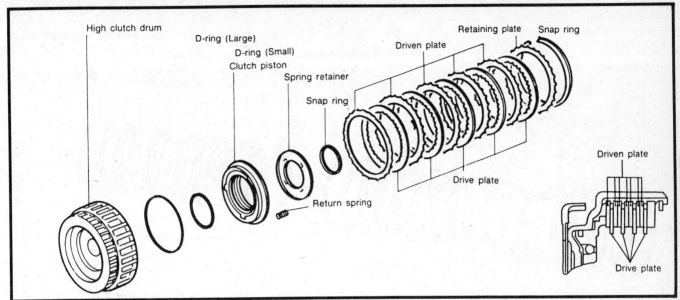

Exploded view of the high clutch assembly

Inspection

1. Inspect the clutch snapring and spring retainer for deformation, fatigue or damage.
2. Inspect the clutch return springs for deformation or damage. The spring length should be 0.77 in. (19.70mm) and the diameter should be 0.45 in. (11.6mm).
3. Inspect the reverse clutch drive plates facing for burns, cracks or damage. The drive plate thickness should be 0.079 in. (2.0mm); if under 0.071 in. (1.8mm), replace the drive plate.
4. Inspect the reverse clutch dish plate for deformation or damage.
5. Shake the reverse clutch piston to make sure the balls are not seized. Using compressed air, lightly, apply it to the check ball oil hole (opposite the return spring) to assure there is no air leakage. Also, apply compressed air to the oil hole (return spring side) to assure air leaks past the ball.

Assembly

1. Lubricate the parts and install the D-ring and oil seal onto the piston.
2. Lubricate the inner surface of the drum and install the piston assembly by turning it slowly and evenly.
3. Install the return springs and the spring retainer.
4. Using a clutch spring compressor tool, attach it to the drum, compress the clutch springs and install the snapring; do not align the snapring gap with the spring retainer stopper.
5. Install the dish plate, the drive plates, the driven plates, the retaining plate and the snapring.
6. Using a feeler gauge, measure the retaining plate-to-snapring clearance; the clearance should be 0.020–0.031 in. (0.5–0.8mm).
7. Check the reverse clutch operation by perform the following procedures:
    a. Install the seal ring and the reverse clutch onto the oil pump cover.
    b. Lightly, apply compressed air into the oil hole; the retaining plate should move to the snapring.
    c. If the retaining plate does not move to the snapring, the D-ring or oil seal may be damaged or fluid may be leaking at the piston check ball.

HIGH CLUTCH

Disassembly

1. Remove the large snapring, the retaining plate, the drive plates and the driven plates.
2. Using a clutch spring compressor tool, attach it to the high clutch assembly and compress the clutch springs.
3. Remove the small snapring, the spring retainer and the clutch springs.
4. Remove the clutch piston and the D-rings.

Inspection

1. Inspect the clutch snapring and spring retainer for deformation, fatigue or damage.
2. Inspect the clutch return springs for deformation or damage. The spring length should be 0.86 in. (22.06mm) and the diameter should be 0.45 in. (11.6mm).
3. Inspect the drive plate thickness; it should be 0.063 in. (1.6mm); if less than 0.055 in. (1.4mm), replace the plate.

Assembly

1. Install the D-rings and the clutch piston into the clutch drum.
2. Install the clutch springs and the spring retainer.
3. Using a clutch spring compressor tool, install it to the clutch drum, compress the clutch springs and install the snapring.
4. Install the drive plates, the driven plates, the retaining plate and the snapring.
5. Using a feeler gauge, measure the retaining plate-to-snapring clearance; the clearance should be 0.071–0.087 in. (1.8–2.2mm).
6. Check the high clutch operation by perform the following procedures:
    a. Install the seal ring and the high clutch onto the oil pump cover.
    b. Lightly, apply compressed air into the oil hole; the retaining plate should move to the snapring.
    c. If the retaining plate does not move to the snapring, the D-ring(s) or oil seal may be damaged or fluid may be leaking at the piston check ball.

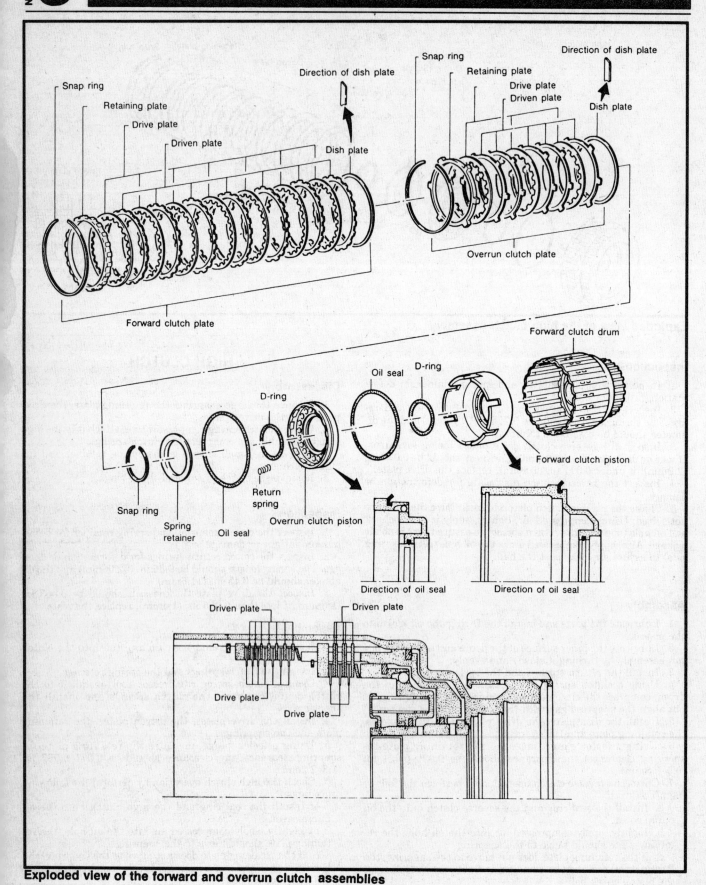

Exploded view of the forward and overrun clutch assemblies

FORWARD AND OVERRUN CLUTCHES

Disassembly

1. From the forward clutch drum, remove the forward clutch plate snapring, the retaining plate, the drive plates, the driven plates and the dish plate.

2. Using compressed air and supporting forward clutch piston, gradually, apply to the forward clutch drum oil hole to drive out the forward clutch piston.

CAUTION

Be careful when applying air pressure, bodily harm could result.

---

3. From the forward clutch piston, remove the snapring, the retaining plate, the drive plates, the driven plates and the dish plate.

4. Using a clutch spring compressor tool, attach it to the forward clutch piston and compress the clutch springs. While compressing the clutch springs, remove the snapring from the overrun clutch piston; do not expand the snapring excessively.

5. Remove the spring retainer and return springs.

6. Remove the D-ring and oil seal from the piston.

Inspection

1. Inspect the snaprings and spring retainer for deformation, fatigue or damage.

2. Inspect the clutch return springs for deformation or damage. The spring length should be 1.40 in. (35.77mm) and the diameter should be 0.38 in. (9.7mm).

3. Inspect the forward and overrun clutch drive plates facing for burns, cracks or damage. The drive plate thickness should be 0.079 in. (2.0mm); if under 0.071 in. (1.8mm), replace the drive plates.

4. Inspect the dish plates for deformation or damage.

Assembly

1. Lubricate the parts and install the D-ring and oil seal onto the piston.

2. Lubricate the inner surface of the drum and install the forward clutch piston by turning it slowly and evenly.

3. Align the notch in the forward clutch piston with the groove in the forward clutch drum.

4. Lubricate the inner surface of the forward clutch piston and install the overrun clutch piston by turning it slowly and evenly.

5. Install the return springs and the spring retainer.

6. Using a clutch spring compressor tool, attach it to the overrun clutch piston, compress the clutch springs and install the snapring; do not align the snapring gap with the spring retainer stopper.

7. Install the overrun clutch dish plate, the drive plates, the driven plates, the retaining plate and the snapring.

8. Using a feeler gauge, measure the overrun clutch retaining plate-to-snapring clearance; the clearance should be 0.039–0.055 in. (1.0–1.4mm).

9. Install the forward clutch dish plate, the drive plates, the driven plates, the retaining plate and the snapring.

10. Using a feeler gauge, measure the forward clutch retaining plate-to-snapring clearance; the clearance should be 0.017–0.033 in. (0.45–0.85mm).

LOW AND REVERSE BRAKE

Disassembly

1. From inside the transmission case, remove the low/reverse brake snapring.

2. Remove the retaining plate, the drive plates, the driven plates and dish plate.

3. From the rear of the transmission case, remove the low one-way clutch inner race-to-case bolts, the low one-way clutch inner race, the spring retainer, and return springs.

4. Remove the seal rings and the needle bearing from the low/one-way clutch inner race.

5. Using compressed air and supporting the low/reverse brake piston, gradually, apply the air to the oil hole (in the case) to remove the low/reverse brake piston.

6. Remove the oil seal and D-ring from the piston.

Inspection

1. Inspect the snapring and spring retainer for deformation or damage.

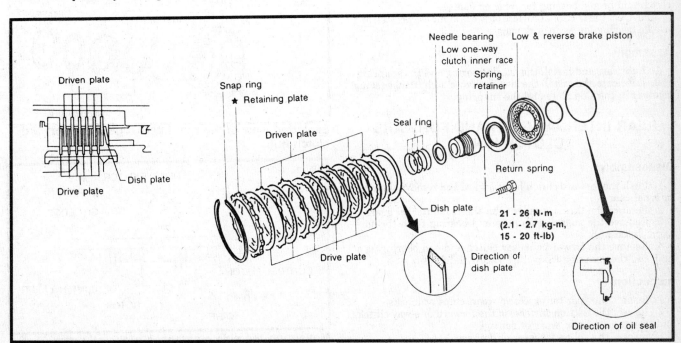

Exploded view of the low and reverse brake clutch assembly

2. Inspect the return springs for deformation or damage. The spring length should be 0.93 in. (23.70mm) and the diameter should be 0.45 in. (11.6mm).

3. Inspect the drive plate thickness; it should be 0.079 in. (2.0mm); if less than 0.071 in. (1.8mm), replace the plate.

4. Inspect the frictional surface of the low one-way clutch inner race for wear or damage. Install new seals and measure the seal-to-groove clearance; it should be 0.0039–0.0098 in. (0.10–0.25mm). If the measurement is greater than 0.0098 in. (0.25mm), replace the low one-way clutch inner race.

Assembly

1. Lubricate the needle bearing with petroleum jelly and install it onto the one-way clutch inner race; the black surface goes toward the rear side.

2. Lubricate the oil seal and D-ring and install them onto the piston.

3. Lubricate the inner surface of the transmission case and install the piston by turning it slowly and evenly.

4. Install the return spring, the spring retainer and the low one-way clutch inner race into the transmission case. Torque the inner race-to-case bolts to 15–20 ft. lbs. (21–26 Nm).

5. Install the dish plate, the drive plates, the driven plates, the retaining plate and the snapring.

6. Using a feeler gauge, measure the retaining plate-to-snapring clearance; the clearance should be 0.049–0.059 in. (1.1–1.5mm).

7. Lubricate with petroleum jelly and press the one-way inner clutch race seal ring firmly into place.

FORWARD CLUTCH DRUM ASSEMBLY

Disassembly

1. From the forward clutch drum, remove the snapring, the side plate and the low/one-way clutch.

2. Remove the snapring and the needle bearing.

Inspection

1. Inspect the drum's spline portion for wear or damage.

2. Inspect the drum's frictional surfaces of the low/one-way clutch and needle bearing for wear or damage.

3. Inspect the frictional surface of the low/one-way clutch and needle bearing for wear or damage.

Assembly

1. Lubricate and install the needle bearing and the snapring.

2. Lubricate and install the low/one-way clutch (flange facing rearward), the side plate and the snapring.

REAR INTERNAL GEAR AND FORWARD CLUTCH HUB

Disassembly

1. Push the forward clutch hub forward and remove the rear internal gear.

2. Remove the thrust washer from the rear internal gear.

3. Remove the snapring and the end bearing from the forward clutch hub.

4. Remove the forward one-way clutch and end bearing as a unit and the snapring from the forward clutch hub.

Inspection

1. Inspect the gear for excessive wear, chips or cracks.

2. Inspect the friction surfaces of the forward one-way clutch and thrust washer for wear or damage.

3. Inspect the spline for wear or damage.

4. Inspect the snaprings for deformation or damage.

Assembly

1. Install the snapring onto the forward clutch hub.

2. Install the end bearing and the forward one-way clutch onto the clutch hub; be sure to install the clutch with the flange facing rearward.

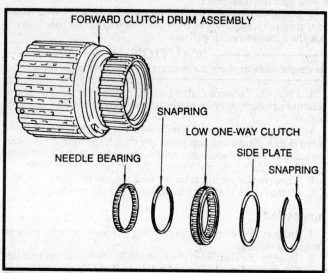

Exploded view of the forward clutch drum assembly

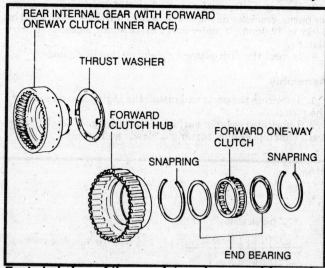

Exploded view of the rear internal gear and forward clutch hub

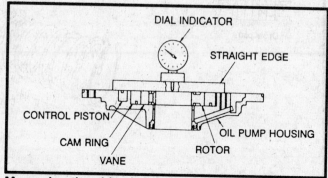

Measuring the side clearances of the oil pump housing

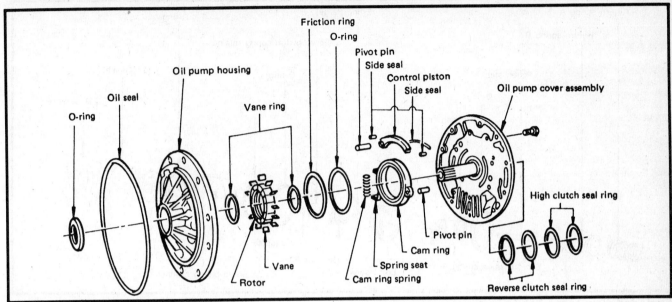

Exploded view of the oil pump assembly

3. Install the end bearing and the snapring.

4. Lubricate the thrust washer with petroleum jelly and install it onto the rear internal gear; be sure to install the thrust washer pawls into gear holes.

5. Install the rear gear into the clutch hub.

6. Make sure the clutch hub rotates clockwise.

OIL PUMP

Disassembly

1. Diagonally, loosen the oil pump bolts and remove the cover.

2. Remove the rotor, the vane rings and vanes; scribe a mark on the back side of the rotor for reassembly purposes.

3. While pushing on the cam ring, remove the pivot pin; be carefully not to scratch the oil pump housing.

4. While holding the cam ring and spring, lift out the cam ring spring; be careful not to damage the oil pump housing and hold the cam ring spring to prevent it from jumping out.

5. Remove the cam ring and the spring from the oil pump housing.

6. Remove the pivot pin from the control piston and the control piston assembly.

7. Using a small pry bar, remove the oil seal from the oil pump housing; be careful not to damage the housing.

Inspection

1. Inspect the oil pump cover, the rotor, the vanes, the control piston, the side seats, the cam ring and the friction ring for wear and/or damage.

NOTE: Before measuring the side clearances, make sure the friction rings, the O-ring, the control piston side seals and the cam ring spring are removed.

2. Using a dial micrometer and a straight edge, measure the side clearances between the end of the pump housing and the cam ring, the rotor, the vanes and the control piston in at least 4 places along their circumferences. Clearance for the cam ring is 0.0004–0.0009 in. (0.01–0.024mm) and for the rotor, vanes and control piston is 0.0012–0.0017 in. (0.03–0.044mm); if not within specifications, replace the oil pump assembly, except the oil pump cover assembly.

3. Using feeler gauges, measure the seal ring-to-ring groove clearance of the oil pump cover. The clearance should be 0.0039–0.0098 in. (0.10–0.25mm); if not within specifications, replace the oil pump cover assembly.

Assembly

1. Using an oil seal installation tool, lubricate the new oil seal with transmission fluid and drive it into the oil pump housing.

2. Install the cam ring by performing the following procedures:

   a. Using petroleum jelly, lubricate the side seal and install it onto the control piston by positioning the black surface toward the piston.

   b. Install the control piston onto the oil pump.

   c. Using petroleum jelly, lubricate the new O-ring. Install the O-ring and the friction ring onto the cam ring.

   d. Assemble the cam ring, the spring and the spring seat; the spring must be installed by pushing it against the pump housing.

   e. Using a pry bar to press on the cam ring, install the pivot pin.

3. Install the rotor, the vanes and the vane rings; be sure to install the rotor in the correct direction.

4. Assemble the oil pump housing by performing the following procedures:

   a. Using masking tape, wrap it around the oil pump cover splines to protect the seal.

   b. Position the oil pump cover assembly into the oil pump housing and remove the masking tape.

   c. Tighten the oil pump cover-to-housing bolts in a crisscross pattern.

NOTE: Seal rings come in 2 sizes: small diameter (no mark) or large diameter (yellow dot); be sure to check the fit in each groove. Be careful not to spread the ring gap excessively for it may become deformed.

5. Using petroleum jelly, pack the oil pump shaft grooves. Carefully, install the seal rings by pressing them into the grooves.

BAND SERVO PISTON ASSEMBLY

Disassembly

1. Block the center hole of the O.D. servo piston and an oil

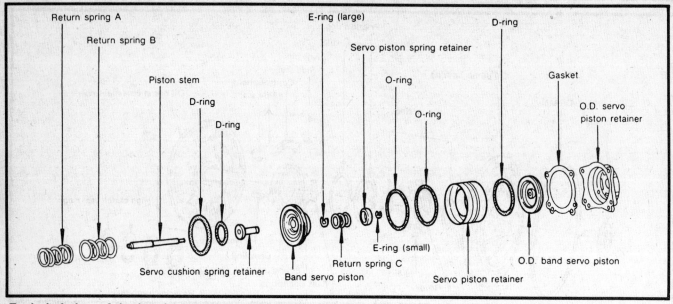

Exploded view of the band servo piston assembly

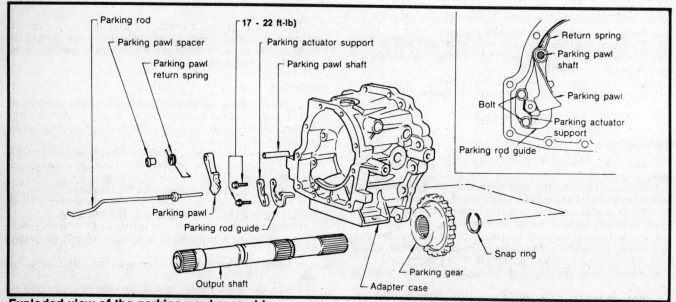

Exploded view of the parking pawl assembly

hole of the O.D. servo piston retainer.

2. Using compressed air, gradually, apply air to the other oil hole in the piston retainer to separate the piston from the retainer.

3. Remove the D-ring from the O.D. band servo piston.

4. Push the band servo piston forward and separate it from the servo piston retainer.

5. Position the piston stem end on a wooden block, push the servo piston spring retainer downward and remove the E-ring. Remove the spring retainer, the return spring C and the piston stem.

6. From the band servo piston, remove the E-ring and the servo cushion spring retainer. Remove the D-rings from the piston and the O-rings from the retainer.

Inspection

1. Inspect the frictional surfaces of the pistons, the retainers and the piston stem for abnormal wear or damage.

2. Inspect the return springs for deformation or damage. Measure the spring length, it should be 1.795 in. (45.6mm) for spring **A**, 2.12 in. (53.8mm) for spring **B** and 1.14 in. (29.0mm) for spring **C**. Measure the spring diameter, it should be 1.35 in. (34.3mm) for spring **A**, 1.59 in. (40.3mm) for spring **B** and 1.09 in. (27.6mm) for spring **C**.

Assembly

1. Lubricate the O-rings and install them onto the servo piston retainer.

2. Install the servo cushion spring retainer onto the band servo piston and the E-ring onto the servo cushion spring retainer.

3. Lubricate the D-rings and install them onto the band servo piston. Install the servo piston retainer, the return spring C and the piston stem onto the band servo piston.

4. Position the piston stem onto a block of wood, push the spring retainer downward and install the E-ring.

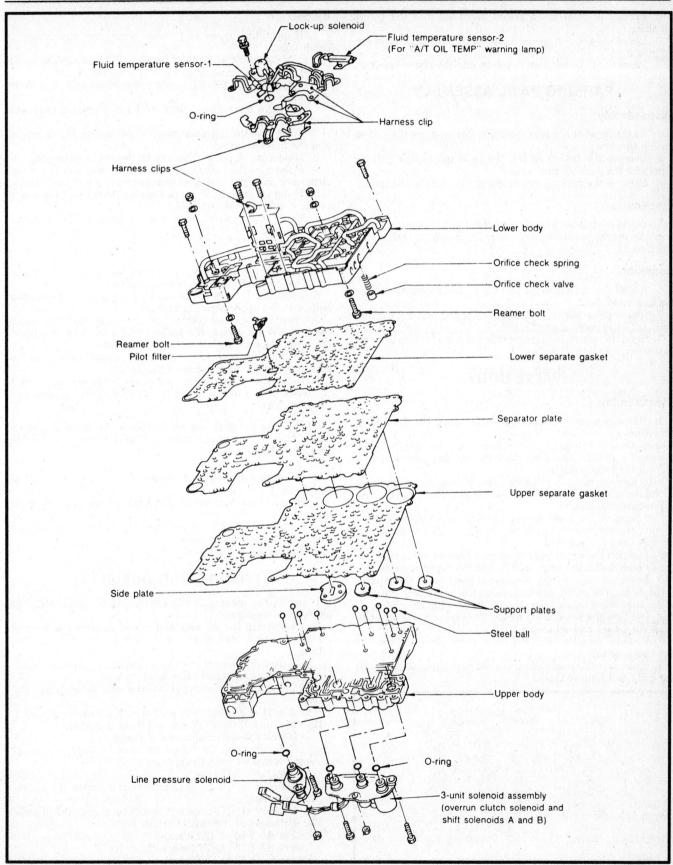

Lock-up solenoid

Fluid temperature sensor-2
(For "A/T OIL TEMP" warning lamp)

Fluid temperature sensor-1

O-ring

Harness clip

Harness clips

Lower body

Orifice check spring

Orifice check valve

Reamer bolt

Reamer bolt

Pilot filter

Lower separate gasket

Separator plate

Upper separate gasket

Side plate

Support plates

Steel ball

Upper body

O-ring

O-ring

Line pressure solenoid

3-unit solenoid assembly
(overrun clutch solenoid and
shift solenoids A and B)

Exploded view of the control valve assembly

5. Press the band servo piston assembly into the piston retainer.

6. Lubricate the D-ring and install it onto the O.D. band servo piston.

7. Press the O.D. band servo piston into the piston retainer.

PARKING PAWL ASSEMBLY

Disassembly

1. At the front of the rear extension flange, move the return spring forward.

2. Remove the return spring, the pawl spacer, the parking pawl and the parking pawl shaft.

3. Remove the parking actuator support and the rod guide.

Inspection

Inspect the contact surface of the parking rod, the parking pawl and the actuator support for wear; if necessary, replace the worn parts.

Assembly

1. Install the rod guide, the parking actuator support and the parking pawl shaft.

2. Install the return spring, the pawl spacer and the parking pawl onto the parking pawl shaft.

3. Bend the return spring upwards and install it into the rear extension.

VALVE BODY

Disassembly

1. Remove the solenoids by performing the following procedures:

   a. Remove the lockup solenoid-to-lower body bolt(s), the solenoid and the side plate. Remove and discard the O-ring from the lockup solenoid.

   b. Remove the line pressure solenoid-to-upper body nut(s) and the solenoid. Remove and discard the O-ring from the line pressure solenoid.

   c. Remove the 3-unit solenoid assembly-to-upper body nut/bolts and the solenoid assembly. Remove and discard the O-rings from the solenoids.

2. Position the upper body facedown. Remove lower body-to-upper body bolts, the reamer bolts and the support plates.

3. From the upper body, remove the lower body, the separator plate and the gasket as a unit; be careful not to drop the pilot filter, the orifice check valve, the spring and the steel balls.

4. Position the lower body assembly facedown. Remove the separate gasket and separator plate.

5. Remove the pilot filter, the orifice check valve and the orifice check spring.

6. Make sure the steel balls are correctly positioned in the upper body and remove them.

View of the steel ball locations in the upper body

Inspection

1. Inspect the upper and lower bodies for the following conditions:

   a. Make sure the pins and retainer plates are in the upper and lower bodies; be careful not to loose these parts.

   b. Make sure the oil circuits are clean and free from damage.

   c. Make sure the tubes and tube connectors are undamaged.

2. Make sure the separator plate is not damaged or deformed and the holes are clean.

3. Make sure the pilot filter is not clogged or damaged.

4. Make sure the lockup and line pressure solenoids are not clogged or damaged. Using an ohmmeter, check the resistance.

5. Using an ohmmeter, check the resistance of each solenoid in the 3-unit solenoid assembly.

6. Using an ohmmeter, check the resistance of the fluid temperature sensor.

Assembly

1. Position the upper body oil circuit facing upwards and install the steel balls in their proper positions.

2. From the bottom of the upper body, install the reamer bolts and the upper separate gasket.

3. Position the lower body oil circuit facing upwards. Install the orifice check spring, the orifice check valve, the pilot filter, the lower separate gasket and separator plate.

4. Install and temporarily tighten the support plates, the fluid temperature sensor and tube brackets.

5. Using the reamer bolts as a guide, temporarily assemble the lower body onto the upper body and tighten the bolts and tube brackets.

NOTE: Be careful not to dislocate or drop the steel balls, the orifice check spring, the orifice check valve and pilot filter.

6. Using new O-rings, lubricate and install them onto the solenoids.

7. Install the lockup solenoid and side plates onto the lower body.

8. Install the 3-unit solenoid assembly and the line pressure solenoid onto the upper body.

9. Tighten all of the bolts.

Transmission Assembly

1. Install the manual shaft components by performing the following procedures:

   a. Lubricate the oil seal and install it onto the manual shaft; be sure to wrap the manual shaft threads with masking tape.

   b. Insert the manual shaft/oil seal assembly into the transmission case and remove the masking tape.

   c. Using a wooden wedge, press the oil seal firmly into the case.

   d. Align the manual shaft groove with the drive pin hole in the case. Install the drive pin and drive it into place.

   e. Install the detent spring and spacer.

   f. Manually push the detent spring downward and install the manual plate onto the manual shaft.

   g. Install the locknuts.

2. Install the accumulator pistons by performing the following procedures:

   a. Lubricate the O-rings and install them onto the pistons. The diameters of the small O-rings are:

   Piston A—1.14 in. (29.0mm)
   Piston B—1.26 in. (32.0mm)
   Piston C—1.77 in. (45.0mm)
   Piston D—1.14 in. (29.0mm)

The diameters of the large O-rings are:
    Piston A – 1.77 in. (45.0mm)
    Piston B – 1.97 in. (50.0mm)
    Piston C – 1.97 in. (50.0mm)
    Piston D – 1.77 in. (45.0mm)

b. Measure the return spring's free length, for accumulator A, and install it into the transmission case; the free length should be 1.69 in. (43.0mm).

c. Lubricate the other accumulator piston bores and install the pistons.

3. Install the band servo piston by performing the following procedures:

a. Install the return springs onto the servo piston.

b. Lubricate the piston's O-ring and the piston bore in the case. Install the band servo piston.

c. Install the band servo retainer into the case.

4. Install the rear side clutch and gear assembly by performing the following procedures:

a. Position the transmission case in a vertical position.

b. Lower the forward clutch drum assembly into the transmission case and move it, slowly, clockwise until the hub passes over the clutch inner race.

NOTE: Be sure the rotation of the forward clutch assembly is clockwise.

c. Lubricate the thrust washer with petroleum jelly and install it onto the front of the overrun clutch hub so the pawls fit into the holes of the overrun clutch hub.

d. Install the overrun clutch hub onto the rear internal gear assembly.

e. Lubricate the needle bearing with petroleum jelly and install it onto the rear of the overrun clutch hub.

f. While holding the overrun clutch hub, facing downward, make sure the forward clutch hub rotates counter-clockwise.

g. Position the transmission case on the transmission stand so it is in the horizontal position with the bottom facing upwards.

h. Install the rear internal gear, the forward clutch hub and the overrun clutch hub as a unit into the transmission case.

i. Lubricate the needle bearing with petroleum jelly and install it onto the rear internal gear.

j. Lubricate the bearing race with petroleum jelly and install it onto the rear of the front internal gear so the pawls fit into the holes of the front internal gear.

k. Install the front internal gear into the transmission case.

5. Install the front side clutch and gear components by performing the following the procedures:

a. While paying attention to it's direction, install the rear sun gear into the transmission case.

b. Lubricate the needle bearing with petroleum jelly and install it onto the front of the front planetary carrier.

c. Lubricate the needle bearing with petroleum jelly and install it onto the rear of the front planetary carrier; the black side faces forward.

d. While rotating the forward clutch drum clockwise, install the front planetary carrier onto the forward clutch drum.

NOTE: Make sure that a portion of the front planetary carrier, protrudes about 0.08 in. (2mm) beyond the surface of the forward clutch assembly.

e. Lubricate the bearing races with petroleum jelly and install them onto the rear of the clutch pack so the pawls fit into the holes of the clutch pack.

f. Move the transmission case into the vertical position.

g. Install the clutch pack into the transmission case.

6. Adjust the total endplay by performing the following procedures:

a. Using a shim setting gauge tool set, attach the long ends of the legs, firmly, on the machined surface of the oil pump assembly. Allow the gauging cylinder to rest on top of the needle bearing and lock it into place with the set screw.

b. Install a gauging plunger into the gauging cylinder.

c. Invert the gauging tool and install it into the transmission case by allowing its legs to rest on the machined surface (no gasket) of the transmission case; allow the gauging plunger to rest on the bearing race. Turn the set screw to lock the gauging plunger into place.

d. Remove the gauging tool.

e. Using a feeler gauge measure the gauging cylinder-to-plunger gap; it should be 0.0098–0.0217 in. (0.25–0.55mm). If the endplay is out of specifications, increase or decrease the thickness of the oil pump cover bearing race.

7. Adjust the reverse clutch drum endplay by performing the following procedures:

a. Using a shim setting gauge tool set, attach the short ends of the legs, firmly, on the machined surface (no gasket)

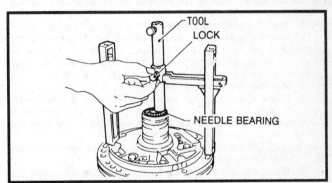

Adjusting the gauging tool on the oil pump assembly to check the total endplay

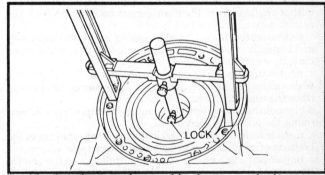

Positioning the gauging tool in the transmission case to check the total endplay

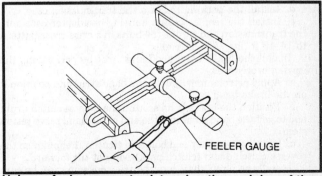

Using a feeler gauge to determine the endplay of the oil pump cover bearing race

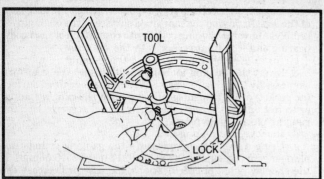

Positioning the gauging tool in the oil pump assembly to check the reverse clutch drum endplay

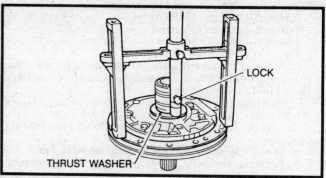

Adjusting the gauging tool on the transmission case to check the reverse clutch drum endplay

of the transmission case. Allow the gauging cylinder to rest on front thrust surface of the reverse clutch drum and lock it into place with the set screw.

    b. Install a gauging plunger into the gauging cylinder.

    c. Invert the gauging tool and install it onto the oil pump assembly, allowing its legs to rest on the machined surface; allow the gauging plunger to rest on the thrust washer. Turn the set screw to lock the gauging plunger into place.

    d. Remove the gauging tool.

    e. Using a feeler gauge measure the gauging cylinder-to-plunger gap; it should be 0.0217–0.0354 in. (0.55–0.90mm). If the endplay is out of specifications, increase or decrease the thickness of the oil pump thrust washer.

8. Install the output shaft and parking gear by performing the following procedures:

    a. While slightly lifting the front internal gear, insert the output shaft into the rear of the transmission; do not force the output shaft against the front of the transmission.

    b. Carefully, push the output shaft against the front of the transmission case and install the snapring at the front of the output shaft; be sure the shaft cannot be removed from the rear direction.

    c. Lubricate the rear needle bearing with petroleum jelly and install it over the output shaft and into the transmission case; be sure the black side faces forward.

    d. Install the parking gear on the output shaft and secure it with a snapring; be sure the output shaft cannot be removed from the rear direction.

9. Install the rear extension housing or adapter case by performing the following procedures:

    a. Lubricate the new oil seal and drive it into the rear of the housing or adapter case using a seal driver tool.

    b. Lubricate the new O-ring and install it onto the revolution sensor. Install the revolution sensor into the housing or adapter case and torque the bolt to 3.6–5.0 ft. lbs. (5–7 Nm).

    c. Install a new housing or adapter case gasket onto the rear of the transmission case.

    d. Install the parking rod into the transmission case.

    e. Install the rear extension housing or adapter case onto the transmission and torque the bolts in a criss-cross pattern to 14–18 ft. lbs. (20–25 Nm).

10. Install the brake band and band strut by performing the following procedures:

    a. Apply petroleum jelly onto the band strut and position it on the brake band.

    b. Position the brake band around the reverse clutch drum and insert the band strut into the end of the band servo piston stem.

    c. Install the anchor end bolt and tighten it enough so the reverse clutch drum (clutch pack) will not tilt forward.

11. Install the input shaft into the transmission case; be sure to position the O-ring groove facing forward.

12. Install a new front case gasket.

13. Install the oil pump assembly by performing the following procedures:

    a. Lubricate the needle bearing and thrust washer with petroleum jelly and install it onto the oil pump assembly.

    b. Lubricate the seal rings with petroleum jelly and press them into the grooves of the oil pump assembly so they are a tight fit.

    c. Lubricate the new large O-ring with petroleum jelly and install it onto the outer edge of the oil pump assembly.

    d. Lubricate the mating surfaces of the transmission and oil pump assembly with petroleum jelly.

    e. Position the oil pump assembly into the transmission case and align the bolt holes; the oil pump should project about 0.04 in. (1mm) from the edge of the transmission case.

14. Lubricate the new O-ring and install it onto the end of the input shaft.

15. Install the converter housing by performing the following procedures:

    a. Install the new small O-rings on the lower portion of the housings mounting surface (transmission side).

    b. Using RTV sealant, apply it to both sides of the housing-to-transmission bolt holes, around the outer circumference of the bolt holes; do not use too much sealant.

    c. Install the converter housing. Torque the housing-to-transmission bolts, in a criss-cross pattern to 45–47 ft. lbs. (61–64 Nm).

16. Torque the brake band anchor end bolt to 2.9–4.3 ft. lbs. (4–6 Nm) and back it off 2½ turns. While holding the anchor end pin, tighten the locknut.

17. Lubricate the terminal cord assembly's O-ring with petroleum jelly, compress the stopper and install the assembly into the transmission case.

18. Install the control valve assembly by performing the following procedures:

    a. Measure the free length of the accumulator piston return springs and install them into the accumulators. The free length should be 2.60 in. (66mm) for **B**, 1.77 in. (45mm) for **C** and 2.30 in. (58.4mm) for **D**.; if not, replace them.

    b. Lubricate the manual valve and install it into the control valve assembly.

    c. Position the control valve assembly on the transmission case and connect the upper body solenoid connector and the connector clip.

    d. Install the control valve assembly and the connector tube brackets. Torque the control valve-to-transmission bolts to 5.1–6.5 ft. lbs. (7–9 Nm); make sure the terminal assembly harness does not catch.

    e. Lubricate the new O-ring with petroleum jelly and install it onto the oil strainer.

    f. Install the oil strainer-to-control valve and torque the bolts to 5.1–6.5 ft. lbs. (7–9 Nm).

    g. Securely fasten the terminal harness with clips.

    h. Connect, the lockup solenoid and fluid temperature sensor connectors.

19. Attach the magnet to the oil pan. Install a new oil pan gasket, the oil pan and bracket. Torque the oil pan-to-transmission bolts, in the criss-cross pattern, to 3.6–5.8 ft. lbs. (5–8 Nm).

20. Install the inhibitor switch by performing the following procedures:

a. Position the manual shaft into **1** range.

b. Temporarily install the inhibitor switch onto the manual shaft.

c. Move the manual shaft into **N**.

d. Using a 0.16 in. (4mm) drill bit, insert it into the manual shaft-to-inhibitor switch adjustment holes, in the vertical position.

e. Tighten the inhibitor switch bolts and remove the adjustment pin.

21. Install the torque converter by performing the following procedures:

a. Using 2⅛ qts. (2L) of automatic transmission fluid, pour it into the torque converter.

NOTE: When reusing an old torque converter, be sure to add the same amount of fluid that was removed.

b. Align the torque converter and oil pump notches and install the converter.

c. Position a straight edge across the front of the torque converter housing and measure the distance from the straight edge to the bosses on the torque converter; the distance should be at least 1.02 in. (26mm).

SPECIFICATIONS

TORQUE SPECIFICATIONS

Part	ft. lbs.	Nm
Case-to-converter housing bolts	45–47	61–64
Oil pump assembly bolts	12–15	16–21
Torque converter-to-flywheel bolts	29–36	39–49
Low one-way clutch inner race bolts	15–20	21–26
Case-to-extension housing bolts	14–18	20–25
Brake servo-to-case bolts	5.1–6.5	7–9
Control valve-to-case bolts	5.1–6.5	7–9
Manual plate locknuts	22–29	29–39
Oil pan-to-case bolts	3.6–5.8	5–8
Case-to-adapter case bolts	14–18	20–25
Revolution sensor bolt	3.6–5.1	5–7

SPECIAL TOOLS

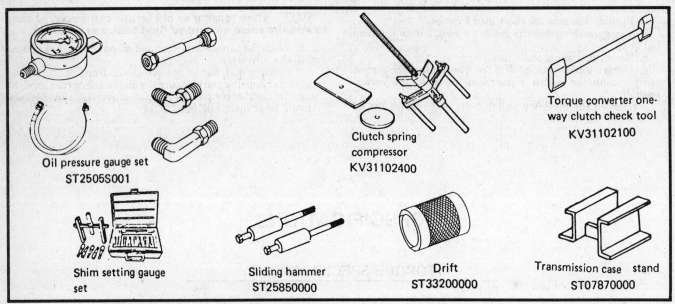

Oil pressure gauge set
ST2505S001

Clutch spring
compressor
KV31102400

Torque converter one-
way clutch check tool
KV31102100

Shim setting gauge
set

Sliding hammer
ST25850000

Drift
ST33200000

Transmission case   stand
ST07870000

View of the special transmission tools

Section 3

A440F and A440L Transmissions
Toyota

APPLICATION

1984–89 Toyota Land Cruiser

GENERAL DESCRIPTION

The A440 automatic transmission is a 4 speed automatic transmission with a 2 speed transfer, developed with the aim of producing an easy driving 4WD vehicle. This transmission is mainly composed of the torque converter, an overdrive planetary gear unit, a 3 speed planetary gear unit, a 2 speed transfer case and the hydraulic control system.

Transmission and Converter Identification

TRANSMISSION

The transmission can be identified by using the vehicle information plate located on the driver's door post. This plate contains the vehicle identification number and all other vehicle information.

CONVERTER

A lockup mechanism is built into the torque converter. The torque converter is a welded unit and is not repairable. If internal problems exist, the torque converter must be replaced.

Metric Fasteners

Metric tools will be required to service this transmission. Due to the large number of alloy parts used in this transmission, torque specifications should be strictly observed. Before installing bolts into aluminum parts, dip the bolts into clean transmission fluid as this will prevent the screws from galling the aluminum threads, thus causing damage.

Metric fastener dimensions are very close to the dimensions of the familiar inch system fasteners. For this reason replacement fasteners must have the same measurement and strength as the original fastener.

Do not attempt to interchange metric fasteners for inch system fasteners. Mismatched or incorrect fasteners can cause damage to the automatic transmission unit and possible personal injury. Care should be taken to reuse fasteners in their original locations.

Capacities

This transmission uses Dexron® II type automatic transmission fluid. The total fluid capacity is 15.9 qts. (15.0L) without an oil cooler. If the vehicle is equipped with an oil cooler, it takes 16.3 qts. (15.4L) of fluid. The oil pan capacity is 6.3 qts. (6.0L) of fluid.

Checking Fluid Level

NOTE: The engine and transmission must be at normal operating temperature (158–176° F) when checking the fluid level. Use only the COOL range on the dipstick as a rough reference when the fluid is replaced or the engine does not run.

1. Park the vehicle on a level surface and set the parking brake.
2. With the engine idling, shift the shift lever into all positions from **P** to **L** and return to the **P** position.
3. Remove the transmission dipstick and wipe it clean.
4. Push the dipstick back fully into the tube.
5. Pull it out and check that the fluid level is in the **HOT** range.
6. If the level is at the low side, add the required amount of Dexron® II automatic transmission fluid.

TROUBLE DIAGNOSIS

CHILTON'S THREE C's TRANSMISSION DIAGNOSIS

Condition	Cause	Correction
Fluid discolored or smells burnt	a) Fluid contaminated b) Torque converter faulty c) Transmission faulty	a) Replace fluid b) Replace torque converter c) Disassemble and inspect transmission
Vehicle does not move in any forward range or reverse	a) Manual linkage out of adjustment b) Valve body or primary regulator faulty c) Parking lock pawl faulty d) Torque converter faulty e) Converter drive plate broken f) Oil pump intake strainer blocked g) Transmission faulty	a) Adjust linkage b) Inspect valve body c) Inspect parking lock pawl d) Replace torque converter e) Replace drive plate f) Clean strainer g) Disassemble and inspect transmission
Shift lever position incorrect	a) Manual linkage out of adjustment b) Manual valve and lever faulty c) Transmission faulty	a) Adjust linkage b) Inspect valve body c) Disassemble and inspect transmission

CHILTON'S THREE C's TRANSMISSION DIAGNOSIS

Condition	Cause	Correction
Harsh engagement into any drive range	a) Throttle cable out of adjustment b) Valve body or primary regulator faulty c) Accumulator pistons faulty d) Transmission faulty	a) Adjust throttle cable b) Inspect valve body c) Inspect accumulator pistons d) Disassemble and inspect transmission
Delayed 1-2, 2-3 or 3-O/D up-shift, or down-shifts from O/D-3 or 3-2 and shifts back to O/D or 3	a) Throttle cable out of adjustment b) Throttle cable and cam faulty c) Governor faulty d) Valve body faulty	a) Adjust throttle cable b) Inspect throttle cable and cam c) Inspect governor d) Inspect valve body
Slips on 1-2, 2-3 or 3-O/D up-shift, or slips or shudders on acceleration	a) Manual linkage out of adjustment b) Throttle cable out of adjustment c) Valve body faulty d) Transmission faulty	a) Adjust linkage b) Adjust throttle cable c) Inspect valve body d) Disassemble and inspect transmission
Drag, binding or tie-up on 1-2, 2-3 or 3-O/D up-shift	a) Manual linkage out of adjustment b) Valve body faulty c) Transmission faulty	a) Adjust linkage b) Inspect valve body c) Disassemble and inspect transmission
No lockup	a) Valve body faulty b) Torque converter faulty c) Transmission faulty	a) Inspect valve body b) Replace torque converter c) Disassemble and inspect transmission
Harsh downshift	a) Throttle cable out of adjustment b) Throttle cable and cam faulty c) Accumulator pistons faulty d) Valve body faulty e) Transmission faulty	a) Adjust throttle cable b) Inspect throttle cable and cam c) Inspect accumulator pistons d) Inspect valve body e) Disassemble and inspect transmission
No downshift when coasting	a) Governor faulty b) Valve body faulty	a) Inspect governor b) Inspect valve body
Downshift occurs too quickly or too late while coasting	a) Throttle cable out of adjustment b) Governor faulty c) Valve body faulty d) Transmission faulty	a) Adjust throttle cable b) Inspect governor c) Inspect valve body d) Disassemble and inspect transmission
No O/D-3, 3-2 or 2-1 kick-down	a) Throttle cable out of adjustment b) Governor faulty c) Valve body faulty	a) Adjust throttle cable b) Inspect governor c) Inspect valve body
No engine braking in 2 or L range	a) Valve body faulty b) Transmission faulty	a) Inspect valve body b) Disassemble and inspect transmission
Vehicle does not hold in P	a) Manual linkage out of adjustment b) Parking lock pawl cam and spring faulty	a) Adjust linkage b) Inspect cam and spring

CLUTCH AND BAND APPLICATION

Shift Lever Position	Gear position	C_0	C_1	C_2	B_0	B_2	B_3	F_0	F_2
P	Parking	Applied	—	—	—	—	—	Applied	—
R	Reverse	Applied	—	Applied	—	—	Applied	Applied	—
N	Neutral	Applied	—	—	—	—	—	Applied	—
D	1st	Applied	Applied	—	—	—	—	Applied	Applied
	2nd	—	Applied	—	—	Applied	—	Applied	—
	3rd	Applied	Applied	Applied	—	—	—	Applied	—
	O/D	—	Applied	Applied	Applied	—	—	—	—
3	1st	Applied	Applied	—	—	—	—	Applied	Applied
	2nd	—	Applied	—	—	Applied	—	Applied	—
	3rd	Applied	Applied	Applied	—	—	—	Applied	—
2	2nd	Applied	Applied	—	—	Applied	—	Applied	—
L	1st	Applied	Applied	—	—	—	Applied	Applied	Applied

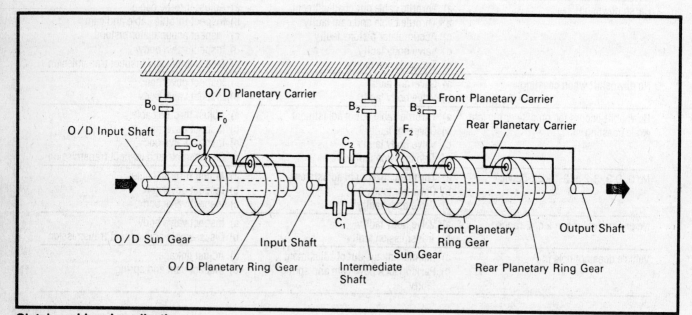

Clutch and band application

Hydraulic Control System

The hydraulic control system is composed of the oil pump, the valve body and the clutches and brakes, as well as the fluid passages which connect all of these components. Based on the hydraulic pressure created by the oil pump, the hydraulic control system governs the hydraulic pressure acting on the torque converter, clutches and brakes in accordance with the vehicle driving conditions.

Hydraulic pressure supplied by the oil pump is controlled by the regulator valve; the resulting oil pressure controlled by the regulator valve is called the line pressure. Line pressure produces the hydraulic pressure for throttle pressure and governor pressure. Line pressure also produces hydraulic pressure for the operation of each brake and clutch in the planetary gear unit.

The throttle valve acts to produce hydraulic pressure called the throttle pressure, which responds to accelerator pedal modulation. Throttle pressure increases as the accelerator pedal is depressed. The governor valve produces hydraulic pressure called governor pressure, in response to vehicle speed. Governor pressure increases as vehicle speed increases.

In accordance with difference between throttle pressure and governor pressure, each shift valve shifts, the fluid passages to the clutches and brakes in the planetary gear unit are opened and the clutches and brakes operate and shift change occurs.

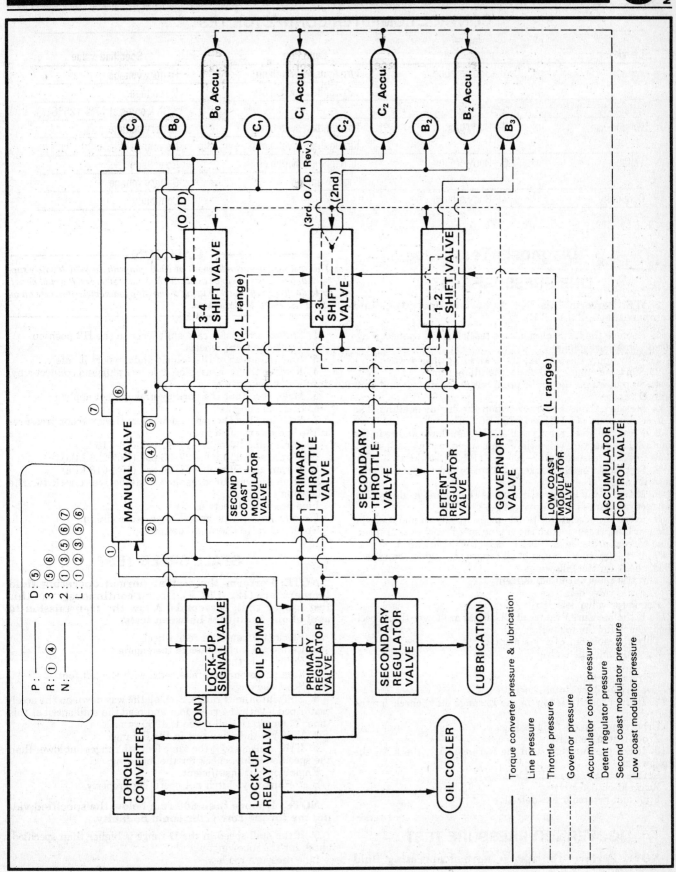

Hydraulic circuitry

CONTROL COMPUTER CONNECTOR TEST

Check for	Tester connection	Condition	Specified value
Voltage	1—Body ground	Turn ignition switch on	Battery voltage
		Turn ignition switch off	No voltage
Continuity	2–5	—	3.38 k ohms at 77°F (25°C)
Voltage	3—Body ground	Turn ignition switch on	Battery voltage
		Turn ignition switch off	No voltage
Voltage	6—Body ground	Turn ignition switch on	No voltage
		Engine running	Battery voltage
Continuity	7—Body ground	—	Continuity

Diagnosis Tests

LINE PRESSURE TEST

NOTE: Perform this test at normal operating fluid temperature (122–176° F).

1. Remove the transmission case test plug and connect a hydraulic pressure gauge.
2. Fully apply the parking brake and block the 4 wheels.
3. Start the engine and check the idling rpm.
4. Step down on the brake pedal with the left foot and shift into **D** range.
5. Measure the line pressure when the engine is idling. The correct pressure is 53–61 psi. (363–422 kPa).
6. Press the accelerator pedal all the way down and read the highest line pressure when the engine speed reaches stall speed. The correct pressure is 158–193 psi. (1089–1344 kPa).
7. Step down on the brake pedal with the left foot and shift into **R** range.
8. Measure the line pressure when the engine is idling. The correct pressure is 64–78 psi. (441–539 kPa).
9. Press the accelerator pedal all the way down and read the highest line pressure when the engine speed reaches stall speed. The correct pressure is 199–242 psi. (1373–1667 kPa).
10. If the measured values at all ranges are higher than specified, check for the following:
    Throttle cable out of adjustment
    Throttle valve defective
    Regulator valve defective
11. If the measured values at all ranges are lower than specified, check for the following:
    Throttle cable out of adjustment
    Throttle valve defective
    Regulator valve defective
    Oil pump defective
    Overdrive direct clutch defective
12. If the pressure is low in the **D** range only, check for the following:
    Drive range circuit fluid leakage
    Front clutch defective
13. If the pressure is low in the **R** range only, check for the following:
    Reverse range circuit fluid leakage
    Rear clutch defective
    First and reverse brake defective

GOVERNOR PRESSURE TEST

NOTE: Perform the test at normal operating fluid temperature (122–176° F).

──────── CAUTION ────────

This measurement can be made at 1000 rpm with the vehicle safely supported, but if tests are to be made at 1800 and 3500 rpm, it would be safer to do this on the road or using a chassis dynamometer because an on stand test could be hazardous.

1. Shift the transfer case shift lever to the **H2** position.
2. Block the front wheels.
3. Raise the rear of the vehicle and support it safely.
4. Remove the transmission case test plug and connect a hydraulic pressure gauge.
5. Make sure that the parking brake is not applied.
6. Start the engine.
7. Shift into the **D** range and measure the governor pressures at the speeds specified below:
   1000 rpm and 20 mph – 11–17 psi. (78–118 kPa)
   1800 rpm and 35 mph – 27–33 psi. (186–226 kPa)
   3500 rpm and 69 mph – 81–90 psi. (559–618 kPa)
8. If the governor pressure is defective, check for the following:
   Line pressure defective
   Fluid leakage in the governor pressure circuit
   Governor valve operation defective

STALL SPEED TEST

NOTE: Perform the test at normal operating fluid temperature (122–176° F). Do not continuously run this test longer than 5 seconds. Allow the transmission to cool about 2 minutes between tests.

1. Block the front and rear wheels.
2. Connect a tachometer to the engine.
3. Fully apply the parking brake.
4. Step down on the brake pedal with the left foot.
5. Start the engine.
6. Shift into the **D** range. Step all the way down on the accelerator pedal with the right foot and read the stall speed at this time. The correct stall speed is 1950 rpm.
7. Perform the same test in the **R** range.
8. If the stall speed is the same for both ranges but lower than the specified value, check for the following:
   Engine output insufficient
   Stator one-way clutch not operating properly

NOTE: If more than 600 rpm below the specified value, the torque converter could be faulty.

9. If the stall speed in the **D** range is higher than specified, check for the following:
   Line pressure too low
   Front clutch slipping

No. 2 one-way clutch not operating properly
Overdrive one-way clutch not operating properly
10. If the stall speed in the **R** range is higher than specified, check for the following:
Line pressure too low
Rear clutch slipping
first and reverse brake slipping
Overdrive one-way clutch not operating properly
11. If the stall speed in both **D** and **R** ranges are higher than specified, check for the following:
Line pressure too low
Improper fluid level
Overdrive one-way clutch not operating properly

TIME LAG TEST

If the shift lever is shifted while the engine is idling, there will be a certain time lapse or lag before the shock can be felt. This test is used for checking the condition of the overdrive direct clutch, front clutch, rear clutch and first and reverse brakes.

NOTE: Perform the test at normal operating fluid temperature (122–176° F). Be sure to allow 1 minute intervals between tests. Make 3 measurements and take the average value.

1. Fully apply the parking brake.
2. Start the engine and check the idle speed. It should be 650 rpm in the **N** range.
3. Shift the shift lever from the **N** to **D** position. Using a stop watch, measure the time it takes from shifting the lever until the shock is felt. The time lag should be less than 0.7 seconds.
4. Following the same procedure, measure the time lag for **N** to **R**. It should be less than 1.2 seconds.
5. If the **N** to **D** time lag is longer than specified, check for the following:
Line pressure too low
Front clutch worn
O/D one-way clutch not operating properly
6. If the **N** to **R** time lag is longer than specified, check for the following:
Line pressure too low
Rear clutch worn
First and reverse brake worn
O/D one-way clutch not operating properly

ROAD TEST

NOTE: Perform the test at normal operating fluid temperature (122–176° F).

D RANGE TEST

1. Shift into the **D** range and drive the vehicle with the accelerator pedal held constant at full throttle valve opening position.
2. Check that the 1–2, 2–3 and 3–O/D up-shifts take place and that the shift points conform to those shown in the automatic shift schedule.
  a. If there is no 1–2 up-shift, check for the following:
Governor valve defective
1–2 shift valve stuck

  b. If there is no 2–3 up-shift, check for the following:
2–3 shift valve stuck
  c. If there is no 3–O/D up-shift, check for the following:
3–4 shift valve stuck
  d. If the shift point is defective, check for the following:
Throttle cable out of adjustment
Throttle valve, 1–2 shift valve, 2–3 shift valve, 3–4 shift valve etc. are defective
3. In the same manner, check the shock and slip at the 1–2, 2–3 and 3–O/D up-shifts. If the shock is excessive, check for the following;
Line pressure too high
Accumulator defective
Check ball defective
4. Drive in the overdrive gear or lockup of the **D** range and check for abnormal noise and vibration.
5. While driving in the 2nd, 3rd or O/D gear of the **D** range, check that the possible kickdown vehicle speed limits for 2–1, 3–2 or O/D–3 kickdowns conform to those indicated in the automatic shift schedule.
6. Check for abnormal shock and slip at the kickdowns.
7. Check for the lockup mechanism by driving in the overdrive gear if the **D** range at a steady speed (lockup **ON**) of about 53 mph. Lightly depress the accelerator pedal and check that the engine rpm does not change abruptly. If there is a big change in engine rpm, there is no lockup.

3 RANGE TEST

1. While driving in 3rd gear of the **3** range, check that there is no up-shift to the overdrive gear.
2. Check for abnormal noise at acceleration and deceleration and for shock at up-shift and downshift.

2 RANGE TEST

1. While driving in the 2nd gear of the **2** range, make sure that there is no up-shift to the 3rd gear.
2. While driving in the 2nd gear of the **2** range, make sure that there is no down-shift to the 1st gear.
3. While driving in the 2nd gear of the **2** range, release the accelerator pedal and check the engine braking effect.
4. Check for abnormal noise during acceleration and deceleration.

L RANGE TEST

1. While driving in the **L** range, check for an up-shift to the 2nd gear.
2. While driving in the **L** range, release the accelerator pedal and check the engine braking effect. If there is no engine braking effect, the 1st and reverse brake is defective.
3. Check for abnormal noise during acceleration and deceleration.

R RANGE TEST

Shift into the **R** range and while starting at full throttle, check for slipping.

P RANGE TEST

Stop the vehicle on a hill and after shifting into the **P** range, release the parking brake. Then check that the parking lock pawl holds the vehicle in place.

OPERATIONAL SPECIFICATIONS

Shift point schedule mph (km/h)	D range (throttle valve fully open)						(fully closed)		2 range	L range
	1→2	2→3	3→O/D	O/D→3	3→2	2→1	Lockup ON	Lockup OFF	3→2	2→1
	17–25 (28–41)	45–53 (72–85)	68–76 (109–122)	63–71 (101–114)	39–47 (63–75)	14–22 (23–36)	48–56 (77–90)	45–53 (73–86)	50–57 (80–92)	2–28 (32–45)

Converter Clutch Operation and Diagnosis

TORQUE CONVERTER CLUTCH

The torque converter is composed of the pump impeller which is rotated by the engine, the turbine runner and lockup clutch is fixed to the transmission input shaft and the stator which is attached to the stator shaft by the one-way clutch. The torque converter is filled with automatic transmission fluid.

The pump impeller is rotated by the engine, which causes a flow of automatic transmission fluid inside the torque converter. The flow of automatic transmission fluid caused by the pump impeller strikes the turbine runner, providing a force to rotate the turbine runner and transmits torque to the input shaft.

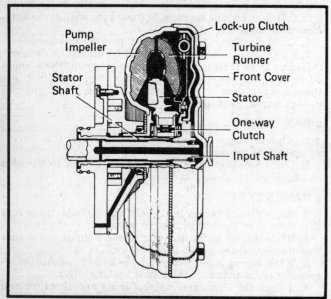

Torque converter crossectional view

The flow of automatic transmission fluid which has hit the turbine runner rebounds and tries to flow in the direction opposite to the direction of rotation of the pump impeller, but the stator returns the flow to the original direction of rotation. So the automatic transmission fluid becomes a force which supports the pump impeller and increases torque.

NOTE: Although the stator is immobilized by the one-way clutch, should the one-way clutch become defective, the stator will be rotated by the flow of automatic transmission fluid. The flow of automatic transmission fluid will not be reversed, torque will not be increased and the problem of inadequate acceleration will occur.

The lockup clutch is pushed against the front cover by fluid pressure so that the engine revolutions are directly transmitted to the input shaft without the medium of the automatic transmission fluid.

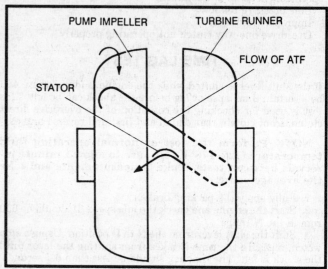

Torque converter operation

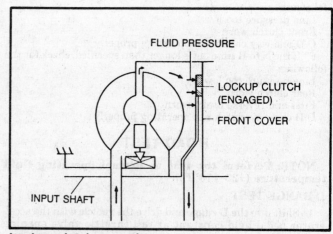

Lockup clutch operation

ON CAR SERVICES

Adjustments

THROTTLE VALVE CABLE

1. Depress the accelerator pedal and check that the throttle valve opens fully. If the throttle valve does not open fully, adjust the accelerator link.
2. Make sure that the throttle cable is installed correctly and not bending.
3. When the throttle valve is fully closed, adjust the cable housing so that the distance between the end of the boot and the stopper on the cable is correct. The correct distance is 0.020–0.059 in. (0.5–1.5mm).
4. If the distance is not correct adjust the cable by the adjusting nuts.

SHIFT LINKAGE

When shifting the shift lever from the **N** position to other positions, check that the lever can be shifted smoothly and accurate-

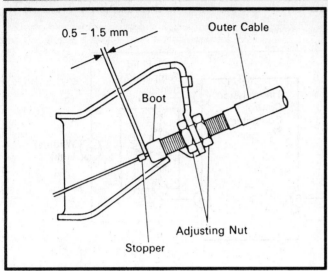

Throttle cable adjustment

ly to each position and that the position indicator correctly indicates the position. If the indicator is not aligned with the correct position, use the following adjustment procedure:
1. Raise the vehicle and support it safely.
2. Loosen the nut on the control rod.
3. Push the control shaft lever fully toward the rear of the vehicle.
4. Return the control shaft lever 2 notches to the **N** position.
5. Set the shift lever to the **N** position.
6. While holding the shift lever lightly toward the **R** position side, tighten the control rod nut.
7. Lower the vehicle.
8. Start the engine and make sure that the vehicle moves forward when shifting the lever from the **N** to **D** position and reverse when shifting it to the **R** position.

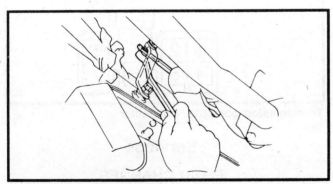

Shift linkage adjustment

NEUTRAL START SWITCH

1. Make sure that the engine can be started with the shift lever only in the **N** or **P** position, but not in other positions.
2. If the engine can be started in other positions, the switch must be adjusted.
3. Loosen the neutral start switch bolts.
4. Set the shift lever to the **N** position.
5. Align the groove and the neutral basic line.
6. While holding it in position, tighten the bolts to 9 ft. lbs. (13 Nm).

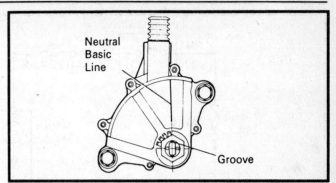

Neutral start switch adjustment and location

Testing

Inspect the neutral start switch using an ohmmeter. Check the continuity of the terminals for each switch position. If the continuity between the terminals is not as specified in the chart, replace the switch.

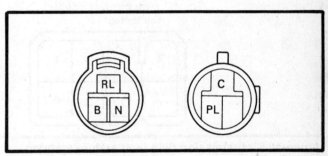

Neutral start switch terminals

NEUTRAL START SWITCH TEST

Shift position	Terminal				
	C	RL	N	B	PL
P range	O———————————————————————————O			O———————O	
R range	O———————O				
N range				O———————O	

AUTOMATIC TRANSMISSION FLUID TEMPERATURE WARNING SYSTEM

Testing

1. To test the temperature warning light, disconnect the connector from the transmission control computer.
2. Connect terminal 1 of the wire harness side connector and body ground.
3. Turn the ignition switch **ON** and check that the light lights.
4. If the warning light does not light, test the bulb.
5. Test the temperature sensor using an ohmmeter. Measure the resistance between terminals. The resistance should be 3.38 ohms at 77° F and 0.55 ohms at 248° F. If the resistance is not as specified, replace the sensor.
6. Test the transmission control computer, by disconnecting the computer connector on the wire harness side following the chart. If the circuit is as specified, replace the computer.

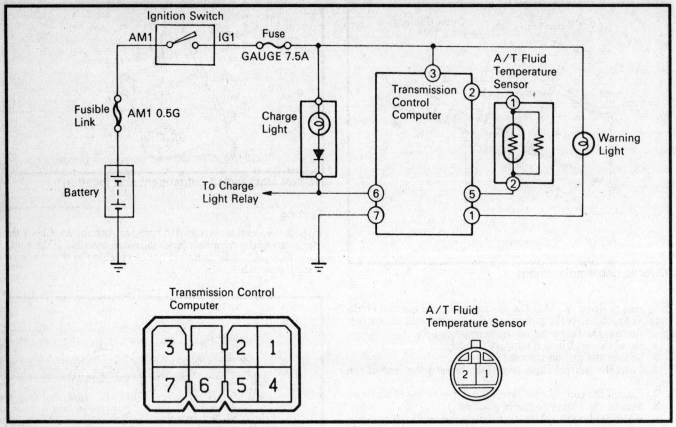

Automatic transmission fluid temperature warning system circuit

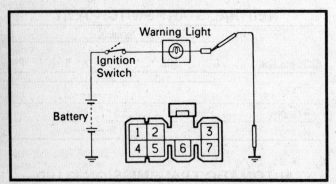

Testing the fluid temperature warning light

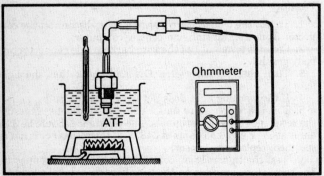

Testing the fluid temperature sensor

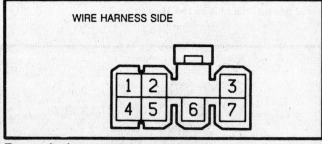

Transmission computer connector

Services

FLUID CHANGES

The conditions under which the vehicle is operated is the main consideration in determining how often the transmission fluid should be changed. Different driving conditions result in different transmission fluid temperatures. These temperatures affect change intervals.

If the vehicle is driven under severe conditions, change the transmission fluid every 15,000 miles. If the vehicle is not used under severe conditions, change the fluid and replace the filter every 30,000 miles.

Do not overfill the transmission. It takes about a pint of automatic transmission fluid to raise the level from the **ADD** to the **FULL** mark on the transmission indicator dipstick. Overfilling the unit can cause damage to the internal components of the automatic transmission.

OIL PAN

Removal and Installation

1. Raise the vehicle and support it safely.
2. Position a suitable drain pan under the transmission oil pan drain plug.
3. Remove the drain plug and drain the fluid.
4. Remove the 6 bolts and the oil pan protector.

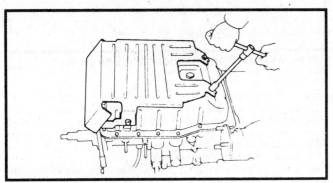

Oil pan protector removal

5. Remove the 20 bolts and the oil pan and gasket.
6. Remove the oil filter.
7. Remove the magnets and use them to collect any steel particles.
8. Inspect and clean the oil pan.
9. Installation is the reverse of the removal procedure. Tighten the oil pan bolts to 61 inch lbs. (6.9 Nm).
10. After the oil pan is installed, fill it with automatic transmission fluid and lower the vehicle. Use the following procedure to check the fluid level.
11. With the engine idling, shift the shift lever into all positions from **P** to **L** and return to the **P** position.
12. Pull out the transmission dipstick and wipe it clean.
13. Push the dipstick back fully into the tube.
14. Pull it out and check that the fluid level is in the **HOT** range.

15. If the level is at the low side, add Dexron®II automatic transmission fluid.

VALVE BODY

Removal and Installation

1. Raise the vehicle and support it safely.
2. Position a suitable drain pan under the transmission oil pan drain plug.
3. Remove the drain plug and drain the fluid.
4. Remove the 6 bolts and the oil pan protector.
5. Remove the 20 bolts and the oil pan and gasket.
6. Remove the 7 bolts, 4 wave washers, lockup relay valve body plate and gasket.

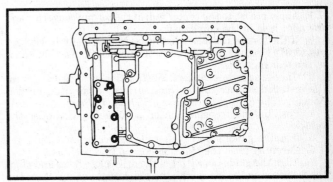

Lockup relay valve body plate

7. Remove the oil tube by prying both tube ends.
8. Temporarily install the lockup relay valve body plate with the 4 short bolts.
9. Remove 10 bolts, oil strainer and gasket.
10. Remove the 15 bolts. Disconnect the throttle cable from the cam and remove the valve body.
11. Installation is the reverse of the removal procedure.
12. When installing the valve body, align the groove of the manual valve with the pin of the manual valve lever.
13. Tighten the valve body bolts to 7 ft. lbs. (10 Nm).

REMOVAL AND INSTALLATION

TRANSMISSION REMOVAL

1. Disconnect the negative battery cable.
2. Open the radiator drain cock and drain the coolant into a suitable drain pan.
3. Disconnect the upper radiator hose.
4. Loosen the adjusting nuts and disconnect the throttle cable housing from the bracket.
5. Disconnect the cable from the throttle linkage.
6. Disconnect the connectors located near the starter.
7. Remove the shift lever knob.
8. Remove the 4 bolts and the shift lever boot.
9. Raise the vehicle and support it safely.
10. Remove the transmission and transfer case undercover pans.
11. Remove the drain plug and drain the automatic transmission fluid into a suitable pan.
12. Remove the clip and pin and disconnect the shift rod from the transfer case.
13. Remove the nut, then remove the washers and the transfer case shift lever with the control rod.

14. Remove the nut and disconnect the control rod from the control shaft lever.
15. Remove the power take-off shift lever knob button, spring and knob.
16. Remove the 4 bolts and the shift lever boot.
17. Remove the nut and disconnect the shift rod from the power take-off.
18. Remove the bolt and then remove the shift lever with the shift rod.
19. Remove the driveshaft.
20. Remove the engine undercover.
21. Matchmark the yoke and flange. Remove the bolts and nuts and disconnect the driveshaft from the power take-off.
22. Remove the front and rear bracket set bolts and then remove the driveshaft.
23. Disconnect the speedometer cable.
24. Disconnect the 2 vacuum hoses.
25. Remove the oil cooler tube clamps and disconnect the 2 oil cooler tubes.
26. Remove the starter.
27. Remove the oil filler tube.

28. Remove the torque converter end plate hole plug.
29. Turn the crankshaft to gain access to each bolt and remove the 6 torque converter mounting bolts.
30. Support the transmission with a suitable transmission jack. Remove the 8 bolts then remove the frame crossmember.
31. Remove the front exhaust pipe.
32. Install a wooden block between the jack and the engine oil pan to prevent damage. Support the oil pan with a jack.
33. Lower the rear end of the transmission.
34. Remove the 9 transmission to engine mounting bolts.
35. Remove the transmission rearward and down.
36. Pull the torque converter straight off and allow the fluid to drain into a suitable drain pan.

TRANSMISSION INSTALLATION

1. Apply grease to the center hub of the torque converter and the pilot hole in the crankshaft.
2. If the torque converter has been drained, refill it with 2.1 qts. (2.0L) Dexron®II automatic transmission fluid and install it in the transmission.
3. Check the torque converter installation by measuring from the installed surface to the front surface of the transmission housing. The correct distance is 0.650 in. (16.5mm).
4. Position the transmission on a suitable jack under the vehicle.
5. Install a guide pin in the torque converter.
6. Carefully raise the transmission up into position.
7. Align the guide pin with 1 of the drive plate holes and align the 2 sleeves on the block with the converter housing. Move the transmission forward into place.

NOTE: Be careful not to tilt the transmission forward because the torque converter could slide out.

8. Install the 9 transmission to engine mounting bolts and torque them to the following specifications:
   8mm bolts – 13 ft. lbs. (18 Nm)
   10mm bolts – 27 ft. lbs. (37 Nm)
   12mm bolts – 53 ft. lbs. (72 Nm)
9. Install the front exhaust pipe.
10. Install the frame crossmember. Tighten the 8 bolts to 29 ft. lbs. (39 Nm) and the nut to 43 ft. lbs. (59 Nm).
11. Remove the transmission jack and remove the jack from

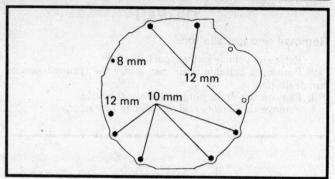

Transmission to engine mounting bolt pattern

under the engine oil pan.
12. Remove the guide pin from the torque converter.
13. Install the 6 torque converter bolts turning the crankshaft to gain access to each bolt. Tighten the bolts evenly. Torque the bolts to 21 ft. lbs. (28 Nm).
14. Install the end plate hole plug.
15. Install a new O-ring on the oil filler tube. Install the filler tube in the transmission.
16. Install the starter and connect the cable and connector.
17. Connect the oil cooler tubes.
18. Connect the 2 vacuum hoses.
19. Connect the speedometer cable.
20. Install the power take-off driveshaft.
21. Install the engine undercover.
22. Install the driveshafts.
23. Install the power take-off shift lever.
24. Connect and adjust the transmission control rod.
25. Install the transfer case shift lever.
26. Install the transmission and transfer case undercovers.
27. Lower the vehicle and connect the upper radiator hose. Fill the radiator to the proper level with coolant.
28. Connect all electrical connectors.
29. Connect and adjust the throttle cable.
30. Connect the negative battery cable.
31. Fill the transmission with automatic transmission fluid and check the fluid level.
32. Perform road test.

BENCH OVERHAUL

Before Disassembly

Cleanliness is an important factor in the overhaul of the automatic transmission. Before opening up this unit, the entire outside of the transmission assembly should be cleaned, preferable with a high pressure washer such as a car wash spray unit. Dirt entering the transmission internal parts will negate all the time and effort spent on the overhaul. During inspection and reassembly all parts should be thoroughly cleaned with solvent then dried with compressed air. Wiping cloths and rags should not be used to dry parts since lint will find its way into the valve body passages.

Wheel bearing grease, long used to hold thrust washers and lube parts, should not be used. Lube seals with clean transmission fluid and use ordinary unmedicated petroleum jelly to hold the thrust washers and to ease the assembly of seals, since it will not leave a harmful residue as grease often will. Do not use solvent on neoprene seals, friction plates if they are to be reused, or thrust washers. Be wary of nylon parts if the transmission failure was due to failure of the cooling system. Nylon parts exposed to water or antifreeze solutions can swell and distort and

must be replaced.

Before installing bolts into aluminum parts, always dip the threads into clean transmission fluid. Antiseize compound can also be used to prevent bolts from galling the aluminum and seizing. Always use a torque wrench to keep from stripping the threads. Take care when installing new O-rings, especially the smaller O-rings. The internal snaprings should be expanded and the external rings should be compressed, if they are to be reused. This will help insure proper seating when installed.

Converter Inspection

1. Measure the torque converter sleeve runout by temporarily mounting the torque converter to the drive plate.
2. Set up a dial indicator.
3. If the runout exceeds 0.0118 in. (0.30mm), try to correct it by reorientating the installation of the converter.
4. If excessive runout cannot be corrected, replace the torque converter.
5. Mark the position of the converter to ensure correct installation.

Transmission Disassembly

1. Position the transmission assembly in a suitable holding fixture.
2. Disconnect the 4 connectors and remove the transmission wire.
3. Pry out the breather plug from the top of the housing. Remove the O-ring from the breather plug.
4. Remove the control shaft lever.
5. Remove the 2 oil cooler pipes.
6. Remove the neutral start switch.
7. Remove the 2 oil cooler unions and discard the O-rings.
8. Remove the automatic transmission fluid temperature sensor.
9. Remove the throttle cable clamp bolt.
10. Remove the 8 bolts and the transmission housing.
11. Remove the oil pan protector. Remove the oil pan.

NOTE:Do not turn the transmission over to remove the oil pan. This will contaminate the valve body with any foreign matter at the bottom of the pan.

12. Remove the magnets and use them to collect any steel particles.
13. Remove the 7 bolts, 4 wave washers, lockup relay valve body plate and gasket.
14. Remove the oil tube by prying both tube ends.
15. Temporarily install the lockup relay valve body plate with the 4 short bolts.
16. Remove 10 bolts, oil strainer and gasket.
17. Remove the 15 bolts. Disconnect the throttle cable from the cam and remove the valve body.
18. Remove the 4 center support apply gaskets.
19. Remove the throttle cable.
20. Remove the accumulator pistons and springs by applying compressed air to the oil holes.
21. Check the thrust clearance of the overdrive input shaft by pushing the shaft toward the rear of the transmission by applying a force of 11–22 lbs. (49–98 N). Using a dial indicator, mea-

sure the thrust clearance. The standard clearance is 0.0157–0.0354 in. (0.40–0.90mm).
22. Remove the oil pump.
23. Remove the overdrive planetary gear, overdrive direct clutch and one-way clutch assembly.
24. Remove the overdrive planetary ring gear from the overdrive case.
25. Remove the transfer case No. 2 cover.
26. Remove the overdrive case assembly.
27. Remove the front clutch assembly.
28. Insert 2 wires into the flukes of the clutch discs and remove the rear clutch assembly.
29. Remove the center support assembly.
30. Remove the transfer case component parts.
31. Remove the transfer case adaptor and the output shaft rear bearing.
32. Remove the output shaft spacer.
33. Remove the governor body assembly.
34. Remove the planetary gears, one-way clutch and output shaft assembly.
35. Remove the 1st and reverse brake piston.
36. Remove the C_1 accumulator piston and spring.
37. Remove the transmission rear cover and gasket.
38. Remove the manual valve lever, shaft and oil seals.

Unit Disassembly and Assembly

OIL PUMP

Disassembly

1. Use the torque converter as a work stand.
2. Remove the 2 oil seal rings.
3. Using the proper tool, compress the spring and remove the spring seat. Remove the spring and check ball.
4. Remove the oil pump cover.
5. Remove the oil pump drive and driven gears.

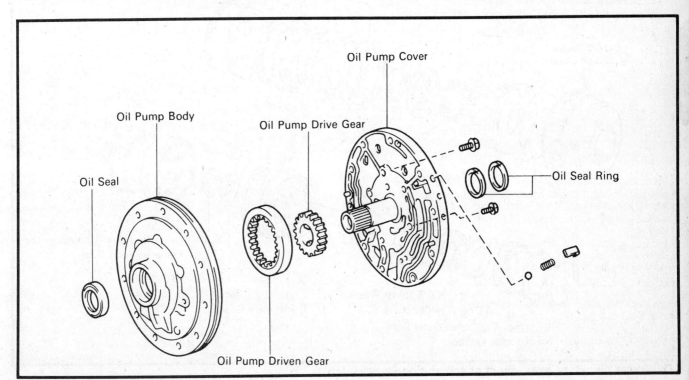

Oil pump and related components

Inspection

1. Using a dial indicator, measure the inside diameter of the oil pump body bushing. The standard diameter is 1.6555–1.6565 in. (42.050–42.075mm). If the inside diameter is greater than specified, replace the pump body.
2. Using a dial indicator, measure the inside diameter of the oil pump cover bushings. The standard inside diameters are:
Front — 0.9449–0.9457 in. (24.000–24.021mm)
Rear — 1.0433–1.0441 in. (26.500–26.521mm)
3. If the inside diameter is greater than specified, replace the pump cover.
4. Push the driven gear to 1 side of the body. Using a feeler gauge, measure the clearance between the driven gear and the body. The standard body clearance is 0.0028–0.0059 in. (0.07–0.15mm). If the body clearance is greater than specified, replace the gears and the pump body as a set.
5. Using a feeler gauge, measure the clearance between the gear teeth and the cresent shaped part of the pump body. The standard tip clearance is 0.0055–0.0094 in. (0.14–0.24mm). If the tip clearance is greater than specified, replace the gears and pump body as a set.
6. Using a steel straight edge and a feeler gauge, measure the clearance between the gears and the steel straight edge. The standard side clearance is 0.0008–0.0020 in. (0.02–0.05mm). If the side clearance is greater than specified, select and replace the gears as a set.
7. There are 2 different thicknesses for drive and driven gears, they are: 0.7258–0.7264 in. (18.435–18.450mm) and 0.7264–0.7278 in. (18.451–18.486mm).
8. Pry off the oil seal and tap in a new oil seal. The seal end should be flushed with the outer edge of the pump body. Apply grease to the oil seal lip.

Assembly

1. Position the oil pump body onto the torque converter.
2. Coat the driven and drive gears with automatic transmission fluid and install them in the oil pump body.
3. Install the oil pump cover on the oil pump body with the 8 bolts.
4. Install the check ball and spring, compress the spring and install the spring seat.
5. Coat the oil seal rings with automatic transmission fluid. Contract the oil seal rings, then install them onto the stator shaft.
6. Make sure that the oil pump drive gear rotates smoothly when installed to the torque converter.

OVERDRIVE PLANETARY GEAR, DIRECT CLUTCH AND ONE-WAY CLUTCH

Disassembly

1. Hold the overdrive clutch drum and turn the input shaft. The input shaft should turn freely clockwise and should turn counterclockwise.
2. Remove the overdrive direct clutch assembly from the overdrive planetary gear.
3. Remove the flange, plates and discs.
4. Remove the piston return spring.
5. Remove the overdrive direct clutch piston by applying compressed air into the oil hole of the oil pump.
6. Remove the oil seal ring from the ring gear flange.
7. Remove the ring gear flange.
8. Remove the snapring from the overdrive planetary gear. Remove the No. 4 thrust washer.

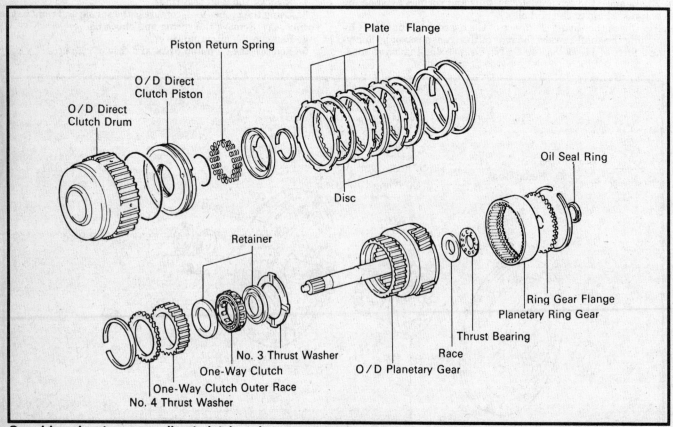

Overdrive planetary gear, direct clutch and one-way clutch

9. Remove the one-way clutch together with the outer race. Remove the No. 3 thrust washer.

10. Remove the 2 retainers and the one-way clutch from the outer race.

Inspection

1. Check the sliding surface of the disc, plate and flange for worn or burnt condition.

2. Check the overdrive direct clutch piston check ball for free movement by shaking the piston.

3. Check for leakage at the valve by applying low pressure compressed air.

4. Using a dial indicator, measure the inside diameter of the overdrive direct clutch drum bushings. The standard inside diameter is 1.0433–1.0441 in. (26.500–26.521mm). If the inside diameter is greater than specified, replace the clutch drum.

5. Using a dial indicator, measure the inside diameter of the overdrive planetary gear bushing. The standard inside diameter is 0.4724–0.4731 in. (12.000–12.018mm). If the inside diameter is greater than specified, replace the planetary gear.

6. Using a feeler gauge, measure the thrust clearance between the pinions and carrier. The standard clearance is 0.0079–0.0232 in. (0.20–0.59mm). If the thrust clearance is greater than specified, replace the planetary gear.

Assembly

1. Install the No. 3 thrust washer, facing the grooved side upward.

2. Install the one-way clutch and 2 retainers into the outer race.

3. Install the one-way clutch and outer race assembly, facing the flanged side of the one-way clutch upward.

4. Install the No. 4 thrust washer and the snapring.

5. Install the ring gear flange to the overdrive planetary ring gear.

6. Coat the oil seal ring with automatic transmission fluid and install it to the ring gear flange.

7. Coat new O-rings with automatic transmission fluid and install them on the direct clutch piston.

8. Push in the clutch piston into the clutch drum with both hands.

9. Install the piston return spring.

10. Install the plates and discs in the following order: plate–disc–plate–disc–plate–disc.

11. Install the flange facing the rounded edge upward.

12. Install the overdrive direct clutch assembly onto the oil pump. Using a dial indicator, measure the piston stroke by applying and releasing compressed air. The piston stroke should be 0.0433–0.0669 in. (1.10–1.70mm). If the piston stroke is less than specified, the parts may have been assembled incorrectly.

13. Install the direct clutch assembly onto the overdrive planetary gear.

NOTE: Mesh the spline of the overdrive planetary gear with the flukes of the discs by rotating and pushing the overdrive direct clutch counterclockwise.

14. Hold the overdrive direct clutch drum and turn the input shaft. The input shaft should turn freely clockwise and should lock counterclockwise.

OVERDRIVE BRAKE

Disassembly

1. Using needle nose pliers, remove the the 3 ring retainers from the oil holes of the overdrive case.

2. Install the overdrive case assembly onto the rear clutch assembly to check the piston stroke of the overdrive brake. Using a dial indicator, measure the piston stroke by applying and re-

leasing 57–114 psi. (392–785 kPa) of compressed air. The piston stroke should be 0.0492–0.0728 in. (1.25–1.85mm).

3. If the piston stroke is greater than specified, inspect the discs.

4. Remove the flange, discs and plates.

5. Compress the piston return spring with a suitable press.

6. Remove the snapring then remove the return spring.

7. Place the return spring on the brake piston and place a suitable spring compressor on the return spring.

8. Hold the spring compressor so it does not slant and apply compressed air into the oil hole of the overdrive case to remove the brake piston.

9. Remove the O-rings from the brake piston. Remove the 2 seal rings from the overdrive case.

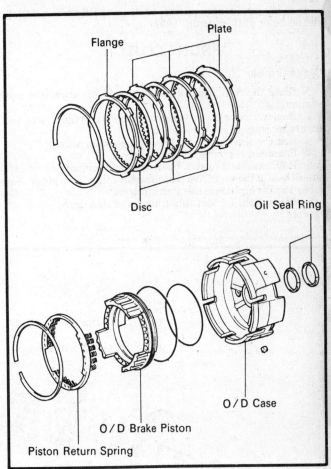

Overdrive brake and related components

Inspection

1. Check the sliding surface of the disc, plate and flange for a worn or burnt condition.

2. Using dial indicator, measure the inside diameter of the overdrive case bushing. The standard inside diameter is 1.3031–1.3051 in. (33.100–33.150mm).

3. If the inside diameter is greater than specified, replace the overdrive case.

Assembly

1. Coat the 2 oil seal rings with automatic transmission fluid and install them onto the overdrive case.

2. Coat the 2 new O-rings with automatic transmission fluid and install them on the brake piston.

3. Align the protrusions of the brake piston with the grooves of the overdrive case. Push the brake piston into the overdrive case.

4. Install the piston return spring on the brake piston.

5. Install the 3 plates and 3 discs in the following order: plate–disc–plate–disc–plate–disc.

6. Install the flange facing the rounded edge upward.

7. Install the overdrive case assembly onto the rear clutch assembly.

8. Using a dial indicator, measure the piston stroke by applying and releasing 57–114 psi. (392–785 kPa) of compressed air. The piston stroke should be 0.0492–0.0728 in. (1.25–1.85mm).

9. If the piston stroke is less than specified, the parts may have been assembled incorrectly, check and reassemble them again.

10. Using needle nose pliers, install the 3 ring retainers into the oil holes of the overdrive case.

FRONT CLUTCH

Disassembly

1. Place the front clutch assembly onto the overdrive case assembly.

2. Remove the rear and front clutch hubs and the 2 races and thrust bearing.

3. Remove the 6 discs, 6 plates and cushion plate.

4. Remove the piston return springs.

5. Hold the clutch piston by hand, apply compressed air into the oil hole of the overdrive case to remove the clutch piston. Remove the O-rings from the clutch piston.

6. Remove the oil seal ring from the clutch drum.

Inspection

1. Check the sliding surface of the disc, plate and flange for a worn or burnt condition.

2. Make sure that the front clutch piston ball is free by shaking the piston.

3. Make sure that the valve does not leak by applying low pressure compressed air.

Assembly

1. Coat the oil seal ring with automatic transmission fluid and install it onto the clutch drum.

2. Coat 2 new O-rings with automatic transmission fluid and install them on the clutch piston. Push the clutch piston into the clutch drum.

3. Install the piston return springs.

4. Install the cushion plate, facing the rounded edge downward.

5. Install the 6 plates and the 6 discs in the following order: plate–disc–plate–disc–plate–disc-plate–disc–plate–disc–plate–disc.

6. Coat the 2 races and thrust bearing with petroleum jelly and install them into the front clutch drum.

7. Install the front clutch hub into the clutch drum.

NOTE: Mesh the spline of the front clutch hub with the flukes of the discs by rotating the front clutch hub clockwise or counterclockwise.

8. Install the rear clutch hub onto the clutch drum. Install the snapring.

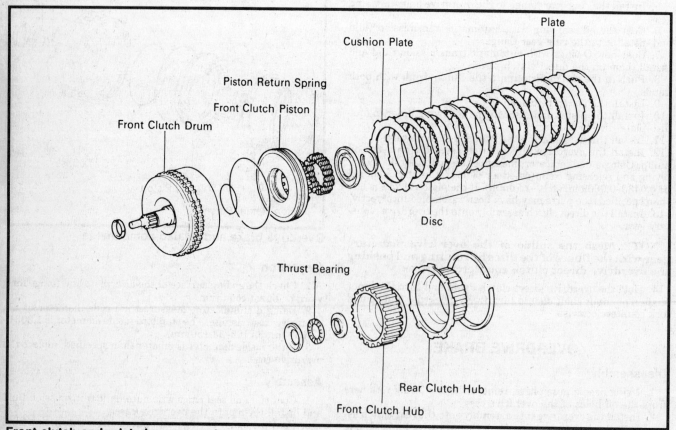

Front clutch and related components

REAR CLUTCH

Disassembly

1. Remove the snapring and remove the flange, 5 discs and 5 plates.
2. Remove the piston return springs.
3. Place the center support assembly on wooden blocks.
4. Place the clutch drum onto the center support assembly.
5. Hold the piston and apply compressed air into the oil hole of the center support to remove the clutch piston.
6. Remove the O-rings from the clutch piston.

Inspection

1. Check the sliding surface of the disc, plate and flange for a worn or burnt condition.
2. Make sure that the front clutch piston ball is free by shaking the piston.
3. Make sure that the valve does not leak by applying low pressure compressed air.

Assembly

1. Coat the 2 new O-rings with automatic transmission fluid and install them on the clutch drum. Push the clutch piston into the clutch drum.
2. Install the piston return springs.
3. Install the 5 plates and the 5 discs in the following order: plate–disc–plate–disc–plate–disc-plate–disc–plate–disc.
4. Install the flange facing the rounded edge upward. Install the snapring.

SECOND BRAKE

Disassembly

1. Using needle nose pliers, remove the 3 ring retainers from the oil holes of the center support.
2. Remove the front planetary sun gear.
3. Remove the flange, 4 discs and 4 plates.
4. Remove the piston return spring.
5. Place the return spring on the brake piston, then place a suitable compressor on the return spring.
6. Hold the spring compressor so that it does not slant and apply compressed air into the oil of the center support to remove the brake piston.
7. Remove the O-rings from the brake piston.
8. Remove the 2 oil seal rings from the center support.

Inspection

1. Check the sliding surface of the disc, plate and flange for a worn or burnt condition.
2. Using dial indicator, measure the inside diameter of the center support bushing. The standard inside diameter is 1.3780–1.3789 in. (35.000–35.025mm).
3. If the inside diameter is greater than specified, replace the center support.
4. Using a dial indicator, measure the inside diameter of the front planetary sun gear bushings. The standard inside diameter is 0.9449–0.9457 in. (24.000–24.021mm).
5. If the inside diameter is greater than specified, replace the front planetary sun gear.

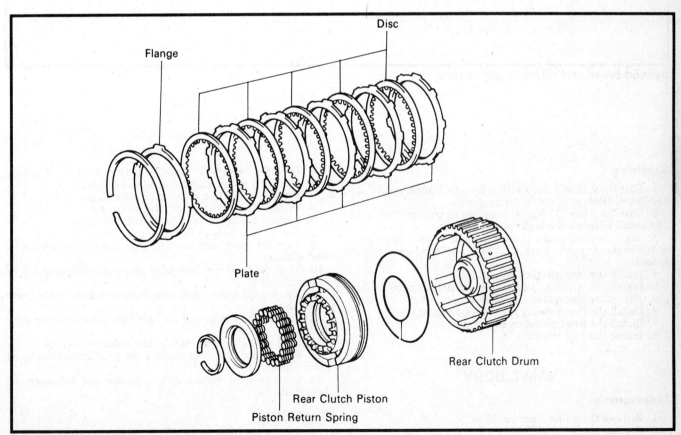

Rear clutch and related components

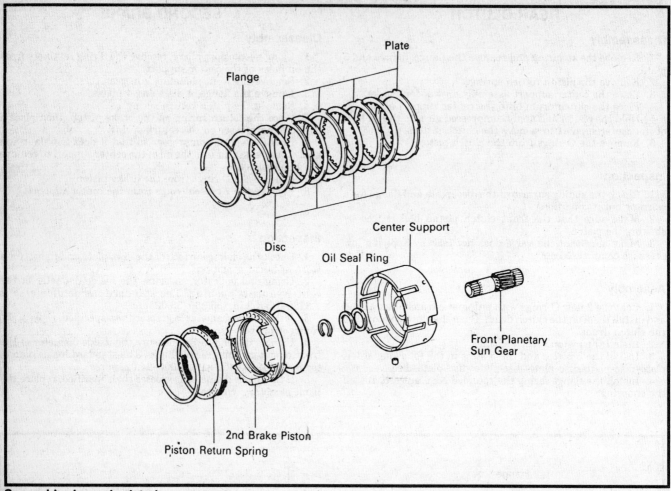

Second brake and related components

Assembly

1. Coat the 2 oil seal rings with automatic transmission fluid and install them onto the center support.
2. Coat the 2 new O-rings with automatic transmission fluid and install them on the brake piston.
3. Align the protrusions of the brake piston with the grooves of the center support. Push the brake piston into the center support.
4. Install the piston return spring.
5. Install the 4 plates and 4 discs in the following order: plate–disc–plate–disc–plate–disc–plate–disc.
6. Install the flange facing the rounded edge upward.
7. Install the front planetary sun gear.
8. Install the ring retainers.

VALVE BODY

Disassembly

1. Remove the 2 line pressure tubes.
2. Remove the bolts and washers and pry out the oil tube.
3. Remove the manual valve. Remove the clamp.
4. Turn the valve body assembly over and remove the bolt, washer, spring cover, detent spring and spacer.
5. Remove the lockup relay valve body plate.
6. Remove the lockup relay valve sleeve pin.
7. Remove the lower valve body cover and plate.
8. Remove the 2 check balls from the lower valve body.
9. Turn the valve body assembly over and remove the 7 bolts and washers.
10. Turn the valve body assembly over and remove the 3 bolts and washers.
11. Remove the front upper valve body by lifting up the lower valve body.
12. Remove the 6 bolts and washers from the rear upper valve body.
13. Hold the valve body plate to the lower valve plate.
14. Remove the rear upper valve body by lifting up the lower valve body.
15. Turn over the valve body and remove the 2 gaskets and body plate.

Inspection

1. All disassembled parts should be washed clean with any fluid passages and holes blown through with compressed air.

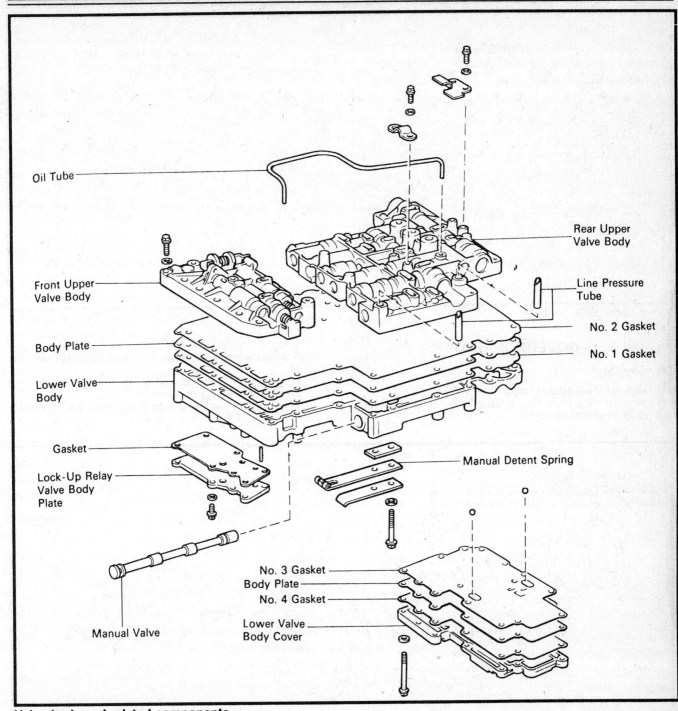

Oil Tube

Front Upper Valve Body

Body Plate

Lower Valve Body

Gasket

Lock-Up Relay Valve Body Plate

Manual Valve

Rear Upper Valve Body

Line Pressure Tube

No. 2 Gasket

No. 1 Gasket

Manual Detent Spring

No. 3 Gasket

Body Plate

No. 4 Gasket

Lower Valve Body Cover

Valve body and related components

2. The recommended automatic transmission fluid or kerosene should be used for cleaning.

3. When disassembling a valve body, be sure to keep each valve together with the corresponding spring.

Assembly

1. Install the new No. 1 gasket and the body plate on the lower valve body. Temporarily secure the body plate with the 2 oil tube clamp bolts.

2. Install a new No. 2 gasket on the body plate.

3. Install the lower valve body on the rear upper valve body.

4. Remove the 2 temporarily installed bolts and install the lower valve body on the front upper valve body.

5. Install the 2 check balls into the lower valve body.

6. Install the lockup relay valve sleeve pin.

7. Temporarily install the lockup relay valve body plate.

8. Install the manual detent spring.

9. Install the manual valve and the clamp.

10. Install the oil tube.

11. Install the 2 line pressure tubes.

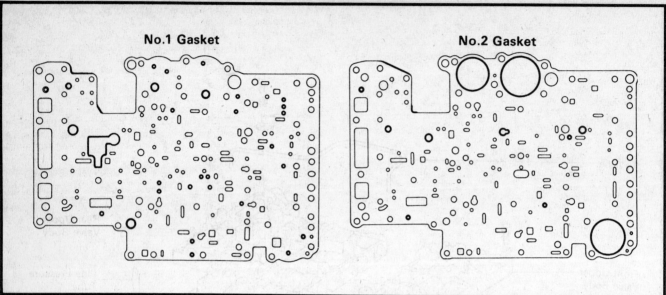

No.1 Gasket **No.2 Gasket**

Valve body plate gaskets

GOVERNOR BODY

Disassembly

1. Remove the 3 oil seal rings.
2. Remove the 8 bolts, the governor body and the gasket.
3. Remove the oil strainer.

4. Remove the governor weight from the outside of the governor body.
5. Remove the valve shaft, spring and No. 1 governor valve from the inside of the governor body.
6. Remove the valve shaft, spring and No. 2 governor valve from the inside of the governor body.

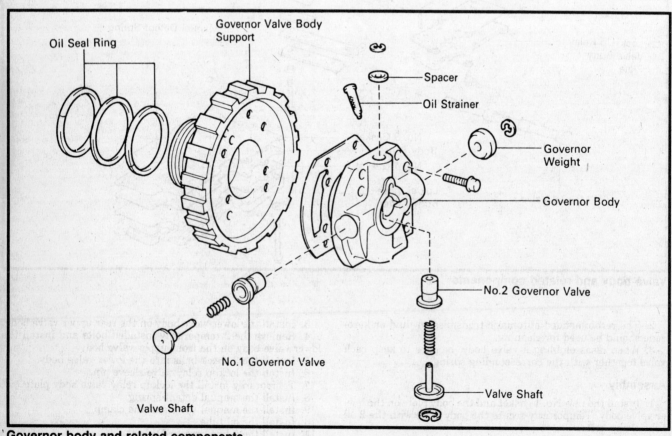

Oil Seal Ring

Governor Valve Body Support

Spacer

Oil Strainer

Governor Weight

Governor Body

No.2 Governor Valve

No.1 Governor Valve

Valve Shaft

Valve Shaft

Governor body and related components

Inspection

1. All disassembled parts should be washed clean with any fluid passages and holes blown through with compressed air.
2. The recommended automatic transmission fluid or kerosene should be used for cleaning.
3. When disassembling the governor body, be sure to keep each valve together with the corresponding spring.

Assembly

1. Coat the governor valve and shaft with automatic transmission fluid.
2. Install the valve shaft, spring and No. 2 governor valve into the inside of the governor body.
3. Coat the governor valve and shaft with automatic transmission fluid.
4. Install the valve shaft, spring and No. 1 governor valve into the inside of the governor body.
5. Install the governor weight on the outside of the governor body.
6. Install the oil strainer.
7. Install the 8 bolts, the governor body and the gasket.
8. Install the 3 oil seal rings.

Transmission Assembly

1. Apply grease to the manual valve oil seal lip.
2. Install a new spacer on the manual valve lever.
3. Connect the parking lock rod to the manual valve lever.
4. Install the manual valve lever shaft to the transmission case through the plate, wave washer, manual valve lever and plate.
5. Install the transmission rear cover and gasket.
6. Coat the new O-rings with automatic transmission fluid and install them on the C_1 accumulator piston.
7. Install the C_1 accumulator piston and spring into the bore of the transmission case.
8. Coat 2 new O-rings with automatic transmission fluid and install them on the first and reverse brake piston.
9. Push in the brake piston and install the return spring. Compress the return spring and install the snapring.
10. Install the cushion plate, facing the rounded edge inward.
11. Install the 6 plates and 6 discs in the following order: plate–disc–plate–disc–plate–disc–plate–disc–plate–disc–plate–disc.
12. Install the flange facing the rounded edge outward.
13. Using a dial indicator, measure the first and reverse brake piston stroke by applying and releasing 57–114 psi. (392–785 kPa) of compressed air. The piston stroke should be 0.059–0.118 in. (1.5–3.0mm).
14. If the piston stroke is less than specified, the parts may have been assembled incorrectly.
15. Install the 1st and reverse brake piston.
16. Install the planetary gears, one-way clutch and output shaft assembly.
17. Install the governor body onto the output shaft.
18. Insert a 0.0004 in. (0.01mm) feeler gauge between the output shaft and governor body and temporarily tighten the bolts. Check that the clearance between the output shaft and the governor body is even all the way around. Tighten the bolts.
19. Install a new gasket on the transmssion case.

20. Insert the parking lock rod between the parking lock pawl and bracket and attach the transfer adapter on the transmission case.
21. Install a new gasket and the transfer adaptor with the 10 bolts.
22. Install the output shaft spacer facing the cutout portion outward.
23. Install the output shaft rear bearing.
24. Install the transfer case component parts.
25. Coat the center support thrust washer with petroleum jelly and install it into the rear side of the center support.
26. Align the oil holes and bolt holes of the center support to the transmission case.
27. Install the center support assembly into the transmission case.
28. Mesh the spline of the rear clutch drum with the flukes of the clutch discs by rotating and pushing the rear clutch drum clockwise or counterclockwise.
29. Install the front clutch assembly.
30. Push the transmission output shaft toward the front of the transmission by applying a force of 11.0–22.0 lbs. (49–98 N). Push the overdrive case toward the rear of the transmission by applying a force of 11.0–22.0 lbs. (49–98 N). Using a dial indicator, measure the thrust clearance of the input shaft. The standard thrust clearance is 0.0118–0.0276 in. (0.30–0.70mm).
31. If the thrust clearance is greater than specified, adjust with a spacer.
32. Install the overdrive case assembly.
33. Install the transfer case No. 2 cover.
34. Install the overdrive planetary ring gear into the overdrive case.
35. Install the overdrive planetary gear, overdrive direct clutch and one-way clutch assembly.
36. Install the oil pump.
37. Check the thrust clearance of the overdrive input shaft by pushing the shaft toward the rear of the transmission by applying a force of 11–22 lbs. (49–98 N). Using a dial indicator, measure the thrust clearance. The standard clearance is 0.0157–0.0354 in. (0.40–0.90mm).
38. Install the accumulator pistons and springs.
39. Install the throttle cable.
40. Install the 4 center support apply gaskets facing the pitted side toward the transmission case.
41. Align the groove of the manual valve with the pin of the manual valve lever.
42. Connect the throttle cable to the cam and install the valve body. Install the 15 bolts.
43. Install oil strainer, gasket and 10 bolts.
44. Install the lockup relay valve body plate.
45. Install the oil tube.
46. Install lockup relay valve body plate and gasket. Install the 7 bolts and 4 wave washers.
47. Install the magnets in the oil pan.
48. Install the oil pan and protector.
49. Install the transmission housing with 8 bolts.
50. Install the throttle cable clamp bolt.
51. Install the automatic transmission fluid temperature sensor.
52. Install the 2 oil cooler unions and O-rings.
53. Install the neutral start switch.
54. Install the 2 oil cooler pipes.
55. Install the control shaft lever.
56. Install the O-ring on the breather plug. Install the breather plug on the top of the housing.

SPECIFICATIONS

OIL PRESSURE SPECIFICATIONS

Item			psi	kPa
Line pressure (wheel locked)	Engine idling	D range	53–61	363–422
		R range	64–78	441–539
	At stall	D range	158–193	1089–1334
		R range	199–242	1373–1667
Governor pressure	Output shaft rpm 1000	(Vehicle speed reference) Approx. 20 mph, 32 km/h	11–17	78–118
	1800	Approx. 35 mph, 57 km/h	27–33	186–226
	3500	Approx. 69 mph, 111 km/h	81–90	559–618

SPRING SPECIFICATIONS

Assembly	Spring	Free Length in. (mm)	Coil Outer Diameter in. (mm)	Total No. of coils	Color
Front upper valve body	Check ball	0.512 (13.0)	0.331 (8.4)	8.0	None
	Primary throttle valve	0.996 (25.3)	0.362 (9.2)	9.5	White
	Primary downshift plug	1.059 (26.9)	0.354 (9.0)	10.5	Blue
	Secondary regulator valve	1.811 (46.0)	0.524 (13.3)	15.0	None
	Secondary throttle valve	0.996 (25.3)	0.362 (9.2)	9.5	White
	Secondary downshift plug	1.283 (32.6)	0.382 (9.7)	13.0	White
	Throttle valve sleeve	0.425 (10.8)	0.717 (18.2)	4.0	None
Rear upper valve body	2-3 shift valve	1.705 (43.3)	0.350 (8.9)	22.0	Brown
	2-3 shift timing valve	1.543 (39.2)	0.362 (9.2)	18.0	Pink
	3-4 shift valve	1.508 (38.3)	0.382 (9.7)	17.0	None
	Detent regulator valve	1.197 (30.4)	0.291 (7.4)	16.0	White
	Lockup signal valve	2.102 (53.4)	0.539 (13.7)	16.0	Green
	O/D clutch exhaust valve	1.311 (33.3)	0.323 (8.2)	14.0	Yellow
	Intermediate modulator valve	0.886 (22.5)	0.303 (7.7)	12.0	Pink
Lower valve body	Check valve	1.091 (27.7)	0.323 (8.2)	13.0	None
	Check ball	0.512 (13.0)	0.331 (8.4)	8.0	None
	1-2 shift valve	1.047 (26.6)	0.272 (6.9)	16.0	None
	3-2 kickdown orifice control valve	1.280 (32.5)	0.327 (8.3)	14.0	Blue
	2nd lock valve	1.158 (29.4)	0.327 (8.3)	14.0	Brown
	Lockup relay valve	1.278 (32.4)	0.366 (9.3)	15.0	Pink
	Primary regulator valve	2.291 (58.2)	0.823 (20.9)	11.0	None
	Accumulator control valve	0.988 (25.1)	0.492 (12.5)	8.5	Red
	Low coast modulator valve	1.181 (30.0)	0.287 (7.3)	16.0	Yellow
	1-2 relay valve	0.902 (22.9)	0.205 (5.2)	15.0	None
Accumulator	B_0	2.524 (64.1)	0.831 (21.1)	13.0	None
	B_2	2.559 (65.0)	0.988 (25.1)	8.5	Yellow
	C_1	3.634 (92.3)	0.708 (17.9)	20.0	None
	C_2	3.437 (87.3)	0.858 (21.8)	15.0	Red

OIL PUMP SPECIFICATIONS

Item			in.	mm
Body clearance	Standard		0.0028–0.0059	0.07–0.15
	Limit	0.012	0.3	
Tip clearance	Standard		0.0055–0.0094	0.14–0.24
	Limit	0.012	0.3	
Side clearance	Standard		0.0008–0.0020	0.02–0.05
	Limit	0.004	0.1	
Drive and driven gear thickness			0.7258–0.7264	18.435–18.450
			0.7264–0.7278	18.451–18.486
Pump body bushing inside diameter	Standard	Front	24.021	24.000
		Rear	1.0433–1.0441	26.500–26.521
	Limit	Front	0.9476	24.07
		Rear	1.0461	26.57
Pump cover bushing inside diameter	Standard	Front	24.021	24.000
		Rear	1.0433–1.0441	26.500–26.521
	Limit	Front	0.9476	24.07
		Rear	1.0461	26.57

TORQUE SPECIFICATIONS

Part	ft. lbs.	Nm
Engine to transmission		
14 mm head bolt	27	37
17 mm head bolt	53	72
Torque converter to drive plate	21	28
Frame crossmember set bolt	29	39
Frame crossmember set nut	43	59
Oil cooler pipe union nut	25	34
Exhaust front pipe to exhaust manifold	46	62
Exhaust front pipe to exhaust tail pipe	29	39
Propeller shaft to transfer	65	88
Driveshaft to differential	65	88
Oil pump cover to oil pump body		
10 mm head bolt	78 ①	8.8
12 mm head bolt	15	21
Lower valve body cover to lower valve body	48	5.4
Front upper valve body to lower valve body	48 ①	5.4
Rear upper valve body to lower valve body	48	5.4
Manual detent spring to lower valve body	48	5.4
Parking lock pawl to transfer adaptor	14	19
Transmission rear cover to transmission case	69 ①	7.8
Front accumulator cover to transmission case	69 ①	7.8
Governor cover to governor valve body support	7	10

TORQUE SPECIFICATIONS

Part	ft. lbs.	Nm
Transfer case adaptor to transmission case	27	37
Center support set bolt	18	25
O/D case set bolt	18	25
Oil pump to transmission case	16	21
Valve body to transmission case	7	10
Oil strainer to valve body		
8 mm head bolt	48 ①	5.4
10 mm head bolt	7	10
Lockup relay valve body plate to valve body		
8 mm head bolt	48 ①	5.4
10 mm head bolt	7	10
Oil pan to transmission case	61 ①	6.9
Transmission housing to transmission case	47	64
Automatic transmission fluid temperature sensor to transmission case	25	34
Oil cooler union to transmission case	22	29
Neutral start switch to transmission case	9	13
Neutral start switch to manual valve shaft	61 ①	6.9
Oil cooler pipe to oil cooler union	25	34
Control shaft to transmission case	9	13

① inch lbs.

SPECIAL TOOLS

SERVICE TOOL SELECTION

Description	
TRANSMISSION BEARING REPLACER	09309-36033
NO. 2 PISTON SPRING COMPRESSOR	09350-06010
NO. 3 PISTON SPRING COMPRESSOR	09350-06020
NO. 1 PISTON SPRING COMPRESSOR	09350-06030
OIL SEAL REPLACER	09350-06040
HANDLE	09350-06050
TRANSMISSION REAR BEARING REPLACER	09350-06060
PLATE	09350-06090
CHECK BALL SPRING COMPRESSOR	09350-06100
NO. 1 MEASURE TERMINAL	09350-06110
NO. 2 MEASURE TERMINAL	09350-06120
EXTENSION BAR	09350-06130
OIL PUMP PULLER	09350-06140

OIL FLOW CIRCUIT—P RANGE—A 440F AND A 440L TRANSMISSIONS

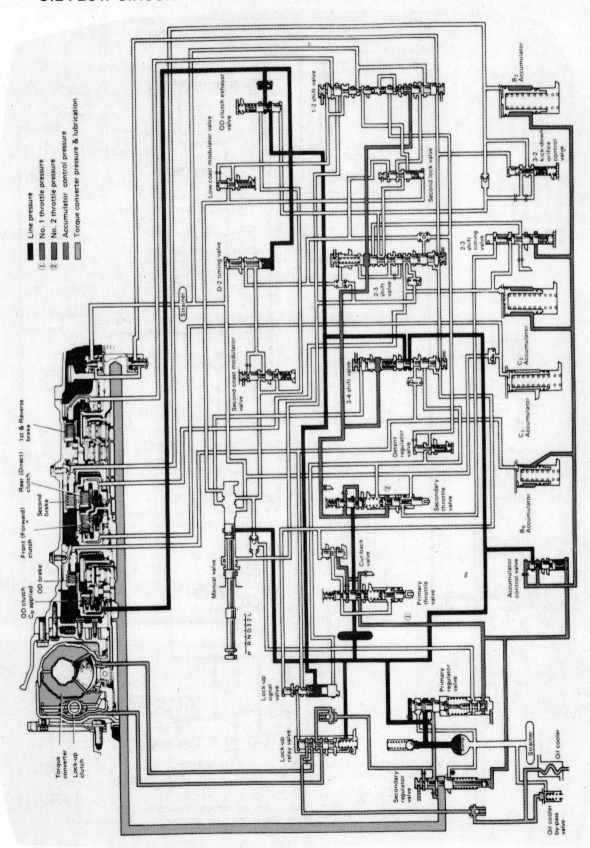

OIL FLOW CIRCUIT—N RANGE—A 440F AND A 440L TRANSMISSIONS

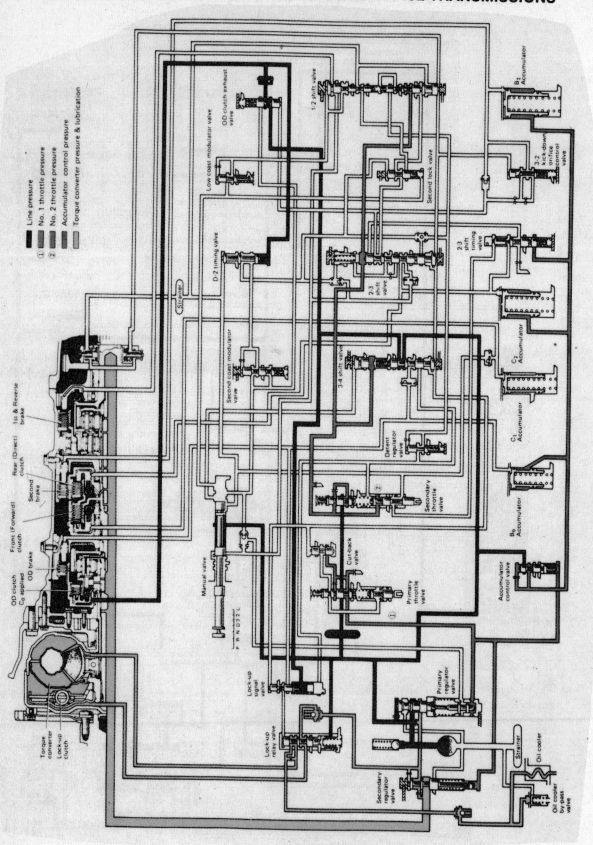

OIL FLOW CIRCUIT – R RANGE – A 440F AND A 440L TRANSMISSIONS

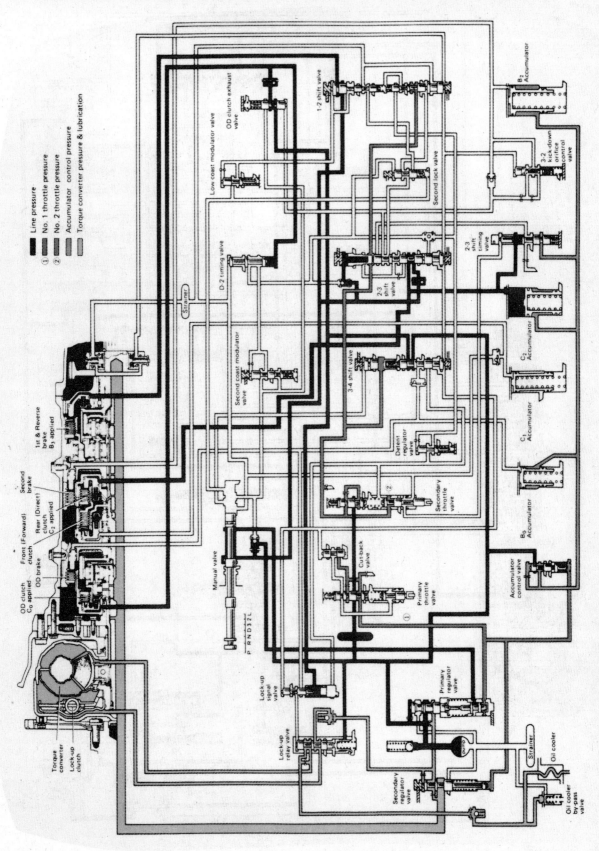

OIL FLOW CIRCUIT — D RANGE FIRST SPEED — A 440F AND A 440L TRANSMISSIONS

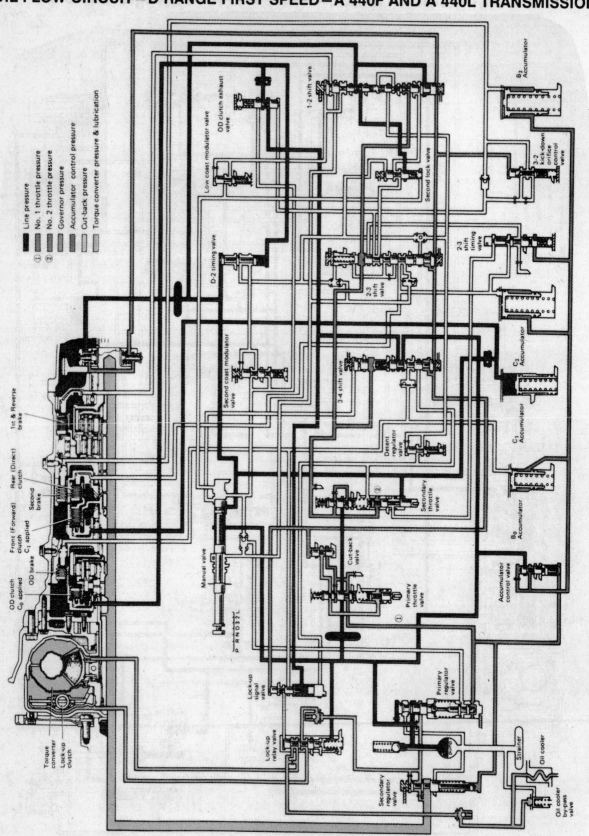

OIL FLOW CIRCUIT—D RANGE SECOND SPEED
A 440F AND A 440L TRANSMISSIONS

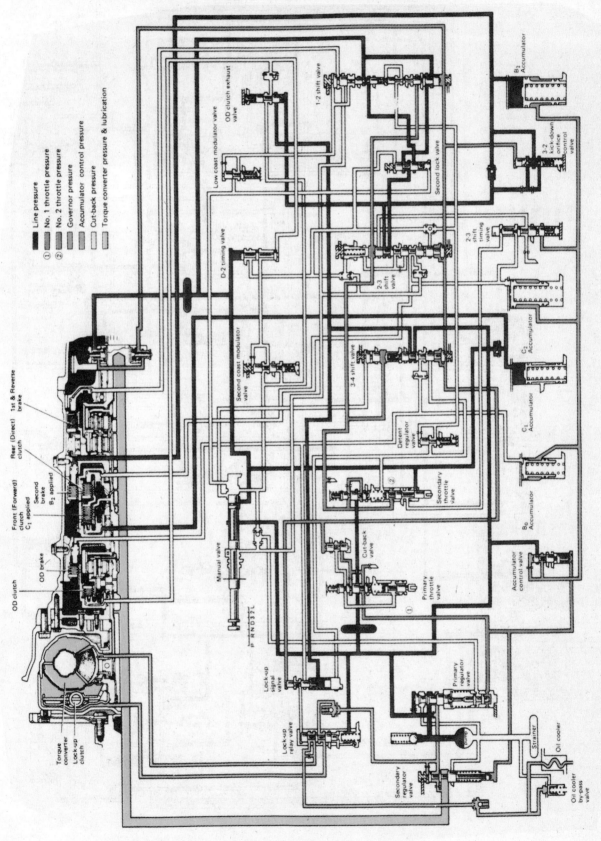

OIL FLOW CIRCUIT—D RANGE THIRD SPEED—A 440F AND A 440L TRANSMISSIONS

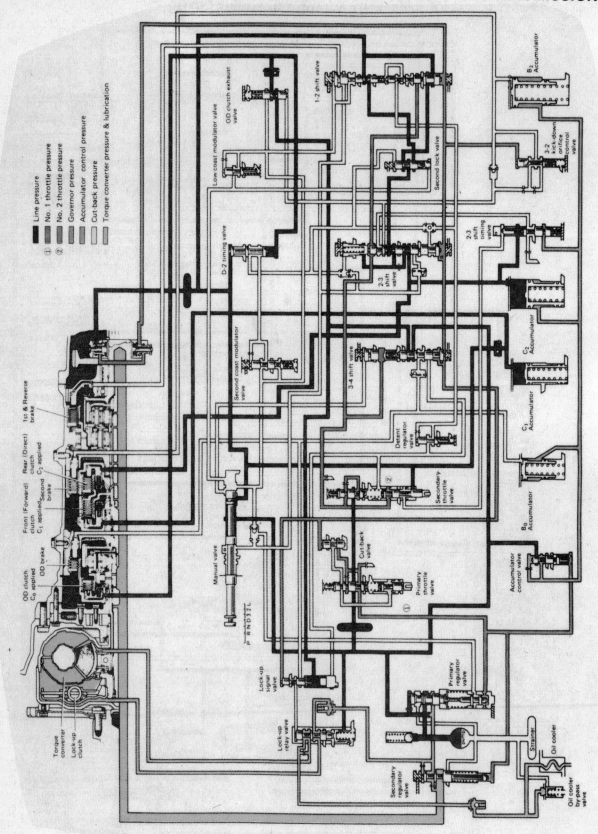

OIL FLOW CIRCUIT—D RANGE THIRD SPEED TV VALVE CLOSED
A 440F AND A 440L TRANSMISSIONS

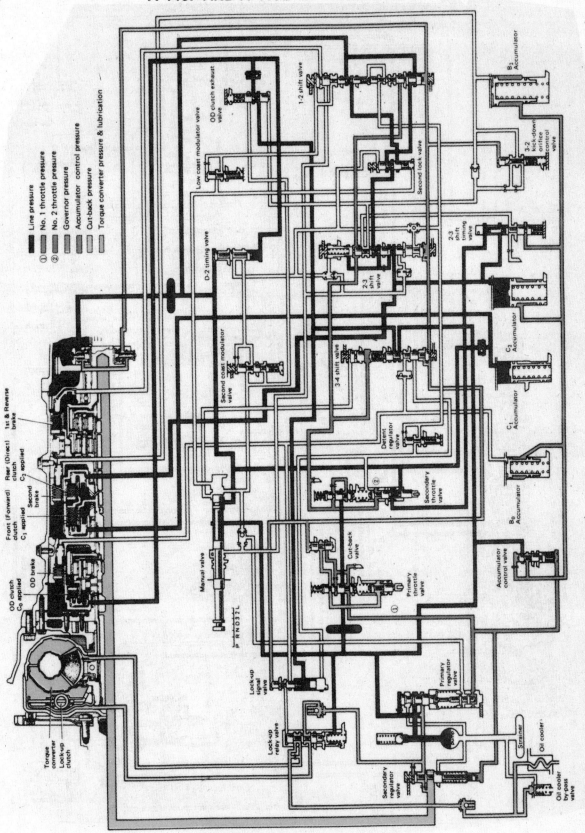

OIL FLOW CIRCUIT—D RANGE OVERDRIVE LOCKUP OFF
A 440F AND A 440L TRANSMISSIONS

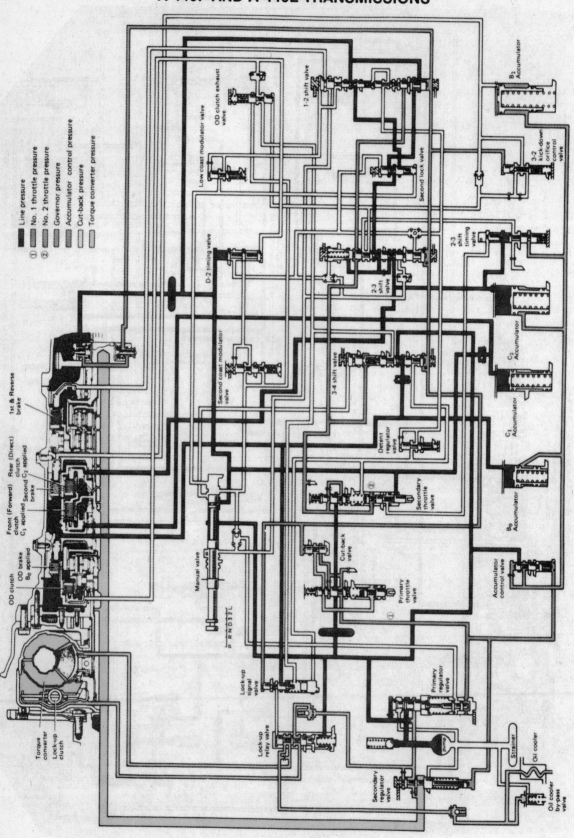

OIL FLOW CIRCUIT—D RANGE OVERDRIVE LOCKUP ON A 440F AND A 440L TRANSMISSIONS

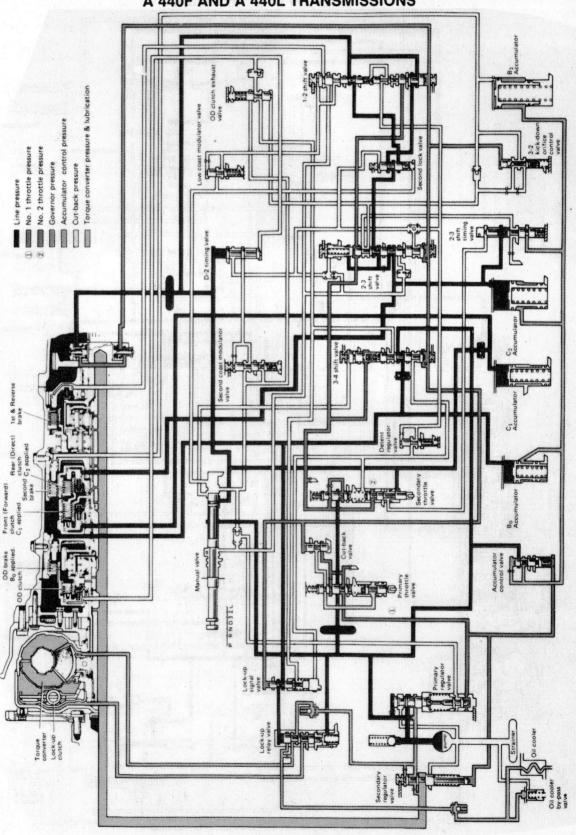

OIL FLOW CIRCUIT—D RANGE KICKDOWN OVERDRIVE TO 3
A 440F AND A 440L TRANSMISSIONS

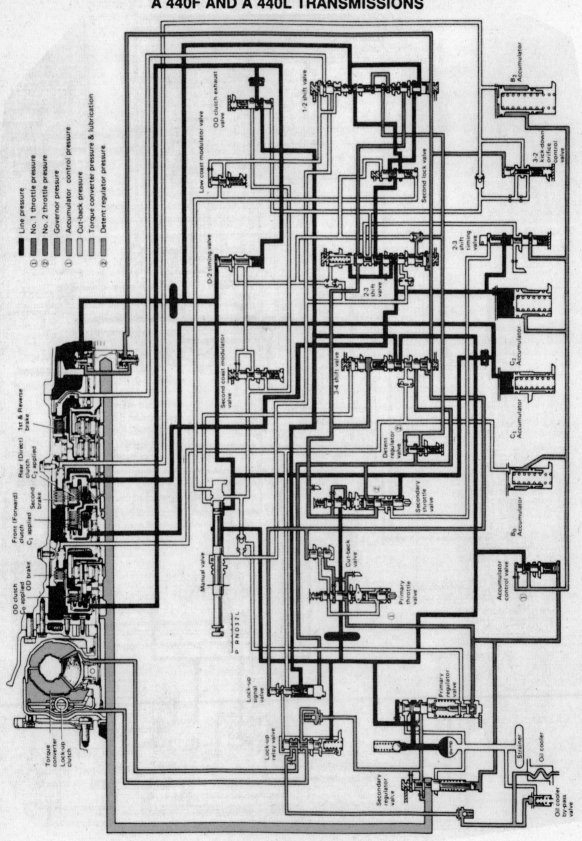

OIL FLOW CIRCUIT—3 RANGE THIRD SPEED—A 440F AND A 440L TRANSMISSIONS

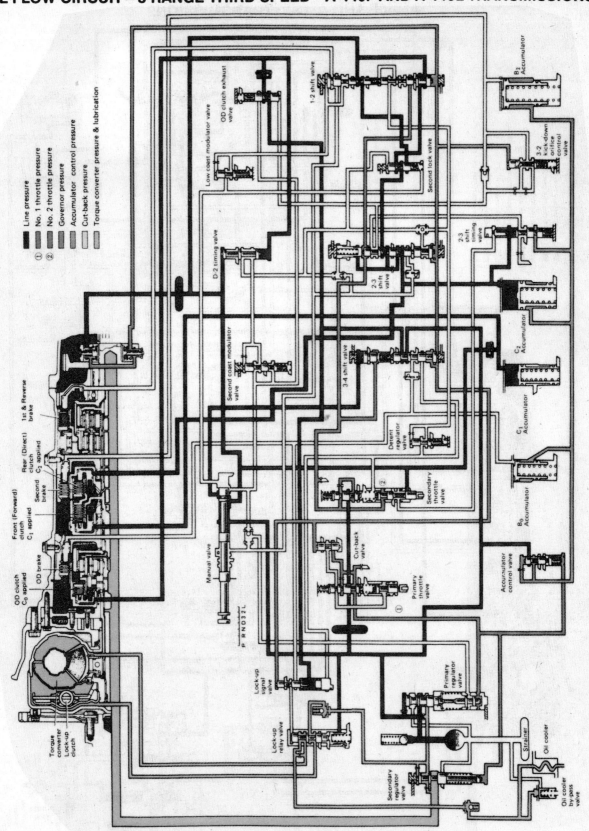

OIL FLOW CIRCUIT — 2 RANGE SECOND SPEED
A 440F AND A 440L TRANSMISSIONS

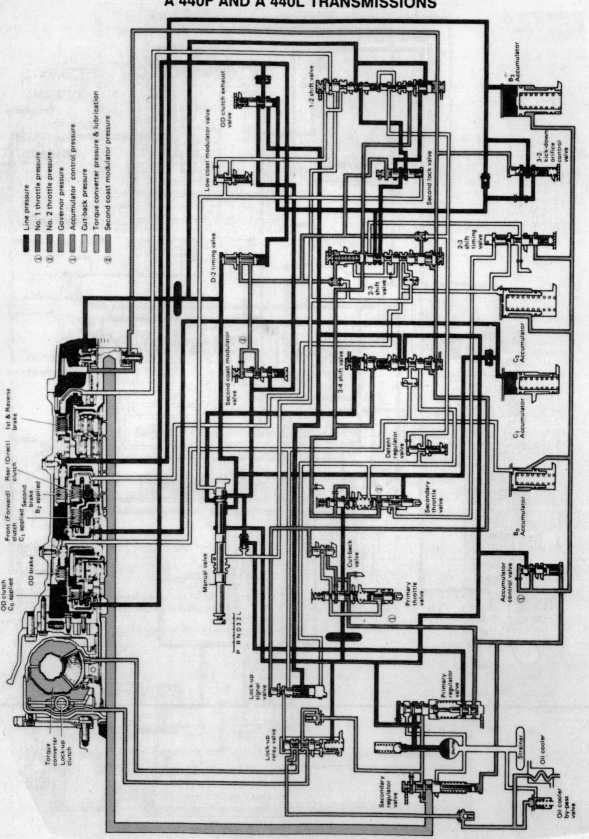

OIL FLOW CIRCUIT—L RANGE FIRST SPEED—A 440F AND A 440L TRANSMISSIONS

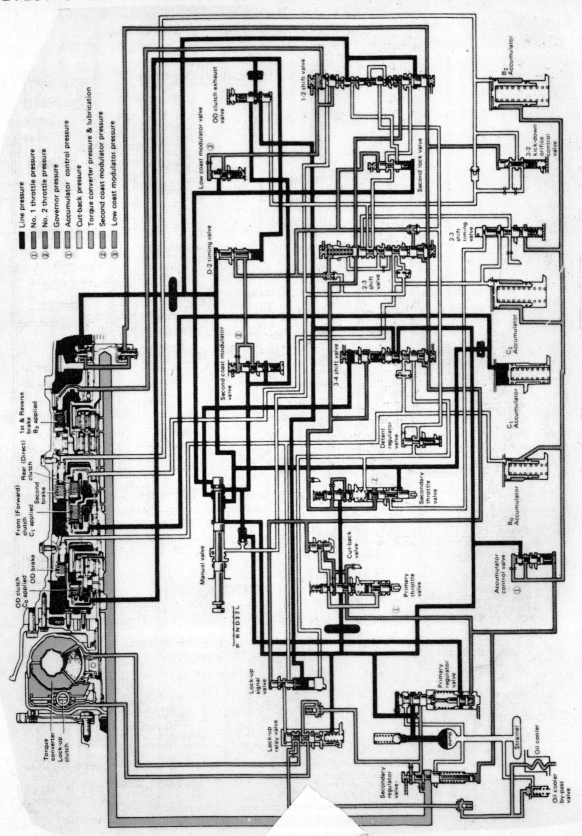

OIL FLOW CIRCUIT—LOCKUP SOLENOID VALVE—A 440L TRANSMISSION

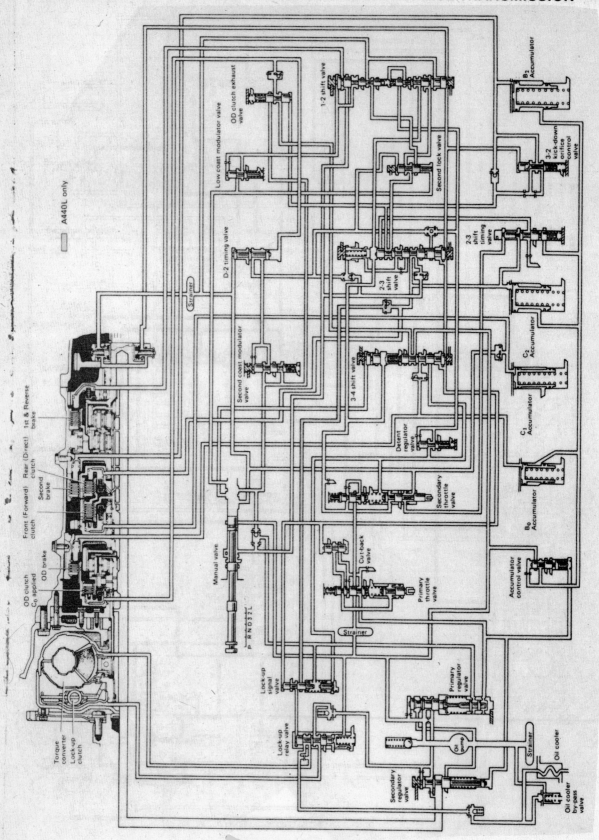